Mexico

John Noble

Wayne Bernhardson

Tom Brosnahan

Scott Doggett

Susan Forsyth

Mark Honan

Nancy Keller

James Lyon

Mexico

6th edition

Published by
  Lonely Planet Publications
  Head Office: PO Box 617, Hawthorn, Vic 3122, Australia
  Branches: 155 Filbert St, Suite 251, Oakland, CA 94607, USA
                  10A Spring Place, London NW5 3BH, UK
                  71 bis rue du Cardinal Lemoine, 75005 Paris, France

Printed by
  The Bookmaker Pty Ltd
  Printed in Hong Kong

Photographs by

Ross Barnet	Robert Frerck/Odyssey	Susan Kaye	Anthony Pidgeon
Wayne Bernhardson	Rick Gerharter	Nancy Keller	Peter Ptschelinzew
Tom Brosnahan	Robert Holmes	James Lyon	Erin Reid
Jan Butchofsky-Houser	Mark Honan	Richard Nebesky	James Simmons
Scott Doggett	Dave G Houser	John Noble	F Stoppelman
Mark Downey	Bonnie Kamin	Allan A Phibiba	Tony Wheeler
Lee Foster			

Front cover: Kevin Schafer

First Published
  1982

This Edition
  April 1998

National Library of Australia Cataloguing in Publication Data

  Mexico.

  6th ed.
  Includes index.
  ISBN 0 86442 429 9.

  1. Mexico – Guidebooks. I. Noble, John, 1951- .

917.204835

text & maps © Lonely Planet 1998
photos © photographers as indicated 1998
climate charts compiled from information supplied by Patrick J Tyson, © Patrick J Tyson, 1998

John Noble

John grew up in the cool, green valley of the River Ribble, England. He escaped intermittently from a career in newspaper journalism by taking lengthy trips around Europe, North and Central America and Southeast Asia, before Lonely Planet answered his call and sent him to update their guide to *Sri Lanka*, where he met his wife and co-author Susan Forsyth. Since then John has co-authored four editions of *Mexico* for Lonely Planet and one each of *Spain, Australia, Indonesia, USSR, Baltic States, Central Asia* and *Russia, Ukraine & Belarus*. John and Susan and their children Isabella and Jack (also experienced Mexico travelers) now live in southern Spain.

Wayne Bernhardson

Born in Fargo, North Dakota, Wayne Bernhardson grew up in Tacoma, Washington, and earned a PhD in geography at the University of California, Berkeley. He has traveled widely in Latin America and lived for extended periods on Chile, Argentina and the Falkland (Malvinas) Islands. His other LP credits include *Argentina, Uruguay & Paraguay*, *Buenos Aires*, *Chile & Easter Island*, *South America* and *Rocky Mountains*. Wayne resides in Oakland, California, with his affectionate Alaskan malamute, Gardel.

Tom Brosnahan

Tom was born and raised in Pennsylvania, went to college in Boston, then set out on the road. After traveling in Europe he joined the Peace Corps, and saw Mexico for the first time as part of the Peace Corps training program. A short term of teaching English in a Mexico City school whetted his appetite for more exploration. After graduate school he traveled throughout Mexico, Guatemala and Belize writing travel articles and guidebooks for various publishers, and in the past two decades his 20 books covering numerous destinations have sold over 2 million copies in 12 languages. For Lonely Planet, Tom has worked on *Turkey, Guatemala, Belize & Yucatan – La Ruta Maya, Central America, Mediterranean Europe*, and *New England*.

Scott Doggett

Scott's interest in Latin America became personal when, in 1983, as a recent graduate of the University of California at Berkeley, he packed up his cameras and moved to El Salvador. His initial career as a photojournalist was followed by postgraduate study at Stanford University, reporting assignments for United Press International in Los Angeles, Pakistan and Afghanistan, and, most recently, seven years on the editorial staff of the *Los Angeles Times*. During his free time, Scott travels and writes about his adventures for newspapers and magazines. He is an author and co-editor of *Travelers' Tales: Brazil*. At the time this book went to press, Scott was writing Lonely Planet's guide on Panama.

Susan Forsyth

Susan hails from Melbourne where she survived a decade teaching in the Victorian state education system before heading off for a year as a volunteer lecturer in Sri Lanka. There she met her future husband and co-author, John Noble. Susan has since helped update LP's *Australia*, *Indonesia*, *Mexico* and *Sri Lanka* guides and *Travel With Children*, traveled lengthily in the ex-USSR, given birth to and nurtured two little *güeros* (blondies) and worked on the first edition of LP's *Spain* guide. For the past three years, she and the family have been living in southern Spain where they all enjoy the semi-tropical climate and improving their Spanish.

Mark Honan

After a university degree in philosophy opened up a glittering career as an office clerk, Mark soon decided that there was more to life than form-filling and data-entry. He set off on a two-year trip round the world, armed with a backpack and a vague intent to sell travel stories and pictures upon his return to England. Astonishingly, this barely-formed plan succeeded and Mark has since contributed regularly to magazine travel pages. He has written guides to *Switzerland, Austria*, and *Vienna*, and contributed to LP's *Western Europe*, *Central America on a shoestring* and *Solomon Islands*.

Nancy Keller

Nancy was born and raised in Northern California, and worked in the alternative press for several years, doing every aspect of newspaper work from editorial and reporting to delivering the papers. She returned to university to earn a master's degree in journalism, finally graduating in 1986 after many breaks for extended stays on the west coast of Mexico. Since then she's been traveling and writing in Mexico, Israel, Egypt, Europe, various South Pacific islands, New Zealand and Central America. She has worked on several LP books, including *Central America*, *Rarotonga & the Cook Islands*, *New Zealand*, and *California & Nevada*.

James Lyon

James is an Australian by birth, a skeptic by nature and a social scientist by training. He was unsuccessful as a government bureaucrat because of an unfortunate tendency to put his itchy foot in his mouth. James eventually became an editor at Lonely Planet's Melbourne office, where the time he has spent traveling was not regarded as a black spot on his CV. After a couple of years, James jumped at the chance to update LP's *Bali & Lombok* guide. James has since worked on LP's *California & Nevada*, and he is currently heading up LP's *USA* guide.

From the Authors

John Noble & Susan Forsyth John Noble and Susan Forsyth would jointly like to thank: Bob Merideth and Diana Liverman of the University of Arizona, and friends, for exceedingly generous help and good company in Puerto Ángel; *everybody* at the Buena Vista; Marie Copozzi, New York; Sr González and family, Casa González, Mexico City; Jorge, Guillermina and staff at Las Golondrinas; Tom Downs and Jacqueline Volin for good-humored, professional and patient editing; and Alex Guilbert and the mapping crew for a huge amount of work and some lovely maps.

Susan would also like to thank: Ana Márquez, Puerto Escondido; Mari Seder, Worcester, MA, USA; Jason 'J Roc' Cuthbert, Guelph, Ontario; Gina DeLuca, Windsor, Ontario; Tangie Rowland, Capitola, CA; Sara Pope, Aptos, CA; Jackie Jett, Ferndale, CA; Elizabeth Riley, Capitola, CA; Cathy Le Jehan, Brittany, France; Marcelino, San Ciro de Acojta, San Luis Potosí; Yolanda and Ricardo, San Miguel de Allende; Raúl Torres Sandoval, Aguascalientes; and the staff of the Guanajuato State Tourist Office.

John adds thanks to: everybody at the Casa de los Amigos, Mexico City; Paco Ramos, Carolina and Ramya in Mexico City; staff at many tourist offices in Mexico who were generous with their time and knowledge; Mark, Scott, Susan, Tom and Wayne for being ever cooperative, committed and able colleagues; Sacha Pearson for indefatigable and invaluable research into North American matters; Margarita Guillen for helping me understand Mexican slang; Carolyn Hubbard for consistent positive thinking and a unique email style; Leonie Mugavin for checking out airfares from Australia; and, not least, all the travelers who took the trouble to write in with so many valuable tips (you make a big difference!).

Wayne Bernhardson Reynaldo and Marta Ayala of Calexico, California, deserve special mention for their hospitality and for their knowledge of the border area in general and Mexicali in particular. Sergio Gracia Valencia and Carlos Guillén of Secture's Mexicali office promptly and conscientiously replied to numerous supplementary requests for information.

Carolina Shepard of the Museo de la Naturaleza y de la Cultura in Bahía de los Angeles graciously reviewed the section on her adopted home and allowed me to work in the museum during closing hours. Serge Dedina of The Nature Conservancy brought me up to date on conservation issues in the Desierto Central. Lucero Gutiérrez of INAH reviewed the material on Desierto Central rock art and offered several other useful comments.

Other notable contributions came from Steve and Linda Sullivan of the The People's Gallery in San Felipe, Miguel and Claudia Quintana of Mulegé Divers, Roy Mahoff and Becky Aparicio of Baja Tropicales at Bahía Concepción, Trudi Angell of Las Parras Tour in Loreto, Oscar Padilla of the Coordinación Estatal de Turismo in La Paz, Janet Howey of El Tecolote Libros in Todos Santos, and Pepe and Libby Merrieta and Fidencio Romero of Cabo Pulmo.

Scott Doggett Those of us whose mugs appear on the preceding page account for only a fraction of the Lonely Planet force that rallied to produce the tome you hold in your hands. The larger and altogether better-looking fraction does excellent work and deserves lost of credit. It's made up of people such as Caroline Liou, who heads the editorial side of Lonely Planet for the Americas and is a total joy to work for; Carolyn Hubbard, a senior editor whose humor and voice of reason are a godsend to stressed-out authors; Tom Downs and Jacqueline Volin, the hawk-eye line editors who took the heaps of text thrown at them and made sense of it all; production manager Scott Summers; Alex Guilbert and his team of cartographers; and designers Henia Miedzinski and Diana Nankin. Thank you all. And to my fiancée, Annette, a special thanks for saying yes.

Mark Honan Thanks to the travelers, expats and Mexicans I met who helped make my research trip both enjoyable and successful. Special thanks to the creators of Bohemia and Negra Modelo – the perfect Mexican beers! Meanwhile, the worldwide search for the perfect chili con carne (a non-Mexican dish) continues . . . .

From the Publisher
The nearly 1000 pages of text and over 150 maps for this edition were edited by Carolyn Hubbard, Tom Downs, Jacqueline Volin, Joan Saunders, Kim Zetter, Julie Connery, Ben Greensfelder, Valerie Perry and Jeff Campbell. JoAnne Cabello helped with indexing. Maps were drawn and corrected by Diana Nankin, Henia Miedzinski, Rini Keagy and Margaret Livingston. Typesetting and layout were done by Henia Miedzinski, Diana Nankin, Richard Wilson and Scott Summers. Hugh D'Andrade designed the cover and drew illustrations. Ann Jeffree, Trudi Canavan, Jacqui Saunders and Lisa Summers also contributed illustrations.

This Book
This is the sixth edition of Lonely Planet's *Mexico*. Past authors have included Doug Richmond, Dan Spitzer, Scott Wayne and Mark Balla (among authors of this edition who have covered Mexico before).

John Noble has been coordinating author for the past two editions. He wrote the intro chapters and Mexico City. He and Susan Forsyth co-wrote Oaxaca, and Susan wrote all of Northern Central Highlands, except Querétaro, which John did.

Scott Doggett wrote Around Mexico City, Central North Mexico, Northeast Mexico, Western Central Highlands and Central Gulf Coast. Tom Brosnahan wrote Tabasco & Chiapas and Yucatán, Mark Honan wrote Northwest Mexico and Central Pacific Coast, and Wayne Bernhardson wrote Baja California. Nancy Keller and James Lyon wrote subtstantial portions of the fifth edition and their efforts are reflected in the quality of this edition.

Warning & Request
Things change – prices go up, schedules change, good places go bad and bad places go bankrupt – nothing stays the same. So, if you find things better or worse, recently opened or long since closed, please tell us and help make the next edition even more accurate and useful.

We value all of the feedback we receive from travelers. A small team reads and acknowledges every letter, postcard and email, and ensures that every morsel of information finds its way to the appropriate authors, editors and publishers. Everyone who writes to us will find their name in the next edition of the appropriate guide and will also receive a free subscription to our quarterly newsletter, *Planet Talk*. The very best contributions will be rewarded with a free Lonely Planet guide.

Excerpts from your correspondence may appear in updates (which we add to the end pages of reprints); new editions of this guide; in our newsletter, *Planet Talk*; or in the Postcards section of our Website – so please let us know if you don't want your letter published or your name acknowledged.

Thanks
Many thanks to the travelers who used the last edition and wrote to us with helpful hints, useful advice and interesting anecdotes. Your names appear in the back of this book.

Contents

Map Legend

BOUNDARIES

— · — · — · — International Boundary

— · · — · · — State Boundary

AREA FEATURES

Park, Parque

National Park

National Refuge

HYDROGRAPHIC FEATURES

Water
Reef
Coastline
Beach, Playa
Swamp
River, Waterfall
Mangrove, Spring

ROUTES

Freeway

Toll Freeway

Primary Road

Secondary Road

Tertiary Road

Poorly Maintained Road

Trail

Ferry Route

Metro Line, Metro Station

Railway, Train Station

ROUTE SHIELDS

$\overset{MEX}{1}$ Mexican Highway

$\overset{MEX}{1D}$ Mexican Toll Highway

(19) State Highway

SYMBOLS

✪ NATIONAL CAPITAL	✦ Airfield	▐ Gas Station	)(Pass
◉ State Capital	✈ Airport	⸪ Archaeological Site, Ruins	⚲ Hospital, Clinic	⊓ Picnic Area
● City	⚲ Hospital, Clinic	★ Police Station
● City, Small	❸ Bank, ATM	❶ Information	▭ Pool
● Town	◳ Baseball Diamond	査 Lighthouse	✉ Post Office
	➶ Beach, Playa	☀ Lookout	❶ Public Toilets
	✦ Border Crossing	☵ Mines	⤫ Shipwreck
▪ Hotel, B&B	▭ Cathedral, Catedral	▲ Mission	❖ Shopping Mall
▲ Campground	⌒ Cave	🅰 Monument	▥ Stately Home
⌷ RV Park	✝ Church, Iglesia	▲ Mountain	☎ Telephone
⌂ Shelter, Refugio	◣ Dive Site	🏛 Museum	▣ Tomb, Mausoleum
▼ Restaurant	◗ Embassy, Consulate	⌂ Observatory	🚶 Trailhead
❚ Bar (Place to Drink)	➴ Fishing	← One-Way Street	◒ Transportation
▰ Cafe	⊁ Footbridge	♠ Park, Parque	⚇ Winery
	✣ Garden	🅿 Parking	🐃 Zoo

Note: Not all symbols displayed above appear in this book.

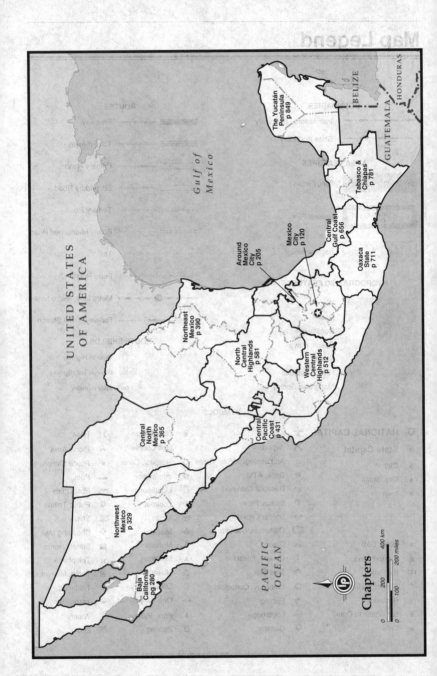

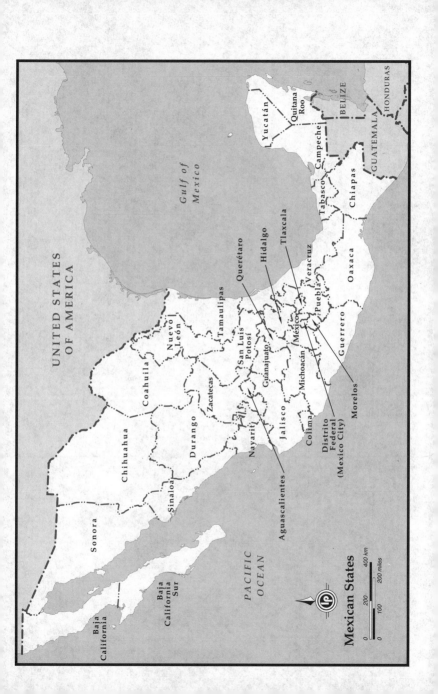

Introduction

To explore Mexico is to traverse vast deserts, journey around (or up) snow-capped volcanoes, wade along tropical jungle-clad beaches and hike through ancient ruins; and it is to walk the streets of teeming modern cities, timeless villages and posh resorts. Mexico is an experience that offers a multitude of cultures, cuisines, environments, handicrafts, art and history.

The country's diversity stems partly from topography. (The Spanish conquistador Hernán Cortés, when asked to describe Mexico, simply crumpled a piece of paper and set it on a table.) The country's endless mountain ranges have always allowed its people to pursue their destiny in some degree of isolation.

Great cultures and empires, among them the Aztecs and the Maya, flourished here centuries ago. Their direct descendants –

over 50 distinct Indian peoples, each with their own language – remain culturally isolated among the country's *mestizo* (mixed-blood) majority, and maintain diverse ancient traditions despite the country's ongoing modernization. Such contrasts are common in Mexico: traditional sources of livelihood, such as mining, fishing and agriculture, coexist with modern manufacturing, services and an important tourism industry. Everywhere, considerable wealth and severe poverty rub shoulders.

But even as modern roads, airplanes, radio and television have knitted the various regions together and helped to forge a national consciousness, being Mexican continues to mean very different things to the distinct peoples of Mexico's many regions. If you're looking for the 'real' Mexico, don't expect just one conclusion.

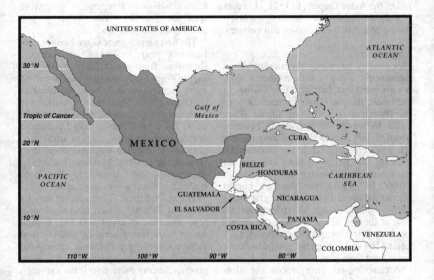

Facts about the Country

HISTORY

There is nothing new about the 'New World,' as a look at Mexico's history reveals. The first people in this land may have arrived more than 20,000 years before Columbus. Their descendants built a succession of highly developed civilizations, which flourished from 1200 BC to 1500 AD. Among these, the Maya and Aztec cultures are the best known. But in your travels through Mexico you'll have the opportunity to explore the achievements of the mysterious Olmecs of the Gulf Coast, the Zapotecs of Oaxaca, the great imperial city of Teotihuacán (near Mexico City), the warlike Toltecs, from Tula, and others.

Historians traditionally divide Mexico's history before the Spanish conquest (the pre-Hispanic era) into four periods – Archaic, before 1500 BC; Preclassic or Formative, 1500 BC to 250 AD; Classic, 250 to 900 AD; and Postclassic, 900 to the fall of the Aztec Empire, in 1521. However you divide it, Mexico's history is a fascinating procession of peoples and cultures.

Beginnings

Discounting beguiling theories of direct transpacific contacts with southeast Asia, it's accepted that, barring a few Vikings in the north, the pre-Hispanic inhabitants of the Americas arrived from Siberia. They came in waves of migrations between about 60,000 and 8000 BC, during the last ice age, crossing land now submerged beneath the Bering Strait. The earliest human traces in Mexico date from about 20,000 BC. These first Mexicans hunted big animal herds that grazed the grasslands of the highland valleys. When temperatures rose at the end of the Ice Age the valleys became drier, ceasing to support such animal life and forcing the people to derive more food from plants.

Archaeologists have traced the slow beginnings of agriculture in the Tehuacán valley in Puebla state, where, soon after 6500 BC, people were planting seeds of chili pepper and a kind of squash. Between 5000 and 3500 BC they started to plant mutant forms of a tiny wild maize and to grind the maize into meal. After 3500 BC a much better variety of maize, and also beans, enabled the Tehuacán valley people to live semipermanently in villages and spend less time in seasonal hunting camps. Pottery appeared by 2300 BC.

The Olmecs

Mexico's first civilization arose near the Gulf Coast, in the humid lowlands of southern Veracruz and neighboring Tabasco. These were the Olmecs, or People from the Region of Rubber, a name coined in the 1920s. Olmec civilization is famed for its awesome 'Olmec heads,' stone sculptures up to three meters high with grim, pug-nosed faces combining the features of human babies and jaguars – a mixture referred to as the 'were-jaguar' – and wearing curious helmets.

The first known great Olmec center, San Lorenzo, near Acayucan, in Veracruz, flourished from about 1200 to 900 BC. Eight Olmec heads and many other carved stone monuments have been identified as originating here. Their basalt material was probably dragged, rolled or rafted from 60 to 80 km away. Finds at San Lorenzo of objects from far away, such as artifacts of obsidian, a glasslike volcanic stone, from Guatemala and the Mexican highlands, suggest that San Lorenzo may have controlled trade over a very large area.

The second great Olmec center was La Venta, in Tabasco, which flourished for a few centuries, to about 600 BC. Several tombs were found here. In one of them jade, a favorite pre-Hispanic ornamental material, makes its appearance. La Venta produced many more fine stone carvings, including at least five Olmec heads.

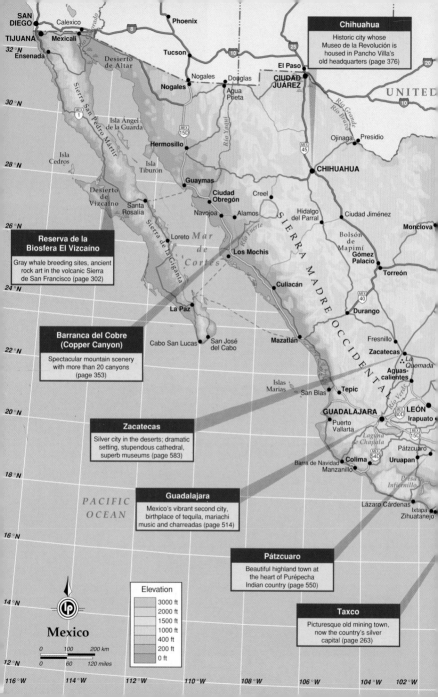

SAN DIEGO
TIJUANA
Ensenada
Calexico
Mexicali

Phoenix

32°N

30°N

Tucson

Nogales
Nogales
Douglas
Agua Prieta

El Paso
CIUDAD JUÁREZ

UNITED

Chihuahua

Historic city whose
Museo de la Revolución is
housed in Pancho Villa's
old headquarters (page 376)

Desierto
de Altar

Isla Ángel
de la Guarda

Hermosillo

Ojinaga
Presidio

CHIHUAHUA

28°N

Isla
Cedros

Isla
Tiburón

Guaymas

Creel

Ciudad
Obregón

Hidalgo
del Parral
Ciudad Jiménez

Monclova

Desierto
de
Vizcaíno
Santa
Rosalía

Navojoa
Alamos

Bolsón
de
Mapimí

26°N

**Reserva de la
Biosfera El Vizcaíno**

Gray whale breeding sites, ancient
rock art in the volcanic Sierra
de San Francisco (page 302)

Loreto
*Mar
de
Cortés*

Los Mochis

Gómez
Palacio
Torreón

Culiacán

24°N

La Paz

Durango

Fresnillo

**Barranca del Cobre
(Copper Canyon)**

Spectacular mountain scenery
with more than 20 canyons
(page 353)

Cabo San Lucas
San José
del Cabo

Mazatlán

22°N

Zacatecas
La
Quemada

Aguas-
calientes

Islas
Marías
San Blas
Tepic

Zacatecas

Silver city in the deserts; dramatic
setting, stupendous cathedral,
superb museums (page 583)

GUADALAJARA
Puerto
Vallarta

LEÓN
Irapuato

20°N

*Laguna
de Chapala*

Pátzcuaro

*PACIFIC
OCEAN*

Guadalajara

Mexico's vibrant second city,
birthplace of tequila, mariachi
music and charreadas (page 514)

Barra de Navidad
Manzanillo
Colima

Uruapan

18°N

*Presa
Infiernillo*

Lázaro Cárdenas

Ixtapa
Zihuatanejo

16°N

Pátzcuaro

Beautiful highland town at
the heart of Purépecha
Indian country (page 550)

14°N

Mexico

0   100   200 km

0   60   120 miles

Elevation

3000 ft
2000 ft
1500 ft
1000 ft
400 ft
200 ft
0 ft

Taxco

Picturesque old mining town,
now the country's silver
capital (page 263)

12°N

116°W   114°W   112°W   110°W   108°W   106°W   104°W   102°W

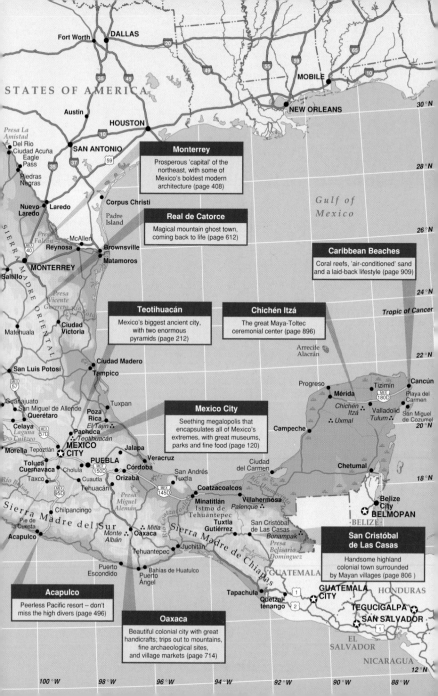

Monterrey
Prosperous 'capital' of the northeast, with some of Mexico's boldest modern architecture (page 408)

Real de Catorce
Magical mountain ghost town, coming back to life (page 612)

Caribbean Beaches
Coral reefs, 'air-conditioned' sand and a laid-back lifestyle (page 909)

Teotihuacán
Mexico's biggest ancient city, with two enormous pyramids (page 212)

Chichén Itzá
The great Maya-Toltec ceremonial center (page 896)

Mexico City
Seething megalopolis that encapsulates all of Mexico's extremes, with great museums, parks and fine food (page 120)

San Cristóbal de Las Casas
Handsome highland colonial town surrounded by Mayan villages (page 806)

Acapulco
Peerless Pacific resort – don't miss the high divers (page 496)

Oaxaca
Beautiful colonial city with great handicrafts; trips out to mountains, fine archaeological sites, and village markets (page 714)

Olmec sites far from the Gulf Coast may well have been trading posts-cum-garrisons to ensure the supply of jade, obsidian and other luxuries for the Olmec elite. The most impressive is Chalcatzingo, in Morelos.

Both San Lorenzo and La Venta were violently destroyed. But the Olmecs secured their place as Mexico's ancestral civilization. Their art, their religion and quite possibly their social organization strongly influenced those that followed. Apart from the were-jaguar, which seems to have been linked with rain, Olmec gods included fire and maize deities and the feathered serpent, all of which persisted throughout the pre-Hispanic era.

Early Monte Albán

By 300 BC settled village life, based on agriculture and hunting, had developed throughout the southern half of Mexico. Monte Albán, the hilltop center of the Zapotec people of Oaxaca, was growing into a town of perhaps 10,000. Some of the stone carvings known as Danzantes (Dancers) from this era at Monte Albán show figures with Olmec-like downturned mouths. Many of them have also hieroglyphs or dates in a dot-and-bar system, which quite possibly means that the elite of Monte Albán were the inventors of writing and the written calendar in Mesoamerica.

Izapa & the Early Maya

The large temple center of Izapa, in Chiapas near the Pacific Coast, almost on the border of Guatemala, flourished from about 200 BC to 200 AD. Among its pyramids stood many tall stone slabs, called stelae, fronted by round altars and carved with mythological scenes showing Olmec-derived gods.

Izapan culture is considered the link between the Olmecs and the next great civilization in southern Mexico, the Maya. Izapa and the early Maya shared several characteristics such as the stela-altar pairing and 'Long Count' dates (see Mayan Writing & the Calendar later in this chapter).

Izapan civilization may have been carried to the Maya by way of Kaminaljuyú, an ancient center on the outskirts of modern Guatemala City. By the close of the Preclassic period, in 250 AD, the Maya in the Yucatán Peninsula and the Petén forest of Guatemala were already building stepped temple pyramids and using the corbeled vault – the Mayan version of an arch: two straight stone surfaces leaning against one another and meeting at the top.

Teotihuacán

The first great civilization of central Mexico emerged in a valley about 50 km northeast of the center of modern Mexico City. Teotihuacán grew into Mexico's biggest pre-Hispanic city, with an estimated population of 200,000 at its height in the 6th century AD, and it controlled probably the biggest pre-Hispanic empire. Teotihuacán had writing and books, the bar-and-dot number system and the 260-day sacred year (see Mayan Writing & the Calendar).

The building of a magnificent planned city began about the time of Christ. The greatest of its buildings, the 70-meter-high, 220-meter-square Pirámide del Sol (Pyramid of the Sun), was constructed within the first 150 years AD. Most of the rest of the city, including the almost-as-big Pirámide de la Luna (Pyramid of the Moon), was built between about 250 and 600 AD.

Empire Teotihuacán probably became an imperialistic state after 400 AD. At its peak it may have controlled the southern two-thirds of Mexico, all of Guatemala and Belize, and bits of Honduras and El Salvador. But it was an empire probably geared toward tribute-gathering, to feed the mouths and tastes of its big home population, rather than to full-scale occupation.

Cholula, near Puebla, with a pyramid even bigger than the Pirámide del Sol, was within Teotihuacán's cultural sphere. Teotihuacán may have had hegemony over the Zapotecs of Oaxaca during the zenith of their capital, Monte Albán, which grew into a city of perhaps 25,000 between about 300 and 600 AD. In about 400 AD invaders from Teotihuacán built almost a miniature replica of their home city in Kaminaljuyú, Guatemala. From there they probably extended their sway over some of the Maya in the Petén.

Fall of Teotihuacán In the 7th century Teotihuacán was burned, plundered and abandoned. It is likely that the state had already been economically weakened – perhaps by the rise of rival powers in central Mexico or by desiccation caused by the denuding of the surrounding hillsides of forest.

But Teotihuacán's influence on Mexico's later cultures was huge. Many of its gods, such as the feathered serpent Quetzalcóatl, an all-important symbol of fertility and life itself, and Tláloc, the rain and water god, were still being worshipped by the Aztecs a millennium later.

The Classic Maya

The Classic Maya region falls into three areas. The northern area is the Yucatán Peninsula; the central area is the Petén forest of northern Guatemala and adjacent lowlands in Mexico (to the west) and Belize (to the east); the southern area consists of the highlands of Guatemala and Honduras and the Pacific coast of Guatemala. It was the northern and central areas – the lowlands – that produced pre-Hispanic America's most brilliant civilization, the Classic Maya, which thrived between about 250 and 900 AD. Many of the major Mayan ruins sites are outside Mexico, with Tikal in the Petén supreme in terms of its splendor.

Until recently scholars thought that the Classic Maya were organized into about 20 independent, often warring city-states. Recent advances in the understanding of Maya writing, however, have yielded a new theory that in the first part of the Classic period most of the city-states were grouped into two loose military alliances centered on Tikal and the now hard-to-reach site of Calakmul, in Mexico's Campeche state.

Tikal is believed to have conquered Calakmul in 695, but was then unable to exert any unified control over Calakmul's former subject states.

Mayan Cities A typical Mayan city functioned as the ceremonial, political and market hub for the surrounding farming hamlets. Its ceremonial center focused on plazas surrounded by tall temple pyramids (usually the tombs of probably deified rulers) and lower buildings, so-called palaces, with warrens of small rooms. Stelae and altars were carved with dates, histories, and elaborate human and divine figures. Stone causeways called *sacbeob*, probably built for ceremonial use, led out from the plazas.

Classic Mayan centers in Mexico fall into any of four zones: Chiapas, in the central Mayan area, and Río Bec, Chenes and Puuc, all on the Yucatán Peninsula.

Chiapas The chief Chiapas sites are Yaxchilán, its tributary, Bonampak (where vivid battle murals were found in 1948), and Palenque, which to many people is the most beautiful of all Mayan sites. Palenque rose to prominence under the 7th-century ruler Pakal, whose treasure-loaded tomb deep inside the fine Templo de las Inscripciones was discovered in 1952.

Río Bec & Chenes In Campeche state are the wild, little-investigated Río Bec and Chenes zones, noted for their lavishly carved buildings. These sites, including Calakmul draw few visitors. They are covered in this book's Xpujil & Vicinity section, in the Yucatán chapter.

Puuc The Puuc zone, in Yucatán state, was the focus of northern Classic Mayan culture. The most important city was Uxmal, south of Mérida. Puuc ornamentation, which reached its peak on the Governor's Palace at Uxmal, featured intricate stone mosaics, part geometric but also incorporating faces of the hook-nosed sky-serpent-cum-rain-god, Chac. The amazing Codz Poop (Palace of Masks) at Kabah, south of Uxmal, is covered with nearly 300 Chac faces. The splendid Chichén Itzá, about 116 km east of Mérida, is another Puuc site, though it also owes much to a later era (see the Toltecs section later in this chapter).

Mayan Art Art was typically elegant but cluttered, and narrative in content. Fine carved stelae showing historical and mythological events have survived, with those in the central area generally superior to those in the north and south. Mayan potters achieved marvelous multicolored effects on grave vessels, created to accompany the dead to the next world. Jade, the most precious substance, was turned into beads or thin carved plaques.

Mayan Writing & the Calendar Among the Maya's greatest achievements were intellectual advances. They had a complex, partly pictorial, partly phonetic writing system with 300 to 500 symbols, whose decipherment in the 1980s greatly

advanced modern understanding of the Maya.

The Maya refined a calendar used by other pre-Hispanic peoples into a tool for the exact recording of earthly and heavenly events. They could predict eclipses of the sun and the movements of the moon and Venus, and they measured time in three ways:

• in tzolkins (sacred or almanac years) composed of 13 periods of 20 days;

• in haabs ('vague' solar years) of 18 20-day 'months' followed by a special five-day 'portentous' period called the Uayeb; the last day of each 'month' was known as the 'seating' of the next month, in line with the Mayan belief that the future influences the present;

• in units of one, 20, 360, 7200 and 144,000 days.

All of Mexico's pre-Hispanic civilizations used the first two counts, whose interlocking enabled a date to be located precisely within a period of 52 years called a

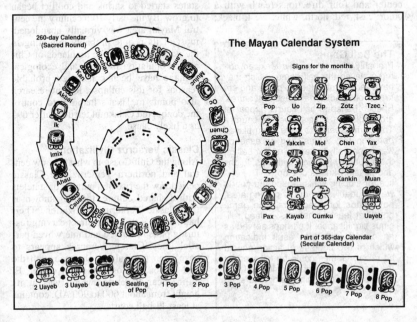

260-day Calendar (Sacred Round)

Chicchan / Cimi / Manik / Lamat / Muluc / Oc / Chuen / Eb / Ben / Ix / Men / Cib / Caban / Etz'nab / Cauac / Ahau / Imix / Ik / Akbal / Kan

The Mayan Calendar System

Signs for the months

Pop   Uo   Zip   Zotz   Tzec

Xul   Yakxin   Mol   Chen   Yax

Zac   Ceh   Mac   Kankin   Muan

Pax   Kayab   Cumku   Uayeb

Part of 365-day Calendar (Secular Calendar)

2 Uayeb   3 Uayeb   4 Uayeb   Seating of Pop   1 Pop   2 Pop   3 Pop   4 Pop   5 Pop   6 Pop   7 Pop   8 Pop

Calendar Round. But the Maya were the preeminent users of the third count, known as the Long Count, which was infinitely extendable. Their inscriptions enumerate the Long Count units elapsed from a starting point (Creation) that corresponds to August 13, 3114 BC. Numbers were written in a system of dots (counted as one) and bars (counted as five).

Mayan Religion Religion permeated every facet of Mayan life. The Maya believed in predestination and had a complex astrology. But to win the gods' favors they also carried out elaborate rituals involving the alcoholic drink *balche*; bloodletting from ears, tongues or penises; and dances, feasts and sacrifices. The Classic Maya seem to have practiced human sacrifice on a small scale, the Postclassic on a larger scale. Beheading was probably the most common method. At Chichén Itzá, victims were thrown into a deep *cenote* (well) to bring rain.

The Maya inhabited a universe with a center and four directions (each with a color: east, red; north, white; west, black; south, yellow; the center, green), 13 layers of heavens, and nine layers of underworld to which the dead descended. The earth was the back of a giant reptile floating on a pond. (It's not *too* hard to imagine yourself as a flea on this creature's back as you look across a Mayan landscape!) The current world was just one of a succession of worlds destined to end in cataclysm and be succeeded by another. This cyclical nature of things enabled the future to be predicted by looking at the past.

Mayan gods included Itzamná, the fire deity and creator; Chac, the rain god; Yum Kaax, the maize and vegetation god; and Ah Puch, the death god. The feathered serpent, known to the Maya as Kukulcán, was introduced from central Mexico in the Postclassic period. Also worshipped were dead ancestors, particularly rulers, who were believed to be descended from the gods.

The Mayan Collapse In the second half of the 8th century, trade between Mayan states started to shrink and conflict began to grow. By the early 10th century the central Mayan area was virtually abandoned, most of its people probably migrating to the northern area or the highlands of Chiapas. Population pressure and ecological damage have been considered probable reasons for this collapse. Recent research also points to Tikal's inability to control the conquered Calakmul territory after 695 as a likely cause.

Classic Veracruz Civilization

Along the Gulf Coast, in what are now central and northern Veracruz, the Classic period saw the rise of a number of statelets with a shared culture, together known as the Classic Veracruz civilization. Their hallmark is a style of abstract carving featuring pairs of curved and interwoven parallel lines. Classic Veracruz appears to have been particularly obsessed with the ball game; its most important center, El Tajín, near Papantla, which was at its height from about 600 to 900 AD, contains at least 11 ball courts.

The Ball Game

Probably all pre-Hispanic Mexican cultures played the ball game, which may have varied from place to place and era to era but had certain lasting features. Special I-shaped ball courts appear at archaeological sites all over the country. The game seems to have been played between two teams, and its essence was apparently to keep a rubber ball off the ground by flicking it with hips, thighs and possibly knees or elbows. The vertical or sloping walls around the courts were probably part of the playing area, not stands for spectators. The game had – at least sometimes – deep religious significance. It perhaps served as an oracle, with the result indicating which of two courses of action should be taken. Games could be followed by the sacrifice of one or more of the players – whether winners or losers, no one is sure. ■

The Toltecs

In central Mexico one chief power center after the decline of Teotihuacán was Xochicalco, a hilltop site in Morelos with Mayan influences and impressive evidence of a feathered-serpent cult. Another may have been Cholula. A third was Tula, 65 km north of Mexico City. Tula is widely thought to have been the capital of a great empire referred to by later Aztec 'histories' as that of the Toltecs (Artificers).

Tula It is particularly hard to disentangle myth and history in the Tula/Toltec story. A widely accepted version is that the Toltecs were one of a number of semi-civilized tribes from the north who moved into central Mexico after the fall of Teoti-huacán. Tula became their capital, probably in the 10th century, growing into a city of 30,000 or 40,000. The Tula ceremonial center is dedicated primarily to the feathered serpent god Quetzalcóatl, but the annals relate that Quetzalcóatl was displaced by Tezcatlipoca (Smoking Mirror), a newcomer god of warriors and sorcery who demanded a regular diet of the hearts of sacrificed warriors. A king identified with Quetzalcóatl fled to the Gulf Coast and set sail eastward on a raft of snakes, promising one day to return.

Tula seems to have become the capital of a militaristic kingdom that dominated central Mexico, with warriors organized in orders dedicated to different animal-gods – the coyote, jaguar and eagle knights. Mass human sacrifice may have started at Tula.

The influence of Tula on contemporary and subsequent civilizations was enormous. It is seen at Paquimé in Chihuahua, at Castillo de Teayo on the Gulf Coast, and in western Mexico. Pottery from as far south as Costa Rica has been found at Tula, and there's even probable Tula influence found in Tennessee and Illinois.

Tula was abandoned about the start of the 13th century, seemingly destroyed by Chichimecs, as the periodic hordes of barbarian raiders from the north came to be known. Many later Mexican peoples revered the Toltec era as a golden age.

Chichén Itzá Mayan scripts relate that toward the end of the 10th century much of the northern Yucatán Peninsula was conquered by Kukulcán. The Mayan site of Chichén Itzá, in northern Yucatán, contains many Tula-like features, from flat beam-and-masonry roofs (contrasting with the Mayan corbeled roof) to gruesome chac-mools – reclining human figures holding dishes that were probably receptacles for human hearts torn out in sacrifices. There is a resemblance that can hardly be coincidental between Tula's Pirámide B (Pyramid B) and Chichén Itzá's Temple of the Warriors. Many writers therefore believe Toltec exiles invaded Yucatán and created a new, even grander version of Tula at Chichén Itzá.

To confuse matters, however, there's a respectable body of opinion that believes the Tula-style features at Chichén Itzá *pre-dated* Tula, implying that Chichén Itzá, not Tula, was the epicenter of whatever culture this was.

MICHAEL PETTYPOOL
Chac-mool at Chichén Itzá

The Aztecs

Rise of the Aztecs The Aztecs' own legends relate that they were the chosen people of their tribal god Huizilopochtli. Originally nomads from the north or west of Mexico who were led to the Valle de México by their priests, they settled on islands in the series of lakes that then filled much of the valley.

The Aztec capital, Tenochtitlán, was founded on one of those islands in the first half of the 14th century. For half a century or more the Aztecs served Azcapotzalco, on the lakeshore, the rising star among the rival statelets in the valley. Then, around 1427, Aztecs rebelled and became the most powerful people in the valley.

The Aztec Empire In the mid-15th century the Aztecs formed the Triple Alliance with two other valley states, Texcoco and Tlacopan, to wage war against Tlaxcala and Huejotzingo, east of the valley. The prisoners they took would form the diet of sacrificed warriors that Huizilopochtli demanded. For the dedication of Tenochtitlán's Templo Mayor (Great Temple) in 1487, the Aztec king Ahuizotl had 20,000 captives sacrificed.

The Triple Alliance brought most of central Mexico from the Gulf Coast to the Pacific (though not Tlaxcala) under its control. The total population of the empire's 38 provinces may have been about 5 million. The empire's purpose was to exact tribute of resources absent from the heartland – jade, turquoise, cotton, paper, tobacco, rubber, lowland fruits and vegetables, cacao, precious feathers – which were needed for the glorification of its elite and to support the many nonproductive servants of its war-oriented state.

A Historical Who's Who

Ahuizotl (d. 1502) Aztec emperor from 1486 to 1502, who expanded the empire.

Allende, Ignacio (1779-1811) One of the instigators of the independence struggle in 1810.

Alvarado, Pedro de (1486-1541) One of the leading conquistadors who accompanied Cortés; later he conquered Guatemala and El Salvador.

Axayacatl Aztec emperor from 1469 to 1481, father of Moctezuma II Xocoyotzin.

Calles, Plutarco Elias (1877-1945) Mexican Revolution leader, and president from 1924 to 1928.

Cárdenas, Cuauhtémoc (b. 1933) Son of Lázaro Cárdenas, he stood for the presidency as an opposition candidate in 1988 and is thought to have been cheated out of victory by PRI fraud; elected Mexico City mayor in 1997.

Cárdenas, Lázaro (1895-1970) A general and a statesman, he was considered a true president of the people, serving from 1934 to 1940. Cárdenas carried out major land reforms and expropriated foreign oil company operations.

Carlota Marie Charlotte Amélie (1840-1927) Daughter of King Leopold I of Belgium, she married Archduke Maximilian of Hapsburg (1857) and accompanied him to Mexico in 1864 to become empress. After her husband's execution in 1867 she lived on for 60 years, mentally unstable, a ward of the Vatican.

Carranza, Venustiano (1859-1920) Leader of the Constitutionalist side, opposed to Pancho Villa and Emiliano Zapata, in the revolution. President from 1917 to 1920, he was overthrown by an alliance led by Alvaro Obregón and assassinated, which effectively ended the revolution.

Ahuizotl's successor was Moctezuma II Xocoyotzin, a reflective character who believed – perhaps fatally – that the Spaniard Hernán Cortés, who arrived on the Gulf Coast in 1519, might be the feathered serpent god Quetzalcóatl, returned from the east to reclaim his throne (see Cortés & the Aztecs).

Economy & Society By 1519 Tenochtitlán and the adjoining Aztec city of Tlatelolco probably had more than 200,000 inhabitants, and the Valle de México as a whole probably well over a million. They were supported by a variety of intensive farming methods using only stone and wooden tools, including irrigation, terracing and lake and swamp reclamation.

The basic unit of Aztec society was the *calpulli*, consisting of a few dozen to a few hundred extended families, owning land communally. The Aztec king held absolute power but delegated important roles such as priest or tax collector to members of the *pilli* (nobles). Military leaders were usually *tecuhtli*, elite professional soldiers. Another special group was the *pochteca*, militarized merchants who helped extend the empire, brought goods to the capital and organized large markets, which were held daily in big towns. At the bottom of society were pawns (paupers who could sell themselves for a specified period), serfs and slaves.

Culture & Religion Tenochtitlán-Tlatelolco had hundreds of temple complexes. The greatest, located on and around modern Mexico City's Zócalo, had its main temple pyramid dedicated to Huizilopochtli and the rain god, Tláloc.

Cortés, Hernán (1485-1547) Spanish conquistador, sometimes known as Hernando or Fernando, who invaded Mexico and conquered the Aztecs. Much maligned today in Mexico, Cortés was the person chiefly responsible for introducing Hispanic civilization into Mexico.

Cuauhtémoc (c. 1495-1525) Last Aztec emperor, defeated and later executed by Cortés.

Cuitláhuac (d. 1520) Aztec emperor who succeeded Moctezuma II Xocoyotzin in 1520, but died the same year.

Díaz, Porfirio (1830-1915) Elected president in 1877 and reelected on numerous occasions on a slogan of 'order and progress,' he became a dictator who pursued public-works projects and encouraged foreign investment at the expense of the poor and of civil liberties. His policies precipitated the Mexican Revolution in 1910.

Díaz del Castillo, Bernal (1492-1581) Captain in the army of Cortés and author of *History of the Conquest of New Spain*, an eyewitness account of the Spanish conquest of Mexico and Guatemala.

Echeverría, Luis (1922) A left-leaning president from 1970 to 1976, he aided the agricultural sector and expanded rural social services, but his term was blighted by violent unrest and the beginnings of severe corruption.

Guerrero, Vicente (1782-1831) A leader in the later stages of the struggle for independence from Spain. Subsequently a liberal president but deposed by the conservative Anastasio Bustamante in 1829 and executed in 1831.

A Historical Who's Who continues on the following page ☞

A Historical Who's Who continued from previous page

Hidalgo y Costilla, Miguel (1753-1811) Parish priest of Dolores who sparked the independence struggle in 1810 with his famous *grito*, or call for independence.

Huerta, Victoriano (1854-1916) Leader of Madero's forces against a 1913 counter-revolution, he switched sides to become president himself. One of Mexico's most disliked and ineffective leaders, he was forced to resign in 1914.

Iturbide, Agustín de (1783-1824) An officer in the royalist army against Guerrero, he switched sides to negotiate with the rebels and achieve independence from Spain (1821). Iturbide set himself up as Emperor Agustín I of Mexico, but his reign lasted less than a year (1822-23).

Juárez, Benito (1806-72) A Zapotec Indian lawyer from Oaxaca, Juárez was prominent in the group of liberals who deposed Santa Anna and then passed laws against the church, which precipitated the three-year War of the Reform. Elected president in 1861, he was forced to flee because of the French takeover by Napoleon III and Emperor Maximilian. After the French left, Juárez resumed the presidency until his death.

Las Casas, Bartolomé de (1474-1566) Spanish missionary and a leading campaigner for Indian rights; Bishop of Chiapas in the 1540s.

Madero, Francisco (1873-1913) A liberal politician, Madero began the Mexican Revolution, leading the first major opposition to Porfirio Díaz and forcing him to resign. But he proved unable to quell factional fighting, and his presidential term (1911-13) ended in front of a firing squad.

Malinche, La (Doña Marina) (c. 1501-50) Cortés' Indian mistress and interpreter, she is considered to have had a major influence on Cortés' strategy in subduing the Aztecs.

Ferdinand Maximilian (1832-67) Hapsburg archduke sent by Napoleon III of France to rule as emperor of Mexico. His rule was short-lived (1864-67), and he was forced to surrender to Juárez's forces, who executed him by firing squad in 1867.

Moctezuma I Ilhuicamina Aztec emperor from 1440 to 1469.

Moctezuma II Xocoyotzin (1466-1520) Aztec emperor from 1502 to 1520. An indecisive leader, he failed to fend off the Spanish invasion led by Cortés.

Much of Aztec culture was drawn from earlier Mexican civilizations. They had writing, bark-paper books and the Calendar Round. They observed the heavens for astrological purposes. A routine of great ceremonies, many of them public, was performed by celibate priests. Typically these ceremonies would include sacrifices and masked dances or processions enacting myths.

The Aztecs believed they lived in a world whose predecessors had been destroyed – in their case the fifth world. The previous four each had been ended by the death of the sun and of humanity. Aztec human sacrifices were designed to keep the sun alive. Like the Maya, the Aztecs saw the world as having four directions, 13 heavens and nine hells. Those who died by drowning, leprosy, lightning, gout, dropsy or lung disease went to the paradisiac gardens of Tláloc, the god who had killed them; warriors who were sacrificed or died in battle, merchants killed while traveling far away, and women who died giving birth to their first child all went to heaven as companions of the sun; everyone else traveled for four years under the northern deserts, in the subterranean abode of the death god, Mictlantecuhtli, before reaching the ninth hell, where they vanished altogether.

Morelos y Pavón, José María (1765-1815) A liberal priest like Hidalgo, he assumed leadership of the independence movement after Hidalgo's execution and proved a brilliant leader and strategist, but was captured and executed in 1815.

Obregón, Alvaro (1880-1928) An enlightened farmer and revolutionary leader, he supported Madero, then Carranza, but rebelled when Carranza tried to keep power illegally. Obregón's presidency (1920-24) saw revolutionary reforms, especially in education. He was assassinated in 1928.

Salinas de Gortari, Carlos (b. 1948) President from 1988 to 1994, Salinas revived the economy, but his final year in power was clouded by a peasant uprising in Chiapas and the assassination of his chosen successor, Luis Donaldo Colosio. Salinas' reputation disintegrated after he left power when he was blamed for the 1994-95 peso crash and suspected of links with drug mobs. He took up residence in Ireland.

Santa Anna, Antonio López de (1794-1876) Santa Anna unseated Iturbide in 1823 and headed 11 of the 50 governments in Mexico's first 35 years of independence, a period of chronic economic decline and corruption. He was a leading player in conflicts with the USA in which Mexico lost huge tracts of territory.

Victoria, Guadalupe (1786-1843) Fought alongside Hidalgo and Morelos and contested (along with Santa Anna) Iturbide's accession as emperor. After Iturbide's removal in 1823, he was the first president (1824-28) of the Mexican republic.

Villa, Francisco 'Pancho' (1878-1923) Bandit in Chihuahua and Durango who became a charismatic fighting leader in the revolution but fell out with Carranza. He was assassinated in 1923.

Zapata, Emiliano (1879-1919) A peasant leader from Morelos state, Zapata was the most radical of the revolution leaders, fighting principally for the return of land to the peasants. He was at odds both with the conservative supporters of the old regime and their liberal opponents. After winning numerous battles (some in association with Pancho Villa), he was ambushed and killed in 1919 on Carranza's orders.

Zedillo Ponce de León, Ernesto (b. 1951) President since 1994, Zedillo steered Mexico out of the peso crisis and has taken serious measures to counter corruption and democratize Mexico. Perceived as unusually honest for a PRI president. ■

Other Postclassic Civilizations

On the eve of the Spanish conquest most Mexican civilizations shared deep similarities. Each was politically centralized and divided into classes, with many people occupied in specialist tasks, including professional priests. Agriculture was productive despite the lack of draft animals, metal tools and the wheel. Maize tortillas and *pozol* (maize gruel) were staple foods. Beans provided important protein, and a great variety of other crops were grown in different regions: squashes, tomatoes, chilies, avocados, peanuts, papayas, pineapples. Luxury foods for the elite included turkey, domesticated hairless dog, game, and chocolate drinks. War was widespread, often in connection with the need to take prisoners for sacrifice to a variety of powerful gods.

Yucatán The 'Toltec' phase at Chichén Itzá lasted until about 1200. After that, the city of Mayapán dominated most of the Yucatán Peninsula until the 15th century, when rebellions broke out and the peninsula became a quarreling-ground of numerous city-states, with a culture much decayed from Classic Mayan glories.

Oaxaca After about 1200 the remaining Zapotec settlements, such as Mitla and

Yagul, were increasingly dominated by the Mixtecs, famed metal smiths and potters from the uplands around the Oaxaca-Puebla border. Mixtec and Zapotec cultures became entangled before much of their territory fell to the Aztecs in the 15th and 16th centuries.

Gulf Coast The Totonacs, a people who may have occupied El Tajín in its later years, established themselves in much of Veracruz state. To their north, the Huastecs, who inhabited another web of probably independent statelets, flourished from 800 to 1200. In the 15th century the Aztecs subdued most of these areas.

The West One civilized people who avoided conquest by the Aztecs were the Tarascans, who ruled modern Michoacán from their capital, Tzintzuntzan, about 200 km west of Mexico City. They were skilled artisans and jewelers; fire and the moon were among their chief deities.

The Spanish Conquest

Ancient Mexican civilization, nearly 3000 years old, was shattered in two short years, from 1519 to 1521. A tiny group of invaders destroyed the Aztec empire, brought a new religion and reduced the native people to second-class citizens and slaves. So alien to each other were the newcomers and the Indians that each doubted whether the other was human (the Pope gave the Indians the benefit of the doubt in 1537).

From this traumatic encounter arose modern Mexico. Most Mexicans are mestizo, of mixed Indian (or African) and European blood, and thus descendants of both cultures. But while Cuauhtémoc, the last Aztec emperor, is now an official hero, Cortés, the leader of the Spanish conquerors, is a villain, and Indians who helped him are seen as traitors.

Early Expeditions The Spaniards had been in the Caribbean since Christopher Columbus arrived in 1492, with their main bases on the islands of Hispaniola and Cuba. Realizing that they had not reached the East Indies, they began looking for a passage through the land mass to their west but were distracted by tales of gold, silver and a rich empire there.

Early expeditions from Cuba, led by Francisco Hernández de Córdoba in 1517 and Juan de Grijalva in 1518, were driven back from Mexico's Gulf Coast by hostile Indians. In 1518 the governor of Cuba, Diego Velázquez, asked Hernán Cortés, a Spanish colonist on the island, to lead a new expedition westward. As Cortés gathered ships and men, Velázquez became uneasy about the costs and Cortés' loyalty and canceled the expedition. Cortés ignored him and set sail on February 15, 1519, with 11 ships, 550 men and 16 horses.

Cortés' cunning and Machiavellian tactics are legendary, but the Aztecs played military politics too. The story of their confrontation is one of the most bizarre in history.

Cortés & the Aztecs The Spaniards landed first at Cozumel, off the Yucatán Peninsula, then moved around the coast to Tabasco, where they defeated some hostile Indians and Cortés delivered the first of many lectures to Indians on the importance of Christianity and the greatness of King Carlos I of Spain. The Indians gave him 20 maidens, among them Doña Marina (La Malinche), who became his interpreter, aide and lover.

The expedition next put in near the present city of Veracruz. In the Aztec capital of Tenochtitlán, tales of 'towers floating on water' and bearing fair-skinned beings reached Moctezuma II, the Aztec god-king. Lightning struck a temple, a comet sailed through the night skies, and a bird 'with a mirror in its head' was brought to Moctezuma, who saw warriors in it. According to the Aztec calendar, 1519 would see the legendary god-king Quetzalcóatl's return from the east. But, unsure if Cortés really was the god returning, Moctezumaa tried to discourage Cortés from traveling to Tenochtitlán by sending messages about the difficult terrain and hostile tribes that lay between them.

The Spaniards were well received at the Totonac towns of Zempoala and Quiahuiztlán, which resented Aztec dominion. Cortés thus gained his first Indian allies. He set up a coastal settlement called Villa Rica de la Vera Cruz and then apparently scuttled his ships to prevent his men from retreating. Leaving about 150 men at Villa Rica, Cortés set off for Tenochtitlán. On the way he won over the Tlaxcalan Indians, who became valuable allies.

After considerable vacillation about how to deal with the Spaniards, Moctezuma finally invited Cortés to meet him, denying responsibility for an ambush at Cholula that had resulted in the Spanish massacring many of that town's inhabitants. The Spaniards and 6000 Indian allies thus approached the Aztecs' lake-island capital – a city bigger than any in Spain. Entering Tenochtitlán on November 8, 1519, along one of the causeways that linked it to the lakeshore, Cortés was met by Moctezuma, who was carried by nobles in a litter with a canopy of feathers and gold. The Spaniards were lodged – as befitted gods – in the palace of Axayacatl, Moctezuma's father.

Though entertained in luxury, the Spaniards were trapped. Some Aztec leaders advised Moctezuma to attack them, but Moctezuma hesitated and the Spaniards took him hostage instead. Moctezuma, believing Cortés a god, told his people he went willingly, but hostility rose in the city, aggravated by the Spaniards' destruction of Aztec idols.

The Fall of Tenochtitlán

After the Spaniards had been in Tenochtitlán about six months, Moctezuma informed Cortés that another fleet had arrived on the Veracruz coast. It was led by Pánfilo de Narváez, sent by Diego Velázquez to arrest Cortés. Cortés left 140 Spaniards under Pedro de Alvarado in Tenochtitlán and sped to the coast with his remaining forces. They routed Narváez's much bigger force, and most of the defeated men joined Cortés.

Hernán Cortés

But meanwhile, things boiled over in Tenochtitlán. Apparently fearing an attack, the Spaniards struck first and killed about 200 Aztec nobles trapped in a square during a festival. Cortés and his enlarged force returned to the Aztec capital and were allowed to rejoin their comrades – only then to come under fierce attack. Trapped in Axayacatl's palace, Cortés persuaded Moctezuma to try to pacify his people. According to one version, the king went up to the roof to address the crowds but was wounded by missiles and died soon afterward; other versions have it that the Spaniards killed him.

The Spaniards fled on the night of June 30, 1520, but several hundred of them, and thousands of their Indian allies, were killed on this Noche Triste (Sad Night). The survivors retreated to Tlaxcala, where they prepared for another campaign by building boats in sections, which could be carried across the mountains for a waterborne assault on Tenochtitlán. When the 900 Spaniards reentered the Valle de México they were accompanied by some 100,000 native allies. For the first time, the odds were in their favor.

Moctezuma had been replaced by his nephew, Cuitláhuac, who then died of smallpox, brought to Mexico by one of Narváez's soldiers. He was succeeded by another nephew, the 18-year-old Cuauhtémoc. The attack started in May 1521. Cortés had to resort to razing Tenochtitlán building by building. By August 13, 1521, the resistance ended. The captured Cuauhtémoc asked Cortés to kill him but was denied his request. (Cortés killed him later.)

The Colonial Era
The Encomienda System Establishing their headquarters at Coyoacán, on the southern shore of the lake, the Spaniards had Tenochtitlán rebuilt as the capital of Nueva España (New Spain), as the new colony was called. By 1524 virtually all the Aztec empire, plus outlying regions such as Colima, the Huasteca area and the Isthmus of Tehuantepec, had been brought under at least loose Spanish control.

To reward his soldiers, Cortés granted them *encomiendas* - rights to the labor or tribute of groups of Indians. The settlers were also supposed to convert, protect and 'civilize' their Indians, but in reality the system often produced little more than

slavery. In 1528 Cortés was himself granted 22 towns as encomiendas and given the title Marqués del Valle de Oaxaca by the Spanish Crown, but he was denied the role of governor. He returned to Spain in 1540 and died near Seville in 1547. The rest of the 16th century saw a long, eventually successful struggle by the Spanish crown to restrict the power of the conquistadors in the colony. By the 17th century the number of encomiendas had fallen drastically (partly because of an appalling decline in the Indian population); the system was abolished in the 18th century.

Nueva España In 1527 the Spanish king set up Nueva España's first *audiencia*, a high court with government functions. Its leader, Nuño de Guzmán, was among the worst of Mexican history's long list of corrupt, violent leaders. After a bloody expedition to western Mexico, from Michoacán up to Sonora, he was eventually recalled to Spain.

The second audiencia (1530-35) brought some order to the colony. The king subsequently appointed Antonio de Mendoza as Nueva España's first viceroy – his personal

A Different Sort of Liberator
The Spanish invaders of the New World acquired, and in many cases earned, a reputation for brutality toward the peoples of the Americas, giving rise to the notorious 'Black Legend' of their deliberate sadism.

While the Black Legend allowed northern Europeans such as the British to claim a moral high ground to which they probably had no right, there is no lack of evidence for the legend. For instance, the Spaniards imported vicious mastiffs for combat, intimidation, punishment, torture, blood sports, guard duty and tracking Indian fugitives. In the invaders' footsteps followed representatives of the Catholic Church, enforcing 'Christian principles' among peoples they regarded as pagans. Since those early days, the official church has often been identified with brutal authority, but a strong counter-current of thought began in early colonial times and has survived to the present.

Of several figures, the outstanding one was Father Bartolomé de Las Casas though he was at first glance an unlikely figure to protest maltreatment of the Indians. Born in Seville in 1474, he joined a 1502 expedition against the Indians of Higuey, on the island of Hispaniola; he soon held encomiendas there and in Cuba. However, he experienced a conversion that convinced him of the evils of the system and devoted the rest of his life to the cause of justice for the indigenous peoples of Spanish America.

Renouncing his encomiendas, Las Casas returned to Spain to argue passionately for reform of the abuses he had observed in the Indies. His polemical *Very Brief Account of the Destruction of the Indies* persuaded King Carlos I to enact the New Laws of 1542, which included a major reform of the encomienda system. Though the New Laws proved representative to govern the colony. Mendoza, who ruled for 15 years, brought badly needed stability, limited the worst exploitation of the Indians, encouraged missionary efforts and ensured steady revenue to the Spanish crown.

The subjection of the Yucatán Peninsula in the 1540s, by two men both named Francisco de Montejo, meant that the entire southern half of Mexico was in Spanish hands. Central America had been conquered in the 1520s by Spanish forces from Mexico and Panama. That left the huge 'Chichimec frontier' – roughly the area north of a line between modern Tampico and Guadalajara – inhabited by fierce seminomads. Big finds of silver in Zacatecas in the mid-1540s, followed by more finds at Guanajuato, San Luis Potosí and Pachuca, spurred Spanish attempts to subdue the north. They were not successful till the 1590s, when the Spanish offered the Chichimecs food and clothing in return for peace. By then Nueva España, the area governed by the viceroy in Mexico City, stretched from these northern frontiers to the border of Panama in the south, and by 1700 it would also officially include

Spain's Caribbean islands and the Philippines. In practice, Central America, the Caribbean and the Philippines were governed separately.

The northern borders were slowly extended by missionaries and a few settlers, and by the early 19th century Nueva España included most of the modern US states of Texas, New Mexico, Arizona, California, Utah and Colorado, though control there was often tenuous.

Indians & Missionaries Despite the efforts of Viceroy Mendoza and Mexico City's first bishop, Juan de Zumárraga, the populations of the conquered peoples declined disastrously, less because of harsh treatment than because of a series of plagues, many of them new diseases brought by the Spaniards. The Indian population of Nueva España fell from an estimated 25 million at the conquest to little over a million by 1605.

The Indians' only real allies were some of the monks who started arriving in Nueva España in 1523 to convert them. Many of the monks were compassionate, brave men; the Franciscan and Dominican orders

---

difficult to enforce, Las Casas continued to speak out against corrupt officials and encomenderos from his position as bishop of Chiapas (Mexico), and then as Protector of the Indians at the Spanish court in Madrid, until his death in 1566.

Before the court, the audacious Dominican reported one cacique's statement that if Spaniards went to heaven, the Indians would prefer hell. Las Casas went so far as to defend the practice of cannibalism, to advocate restitution for all the wealth that Spain had plundered from the Americas, and even to imply that the lands themselves should be returned to the Indians in the interests of good government:

When we entered there . . . would we have found such great unions of peoples in their towns and cities if they had lacked the order of a good way of life, peace, concord and justice?

While Las Casas never achieved his utopian goals, his advocacy undoubtedly mitigated some of the worst abuses against the Indians. In this sense, he was a role model for the Latin American activist clergy of recent decades, which, inspired by liberation theology, has worked to alleviate poverty and human rights abuses despite great personal risk. Las Casas was the original liberation theologist.

Las Casas also left valuable observations of Indian customs and history. His estimates of the dense population of Hispaniola, which according to his count was about 4 million, have been confirmed and even augmented by modern researchers. His is a broad and complex legacy with great modern relevance. ∎

Wayne Bernhardson

distinguished themselves by protecting the Indians from the colonists' worst excesses. One Dominican monk, Bartolomé de Las Casas, persuaded the king to enact new laws in the 1540s to protect the Indians. But when that nearly caused a rebellion among encomienda holders the laws went unenforced.

The monks' missionary work helped extend Spanish control over Mexico. By 1560 they had built more than 100 monasteries, some fortified, and had carried out millions of conversions. Under the second viceroy, Luis de Velasco, Indian slavery was abolished in the 1550s, to be partly replaced by black slavery. Forced labor on encomiendas was also stopped, but a new system of about 45 days' forced labor a year (the *cuatequil*) was introduced for all Indians. That system too was widely abused by the Spaniards until abolished about half a century later.

The Criollos In colonial times a person's place in society was determined by skin color, parentage and birthplace. Spanish-born colonists – known as *peninsulares* or, derisively, *gachupines* – were a minuscule part of the population but were at the top of the tree and considered nobility in Nueva España, however humble their status in Spain.

Next on the ladder were *criollos*, people born of Spanish parents in Nueva España. By the 18th century some criollos had acquired fortunes in mining, commerce, ranching or agriculture *(haciendas*, large landed estates, had begun to grow up as early as the 16th century). Not surprisingly, criollos sought political power commensurate with their wealth.

Below the criollos were the mestizos, and at the bottom of the pile were the remaining Indians and the Africans. Though the poor were, by the 18th century, paid for their labor, they were paid very little. Many were *peones*, bonded laborers tied by debt to their employers. Indians still had to pay tribute to the crown.

Aware of the threat to Nueva España from British and French expansion in

North America, King Carlos III (1759-88) sought to bring the colony under firmer control and improve the flow of funds to the crown. He reformed the colonial administration and, equally significant, expelled the Jesuits, whom he suspected of disloyalty, from the entire Spanish empire. The Jesuits in Nueva España had played major roles in missionary work, education and administration, and two-thirds of them were criollos.

Continuing its attack on the powerful Catholic Church in Nueva España, the Spanish crown in 1804 decreed the transfer of many church assets to the royal coffers. As a result the church had to call in many debts, which hit criollos hard and created widespread discontent.

The catalyst for rebellion came in 1808, when Napoleon Bonaparte occupied most of Spain, forcing King Carlos IV to abdicate. Napoleon put his brother Joseph on the Spanish throne, and direct Spanish control over Nueva España evaporated. Rivalry between peninsulares and criollos in the colony intensified.

Independence
War of Independence In 1810 a criollo coterie based in Querétaro began planning a rebellion. News of the plans leaked to the government, so the group acted immediately. On September 16 one of its members, Miguel Hidalgo y Costilla, parish priest of the town of Dolores, summoned his parishioners and issued his now-famous call to rebellion, the Grito de Dolores, whose exact words have been lost to history but whose gist was:

My children, a new dispensation comes to us this day. Are you ready to receive it? Will you be free? Will you make the effort to recover from the hated Spaniards the lands stolen from your forefathers 300 years ago? We must act at once . . . Long live Our Lady of Guadalupe! Death to bad government!

A mob formed and marched quickly on San Miguel, Guanajuato and Celaya, massacring peninsulares in Guanajuato. Over the next month and a half the rebels captured Zacatecas, San Luis Potosí and Valladolid (now called Morelia). On October 30 their army, numbering about 80,000, defeated loyalist forces at Las Cruces outside Mexico City, but Hidalgo hesitated to attack the capital. The rebels occupied Guadalajara but thereafter they were pushed northward by their opponents, their numbers shrank, and in 1811 their leaders, including Hidalgo, were captured and executed.

José María Morelos y Pavón, a former student of Hidalgo and also a parish priest, assumed the rebel leadership, blockading Mexico City for several months. Meanwhile he convened a congress at Chilpancingo, which adopted guiding principles for the independence movement. They included abolition of slavery and royal monopolies, universal male suffrage and popular sovereignty. Morelos was captured and executed in 1815, and his forces split into several guerrilla bands, the most successful of which was led by Vicente Guerrero in the state of Oaxaca.

Emperor Agustín I Sporadic fighting continued until 1821, when the royalist general Agustín de Iturbide defected during an offensive against Guerrero and conspired with the rebels to declare independence from Spain. Iturbide and Guerrero worked out the Plan de Iguala, which established three guarantees – religious dominance by the Catholic Church, a constitutional monarchy and equal rights for criollos and peninsulares. The plan won over all influential sections of society, and the incoming Spanish viceroy in 1821 agreed to Mexican independence. Iturbide, who had command of the army, soon arranged his own nomination to the throne, which he ascended as Emperor Agustín I in 1822.

The Mexican Republic

Iturbide was deposed in 1823 by a rebel army led by another opportunistic soldier, Antonio López de Santa Anna. A new constitution was drawn up in 1824, establishing a federal Mexican republic of 19 states and four territories. Guadalupe Victoria, a former independence fighter, became its first president. Mexico's southern boundary was the same as it is today, Central America having set up a separate federation in 1823. In the north, Mexico stretched as far as Nueva España had, to include much of what's now the southwestern USA.

Vicente Guerrero stood as a liberal candidate in the 1828 presidential elections and was defeated, but he eventually was awarded the presidency after another Santa Anna-led revolt. Guerrero abolished slavery but was deposed and executed by his conservative vice-president, Anastasio Bustamante. The struggle between liberals, who favored social reform, and conservatives, who opposed it, would be a constant theme in 19th-century Mexican politics.

Santa Anna Intervention in politics by ambitious military men was also becoming a habit. Santa Anna, a national hero after defeating a small Spanish invasion force at Tampico in 1829, overthrew Bustamante and was elected president in 1833. Thus began 22 years of chronic instability in which the presidency changed hands 36 times; 11 of those terms went to Santa Anna. Economic decline and corruption became entrenched, and Santa Anna quickly turned into a conservative. His main contributions to Mexico were manifestations of his megalomaniacal personality. Most memorably, he had his amputated, mummified leg (which he lost in an 1838 battle with the French) disinterred in 1842 and paraded through Mexico City.

Santa Anna is also remembered for helping to lose large chunks of Mexican territory to the USA. North American settlers in Texas, initially welcomed by the Mexican authorities, grew restless and declared Texas independent in 1836. Santa Anna led an army north and wiped out the defenders of an old mission called the Alamo in San Antonio, but he was routed on the San Jacinto River a few weeks later. Texan independence was recognized by the USA, but not by Mexico.

In 1845 the US congress voted to annex Texas, and US President Polk demanded further Mexican territory. That led, in 1846, to the Mexican-American War, in which US troops captured Mexico City. At the end of the war, by the Treaty of Guadalupe Hidalgo (1848), Mexico ceded modern Texas, California, Utah, Colorado, and most of New Mexico and Arizona to the USA. A Santa Anna government sold the remaining bits of New Mexico and Arizona to the USA in 1853 for US$10 million, in the Gadsden Purchase. This loss precipitated the liberal-led Revolution of Ayutla, which ousted Santa Anna for good in 1855.

Mexico almost lost the Yucatán Peninsula, too, in the so-called War of the Castes in the late 1840s, when the Mayan Indians rose up against their criollo overlords and narrowly failed to drive them off the peninsula.

Juárez & the French Intervention The new liberal government ushered in the era known as the Reform, in which it set about dismantling the conservative state that had developed in Mexico. The key figure was Benito Juárez, a Zapotec Indian from Oaxaca who had become a leading lawyer and politician. Laws requiring the church to sell much of its property helped precipitate the internal War of the Reform (1858-61) between the liberals, with their 'capital' at Veracruz, and conservatives, based in Mexico City. The liberals eventually won, and Juárez became president in 1861. But the country was a shambles and heavily in debt to Britain, France and Spain. These three countries sent a joint force to Mexico to collect their debts, but France's hawkish Napoleon III decided to go further and take over Mexico, leading to yet another war.

Though the French were defeated at Puebla by General Ignacio Zaragoza on May 5, 1862, they took Puebla a year later and went on to capture Mexico City. In 1864 Napoleon invited the Austrian archduke, Maximilian of Hapsburg, to become emperor of Mexico. The French army drove Juárez and his government into the provinces.

Maximilian and Empress Carlota entered Mexico City on June 12, 1864, and moved into the Castillo de Chapultepec. But their reign was brief. In 1866, under pressure from the USA, Napoleon began to withdraw the troops who sustained Maximilian's rule. Maximilian – in some ways a noble, tragic figure who refused to abandon his task even after Napoleon abandoned him – was defeated in May 1867 at Querétaro by forces loyal to Juárez and was executed there by firing squad on June 19.

Juárez immediately set an agenda of economic and educational reform. The education system was completely revamped, and for the first time, schooling was made mandatory. A railway was built between Mexico City and Veracruz. A rural police force, the *rurales*, was organized to secure the transport of cargo through Mexico.

The Porfiriato Juárez died in 1872. When his successor, Sebastián Lerdo de Tejada, stood for reelection in 1876, Porfirio Díaz, an ambitious liberal from Oaxaca, launched a rebellion on the pretext that presidents should not serve more than one term of office. (At the time, presidential terms were four years long.) The following year Díaz, the sole candidate, won the presidential elections, and for the next 33 years he ran Mexico, brushing aside old principles to serve six successive presidential terms from 1884. Díaz brought Mexico into the industrial age, launching public works projects throughout the country, particularly in Mexico City. Telephone and telegraph lines were strung, the railway network grew and spread, and stability attracted foreign investors.

Díaz kept Mexico free of the civil wars that had plagued it for more than 60 years, but at a cost. Political opposition, free elections and a free press were banned. Many of Mexico's resources went into foreign ownership, peasants were cheated out of their land by new laws, workers suffered appalling conditions, and the country was kept quiet by a ruthless army and the now-feared rurales. Land and wealth became concentrated with a small minority. Some hacienda owners amassed truly vast landholdings – in Chihuahua Don Luis Terrazas, for instance, had at least 14,000 sq km – and commensurate political power. Many rural workers were tied by debt to their bosses, just like their colonial forebears.

In the early 1900s a liberal opposition formed, but it was forced into exile in the USA. In 1906 the most important group of exiles issued a new liberal plan for Mexico from St Louis, Missouri. Their actions precipitated strikes throughout Mexico – some violently suppressed – which led, in late 1910, to the Mexican Revolution.

The Mexican Revolution

The revolution was no clear-cut struggle between oppression and liberty, but a 10-year period of shifting allegiances between a spectrum of leaders in which successive attempts to create stable governments were wrecked by new outbreaks of devastating fighting.

Madero & Zapata In 1910 Francisco Madero, a wealthy liberal from Coahuila, campaigned for the presidency and probably would have won if Díaz hadn't jailed him. On his release Madero drafted the Plan de San Luis Potosí, which called for the nation to rise in revolution on November 20. The call was heard, and the revolution spread quickly across the country. When revolutionaries under the leadership of Francisco 'Pancho' Villa took Ciudad Juárez in May 1911, Díaz resigned. Madero was elected president in November 1911.

But Madero was unable to contain the factions fighting for power throughout the country. The basic divide that would dog the whole revolution was between liberal reformers like Madero and more radical leaders, such as Emiliano Zapata, from the state of Morelos, who was fighting for the transfer of hacienda land to the peasants with the cry *'Tierra y Libertad!'* ('Land

and Liberty!'). Madero sent federal troops to Morelos to disband Zapata's forces, which triggered the birth of the Zapatista movement.

In November 1911 Zapata promulgated the Plan de Ayala, calling for restoration of all land to the peasants. Zapatistas won several battles against government troops in central Mexico. Other forces of varied political complexion took up local causes elsewhere. Soon all Mexico was plunged into military chaos.

Huerta In February 1913 two conservative leaders – Félix Díaz, nephew of Porfirio, and Bernardo Reyes – were sprung from prison in Mexico City and commenced a counterrevolution that brought 10 days of fierce fighting, the 'Decena Trágica,'to the capital. Thousands were killed or wounded, and many buildings destroyed. The fighting ended only after the US ambassador to Mexico, Henry Lane Wilson, negotiated for Madero's general, Victoriano Huerta, to switch to the rebel side and help depose Madero's government. Huerta himself became president; Madero and his vice president, José María Pino Suárez, were executed.

But Huerta only fomented greater strife. In March 1913 three revolutionary leaders in the north united against him under the Plan de Guadalupe: Venustiano Carranza, a Madero supporter, in Coahuila; Pancho Villa, in Chihuahua; and Alvaro Obregón, in Sonora. Zapata too was fighting against Huerta. Terror reigned in the countryside as Huerta's troops fought, pillaged and plundered. Finally he was defeated and forced to resign in July 1914.

Constitutionalists vs Radicals Carranza called the victorious factions to a conference in Aguascalientes, but when he failed to unify them, war broke out again. This time Obregón and the far-from-radical Carranza – who formed the 'Constitutionalists,' with their capital at Veracruz – were pitted against the populist Villa and the radical Zapata. But Villa and Zapata, despite a famous meeting in

Mexico City, never formed a serious alliance, and the fighting became increasingly anarchic. Villa never recovered from a defeat by Obregón in the battle of Celaya (1915), and Carranza eventually emerged the victor, to form a government that was recognized by the USA. A new reformist constitution, still largely in force today, was enacted in 1917.

In Morelos the Zapatistas continued to demand reforms. Carranza had Zapata assassinated at Chinameca on April 10, 1919, but the following year Obregón turned against him and, together with fellow Sonorans Adolfo de la Huerta and Plutarco Elías Calles, raised an army, chased Carranza out of office and had him assassinated.

The 10 years of violent civil war cost an estimated 1.5 to 2 million lives – roughly one in eight Mexicans – and shattered the economy.

From Revolution to WWII
Obregón & Calles As president (1920-24), Obregón turned to national reconstruction. More than 1000 rural schools were built, and some land was redistributed from big landowners to the peasants. Education minister José Vasconcelos commissioned top artists, such as Diego Rivera, David Alfaro Siqueiros and José Clemente Orozco, to decorate important public buildings with large, vivid murals on social and historical themes.

Plutarco Elías Calles, who succeeded Obregón, built 2000 rural schools and distributed more land to small farmers. He also closed monasteries, convents and church schools, deported foreign priests and nuns, and prohibited religious processions. These measures precipitated the bloody Cristero Rebellion by Catholics, which lasted until 1929.

At the end of Calles' term, in 1928, Obregón was elected president again but was assassinated by a Cristero. Calles reorganized his supporters to found the Partido Nacional Revolucionario (PNR, National Revolutionary Party), the initiator of a long tradition of official acronyms.

Cárdenas In 1934 Lázaro Cárdenas, former governor of Michoacán, won the presidency with the support of the PNR and stepped up the reform program. Cárdenas redistributed almost 200,000 sq km of land – nearly double the amount distributed by his predecessors since 1920 – mostly through the establishment of *ejidos* (peasant landholding cooperatives). Thus, most of Mexico's arable land had been redistributed, and nearly one-third of the population had received land. Cárdenas also set up the million-member Confederación de Trabajadores Mexicanos (CTM, Confederation of Mexican Workers, a labor organization) and boldly expropriated foreign oil-company operations in Mexico (1938), forming Petróleos Mexicanos (Pemex, the Mexican Petroleum Company). After the oil expropriation foreign investors avoided Mexico, which slowed the economy.

Cárdenas reorganized the PNR into the Partido de la Revolución Mexicana (PRM, Party of the Mexican Revolution), a coalition of representatives from four sectors of Mexican society – agrarian, military, labor and the people at large.

The transition from Cárdenas to Manuel Ávila Camacho tipped the scales toward more conservative government at the end of the first two postrevolutionary decades. WWII was the key event of Camacho's presidency (1940-46). He sent Mexican troops to help the Allies in the Pacific and supplied raw materials and labor to the USA. The drying up of manufactured imports proved a boost to Mexican industry and exports.

After WWII
As the Mexican economy expanded, new economic and political groups demanded influence in the ruling PRM. To recognize their inclusion, the party was renamed the Partido Revolucionario Institucional (PRI, Institutional Revolutionary Party, 'El pree'). President Miguel Alemán (1946-52) continued development by building hydroelectric stations, irrigation projects and UNAM, the

National Autonomous University of Mexico, and by expanding the road system. Pemex grew dramatically and, with the rise of other industries, spawned some of Mexico's worst corruption.

Alemán's successor, Adolfo Ruiz Cortines (1952-58), began to confront a new problem – explosive population growth. In two decades Mexico's population had doubled, and many people began migrating to urban areas to search for work. Adolfo López Mateos (1958-64), one of Mexico's most popular post-WWII presidents, redistributed 120,000 more sq km of land to small farmers, nationalized foreign utility concessions, implemented social welfare and rural education programs, and launched health campaigns. These programs were helped by strong economic growth, particularly in tourism and exports.

Unrest, Boom & Bust

President Gustavo Díaz Ordaz (1964-70) was a conservative with an agenda that emphasized business. Though he fostered education and tourism and the economy grew by 6% a year during his term, he is better remembered for his repression of civil liberties. He sacked the president of the PRI, Carlos Madrazo, who had tried to democratize the party. University students in Mexico City were the first to express their outrage with the Díaz Ordaz administration.

Discontent came to a head in the months preceding the 1968 Mexico City Olympic games, the first ever held in a Third World country. Single-party rule, restricted freedom of speech, and spending on the Olympics were among the objects of protest. More than half a million people rallied in Mexico City's Zócalo on August 27; in mid-September troops seized the UNAM campus to break up a student occupation. On October 2, with the Olympics only a few days away, a rally was organized in Tlatelolco, Mexico City. The government sent in heavily armed troops and police. Several hundred people died in the ensuing massacre.

President Luis Echeverría (1970-76) sought to distribute wealth more equitably than it had been in the past. He instituted government credit for the troubled agricultural sector, launched family-planning programs and expanded rural clinics and the social security system. But unrest increased, and there was a guerrilla insurrection in Guerrero, all fueled partly by the corruption that was now rife among government officials.

José López Portillo (1976-82) presided during the jump in world oil prices caused by the OPEC embargo of the early 1970s. He announced that Mexico's main problem now was how to manage its enormous prosperity: on the strength of the country's vast oil reserves, international institutions began lending Mexico billions of dollars. Then, just as suddenly, a world oil glut sent prices plunging. Mexico's worst recession for decades began.

Miguel de la Madrid (1982-88) was largely unsuccessful in coping with the problems he inherited. The population continued to grow at Malthusian rates; the economy made only weak progress, crushed by the huge debt burden from the oil boom years; and the social pot continued to simmer. Things were not helped by the 1985 Mexico City earthquake, which killed at least 10,000 people, destroyed hundreds of buildings and caused more than US$4 billion in damage.

In this climate of economic helplessness and rampant corruption, dissent grew on both the left and the right and even within the PRI. There were sometimes violent protests over the PRI's now-routine electoral fraud and strong-arm tactics.

Salinas

Discontent mounted to the point where, in 1988, it finally made an impact on the presidential election. Cuauhtémoc Cárdenas, son of 1930s president Lázaro Cárdenas, walked out of the PRI to stand as a presidential candidate for the new, center-left Frente Democrático Nacional (FDN, National Democratic Front). It's widely believed that more voters chose Cárdenas than the PRI candidate, Carlos Salinas de Gortari, but as counting proceeded after the voting, a mysterious computer failure halted the tallying of results. In the end Cárdenas was awarded 31% of the vote, while Salinas received 50.7% – still the lowest up to that point of any PRI candidate.

Reform Harvard-educated Salinas (1988-94) set about transforming Mexico's state-dominated economy into one of private enterprise and free trade. The apex of his program was NAFTA, the North American Free Trade Agreement, known to Mexicans as the TLC, or Tratado de Libre Comercio. The product of several years of negotiations, NAFTA came into effect on January 1, 1994.

Salinas also brought an end to the conflict between the Mexican state and the Catholic Church, which since 1917 had been officially banned from owning property or running schools or newspapers. Mexico and the Vatican established full diplomatic relations in 1992.

Drugs Mexico had long been a marijuana and heroin producer, but a huge impetus was given to its drug gangs by a mid-1980s US crackdown on drug shipments from Colombia through the Caribbean to Florida. Three main Mexican cartels emerged: the Pacific or Tijuana cartel, headed by the Arellano Félix brothers; the (Ciudad) Juárez cartel, run by Amado Carrillo Fuentes; and the Gulf cartel of Juan García

Family Affairs – A Salinas Postscript

Early in 1995, Raúl Salinas de Gortari, brother of then ex-president Carlos, was arrested on suspicion of masterminding the murder of José Francisco Ruiz Massieu. The dead man, it emerged, had once been married to Raúl's (and Carlos') sister Adriana. Some said he and Raúl had fallen out over the divorce. Others posited deeper motives. There was talk of Raúl being linked to Mexico's Gulf drug cartel.

Following Raúl's arrest, Carlos Salinas de Gortari, vilified for the economic crisis that Mexico had plunged into soon after he left office, went on a brief hunger strike in Monterrey, demanding that new president Ernesto Zedillo clear his name. When Zedillo failed to comply, Carlos fled to the USA, then Canada, then the Caribbean.

In November 1995 Swiss investigators announced they had found more than US$80 million in Swiss bank accounts controlled by Raúl. The widespread suspicion was that this money had come from selling influence with his brother's presidential administration and/or selling protection to Mexican drug lords. In 1997 Mexican authorities announced they were investigating his alleged drug links. They also have reportedly investigated his possible connections to the 1994 murder of Luis Donaldo Colosio.

Carlos, meanwhile, had resurfaced in Dublin, Ireland – a country that has no extradition treaty with Mexico. Carlos too is suspected by many of having mingled with or protected drug chiefs for vast sums of money, though like Raúl he has denied any such links. In 1996 and '97 Carlos was questioned by Mexican agents investigating the Colosio and Ruiz Massieu murders.

A hint of what it might all add up to was provided in April 1997, when Mexican prosecutors released testimony suggesting that Carlos Salinas took part in a cover-up of Raúl Salinas' alleged role in the Ruiz Massieu murder. One conveniently simple theory is that both Salinas brothers *and* their sister *and* their father *and* Ruiz Massieu and *his* brother Mario were all in it together with the top Mexican drug lords.

And Colosio? One story has it that before his murder he had broken with Salinas but refused to give up his candidacy. Another is that his murder was a drug killing of some kind (either because Colosio was feared by the drug lords or because he was somehow mixed up with them – though it should be said that the latter version has strident detractors). Yet another story is that the PRI old guard just could not contemplate the prospect of a reforming Mr Clean, which Colosio had promised to be, at the helm. ■

Ábrego. These cartels bought up politicians, top antidrug officials, even whole police forces. Several big traffickers were caught but then released by corrupt police or judges.

Rebellion Mexican opinion, meanwhile, was divided over Salinas' economic policies. The middle class had benefited from them, but fears for the poor were in the background of the event that kicked off the disastrous final year of Salinas' presidency: the uprising in Chiapas by the Ejército Zapatista de Liberación Nacional (EZLN, Zapatista National Liberation Army). The day NAFTA took effect, this group of 2000 or so Indian-peasant rebels shocked Mexico by taking over San Cristóbal de Las Casas and other towns. They were fighting to end decades of evictions, discrimination and disappearances in their impoverished state, on which a wealthy minority had maintained a near-feudal grip since before the Mexican Revolution. About 150 people were killed in the uprising.

Though the EZLN was driven out of the towns within a few days, the uprising struck a chord nationally among all who felt that the Mexican system prevented real social or political change. The rebels were able to retreat under a truce to a base in the Chiapas jungle, and the uprising precipitated a social upheaval in Chiapas, with peasants forcibly taking over hundreds of estates, farms and ranches. The rebel leader, a balaclava-clad figure known as Subcomandante Marcos, became something of a national folk hero.

Assassinations & Elections Things took a further turn for the worse when Luis Donaldo Colosio, Salinas' chosen successor as PRI presidential candidate, was assassinated in Tijuana in March 1994. Conspiracy theories abound about the killing, but by 1997 nobody except one man who had been captured on the spot (and later sentenced to 43 years in jail) had been convicted.

After the EZLN uprising Salinas pushed through some electoral reforms against ballot-stuffing and double voting, and the 1994 presidential election was regarded as the cleanest ever – though on polling day at least a million voters still mysteriously found they were not on the electoral roll. The left-wing Partido de la Revolución Democrática (PRD, Democratic Revolution Party) claimed that thousands of its members had been murdered during Salinas' term. The PRI had also, no doubt, won many votes through subsidies, bribes, threats and its control of trade unions and peasant organizations.

Colosio's replacement as PRI candidate, 43-year-old Ernesto Zedillo, won the election with 50% of the vote. Before he took office in December, another PRI chief, José Francisco Ruiz Massieu, the party's secretary-general, was assassinated in September outside a Mexico City hotel.

Zedillo
Peso Crash Within days of President Zedillo's taking office in late 1994 the peso suddenly collapsed, leaving Mexico almost bankrupt and dependent on an emergency multibillion-dollar credit package from US and international financial bodies. The crisis was made worse by Zedillo's inexpert handling of it, but its roots lay in actions taken (or not taken) earlier, by Salinas.

The peso crash brought on a rapid recession that hit everyone hard, and the poor hardest, leading to, among other things, a big increase in crime, intensified discontent with the PRI, and large-scale Mexican immigration to the US. By 1997 more than 2.5 million Mexicans a year, it is estimated, were entering the US illegally despite intensified US efforts to keep them out. Zedillo pursued policies that, fairly quickly, started to bring Mexico out of recession, though the recovery wasn't quickly apparent to very many Mexicans.

Political Reform Zedillo is an uncharismatic figure but is perceived in Mexico to be more honest than his predecessors.

Hailing from outside the country's circle of privileged political families, he owes few debts to Mexico's corrupt traditional ruling elite. The arrest of Raúl Salinas, the wholesale replacement of the notoriously partial supreme court, and the sacking of more than 1000 corrupt police were early signs that Zedillo might work serious change. Zedillo set his sights on genuine democratic reform and set up a new, independent electoral apparatus that achieved Mexico's freest and fairest elections since 1911 when voting took place in 1997 for the federal Chamber of Deputies and the Mexico City mayoralty. These elections, like many others during Zedillo's term, went badly for the PRI (see Government & Politics).

The human rights picture, however, seems as bleak as ever. The most notorious incident was the 1995 Aguas Blancas massacre of 17 peasant political activists by police in Guerrero state. Mexican and foreign human rights organizations frequently draw attention to continuing abuses, including torture and executions by troops and police seeking EPR rebels (see below) in Oaxaca state.

More Rebels In Chiapas Zedillo at first negotiated with the EZLN, but then in February 1995 he sent in the army to 'arrest' Subcomandante Marcos and other leaders. They escaped deeper into the jungle, accompanied by thousands of peasants. On-and-off negotiations eventually brought an agreement on indigenous rights in February 1996 (see the Zapatistas sidebar in the Tabasco & Chiapas chapter), but Zedillo balked at turning the agreement into this law. In response, the Zapatistas refused to move on to further talks that could lead to formal peace.

In mid-1996 a new left-wing rebel movement, the Ejército Popular Revolucionario (EPR, People's Revolutionary Army) emerged in the impoverished southern states of Guerrero and Oaxaca. After a wave of attacks against police and military posts in several states, in which some 20 people died, the EPR seemed to revert to propaganda and publicity. One effect of its activities was a further intensification of the military presence already evident around the country as a result of the Zapatista uprising and the drug problem.

More Drugs By 1997 most illegal drugs entering the USA were coming through Mexico – an annual flow of about 770 tons of cocaine, 7700 tons of marijuana, and six tons of heroin, plus quantities of methamphetamine (speed). The Mexican cartels were taking up to half the Colombian cocaine shipments themselves and rapidly developing their own production of heroin and speed. The drug gangs' profits amounted to US$15 billion or more a year.

Zedillo brought the armed forces into the fight against the drug mobs, but in 1997 his trusted top drug fighter, General Jesús Gutiérrez Rebollo, was himself arrested on charges of being in the pay of the Juárez mob. There were some successes. In 1996 Juan García Ábrego, of the Gulf cartel, was captured, deported to the US and jailed for life in Houston. In 1997 Amado Carrillo Fuentes, head of the Juárez mob, died under mysterious circumstances in a Mexico City hospital after plastic surgery – but his death only unleashed a succession war, which brought dozens of murders. Meanwhile, other traffickers stayed free because they were tipped off about raids or allowed to slip through the fingers of corrupt officials. Numerous drug investigators, judges and witnesses were murdered, most notoriously in Tijuana.

GEOGRAPHY

Covering almost 2 million sq km, Mexico is big: it's nearly 3500 km as the crow flies from Tijuana, in the northwest, to Cancún in the southeast, or about 4600 km by road. To travel from the US border at Ciudad Juárez to Mexico City, you must ride 1900 km (about 26 hours by bus). From Mexico City to the Guatemalan border at Ciudad Cuauhtémoc is 1200 km.

Mexico curves from northwest to southeast, narrowing to the Isthmus of Tehuantepec in the south and then continuing northeast to the Yucatán Peninsula. To the west and south it's bordered by the Pacific Ocean. The Gulf of California (also called the Sea of Cortés) lies between the mainland and Baja California, the world's longest peninsula – 1300 km of mountains, deserts, plains and beaches. Mexico's east coast is bordered by the Gulf of Mexico all the way from the US border to the northeastern tip of the Yucatán Peninsula. The eastern Yucatán Peninsula faces the Caribbean Sea.

Mexico has a 3326-km northern border with the US, the eastern half of which is formed by the Río Bravo del Norte (Rio Grande, as it's called in the US). In the south and southeast are a 962-km border with Guatemala and a 250-km border with Belize.

Topography
Altiplano Central & Sierra Madre
Northern and central Mexico – as far south as Mexico City – have coastal plains on the east and west and two north-south mountain ranges framing a group of broad central plateaus known as the Altiplano Central.

On the west coast a relatively dry coastal plain stretches south from Mexicali, on the US border, almost to Tepic, in Nayarit state. Inland from this plain is the rugged Sierra Madre Occidental, a mountain range crossed by only two main transport routes – the Barranca del Cobre (Copper Canyon) railway, from Chihuahua to Los Mochis, and the dramatic highway from Durango to Mazatlán.

The Altiplano Central is divided into northern and central parts, themselves split by minor ranges, and varies in altitude from about 1000 meters in the north to more than 2000 meters in the center of the country. The northern plateau extends northward into Texas and New Mexico. The central plateau is mostly a series of rolling hills and broad valleys and includes some of the best farm and ranch land in the country.

The altiplano is bound on the east by the Sierra Madre Oriental, a mountain range that runs as far south as the state of Puebla

and includes peaks as high as 3700 meters. The Gulf Coast plain is an extension of a similar coastal plain in Texas. In northeastern Mexico the plain is wide and semi-marshy near the coast, but it narrows as it nears the port of Veracruz.

Cordillera Neovolcánica
South of the Altiplano Central and the two Sierra Madres, the Cordillera Neovolcánica runs east-west across the country. This range includes the active volcanoes Popocatépetl (5452 meters) and Volcán de Fuego de Colima (3960 meters), as well as Mexico's other highest peaks – Pico de Orizaba (5611 meters) and Iztaccíhuatl (5286 meters) – and its youngest volcano, Paricutín (2800 meters), which appeared only in 1943. Mexico City lies in the heart of the volcanic country, 60 km northwest of Popocatépetl.

The South
South of Cabo Corrientes (in Jalisco state, west of Guadalajara), the Pacific lowlands narrow to a thin strip. The main mountain range in the south of Mexico is the Sierra Madre del Sur, which stretches across the states of Guerrero and Oaxaca to the low Isthmus of Tehuantepec, the narrowest part of Mexico at just 220 km wide. The north side of the isthmus is part of a wide, marshy plain stretching from Veracruz to the Yucatán Peninsula.

In the southernmost state, Chiapas, the Pacific lowlands are backed by the Sierra Madre de Chiapas, behind which is the Río Grijalva basin and then the Chiapas highlands. East of these highlands is a tropical rainforest area stretching into northern Guatemala. The jungle melts into a region of tropical savanna on the flat, low Yucatán Peninsula and, at the tip of the peninsula, an arid desertlike region.

CLIMATE
The tropic of Cancer cuts across Mexico north of Mazatlán and Tampico. South of the tropic it's hot and humid along the coastal plains on either side of the country. Inland, at higher elevations, such as at Guadalajara or Mexico City, the climate is

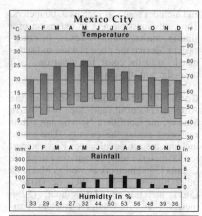

Mexico City

Temperature

Rainfall

Humidity in %

33	29	24	27	32	44	50	53	56	48	39	36

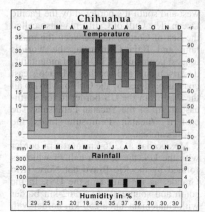

Chihuahua

Temperature

Rainfall

Humidity in %

29	25	21	20	18	24	35	37	36	30	30	30

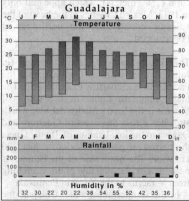

Guadalajara

Temperature

Rainfall

Humidity in %

32	30	22	20	22	38	54	55	52	42	35	36

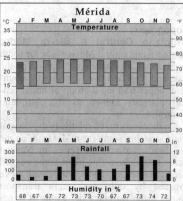

Mérida

Temperature

Rainfall

Humidity in %

68	67	67	72	73	73	70	67	67	73	74	72

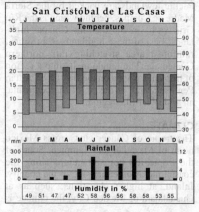

San Cristóbal de Las Casas

Temperature

Rainfall

Humidity in %

49	51	47	47	52	58	56	56	58	58	53	55

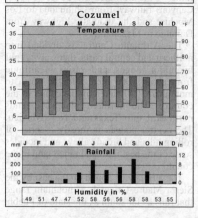

Cozumel

Temperature

Rainfall

Humidity in %

49	51	47	47	52	58	56	56	58	58	53	55

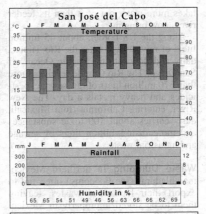

San José del Cabo

Temperature

Rainfall

| Humidity in % |
| 65 | 65 | 54 | 51 | 49 | 46 | 56 | 63 | 66 | 66 | 62 | 69 |

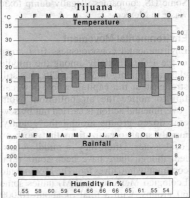

Tijuana

Temperature

Rainfall

| Humidity in % |
| 55 | 58 | 60 | 59 | 64 | 66 | 66 | 66 | 65 | 61 | 55 | 54 |

much more dry and temperate, and the mountain peaks are often capped with snow.

The hot, wet season is May to October, with the hottest and wettest months falling between June and September for most of the country. Low-lying coastal areas are wetter and hotter than elevated inland ones, but there's considerable local variation: among coastal resorts, Acapulco receives twice as much rain as Mazatlán does (nearly all of it, more than 170 cm, from May to October); Acapulco and Cancún share similar temperatures, but Mazatlán and Cozumel are a few degrees cooler.

Mexico City's rainfall and temperatures are both on the low side for an inland city: Taxco and Pátzcuaro both get about twice as much rain as the capital and are a few degrees warmer; Oaxaca is also a few degrees warmer but similarly dry.

Northwestern Mexico and inland northern areas are drier than the rest of the country. In the east rainfall is particularly high on the eastern slopes of the Sierra Madre Oriental and on the northern side of the Isthmus of Tehuantepec. North winds can make inland northern Mexico decidedly chilly in winter, with temperatures sometimes approaching freezing.

ECOLOGY & ENVIRONMENT

Bridging temperate and tropical regions and lying in the latitudes that contain most of the world's deserts, Mexico has an enormous range of natural environments. Its rugged, mountainous topography adds to the variety by creating countless microclimates, which support one of the most diverse arrays of plant and animal species of any country on the planet. Yet many of Mexico's species are endangered. The human impact on Mexico's environment has been enormous, and the country has a litany of environmental problems as long as a rain forest liana – problems that threaten not only the fauna and flora but the people too.

Problems

Mexico's environmental crises are typical of a poor country with an exploding population struggling to develop in the second half of the 20th century. While city-based industrial growth, intensive chemical-based agriculture and forest clearance were seen as paths toward prosperity, there was a lack both of awareness about their environmental effects and of money or will to mitigate them.

Most infamous is the pollution from traffic and industry, which chokes the air of Mexico's ever-growing cities, above all Mexico City, where residents are plagued by a host of smog-related health problems (see the sidebar Mexico City's Air, in the Mexico City chapter).

Forests Before the Spanish conquest, about two-thirds of Mexico was forested, from cool pine-clad highlands to tropical jungle. Today somewhere around 15% (or 300,000 sq km) is forested, and this is being reduced at a rate of about 5000 sq km a year for grazing, logging and new farming settlements. The southern states of Chiapas and Tabasco are said to have lost more than half their tropical jungles since 1980, and by some estimates only 2% of Mexico's tropical jungles remain.

Erosion An estimated 13% of Mexican soil is severely eroded (with more than 1000 tons of soil lost per sq kilometer per year in such areas), and 66% is moderately eroded. Erosion is mainly the result of deforestation followed by cattle grazing or intensive agriculture on unsuitable terrain. Some 2000 sq km of fertile land are reckoned to be desertified annually. In the Mixteca area of Oaxaca, around 80% of the arable land is gone.

Agricultural Pollution Some rural areas and watercourses have been contaminated by careless, excessive use of chemical pesticides and defoliants, including some that have been banned in other countries. Agricultural workers have suffered health problems related to these chemicals as well.

Water Sewage and industrial and agricultural wastes contaminate most Mexican rivers, and some have turned into real health hazards. The Río Pánuco carries some 2000 tons of untreated sewage a day, mainly from Mexico City, which gets rid of it via a 50-km tunnel.

Mexico City, despite extracting groundwater at a rate that causes the earth to sink all over the city, has to pump about one-third of its water up from outside the Valle de México. One of the rivers from which the capital and other cities take water is the Lerma, which receives raw sewage and industrial effluent from 95 towns on its way to the Lago de Chapala, Mexico's biggest natural lake, near Guadalajara. Chapala itself is shrinking because Guadalajara takes more water out of it than its feeder rivers now bring in.

Along the US border, about 45 million liters of raw sewage enter the Río Tijuana daily and flow into the Pacific Ocean off San Diego. The Rio Grande receives more than 370 million liters of raw sewage, pesticides and heavy metals a day. The New River, entering California from Mexicali, daily carries about 100 toxic substances and more than 1 billion liters of sewage and industrial waste.

Waste Dumping In northern Mexico, maquiladoras (see Economy) often fail to export their hazardous wastes, leaving them to be stored improperly in Mexico. Some US companies illegally dump toxic waste in Mexico.

Environmental Movement

Environmental consciousness first arose in the 1970s, initially among the middle class and mainly in Mexico City. It's still strongest in the capital, where few can fail to notice the air pollution. Nongovernmental action is carried out by several dozen groups around the country, mainly small organizations that work on local issues. Often they're middle-class-led, though there have been some rural community initiatives too. The Movimiento Ecológico Mexicano (MEM) unites some 60 groups, with a total of about 10,000 members. The Grupo de Cien is a group of 100 intellectuals who manage to keep ecological issues in the public mind through their high profile and media access. A popular campaign against Mexico's first nuclear power plant, at Laguna Verde, Veracruz, did not prevent Laguna Verde from opening but did make the government shelve plans for follow-up plants elsewhere in the country.

The government is routinely criticized for lacking the will, as well as the money, to tackle environmental problems seriously. Since the mid-1980s the federal government has – in public at least – recognized the need for economic development to be environmentally sustainable.

President Salinas made significant – though still, it seems, inadequate – efforts to tackle Mexico City's air pollution problem and banned the hunting of sea turtles, which are endangered. President Zedillo in 1994 placed most government environmental agencies under the new Secretaría de Medio Ambiente, Recursos Naturales y Pesca (SEMARNAP, Secretariat of Environment, Natural Resources & Fisheries). SEMARNAP's mandate is to foster environmental protection and the orderly use of natural resources, with an emphasis on sustainable development.

FLORA & FAUNA

As one of the dozen or so tropical countries that harbor two-thirds of the earth's plant and animal species, Mexico is one of the planet's most biologically diverse nations. It has 1041 bird species, 439 mammals, 989 amphibians and reptiles and about 26,000 plants – in each case, about 10% of the world's total on just 1.4% of the earth's land. Many of these species are endemic (found nowhere else), including more than half the reptiles and amphibians and 139 of the mammals. More than one-third of all the world's marine mammals have been found in the Gulf of California. The state of Chiapas alone has some 10,000 plant species, more than 600 birds (twice as many as the US) and 1200 butterflies (more than twice as many as the US and Canada combined).

Vegetation Zones

Northern Mexico is dominated by two deserts – the Desierto Sonorense (Sonoran Desert), west of the Sierra Madre Occidental, and the Desierto Chihuahuaense (Chihuahuan Desert), occupying much of the Altiplano Central. The deserts are sparsely vegetated with cacti, agaves, yucca, scrub and short grasses. Just west of Monclova (in Coahuila state), a big marsh called Cuatrociénegas is an oasis in the desert, renowned for its plentiful wildlife. Both deserts stretch north into the USA; the Sonoran Desert also extends down into Baja California (although Baja has a sur-

prising range of other habitats too, and because of its isolation, a rather specialized flora and fauna). Most of the world's estimated 800 to 1500 species of cacti are found in Mexico.

The Sierra Madre Occidental and Oriental, the Cordillera Neovolcánica (running east-west across the middle of the country), and the Sierra Madre del Sur still have some big stretches of pine- and (at lower elevations) oak-dominated forest, though human occupation has stripped away much of the forest around the valleys. Between the Chihuahuan Desert and the Sierras, as well as in the northeast, much of the land has been turned over to irrigation, grazing or wasteland, but there are also still natural grasslands dotted with mesquite, a hardy bush of the bean family.

The natural vegetation of much of low-lying southeast Mexico – from southern Veracruz to eastern Chiapas and on to Quintana Roo – is evergreen tropical forest – rain forest in parts. The forest is dense and highly diversified, with ferns, epiphytes, palms, tropical hardwoods such as mahogany, and fruit trees such as the mamey and the *chicozapote* (sapodilla), which yields *chicle* (natural chewing gum). Again, human impact has destroyed much: the largest remaining tropical forest area is the Selva Lacandona (Lacandón Forest) in eastern Chiapas, and it too is vanishing – perhaps Mexico's biggest ecological tragedy of all. The Yucatán Peninsula changes from rain forest in the south to dry thorny forest in the north.

On the drier, Pacific side of Mexico – the western slopes of the Sierra Madre Occidental, the western and southern portions of the Cordillera Neovolcánica, and in much of the southern states of Oaxaca and Chiapas – is deciduous or semideciduous tropical forest, less varied than the eastern tropical forests. Much of this plant community has been turned into ranches and cropland.

Here and there in the southern half of the country, mountaintop pine forest that's often covered in clouds turns into cloud forest, with lush, damp vegetation and epiphytes growing on the tree branches.

The Reserva Ecológica Huitepec, near San Cristóbal de Las Casas, has many cloud forest features.

Along the dry Pacific coastal plain, from the southern end of the Sonoran Desert to the state of Guerrero, as well as on the northern Gulf Coast plain and in the northern Yucatán Peninsula, the predominant vegetation is thorn forest, composed of thorny bushes and small trees, including many acacias. Some of this terrain occurs naturally, some is the result of overgrazed grassland or abandoned slash-and-burn farmland.

Fauna

Land In the north, domesticated grazing animals have pushed the larger wild beasts, such as puma (mountain lion), wolf, deer and coyote, into isolated, often mountainous, pockets. Raccoons, armadillos, skunks, rabbits and snakes are still fairly common, however. The last four are found in much of the rest of the country too. Vampire bats live in deep sinkholes known as *sótanos* in the northeast and emerge at night to drink the blood of cattle and horses. They are harmless, except when they carry diseases such as rabies.

The remaining tropical forests of the south and east – the Pacific Coast and the Yucatán Peninsula, as well as the Gulf Coast and Chiapas – still harbor (in places) howler and spider monkeys, jaguars, ocelots, tapirs, anteaters, peccaries (a type of wild pig), deer, and some mean tropical reptiles, such as boa constrictors. The big cats are reduced to isolated pockets mainly in eastern Chiapas, though they also exist around Celestún in Yucatán. You may well hear howler monkeys (early in the morning) and see spider monkeys near the ruins at Palenque.

In all warm parts of Mexico you'll come across two harmless though sometimes alarming reptiles: the iguana, a lizard that can grow a meter or so long and comes in many different colors, and the gecko, a tiny, usually green lizard that may shoot out from behind a curtain or cupboard when disturbed. Geckos might make you jump, but they're good news – they eat mosquitoes. Less welcome are scorpions, also common in warmer parts of the country.

Sea & Coast Mexico's coasts – from Baja California to Oaxaca and from the northeast to the Yucatán Peninsula – are among the world's chief breeding grounds for sea turtles – for more information see the sidebar Mexico's Turtles: Not Saved Yet, in the Oaxaca chapter.

Dolphins can be seen in the seas off much of the Pacific Coast, while some wetlands, mainly in the south of the country, harbor crocodiles or caimans.

Baja California is famous for whale watching in the early months of the year, but it's also a breeding ground for other big sea creatures such as sea lions and elephant seals.

Underwater life is richest along the Yucatán Peninsula's Caribbean Coast, where there are coral reefs.

Birds Coastal Mexico is a major bird habitat, especially on the estuaries, lagoons, islands, mangroves and wetlands in the northeast, the Yucatán Peninsula and the Pacific Coast. Mexico abounds with eagles, hawks and buzzards, while innumerable ducks and geese winter in the northern Sierra Madre Occidental.

Tropical species – hummingbirds, trogons, parrots, parakeets, tanagers and many others – start to appear south of Tampico in the east of the country and from about Mazatlán in the west. The forests of the southeast are still home to colorful macaws, toucans, parrots and even a few quetzals. The Yucatán is home to some spectacular flamingo colonies.

Protected Areas

Sadly, one feature that's common to many protected areas in Mexico is that they're not very well protected. Governments have never had the money to properly police their protected areas against unlawful hunting, logging, farming, grazing or animal and plant collection.

Officially, more than 35% of Mexico (700,000 sq km) is under some kind of protection. The two most important protective categories are Parque Nacional (National Park) and Reserva de la Biosfera (Biosphere Reserve).

National Parks There are 40-odd national parks, totaling around 7000 sq km. Many are tiny – smaller than 10 sq km – and most were created between 1934 and 1940, often for their archaeological, historical, scenic or recreational value rather than for biological or ecological reasons. Some have no visitor infrastructure and draw few people, others are alive with weekend picnickers.

Mexico's national parks officially restrict many forms of human exploitation, but little attempt has ever been made to find alternative sources of income for the local people. Consequently, tree-cutting, hunting, grazing, etc, have carried on illegally. Nevertheless, national parks have succeeded in giving some protection to some big tracts of forest – especially the high coniferous forests of central Mexico.

Among the better-known and most interesting national parks are Constitución de 1857, in Baja California; Pico de Orizaba, La Malinche, Iztaccíhuatl-Popocatépetl, Nevado de Toluca and Nevado de Colima, all in the central volcanic belt; Lagunas de Chacahua, in Oaxaca; Palenque, Cañon del Sumidero and Lagunas de Montebello, all in Chiapas; and Dzibilchaltún and Tulum (on the Yucatán Peninsula). Marine national parks, created in the 1990s to protect aquatic ecosystems, include the Cozumel reefs, the west coast of Isla Mujeres, and the Bahía de Loreto in Baja California Sur.

Biosphere Reserves Biosphere reserves came into being as a result of a 1970s initiative by UNESCO, the United Nations Educational, Scientific & Cultural Organization, which recognized that it was impractical for developing countries to take productive areas out of economic use. Biosphere reserves take account of local people's needs and encourage them to take part in planning and developing sustainable economic activities outside strictly protected *zonas núcleo* (core areas). Today there are about 20 biosphere reserves in Mexico, covering more than 70,000 sq km. They focus on whole ecosystems with genuine biodiversity, ranging from deserts through dry and temperate forests to tropical forests and coastal areas. One, Sian Ka'an on the Yucatán Peninsula, is a UNESCO World Heritage Site.

Mexican biosphere reserves have had varied success. Sian Ka'an is one of the most successful: here some villagers have turned from slash-and-burn farming and cattle grazing to drip irrigation and multiple crops, conserving the forest and increasing food yields; lobster fishers have seen lobster numbers cease to fall after they accepted a two-month close-season for egg-laying and began returning pregnant females to the sea. Controlled tourism is now seen as an important new source of income in several biosphere reserves.

Biosphere reserves tend to be harder to access than national parks. Among the most visited or most interesting ones are El Vizcaíno and Sierra de la Laguna, in Baja California Sur; El Pinacate y El Gran Desierto de Altar, in Sonora; El Cielo, in Tamaulipas; El Triunfo, in Chiapas; and Calakmul and Sian Ka'an, on the Yucatán Peninsula.

Other Areas Until 1996 there existed a category of Reservas Especiales de la Biosfera (Special Biosphere Reserves). They were smaller and less biologically diverse than biosphere reserves but were managed in a similar way. They included the Cascadas de Agua Azul, in Chiapas; Ría Celestún and Ría Lagartos (the Celestún and Lagartos estuaries) and Isla Contoy, all on the Yucatán Peninsula; and the Mariposa Monarca (monarch butterfly) sanctuaries in Michoacán and México states, of which El Rosario, covered in this book's Western Central Highlands chapter, is the only section open to the public. All these reserves, however, are being recategorized.

There are nine Áreas de Proteccion de Flora y Fauna, intended to protect habitats of specific species rather than whole ecosystems. Reservas Campesinas, created by rural communities without government involvement, are intended to preserve the communities' forests or agricultural ecosystems. One of the best known is Mazunte, in Oaxaca.

Seeing Wildlife

You're not likely to bump into much of Mexico's terrestrial wildlife unless you make the effort to visit remote areas. Probably the most concentrated selection of purely Mexican wildlife is to be found at the zoo in Tuxtla Gutiérrez, Chiapas, which is devoted mainly to endangered species among the wide variety of fauna in that state. Parque-Museo La Venta, in Villahermosa, Tabasco, also has a good range of local wildlife. But as interest in Mexican nature increases the possibilities for visiting interesting natural areas are growing. Here's a selection of good places to see Mexican fauna in the wild (you'll find more information on most of them in the regional chapters):

Birds – Parque Nacional Constitución de 1857, Baja California, and Laguna San Ignacio, Baja California Sur; Alamos area, Sonora; Creel area, Chihuahua; coastal lagoons and wetlands, Tamaulipas and northern Veracruz; Mexcaltitán and San Blas, Nayarit; lagoons near Manzanillo, Colima; Pie de la Cuesta, Acapulco; Laguna Manialtepec and Lagunas de Chacahua, Oaxaca; Reserva de la Biosfera El Triunfo, near Ángel Albino Corzo, Chiapas (quetzal birds, tanagers, horned guan and many other tropical forest birds; see note below); Celestún and Río Lagartos, Yucatán (especially for flamingos); Isla Contoy and Cayo Colibrí, Quintana Roo

Crocodiles – Playa Ventanilla, near Mazunte, Oaxaca

Elephant Seals – Isla Cedros and Islas San Benito, Baja California

Monarch Butterflies – Santuario de Mariposas El Rosario, Michoacán

Sea Lions – Isla Cedros, Baja California

Tropical Forest Fauna (howler monkeys, pumas, crocodiles, ocelots, jaguars) – Reserva de la Biosfera Sian Ka'an, Quintana Roo

Whales – Laguna Ojo de Liebre, Laguna San Ignacio, Puerto López Mateos, all Baja California Sur; Bahía de las Banderas, Jalisco

For information on some companies and organizations that run tours to interesting natural areas, see the Organized Tours section of the Getting Around chapter. For information on visits to the Reserva de la Biosfera El Triunfo, contact the Instituto de Historia Natural (☎ 961-1-39-04, fax 961-2-36-63), Apartado Postal 391, 29000 Tuxtla Gutiérrez, Chiapas.

Information Sources

Some useful and interesting books on Mexico's environment and plant and animal life are mentioned under Books in Facts for the Visitor. For relevant Internet sites, see the Website Directory in the back of the book.

GOVERNMENT & POLITICS

Mexico is a federal republic of 31 states and one federal district, with the states further divided into 2394 *municipios* (municipalities). A two-chamber federal congress, with a 128-member upper chamber, the Cámara de Senadores (Senate), and a 500-member lower chamber, the Cámara de Diputados (Chamber of Deputies), makes the laws. A directly elected president carries the laws out, and an independent judiciary decides disputes according to Napoleonic law. Women gained the vote in 1954, and an Equal Rights Amendment was added to the constitution in 1974. The legislatures and governors of Mexico's states are elected by their citizens, as are the *ayuntamientos* (town councils), which run municipios, and their presidents.

That is the theory. In practice Mexican political life has been dominated for decades by one party, the Partido Revolucionario Institucional (PRI, Institutional Revolutionary Party) and its predecessors, and the president of Mexico has ruled in the tradition of strong, centralized leadership going back to Moctezuma. Though the Chamber of Deputies has, on paper, the power of the purse and weighty powers to oversee the executive, the president's will has rarely been denied.

What's more, the fiscal and political power of the states has been very much subordinate to the federal government, and elections at all levels have routinely raised accusations of fraud, bribery, intimidation and also violence on the part of the all-conquering PRI.

No significant challenge from opposition parties arose till the 1980s. Carlos Salinas de Gortari, president from 1988 to 1994, signaled the tentative beginnings of democratization. Limited anticorruption measures were introduced for the election of his successor in 1994, and during his term governors belonging to the center-right Partido de Acción Nacional (PAN) were elected in three Mexican states (Baja California, Chihuahua and Guanajuato) – the first time ever that the PRI conceded any state governorship.

The first real cracks in the monolith of PRI dominance have opened up since 1994, during the presidency of Ernesto Zedillo. Responding to growing dissatisfaction with PRI corruption and economic failure, to mounting clamor in Mexico for real democratic change, and to pressure from other countries that came with NAFTA, Zedillo began reforms that may lead Mexico to a genuinely pluralist democracy – despite a huge weight of opposition from the PRI old guard.

Most important, Zedillo freed from government control the body that organizes elections, the Instituto Federal Electoral (IFE), and let it spend hundreds of millions of dollars to build an electoral apparatus transparent enough to overcome fraud.

The first elections under this new regime, in 1997, were for all 500 seats in the Chamber of Deputies, a quarter of the Senate, six state governorships, and the Mexico City mayoralty, a new post created after decades of the capital's being run directly by the federal government. The PRI, unprecedentedly, lost overall control of the Chamber of Deputies, with the PAN and the center-left Partido de la Revolución Democrática (PRD) each winning about a quarter of the seats. The Mexico City mayoralty went to Cuauhtémoc Cárdenas, of the PRD, who had lost the 1988 presidential election to Salinas. The PAN won the governorship of the industrially important state of Nuevo León. The elections were not flawless, but they were hailed as the freest and fairest in Mexico since 1911, and they left a majority of Mexicans under a non-PRI government at either the state or local level.

The biggest test will come when it's time to elect Zedillo's replacement, at the end of his *sexenio* (six-year presidential term) in 2000. Under Mexican law, no president may serve consecutive terms in office. Instead, the PRI has developed the tradition of the *dedazo* (fingering), by which the outgoing president picks a candidate to succeed him from within PRI ranks. Since the 1930s that candidate has invariably won. Whether the unhappy dinosaurs in the PRI will allow the ultimate prize to slip from their hands, and how governable Mexico would be for a non-PRI president, remains to be seen.

ECONOMY
Resources & Products

Mexico, almost entirely agricultural before the 1910 revolution, is now one of Latin America's most industrialized nations. Manufacturing, largely concentrated in the major cities, employs about 18% of the work force and produces about a quarter of the gross national product and most of the country's exports. Motor vehicles, processed food, steel, chemicals, paper and textiles have joined more traditional sources of income such as sugar, coffee, silver, lead, copper and zinc. Among Mexico's biggest national assets are its oil reserves, the fifth largest in the world, and its gas reserves. Concentrated primarily along the Gulf Coast, Mexico's oil and gas industries yield about one-tenth of export earnings.

Half of Mexico's output is produced within 150 km of Mexico City, though northern states such as Nuevo León and Baja California are becoming increasingly important, aided by their proximity to that major export market, the USA, and by maquiladoras – factories where foreign companies are allowed to import raw materials duty-free for processing or assembly by inexpensive Mexican labor, then re-export the finished products. Maquiladoras employ some 600,000 Mexicans.

Mining, the source of most of Mexico's income in the colonial era, remains significant in the northern half of the country and accounts for about 3% of the national product. Mexico is still the world's largest silver producer.

About 30% of the work force is in service industries, of which tourism is one of the most important, generating around US$7 billion a year (compared to about US$10 billion for petrochemical exports). Agriculture occupies about 25% of the country's workers but produces only about 8% of the national product. Around 10% to 12% of Mexico is planted with maize, wheat, rice and beans, but the country still imports more grain than it exports. Small farming plots became prevalent after the redistribution of hacienda land to ejidos following the revolution. These plots are often farmed at subsistence level, their owners lacking the technology and capital to render them more productive. Larger-scale farming goes on primarily along the Gulf Coast (coffee and sugar cane), in the north and northwest (livestock, wheat and cotton), and in the Bajío area, north of Mexico City (wheat and vegetables).

Policy

Salinas The oil boom of the 1970s encouraged Mexico to undertake ambitious spending projects, piling up a big burden of national debt that could not be paid when revenues slumped in the early-1980s oil bust. In response to that, particularly from 1988 to 1994 under President Salinas, debt was rescheduled, austerity measures were introduced, and government enterprises from banks to utilities to steel mills were sold off (some to Salinas' cronies). Inflation was cut from well over 100% to less than 10% under Salinas. By the early 1990s Mexico was showing healthy growth again, and the peso, which had slumped disastrously through the 1980s, had been stabilized.

The key to Salinas' program was the North American Free Trade Agreement (NAFTA), which took effect in 1994.

NAFTA eliminates restrictions on trade and investment between the US, Mexico, and Canada step by step over a 15-year period. The hope was that NAFTA would bring Mexico, with its cheap labor, increased employment and growing exports, as well as cheaper imports.

By the end of 1993 Salinas' policies were widely seen as a success, at least by the rich and middle class, who definitely benefited from them. But the 1994 Zapatista rebellion drew the spotlight back to the gap between rich and poor – a gap some feared would be further widened as imports under NAFTA damaged uncompetitive sectors of the Mexican economy.

Peso Crisis Then came the peso collapse of late 1994 and 1995. It happened after Salinas left office but was a consequence of his policies. The foreign investment that had poured into Mexico in the early 1990s slowed to a trickle in 1994, partly because of political alarms in Mexico, partly because of rising US interest rates, and partly because of fears that the peso, which was pegged to the US dollar as part of Salinas' anti-inflation program, was overvalued. The government had to spend more and more of its foreign reserves to support the peso. Salinas hoped that the flow of foreign capital would resume before Mexico's reserves ran out. It didn't.

The devaluation that had to come was left for the unfortunate President Zedillo to carry out soon after he replaced Salinas in late 1994. With its foreign reserves nearly exhausted, Mexico was unable to hold the peso even at the new rate of four to the dollar (a 15% devaluation), and the currency was floated to find its own level. It fell fast to nearly eight to the dollar, and Mexico had to be bailed out by a multibillion-dollar package of emergency credit from the US, Canada and international financial bodies.

The government raised taxes and interest rates, cut spending, and announced new privatizations. Prices leapt upward; production and standards of living fell; more than 1.5 million people lost their jobs; crime rose; borrowers of all kinds faced crippling debts or went broke; more Mexicans looked to (usually illegal) migration to the USA as the only way out of poverty.

Recovery – of a Sort The government's austerity measures and its successful raising of new capital on private markets, coupled with big help for exports from NAFTA and the cheap peso, began to pull Mexico out of the slump surprisingly quickly. In 1996 production started growing again, and unemployment (according to official figures) fell. Foreign investment revived, and Mexico repaid ahead of schedule most of its emergency debt. By mid-1997 price increases were down to a rate of around 20% a year.

But for most people, government austerity translated into less money for basic necessities. One 1997 study concluded that more than one-fifth of the people in the Distrito Federal (which encompasses about half of Mexico City) were living in extreme poverty, on 'marginal levels of basic subsistence,' with a further two-thirds barely able to pay for material necessities. Yet the *Economist* had reported in 1996 that about two-thirds of Mexico's 20 to 25 million 'really poor' lived in *rural* areas, which received much less welfare spending than cities. The poorest states are Guerrero, Oaxaca, Chiapas, Veracruz, Puebla and Hidalgo.

The minimum wage in 1997 was around just US$3 a day. That is what many people in unskilled jobs were actually paid, and few workers earned more than twice that. Then there are the millions in the so-called informal economy: street hawkers, traffic signal fire-eaters, buskers, home workers, criminals – anybody whose work is not officially registered and who doesn't pay taxes. Perhaps one-third of Mexico's work force was 'informal' even before the peso crisis, and the number has only grown since then. Few of these people scrape together much more than the minimum wage. Meanwhile, Mexico's growing population adds

more than a million people to the labor market every year.

POPULATION & PEOPLE

Mexico's population, according to the 1995 census, was 91.2 million. In 1940 it was counted at 20 million, in 1960 at 35 million, in 1970 at 49 million, in 1980 at 67 million and in 1990 at 81 million.

About two-thirds of Mexicans live in towns or cities of more than 5000 people, and more than one-third are age 15 or younger. The biggest cities are Mexico City (with perhaps 20 million people), Guadalajara (estimated at 5 million) and Monterrey (3 million). Tijuana, Acapulco, Puebla and Ciudad Juárez all have estimated populations of 1 to 1.5 million. The most populous state is the state of México, which includes the rapidly growing outer areas of Mexico City and has about 12 million people.

The population is growing by about 1.9% a year, which is down from rates of more than 3% between 1950 and 1980 but still means an extra 1.8 million mouths to feed every year. Of even more concern is the growth of the cities, which attract thousands of newcomers from the impoverished countryside every day. Mexico City alone receives an estimated 2000 migrants daily.

Ethnic Groups

The major ethnic division is between mestizos and *indígenas* (Indians). Mestizos are people of mixed ancestry – usually Spanish and Indian, although African slaves and other Europeans were also significant elements. Indians are descendants of Mexico's pre-Hispanic inhabitants who have retained their sense of distinct identity. Mestizos are the overwhelming majority, and together with the few people of supposed pure Spanish descent they hold most positions of power in Mexican society.

Researchers have listed at least 139 vanished Indian languages. The 50 or so Indian cultures that have survived, some now with only a few hundred people, have done so largely because of their rural isolation. Indians in general remain second-class citizens, often restricted to the worst land or forced to migrate to city slums or the USA in search of work. Their main wealth is traditional and spiritual, their way of life imbued with communal customs and rituals bound up with nature. Indian traditions, religion, arts, crafts and costumes are fascinating subjects of study. There is more information on them in the various regional chapters, in this chapter under Arts and Religion, and in the color Artesanías section at the back of the book.

Official figures count as Indians only those who list themselves in censuses as speakers of Indian languages. They number about 7 million, though people of predominantly Indian ancestry may total as many as 25 million. The biggest Indian group is the Nahua, descendants of the Aztecs. At least 1.7 million Nahua speakers are spread around central Mexico, with the greatest concentration in Puebla, Veracruz, Hidalgo, Guerrero and San Luis Potosí states. There are approximately 1 million Mayan speakers, from the Yucatán Peninsula; 500,000 Zapotecs, from Oaxaca; 500,000 Mixtecs, from Oaxaca, Guerrero and Puebla; 260,000 Totonacs, in Veracruz and Puebla; and 130,000 Tarascos or Purépecha, in Michoacán – each group descended from a well-known pre-Hispanic people of the same name (Purépecha is now the more common name for the modern descendants of the pre-Hispanic Tarascos).

Descendants of lesser-known pre-Hispanic peoples include the approximately 330,000 Otomí, mainly in Hidalgo and México states; 150,000 Mazahua, in México state; and 150,000 Huastecs, in San Luis Potosí and northern Veracruz. The Tzotzils and Tzeltals of Chiapas are probably descendants of lowland Maya who migrated into the hills at the time of the Classic Maya downfall. Among smaller Indian peoples, the Huichol of Jalisco and Nayarit are renowned for the importance of the hallucinogenic plant peyote in their spiritual life, and the Mazatecs of northern Oaxaca for their use of hallucinogenic mushrooms.

ARTS
Painting & Sculpture
Mexicans have had a talent for painting – and an excitement about bright colors – since pre-Hispanic times. Today Mexico is spattered with murals and littered with galleries of contemporary and historic art, which are a highlight for many visitors. On another level, Mexican creativity is expressed in its myriad folk arts, which are still very much a living tradition – see the Artesanías color section for more on them.

Pre-Hispanic Art The Olmecs of the Gulf Coast produced some of the most remarkable pre-Hispanic stone sculpture, depicting deities, animals, and wonderfully lifelike human forms. Most awesome are the huge Olmec heads, which combine the features of human babies and jaguars. The earliest outstanding Mexican murals are found at Teotihuacán, where the colorful *Paradise of Tláloc* depicts in detail the delights awaiting those whose died at the hands of the water god, Tláloc. The Teotihuacán mural style spread to other parts of Mexico, such as Monte Albán, in Oaxaca. The Classic Maya of southeast Mexico, at their cultural height from about 250 to 900 AD, were perhaps ancient Mexico's most artistic people and have left countless beautiful stone carvings of complicated design and meaning but with an easily appreciable delicacy of touch – a talent also expressed in their unique architecture. Subjects are typically rulers, deities and ceremonies. The Maya also created some marvelous multicolored murals and pottery, most famously the murals of Bonampak, in Chiapas. The art of the Aztecs (whose civilization lasted from about 1350 to 1521) reflects their harsh world-view, with many carvings of skulls and complicated, symbolic representations of gods.

Other pre-Hispanic peoples who left major artistic legacies include the Toltecs of central Mexico (10th to 13th centuries), who had a fearsome, militaristic style of carving; the Mixtecs of Oaxaca and Puebla (13th to 16th centuries), who were excellent goldsmiths and jewelers; and the Classic Veracruz civilization (about 400 to 900 AD), which left a wealth of pottery and stone carving.

Pre-Hispanic art can be found at archaeological sites and museums throughout Mexico. The Museo Nacional de Antropología, in Mexico City, provides an excellent overview, with fine reproductions as well as original works.

Colonial Period Mexican art during Spanish rule was heavily Spanish-influenced and chiefly religious in subject, though portraits grew in popularity under wealthy patrons later in the period. The influence of Indian artisans is seen in the elaborate altarpieces and sculpted walls and ceilings, overflowing with tiny detail, in churches and monasteries, as well as in some fine frescoes, such as those at Actopan monastery in Hidalgo state. Miguel Cabrera (1695-1768), a Zapotec Indian from Oaxaca, was probably the leading painter of the era – his scenes and figures have a sureness of touch lacking in the more labored efforts of others. His work can be seen in churches and museums scattered all over Mexico.

Independent Mexico Juan Cordero (1824-84) began the modern Mexican mural tradition, expressing historical and philosophical ideas on public buildings such as the Escuela Nacional Preparatoria (now the Museo de San Ildefonso) in Mexico City. The landscapes of José María Velasco (1840-1912) capture the magical qualities of the country around Mexico City and areas farther afield, such as Oaxaca.

The years before the 1910 revolution saw the beginnings of socially conscious art and of a real break from European traditions. Slums, brothels and Indian poverty began to appear on canvases. The cartoons and engravings of José Guadalupe Posada (1852-1913), with their characteristic *calavera* (skull) motif, satirized the injustices of the Porfiriato period and were aimed at a wider audience than most

previous Mexican art. Gerardo Murillo (1875-1964), who took the name Dr Atl (from a Nahuatl word meaning 'water'), displayed some scandalously orgiastic paintings at a show marking the 1910 centenary of the independence movement.

The Muralists Immediately after the revolution, in the 1920s, education minister José Vasconcelos commissioned leading young artists to paint a series of murals on public buildings to spread awareness of Mexican history and culture and the need for social and technological change. The trio of great muralists were Diego Rivera (1885-1957), José Clemente Orozco (1883-1949) and David Alfaro Siqueiros (1896-1974).

Rivera's work carried a clear left-wing message, emphasizing past oppression suffered by Indians and peasants. He had an intense interest in Indian Mexico and tried hard to pull the country's Indian and Spanish roots together into one national identity. Typically, his murals are colorful, crowded tableaus depicting historical people and events or symbolic scenes of Mexican life, with a simple, clear-cut moral message. They're realistic, if not always lifelike. To appreciate them you need a bit of knowledge of Mexican history and, preferably, an explanation of the details. Some of Rivera's greatest works can be seen in Mexico City (see the Diego & Frida sidebar in that chapter) and at the Palacio de Cortés, Cuernavaca.

Siqueiros, who fought on the Constitutionalist side in the revolution (while Rivera was in Europe), remained a political activist afterward, spending time in jail as a result and leading an attempt to kill Leon Trotsky in Mexico City in 1940. His murals lack Rivera's realism but convey a more clearly Marxist message through dramatic, symbolic depictions of concepts such as the oppressed and the people, and through grotesque caricatures of the oppressors. Some of his best works can be seen at the Palacio de Bellas Artes, Castillo de Chapultepec and Ciudad Universitaria, all in Mexico City.

Orozco was less of a propagandist, conveying emotion, character and atmosphere and focusing more on the universal human condition than on historical or political specifics. By the 1930s Orozco grew disillusioned with the revolution. Some of his most powerful works, such as those in the Palacio de Bellas Artes, depict oppressive scenes of degradation, violence or injustice but do not offer any simplistic political solution. His work is reckoned to have reached its peak in Guadalajara from 1936 to 1939, particularly in the 50-odd frescoes in the Instituto Cultural Cabañas.

Rivera, Siqueiros and Orozco were also great artists on a smaller scale. Some of their portraits, drawings and other works can be seen in the Museo de Arte Moderno, Museo de Arte Carrillo Gil and Museo Dolores Olmedo Patiño, all in Mexico City, and in personal museums devoted to Siqueiros and Rivera in Mexico City and Guanajuato.

The mural movement continued long after WWII. Rufino Tamayo (1899-1991), a Zapotec Indian from Oaxaca, also represented in the Palacio de Bellas Artes, was relatively unconcerned with politics and history but was absorbed by abstract and mythological scenes and effects of color. Juan O'Gorman (1905-81), a Mexican of Irish ancestry, was even more realistic and detailed than Rivera. His mosaic on the Biblioteca Central at Mexico City's Ciudad Universitaria is probably his best-known work, but is atypical of his overall style.

Other 20th Century Artists Frida Kahlo (1907-54), physically crippled by a road accident and mentally tormented in her tempestuous marriage to Diego Rivera, painted anguished, penetrating self-portraits and grotesque, surreal images that expressed her left-wing views and externalized her inner tumult. After several decades of being seen as an interesting oddball, Kahlo suddenly seemed to strike an international chord in the late 1980s, almost overnight becoming hugely popular and as renowned as Rivera (see the Diego & Frida sidebar, in the Mexico City chapter).

After WWII, young Mexican artists reacted against the muralist movement, which they saw as too didactic and too obsessed with *Mexicanidad* (Mexicanness). They opened Mexico up to world trends such as abstract expressionism and op art. The Museo José Luis Cuevas, in Mexico City, is named after and partly devoted to one of the leaders of this movement. Other interesting artists to look for include Zacatecans Francisco Goitia and Pedro Coronel, and Francisco Toledo, from Oaxaca.

Architecture

Pre-Hispanic The ancient civilizations of Mexico produced some of the most spectacular and eye-pleasing architecture ever built. At sites such as Teotihuacán, near Mexico City; Monte Albán, in Oaxaca; and Chichén Itzá and Uxmal, in Yucatán, you can still see fairly intact pre-Hispanic cities. Their spectacular ceremonial centers, used by the religious and political elite, were designed to impress, with great stone pyramids, palaces and ball courts. Pyramids usually functioned as the bases for small shrines on their summits. Mexico's three biggest pyramids are the Pirámide del Sol and Pirámide de la Luna, at Teotihuacán, and the Great Pyramid of Cholula, near Puebla.

There are many differences in style between pre-Hispanic civilizations: while Teotihuacán, Monte Albán and Aztec buildings were relatively simple, designed to awe by their grand scale, Mayan architecture paid more attention to aesthetics, with intricately patterned façades, delicate 'combs' on temple roofs, and sinuous carvings. Buildings at Mayan sites such as Uxmal, Chichén Itzá, and Palenque are undoubtedly some of the most beautiful human creations in Mexico.

Colonial One of the Spaniards' first preoccupations was to replace pagan temples with Christian churches. A classic case is the Great Pyramid of Cholula, now topped by a small colonial church. Many of the fine mansions, churches, monasteries and plazas that today contribute so much to the country's beauty were created during the 300 years of Spanish rule. Most were in basically Spanish styles, but with unique local variations.

Gothic & Renaissance These styles dominated in Mexico in the 16th and early 17th centuries. Gothic, which originated in medieval Europe, is typified by soaring buttresses, pointed arches, clusters of round columns and ribbed vaults (ceilings). The Renaissance style saw a return to the disciplined ancient Greek and Roman ideals of harmony and proportion: columns and shapes such as the square and circle predominated. The usual Renaissance style in Mexico was plateresque – from *platero* (silversmith), because its decoration resembled the elaborate ornamentation that went into silverwork. Plateresque was commonly used on the façades of buildings, particularly church doorways, which had round arches bordered by classical columns and stone sculpture. A later, more austere Renaissance style was called Herreresque, after the Spanish architect Juan de Herrera. Two of Mexico's outstanding Renaissance buildings are Mérida's cathedral and Casa de Montejo. Mexico City and Puebla cathedrals mingle Renaissance and baroque styles.

Gothic and Renaissance influences were combined in many of the fortified monasteries that were built as Spanish monks carried their missionary work to all corners of the country. Monasteries usually had a large church, a cloister where the monks lived and worked, a big atrium (churchyard) and often a *capilla abierta* (open chapel), from which priests could address large crowds of Indians. Notable monasteries include Actopan and Acolman in central Mexico, and Yanhuitlán, Coixtlahuaca and Teposcolula, in Oaxaca.

The influence of the Muslims, who had ruled much of Spain until the 15th century, was also carried to Mexico. Examples of the Muslim-influenced Spanish Christian style, known as Mudéjar, can be seen in some beautifully carved wooden ceilings and in the *alfíz*, a rectangle framing a round arch. The 49 domes of the Capilla Real in Cholula almost resemble a mosque.

Baroque Baroque style, which reached Mexico in the early 17th century, was a reaction against the strictness of Renaissance styles, combining classical influences with other elements and aiming at dramatic effect rather than pure proportion. Curves, color, contrasts of light and dark, and increasingly elaborate decoration were among its hallmarks. Painting and sculpture were integrated with architecture for further elaborate effect – most notably in ornate, often enormous altarpieces.

Early, more restrained baroque buildings include the churches of Santiago Tlatelolco in Mexico City, San Felipe Neri in Oaxaca and San Francisco in San Luis Potosí. Among later baroque structures are the churches of San Cristóbal in Puebla and La Soledad in Oaxaca, and the Zacatecas cathedral façade.

Mexican baroque reached its final form, Churrigueresque, between 1730 and 1780. Named after a Barcelona carver and architect, José Benito Churriguera, this style was characterized by riotous surface ornamentation of which the hallmark is the *estípite* – a pilaster (a vertical pillar projecting only partly from the wall) in the form of a very narrow upside-down pyramid. The estípite helped give Churrigueresque its typical 'top-heavy' effect.

Outstanding Churrigueresque churches include the Sagrario Metropolitano in Mexico City; San Martín in Tepotzotlán; San Francisco, La Compañía and La Valenciana in Guanajuato; Santa Prisca and San Sebastián in Taxco; and the Ocotlán sanctuary at Tlaxcala.

Mexican Indian artisans added a profusion of detailed sculpture in stone and colored stucco to many baroque buildings. Among its most exuberant examples are the Capilla del Rosario in Santo Domingo church, Puebla, and the nearby village church of Tonantzintla. Arabic influence continued with the popularity of *azulejos* (colored tiles) on the outside of buildings, particularly in and around Puebla.

Neoclassical Neoclassical style was another return to Greek and Roman ideals. In Mexico it lasted from about 1780 to 1830. Outstanding examples include the Colegio de Minería in Mexico City, the Alhóndiga de Granaditas in Guanajuato and the second tiers of the Mexico City cathedral towers. Eduardo Tresguerras and Spanish-born Manuel Tolsá were the most prominent neoclassical architects.

19th & 20th Centuries Independent Mexico saw revivals of Gothic and colonial styles. Toward the end of the 19th century many buildings copied contemporary French or Italian styles. The Palacio de Bellas Artes in Mexico City is one of the finest buildings from this era.

After the revolution of 1910 to 1921, art deco appeared in buildings such as the Lotería Nacional and Frontón México in Mexico City, but more important was an attempt to return to pre-Hispanic roots in the search for a national identity. This trend was known as Toltecism, and many public buildings exhibit the heaviness of Aztec or Toltec monuments. It culminated in the 1950s with the UNAM campus in Mexico City, where many buildings are covered with colorful murals.

Music

In Mexico live music may start up at any time on streets, plazas or even buses. The musicians play for a living and range from marimba (wooden xylophone) teams and mariachi bands (trumpeters, violinists, guitarists and a singer, all dressed in smart cowboy-like costumes) to ragged lone buskers with out-of-tune guitars and sandpaper voices. Mariachi music – perhaps the most 'typical' Mexican music of all – originated in the Guadalajara area but is played nationwide. Marimbas are particularly popular in the southeast and on the Gulf Coast.

On a more organized level, Mexico has a thriving popular music business. Its outpourings can be heard live at fiestas, nightspots and concerts or bought from music shops or cheap bootleg-tape vendors.

(Ask bootleg sellers if you can try out the cassette you're buying, as there are many defective or even blank copies.)

Popular music ranges from the simple melodies accompanying Indian traditional dances through Mexican regional styles to foreign imports such as Latin *música tropical* and Western rock and pop. Indian dance music is typically played on flute, drum and perhaps guitar or violin and tends to be solemn, even stately.

Most regional popular music is rooted in a strong rhythm from several guitars, with voice, accordion, violin or brass providing the melody. *Música ranchera* is Mexico's version of country music – it's vocalist-and-combo music, maybe with a mariachi backing, and sentimental. Lola Beltrán, the 'Queen of Ranchera' and darling of the older generation, died in 1996 and was accorded a lying-in-state at Mexico City's Palacio de Bellas Artes. More contemporary ranchera bears the label *groupera*, and leading exponents include the groups Limite, Los Bukis and Los Tigres del Norte.

Norteña is country music with a cowboy flavor from northern Mexico. Norteña groups go for 10-gallon hats, and backing for the singer tends to consist of accordion, bass, rhythm guitars and drums. *Banda* is the big-band version of norteña, substituting large brass sections for guitar and accordion.

Pop and rock are big news, and concerts by homegrown and international stars draw large crowds. The Mexican rock scene is varied, and top groups range from El Tri, a kind of Mexican AC/DC (but better), through folk-rockers Café Tacuba to the psychedelic Fobia. Other names to look out for are *metálica* heavies Ángeles del Infierno, mystical Def Leppard-type rockers Jaguares, Police-sound-alikes Maná, and eclectic newcomers Luna Limón, a keyboards, guitar and vocals threesome who combine reggae, jazz, pop and Latin influences with poetic lyrics.

Jazz and classical music are far from neglected, with frequent concerts and festivals in Mexico City and elsewhere.

Dance

Indian Dance Colorful traditional Indian dances are an important part of many Mexican fiestas. Many bear traces of pre-Hispanic ritual. There are hundreds of them, some popular in many parts of the country, others danced only in a single town or village. Nearly all require special costumes, often including masks. Among the most superb costumes are those of the Zapotec feather dance, in Oaxaca, and the Nahua quetzal dance, in Puebla, which feature enormous feathered headdresses or shields.

Some dances have evolved from old fertility rites. Others tell stories that are Spanish or colonial in origin. The Zapotec feather dance represents the Spanish conquest of Mexico. *Moros y Cristianos* is a fairly widespread dance that reenacts the victory of Christians over Muslims in 15th-century Spain. The costumes of Los Viejitos (The Old Men), which can be seen in Pátzcuaro, Michoacán, originated in mockery of the Spanish, whom the local Tarasco Indians thought aged very fast.

Some dances are these days performed outside their religious context as simple spectacles. The Ballet Folklórico in Mexico City brings together traditional dances from all over the country. Other folkloric dance performances can be seen in several cities and at annual festivals such as the Guelaguetza, in Oaxaca, and the Atlixcáyotl, in Atlixco, Puebla, which gather performers from wide areas.

Latin Dance Latin and Caribbean dance and its music – broadly described as *música Afro-Antillana* or *música tropical* – didn't originate in Mexico but both have become highly popular. Basically it's tropical-style ballroom dancing, with percussion and often electric guitars or brass providing infectious rhythms. Mexico City has a dozen or more clubs and large dance halls devoted to this scene; aficionados can go to a different hall each night of the week. One of the more formal, old-fashioned varieties of Latin dance is *danzón*, associated particularly with the city of Veracruz. For danzón, high heels and a dress are de rigueur for women, and a Panama hat is for men. Steps are small, movement is from the hips down, and danzón can be danced only to danzón music. *Cumbia* has set steps too but is livelier and less structured than danzón: you move the top half of your body too. *Merengue*, mainly from Colombia and Venezuela, has a hopping step: the rhythm catches the shoulders, and the arms go up and down. Merengue music is strong on maracas, and its musicians go for puffed-up sleeves. *Salsa* is hot New York Cuban stuff with a lot of exciting turns.

Literature

Mexico's best-known novelist internationally is probably Carlos Fuentes, and his most highly regarded novel is *Where the Air is Clear*, written in the 1950s. Like his *Death of Artemio Cruz*, it's an attack on the failure of the Mexican Revolution. Fuentes' *Aura* is a magical book with one of the most stunning endings of any novel.

In Mexico, Juan Rulfo is generally regarded as the country's supreme novelist. His *Pedro Páramo*, set before and during the revolution, has been described as 'Wuthering Heights' set in Mexico and written by Kafka.' Laura Esquivel's *Like Water for Chocolate* is a passionate love story, interwoven with both fantasy and recipes (!) and set in rural Mexico at the time of the revolution.

Octavio Paz, a master of Mexican letters and winner of the 1990 Nobel Prize in Literature, has written perhaps the most probing examination of Mexico's myths and the Mexican character in *The Labyrinth of Solitude*.

For information on fiction and books about Mexico by non-Mexican authors, see Books in Facts for the Visitor.

SOCIETY & CONDUCT

Despite strong currents of machismo and nationalism, Mexicans are in general friendly, humorous, and helpful to visitors – the more so if you address them in Spanish, however rudimentary.

Machismo & the Family

Machismo is an exaggerated masculinity, aimed perhaps at impressing other males rather than women. Its manifestations range from aggressive driving and the carrying of weapons to heavy drinking. On the other side of this coin are women who emphasize their femininity. Such stereotyping, however, is far from universal and is under pressure from more modern influences. The women's movement has made some advances since it began in the 1970s as a small middle-class affair, but abortion, for instance, remains illegal in most cases.

The macho image may have roots in Mexico's often violent past and seems to hinge on a curious network of family relationships. Since it's not uncommon for Mexican husbands to have mistresses, wives in response lavish affection on their sons, who end up idolizing their mothers and, unable to find similar perfection in a wife, take a mistress . . . The strong mother-son bond also means that it's crucial for a Mexican wife to get along with her mother-in-law. And while the virtue of daughters and sisters has to be protected at all costs, other women – including foreign tourists without male companions – may be seen as fair game by Mexican men.

Despite tensions, family loyalty is strong. One gringo who lived in Mexico for several years commented that Mexicans never really reveal their true selves outside the family: 'However well you think you know someone, you eventually realize that everything they say or do is an act of one kind or another – but that doesn't stop them from being friendly, loyal or charming.' An invitation to a Mexican home is quite an honor for an outsider; as a guest you will be treated royally and will enter a part of real Mexico to which few outsiders are admitted.

Nationalism

This stems from Mexico's 11-year war for independence from Spain in the early 19th century and subsequent struggles against US and French invaders. Foreign economic domination – by the British and Americans around the beginning of the 20th century and more recently by the US again – has also been impossible to forget. The classic Mexican attitude toward the US is a combination of the envy and resentment that a poor neighbor feels for a rich one. The word 'gringo' isn't exactly a compliment, but it's not usually an insult either.

Making Contact

Most tourists and travelers in Mexico are assumed to be citizens of the USA. Away from tourist destinations, your presence may bring any reaction from curiosity or wonder to fear or, very occasionally, brusqueness. But any negative response will usually evaporate as soon as you show that you're friendly.

Language difficulties may be the biggest barrier to friendly contact: some people are shy or will ignore you because they don't imagine a conversation is possible; just a few words of Spanish will often bring smiles and warmth, not to mention lots of questions. Then someone who speaks a few words of English will pluck up the courage to try them out.

Indian Peoples Some Indian peoples adopt a cool attitude toward visitors: they have learned to mistrust outsiders after five centuries of exploitation. They don't like being gaped at by tourists and are sensitive about cameras.

Time

The fabled Mexican attitude toward time – *'mañana, mañana . . .'* – has probably become legendary simply from comparison with the USA. But it's still true, especially outside the big cities, that the urgency Europeans and North Americans are used to is lacking. Most Mexicans value *simpatía* (congeniality) over promptness. If something is really worth doing, it gets done. If not, it can wait. Life should not be a succession of pressures and deadlines. According to many Mexicans, life in the 'businesslike' cultures has been de-sympathized. You may come away from Mexico convinced that the Mexicans are right!

RELIGION
Roman Catholicism

Almost 90% of Mexicans profess Catholicism. Its dominance is remarkable, considering the rocky history that the Catholic Church has had in Mexico, particularly in the last two centuries.

The church was present in Mexico from the very first days of the Spanish conquest. Until independence it remained the second most important institution after the crown's representatives and was really the only unifying force in Mexican society. Almost everyone belonged to the church because, spirituality aside, it was the principal provider of social services and education.

The Jesuits were among the foremost providers and administrators, establishing missions and settlements throughout Mexico. Their expulsion from the Spanish empire in the 18th century marked the beginning of stormy church-state relations in Mexico. In the 19th and 20th centuries (up to 1940), Mexico passed numerous measures restricting the church's power and influence. The bottom line was money and property, both of which the church was amassing faster than the generals and political bosses. The 1917 Mexican constitution prevented the church from owning property or running schools or newspapers and banned clergy from wearing clerical garb or speaking out on government policies and decisions. In practice most of these provisions ceased to be enforced in the second half of the 20th century, and in the early 1990s President Salinas had them removed from the constitution.

The Mexican Catholic Church is one of Latin America's more conservative. Only in the south of the country have its leaders – notably Bishop Samuel Ruiz García of San Cristóbal de Las Casas – gotten involved in political issues such as human rights and poverty.

The church's most binding symbol is *Nuestra Señora de Guadalupe*, the dark-skinned Virgin of Guadalupe, a manifestation of the Virgin Mary who appeared to a Mexican Indian in 1531 on a hill near Mexico City. The Guadalupe Virgin

The Virgin of Guadalupe

became a crucial link between Catholic and Indian spirituality, and as Mexico grew into a mestizo society she became the most potent symbol of Mexican Catholicism. Today she is the country's patron, her blue-cloaked image is ubiquitous, and her name is invoked in religious ceremonies, political speeches and literature.

Other Christians

Around 5% of Mexicans profess other varieties of Christianity. One group encompasses the Methodist, Baptist, Presbyterian and Anglican churches set up by American missionaries in the 19th century. Another results from a new wave of North American missionaries, this time of evangelical leanings, entering Mexico in the 20th century – among them the Wycliff Bible Translators, also known as the Summer Institute of Linguistics. In recent decades Pentecostal evangelical churches such as the Assembly of God and Church of God have gained many converts, particularly among the rural and Indian peoples of southeast Mexico, sometimes leading to strife with Catholics.

Indian Religion

The missionaries of the 16th and 17th centuries won the indigenous people over to Catholicism as much by grafting it on to pre-Hispanic religions as by deeper conversion. Often old gods were simply identified with Christian saints, and the old festivals continued to be celebrated, much as they had been in pre-Hispanic times, on the nearest saint's day. Acceptance of the new religion was greatly helped by the appearance of the Virgin of Guadalupe in 1531.

Today, despite modern inroads into Indian life, Indian Christianity is still fused with more ancient beliefs. In some remote regions Christianity is only a veneer at most. The Huichol Indians of Jalisco have two Christs but neither is a major deity. Much more important is Nakawé, the fertility goddess. The hallucinogenic plant peyote is a crucial source of wisdom in the Huichol world. Elsewhere, notably among the Tarahumara, drunkenness is an almost sacred element at festival times.

Even among the more orthodox Christian Indians it is not uncommon for spring saints' festivals, or the pre-Lent carnival, to be accompanied by remnants of fertility rites. The famous Totonac voladores (see the Voladores sidebar, in the Central Gulf Coast chapter) enact one such ritual. The Guelaguetza dance festival, which draws thousands of visitors to Oaxaca every summer, has roots in pre-Hispanic maize-god rituals.

In the traditional Indian world almost everything has a spiritual dimension – trees, rivers, plants, wind, rain, sun, animals and

hills have their own gods or spirits. Even Coca-Cola bottles can be seen among the offerings in the Tzotzil Indian church at San Juan Chamula, Chiapas.

Witchcraft and magic survive. Illness may be seen as a 'loss of soul' caused by the sufferer's wrongdoing or by the influence of someone with magical powers. A soul can be 'regained' if the appropriate ritual is performed by a *brujo* (witch doctor).

Judaism

Jews make up 0.1% of Mexico's population. Most of them live in the state of México and in Mexico City, where there are several synagogues.

LANGUAGE

The predominant language of Mexico is Spanish. Mexican Spanish is unlike Castilian Spanish, the language of Spain, in two respects: in Mexico the Castilian lisp has more or less disappeared and numerous Indian words have been adopted.

Travelers in cities, towns and larger villages can almost always find someone who speaks at least some English. All the same, it is advantageous and courteous to know at least a few words and phrases of Spanish. Mexicans will generally respond much more positively to you if you attempt to speak to them in their own language.

About 50 Indian languages are spoken by 7 million or more people in Mexico, of whom about 15% don't speak Spanish.

For a guide to Spanish pronunciation, vocabulary and some useful phrases, see the Spanish for Travelers section at the back of this book.

Facts for the Visitor

PLANNING

When to Go

Any time is a good time to visit Mexico, though the coastal and lowland regions, particularly in the southern half of the country, are pretty hot from May to September and can get unpleasantly humid. The interior of the country has a more moderate climate than the coasts, though it's sometimes decidedly chilly in the north in winter.

July and August are peak holiday months for both Mexicans and foreigners; the coastal resorts attract big tourist crowds, and room prices are likely to go up.

Mexico's other peak holiday seasons are between mid-December and early January (for both foreigners and Mexicans), and a week either side of Easter (for Mexicans). Room prices rise in popular places, and rooms and public transportation are heavily booked, so advance reservations are often advisable.

Maps

Good country maps include International Travel Map Productions' (ITM) 1 cm:33 km *México*, which has considerable detail but is fairly easy to read, and *Mexico* in the Bartholomew World Travel Map series, which is strong on geographical features such as altitudes and rivers. The AAA's (American Automobile Association's) *Mexico* is also useful. (For road atlases, see Car & Motorcycle in the Getting Around chapter).

ITM also produces the 1 cm:10 km regional maps *Baja California*, *Mexico South* and *Yucatán Peninsula*, and a *Mexico City* map.

Mapa de la República Mexicana 9600, available at some Sanborn's stores and a few other outlets in Mexico, shows 9600 towns and villages, all indexed.

City, town and regional maps of varying quality are available, almost always free, from local tourist offices in Mexico, and you can often find commercially published ones at bookstores or newsstands. INEGI, the Instituto Nacional de Estadística, Geografía e Informática, publishes a large-scale series of 1:50,000 (1 cm: 500 meters) maps covering the whole of Mexico. INEGI has an office in every Mexican state capital, and in Mexico City it has a conveniently located shop just outside the Insurgentes metro station (see the Maps section in the Mexico City chapter).

What to Bring

The clothing you bring should depend on how, when and where you want to travel, and how you would like to be perceived by Mexicans. You might want to conform to Mexican norms.

Mexicans tend to dress informally but conservatively. Even in the hot regions, men wear long trousers. A *guayabera* – a fancy shirt decorated with tucks and worn outside the belt – substitutes for a jacket and tie on more formal occasions. Many women wear stylish dresses, or blouses and skirts.

The local people do not expect you to dress as they do, but you should know that, except in beach resorts, shorts and T-shirts are the marks of the tourist. In the hotter regions, these plus light cotton trousers or skirts, trainers or sandals, and light blouses or shirts should see you through. Jeans are often uncomfortably heavy in warm, humid areas but are good for upland areas in the cooler months. Bring a light sweater or jacket – even on the coast you may want it for evening boat rides. A light rain jacket, preferably a loose-fitting poncho, is good to have from October to May and is a necessity from May to October.

In general, it is better for women to dress conservatively in towns (except seaside resorts) and in off-the-beaten-track villages unaccustomed to tourists – no shorts, sleeveless tops, etc. Lean toward the more respectful end of the dress spectrum when visiting churches.

In lowland areas such as the Pacific and Gulf Coasts, Yucatán and Tabasco, everyone should have a hat and sun block. If your complexion is particularly fair or you burn easily, consider wearing long sleeves and long pants.

Toiletries such as shampoo, shaving cream, razors, soap and toothpaste are readily available throughout Mexico in all but the smallest villages. You should bring your own contact lens solution, tampons, contraceptives and insect repellent – they are available in Mexico, but not always readily so.

Other recommended items are sunglasses, a torch (flashlight), a pocket knife, two to three meters of cord, a small sewing kit, a money belt or pouch that you can wear under your clothes, a drain plug, a small padlock, and a small Spanish dictionary. You can pick up a hat when you get to Mexico.

For carrying it all, a backpack is the most convenient if you'll be doing much traveling. You can make it reasonably theft-proof with small padlocks. A light daypack, too, is useful.

TOURIST OFFICES
Local Tourist Offices
Just about every place of interest to tourists has a national, state or city/town tourist office. They can be helpful with maps and brochures, and often the staff members speak English.

You can call the Mexico City office of SECTUR, the Mexican tourism ministry (☎ 5-250-01-23, 800-90392), at any time – 24 hours a day, seven days a week – for information or help.

Tourist Offices Abroad
In the USA and Canada you can call ☎ 800-446-3942 for Mexican tourist information. You can also contact a Mexican Government Tourism Office, at the following locations:

Chicago
  70 East Lake St, Suite 1413, Chicago, IL 60601 (☎ 312-606-9015)
Houston
  5075 Westheimer Blvd, Suite 975W, Houston, TX 77056 (☎ 713-629-1611)
Los Angeles
  1801 Century Park East, Suite 1080, Los Angeles, CA 90067 (☎ 310-203-8191)
Miami
  2333 Ponce de Leon Blvd, Suite 710, Coral Gables, FL 33134 (☎ 305-443-9160)
Montreal
  1 Place Ville Marie, Suite 1526, Montreal, QC H3B 2B5 (☎ 514-871-1052)
New York
  405 Park Ave, Suite 1401, New York, NY 10022 (☎ 212-755-7261)
Toronto
  2 Bloor St West, Suite 1801, Toronto, ON M4W 3E2 (☎ 416-925-0704)
Vancouver
  999 West Hastings St, Suite 1610, Vancouver, BC V6C 2W2 (☎ 604-669-2845)
Washington DC
  1911 Pennsylvania Ave NW, Washington, DC 20006 (☎ 202-728-1750/55)

There are these Mexican Government Tourism Offices in Europe:

France
  4 rue Notre Dame des Victoires, 75002 Paris (☎ 01 42 86 56 30)
Germany
  Wiesenhuettenplatz 26, D60329 Frankfurt-am-Main (☎ 069-252-413, 069-253-541)
Italy
  Via Barberini 3, 00187 Rome (☎ 06-487-2182)
Spain
  Calle Velázquez 126, Madrid 28006 (☎ 91-561-3520)

UK
  60-61 Trafalgar Square, 3rd floor, London
WC2N 5DS (☎ 0171-734-1058)

VISAS & DOCUMENTS

Visitors to Mexico should have a valid passport. Some nationalities have to obtain visas, but most Western nationalities require only the easily obtained Mexican government tourist card. Since the regulations sometimes change, it would be wise to confirm them at a Mexican Government Tourism Office or Mexican embassy or consulate before you go.

Passport

Though it is not recommended, US tourists can enter Mexico without a passport if they have official photo identification, such as a driver's license, plus some proof of their citizenship, such as their original birth certificate with an official stamp from the state of birth, a notarized copy of their birth certificate, or their original certificate of naturalization (not a copy). Citizens of other nationalities who are permanent residents in the United States have to present their Permanent Resident Alien card.

Canadian tourists may enter Mexico with official photo identification plus a citizenship card or original birth certificate or notarized affidavit. Canadian landed immigrants, however, require a valid passport and their original landed immigrant document (record of landing).

But it is much better to have a passport, because officials are used to passports and may delay people who have other documents. This applies to officials you have to deal with on reentry to North America as well as to Mexican officials: the only proof of citizenship recognized by US or Canadian immigration is a passport or (for non-naturalized citizens) a certified copy of your birth certificate from the government agency that issued it. In Mexico you will often need your passport when you change money, as well.

Citizens of other countries need to show a passport valid for at least six months after they arrive in Mexico.

Visas & Tourist Cards

Citizens of the USA, Canada, EU countries, Australia, New Zealand, Norway, Switzerland, Iceland, Israel, Japan and Argentina are among those who do not require visas to enter Mexico as tourists. But they must obtain a Mexican government *tarjeta de turista* (tourist card).

Travelers under 18 who are not accompanied by *both* parents must have special documentation – see the Under-18 Travelers section.

Visas Countries whose nationals *do* have to obtain visas include South Africa, Brazil and eastern European nations – check well ahead of travel with your local Mexican embassy or consulate.

Non-US citizens passing through the USA on the way to or from Mexico, or making a visit to Mexico from the USA, should check visa requirements for entering the USA.

Tourist Cards The tourist card – officially the Forma Migratoria de Turista (FMT) – is a brief paper document that you have to get validated (stamped) when you enter Mexico and must keep till you leave. The card is available free of charge at Mexican immigration points at official border crossings, at international airports and at ports, which will also validate it. At the US-Mexico border you won't usually be given one automatically – you have to ask for it.

At many US-Mexico border crossings you don't *have* to get the card validated at the border itself, as there are other immigration offices a little further into Mexico where it's possible to do it – but it's advisable to do it at the border, in case there are difficulties elsewhere.

One section of the card deals with the length of your stay in Mexico. The normal maximum is 180 days, though for French, Austrian, Greek and Argentine passport holders it's 90 days. If you don't fill in this part yourself, Mexican immigration officials will often do it for you, putting '30 days' on the assumption you're there for a short vacation. If you want more time than that, fill in the number of days yourself or tell the officer before he or she does so. In any case it's often advisable to put down more days than you think you'll need, in case you change your plans. Travelers entering Mexico from Guatemala or Belize may find that immigration officers will not put more than 15 or 30 days on their tourist card – at little as five days in some cases – but you should be able to get an extension once you are deeper inside Mexico (see Extensions & Lost Cards, below).

Look after your tourist card, as Mexican law requires you to hand it in when you leave Mexico and carry it with you at all times while you're there. (In large cities it may be a good idea to put your tourist card in the hotel safe and carry a photocopy instead, in case of theft.)

If you overstay the limit on your card you may be subject to a fine (normally around US$50 for up to one month). If no one looks at your tourist card when you leave or reenter Mexico, as often happens at the US border, there would be nothing to stop you from using the same card more than once, provided it's still valid.

Tourist cards are not needed for visits shorter than 72 hours from the US to Mexican towns on the border. From Tijuana this rule extends south to Maneadero (south of Ensenada), and from Mexicali as far as San Felipe.

Extensions & Lost Cards If the limit on your tourist card is for less time than the maximum you're allowed (see previous section), its validity may be extended one or more times, at no cost, up to your maximum. But not everyone is automatically allowed the maximum – especially people applying for a second or subsequent extension. To get a card extended you have to apply to a Delegación de Servicios Migratorios (immigration office). These offices exist in many towns and cities. The procedure should be straightforward; you'll need your passport, tourist card, ticket out of Mexico (if you have one), and some evidence of 'sufficient funds' – a major credit

card is OK, and in Mexico City US$100 in traveler's checks will suffice. Most offices will not extend a card until a few days before it is due to expire – it's not usually worth trying earlier.

If you lose your card or need further information, contact your embassy or consulate. They may be able to give you a letter enabling you to leave Mexico without your card, or at least an official note to take to your local Delegación de Servicios Migratorios, which will have to issue a duplicate. You can also call the SECTUR tourist office in Mexico City (☎ 5-250-01-230, 800-90392) for information.

Under-18 Travelers
Every year numerous parents try to run away from the USA or Canada to Mexico with their children to escape the legal machinations of the children's other parent. To prevent this, minors (people under 18) entering Mexico without one or both of their parents may be – and often are – required to show a notarized consent form, signed by the absent parent or parents, giving permission for the young traveler to enter Mexico. In the case of divorced parents, a custody document may be needed too. If one or both parents are dead, or the traveler has only one legal parent, a notarized statement saying so may be required.

These rules are aimed primarily at North Americans but apparently apply to all nationalities. Procedures vary from country to country; you should contact a Mexican consulate well ahead of your trip to find out exactly what you need to do.

Photocopies
Before you leave for Mexico, it's worth making two photocopies of all important documents you're taking with you – things like the data pages of your passport and any important visas in it, air tickets, insurance papers, traveler's check receipts or serial numbers, driver's license, vehicle papers, numbers of any credit or bank cards you're carrying, and contact telephone numbers for replacing lost documents,

checks or cards. Leave one set with someone at home, take the other with you, and keep it separate from the originals. When you get to Mexico, add a photocopy of your tourist card and, if you're driving, vehicle import papers. The copies can make things a whole lot easier if any of your documents are lost or stolen and you have to replace them.

Travel Insurance
See the Health section later in this chapter.

Driver's License & Permits
If you're thinking of renting a vehicle in Mexico, take your driver's license and a major credit card with you. For more information on rentals, see the Getting Around chapter. For the paperwork involved in taking your own vehicle into Mexico, see the Getting There & Away chapter.

Hostel, Student,
Youth & Teacher Cards
An HI card is good for small discounts at a few Mexican youth hostels.

Notices at museums, archaeological sites and so on usually state that student prices are only for those with Mexican education system credentials, but in practice the ISIC card will sometimes get you a reduction. It may also get you discounts on some bus tickets. Take it along. The GO25 card for any traveler between ages 12 and 25 and the ITIC card for teachers are less recognized in Mexico.

CUSTOMS
Motor vehicles entering Mexico (except Baja California or the border zone, which extends about 25 km into mainland Mexico) must have vehicle permits and should have Mexican insurance – see the Getting There & Away chapter.

Things that visitors are allowed to bring into Mexico duty-free include items for personal use, such as clothing, footwear and toiletries; medicine for personal use, with prescription in the case of psychotropic substances (medicines that can alter perception or behavior); one movie camera and one still camera; up to 12 rolls of film; and, if you're 18 or older, three liters of alcohol or wine and 400 cigarettes or 50 cigars. These limits are not always applied very strictly.

The normal customs inspection routine when you enter Mexico is to complete a customs declaration form, then choose between going through a goods-to-declare channel or a nothing-to-declare channel. Those declaring items have their belongings searched, and duty is collected. Those not declaring items have to pass a full-size traffic signal. The signal responds randomly: a green light lets you pass without inspection, a red light means your baggage will be searched. This random system has largely done away with the curse of La Mordida, the 'bite' (a small bribe or tip) that used to determine the speed and ease with which visitors passed through Mexican customs.

MONEY
Costs
The peso collapse of 1994-95 has made Mexico a somewhat cheaper place to visit than it was a few years ago. Though peso prices roughly doubled between 1994 and '97, the number of pesos you got for your dollar went up even more.

With the main exceptions of Baja California and the Yucatán Peninsula's Caribbean Coast, where rooms can cost double what they do in the rest of Mexico, a single budget traveler either camping or staying in budget accommodations and eating two meals a day in restaurants can expect to pay US$10 to US$20 a day for those basics. Add in other costs (snacks, purified water and soft drinks, entry to archaeological sites, long-distance buses, etc), and you'll spend more like US$15 to US$30 a day. If there are two or more of you sharing rooms, costs per person drop considerably. Double rooms are often only a dollar or two more than singles, and triples or quadruples only slightly dearer than doubles.

Mexican Embassies & Consulates Abroad
Unless otherwise noted, details are for embassies or their consular sections.

Argentina
Larrea 1230
1117 Buenos Aires
(☎ 01-821-7210)

Australia
14 Perth Ave, Yarralumla
Canberra, ACT 2600
(☎ 02-6273-3905)

Consulate: Level 1,
135-153 New South Head Rd
Edgecliff, Sydney, NSW
2027 (☎ 02-9326-1311)

Austria
Turkenstrasse 15
1090 Vienna
(☎ 0222-310-7383)

Belgium
Av Franklin Roosevelt 94
1050 Brussels
(☎ 02-629-0711)

Belize
20 North Park St, Fort
George Area, Belize City
(☎ 02-30-193/194)

Brazil
SES Av Das Nacoes Lote
18, 70412-900 Brasilia DF
(☎ 61-244-6866/1011)

Canada
Embassy consular section:
45 O'Connor St, Suite 1500
Ottawa, Ontario K1P 1A4
(☎ 613-233-8988/6665)

Consulate: 2000 rue
Mansfield, Suite 1015
Montreal, QC H3A 2Z7
(☎ 514-288-2502/2707)

Consulate: Commerce Court
West, 199 Bay St, Suite
4440, Toronto
ON M5L 1E9
(☎ 416-368-2875/1847)

Consulate:
810-1130 West Pender St
Vancouver, BC V6E 4A4
(☎ 604-684-3547/1859)

Costa Rica
Avenida 7a No 1371
San José
(☎ 257-0633, 225-4430)

Denmark
Gammel Vartov Vej 18
2900 Hellerup, Copenhagen
(☎ 3929-5744)

El Salvador
Calle Circunvalación y
Pasaje No 12, Colonia San
Benito, San Salvador
(☎ 243-3458/3190)

France
9 rue de Longchamp
75116 Paris (☎ 01 45 53 99
34, 01 45 53 76 43)

Consulate: 4 rue Notre
Dame des Victoires, 75002
Paris (☎ 01 42 61 51 80)

Germany
Adenauerallee 100, 53113
Bonn (☎ 0228-914-8620)
Consulate: Kurfurstendamm
72, 10709 Berlin
(☎ 030-324-9047)

Consulate: Hochstrasse
35-37, 60330 Frankfurt-am-
Main (☎ 069-299-8750)

Guatemala
Edificio Central Ejecutivo,
7th floor, 15a Calle No 3-20,
Zona 10, Guatemala City
(☎ 333-72-54)

Consulate: 13a Calle No 7-
30, Zona 9, Guatemala City
(☎ 331-81-65, 332-52-49)

Consulate: 9a Avenida No
6-19, Zona 1, Quetzalte-
nango (☎ 763-13-12 to 15)

Honduras
Avenida República de
México 2907, Colonia
Palmira, Tegucigalpa
(☎ 32-64-71, 32-40-39)

Ireland
43 Ailesbury Rd
Ballsbridge, Dublin 4
(☎ 01-260-0699)

Israel
3 Rehov Bograshov
63808 Tel Aviv
(☎ 03-523-0367 to 69)

Italy
Via Lazzaro Spallanzani 16
00161 Rome
(☎ 06-440-2309/4404)
Consulate:Via Cappucini 4
Milan (☎ 02-7602-0541)

Japan
2-15-1 Nagata-cho,
Chiyoda-ku, Tokyo 100
(☎ 3-3580-2961/62,
3-3581-1131 to 35)

Netherlands
Nassauplein 17, 2585 EB
The Hague (☎ 070-360-
2900, 070-345-2569)

New Zealand
8th Floor, 111-115 Custom-
house Quay, Wellington
(☎ 04-472-5555/56)

Nicaragua
Carretera a Masaya Km 4.5,
25 varas arriba (next to
Optica Matamoros),
Altamira, Managua
(☎ 5052-78-1860)

In the middle range you can live well in most of Mexico for US$30 to US$45 per person per day, even in the large cities and expensive resorts. In most places two people can easily find a clean, modern room with private bath and TV for US$15 to US$30 and have the other US$30 or so

pay for food, admission fees, transport and incidentals.

At the top of the scale are a few hotels and resorts that charge upwards of US$200 for a room, and restaurants where you can pay US$50 per person, but you can also stay at very comfortable smaller hotels for US$40

Norway
Drammensveien 108B
0244 Oslo
(☎ 22-43-1165/1477)

South Africa
Southern Life Plaza, 1st
Floor, CNR Schoeman &
Festival Streets, Hatfield,
0083 Pretoria
(☎ 12-342-6190)

Spain
Carrera de San Jerónimo
46, Madrid 28014
(☎ 91-369-4781/2814)

Consulate: Avenida
Diagonal Sur 626, 4th
floor, Barcelona 08021
(☎ 93-201-1822)

Consulate: Calle San
Roque 6, Seville 41001
(☎ 95-456-3944)

Sweden
Grevgatan 3,
11453 Stockholm
(☎ 08-661-2213, 08-663-5170)

Switzerland
Bernestrasse 57, 3005 Bern
(☎ 031-351-4060/1814)

UK
8 Halkin St
London SW1X 7DW
(☎ 0171-235-6393)

USA
1911 Pennsylvania Ave NW,
Washington DC 20006
(☎ 202-728-1633/36/94)
Consulate: 2827 16th St
NW, Washington, DC 20009
(☎ 202-736-1010)

Mexican Consulates in the USA There are consulates in many other US cities
besides Washington DC, particularly in the border states:

Arizona
Douglas (☎ 520-364-3107)
Nogales (☎ 520-287-2521)
Phoenix (☎ 602-242-7398)
Tucson (☎ 520-882-5595)

California
Calexico
(☎ 760-357-3863)
Fresno (☎ 209-233-3065)
Los Angeles
(☎ 213-351-6800)
Sacramento
(☎ 916-441-2987)
San Bernardino
(☎ 909-889-9837)
San Diego
(☎ 619-231-9741)
San Francisco
(☎ 415-392-5554)
San Jose (☎ 408-298-5581)

Colorado
Denver (☎ 303-331-1110)

Florida
Miami (☎ 305-716-4979)

Orlando (☎ 407-894-0514)

Georgia
Atlanta (☎ 404-266-1204)

Illinois
Chicago (☎ 312-855-1380)

Louisiana
New Orleans
(☎ 504-522-3596)

Massachusetts
Boston (☎ 617-426-4942)

Michigan
Detroit (☎ 313-567-7709)

Missouri
St Louis (☎ 314-436-3426)

New Mexico
Albuquerque
(☎ 505-247-2139)

New York
New York (☎ 212-689-0456)

Oregon
Portland (☎ 503-274-1442)

Pennsylvania
Philadelphia
(☎ 215-922-4262)

Texas
Austin (☎ 512-478-9031)
Brownsville
(☎ 956-542-2051)
Corpus Christi
(☎ 512-882-3375)
Dallas (☎ 214-630-1604)
Del Rio (☎ 830-775-2352)
Eagle Pass
(☎ 830-773-9255)
El Paso (☎ 915-533-3644)
Houston (☎ 713-524-1301)
Laredo (☎ 956-723-6369)
McAllen (☎ 956-686-4684)
Midland (☎ 915-687-2334)
San Antonio
(☎ 210-227-9145)

Utah
Salt Lake City
(☎ 801-521-8502)

Washington State
Seattle (☎ 206- 448-8435)

to US$75 a double and eat extremely well
for US$20 to US$40 per person per day.

These figures do not include extra
expenses like internal air fares or car rentals,
which you're more likely to need if you're
on a quick trip, or any souvenirs or clothes
you buy in Mexico.

Carrying Money
Ideally, when you're out and about, carry
only what you'll need that day. Leave the
rest in the *caja fuerte* (hotel safe). If there
isn't a safe, you have to decide whether it's
better to carry your funds with you or try to
secret them in your room. Baggage that

Embassies in Mexico

All embassies are in Mexico City. Many countries also have consulates in other cities around Mexico; details of many are given in this book's city sections.

The following is a selective list of embassies in Mexico City. They often keep limited business hours – usually something like Monday to Friday from 9 or 10 am to 1 or 2 pm – and close on both Mexican and their own national holidays. But many provide 24-hour emergency telephone contact. If you are telephoning from outside Mexico City, dial the long-distance access code 01, then the city code 5, before the number given below. If you're visiting your embassy, it's best to call ahead to check hours and confirm that the address you're heading for is the right one for the service you want. The addresses below include the *colonias* (neighborhoods) of Mexico City in which the embassies are located and any metro stations convenient to them.

Argentina
Boulevard Manuel Ávila Camacho 1, 7th floor, Lomas de Chapultepec (☎ 520-94-32)

Australia
Rubén Darío 55, Polanco (☎ 531-52-25); open Monday to Wednesday 8 am to 2 pm and 3 to 5 pm, Thursday and Friday 8 am to 2 pm; metro: Polanco or Auditorio

Austria
Sierra Tarahumara 420, Lomas de Chapultepec (☎ 251-97-92)

Belgium
Musset 41, Polanco (☎ 280-07-58); metro: Polanco

Belize
Bernardo de Gálvez 215, Lomas de Chapultepec (☎ 520-12-74)

Brazil
Lope de Armendáriz 130, Lomas de Chapultepec (☎ 202-87-37, 202-75-00)

Canada
Schiller 529, Polanco, 400 meters north of the Museo Nacional de Antropología (☎ 724-79-00, 800-70629);

open Monday to Friday 9 am to 1 pm and 2 to 5 pm; metro: Polanco

Costa Rica
Río Po 113, Cuauhtémoc, north of the Monumento a la Independencia (☎ 525-77-64); metro: Insurgentes

Denmark
Tres Picos 43, Polanco (☎ 255-34-05, 255-41-45); open Monday to Friday 9 am to 1 pm; metro: Auditorio

El Salvador
Montes Altai 320, Lomas de Chapultepec (☎ 520-08-56)

you can lock up is an advantage here. It's also a good idea to divide your funds into several stashes in different places. See Dangers & Annoyances, later in this chapter, for more tips on safeguarding your money.

When paying for something, wait till all the change has been counted out before picking it up. A favorite ruse of ticket clerks in particular is to hand over the change slowly, bit by bit, in the hope that you'll pick it up and go before you have it all.

Credit Cards & ATMs

The easiest money in Mexico is a major credit card or bank cash card. Credit cards such as Visa and MasterCard (Eurocard, Access) are accepted by virtually all airlines, car rental companies and travel agents in Mexico, and by many hotels,

restaurants and shops; American Express cards are widely accepted too.

Equally convenient, you can use major credit cards and some bank cards, such as those on the Cirrus and Plus systems, to withdraw cash pesos from ATMs (bank cash machines, which are now very common in Mexico) and over the counter at banks. ATMs are generally the easiest source of cash. Despite the handling charge that will normally appear on your account, you win by using ATMs because you get a good exchange rate and avoid the commission you would pay when changing cash or traveler's checks.

Mexican banks call their ATMs by a variety of names – usually something like *caja permanente* or *cajero automático*. Each ATM displays the cards it will accept.

France
Campos Elíseos 339,
Polanco (☎ 282-97-00);
consulate is around the
corner at Lafontaine 32; open
Monday to Friday 9 am to
1 pm; metro: Auditorio

Germany
Moliere 118, Polanco
(☎ 280-75-44); open
Monday to Friday 7.30 am
to 1.15 pm; metro: Polanco

Guatemala
Avenida Explanada 1025,
Lomas de Chapultepec
(☎ 540-75-20, 282-53-78)

Honduras
Alfonso Reyes 220,
Hipódromo Condesa
(☎211-52-50,

Consulate: (☎515-66-89);
metro: Juanacatlán

Israel
Sierra Madre 215, Lomas de
Chapultepec (☎ 540-63-40)

Italy
Paseo de las Palmas 1994,
Lomas de Chapultepec
(☎ 596-36-55)

Japan
Paseo de la Reforma 395,
Cuauhtémoc, near the
Monumento a la Indepen-
dencia (☎ 211-00-42);
consular section (☎ 211-00-
28) open Monday to Friday
9.30 am to 1 pm; metro: Sevilla

Netherlands
Montes Urales Sur 635, 2nd
floor, Lomas de
Chapultepec
(☎ 202-84-53, 202-83-46)

New Zealand
José Luis Lagrange 103,
10th floor, Los Morales
(☎ 281-54-86)

Nicaragua
Payo de Rivera 120, Lomas
de Chapultepec
(☎ 540-56-25)

Norway
Boulevard Virreyes 1460,
Lomas de Chapultepec
(☎ 540-34-86)

Spain
Galileo 114, Polanco
(☎ 282-22-71, 282-27-63);
metro: Polanco

Sweden
Paseo de las Palmas

Switzerland
Paseo de las Palmas 405,
11th floor, Lomas de
Chapultepec
(☎ 520-30-03, 520-85-35)

UK
Río Lerma 71 between Río
Sena and Río Rhin,
Cuauhtémoc, north of the
Monumento a la Indepen-
dencia (☎ 207-20-89, 207-
24-49); open Monday to
Friday 8.30 am to 3.30 pm;

Consular section at rear
(Río Usumacinta 30) open
Monday to Friday 9 am to
2 pm; metro: Insurgentes

USA
Paseo de la Reforma 305 at
Río Danubio, Cuauhtémoc,
not far from the Monumento
a la Independencia (☎ 211-
00-42, always attended);
open Monday to Friday
8.30 am to 5.30 pm, closed
on Mexican and US holi-
days; visa office (☎ 533-05-
76) at rear, Río Danubio at
Río Lerma, open Monday
to Friday 6 to 10.30 am;
metro: Insurgentes ■

To guard against robbery when using
ATMs, try to use them during working hours
and choose ones that are securely inside a
bank building, rather than the glass-enclosed
ones on the street.

Traveler's Checks & Cash

If you have a credit card or bank card, as a
backup you should still take along some
major-brand traveler's checks (best denomi-
nated in US dollars), or – less desirable for
security reasons – cash US dollars. If you
don't have a credit or bank card, use US-
dollar traveler's checks. American Express
is a good brand to have because it's recognized everywhere, which can prevent delays.
American Express in Mexico City maintains
a 24-hour hot line (☎ 5-326-36-25) for lost
American Express traveler's checks; you
can call it collect from anywhere in Mexico.

International Transfers

If you need money wired to you in Mexico,
an easy and quick method is the Western
Union 'Dinero en Minutos' (Money in
Minutes) service. It's offered by the
approximately 300 Elektra electrical-goods
stores around Mexico (most are open daily
from 9 am to 9 pm), and by the telégrafos
(telegraph) offices in many cities. Your
sender pays the money at their nearest
Western Union branch, along with a fee,
and gives the details on who is to receive it
and where. When you go to pick it up, take
photo identification. Western Union has
offices worldwide; in the USA call ☎ 800-
325-6000.

Currency

Mexico's currency is the peso, officially
the *nuevo peso* (new peso).

The peso is divided into 100 centavos. Coins are issued in denominations of five, 10, 20 and 50 centavos and one, two, five, 10, 20 and 50 pesos. There are notes of 10, 20, 50, 100, 200 and 500 pesos.

Since the peso's exchange value is unpredictable, prices in this book are given in US dollar equivalents.

The $ sign is used to refer to pesos in Mexico. The designations 'N$,' 'NP' (both for nuevos pesos) and 'MN' *(moneda nacional)* all refer to pesos. Prices quoted in US dollars will normally be written 'US$5,' '$5 Dlls' or '5 USD' to avoid misunderstanding.

Currency Exchange

US dollars are the best currency in which to have traveler's checks. Though you should be able to change non-US-dollar checks and currency (especially Canadian dollars) in main cities, it can require some time-consuming hassles, and in smaller cities and towns you may get poor exchange rates or be unable to exchange at all.

The peso has been fairly stable since the currency crisis of 1994-95, when it lost 60% of its value in three months. Exchange rates as this book went to press were:

Australia	A$1	=	5.51	pesos
Canada	C$1	=	5.67	pesos
France	FF1	=	1.38	pesos
Germany	DM1	=	4.60	pesos
Japan	100Y	=	6.34	pesos
New Zealand	NZ$1	=	5.03	pesos
Spain	100pta	=	5.44	pesos
UK	UK£1	=	13.50	pesos
USA	US$1	=	8.10	pesos

Changing Money

You can change money in banks or at *casas de cambio* ('exchange houses,' often single-window kiosks). Banks go through a more time-consuming procedure than casas de cambio and have shorter exchange hours (typically Monday to Friday from 9 or 10 am to 1 or 2 pm). Casas de cambio can easily be found in just about every large or medium-size town and in many smaller ones. They're quick and often open afternoons, evenings or weekends, but they may

not accept traveler's checks, which rarely happens in banks.

Exchange rates vary a little from one bank or casa de cambio to another. Different rates are also often posted for *efectivo* (cash) and *documento* (traveler's checks). On the whole, though not invariably, banks give better rates for traveler's checks than for cash, and casas de cambio do the opposite.

If you have trouble finding a place to change money, particularly on a weekend, you can always try a hotel – though the exchange rate won't be the best.

Tipping & Bargaining

In general, people on staff in the smaller, cheaper places don't expect much in the way of tips, while those in the expensive resort establishments expect you to be lavish in your largesse. Tipping in the resorts frequented by foreigners (Acapulco, Cancún, Cozumel) is up to US levels of 15%; elsewhere 10% is usually sufficient. Taxi drivers don't generally expect tips, but gas station attendants do.

Though you can attempt to bargain down the price of a hotel room, especially in cheaper places and in the off-season, the rates normally are set fairly firmly, particularly during the busy winter season. In markets bargaining is the rule, and you may pay much more than the going rate if you accept the first price quoted. You should also bargain with drivers of unmetered taxis.

Taxes

Mexico's *Impuesto de Valor Agregado* (Value-Added Tax), abbreviated IVA ('EE-bah'), is levied at 15%. By law the tax must be included in virtually any price quoted to you and should not be added afterward. Signs in shops and notices on restaurant menus often state *'IVA incluido'* Occasionally they state instead that IVA must be added to the quoted prices.

Impuesto Sobre Hospedaje (ISH, 'ee-ESSe-AHCH-e,' the Lodging Tax) is levied on the price of hotel rooms. Each Mexican state sets its own level of ISH, but in most places it's 2%.

Most budget and mid-range accommodations include both IVA and ISH in quoted prices (though it's sometimes worth checking). But in top-end hotels a price may often be given as, say, 'US$100 *más impuestos*' ('plus taxes'), in which case you must add about 17% to the figure. When in doubt, ask, '*¿Están incluidos los impuestos?*' ('Are taxes included?')

Prices in this book all, to the best of our knowledge, include IVA and ISH. See the Getting There & Away and Getting Around chapters for details of taxes on air travel.

POST & COMMUNICATIONS
Post

Almost every town in Mexico has an *oficina de correos* (post office) where you can buy stamps and send or receive mail. They're usually open Saturday mornings as well as long hours Monday to Friday.

Sending Mail An air mail letter weighing up to 20 grams costs US$0.50 to North America, US$0.60 to Europe and US$0.70 to Australasia. Post cards are slightly cheaper.

Delivery times are elastic, and packages in particular sometimes go missing. If you are sending something by air mail, be sure to clearly mark it 'Correo Aéreo.' *Certificado* (registered) service helps ensure delivery and costs less than US$1. An air mail letter from Mexico to the USA or Canada can take four to 14 days to arrive (but don't be surprised if it takes longer). Mail to Europe may take between one and three weeks, to Australasia a month or more. The Mexpost express mail service, available at some post offices, supposedly takes three working days to anywhere in the world; it charges US$10.75 for up to 500 grams to North America, or US$16.25 to Europe.

If you're sending a package internationally from Mexico, be prepared to open it for customs inspection – take packing materials with you to the post office.

For assured and speedy delivery, you can use one of the expensive international courier services, such as United Parcel Service, Federal Express, or DHL. Minimum

rates from Mexico (up to 500 grams) are in the region of US$17 to North America or US$23 to Europe.

Receiving Mail You can receive letters and packages care of a post office if they're addressed as follows (for example):

Jane SMITH (last name in capitals)
Lista de Correos
Acapulco
Guerrero 00000 (post code)
MEXICO

When the letter reaches the post office, the name of the addressee is placed on an alphabetical list that is updated daily. If you can, check the list yourself – it's often pinned on the wall – because the letter may be listed under your first name instead of your last. To claim your mail, present your passport or other identification. There's no charge; the snag is that many post offices hold 'Lista' mail for only 10 days before returning it to the sender. If you think you're going to pick mail up more than 10 days after it has arrived, have it sent to (for example):

Jane SMITH (last name in capitals)
Poste Restante
Correo Central
Acapulco
Guerrero 00000 (post code)
MEXICO

Poste Restante may hold mail for up to a month, but no list of what has been received is posted. Again, there's no charge for collection.

If you have an American Express card or American Express traveler's checks, you can have mail sent to you c/o any of the 50-plus American Express offices in Mexico (the Mexico City office holds mail for two months before returning it to the sender). Take along your card or a traveler's check to show when you collect the mail.

Inbound mail usually takes as long to arrive as outbound mail does (see above), and international packages coming into Mexico may go missing, just like outbound ones.

Telephone

Local calls are cheap. International calls can be very expensive – but they needn't be if you call from the right place at the right time.

The Mexican telephone system was in the throes of being opened up to competition in 1997. Companies such as Alestra (a consortium that includes AT&T from the US) and Avantel (in which MCI is involved) were joining the former monopoly holder, Telmex, in the long-distance telephone market.

It was impossible to say as this book was being written exactly how things would shake down. The following information is based mainly on Telmex precompetition services, but it's likely to remain accurate in terms of calling procedures and is at least a useful pointer to price levels.

There are three main types of places you can place a call from. Cheapest is a public pay phone. A bit more expensive is a *caseta de teléfono* or *caseta telefónica* – a call station, maybe in a shop or restaurant, where an operator connects the call for you and you take it in a booth. The third option is to call from your hotel, but hotels can – and do – charge what they like for this service. It's nearly always cheaper to go elsewhere.

Public Pay Phones

These are common in towns and cities: you'll usually find some at airports, bus stations, and around the main square of any sizable town. Most work OK. Those operated by Telmex are usually marked 'Ladatel,' 'Lada 91,' 'Lada 01' or 'Telmex.' 'Lada' stands for *larga distancia* (long distance), but these phones work for both local and long-distance calls.

Nearly all Telmex pay phones work exclusively on *tarjetas telefónicas* or *tarjetas Ladatel* (phone cards). The cards are sold at many kiosks and shops – look for the blue-and-yellow sign reading *'De Venta Aquí Ladatel'* – in denominations of 20, 50 or 100 pesos. As you talk, the display shows you how much credit you have left on the card. Only a few pay phones are still coin-operated.

Casetas

Casetas de teléfono are more expensive than pay phones (anywhere from 10% to 100% more), but you don't need a phone card to use them and they eliminate street noise. Casetas usually have a telephone symbol outside, or signs saying *'teléfono,'* 'Lada' or 'Larga Distancia.' In Baja California they are known as *cabinas*.

Prefixes, Codes & Costs

When dialing a call, you need to know what *prefijo* (prefix) and *claves* (country or area codes) to put before the number. Prefixes were all changed in 1997 and are likely to be the same for all companies in the competitive new Mexican telephone market.

If you are making a call in Mexico, the prefixes, codes and approximate costs of local and long distance calls vary depending on where you are calling to. General guidelines are as follows:

Calls to city/town you are in – no need to dial a prefix or code; US$0.04 per minute
Calls to other citys/towns in Mexico – dial 01 + area code; US$0.40 per minute
Calls to USA or Canada – dial 00 + country code + area code; US$1.30 per minute (Calls from northern Mexico to the southern USA are cheaper.)
Calls to Europe – dial 00 + country code + area code; US$2.75 per minute
Calls to Australasia – dial 00 + country code + area code; US$3.50 per minute

So if you're in Mexico City and you want to call the Mexico City number 876-54-32, just dial 876-54-32. To call from Mexico City to the Oaxaca number 7-65-43, dial 01, then the Oaxaca area code 951, then 7-65-43. (If you're calling from one town to another with the same area code, you still have to dial 01 and the area code.)

To call the New York City number 987-6543 from Mexico, dial 00, then the US country code 1, then the New York City area code 212, then 987-6543. Other country codes include: Canada, 1; UK, 44; Australia, 61; New Zealand, 64; France, 33; Germany, 49; Italy, 39; Spain, 34; Guatemala, 502; Belize, 501.

Telmex international calls are 33% cheaper at the following times:

Calls to the USA (except Alaska and Hawaii) and Canada: Monday to Friday 7 pm to 6.59 am, Saturday all day, Sunday till 4.59 pm

Calls to Europe or Australasia: Monday to Friday 6 pm to 5.59 am (Europe), 5 am to 4.59 pm (Australasia), Saturday and Sunday all day (both)

If you need to speak to a domestic operator, call ☎ 020; for an international operator, call ☎ 090. For Mexican directory information, call ☎ 040. The country code for Mexico is 52.

Toll-Free Numbers Mexican toll-free numbers – all ☎ 800 followed by five digits – always require the 01 prefix. Most US toll-free numbers are ☎ 800 or 888 followed by seven digits. In general you cannot call a toll-free number from outside the country where it is based, but in the US and Canada you can call any toll-free number in either of those two countries.

North American Calling Cards If you have an AT&T, MCI or Sprint card, or a Canadian calling card or HELLO! phone pass or Call-Me service, you can use them for calls from Mexico to the USA or Canada by dialing the access numbers below. You can check with your phone company before going to Mexico (in Canada or the US call Canada Direct at ☎ 800-561-8868 or visit their website – see the Website Directory for the address) to ask about costs and exactly what procedures you'll have to follow. Normally, after dialing the access number you either have to enter your calling card number or follow voice prompts or operator instructions:

AT&T	001-800-462-4240
MCI	91-800-021-8000
Sprint	001-800-877-8000
Canada Direct	01-800-123-0200

If you get an operator who asks for your Visa or MasterCard number instead of your calling card number, or says the service is unavailable, hang up and dial again. There are scams in which calls are rerouted to credit-card phone services (see below).

Collect Calls A *llamada por cobrar* (collect call) can cost the receiving party much more than if *they* call *you*, so it's cheaper for them if you find a phone where you can receive an incoming call, then pay for a quick call to the other party to ask them to call you back.

If you do need to make a collect call, you can do so from pay phones without a card. Call an operator on ☎ 020 for domestic calls, or ☎ 090 for international calls, or use a Home Country Direct service (see below). Mexican international operators can usually speak English.

Some telephone casetas and hotels will make collect calls for you, but they usually charge for the service.

Home Country Direct This service, by which you make an international collect call via an operator in the country you're calling, is available for several countries. You can get information on Home Direct services and their costs from your phone company before you leave for Mexico, and you can make the calls from pay phones without any card. For Home Direct calls to the USA through AT&T, MCI or Sprint, and to Canada via Canada Direct, dial the numbers given above under North American Calling Cards. Mexican international operators may be able to tell you access numbers for other countries. The Mexican term for Home Country Direct is *País Directo*.

Area Codes

Mexican area codes are given at the beginning of each city or town section in this book and thus are not repeated with each number in that section. But in the introductory chapters, and for telephone numbers outside the section they appear under, the area code is included. ∎

Credit Card Phones In some parts of Mexico – mainly those frequented by many North American tourists, such as Baja California and the big resorts further south – you'll find phones with signs urging you to charge calls to MasterCard, Visa or American Express. Some of them resemble Pacific Bell or AT&T phones. Be aware that very high rates – as high as US$23 for the first minute, US$8 per minute after that – are charged on these devices, which require dialing only 0 to contact an international operator.

Calling Mexico To call a number in Mexico from another country, dial your international access code, then the Mexico country code – 52 – then the area code and number.

Fax, Email & Internet
Public fax service is offered in many Mexican towns by the *telégrafos* (telegraph) office, which may go under the name Telecomm. Also look for *'Fax Público'* signs on shops, businesses and telephone casetas, and in bus stations and airports.

Some places in Mexico – among them Mexico City, Puerto Vallarta, Oaxaca and San Miguel de Allende – have Internet cafés where you can send and receive email or browse the Internet. They typically charge around US$3 for 30 minutes on a computer.

For those traveling with their own computers, CompuServe has 28,800 bps nodes (access numbers) in Guadalajara, León, Mexico City and Puebla, and also a nationwide toll-free number (modem 800-72000).

America Online has AOL GlobalNet nodes in Mexico City (modem 5-628-93-93), Guadalajara (modem 3-827-05-90), Monterrey (modem 8-340-37-24) and Cancún (modem 98-84-12-12). The Cancún node is at 9600 bps, the others at 28,800 bps.

Some hotel rooms have direct-dial phones and phone sockets that allow you to unplug the phone and insert a phone jack that runs directly to your computer. In others you're confronted with switchboard phone systems and/or room phones with a cord running directly into the wall, both of which make it impossible to go online from your room. In such cases you can ask to borrow reception's fax line for a couple of minutes – nine times out of 10 they'll comply, especially if you wait till nighttime, when the boss is away.

It's also possible to plug in your computer at some telephone casetas.

For addresses of some useful Mexican and Mexico-related websites, see the Website Directory.

BOOKS
Although you can buy books in English in most major centers, only Mexico City has an extensive choice. The Mexican-published titles mentioned here – such as the guides to archaeological sites – are widely available in Mexico, but it's wise to obtain other books before arriving in the country. Some libraries in places such as Mexico City, San Miguel de Allende and Oaxaca have good collections of English-language books on Mexico.

History & Society
General One of the best general books on Mexico is Lesley Byrd Simpson's *Many Mexicos*, a classic collection of short essays ranging from pre-Columbian times to the present. *Sons of the Shaking Earth*, by Eric Wolf, is a wonderfully readable introduction to Mexican history and Mesoamerican ethnology. Michael C Meyer & William L Sherman's *The Course of Mexican History* is one of the best general accounts of Mexican history and society.

Ancient Mexico Two books by Michael D Coe give a learned and well-illustrated but not overly lengthy picture of the great cultures of ancient Mexico: *The Maya* traces the history, art and culture of the Maya, while *Mexico* concentrates on Mexico's other pre-Hispanic civilizations. Both have gone through several editions. Coe's 1992 book *Breaking the Maya Code* tells the fascinating story of the decipherment of Mayan writing – an achievement that has added hugely to our understanding of the Maya.

Nigel Davies' *Ancient Kingdoms of Mexico* is a succinct but scholarly study of the Olmec, Teotihuacán, Toltec and Aztec civilizations. Diagrams, illustrations, plans and maps complement the text.

Jacques Soustelle's *Daily Life of the Aztecs* (1962) is a classic on its subject. Also good is *The Aztecs*, by Richard F Townsend (1992).

Spanish Conquest William Henry Prescott's mammoth *History of the Conquest of Mexico* remains a classic, even though it was published in 1843 by an author who never went to Mexico. Only with Hugh Thomas' *Conquest: Montezuma, Cortes & The Fall of Old Mexico* has the 20th century produced an equivalent tome. This book, the product of meticulous research, was published in Britain as *The Conquest of Mexico* in 1993. *History of the Conquest of New Spain*, by Bernal Díaz del Castillo, is an eyewitness account of the Spanish arrival by one of Cortés' lieutenants.

Modern Mexico First published in 1984, *Distant Neighbors*, by Alan Riding, remains a good introduction to modern Mexico and its love-hate relationship with the United States. In Britain it's published as *Mexico, Inside the Volcano*. The more recent *Mexico: A Country Guide*, edited by Tom Barry (1992), is a fine background fact book on how Mexico works, covering all sorts of issues, from the political system to human rights to feminism to the ecology movement. *The Mexicans*, by Patrick Oster, is a sort of microcosmic counterpart to *Distant Neighbors*, focusing on the lives of 20 individual Mexicans.

Oscar Lewis' *The Children of Sánchez* is essential reading on the family dynamics that are crucial to Mexican society. *Mexico under Salinas*, by Philip E Russell, is an absorbing portrait of the country as well as a chronicle of the Salinas presidency; unfortunately, it was published in 1994, before Salinas left office and his name became mud (see the Family Affairs sidebar in Facts about the Country).

Art, Architecture & Crafts

The Art of Mesoamerica, by Mary Ellen Miller in the Thames & Hudson World of Art series, is a good survey of pre-Hispanic art and architecture. On colonial architecture the most important single book is George Kubler's *Mexican Architecture of the Sixteenth Century* (1948).

Good books on Mexico's great 20th-century artists include Diego Rivera's autobiography *My Art, My Life*; *The Fabulous Life of Diego Rivera*, by BD Wolfe; *Frida: A Biography of Frida Kahlo*, by Hayden Herrera; *Frida Kahlo*, another biography, by Malka Drucker; and *The Mexican Muralists*, by Alma M Reed.

Mexico City bookstores are full of beautifully illustrated coffee-table books in English on Mexican arts, archaeology and anthropology. Many are written by experts, and though they're often very expensive, you might want to take one home with you or note its details so you can order it back home. One such is *Mask Arts of Mexico*, by Ruth D Lechuga and Chloe Sayer, a finely illustrated work by two experts. Sayer has also written two fascinating books tracing the evolution of crafts from pre-Hispanic times to the present, with dozens of beautiful photos. *Arts & Crafts of Mexico* is a wide-ranging overview, while *Mexican Textiles*, originally published in Britain as *Mexican Costume*, is a comprehensive treatment of its absorbing topic, with a wealth of detail about Mexican life.

Flora, Fauna & Environment

Roland H Wauer's *Naturalist's Mexico* (1992) is a guide to dozens of areas of natural interest all around Mexico based on the author's three decades of annual trips exploring what he calls 'a biological paradise of enormous natural diversity.' *Mexico – A Hiker's Guide to Mexico's Natural History*, by Jim Conrad (1995), focuses in detail on about 20 day hikes in varied regions, with interesting background information.

Defending the Land of the Jaguar, by Lane Simonian (1995), is the detailed but absorbing story of Mexico's long, if weak, tradition of conservation, from pre-Hispanic forest laws to the modern environmental movement.

Dedicated birders should seek out the Spanish-language *Aves de México*, by Roger Tory Peterson and Edward L Chalif, published by Mexico's Editorial Diana. The English-language version of this book, *A Field Guide to Mexican Birds*, omits pictures of birds that also appear in Peterson's guides to US birds. An alternative is *A Guide to the Birds of Mexico & Northern Central America*, by Steve NG Howell and Sophie Webb.

Brimming with bright color photos, *The Pisces Guide to Caribbean Reef Ecology*, by William S Alevizon, introduces its subject with lively text.

Travel Guides

Lonely Planet has three guides covering specific parts of Mexico in detail: *Guatemala, Belize & Yucatán – La Ruta Maya*, *Baja California*, and *Mexico City*. A handy companion for anyone traveling in Mexico is Lonely Planet's *Latin American Spanish phrasebook*, which contains practical, up-to-date words and expressions in Latin American Spanish.

The People's Guide to Mexico and *The People's Guide to RV Camping in Mexico*, by Carl Franz, have long been invaluable, amusing resources for anyone on an extended trip. They don't try to give hotel, transport, or sightseeing specifics but do provide an all-around general introduction to Mexico.

Those with a big interest in pre-Hispanic sites should find *A Guide to Ancient Mexican Ruins* and *A Guide to Ancient Maya Ruins*, both by C Bruce Hunter. Between them, the two books provide maps and details on more than 40 sites.

Several useful series of straightforward guides to single sites or regions are fairly widely available in Mexico. One is the INAH-SALVAT *Official Guide* booklets on important museums and archaeological sites. Most cost US$5 to US$8. Also useful, and cheaper, are the books in the *Easy Guide* series by Richard Bloomgarden.

If you're a diver, the *Pisces Watersports Guide to Cancún*, by Susanne and Stuart Cummings, is worth seeking out. It includes Isla Mujeres, Playa del Carmen, Akumal, and Tulum. There's also the *Pisces Guide to Diving & Snorkeling Cozumel*, by George Lewbel.

A few guides cater to travelers who want to get out into back-country Mexico. Jim Conrad's *No Frills Guide to Hiking in Mexico* (1992) details 33 walks, more than half of them in Baja California and the northwest. *Mexico's Volcanoes*, by RJ Secor (1981), covers routes up the seven main peaks of Mexico's central volcanic belt. (Also see the preceding Flora, Fauna & Environment section.)

Travel & Description

Incidents of Travel in Central America, Chiapas & Yucatán and *Incidents of Travel in Yucatán*, by John L Stephens, are fascinating accounts of adventure and discovery by the enthusiastic 19th-century amateur archaeologist.

Graham Greene's *Lawless Roads* traces his wanderings down the eastern side of Mexico to Chiapas in the 1930s, a time of conflict between Catholics and the atheistic state. Greene wasn't impressed with Mexican food, which he found to be 'all a hideous red and yellow, green and brown.' Aldous Huxley's *Beyond the Mexique Bay*, first published in 1934, has interesting observations on the Maya. It's also worth reading if you're going to be staying long in Oaxaca.

So Far from God, by Patrick Marnham, is an amusing account of a 1980s journey from Texas through Mexico into Central America. Paul Theroux rides the rails through Mexico on *The Old Patagonian Express*.

Travelers' Tales Mexico is an anthology of some 50 recent articles and essays on all sorts of Mexican places and experiences – good reading while you're there.

Fiction

Many foreign novelists have been inspired by Mexico. *The Power and the Glory*, by Graham Greene, dramatizes the state-church conflict that followed the Mexican Revolution. *Under the Volcano*, by the British dipsomaniac Malcolm Lowry, follows a British diplomat who drinks himself to death on the Day of the Dead in a fictionalized Cuernavaca. Sounds simplistic, but it delves deeply into the Mexican psyche, as well as into Lowry's own, at a time of deep conflict (1938). DH Lawrence's *Plumed Serpent* is heavy going even for Lawrence fans. His *Mornings in Mexico* is a collection of short stories set in both Mexico and New Mexico.

Carlos Castaneda's *Don Juan* series, which reached serious cult status in the 1970s, tells of a North American's experiences with a peyote guru somewhere in northwestern Mexico.

The 1990s have brought a crop of fine new English-language novels set in Mexico. Cormac McCarthy's marvelous *All the Pretty Horses* is the laconic, tense and poetic tale of three young latter-day cowboys riding south of the border. James Maw's thrilling and topical *Year of the Jaguar* takes its youthful English protagonist, in search of the father he has never met, from the US border to Chiapas, where all is revealed. *Consider This, Señora*, by Harriet Doerr, tells of a handful of North Americans who settle in a well-evoked rural Mexico. Their lives unfold dramatically against an exotic landscape and alien culture.

For information about Mexican literature, see the Arts section in Facts about the Country.

Books Published in Mexico

Mexican publisher Minutiae Mexicana produces a range of interesting booklets, including *A Guide to Mexican Witchcraft, A Guide to Mexican Mammals & Reptiles, The Maya World, The Aztecs Then and Now, A Guide to Mexican Ceramics* and even *A Guide to Tequila, Mezcal & Pulque*. They're widely available at about US$3 each.

A similar Mexican-produced paperback series with many titles in English is Panorama.

NEWSPAPERS & MAGAZINES
English Language

Two daily English-language papers – *The News*, which is long established, and the *Mexico City Times*, founded in 1995 – are published in Mexico City and distributed throughout Mexico. They cover the main items of Mexican and foreign news, have long stock exchange listings and some interesting Mexico features, and will keep you in touch with North American and European sports. Most cities that attract long-stay English-speakers – San Miguel de Allende, Guadalajara, Oaxaca and Puerto Vallarta, for example – have an English-language newspaper or newsletter.

You can find North American papers and magazines, and sometimes European ones, all a few days old, in the major cities and tourist towns.

Spanish Language

Mexico has a thriving local press, as well as national newspapers such as *Excelsior*, *El Universal* and *Uno más Uno*. Even small cities often have two or three newspapers of their own. In theory the press is free. In practice it's subject to pressure from politicians and even drug barons, but it does seem to have become more open in the past few years. *La Jornada* is a good national daily with a nonestablishment viewpoint; it covers a lot of stories other papers don't.

México Desconocido (Unknown Mexico) is a colorful monthly magazine with intelligent coverage of many interesting places. Buy it at newsstands for US$2. You can often find back issues or special supplements with features about local areas.

RADIO & TV

Mexican TV is dominated by Televisa, the biggest TV company in the Spanish-speaking world, which runs four of the six main national channels (Nos 2, 4, 5 and 9) and until recently always backed the establishment without much questioning.

TV Azteca, which began transmissions in 1993, has two channels (TV7 and TV13), livelier programs, around 15% of viewers, and a more independent stance. Mexican airtime is devoted mainly to ads, low-budget and popular *telenovelas* (soap operas), soccer, game/talk/variety shows, movies (dubbed if they're foreign) and comedy. If nothing else, it can help you to improve your Spanish. Nudity, graphic violence and offensive language are pretty much kept off the screen.

Cable and satellite TV are widespread, and you'll find at least a few channels on many midrange and top-end hotel room TVs. The main providers are Multivisión and Cablevision, each offering around 25 Mexican and foreign (mainly US) channels. Both offer CNN. Multivisión has the popular sports channel ESPN. Cablevision's Ritmo Son channel is devoted to Latin music.

Mexico has around 1000 AM and FM radio stations, most of them privately run (many by Televisa). Radio announcers are much given to the use of the dramatic echo chamber. Apart from that they offer a variety of music, often that of the region where you're listening. In the evening you may be able to pick up US stations on the AM (medium wave) band.

PHOTOGRAPHY & VIDEO
Film & Equipment
According to Mexican customs laws you are allowed to bring in no more than one still camera, with up to 12 rolls of film, and one movie or video camera, with 12 rolls or cassettes, but these limits are rarely applied strictly.

Camera and film processing shops, pharmacies and hotels all sell film. Most types of film are available in larger cities and resorts at prices similar to those in North America. Film being sold at lower prices may be outdated. If the date on the box is obscured by a price sticker, look under the sticker. Avoid film from sun-exposed shop windows.

Wide-angle and zoom lenses are useful, and it helps to have a polarizing filter to cut down the glare from reflections of sunlight on the ocean.

If your camera breaks down, you'll be able to find a repair shop in most sizable towns, and prices will be agreeably low.

To avoid damage by x-ray machines, carry your film in a lead-lined pouch or have it hand-inspected.

Photography
Mexico is a photographer's paradise. You'll get better results if you take pictures in the morning or afternoon rather than at midday, when the bright sun bleaches out colors and contrast. Be sensitive about photographing people; if in doubt, ask first. Indian people in particular can be reluctant to be photographed.

TIME
Daylight-saving time runs from the first Sunday in April to the last Sunday in October. Most of the country observes Hora del Centro, the same as US Central Time – GMT minus six hours in winter, and GMT minus five hours during daylight-saving. The western states of Nayarit, Sinaloa, Sonora and Baja California Sur are on Hora de las Montañas, the same as US Mountain Time – GMT minus seven hours in winter, GMT minus six hours during daylight-saving. Baja California (Norte) observes Hora del Pacífico, the same as US Pacific Time – GMT minus eight hours in winter, GMT minus seven hours during daylight-saving.

If you enter Mexico from New Mexico or El Paso, Texas, or from Arizona between the first Sunday in April and the last Sunday in October, put your watch forward one hour. Otherwise, there's no time change entering Mexico from the USA.

ELECTRICITY
Electrical current in Mexico is the same as in the USA and Canada: 110 volts, 60 cycles. Though most plugs and sockets are the same as in the US, Mexico actually has three different types of electrical socket: older ones with two equally sized flat slots, newer ones with two flat slots of

differing sizes, and a few with a round hole for a grounding (earth) pin. If your plug doesn't fit the Mexican socket, the best thing to do is get an adapter or change the plug. Fortunately, Mexican electrical-goods stores have a variety of adapters and extensions, which should solve the problem.

WEIGHTS & MEASURES

Mexico uses the metric system. For conversion between metric and US or Imperial measures, see the back of this book.

HEALTH
Predeparture Planning

Insurance Mexican medical treatment is generally inexpensive for common diseases and minor treatment, but if you suffer some serious disease or injury, you may want to find a private hospital or fly out for treatment. Travel insurance can cover the costs of that. Insurance against theft, loss (including plane tickets), and delay or cancellation of a flight is also worth considering. Many US health insurance policies stay in effect, at least for a limited time, if you travel abroad, but it's worth checking exactly what you'll be covered for in Mexico.

For people whose medical insurance or national health systems don't extend to Mexico – which means most non-Americans – a travel policy is advisable. Your travel agent will be able to make recommendations. The international student travel policies handled by STA Travel or other student travel organizations are usually a good value. Check the fine print:

- Some policies specifically exclude 'dangerous activities,' which can mean scuba diving, for instance.
- You may prefer a policy that pays doctors or hospitals directly, rather than your having to pay on the spot and getting reimbursed later. If you have to claim later, make sure you keep all documentation.
- Check if the policy covers ambulances or an emergency flight home.

Medical Kit It is always a good idea to travel with a small first-aid kit. Items it should contain include: antihistamine (such as Benadryl) – useful as a decongestant for colds and allergies, or to ease the itch from insect bites or stings; kaolin preparation, Imodium or Lomotil for stomach upsets; rehydration mixture for severe diarrhea (particularly important for children); antiseptic such as Dettol or Betadine; bandages and Band-Aids; scissors, tweezers and a thermometer (but mercury thermometers are prohibited by airlines); insect repellent (see Protection against Mosquitoes); sunscreen; burn cream (Caladryl is good); and a couple of syringes, in case you need injections and you're dubious about hygiene.

Don't forget an adequate supply of any medication you're already taking: the prescription may be difficult to match in Mexico.

Medical Information Services For advice on immunizations or other matters, talk to your doctor or an appropriate information service. In the USA you can call the Centers for Disease Control & Prevention's international travelers hot line at ☎ 404-332-4559, or visit their website – see the Website Directory for the address. In Canada there's Health Canada (☎ 613-957-8739). In the UK you can obtain a printed health brief for any country by calling MASTA (Medical Advisory Services for Travellers Abroad – ☎ 0891-224100). In Australia call the Australian Government Health Service or consult a clinic such as the Travelers Medical & Vaccination Centre, Level 2, 393 Little Bourke St, Melbourne (☎ 03-9670-3969).

Immunizations It's a good idea to be up to date on your tetanus, typhoid, polio and diphtheria shots and to check your immunity to measles (catching measles is not a pleasant prospect for an adult; those who had it as children are definitely immune). You may want to take antimalarial medicine and get vaccinations against hepatitis A, tuberculosis (for children), or even rabies. See the later sections on individual diseases for more information. Consult a doctor: much depends on which parts of Mexico you're going to and what you'll be doing there.

You need a yellow fever certificate to enter Mexico only if you are coming from an infected country.

Basic Rules
Food & Water Food can be contaminated when it is harvested, shipped, handled, washed or prepared. Cooking, peeling – with clean hands and knife – and/or washing food in pure water is the way to get rid of the germs. Make sure the food you eat is freshly cooked and still hot. Steer clear of salads; uncooked vegetables; raw or rare meat, fish or shellfish; and unpasteurized milk or milk products (including cheese). Squeezing lime on salads may help, as may eating lots of raw garlic, but these habits are far from foolproof. In general, restaurants that are packed with customers will be fine; empty ones are questionable.

Don't trust any water unless it has been boiled for at least five minutes, treated with purifiers or comes in an unopened bottle labeled *agua purificada*. Simple filtering will not remove all dangerous organisms. Most hotels have large bottles of purified water from which you can fill your water bottle or canteen. Inexpensive purified water is available from supermarkets, grocery shops and liquor stores.

If the waiter swears that the ice in your drink is made from agua purificada, you may feel you can take a chance with it. Canned or bottled carbonated beverages, including carbonated water, are usually safe, as are beer, wine and liquor.

If you plan to travel off the beaten track, you may have to purify water yourself. Tincture of iodine (2%), or water purification drops or tablets containing tetraglycine hydroperiodide are sold under brand names such as Globaline, Potable Aqua or Coghlan's in pharmacies and US sporting goods stores such as REI (☎ 800-426-4840), LL Bean (☎ 800-441-5713) or Campmor

(☎ 800-526-4784). In Mexico ask for *gotas* (drops) or *pastillas* (tablets) *para purificar agua* in pharmacies and supermarkets. For tincture of iodine, four drops per liter or quart of clear water is the recommended dosage; let the treated water stand for 20 to 30 minutes before drinking. Vigorously boiling water for five minutes is another way to purify the water, but at high altitudes water boils at a lower temperature, so germs are less likely to be killed. Boil it for longer in those environments.

Heat You can avoid heat problems by drinking lots of fluids and generally not overdoing things. Take time to acclimatize: avoid excessive alcohol intake or strenuous activity when you first arrive. Remember that the sun is much fiercer in the middle of the day than in the morning or afternoon.

Take it easy climbing pyramids and hiking through the jungle. Carry water and wear a hat and light, loose cotton clothing. Take frequent rest breaks in the shade. Use sun block. You can get burned surprisingly quickly, even through clouds. Near water the glare from the sand and water can double your exposure to the sun; you may want to wear a T-shirt and hat while swimming or boating. Calamine lotion is good for treating mild sunburns.

Dehydration or salt deficiency can cause heat exhaustion. Salt deficiency is characterized by fatigue, lethargy, headaches, giddiness and muscle cramps, and in this case salt tablets may help. In extreme cases you may develop heat stroke – see the section below.

Protection against Mosquitoes Some serious tropical diseases are spread by infected mosquitoes. In general, mosquitoes are most bothersome between dusk and dawn and most prevalent in lowland and coastal regions and during the rainy season (May to October). You can discourage them by:

- wearing light-colored clothing, long pants and long-sleeved shirts
- using mosquito repellents containing the compound DEET on exposed areas (overuse of DEET may be harmful, especially to children)

- avoiding highly scented perfume or aftershave
- making sure your room has properly fitting mosquito screens over the windows
- using a mosquito net (it may be worth taking your own

Medical Problems & Treatment

Before presenting the following somewhat alarming catalog of potential illnesses, we can say from our own experience that it is possible to take dozens of journeys in every region of Mexico, climbing volcanoes, trekking to pyramids in remote jungle, camping out, staying in cheap hotels and eating in all sorts of markets and restaurants without getting anything worse than occasional traveler's diarrhea. But some of us *have* experienced hepatitis and dysentery, and we have known people who caught dengue fever and typhoid, so we know that these things can happen.

If you come down with a serious illness, be careful to find a competent doctor, and don't be afraid to get second opinions. You may want to telephone your doctor at home as well.

Hospitals & Clinics

Almost every Mexican town and city has either a hospital or a clinic, as well as Cruz Roja (Red Cross) emergency facilities, all of which are indicated by road signs showing a red cross. Most major hotels have a doctor available. Hospitals are generally inexpensive for common ailments (diarrhea, dysentery) and minor treatments (stitches, sprains). Clinics are often too overburdened with local problems to be of much help, but they are linked by radio to emergency services.

If you use these services, try to ascertain the competence of the staff treating you. In big cities and major tourist resorts you should be able to find an adequate hospital. Care in more remote areas is limited.

Most hospitals have to be paid at the time of service, and doctors usually require immediate cash payment. Some facilities may accept credit cards.

If you have questions, call your embassy or consulate for recommendations of a doctor or hospital, or call your own doctor back home. In some serious cases it may be best to fly home for treatment, difficult as that may be. Medical treatment in Mexico is not always what it should be.

If you should need an air ambulance to fly you to Mexico City or another city with top-notch medical facilities, the Mexico City-based Aeromed (☎ 5-294-4286) has been recommended by travelers. You're looking at thousands of dollars for the service.

Medicines Not to Take Pharmacies in Mexico may sell medicines – often without a prescription – that might be banned for good reason in your home country. Incompetent doctors or pharmacists might recommend such medicines for gastrointestinal ailments, but these drugs may cause other sorts of harm, such as neurological damage. Medicines called halogenated hydroxyquinoline derivatives are among these; they may bear the chemical names clioquinol or iodoquinol, or the brand names Entero-Vioform, Mexaform or Intestopan, or something similar.

Climatic & Geographical Considerations

Heat Stroke Long, continuous periods of exposure to high temperatures can leave you vulnerable to this serious, sometimes fatal condition. The symptoms are feeling unwell, not sweating very much or at all, and a high body temperature (39°C to 41°C, or 102°F to 106°F). Where sweating has ceased, the skin becomes flushed and red. Severe, throbbing headaches and lack of coordination will occur. The victim will become delirious or convulse. Hospitalization is essential, but meanwhile get victims out of the sun, remove their clothing, cover them with a wet sheet or towel and fan them continually.

Altitude Sickness Acute Mountain Sickness (AMS) occurs at high altitudes and can be fatal. The lack of oxygen at high altitudes affects most people to some extent. There is no firm rule on how high is too high: AMS has been fatal at 3000 meters, although 3500 to 4500 meters is the usual range. Several Mexican mountains are well above 3500 meters.

To prevent AMS, it helps to acclimatize and ascend slowly – take rest days, spending two to three nights at each rise of 1,000 meters; drink extra fluids (not alcohol) and eat light, high-carbohydrate meals for energy. It is always wise to sleep at a lower altitude than the greatest height reached during the day.

Danger signs include breathlessness; a dry, irritative cough (which may progress to production of pink, frothy sputum); severe headache; loss of appetite; nausea; and sometimes vomiting. Increasing fatigue, confusion, and lack of coordination and balance are real danger signs. Mild altitude sickness will generally abate after a day or so, but if the symptoms persist or become worse the only treatment is to descend – even 500 meters can help.

Infectious Diseases

Diarrhea A change of water, food or climate can all cause the runs, but diarrhea caused by contaminated food or water is more serious. Despite precautions, you may still have a mild bout of traveler's diarrhea – known informally in Mexico as Montezuma's revenge or *turista* – but a few rushed toilet trips with no other symptoms are not indicative of a serious problem.

Moderate diarrhea, involving half a dozen loose movements in a day, is more of a nuisance. Dehydration is the main danger with any diarrhea, particularly for children, in whom it can occur quite quickly, and fluid replacement is the mainstay of management. Soda water, weak black tea with a little sugar, or soft drinks allowed to go flat and diluted 50% with water are all good. With severe diarrhea a rehydrating solution is necessary to replace minerals and salts. Commercially available oral rehydration salts are very useful; add the contents of one packet to a liter of boiled or bottled water. In an emergency you can make up a solution of six teaspoons of sugar and a half teaspoon of salt to a liter of boiled or bottled water. Stick to a bland diet as you recover.

Lomotil or Imodium can be used to bring relief from the symptoms, though they do not cure the problem. Use these drugs only if absolutely necessary – for example, if you *must* travel. Do not use them if you have a high fever or are severely dehydrated.

In the following situations antibiotics may be indicated (gut-paralyzing drugs such as Imodium or Lomotil should be avoided):

- Watery diarrhea with blood and mucus
- Watery diarrhea with fever and lethargy
- Persistent diarrhea for more than five days
- Severe diarrhea, if it is logistically difficult to stay in one place

Diarrhea can also be a sign of giardiasis, dysentery, cholera or typhoid – see the following sections on those diseases.

Giardiasis The parasite causing this intestinal disorder is present in contaminated water. The symptoms are stomach cramps, nausea, a bloated stomach, frequent gas and watery, foul-smelling diarrhea. Giardiasis can appear several weeks after you have been exposed to the parasite. The symptoms may disappear for a few days and then return; this can go on for several weeks. Tinidazole, also known as Fasigyn, or metronidazole (Flagyl) are the recommended treatments.

Dysentery This serious illness is caused by contaminated food or water and is characterized by severe diarrhea, often with blood or mucus in the stool.

Bacillary dysentery is characterized by a high fever and rapid onset of illness; headache, vomiting and stomach pains are also symptoms. It generally does not last longer than a week, but it is highly contagious.

Amebic dysentery ('amoebas') is often more gradual in onset, with cramping abdominal pain and vomiting less likely; fever may not be present. It will persist until treated and can recur and cause long-term health problems.

A stool test is necessary to diagnose which kind of dysentery you have, so you should seek medical help urgently. In an emergency, norfloxacin 400 mg twice daily for three days or ciprofloxacin 500 mg twice daily for five days can be used as presumptive treatment for bacillary dysentery.

For amebic dysentery, metronidazole (Flagyl) can be used as presumptive treatment in an emergency. An alternative is Fasigyn. Avoid alcohol during treatment and for 48 hours afterward.

Cholera Cholera vaccination is not very effective. The bacteria responsible for cholera are waterborne, so attention to the rules of eating and drinking should protect you. Parts of Mexico do suffer occasional epidemics of cholera, but they're usually fairly widely reported, so you can avoid problem areas. Cholera spreads quickly where sewage systems and water supplies are rudimentary. Beware of foods that are partly cooked or uncooked, such as the popular *ceviche*, made from marinated raw fish, as well as salads and raw vegetables.

The disease is characterized by a sudden onset of acute diarrhea with 'rice water' stools, vomiting, muscular cramps, and extreme weakness. You'll need medical help – but treat for dehydration, which can be extreme, and if there is an appreciable delay in getting to a hospital, begin taking tetracycline. The adult dose is 250 mg four times daily; it is not recommended for children age eight or younger, nor for pregnant women. Fluid replacement is by far the most important aspect of treatment.

Hepatitis Hepatitis is a general term for inflammation of the liver. It has many causes: drugs, alcohol and injections are but a few.

The letters A, B, C, D, E and a rumored G identify specific agents that cause viral hepatitis, which is an infection of the liver that can lead to jaundice (yellow skin),

fever, lethargy and digestive problems. It can have no symptoms at all, with the infected person not knowing they have the disease. Hep D, E and G are fairly rare (so far), and following the same precautions as for A, B and C should be all that's necessary to avoid them.

Hepatitis A This is common in countries with poor sanitation. It's transmitted by contaminated water or food, including shellfish contaminated by sewage. Taking care with what you eat and drink can go a long way toward preventing hepatitis A, but it's a very infectious virus, so additional precautions are recommended. Protection can be provided in two ways – either with the antibody gamma globulin, or with the vaccine Havrix 1440, which provides long-term immunity (possibly longer than 10 years) after an initial injection and boosters at six and 12 months. Gamma globulin should not be given until at least 10 days after administration of the last vaccine needed; it is at its most effective in the first few weeks after administration. Havrix takes about three weeks to provide satisfactory protection.

The symptoms of hepatitis A are fever, chills, headache, fatigue, aches and pains, followed by loss of appetite, nausea, vomiting, abdominal pain, dark urine, light-colored feces, and jaundiced skin. The whites of the eyes may turn yellow. You should seek medical advice, but in general there is not much you can do apart from rest, drink lots of fluids, eat lightly and avoid fatty foods. People who have had hepatitis must forgo alcohol for six months after the illness.

Hepatitis B Incidence of this is low in Mexico, and vaccination is not considered necessary. It's spread through contact with infected blood, blood products or bodily fluids, for example through sexual contact, unsterilized needles or blood transfusions. Other risk situations include getting a shave or tattoo or getting your ears pierced.

The symptoms are much the same as for hepatitis A, except that they are more severe and may lead to irreparable liver damage or even liver cancer.

Hepatitis C This is a concern because it seems to lead to liver disease more rapidly than does hepatitis B. The virus is spread by contact with blood – usually via contaminated transfusions or shared needles. Avoiding both is the only means of prevention, as there is no available vaccine.

Typhoid Typhoid fever is a gut infection spread by contaminated water and food. Vaccination is not totally effective, and typhoid is one of the most dangerous infections, so medical help must be sought.

Early symptoms are headache, sore throat, and a fever that rises a little each day until it is around 40°C (104°F) or higher. The victim's pulse often gets slower as the fever rises – unlike a normal fever, with which the pulse increases. There may be vomiting, diarrhea or constipation.

In the second week the high fever and slow pulse continue and a few pink spots may appear on the body; trembling, delirium, weakness, weight loss and dehydration are other symptoms. If there are no further complications, the fever and other symptoms will slowly diminish during the third week. However, you must get medical help before then, because pneumonia or peritonitis (perforated bowel) are common complications and because typhoid is very infectious.

The victim should be kept cool; watch for dehydration. The drug of choice is ciprofloxacin at 750 mg twice a day for 10 days, but it's quite expensive and may not be available. Alternatives are chloramphenicol and Ampicillin. Ampicillin has fewer side effects, but people who are allergic to penicillin should not be given it.

Tetanus This potentially fatal disease is found in undeveloped tropical areas. It is difficult to treat but preventable with immunization. Tetanus occurs when a wound becomes infected by a germ that lives in the feces of animals or people, so clean all cuts, punctures or animal bites

well. Tetanus is also known as lockjaw, and its first symptom may be discomfort in swallowing, or stiffening of the jaw and neck; this is followed by painful convulsions of the jaw and whole body.

Rabies Rabies is caused by a bite or scratch by an infected animal. Dogs are noted carriers, as are monkeys and cats. Any bite, scratch or even lick from a warm-blooded furry animal should be cleaned immediately and thoroughly. Scrub with soap and running water, then clean with an alcohol solution. If there is any possibility that the animal is infected, medical help should be sought immediately. Even if the animal is not rabid, bites should be treated seriously, as they can become infected or result in tetanus. A rabies vaccination is available and should be considered if you are in a high-risk category – for example, if you intend to explore caves (bat bites can be dangerous) or work with animals.

Sexually Transmitted Diseases Sexual contact with an infected partner spreads these diseases. While abstinence is the only sure-fire preventive, using condoms is also effective. (Only latex condoms have proved effective in preventing the transmission of HIV; see the following section for more information.)

Gonorrhea and syphilis are the most common sexually transmitted diseases; their usual symptoms are sores, blisters or rashes around the genitals, discharges, or pain when urinating. Symptoms may be less marked or not observed at all in women. Syphilis symptoms eventually disappear, but the disease continues and can cause severe problems in later years. The treatment for gonorrhea and syphilis is by antibiotics. There is no cure for either, and there is currently no cure for AIDS.

HIV/AIDS HIV, the Human Immunodeficiency Virus, may develop into AIDS, Acquired Immune Deficiency Syndrome. Any exposure to blood, blood products or bodily fluids may put the individual at risk. Transmission can be by sexual activity or via contaminated needles shared by intravenous drug users. Blood transfusions, vaccinations, acupuncture, tattooing and ear or nose piercing are also potentially dangerous if the equipment is not clean. If you need an injection, ask to see the syringe unwrapped in front of you, or better still, take a needle and syringe pack with you.

Without a blood test it is impossible to detect if an individual, however healthy looking, is HIV-positive.

More than 28,000 AIDS cases had been reported in Mexico by 1997, with the highest rates being in the center of the country, including Mexico City. An estimated 200,000 people in Mexico are HIV-positive. Foreigners applying for permanent residence in Mexico need an HIV-negative certificate.

Insect-Borne Diseases

Malaria This serious disease is spread by mosquito bites; you can greatly reduce your risk by following the antimosquito measures outlined in the earlier Protection against Mosquitoes section. Most visitors to Mexico do not take antimalarial medicine, and do not get malaria, but there's risk in some rural areas of Oaxaca, Chiapas, Guerrero, Campeche, Quintana Roo, Sinaloa, Michoacán, Nayarit, Colima and Tabasco.

If you are traveling in areas where malaria is endemic, it is advisable to take malarial prophylactics – none is 100% effective, but the appropriate drug significantly reduces the risk of contracting the disease. Consult a doctor or one of the medical information services mentioned earlier in this section.

Chloroquine (under various brand names) is the most commonly used antimalarial drug for Mexico. Chiapas is the only state where chloroquine-resistant strains of malaria are suspected. You will usually be told to start taking the medicine one or two weeks *before* you arrive in a malarial area and continue taking it while you're there and for a month after you've left.

Symptoms of malaria range from fever, chills and sweating, headache and abdom-

inal pains to a vague feeling of ill-health, so seek examination immediately if there is any suggestion of the disease. It can be diagnosed by a simple blood test and is curable, as long as you seek medical help when symptoms occur. Without treatment malaria can develop more serious, potentially fatal effects.

Dengue Fever There is no prophylactic for this mosquito-spread disease; the main preventive measure is to avoid mosquito bites. A sudden onset of fever, headaches and severe joint and muscle pains are the first signs before a rash starts on the trunk of the body and spreads to the limbs and face. After another few days, the fever will subside and recovery will begin. Serious complications are not common, but full recovery can take up to a month or more.

Cuts, Bites & Stings

Skin punctures can easily become infected in hot climates. Treat any cut with an antiseptic such as Betadine. Avoid bandages and Band-Aids, which can keep wounds wet. When walking on reefs, shoes will prevent coral cuts, which are slow to heal. An effective folk remedy for jellyfish stings is immediate application of fresh urine.

Scorpion stings are notoriously painful and in Mexico can even be fatal. Scorpions may hide in shoes or clothing, so in rural areas shake these out before you put them on. When walking through undergrowth where snakes may be present, wear boots, socks and long trousers. Snake bites do not cause instantaneous death, and antivenins are usually available.

Women's Health

Gynecological Problems Poor diet, antibiotics for stomach upsets and even contraceptive pills can lead to vaginal infections in hot climates. Wearing skirts or loose-fitting trousers and cotton underwear will help to prevent them.

Yeast infections, characterized by a rash, itch and discharge, can be treated with a vinegar or lemon-juice douche, or with yogurt. Nystatin suppositories are the usual medical prescription. Trichomoniasis is a more serious infection; symptoms are a discharge and a burning sensation when urinating. Male sexual partners must also be treated, and if a vinegar-water douche is not effective medical attention should be sought. Metronidazole (Flagyl) is the prescribed drug.

Pregnancy Most miscarriages occur during the first three months of pregnancy, so that is the most risky time to travel. Miscarriage is not uncommon and can occasionally lead to severe bleeding. Pregnant women should avoid all unnecessary medication, but needed vaccinations and malarial prophylactics should still be taken when possible. Extra care should be taken to prevent illness, and particular attention should be paid to diet and nutrition.

WOMEN TRAVELERS
In this land that invented machismo, women have to make some concessions to local custom – but don't let that put you off going to Mexico. In general, Mexicans are great believers in the *difference* (rather than the equality) between the sexes. Lone women have to expect some catcalls and attempts to chat them up. Normally these men only want to talk to you, but it can get tiresome; the best way to discourage unwanted attention is to avoid eye contact and, if possible, ignore the attention altogether. Otherwise use a cool but polite initial response and a consistent, firm 'No.' It is possible to turn uninvited attention into a worthwhile conversation by making clear that you *are* willing to talk, but no more.

Don't put yourself in peril by doing things Mexican women would not do, such as challenging a man's masculinity, drinking in a cantina, hitchhiking without a male companion, or going alone to isolated places.

Wearing a bra will spare you a lot of unwanted attention. A wedding ring and talk of your husband may help too. Except in beach resorts, it's advisable to wear shorts only at a swimming pool. You might even consider swimming in shorts and a T-shirt, as many Mexican women do.

Recommended reading is the *Handbook for Women Travellers*, by Maggie Moss and Gemma Moss.

GAY & LESBIAN TRAVELERS
Mexico is one of the world's more heterosexual countries, but more broad-minded than you might expect. Gays and lesbians tend to keep a low profile, but they rarely attract open discrimination or violence. There are active scenes in cities such as Puerto Vallarta, Acapulco, Mexico City and Ciudad Juárez (see Entertainment in those cities' sections).

The annual *Women's Traveller*, with listings for lesbians, and *The Damron Address Book*, for men, are both published by Damron Company (☎ 415-255-0404, 800-462-6654), PO Box 422458, San Francisco, CA 94142-2458 USA. *Ferrari's Places for Women*, *Ferrari's Places for Men*, *Women's Travel in Your Pocket*, and *Ferrari Guides' Gay Travel A to Z* (for men and women), all published by Ferrari Publications, are also useful. They can be obtained at any good bookstore.

DISABLED TRAVELERS
Mexico doesn't yet make many concessions to the disabled, though a few new public buildings are starting to provide wheelchair access. Mobility is easiest in the major tourist resorts and the more expensive hotels. Public transportation is mainly hopeless; flying and taxi or car are easiest.

Mobility International USA (☎ 541-343-1284, fax 541-343-6812, miusa@igc.apc.org), PO Box 10767, Eugene, OR 97440 USA, runs exchange programs (including in Mexico) and publishes *A World of Options: A Guide to International Exchange, Community Service & Travel*. In Europe, Mobility International is at rue de Manchester 25, Brussels B1070, Belgium (☎ 02-410 6274, fax 02-410 6297).

The Council on International Educational Exchange (see Courses later in this chapter) can help disabled people interested in working, studying or volunteering abroad.

Twin Peaks Press (☎ 360-694-2462, 800-637-2256), PO Box 129, Vancouver, WA 98666 USA, publishes access guides, directories and a quarterly newsletter.

SENIOR TRAVELERS

The American Association of Retired Persons (AARP, ☎ 800-424-3410), 601 E St NW, Washington, DC 20049 USA, is an advocacy group for Americans 50 years and older and a good resource for travel bargains. Membership for one/three years is US$8/20.

Membership in the US's National Council of Senior Citizens (☎ 301-578-8800), 8403 Colesville Road, Silver Spring, MD 20910 USA, gives access to discount information and travel-related advice.

Grand Circle Travel (☎ 617-350-7500, fax 617-350-6206), 347 Congress St, Boston, MA 02210 USA, offers escorted tours and travel information in a variety of formats and distributes a useful free booklet, *Going Abroad: 101 Tips for Mature Travelers*.

TRAVEL WITH CHILDREN

Mexicans as a rule like children. Any child whose hair is less than jet black will get called *güera* (blond) if she's a girl, *güero* if he's a boy. Children are welcome at all kinds of hotels and in virtually every café and restaurant.

Most children are excited and stimulated by the colors, sights and sounds of Mexico, but younger children especially don't like traveling all the time – they're happier if they can settle in to places and find other children to make friends with.

Children are likely to be more affected than adults by heat or disrupted sleeping patterns. They need time to acclimatize and extra care to avoid sunburn. Take care to replace fluids if a child gets diarrhea (see the Health section).

Bring some of the kids' own toys and books, and give them time to get on with some of the activities they are used to back home. Otherwise, apart from the obvious attractions of beaches, coasts and swimming

pools, in some places you can find excellent special attractions, such as amusement parks, zoos, aquariums and boat rides. In Mexico City don't miss the marvelous hands-on children's museum, Papalote Museo del Niño. Archaeological sites can be fun if the kids are into climbing pyramids and exploring tunnels.

Diapers (nappies) are widely available, but you may not easily find creams, lotions, baby foods or familiar medicines outside larger cities and tourist towns. Bring at least some of any of those that you need.

It's usually not hard to find an inexpensive baby sitter if the grownups want to go out on their own; just ask at your hotel.

On flights to and within Mexico children under two generally travel for 10% of the adult fare, and those between two and 12 normally pay 67%. Children pay full fare on Mexican long-distance buses unless they're small enough to sit on your lap.

Lonely Planet's *Travel with Children*, by Maureen Wheeler, has lots of practical advice on the subject, as well as firsthand stories from many Lonely Planet authors, and others, who have done it.

DANGERS & ANNOYANCES

There has been a big increase in crime, including violent crime, stemming from Mexico's economic crisis of the mid-1990s. With a few precautions you can minimize any danger to your physical safety. More at risk are your possessions, particularly those you carry around with you – but again, a few sensible steps reduce the risk.

For information on the potential risks of Mexico travel – though such official information can make Mexico sound more alarming than it really is – you can contact your country's foreign affairs department: Australia (☎ 02-6261-3305); Canada (☎ 613-944-6788, 800-267-6788); UK (☎ 0171-238-4503); USA (☎ 202-647-5225). Most of these services also make their information available on the Internet – see the Website Directory. If you're already in Mexico, you can contact your embassy.

Theft & Robbery

Theft, particularly pocket-picking and purse-snatching, is common in all large Mexican cities and epidemic in Mexico City. Tourists are singled out, as they are presumed to be wealthy (by Mexican standards) and to be carrying valuables. Crowded buses, bus stops, bus stations, airports, the Mexico City metro, markets, pedestrian underpasses, thronged streets and plazas, remote beach spots and anywhere frequented by large numbers of tourists are all prime locations for theft.

Pickpockets often work in teams: one or two of them may grab your bag or camera (or your arm and leg), and while you're trying to get it free another will pick your pocket. Or one may 'drop' something as a crowd jostles onto a bus and as he or she 'looks for it,' a pocket will be picked or a bag slashed. Pickpockets often carry razor blades, with which they slit pockets, bags or straps. The operative principle is to outnumber you, confuse you, and get you off balance. If your valuables are *underneath* your clothing, the chances of losing them are greatly reduced.

Robberies and muggings are less common than pocket-picking and purse-snatching, but they are on the increase, and resistance may be met with violence. Mexico City taxis have become notorious for robberies. Robbers may be armed. One of this book's authors was robbed at gun and knifepoint in Mexico City on a quiet Sunday afternoon – he was not harmed and he lost little, as his valuables were in the hotel safe. Robbery is easier to avoid than theft, but more serious when it happens, as the robbers may force you to remove your money belt or neck-strap pouch, watch, rings, etc. Usually robbers will not harm you. What they want is your money, fast. There have, however, been a few cases of robbers beating victims to extract credit or bank card PIN numbers.

Precautions To avoid being robbed in cities, do not go where there are few other people. This includes empty streets or empty metro cars at night, little-used pedestrian underpasses, and similarly lonely places.

On beaches and in the countryside, do not camp overnight in lonely places unless you can be absolutely sure it's safe.

You must protect yourself, or you can expect to lose a considerable amount. In Mexican cities follow the precautions listed below *without fail*.

- Unless you have immediate need of them, leave most of your cash, traveler's checks, passport, jewelry, air tickets, credit cards, watch, and perhaps your camera in a sealed, signed envelope in your hotel's safe. Virtually all hotels except the very cheapest provide safekeeping for guests' valuables. You may have to provide the envelope.

- Leaving valuables in a locked suitcase in your hotel room is often safer than carrying them on the streets of a Mexican city.

- Wear a money belt, shoulder wallet, or a pouch on a string around your neck, *underneath your clothing*, and place your remaining valuables in it. Visible round-the-waist money belts are an invitation, and an easy target, for thieves. Carry a small amount of money in a pocket.

- Don't keep money (cash or plastic), purses or bags in open view any longer than you have to. At ticket counters in bus stations and airports, keep your bag between your feet, particularly when you're busy with a ticket agent.

- On trains and lower-grade buses, keep your baggage with you if you can. If you let it disappear into the baggage hold of a 2nd-class bus, the chances of not seeing it again increase.

- Do not leave anything valuable-looking visible in your vehicle when you park it in a city.

Highway & Railway Robbery Bandits sometimes hold up buses and other vehicles on intercity routes, especially at night, taking luggage or valuables. Sometimes buses are robbed by people who board as passengers. The best way to avoid highway robbery is not to travel at night. Risky areas at the time of writing included the states of Campeche and Sinaloa (where some holdups have involved violence and bandits have also operated by day), and Michoacán, Guerrero, Oaxaca and Chiapas. In Sinaloa some bandits have disguised themselves as police or other officials. Robberies are also a risk on trains east of the Isthmus of Tehuantepec. If the situation in Chiapas remains tense, seek local advice before venturing off major roads.

Reporting a Theft or Robbery Unless you have been physically mistreated or otherwise feel that the gravity of an offense is such that the police ought to know about it, there's usually little to gain by going to them unless you need a police statement to present to your insurance company. In serious cases you may want to seek your embassy or consulate's help or advice. You can also contact SECTUR, the national tourism ministry, in Mexico City, which maintains two 24-hour phone lines (☎ 5-250-01-23, 800-90392).

If you go to the police and your Spanish is poor, take a more fluent speaker. Also take your passport and tourist card, if you still have them. If you just want to report a theft for insurance purposes, say you want to *'poner una acta de un robo'* (make a record of a robbery). This should make it clear that you merely want a piece of paper and you should get it without much trouble.

BUSINESS HOURS

Shops are generally open Monday to Saturday from 9 am to 2 pm, close for siesta, then reopen from 4 to 7 pm. Stores in hot regions sometimes take a longer siesta but stay open later in the evening. Some may not be open Saturday afternoon.

Offices have similar Monday to Friday hours; those with tourist-related business might be open for a few hours on Saturday.

Some Mexican churches – particularly those that contain valuable works of art – are locked when not in use. But most churches are in frequent use – be careful not to disturb services when you visit them.

Archaeological sites are usually open seven days a week from 8, 9 or 10 am to 5 pm. This is unfortunate, because in many hot regions the hours before 8 am and after 5 pm, especially in summer, are cooler and much more pleasant, and there's plenty of golden light. Most museums have one closing day a week, often Monday. On Sunday nearly all archaeological sites and museums are free, and the major ones can get very crowded.

PUBLIC HOLIDAYS & SPECIAL EVENTS

Mexico's frequent fiestas are full-blooded, highly colorful affairs that often go on for several days and add a great deal of spice to life. There's a major national holiday or celebration almost every month, to which each town adds nearly as many local saints' days, fairs, arts festivals and so on.

Christmas-New Year and Semana Santa, the week leading up to Easter, are the chief Mexican holiday periods. If you're traveling at either time, try to book transport and accommodations in advance.

National Holidays

Banks, post offices, government offices and many shops throughout Mexico are closed on the following days:

January 1
   Año Nuevo – New Year's Day
February 5
   Día de la Constitución – Constitution Day
March 21
   Día de Nacimiento de Benito Juárez –
   Anniversary of Benito Juárez's Birth
May 1
   Día del Trabajo – Labor Day
May 5
   Cinco de Mayo – anniversary of Mexico's
   1862 victory over the French at Puebla,
   celebrated grandly in Puebla
September 16
   Día de la Independencia – commemoration
   of the start of Mexico's war for indepen-
   dence from Spain; the biggest celebrations
   are in Mexico City.
October 12
   Día de la Raza – commemorating
   Columbus' discovery of the New World
   and the founding of the Mexican (mestizo)
   people
November 20
   Día de la Revolución – anniversary of the
   Mexican Revolution of 1910
December 25
   Día de Navidad – Christmas Day; the
   Christmas feast traditionally takes place
   in the early hours of December 25, after
   midnight mass.

Other National Celebrations

Though not official holidays, some of these are among the most important festivals on the Mexican calendar. Many offices and businesses close.

January 6
Día de los Reyes Magos – Three Kings' Day (Epiphany); Mexican children traditionally receive gifts this day, rather than at Christmas (but some get two loads of presents!).

February 2
Día de la Candelaría – Candlemas; processions, bullfights, and dancing in many towns commemorate the presentation of Jesus in the temple 40 days after his birth.

Late February or early March
Carnaval – Carnival; takes place the week or so before Ash Wednesday (which falls 46 days before Easter Sunday), this is the big bash prior to the 40-day penance of Lent; it's celebrated most festively in Mazatlán, Veracruz and La Paz, with huge parades and masses of music, food, drink, dancing, fireworks and fun.

March or April
Semana Santa – Holy Week, starting on Palm Sunday (Domingo de Ramos); closures are usually from Good Friday (Viernes Santo) to Easter Sunday (Domingo de Resurrección); particularly colorful celebrations are held in San Miguel de Allende, Taxco and Pátzcuaro; most of Mexico seems to be on the move at this time.

September 1
Informe Presidencial – the president's state of the nation address to the legislature

November 1
Día de Todos los Santos – All Saints' Day

November 2
Día de los Muertos – Day of the Dead, Mexico's most characteristic fiesta; the souls of the dead are believed to return to earth this day. Families build altars in their homes and visit graveyards to commune with their dead on the preceding night and the day itself, taking garlands and gifts of, for example, the dead one's favorite foods. A happy atmosphere prevails. The souls of dead children, called *angelitos* because they are believed to have automatically become angels, are celebrated the previous day, All Saints' Day. Like many Mexican rituals, these events have pre-Hispanic roots. Those around Pátzcuaro are most famous, but every cemetery in the country comes alive this day.

December 12
Día de Nuestra Señora de Guadalupe – Day of Our Lady of Guadalupe, Mexico's national patron, the manifestation of the Virgin Mary who appeared to a Mexican Indian, Juan Diego, in 1531; a week or more of celebrations leads up to the big day, with children taken to church dressed as little Juan Diegos or Indian girls; festivities take place nationwide, but the biggest are at the Basílica de Guadalupe in Mexico City.

December 16-24
Posadas – Candlelit parades of children and adults, reenacting the journey of Mary and Joseph to Bethlehem, held for nine nights (the tradition is more alive in small towns than in cities); the ninth procession, on Christmas Eve, goes to the church. Also around Christmas, *pastorelas* – dramas enacting the journey of the shepherds to see the infant Jesus – are staged.

Local Fiestas

Every city, town, *barrio* (neighborhood) and village has its own fiestas, often in honor of its patron saint(s). Street parades of holy images, special costumes, fireworks, dancing, lots of music, plenty of drinking – even bull-running through the streets in some places – are all part of the scene. There are festivals of arts, dance, music and handicrafts, and celebrations for harvests of avocados, grapes, even radishes. Even trade and business fairs often serve as a focus for wider festivities.

ACTIVITIES

A source of information on organizations and firms involved in active tourism in Mexico is the website Eco Travels in Mexico (see the Website Directory). See also the Organized Tours sections in this book's Getting Around chapter.

Hiking, Cycling & Horseback Riding

Interest in the wilderness experience has only recently started to take off among Mexicans. For the urban middle class, the countryside has traditionally been a place where *campesinos* work and *bandidos* roam. Some picturesque spots are popular for an outing in the car, a family picnic and a look at the view. There is a also small mountaineering community (see below), but fishing and hunting are bigger news.

That doesn't stop intrepid gringos from trekking off into rough country. Trails in the Barranca del Cobre (Copper Canyon) area and Baja California are among the most popular. There's also a variety of long and short day-hike possibilities elsewhere, though in many coastal regions heat and humidity are a deterrent. Long-distance cycling and mountain biking are similarly infrequent activities for Mexicans, but that doesn't stop some gringos from enjoying cycling trips in Mexico. In a few places you'll find horses or bicycles – very occasionally mountain bikes – for rent, mainly to reach specific sites. There are also some riding ranches for trail or beach rides.

See the Flora & Fauna section in Facts about the Country for more on visiting places of natural interest. The Books section earlier in this chapter mentions some useful guides for hikers and nature lovers.

Mountain Climbs & Guides A number of Mexico City organizations conduct hiking and climbing trips on Mexico's volcanoes. Popocatépetl was off-limits at the time of writing because of a spell of volcanic activity that began in 1994. For a guided mountain trip – and a guide is certainly recommended for Iztaccíhuatl or Pico de Orizaba – you should book at least a week ahead, and you will probably need at least two people.

One professional organization that provides qualified guides for most Mexican mountain peaks is Coordinadores de Guías de Montaña (☎ /fax 5-584-46-95), Tlaxcala 47, Colonia Roma, Mexico City. A two-day, one-night trip for two people from Mexico City to the top of Iztaccíhuatl and back is around US$350 per person, including transportation and two meals.

Water Sports

Most imaginable water sports can be found along Mexico's coasts. You'll find more information on sites and facilities in the

JENNIFER JOHNSEN

Mountainscape inland from Puerto Escondido

regional chapters. Most coastal resorts have shops that will rent equipment such as snorkels, masks and fins, and outfits that can arrange boat and fishing trips. Waterskiing, parasailing and 'banana' riding (in which you sit on a long, inflated bananalike thing and are towed at a rapid clip by a boat) are easy to find at many resorts. You might want to check on the safety of the equipment before taking off. Inland are many *balnearios*, bathing places with swimming pools, often centered on hot springs in picturesque surroundings.

Snorkeling & Diving There are some wonderful waters on both the Caribbean and Pacific Coasts, but visibility is more predictably good on the Caribbean. Fine Caribbean diving spots include Isla Mujeres, Playa del Carmen, Cozumel, Akumal and Xcalak. There's good snorkeling at the same places, plus at Puerto Morelos, Laguna Yal-Xu, Chemuyil and Xcacel. On the Pacific Coast, Puerto Vallarta, Zihuatanejo, Acapulco and Huatulco are among the best places for both diving and snorkeling. There are many spots in Baja California too: Mulegé and Cabo San Lucas are particularly popular with divers.

Surfing & Windsurfing The Pacific Coast has some superb waves. Among the best are the summer breaks at spots between San José del Cabo and Cabo San Lucas (Baja California); the 'world's longest wave,' on Bahía de Matanchén (near San Blas); and the 'Mexican Pipeline,' at Puerto Escondido. Other spots include Ensenada, Mazatlán, Barra de Navidad, Manzanillo, Troncones Point (near Zihuatanejo), and Playa Revolcadero (near Acapulco). Many surf beaches are easiest reached with your own vehicle. Fishermen are often the best people to tell you where *'las olas'* (the waves) are to be found.

Los Barriles is Baja California's windsurfing capital. Further south, Puerto Vallarta and Manzanillo can be good.

Fishing There are opportunities for lake and reservoir fishing inland, and lagoon and sea fishing on the Gulf and Caribbean Coasts, but it's sport fishing off the Pacific Coast that Mexico is justifiably famous for. See destination sections in the Baja California and Central Pacific Coast chapters for more detail on what you can fish for – for example, marlin, swordfish, sailfish and tuna – and when. Contact a Mexican Government Tourism Office or a Mexican consulate for information on fishing permits.

COURSES

Taking classes in Mexico can be a great way to meet people and get an inside angle on local life as well as study the language or history of the country. There are Spanish language schools in many of Mexico's most attractive cities; some are private, some affiliated with universities. Course lengths range from a week to a year. In some places you can enroll on the spot and start any Monday.

You may be offered accommodations with a local family as part of the deal. Living with Spanish speakers will help your language skills as much as any formal tuition. Mexico City, Guadalajara, Guanajuato, Cuernavaca, San Miguel de Allende, Morelia, Taxco, Oaxaca and Puerto Vallarta are all among the cities with college courses or private language schools. In some places courses in art, crafts or indepth study of Mexico are also available.

Mexican universities and colleges often offer tuition to foreigners to complement courses they are taking back home. If you're studying long term in Mexico you'll need a student visa – contact a Mexican consulate for information.

Information about Spanish language programs in Mexico is available from the National Registration Center for Study Abroad (☎ 414-278-7410, inquire@nrcsa.com), PO Box 1393, Milwaukee, WI 53201 USA. The Council on International Educational Exchange (☎ 888-268-6245, info@ciee.org), 205 East 42nd St, New York, NY 10017 USA, also has information on studying in Mexico.

The Institute of International Education (☎ 5-211-0042, fax 5-535-5597, iie@profmexis.sar.net), Londres 16, 2nd floor, Colonia Juárez, 06600 México DF, Mexico, publishes *Spanish Study in Mexico*, profiling 43 Spanish language schools in Mexico, and *An International Student's Guide to Mexican Universities*. For a copy of either, send a check or money order payable to the Institute of International Education – US$5.95 for the first book, US$19.95 for the second – to IIE-Mexico at the above Mexico City address or IIE-Mexico, PO Box 3087, Laredo, TX 78041 USA.

The Casa de los Amigos in Mexico City (see Mexico City – Places to Stay) holds several open seminars a year – usually one to two weeks – on social issues such as women, children and health in Mexico; the Mexico City environment; and urban popular movements. The seminars include visits to local service organizations and work on community projects. The fee of around US$35 a day includes lodging and most meals. The Casa de los Amigos also has useful files on language schools in Mexico and Central America.

WORK

Mexicans themselves need jobs, and by law people who enter Mexico as tourists are not allowed to take employment.

English-speakers may find teaching work in language schools, *preparatorias* (high schools), or universities, or can offer personal tutoring. Mexico City is the best place to pick up English-teaching work; Guadalajara is also good. It should also be possible in other major cities. The pay is low, but you can live on it.

The News and the telephone yellow pages in large towns are good sources of job opportunities. Positions in high schools or universities are more likely to become available with the beginning of each new term – contact institutions that offer bilingual programs or classes in English; for universities, arrange an appointment with the director of the language department. Language schools tend to offer short courses, so teaching opportunities with them come up more often and

your commitment is for a shorter time, but they pay less than high schools and universities do.

A foreigner working in Mexico must have a permit or government license, but a school will often pay a foreign teacher in the form of a *beca* (scholarship), and thus circumvent the law, or the school's administration will procure the appropriate papers.

It's helpful to know at least a little Spanish, even though some institutes insist that only English be spoken in class.

Volunteer Work

The Council on International Educational Exchange (see Courses), has information on volunteer programs in Mexico. *Volunteer Vacations*, by Bill McMillon (Chicago Review Press, 1995), lists lots of volunteer work organizations and other information sources.

The Casa de los Amigos (see Mexico City – Places to Stay) has files on volunteer opportunities in Mexico and other parts of Latin America and can place Spanish-speaking volunteers on projects in Mexico City focusing on issues such as education, street children, AIDS, refugees, or democratic struggle. Most of its openings are for full-time work of six months or longer.

For work focused on the environment, Earthwatch runs several projects in Mexico that you pay to take part in. It has three offices:

Australia
Level One, 457 Elizabeth St, Melbourne 3000, Australia (☎ 03-9600-9100, fax 03-9600-9066, earth@earthwatch.org)
UK
57 Woodstock Rd, Oxford, OX2 6HJ, UK (☎ 01865-311600, fax 01865-311383, info@uk.earthwatch.org)
USA
680 Mount Auburn St, PO Box 9104, Watertown, MA 02272 USA (☎ 800-776-0188; fax 617-926-8532, info@earthwatch.org)

One World Workforce (☎ /fax 520-779-3639), Rt 4, Box 963A, Flagstaff, AZ 86001, USA, sends paying volunteers to work on environmental conservation projects in Mexico such as protecting sea turtle nests.

Amigos de las Americas (☎ 800-231-7796; fax 713-782-9267), 5618 Star Lane, Houston, TX 77057, sends volunteers to work on public health projects in Latin America. Volunteers are normally involved in fundraising to defray project costs.

ACCOMMODATIONS
Accommodations in Mexico range from campsites, *casas de huéspedes* (guesthouses) and hostels through budget hotels and motels to world-class luxury high-rise hotels and lavish resorts.

Reservations
It's often advisable to reserve a room in advance at particularly popular hotels or if you plan to visit busy areas during the Christmas-New Year holidays, Semana Santa, or during July and August. You should request a reservation by telephone or fax, asking whether a deposit is required and how to send it, and requesting confirmation.

Camping
All Mexican beaches are public property. You can camp for nothing on most of them, but any beach can be a risky place for your belongings.

Most equipped campgrounds are actually trailer parks, set up for RVs (camper vans) and trailers (caravans), but they accept tent campers at lower rates. Some are very basic, others quite luxurious. Expect to pay about US$3 to US$5 to pitch a tent, and US$8 to US$15 for two people to use the full facilities of a good campground. Some restaurants or guesthouses in small beach spots will let you pitch a tent on their patch of land for a dollar or two per person.

Tent camping is more practicable on the Yucatán Peninsula, in Baja California and along the Pacific Coast than in most other areas, where campgrounds are rarer. If you plan to camp much, we recommend *The People's Guide to RV Camping in Mexico*,

by Carl Franz (see Books, earlier in this chapter).

Hammocks & Cabañas
Both these forms of accommodations are mainly found in low-key beach spots in the south of the country.

Hammocks are a very cheap way of sleeping. You can rent one and a place to hang it – usually under a palm roof outside a small casa de huéspedes or beach restaurant – for US$2 in some places, though it may be more like US$5 to US$10 on the Caribbean Coast, where all accommodations are more expensive. If you have your own hammock the cost comes down a bit. It's easy enough to buy hammocks in Mexico; Mérida specializes in them, and you'll find them offered for sale in beach spots on the Yucatán Peninsula and in Oaxaca.

Cabañas are palm-thatched huts – some have dirt floors and nothing inside but a bed; others are deluxe, with electric light, mosquito nets, fans, fridge, bar and tasteful decor. Generally, prices for simple cabañas range from US$6 to US$20, with the more expensive ones being on the Caribbean – where you'll also find luxury cabañas costing US$100!

Hostels
Villas juveniles or *albergues de juventud* (youth hostels) exist in about 20 university and resort towns. Many are attached to sports centers. Sometimes they are of use to travelers; other times cheap hotels are preferable. Hostels have basic but usually clean single-sex dormitories and a variety of other facilities (but not necessarily a kitchen). A bed usually costs about US$4. You may get a small discount with an HI card.

In a few places, such as Oaxaca, Palenque and San Miguel de Allende, there are privately run hostels aimed at international backpackers.

Casas de Huéspedes & Posadas
The cheapest and most congenial lodging is often a casa de huéspedes – that is, a

home converted into simple guest lodgings. Good casas de huéspedes are usually family run and have a relaxed, friendly atmosphere. Rooms may or may not have a private bathroom. A double typically costs US$8 to US$12, though a few places are more comfy and more expensive. Some *posadas* (inns) are like casas de huéspedes; others are small hotels.

Cheap Hotels

These exist in every Mexican town. There are many clean, friendly ones; there are also dark, dirty ones. You can get a decent double room with private shower and hot water in most of the country for US$10 to US$15, or even less, but in Baja California or on the Caribbean Coast you may have to pay double that. Many hotels have rooms for three, four or five people that cost little more than a double.

Note that *cuarto sencillo* usually means a room with one bed, which is often a *cama matrimonial* (double bed). One person can usually occupy such a room for a lower price than two people. A *cuarto doble* is usually a room with two beds, often both 'matrimonial.'

Middle & Top-End Hotels

Mexico specializes in good middle-range hotels where two people can usually get a room with a private bathroom, TV, perhaps air-con and an elevator, and often a restaurant and bar, for between US$20 and US$40. These places are generally pleasant, respectable, safe, and comfortable without being luxurious.

Among the most charming hotels are many old mansions, inns, even convents, turned into hotels. Some date from colonial times, others from the 19th century. Most are wonderfully atmospheric, with fountains gurgling in old stone courtyards. Some are a bit spartan (but relatively low in price), others have been modernized and can be posh and expensive. These are often the lodgings you will remember most fondly after your trip.

Mexico has plenty of large, modern hotels, particularly in the largest cities and resorts. They offer the expected levels of luxury at expectedly lofty prices. If you like to stay in luxury but also enjoy saving some money, choose a Mexican hotel, not one that's part of an international chain.

Apartments

In some places there are apartments with fully equipped kitchens designed for tourists. Some are very comfortable, and they can be a good value for three or four people.

FOOD

Mexican cuisine is enormously varied, full of regional differences and subtle surprises. You'll eat well in Mexico, and the choice is wide in all sizable towns. In addition to the Mexican fare that we describe here, you'll find all sorts of international food too, even some good vegetarian restaurants. If you crave familiar flavors and familiar ambiance, there are many international-style eateries, including reliable chain restaurants like VIPS and Sanborn's. For fresh fruit, vegetables, tortillas, cheese and bread, pop into the local market.

Staples

Mexicans eat three meals a day: *desayuno* (breakfast), *comida* (lunch), and *cena* (supper). Each includes one or more of three national staples: *tortillas, frijoles* and *chiles*.

Tortillas are thin round patties of pressed corn *(maíz)* or wheat-flour *(harina)* dough cooked on griddles. Both can be wrapped around or served under any type of food. Frijoles are beans, eaten boiled, fried or refried in soups, on tortillas, or with just about anything.

Chiles are spicy-hot chili peppers; they come in dozens of varieties and are consumed in hundreds of ways. Some types, such as the *habanero* and *serrano*, are always very hot, while others, such as the *poblano*, vary in spiciness according to when they were picked. If you are unsure about your tolerance for hot chilies, ask if they are *dulce* (sweet), *picante* (hot), or *muy picante* (very hot).

Street & Market Meals

The cheapest food in Mexico is served up by the thousands of street stands selling all manner of hot and cold food and drinks. At these places you can often get a taco or a glass of orange juice for less than US$0.20. Many are very popular and well patronized, but hygiene can be a risk. Deciding whether to use them is a matter of personal judgment; those with a lot of customers are likely to be the best and safest.

A step up from street fare are the *comedores* found in many markets. They offer Mexico's cheapest sit-down meals – you sit on benches at long tables and the food is prepared in front of you. It's usually typical local fare, and at good comedores it's like home cooking. It's best to go at lunchtime, when ingredients are fresher, and pick a comedor that's busy – which means it's good.

Breakfast

The simplest breakfast is coffee or tea and *pan dulce* (sweet rolls), a basket of which is set on the table; you pay for the number consumed. Many restaurants offer combination breakfasts for about US$1.50 to US$2.50, typically composed of *jugo de fruta* (fruit juice), *café* (coffee), *bolillo* or *pan tostado* with *mantequilla* and *mermelada* (roll or toast with butter and jam), and *huevos* (eggs), which are served in a variety of ways:

huevos pasados por agua – lightly boiled eggs (too lightly for many visitors' tastes)
huevos cocidos – harder-boiled eggs (specify the number of minutes if you're in doubt)
huevos estrellados – fried eggs
huevos fritos (con jamón/tocino) – fried eggs (with ham/bacon)
huevos mexicanos – eggs scrambled with tomatoes, chilies and onions (representing the red, green and white of the Mexican flag)
huevos motuleños – tortilla topped with slices of ham, then fried eggs, cheese, peas and tomato sauce

huevos rancheros – fried eggs on tortillas, covered in salsa
huevos poches – poached eggs

Mexicans usually eat meat for breakfast, but in many places frequented by travelers, granola, *ensalada de frutas* (fruit salad), *avena* (porridge) and even Corn Flakes are available.

Lunch

La comida, the biggest meal of the day, is usually served between 1 and 3 or 4 pm. Most restaurants offer not only à la carte fare but also special fixed-price menus called *comida corrida, cubierto* or *menú del día*. These menus constitute the best food bargains, because you get several courses (often with some choice) for much less than such a meal would cost à la carte. Prices typically range from US$1.50 or less at a market comedor for a simple meal of soup, a meat dish, rice and coffee to US$8 or more for elaborate repasts beginning with oyster stew and finishing with profiteroles – but typically you'll get four or five courses for US$2.50 or so. Drinks usually cost extra.

Dinner/Supper

La cena, the evening meal, is usually lighter than the comida. Fixed-price meals are rarely offered, so plan to eat your main meal at lunchtime.

Snacks

Antojitos, or 'little whims,' are traditional Mexican snacks or light dishes. Some are actually small meals in themselves. They can be eaten at any time, on their own or as part of a larger meal. There are many, many varieties, some peculiar to local areas, but here are some of the more common ones:

burrito – any combination of beans, cheese, meat, chicken or seafood seasoned with salsa or chili and wrapped in a wheat-flour tortilla
chilaquiles – fried tortilla chips with scrambled eggs or sauce, often with grated cheese on top

chiles rellenos – chilies stuffed with cheese, meat or other foods, deep fried and baked in sauce

empanada – small pastry with savory or sweet filling

enchilada – ingredients similar to those used in burritos and tacos rolled up in a tortilla, dipped in sauce and then baked or partly fried; *enchiladas Suizas* (Swiss enchiladas) come smothered in a blanket of thick cream

enfrijolada – soft tortilla in a frijole sauce with cheese and onion on top

entomatada – soft tortilla in a tomato sauce with cheese and onion on top

gordita – fried maize dough filled with refried beans, topped with cream, cheese and lettuce

guacamole – mashed avocados mixed with onion, chili, lemon, tomato and other ingredients

quesadilla – flour tortilla topped or filled with cheese and occasionally other ingredients and then heated

queso fundido – melted cheese served with tortillas

sincronizada – a lightly grilled or fried tortilla 'sandwich,' usually with a ham and cheese filling

sope – thick patty of corn dough lightly grilled then served with salsa verde or salsa roja (see Other Foods) and frijoles, onion and cheese

taco – the Número Uno Mexican snack: soft corn tortilla wrapped or folded around the same fillings as a burrito

tamale – corn dough stuffed with meat, beans, chilies or nothing at all, wrapped in corn husks or banana leaves and then steamed

torta – Mexican-style sandwich in a roll

tostada – crisp-fried, thin tortilla that may be eaten as a nibble while you're waiting for the rest of a meal or can be topped with meat or cheese, tomatoes, beans and lettuce

Soup

There are many *sopas* (soups) made from meats, vegetables and seafoods, including:

caldo – broth

gazpacho – chilled vegetable soup spiced with hot chilies

menudo – tripe soup made with the spiced entrails of various four-legged beasts

pozole – rich, spicy stew of hominy (large maize kernels) with meat and vegetables

Note that *sopa de arroz* is not soup at all but rice pilaf.

Seafood

Seafood is good along the coasts and in the major cities, where customers abound. Be suspicious of seafood in out-of-the-way mountain towns, and take care with uncooked seafood.

Fish is often eaten as a *filete* (filet), *frito* (fried whole fish), or *al mojo de ajo* (fried in butter and garlic). *Ceviche*, the popular Mexican cocktail, is raw seafood (fish, shrimp, etc) marinated in lime and mixed with onions, chilies, garlic and tomatoes. There are other seafood *cocteles* (cocktails) as well.

Fish

atún – tuna

corvina – bass

filete de pescado – fish filet

huachinango – red snapper

mojarra – perch

pescado – fish after it has been caught

pez espada – swordfish

pez – fish that is alive in the water

robalo – sea bass

salmón (ahumada) – (smoked) salmon

tiburón – shark

trucha – trout

Other Seafood

abulón – abalone

almejas – clams

calamar – squid

camarones – shrimp

camarones gigantes – prawns

cangrejo – large crab

caracol – snail

jaiba – small crab

langosta – lobster

mariscos – shellfish
ostiones – oysters

Meat & Poultry
Meat and poultry are often listed separately as *carnes* and *aves* on Mexican menus.

Meat
bistec, bistec de res (also spelled bisteck) – beefsteak
cabra – goat
cabrito – kid (young goat)
carne – meat, usually beef if not otherwise specified
carnero – mutton
carnitas – deep-fried pork
cerdo – pork
chicharrón – deep-fried pork rind; pigskin cracklings
chorizo – spicy pork sausage
cochinita – suckling pig
conejo – rabbit
cordero – lamb
costillas – ribs
hamburguesa – hamburger
hígado – liver
jamón – ham
puerco – pork
res – beef
salchicha – spicy pork sausage
ternera – veal
tocino – bacon
venado – deer (venison)

Poultry
faisán – pheasant; turkey
guajolote – turkey
pato – duck
pavo – turkey
pechuga – chicken breast
pollo – chicken

Cuts & Preparation
You'll come across meat, poultry and seafood prepared and served in many ways, including the following:

adobado – marinated, seasoned and dried
ahumado – smoked
a la parrilla – grilled, perhaps over charcoal
a la plancha – 'planked,' split and roasted
a la tampiqueña – sautéed thinly sliced meat, officially also marinated in garlic, oil and oregano
a la veracruzana – topped with tomato, olive and onion sauce
al carbón – charcoal-grilled
al horno – baked
al mojo de ajo – in garlic sauce
alambre – shish kebab, 'en brochette'
asada – grilled
barbacoa – literally 'barbecued,' but meat is covered and placed under hot coals
bien cocido – well done
birria – stew-cum-broth of kid or mutton and chopped onion
cabeza – head
cecina – thin-sliced beef, soaked in lemon or orange and salt, then grilled
chuleta – chop (such as a lamb chop)
cocido – boiled
coctel – appetizer (seafood, fruit, etc) in sauce
empanizado – breaded
filete – filet of fish or meat
frito – fried
lengua – tongue
lomo – loin
milanesa – breaded Italian-style
mixiotes – stew of sliced lamb
mole – sauce made from chilies and other ingredients, often served over chicken or turkey
mole poblano – Puebla-style mole, especially delicious, with many ingredients, including hot chilies and bitter chocolate
patas – trotters (feet)
pibil – meat (usually suckling pig or chicken) flavored with ingredients such as garlic, pepper, chili, oregano and orange juice, then baked (best the traditional way – in a pit in the ground called a *pib*)
pierna – leg
poco cocido – rare

Vegetables & Fruit
Legumbres (legumes) and *verduras* (vegetables) are usually mixed into salads, soups and sauces or used as garnishes. Vegetarians needn't worry: there are usually

plenty of options for them, and many Mexican towns have good vegetarian restaurants.

Vegetables

aguacate – avocado
betabel – beet
calabaza – squash or pumpkin
cebolla – onion
champiñones – mushrooms
chícharos – peas
col – cabbage
coliflor – cauliflower
ejotes – green beans
elote – corn on the cob; commonly served from steaming bins on street carts
ensalada verde – green salad
espárragos – asparagus
espinaca – spinach
frijoles – beans, usually black
hongos – mushrooms
lechuga – lettuce
lentejas – lentils
nopales – green prickly-pear cactus ears
papas – potatoes
papas fritas – French fries (chips)
pepino – cucumber
rábano – radish
tomate – tomato
zanahoria – carrot

Fruit

chabacano – apricot
coco – coconut
durazno – peach
ensalada de frutas – plain mixed seasonal fruits
fresas – strawberries, but also used to refer to any berries
fruta – fruit
granada – pomegranate
guanabana – green pearlike fruit
guayaba – guava (yellow ones are better than pink ones)
higo – fig
limón – lime or lemon
mamey – sweet, orange tropical fruit
mango – mango
manzana – apple
melón – melon
naranja – orange

papaya – papaya
pera – pear
piña – pineapple
plátano – banana
toronja – grapefruit
tuna – nopal (prickly-pear) cactus fruit
uva – grape
zapote – sweet fruit of the chicle tree, best liquidized with, for example, orange juice or Kahlua

Desserts

Most *postres* (desserts) are small after-thoughts to a meal.

arroz con leche – rice pudding
crepa – crêpe; thin pancake
flan – custard; crème caramel
galletas – cookies/biscuits
gelatina – Jell-O (jelly)
helado – ice cream
nieve – sorbet
pastel – pastry or cake
pay – fruit pie

Other Foods

You may find a number of other food words useful:

aceite – oil
aceitunas – olives
arroz – rice
azúcar – sugar
catsup – ketchup; US-style spiced tomato sauce
chipotle – chilies dried, then fermented in vinegar; many Mexicans feel a meal is not complete without it
cilantro – fresh coriander leaf
crema – cream
entremeses – hors d'oeuvres
huitlacoche – a kind of mold that grows on maize, considered a delicacy since Aztec times
leche – milk
mantequilla – butter
margarina – margarine
paleta – flavored ice on a stick
pan (integral) – (whole-grain) bread
pimienta – pepper
queso – cheese

salsa roja/verde – red/green sauce made with chilies, onions, tomato, lemon or lime juice and spices

sal – salt

At the Table

Note that *el menú* can mean either the menu or the special fixed-price meal of the day. If you want the menu, ask for *la lista* or *la carta* or you may inadvertently order the fixed-price meal.

copa – wineglass
cuchara – spoon
cuchillo – knife
cuenta – check (bill)
mesero/a – waiter
plato – plate
propina – tip
servilleta – napkin
taza – cup
tenedor – fork
vaso – glass

DRINKS

A variety of *bebidas* (drinks), both alcoholic and nonalcoholic, is available – as befits a country with such a warm climate. Don't drink any water unless you know it has been purified or boiled (see Health). You can buy bottles of inexpensive purified or mineral water everywhere.

Tea & Coffee

Ordinary Mexican *café*, grown mostly near Córdoba and Orizaba and in Chiapas, is flavorful but often served weak. Those addicted to stronger caffeine shots should ask for 'Nescafé' – unless they're lucky enough to come upon one of the few real coffeehouses that have emerged in recent years. A few of these even serve Mexican organic coffee, from Oaxaca or Chiapas. Tea, invariably in bags, is a profound disappointment to any real tea drinker.

café americano – black coffee
café con leche – coffee with hot milk, half-and-half
café con crema – coffee with cream, each served separately
café instantaneo – instant coffee

café negro – black coffee
espresso – espresso, brewed by steam pressure
Nescafé – any instant coffee *(agua para Nescafé* is a cup of boiled water presented with a jar of instant coffee)
té de manzanilla – chamomile tea
té negro – black tea, to which you can add *leche* (milk) if you wish

Fruit & Vegetable Drinks

Jugos (pure fresh juices) are popular in Mexico and readily available from streetside stalls and juice bars, where the fruit normally is squeezed before your eyes. Every fruit and a few of the squeezable vegetables are used. Ever tried pure beet juice?

Licuados are blends of fruit or juice with water and sugar. *Licuados con leche* use milk instead of water. Possible additions include raw egg, ice, and flavorings such as vanilla or nutmeg. The delicious combinations are practically limitless. In Mexico's many juice bars you can expect the water that is used to be purified – but don't assume the same for street-side juice stalls.

Aguas frescas or *aguas de fruta* are made by mixing fruit juice or a syrup made from mashed grains or seeds with sugar and water. You will usually see them in big glass jars on the counters of juice stands. *Agua fresca de arroz* (literally, 'rice water') has a sweet, nutty taste.

Refrescos

Refrescos are bottled or canned soft drinks, and there are some interesting and tasty local varieties. Sidral and Manzanita are two reasonable apple-flavored fizzy drinks. There's also a nonalcoholic variety of sangría (see Wine & Brandy).

There are many brands of *agua mineral* (mineral water) from Mexican springs – Tehuacán and Garci Crespo are two of the best and can sometimes be obtained with refreshing flavors, as well as plain.

Alcohol

Mexico produces a fascinating variety of intoxicating drinks made from grapes, grains and cacti. Foreign liquors are widely available too.

Drinking Places Everyone knows about Mexican cantinas, those pits of wild drinking and even wilder displays of machismo. One of this book's authors was once in a cantina in Mexico City where it was hardly noticed when a man drew his pistol and fired several rounds into the ceiling. Cantinas are generally loud, but not necessarily that loud.

Cantinas are usually for men only – no women or children are allowed. They're not usually marked as cantinas, but can be identified by Wild West-type swinging half-doors, signs prohibiting minors, and the generally raucous atmosphere. Those who enter must be prepared to drink hard. Chances are you will be challenged by a regular to go one-for-one at a bottle of tequila, mezcal or brandy. If you're not up to that, excuse yourself and beat a retreat.

Some of the nicer cantinas don't get upset about the presence of a woman if she is accompanied by a regular patron. Leave judgment of the situation up to a local, though.

Besides cantinas, Mexico has lots of bars, lounges, 'pubs' and cafés in which all are welcome.

Mezcal, Tequila & Pulque Mezcal can be made from the sap of several species of the maguey plant, a spray of long, thick spikes that stick out of the ground. Tequila is made only from the maguey *Agave tequilana weber*, grown in Jalisco and a few other states. The production method for both is similar (see the Tequila sidebar, in the Western Central Highlands chapter), except that for mezcal the chopped up *piña* (core) of the plant is baked, whereas for tequila it's steamed. The final product is a clear liquid (sometimes artificially tinted) which is at its most potent as tequila. The longer the aging process, the smoother the drink and the higher the price. A repugnant *gusano* (worm) is added to each bottle of mezcal.

The traditional steps in drinking mezcal or tequila are:

1) lick the back of your hand and sprinkle salt on it
2) lick the salt
3) suck on a wedge of lime
4) down the shot in one gulp
5) lick more salt

When the bottle is empty you are supposed to eat the worm.

For foreigners not used to the potency of straight tequila, Mexican bartenders invented the margarita, a concoction of tequila, lime juice and liqueur served in a salt-rimmed glass.

Pulque is a cheap, mainly working-class drink, much less potent than tequila or mezcal, that is derived directly from the sap of the maguey. The foamy, milky, slightly sour liquid spoils quickly and thus cannot easily be bottled and shipped. Most pulque is produced around Mexico City and served in male-dominated *pulquerías*.

Beer Breweries were established in Mexico by German immigrants in the late 19th century. Mexico's several large brewing companies now produce more than 25 brands of *cerveza* (beer), many of which are excellent. Each major company has a premium beer, such as Bohemia and Corona de Barril (usually served in bottles); several standard beers, such as Carta Blanca, Superior and Dos Equis; and 'popular' brands, such as Corona, Tecate and Modelo. All are blond lagers meant to be served chilled – it's a good idea to ask for *una cerveza fría* (a cold beer). Each of the large companies also produces an *oscura* (dark) beer, such as Modelo Negro and Tres Equis. There are some regional beers too, brewed to similar tastes.

Wine & Brandy Wine is not as popular in Mexico as beer and tequila, but the country's three large wine growers, all around Ensenada in Baja California, produce some quite drinkable vintages.

Pedro Domecq is best known for Los Reyes, its table wines, and various brandies. Formex-Ybarra is known for its Terrasola table wine. Bodegas de Santo Tomás, run by the Tchelistcheffs, a California-based wine-growing family, hopes eventually to make wines that can compete with California's; it produces pinot noir, chardonnay and cabernet wines, which are worth a try.

Wine mixed with fruit juice makes the tasty *sangría*.

ENTERTAINMENT

Nothing beats a Mexican fiesta for entertainment, but if none is being celebrated, you have alternatives. People-watching from a café on a plaza is high on the list. In the larger cities and resorts the range of entertainment is broad, with music clubs (jazz, salsa, mariachi, rock, etc), discos, bars and lounges abounding. In the big cities you'll also find opera, classical concerts, and theater (in Spanish). Cinemas screen both local and foreign films. Foreign ones may be dubbed into Spanish or may have subtitles. Small-town Mexico is a fairly early-to-bed zone: the best you can expect is a primitive cinema and a bar, perhaps with entertainment, in the best local hotel.

One location worth making an effort to see is a performance of folk dance, always colorful and interesting (see the Arts section in Facts about the Country). If you can't catch dance in its natural setting – at a fiesta – some good regular shows are put on in theaters and hotels. The most dazzlingly elaborate is Mexico City's Ballet Folklórico.

SPECTATOR SPORTS

Events such as soccer games, bullfights and charreadas can be fascinating: even if the action doesn't especially grab you, the crowd probably will.

Soccer (Football)

Fútbol is at least as popular as bullfighting. There is an 18-team national *primera división*, and there are several impressive

stadiums. Mexico hosted the World Cup finals in 1970 and 1986.

The two most popular teams in the country are América, of Mexico City (nicknamed Las Águilas), and Guadalajara (Las Chivas). They attract large followings wherever they play. The two major cities also are home to several other teams usually to be found in the primera división, including UNAM (the Universidad Autónoma de Mexico, nicknamed Las Pumas), Cruz Azul, Atlante, and Necaxa, all from Mexico City, and Universidad de Guadalajara, Universidad Autónoma de Guadalajara (Los Tecos), and Atlas, all from Guadalajara. Leading provincial clubs include Santos of Torreón, Monterrey, and Universidad de Nuevo León, also of Monterrey.

The biggest games of the year are those between América and Guadalajara, known as 'Los Superclásicos.' These teams attract crowds of 100,000 when they meet at the Estadio Guillermo Cañedo in Mexico City. Crowds at other games range from a few thousand to around 70,000. Games are spaced over the weekend from Friday to Sunday; details are printed in *The News*, the *Mexico City Times* and the Spanish-language press. Recently the annual soccer calendar was divided into a *torneo de invierno* (winter season, August to December) and a *torneo de verano* (summer season, January to May), each ending in playoffs and eventually a two-leg final to decide the champion.

Attending a game is fun: rivalry between opposing fans is generally good-humored. Tickets can be bought at the gate and can cost from less than US$1 to US$10, depending on the quality of your seat.

Other Sports

Professional *beisbol* (baseball) is popular, especially in the northwest. The winner of the October-to-January Liga Mexicana del Pacífico represents Mexico in the February Serie del Caribe, the Caribbean World Series, the biggest event in Latin American baseball. Some Mexican stars move to the

Bullfighting

To many gringo eyes the *corrida de toros* (bullfight) hardly seems to be sport or, for that matter, entertainment. Mexicans, however, see it as both and more. It's as much a ritualistic dance as a fight, and readily lends itself to a variety of symbolic interpretations, mostly related to machismo. It's said that Mexicans arrive on time for only two events – funerals and bullfights.

The corrida de toros (literally, running of the bulls) or *fiesta brava* (wild festival) begins promptly at 4, 4.30 or 5 pm on a Sunday. To the sound of music, usually a Spanish *paso doble*, the matador, in his *traje de luces* (suit of lights), and the toreros (his assistants) give the traditional *paseillo* (salute) to the fight authorities and the crowd. Then the first of the day's six bulls is released from its pen for the first of the ritual's three *suertes* (acts) or *tercios* (thirds).

The cape-waving toreros tire the bull by luring him around the ring. After a few minutes two picadores, on heavily padded horses, enter and jab long lances called *picas* into the bull's shoulders to weaken him. Somehow this is often the most gruesome part of the whole process.

After the picadores leave the ring the *suerte de banderillas* begins, as the toreros attempt to stab three pairs of elongated darts into the bull's shoulders without getting impaled on his horns. After that the *suerte de muleta* is the climax, in which the matador has exactly 16 minutes to kill the bull. Starting with fancy cape work to tire the animal, the matador then exchanges his large cape for the smaller muleta and takes sword in hand, baiting the bull to charge before delivering the fatal *estocada* (lunge) with his sword. The matador must deliver the estocada into the neck from a position directly in front of the animal.

If the matador succeeds, and he usually does, the bull collapses and an assistant dashes into the ring to slice its jugular. If the applause from the crowd warrants, he will also cut off an ear or two and sometimes the tail for the matador. The dead bull is dragged from the ring to be butchered for sale.

A 'good' bullfight depends not only on the skill and courage of the matador but also the spirit of the bulls. Animals lacking heart for the fight bring shame on the ranch that bred them. Very occasionally, a bull that has fought outstandingly is *indultado* (spared) – an occasion for great celebration – and will then retire to stud.

The veteran Eloy Cavasos, from Monterrey, and Miguel 'Armillita' Espinosa are widely reckoned to be Mexico's two best matadors, with Rafael Ortega the rising young star. *The News* carries an informative weekly bullfighting column called Blood on the Sand, usually on Saturday. ■

TOROS

BULLFIGHTS in TIJUANA
EL TOREO
DOWNTOWN BULLRING

May 6, 1990 – At 4 P.M.
Grand Inaugural Corrida of
1990 Season !

EL TOREO de TIJUANA
Domingo 6 de Mayo, 1990 - 4 P.M.
Gran Corrida Inaugural de
la Temporada '90

United States, and younger Americans on the way up often play in the Pacific league.

The **charreada** is the rodeo, held particularly in the northern half of the country both during fiestas and at regular venues often called *lienzos charros*.

Several *hipódromos* (racetracks) around the country have **horse racing**. It's popular in some towns on the US border and at the Hipódromo de las Américas, in Mexico City.

The Basque game *pelota*, brought by the Spanish, is played in Mexico as *jai alai* ('HIGH-lie'). It is a bit like squash, played on a very long court with a hard ball and with curved baskets attached to the arm, and it can be fast and exciting. You can see it played by semiprofessionals in Mexico City and Tijuana, among other places.

As much showbiz as sport is *lucha libre*, a type of freestyle wrestling. Participants wear lurid masks and sport attractive names like Bestia Salvaje, Shocker, Los Karate Boy and Heavy Metal.

THINGS TO BUY

See the Artesanías color section for information on Mexico's wonderful range of *artesanías* (handicrafts). It's worth bearing in mind that if you buy crafts in the villages where they are made, from individual vendors on the streets or in small markets, rather than from shops or large centralized craft markets, then a lot more of the profit will go to the usually poor people who make them, instead of to entrepreneurs.

46
EL SOL

28
LA SANDIA

1
EL GALLO

17
EL BANDOLÓN

30
EL CAMARON

35
LA ESTRELLA

Getting There & Away

Most visitors to Mexico arrive by air. You can also approach by road from the USA, Guatemala or Belize and reach either side of the US-Mexican border (but not actually cross it) by rail. There are backcountry jungle routes by bus and riverboat between Flores, in Guatemala, and Palenque, in Chiapas. However you're traveling, give serious thought to taking out travel insurance, and buy it as early as possible. If you buy it the week before you fly, you may find, for example, that you're not covered for delays to your flight caused by strikes. See Health in Facts for the Visitor for more on insurance.

AIR

If you have access to the Internet, it's a good source of quotes and often bookings for cheap airfares. A Web search for 'discount airfares' will bring hundreds of responses, which you can then refine to your own needs. One good site for fares from North America, Europe or Australia is the Discount Airfares Home Page, but there are others. Two sites to check out for fares from North America are Travelocity and Expedia. For fares in the US or the UK, try Flifo. (See the Website Directory for all addresses.)

Travelers with Special Needs

If you have special needs of any sort – you're vegetarian, traveling in a wheelchair, taking the baby – you should let the airline know as soon as possible so that they can make arrangements accordingly. Remind them when you reconfirm your booking (at least 72 hours prior to departure) and again when you check in at the airport. Don't trust a travel agent to do this for you.

Round-the-World Tickets

Round-the-World (RTW) tickets – either ones sold by airlines or ones put together by travel agents – are often real bargains, and from Australasia they can work out to be no more expensive – or can even be cheaper – than an ordinary roundtrip ticket to Mexico. Prices start at about UK£850 or A$1800, though they tend to be more expensive if you want to include Mexico.

The USA & Canada

The airlines with the most services to Mexico include Alaska Airlines, American, Canadian Airlines International, Continental, Delta, TWA, United and the two main Mexican airlines, Aeroméxico and Mexicana. You can fly without changing planes to at least somewhere in Mexico from at least these North American cities: Atlanta, Chicago, Dallas/Fort Worth, Denver, El Paso, Houston, Las Vegas, Los Angeles, McAllen (Texas), Miami, Montreal, New Orleans, New York, Oakland, Orlando, Phoenix, San Antonio, San Diego, San Francisco, San Jose, Seattle, Toronto and Tucson. There are one-stop connecting flights from many others.

About 30 Mexican cities receive direct flights from North America. Mexico City receives the most, followed by Guadalajara, Cancún, Monterrey and Acapulco. There are connections to many other places in Mexico, the majority through Mexico City. See the relevant city sections of this book for more information.

Fares There are dozens of airfares for any given route. Consult travel agents or the Internet about fares and routes. Once you've discovered the basics of airlines, routes and the various discounted tickets available, you can consult your favorite discount ticket agent, consolidator or charter airline to see if their fares are better. Good fares are offered by well-known student travel agencies with branches in major cities, including Council Travel, STA Travel and, in Canada, Travel CUTS.

Consolidators buy seats in bulk from airlines at considerable discounts and resell them to the public, usually through travel agents, sometimes directly through newspaper and magazine ads. Though there are some shady dealers, most consolidators are quite legitimate. Ask your travel agent about buying a consolidator ticket, or look for the consolidator ads in the travel section of the newspaper (they're the ones with tables of destinations and fares and toll-free numbers to call).

Fares depend, among other things, on what time of year you fly (expect to pay more around Christmas and New Year's and during the summer), how far ahead you book, and how long you're traveling for (usually the longer the dearer). Here are some typical examples of full/cheap roundtrip fares:

From	To Mexico City	To Cancún
Chicago	US$490/170	US$490/340
Dallas/Fort Worth	US$400/140	US$530/340
Los Angeles	US$450/140	US$620/370
Miami	US$540/170	US$430/290
New York	US$480/190	US$730/280
Toronto	US$530/230	US$690/380

Another possibility is a package tour flight. Check newspaper travel ads and call a package tour operator, or a travel agent who sells such tours, and ask if you can buy 'air only' (just the roundtrip air transportation, not the hotel or other features). This is often possible, and it's usually cheaper than buying a discounted roundtrip ticket.

Europe
Only a few airlines fly nonstop from Europe to Mexico, among them Aeroméxico, Air France, British Airways, Iberia, KLM and Lufthansa. On some of them you can fly to Cancún instead of Mexico City, if you wish. US airlines take you to a US city, where you will at least touch down and may change planes, perhaps to another airline.

The most common type of ticket from Europe to Mexico is a three-month or six-month return. You can often change the date of the return leg, subject to availability, at no cost. One-ways, open returns, circle trips and 'open jaws' (see below) are also possible. Most types of ticket are available at discount rates from cheap ticket agencies in Europe's bargain flight centers, such as London, Amsterdam, Paris and Frankfurt. Typically, a roundtrip fare from western Europe to Mexico for up to six months costs between UK£350 and UK£450. The sooner you buy, the cheaper the ticket may be. Fares can also vary between high and low seasons.

Circle trips and open jaws are useful if you want to hop from one part of Mexico to another, or between Mexico and elsewhere in the Americas, without backtracking. You usually depart from, and return to, the same city in Europe. Circle trips give you flights between your different destinations en route; with open-jaw tickets you make your own way between your arrival and departure points.

Ticket Agents in the UK For cheap tickets, search the Internet or pick up a good weekend newspaper travel section, such as the Saturday *Independent*, or look in *Time Out* or any of the other London magazines that advertise discount or bucket shop flights, and check out a few of the advertisers. Most bucket shops are trustworthy and reliable, but the occasional sharp operator appears. If a travel agent is registered with the ABTA (Association of British Travel Agents), as most are, ABTA will guarantee a refund or an alternative if the agent goes out of business after you have paid for your flight.

Reputable agents offering good-value fares to Mexico include Journey Latin America (☎ 0181-747-3108), 16 Devonshire Rd, Chiswick, London W4 2HD; Campus Travel (☎ 0171-730-8111), 52 Grosvenor Gardens, London SW1W 0AG; STA (☎ 0171-937-9962 for both addresses), 86 Old Brompton Rd, London SW7 3LQ, or 117 Euston Rd, London NW1 2SX; and Trailfinders (☎ 0171-937-5400), 194 Kensington High St, London W8 7RG, or (☎ 0171-937-5400), 42-50 Earls Court Rd,

London W8 6FT. All these agencies have branches in other cities too.

Ticket Agents Elsewhere in Europe

Agencies specializing in cheap tickets and youth/student travel include:

France – The main Paris office of Council Travel, the USA's biggest student and budget travel agency (☎ 01 44 55 55 65), is at 22 rue des Pyramides, Paris 1er.

Germany – Cheap flights are advertised in the Berlin magazine *Zitty*. Agents include SRID Reisen (☎ 069-430-191), Berger Strasse 118, Frankfurt; SRS Studenten Reise Service (☎ 030-283-3074), Marienstrasse 25, Berlin; and Flugbörse with branches in many towns.

Ireland – USIT Travel Office (☎ 01-679-8833), 19 Aston Quay, Dublin

Italy – CTS (☎ 06-46791), Via Genova 16, off Via Nazionale, Rome; branches all over Italy

Netherlands – NBBS Reizen (☎ 020-624-0989), Rokin 38, Amsterdam; Malibu Travel (☎ 020-626-6611), Damrak 30, Amsterdam

Scandinavia – Kilroy Travels, with branches in Copenhagen, Stockholm, Oslo, Helsinki and several other cities, is a well-established cheap-flight agent; fares are often especially good if you're under 26 or a student under 35.

Spain – Halcón Viajes, with branches in many cities, has some respectable fares; Viajes Zeppelin (☎ 91-547-79-03), Plaza de Santo Domingo, Madrid, has good deals; for youth and student fares try TIVE (☎ 91-347-77-00), Calle José Ortega y Gasset 71, Madrid.

Switzerland – SSR (☎ 01-297-1111), Leonhardstrasse 10 and Bäckerstrasse 40, Zurich; branches in several other Swiss cities

Australasia

There are no direct flights from Australia or New Zealand to Mexico. Often the cheapest way to get there is via the USA (usually Los Angeles) or Japan. From Sydney/Melbourne to Mexico City via Los Angeles, typical low/high-season roundtrip fares are around A$1950/2300. You might be able to do it more cheaply by buying a ticket to Los Angeles, then getting your Los Angeles-Mexico ticket there (check the US visa requirements if you're thinking of doing this).

STA Travel and Flight Centres International are major dealers in cheap airfares in both Australia and New Zealand, with offices in numerous main towns and cities. Check the Internet or travel agents' ads in the yellow pages and the newspapers and call around.

Central & South America & the Caribbean

Aviateca (Guatemala's national airline) and Mexicana fly between Guatemala City and Mexico City. Flights from Guatemala City or Flores (Tikal) to places like Mérida, Cancún, Chetumal, Palenque and Tuxtla Gutiérrez come and go. They're usually by Aviateca, Aerocaribe or Aviacsa.

Mexicana flies to Mexico City from Bogotá, Santiago and San José (Costa Rica), and to Cancún from Buenos Aires and Lima. Aerocaribe, a subsidiary of Mexicana, has daily flights linking Havana, Cancún, Mérida, Villahermosa, Tuxtla Gutiérrez and Oaxaca. Aeroméxico and Aeroperú fly from Lima and São Paulo to Mexico City. Servivensa of Venezuela links Caracas, Panama and Mexico City. The airlines of many other Central and South American countries fly to and from Mexico City.

Airline Toll-Free Numbers

Many airlines have telephone numbers you can call toll free from anywhere in Mexico. They include:

Aerolíneas Internacionales	
Guadalajara	☎ 800-36546
Tijuana	☎ 800-66805
Aerolitoral	☎ 800-36202
Aeroméxico	☎ 800-90999
American Airlines	☎ 800-90460
Aviacsa/Aeroexo	
Mexico City	☎ 800-00672
Tijuana	☎ 800-66446
Villahermosa	☎ 800-23080
Continental Airlines	☎ 800-90050
Delta Airlines	☎ 800-90221
Mexicana	
Cancún	☎ 800-21654
Guadalajara	☎ 800-36654
Mexico City	☎ 800-50220
Monterrey	☎ 800-83654

Northwest Airlines	☎ 800-90008
TAESA	☎ 800-90463
United Airlines	☎ 800-00307

LAND

You can enter Mexico by road from the USA, Guatemala or Belize. By train you can reach a few US or Mexican border towns, but you cannot cross the border.

The USA

There are at least 18 official road crossing points on the US-Mexico border:

Arizona: Douglas/Agua Prieta, Lukeville/Sonoita, Nogales/Nogales, and San Luis/San Luis Río Colorado (all open 24 hours); Naco/Naco, Sasabe/El Sásabe

California: Calexico/Mexicali (two crossings, one open 24 hours); San Ysidro/Tijuana (open 24 hours); Otay Mesa/Mesa de Otay (near the Tijuana airport; open 6 am to 10 pm); Tecate/Tecate (open 6 am to midnight)

New Mexico: Columbus/General Rodrigo M Quevedo (also called Palomas, open 24 hours)

Texas: Brownsville/Matamoros, McAllen/Reynosa, Laredo/Nuevo Laredo, Del Rio/Ciudad Acuña, and El Paso/Ciudad Juárez (all open 24 hours); Eagle Pass/Piedras Negras, Presidio/Ojinaga

More information on many of these crossings can be found in the regional chapters.

Bus A new Mexican law in 1997 permitted bus services for the first time to link cities in the US *interior* with cities in the Mexican *interior*. Until these services get going, you must take one bus to the border, then another onward. A few buses from US cities cross to Mexican border towns; routes include Los Angeles to Tijuana, Mexicali and Ciudad Juárez, and Albuquerque or Denver to Ciudad Juárez. Greyhound buses (☎ 800-231-2222) serve Brownsville, Del Rio, Eagle Pass, El Paso, Laredo, McAllen and Presidio, Texas, and Calexico and San Diego, California. To reach other border cities, transfer from Greyhound to a smaller line.

A few buses start for destinations in the Mexican interior from US border towns, but you'll find a much better selection of companies and routes (and usually significantly better fares) by crossing to the Mexican bus terminal.

Train You can reach some US border cities by train, and you can travel on from some Mexican border cities by train, but you can't cross the border by train.

Taking a train to the Mexican border may not be much cheaper than flying when you add in meals and other expenses. Trains tend to be a little slower, a little cheaper, and less frequent than buses. Amtrak (☎ 800-872-7245) serves three US cities from which access to Mexico is easy: from El Paso, Texas, cross to Ciudad Juárez; from San Antonio, Texas, take a bus to the border at Eagle Pass/Piedras Negras, Del Rio/Ciudad Acuña, or Laredo/Nuevo Laredo; from San Diego, California, cross to Tijuana.

Mexican railways are not for those in a hurry or those in need of a great deal of comfort. The main services from Mexican border cities, all daily but none with sleeper cars, are from Nuevo Laredo to Mexico City via Monterrey, San Luis Potosí and San Miguel de Allende; from Ciudad Juárez to Mexico City via Chihuahua, Zacatecas and Querétaro; and from Nogales and Mexicali to Guadalajara via Hermosillo, Sufragio and Mazatlán. See the Mexico City and Guadalajara Getting There & Away sections for schedules, and the Getting Around chapter for information on bookings and Mexican train classes.

Car & Motorcycle Driving into Mexico is not for everyone – you should know some Spanish and have basic mechanical aptitude, large reserves of patience, and access to some extra cash for emergencies. You should also note warnings about risk areas for highway robbery (see the Dangers & Annoyances section in Facts for the Visitor) and try to avoid intercity driving at night. Cars are most useful for travelers who:

- have plenty of time
- plan to go to remote places
- will be camping out a lot
- have surfboards, climbing gear, diving equipment or other cumbersome luggage
- will be traveling with a group or family of four or more
- want to buy lots of bulky handicrafts

Don't take a car if you:

- are on a tight schedule
- have a low budget
- plan to spend most of your time in urban areas
- will be traveling alone
- want a relaxing trip with minimum risks

Cars are expensive to buy or rent in Mexico, so your best option may be to take one in from North America. If that means buying it first, you may need several weeks to find a good vehicle at a reasonable price. It may also take some time at the end of your trip to sell the thing. So it's not worth buying a car for a short trip.

The best makes of car to take to Mexico are Volkswagen, Nissan/Datsun, Chrysler, General Motors or Ford, which have manufacturing or assembly plants in Mexico and dealers in most big Mexican towns. Big cars are unwieldy on narrow roads and streets and use a lot of gasoline. A sedan with a trunk (boot) provides safer, more discreet storage than a station wagon or a hatchback. Volkswagen camper vans are economical, and parts and service are easy to find. For any vehicle, you should take as many spare parts as you can manage and know what to do with. Tires (including spare), shock absorbers and suspension should be in good condition. For security, at least have something to immobilize the steering wheel, such as 'The Club'; you also might want to consider getting a kill switch installed.

Motorcycling in Mexico is not for the faint-hearted. Roads and traffic can be rough, and parts and mechanics generally hard to come by. The only parts you'll find at all will be for Kawasaki, Honda and Suzuki bikes.

The rules for taking a vehicle into Mexico, described in the sections that follow, have in the past changed from time to time. You can check with the American Automobile Association (AAA), a Mexican consulate, a Mexican government tourist office or the information number ☎ 800-446-3942. For more on driving in Mexico, see the Getting Around chapter.

Buying a Car in the USA The border states, particularly California and Texas, are good places to buy – they have many car lots, and every town has magazines and newspapers with ads from private sellers. Cars there are also likely to have air-con – desirable in Mexico. Most libraries have copies of the *Kelley Blue Book*, which lists retail prices (what a dealer would charge) and the trade-in value (what private sellers might charge) for used cars. About US$1300 to US$2300 should buy a car that will take you around Mexico and still be worth something at the end.

To avoid delay in getting your certificate of title or ownership for the vehicle – which you must take with you to Mexico – you can ask the state's department of motor vehicles for rush service on the transfer of ownership. Alternatively, ask for an official letter stating that you have bought the vehicle and applied for a transfer. If a lien holder's name (for example, a bank that has lent money for the vehicle) is shown on the certificate of title, you'll need a notarized affidavit giving their permission for the vehicle to be taken into Mexico.

Car Insurance It is foolish to drive in Mexico without Mexican liability insurance. If you are involved in an accident, you can be jailed or forbidden to leave the immediate area until all claims are settled, which could take weeks or months. A valid Mexican insurance policy is regarded as a guarantee that restitution will be paid, and it will expedite release of the driver. Mexican law recognizes only Mexican *seguro* (car insurance), so a US or Canadian policy won't help.

Mexican insurance is sold in US border towns; as you approach the border from the USA you will see billboards advertising offices selling Mexican policies. At the busiest border crossings (Tijuana, Mexicali, Nogales, Agua Prieta, Ciudad Juárez, Nuevo Laredo, Reynosa and Matamoros), there are insurance offices open 24 hours a day. Some deals are better than others. Check the yellow pages in US border towns. Three organizations worth looking into are the American Automobile Association (AAA), International Gateway Insurance Brokers and Sanborn's (the last offers lots of useful free travel information). Short-term insurance is about US$6 a day for full coverage on a car worth US$5000, but there are big discounts for longer periods.

Driver's License To drive a motor vehicle – car, RV (camper van), motorcycle or truck – in Mexico, you need a valid driver's license from your home country. Mexican police are familiar with US and Canadian licenses; those from other countries may be scrutinized more closely, but they are still legal.

Vehicle Permit You will need a *permiso de importación temporal de vehículos* (a temporary import permit for vehicles) if you want to take a vehicle beyond Baja California or the border zone, which extends about 25 km into Mexico (farther in some places). Customs officials at posts south of each Mexican border town (usually just a few km south but in some cases as many as 100 km), and at the Baja California ports for ferries to the mainland, will want to see the permit for your vehicle. You must get one at the *aduana* (customs) office at a border crossing or, in Baja, at the Pichilingue (La Paz) ferry terminal (permits are not available at Santa Rosalía, the other Baja ferry port).

In addition to a passport or proof of US or Canadian citizenship, the person importing the vehicle will need originals of the following documents, which must all be in his/her own name: a tourist card

(go to *migración* before you go to the aduana), a certificate of title or ownership for the vehicle, a current registration card or notice, a driver's license (see above), and either a valid international credit card (Visa, MasterCard, American Express or Diner's Club) issued by a non-Mexican bank or cash to pay a very large bond (see below). You need at least one photocopy of each of these documents as well as the original, but people at the office may make photocopies for a small fee.

If the vehicle is not fully paid for, you need a letter from the lender authorizing its use in Mexico for a specified period. If it's a company car and you do not have a certificate of ownership in your own name, bring a notarized affidavit certifying that you work for the company and are allowed to take the car into Mexico. If the vehicle is leased or rented, bring the original contract (plus a copy), which must be in the name of the person importing the car, and a notarized affidavit from the rental firm authorizing the driver to take it into Mexico.

One person cannot bring in two vehicles. If, for example, you have a motorcycle attached to your car, you'll need another adult traveling with you to obtain a permit for the motorcycle, and he/she will need to have all the right papers for it. If the motorcycle is registered in your name, you'll need a notarized affidavit authorizing the other person to take it into Mexico. A special permit is needed for vehicles weighing more than about 3.3 US tons (three British tonnes).

At the border there will be a building with a parking area for vehicles awaiting permits. Go inside and find the right counter at which to present your papers. After some signing and stamping of papers, you sign a promise to take the car out of the country, the Banco del Ejército (also called Banjército; it's the army bank) charges US$11 to your credit card, and you are sent out to wait with your vehicle. Make sure you get back the originals of all documents. Eventually someone will come out, check the details of your vehicle, put a hologram sticker on the top corner of the windshield, and give you a permit (with another hologram sticker) and your tourist card, stamped *'con automóvil.'*

If you don't have an international credit card, you will have to deposit a cash bond (not a check) with the Banco del Ejército or an authorized Mexican *afianzadora* (bonding company) – unless you're just visiting the state of Sonora and you enter at Nogales, in which case no credit card or bond is needed (call Sonora Turismo at ☎ 800-476-6672 to find out more about this program). The required bond amounts for medium or small cars in 1997 were US$6000 for a vehicle up to two years old, US$3000 (three or four years old), US$1000 (five or six years old), US$750 (seven to 14 years old), and US$500 (15 years or older). There may be taxes and processing fees to pay too. The bond should be refunded, plus any interest, when the vehicle finally leaves Mexico and the temporary import permit is canceled. If you plan to leave Mexico at a different border crossing, make sure that the bonding company will give you a refund there. There are offices for Banco del Ejército and authorized Mexican bonding companies at or near all the major border points; Banco del Ejército offices at major crossings are always open, except at Tijuana (Monday to Friday 8 am to 10 pm, Saturday 8 am to 6 pm, Sunday noon to 4 pm) and Tecate (open daily from 8 am to 4 pm).

The permit entitles you to take the vehicle in and out of Mexico for the period shown on your tourist card. If the car is still in Mexico after that time, aduana will start charging fines to your credit card. Cars in Mexico without a current permit can be confiscated. The permit allows the vehicle to be driven by the owner's spouse or adult children or by other people if the owner is in the vehicle.

When you leave Mexico for the last time you must have the permit canceled by the Mexican authorities, no later than the day before it expires. An official may cancel the permit as you enter the border zone, usually about 25 km before the border itself. If not, you will have to find the right official from aduana and/or Banco del Ejército at the border crossing. If you leave Mexico without having the permit canceled, once the permit expires the authorities will assume that you've left the vehicle in the country illegally and will start charging fines to your credit card.

Only the owner can take the vehicle out of Mexico – and as a rule, the owner cannot leave Mexico without it. If it's wrecked in an accident, you must obtain permission to leave it in the country from either the Registro Federal de Vehículos (Federal Registry of Vehicles) in Mexico City, or a Hacienda (Treasury Department) office in another city or town; your insurance company can help with this. If you have to leave the country in an emergency, the vehicle can be left in temporary storage at an airport or seaport or with an aduana or Hacienda office.

Guatemala & Belize

For detailed information on travel in and through Central America, see *Guatemala, Belize & Yucatán – La Ruta Maya* or *Central America*, both published by Lonely Planet.

There are three official highway border crossings between Guatemala and Mexico. La Mesilla/Ciudad Cuauhtémoc is on the Pan-American Highway in the highlands (on the way to San Cristóbal de Las Casas). Ciudad Tecún Umán/Ciudad Hidalgo and El Carmen/Talismán are both on the Pacific slope, near Tapachula; Tecún Umán is preferred to El Carmen, as there are fewer hassles.

There is one official crossing point between Belize and Mexico, at Santa Elena/Subteniente López (near Corozal and Chetumal, respectively).

Bus Transportes Velásquez, 20a Calle & 2a Avenida, Zona 1, Guatemala City, runs hourly buses to La Mesilla (380 km, seven hours, US$4.50) from 8 am to 4 pm.

Transportes Fortaleza (☎ 230-3390, 220-6372), 19 Calle 8-70, Zona 1, Guatemala City, has hourly buses to Ciudad Tecún Umán (253 km, five hours, US$5) from 1.30 am to 6 pm, stopping at

Escuintla, Mazatenango, Retalhuleu and Coatepeque.

Transportes Galgos (☎ 253-4868, 232-3661), 7a Avenida 19-44, Zona 1, Guatemala City, has direct buses via the crossing at El Carmen/Talismán to Tapachula (295 km, five hours, US$19) at 7.30 am and 1.30 pm. From Tapachula they depart for Guatemala City at 9.30 am and 1.30 pm.

One daily 1st-class bus by Servicio San Juan runs between Flores and Tikal, in Guatemala's Petén province, and Chetumal, in Mexico (350 km, nine hours, US$35). To go 2nd-class you must go via the Guatemala/Belize border at Benque Viejo to Belize City and change buses there – a slower and less comfortable but much cheaper trip.

Between Belize City and Chetumal (160 km, three to four hours, US$5 to US$6) there are frequent buses. These and other buses link Chetumal with Orange Walk and Corozal, in Belize.

There's more information on border points and buses in the Tabasco & Chiapas and Yucatán Peninsula chapters.

RIVER

There are currently three routes through the jungle from Flores (El Petén, Guatemala) to Palenque (Chiapas, Mexico).

The El Naranjo route takes you by bus to El Naranjo, then by boat down the Río San Pedro to La Palma, then by taxi and/or bus via Tenosique to Palenque.

Another route is by bus to Bethel, then down the Río Usumacinta to Frontera Corozal (from which you can reach the Mayan ruins of Bonampak and Yaxchilán), then by bus to Palenque.

The third route takes you to Sayaxché by bus, then down the Río de la Pasión via Pipiles to Benemerito, where you can catch a bus to Palenque.

For details on these routes, see the Tabasco & Chiapas chapter.

DEPARTURE TAXES

A departure tax equivalent to about US$13 is levied on international flights from Mexico. If you buy your ticket in Mexico, the tax will be included in your ticket cost; if you bought it outside Mexico, it may or may not have been included. If the letters XD appear on your ticket, they prove that the tax has already been paid. If it hasn't, you will have to pay the tax in cash at the airport check-in.

ORGANIZED TOURS

If you just want a short holiday in Mexico, consider signing up for one of the many package deals offered by travel agents and in newspaper travel sections. Mexican government tourist offices can give you armfuls of brochures about these trips. Costs depend, among other things, on where and when you go (peak time is usually December to February), but some packages give you flights and accommodations for little more than the cost of an individually bought discount airfare. A typical seven-night off-season trip from southern California, for example, costs around US$300 to US$400 to Puerto Vallarta or US$400 to US$600 to Cancún. Some packages also include a rental car and airport transportation.

If you are looking for an adventure- or activity-focused group trip to Mexico you'll find a wide selection, especially from the USA. See the Organized Tours section in Getting Around for more information.

WARNING

The information in this chapter is particularly vulnerable to change: prices for international travel are volatile, routes are introduced and canceled, schedules change, special deals come and go. Price structures and regulations can be complicated; you should check directly with the airline or a travel agent to make sure you understand how a fare (and ticket you may buy) works. In sum, try to get opinions, quotes and advice from as many airlines and agents as possible before you part with your hard-earned cash. The details given in this chapter should be regarded as pointers and are not a substitute for your own careful, up-to-date research.

Getting Around

The peak travel periods of Semana Santa (the week before Easter) and the Christmas-New Year holiday period of about 10 days are hectic and heavily booked throughout Mexico; try to book transport in advance for those periods.

For some useful words and phrases when traveling, see Spanish for Travelers at the back of this book.

AIR

All sizable cities in Mexico, and many smaller ones, have passenger airports. Aeroméxico and Mexicana are the country's two largest airlines. There are also numerous smaller ones, often flying useful routes between provincial cities that the big two don't bother with. These airlines include Aero California (serving Mexico City and northern and western Mexico, including Baja California), Aerocaribe and Aerocozumel (southeast and Gulf Coast), Aeroexo (Mexico City, Monterrey, Guadalajara and Tijuana), Aerolíneas Internacionales (Mexico City, Cuernavaca and northern and western Mexico), Aerolitoral (central highlands and Gulf Coast), Aeromar (central highlands), Aviacsa (southeast), and TAESA (about 20 cities around the country).

Most of these airlines will be included in travel agents' computerized reservation systems in Mexico and abroad, but you may find it impossible to get information on smaller ones until you reach a city served by them.

Aerolitoral and Aeromar are feeder airlines for Aeroméxico and normally share its ticket offices. A similar arrangement applies between Aerocaribe, Aerocozumel and Mexicana.

Fares

Information on specific flights is given in the city sections of this book. Fares can vary a lot depending on airline, whether you fly at a busy or quiet time of the day or week, and how far ahead you book and pay. For the cheapest fares you may have to buy the ticket seven days ahead and be prepared to fly late in the evening. Aeroméxico and Mexicana work in tandem, with identical fare structures, but other airlines may offer cheaper fares – often with the same comfort, service and safety standards as the big two. Though some roundtrip excursion fares exist, roundtrip fares are usually twice the price of one-ways.

Depending on what fare you get, flying can be a good value for the money, especially considering the long bus trip that may be the alternative. Here are some examples of the cheapest one-way fares from Mexico City, including taxes:

Destination	Aeroméxico/Mexicana	TAESA
Acapulco	US$83	US$77
Cancún	US$126	US$121
Guadalajara	US$103	US$95
Mérida	US$120	US$113
Monterrey	US$121	US$112
Oaxaca	US$77	N/A
Puerto Vallarta	US$112	US$112
Tijuana	US$210	US$217
Zacatecas	US$106	US$106

See the Getting There & Away chapter for some airline toll-free numbers in Mexico.

Taxes There are two taxes on domestic flights: IVA, the consumer tax (15%), and TUA, an airport tax of about US$8.50. In Mexico they are normally included in quoted fares and paid when you buy the ticket. If you bought the ticket outside Mexico, TUA will not have been included and you will have to pay it at check-in.

BUS

Mexico has a good and improving intercity road and bus network. Intercity buses offer frequent service and go almost everywhere, typically for US$3 or US$4 an

JOHN NOBLE

hour (60 to 80 km) on deluxe or 1st-class buses. For trips of up to three or four hours on busy routes, you can usually just go to the bus terminal, buy a ticket and head out without too much delay. For longer trips, or trips on routes with infrequent service, book a ticket at least a day in advance, preferably two or three.

Immediate cash refunds of 80% to 100% are often available if you cancel your ticket more than three hours before the listed departure time. To check whether refunds apply, ask '¿Hay cancelaciones?'

All deluxe and most 1st-class buses are air-conditioned, so bring a sweater or jacket. Most deluxe and 1st-class bus companies have computerized ticket systems that allow you to select your seat from an on-screen diagram. Try to avoid the back of the bus, which is where the toilets are and tends to give a bumpier ride. For a long journey, it helps to work out which side the sun will be on and sit on the other side. If the bus is not air-con, it's a particularly good idea to get a window seat so that you have some control over the window – Mexicans often have different ideas from yours about what's too warm or too cool.

Conventional wisdom on luggage is of two minds. One says you should keep your luggage with you in the passenger compartment, where, under your watchful eye, it will be safer. The other says you should have it locked in the luggage compartment below. In practice many bus companies don't allow big baggage, such as backpacks, to be carried into the cabin. We suggest that you carry your valuables on your person in a money belt or pouch and store most of your stuff in the luggage compartment on deluxe and 1st-class buses. Don't allow it to be hoisted onto the open luggage rack atop a 2nd-class bus unless you feel you can keep an eye on it (which is nearly impossible).

Food and drinks in bus stations are overpriced; you'd do well to bring your own. Drinks and snacks are provided on some deluxe services. The better buses have toilets, but it's worth carrying some toilet paper.

Highway robbery has increased in some parts of Mexico. The danger is greatest at night, on isolated stretches of highway far from cities. See Dangers & Annoyances in Facts for the Visitor for more information.

Terminals & Schedules

Most cities and towns have a single, modern, main bus station where all long-distance buses arrive and depart. It's called the *Central Camionera, Central de Autobuses, Terminal de Autobuses, Central de Camiones* or simply *El Central*, and it is usually a long way from the center of town. Frequent local buses link bus stations with town centers. Note the crucial difference between the *Central* (bus station) and the *Centro* (city center).

If there is no single main terminal, different bus companies will have their own terminals scattered around town.

Most bus lines have schedules posted at their ticket desks in the bus station, but they aren't always comprehensive. If your destination isn't listed, ask: it may be en route to one that is. From big towns, many different bus companies may run on the same routes, so compare fares and classes of service.

Classes

Long-distance buses range enormously in quality, from comfortable, nonstop, air-con deluxe services to decaying, suspension-less ex-city buses grinding out their dying years on dirt roads to remote settlements. The differences between classes are no longer clear-cut, and terms such as *de lujo* and *primera clase* can cover quite a wide range of comfort levels. All of them offer a combination of features, such as extra legroom, reclining seats, drinks, snacks or videos. But broadly, buses fall into three categories:

De lujo – Deluxe services run mainly on the busy routes. They bear names such as 'Plus,' 'GL' or 'Ejecutivo.' The buses are swift, new, comfortable and air-con; they may cost just 10% or 20% more than 1st-class, or twice the 1st-class rate for the most luxurious lines, such as ETN and UNO, which offer reclining seats, plenty of legroom, few or no stops, and snacks, hot and cold drinks, videos and toilets on board.

Primera (1a) clase – 1st-class buses have a comfortable *numerado* (numbered) seat for each passenger and often show videos. Their standards of comfort are usually perfectly adequate. They usually have air-con and a toilet. They stop infrequently and serve all sizable towns. As with deluxe buses, you must buy your ticket in the bus station before boarding.

Segunda (2a) clase – 2nd-class buses serve small towns and villages and also offer cheaper, slower travel on some intercity routes. A few are old, tatty, uncomfortable, liable to break down, and will stop anywhere for someone to get on or off. Except on some major runs, there's usually no apparent limit on capacity, which means that if you board mid-route you might make the trip *parado* (standing) rather than *sentado* (seated). (Don't confuse parado with *parada*, bus stop.) If you board mid-route you pay your fare to the conductor. Fares are about 10% or 20% lower than for 1st-class.

Types of Service

It is also important to know the types of service offered.

Sin escalas – Nonstop

Directo – Very few stops

Semi-directo – A few more stops than directo

Ordinario – Stops wherever passengers want to get on or off; deluxe and 1st-class buses are never ordinario

Express – Nonstop on short to medium trips, very few stops on long trips

Local – Bus that starts its journey at the bus station you're in and usually leaves on time; preferable to *de paso*

De paso – Bus that started its journey somewhere else but is stopping to let off and take on passengers. A de paso bus may be late and may or may not have seats available; you also may have to wait until it arrives before any tickets are sold. If the bus is full, you may have to wait for the next one.

Viaje redondo – Roundtrip, available only on some journeys, most starting in Mexico City

TRAIN

Service offered by Ferrocarriles Nacionales de México (FNM, Mexican National Railways) has been in decline for a long time. Trains are slow even when they run on schedule, sleeper and restaurant services are disappearing, ticket offices may be open only for brief periods, and it can be difficult to find out just when a train is leaving or what accommodations it carries at what fares. At least rail travel is cheap – unless you take the reasonably comfortable *coches dormitorios* (sleeper cars). They are available on just a handful of trains and can cost as much as a deluxe bus.

One Mexican rail trip, the spectacular Barranca del Cobre (Copper Canyon) railway between Chihuahua and Los Mochis, is deservedly a major visitor attraction in its own right. Some other trains are mediocre to unpleasant; still others are downright unsafe. That said, most major trains north and west of the Isthmus of Tehuantepec (Mexico's narrow 'waist') are worth considering if you're not in a big hurry. Trains can be fun, even romantic, and they travel picturesque backcountry that you don't see from the highways. East of the Isthmus of Tehuantepec service is poor, and the trains are renowned for theft and robbery. Take a bus or the plane or prepare for unpleasantness.

Classes

Most travelers go 1st-class; 2nd-class is strictly for the more adventurous – though it has a few devotees.

Primera preferente – This is the only type of 1st-class seating on nearly all trains, equivalent to the former *primera especial* (and still called that by many people); you get a reclining numbered seat, and the car is normally air-con. Fares are cheaper than 2nd-class bus fares. Seats can be booked in advance.

Segunda (2a) clase – The poorest Mexicans walk; the next poorest ride segunda. Second-class cars are usually hot and uncomfortable, with vile toilets and no lights at night; they may be overcrowded or they may be nearly empty. At least the floors are swept and mopped regularly. Fares are little more than half those of primera preferente. If you're an adventurous sort with more time than money at your disposal, you might consider segunda. Many of the better trains don't have 2nd-class carriages; some 2nd-class trains are *mixto* (hauling both passengers and freight).

Coche dormitorio – Sleeper car, available only on a handful of trains. The fare includes fairly presentable meals in a dining car. There are two types of accommodations, Camarín and Alcoba (see below), both of acceptable but not exceptional cleanliness:

Camarín – Private 'roomette' with washbasin and toilet (under the seat/bed, which must be moved for use). At night a berth folds out to fill the entire compartment. Camarines can take one or two people, each paying around double the cost of a primera preferente seat.

Alcoba – Private 'bedroom' with two berths (upper and lower) that convert to seats during the day and are comfortable for one adult each. Minimum occupancy is two adults, but up to four adults and one child are permitted. Washbasin and toilet are always accessible. The fare per person is a little more than in a camarín.

Schedules & Ticketing

Information about rail services to and from particular cities is given in this book's city sections. Since nearly all the better trains terminate in Mexico City or Guadalajara, the fullest schedule and fare information is given in those cities' Getting There &

Away sections. The details of schedules change quite often, but the basics are fairly constant.

Mexico's top trains are listed in the *Thomas Cook Overseas Timetable*, perhaps the most convenient way to check current schedules outside Mexico. The timetable, published six times a year, is available in the UK from bookstores or from Thomas Cook Publishing (☎ 01733-268943), PO Box 227, Peterborough PE3 8BQ. In the US it is on sale in good travel bookstores or by mail from Forsyth Travel Library (☎ 913-384-3440), PO Box 480800, Kansas City, MO 64148-0800 USA, for US$27.95 plus US$4.50 for shipping and handling.

In Mexico you can get train schedule and ticketing information in English by calling ☎ 800-90392, a toll-free number operated by the tourism ministry SECTUR. At Mexico City's Buenavista Station you can pick up *Rutas Ferroviarias*, a free schedule and fare list for the country's main trains, from the Departamento Tráfico de Pasajeros.

Coche dormitorio and primera clase tickets can be bought up to one month ahead; for some trains they will still be available on the day of travel, but it's advisable to buy them in advance if you can. You can buy tickets for trains from Mexico City at stations in other main Mexican cities – allow two or three days. Segunda clase tickets are sold only on the day of departure.

In the USA you can book Mexican train tickets in advance (coche dormitorio or primera clase only), at some extra cost, through Mexico by Train (☎ 956-725-3659, 800-321-1699), PO Box 2782, Laredo, TX 78044 USA.

CAR & MOTORCYCLE

Driving in Mexico is not as easy as it is in North America, but it is often easier and more convenient than the bus and sometimes the only way to get to some of the most beautiful places or isolated towns and villages. See Dangers & Annoyances in Facts for the Visitor for a warning about risks of highway robbery in some areas, and the Getting There & Away chapter for information about the requirements for bringing a vehicle into Mexico. The Spanish for Travelers section in the back of the book has some useful Spanish words and phrases for drivers.

Traffic laws and speed limits rarely seem to be enforced on the highways. In the cities you'll want to obey the laws strictly so as not to give the police an excuse to hit you with a 'fine' payable on the spot.

Fuel & Service

All *gasolina* (gasoline) and diesel fuel in Mexico is sold by the government's monopoly, Pemex (Petróleos Mexicanos), for cash (no credit cards). Most towns, even small ones, have a Pemex station, and the stations are pretty common on most major roads. Nevertheless, in remote areas it's better to fill up when you can.

Unleaded gas is available at just about every Pemex station. It's called Magna Sin and is sold from green pumps. It's 92 octane by Mexican standards but 87 octane by US standards (equivalent to US regular unleaded). Mexico has plans to eliminate leaded fuel, but at the time of writing Nova leaded fuel was still available, from blue pumps. It's 82 octane by Mexican standards, 80 by US standards. Diesel fuel, in red or purple pumps, is also widely available.

At 1997 rates Magna Sin and Nova both cost a little under US$0.40 a liter (US$1.50 a US gallon), with Nova slightly cheaper; those prices were a bit higher than the typical US prices. Mexican fuel prices are low compared with European, Asian or Australian prices.

All stations have pump attendants (who expect tips), but they are not always trustworthy. When buying fuel, it's better to ask for a peso amount than to say *lleno* (full) – lleno usually finishes with fuel gushing down the side of your car. Check that the pump registers zero pesos to start with, and be quick to check afterward that you have been given the amount you requested – the attendants often reset the pump immedi-ately and start to serve another customer. Don't have the attendants do your gas, oil and water all at once, or you may not get what you paid for. Pressure gauges on air hoses are often absent, so carry and use your own.

Road Conditions

Mexican highways, even some toll highways, are not up to the standards of European or North American ones. Still, the main roads are serviceable and fairly fast when traffic is not heavy. A common problem is steep shoulders, so if your wheels go off the road surface the car tilts alarmingly. Sometimes there's a deep gutter, and if you go into it you may roll the car. Driving at night is especially dangerous – unlit vehicles, rocks and livestock on the roads are common. Hijacks and robberies do occur. Especially on roads heading south from the US border, be prepared for fairly frequent drug and weapon searches by the army and police.

In towns and cities you must be especially wary of *alto* (stop) signs, *topes* (speed bumps) and potholes. They are often not where you'd expect, and missing one can cost you in traffic fines or car damage. One-way streets are the rule in towns: usually alternating streets run in opposite directions, so if you cross one that's westbound only, the next one will probably go east.

Toll Roads Mexico has more than 6000 km of toll roads. Some are run by the federal government, some by private concessions. *Cuotas* (tolls) fluctuate: some on the privatized highways have been exorbitant – most notoriously the 400-km Mexico City to Acapulco run, which at one time cost US$75. In 1997 the government took back control of 23 of the 52 privatized routes – including Mexico City-Acapulco – and promised to reduce tolls on them.

On a government toll road you can expect to pay about US$1 per 20 km. There are usually alternative free roads, but if the toll road is overpriced, the free road will often be overloaded – a four-lane *autopista* (highway) might be deserted while a parallel road is breaking up under the burden of every truck, bus and car on the route.

Motorcycle Hazards Certain aspects of Mexican roads make them more hazardous for bikers than for drivers. They include:

- poor signage of road or lane closures (there may be nothing more than a rock placed 20 meters before where the work is being done)
- lots of dogs on the roads
- lack of hotels/motels on some stretches of highway
- debris and deep potholes
- vehicles without taillights; lack of highway lighting

Maps

Town and country roads are often poorly or idiosyncratically signposted. It pays to get the best road maps you can. The Mexican *Guía Roji Por Las Carreteras de México* road atlas is a good investment, at US$6.50 from decent bookstores and some city newsstands in Mexico. It's updated annually and keeps tabs on new highways, though it's not perfect on minor roads. There's also the similar *Guía Verdi México Atlas de Carreteras*. The 'Travelogs' that Sanborn's insurance supplies free to its customers are very detailed and can be quite useful.

Parking

It's inadvisable to park on the street overnight, and most cheap city hotels don't provide parking. Sometimes you can leave a car out front and the night porter will keep an eye on it. Usually you have to use a commercial *estacionamiento* (parking lot), which might cost US$2.50 overnight and US$0.50 per hour during the day. Hotels that offer parking tend to be the more expensive ones.

If you're just overnighting and moving on in the morning, you can often find decent motels on highways just outside cities. These have easy parking.

Breakdown Assistance

The Mexican tourism ministry, SECTUR, maintains a network of *Ángeles Verdes* (Green Angels) – bilingual mechanics in bright green trucks who patrol each major stretch of highway in Mexico at least twice daily during daylight hours searching for motorists in trouble. They make minor repairs, replace small parts, provide fuel and oil, and arrange towing and other assistance by radio if necessary. Service is free; parts, gasoline and oil are provided at cost. If you are near a telephone when your car has problems, you can call them on their 24-hour hot line in Mexico City (☎ 5-250-82-21) or through the national 24-hour tourist assistance numbers in Mexico City (☎ 5-250-01-23, 800-90392).

Most serious mechanical problems can be fixed efficiently and inexpensively by mechanics in towns and cities as long as the parts are available. Volkswagen, Ford, Nissan/Datsun, Chrysler and General Motors parts are the easiest to obtain; others may have to be ordered from the USA. For parts suppliers, consult the telephone directory's yellow pages under *Refacciones y Acesorios para Automóviles y Camiones*. For authorized dealer service, look under *Automóviles – Agencias*.

Accidents

Under Mexico's legal system, people involved in an incident are assumed to be guilty until proven innocent. They can be detained until the matter is resolved, perhaps weeks or months later. For minor accidents, drivers will probably be released if they have insurance to cover any property damage they may have caused. If it's a serious accident, involving injury or death, the drivers may be held until the authorities determine who is responsible. The guilty party will not be released until he/she guarantees restitution to the victims and payment of any fines. Your embassy can help only by recommending a lawyer and contacting friends or family at home. Adequate insurance coverage is the only real protection.

Rental

Car rental in Mexico is expensive by North American or European standards, but it can be worthwhile if you want to visit several places in a short time and have three or four people to share the cost. It can also be useful for getting off the beaten track, where public transport is slow or scarce.

Cars can be rented in most of Mexico's cities and resorts, at airports and sometimes at bus and train stations. Most big hotels can arrange a car. Sometimes it's necessary to book a few days ahead.

Renters must have a valid driver's license (your license from home is OK) and passport, and are usually required to be at least 25 years old. Sometimes age 21 is acceptable, but you may have to pay more. A major credit card is needed, or a huge cash deposit. You should get a signed rental agreement and read its small print.

In addition to the basic daily or weekly rental rate, you must pay for insurance, tax and fuel. Ask about just what the insurance covers – the insurance on one car we rented from Budget while researching this edition covered only 90% of the car's value in case of theft, and gave no coverage at all for 'partial theft' (which turned out to be theft of part of the vehicle, such as wiper blades or tires). Fortunately, nothing was either completely or partially stolen.

Most agencies offer a choice between a per-km deal or unlimited km. The latter is usually preferable if you intend to do some hard driving. (If you don't, why are you renting a car?) Local firms are often cheaper than the big international ones. You can usually find a Volkswagen Beetle – often the cheapest car available – for US$40 to US$50 a day with unlimited km and including insurance and tax. The weekly rate is often equivalent to six single days. The extra charge for drop-off in another city is usually about US$0.30 per km.

You can book cars in Mexico through the large international agencies in other countries. Doing this may sometimes get you lower rates. Here are toll-free telephone numbers for some international firms:

Company	In the USA	In Mexico
Avis	☎ 800-331-2112	☎ 800-70777
Budget	☎ 800-527-0700	☎ 800-70017
Dollar	☎ 800-800-4000	☎ 800-90010
Hertz	☎ 800-654-3131	☎ 800-70016
National	☎ 800-328-4567	☎ 800-00395
Thrifty	☎ 800-367-2277	☎ 800-01859

HITCHHIKING

Travelers who decide to hitchhike should understand that they are taking a small but potentially serious risk. A woman alone certainly should not hitchhike in Mexico, and two women alone are not advised to either. However, some people do choose to hitchhike, and it's not an uncommon way of getting to off-the-beaten-track archaeological sites and other places that are poorly served by bus. Hitching is less common along the highways and main roads, but it's possible if you have a sign and don't look scruffy. Be alert to possible dangers wherever you are. If in doubt, ask local advice about safety.

If the driver is another tourist or a private motorist, you may get the ride for free. If it is a work or commercial vehicle, you should expect (and offer) to pay.

BOAT

Vehicle and passenger ferries connect Baja California with the Mexican mainland at Santa Rosalía/Guaymas, La Paz/Mazatlán and La Paz/Topolobampo. Ferries also run to the islands Isla Mujeres, Cozumel and Isla Holbox, off the Yucatán Peninsula. For details, see the relevant city and island sections.

LOCAL TRANSPORT

Bus

Generally known as *camiones*, local buses are the cheapest way of getting around cities and to nearby villages. They run everywhere, frequently, and are dirt cheap (fares in cities are rarely more than US$0.20). Older buses are often noisy, dirty and crowded, but in some cities there are fleets of small, modern microbuses, which are more pleasant. In cities, buses halt only at specific *paradas* (bus stops), which may or may not be marked.

Colectivo, Combi & Pesero

Colectivos are minibuses or big cars that function as something between a taxi and a bus. (A *combi* is a VW minibus; a *pesero* is Mexico City's word for colectivo.) They're cheaper than taxis, quicker and less crowded than buses. They run along set routes – sometimes displayed on the windshield – and will pick you up or drop you off on any corner along that route.

If you're not at the start of a colectivo's route, go to the curb and wave your hand when you see one. As the driver approaches he may indicate how many places are free by holding up the appropriate number of fingers. Tell the driver where you want to go; you normally pay at the end of the trip, and the fare usually depends on how far you go.

Taxi

Taxis are common in towns and cities. They're often surprisingly economical, and they're useful if you have a lot of baggage, need to get from point A to point B quickly or are worried about theft on public transport. (But see the Mexico City Information section for a warning on that city's taxi crime epidemic.) In many cities most taxis are Volkswagen Beetles. If a taxi has a meter, ask the driver if it's working *('¿Funciona el taxímetro?')*. If it's not, or if the taxi doesn't have a meter, establish the price of the ride *before* getting in (this usually involves a bit of haggling).

Some airports and big bus stations have taxi *taquillas* (kiosks), where you buy a fixed-price ticket to your destination, then hand it to the driver instead of paying cash. This can save haggling and major rip-offs, but fares are usually higher than you could get outside on the street.

Finding Your Way in Cities

Mexican street naming and numbering can be confusing. When asking directions, it's better to ask for a specific place, such as the Hotel Central or the Museo Regional, than for the street it's on. To achieve a degree of certainty, ask three people.

ORGANIZED TOURS

Taking a guided tour can be an easy way of getting a quick introduction to big cities such as Mexico City or Guadalajara, or of exploring out-of-the-way places where public transportation isn't the greatest, such as the Barranca del Cobre (Copper Canyon), villages around San Cristóbal de Las Casas or the Bonampak and Yaxchilán ruins (in Chiapas), or some archaeological sites on the Yucatán Peninsula. There are also pleasant walking tours of historic towns such as Morelia, San Miguel de Allende and Alamos. You'll find details on all these in the regional chapters.

If you're looking for an adventure- or activity-focused group trip, the following lists just a few of the companies you might like to check out. See the Website Directory for some sources on others – many Mexican tour companies and organizations are linked to some of the Internet sites listed. Mexican Government Tourism Offices can help you too.

Adventure Center (☎ 510-654-1879), 1311 63rd St Suite 200, Emeryville, CA 94608, USA, runs ecologically minded adventure trips through Mexico, including a trek in the mountains of Oaxaca.

Adventure Specialists (☎ 719-783-2519 May to November, 719-630-7687 December to April), Bear Basin Ranch, Westcliffe, CO 81252 USA, specializes in Barranca del Cobre (Copper Canyon) expeditions.

AMTAVE (☎ 5-661-91-21, fax 5-662-73-54, 74174.2424@compuserve.com), Avenida Insurgentes Sur 1971, Nivel Paseo loc 251, Colonia Guadalupe Inn, 01020 Mexico DF, is a Mexico City-based group of about 40 Mexican adventure travel and ecotourism companies and organizations.

Biodiversidad Mexicana (☎ 210-283-5142), 384 Treeline Park No 613, San Antonio, TX 78209, USA, offers tours of cacti in their natural habitats.

Ceiba Adventures (☎ 520-527-0171), PO Box 2274, Flagstaff, AZ 86003, USA, does rain forest and archaeological river trips in the Maya regions.

Explore Worldwide runs small-group land trips with interesting itineraries. It has offices and agents in several countries, including Britain (☎ 01252-344161), Australia (☎ 02-9956-7766), and the USA (☎ 800-227-8747).

Journey Latin America (☎ 0181-747-3108), 16 Devonshire Rd, Chiswick, London W4 2HD, UK, runs some small-group tours using local transport and budget hotels.

Mayan Adventures (☎ 206-523-5309, fax 206-524-6309), PO Box 15204, Seattle, WA 98115, USA, offers small-group trips to off-the-beaten-track Mayan sites.

Río y Montaña Expediciones (☎ 5-520-2041, fax 5-540-78-70), Prado Norte 450, Lomas de Chapultepec, 11000 Mexico DF, is a Mexico City firm recommended by readers that runs canoe and rafting trips on rivers and lakes in various parts of Mexico, and also some guided hiking trips.

The Touring Exchange (☎ 360-385-0667), Box 265, Port Townsend, WA 98368, USA, organizes Pacific Coast bicycle tours and adventure trips in Baja California.

TrekAmerica (☎ 973-983-1144, 800-221-0596), PO Box 189, Rockaway, NJ 07866 USA, takes international small group camping expeditions through several parts of Mexico.

Victor Emmanuel Tours (☎ 512-328-5221, 800-328-8368), PO Box 33008, Austin, TX 78764, USA, runs birding and natural history tours.

Mexico City

pop 20 million (approx); alt 2240m; ☎ *5*

Mexico City is a place to love and loathe. Spread across more than 2000 sq km of a single highland valley, it encapsulates the best and worst of Mexico the country. The result is a seething, cosmopolitan city that is by turns exhilarating and overpowering. One moment Mexico City is music, glamour and excitement; the next it's drabness, poverty, overcrowding and foul smells. This is a city of colonial palaces, world-renowned cultural treasures and sprawling slums; of ear-splitting traffic and quiet, peaceful plazas; of huge wealth and miserable poverty; of green parks and brown air.

Despite its problems, Mexico City is a magnet for Mexicans and visitors alike, because with nearly a quarter of the country's population, it far outstrips the rest of the country in economic, cultural and political importance. As one Mexican acquaintance put it, *'Lo que ocurre en México, ocurre en el DF'* – 'What happens in Mexico, happens in Mexico City.'

The city is known to Mexicans simply as México – pronounced, like the country, 'MEH-hee-ko.' If they want to distinguish it from Mexico the country, they call it either *la ciudad de México* or *el DF* ('el de EFF-ay'). The DF is the Distrito Federal (Federal District), in which half the city, including all its central areas, lies. The outlying parts of Mexico City are in the state of México, which surrounds the Distrito Federal on three sides.

HISTORY

As early as 10,000 BC, humans and animals were attracted to the shores of Lago de Texcoco, the lake that then covered much of the Valle de México. After 7500 BC the lake began to shrink and hunting became more difficult, so the inhabitants turned to agriculture. A loose federation of farming villages had evolved around Lago de Texcoco by approximately 200 BC. The

HIGHLIGHTS

- The world-class Museo Nacional de Antropología, a treasure house of Mexican archaeological marvels
- The Bosque de Chapultepec, a large woodland expanse in the midst of the city, with a fine zoo and several good museums
- The old suburbs of Coyoacán and San Ángel, full of colonial atmosphere and memories of Diego Rivera and Frida Kahlo, vibrant with weekend markets
- The Zócalo, one of the world's biggest plazas, surrounded by the presidential palace, the city's cathedral and the remains of the main temple of Aztec Tenochtitlán
- Marvelous murals by 20th century Mexican masters in the Palacio Nacional, the Palacio de Bellas Artes, the Museo Mural Diego Rivera and elsewhere
- A gondola ride along the ancient canals of Xochimilco and a visit to the beautiful nearby Museo Dolores Olmedo Patiño, with its superb Rivera collection

biggest, Cuicuilco, was destroyed by a volcanic eruption about 100 AD.

After that the big influence in the area was Teotihuacán, 25 km northeast of the lake. For centuries it was the capital of an empire stretching to Guatemala and beyond, but it fell in the 7th century AD. Among the several city-states in the region in the following centuries, the Toltec empire, based at Tula, 65 km north of modern Mexico City, was probably the most important.

The Aztecs

By the 13th century the Tula empire had also collapsed, leaving a number of small statelets around the lake to compete for control of the Valle de México. It was the Mexica ('meh-SHEE-kah'), or Aztecs, a wandering Chichimec tribe from northern or western Mexico, who eventually came out on top.

The Aztecs had settled on the western shore of Lago de Texcoco, but other valley inhabitants objected to Aztec interference in their relations and to Aztec habits such as human sacrifice (done to appease their guardian god, Huizilopochtli) and wife-stealing. In the early 14th century, fighting as mercenaries for Coxcox, ruler of Culhuacán, on the southern shore of the lake, the Aztecs defeated nearby Xochimilco and sent Coxcox 8000 human ears as proof of their victory. Coxcox granted them land and rashly agreed that they could make his daughter an Aztec goddess. As described in *The Course of Mexican History*, by Michael Meyer & William Sherman:

The princess was sacrificed and flayed. When her father attended the banquet in his honor, he was horrified to find that the entertainment included a dancer dressed in the skin of his daughter . . . Coxcox raised an army which scattered the barbarians.

Sometime between 1325 and 1345 the Aztecs, wandering around the swampy fringes of the lake, finally founded their own city, Tenochtitlán, on an island near the lake's western shore. (Today the island site is the downtown area around the main square, the Zócalo.) The site was chosen, according to legend, because there the Aztecs saw an eagle standing on a cactus, eating a snake – a sign, they believed, that they should stop their wanderings and build a city.

About 1370 the Aztecs began to serve as mercenaries for the kingdom of Azcapotzalco, on the western shore of the lake. When they rebelled against Azcapotzalco about 1427, they became the greatest power in the valley.

Tenochtitlán rapidly grew into a sophisticated city-state whose empire would, by the early 16th century, stretch across most of central Mexico from the Pacific to the gulf and down into far southern Mexico. The Aztecs' sense of their own importance as the chosen people of the voracious Huizilopochtli grew too. In the mid-15th century they formed the Triple Alliance with the lakeshore states Texcoco and Tlacopan to conduct wars against Tlaxcala and Huejotzingo, which lay east of the valley. The purpose was to gain a steady supply of the prisoners needed to sate Huizilopochtli's vast hunger for sacrificial victims, so that the sun would continue to rise each day and floods and famines could be avoided. In four days in 1487, no less than 20,000 prisoners were sacrificed to dedicate Tenochtitlán's newly rebuilt main temple.

The prosperity at the heart of the empire allowed the Aztecs to build a large city on a grid plan, with canals as thoroughfares. In the more marshy parts they created raised gardens by piling up vegetation and mud from the lake and stabilizing the resulting plots by planting willows. These *chinampas* – versions of which can still be seen at Xochimilco in southern Mexico City – gave three or four harvests a year but were still not enough to feed the growing population. The Aztecs also needed to extract tribute from conquered tribes to supplement the resources of the Valle de México – another reason for their rapid imperial expansion in the 15th century.

At the city's heart stood the main *Teocalli* (sacred precinct), with its double-pyramid temple dedicated to Huizilopochtli and the water god, Tláloc. The remains of this temple, the Templo Mayor, can be seen today just off the Zócalo. Three main causeways linked the city to the lakeshore. This was the city that amazed the Spanish when they arrived in 1519, by which time its population was an estimated 200,000. (That of the whole Valle de México at the time was perhaps 1.5 million, making it even then one of the world's biggest and densest urban areas.)

Capital of Nueva España
Wrecked during and after the Spanish conquest (see History in Facts about the Country), Tenochtitlán was rebuilt as a Spanish city. The native population of the Valle de México shrank drastically – to fewer than 100,000 within a century of the conquest, by some estimates. But the city itself had emerged by 1550 as the prosperous and elegant, if somewhat insanitary, capital of a politically centralized Nueva España. Broad, straight streets were laid out and buildings constructed to Spanish designs with local materials such as *tezontle*, a light-red, porous volcanic rock that the Aztecs had used for their temples. Hospitals, schools, churches, palaces, parks, a university and even an insane asylum were built. But right up to the late 19th century it suffered floods caused by the partial destruction in the 1520s of the Aztecs' canals. Lago de Texcoco often overflowed into the city, damaging streets and buildings, bringing disease and forcing the relocation of thousands of people.

Independence
On October 30, 1810, some 80,000 independence rebels, led by the priest Miguel Hidalgo, had Mexico City at their mercy after defeating Spanish loyalist forces at Las Cruces, outside the capital. But Hidalgo decided against advancing on the city – a mistake that cost Mexico 11 more years of fighting before independence was achieved. By 1821 the city had a population of 160,000, which made it the biggest in the Americas.

Mexico City entered the modern age under the despotic Porfirio Díaz, who ruled Mexico for most of the period from 1877 to 1911 and attracted a great deal of foreign investment. Díaz ushered in a construction boom in the city and had railways built to the provinces and the USA. Some 150 km

of electric tramways threaded through the streets, industry expanded, and by 1910 the city had 471,000 inhabitants. A drainage canal with two tunnels finally succeeded in drying up a large part of the Lago de Texcoco, allowing the city to expand farther, but that brought a host of new problems by causing ground levels to sink – which they continue to do today, with damage to many notable buildings.

The 20th Century
After Díaz fell in 1911, the chaos of the Mexican Revolution brought warfare and hunger to the city's streets. The 1920s ushered in peace and a modicum of prosperity. The postrevolution minister of education, José Vasconcelos, commissioned Mexico's top artists – among them Diego Rivera, David Alfaro Siqueiros and José Clemente Orozco – to decorate numerous public buildings in the city with dramatic, large-scale murals conveying a clear sense of Mexico's past and future.

Growth was halted by the Great Depression, but afterward a drive to industrialize attracted more and more money and people to the city. By 1940 the population was 1,726,858; Mexico City was growing into the urban monster that we know today.

In the 1940s and '50s factories and skyscrapers rose almost as quickly as the population, which was increasing by an average of 7% a year. The supply of housing, jobs and services could not keep pace with the influx of people; shantytowns started to appear at the city's fringes, and Mexico City's modern problems began to take shape.

Despite continued economic growth into the 1960s, political and social reform lagged far behind. Student-led discontent came to a head as Mexico City prepared for the 1968 Olympic Games. On October 2, 10 days before the games started, about 5000 to 10,000 people gathering in Tlatelolco, north of the city center, were encircled by troops and police. To this day, no one is certain how many people died in the ensuing massacre, but estimates have been put at several hundred.

Megalopolis

Mexico City continued to grow at a frightening rate in the 1970s, spreading beyond the Distrito Federal into the state of México and developing some of the world's worst traffic and pollution problems, only partly alleviated by the metro system (opened in 1969) and by more recent attempts to limit traffic.

People have continued to pour into Mexico City despite the earthquake of September 19, 1985, which registered more than eight on the Richter scale, killed at least 10,000 (possibly 20,000) people, displaced thousands more and caused more than US$4 billion in damage.

Today an estimated 2000 newcomers arrive in the city daily, and its population is estimated at 20 million. Efforts to move industry and government jobs away from the overcrowded capital have had little success. Since 1940 Mexico City has multiplied in area more than 10 times, yet it's still one of the world's most crowded metropolitan areas, as well as one of the most polluted. It is the industrial, retail, financial, communications and cultural center of the country; its industries generate more than one-third of Mexico's wealth, and its people consume 66% of Mexico's energy. Its cost of living is the highest in the nation.

Heavy subsidies are needed to keep the place from seizing up, and more than half the country's spending on social welfare goes to the capital. Extraction of water from the subsoil makes the city sink steadily – by about six cm a year in the center (where some areas have sunk nine meters in the 20th century) and as many as 15 to 40 cm a year on the city's fringes. Even so, about one-third of the city's water has to be pumped in at great cost from outside the Valle de México.

The poverty and overcrowding that have always existed alongside the wealth have been exacerbated by the recession of the mid-1990s. In 1996 it was estimated that more than one-fifth of the people in the Distrito Federal were living on marginal levels of basic subsistence, and another two-thirds were barely able to cover the expense of material necessities. Those figures did not include the outer parts of the city in the state of México, where most of the newer shantytowns lie. One effect of the crisis has been a big rise in crime.

In 1997 the city was given permission for the first time to elect its own mayor, after being ruled directly by the federal government since 1928. The winner, Cuauhtémoc Cárdenas, of the left-of-center PRD party, carries the hopes of millions that he can somehow prevent Mexico City's difficulties from getting worse.

ORIENTATION

Mexico City's 350 *colonias* (neighborhoods) sprawl across the ancient bed of Lago de Texcoco and beyond. Though this vast urban expanse is daunting at first, the main areas of interest to visitors are fairly well defined and easily traversed.

Centro Histórico

The historic heart of the city is the wide plaza known as El Zócalo, surrounded by the Palacio Nacional, the Catedral Metropolitana and the excavated site of the Templo Mayor, the main temple of Aztec Tenochtitlán. The Zócalo and its surrounding neighborhoods are known as the Centro Histórico (Historic Center) and are full of notable old buildings and interesting museums. North, west and south of the Zócalo are many good, economical hotels and restaurants.

Alameda Central & Bellas Artes

Avenida Madero and Avenida Cinco de Mayo (or 5 de Mayo) link the Zócalo with the verdant park named the Alameda Central, eight blocks to the west. On the east side of the Alameda stands the magnificent Palacio de Bellas Artes. The landmark Torre Latinoamericana (Latin American Tower) pierces the sky a block south of the Bellas Artes, beside one of the city's main north-south arterial roads, the Eje Central Lázaro Cárdenas, also called Juan Ruiz de Alarcón at this point.

Plaza de la República

Some 750 meters west of the Alameda, across Paseo de la Reforma, is the Plaza de la República, marked by the somber, domed art deco-style Monumento a la Revolución. This is a fairly quiet, mostly residential area with many decent, moderately priced hotels.

Paseo de la Reforma

Mexico City's grandest boulevard runs for many kilometers across the city's heart, connecting the Alameda to the Zona Rosa and the Bosque de Chapultepec. Major hotels, embassies and banks rise on either side.

Zona Rosa

The glitzy Zona Rosa (Pink Zone) is the highlife and nightlife district bound by Paseo de la Reforma to the north, Avenida Insurgentes to the east, and Avenida Chapultepec to the south. Many top hotels, restaurants, clubs and boutiques cluster here. It's a fascinating place for a stroll and can yield some good budget surprises as well.

Bosque de Chapultepec

The Wood of Chapultepec, known to gringos as Chapultepec Park, is to the west of the aforementioned districts. It's Mexico City's 'lungs,' a large expanse of greenery and lakes, and holds many of the city's major museums, including the renowned Museo Nacional de Antropología.

North of the Center

Estación Buenavista, the city's train station, is 1.2 km north of Plaza de la República along Avenida Insurgentes, the city's major north-south axis. Five km north of the center is the Terminal Norte, the largest of the city's four major bus terminals. Six km north of the center is the Basílica de Guadalupe, Mexico's most revered shrine.

South of the Center

Avenida Insurgentes connects Paseo de la Reforma to most points of interest in the south. Ten to 15 km south of the Alameda are the atmospheric former villages of San Ángel and Coyoacán and the vast campus of UNAM, the National Autonomous University of Mexico. Also down here is the Terminal Sur, the southern intercity bus station. Further south, about 20 km from the Alameda, are the canals and gardens of Xochimilco.

The Eje System

Besides their regular names, many major streets in Mexico City are termed Eje (axis). The Eje system superimposes a grid of priority roads on this sprawling city's maze of smaller streets, making transport easier and quicker. The key north-south Eje Central Lázaro Cárdenas passes just east of the Palacio de Bellas Artes, at which point it's also called Juan Ruiz de Alarcón. (For two blocks north of the Bellas Artes it's called Aquiles Serdán, and a block south of the Bellas Artes it becomes San Juan de Letrán.) Major north-south roads to the west of the Eje Central are termed Eje 1 Poniente (also called Guerrero, Rosales and Bucareli as it passes through the central area), Eje 2 Poniente (Avenida Florencia, Monterrey), etc. Major north-south roads to the east of the Eje Central are called Eje 1 Oriente (Alcocer, Anillo de Circunvalación), Eje 2 Oriente (Avenida Congreso de la Unión) and so on. The same goes for major east-west roads to the north and south of the Alameda Central and Zócalo: Rayón is Eje 1 Norte, and Fray Servando Teresa de Mier is Eje 1 Sur.

Maps

Maps handed out by tourist offices in Mexico City are very basic. You can buy better maps of the city and country in many bookstores (including those in the Sanborn's store chain and at top-end hotels), from street hawkers (some of those on Avenida Juárez facing the south side of the Alameda Central specialize in maps), and at the shop of INEGI (the Instituto Nacional de Estadística, Geografía e Informática, or National Institute of Statistics, Geography & Information Technology) at

Local (Office) CC23, Glorieta Insurgentes, just outside Insurgentes metro station. The INEGI shop not only has maps of Mexico City and the whole country, but also stocks a good range of other Mexican city and state maps, plus INEGI's own large-scale series of 1:50,000 (1 cm: 500 meters) maps covering the whole of Mexico. It's open Monday to Friday 8 am to 8 pm, Saturday 8.30 am to 4 pm.

Among the best maps of Mexico City is the *Guía Roji Ciudad de México* street atlas, costing US$8.50, which has a comprehensive index and is updated annually. The same maps are available in five large sheets – updated less frequently – as *Guía Roji Infocalles Ciudad de México*. Each sheet costs around US$3. The *Área Metropolitana* sheet covers all central parts of the city and includes a plan of the metro system. The scale on both the atlas and the sheets is around 1:22,500 (1 cm:225 meters).

Finding an Address
Some major streets, such as Avenida Insurgentes, keep the same name for many kilometers, but the names – and numbering systems – of many lesser streets change every few blocks. Full addresses normally include the name of a colonia (neighborhood). Except for well-known city center districts, you may need help in finding a particular colonia. Often the easiest way to find an address is by asking where it is in relation to the nearest metro station.

INFORMATION
Tourist Offices
Mexico City has three tourist information offices in central areas. There's also one at the airport (see Getting There & Away). None of them has much giveaway material, and they offer only very basic city maps.

The tourist office of SECTUR, the national tourism ministry (☎ 250-01-23, 800-90392), is located, not very conveniently, at Avenida Presidente Masaryk 172, on the corner of Hegel in the Polanco district, about 700 meters north of the Bosque de Chapultepec (metro: Polanco). It has multilingual staff who willingly answer queries on Mexico City and the rest of the country and can provide computer printouts on some specific subjects.

SECTUR's two phone lines are staffed 24 hours, seven days a week, to provide tourist information and help with tourist problems and emergencies. The office itself is open Monday to Friday 9 am to 9 pm, Saturday 10 am to 3 pm.

The easier-to-reach Oficina de Turismo de la Ciudad de México (☎ 525-93-80), Amberes 54, at Londres, in the Zona Rosa (metro: Insurgentes), provides information on Mexico City only. Some English is spoken. Hours are daily 9 am to 8 pm.

The Cámara Nacional de Comercio de la Ciudad de México (Mexico City National Chamber of Commerce), Paseo de la Reforma 42, between Avenida Juárez and Guerra, (metro: Hidalgo or Juárez) also has a tourist office (☎ 592-26-77, ext 1015 or 1016), providing information on the city only. It's on the 4th floor and open Monday to Friday 9 am to 2 pm and 3 to 6 pm.

Tourist Card Extensions
Subject to the general rules on tourist card extensions (see Visas & Documents in Facts for the Visitor), cards can be extended at the Instituto Nacional de Migración (☎ 626-72-00), Avenida Chapultepec 284, Monday to Friday from 9 am

Shantytowns
Mexico City's notorious shantytowns are on its fringes, where most of the city's expansion is taking place. You may glimpse some as you enter or leave the city by road, though most of the main routes are lined by more established communities. Many of the oldest shantytowns – such as the vast Ciudad Nezahualcóyotl, east of the airport and home to well over a million people – are no longer really shantytowns, as they have succeeded in gaining services such as running water and electricity, and many of their inhabitants have earned enough money to build themselves relatively comfortable homes. ■

to 2 pm. Bring your card there a few days before it is due to expire, along with your passport and a major international credit card or US$100 in traveler's checks. To get there, take the metro to Insurgentes station and leave the plaza outside the station by the 'Ave Chapultepec Sur-Ote' exit. Enter the building in front of you at the top of the steps and go up to the 'Ampliación de Estancia a Turistas' section on the second floor. The process takes about half an hour.

Money

Exchange rates vary a bit between Mexico City's numerous money-changing outlets, so if you have time, it's worth checking two or three before you part with your money. Most banks and *casas de cambio* (exchange offices) will change both cash and traveler's checks; some give a better rate for cash, others for traveler's checks. Some will change only US or Canadian dollars.

The greatest concentration of banks, ATMs and casas de cambio is on Paseo de la Reforma between the Monumento a Cristóbal Colón and the Monumento a la Independencia, but there are many others all over the city, including at the airport, where some casas de cambio are open 24 hours. Casas de cambio are also numerous in the Zona Rosa.

Banks & ATMs Mexico City is full of banks, most open Monday to Friday 9 am to 1.30 pm, some for longer hours. Many banks have ATMs, so if you have a major international credit card or an ATM card you can usually withdraw money quickly and easily.

Casas de Cambio The city's dozens of casas de cambio have longer hours and quicker procedures than banks. For that you may get a less favorable exchange rate, but the better ones are as good as bank rates. A useful casa de cambio near the downtown area is Casa de Cambio Plus, on Avenida Juárez facing the Alameda, which is open Monday to Friday 9 am to 4 pm, Saturday 9.30 am to 1.30 pm, and gives good rates for cash and traveler's checks.

On the edge of the Zona Rosa, at Paseo de la Reforma and Avenida Florencia, Casa de Cambio Bancomer, open Monday to Friday 9 am to 7 pm, Saturday and Sunday 10 am to 5 pm, gives excellent rates for cash and traveler's checks.

American Express On the edge of the Zona Rosa, at Paseo de la Reforma 234, on the corner of Havre (metro: Insurgentes), is American Express (☎ 207-72-82). It's open Monday to Friday 9 am to 6 pm, Saturday 9 am to 1 pm. You can change American Express traveler's checks here, though the rate is poor. The office also has other financial and card services, a travel bureau and a mail pickup desk.

Wire Transfers The Western Union 'Dinero en Minutos' money wiring service (see Money in Facts for the Visitor) is available at several places, including:

Central de Telégrafos
   Tacuba 8 (open daily 9 am to 9 pm; metro: Allende)
Telecomm
   Insurgentes 114, 1½ blocks north of Reforma (nearest metro: Revolución)
Elektra
   Pino Suárez at El Salvador, three blocks south of the Zócalo (metro: Pino Suárez)
   Balderas at Artículo 123, two blocks south of the Alameda Central (metro: Juárez)
   East side of Insurgentes Sur, two blocks south of Insurgentes metro

(Elektra is a chain of electrical-goods stores, all open daily 9 am to 9 pm.)

Post

The Correo Mayor, the central post office of Mexico City, is a lovely early 20th century building in Italian Renaissance style on Juan Ruiz de Alarcón (Eje Central Lázaro Cárdenas) at Tacuba, across from the Palacio de Bellas Artes. (metro: Bellas Artes). The stamp windows, open Monday to Friday 8 am to 9.30 pm, Saturday 9 am to 8 pm, are marked 'estampillas.' The poste restante and lista de correos window, No 3, is open Monday to Friday 8 am to 5 pm, Saturday 9 am to

5 pm, Sunday 9 am to 1 pm. Have poste restante or lista de correos mail addressed this way:

Albert JONES (last name in capitals)
Poste Restante (or Lista de Correos)
Oficina Central de Correos
México 06002 DF
MEXICO

For other information, go to window No 49.

Other post offices are generally open Monday to Friday 8 am to 5 pm, Saturday 8 am to 1 pm. Here are a few:

Zócalo
Inside Plaza de la Constitución 7 (the west side of the Zócalo), open Monday to Friday 8.30 am to 2.30 pm
Near Plaza de la República
Corner of Ignacio Mariscal and Arriaga (metro: Revolución)
Zona Rosa
Corner of Varsovia and Londres (metro: Insurgentes or Sevilla)

If you carry an American Express card or American Express traveler's checks, you can use the American Express office (see Money) as your mailing address in Mexico City. Have mail addressed this way:

Lucy CHANG (last name in capitals)
Client Mail
American Express
Paseo de la Reforma 234
México 06600 DF
MEXICO

The office holds mail for two months before returning it to the sender.

Courier Services
These include:

DHL
Reforma 76 at Versalles (☎ 227-02-99); Niza just south of Reforma in the Zona Rosa
Federal Express
Reforma 308, west of Belgrado (☎ 228-99-04); Avenida Madero 70, half a block from the Zócalo (☎ 228-99-04)
United Parcel Service (UPS)
Reforma 404, between Praga and Sevilla (☎ 228-79-00)

Telephone
See Post & Communications in Facts for the Visitor for information on the various sorts of telephones, rates and how to place calls.

There are thousands of pay phones on the streets of Mexico City. Phone-card sales points are also plentiful, including at the airport – look for blue-and-yellow 'De Venta Aqui Ladatel' signs.

Fax, Email & Internet
You can send faxes from the Central de Telégrafos, Tacuba 8 (metro: Bellas Artes). It's open daily 9 am to 9 pm. Many private businesses offer public fax service – look for 'fax público' signs. Fax service is also available at the airport and at the long-distance bus stations.

Mexico City has several Internet cafés where you can send and receive email or access the Internet. The most central is the small Cybercafe, Bolívar 66, about 600 meters southwest of the Zócalo (metro: San Juan de Letrán). The minimum charge here – for up to 30 minutes online – is US$4. One hour costs US$6.50. Hours are Monday to Saturday 10 am to 7 pm.

Travel Agencies
Many mid-range and top-end hotels have a travel agent's desk or can recommend agencies nearby. The following are worth trying for reasonably priced air tickets:

Ibermex
Paseo de la Reforma 237 (☎ 721-51-54)

Mundo Joven (youth and student tickets)
Avenida Insurgentes Sur 1510, just south of Avenida Río Mixcoac, 1.3 km northeast of Barranca del Muerto metro station (☎ 662-35-36)

Russvall Viajes
Arriaga 23A at Édison, near Plaza de la República (☎ 592-83-83)

Tony Pérez
Río Volga 1 at Río Danubio, behind the María Isabel-Sheraton Hotel (☎ 533-11-48)

Bookstores
All the following stores, except the Gandhi branch in San Ángel, have a good range of

English-language books. Top-end hotels, Sanborn's stores and major museums often have stalls selling English-language books and other print media.

Downtown All of the following stores, except Librería Británica, are near Bellas Artes metro station.

American Bookstore, Avenida Madero 25 – Has a wide range of books on Mexico, plus magazines and newspapers

Gandhi, Avenida Juárez 4 – A good source of books about Mexico and Mexico City; sells Lonely Planet guides

Librería Británica, Avenida Madero west of Isabel la Católica – A specialist in English-language books; sells Lonely Planet guides (metro: Zócalo or Allende)

Palacio de Bellas Artes – An excellent arts bookstore

Near the Jardín del Arte Librería Británica (☎ 705-05-85), Serapio Rendón 125 (metro: San Cosme), has many novels and books on Mexico, plus some Lonely Planet guides.

San Ángel & Coyoacán Gandhi, Avenida M A de Quevedo 128 to 132, San Ángel (metro: M A de Quevedo), is a Mexico City institution with a big range of books on most subjects, mostly in Spanish, and a popular upstairs café. It's open Monday to Friday 9 am to 9 pm, Saturday and Sunday 10 am to 8 pm.

Librería Británica has branches at Avenida Coyoacán 1955 (by Coyoacán metro), and at Avenida Robles 53, San Ángel.

Libraries

There are several useful foreign-run libraries in Mexico City:

Biblioteca Benjamín Franklin (Benjamin Franklin Library, ☎ 211-00-42), Londres 16, west of Berlín (metro: Cuauhtémoc), is run by the US embassy. A wide range of books about Mexico is available, plus English-language periodicals. You must be 20 or older to use the library. Hours are Monday and Friday 3 to 7.30 pm, Tuesday to Thursday 10 am to 3 pm.

Canadian Embassy Library (☎ 724-79-00), Schiller 529, Polanco, in the embassy (metro: Polanco), has many Canadian books and periodicals in English and French. It's open Monday to Friday 9 am to 12.30 pm.

Consejo Británico (British Council, ☎ 566-61-44), Antonio Caso 127 (metro: San Cosme), has lots of books and magazines in English, plus British newspapers a couple of weeks old. Hours are Monday to Friday 8.30 am to 7.30 pm, Saturday 10 am to 1 pm.

Institut Français d'Amérique Latine (☎ 566-07-77), Río Nazas 43 (metro: San Cosme or Insurgentes), has a library with French newspapers, magazines and many books. It's open Monday to Friday 9 am to 7 pm, Saturday 10 am to 1 pm.

Instituto Goethe (☎ 207-04-87), Tonalá 43, Colonia Roma (metro: Insurgentes), has a German library open Monday to Thursday 9 am to 1 pm and 4 to 7 pm.

Media

Mexico's English-language daily newspapers, *The News* and the *Mexico City Times*, are sold at many downtown and Zona Rosa newsstands, as well as by several of the bookstores mentioned above. The essential Spanish-language what's-on directory for entertainment in Mexico City is the weekly magazine *Tiempo Libre*.

Some North American and European newspapers and magazines are sold at hotel newsstands and at the above bookstores. La Casa de la Prensa, in the Zona Rosa at Avenida Florencia 59 and Hamburgo 141 (metro: Insurgentes), sells major British and American newspapers and magazines, plus a few French and German ones; both branches are closed Sunday.

Cultural Centers

The Consejo Británico, Institut Français d'Amérique Latine and Instituto Goethe (see Libraries) all have programs of events, such as films, exhibitions and concerts, from their home countries.

Laundry & Dry Cleaning

Lavandería Automática Edison, at Édison 91, near Plaza de la República (metro: Revolución), charges US$1.70 for 3kg of washing, the same for drying. They will do your laundry for you for a further US$1.70.

MEXICO CITY
Top: Satellite City
Bottom Left: 'El Ángel' Monumento a la Independencia, Paseo de la Reforma
Bottom Right: Catedral Metropolitana on the Zócalo

MEXICO CITY
Top: Aztec Dancer scans the Zócalo
Bottom Left: Mother and child in a procession honoring the Virgin of Guadalupe
Bottom Right: Casa de Cortés, Coyoacán

Opposite Page
Top Left: Sagrario Metropolitano
Top Right: A produce market on the stairs
Bottom: Strumming and munching

RICHARD NEBESKY

RICK GERHARTER

RICK GERHARTER

F STOPPELMAN

RICK GERHARTER

RICHARD NEBESKY

Top Left: Newspaper delivery, Mexico City
Top Right: A young clown takes a break
Bottom: Overview of the Zócalo, Mexico City

Hours are Monday to from Friday 10 am to 7 pm, Saturday 10 am to 6 pm.

Lavandería Automática, at Río Danubio 119B, not far north of the Zona Rosa, has similar prices. It's open Monday to Friday 8.15 am to 6 pm, Saturday 8.15 am to 5 pm.

Two reliable dry cleaners are Dryclean USA, at Paseo de la Reforma 32 (metro: Juárez or Hidalgo), and Jiffy ('HEE-fee'), on the corner of Río Tíber and Río Lerma, two blocks north of the Monumento a la Independencia (metro: Insurgentes).

Medical Services

For recommendation of a doctor, dentist or hospital, you can call your embassy (see Embassies in Facts for the Visitor) or the 24-hour SECTUR help line (☎ 250-01-23). A private doctor's consultation generally costs between US$25 and US$40.

One of the best hospitals in all Mexico is the Hospital ABC (American British Cowdray Hospital, ☎ 232-80-00, 272-85-00, emergencies 515-83-59), at Calle Sur 136 No 116, just south off Avenida Observatorio in Colonia Las Américas, south of the Bosque de Chapultepec. There's an outpatient section, and many of the staff speak English – but fees can be steep, so medical insurance is a big help. Observatorio, about one km southeast, is the nearest metro station.

For an ambulance, you can call the Cruz Roja (Red Cross, ☎ 557-57-58/59), or the general emergency number for ambulance, fire and police (☎ 080).

Emergency

SECTUR (see Tourist Offices) is available by phone 24 hours a day to help tourists with problems and emergencies.

Reporting Crimes The Procuraduría General de Justicia del Distrito Federal (Attorney General of the Federal District) maintains two police offices to aid tourists with legal questions and problems. If you need to report a crime, you can do so at either one. Offices are at Avenida Florencia 20, in the Zona Rosa (metro: Insurgentes; ☎ 625-87-61), and at the airport (☎ 625-

87-63). The Florencia office is always open and has English-speaking staff present from 8 am to 10 pm and available by telephone at other times.

Dangers & Annoyances

Crime The recession of the mid-1990s brought a big increase in crime in Mexico City, with foreigners among the juicier and often easier targets for pickpockets, thieves and some armed robbers. But there's no need to walk in fear whenever you step outside your hotel: a few precautions greatly reduce the risks. Please read Dangers & Annoyances in Facts for the Visitor for general hints applicable throughout Mexico, including the capital.

Mexico City's metro and buses are notorious for pickpockets and thieves, particularly when crowded. Taxis are now notorious for robberies.

The riskiest time is after dark, and the riskiest places are those where foreigners most often go: central metro stations – notably Hidalgo, where pickpockets and bag snatchers wait for foreigners and follow them onto crowded trains – and places such as the Bosque de Chapultepec, buses along Paseo de la Reforma, around the Museo Nacional de Antropología, the Zona Rosa and the area around the US embassy. Steer clear of empty streets after dark. The US State Department warned in 1997: 'In several cases, tourists report that uniformed police are the crime perpetrators, stopping vehicles and seeking money or assaulting and robbing tourists walking late at night.'

Using the metro only at less busy times enables you to find a less crowded car (usually at one end of the train), where would-be thieves will find it harder to get close to you without being noticed (but avoid empty or near-empty cars.) During peak hours (roughly 7.30 to 10 am and 5 to 7 pm) all trains and buses in the central area are sardine cans, which suits pickpockets. Hold on to bags or any other belongings tightly. Our advice is to avoid getting on or off a train, or even changing trains, at Hidalgo – and if you're on a train that's going through Hidalgo, use only the last cars, so that thieves waiting in the station are less likely to spot you.

Do not use guides who are not properly licensed or officially authorized.

Do not walk into a pedestrian underpass that is empty or nearly so; robbers may intercept you in the middle.

If you participate in any Mexican festivities (rallies or celebrations in the Zócalo, etc) be aware that half the pickpockets in the city will be there too.

Be on your guard at the airport and bus stations, and keep your bag or pack between your feet when checking in.

Perhaps most important, don't risk injury by resisting robbers.

Taxi Crime Robberies and hijackings in taxis - once a secure form of transportation in Mexico City – have mounted to alarming levels, with foreigners often the victims. Some robbers are armed. In 1997 the US State Department warned Americans against hailing Volkswagen Beetle taxis on Mexico City's streets or using taxis cruising tourist areas or waiting outside the Palacio de Bellas Artes, nightclubs or restaurants. Instead you can use cabs from *sitios* (taxi stands) or call a radio cab (☎ 271-91-46, 271-90-58, 273-61-25). Sitio and radio cabs are a bit more expensive than regular *(libre,* or free) cabs, but they probably are worth the extra security. If you do need to hail a cab on the street, sitio cabs are identifiable by the letter S at the beginning of the number on their license plate and an orange stripe along the bottom of the plate. Libre taxis have the letter L and a green stripe. Advice from the US embassy in 1997 included:

- When entering a taxi note the taxi number, the driver's name and a physical description of the driver. (The number, name and a photo of the driver should be displayed on a card inside the cab – if they aren't, it's better to get another vehicle.)
- Lock the doors and keep windows rolled up.
- Do not carry large amounts of cash, ATM cards or credit cards. (A growing practice has been to force hijack victims to withdraw money from ATMs.)

Mexico City's Air

Mexico City has some of the world's worst air. Severe pollution from traffic and industry is intensified by the mountains that ring the Valle de México and prevent air from dispersing, and by the city's altitude and consequent lack of oxygen. (Air at high altitudes contains less oxygen than air at sea level.)

Pollution is at its worst in the cooler months, especially November to February, which is when an unpleasant phenomenon called thermal inversion is most likely to occur: warm air passing over the Valle de México stops cool, polluted air near ground level from rising and dispersing. But at any time the pollution and altitude may make a visitor feel breathless and tired or may cause a sore throat, headache, runny nose or insomnia. People with serious lung, heart, asthmatic or respiratory problems are advised to consult a doctor before coming.

The major culprit is ozone, too much of which causes respiratory and eye problems in humans and corrodes rubber, paint and plastics. Recent research suggests that leaks of unburned LPG (liquefied gaseum gas), used for cooking and heating, play a big role in raising ozone levels. But the primary factor is still generally reckoned to be low-lead gasoline, introduced in 1986 to counter lead pollution, which until then was the city's worst atmospheric contaminant. The reaction between sunlight and combustion residues from low-lead gasoline produces a great deal of ozone.

In an attempt to reduce traffic pollution, since 1989 every car in the city has been banned from the streets on one day each week by a program called Hoy No Circula (Don't Drive Today), and catalytic converters have been compulsory in all new cars in Mexico since the early 1990s. But ozone levels have remained high. Hoy No Circula has unwittingly encouraged people to buy or rent extra cars to get around the once-a-week prohibition. Today there are around 4 million cars in the city – the number has doubled since 1980.

- Never travel alone after dark.
- If you become a robbery victim, give the perpetrator your valuables. They are not worth risking injury or death.

The warning also says, 'Tourists are not only robbed, but often beaten.' Your embassy should be able to tell you whether extra precautions still need to be taken. For more information on taxis, see this chapter's Getting Around section.

CENTRO HISTÓRICO

A good place to start your explorations of the city is where it began. The area known as the Centro Histórico focuses on the large downtown plaza known as El Zócalo and stretches for several blocks in each direction from there.

The Centro Histórico is full of historic sites and buildings from the Aztec and colonial eras, contains some of the city's finest art and architecture and is home to a number of absorbing museums. It also bustles with modern-day street life.

Sunday is a particularly good day to explore this innermost part of the inner city. Traffic and street crowds are thinner, a relaxed atmosphere prevails and museums are free.

By a few years ago the Centro Histórico had become rather rundown, but since then it has undergone a spruce-up to make it better fit the image of the hub of a proud nation. Some streets have been pedestrianized, attractive new museums have opened and a growing number of glossy eateries and fashionable bars and stores are appearing. The city authorities have also fought a long-running battle with the many street vendors who operate small sidewalk stalls in the Centro Histórico. Attempts to ban them from the area – which made it an easier place to walk around and pleased shopkeepers – brought protests and riots and succeeded only temporarily. In 1997 the authorities came up with a new plan to move some vendors into public markets and commercial plazas and to charge the others up to US$2 a day for the use of

---

Mexico City's average ozone level is almost twice the maximum permitted in the USA and Japan; readings were within World Health Organization limits on fewer than 30 days a year from 1993 to 1996. Ozone concentrations are worst around midday on sunny days.

The News publishes daily pollution reports and forecasts. Air contamination is measured by the Índice Metropolitana de Calidad de Aire (IMECA, Metropolitan Air Quality Index). IMECA assesses five pollutants – ozone, sulfur dioxide, nitrogen dioxide, carbon monoxide and suspended particles. Readings below 100 are classed as 'satisfactory,' 101 to 200 is 'unsatisfactory,' 201 to 300 is 'bad,' and over 300 is 'very bad.' Ozone readings of more than 250 – which occur several times a year – trigger phase one of the city's environmental contingency plan, including a ban on outdoor activities at schools, a 30% reduction in activity at more than 200 big industrial plants, and the 'Doble Hoy No Circula' (Double Don't Drive Today) rule, which takes about 40% of the vehicles off the streets. Higher IMECA readings lead to phases two and three of the plan. Phase three, which is rarely instituted, stops all industry and permits only emergency traffic.

The more exotic remedies suggested for the pollution crisis have included fleets of helicopters to sweep the smog away, and exploding a hole in the ring of mountains around the city, then using giant fans to blow the smog through it. More feasible, perhaps, is the idea of ionizing the air to create winds that would disperse pollution. This proposal is being tested at Tuxtla Gutiérrez airport, in Chiapas. Five 25-kilowatt antennae would be needed to break down ozone, water vapor and other molecules in Mexico City's air into positive hydrogen atoms and negative oxygen particles. These would, it is hoped, align to create strong winds that would carry pollutants into the upper atmosphere, and rainstorms would often follow, further cleaning the air. ■

sidewalk space. Such 'rent' could approach half a vendor's earnings.

El Zócalo

The heart of Mexico City is the Plaza de la Constitución, more commonly known as the Zócalo (metro: Zócalo).

The Aztec word *zócalo*, which means plinth or stone base, was adopted in 1843 when a tall monument to independence was constructed only as far as the base. The plinth is long gone, but the name remains and has been adopted informally by a lot of other Mexican cities for their main plazas.

The center of Aztec Tenochtitlán, the ceremonial precinct known as the Teocalli, lay immediately north and northeast of the Zócalo. *Conchero* dancers remind everyone of this heritage with daily get-togethers in the Zócalo to carry out a sort of aerobics, in feathered headdresses and shell *(concha)* anklets and bracelets, to the rhythm of booming drums.

In the 1520s Cortés paved the plaza with stones from the ruins of the Teocalli and other important Aztec buildings. Until the early 20th century, the Zócalo was more often a maze of market stalls than an open plaza. With each side measuring more than 200 meters, today it's one of the world's largest city squares.

The Zócalo is the home of the powers-that-be in Mexico City. On its east side is the Palacio Nacional, on the north the Catedral Metropolitana, on the south the Departamento del Distrito Federal (the government department that runs the Distrito Federal). The plaza is also a place for political protesters to make their points – it's often dotted with makeshift camps of strikers or indigenous rights campaigners.

Each day the huge Mexican flag flying in the middle of the Zócalo is ceremonially – and sometimes with some difficulty – lowered by the Mexican army at 6 pm and carried into the Palacio Nacional.

Palacio Nacional

Home to the offices of the president of Mexico, the Federal Treasury and dramatic murals by Diego Rivera, the National Palace fills the entire east side of the Zócalo. Bring your passport or other photo ID if you want to see the murals inside the palace.

The first palace on this spot was built of tezontle by Aztec emperor Moctezuma II in the early 16th century. Cortés destroyed the palace in 1521 and rebuilt it with a large courtyard so that he could entertain visitors with Nueva España's first recorded bullfights. The palace remained in Cortés' family until the king of Spain bought it in 1562 to house the viceroys of Nueva España. It was destroyed during riots in 1692, rebuilt again and continued to be used as the viceregal residence until Mexican independence in the 1820s.

As you face the palace you see three portals. On the right (south) is the guarded entrance for the president and other officials. High above the center door hangs the **Campana de Dolores** (Bell of Dolores), rung in the town of Dolores Hidalgo by Padre Miguel Hidalgo in 1810 to signal the start of the Mexican War of Independence, and later moved to this place of honor.

Enter the palace through the center door. The colorful **Diego Rivera murals** around the courtyard present Rivera's view of Mexican civilization from the arrival of Quetzalcóatl – the Aztec plumed serpent god whom some believed to be personified in Hernán Cortés – to the 1910 revolution. Painted between 1929 and 1935, the murals are open for public viewing daily from 9 am to 5 pm. Admission is free. Detailed guides to the murals (in English) are sold at the foot of the stairs just inside the entrance gate.

Catedral Metropolitana

The Metropolitan Cathedral, on the north side of the Zócalo, was built between 1573 and 1813. Though its inside is disfigured by scaffolding as builders struggle to arrest its uneven descent into the soft ground on which it's built, the cathedral is still impressive. (Extraction of water from the subsoil – the source of two-thirds of Mexico City's water – is the main reason for the subsidence.) In Aztec times the

Teocalli's main *tzompantli* (rack for the skulls of sacrifice victims) stood on part of the cathedral site. Cortés reportedly found more than 136,000 skulls of sacrificial victims here and nearby.

Exterior With a three-naved basilica design of vaults on semicircular arches, the cathedral was built to resemble those in the Spanish cities of Toledo and Granada. Parts were added or replaced over the years, and as a result the cathedral is a compendium of the architectural styles of colonial Mexico. The grand portals facing the Zócalo were built in the 17th century in baroque style. They have two levels of columns and marble panels with bas-reliefs. The central panel shows the Assumption of the Virgin Mary, to whom the cathedral is dedicated. The tall north portals facing Tacuba, dating from 1615, are in pure Renaissance style.

The upper levels of the towers, with their unique bell-shaped tops, were not added till the end of the 18th century, and the exterior was finally completed in 1813, when architect Manuel Tolsá added the clock tower, topped by statues of Faith, Hope and Charity, and a great central dome, all in neoclassical style, to create some unity and balance.

Interior Much of the interior is a forest of scaffolding. A plumb line hanging from the dome above the central nave graphically demonstrates the building's subsidence problem.

The cathedral's chief artistic treasure is the gilded 18th century Altar de los Reyes (Altar of the Three Kings), behind the main altar, a masterly exercise in controlled elaboration and a high point of the Churrigueresque style. The two side naves are lined by 14 richly decorated chapels. The Capilla de los Santos Ángeles y Arcángeles (Chapel of the Holy Angels and Archangels), at the southwest corner, is an exquisite example of baroque sculpture and painting, with a huge main altarpiece and two smaller altarpieces decorated by the 18th century painter Juan Correa. Four oval

paintings by another leading 18th century Mexican artist, Miguel Cabrera, grace the cathedral's side entrances.

A lot of other art in the cathedral was damaged or destroyed in a 1967 fire. The intricately carved late 17th century wooden choir stalls by Juan de Rojas and the huge, gilded Altar de Perdón (Altar of Pardon), all in the central nave, have been restored, and work continues.

Sagrario Metropolitano Adjoining the east side of the cathedral is the 18th century sacristy, built to house the archives and vestments of the archbishop. Its exterior is a superb example of the ultradecorative Churrigueresque style. It's not open to visitors.

Templo Mayor

The Teocalli of Aztec Tenochtitlán, demolished by the Spaniards in the 1520s, stood on the site of the cathedral and the blocks to its north and east. The decision to excavate the Teocalli's Templo Mayor (Main Temple), with the demolition of colonial buildings that it entailed, wasn't made until 1978, after electricity workers digging northeast of the cathedral happened upon an eight-ton stone-disc carving of the Aztec goddess Coyolxauhqui, She of Bells on her Cheek. The temple is thought to be on the exact spot where the Aztecs saw their symbolic eagle with a snake in its beak perching on a cactus – still the symbol of Mexico today. In Aztec belief the spot was, literally, the center of the universe.

The entrance to the temple site is just east of the cathedral, on pedestrianized Calle Seminario. The site is open Tuesday to Sunday 9 am to 5 pm (☎ 542-06-06; US$2.25, free on Sunday).

A walkway around the site reveals the temple's multiple layers of construction. There's plenty of explanatory material, though it's all in Spanish. Like many other sacred buildings in Tenochtitlán, the temple, first begun in 1375, was enlarged several times, with each rebuilding accompanied by the sacrifice of captured warriors.

In 1487 these rituals were performed at a frenzied pace to rededicate the temple after one major reconstruction. Michael Meyer and William Sherman write in *The Course of Mexican History*:

In a ceremony lasting four days sacrificial victims taken during campaigns were formed in four columns, each stretching three miles. At least twenty thousand human hearts were torn out to please the god . . . In the frenzy of this ghastly pageant, the priests were finally overcome by exhaustion.

What we see today are sections of several of the temple's different phases, though hardly anything is left of the seventh and final version, built about 1502 and seen by the Spanish conquistadors. A replica of the Coyolxauhqui stone lies near the west side of the site. At the center of the site is a platform dating from about 1400; on its southern half, a sacrificial stone stands in front of a shrine to Huizilopochtli, the Aztec tribal god. On the northern half is a *chac-mool* figure before a shrine to the water god, Tláloc. By the time the Spanish arrived, a 40-meter-high double pyramid towered above this spot, with steep twin stairways climbing to shrines to the two gods.

Other highlights of the site are a late 15th century stone replica of a tzompantli, carved with 240 stone skulls, and the mid-15th century Recinto de los Guerreros Águila (Sanctuary of the Eagle Warriors, an elite band of Aztec fighters), decorated with colored bas-reliefs of military processions.

Museo del Templo Mayor The excellent museum within the Templo Mayor site houses artifacts from the site and gives a good overview (in Spanish) of Aztec civilization. Pride of place is given to the great wheel-like stone of Coyolxauhqui. She is shown decapitated – the result of her murder by Huizilopochtli, her brother, who also killed his 400 brothers en route to becoming top god. Other outstanding exhibits include full-size terra-cotta eagle

warriors. (Admission to the Templo Mayor includes the museum.)

Here is an outline of the exhibit rooms:

Sala 1, Antecedentes – The early days of Tenochtitlán

Sala 2, Guerra y Sacrificio – Aztec beliefs, war and human sacrifice

Sala 3, Tributo y Comercio – Government and trade

Sala 4, Huizilopochtli – Lord of the Templo Mayor and demander of sacrifices

Sala 5, Tláloc – The water and fertility god

Sala 6, Fauna – Animals of the Aztecs and their empire

Sala 7, Agricultura – The chinampa system and its products

Sala 8, Arqueología Histórica – Archaeological finds from the postconquest era

Calle Moneda

As you walk back down Seminario toward the Zócalo from the Templo Mayor, Moneda is the first street on your left. Many of its buildings are made of tezontle.

The **Museo de la Secretaría de Hacienda y Crédito Público** (Museum of the Secretariat of Finance & Public Credit), Moneda 4, houses a good collection of Mexican art, ranging from works by the 18th century master Juan Correa to 20th century giants Diego Rivera and Rufino Tamayo to interesting contemporary artists. The setting, a colonial archbishop's palace with two lovely courtyards, adds to its attraction. It's open Tuesday to Sunday 10 am to 5 pm (US$1.10, free on Sunday).

The **Museo Nacional de las Culturas** (National Museum of Cultures, ☎ 512-74-52), Moneda 13, in a fine courtyarded building constructed in 1567 as the colonial mint, has a collection of exhibits showing the art, dress and handicrafts of several world cultures. Hours are Tuesday to Sunday 10 am to 5 pm (free).

A block farther east, then a few steps north to Academia 13, is a former convent housing the **Museo José Luis Cuevas** (☎ 542-61-98), founded by Cuevas, a leading modern Mexican artist. There are engravings by Picasso, sketches and drawings by Rembrandt, and work by Cuevas himself, and other moderns. Hours are Tuesday to Sunday 10 am to 5.45 pm (US$0.70, free on Sunday).

Nacional Monte de Piedad

Facing the west side of the cathedral on the corner of Avenida Cinco de Mayo is Mexico's national pawnshop, founded in 1775. As one of the world's largest secondhand shops, it's worth a look. Who knows – you may pick up a bargain. Housed in a large, dark building, it's open Monday to Friday 8.30 am to 6 pm, Saturday 8.30 am to 3 pm.

Plaza Santo Domingo

Plaza Santo Domingo, two blocks north of the cathedral on the corner of Brasil and Cuba, is a scruffier affair than the Zócalo. Modern-day scribes, with typewriters and antique printing machines, work beneath the **Portal de Evangelistas**, along its west side.

The **Iglesia de Santo Domingo**, dating from 1736, is a beautiful baroque church, decorated on its east side with carved stone figures of Santo Domingo (Saint Dominic) and San Francisco (Saint Francis). Below the figures, the arms of both saints are symbolically entwined as if to convey a unity of purpose in their lives. The front, or southern, façade is equally beautiful, with 12 columns around the main entrance. Between the columns are statues of San Francisco and San Agustín (Saint Augustine), and in the center at the top is a bas-relief of the Assumption of the Virgin Mary.

On the corner of Brasil and Venezuela, opposite the church, is the 18th century Palacio de la Escuela de Medicina, built as the headquarters of the Inquisition in Mexico. It houses the interesting **Museo de la Medicina Mexicana**, whose displays range from a model of a *baño de temazcal* – a kind of indigenous sauna, used for spiritual purification – to collections of plants used in modern folk medicine to a reconstruction of a 19th century pharmacy. It's open daily from 9 am to 6 pm (free).

Murals

The **Secretaría de Educación Pública** is on Argentina 3½ blocks north of the Zócalo. As it houses government offices, it's only open Monday to Friday from 9 am to 3 pm. Admission is free, but sometimes the door attendants ask for ID, so it's best to take along your passport. The two courtyards are lined with 235 mural panels done by Rivera in the 1920s. The paintings range over a host of subjects covering the lives, work, traditions and struggles of the Mexican people. Frida Kahlo can be spotted in a red shirt in one, called *El Arsenal*, on the upper floor of the second courtyard. There are also panels by Jean Charlot, Juan O'Gorman, Carlos Mérida and others.

A block back toward the Zócalo, then half a block east to Justo Sierra 16, is the **Museo de San Ildefonso** (☎ 702-28-34, 702-32-54), open daily except Monday from 11 am to 5.30 pm (US$2.25, free on Tuesday). Originally the Jesuit college of San Ildefonso, it became the Escuela Nacional Preparatoria, a prestigious college, under President Benito Juárez. Juan Cordero, the first modern Mexican muralist, completed a painting depicting Mexican progress in science and industry on the main staircase in 1874. From 1923 to 1933, Rivera, Orozco, Siqueiros and others were brought in to add many more murals. Most of the work in the main court and on the grand staircase is by Orozco, inspired by the Mexican Revolution (recently ended at the time). In a small patio are Siqueiros' works. The amphitheater holds a gigantic Creation mural by Rivera.

Museo Nacional de Arte

Several blocks west of the Zócalo, at Tacuba 8 (metro: Bellas Artes), the National Museum of Art (☎ 512-32-24) contains exclusively Mexican work. You'll recognize the building by the distinctive bronze equestrian statue in front, of the Spanish king Carlos IV (who reigned from 1788 to 1808) by the sculptor and architect Manuel Tolsá. Called *El Caballito* (The Little Horse), it originally stood in the Zócalo but was moved here in 1852. Note that the name refers to the horse, not the rider, who reigned shortly before Mexico gained its independence. A sign points out that the statue is preserved as a work of art (and not, it's implied, out of respect for the king).

The museum – once the Communications Ministry – was built at the turn of the 20th century in the style of an Italian Renaissance palace. A grand marble staircase greets you as you enter. The collections represent every style and school of Mexican art. The work of José María Velasco, depicting Mexico City and the countryside in the late 19th and early 20th centuries, is among the highlights. One painting shows the city still surrounded by lakes, even in the late 19th century.

Collections upstairs include 17th century religious paintings by Antonio Rodríguez, Juan Correa and José de Ibarra; 18th and 19th century sculptures; portraits by Antonio Poblano; prints of skeletal figures sweeping streets; and anonymous paintings with social and political themes. Hours are Tuesday to Sunday 10 am to 5.30 pm (US$1.30).

Colegio de Minería
Opposite the Museo Nacional de Arte, at Tacuba 5, is the College of Mining, a beautiful neoclassical building designed by Manuel Tolsá and built between 1797 and 1813. Four meteorites found in Mexico are displayed in its entrance.

Casa de Azulejos
A block south of the Museo Nacional de Arte, between Avenida Cinco de Mayo and Avenida Madero, stands one of the city's gems. The Casa de Azulejos (House of Tiles) dates from 1596, when it was built for the counts of the valley of Orizaba. Although the superb tile work, which has adorned the outside walls since the 18th century, is Spanish and Moorish in style, most of the tiles were actually produced in China and shipped to Mexico on the Manila *naos* (Spanish galleons used up to the early 19th century).

The building now houses a Sanborn's store and is a good place to buy a newspaper or have refreshments. The main restaurant (see Places to Eat) is set in a lovely courtyard with a Moorish-style fountain. The staircase on the north side of the restaurant has a 1925 mural by Orozco.

Torre Latinoamericana
The Latin American Tower, the landmark 1950s skyscraper on the corner of Avenida Madero and Juan Ruiz de Alarcón (Eje Central Lázaro Cárdenas), has an observation deck and café on its 43rd and 44th floors, open every day between 9.30 am and 11 pm (US$3). The views are spectacular, smog permitting. Tickets are sold at the street entrance, on the Alarcón side of the building.

Palacio de Iturbide
A block east of the Casa de Azulejos, at Avenida Madero 17, rises the beautiful baroque façade of the Iturbide Palace. Built between 1779 and 1785 for colonial nobility, it was claimed in 1821 by General Agustín Iturbide, a hero of the Mexican struggle for independence from Spain. The general responded favorably to a rent-a-crowd that gathered in front of the palace in 1822, beseeching him to be their emperor. Iturbide proclaimed himself Emperor Agustín I but reigned over Mexico for less than a year, abdicating in 1823 after General Santa Anna announced the birth of a republic.

The palace now houses the Fomento Cultural Banamex (the cultural promotion section of the bank Banamex), and some excellent exhibitions are shown in the fine courtyard (free).

Museo Serfin
A block farther east, at Avenida Madero 33, is the Museo Serfin (☎ 625-56-00), with an interesting and colorful permanent exhibition of Indian costumes from around Mexico. It's open daily except Monday from 10 am to 5 pm (free).

Mexico City Map Section

MEXICO CITY MAP 1

Mexico City

0 1 2 km
0 .5 1 mile

Carretera Xochimilco–Tulyehualco

Carretera a Oaxtepec

Av Tláhuac

Canal de Garay

Anillo Periférico

Av Tláhuac

(Av Periférico)

Ermita Iztapalapa

Meyehualco

Parque Nacional
Cerro de la Estrella

Cerro
de la Estrella

Parque Ecológico
de Xochimilco

Lago
Huetzalin

21

20

Canal El Bordo

Canal Apatlaco

Canal Santa Cruz

XOCHIMILCO

24

23

Bosque de
Nativitas

Av Tenochtitlán

Canal de Cuemanco

Av Tláhuac

Ameses

Armero

Calz Taxqueña

Escuela Naval Militar

Calz del Hueso

Cafetales

Calz Acoxpa

Prolongación División del Norte

22

Camino a Santiago

Country
Club

16

Av Canal de Miramon

Calz de Tlalpan

19

Henríquez Ureña

20

Calz de Tlalpan

Club de
Golf México

Viaducto Tlalpan

Autopista México-Cuernavaca

To Cuernavaca

COYOACÁN

Av MA de Quevedo

Viveros de
Coyoacán

Av Universidad

Av Insurgentes

SAN
ÁNGEL

see Map 6

Av Insurgentes Sur

Av Aztecas

Ciudad
Universitaria

17

18

Av Insurgentes Sur

Anillo Periférico

Carretera México-Cuernavaca

MEX
95

MEX
95D

Carretera Federal Cuernavaca

To Cuernavaca

Estadio
Olímpico

Reserva
Ecológica

Paseo del Pedregal

Parque
Nacional
Ajusco

Carretera México Ajusco

Blvd López Mateos

Carretera Picacho Ajusco

Blvd de la Luz

Av México

Av San Jerónimo

Camino al Desierto de los Leones

San Bernabé

1 Terminal Norte
2 Hotel Brasilia
3 Basílica de Guadalupe
4 New Zealand Embassy
5 La Hacienda de los Morales
6 Estación Buenavista
7 Centro Artesanal Buenavista
8 Terminal Oriente (TAPO)
9 Airport Terminal
10 Hospital ABC
11 Terminal Poniente
12 Meneo
13 Monumental Plaza México
14 Estadio Azul
15 Mundo Joven
16 Terminal Sur
17 Biblioteca Central
18 Centro Cultural Universitario
19 Anahuacalli
20 Estadio Guillermo Cañedo
21 Mercado de Flores y Plantas
22 Embarcadero Cuemanco
23 Museo Dolores Olmedo Patiño
24 Mercado de Xochimilco
25 Embarcaderos

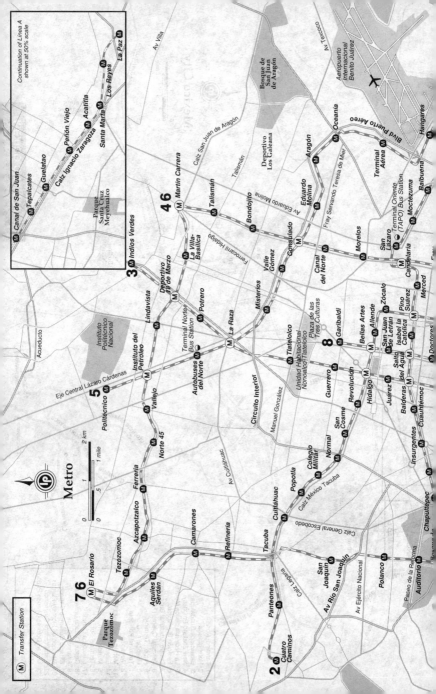

MEXICO CITY MAP 2

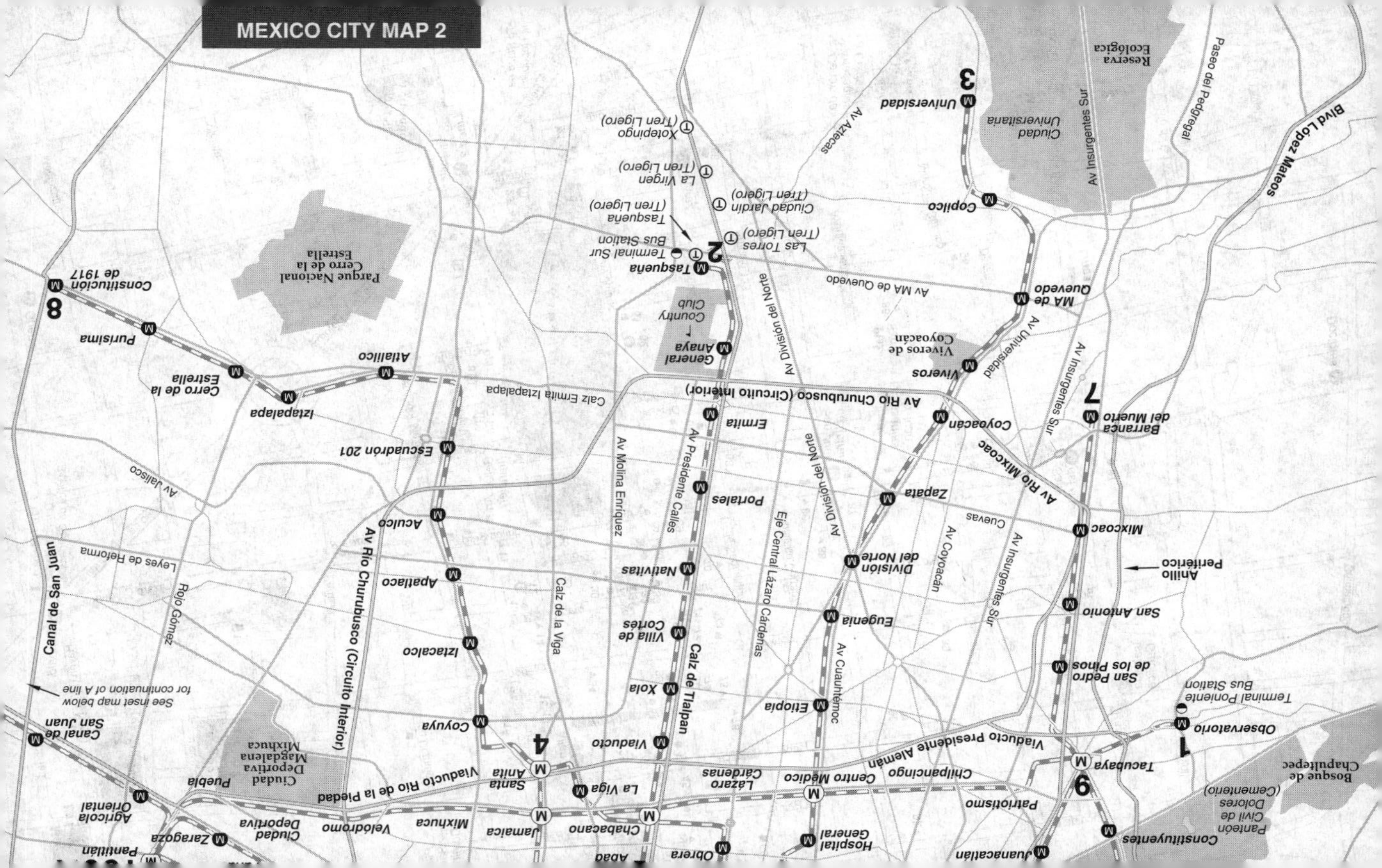

Canal de San Juan

Pantitlán

Agrícola Oriental

Zaragoza

Puebla

Ciudad Deportiva

Velódromo

Mixhuca

Jamaica

Santa Anita

Obrera

Chabacano

La Viga

Viaducto

Adób

Hospital General

Chilpancingo

Centro Médico

Lázaro Cárdenas

Juanacatlán

Patriotismo

Tacubaya

San Pedro de los Pinos

Constituyentes

Observatorio

Panteón Civil de Dolores (Cementerio)

Terminal Poniente Bus Station

Bosque de Chapultepec

San Antonio

Mixcoac

Barranca del Muerto

Av Río Mixcoac

Coyoacán

Anillo Periférico

Av Insurgentes Sur

Av Central Lázaro Cárdenas

Leyes de Reforma

Rojo Gómez

Av Jalisco

Cerro de la Estrella

Iztapalapa

Atlalilco

Purísima

Constitución de 1917

Parque Nacional Cerro de la Estrella

Ecuadrón 201

Aculco

Apatlaco

Iztacalco

Coyuya

Viaducto Río de la Piedad

Av Río Churubusco (Circuito Interior)

Calz de la Viga

Calz Ermita Iztapalapa

Av Molina Enríquez

Xola

Villa de Cortés

Nativitas

Av Presidente Calles

Portales

Ermita

General Anaya

Country Club

Calz de Tlalpan

Eje Central Lázaro Cárdenas

Tasqueña

Terminal Sur Bus Station

Tasqueña (Tren Ligero)

Las Torres (Tren Ligero)

Ciudad Jardín (Tren Ligero)

La Virgen (Tren Ligero)

Xotepingo (Tren Ligero)

Av Aztecas

Etiopía

Av Cuauhtémoc

División del Norte

Zapata

Av Coyoacán

Eugenia

Av División del Norte

Viveros

Viveros de Coyoacán

Av MA de Quevedo

Copilco

Universidad

Ciudad Universitaria

Reserva Ecológica

Paseo del Pedregal

Blvd López Mateos

Av Insurgentes Sur

Cuevas

Av Insurgentes Sur

Av Universidad

MA de Quevedo

See inset map below for continuation of A line

Mercado Tepito

Mercado
Tepito Shoes
Building

Héroe de Granaditas

Costa Rica

Av del Trabajo

Aztecas

Florida

Nicaragua

Centro Histórico &
Alameda Central

| 0 | 150 | 300 m |
| 0 | 150 | 300 yards |

Bolivia

Colombia

🏛 5

Argentina

Venezuela

*Secretaría
de Educación
Pública*

San Ildefonso

🏛 20

Justo Sierra

8   ■ 19

Seminario (Pedestrian)

*Templo
Mayor*
(Ped)

Guatemala

Loreto

Alcocer

**Catedral
Metro-
politana**

54 🏛
(Ped)

56 🏛

Moneda

Zócalo
Ⓜ

Zócalo
aza de la
nstitución)

🏛 55

**Palacio
Nacional**

Correo Mayor

Academia

Zapata

Soledad

To TAPO

❖ 84

**Suprema
Corte de
Justicia**

(Pedestrian)

Corregidora

93 ■

México Millar

Las Cruces

Jesús María

Talavera

Roldán

Santo Tomás

Manzanares

Eje Oriente

Santa Escuela

Rosario

*Candelaria
(transfer)*
Ⓜ

Línea 4

Av Congreso de la Unión (Eje 2 Oriente)

• 94

General Anaya

Candelaria

*Candelaria
(transfer)*
Ⓜ

Línea 2

Pino Suárez

Ⓜ

Pino Suárez
Ⓜ

Línea 1

San Pablo

Carretones

Amilo de Circunvalación

Cabaña

**Mercado
La Merced**

Merced
Ⓜ

Olvera

San Cipriano

San Cipriano

Gurrión

Cuamatzin

Fray Servando Teresa de Mier (Eje 1 Sur)

**Deportivo
Venustiano
Carranza**

**Jardín
Periodistas
Illustres**

98 ●

MAP 3   Centro Histórico & Alameda Central

PLACES TO STAY

2	Hotel Antillas
6	Hotel de Cortés
10	Hotel Hidalgo
19	Hotel Catedral
35	Hotel Ritz
36	Hotel Buenos Aires
40	Hotel Gillow
42	Hotel Rioja
43	Hotel Juárez
44	Hotel Canadá,
46	Hotel Zamora
47	Hotel Washington
48	Hotel San Antonio
59	Hotel Fleming
61	Hotel Bamer
63	Hotel Del Valle
65	Hotel Marlowe
73	Hotel Principal
78	Hotel Majestic
80	Gran Hotel Ciudad de México
90	Hotel Isabel
91	Hotel Montecarlo
93	Hotel Roble
95	Hotel Fornos
96	Hotel San Diego

PLACES TO EAT

3	Hostería de Santo Domingo
11	Restaurant El Correo, Frutería Frutivida
14	Los Girasoles
15	Café de Tacuba
17	Super Soya
21	Sanborn's
24	Café Trevi
28	Café El Popular
32	Restaurante El Vegetariano
34	Restaurante Jampel
37	Restaurante Madero
39	Café La Blanca
44	Jugos Canadá
45	Restaurante El Vegetariano
46	Café El Popular
49	Bertico Café
50	Restaurante México Viejo
51	Flash Taco
52	Shakey's Pizza y Pollo
60	Los Faroles
64	Hong King
66	Centro Naturista de México
68	Taquería Tlaquepaque
70	Pastelería Ideal
75	Comedor Vegetariano
76	La Casa del Pavo
77	VIPS
85	Mercado San Juan
86	Churrería El Moro
87	Restaurant Danubio
88	Restaurant Centro Castellano
89	Cybercafe
92	Pastelería Madrid

OTHER

1	El Tenampa
4	Iglesia de Santo Domingo
5	Museo de la Medicina Mexicana
7	Recinto de Homenaje a Benito Juárez (Temporary Site)
8	Museo Franz Mayer
9	Museo de la Estampa
12	Museo Nacional de Arte
13	Central de Telégrafos
16	Teatro de la Ciudad
18	Restaurante-Bar León
20	Museo de San Ildefonso
22	Exposición Nacional de Arte Popular
23	Museo Mural Diego Rivera
25	Correo Mayor
26	Casa de Azulejos
27	Bar Museo
29	Colegio de Minería
30	La Ópera Bar
31	Bar Mata
33	Bar Roco
38	Dulcería de Celaya
41	Librería Británica
53	Federal Express
54	Museo de la Secretaría de Hacienda y Crédito Público
55	Museo Nacional de las Culturas
56	Museo José Luis Cuevas
57	Mexicana
58	Elektra
62	Casa de Cambio Plus
67	Gandhi
69	Torre Latinoamericana
71	Palacio de Iturbide
72	American Bookstore
74	Museo Serfin
79	Post Office
81	El Nuevo Mundo
82	El Palacio de Hierro
83	Departamento del Distrito Federal
84	Liverpool
94	Elektra
97	Butterfly
98	Mercado Sonora

MAP 4 Plaza de la República & Zona Rosa

PLACES TO STAY
4   Hotel Texas
6   Hotel Pensylvania
7   Casa de los Amigos
10   Hotel Ibiza
11   Hotel Édison
14   Hotel Carlton
16   Hotel Oxford
19   Hotel Jena
20   Hotel Frimont
21   Hotel Crowne Plaza
27   Hotel Mallorca
29   Hotel Compostela
30   Hotel Sevilla
34   Hotel Corinto
35   Palace Hotel
38   Hotel Mayaland
39   Hotel Sevilla Palace
40   Fiesta Americana
46   Hotel María Cristina
52   Casa González
56   Hotel Marquis Reforma
69   Hotel Aristos
73   Hotel Internacional Havre
76   Hotel Westin Galería Plaza
80   Hotel Marco Polo
106 Hotel Plaza Florencia
110 Hotel Krystal Rosa
113 Hotel Century
114 Hotel Calinda Geneve

PLACES TO EAT
2   Super Tortas Gigantes
3   Super Cocina Los Arcos &
     Restaurante Costillas El
     Sitio
13   Restaurant Cahuich
17   Seafood Cocktail Stand
18   Restaurante Samy
33   Sanborn's
36   VIPS
37   Tacos El Caminero
44   Sanborn's
48   Restaurante Vegetariano
     Las Fuentes
60   Restaurante Vegetariano
     Yug
61   Sanborn's

78   Auseba
79   Sushi Itto
82   La Taba
84   Freedom
85   El Perro d'Enfrente
86   Angus Butcher House
87   Mesón del Perro Andaluz
89   Salón de Te Duca d'Este
91   Parri
92   Sanborn's
95   Konditori
97   Pizza Pronto
98   Taco Inn
99   Carrousel Internacional
100 Chalet Suizo
101 Sanborn's
102 Luaú
104 La Beatricita
105 Restaurante Don Luca's
108 Ricocina
109 Mercado Insurgentes
115 Sanborn's

OTHER
1   Antillanos
5   Post Office
8   Lavandería Automática
     Édison
9   Russvall Viajes
12   Monumento a la Revolución
     & Museo Nacional de la
     Revolución
15   Museo de San Carlos
22   Cámara Nacional de
     Comercio de la Ciudad de
     México
23   Dryclean USA
24   TAESA
25   Iberia
26   Consejo Británico
28   Librería Británica
31   Bulldog Café
32   Telecomm
41   Aeroméxico
42   Monumento a Cristóbal
     Colón
43   DHL
45   Institut Français d'Amérique
     Latine

47   Monumento a Cuauhtémoc
49   Jiffy
50   Lavandería Automática
51   Tony Pérez
53   UK Embassy
54   Centro Bursátil
55   Ibermex
57   Aeroméxico
58   Thrifty Rent a Car
59   Air France & UPS
62   Monumento a la
     Independencia (El Ángel)
63   Casa de Cambio Bancomer
64   Aero California
65   American Airlines
66   US Embassy
67   Mexicana
68   Federal Express
70   Rockstock
71   DHL
72   American Express
74   Biblioteca Benjamín Franklin
75   Alaska Airlines & United
     Airlines
77   Procuraduría General de
     Justicia del Distrito Federal
81   La Casa de la Prensa
83   Yuppie's Sports Bar
88   El Taller
90   Casa Rasta
93   Oficina de Turismo de la
     Ciudad de México
94   El Chato
96   Mekano
103 Post Office
107 La Casa de la Prensa
111 Grey Line
112 Cantina Las Bohemias
116 INEGI Map Shop
117 Instituto Nacional de
     Migración
118 Casanova Chapultepec
119 Mocamboo
120 Elektra
121 Instituto Goethe
122 Enigma

MEXICO CITY MAP 4

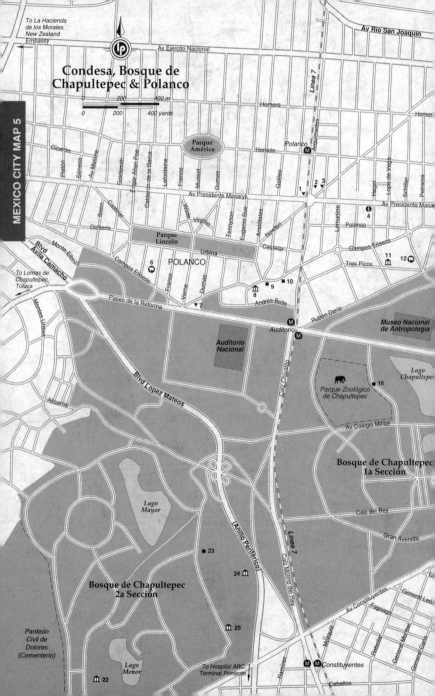

Condesa, Bosque de Chapultepec & Polanco

To La Hacienda de los Morales, New Zealand Embassy

Av Río San Joaquín

Av Ejército Nacional

Homero

Homer

Parque América

Horacio

Av Presidente Masaryk

Av Presidente Masa

Parque Lincoln

Urbina

Castelar

PParque Lincoln

POLANCO

Paseo de la Reforma

Andrés Bello

Rubén Darío

Auditorio

Auditorio Nacional

Museo Nacional de Antropología

Parque Zoológico de Chapultepec

Lago Chapultepe

Av Colegio Militar

Bosque de Chapultepec 1a Sección

Blvd López Mateos

Lago Mayor

Calz del Rey

Gran Avenida

(Anillo Periférico)

Línea 7

Calz Molino del Rey

Bosque de Chapultepec 2a Sección

Av Constituyentes

General Leó

Panteón Civil de Dolores (Cementerio)

Lago Menor

To Hospital ABC Terminal Poniente

Constituyentes

Ceballos

Blvd Avila Camacho

To Lomas de Chapultepec, Toluca

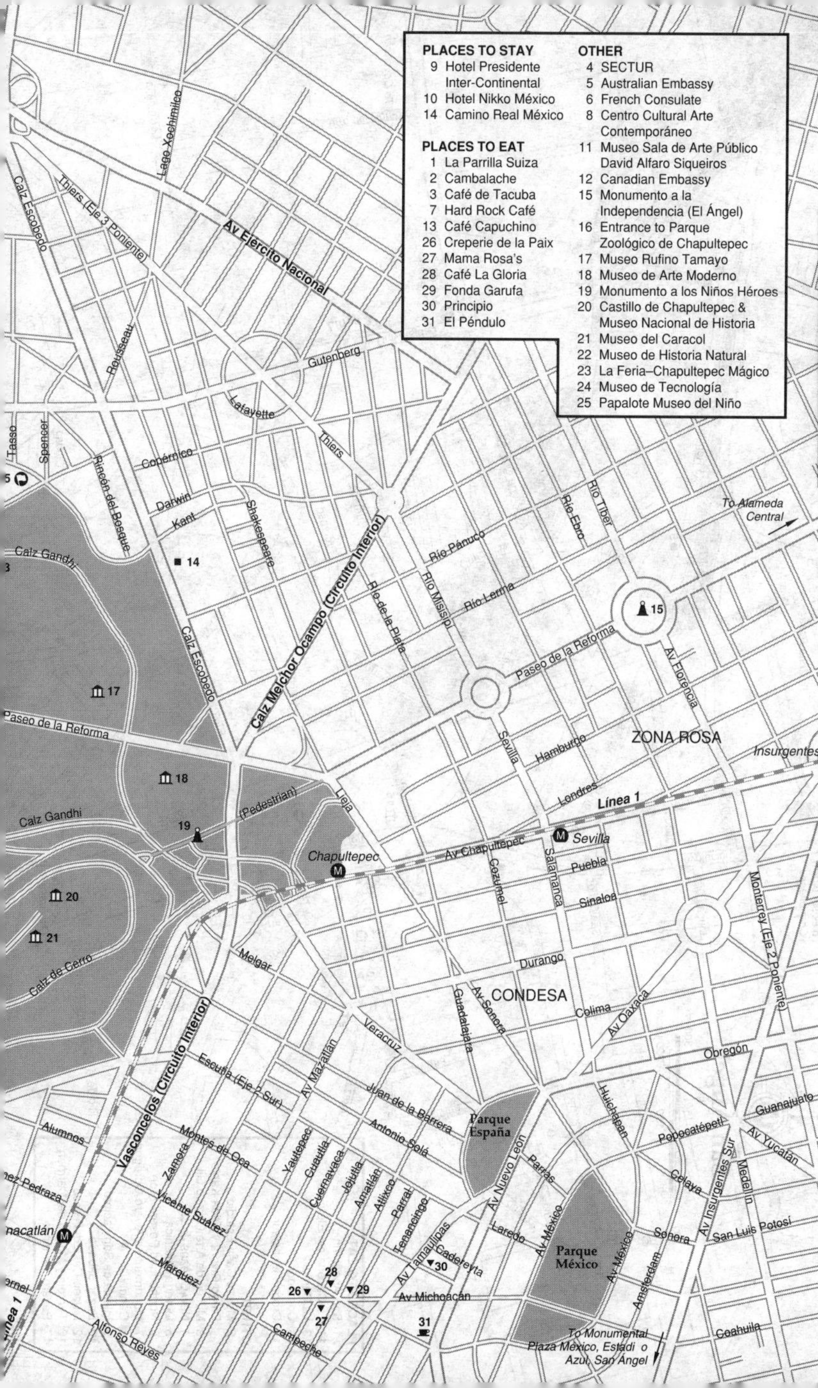
PLACES TO STAY
9 Hotel Presidente Inter-Continental
10 Hotel Nikko México
14 Camino Real México
PLACES TO EAT
1 La Parrilla Suiza
2 Cambalache
3 Café de Tacuba
7 Hard Rock Café
13 Café Capuchino
26 Creperie de la Paix
27 Mama Rosa's
28 Café La Gloria
29 Fonda Garufa
30 Principio
31 El Péndulo
OTHER
4 SECTUR
5 Australian Embassy
6 French Consulate
8 Centro Cultural Arte Contemporáneo
11 Museo Sala de Arte Público David Alfaro Siqueiros
12 Canadian Embassy
15 Monumento a la Independencia (El Ángel)
16 Entrance to Parque Zoológico de Chapultepec
17 Museo Rufino Tamayo
18 Museo de Arte Moderno
19 Monumento a los Niños Héroes
20 Castillo de Chapultepec & Museo Nacional de Historia
21 Museo del Caracol
22 Museo de Historia Natural
23 La Feria–Chapultepec Mágico
24 Museo de Tecnología
25 Papalote Museo del Niño
Lago Xochimilco
Calz Escobedo
Thiers (Eje 3 Poniente)
Av Ejército Nacional
Rousseau
Gutenberg
Lafayette
Thiers
Tasso
Spencer
Rincón del Bosque
Copérnico
Darwin
Kant
Shakespeare
Calz Gandhi
Río Pánuco
Río Lerma
Río Misisipi
Río de la Plata
Río Ebro
Río Tiber
To Alameda Central
Calz Melchor Ocampo (Circuito Interior)
Paseo de la Reforma
Av Florencia
ZONA ROSA
Sevilla
Hamburgo
Londres
Insurgentes
Línea 1
Lieja
(Pedestrian)
Chapultepec
Av Chapultepec
Sevilla
Cozumel
Salamanca
Puebla
Sinaloa
Monterrey (Eje 2 Poniente)
Calz de Cerro
Melgar
Durango
CONDESA
Guadalajara
Av Sonora
Colima
Av Oaxaca
Veracruz
Obregón
Vasconcelos (Circuito Interior)
Escutia (Eje 2 Sur)
Av Mazatlán
Juan de la Barrera
Antonio Solá
Parque España
Huichapan
Popocatépetl
Guanajuato
Av Yucatán
Alumnos
Montes de Oca
Zamora
Yautepec
Cuautla
Cuernavaca
Jojutla
Amatlán
Atlixco
Parral
Tenancingo
Av Nuevo León
Parras
Celaya
Av Insurgentes Sur
Medellín
Vicente Suárez
Av Tamaulipas
Laredo
Av México
Parque México
Sonora
San Luis Potosí
Cadereyta
Márquez
Amsterdam
Av Michoacán
Alfonso Reyes
Campeche
To Monumental Plaza México, Estadi o Azul, San Ángel
Coahuila

San Angel

0   150   300 m
0   150   300 yards

RICK GERHARTER

RICK GERHARTER

PLACES TO EAT
5 El Jardín del Pulpo
7 El Tizoncito
9 El Hijo del Cuervo
10 Los Bigotes de Villa
12 Sanborn's
14 Café El Parnaso
16 Restaurante Caballocalco
17 Quesadilla Stands

OTHER
1 Librería Británica
2 Cineteca Nacional
3 Museo Léon Trotsky
4 Museo Frida Kahlo
6 Pasaje Coyoacán
8 Casa de Cortés
11 Bazar Artesanal de
   Coyoacán
13 Museo Nacional de
   Culturas Populares
15 Parroquia de
   San Juan Bautista
18 Casa Colorada
19 El Ángel
20 Terminal Sur Bus Station

Real Mayorazgo
Coyoacán

Av Popocatapetl (Eje 8 Sur)

Av Universidad

Manzana (Eje 2 Poniente

Av Coyoacán (Eje 3 Poniente

Av Camillo Puerto

Av México-Coyoacán (Eje 1 Poniente)

San Felipe

Av Mayorazgo

Travon

Av Río Churubusco (Circuito Interior)

Matamoros

Mina

Bruselas

Guerrero

Madrid

Aldama

Abasolo

Gómez Farías

Viena

Allende

Berlín

Centenario

Museo Frida Kahlo

Londres

Aguayo

París

Xicoténcatl

Melitzin

Av Universidad

Línea 3

Viveros de Coyoacán

Viveros

Ocampo

Av México

Lerdo de Tejada

Mercado

Cuauhtém

Juárez

Moctezu

Belisario Domínguez

Valenzuela

To Ciudad
Universitaria

Av Progreso

Av Sosa

Plaza
Santa
Catarina

Jardín del
Centenario

Plaza
Hidalgo

Av Hida

Higuera

Yautepec

Dulce Oliva

Ortega

Carranza

San Gregorio

Plaza
Conc

Camilo Puerto

Xochicalilla

To San Ángel

Av MA de Quevedo

Aguayo

Centenario

Real

Parque
Dos
Conejos

Coyoacán

0   200   400 m

0   200   400 yards

To Alameda Central, Zócalo

Municipio Libre

Av General Emiliano Zapata

Panama (Eje Central Lázaro Cárdenas)

Oriente 172

Calz de Tlalpan

Av Popocatépetl

M Ermita

Av Presidente Calles

Calz Ermita Iztapalapa

Aniceto

Av Río Churubusco (Circuito Interior)

Privada Corina

Corina

Av División del Norte

Ex-Convento de
Churubusco
(Museo Nacional de
las Intervenciones)

20 de Agosto

Calz de Tlalpan

General
Anaya M

Av del Convento

Calz General Anaya

Mártires Irlandeses

Irlanda

Línea 2

Country Club

García Torres

Canadá

Pallares y Portillo

Cerro de Jesús

Tepalcatitla

América

Inglaterra

Av MA de Quevedo

Pacífico

M Tasqueña
Tasqueña T

20

Av División del Norte

Av Tasqueña

Canal de Miramontes

Las Torres T

Pinos   To Anahuacalli

Calz de Tlalpan

To Estadio
Guillermo
Cañedo

AROUND THE ALAMEDA CENTRAL

A little less than one km west of the Zócalo is the pretty Alameda Central, Mexico City's only sizable downtown park. In the blocks around the Alameda are some of the city's most interesting buildings and museums.

Bellas Artes and Hidalgo metro stations are at the northeast and northwest corners of the Alameda, respectively. You can also reach the Alameda from the Zócalo area by catching a westbound 'M(etro) Chapultepec' *pesero (colectivo*, or minibus) on Avenida Cinco de Mayo at Isabel la Católica.

Alameda Central

What is now a pleasant, verdant park was once an Aztec marketplace. In early colonial times it became the site of autos-da-fé, in which heretics were burned or hanged. Then, in 1592, Viceroy Luis de Velasco decided the growing city needed a pleasant area of pathways, fountains and trees. It took its name from the poplar trees (*álamos*) with which it was planted. By the late 19th century the park was dotted with European-style statuary, a bandstand was the venue for free concerts, and gas lamps illuminated it at night. Today the Alameda is a popular, easily accessible refuge from the city streets. It's particularly busy on Sunday, when you may catch a rock or salsa band playing open-air.

Palacio de Bellas Artes

This splendid white marble concert hall and arts center, commissioned by President Porfirio Díaz, dominates the east end of the Alameda. Construction of the Palace of Fine Arts (☎ 709-31-11) began in 1904 under Italian architect Adamo Boari, who favored neoclassical and art nouveau styles. It was supposed to be completed by 1910 for the centennial of Mexican independence. But the heavy marble shell of the building began to sink into the spongy subsoil, and work was halted. Then came the Mexican Revolution, which delayed completion until 1934. Architect Federico Mariscal finished

the interior with new designs reflecting the art deco style of the 1920s and 1930s.

The palace houses some of Mexico's finest murals, which dominate immense wall spaces on the second and third levels. On the second level are two large, striking early 1950s works by Rufino Tamayo: *México de Hoy* (Mexico Today), and *Nacimiento de la Nacionalidad* (Birth of Nationality), a symbolic depiction of the creation of the Mexican mestizo identity.

At the west end of the third level is Diego Rivera's famous *El Hombre, Contralor del Universo* (Man, Controller of the Universe), which was first commissioned for Rockefeller Center in New York. The Rockefeller family had the original destroyed because of its anticapitalist themes, but Rivera re-created it even more dramatically here in 1934. Capitalism, with accompanying death and war, is shown on the left; socialism, with health and peace, is on the right.

On the north side of the third level are David Alfaro Siqueiros' three-part *La Nueva Democracía* (New Democracy), painted in 1944-45, and Rivera's four-part *Carnaval de la Vida Mexicana* (Carnival of Mexican Life), from 1936. At the east end is José Clemente Orozco's eye-catching *La Katharsis* (Catharsis), from 1934-35. Contradictory 'natural' and 'social' poles of human nature are symbolized by naked and clothed figures fighting each other. Violence and degradation result from this conflict, and a giant bonfire threatens to consume all and provide a spiritual rebirth.

Another highlight of the palace is the beautiful stained-glass stage curtain in the theater, depicting the highlands of Mexico, based on a design by Mexican painter Gerardo Murillo (also known as Dr Atl). Tiffany Studios of New York assembled the curtain from almost a million pieces of colored glass. On Sunday mornings and just before performances it is lit up for public viewing.

You can view the murals and look around the palace Tuesday to Sunday 10 am to 6 pm (US$1.30, free on Sunday).

Museo Franz Mayer

The Franz Mayer Museum (☎ 518-22-71), a sumptuous collection of mainly Mexican art and crafts, is housed in the lovely 16th century Hospital de San Juan de Dios, at Avenida Hidalgo 45, on little Plaza de Santa Veracruz, opposite the north side of the Alameda. This oasis of calm and beauty is the fruit of the efforts of Franz Mayer, who was born in Mannheim, Germany, in 1882, moved to Mexico, became a citizen, earned the name Don Pancho, and amassed a collection of Mexican silver, textiles, ceramics and furniture masterpieces.

The museum is open Tuesday to Sunday 10 am to 5 pm (US$1.10, US$0.60 on Sunday). The way into the main part of the museum is to the right as you enter. To the left is a gorgeous colonial garden courtyard. The suite of rooms on the courtyard's west side is done in antique furnishings and is very fine, especially the lovely chapel. On the north side is the delightful Cafetería del Claustro (see Places to Eat).

Museo de la Estampa

Also on Plaza de Santa Veracruz is the Museum of Engraving (☎ 521-22-44), with a permanent collection of engravings, lithographs, etc, by top Mexican artists, as well as the tools of these techniques and changing graphic arts exhibits. Hours are Tuesday to Sunday 10 am to 6 pm (US$1.10).

Recinto de Homenaje a Benito Juárez

The Place of Homage to Benito Juárez is normally housed in the Palacio Nacional, but for several years, owing to rebuilding there, it has had a temporary home at Avenida Hidalgo 79, west of the Museo Franz Mayer. Juárez, one of Mexico's most respected heroes, was born into poverty in the state of Oaxaca but rose to lead the reform movement in the 1850s and the fight against the French invaders in the 1860s. He served as president until his death in 1872. The exhibit includes various personal effects and displays on his life and times. It's open daily 10 am to 6 pm (free).

Museo Mural Diego Rivera

Among Diego Rivera's most famous murals is *Sueño de una Tarde Dominical en la Alameda* (Dream of a Sunday Afternoon in the Alameda), 15 meters long by four meters high, painted in 1947. The artist imagines many of the figures who walked in the city from colonial times onward, among them Cortés, Juárez, Santa Anna, Emperor Maximilian, Porfirio Díaz, and Francisco Madero and his nemesis, General Victoriano Huerta. All are grouped around a skeleton dressed in prerevolutionary lady's garb. Rivera himself (as a rather pug-faced child), and his artist wife Frida Kahlo appear next to the skeleton.

The museum housing this work (☎ 510-23-29) is just west of the Alameda, fronting the Jardín de la Solidaridad. It was built in 1986 specifically to house this mural – which had stood in the Hotel del Prado, nearby on Avenida Juárez, until the hotel was wrecked in the 1985 earthquake.

Charts in English and Spanish identify all the characters. There are also photos and other material on Rivera's life and work, and temporary exhibitions. The museum is open Tuesday to Sunday 10 am to 6 pm (US$1).

AROUND PLAZA DE LA REPÚBLICA

This plaza, 600 meters west of the Alameda Central, is dominated by the huge, domed Monumento a la Revolución. Revolución metro station is nearby.

Monumento a la Revolución

Begun in the early 1900s under Porfirio Díaz, the Monument to the Revolution was originally meant to be not a monument at all, but a meeting chamber for senators and deputies. But construction (not to mention Díaz's presidency) was interrupted by the revolution. The structure was modified and given a new role in the 1930s: the tombs of the revolutionary and postrevolutionary heroes Pancho Villa, Francisco Madero, Venustiano Carranza, Plutarco Elías Calles and Lázaro Cárdenas are inside its wide pillars (not open to the public).

MEXICO CITY

Beneath the monument lies the interesting little **Museo Nacional de la Revolución** (☎ 546-21-15), with exhibits on the revolution and the decades leading up to it. It's entered from the northeast quarter of the garden around the monument. Hours are Tuesday to Saturday 9 am to 5 pm, Sunday 9 am to 3 pm (US$0.70, free on Wednesday).

Frontón México
On the north side of Plaza de la República is the Frontón México, Mexico City's grand art deco arena for the sport of jai alai. See Spectator Sports for more on the Frontón.

Museo de San Carlos
The Museum of San Carlos (☎ 566-85-22), Puente de Alvarado 50, at Ramos Arizpe, has a fine collection of European art. It's housed in the former mansion of the Conde (Count) de Buenavista, designed by Manuel Tolsá in the early 1800s, which for a long time also housed the country's leading art academy. Rivera, Siqueiros and Orozco all studied there. The rooms on the 1st floor hold temporary exhibits. The museum's permanent collection of European paintings from the 14th to 19th centuries, upstairs, includes works by Bruegel,

Goya, Rembrandt and Titian. There's also a collection of Mexican and international contemporary art. Hours are Wednesday to Monday 10 am to 6 pm (US$1, free on Sunday).

Lotería Nacional
Mexico's national lottery is a national passion. The tall art deco tower on the west side of Paseo de la Reforma opposite Avenida Juárez (metro: Hidalgo) is the game's headquarters. Walk into the building and up the stairs almost any Sunday, Tuesday or Friday after 7.30 pm, take a seat in the cozy auditorium, and at exactly 8 pm the *sorteo*, the ceremony of picking the winning numbers, begins. Cylindrical cages spew out numbered wooden balls, which are plucked out by uniformed pages who announce the winning numbers and the amounts they have won. Admission is free.

PASEO DE LA REFORMA & ZONA ROSA
Paseo de la Reforma, Mexico City's main boulevard and status address, runs southwest across the city from the Alameda Central and through the Bosque de Chapultepec. It's said that Emperor Maximilian of Hapsburg laid out the boulevard to connect his castle on Chapultepec Hill with the older

---

The Lottery
Lottery tickets are sold all over Mexico by street vendors and at kiosks, and normally they cost US$0.70 or US$1.30. Anyone can buy them. Each ticket is for a particular draw *(sorteo)* on a specific date. Prizes range from around US$100 to more than US$250,000. The winning numbers are posted at ticket sales points.

Buying a ticket enables you to at least fantasize for a day or two about what you would do with US$250,000. Retire to Mexico? Travel the world for a few decades? Give it to charity? Buy a lifetime supply of Bohemia lager? Since the ticket numbering system is a bit complicated, get a ticket seller or someone else who understands it to check your ticket against the list of winners. Each draw usually has several series of tickets, each of which gets a share of the many prizes.

Mexicans resort to all sorts of calculations, hunches and superstitions to decide which numbers may be lucky. Added spice is provided by regular *zodiaco* draws, wherein each ticket bears a sign of the zodiac as well as a number. Four times a year, at times such as Christmas, there are *sorteos especiales*, with tickets costing US$3.25 or US$6.50, and prizes as generous as more than US$1 million. Other draws may be suspended for a couple of weeks beforehand to ensure good sales for the big one.

Profits from the lottery go to government charity projects. ■

section of the city. He could look eastward straight along it from his bedroom and ride along it to work in the Palacio Nacional, on the Zócalo.

Today the traffic along Reforma means that it's not a very pleasant place for a prolonged stroll, but you're likely to pass along it at some point, or to call at one of the banks, shops, hotels, restaurants or embassies on or near it. The Zona Rosa, Mexico City's high-life and nightlife district, lies on the south side of Reforma west of Avenida Insurgentes, roughly two km from the Alameda Central.

Many modern skyscrapers have now joined the older buildings on Reforma, which is also dotted with noteworthy pieces of art. A few blocks due south of Plaza de la República on Reforma is the **Glorieta Cristóbal Colón**, a traffic circle with a statue of Christopher Columbus at its center, created by French sculptor Charles Cordier in 1877.

Reforma's busy intersection with Avenida Insurgentes is marked by the **Monumento a Cuauhtémoc**, the last Aztec emperor. Two blocks northwest of this intersection is the **Jardín del Arte**, a sliver of shady park that becomes an interesting open-air artists' bazaar on Sunday.

The most striking of the modern buildings on Reforma is the **Centro Bursátil**, Mexico City's stock exchange, an arrow of reflecting glass at Reforma 255, about 4½ blocks southwest of Insurgentes.

The glossy **Zona Rosa** is an integral piece of the Mexico City jigsaw and people-watching from its sidewalk cafés reveals a fascinating variety among the passing parade of pedestrians. For details of how to spend money here, see Places to Stay, Places to Eat, Entertainment and Things to Buy.

On the northwest flank of the Zona Rosa, at Reforma's intersection with Avenida Florencia, stands the symbol of Mexico City, the **Monumento a la Independencia**, a gilded statue of Winged Victory on a tall pedestal, called by locals simply El Ángel. The statue was created by sculptor Antonio Rivas Mercado and erected in 1910, just as

the Mexican revolution got under way. Southwest from the Angel, Reforma reaches the Bosque de Chapultepec then continues through the park to become the start of the main road to Toluca.

Getting There & Away

Hidalgo metro station is on Reforma at the Alameda Central; Insurgentes station is at the southern tip of the Zona Rosa, about 500 meters south of Reforma; Chapultepec station is just south of Reforma at the east end of the Bosque de Chapultepec; Sevilla station is on Avenida Chapultepec at the southwest corner of the Zona Rosa.

Westbound 'M(etro) Chapultepec' peseros, which you can catch on Avenida Cinco de Mayo at Isabel la Católica, go along Reforma to Chapultepec metro station. Any 'M(etro) Auditorio,' 'Reforma Km 13' or 'Km 15.5 por Reforma' pesero or bus heading west on Reforma will continue along Reforma through the Bosque de Chapultepec.

Going in the opposite direction, 'M(etro) Hidalgo,' 'M(etro) Garibaldi,' 'M(etro) Villa,' 'M(etro) La Villa' and 'M(etro) Indios Verdes' buses and peseros all head northeast up Reforma to the Alameda Central or beyond.

CONDESA

South of the Zona Rosa, Condesa is a relaxed, middle class, vaguely trendy neighborhood without any major sights but with a couple of pleasant parks, some attractive early 20th century houses, and a number of enjoyable little restaurants and coffee bars. It's worth a wander if you're looking for some place off the tourist trail.

The main focus is the peaceful and beautifully kept **Parque México**, full of trees, well-maintained paths, benches with cute little roofs, and signs exhorting everyone to demonstrate their eco-consciousness and treat their *parque* nicely. **Parque España**, two blocks northwest, has a children's fun fair and is a bit less laid back. Parque México is a one-km walk south from the Sevilla metro station, or you can get a pesero south on Avenida

Insurgentes from the Insurgentes metro station to the intersection with Avenida Michoacán and walk two blocks west to the park.

BOSQUE DE CHAPULTEPEC

According to legend, one of the last kings of the Toltecs took refuge in the Chapultepec woods after fleeing from Tula. Later, the hill in the park served as a refuge for the wandering Aztecs before eventually becoming a summer residence for Aztec nobles. Chapultepec means Hill of Grasshoppers in the Aztec language, Nahuatl. In the 15th century Nezahual-cóyotl, ruler of nearby Texcoco, gave his sanction for the area to be made a forest reserve. At that time Chapultepec was still separated from Tenochtitlán, the site of modern central Mexico City, by the waters of Lago de Texcoco.

The Bosque de Chapultepec has remained Mexico City's largest park for 500 years. Today it covers more than four sq km and has lakes, a good zoo and several excellent museums. It attracts thousands of visitors daily, particularly on Sunday, when vendors line its main paths and throngs of families come to picnic, relax and crowd into the museums. The park is divided into two main sections by two big roads – Calzada Molino del Rey and Boulevard López Mateos – which run north-south across the middle. Most of the major attractions are in or near the eastern, or first, section (1a sección), which is open daily from 5 am to 5 pm.

Monumento a los Niños Héroes

The six columns of the Monument to the Boy Heroes, near Chapultepec metro, mark the main entrance to the park. Vaguely resembling sprigs of asparagus, they commemorate six brave cadets at the national military academy, which was once housed in the Castillo de Chapultepec. On September 13, 1847, when invading American troops reached Mexico City, the six cadets, having defended their school as long as they could, wrapped themselves in Mexican flags and leapt to their deaths rather than surrender.

Castillo de Chapultepec

Part of the castle on Chapultepec Hill was built in 1785 as a residence for the viceroys of Nueva España. The building was converted into a military academy in 1843. When Emperor Maximilian and Empress Carlota arrived in 1864, they refurbished the castle as their main residence. After their fall from power the castle became a residence for Mexico's presidents, remaining so until 1940, when President Lázaro Cárdenas converted it into the **Museo Nacional de Historia** (National History Museum, ☎ 553-62-02).

Today two floors of exhibits chronicle the rise and fall of Nueva España, the establishment of independent Mexico, the dictatorship of Porfirio Díaz and the Mexican Revolution. Several of the 1st floor rooms are decorated with impressive murals on historical themes by famous Mexican artists. These include O'Gorman's *Retablo de la Independencia* (Thanksgiving Panel for Independence), in room 5; Orozco's *La Reforma y la Caída del Imperio* (The Reform and Fall of the Empire), in room 7; and Siqueiros' *Del Porfirismo a la Revolución* (From Porfirism to the Revolution), in room 13. Don't miss the rooms entered from a garden walkway around the east end of the castle – this is the portion where Maximilian and Carlota lived, and it is furnished in period style, including Carlota's marble bath. Above them, reached by a staircase at the side of the building, are Porfirio Díaz's sumptuous rooms, flanking a patio with expansive views.

The museum is open Tuesday to Sunday 9 am to 5 pm (the last tickets are sold at 4 pm). Admission is US$1.90, free on Sunday. To reach the castle, walk up the road that curves up the right-hand side of the hill behind the Monumento a los Niños Héroes. Alternatively, a little road-train runs up this road every 10 minutes while the castle is open, for US$0.40 roundtrip.

Museo del Caracol

From the Castillo de Chapultepec, the Museo del Caracol (☎ 553-62-85) is just a short distance back down the approach road. Shaped somewhat like a snail shell (*caracol*), this is officially a 'Galería de Historia' on the subject of the Mexican people's struggle for liberty. Displays cover social and political life from Spanish colonial days, the divisions of Nueva España in the 18th century, Miguel Hidalgo's leadership in the struggle for independence, and Francisco Madero's leadership in the revolution. The self-guided tour ends in a circular hall that contains only one item – the 1917 Constitution of Mexico. The museum's hours are Tuesday to Saturday 9 am to 4.30 pm, Sunday and holidays 10 am to 3.30 pm (US$1, free on Sunday and holidays).

Museo de Arte Moderno

The two rounded buildings of the Museum of Modern Art (☎ 211-83-31) stand in their own sculpture garden just north of the Monumento a los Niños Héroes. The entrance is on the north side of the museum, facing Paseo de la Reforma. The museum's permanent collection of work by Mexico's most famous 20th century artists, including Dr Atl, Rivera, Siqueiros, Orozco, Kahlo, Tamayo and O'Gorman. In contrast to the large murals for which many of these artists are best known, some of their more intimate work, such as portraiture, is shown here. In addition, the museum always has temporary exhibitions by prominent artists from Mexico and abroad. The museum's hours are Tuesday to Sunday 10 am to 5.30 pm (US$1.30, free on Sunday).

Parque Zoológico de Chapultepec

The first zoo in Chapultepec – and the Americas – is said to have been established by King Nezahualcóyotl well before the Spanish arrived. In 1975 a gift from China brought pandas. Completely rebuilt a few years ago for US$30 million, the Chapultepec Zoo (☎ 553-62-29) is an enjoyable open-air place with a wide range of the world's creatures in relatively large enclosures. The four pandas apparently don't like bright sun and stay indoors – though visible through large windows – from 11 am to 3.30 pm. The zoo is open Tuesday to Sunday 9 am to 4 pm (free). You have to leave bags at a storeroom outside the entrance, and you're not allowed to eat or drink inside the zoo, except in the snack bar area, which is expensive.

Museo Nacional de Antropología

The National Museum of Anthropology (☎ 553-63-81) is one of the finest museums of its kind in the world. It stands in an extension of the Bosque de Chapultepec, on the north side of Paseo de la Reforma. Hours are Tuesday to Saturday 9 am to 7 pm, Sunday and holidays 10 am to 6 pm (US$2.25, free on Sunday, you pay extra for cameras).

The museum is fascinating and very large, with more than most people can absorb (without brain strain) in a single visit. A good plan is to concentrate on the regions of Mexico that you plan to visit or have visited, with a quick look at some of the other eye-catching exhibits. Labeling is in Spanish, but some of the spectacular exhibits justify a visit even if you can't decipher a word.

In a clearing in the park about 100 meters in front of the museum's entrance, Totonac Indians perform their spectacular *voladores* rite – 'flying' from a 20-meter-high pole – several times a day, collecting money from onlookers afterward. See the Voladores sidebar in the Central Gulf Coast chapter for more information.

The spacious museum building is the work of Mexican architect Pedro Ramírez Vásquez and was constructed in the early 1960s. Its long, rectangular courtyard is surrounded on three sides by the museum's two-story display halls. An immense umbrella-like stone fountain rises from the center of the courtyard.

The museum's ground-floor halls are dedicated to pre-Hispanic Mexico. Rooms on the upper level cover the way modern

Mexico's Indian peoples, the descendants of those pre-Hispanic civilizations, live today. With a few exceptions, each ethnological section upstairs covers the same territory as the archaeological exhibit below it, so you can see the great Mayan city of Palenque as it was in the 700s, then go upstairs and see how Mayan people live today. Here's a brief guide to the ground-floor halls, in counterclockwise order around the courtyard:

Introducción a la Antropología – An introduction to anthropology, ethnology, and pre-Hispanic culture in general.

Sala Origenes – The Origins Room shows evidence of the first people in the Americas, explaining their arrival from Asia, and displays early findings from the Valle de México.

Sala Preclásica – The preclassic period lasted from about 1500 BC to 250 AD. These exhibits highlight the transition from a nomadic hunting life to a more settled farming life around 1000 BC.

Sala Teotihuacana – The Teotihuacán Room has models of the awesome city of Teotihuacán, near Mexico City, the Americas' first great and powerful state. A highlight is the full-size color model of part of the Templo de Quetzalcóatl.

Sala Tolteca – This hall covers cultures of central Mexico between about 650 and 1250 AD and is named for one of the most important of these, the Toltecs. Exhibits include a huge stone statue of Quetzalcóatl from Tula.

Sala Mexica – At the west end of the courtyard is the hall devoted to the Mexica, or Aztecs. Come here to see the famous sun, or 'calendar,' stone, with the face of the sun god, Tonatiuh, at the center of a web of symbols representing the five worlds, the four directions, the 20 days and more; the statue of Coatlicue ('She of the Skirt of Snakes'), the mother of the Aztec gods, found – like the sun stone – beneath the Zócalo in 1790; a replica of a carved stone tzompantli; an 'aerial view' painting of Tenochtitlán; and other graphic evidence of this awesome culture.

Sala Oaxaca – In the southern state of Oaxaca, artistic heights were reached by the Zapotecs (about 300 BC to 700 AD) and the Mixtecs (about 1200 to 1500 AD). Two tombs from the great hilltop site of Monte Albán are reproduced full-size.

Sala Golfo de México – Important ancient civilizations along the Gulf of Mexico included the Olmec, Classic Veracruz, Totonac and Huastec. There are very fine stone carvings here, including two awesome Olmec heads.

Sala Maya – The Maya Room has wonderful exhibits not only from southeast Mexico, but from Guatemala, Belize and Honduras too. The full-scale model of the tomb of King Pakal, discovered deep in the Templo de los Inscripciones at Palenque, is breathtaking. On the outside patio are replicas of the famous wall paintings of Bonampak (looking much better than the damaged originals) and of Edificio II at Hochob, in Campeche, constructed as a giant mask of the rain god, Chac.

Cafetería – Just past the Sala Maya is a flight of stairs down to the museum's cafeteria. On some days musicians playing copies of pre-Hispanic instruments give recitals on the stairs.

Sala Norte – The Northern Mexico Room covers the Casas Grandes (Paquimé) site, in Chihuahua, and other cultures from the dry north. Similarities can be seen with Indian cultures of the American southwest.

Sala Occidente – The Western Mexico Room deals with cultures of Nayarit, Jalisco, Michoacán, Colima and Guerrero states. The Tarascans, of Michoacán, were one of the few peoples able to repel the invading Aztecs.

Museo Rufino Tamayo

The Tamayo Museum (☎ 286-65-99), a multilevel concrete and glass structure about 250 meters east of the Museo Nacional de Antropología, was built to house the fine collection of international modern art donated by Rufino Tamayo and his wife, Olga, to the people of Mexico. More than 150 artists, including Picasso, Warhol and Tamayo himself, are represented in the permanent collection, but you may find that their works have all been put away to make room for temporary exhibitions. The museum is open Tuesday to Sunday 10 am to 6 pm (US$1.30, free on Sunday).

Segunda (2a) Sección

The second section of the Bosque de Chapultepec lies west of Boulevard López

Mateos. The nearest metro station is Constituyentes, near its southern perimeter.

One of the highlights here is **La Feria – Chapultepec Mágico**, a large amusement park with some hair-raising rides, open Tuesday to Friday 11 am to 7 pm, Saturday and Sunday 10 am to 9 pm (US$0.80, includes 30 free rides). Another is **Papalote Museo del Niño** (☎ 237-17-00), a hands-on children's museum that is a sure-fire hit if you have children in tow. Activities range from a tunnel slide and a conventional playground to giant-soap-bubble making, a 'supermarket' where kids can play shop in earnest, and all manner of technical/scientific gadget-games. Everything is attended by young, child-friendly supervisors, and you can be sure that your kids will not want to leave. Hours are Monday to Friday 9 am to 1 pm and 2 to 6 pm (plus Thursday 7 to 11 pm), Saturday and Sunday 10 am to 2 pm and 3 to 7 pm. Each four-hour session costs US$2.75 for children (ages two to 12), US$3.25 for others.

Also in Chapultepec's Segunda Sección you'll find two lakes, some large fountains, and the **Museo de Tecnología** (☎ 516-09-64) and **Museo de Historia Natural** (☎ 515-22-22).

Getting There & Away

Chapultepec metro station is at the east end of the Bosque de Chapultepec, near the Monumento a los Niños Héroes and the Castillo de Chapultepec. Auditorio metro station is on the north side of the park, 500 meters west of the Museo Nacional de Antropología.

You can also reach the park from the Zócalo area by catching a westbound 'M(etro) Chapultepec' pesero at Avenida Cinco de Mayo and Isabel la Católica. From anywhere on Paseo de la Reforma west of the Alameda Central you can catch a pesero or bus saying 'M(etro) Chapultepec,' 'M(etro) Auditorio,' 'Km 15.5 por Reforma' or 'Reforma Km 13.' The last three cross the park on Reforma – you can get off outside the Museo Nacional de Antropología (but watch for pickpockets).

To return downtown take any 'M(etro) Hidalgo,' 'M(etro) Garibaldi,' 'M(etro) Villa,' 'M(etro) La Villa' or 'M(etro) Indios Verdes' pesero or bus from Chapultepec metro station or heading east on Reforma. All go along Reforma at least as far as the Hidalgo metro station.

POLANCO

This smart residential quarter north of Bosque de Chapultepec contains a couple of interesting museums, numerous art galleries and restaurants, several embassies, some expensive hotels and shops, and the SECTUR tourist office. You could visit Polanco before or after the Museo Nacional de Antropología, which is close by.

Centro Cultural Arte Contemporáneo

The Contemporary Art Cultural Center (☎ 282-03-55), on Campos Elíseos at Eliot (metro: Auditorio), focuses on avant-garde art – a generation or two more recent than that displayed in the Museo de Arte Moderno. Some of the exhibits are beautiful or arresting, others may make you wonder why the artists bothered! The two lower floors display varied visiting exhibitions; above are permanent collections of Mexican and international art and photographs; the top floor is devoted to 'electronic art' – strange (or just boring?) arrangements of light and screens.

Hours are Tuesday to Sunday 10 am to 6 pm (Wednesday 10 am to 8 pm). Admission is US$0.70 on Tuesday, Thursday and Saturday and is free the other days.

Museo Sala de Arte Público David Alfaro Siqueiros

Shortly before his death in 1974, Siqueiros donated his house and studio at Tres Picos 29 (metro: Auditorio or Polanco) as a museum. His private papers and photographs, along with a lot of his art, are on display. Hours are Tuesday to Sunday 10 am to 6 pm (US$1, free on Sunday).

LOMAS DE CHAPULTEPEC

West of Polanco and Bosque de Chapultepec is Lomas de Chapultepec, one of

Mexico City's wealthiest residential areas, full of large houses protected by high walls. You can take a quick tour of the area by boarding bus 'Km 15.5 por Palmas' at the Chapultepec metro station or westbound on Paseo de la Reforma in the Bosque de Chapultepec. The bus goes along Paseo de las Palmas, the main boulevard of Lomas de Chapultepec, before reemerging on Paseo de la Reforma four or five km west of Bosque de Chapultepec. Here you can either take a 'M(etro) Auditorio' or 'M(etro) Chapultepec' bus or pesero back toward the city center, or stay on the bus as it climbs toward the city's fringes, past exclusive housing precincts where ID is needed to enter.

TLATELOLCO & GUADALUPE
Tlatelolco – Plaza de las Tres Culturas
About two km north of the Alameda Central, up Eje Central Lázaro Cárdenas, is the Plaza de las Tres Culturas, so called because it symbolizes the fusion of pre-Hispanic and Spanish roots into the modern Mexican mestizo identity. The Aztec pyramids of Tlatelolco, the 17th century Spanish Templo de Santiago, and the modern Secretaría de Relaciones Exteriores (Foreign Ministry) building, on the plaza's south side, represent the three cultures.

Founded by Aztecs in the 14th century on what was then a separate island, Tlatelolco was annexed by Tenochtitlán in 1473. In pre-Hispanic times it was the scene of the largest market in the Valle de México. Spaniards under Cortés defeated Tlatelolco's Aztec defenders, led by Cuauhtémoc, here in 1521. An inscription about that battle in the plaza translates: 'This was neither victory nor defeat. It was the sad birth of the mestizo people which is Mexico today.'

Tlatelolco is also a symbol of more modern troubles. On October 2, 1968, several hundred people among a crowd of political protesters were massacred by government troops on the eve of the Mexico City Olympic Games. In 1985 the area suffered some of the worst damage and casualties of the Mexico City earthquake when apartment blocks collapsed, killing hundreds of people.

The plaza is a calm oasis amid the hurly-burly of the city, but it is haunted by echoes of its somber history. You can view the ruins of Tlatelolco's Aztec buildings from a walkway around them. The Spanish, recognizing the religious significance of the place, built a monastery and then, in 1609, the Templo de Santiago. Just inside the main (west) doors of this church is the baptismal font of Juan Diego (see Basílica de Guadalupe). Outside the north wall of the church stands a monument to the victims of the 1968 massacre, erected in 1993. The full truth about the massacre has never emerged; the site was hastily cleaned up, and not until 1993 were Mexican schoolbooks permitted to refer to it.

You can catch northbound 'Eje Central, Central Camionera, Tenayuca' peseros or buses on Aquiles Serdán at Donceles, one block north of the Palacio de Bellas Artes; they pass right by the Plaza de las Tres Culturas. Alternatively, take the metro to Tlatelolco station, exit onto the busy Manuel González, and turn right. Walk to the first major intersection (Avenida Lázaro Cárdenas), turn right, and you will soon see the plaza on the far (east) side of the road.

Basílica de Guadalupe
On December 9, 1531, a Mexican Indian Christian convert named Juan Diego, standing on Cerro del Tepeyac (Tepeyac Hill), site of an old Aztec shrine, saw a vision of a beautiful lady in a blue mantle trimmed with gold. He told the local priest that he had seen the Virgin Mary, but the priest didn't believe him. Juan returned to the hill, saw the vision again, and an image of the lady was miraculously emblazoned on his cloak. Eventually the church authorities believed his story, and a cult grew up around the place.

Over the following centuries Nuestra Señora de Guadalupe (Our Lady of Guadalupe), as this Virgin became known, came to receive credit for all manner of miracles, hugely aiding the acceptance of

Catholicism by Mexican Indians. In 1737, after she had extinguished an outbreak of typhoid in Mexico City, she was officially declared the Patrona Principal (Principal Patroness) of Nueva España. Today her image is seen throughout the country, and her shrines around the Cerro del Tepeyac are the most revered in Mexico, attracting thousands of pilgrims daily from all over the country – and hundreds of thousands on the days leading up to her feast day, December 12. See Special Events for more on these festivities.

The pilgrims' main goal is the modern **Basílica de Nuestra Señora de Guadalupe**, at the foot of the Cerro del Tepeyac. Some pilgrims travel the last meters to this church on their knees. By the 1970s the old yellow-domed basilica here, built around 1700, was being swamped by the numbers of worshippers and was leaning alarmingly as it slowly sank into the soft earth beneath it. So the new basilica was built next door. Designed by Pedro Ramírez Vásquez, architect of the Museo Nacional de Antropología, it's a vast, rounded, open-plan structure able to hold thousands of worshippers. The sound of so many people singing together is quite thrilling. The image of the Virgin, renowned for the miracles it has performed, hangs above the main altar, with moving walkways beneath it to bring visitors as close as possible.

The rear of the **Antigua Basílica** (old basilica) is now the **Museo de la Basílica de Guadalupe** (☎ 577-60-22, ext 137), with a fine collection of *retablos*, plus plenty of colonial religious art. It's open Tuesday to Sunday from 10 am to 6 pm (US$0.30).

Stairs behind the Antigua Basílica climb about 100 meters to the hilltop **Capilla del Cerrito** (Hill Chapel), on the spot where Juan Diego saw his vision. From here, stairs lead down the east side of the hill to the **Jardín del Tepeyac** (Tepayac Garden), from which a path leads back to the main plaza, reentering it beside the 17th century **Capilla de Indios** (Chapel of Indians), next to the spot

where, according to tradition, Juan Diego lived from 1531 to his death, in 1548.

An easy way to reach the Basílica de Guadalupe is to take the metro to La Villa-Basílica station (formerly called La Villa, a name that still crops up on older maps), then follow the crowds two blocks north along Calzada de Guadalupe. You can also reach the metro station by taking any 'M(etro) La Villa' pesero or bus northeast on Paseo de la Reforma from central areas of the city. A 'M(etro) Hidalgo' or 'M(etro) Chapultepec' pesero or bus south down Calzada de los Misterios, a block west of Calzada de Guadalupe, will return you to downtown.

SAN ÁNGEL

Sixty years ago San Ángel ('san ANN-hell'), 8.5 km south of the Bosque de Chapultepec, was a village separated from Mexico City by open fields. Today it's one of the city's more charming suburbs, with many quiet cobbled streets lined by both old colonial houses and expensive modern ones. San Ángel is best known for its weekly arts and crafts market, the Bazar Sábado, but there's plenty to do on other days too (except Monday, when the museums are closed).

Avenida Insurgentes Sur runs north-south through eastern San Ángel.

Plaza San Jacinto & Bazar Sábado

Every Saturday the Bazar Sábado (see Things to Buy) brings a festive atmosphere, masses of color and crowds of people to San Ángel's pretty little Plaza San Jacinto.

The 16th century **Iglesia de San Jacinto**, off the west side of the plaza, has a peaceful garden where you can take refuge from the crowded market areas. It's entered from Juárez. The **Museo Casa del Risco**, Plaza San Jacinto 15, in an 18th century mansion with two courtyards, each with a beautiful tiled fountain, has a hall for temporary exhibitions on the 1st floor and, upstairs, a permanent exhibition of 14th to 19th century European art and 17th to 19th century Mexican art. It's open daily except Monday from 10 am to 5 pm (free).

Museo Casa Estudio Diego Rivera y Frida Kahlo & San Ángel Inn

One km northwest of Plaza San Jacinto, at Calle Diego Rivera 2, on the corner of Altavista, is the Diego Rivera & Frida Kahlo Studio Museum (☎ 280-87-71). The famous pair lived in this 1930s avant-garde abode – with a separate house for each of them – from 1934 to 1940, when they divorced. Rivera stayed on until his death, in 1957 (see the Diego & Frida sidebar). Rivera's house (the pink one) has an upstairs studio. The museum is packed with mainly Rivera art and memorabilia, including the bed in which he died, and also stages temporary exhibitions. It's open daily except Monday from 10 am to 6 pm (US$1).

Across the street from the museum is the San Ángel Inn restaurant, in the 18th century Ex-Hacienda de Goicoechea, once the home of the marquises of Selva Nevada and the counts of Pinillos, with a beautiful verdant courtyard, a chapel and colonial gardens. If your budget won't allow an expensive meal here (see Places to Eat),

---

Diego & Frida

Diego Rivera, born in Guanajuato in 1886, first met Frida Kahlo, 21 years his junior, when he was working on a mural at Mexico City's prestigious Escuela Nacional Preparatoria (National Preparatory School), which she was attending in the early 1920s. Rivera was already at the forefront of Mexican art and a socialist; his commission at the Escuela Nacional Preparatoria was the first of many semipropagandistic murals on public buildings that he was to execute over the next 30 years. He was also already an inveterate womanizer: he had fathered children by two Russian women in Europe and in 1922 married Lupe Marín in Mexico. She bore him two more children before their marriage broke up, in 1928.

Kahlo, born in Coyoacán in 1907, had contracted polio at the age of six, which left her right leg permanently thinner than her left. Nevertheless, at school she was a tomboyish character. In 1925 Kahlo was horribly injured in a bus accident that left her with multiple fractures in her back and right leg, plus broken ribs and a broken collarbone and pelvis. She made a miraculous recovery but suffered much pain thereafter and underwent many operations to try to alleviate it. It was during convalescence from her accident that she began painting. Pain, both physical and emotional, was to be a dominating theme of her art.

Kahlo and Rivera both moved in left-wing artistic circles and met again in 1928. They married the following year. The liaison, which has been described as a union between an elephant and a dove (he was big and fat, she short and thin), was always a passionate love-hate affair. Rivera wrote: 'If I ever loved a woman, the more I loved her, the more I wanted to hurt her. Frida was only the most obvious victim of this disgusting trait.' Both had many extramarital affairs. In fact Kahlo was bisexual.

Kahlo's beauty and unconventional behavior – she drank tequila, told dirty jokes and held wild parties – fascinated many people. In 1934 the pair, after a spell in the USA, moved into a new home built by Juan O'Gorman in San Ángel; the place had a separate house for each of them. In 1937 exiled Russian revolutionary Leon Trotsky arrived in Mexico with his wife, Natalia, after Rivera persuaded President Lázaro Cárdenas to allow them refuge. The Trotskys moved into the 'Blue House' in Coyoacán, where Kahlo had been born, a few kilometers from San Ángel. Kahlo and Trotsky wound up having an affair. In 1939 Rivera quarreled with Trotsky, and the Trotskys moved to a different house in Coyoacán.

The following year Rivera and Kahlo divorced, and Rivera went to San Francisco. Soon afterward, Trotsky was assassinated at his Coyoacán home. Kahlo and Rivera remarried in San Francisco, but, back in Mexico, she moved into the Blue House and he stayed at San Ángel – a state of affairs that endured for the rest of their lives, though their relationship endured too. Kahlo remained Rivera's most trusted critic, and Rivera was Kahlo's biggest fan.

you can still have a peek inside and maybe a drink in the bar.

Museo de Arte Carrillo Gil

The Carrillo Gil Art Museum (☎ 550-39-83), Avenida Revolución 1608, has a permanent collection by Mexican artists of the first rank, with many works by Rivera, Siqueiros and Orozco (including some of Orozco's grotesque, satirical early drawings and watercolors). Temporary exhibits are excellent, too. Hours are Tuesday to Sunday 10 am to 6 pm (US$1, free on Sunday). There's also a pleasant bookstore and café in the basement.

Templo y Museo del Carmen

The cool, peaceful, tile-domed 17th century Templo del Carmen (☎ 616-28-16) is at Avenida Revolución 4. The museum occupies the former monastic quarters to one side of the church and is mainly devoted to colonial-era furniture and religious art – but its big tourist attraction is the mummified bodies in the crypt, which are thought to be 18th century monks, nuns and gentry. You

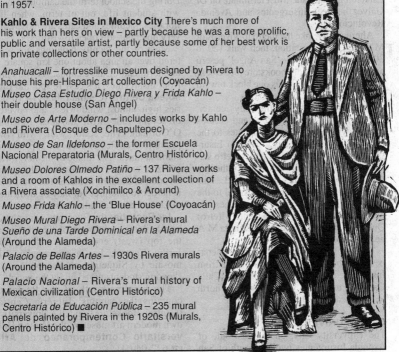

Kahlo had only one exhibition in Mexico in her lifetime, in 1953. She arrived at the opening on a stretcher. Rivera said of the exhibition, 'Anyone who attended it could not but marvel at her great talent.' She died, at the Blue House, in 1954. The final words in her diary were, 'I hope the leaving is joyful and I hope never to return.' Rivera called the day of her death 'the most tragic day of my life....Too late I realized that the most wonderful part of my life had been my love for Frida.'

In 1955 Rivera married Emma Hurtado, his dealer. He died in 1957.

Kahlo & Rivera Sites in Mexico City There's much more of his work than hers on view – partly because he was a more prolific, public and versatile artist, partly because some of her best work is in private collections or other countries.

Anahuacalli – fortresslike museum designed by Rivera to house his pre-Hispanic art collection (Coyoacán)

Museo Casa Estudio Diego Rivera y Frida Kahlo – their double house (San Ángel)

Museo de Arte Moderno – includes works by Kahlo and Rivera (Bosque de Chapultepec)

Museo de San Ildefonso – the former Escuela Nacional Preparatoria (Murals, Centro Histórico)

Museo Dolores Olmedo Patiño – 137 Rivera works and a room of Kahlos in the excellent collection of a Rivera associate (Xochimilco & Around)

Museo Frida Kahlo – the 'Blue House' (Coyoacán)

Museo Mural Diego Rivera – Rivera's mural *Sueño de una Tarde Dominical en la Alameda* (Around the Alameda)

Palacio de Bellas Artes – 1930s Rivera murals (Around the Alameda)

Palacio Nacional – Rivera's mural history of Mexican civilization (Centro Histórico)

Secretaría de Educación Pública – 235 mural panels painted by Rivera in the 1920s (Murals, Centro Histórico) ∎

can also walk out into the pretty garden, once much bigger, which was a source for cuttings and seeds sent all over colonial Mexico, including California. The museum is open Tuesday to Sunday 10 am to 4.45 pm (US$1.90, free on Sunday).

Parque de la Bombilla

This pleasant park lies just east of Avenida Insurgentes. The **Monumento a Álvaro Obregón** marks the spot where the Mexican revolutionary and president was assassinated during a banquet in 1928. Obregón's killer was a young Christian fanatic, José de León Toral, who was involved in the Cristero rebellion against the government's anti-Church policies.

Getting There & Away

'San Ángel' peseros and buses run south on Insurgentes from at least as far north as Estación Buenavista. Most terminate on Dr Gálvez between Insurgentes and Avenida Revolución.

Alternatively, take the metro to Viveros or M A de Quevedo station, then walk (20 to 30 minutes) or board a 'San Ángel' pesero at either place. Gandhi bookstore (see Bookstores and Places to Eat) is one block toward San Ángel from Quevedo station.

Returning north to the city center, 'M(etro) Indios Verdes' buses and peseros run the whole length of Insurgentes to the northern part of the city; 'M(etro) Insurgentes' vehicles go to Insurgentes metro station. A good place to catch either of these is the corner of Insurgentes and Avenida La Paz.

Returning from central San Ángel to the metro stations, 'M(etro) Viveros' peseros head east on Avenida Robles, and 'M(etro) Quevedo' peseros go east on Avenida M A de Quevedo, both from Insurgentes.

To Coyoacán, take a 'M(etro) Tasqueña' pesero or bus east on Avenida La Paz from Insurgentes. After 2.5 km, get off at Calle Carrillo Puerto and walk five blocks north to Coyoacán's Jardín del Centenario.

CIUDAD UNIVERSITARIA

The University City, on the east side of Avenida Insurgentes two km south of San Ángel, is the main campus of Latin America's biggest university, the Universidad Nacional Autónoma de México (UNAM), and one of the nation's modern architectural showpieces.

The university was originally founded in the 1550s but was suppressed from 1833 to 1910. Most of the Ciudad Universitaria was built between 1950 and 1953 by a team of 150 young architects and technicians headed by José García Villagrán, Mario Pani and Enrique del Moral. It's a monument both to national pride, with its buildings covered in optimistic murals linking Mexican and global themes, and to an idealistic education system in which almost anyone is entitled to university tuition.

UNAM has some 250,000 students and 28,000 teachers. It has often been a center of political dissent, most notably in the lead-up to the 1968 Mexico City Olympics. During the school term the campus is busy with student life; out of term, when the libraries, faculties and cafés are closed, it's very quiet but still open to visitors.

Most of the faculty buildings are scattered over an area about one km square at the north end of the campus. As you enter from Insurgentes, it's easy to spot the **Biblioteca Central** (Central Library) – 10 stories high, almost windowless, and covered on every side with mosaics by Juan O'Gorman. The south wall, with two prominent circles toward the top, covers colonial times. The theme of the north wall is Aztec culture. The east wall shows the creation of modern Mexico. The west wall is harder to interpret but may be dedicated to Latin American culture as a whole.

La Rectoría, the Rectorate administration building, southwest of the library, at the top (west) end of the wide, grassy Jardín Central, has a spectacular 3-D mosaic by Siqueiros on its south wall, showing students urged on by the people.

The building south of the Rectorate contains the campus' Librería Central (Central Bookstore) and the university's own modern art museum, the **Museo Universitario Contemporáneo de Arte** (☎ 622-04-04).

The **Auditorio Alfonso Caso**, at the bottom (east) end of the Jardín Central, has on its north end a mural by José Chávez Morado showing the conquest of energy. Humanity progresses from the shadow of a primitive jaguar god to the use of fire and then the atom before emerging into an ethereal, apparently female, future. A little farther east, on the west wall of the **Facultad de Medicina**, a mosaic in Italian stone by Francisco Eppens interprets the theme of life and death. The central mask has a Spanish profile on the left, an Indian one on the right, together making up a mestizo face in the middle. A maize cob and symbols of Aztec and Mayan gods represent forces of life and death.

The **Estadio Olímpico** (Olympic Stadium), on the west side of Insurgentes opposite the northern part of the campus, is designed to resemble a volcano cone and holds 80,000 people. There's a Rivera mosaic over its main entrance. The stadium is home to UNAM's soccer team, Las Pumas. You can peek inside when it's closed by going to Gate 38, which is at the south end.

A second main section of the campus, about two km farther south, contains the **Centro Cultural Universitario**, with several concert halls, theaters and cinemas, the **Unidad Bibliográfica**, housing part of Mexico's National Library, and the **Espacio Escultórico** (Sculptural Space), focused on a striking work by Mathias Goeritz that consists of concrete shapes around a round platform, set on a bare lava bed.

There are student cafés, open to visitors when school is in session, in the Facultad de Economía and the Unidad Posgrado (Economics Faculty, Postgraduate Unit), both off the east end of the Jardín Central in the northern section, and in the Centro Cultural Universitario.

Getting There & Away

Any pesero or bus marked 'Imán,' 'Tlalpan,' 'Villa Olímpica' or 'Perisur' traveling south on Insurgentes from the city center or San Ángel will take you to the

Ciudad Universitaria. If none of these shows up, take one marked 'San Ángel' and change to an 'Imán,' 'Tlalpan,' 'Villa Olímpica' or 'Perisur' vehicle in San Ángel (on Avenida Insurgentes or at the pesero terminal on Dr Gálvez).

For the northern part of the campus, get off at the first yellow footbridge crossing Insurgentes, a little more than one km from San Ángel, just before the Estadio Olímpico. For the southern part of the campus, get off at the second yellow footbridge *after* the Estadio Olímpico.

Returning north, 'San Ángel,' 'M(etro) Insurgentes' or 'M(etro) Indios Verdes' buses or peseros go along Insurgentes as far as their respective destinations.

Copilco metro station is near the northeast edge of the campus, one km east of the Biblioteca Central.

COYOACÁN

About 10 km south of downtown Mexico City, Coyoacán ('Place of Coyotes' in the Aztec language, Nahuatl) was Cortés' base after the fall of Tenochtitlán. It remained a small town outside Mexico City until urban sprawl reached it 50 years ago. Close to the university and once home to Leon Trotsky and Frida Kahlo (whose old houses are among several excellent museums in the area), it still has its own identity, with narrow colonial-era streets, plazas, cafés and a lively atmosphere. Especially on Saturdays and Sundays, assorted musicians, mimes and craft markets (see Things to Buy) draw large but relaxed crowds from all walks of life to Coyoacán's central plazas.

Viveros & Jardín de Santa Catarina

A pleasant way of approaching Coyoacán is via the Viveros de Coyoacán. The Viveros (plant nurseries) are a swath of greenery, popular with joggers, about one km west of Coyoacán's central plazas. You can stroll here any day between 6 am and 6 pm free. From Viveros metro station, walk south along Avenida Universidad, then take the first street on the left, Valenzuela, which runs along the south side of the

Viveros. An entrance to the Viveros is a short distance along Valenzuela, on the left.

A block south of the Viveros, along Ocampo, is pretty little Plaza Santa Catarina. The 700-meter walk east from here along Avenida Sosa to Coyoacán's central plazas takes you past some fine 16th and 17th century houses.

Plaza Hidalgo & Jardín del Centenario

The focuses of Coyoacán life, and scene of most of the weekend festivities, are its twin central plazas – the eastern Plaza Hidalgo, with a statue of Miguel Hidalgo, and the western Jardín del Centenario, with a coyote fountain.

The former town hall (ayuntamiento) of Coyoacán, on the north side of Plaza Hidalgo, is also called the **Casa de Cortés**. It's said that on this spot the Spanish tortured the defeated Aztec emperor Cuauhtémoc to try to make him reveal the whereabouts of treasure. The building was the headquarters of the Marquesado del Valle de Oaxaca, the Cortés family's lands in Mexico, which included Coyoacán.

The **Parroquia de San Juan Bautista**, Coyoacán's church, and the adjacent ex-monastery, on the south side of Plaza Hidalgo, were built for Dominican monks in the 16th century. Half a block east of Plaza Hidalgo, at Avenida Hidalgo 289, is the **Museo Nacional de Culturas Populares** (☎ 658-12-65), which has good exhibitions on popular cultural forms such as *lucha libre* (freestyle wrestling), *nacimientos* (nativity models) and circuses. It's open Tuesday to Sunday right through from 9 am to 11 pm (usually free).

Plaza de la Conchita

Formally called Plaza de la Concepción, this peaceful little square is two blocks southeast on Higuera from Plaza Hidalgo. The red house on the corner of Higuera (not open to the public) is called the 'Casa Colorada.' Cortés is said to have built it for La Malinche, his Mexican interpreter and mistress, and to have had his Spanish wife, Catalina Juárez de Marcaida, murdered here.

Museo Frida Kahlo

The 'Blue House,' at Londres 247, six blocks north of Plaza Hidalgo, was the long-time home of artist Frida Kahlo (see the sidebar Diego & Frida).

Kahlo and her husband, Diego Rivera, were part of a glamorous but far from harmonious leftist intellectual circle (which included, in the 1930s, Leon Trotsky), and the house is littered with mementos of the couple. As well as some of their own and other artists' work, it contains pre-Hispanic objects and Mexican folk art collected by them.

The Kahlo art on display consists mostly of lesser works, but it still expresses the anguish of her existence: one painting, *El Marxismo Dará la Salud* (Marxism Will Give Health), shows her casting away her crutches. In the upstairs studio an unfinished portrait of Stalin, who became a Kahlo hero after Rivera had fallen out with Trotsky, stands before a poignantly positioned wheelchair. The folk art collection includes Mexican regional costumes worn by Kahlo and Rivera's collection of small retablo paintings done by Mexicans to give thanks for miracles.

The house and its garden (☎ 554-59-99) are open Tuesday to Sunday from 10 am to 5.45 pm (US$1.30).

Museo Léon Trotsky

Having come in second to Stalin in the power struggle in the Soviet Union, Trotsky was expelled from that country in 1929. Condemned to death in absentia, in 1937 he found refuge in Mexico thanks to the support of Diego Rivera. At first Trotsky and his wife, Natalia, lived in Frida Kahlo's Blue House, but after a falling out with Rivera in 1939 they moved a few streets away, to the house at Viena 45.

The house has been left pretty much as it was on the day in 1940 when a Stalin agent finally caught up with Trotsky and killed him here. High walls and watchtowers – once occupied by armed guards – surround the house and small garden. These defenses were built after a first attempt on Trotsky's life, on May 24, 1940, when attackers led by the Mexican artist Siqueiros pumped bullets into the house. Trotsky and Natalia survived by hiding under their bedroom furniture. The bullet holes remain.

The final, fatal attack took place in Trotsky's study. The assassin had several identities but is usually known as Ramón Mercader, a Spaniard. He had managed to become the lover of Trotsky's secretary and gain the confidence of the household. On August 20, 1940, Mercader went to Trotsky at his desk and asked him to look at a document. Mercader then pulled an ice ax from under his coat and smashed it into Trotsky's skull. Trotsky died the next day; Mercader was arrested and spent 20 years in prison. Trotsky's desk has been left much as it was at the time of his death; the books and magazines lying on it give an intriguing glimpse of his preoccupations.

The garden contains a tomb holding the Trotskys' ashes.

To enter the house (☎ 554-06-87), go to its northern entrance, at Avenida Río Churubusco 410, near the corner of Morelos. Hours are Tuesday to Sunday 10 am to 5 pm; US$1.30, half-price for ISIC cardholders.

Ex-Convento de Churubusco

Less than 1.5 km east of the Trotsky Museum stands the 17th century former Monastery of Churubusco, scene of one of Mexico's heroic military defeats. It's on Calle 20 de Agosto, east of Avenida División del Norte.

On August 20, 1847, an invading American army was advancing on Mexico City from Veracruz. Mexicans who had fortified the old monastery fought until they ran out of ammunition and were finally beaten only after hand-to-hand fighting. General Pedro Anaya, asked by US general David Twiggs to surrender his ammunition, is said to have answered, 'If there was any, you wouldn't be here.' Cannon and memorials outside the monastery recall these events.

The monastery's church, on its west side, still functions, but most of the monastery is currently occupied by the interesting **Museo Nacional de las Intervenciones** (National Interventions Museum, ☎ 604-06-99), open Tuesday to Sunday 9 am to 6 pm (US$1.90). Displays include an American map showing operations in 1847 (note how far outside the city Churubusco was then), and material on the French occupation in the 1860s and the plot by US ambassador Henry Lane Wilson to bring down the Madero government in 1913. Parts of the peaceful old monastery gardens are also open.

You can reach Churubusco on an eastbound 'M(etro) Gral Anaya' pesero or bus – catch it on Xicoténcatl at Allende, a few blocks north of Coyoacán's Plaza Hidalgo. Alternatively, it's about a 500-meter walk from the General Anaya metro station.

Anahuacalli

This dramatic museum was designed by Diego Rivera to house his excellent collection of pre-Hispanic art. It also contains one of his studios and some of his work. It's at Calle del Museo 150, 3.5 km south of central Coyoacán.

The fortresslike building is made of dark volcanic stone and incorporates many pre-Hispanic stylistic features. Its name means House of Anáhuac (Anáhuac was the Aztec name for the Valle de México). If the air is clear, there's a great view over the city from the roof.

The archaeological exhibits are mostly of pottery and stone figures, chosen primarily for their artistic qualities. Among Rivera's own art, the most interesting are studies for major murals such as *El Hombre en el Cruce de los Caminos* (Man at the Crossroads), whose final version, *El Hombre, Contralor del Universo*, is in the Palacio de Bellas Artes. The Anahuacalli (☎ 617-37-97) is open daily except Monday 10 am to 6 pm (US$1.30).

To get there from Coyoacán, catch a 'Huipulco' or 'Espartaco' bus or pesero south down Avenida División del Norte. Get off after three km at Calle del Museo (there are traffic lights and a church at the intersection), and walk 600 meters southwest along Calle del Museo, curving to the left at first, then going slightly uphill. Returning northward, take a 'M(etro) División del Norte' pesero or bus along Avenida División del Norte.

From central Mexico City you can take the metro to Tasqueña, then the Tren Ligero (streetcar, US$0.20) from the Tasqueña metro station to Xotepingo. Follow 'Salida a Museo' signs at Xotepingo station and go three short blocks west along Calle Xotepingo to the traffic lights at Avenida División del Norte. Then continue ahead along Calle del Museo for 600 meters, as in the previous paragraph.

Getting There & Away

The nearest metro stations to Coyoacán are Viveros, Coyoacán and General Anaya, all 1.5 to two km away. If you don't fancy a walk (or a taxi), from Viveros station, walk south to Valenzuela and catch an eastbound 'M(etro) Gral Anaya' pesero to Allende; from Coyoacán station take the 'Coyoacán' exit, walk a few meters south along Avenida Universidad, and catch a 'Coyoacán' pesero going southeast (half left) on Avenida México; from General Anaya station, many peseros and buses go to central Coyoacán.

To return to these metro stations from central Coyoacán, there are 'M(etro) Viveros' peseros going west on Malitzin at Allende, 'M(etro) Coyoacán' peseros north on Aguayo, and 'M(etro) Gral Anaya' peseros east on Xicoténcatl at Allende.

To reach San Ángel from Coyoacán, 'San Ángel' peseros head west on Malitzin at Allende, and 'San Ángel' peseros or buses head west on Avenida M A de Quevedo, five blocks south of Plaza Hidalgo. To reach the Ciudad Universitaria, take a 'M(etro) Copilco' pesero west on Malitzin at Allende.

XOCHIMILCO & AROUND

About 20 km south of downtown Mexico City, the urban sprawl is strung with a network of canals lined by plant nurseries and houses with patches of waterside lawn. These are the 'floating gardens' of Xochimilco ('so-chi-MEEL-co'), remnants of the chinampas where the Aztecs grew much of their food. A boat trip along the canals is an enjoyable, if not often tranquil, experience. A little more than two km west of Xochimilco is one of the city's best art museums, the Museo Dolores Olmedo Patiño.

Museo Dolores Olmedo Patiño

Opened in 1994 at Avenida México 5843, the Olmedo Patiño museum (☎ 555-08-91) claims to have the biggest and most important Diego Rivera collection of all. It's a fascinating place, set in a peaceful 16th century hacienda with extensive gardens.

Dolores Olmedo Patiño, who still lives in part of the mansion, is a rich socialite and was a patron of Diego Rivera, amassing a large collection of his art which, late in life, she decided to put on public display. The museum's 137 Rivera works – oils, watercolors, drawings and lithographs – are drawn from many periods of his life, including Cubist works from 1916, paintings done in Russia in 1956, and 20 sunsets painted on the balcony of Dolores Olmedo's house in Acapulco. They're displayed together with a fine collection of pre-Hispanic pottery figures and metalwork, as well as memorabilia that include a photograph of Dolores and Diego, signed by Rivera in 1955 with the message 'I adore you . . . '

There's also a room of Frida Kahlo paintings, including an especially anguished self-portrait depicting her spine as a stone column broken in several places. Elsewhere in the museum you'll find Emperor Maximilian's 365-piece silver cutlery set and an impressive and colorful collection of Mexican folk art.

The museum is open daily except Monday from 10 am to 6 pm (US$1.30). To get there, take the metro to Tasqueña, then the Tren Ligero (streetcar, US$0.20) from the Tasqueña metro station to La Noria. Leaving La Noria station, turn left at the top of the steps, walk down to the street and continue ahead to an intersection with a footbridge over it. Here turn a sharp left, almost doubling back on yourself, onto

Antiguo Camino Xochimilco. The museum is 300 meters along here, just past the first intersection. Altogether the trip is about one hour from the city center.

Xochimilco

The name Xochimilco means 'place where flowers grow' in Nahuatl, the language spoken by the Aztecs and their Nahua Indian descendants. Pre-Hispanic inhabitants here piled up vegetation and lake mud in the shallow waters of Lago de Xochimilco, a southern offshoot of the Lago de Texcoco, to make fertile gardens called chinampas, which became an economic base of the Aztec empire. As the chinampas proliferated, much of the lake was transformed into a series of canals. About 100 km of these canals are still navigable.

An environmental recovery program begun in the late 1980s has eliminated much of the pollution resulting from urban sprawl in this corner of the city, and the canals of Xochimilco remain one of Mexico City's favorite places for a bit of fun and relaxation. If you want to take a ride along the canals, you have a choice of several places to board your boat, and between a regular tourist ride or an ecologically oriented ride.

The standard tourist ride begins at one of the *embarcaderos* (boat landings) near the center of Xochimilco. Hundreds of colorful *trajineras* (gondolas), each punted along by one man with a pole, wait to cruise the canals with parties of merrymakers or tourists. There are also boatborne mariachi and marimba bands, photographers, and hawkers of food, drink and handicrafts. On the weekends, especially Sunday, a fiesta atmosphere takes over as the town and waterways of Xochimilco become jammed with people arranging boats, cruising the canals or trying to talk you into buying something. If you fancy a more relaxed atmosphere, come on a weekday, when there are far fewer visitors and hawkers.

Official prices for the boats are posted up at the embarcaderos, and you needn't pay more. At our last check a four-person boat

(yellow roof) was US$5.25 an hour, an eight-person boat (red) US$6.50. Though you can get a taste of Xochimilco in an hour, it's worth going for longer: you can go farther, see more, and get a chance to relax.

To reach Xochimilco, take the metro to Tasqueña station, then take the Tren Ligero (streetcar, US$0.20), which starts there, to its last stop, Embarcadero. From Embarcadero station walk two blocks to the left along Avenida Morelos, then turn right along Netzahualcóyotl beside Xochimilco's bustling daily market. Netzahualcóyotl leads straight for 650 meters to a canal where boats wait.

Alternatively, 'Xochimilco' buses and peseros run from outside Tasqueña metro station. It's about 45 minutes from Tasqueña to Xochimilco either way.

Parque Ecológico de Xochimilco About four km north of downtown Xochimilco, this recently created park (☎ 673-80-61, 673-78-90) of nearly two sq km contains lakes, pathways and a botanical garden. On the north side of the Anillo Periférico ring road, which splits the park in two, is a large flower, plant and handicraft market, the Mercado de Flores y Plantas. To reach Parque Ecológico de Xochimilco, take a 'Cuemanco' or 'Colonia Del Mar' pesero from General Anaya metro station and get off at the park's Centro de Información on the south side of the Anillo Periférico (about 30 minutes).

Ecologically oriented boat tours, focusing on chinampa farming and the surprisingly abundant bird life, leave from Embarcadero Cuemanco, near the southwest corner of the park. These hour-long trips cost US$7.75. You'll need to take a taxi from the Centro de Información to Embarcadero Cuemanco.

COURSES

The Centro de Enseñanza Para Extranjeros (Foreigners' Teaching Center) at UNAM offers six-week intensive courses in Spanish language and Latin American culture five times a year. Beginners and others will find courses that cater to them. Though classes can be quite large, the courses have received good reports from students we have met. For a cost of US$265 (US$375 for summer courses), you get three or more hours in the classroom five days a week. UNAM also runs other courses on Latin American culture, history and society. For more information contact CEPE (☎ 622-24-70, fax 616-26-72, cepe@servidor.unam.mx), Avenida Universidad 3002, Ciudad Universitaria, 04510 México DF, México, or visit the UNAM website (see the Website Directory).

ORGANIZED TOURS

Many travel agencies, including those in most top-end and mid-range hotels, offer bus tours with foreign-language guides within and out of the city. A five-hour whiz around the Zócalo area, the Museo Nacional de Antropología and the Centro Artesanal Buenavista (see Markets under Things to Buy) costs around US$25. The price for a trip to Tlatelolco, the Basílica de Guadalupe and Teotihuacán is similar. Grey Line (☎ 208-11-63), at Londres 166 in the Zona Rosa, is one well-established agency offering such tours.

SPECIAL EVENTS

Every major festival described in Facts for the Visitor is celebrated in Mexico City. Those with a special flavor in the capital are described below.

Semana Santa

The most evocative events of Holy Week, the week leading up to Easter, are in the humble barrio of Iztapalapa, about nine km southeast of the Zócalo (metro: Iztapalapa), where more than 150 locals act out realistic scenes from the Passion and death of Christ. Palm Sunday sees the triumphal entry into Jerusalem. On Holy Thursday the betrayal by Judas and the Last Supper are played out in Iztapalapa's plaza, and Christ's address in Gethsemane is enacted on Cerro de la Estrella, the hill rising to the south. The most emotive scenes begin at noon in the plaza on Good Friday. Christ is sentenced, beaten, and

has a crown of thorns placed on his head (drawing real blood), then carries his 90-kg cross four km up Cerro de la Estrella, where he is tied to the cross and 'crucified.' Afterward he is carried down the hill and taken to a hospital.

Día de la Independencia

On the evening of September 15 thousands of people gather in the Zócalo to hear the president of Mexico recite a version of the Grito de Dolores (Cry of Dolores), Miguel Hidalgo's famous rallying call to rebellion against the Spanish in 1810, from the central balcony of the National Palace at 11 pm. The president then rings the ceremonial Campana de Dolores (Bell of Dolores), and there's lots of cheering, fireworks and throwing of confetti, usually in the faces of other merrymakers. If you go, leave your valuables in the hotel safe.

Día de Nuestra Señora de Guadalupe

At the Basílica de Guadalupe in the northern part of the city, December 12, the Day of Our Lady of Guadalupe, caps 10 days of festivities celebrating Mexico's religious patron, the Virgin of Guadalupe. From December 3 onward, ever growing crowds flood toward the basilica and its huge plaza. On December 11 and 12 groups of Indian dancers and musicians from all over Mexico perform on the plaza in uninterrupted succession for two days. The numbers of pilgrims reach the millions by December 12, when religious services go on in the basilica almost round the clock.

Christmas & Día de los Reyes Magos

For the couple of weeks before Christmas the Alameda Central is ringed with brightly lit fairy-tale castles and polar grottoes, where children pose for photos with Mexican Santa Clauses and their reindeer. Between Christmas and January 6 – the Day of the Three Kings (los Reyes Magos) – Santa Claus is replaced by the Three Kings, who are equally popular and look, if anything, even more ill at ease than the Santas. Families flock in, and hosts of stalls selling anything from tacos to music tapes pop up.

PLACES TO STAY

Mexico City has a full range of hotels, from basic but centrally located places (up to US$15 a double) through comfortable mid-range hostelries (US$15 to US$45 a double) to a wide range of top-end hotels costing from US$50 up to the sky. In general, the best cheap and moderately priced rooms are in the areas west of the Zócalo, near the Alameda Central or Plaza de la República; luxury hotels are mostly in the Zona Rosa, along Paseo de la Reforma, and in the Polanco district.

Hotels are described here in order of preference. Where two prices are given for double rooms, the lower is for two people in one bed, the higher for twin beds. Many hotels have rooms for three or four people, costing not very much more than a double.

Places to Stay – budget

Rooms in these hotels have private baths unless otherwise mentioned. Many also have TV and carafes or bottles of purified water.

Centro Histórico There are many suitable hotels on Avenida Cinco de Mayo and the streets to its north and south. Hot water supplies are erratic in some places.

Hotel Juárez (☎ 512-69-29), at 1a Cerrada de Cinco de Mayo 17, has 39 rooms on a quiet side street off Avenida Cinco de Mayo only 1½ blocks west of the Cathedral (metro: Zócalo or Allende). It's simple but very clean and presentable, with 24-hour hot water, a fountain in the little courtyard, and low prices of US$9.25 a single, US$9.75 or US$10.50 a double. Rooms all have TV, but only a few have windows. It's a popular place, but if you're there by 2 pm you should get a room.

Hotel Isabel (☎ 518-12-13, fax 521-12-33), Isabel la Católica 63, at El Salvador (metro: Isabel la Católica), is popular for its convenient location, comfy if old-fashioned rooms, and moderately priced

little restaurant. All rooms have TV, and some are very large; those overlooking the street are noisy but bright. Singles/doubles cost US$12.50/14.50, or US$7.75/8.50 on the upper floors, with shared bath and good views from some rooms.

Hotel San Antonio (☎ 512-99-06), at 2a Cerrada de Cinco de Mayo 29, is just south of Hotel Juárez, across Avenida Cinco de Mayo on the corresponding side street (metro: Zócalo or Allende). All 40 small, clean rooms have TV, and it's quiet and convenient. Rooms are US$9.25 with one double bed and shared bathrooms, US$10.50 with two beds and private bath. Those on the street side are brighter.

Hotel Zamora (☎ 512-82-45), at Avenida Cinco de Mayo 50, between La Palma and Isabel la Católica (metro: Allende or Zócalo), has absolutely no frills, and rooms can be noisy and/or dark, but it's clean, friendly and cheap, with hot showers and a safe. One-bed rooms are US$5.25 with shared bath, US$6.50 with private bath; two-bed doubles are US$7.25 with shared bath, US$9.25 with private bath.

Hotel Buenos Aires (☎ 518-21-04), Motolinía 21 (metro: Allende), has good prices, too: US$6.50 single/double with shared bath, US$7.75 with private bath and TV (US$9.25 for twin-bed doubles). Rooms are plain but clean and adequate, and management is friendly.

Hotel Principal (☎ 521-13-33), at Bolívar 29, between Avenida Madero and 16 de Septiembre (metro: Allende or Zócalo), is a friendly place, with most rooms opening onto a plant-draped central hall. Singles/doubles with shared bath are US$6.50/7.75. With private bath it's US$11.75 a single, US$13 or US$15.75 for doubles. The twin rooms are quite large.

Hotel Washington (☎ 512-35-02), Avenida Cinco de Mayo 54 at La Palma, near the aforementioned Hotels Juárez and Zamora (metro: Allende or Zócalo), has noisy front rooms but is well situated. Singles are US$11, doubles US$12.50 or US$14.25.

Hotel Montecarlo (☎ 518-14-18) at Uruguay 69 (metro: Zócalo), is where DH

Lawrence once stayed. Though renovated and clean, it's rather gloomy and devoid of atmosphere. But its handy location and prices – US$9.25 single/double with shared bath, US$11/11.75 for singles/doubles with private bath – make it worth considering.

Hotel Rioja (☎ 521-83-33), Avenida Cinco de Mayo 45, at Isabel la Católica (metro: Allende), is in an ongoing state of reconstruction. Rooms are all small. The modernized ones are bare but clean, with tiled bathrooms; the others are similar but worn. Prices depend on whether rooms are interior or exterior, have private or shared bath, and are modernized or not: singles are from US$7.25 to US$10.75, doubles from US$8 to US$16.

Near the Alameda Central This is a convenient, if drab, area.

Hotel Del Valle (☎ 521-80-67), Independencia 35, just a block from the Alameda (metro: San Juan de Letrán or Juárez), is a friendly place whose medium-size, slightly worn rooms have TV and are reasonably priced at US$9.25 for singles, US$9.25 or US$11.25 for doubles.

Hotel San Diego (☎ 521-60-10), Luis Moya 98, is 5½ blocks from the Alameda (metro: Salto del Agua) but offers a good value. The 87 spacious, modern rooms boast satellite TV, tiled bathrooms, and prices of US$10.50 a single, US$11.75 or US$15.50 a double. There's a good restaurant, a bar and a garage.

Hotel Fornos (☎ 510-47-32), at Revillagigedo 92, 700 meters from the Alameda (metro: Balderas), has smallish but pleasant rooms with tiled bathrooms and carpets. One or two people in a double bed pay US$11 or US$12.50; a twin room is US$19.50. The hotel has a parking lot and restaurant.

Near Plaza de la República This area, about one km west of the Alameda, is slightly less convenient, but prices are good and the neighborhood is quiet and residential, with an amiable feel. The metro station is Revolución.

Casa de los Amigos (☎ 705-05-21, fax 705-07-71, amigos@laneta.apc.org), at Ignacio Mariscal 132, is run by Quakers, but anyone can stay here and there's no religious pressure on guests. Many people involved in social justice projects in Mexico and Central America stay here, so it's a good place for meeting people with an informed interest in the region. Facilities include a kitchen, information files on volunteer opportunities and language schools, and a library. A US$1.30 breakfast is served Monday to Friday. There's room for 40 people in single-sex dormitories and private rooms. Dorm beds cost US$5.25; singles/doubles with shared bath are US$7.25/10.50; doubles with private bath are US$11.75. Reservations are advisable, especially in August and September and from December to February. Minimum stay is two nights. Alcohol and smoking are banned inside the building.

The small *Hotel Ibiza* (☎ 566-81-55), Arriaga 22, at Édison, is a good value. Nice clean little singles/doubles, with bright bedspreads and TV, are US$7.75/10.50.

For a bit more comfort, a good bet is the *Hotel Édison* (☎ 566-09-33), Édison 106. It has 45 pleasant, clean rooms around a small, plant-filled courtyard, costing US$13 for singles, US$14.25 or US$15.50 for doubles. There's a garage, and a bakery just across the street.

Hotel Pensylvania (☎ 703-13-84), Ignacio Mariscal 101, at Arriaga, was modernized a few years ago and has 82 decent lilac-painted rooms, all with TV and tiled bathrooms. Standard singles/doubles cost US$6.50/9.25, but there's also a *'zona de kingsize,'* with bigger beds in mostly bigger rooms, at US$9.25/10.50. Parking is available.

Hotel Carlton (☎ 566-29-11), Ignacio Mariscal 32B, at Ramos Arizpe, is still popular among budget travelers, though it's getting pretty worn and is due for a spot of refurbishment. The rooms, US$9.25/10.50 single/double, are carpeted, have TV and are vaguely cozy.

Hotel Oxford (☎ 566-05-00), Ignacio Mariscal 67, at Alcázar, is in a similar state – the carpets don't appear to have been washed for at least a decade – but it has large singles or doubles with TV for US$6.50 to US$10.50.

Places to Stay – middle

Hotels in this range provide comfortable and attractive, if sometimes small, rooms in well-located modern or colonial buildings. All rooms have private bath (usually with shower, sometimes with tub) and color TV.

Centro Histórico *Hotel Catedral* (☎ 518-52-32, fax 512-43-44), Donceles 95 (metro: Zócalo), just around the corner from the Templo Mayor and a block north of the cathedral, is shiny, bright and efficient, with a good restaurant off the bright lobby. The 120 rooms are well kept, pleasant and comfortable, at US$23.50 a single, US$28.25 or US$32.50 a double. There's parking nearby.

Hotel Canadá (☎ 518-21-06, fax 521-93-10), Avenida Cinco de Mayo 47, east of Isabel la Católica (metro: Allende), is bright, modern and tidy, and the location is excellent, though most of the 100 rooms are modestly sized and the exterior ones get some street noise. They cost US$20.75 a single, US$23.25 or US$25.25 a double, and all have safes.

Hotel Gillow (☎ 518-14-40, fax 512-20-78), handily located at Isabel la Católica 17, on the corner of Avenida Cinco de Mayo (metro: Allende), has a pleasant leafy lobby and clean, cheerful, up-to-date rooms. Singles are US$23.25, doubles US$26 or US$32.50. There's a popular, moderately priced restaurant too.

Hotel Roble (☎ 522-78-30), Uruguay 109, at Pino Suárez (metro: Zócalo or Pino Suárez), is two blocks south of the Zócalo on a noisy corner. Used mostly by Mexicans with dealings in the nearby shops and markets, it's at the cheap end of the middle range, with singles at US$13 and doubles from US$15.75 to US$17.75. The rooms are reasonably sized and clean – better than the building's outside suggests. A bright, busy restaurant adjoins the hotel.

Hotel Antillas (☎ /fax 526-56-74), Belisario Domínguez 34, east of Allende (metro: Allende), seven blocks northwest of the Zócalo, has 100 good-size rooms with carpeting and bright bedspreads for US$15 a single, US$18 or US$20.25 a double. The staff are agreeable, and there's an attractive restaurant off the lobby. Parking is available.

Near the Alameda Central *Hotel Bamer* (☎ 521-90-60, fax 510-17-93) faces the Alameda at Avenida Juárez 52 (metro: Bellas Artes). Many of the 111 comfortable, air-con rooms are very large and have fantastic views of the Alameda. Singles/doubles cost US$31/38.75. There are some smaller rooms at the sides, without Alameda views or bathtub (but with shower), for US$22/23.25. The first-floor cafeteria serves good, reasonably priced breakfasts and lunches.

In the streets south of the Alameda, an area not quite fully recovered from the ravages of the 1985 earthquake, are a few good, modernized hotels. *Hotel Fleming* (☎ 510-45-30, fax 512-02-84), at Revillagigedo 35, 2½ blocks from the Alameda (metro: Juárez), has 100 comfortable rooms with large tiled bathrooms; some on the higher floors have great views. Singles are US$24.25, doubles US$28.75 or US$31.75. There's a nice restaurant, and parking.

Hotel Marlowe (☎ 521-95-40, fax 518-68-62), Independencia 17, between Dolores and López (metro: San Juan de Letrán), is one short block from the Alameda. It's bright and comfortable, and the 120 rooms are pleasant, tasteful and quite big. Corner rooms – especially those higher up – tend to be brightest. Singles are US$25.75, doubles US$28.75 or US$31.75.

One block north of the Alameda, *Hotel Hidalgo* (☎ 521-87-71), Santa Veracruz 37, at Dos (2) de Abril (metro: Bellas Artes), is on a grungy street, but the 100 rooms are modern and excellent. There's a restaurant and a garage. Singles/doubles are US$17.50/20.75.

Near Plaza de la República The nearest metro station to these hotels, unless otherwise specified, is Revolución.

Hotel Frimont (☎ 705-41-69), Terán 35, is a good value, with 100 clean, carpeted, decent-size rooms costing US$16.50 a single, US$18 or US$21 a double, and a restaurant where you can get a fruit, eggs and coffee breakfast for US$1.60 to US$2.25.

The recently rebuilt *Hotel Texas* (☎ 705-57-82, fax 566-97-24), Ignacio Mariscal 129, has helpful staff and 60 cozy, clean rooms with free bottled drinking water. Singles are US$15, doubles US$16.25 or US$17.50, and there's a garage.

In the streets south of Plaza de la República are several more upmarket hotels offering good values. One is *Hotel Corinto* (☎ 566-65-55, fax 546-68-88), Ignacio Vallarta 24, a sleek, modern, polished place with a good restaurant, a bar, helpful staff, and even a small swimming pool on the roof. The 155 air-con rooms, though small, are comfortable and quiet. Singles cost US$24.25, doubles US$26 or US$31.25.

Palace Hotel (☎ 566-24-00, fax 535-75-20), Ramírez 7, always has lots of bustle in its lobby as guests arrive and depart. The 200 rooms are modern and comfortable, at US$22.75 for singles, US$24.25 or US$27.25 for doubles. There's a restaurant, bar and garage.

In a similar bracket is the *Hotel Mayaland* (☎ 566-60-66, fax 535-12-73), Antonio Caso 23. The 100 rooms are small but clean, with air-con and drinking water, and cost US$22.75 or US$24 for singles, US$26.50 for doubles. There's a restaurant and parking.

Back north and east of Plaza de la República, *Hotel Jena* (☎ 566-02-77, fax 566-04-55), Terán 12 (metro: Hidalgo), is a modern, gleaming building with a posh feel. Its 120-plus rooms are ultraclean and among the most luxurious in the middle range. Singles are US$36.25, doubles US$39.25 to US$44. There's a piano bar, open till 2 am, and a slightly pricey restaurant.

Near the Jardín del Arte The Jardín del Arte is a small park about one km north of the Zona Rosa, close to the Reforma/Insurgentes intersection. Three decent midsize hotels, all with parking, are on Calle Serapio Rendón within a block of the park. Buses and peseros pass nearby on Insurgentes and Reforma.

Hotel Mallorca (☎ 566-48-33), Serapio Rendón 119, has clean, pleasant, carpeted rooms with singles at US$17.75 and doubles from US$19.50. It's popular with Mexican couples and families. The '*doble chico*' and '*doble grande*' doubles (US$21 and US$22.75) are large.

Hotel Sevilla (☎ /fax 566-18-66), Serapio Rendón 126, is in the throes of renovation but the already completed rooms are nice, if a bit smaller than the Mallorca's. The hotel also has a travel agency and a small restaurant/bar. Singles are US$17.50, doubles US$19.25 or US$22.75.

Hotel Compostela (☎ 566-07-33, fax 566-26-71), Sullivan 35, at Serapio Rendón, has smallish but pleasant rooms starting at US$15.25 for singles, and US$16.75 or US$19.25 for doubles.

Near the Zona Rosa Accommodations right in the posh Zona Rosa are expensive, but there are a couple of good mid-range places nearby. The nearest metro station to both is Insurgentes (800 meters south).

Casa González (☎ 514-33-02), Río Sena 69, is a 500-meter walk north from the heart of the Zona Rosa, in a quieter neighborhood. Two beautiful houses set in small plots of lawn have been converted into a lovely guesthouse. It's an exceptional place run by a charming family, perfect for those staying more than one or two nights, and a good value at US$23 to US$31 a single and US$26.50 to US$31 a double (plus one double at US$57.50). Good home-cooked meals are available in the pretty dining room. They may have parking. Reserve in advance if you can. No sign marks the houses, and the gate is kept locked. Ring the bell to enter.

Hotel María Cristina (☎ 703-17-87, fax 566-91-94), Río Lerma 31, 600 meters north of the center of the Zona Rosa, is a colonial-style gem. It has 150 comfy rooms, small manicured lawns, baronial public rooms, and a patio with a fountain. There's a fine restaurant (comida for US$5.25), a bar and parking. Singles/doubles are US$33.25/36.25, suites US$44 and up. The hotel is popular with Mexican businesspeople, families, and foreign tourists, so book in advance if you can.

Near Terminal Norte *Hotel Brasilia* (☎ 587-85-77), Avenida de los Cien Metros 4823 (metro: Autobuses del Norte), is a five- to eight-minute walk south of the northern bus terminal; turn left out of the terminal's front door. It has 200 decent rooms at US$15.50 or US$20.75, single or double. There's a restaurant and bar.

Places to Stay – top end
Top-end accommodations range from comfortable medium-size tourist-oriented hotels, some with rooms for well under US$100, to modern luxury high-rises geared toward international business travelers where the cheapest rooms are more than US$300. For the hotels in the Best Western group call ☎ 800-528-1234 in the USA or Canada for reservations.

Centro Histórico The long-established *Hotel Majestic* (☎ 521-86-00, fax 512-62-62), Avenida Madero 73, on the west side of the Zócalo (metro: Zócalo), has lots of colorful tiles in the lobby, and a few rooms (the more expensive ones) overlooking the vast plaza. Avoid the rooms facing Madero (too noisy) and around the inner glass-floored courtyard (unless you don't mind people looking in your windows). Rates are US$93.75 a room or US$140.50 a suite, single or double. The 7th-floor café/restaurant has a great view of the Zócalo. This hotel is in the Best Western group.

Gran Hotel Ciudad de México (☎ 510-40-40, fax 512-67-72), 16 de Septiembre 82, just off the Zócalo (metro: Zócalo), is a feast of art nouveau style. Sit on one of the plush settees in the spacious lobby, listen to the songbirds in the large cages, and watch the open ironwork elevator glide toward the brilliant canopy of stained glass high above you. The 124 large, comfortable rooms are US$87 single or double. There's a branch of the Delmonico's restaurant chain, plus a 4th-floor restaurant overlooking the Zócalo.

The Best Western *Hotel Ritz* (☎ 518-13-40, fax 518-34-66), 3½ blocks west of the Zócalo, at Avenida Madero 30 (metro: Allende), caters to business travelers and North American tour groups, offering 140 comfortable rooms with minibars at US$57 a single or double. There's a restaurant, a good little bar, and parking.

Near the Alameda Central *Hotel de Cortés* (☎ 518-21-84, fax 512-18-63), Avenida Hidalgo 85, facing the Alameda Central (metro: Hidalgo), has a somewhat forbidding façade of dark tezontle, but inside is a charming little colonial courtyard hotel. Built in 1780 as a hospice for Augustinian friars, it now has modern and comfortable rooms with TV and small windows that look out onto the courtyard restaurant. Noise can be a problem, though. Singles/doubles are US$82.50/94.25; there are also some more expensive suites. The four-course lunch is US$7.75. This is another Best Western hotel.

Near Plaza de la República Several mainly business-oriented hotels on Paseo de la Reforma provide a convenient location between the Alameda and Zona Rosa. They include:

Fiesta Americana (☎ 705-15-15, fax 705-13-13), Reforma 80 (nearest metro: Revolución) – a 26-story, 610-room slab with stylish singles/doubles for US$120.25/132.25.

Hotel Crowne Plaza (☎ 128-50-00, fax 128-50-50), Reforma 1 (metro: Hidalgo) – a smooth new 490-room luxury hotel; standard rooms US$233

Hotel Sevilla Palace (☎ 566-88-77, in USA 800-732-9488; fax 535-38-42), Reforma 105 (nearest metro: Revolución) – helpful service and good, modern rooms at US$99.75 single or double

Zona Rosa & Nearby The nearest metro station here is Insurgentes, unless stated otherwise.

Hotel Internacional Havre (☎ 211-00-82, fax 533-12-84), at Havre 21, has 48 very big and comfy rooms with nice furniture and TV, and fine views from the top floors. Singles/doubles are US$64/71.25. Management is helpful, and there's free guarded parking and a restaurant.

Hotel Plaza Florencia (☎ 211-31-89, fax 511-15-42), Avenida Florencia 61, is a pleasant, modern hotel with 142 tasteful – though not huge – air-con rooms with minibar and cable TV. Standard rooms are US$106 for one to four people; better ones go up to US$171. There's a restaurant too.

Hotel Calinda Geneve (☎ 211-00-71, in USA 800-221-2222; fax 208-74-22), Londres 130, near Génova, is the dowager of Zona Rosa hotels – old but well kept – with a formal colonial lobby from which you can walk into a glass-canopied Sanborn's restaurant or, at the other end, the popular Café Jardín (see Places to Eat). The 320 rooms are pleasant, with a bit of period style, air-con, minibar and cable TV, and cost US$100.50. There's also a spa.

The 400-room *Hotel Aristos* (☎ 211-01-12, fax 525-67-83) is at Reforma 276, on the corner of Copenhague. Rooms are not huge, but they're comfortable and pleasant enough, with typical top-end touches. The hotel sports two restaurants, a bar and two nightclubs. Rooms are US$118.75 Monday through Thursday but come down to just US$44.75 Friday through Sunday.

Hotel Marquis Reforma (☎ 211-36-00, in USA 800-223-6510; fax 211-55-61), Paseo de la Reforma 465, at Río de la Plata (metro: Sevilla), opened in 1991 with design and decor that draw from the city's rich art deco heritage and update it for the 21st century. It has lots of colored marble, well-trained multilingual staff, and facilities such as an outdoor spa with whirlpool baths. The 125 deluxe rooms and 85 lavish executive suites cost from US$275 to US$489.

María Isabel-Sheraton Hotel (☎ 207-39-33, in USA 800-325-3535; fax 207-06-84),

Paseo de la Reforma 325, at the Monumento a la Independencia (El Ángel), is older (1962), but as attractive and solidly comfortable as ever with spacious public rooms, excellent food and drink, nightly mariachi entertainment, and all the services of a top-class hotel, including pool, saunas, and two lighted tennis courts. The 752 deluxe rooms and suites offer all the comforts and start at US$287/305 for singles/doubles.

Other Zona Rosa hotels include:

Hotel Century (☎ 726-99-11, fax 525-74-75), Liverpool 152 – 142 small rooms in outspoken modern style for US$178, single or double

Hotel Krystal Rosa (☎ 228-99-28, fax 511-34-90), Liverpool 155 – a glitzy place with 302 plush rooms, many affording good city views; singles or doubles US$175 and up

Hotel Marco Polo (☎ 207-18-93, fax 533-37-27, marcopolo@data.net.mx), Amberes 27 – this trendy lodging attracts arts and entertainment types; 60 stylishly modern rooms at US$165, single or double

Hotel Westin Galería Plaza (☎ 230-17-17, fax 207-58-67), Hamburgo 195 – a classy hotel with a reputation for good, varied cuisine; 439 rooms at US$233 a single or double, except on weekends, when the price is halved

Polanco The Polanco area just north of Bosque de Chapultepec has some of the city's best business hotels – including three high-rises in a row along Campos Elíseos. They include the following (metro: Auditorio, unless stated):

Camino Real México (☎ 203-21-21, fax 250-68-97), Calzada General Escobedo 700 (metro: Chapultepec) – bold modern architecture, 713 rooms from US$212, single or double (Friday and Saturday US$88.75)

Hotel Nikko México (☎ 280-11-11, fax 280-91-91), Campos Elíseos 204 – a 746-room high-rise blending modern luxury with excellent service in a dramatically designed building; very comfortable standard rooms are US$287.50, single or double (US$155.25 weekends, including breakfast)

Hotel Presidente Inter-Continental (☎ 327-77-77/00, fax 327-77-83), Campos Elíseos 218 – has 'Centro Gourmet,' with seven varied high-quality restaurants, and 659 rooms from US$353.25

PLACES TO EAT

This cosmopolitan capital has eateries for all tastes and budgets, with plenty of European, North American, Argentine and Asian restaurants, as well as Mexican ones. Some of the best places are cheap, but some of the more expensive ones are well worth the extra money. In the few restaurants we describe as formal, men should wear a jacket and tie, and women something commensurate. Phone numbers are given for places where it's worth reserving a table.

The city's cheapest food is at the thousands of street stands – see Food in Facts for the Visitor for a word on these.

Chain Restaurants

The city is liberally provided with modern chain restaurants whose predictable food is a sound fallback if you fancy somewhere easy and reliable to eat. Prices may be slightly higher than you'd like, but many of these places are popular with both locals and visitors. Numerous branches of *VIPS* and the *Sanborn's* chain, with Mexican and international food and main dishes at around US$3.50 to US$6, can be found in affluent and touristed parts of the city such as the Zona Rosa, the Alameda area and Paseo de la Reforma.

Centro Histórico

Budget *Café El Popular*, just 1½ blocks west of the Zócalo at Avenida Cinco de Mayo 52, sharing a spot with the Hotel Zamora, is a good neighborhood place with tightly packed tables, open 24 hours a day. A second, newer branch at Avenida Cinco de Mayo 10 has the same menu, more space and bright yellow plastic furnishings. Both serve good breakfasts (fruit, eggs, frijoles, roll and coffee for US$1.80) and all sorts of other food, such as vegetarian fried rice or a quarter chicken with mole (both US$2.50). Good, strong café con leche is US$0.70.

Café La Blanca, Avenida Cinco de Mayo 40, west of Isabel la Católica, is big, always busy, and good for people-watching over a café con leche (US$1). Prices are

not the lowest, but you can have a three-course lunch for US$3.25. It's open every day from 6.30 am to 11.30 pm.

At *La Casa del Pavo*, three blocks west of the Zócalo at Motolinía 40A, chefs in white aprons slice roast turkeys all day long and serve them up at low prices. The four-course comida corrida is an excellent value at US$2.25, and there are turkey tacos and tortas, too. For bargain-basement food, wander up to the northern half of Motolinía, toward Allende metro station, where several big, bare eateries sell tacos, enchiladas and other Mexican snacks at low prices (around US$0.30 a taco).

Restaurante Madero, on Avenida Madero at Motolinía, is popular for its five-course lunch (US$4), which includes a choice of main courses such as mole poblano, paella or cabrito al horno (roast kid).

Vegetarian Restaurants To get to the *Restaurante El Vegetariano* go up a flight of stairs at Avenida Madero 56, west of La Palma. Don't be put off by the unimpressive entrance: upstairs are three busy, high-ceilinged rooms where a pianist plunks out old favorites as you dine. The food is tasty, filling, and an excellent value: five-course lunches go for US$2.75 or US$3.25. Breakfasts and à la carte main dishes are around US$2. It's open daily except Sunday from 8.30 am to 12.30 pm and 1.30 to 6.30 pm. There's also a more modern, street-level branch a few blocks away, at Mata 13.

Comedor Vegetariano, Motolinía 31, serves up a good US$2.75 comida daily from 1 to 5 pm.

Juice Bars *Jugos Canadá*, in the Hotel Canadá on Avenida Cinco de Mayo at 2a Cerrada de Cinco de Mayo, is good to pop into for a refreshing pure fruit juice, licuado, or fruit salad. A big orange or carrot juice, squeezed before your eyes, is yours for US$0.80; a 'cóctel biónico,' which includes five fruit juices, condensed milk, granola and cocoa, is US$1.30. *Super Soya*, on Tacuba opposite the end of Motolinía, is in a similar vein, with an array of gaudy colored signs listing all the varieties of juice, licuado, fruit salad, torta and taco it can manage. You could wash down a couple of vegetarian tacos at US$0.60 each with a 'Dracula' – mixed beet, pineapple, celery and orange juice (US$1.10). It's open Monday to Saturday 9 am to 9 pm, Sunday 10 am to 7 pm.

Bakeries & Pastry Shops There are always good snacks or light breakfast fare to be bought at *pastelerías* (pastry shops). You enter the pastelería, take a tray and tongs, fill the tray with what you like, and an attendant will price and bag it.

Pastelería Madrid, Cinco de Febrero 25 at El Salvador, 2½ blocks south of the Zócalo, is huge, with breads and pastries fresh from the ovens all the time. Open from 7.30 am, it has a café section where you can get a coffee with a croissant or Danish pastry for US$0.80.

Pastelería Ideal, 16 de Septiembre 14, west of Gante, looks fancy but its prices are still low. All the breads and rolls are at the back. Upstairs, Mexico's ultimate array of wedding cakes is on offer: this is the place to come if you need a US$300, multistory gâteau for your nuptials.

Middle & Top End Two eateries facing the northwest corner of the Zócalo have sidewalk tables for watching the city in action. *Shakey's Pizza y Pollo* does pizza slices for US$1.50 to US$3, or whole pies for US$5 or more – also burgers, chicken nuggets and so on. *Flash Taco* offers Mexican and Tex-Mex staples (two tacos US$1 to US$3, fajitas US$4).

For an even better view, head up to the *Restaurante Terraza*, which overlooks the Zócalo from the 7th floor of the Hotel Majestic, at Avenida Madero 73. Monday to Friday there's a set lunch for US$4, but you can have something lighter or à la carte if you wish.

Facing the Catedral Metropolitana, at Tacuba 87 on the corner of Monte de Piedad, the amiable *Restaurante México Viejo* sports bright blue tablecloths and sepia photos of old Mexico City and

serves up decent Mexican and international food, from fettuccine Montezuma (pasta with a huitlacoche sauce, US$3.50) to steaks for around US$7; there's also a four-course *menú ejecutivo* lunch for US$6. It's open Monday to Saturday 8 am to 9.30 pm, Sunday 10 am to 6 pm.

Bertico Café, Avenida Madero 66, less than a block from the Zócalo, is a bright continental-style newcomer, serving pasta dishes for US$4.50, baguettes for US$2, and good coffee.

Café de Tacuba, Tacuba 28, just west of the Allende metro station, is a gem of old-time Mexico City, opened in 1912. Colored tiles, brass lamps and oil paintings set the mood. The cuisine is traditional Mexican and delicious. There's a five-course prix fixe lunch for US$7.75. À la carte, main dishes are US$4 to US$6.50. It's open daily 8 am to 11.30 pm.

Hostería de Santo Domingo, Belisario Domínguez 72, six blocks northwest of the Zócalo, is small but intense. Handicrafts crowd the walls and ceiling, and good, unusual regional cooking fills the menu and the customers. Three-course à la carte meals cost US$10 to US$12, though you could eat for US$6 or so. If you want somewhere atmospheric, this is it. Come any day between 9 am and 10.30 am. A pianist or trio plays from 3 pm.

Restaurante Jampel, Bolívar 8, north of Avenida Cinco de Mayo, is a large cafeteria with quick, smooth service and three-course comidas priced at US$3.25 to US$6, plus an à la carte menu. Daily except Saturday a US$3 lunch buffet is served in the room upstairs at the back. Jampel is open Monday to Saturday 7.30 am to 11 pm, Sunday 1 to 6 pm.

Several hotels have good-value restaurants. Two bright, very popular ones are at the *Hotel Catedral*, Donceles 95, a block north of the cathedral, with breakfasts from US$1.60 to US$3 and a set-price lunch for US$4.25, and the *Restaurante-Bar Maple* at the Hotel Roble, Uruguay 109, two blocks south of the Zócalo, where a four-course lunch costs US$3 or US$3.50.

Near the Alameda Central
Budget One of the prettiest, most peaceful restaurants in the city is the *Cafetería del Claustro* (Cloister Café), in the Museo Franz Mayer, opposite the north side of the Alameda at Avenida Hidalgo 45. The museum and café are open Tuesday to Sunday from 10 am to 5 pm: if you want to visit only the café, you need a US$0.30 ticket for the cloister. Marble-top tables are set in the lovely courtyard, with recorded baroque music setting the mood. The good, self-service food includes sandwiches, salads and quiche for US$0.60 to US$1.60; there are also juices, coffee, yogurt, and excellent cakes at US$1.10.

Facing the west side of the Alameda, *Café Trevi*, on Dr Mora, is a good, popular Italian and Mexican restaurant open daily from 8 am to 11.30 pm. It serves breakfasts till noon for US$1.70 to US$2.75, and its six-course set-price daily meal costs just US$2.75. Pasta dishes and one-person pizzas range from US$2.75 to US$4.

One block south of the southeast corner of the Alameda there's a cluster of bright, inexpensive eateries around the intersection of Independencia and López. Pick of the bunch is the clean, bustling *Taquería Tlaquepaque*, at Independencia 4, east of López. Bow-tied waiters serve up several dozen types of taco, priced at US$1 to US$2.75 a trio. Try the delicious chuletas, nopales y queso variety (chopped pork, cactus tips and cheese), at the top of the range.

Not far away, at Luis Moya 41, is *Los Faroles*. Beneath the brick arches, white-aproned señoras ladle steaming caldo (stew) from huge earthenware *cazuelas* (cooking pots) and prepare authentic and tasty tacos and enchiladas. The dining room can be dark and hot, but prices are low. There's a five-course comida corrida for just US$2. Hours are from 8 am to 7 pm every day.

For cheap eats close to the Palacio de Bellas Artes, head to the intersection of Eje Central Lázaro Cárdenas and Donceles, where *Restaurant El Correo* (its awning actually says *Antojitos Mexicanos, La Casa de la Birria*) serves a wide variety of tacos – from US$0.20 each for the cheapest fillings up to US$2 for three superior tacos. Next door is *Frutería Frutivida*, with lots of fresh juices, licuados, fruit salads, tortas – and more tacos. There are several other inexpensive *taquerías* (taco places) nearby, most open till 3 am.

For a taste of lingering Spanish influence in Mexico, you can't beat a dose of churros y chocolate. Churros are long, thin, deep-fried doughnuts, just made to be dipped in a cup of thick hot chocolate. A fine spot for this experience is *Churrería El Moro*, San Juan de Letrán 42, 2½ blocks south of the Torre Latinoamericana, where chocolate with four churros sets you back US$2.50. It's always open and often busy in the wee hours with people mellowing out after a night on the town.

Vegetarian Restaurants The *Centro Naturista de México*, Dolores 10B, half a block south of Avenida Juárez, is a health food shop with a vegetarian restaurant serving lunches of soup, main course, salad, dessert, bread, water and tea for US$1.30, or an all-you-can-eat buffet for US$2.50, every day from 12.30 to 5.30 pm.

Markets The best and freshest produce in the city is generally agreed to be at *Mercado San Juan*, on Pugibet west of Plaza de San Juan, 500 meters south of the Alameda, open daily from 9 am to 5 pm. Here you'll find rarities such as tofu or chapulines (grasshoppers), from Oaxaca, as well as good fruit, vegetables, cheese, meat and fish. It's not the cheapest market, but it does have a number of low-priced comedores (closed Sunday) where you can sit down for prepared meals: No 305-7 is a favorite for its pechuga empanizada (breaded chicken breast) and pollo con mole rojo; it also does a comida corrida for just US$1.60.

Middle & Top End *Sanborn's Casa de Azulejos*, Avenida Madero 4, is worth a visit just to see its superb 16th century tile-bedecked building (see the Centro Histórico section). The restaurant is in a courtyard around a Moorish-style fountain, with odd murals of mythical landscapes. The food is Mexican and good, if not exceptional, at about US$4 to US$7 per main dish. It's open daily 7.30 am to 10 pm.

Los Girasoles (☎ 510-06-30), on Plaza Tolsá, the space beside Tacuba in front of the Museo Nacional de Arte, is one of the best of a new wave of restaurants specializing in *alta cocina Mexicana* (Mexican haute cuisine). Recipes are either traditional or innovative, but all have a very Mexican flavor. You might start with a 'tricolor' (eggplant stuffed with spinach, cheese and a tomato sauce), and follow up with 'Sabados 1 a 3' (Sonora ranch-style beef medallions with chipotle sauce) or a Baja California-style shrimp and bacon stew. Starters and soups are mostly US$3 to US$5, main courses US$6.50 to US$8. Los Girasoles is open Monday to Saturday 1 pm to 1 am, Sunday 1 to 11 pm, and busy most of the time. There are pleasant outside tables as well as indoor seating.

Restaurant Danubio (☎ 512-09-12), Uruguay 3, at San Juan de Letrán, is a city tradition. It has been here, specializing in seafood, for half a century and still does it well. It serves a huge and excellent six-course set-price menú – including fish *and* meat courses – for US$9.25. Langosta (lobster) and langostinos (crayfish) are the specialties, but prices for them are stratospheric. The Danubio is open daily from 1 to 10 pm.

Restaurant Centro Castellano (☎ 518-29-37), close to the Danubio at Uruguay 16, is huge, occupying three floors of its building. The decor is colonial, and the long, varied menu includes several Spanish specialties such as paella, pulpo a la gallega (Galicia-style octopus) and fabiada asturiana (Asturias-style bean and meat stew), all between US$6 and US$7.75. The six-course comida corrida costs US$8.50. Hours are daily 1 to 10 pm (1 to 7 pm on Sunday).

Mexico City has a small Chinatown district centered on Calle Dolores south of the Alameda. One of the best restaurants on the street is the small and attractive *Hong King*, Dolores 25, with set-price meals from US$5.25 to US$10.50 per person (minimum two people) and menus in Chinese, Spanish and English. It's open daily 11.30 am to 11 pm.

Near Plaza de la República

There are several small, homey, neighborhood restaurants here. *Restaurante Samy*, Ignacio Mariscal 42, just southwest of the Hotel Jena, doesn't look like much from the outside, but inside it's clean and pleasant, offering fixed-price breakfasts for US$1.10 to US$2 and a four-course comida corrida for US$2.25.

Restaurant Cahuich, Ramos Arizpe 30, at Édison, is a good, clean little neighborhood place where a breakfast of juice, eggs and coffee, or a comida of soup, rice or pasta and a meat main course, will set you back just US$1.60. There's well-priced à la carte fare too, and it's open daily from 8 am to 12.30 am.

Another pair of decent, basic little eateries sits side by side on Iglesias at Ignacio Mariscal. *Super Cocina Los Arcos* can prepare bisteck various ways from just US$1.30, or three tacos for US$2, or tortas, eggs, juices, licuados or other staples. Next door, *Restaurante Costillas El Sitio* does breakfasts of eggs or bisteck with chilaquiles, frijoles, coffee and tortillas or bread for just US$1.10. Across the corner is *Super Tortas Gigantes*, serving tasty hot tortas with fillings of ham, egg, cheese and so on for US$1.30; they also have tacos, sincronizadas, juices and licuados.

A great place for a quick lunch is the *seafood cocktail stand* on Emparán just north of Édison. It has stood here daily (except Sunday) for at least a decade and includes many office workers in suits among its regular customers. A *mediano* (medium-size) prawn or crab cocktail at US$2.25 is filling.

About 100 meters south of Plaza de la República on Ramírez, next door to a branch of VIPS, *Tacos El Caminero* is a busy, slightly upscale taco joint doling out three good tacos for US$2.25, or six for US$3.50. There's *cerveza de barril* (draft beer) at US$1.10 a mug. El Caminero's hours are Monday to Friday 10 am to 1 am, Saturday 1 pm to 1 am, Sunday 1 to 11 pm.

Near Estación Buenavista

El Portón, out the front of the station and across Mosqueta, serves Mexican food at moderate prices (breakfasts or light dishes US$2.25 to US$3.50, main dishes US$3.50 to US$5.75). Across Insurgentes from El Portón is a branch of *Shakey's Pizza y Pollo*.

Zona Rosa

The Zona Rosa is packed with places to eat and drink. Some streets are closed to traffic, making the sidewalk cafés very pleasant.

Budget The cheapest meals of all are at the *Mercado Insurgentes*, on Londres. One corner of this crafts market is given over to typical Mexican market *comedores*, serving up hot lunches daily to customers who sit on benches in front of the cooks and their stoves. You'll find many of the same typical Mexican dishes as you would in restaurants, but at much lower prices – around US$1.70 for a comida corrida. Pick a comedor that's busy.

A bit further west along Londres are the area's most economical restaurants, the best of them packed with customers at lunchtime. *Ricocina*, at No 168, does a three-course comida including drinks for US$2.50, and breakfasts such as juice, coffee, and eggs, hotcakes, or French toast for US$1.60. At No 178, *Restaurante Don Luca's* does a good comida for US$2. The four-course comida at *La Beatricita*, Londres 190D, includes drinks and offers lots of main course choices, for US$3.

Near the hub of the Zona Rosa, *Taco Inn*, Hamburgo 96, opposite Copenhague, is a branch of a cheery chain eatery turning out more than 30 taco choices from US$1.30 to US$3.25 a serve.

Middle *Konditori*, Génova 61, between Londres and Hamburgo, serves a mixture of Italian, Scandinavian and Mexican fare

in its elegant small dining rooms and spacious sidewalk café, which is a great place to observe the passing parade on the Zona Rosa's busiest pedestrian street. Pasta or good crepa (pancake) dishes cost around US$5, meat or fish US$7 or so. Coffee is US$1.20. There are good cakes and pastries too. It's open daily 8 am to 11.30 pm.

Parri, Hamburgo 154, between Amberes and Avenida Florencia, is a busy, barnlike place serving grilled beef, pork and chicken in various ways – from tacos to steaks or whole birds. Chefs tend the grill and waiters scurry about. Three tacos cost US$1.70, but you're more likely to spend US$4 to US$8. It's open Monday to Thursday 9 am to 1 am, Friday and Saturday 8 am to 3 am, and Sunday 9 am to midnight.

If Japanese food is your fancy, try *Sushi Itto*, Hamburgo at Estocolmo, a branch of a no-fuss, popular little chain eatery with moderately priced sushi and sashimi and combination meals from US$5.25 to US$11.

The pleasant, modern *Café Jardín*, attached to the Hotel Calinda Geneve, Londres 130, does a reasonable-value US$6.50 buffet lunch, as well as à la carte fare from burgers or enchiladas (around US$3.50) to meat or fish (from US$4.50 to US$7.75).

The straightforward *Pizza Pronto*, on Hamburgo just east of Génova, serves up acceptable one-person pizzas for US$3.75 to US$6, two-person size for US$4.75 to US$8.75 and pasta for US$3 to US$4.75.

Freedom, at Copenhague 25 – on a street full of generally more expensive restaurants – is both a lively bar (see Bars, in Entertainment) and a restaurant serving good US-style and Tex-Mex fare like barbecued ribs, nachos, pasta, burgers, salads and chicken. Most main dishes are between US$5 and US$6.50.

Carrousel Internacional, Niza 33, at Hamburgo, is a lively bar/restaurant with mariachis performing energetically most of the time. Come for spaghetti or a salad (around US$3.25), a grill or fish (US$5.25) or a drink, and enjoy the music. It's open daily from 11.30 am to midnight.

MEXICO CITY

Chalet Suizo, Niza 37, between Hamburgo and Londres, has dependably good food served in pseudo-Swiss rusticity. They have fondues (US$5.75 to US$9 for two), pasta plates (US$4) and a range of meat dishes between US$4.75 and US$7.50, including pig's knuckles with sauerkraut and duck in orange sauce. Full meals will cost around US$8 to US$14. It's open daily 12.30 to 11.45 pm.

Across the street at Niza 38, *Luaú* is an elaborate Chinese-Polynesian fantasy with fountains and miniature gardens. The best bargains are the set-price Cantonese meals at US$5 to US$7 per person. It's open Monday to Thursday noon to 10 pm, Friday and Saturday noon to midnight.

Vegetarian Restaurants The good *Restaurante Vegetariano Yug*, Varsovia 3, just south of Reforma, does a lunch buffet (upstairs) for US$3.75 from 1 to 5 pm daily except Saturday, and daily four-course comidas corridas (downstairs), with good whole-wheat bread, for US$2.50 or US$3.25. The clientele are mostly local office workers. Hours are Monday to Friday 7 am to 10 pm, Saturday 8.30 am to 8 pm, Sunday 1 to 8 pm.

A couple of blocks outside the Zona Rosa, *Restaurante Vegetariano Las Fuentes*, Río Pánuco 127, at Río Tíber, is big and attractive, serving tasty food in big portions. Full meals of soup, salad bar, main course and a drink cost US$6.50; big breakfasts are US$3.75. Wine and beer are served too. It's open daily 8 am to 6 pm.

Tearooms The Zona Rosa has two fine tearooms serving good drinks, pastries, breakfasts and light meals.

Auseba, Hamburgo 159B, east of Avenida Florencia, has glass cases filled with enticing sweet offerings and large windows for watching Hamburgo go by. Most cakes and pastries are around US$2 each, but you can get a pan danés (Danish pastry) for US$0.70. Tea or coffee is about US$1.20.

Salón de Te Duca d'Este, at Hamburgo 164B, almost facing the Auseba, has

formal decor, polite service and some delicious cakes. A tea or coffee and a pastry, cake or cookies costs US$2.75 or more. A breakfast is around the same price, or there's a four-course lunch for US$5. Hours are from 7 am to 11 pm every day.

Top End One of the Zona Rosa's busiest restaurant strips is Copenhague, a short street lined with bustling upscale eateries. At Copenhague 31, right on the corner of Hamburgo, the *Angus Butcher House* (☎ 207-68-80) serves some of the best steaks in the city, for which you can pay anywhere from US$8 to US$32, and it's always packed. There's a good outdoor area under an awning, as well as indoor tables. It's open daily from 1 pm to 1 am.

Also good and popular on Copenhague are the *Mesón del Perro Andaluz* (☎ 533-53-06), serving meat and seafood – with some Spanish dishes, as the name suggests – on the east side of the street, and *El Perro d'Enfrente* (☎ 511-89-37), opposite, with good Italian food. Main dishes in both are mostly in the US$6.50 to US$9.50 range (though pasta and pizza at d'Enfrente are a little cheaper).

La Taba (☎ 208-74-36), Amberes 12, is a good Argentine steak house; steaks are around US$9.25, but salads and pasta go for US$5 or less. It's open Monday to Friday 1 to 10 pm, Saturday and Sunday from 1 to 6 pm. Across the street at Amberes 27, *Il Caffe Milano*, at the Hotel Marco Polo, serves up good Italian food amid stylishly Italian design, with some sidewalk tables. You pay US$5 to US$8.50 for pasta, meat or seafood main dishes. It's open daily from 8 am to 2 am.

Condesa
This pleasant area south of the Zona Rosa has a number of small bistro-type restaurants and coffee bars where you can enjoy good food in a relaxed atmosphere among a mainly local crowd. *Fonda Garufa*, Avenida Michoacán 93, just east of Vicente Suárez, serves up a big range of pasta for US$3.50 to US$5, as well as salads, chicken and meat; it's open daily

from 1 to 11 pm or later. *Mama Rosa's* and *Café La Gloria*, both on the Michoacán/Vicente Suárez intersection, are in a similar vein. *Creperie de la Paix*, also on the same intersection, is popular for its variety of sweet and savory crepes from US$1.60 to US$3. *Principio*, a couple of blocks northeast, at Avenida Tamaulipas and Montes de Oca, is good for varied Mediterranean food, from lentil soup with banana at US$1.90 to tabbouleh at US$2.75, couscous for US$5, or pasta for US$4.25.

Good for a coffee or something light to eat is *El Péndulo*, at Avenida Nuevo León 115, which is combined with a bookstore and music store that sometimes has live music; it's open daily from 9 am (10 am Saturday and Sunday) to 10 pm.

Chapultepec & Polanco
Budget & Middle There's a reasonable cafeteria inside the *Museo Nacional de Antropología* with hours the same as the museum's, but it's not cheap: a lunch buffet costs US$6.25 (excluding drinks), and individual Mexican and international main dishes are mostly between US$4 and US$6.50. The nearest cheap food is at *Café Capuchino*, beside Calzada Gandhi, 100 meters north of the museum entrance – a basic, open-air eatery with tortas at US$1.10 or chicken, frijoles and fries at US$2.50.

For something meaty, a good economical choice in Polanco is *La Parrilla Suiza*, on the traffic circle at Avenida Presidente Masaryk and Arquímedes. It gets packed at lunchtime. A chicken alambre (kebab on a skewer), served with sausage, Swiss cheese, rice, salad and frijoles, costs US$3.50; larger grills are around US$6, or there are set meals for US$3 or US$3.50. It's open daily noon till midnight or later.

Café de Tacuba, Newton 88, northeast of the intersection with Arquímedes, is a pleasant little place with colored windows, a beamed ceiling and a bit of character, serving Mexican and international fare. Polanco metro station is 2½ blocks away.

Set-price lunches cost US$3.50 or US$6.50, and good breakfasts are served too.

For other moderately priced fare, head for the string of sidewalk cafés on Avenida Presidente Masaryk between Dumas and France.

Top End The *Hard Rock Café* (☎ 327-71-00), Campos Elíseos 290, at Paseo de la Reforma, is favored by groups of Mexicans, plus a few foreigners, who come to enjoy the background rock music, rock-paraphernalia decor, lively scene and good burgers (around US$7). Grills cost US$8 and up. Hours are 1 pm to 2 am daily, and it's always busy, but you should be able to walk in before about 6 pm.

Cambalache (☎ 280-20-80), Arquímedes 85, just north of Avenida Presidente Masaryk, is a cozy Argentine steak house, serving up great steaks from US$10.50, chicken around US$7.75 and pasta around US$5. You might like to try the soufflé French fries (!) for US$4. There's an ample wine list too. Cambalache is open daily from 1 pm to 1 am.

La Hacienda de los Morales (☎ 281-45-54), Vázquez de Mella 525, is about 1.5 km northwest of the middle of Polanco, just south of Avenida Ejército Nacional. It's easiest to get there by taxi. Once a grand colonial country house, it's now surrounded by the city, which makes the spacious rooms and pretty gardens all the more appealing. Excellent Mexican, American and European dishes are served in numerous dining rooms by experienced waiters. A full meal costs around US$12 to US$20. Reservations are advisable, and dress is formal. It's open daily from 1 pm to 1 am.

Polanco's luxury hotels contain some of the city's best restaurants – among them three French highlights, all open from Monday to Saturday: *Maxim's de Paris* (☎ 327-77-00), in the Hotel Presidente Inter-Continental, Campos Elíseos 218; *Les Célébrités* (☎ 280-11-11), in the Hotel Nikko México, Campos Elíseos 204; and *Fouquet's de Paris* (☎ 203-21-21), in the Camino Real México, Calzada General

Escobedo 700. All are formal, with reservations recommended, and a full dinner at any of them runs US$30 to US$50 (maybe more at Maxim's).

San Ángel

Budget & Middle *La Casona del Elefante*, next door to the Bazar Sábado at Plaza San Jacinto 9, is an Indian restaurant with a few pleasant outdoor tables, and is not a bad value, with a tali (vegetarian plate) at US$3.75 or chicken curry for US$3.50. You may have to wait a while for a table on Saturdays.

The nameless little *comedor* on the east side of Plaza San Jacinto, next to the unremarkable Café La Finca, offers a good comida corrida for US$1.90 or US$3.25, and on weekends great caldo de camarón (prawn soup) for US$2.50 or US$3.75. *Croque-Monsieur*, down toward the Avenida Revolución end of Madero, near the Plaza del Carmen, does good hot baguettes with cheese and other fillings for around US$3.50.

San Ángel's most famous café is upstairs in the *Gandhi* bookstore at Avenida M A de Quevedo 128 to 132, 400 meters east of Parque de la Bombilla. Customers linger over coffee, snacks, books, newspapers and chess in this haunt of Mexico City's intelligentsia. It's open Monday to Friday 9 am to 9 pm, Saturday and Sunday 10 am to 8 pm. The M A de Quevedo metro station is one block away.

Top End On the north side of Plaza San Jacinto, *La Camelia* is the liveliest place on the square, with people waiting in line to enjoy its expensive seafood and trendy atmosphere.

For fancier meals, head for the *San Ángel Inn* (☎ 616-22-22), Diego Rivera 50, at Avenida Altavista, one km northwest of Plaza San Jacinto. This is a lovely ex-hacienda transformed into a restaurant serving delicious traditional Mexican and European cuisine. If you order carefully you can eat two courses for US$8, but you could easily spend US$25 or more on a full meal. It's open daily from 1 pm to 1 am.

Coyoacán

Many places are on or near Coyoacán's central plazas. For cheap Mexican snacks, leave Plaza Hidalgo along Higuera. The municipal building on the left is filled with stands charging US$0.60 apiece for quesadillas with various tasty fillings. Or go half a block north to Aguayo 3, where the cheerful, bustling *El Tizoncito* serves up several varieties of taco at US$0.70 each. One excellent choice here is nopalqueso (cactus tips and cheese).

There are several pleasant sidewalk cafés around the Jardín del Centenario. *Café El Parnaso*, on the south side, has a bookstore in the back. Good burritos and ham-and-cheese croissants cost US$3.25. It's open daily from 9 am to 10 pm. On the north side are *El Hijo del Cuervo*, a fashionable café/bar with a young clientele, and *Los Bigotes de Villa*, with outdoor and indoor tables, offering enchiladas, quesadillas or chile relleno for US$2.25.

Restaurante Caballocalco, at Higuera 2 facing the east side of Plaza Hidalgo, is a touch more refined, but still relaxed and not too expensive, with good food. Soups are around US$2.50, meat and seafood mostly US$4 to US$5. It's open daily from 8.30 am to 11 pm.

On the corner of Coyoacán's main market, on Allende 2½ blocks north of Plaza Hidalgo, is the excellent and very popular *El Jardín del Pulpo* (The Octopus' Garden), which serves fish platters at US$5.25 and seafood cocktails at US$2.50 or US$4.75. Everyone sits on benches at long tables.

ENTERTAINMENT

There's a vast choice of entertainment in Mexico City, as a glance through *Tiempo Libre*, the city's wide-ranging what's-on magazine, will show. *Tiempo Libre* is published every Thursday and sold at newsstands for US$0.70. Even with limited Spanish, it's not too hard to work out what's going on, from music and movies to exhibitions and lots of entertainment for children. *The News* and the *Mexico City Times* also carry some arts and entertainment listings.

Dance, Classical Music & Theater

The *Palacio de Bellas Artes* (☎ 512-25-93, 529-93-20), beside the Alameda Central, is home to the Orquesta Sinfónica Nacional (National Symphony Orchestra) and a main venue for classical music in general, but its most famous show is the Ballet Folklórico de México, a two-hour festive blur of colored lights and costumes, music, and dance from all over Mexico. This famous company has been performing such shows for decades. Tickets are expensive, however, at US$12 to US$29. Performances are normally on Wednesday at 8.30 pm, Sunday at 9.30 am and 8.30 pm. Tickets are usually available the day of or the day before the show at the *taquillas* (ticket windows) in the Bellas Artes lobby, open Monday to Saturday 11 am to 7 pm, Sunday 9 am to 7 pm. Travel agencies and hotels also have tickets but mark up the prices.

A second Mexican folk dance spectacular, cheaper but said to be just as good, is staged twice a week by the *Ballet Folklórico Nacional de México Aztlán*, based at the Teatro de la Ciudad, Donceles 36 (☎ 521-23-55; metro: Allende).

The city also offers a big choice of other classical concerts, ballet and contemporary dance, as well as Spanish-language theater. Check *Tiempo Libre*.

Cinema

Many non-Mexican movies are dubbed into Spanish, though some have subtitles. Tickets are usually around US$2, half-price in most cinemas on Wednesdays. Classic and art-house films are shown at the *Cineteca Nacional* (☎ 688-32-72), at Avenida México-Coyoacán 389, 700 meters east of the Coyoacán metro station; at *cineclubes* in the *Centro Cultural Universitario* (☎ 665-25-80) at the Ciudad Universitaria; and elsewhere. *Tiempo Libre* carries full listings.

Mariachis

Plaza Garibaldi, five blocks north of the Palacio de Bellas Artes (metro: Bellas Artes or Garibaldi), is where the city's mariachi bands gather in the evenings. Outfitted in their fancy costumes, they tune their guitars and stand around with a drink until approached by someone who's ready to pay for a song (about US$5) or whisk them away to entertain at a party. You can wander and listen to the mariachis in the plaza for free and stay on in one of the bars or clubs around the plaza, some of which have live Latin dance music as a change from the mariachis. The bars usually have no entry fee but charge around US$2 for a shot of tequila or US$20 for a bottle.

El Tenampa bar, on the north side of the plaza, has in-house mariachis and is daubed with murals of famous mariachi musicians. For food, you can find taquerías in the northeast corner of the plaza.

Don't bring valuables to Plaza Garibaldi, and look out for pickpockets. The place gets going by about 8 pm and stays busy till around midnight.

Nightlife

Try to check not only cover charges but also drink prices before you enter a club or fancy bar.

SUSAN KAYE

There are dozens of live music venues around the city. For rock and pop concerts, check the 'Espectáculos Nocturnos' and 'Espectáculos Populares' sections in *Tiempo Libre*.

Centro Histórico & Alameda Area

A number of buzzing, youthful music bars have sprung up in the past few years in the Centro Histórico, and there's a convenient cluster of them around the corner of Mata and Avenida Cinco de Mayo (metro: Bellas Artes or Allende). Pick of the bunch is *Bar Mata* (☎ 518-02-37), on the 4th floor at Mata 11. It's full of beautiful people but has a casual atmosphere, and it has good music and a roof terrace with great views over nocturnal Mexico City. Most drinks are around US$2.75, and there's no cover charge. It's open Tuesday to Thursday 8 pm to 1 am, Friday to Saturday 8 pm to 2 am. Thursday is gay and lesbian night.

A few doors away, at Mata 17, trendy *Bar Roco* (☎ 521-33-05) has a selective door policy, kitschy décor and varied dance music. It's open daily from 8 pm (men US$6.50, women free). *Bar Museo* (☎ 510-40-20), entered from an arcade off Avenida Cinco de Mayo just west of Mata, is another jumping place, with enough space for dancing if the mood takes you. It's open Thursday to Saturday 10 pm to 2 am (men US$6.50, women free).

A rather different type of place, much less flashy but still lively, is the little *Restaurante-Bar León* (☎ 510-30-93), at Brasil 5 (metro: Allende or Zócalo). Live salsa, merengue and rumba rhythms drive customers to the tightly packed dance floor. Open Wednesday to Saturday from 9 pm to 3 am, it has a cover charge of US$4.75; drinks are US$2.25 and up.

La Ópera Bar, Avenida Cinco de Mayo 14, a block east of the Palacio de Bellas Artes (metro: Bellas Artes), is an ornate early 20th century watering hole that opened its doors to women in the 1970s. Dark wood booths and a massive bar are all original, and there's a hole in the gilded ceiling said to have been made by a bullet from Pancho Villa. Drinks cost US$1.50

and up, lots of food is served at middling prices, and musicians serenade the tables. It's a fun place to spend a couple of hours, open Monday to Saturday 1 to 11 pm, Sunday 1 to 6 pm.

Zona Rosa & Nearby

The biggest magnet for night owls is the glitzy Zona Rosa (metro: Insurgentes). This is where the city's non-poor converge for a good time. Friday and Saturday are the busiest nights, peaking from about 11 pm to 2 or 3 am.

Bars You can start an evening here with a meal in one of the many restaurants, or a drink in one of the numerous cafés or bars. *Cantina Las Bohemias*, on Londres west of Amberes, is a bright, jolly one, popular with women as well as men, as it's not a *real* cantina. A beer is US$0.80, spirits US$1.30 and up. *El Chato*, Londres 117 east of Amberes, has a calm if smoky piano bar, open nightly except Sunday from 6 pm.

Freedom, Copenhague 25, gets packed in the evening with a youngish after-work crowd. It has at least three bars on two levels, plays loud disco music, and is fun. A beer is US$1.90. There's just enough room to dance upstairs, and downstairs there's good food. Another popular but more expensive bar-cum-restaurant is *Yuppie's Sports Bar*, Génova 34, at Hamburgo.

Live Music *Casa Rasta*, on Avenida Florencia, is open Wednesday to Sunday from about 10 pm to 3 am, thumping out reggae all the time, with a live band Thursday to Saturday nights from about 12.30 am. It pulls in an international crowd and is fun – but it's not a place for the penniless: entry is US$13 for men and free for women, rising to US$18.25 and US$4 on Friday and Saturday. Drinks are free, at least.

The *Carrousel Internacional* restaurant/bar, Niza 33 at Hamburgo (see Places to Eat), has mariachis singing energetically most of the time.

Outside the Zona Rosa proper, *Bulldog Café* (☎ 566-81-77), Insurgentes Centro 149, at Sullivan, two blocks north of Reforma, is a fairly trendy club playing good music, ranging from U2 to Mexican bands such as Café Tacuba. It's open Thursday to Saturday 10 pm to 4 am, with live bands around 1 to 2.30 am. Entry is a hefty US$18.25 for men, free for women, and drinks are free. Spot Bulldog by its five entrance columns, on Sullivan next to a yellow 'Farmacia' sign.

Discos *Rockstock* (☎ 533-09-07), on the southwest side of the Reforma/Niza intersection, is the premier Zona Rosa disco. Open Thursday to Saturday 10.30 pm to 4 am, it plays mainly rock and disco, often with live bands. Officially there's no dress code, but if there's a big crowd waiting to get in, the bouncers may look unfavorably on sneakers. It attracts an international crowd, and entry is usually US$15.75 for men, US$2.75 for women, with free drinks.

Mekano (☎ 208-95-11), Génova 44, has a more techno sound and a younger crowd. It's open Wednesday to Saturday 9.30 pm to 3 or 4 am, with a cover of US$5.25 on Wednesday and Thursday (when you pay for drinks), and US$15.75 for men, free for women, on Friday and Saturday, when drinks are free.

There are several more discos and music bars around the Zona Rosa, especially on Niza and Avenida Florencia. Places you'll probably want to avoid are the 'ladies' bars' and 'table dance' clubs, which touts try to talk men into. These apparently are striptease joints, also with women who will dance with male customers for a fee.

Southern Suburbs For free entertainment, you can't beat the musicians, comedians and mimes who turn Coyoacán's central plazas into a big open-air party most evenings and all day Saturday and Sunday. There are also good cafés and bars around the plaza where you can take in the atmosphere. *El Hijo del Cuervo*, with a youngish student/arty crowd, plays a mixture of Latin music and US rock and stages occasional theatrical or musical entertainment. A beer is US$1.60, tequila from US$2.25. It's open daily from 1 pm to 2 am. *Los Bigotes de Villa*, next door,

has fairly gentle live music (ballads or classical) Friday to Sunday at 10.30 pm.

El Ángel, at Tres Cruces 95 in Coyoacán, is a funky little bar with good and varied music – rock, reggae, disco – and a studenty, mainly Mexican crowd. It's open Wednesday to Sunday nights till 2 am and has just enough space for a bit of dancing. There's no sign – the building is white and blue outside, black inside. A beer is around US$1.20.

In San Ángel, *New Orleans Jazz* (☎ 550-19-08), Avenida Revolución 1655, serves up good mainstream jazz Tuesday to Saturday from 9 pm. It's a restaurant too (spaghetti, crepes, chicken all US$3.50 to US$5, meat dishes around US$7), and popular with business folk. There's a cover charge of US$4 if you don't dine.

See the earlier Coyoacán and San Ángel sections for how to reach these suburbs.

Dance Halls The city's many Latin dance aficionados have their choice of a whole circuit of large glitzy dance halls (*salones de baile*), some capable of holding thousands of people. You need to dress up a little and know how to dance salsa, merengue, cumbia or danzón to really enjoy these places, and it's best to go in a group, or at least with someone to dance with. One of the best is *Antillanos* (☎ 592-04-39), Pimentel 78, at Velázquez de León in Colonia San Rafael, 1.5 km north of the Zona Rosa (metro: San Cosme). Top bands from Mexico, Cuba and sometimes Puerto Rico or Colombia grind out infectious rhythms Thursday to Saturday from 9 pm to 3 am. Entry is US$6.50, and men without partners aren't admitted. Tequila, rum and whisky are served by the bottle at around US$25. Other salones de baile include:

Meneo (☎ 523-94-48), Nueva York 315, just west of Insurgentes Sur – salsa and merengue bands Tuesday to Sunday 9 pm to 3 am; entry around US$8, jacket required for men; take a 'San Ángel' pesero five km south from Insurgentes metro station

Mocamboo, Puebla 191, just west of Avenida Oaxaca (metro: Insurgentes) – Thursday to Saturday 9 pm to 4 am; entry US$6.50, drinks from US$2.75

Gay & Lesbian Nightspots The biggest, busiest gay men's disco is *Butterfly* (☎ 761-13-51), at Izazaga 5, a few steps east of Avenida Lázaro Cárdenas (metro: Salto del Agua). With a packed dance floor and lighting wizardry, it's open nightly from 9 pm to 4 am, with transvestite shows Friday and Saturday. The US$4.75 cover includes two drinks.

El Taller, Avenida Florencia 37 in the Zona Rosa, is a long-established gay men's disco/bar, less loud and techno-ish than Butterfly. It's open daily except Monday from 9 pm to 4 am, with 'rave' nights on Friday for US$9.25 (free drinks), and a cover of US$4 on Thursday, Saturday and Sunday (free Tuesday and Wednesday). On Tuesdays 'Los Martes del Taller' involve improvised musical, dance and theater shows, and discussions.

Enigma (☎ 207-73-67), Morelia 111 in Colonia Roma, 700 meters south of Cuauhtémoc metro, is a lesbian disco/bar with regular transvestite shows. It's open Tuesday to Saturday 9 pm to 3.30 am, Sunday 6 pm to 2 am. Entry ranges from free to US$3.25, depending on the night (Wednesday by invitation only).

Bar Mata (see Centro Histórico & Alameda Area, earlier in this section) reserves Thursday night for lesbians and gays.

Tiempo Libre magazine has a gay section with information on other venues, and a fuller version of its listings is available on the Internet.

SPECTATOR SPORTS
Soccer (Football)
The capital stages two or three matches in the national Primera División almost every weekend from August to May. *The News* and the *Mexico City Times* carry details on upcoming games. The Mexico City team América, nicknamed Las Águilas (the Eagles), is easily the most popular in the country and usually one of the best. Las Pumas, of UNAM, come second in popularity in the capital, with Cruz Azul (known as Los Cementeros) third.

The biggest crowds flock to games between any two of América, Las Pumas, Cruz Azul, and Guadalajara (Las Chivas), which is the biggest club outside the capital. The biggest match of all is 'El Superclásico,' between América and Guadalajara, which fills the awesome Estadio Guillermo Cañedo (formerly Estadio Azteca, see below) with 100,000 flag-waving fans – an occasion surprising for the friendliness of the rivalry between the two bands of supporters. This is about the only game of the year in the capital where you need to get a ticket in advance.

Most big matches are played at the *Estadio Guillermo Cañedo* (☎ 617-80-80), Calzada de Tlalpan 3465. The metro to Tasqueña station, then the Tren Ligero (streetcar) from Tasqueña to Estadio Azteca station, is the easiest way to reach the stadium from central Mexico City. The Pumas' home is the Estadio Olímpico, at the Ciudad Universitaria, and Cruz Azul's is the Estadio Azul, next door to the Monumental Plaza México, the city's main bullring (see Bullfights). Tickets for games are usually available at the gate right up to kickoff; prices range from less than US$1 to about US$10.

Bullfights
The *Monumental Plaza México* (☎ 563-39-61), a deep concrete bowl holding 48,000 spectators, is one of the largest bullrings in the world. It's at Augusto Rodin 241, a few blocks west of Avenida Insurgentes Sur, 5.5 km south of Paseo de la Reforma (metro: San Antonio).

If you're not put off by the very idea, a *corrida de toros* (bullfight) is quite a spectacle, from the milling throngs and hawkers outside the arena beforehand to the pageantry and drama in the ring itself and the crowd response it provokes. Six bulls are usually fought in an afternoon, two each by three matadors.

From October to March or April, professional fights are held at the Monumental every Sunday, starting at 4.30 pm. From June to October, junior matadors fight young bulls. *The News* carries a bullfighting column, 'Blood on the Sand,' on Saturdays, which will tell you what's in store.

The taquillas (ticket windows) by the bullring's main entrance on Augusto Rodin have printed lists of ticket prices. The cheapest seats, less than US$2, are in the Sol General section – the top tiers of seating on the sunny side of the arena. These are OK if the weather's not too hot – and many of them fall into shade as the afternoon goes on, in any case. The Sombra General – the top tiers on the shady side – costs slightly more. The best seats are in the Barreras, the seven rows nearest the arena, and normally cost US$17 to US$26. Between the Barreras and the General sections are first the Primer (1er) Tendido, then the Segundo (2o) Tendido.

Except for the biggest corridas, tickets are available right up to the time the third bull is killed, though the best may sell out early. You can buy advance tickets Thursday to Saturday from 9.30 am to 1 pm and 3.30 to 7 pm, and Sunday from 9.30 am onward. Most major hotels and many travel agencies also sell tickets at a mark-up.

An easy way to reach the Monumental is to ride the metro to San Antonio station on línea 7, take the Avenida San Antonio exit, turn right, and walk about 10 minutes, crossing the broad Avenida Revolución and Avenida Patriotismo en route. For more information on bullfights, see Spectator Sports in Facts for the Visitor.

Jai Alai

This old Basque game, reminiscent of squash, is fast and elegant when played by experts, and some of the best is played at the *Frontón México* (☎ 546-32-40), on Plaza de la República (metro: Revolución). At this writing the Frontón had been closed for many months by a strike of its workers. When it's in action, the attraction for spectators is not just the game but the chance to bet on it. Normally, games are played nightly except Monday almost all year, starting at 7 pm (5 pm on Sunday). Admission is around US$5. It's something of an upper-class sport: officially, formal dress is required (jacket and tie for men), but in practice visitors may get away with less. However, a notice at the door translates: 'No entry with guns, cellular phones, radios or cameras.' For a little more on jai alai, see Spectator Sports in Facts for the Visitor.

Jai alai players

THINGS TO BUY

For boutiques, art and antiques, stroll the Zona Rosa. For specialty shops with more everyday things, from shoes or screws to fireworks or cakes, wander the streets south of the Zócalo. There are also three large department stores, all open daily, within a block south of the Zócalo: El Nuevo Mundo and El Palacio de Hierro face each other across Cinco de Febrero, and Liverpool is at Venustiano Carranza 92.

Mexican Sweets

For delicate Mexican sweets such as candied fruits, sugared almonds and crystallized strawberries, as well as honey and fruit jams, go directly to Dulcería de Celaya, Avenida Cinco de Mayo 39, west of Isabel la Católica (metro: Allende or Zócalo) These treats cost US$0.40 or more apiece, but anyone can afford at least one or two. The dulcería is open every day from 10.30 am to 7 pm.

Crafts

The Exposición Nacional de Arte Popular, Avenida Juárez 89, a few steps west of the Alameda Central (metro: Hidalgo), is a permanent exhibition selling quality Indian handicrafts from all over Mexico. It's more of a place to admire fine work than to pick up bargains, but worth a look before you dive into some of the markets (see the following section). You'll find colorful glassware, lacquerware and ceramics, hand-woven blankets, wooden animals, baskets and many other items from all over the country. Prices are fixed. It's open Monday to Saturday 10 am to 7 pm.

Markets

There are numerous interesting markets dotted around the city where you can buy all sorts of Mexican handicrafts, souvenirs and everyday goods.

Mercado Insurgentes This stretches from Londres to Liverpool, just west of Amberes in the Zona Rosa (metro: Insurgentes). It's packed with crafts from around the country – silver, textiles, pottery, leather, carved wood figures and more – and is open Monday to Saturday 9 am to 7.30 pm, Sunday 10 am to 4 pm. You need to bargain for sensible prices.

La Ciudadela & San Juan About 600 meters south of the Alameda, on Balderas at Dondé (metro: Balderas), the Centro de Artesanías La Ciudadela, open daily, is full of craft stalls with prices that are fair even before you begin bargaining. You'll find brightly dyed sarapes, pretty lacquerware boxes and trays, masks, silver jewelry, pottery, Huichol bead masks, guitars, maracas – and baskets of every shape and size, some large enough to hide in.

The Mercado de Artesanías San Juan, four blocks east at Dolores and Ayuntamiento (metro: San Juan de Letrán), has a similar range of goods and prices that are, if anything, a little cheaper. It's open Monday to Saturday 9 am to 7 pm, Sunday 9 am to 4 pm.

La Lagunilla & Tepito Two of the city's biggest markets, both open daily, merge into each other along Rayón and Héroe de Granaditas about one km north of the Zócalo. Both deal mainly in everyday things that Mexicans go shopping for, and they're lively, crowded places. Garibaldi metro station is just west of La Lagunilla.

La Lagunilla, the more westerly of the two markets, is centered on three large buildings. Building No 1 is full of clothes and fabrics, No 2 is for furniture, and No 3 is devoted to *comestibles* (food). Tepito takes over where La Lagunilla ends and stretches several hundred meters east along Rayón and Héroe de Granaditas and deep into most of the side streets. Much of what's sold here is said to be *fayuca* (contraband), and the market has a reputation for pickpockets and thieves – so take care. It's composed mainly of street-side stalls and focuses on clothes and leisure goods such as videos, CD players, TVs, Rollerblades and toys – which gives it a fun atmosphere. The only large building, at Héroe de Granaditas and Aztecas, is packed with every kind of shoe and boot you might need or even imagine.

Centro Artesanal Buenavista Just east of the Buenavista train station, at Aldama 187, this large handicrafts 'market' is actually a huge fixed-price store. Much advertised and often visited by tour groups, it has a huge assortment of stuff ('110,000 Mexican typical articles'). Some of it is quality – but bargains can be scarce. It's open Monday to Saturday 9 am to 6 pm.

La Merced & Sonora Mercado La Merced, about one km southeast of the Zócalo, occupies four whole blocks dedicated to the buying and selling of Mexicans' daily needs, which makes for an interesting wander. It's also worth straying a couple of blocks south to Mercado Sonora, on the south side of Fray Servando Teresa de Mier, which has four diverse specialties: toys, caged birds, herbs and folk medicine. Merced metro station is in the middle of La Merced market.

Bazar Sábado The 'Saturday Bazaar,' at Plaza San Jacinto 11 in the southern suburb San Ángel, is a showcase for some of Mexico's very best crafts in fields such as jewelry, woodwork, ceramics and textiles. Prices are high but so is quality. It's held every Saturday from 10 am to 7 pm. At the same time, artists and artisans display work in Plaza San Jacinto itself, in surrounding streets and in nearby Plaza del Carmen. See the earlier San Ángel section for how to reach San Ángel.

Coyoacán On both Saturday and Sunday a colorful jewelry and craft market spreads over much of Coyoacán's central Jardín del Centenario. Hippie jewelry, Mexican Indian crafts, leatherwork and tie-dye clothes are among the stocks-in-trade. The Bazar Artesanal de Coyoacán, on the west side of the adjoining Plaza Hidalgo, and Pasaje Coyoacán, 1½ blocks further north,

at Aguayo and Cuauhtémoc, have more crafts. See the earlier Coyoacán section for information on getting to Coyoacán.

GETTING THERE & AWAY
Air
For information on international flights and domestic and international departure taxes, see the Getting There & Away chapter. For general information on air travel within Mexico and sample fares, see the Getting Around chapter.

Airport Aeropuerto Internacional Benito Juárez (☎ 571-36-00, flight information ☎ 571-32-95), six km east of the Zócalo, is Mexico City's only airport for international and domestic flights (metro: Terminal Aérea).

The single terminal is divided into six *salas*, or halls: Sala A, domestic arrivals; Sala B, check-in for Aeroméxico, Mexicana, Aero California and Aeromar; Salas C and D, check-in for other Mexican airlines; Sala E, international arrivals; Sala F, international airlines check-in.

The terminal has hosts of shops and facilities, including some good bookstores. There are many bank branches and casas de cambio where you can change money: Tamize, between Sala D and Sala E, is one casa de cambio that stays open 24 hours. You can also obtain pesos from several ATMs. There are plenty of pay phones and telephone casetas (call stations), plus shops selling cards for the pay phones. In Sala A you'll find guarded luggage lockers, open 24 hours (US$2.75 for 24 hours); a tourist information office (☎ 762-67-73), open 9 am to 8 pm daily; and post and telegraph offices. Car rental agencies are in Sala E.

Airlines If you already have an onward air ticket from Mexico City, you're all set. If not, a visit to a couple of the city's many travel agencies *(agencias de viajes)* is a good way of finding a suitable ticket. Some are mentioned in this chapter's Information section, or you could ask at your hotel for a full-service agency. Here's where to find the offices of major domestic and international airlines:

Aero California
    Paseo de la Reforma 332 (☎ 207-13-92)
Aeroexo
    Avenida Insurgentes Sur 1292, Colonia Del
    Valle (☎ 559-19-55)
Aerolíneas Argentinas
    Estocolmo 8, Zona Rosa (☎ 208-10-50)
Aerolitoral
    Paseo de la Reforma 445 (☎ 208-38-37)
Aeromar
    Río Nazas 199A, Colonia Cuauhtémoc
    (☎ 627-02-07)
Aeroméxico
    Paseo de la Reforma 80 (☎ 207-49-00),
    Paseo de la Reforma 445 (☎ 228-99-10)
    and eight other offices around the city
Air France
    Paseo de la Reforma 404, 15th floor
    (☎ 627-60-60)
Air New Zealand
    Río Nilo 80, Colonia Cuauhtémoc
    (☎ 208-15-17)
Alaska Airlines
    Hamburgo 213, 10th floor, Zona Rosa
    (☎ 533-17-46)
Alitalia
    Paseo de la Reforma 322 (☎ 533-51-90,
    533-12-40)
Allegro
    Avenida Baja California 128, Colonia Roma
    (☎ 264-84-54)
American Airlines
    Paseo de la Reforma 300 (☎ 209-14-00)
Aviacsa
    Avenida Insurgentes Sur 1292, Colonia Del
    Valle (☎ 559-19-55)
Aviateca (Guatemala)
    Paseo de la Reforma 56 (☎ 592-52-89,
    533-33-66)
British Airways
    Paseo de la Reforma 10, 14th floor
    (☎ 628-05-00)
Canadian Airlines
    Paseo de la Reforma 390 (☎ 208-18-83,
    207-33-38)
Continental Airlines
    Andrés Bello 45, Polanco (☎ 280-34-34)
Cubana
    Temístocles 246, Polanco (☎ 250-63-55,
    255-37-76)
Delta Airlines
    Horacio 1855, Polanco (☎ 557-42-92,
    202-16-08)
Iberia
    Paseo de la Reforma 24 (☎ 705-07-16,
    703-07-09)

Japan Air Lines
    Paseo de la Reforma 295 (☎ 533-55-15,
    553-55-19)
KLM
    Paseo de las Palmas 735, 7th floor, Lomas
    de Chapultepec (☎ 202-44-44)
LACSA (Costa Rica)
    Río Nilo 88, Colonia Cuauhtémoc
    (☎ 525-00-25, 553-33-66)
Lufthansa
    Paseo de las Palmas 239, Lomas de
    Chapultepec (☎ 230-00-00)
Mexicana
    Avenida Juárez at Balderas, near the
    Alameda; Paseo de la Reforma 312, at
    Amberes, in the Zona Rosa; and more than
    a dozen other offices throughout the city
    (☎ 325-09-90)
Qantas
    Paseo de la Reforma 10, 14th floor
    (☎ 628-05-00)
TAESA
    Paseo de la Reforma 30 (☎ 227-07-00)
United Airlines
    Hamburgo 213, Zona Rosa (☎ 627-02-22)
US Airways
    Paseo de la Reforma 10, 14th floor
    (☎ 628-05-00)

Bus

Mexico City has four main long-distance bus terminals, basically serving the four points of the compass: Terminal Norte (north), Terminal Oriente (called TAPO, east), Terminal Sur (south), and Terminal Poniente (west). All terminals have baggage checkrooms or lockers; toilets; newsstands; pay phones or casetas where you can make long-distance calls; post, telegraph and fax offices; and cafeterias.

Here are some long-distance bus travel tips:

• For shorter trips (up to five hours), just go to the bus station, buy your ticket and go.
• For longer trips, many buses leave in the evening or at night, and service (except to Monterrey and Guadalajara) may be limited, so buy your ticket in advance. If you speak some Spanish, you can telephone bus companies to ask about schedules – they're listed in the *sección amarilla* (yellow pages) phone book under 'Camiones y Automóviles Foráneos para Pasajeros.'

- Most destinations are served by just one of the four terminals, but for a few major destinations you have a choice of terminal.
- Large bus companies have ticket counters in several bus stations, so you may be able to buy a ticket at the Terminal Norte for a bus departing later from the Terminal Sur, etc.
- Some companies require you to check in luggage at their counter at least 30 minutes before departure.

Terminal Norte The Terminal Central Autobuses del Norte (☎ 587-59-73), Avenida de los Cien Metros 4907, is about five km north of the Zócalo (metro: Autobuses del Norte). It's the largest of the four terminals, and its name has many variations, including Autobuses del Norte, Central del Norte, Central Camionera del Norte, Camiones Norte, or just CN. It serves places north of Mexico City, plus Guadalajara, Puerto Vallarta and Colima to the west, and Pachuca, Papantla and Tuxpan to the northeast.

More than 30 different bus companies run services from the terminal. The main, deluxe and 1st-class ticket counters are in the southern half of the building (to the right as you enter from the street), and 2nd-class counters are in the northern half.

There are luggage *guarderías* (checkrooms) at the far south end of the terminal and in the central passage. The one at the south end is always open, charging US$1.60 per item per 24 hours. Don't leave valuables in your bags.

Near the middle of the main concourse are a Banamex ATM, giving cash on Visa, Cirrus, MasterCard and Plus System cards, and a casa de cambio with poor rates.

Terminal Oriente (TAPO) The Terminal de Autobuses de Pasajeros de Oriente (☎ 762-59-77), usually known by its acronym TAPO, is at Calzada Ignacio Zaragoza 200, at the intersection with Avenida Eduardo Molina, about two km east of the Zócalo (metro: San Lázaro). This is the terminal for buses serving places east and southeast of Mexico City, including Puebla, central and southern Veracruz, Yucatán, Oaxaca and Chiapas.

There's a Banamex ATM, giving cash on Visa, Cirrus, MasterCard and Plus System cards, in the passage between the metro and the terminal's circular main hall. Luggage lockers are underneath the ticket hall of the Sur bus company.

Terminal Sur The Terminal Central de Autobuses del Sur (☎ 689-97-95), at Avenida Tasqueña 1320, 10 km south of the Zócalo (metro: Tasqueña), is busy with services to Tepoztlán, Cuernavaca, Taxco, Acapulco and a few other destinations. There are no money-changing facilities here.

Terminal Poniente The Terminal Poniente de Autobuses (☎ 271-45-19), on Avenida Sur 122 at Avenida Río de Tacubaya, is south of the Bosque de Chapultepec, eight km southwest of the Zócalo (metro: Observatorio). This is the place to come for frequent shuttle services to nearby Toluca and for most buses to the state of Michoacán. There are no money-changing facilities, and the pay phones take only coins, not cards.

Destinations The table (next page) shows main daily services to a selection of major destinations from Mexico City. More information can be found in other town and city sections of this book. It is all subject to change, of course!

Train
Estación Buenavista The city's central station is the Terminal de Ferrocarriles Nacionales de México (FNM), better known as Estación Buenavista (Buenavista Station). It's a cavernous building at Insurgentes Norte and Mosqueta (Eje 1 Norte), 1.2 km north of Plaza de la República.

The main hall has taquillas for primera clase and coche dormitorio accommodations, open daily from 6 am to 9 pm, and an information desk open daily from 8 am to 9 pm (English not spoken). Downstairs from the main hall are the segunda-clase ticket windows and a *Guarda Equipaje* (luggage checkroom) open from 6.30 am to 9.30 pm daily, charging US$0.70 per item per day.

MEXICO CITY

Buses from Mexico City

Destination	Distance (km)	Journey (hours)	Terminal in Mexico City	Class	Bus Company	No of Daily Departures	Price (US$)
Acapulco	400	5 to 6	Sur	deluxe	Estrella de Oro	a few	26
					Turistar Ejecutivo	a few	26
				1st	Futura	5	19
					Estrella de Oro	15	18.25
				2nd	Cuauhtémoc	15	12.75
			Norte	1st	Futura	10	19
Aguascalientes	521	7	Norte	deluxe	ETN	8	26.75
				1st	Primera Plus	13	21
					Ómnibus de México	14	19.50
				2nd	Flecha Amarilla	6	15.75
Bahías de Huatulco	840 via Salina Cruz	14	Sur	1st	Cristóbal Colón	1	28
	900 via Cuajinicuilapa	15	Sur	1st	Flecha Roja	1	27.50
Campeche	1360	20	Oriente	deluxe	ADO	1	51.50
				1st	ADO	5	44.50
Cancún	1772	22	Oriente	deluxe	ADO	1	57
				1st	ADO	3	48
Chetumal	1450	24	Oriente	1st	ADO	5	45.25
Chihuahua	1500	21	Norte	1st	Futura	5	52
					Transportes Chihuahuenses	9	52
					Ómnibus de México	9	52
Ciudad Juárez	1900	26	Norte	1st	Futura	5	64
					Transportes Chihuahuenses	9	64
					Ómnibus de México	9	64
Cuernavaca	85	1	Sur	deluxe	Pullman de Morelos	frequent	4
				1st	Pullman de Morelos	frequent	3.50
					Cuernavaca	frequent	3.50
				2nd	Cuernavaca	frequent	3
Guadalajara	535	7 to 8	Norte	deluxe	ETN	20	35
				1st	Primera Plus	31	27
					Futura	15	25
				2nd	Flecha Amarilla	22	22
			Poniente	deluxe	ETN	4	35
				2nd	Autobuses de Occidente	8	22
Guanajuato	380	4½	Norte	deluxe	ETN	5	17.50
				1st	Primera Plus	7	14.25
					Futura	4	13.25
Jalapa	315	5	Oriente	deluxe	UNO	6	19.25
				1st	ADO	23	11
				2nd	AU	19	10
			Norte	1st	ADO	2	10.75
Matamoros	1010	15	Norte	deluxe	Turistar Ejecutivo	2	51
				1st	Futura	5	38
				2nd	Transportes Frontera	3	34
Mazatlán	1041	17	Norte	deluxe	Turistar Ejecutivo	1	52.75
				1st	Elite	12	44.75
					Transportes del Pacífico	11	44
				2nd	Transportes del Pacífico	2	38.75
Mérida	1550	20	Oriente	deluxe	ADO	1	53.75
				1st	ADO	5	45

Destination	Distance (km)	Journey (hours)	Terminal in Mexico City	Class	Bus Company	No of Daily Departures	Price (US$)
Mexicali	2667	40	Norte	1st	Futura	3	84
					Elite		84
					Transportes del Pacífico		84
				2nd	Transportes Norte de Sonora		73
Monterrey	934	11 or 12	Norte	deluxe	Turistar Ejecutivo	7	45
					Transportes del Norte	5	45
				1st	Futura	11	34
				2nd	Transportes Frontera	7	29
Morelia	304	4	Poniente	deluxe	ETN	26	22
				1st	Pegasso Plus	16	15
				2nd	Herradura de Plata	12	12
					Autobuses de Occidente	many	11
			Norte	1st	Primera Plus	14	15
				2nd	Flecha Amarilla	32	11.50
Nogales	2227	33	Norte	1st	Elite	3	83.50
				2nd	Transportes del Pacífico	1	71.25
Nuevo Laredo	1158	15	Norte	deluxe	Turistar Ejecutivo	7	59
				1st	Transportes del Norte	4	44
				2nd	Transportes Frontera	7	38
Oaxaca	442	6½	Oriente	deluxe	Cristóbal Colón	6	19.50
				1st	ADO	17	17
				2nd	AU	13	15.75 or 14*
			Norte	deluxe	ADO	1	19.50
				1st	ADO	2	17
			Sur	deluxe	Cristóbal Colón	1	19.50
				1st	Cristóbal Colón	2	17
Palenque	1020	14 to 16	Oriente	1st	ADO	2	35
Papantla	290	5½	Norte	1st	ADO	4	10
Pátzcuaro	370	5	Poniente	1st	Pegasso Plus	9	17
			Norte	1st	Primera Plus	2	15
Playa del Carmen	1840	28	Oriente	1st	ADO	2	47
Puebla	130	2	Oriente	deluxe	Pullman Plus	54	5.75
				1st	Pullman Plus	54	5
					ADO	54	5
				2nd	Estrella Roja	96	4.25
					AU	70	4.25
			Norte	1st	ADO	33	5
			Sur	1st	Cristóbal Colón	32	5
Puerto Escondido	790 via Cuajinicuilapa	13	Sur	1st	Flecha Roja	1	24
	1010 via Salina Cruz	16½	Sur	1st	Cristóbal Colón	1	30
Puerto Vallarta	880	13 to 15	Norte	deluxe	ETN	1	56
					Turistar Ejecutivo	1	49
				1st	Elite	3	42
					Futura	4	
Querétaro	215	2½ to 3	Norte	deluxe	ETN	31	11.75
				1st	Primera Plus	50	8.75
					Futura	48	8
					Ómnibus de México	48	8
				2nd	Flecha Amarilla	80	6.50

*Cheaper fare is for longer nine-hour route

MEXICO CITY

Destination	Distance (km)	Journey (hours)	Terminal in Mexico City	Class	Bus Company	No of Daily Departures	Price (US$)
San Cristóbal de Las Casas	1085	19	Oriente	deluxe	UNO	1	57.50
					Cristóbal Colón	3	44
				1st	Cristóbal Colón	5	38
San Luis Potosí	417	5 to 6	Norte	deluxe	ETN	15	20
				1st	Primera Plus	6	15.75
					Ómnibus de Oriente	24	14.75
				2nd	Flecha Amarilla	9	13
San Miguel de Allende	280	3¼ to 4	Norte	deluxe	ETN	3	15.50
				1st	Primera Plus	3	11
					Pegasso Plus		11
				2nd	Flecha Amarilla	25	8.50
					Herradura de Plata		8.50
Taxco	170	3	Sur	deluxe	Estrella de Oro	2	8
					Cuernavaca	3	7.50
				1st	Estrella de Oro	4	7
					Cuernavaca	12	6 to 7
Teotihuacán	50	1	Norte	2nd	Autobuses Teotihuacán	40**	1.50
Tepoztlán	70	1¼	Sur	1st	Pullman de Morelos	frequent	3
Tijuana	2837	42	Norte	1st	Elite	24	85
					Futura	20	85
Toluca	66	1¼	Poniente	deluxe	ETN	23	3.25
				1st	TMT	204	2.50
				2nd	Flecha Roja	100	2.25
Tula	65	1	Norte	1st	Ovni	15	3.50
				2nd	AVM	60	3
Tuxtla Gutiérrez	1000	17	Oriente	deluxe	UNO	2	54
					Cristóbal Colón	3	42
				1st	Cristóbal Colón	4	37
					ADO	2	37
Uruapan	430	6	Poniente	deluxe	ETN	6	26
				1st	Vía 2000	11	19 or 21
				2nd	Autobuses de Occidente	3	17
			Norte	1st	Primera Plus	5	21
					Vía 2000		19
				2nd	Flecha Amarilla		17
Veracruz	430	5	Oriente	deluxe	UNO	6	27
					ADO	15	18
				1st	ADO	17	15.50
				2nd	AU	17	13.50
			Norte	1st	ADO	4	15.50
Villahermosa	820	14	Oriente	deluxe	UNO	3	43
					ADO	6	35
				1st	ADO	20	30
				2nd	AU	3	26
			Norte	deluxe	ADO	1	35
				1st	ADO	1	30
Zacatecas	651	8 to 9	Norte	deluxe	Turistar Ejecutivo	1	31
					Transportes del Norte	1	31
				1st	Ómnibus de México	15	23
					Transportes Chihuahuaenses	11	23
				2nd	Estrella Blanca	5	19.50
Zihuatanejo	640	9	Sur	deluxe	Estrella de Oro	1	35
				1st	Estrella de Oro	1	22 to 25.75

**7 am to 5 pm; make sure your bus is heading for 'Los Pirámides'

You can make long-distance phone calls from the card and coin phones upstairs, or from the telephone caseta in the main hall (which also has a fax service).

Telephone information in English on train services, ticketing and so on can be obtained by calling ☎ 800-90392, a toll-free number operated by the national tourism ministry, SECTUR. Information in Spanish is available at ☎ 547-10-84 or 547-10-97. If you need help in English at the station, go to the Departamento Tráfico de Pasajeros (Passenger Traffic Department), next to the telephone caseta in the main hall, or the Gerencia de Pasajeros (Passenger Management), upstairs.

For more on Mexican trains, including an explanation of the accommodations class system, see the Train section of the Getting Around chapter.

For places to eat within walking distance of the station, see Places to Eat.

Top Trains Here are the daily schedules of the better trains to/from Mexico City. The schedules and fares will probably change at least slightly by the time you travel, so please confirm these and other details in advance.

Ciudad Juárez División del Norte, train Nos 7 and 8, has primera preferente and segunda clase seats. Fares in primera preferente are US$16.50 to Zacatecas, US$37.50 to Chihuahua, and US$45.75 to Ciudad Juárez.

departs	Train 7
Mexico City	8.00 pm
Querétaro	11.30 pm
León	3.35 am
Aguascalientes	6.30 am
Zacatecas	9.30 am
Torreón	5.10 pm
Chihuahua	1.20 am
arrives	
Ciudad Juárez	6.45 am

departs	Train 8
Ciudad Juárez	10 pm
Chihuahua	3.15 am
Torreón	12 noon
Zacatecas	8.05 pm

Aguascalientes	10.30 pm
León	2.02 am
Querétaro	5.40 am
arrives	
Mexico City	9.30 am

Monterrey & Nuevo Laredo El Regiomontano, train Nos 71 and 72, running between Mexico City and Monterrey, hauls primera preferente and, on Friday, Saturday and Sunday, coche dormitorio coaches. Fares (primera preferente/one-person camarín) are US$10.25/22.25 to San Luis Potosí and US$22/47 to Monterrey.

Train Nos 1 and 2 between Mexico City and Nuevo Laredo have primera preferente and segunda clase seats. Fares in primera preferente are US$7.50 to San Miguel de Allende, US$11.50 to San Luis Potosí, US$23 to Monterrey, and US$30 to Nuevo Laredo.

departs	Train 71	Train 1
Mexico City	6 pm	9 am
Querétaro	–	12.56 pm
San Miguel de Allende	–	2.35 pm
San Luis Potosí	12.01 am	5.10 pm
Saltillo	5.44 am	11.55 pm
Monterrey	–	2.20 am
arrives		
Monterrey	8.10 am	–
Nuevo Laredo	–	7.20 am

departs	Train 72	Train 2
Nuevo Laredo	–	6.55 pm
Monterrey	7.50 pm	11.30 pm
Saltillo	10 pm	2.35 am
San Luis Potosí	3.45 am	10.05 am
San Miguel de Allende	–	1.09 pm
Querétaro	–	2.42 pm
arrives		
Mexico City	10 am	7 pm

Guadalajara El Tapatío, train Nos 5 and 6, hauls segunda clase and primera preferente cars, with coches dormitorios on Friday, Saturday and Sunday. Primera preferente/one-person camarín fares between Mexico City and Guadalajara are US$14.25/31.

departs	Train 5
Mexico City	8.30 pm
arrives	
Guadalajara	8.15 am

MEXICO CITY

departs	Train 6
Guadalajara	9 pm
arrives	
Mexico City	8.25 am

Veracruz El Jarocho, train Nos 53 and 54, hauls segunda clase, primera preferente and coche dormitorio accommodations. Fares from Mexico City (primera preferente/one-person camarín) are US$11/23.50 to Veracruz.

departs	Train 53
Mexico City	9.15 pm
Orizaba	4 am
Fortín de las Flores	4.33 am
Córdoba	4.45 am
arrives	
Veracruz	7.10 am

departs	Train 54
Veracruz	9.30 pm
Córdoba	11.35 pm
Fortín de las Flores	12.08 am
Orizaba	12.30 am
arrives	
Mexico City	7.40 am

Michoacán El Purépecha, train Nos 31 and 32, hauls primera preferente and segunda clase coaches. Primera preferente fares are US$8.75 to Morelia, US$10.25 to Pátzcuaro, US$12 to Uruapan, and US$18.50 to Lázaro Cárdenas.

departs	Train 31
Mexico City	9 pm
Toluca	11.10 pm
Morelia	5.20 am
Pátzcuaro	6.45 am
Uruapan	9 am
arrives	
Lázaro Cárdenas	4 pm

departs	Train 32
Lázaro Cárdenas	12 noon
Uruapan	6.15 pm
Pátzcuaro	9.15 pm
Morelia	10.40 pm
Toluca	5.05 am
arrives	
Mexico City	7.30 am

Oaxaca El Oaxaqueño, train Nos 111-112 and 112-111, hauls primera preferente and segunda clase. The primera preferente fare is US$13.50 to Oaxaca.

departs	Train 111-112
Mexico City	7 pm
Puebla	11.50 pm
arrives	
Oaxaca	9.25 am

departs	Train 112-111
Oaxaca	7 pm
Puebla	4.05 am
arrives	
Mexico City	9.20 am

Car & Motorcycle

Touring Mexico City by car is strongly discouraged, unless you are familiar with the streets and have a healthy reserve of stamina and patience. You may, however, want to rent a car here for travel outside the city. If you're traveling through Mexico by car, pick a hotel that has off-street parking (many do).

Rental Many car rental companies, including the big international names, have offices at the airport and in or near the Zona Rosa; ask at any of the large hotels there. Most hotels can put you in touch with a car rental agent (who may be the hotel owner's brother-in-law). Prices vary quite a lot between agencies. The seemingly better deals offered by some small ones should be compared carefully with a larger international chain before you take the plunge. One local firm offering good rates is Casanova Chapultepec (☎ 514-04-49), at Avenida Chapultepec 442 on the fringe of the Zona Rosa, with VW sedans for US$28.25 a day, including tax, insurance and unlimited mileage (minimum two days, book one day ahead). Among the international firms, Thrifty (☎ 207-75-66), at Sevilla 4 in the Zona Rosa and also at the airport, has VW sedans for US$44.50 a day, or US$266.25 a week.

Experiences related to us by some readers suggest that roads approaching the airport are favorite spots for corrupt traffic police to stop foreigners and try to extract 'fines' for bogus traffic offenses.

For more on car rentals, see the Getting Around chapter.

Ángeles Verdes The Green Angels (see Breakdown Assistance in the Getting Around chapter) can be contacted in Mexico City at ☎ 250-82-21.

GETTING AROUND

A recent increase in crime has made some precautions advisable on all transport (including taxis) – see this chapter's Dangers & Annoyances section.

Mexico City has a good, cheap, easy-to-use metro (underground railway). Peseros (minibuses), buses and/or trolley buses ply all main routes and are also cheap and useful. Taxis are plentiful.

Obvious though it may sound, always look both ways when you cross a street. Some one-way streets have bus lanes running counter to the flow of the rest of the traffic, and traffic on some divided streets runs in the same direction on both sides.

To/From the Airport

Unless you are renting a car, use a taxi or the metro to travel to and from the airport. No bus or pesero runs directly between the airport and the city center.

Metro Officially, you're not supposed to travel on the metro with anything larger than a shoulder bag – and at busy times the crowds make it inadvisable in any case. However, this rule is often not enforced at quieter times, especially before 7 am, after 9 pm and on Sunday.

The airport metro station is Terminal Aérea, on línea 5. It's 200 meters from the terminal: leave the terminal by the exit at the end of Sala A – the domestic flight arrivals area – and continue walking in the same direction until you see the metro logo, a stylized 'M,' and the steps down to the station. One ticket costs US$0.20. To get to the hotel areas in the city center, follow signs for 'Dirección Pantitlán'; at Pantitlán station you have to change trains: follow signs for 'Dirección Tacubaya' (línea 9). Change trains again at Chabacano, where you follow signs for 'Dirección Cuatro Caminos' (línea 2), which takes you to the Zócalo, Allende, Bellas Artes, Hidalgo and Revolución stations (but note the warning about Hidalgo in this chapter's Dangers & Annoyances section).

Taxi Comfortable 'Transportación Terrestre' taxis from the airport terminal give good service and are controlled by a fixed-price ticket system.

Two kiosks in the terminal sell Transportación Terrestre tickets: one is in Sala E (the international flight arrivals area), the

Driving Restrictions

As part of its efforts to combat pollution, Mexico City operates an 'Hoy No Circula' ('Don't Drive Today') program banning all vehicles, wherever they are registered, from being driven in the city on one day each week (except for a few that are specially exempt). The last digit of the vehicle's registration number determines the day. Any car may operate on Saturday and Sunday. Several times a year, when ozone readings in the city top 250 IMECA points (see the sidebar Mexico City's Air), a 'Doble Hoy No Circula' ('Double Don't Drive Today') rule takes effect, banning each vehicle on two weekdays and one weekend day. The system works as follows:

Day	Hoy No Circula Prohibited Last Digits	Doble Hoy No Circula Prohibited Last Digits
Monday	5, 6	3, 4, 5, 6
Tuesday	7, 8	1, 2, 7, 8
Wednesday	3, 4	3, 4, 9, 0
Thursday	1, 2	1, 2, 5, 6
Friday	9, 0	7, 8, 9, 0
Saturday	–	1, 3, 5, 7, 9
Sunday	–	2, 4, 6, 8, 0

other is in Sala A (domestic arrivals). Maps on display by the kiosks divide the city into *zonas* (zones), which determine your fare from the airport. The Zócalo and Alameda Central are in zona 3 (US$6); Plaza de la República and the Zona Rosa are in zona 4 (US$7). One ticket is valid for up to four people and luggage that will fit in the trunk of the cab. If you simply mention a landmark such as 'Zócalo' or 'Plaza de la República' to the ticket clerk, you should receive a ticket for the correct zone – but it's advisable to check the map and count your change, as rip-offs are not unknown.

Walk to the taxi rank, put your luggage in the car's trunk, and hand the ticket to the driver only after getting into the car. (Porters may want to take your ticket and your luggage the few steps to the taxi, and will then importune you for a tip.) At the end of a trip the driver is not supposed to expect a tip.

Going to the airport from the city, you can book a Transportación Terrestre cab by calling ☎ 571-93-44 an hour or more before you want to be picked up.

To/From the Bus Terminals

The metro is the fastest and cheapest way to any bus terminal, but the prohibition against luggage bigger than a shoulder bag may keep you from using it. Each terminal is reachable by bus, pesero and/or trolley bus. They also operate ticket-taxi systems; these *taxis autorizados* are cheaper than those from the airport, with fares similar to street taxis.

Terminal Norte

The metro station (on línea 5) outside the front door is named Autobuses del Norte, but on some maps it's marked Central Autobuses del Norte, or Autobuses Norte, or just 'TAN' (for 'Terminal de Autobuses del Norte'). If you're traveling from the Terminal Norte into the center, enter the metro station and follow signs for 'Dirección Pantitlán,' then change at La Raza, or at Consulado then Candelaria. At La Raza you must walk for seven or eight minutes and negotiate a long flight of steps.

The terminal's Taxi Autorizado kiosk is in the central passageway; a cab to the Plaza de la República, Alameda, Zócalo or Terminal Oriente (TAPO), all in zona 3, costs US$2.75 (US$3.75 between 9 pm and 6 am).

You can also reach the center by trolley bus, pesero or bus. Trolley buses marked 'Eje Central' waiting in front of the terminal head south along Eje Central Lázaro Cárdenas, going within one block of the Alameda Central and six blocks from the Zócalo. Those marked 'Tasqueña' or 'Terminal Sur' take the same route and continue to the southern bus station at Tasqueña, some 15 km south. For peseros or buses going downtown, cross under the road through the underpass. Vehicles heading for central areas include those marked 'M(etro) Insurgentes,' 'M(etro) Revolución,' 'M(etro) Hidalgo,' 'M(etro) Bellas Artes' or 'M(etro) Salto del Agua.'

To reach the Terminal Norte from central areas, there are trolley buses and peseros heading north on Aquiles Serdán at Donceles, one block north of Palacio de Bellas Artes. They're marked with some variation of the terminal's name, such as 'Central Camionera Norte,' 'Central Norte,' 'Terminal Norte' or 'Central Camionera.' On Avenida Insurgentes, anywhere north of Insurgentes metro station, take a northbound 'Central Camionera' bus or pesero or a 'Reclusorio Norte x Cien Metros' bus.

Terminal Oriente (TAPO)

This station is next door to San Lázaro metro station. For peseros or city buses from TAPO, follow the signs to Avenida Eduardo Molina, and when you hit the street the bus stop is 50 meters to the right. Peseros marked 'Zócalo, M(etro) Allende, M(etro) Bellas Artes, Alameda,' or some combination of these run to the city center, passing a few blocks north of the Zócalo and terminating on Trujano opposite the north side of the Alameda Central.

The taxi autorizado fare to the Zócalo (zona 1) is US$1.90; to the Alameda or Plaza de la República (zona 2), US$2.25. Add US$1 between 10.30 pm and 6.30 am.

To get to TAPO from central parts of the city, you can take a 'M(etro) San Lázaro' pesero on Arriaga at Ignacio Mariscal, near Plaza de la República, or heading east on Donceles north of the Zócalo. Or take a 'Santa Martha' bus from the west side of Trujano near the Alameda Central.

Terminal Sur Tasqueña metro station is a two-minute walk through a crowded hawkers' market from the Terminal Sur. 'Eje Central' and 'Central Camionera Norte' trolley buses run north from Terminal Sur along Eje Central Lázaro Cárdenas to the Palacio de Bellas Artes in the city center, then all the way on to the Terminal Norte. Walk to the left from Terminal Sur's main exit, and you'll find the trolley buses waiting on the far side of the main road.

A taxi autorizado from Terminal Sur costs US$3.75 to the Zona Rosa, Alameda or Zócalo (zona 4), and US$4.25 to Plaza de la República (zona 5). Add US$1 between 9 pm and 6 am.

Heading south from the city center to Terminal Sur, trolley buses are marked with some combination of 'Eje Central,' 'Tasqueña/Taxqueña,' 'Autobuses Sur' or 'Terminal Sur.' You can pick them up one block north of the Palacio de Bellas Artes, on Aquiles Serdán at Santa Veracruz. From San Ángel or Coyoacán, you can take a 'M(etro) Tasqueña' pesero or bus east on Avenida Miguel Ángel de Quevedo.

Terminal Poniente Observatorio metro station is a couple of minutes' walk from the terminal. A taxi ticket to the Zócalo costs US$3.75.

To/From the Train Station
Many peseros and buses run along Avenida Insurgentes right past Estación Buenavista. To catch them, turn to the right outside the station and cross to the far side of Insurgentes. Ones marked 'M(etro) Insurgentes' run as far as the intersection with Avenida Chapultepec, one km south of Paseo de la Reforma; ones marked 'San Ángel' continue to the southern suburb of that name.

The taxi fare to the Zócalo or Zona Rosa should be a little over US$1.

The nearest metro station to Estación Buenavista is Guerrero, 900 meters east along Mosqueta, the road in front of the station. 'M(etro) Guerrero,' 'M(etro) Morelos' or 'M(etro) Oceanía' peseros along Mosqueta will take you there.

To reach Estación Buenavista from central areas of the city, there are many buses and peseros going north on Avenida Insurgentes. Any saying 'Buenavista,' 'Central Camionera,' 'M(etro) La Raza' or 'M(etro) Indios Verdes' will do. As you head north on Insurgentes, look for a large Suburbia store on the right and get off at the next stop. The station is topped with the words 'Ferrocarriles Nacionales de México.'

Metro
Mexico City's metro system offers the quickest and most crowded way to get around Mexico City. The fare is US$0.20 a ride, including transfers.

About 4 million people ride the metro on an average day, making it the world's third busiest underground railway, after Moscow's and Tokyo's. It has 150 stations and 178 km of track on 10 lines *(líneas)*.

The stations are generally clean and well organized but often crowded, sometimes fearfully so. The cars at the ends of trains are usually the least crowded. The platforms can become dangerously packed with passengers during the morning and evening rush hours (roughly 7.30 to 10 am and 5 to 7 pm). At these times cars are reserved for women and children on some trains. Boarding for them is done through special *'Solo Mujeres y Niños'* lanes. The best times to ride the metro are late morning, in the evening and Sunday. From Monday to Friday, trains start at 5 am and begin their final runs at midnight; on Saturday the times are 6 am and 1 am; on Sunday 7 am and midnight.

With such crowded conditions, it's not surprising that pickpocketing is rife and that luggage bigger than a shoulder bag is not allowed. Be careful with your belongings. Hidalgo station is particularly notorious for thefts.

The metro is easy to use. Signs in stations reading 'Dirección Pantitlán,' 'Dirección Universida' and so on name the stations at the end of the metro lines. Check a map for the *dirección* you want. Buy a *boleto* (ticket) – or several at once to save queuing next time – at the booth, feed it into the turnstile, and you're on your way.

When changing trains, look for '*Correspondencia*' (Transfer) signs.

Pesero, Bus & Trolley Bus

About 2.5 million people use Mexico City's thousands of peseros and buses daily. They run from about 5 am to midnight and are most crowded during the rush hours – roughly 7.30 to 10 am and 5 to 7 pm. During other hours, the routes of most use to travelers are not too crowded. Pickpockets and thieves are worst on the routes frequented by tourists, especially along Paseo de la Reforma – though the replacement of many larger buses by peseros has reduced this danger.

Peseros are usually gray and green minibuses, but occasionally, in the outer suburbs, they're Volkswagen combi-type vehicles. They run along fixed routes, often starting or ending at metro stations, and will stop to pick up or drop off at virtually any street corner. Route information is displayed on the front of vehicles, often painted in random order on the windshield. Fares are US$0.20 for trips of up to five km, US$0.30 for five to 12 km, and US$0.40 for more than 12 km.

Full-size buses, and the few trolley bus services, are more limited in their stops than peseros; fares are US$0.20. There are a few express buses, which stop only every kilometer or so.

Information on services to specific places around the city is given in the relevant sections of this chapter.

Taxi

Please read first the section on Taxi Crime under Dangers & Annoyances in this chapter's Information section.

Mexico City has several classes of taxi. Cheapest are the regular street cabs – mostly Volkswagen Beetles, but also small Nissans and other Japanese models. They have license plate numbers beginning with the letter L (for *libre*, free) and a green stripe along the bottom of the license plate. Slightly more expensive, and safer, are *sitio* (taxi stand) cars, which are usually larger and which have numbers beginning with S and an orange stripe on their plate. Both these types of vehicle are painted green if they run on unleaded fuel *(taxis ecológicos)*. Most expensive are the large, comfortable Transportación Terrestre vehicles from the airport.

In street and sitio taxis, fares are computed by digital meter. At this writing, the meters in a street taxi ecológico should have shown 3.60 pesos (US$0.50) when you started, then after 90 seconds or 500 meters (whichever came first) should have risen by 0.40 pesos (US$0.10) every 45 seconds or 250 meters. So a 10-minute, 3.5 km ride – from the Zócalo to the Zona Rosa, for instance – was 8.40 pesos (US$1.10). In non-ecológico cabs, strangely, the starting rate is a bit lower. Between 10 pm and 6 am, 20% is added to fares.

Some drivers will try to get you to agree to a fare before you start, or claim that their meter is not working. This will be to your disadvantage, so establish before you get in that you'll be paying what the meter shows *('por el taxímetro')*. If the driver refuses to accept that, walk away and try another cab. At night, however, many drivers just cannot be persuaded to use the meter, so you have no option but to negotiate a fare.

You need not tip taxi drivers unless they have provided some special service.

Around Mexico City

Some of the best things to see and do in Mexico are within a day's travel of the capital. Many of them, such as the ancient city of Teotihuacán or the quaint town of Tepoztlán, can easily be visited as day trips. Other destinations, such as the colonial cities of Puebla and Taxco, are a bit farther away and have so many attractions that you should plan to spend at least one night.

Alternatively, you can stop at most of the places covered in this chapter on your way between the capital and other parts of Mexico. The chapter is divided into four sections – north, east, south and west of Mexico City – and each covers at least one major route to/from the capital. Another option is a circular tour around the capital, which would make a fascinating trip. The roads going around the Distrito Federal generally are not quite as good as those going to and from it, but it is still quite feasible to take this option, either in your own vehicle or on the local buses.

Geographically, the whole area is elevated. South of Mexico City the Cordillera Neovolcánica, with Mexico's highest volcanoes, runs from Pico de Orizaba in the east to Nevado de Toluca in the west (and continues as far west as Colima). North of this range is the Altiplano Central (Central Plateau). The altitude makes for a very pleasant climate, cooler and less humid than the lowlands, with rain falling in brief summer downpours. It also makes for a variety of landscapes, from dramatic gorges to fertile plains, fragrant pine forests and snow-capped peaks. Geologically, it remains an active area, with some still-smoking volcanoes and natural hot springs.

Historically the area was home to a succession of important indigenous civilizations (notably Teotihuacán, Toltec and Aztec), and a crossroads of trade and cultural exchange. By the late 15th century, all

HIGHLIGHTS

- Spectacular Teotihuacán, Mexico's biggest ancient city and the site of two enormous pyramids
- The old mining town of Taxco, a gorgeous colonial antique that is Mexico's picturesque silver capital
- The hilltop ruins of Cacaxtla, with their vividly colored frescos of warriors in battle
- Charming Puebla, which preserves the Spanish imprint as faithfully as any Latin American city
- The remote town of Cuetzalán, famed for a Sunday market that attracts scores of Indians in traditional dress

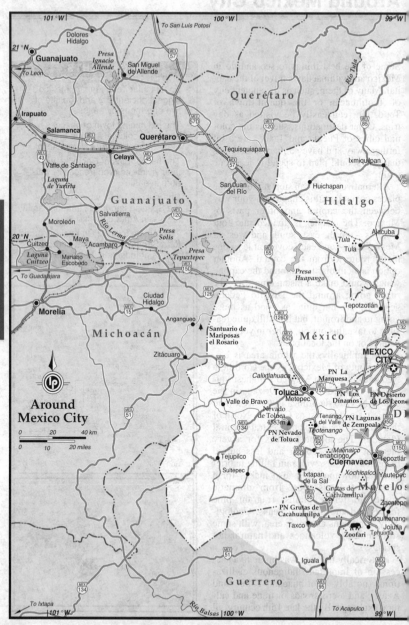

AROUND MEXICO CITY

Around Mexico City

0   20   40 km

0   10   20 miles

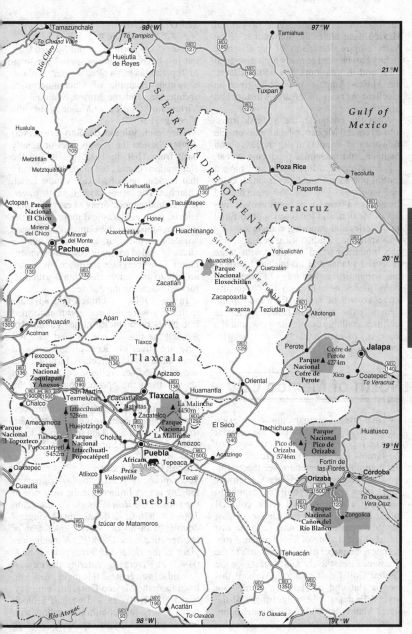

but one of the small states of central Mexico were under the domination of the Aztec empire. Remnants of pre-Hispanic history can be seen at many archaeological sites, and in museums rich with artifacts; the Museo Amparo in Puebla gives an excellent overview of the area's history and culture.

After the conquest, the Spanish transformed central Mexico, establishing ceramic industries at Puebla, mines at Taxco and Pachuca, and haciendas producing wheat, sugar and cattle. Most towns still have a central plaza surrounded by Spanish colonial buildings. The Catholic church used the area as a base for its missionary activities in Mexico, and left a series of fortified monasteries and imposing churches.

Despite the rich historical heritage, this is a modern part of Mexico, with large industrial plants and up-to-date transport and urban infrastructure. On weekends many places near Mexico City typically attract crowds of visitors from the capital. Generally this means that there are ample facilities available during the week, and if a place is crowded it likely won't be with foreigners.

North of Mexico City

Two main routes go to the north of Mexico City. Highway 57D goes past the colonial town of Tepotzotlán, swings northwest past the turnoff for Tula with its Toltec ruins, and continues to Querétaro (see the Northern Central Highlands chapter). Highway 130D goes northeast from the capital to Pachuca, a mining town since colonial times. Highway 132D branches east, past the old monastery at Acolman and the vast archaeological zone of Teotihuacán. From Pachuca, a number of routes go north to the Huasteca or east to the Gulf Coast (see the Central Gulf Coast chapter). Most of this area is flat and not terribly scenic, but beyond Pachuca, where the fringes of the Sierra Madre descend to the coastal plain, it can be quite spectacular.

TEPOTZOTLÁN
pop 54,358; alt 2300m; ☎ 5

About 35 km north of central Mexico City, but just beyond its urban sprawl, the town of Tepotzotlán has a pleasant central plaza, a riotous example of Churrigueresque architecture and the Museo Nacional del Virreinato (National Museum of the Viceregal Period).

The Jesuit **Iglesia de San Francisco Javier**, beside the zócalo, was originally built from 1670 to 1682, but it was the elaborations carried out in the 18th century that made it one of Mexico's most lavish churches. The façade, with its single tower, is a phantasmagoric array of carved saints, angels, people, plants and more, while the interior walls, and the Camarín del Virgen adjacent to the altar, are covered with a circus of gilded and multicolored ornamentation. One sparkling altarpiece gives way artfully to another, each adorned with mirrors accentuating the dazzle.

In the 1960s the church and adjacent monastery were restored and transformed into the **Museo Nacional del Virreinato**. Among the fine art and folk art gathered here are silver chalices, pictures created from inlaid wood, porcelain, furniture and some of the finest religious paintings and statues from the epoch. Don't miss the Capilla Doméstica, whose Churrigueresque main altarpiece is thick with mirrors. The museum is open weekdays from 10 am to 6 pm, weekends 10 am to 5 pm. Admission is US$2 (free Sunday).

Places to Stay & Eat
Tepotzotlán is geared to day-trippers – lodging is *very* limited. On the west side of the zócalo, the *Hotel Posada Familiar San José* (☎ 876-05-20) has small singles/ doubles with no hot water, toilet seat or shower curtain for US$8/12. A much nicer place is the *Hotel San Francisco* (☎ 867-04-43) at Rivera 10; entering the city on Avenida Insurgentes, the main road into town from the Mexico-Querétaro highway, turn right on Rivera and go half a block down. Thirty-four comfortable rooms with hot water fill a two-story brick building

that faces an inviting pool. Rates are US$22/25.

Tepotzotlán has four popular restaurants overlooking the zócalo. The *Restaurant-Bar Pepe* and the *Casa Mago* are a bit pricey and serve mediocre food. *Los Virreyes* and the *Montecarlo*, a few meters away, are similarly priced but serve much better food. Expect to pay US$3 for soup or salad and US$4 or more for beef or chicken. Beside the monastery museum, the *Hostería de Tepotzotlán* serves US$3 soups and US$7 main courses in a pretty courtyard. The street west of the market has cheaper places, including a good taquería.

Getting There & Away

Tepotzotlán is 1.5 km west of the Caseta Tepotzotlán, the first tollbooth on highway 57D from Mexico City to Querétaro and the first from Tula to Mexico City. Avenida Insurgentes leads from the highway, 200 meters south of the tollbooth, to the zócalo.

There are a number of public transport options from Mexico City to Tepotzotlán. Many buses from the Terminal Norte bus station pass the tollbooth. For example, Autotransportes Valle de Mezquital (AVM) buses en route to Tula stop at the tollbooth every 15 minutes. From the tollbooth take a local bus or taxi, or walk along Avenida Insurgentes. You can also take a colectivo or bus to Tepotzotlán from Tacuba or Cuatro Caminos metro stations in Mexico City. From Tacuba it takes one hour (US$2).

TULA

pop 82,247; alt 2060m; ☎ *773*

The probable capital of the ancient Toltec civilization stood 65 km north of what is now Mexico City. Though less spectacular than Teotihuacán, Tula is still an absorbing site, best known for its fearsome 4.5-meter-high stone warrior figures. The modern town has a refinery and cement works on its outskirts, and is generally unexciting.

History

Tula was an important city from about 900 to 1150 AD, reaching a peak population of about 35,000. The Aztec annals tell of a king called Topiltzin – fair-skinned, long-haired and black-bearded – who founded a city in the 10th century as the capital of his Toltec people. There's debate about whether Tula was this capital, though.

The Toltecs were mighty empire-builders to whom the Aztecs themselves looked back with awe, claiming them as royal ancestors. Topiltzin was supposedly a priest-king dedicated to the peaceful, non-human-sacrificing worship of the feathered serpent god Quetzalcóatl. Tula is known to have housed followers of the less likable Tezcatlipoca (Smoking Mirror), god of warriors, witchcraft, life and death. The story goes that Tezcatlipoca appeared in various guises to provoke Topiltzin: as a naked chili-seller he aroused the lust of Topiltzin's daughter and eventually married her; as an old man he persuaded the sober Topiltzin to get drunk.

Eventually the humiliated leader left for the Gulf Coast, where he set sail eastward on a raft of snakes, promising one day to return and reclaim his throne. (This caused the Aztec emperor Moctezuma much consternation when Hernán Cortés arrived on the Gulf Coast in 1519.) The conventional wisdom is that Topiltzin set up a new Toltec state at Chichén Itzá in Yucatán, while the Tula Toltecs built a brutal, militaristic empire that dominated central Mexico. (But see under Chichén Itzá in the History section of the Facts about the Country chapter for a rival theory.)

Tula was evidently a place of some splendor – legends speak of palaces of gold, turquoise, jade and quetzal feathers, of enormous cobs of maize and colored cotton that grew naturally. Possibly its treasures were looted by the Aztecs or Chichimecs.

In the mid-12th century the ruler Huémac apparently moved the Toltec capital to Chapultepec after factional fighting at Tula, then committed suicide. Tula was abandoned about the beginning of the 13th century, seemingly after violent Chichimec destruction.

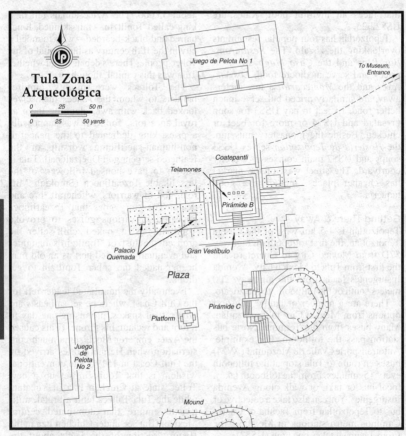

Tula Zona Arqueológica

0   25   50 m
0   25   50 yards

Juego de Pelota No 1

To Museum, Entrance

Coatepantli

Telamones

Pirámide B

Palacio Quemada

Gran Vestíbulo

Plaza

Pirámide C

Platform

Juego de Pelota No 2

Mound

Orientation

The archaeological zone is on the north side of town, with the entrance two km from the center. The town itself is easy paced but unimpressive, generally regarded only as the town near the stone warriors. The main street is Zaragoza, which runs from the outskirts of town to the zócalo. There's a pleasant, block-long pedestrian street, Juárez, that runs parallel to Zaragoza 100 meters from the zócalo. On Juárez there are a couple of banks and places for cheap eats. There's no tourist office in Tula. Payphones abound. See Getting

Around to find out how to get to the Zona Arqueológica from town.

Town Center

The fortress-like church on Zaragoza was part of the 16th-century fortified monastery of San José. Inside, its vault ribs are picked out in gold. On the library wall in the zócalo is a mural of Tula's history.

Zona Arqueológica

The site itself is on a hilltop, with a rural feel and good views over rolling country-side. The old settlement of Tula covered nearly 13 sq km and stretched to the far side of the modern town, but the present focus is the ruins of the main ceremonial center. There's a visitor's center and museum. Tula's ruins are open daily from 9.30 am to 4.30 pm; admission is US$2 (free on Sunday). There are signs at the site in English and Spanish.

Juego de Pelota No 1 This ball court, a copy of an earlier one at Xochicalco, is the first large structure you reach from the museum. It's I-shaped and 37 meters long.

Coatepantli Near the north side of Pirámide B stands the Coatepantli (Serpent Wall), 40 meters long, 2.25 meters high, and carved with rows of geometric patterns and a row of snakes devouring human skeletons. Traces remain of the original bright colors with which most Tula structures were painted.

Pirámide B Also known as the temple of Quetzalcóatl or Tlahuizcalpantecuhtli (the Morning Star), Pyramid B can be scaled via steps on its south side. The four basalt telamones at the top, and the pillars behind, supported the roof of a temple. At the top of the stairway parts of two round columns carved with feather patterns are remains of the temple entrance. They depicted feathered serpents with their heads on the ground and their tails in the air.

The left-hand telamon is a replica of the original, which is in the Museo Nacional de Antropología. Part of the right-hand one was missing and has been reproduced. These warriors symbolize Quetzalcóatl as the morning star. Their headdresses are vertical feathers set in what may be bands of stars; the breastplates are butterfly-shaped. Short skirts cover most of the front of the thighs but leave the buttocks bare. The skirts are held in place by disks at the back representing the sun. The warriors' right hands hold spear-throwers; in their left hands are spears or arrows and incense bags. The columns behind the telamones are engraved with crocodile heads (which symbolize the earth), warriors, symbols of

warrior orders, weapons and the head of Quetzalcóatl.

On the north wall of the pyramid, protected by scaffolding, are some of the carvings that once surrounded all four sides of the structure. These show the symbols of the warrior orders: jaguars, coyotes, eagles eating hearts, and what may be a human head in the mouth of Quetzalcóatl.

Gran Vestíbulo A now roofless colonnaded hall, the Great Vestibule extends along the front of the pyramid, facing the open plaza. The stone bench carved with warriors originally ran the length of the hall, possibly to seat priests and nobles observing ceremonies in the plaza.

Palacio Quemada The 'Burnt Palace' immediately west of Pirámide B is a series of halls and courtyards with more low benches and relief carvings, one showing a procession of nobles. It was probably used for meetings or ceremonies, and the walls were painted with frescos.

Plaza The plaza in front of Pirámide B would have been the scene of religious and military displays. At its center is a small altar or ceremonial platform. **Pirámide C**, on the east side of the plaza, is Tula's biggest structure but is largely unexcavated. To the west is **Juego de Pelota No 2**, the largest ball court in central Mexico at more than 100 meters in length, with alarming chac-mools at each end.

Places to Stay
The best budget place in Tula is the *Auto Hotel Cuéllar* (☎ 2-04-42) at 5 de Mayo 23 (turn left at the east end of Zaragoza). It has smallish rooms with private baths for US$10/11; add US$1.50 for TV. Rooms 31-36 are newer and best. The *Hotel Catedral* (☎ 2-36-33) at Zaragoza 106 has basic rooms with worn carpet and scant fresh air, but they're OK for the price: US$11/13. Rooms 101 and 201 are best.

The *Hotel Lizbeth* (☎ 2-00-45) at Ocampo 200 is a big step up from the Hotel Catedral in quality and price, with bright, clean, comfortable rooms with TV for US$16/23. The best place in town is the multistory *Hotel Sharon* (☎ 2-09-76) at Callejón de la Cruz 1 (at the turnoff to the archaeological site), with singles/doubles at US$24/26 and suites up to US$55.

Places to Eat

The large, clean *Restaurant Casa Blanca* at Zaragoza and Hidalgo is the best restaurant in town and quite reasonable: antojitos for about US$4, meat dishes from US$4.50 to US$6. The tortilla soup (US$2) and the *filete ranchero* (US$6) are tasty. *Cafetería El Cisne*, 100 meters from the zócalo at the end of the pedestrian street Juárez, does US-type snacks and light meals. Burgers are US$1.50, sandwiches about US$2, and beef dishes around US$4.

Getting There & Away

Autotransportes Valle de Mezquital (AVM) runs 2nd-class buses to Tula from Mexico City's Terminal Norte every 15 minutes (US$3). There are a few 'Directo' buses, and more frequent 'Directo vía Refinería' services, and 'Ordinario vía Refinería' buses that are even more frequent but slower; 'Vía Cruz Azul' services take a more indirect route.

Tula's bus depot is on Xicoténcatl. Autotransportes Valle de Mezquital and the 1st-class Ovni line have frequent buses to Mexico City. Buses to Pachuca leave every 15 minutes. From the same terminal, Flecha Amarilla has daily service to Querétaro, Guanajuato, León and Morelia.

Getting Around

If you arrive in Tula by bus, the easiest way to the archaeological zone is to catch a taxi from outside the depot (US$3). If you prefer to walk, turn right from the bus station, go 1½ blocks to Ocampo, turn right, go a few more blocks and cross the river bridge. You'll see the Hotel Sharon on a corner on the left, with a replica warrior statue in the middle of the side road in front of it. Turn left at the statue and follow the road two km to the entrance to the ruins. The car park and museum are 500

meters from the entrance, and it's 700 meters more to the center of the ancient city.

Motorists can reach the site by following 'Parque Nacional Tula' and 'Zona Arqueológica' signs.

ACOLMAN

pop 54,369; alt 2250m; ☎ 595

About 40 km north of Mexico City, just beside highway 132D (the toll road to Teotihuacán), you'll see what look like battlements surrounding the **Ex-Convento de San Agustín Acolman**. The adjacent church of San Agustín, built between 1539 and 1560, has a spacious Gothic interior and one of the earliest examples of a plateresque façade. The old monastery now houses a museum with artifacts and paintings from the early Christian missionary period; it's open Tuesday to Sunday from 10 am to 5 pm (US$2). The historic building, with its massive thick walls, colonnaded courtyards and carved stonework, is the site of many frescos. This is a very pleasant stop on the way to or from Teotihuacán. Buses go to Acolman from Indios Verdes metro station in Mexico City. It's not very far from Teotihuacán; if there's no convenient bus you can get a taxi for about US$4.

TEOTIHUACÁN

pop 39,182; alt 2300m; ☎ 595

If there is any must-see attraction near Mexico City, it is the archaeological zone Teotihuacán ('teh-oh-tih-wah-KAN', 50 km northeast of downtown in a mountain-ringed offshoot of the Valle de México. Site of the huge Pirámides del Sol y de la Luna (Pyramids of the Sun and Moon), Teotihuacán was Mexico's biggest ancient city, with perhaps 200,000 people at its peak, and the capital of probably Mexico's biggest pre-Hispanic empire. If you don't let the hawkers get you down, a day here can be an awesome experience. Using some of the less-trodden paths off the Avenida de los Muertos helps you appreciate the place.

A grid plan for the city was used from the early years AD and the Pyramid of the

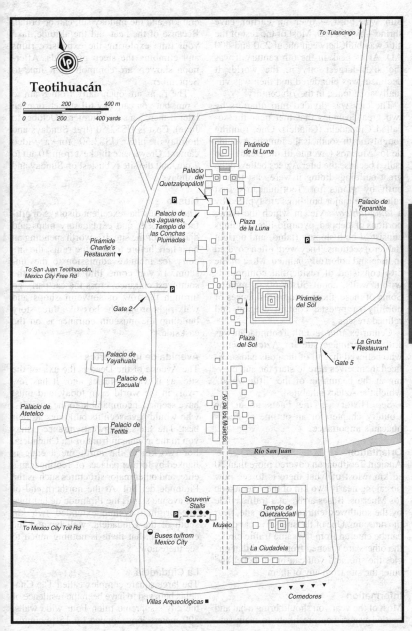

Teotihuacán

0   200   400 m
0   200   400 yards

To Tulancingo

Pirámide de la Luna

Palacio del Quetzalpapálotl

Palacio de los Jaguares, Templo de las Conchas Plumadas

Plaza de la Luna

Palacio de Tepantitla

Pirámide Charlie's Restaurant ▼

To San Juan Teotihuacán, Mexico City Free Rd

Gate 2

Pirámide del Sol

Plaza del Sol

La Gruta Restaurant ▼

Gate 5

Palacio de Yayahuala

Palacio de Zacuala

Palacio de Atetelco

Palacio de Tetitla

Av de los Muertos

Río San Juan

To Mexico City Toll Rd

Souvenir Stalls

P

Buses to/from Mexico City

Museo

Templo de Quetzalcóatl

La Ciudadela

Comedores

Villas Arqueológicas ■

Sun was built – over an earlier cave shrine – by 150 AD. Most of the rest of the city was built between about 250 and 600 AD. At its peak in the 6th century it was the sixth-largest city in the world. It declined, was plundered and then was virtually abandoned in the 7th century.

The city was divided into quarters by two great avenues that met near the so-called Ciudadela (Citadel). One, running roughly north-south, is the famous Avenida de los Muertos (Avenue of the Dead) – so called because the later Aztecs believed the great buildings lining it were vast tombs, built by giants for Teotihuacán's first rulers. The major buildings are typified by a *talud-tablero* style, in which the rising portions of stepped, pyramid-like buildings consist of both sloping (talud) and upright (tablero) sections. They were often covered in lime and colorfully painted. Most of the city consisted of residential compounds within walls, about 50 or 60 sq meters. Some of these, thought to be residences of nobility or priests, contain elegant and refined frescos.

Centuries after its fall, Teotihuacán was still a pilgrimage site for Aztec royalty, who believed that all of the gods had sacrificed themselves here to start the sun moving at the beginning of the 'fifth world,' which the Aztecs inhabited.

See History in the Facts about the Country chapter for an outline of Teotihuacán's importance.

Orientation

Ancient Teotihuacán covered more than 20 sq km. Most of what there is to see now lies along nearly two km of the Avenida de los Muertos. Buses arrive at a traffic circle by the southwest entrance to the site, near the museum. One of the site's five car parks can be entered from the same traffic circle; the others are reached from a road that circles the site, and you can buy a ticket and enter the site from any of them.

Information

Most of the year you should bring a hat and bottled water; you are likely to walk sev-

eral km and the midday sun can be brutal. Because of the heat and the altitude, take your time exploring the expansive ruins and climbing the steep pyramids. Afternoon showers are common from June to September.

The ruins are open daily from 8 am to 5 pm, but you can stay till sunset, or even later if there's a son et lumière (October to June). Cost is US$2.50 (free Sundays and holidays), plus US$3.50 for a video camera. Crowds are thickest from 10 am to 2 pm, and the site is busiest on Sunday and holidays.

Museo

The museum has excellent displays of artifacts, models, and explanatory maps and diagrams of the site. It's worth spending an hour here before touring the ruins; the site entry fee includes admission to the museum. If you come into the site at the southwest entrance, cross the car park, go through the row of souvenir shops and walk right around the box-like three-story building; the museum entrance is on the east side.

Avenida de los Muertos

The Avenue of the Dead is the axis of the site, as it was centuries ago. It has few rivals in the world even today, and must have seemed incomparable to the ancients, who would have seen its buildings at their best. The site's southwest entrance brings you to the avenue in front of La Ciudadela. For two km to the north the avenue is flanked by former palaces of Teotihuacán's elite, and other major structures such as the Pirámide del Sol. At the northern end of the avenue stands the Pirámide de la Luna. The original avenue extended two km south of the Ciudadela, well beyond the current site, but there is nothing much to see there now.

La Ciudadela

The large square complex called The Citadel is believed to have been the residence of the city's supreme ruler. Four wide walls, 390 meters long, topped by 15 pyramids, enclose a huge open space of which the main feature, toward the east side, is a pyramid called the Templo de Quetzalcóatl. The temple is flanked by two large ruined complexes of rooms and patios, which may have been the city's administrative center.

Templo de Quetzalcóatl The fascinating feature of this temple is the façade of an earlier structure from around 250 to 300 AD, which was revealed by excavating the more recent pyramid that had been superimposed on it. The four surviving 'steps' of this façade (there were originally seven) are encrusted with striking carvings. In the upright tablero panels the sharp-fanged feathered serpent deity, its head emerging from a 'necklace' of 11 petals, alternates with a four-eyed, two-fanged creature often identified as the rain god Tláloc but perhaps more authoritatively reckoned to be the fire serpent, bearer of the sun on its daily journey across the sky. On the sloping panels are side views of the plumed serpent, its body snaking along behind its head. Seashells, an important Teotihuacán motif, form part of the background in both sets of panels.

Pirámide del Sol
The world's third-largest pyramid stands on the east side of the Avenida de los Muertos. The Pyramid of the Sun is surpassed in size only by the pyramid of Cholula and Egypt's Cheops. Built around 100 AD and rebuilt in 1908, it has a base of 222 sq meters and is now just over 70 meters high (it originally had a wood- and thatch-temple on top). The pyramid was made from 3 million tons of stone, brick and rubble without the use of metal tools, pack animals or the wheel!

The Aztec belief that the structure was dedicated to the sun god was validated in 1971, when archaeologists uncovered a 100-meter-long underground tunnel leading from near the pyramid's west side to a cave directly beneath its center. Here they found religious artifacts. It is thought the sun was worshipped here before the pyramid was built and that the city's ancient

JOHN NOBLE
Templo de Quetzalcóatl, detail

inhabitants traced the very origins of life to this grotto.

At Teotihuacán's height, the pyramid's plaster was painted bright red, which must have been a radiant sight at sunset. Climb the pyramid's 248 steps for an overview of the entire ancient city.

Pirámide de la Luna
The Pyramid of the Moon, at the north end of the Avenida de los Muertos, is not as big as the Pirámide del Sol, but it is more gracefully proportioned. Its summit is virtually at the same height, because it is built on higher ground. It was completed about 300 AD.

The Plaza de la Luna, in front of the pyramid, is a handsome arrangement of 12 temple platforms. Some experts attribute astronomical symbolism to the total 13 (made by the 12 platforms plus the pyramid). The altar in the plaza's center is thought to have been the site of religious dancing.

Palacio del Quetzalpapálotl

Off the southwest corner of the Plaza de la Luna is the Palace of the Quetzal Butterfly, where it is thought a high priest lived. A flight of steps leads up to a roofed portico with an abstract mural and, just off that, a well-restored patio with thick columns carved with designs representing the quetzal bird or a hybrid quetzal butterfly.

Palacio de los Jaguares & Templo de las Conchas Plumadas

These structures lie behind and below the Palacio del Quetzalpapálotl. On the lower walls of several of the chambers off the patio of the Jaguar Palace are parts of murals showing the jaguar god in feathered headdresses, blowing conch shells and apparently praying to the rain god Tláloc.

The Temple of the Plumed Conch Shells, entered from the Jaguar Palace patio, is a now-subterranean structure of the 2nd or 3rd century AD. Carvings on what was its façade show large shells – possibly used as musical instruments – decorated with feathers, and four-petal flowers. The base on which the façade stands has a green, blue, red and yellow mural of birds with water streaming from their beaks.

Palacio de Tepantitla

Teotihuacán's most famous fresco, the worn *Paradise of Tláloc*, is in the Tepantitla Palace, a priest's residence about 500 meters northeast of the Pirámide del Sol. The mural flanks a doorway in a covered patio in the northeast corner of the building. The rain god Tláloc, attended by priests, is shown on both sides. Below, on the right of the door, appears his paradise, a garden-like place with tiny people, animals and fish swimming in a river flowing from a mountain. Left of the door, tiny human figures are engaged in a unique ball game. Frescos in other rooms show priests with feather headdresses.

Palacio de Tetitla & Palacio de Atetelco

Another group of palaces lies west of the main part of the site, several hundred meters from the southwest entrance. Their many murals, discovered in the 1940s, are often well preserved or restored and perfectly intelligible. The Tetitla Palace is a large complex, perhaps of several adjoining houses. No less than 120 walls have murals, with Tláloc, jaguars, serpents and eagles among the easiest to make out.

Some 400 meters west is the Atetelco Palace, whose vivid jaguar or coyote murals – a mixture of originals and restorations – are in the so-called Patio Blanco in the northwest corner. Processions of these creatures in shades of red perhaps symbolize warrior orders. There are also crisscross designs of priests with Tláloc and coyote costumes.

Places to Stay

If there's one place to splurge on lodging in Mexico, this is it. The Club Med-run *Villas Arqueológicas* (☎ 9-15-95) immediately south of the ancient city has some very charming air-con singles/doubles for US$42/48. It also has a swimming pool, a tennis court, a billiards table and a French-Mexican restaurant.

The next closest place is several km away on the highway linking Mexico City to Tulancingo. Called *Hotel La Cascada* (☎ 6-07-89), its receptionists seem to quote rates based on what they believe you'd be willing to pay. A dumpy single costs US$12 to US$14, a dumpy double US$23 and up.

El Temazcal Hotel (☎ 6-34-13) is seven km from the ruins; follow the signs from the Mexico City-Tulancingo highway. Spacious but dingy rooms go for US$23/44. Its saving grace is its several swimming pools.

Local buses will transport people from the driveways of both the Cascada and the Temazcal to the ruins for US$1.50.

Places to Eat

Except for some dusty eateries on the ring road on the south side of the archaeological site, meals are pricey in the vicinity of the ruins. The most convenient place to eat is on the 3rd floor of the museum building, where there's a relatively expensive restaurant with a great panorama of the site. There's a bar on the 2nd floor with almost as good a view.

On the ring road just north of Gate 2 is *Pirámide Charlie's*, which serves savory but costly meals: US$2 to US$5 for soup, chicken dishes US$5 to US$7, beef dishes around US$9, fish US$9 to US$12.

A very unusual place to dine is *La Gruta* (The Cave), 75 meters east of Gate 5. Meals have been served in this cool, wide-mouthed natural cave since 1929. The food's quite OK and fairly priced: soups and salads around US$3, antojitos US$3 to US$6, and filet mignon and fish dishes about US$8.

Getting There & Away

The 2nd-class buses of Autobuses San Juan Teotihuacán run from Mexico City's Terminal Norte to the ruins every 15 or 20 minutes during the day, costing US$1.50 for the hour-long journey. The ticket office is at the north end of the terminal. Make sure your bus is going to 'Los Pirámides' – not simply the town of Teotihuacán, two km west of the ruins.

Buses arrive and depart from the traffic circle outside the site's southwest entrance. Return buses are more frequent after 1 pm. The last bus back Mexico City from the traffic circle leaves about 6 pm. Some buses terminate at the Indios Verdes metro station on Insurgentes Norte in the north of Mexico City, but most continue to Terminal Norte. If you don't fancy taking the metro from Indios Verdes, you can get a taxi down Insurgentes to the city center.

Numerous tours from Mexico City go to the ruins.

PACHUCA

pop 220,485; alt 2426m; ☎ *771*

Pachuca, capital of the state of Hidalgo, lies 90 km northeast of Mexico City. It has grown rapidly in the last few years and brightly painted houses climb the dry hillsides around the town. There are a few interesting sights, and Pachuca is a good departure point for trips north and east to the dramatic fringes of the Sierra Madre.

Silver was found in the area as early as 1534, and the mines of Pachuca and Real del Monte, nine km northeast, still produce substantial amounts of the metal. Pachuca was also the gateway by which soccer entered Mexico, brought by miners from Cornwall, England, in the 19th century.

Orientation & Information

Pachuca's zócalo is the rectangular Plaza de la Independencia, with its central clock tower. The main market is on Plaza Constitución, a couple of blocks northeast of the zócalo.

Key streets include Matamoros, along the east side of zócalo, and Allende, running south from the zócalo's southwest corner. Guerrero runs parallel to the zócalo, about 100 meters to the west. To the south, by about 700 meters, both Guerrero and Matamoros reach the modern Plaza Juárez.

There's a tourist office (☎ 5-14-11) in the base of the clock tower, open weekdays from 9 am to 3 pm, weekends from 10 am to 6 pm. There are banks (with ATMs) on Plaza de la Independencia. The post office is on the corner of Juárez and Iglesias.

City Center

Two streets east of the zócalo have been pedestrianized and several small, modern plazas now abut the older ones. The central clock tower, the **Reloj Monumental**, was built in 1904 in the French style then popular. Four marble sculptures, one on each side, represent Independence, Liberty, the Constitution and Reform.

The old **Cajas Reales** (Royal Treasuries) are behind the north side of the Plaza Constitución.

Centro Cultural Hidalgo

The ex-monastery of San Francisco has become the Centro Cultural Hidalgo, which embodies two museums, a theater, a library and a gallery. Admission is free, except during performances. The center is open Tuesday to Sunday, 10 am to 6 pm.

From Plaza de la Independencia go three blocks south down Matamoros to a crossroads with a fountain. A fine mural depicting animals and plants, inspired by Hidalgo's Otomí Indian heritage, adorns a wall just south of this fountain. From there go two blocks east along Arista to the monastery, which is behind the San Francisco church beside the Jardín Colón.

The **Museo Nacional de la Fotografía** displays early photographic technology (such as a daguerreotype studio) and selections from the 1.5 million photos in the archives of the Instituto Nacional de Antropología e Historia (INAH). Some of the images are from Europeans and North Americans who worked in Mexico years ago. Many more are from the library of Agustín Victor Casasola, one of Mexico's first photojournalists. The photos provide fascinating glimpses of Mexico from 1873 to the present.

Places to Stay

The *Hotel Grenfell* (☎ 5-08-68) occupies an imposing building on the west side of the zócalo but is much less impressive inside. Sizable but bare singles/doubles cost US$9/10 with private bath, US$7/8 with shared bath.

Much better value is the *Hotel de los Baños* (☎ 3-07-00) at Matamoros 205, half a block southwest of the zócalo. Particularly nice are rooms 26 and 28; these are large, cleanish, have TV, phone and a balcony, and are elegantly furnished. All of the rooms at this lovingly maintained hotel surround a handsome enclosed courtyard, but only these two rooms are so spacious and finely attired. Rates for all rooms are US$10/11 – a bargain no matter which room you get.

Another excellent choice is the *Hotel Plaza El Dorado* (☎ 4-28-08) at Guerrero 721, with 92 very agreeable rooms with TV costing US$11/13. To find it, take the street off the middle of the west side of Plaza de la Independencia, turn left on Guerrero, and go 200 meters. The hotel is on the left.

The *Hotel Noriega* (☎ 5-15-55) at Matamoros 305 two blocks south of the zócalo is a superb-value colonial-style place with

a good restaurant. There's a covered courtyard, a stately staircase and *lots* of tropical plants. Pleasant rooms with TV and private bath cost US$13/15.

The modern *Hotel Emily* (☎ 5-08-68), on the south side of the zócalo, offers rooms comparable to the El Dorado for a lot more: US$20 for one or two people. Similar to the Emily in both cost and quality is *Hotel Ciro's* (☎ 5-40-83) on the north side of the plaza. Get a room facing the clock tower for a lovely night vista.

Places to Eat

The *Mirage* restaurant-bar on Guerrero between the Hotel Plaza El Dorado and the zócalo is the best place in town – and quite affordable: breakfasts from US$2.50, salads US$2 to US$4, chicken dishes for US$3.50, beef for about US$6.50. Even their 'traditional ham and cheese sandwich' is a tasty treat – a triple-decker containing a fine mix of ham and Swiss and avocado, tomato, onion and mild chilies. Their filete de la mexicana is a large slice of beef smothered in salsa and served with potato, beans and tortillas (US$7).

The *Restaurant Noriega* in the Hotel Noriega has a touch of elegance (including prints of old London on the walls), and prices are fair, particularly for the set lunch.

Chip's Restaurant, in the Hotel Emily, feels more like an upscale snack and coffee bar than a restaurant, but it whips up quite decent food and offers it cheap.

Restaurant Ciro's, on the north side of Plaza de la Independencia, is quite popular but it gets quite smoky and its meals don't compare favorably to those at the Mirage although they cost about the same.

Next to the Hotel de los Baños, the *Restaurant-Bar Cabales* is quite lovely, with lots of lightly stained wood, a fine bar ringed with swiveling stools, and good, reasonably priced food (the five-course meal of the day runs US$3.50). It's open till 11 pm.

Getting There & Away

First-class ADO buses leave Mexico City's Terminal Norte for Pachuca every

15 minutes (US$3). From Pachuca, ADO serves the following daily: Mexico City, every 15 minutes, US$3; Poza Rica, three buses, US$7; Tampico, one bus at 8.45 pm, US$17; Tulancingo, every 30 minutes, US$2. Futura also offers 1st-class service to Mexico City every 15 minutes for US$4. Buses serving destinations closer to Pachuca are nearly all 2nd-class; these frequently go to/from Tula, Tulancingo and Tamazunchale, while several go daily to/from Huejutla and Querétaro.

Getting Around

The bus station is several km southwest of downtown, beside the road to Mexico City. Green-and-white colectivos marked 'El Centro' take you to Plaza Constitución (US$0.40), a short walk from Plaza de la Independencia; the trip by taxi costs US$3.

AROUND PACHUCA

Highway 85 – the Pan-American Highway – goes via Actopan and Ixmiquilpan, across the forested, sometimes foggy Sierra Madre to Tamazunchale and Ciudad Valles in the Huasteca (see the Central Gulf Coast chapter). Two other scenic roads descend from the Sierra Madre: highway 105 goes north to Huejutla and Tampico, and highway 130 goes east to Tulancingo and Poza Rica.

Actopan

pop 44,255; alt 2400m; ☎ *772*

Actopan, 37 km northwest of Pachuca on highway 85, has one of the finest of Hidalgo's many 16th century fortress-monasteries. Founded in 1548, the **monastery** is in an excellent state of preservation. Its church has a lovely plateresque façade and a single tower showing Moorish influence. The nave has Gothic vaulting. Mexico's best 16th century frescos are in the cloister: hermits are depicted in the Sala De Profundis, while on the stairs are shown saints, Augustinian monks and a meeting between Fray Martín de Acevedo, an important early monk at Actopan, and two Indian nobles, Juan Inica

Actopa and Pedro Ixcuincuitlapilco. To the left of the church a vaulted capilla abierta is also adorned with frescos.

Wednesday is **market day** in Actopan, and has been for at least 400 years. Local handicrafts are sold, along with regional dishes such as barbecued meat.

Getting There & Away There are frequent 2nd-class buses from Pachuca (45 minutes) and from Mexico City's Terminal Norte.

Ixmiquilpan

pop 73,804; alt 1700m; ☎ *772*

Ixmiquilpan, 75 km from Pachuca on highway 85 (1½ hours by frequent buses), is a former capital of the Otomí Indians, anciently established inhabitants of Hidalgo. The arid Mezquital valley in which the town stands remains an Otomí enclave; about half of Mexico's 350,000 Otomí live in Hidalgo. Traditional Otomí women's dress is a quechquémitl worn over an embroidered cloth blouse. The Mezquital valley Otomí make Mexico's finest *ayates*, cloths woven from *ixtle*, the fiber of the maguey cactus. The Otomí also use maguey to make food, soap and needles.

The **Casa de Artesanías**, on Felipe Ángeles, displays and sells Otomí crafts, but the busy Monday **market** is the best place to find products such as miniature musical instruments made of juniper wood with pearl or shell inlay, colorful drawstring bags or embroidered textiles.

The **church** of Ixmiquilpan's monastery has a huge Gothic vault. In the cloister are frescos by Indian artists showing battle between Indians and mythical pre-Hispanic figures, as well as religious scenes.

Places to Stay The best budget place in town is the *Hotel Palacio Real* (☎ 3-01-81) on the southern corner of the Plaza Juárez. The hotel offers 15 singles/doubles with firm beds, hot water and TV for US$9/13. The *Hotel Jardín* (☎ 3-03-08), 75 meters east of the Palacio Real, was undergoing renovation as this was written but would be worth looking into; its rates had been comparable to the Real's.

The *Hotel Club Alcantara* (☎ 9-17-92) at Peña y Ramirez 8, half a block from the plaza, offers puny thin-walled rooms with TVs for an excessive US$13/15; it has a swimming pool, which some might feel makes up for the hotel's shortcomings.

The best hotel in town is the *Hotel Del Valle Inn* (☎ 3-24-53) at Cardonal 50. It offers 28 standard-size, peach-painted rooms, with firm mattresses, TV and phone, for US$23/30.

Places to Eat The best and most popular restaurant in Ixmiquilpan is *El Sabino* at Insurgentes 111, three blocks from the zócalo. To get there, follow the street on the south side of the zócalo west past the church. The street will curve to the right, and you want to stay with it past the Pemex station; the restaurant-bar is 75 meters farther. El Sabino has a pleasant ambiance and low prices; few menu items top US$5.

The *Restaurant Los Portales* next to the Hotel Palacio Real looks promising enough but the food is thoroughly lousy.

The restaurant at the Hotel Del Valle Inn is large and bright and has a wall of windows facing mountains. The filet of sole, the restaurant's specialty, is very tasty and costs US$4. Breakfasts run to US$2.50, antojitos are US$3 or less, beef under US$5.

North of Pachuca – Highway 105
Nine km north of Pachuca, a road branches northwest (left) off highway 105 and winds 10 km or so to the picturesque old mining town of **Mineral del Chico**, located in **Parque Nacional El Chico**. The park has spectacular rock formations popular with climbers, pine forests with lovely walks, and rivers and dams for fishing. There are places to eat and to camp, but otherwise lodging is limited.

Two km past the park turnoff, **Mineral del Monte** (also known as Real del Monte) was the scene of a miners' strike in 1776 – commemorated as the first strike in the Americas. Most of the town was settled in the 19th century, after a British company took over the mines. Cornish-style cottages line many of the steep cobbled streets, and

there is an English cemetery nearby. There are regular buses to/from Pachuca.

Eleven km north of Mineral del Monte is a turnoff east to **Huasca** (or Huasca de Ocampo), with a 17th century church, balnearios and a variety of local crafts. Some old haciendas have been converted into attractive hotels. Nearby is a canyon with imposing basalt columns and a waterfall.

At **Atotonilco el Grande**, 34 km from Pachuca, there's a 16th century fortress-monastery, and a balneario beside some hot springs. Market day is Thursday. The highway then descends to Metzquititlán, in the fertile Río Tulancingo valley – see Tampico & the Huasteca in the Central Gulf Coast chapter for information about other places on this route.

East of Pachuca – Highway 130
Just 46 km east of Pachuca is **Tulancingo** (population 110,112, altitude 2140 meters), the second-biggest town in Hidalgo. Before Tula, it was the Toltec capital for a short time. There's a Toltec pyramid at the foot of a cliff at **Huapalcalco**, three km north. Market day is Thursday.

The Otomí village of **Tenango de Doria** is 40 rugged km north of Tulancingo by sometimes impassable roads. Indians here make cotton fabric colorfully embroidered with animals and plants. In **Huehuetla**, 50 km north of Tulancingo, one of the few communities of the tiny Tepehua Indian group embroiders floral and geometric patterns on its enredos and quechquémitls.

Beyond Tulancingo, highway 130 descends toward Huauchinango in the state of Puebla – see the section on Northern Veracruz in the Central Gulf Coast chapter.

East of Mexico City

Toll highway 190D goes east to Puebla across a high, dry region studded with volcanic peaks, including Popocatépetl, Iztac-cíhuatl and La Malinche. In the mountains, you can try anything from pleasant alpine strolls to demanding technical climbs – though Popocatépetl is off-limits because of recent volcanic activity. Just north of the highway, the tiny state of Tlaxcala (population 850,000) features a charming capital, and relics from a rich pre-Hispanic and colonial history. Puebla itself is one of Mexico's best preserved colonial cities, a pivot of its history, and a lively modern metropolis with a lot to see. Nevertheless, the state of Puebla is predominantly rural, with about half a million Indians. The Indian presence helps give Puebla a rich handicraft output, including pottery, carved onyx and fine hand-woven and embroidered textiles.

You can continue east from Puebla on highway 150D, past Pico de Orizaba (Mexico's highest mountain), and descend from the highlands to the coast of Veracruz state (see the Central Gulf Coast chapter). Alternatives are to swing north on highway 140 toward the remote Sierra Norte de Puebla, or descend to the Gulf Coast via Jalapa. South and east of Puebla there's a choice of scenic routes through the mountains to the state and city of Oaxaca.

POPOCATÉPETL & IZTACCÍHUATL

The peaks of Mexico's two most famous mountains, Popocatépetl ('po-po-ka-TEH-pettle') and Iztaccíhuatl ('iss-ta-SEE-wattle'), form the eastern rim of the Valle de México, 60 km southeast of Mexico City and 45 km west of Puebla. The peaks are Mexico's second and third highest, and while the craterless Iztaccíhuatl remains dormant, Popocatépetl in recent years has spouted plumes of gas and ash, forced the evacuation of 75,000 people, and spurred experts to issue warnings to the 30 million people who live within striking distance of the volcano. At the time of writing, leading vulcanologists were watching Popocatépetl with grave concern.

Fearing an imminent eruption of Popocatépetl, which means 'Smoking Mountain' in Nahuatl, soldiers on December 22, 1994, evacuated 16 villages close to the 5452-meter volcano. The action was taken after explosions under the mountain the

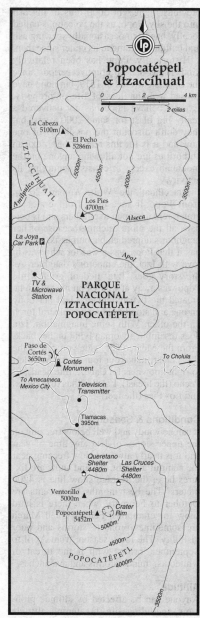

previous night sent 5000 tons of hot ash into the sky. Popo, as the volcano is called locally, has been occasionally spewing ash and building a dome in its crater since then.

Historically, Popo has been relatively kind. It has had 16 eruptive periods since the Spanish arrived in 1519, but none have caused a major loss of life or property. Experts believe Popo has not delivered a really big blast for some 2000 years, but they don't discount the possibility of one now and it is for this reason that Mexican authorities are not allowing anyone on the mountain except scientists monitoring its activity.

Iztaccíhuatl, the 'White Woman,' 20 km from Popo if measured from crater to crater, remains open to climbers and is perhaps all the more fetching because of her neighbor's unpredictable outbursts. Legend has it that Popo was a warrior who was in love with Izta, the emperor's daughter. As the story goes, Izta died of grief while Popo was away at war. Upon his return, he created the two mountains, laid her body on one and stood holding her funeral torch on the other. With some imagination, Izta does resemble a woman lying on her back. From the Mexico City side you can, if the sky's clear, make out four peaks from left to right known as La Cabeza (the head), El Pecho (the breast), Las Rodillas (the knees) and Los Pies (the feet).

Conditions & Seasons

It can be windy and well below freezing on the upper slopes of Izta any time of year and it is nearly always below freezing near the summit at night. Ice and snow are fixtures here; the average snow line is 4200 meters. The best months for ascents are October to February, when there is hard snow for crampons. February and March are sometimes prone to storms and poor visibility. The rainy season, from April to September, brings with it the threat of whiteouts, thunderstorms and avalanches.

Altitude

Anyone can be affected by altitude problems, including life-threatening altitude sickness. Even the Paso de Cortés (3650 meters), the turnoff for Izta, is at a level where you should know the symptoms – see Altitude Sickness in the Health section of the Facts for the Visitor chapter.

Guides

Iztaccíhuatl should be attempted by experienced climbers *only*, and because of hidden crevices on the ice-covered upper slopes, a guide is highly recommended.

Mario Andrade, director of Coordinadores de Guías de Montaña, a professional group that provides qualified guides for most Mexican peaks, has led many Izta ascents. He speaks Spanish and English and can recommend a capable guide when he is unavailable. His fee for leading one or two climbers up Izta is US$350; the cost includes transportation from Mexico City to Izta and back, guide, lodging and national park entry fees, two mountain meals, and the use of rope. Contact Andrade through Coordinadores de Guías (☎ /fax 5-584-46-95) at Tlaxcala 47 in Colonia Roma in Mexico City, or at his Mexico City home (☎ 5-875-01-05). His mailing address is PO Box M-10380, México DF, Mexico.

Climbing Iztaccíhuatl

Izta's highest peak is El Pecho at 5286 meters, and all of the routes to it require a night on the mountain. The usual routes begin at La Joya car park. Between there and Las Rodillas there are several shelter huts that could be used during an ascent of El Pecho. On average, it takes five hours to reach the huts from La Joya, another four hours from the huts to El Pecho, and four hours to descend. There are other huts and other routes on Izta.

If you opt to use Andrade's services, he will pick you up in Mexico City at 8 am and drive you to Amecameca, from which both of you will travel by taxi to La Joya and begin climbing immediately. You will eat and spend the night at a hut at 4700 meters, and begin the final ascent at 4 am. You should reach the summit by 9 am. A taxi will meet you both at La Joya that afternoon to take you back to Amecameca, from which Andrade will drive you back to Mexico City.

Amecameca
pop 41,666; alt 2480m; ☎ *597*

From the Mexico City side, the town of Amecameca, 60 km by road from the city, is the key staging post for an Izta climb. There are a few restaurants around the plaza and a cheap hotel, the *San Carlos* (no phone), in the southeast corner. A lively market is held on the weekends in front of the church.

Getting There & Away
From Mexico City's Terminal Oriente (TAPO), the 2nd-class Sur bus line runs every few minutes to/from Amecameca (1¼ hours; US$1.20) and Cuautla. From Amecameca bus station, turn right and walk two blocks to the plaza.

TLAXCALA
pop 61,514; alt 2252m; ☎ *246*

About 120 km east of Mexico City and 30 km north of Puebla, this quiet colonial town is the capital of Tlaxcala state, Mexico's smallest state. It makes a pleasant day trip from either city.

History
In the last centuries before the Spanish conquest, numerous small warrior kingdoms *(señoríos)* arose in the Tlaxcala area. Some of them formed a loose federation that managed to stay independent of the Aztec empire as it spread from the Valle de México in the 15th century. The most important kingdom seems to have been Tizatlán, now on the edge of Tlaxcala city.

When the Spanish arrived in 1519 the Tlaxcalans fought them fiercely at first, but then became Cortés' staunchest allies against the Aztecs (with the exception of one chief, Xicoténcatl the Younger, who tried at least twice to rouse his people against the Spanish and is now a Mexican hero). The Spanish rewarded the Tlaxcalans with privileges and used them to help pacify and settle Chichimec areas to the north. In 1527 Tlaxcala became the seat of the first bishopric in Nueva España, but a plague in the 1540s decimated the population and the town never played an important role again.

Orientation
Two central plazas meet on the corner of Independencia and Muñoz. The northern one, surrounded by colonial buildings, is the zócalo, called Plaza de la Constitución. The other one, Plaza Xicohténcatl, has a crafts market on Saturday. Tlaxcala's bus station is one km southwest of the plazas.

Information
The Tlaxcala state tourist office (☎ 2-00-27) is on the corner of Juárez and Lardizabal. It's open weekdays from 9 am to 7 pm, weekends from 10 am to 6 pm. Its helpful staff speak some English. The post office is on the west side of the zócalo. Bancomer and Banamex (with ATMs) have branches nearby.

Zócalo
The spacious, shady zócalo is one of the best looking in Mexico. Most of its north side is taken up by the 16th century **Palacio Municipal**, a former grain storehouse, and the **Palacio de Gobierno**; inside the latter are more than 450 sq meters of vivid murals of Tlaxcala's history by Desiderio Hernández Xochitiotzin, one of Mexico's top muralists. It took him 30 years to complete the murals, which are considered his finest. Just off the zócalo's northwest corner is the pretty brick, tile and stucco **Parroquia de San José**.

Ex-Convento San Francisco
This former monastery is up a short, steep path from the southeast corner of Plaza Xicohténcatl. This was one of Mexico's earliest monasteries, built between 1537 and 1540, and its church – the city's cathedral – has a beautiful Moorish-style wooden ceiling. Admission is free. Next to the church is the **Museo Regional de Tlaxcala**, which includes showrooms with permanent exhibits that describe the environment and condition of Tlaxcala through

AROUND MEXICO CITY

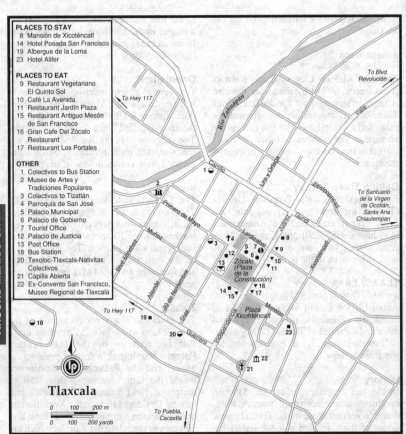

PLACES TO STAY
8   Mansión de Xicoténcatl
14 Hotel Posada San Francisco
18 Albergue de la Loma
23 Hotel Alifer

PLACES TO EAT
9   Restaurant Vegetariano
    El Quinto Sol
10 Café La Avenida
11 Restaurant Jardín Plaza
15 Restaurant Antiguo Mesón
    de San Francisco
16 Gran Cafe Del Zócalo
    Restaurant
17 Restaurant Los Portales

OTHER
1   Colectivos to Bus Station
2   Museo de Artes y
    Tradiciones Populares
3   Colectivos to Tizatlán
4   Parroquia de San José
5   Palacio Municipal
6   Palacio de Gobierno
7   Tourist Office
12 Palacio de Justicia
18 Post Office
18 Bus Station
20 Texoloc-Tlaxcala-Nativitas
    Colectivos
21 Capilla Abierta
22 Ex-Convento San Francisco,
    Museo Regional de Tlaxcala

Tlaxcala

0   100   200 m
0   100   200 yards

To Blvd Revolución

To Hwy 117

Río Zahuapan

To Santuario
de la Virgen
de Ocotlán,
Santa Ana
Chiautempan

Zócalo
(Plaza
de la
Constitución)

Plaza
Xicohténcatl

To Hwy 117

To Puebla,
Cacaxtla

the pre-Hispanic, colonial, independent, reform and revolutionary periods. The museum is open Tuesday through Sunday from 10 am to 5 pm.

Museo de Artes y Tradiciones Populares

This museum, on Sánchez near Lardizabal, has displays on Tlaxcalan village life, mask carving, weaving and pulque-making, sometimes with demonstrations. It's open from 10 am to 5 pm except on Monday (US$1). Next door, the Casa de Artesanías has handicrafts such as pottery

and textiles that are worth a look if you're in the market.

Santuario de la Virgen de Ocotlán

This is one of Mexico's most spectacular churches, and an important pilgrimage site because the Virgin is believed to have appeared here in 1541. The 18th century façade is a classic example of the Churrigueresque style, with white stucco 'wedding cake' decoration contrasting with plain red tiles. Inside, the 18th century Indian Francisco Miguel spent 25 years decorating the altarpieces and the chapel beside the main altar with a riot of color and gilding. An image of the Virgin stands on the main altar in memory of the 1541 apparition, and on the third Monday in May it is carried round other churches in a procession that attracts scores of pilgrims and onlookers.

The church is on a hill one km northeast of the zócalo. Walk north on Juárez for three blocks, then turn right up Zitlalpopocatl, or take an Ocotlán bus or colectivo from the bus station.

Santa Ana Chiautempan

This adjoining town, just east of Tlaxcala (and slightly bigger, with 63,000 people), is known for its weaving and embroidery. There's a market on Sunday, but you can see examples in shops any time. Take a local bus, or keep walking east of Ocotlán.

Tizatlán

These ruins are the scant remains of Xicoténcatl's palace. Under a shelter are two altars with some faded frescos showing gods such as Tezcatlipoca (Smoking Mirror), Tlahuizcalpantecuhtli (Morning Star) and Mictlantecuhtli (Underworld). Templo San Estéban, next to the ruins, has a 16th century Franciscan capilla abierta and frescos showing angels playing medieval instruments. The site is on a small hill four km north of the town center; take a 'Tizatlán' colectivo from the corner of Primero de Mayo and 20 de Noviembre.

Places to Stay

The best centrally located budget place is the *Hotel Alifer* (☎ 2-56-78) at Morelos 11, which has clean singles/doubles, with TV and phone, around a paved car park for US$13/15. The hillside hotel is less than two blocks from the zócalo, but the last 50 meters may be too steep for some people.

Another good option is the modern *Albergue de la Loma* (☎ 2-04-24), up the slope at Guerrero 58, which has big, clean rooms with tiled bathrooms for US$18/21. Some rooms and all of the restaurant offer views of the city, but the 61 steps to the hotel may be too many for weak-kneed

people. Some beds are better than others; check before registering.

The cheapest option in Tlaxcala is the *Mansión de Xicoténcatl* (☎ 2-19-00) at Juárez 15, with big but basic rooms for US$7/8. At the opposite end of the spectrum is the ritzy *Hotel Posada San Francisco* (☎ 2-60-22), on the south side of the zócalo in a restored 19th century mansion, with a fine restaurant and an inviting pool; prices start at US$58/68.

Places to Eat

For breakfast and healthy snacks and meals, try the popular *Restaurant Vegetariano El Quinto Sol* on Juárez, next to the Mansión de Xicoténcatl hotel. Fixed-price meals (from US$2 to US$4) are good value, with fresh salads, fish and veggie burgers available, as well as yogurt, fruit, granola and a large variety of juices. A filling portion of yogurt with papaya, banana, pineapple and melon, topped off with granola, costs just US$2.50.

There's a row of places under the arcades on the east side of the zócalo. *Restaurant Jardín Plaza* is the best of the bunch, with delicious food served in a pleasant indoor-outdoor setting. One dish, the 'molcajete jardín plaza,' combines strips of beef, chicken and pan-fried bell peppers, and black beans, guacamole and string cheese. It's served in a large clay bowl and is quite tasty and reasonable (US$5.50). The *Restaurant Los Portales* is equally popular and equally priced, but the service isn't as good. Between these two is the *Gran Cafe Del Zócalo Restaurant*, which takes a step down from the others in service and quality.

Just north of the arcades is the popular *Café La Avenida*, where any time of day well-dressed patrons can be seen sipping good coffee (29 coffee drinks are available). Mealwise, the Avenida's strongest suits are its set breakfasts (US$3.50), its salads (around US$4) and its soups (US$2.50).

Just south of the arcades is the *Restaurant Antiguo Mesón de San Francisco*, on the corner of Muños and Juárez. The

Mesón specializes in seafood and offers an excellent tortilla soup for US$1.50, seafood cocktails for US$1.50 to US$4 and seafood entrees for US$4 to US$9.

Tlaxcala's priciest (and some would say finest) cuisine can be found in the restaurants at *Hotel Posada San Francisco* on the south side of the zócalo.

Getting There & Away
Flecha Azul provides hourly 2nd-class direct service to/from Puebla for US$1. Autobuses Tlaxcala-Apizaco-Huamantla (ATAH) runs 1st-class 'expresso' buses (US$5) every 30 minutes and 'ordinario' buses (US$4.50) every hour to/from Mexico City's Terminal Oriente (TAPO) – a two-hour trip.

Getting Around
Buses and white colectivos in Tlaxcala cost US$0.30. Gray colectivos, which are faster and less crowded, cost US$0.50. Most colectivos at the bus station go to the town center. From the center to the bus station, catch a white or gray colectivo on the southwest corner of Carrillo and Allende.

CACAXTLA & XOCHITÉCATL
The hilltop ruins at Cacaxtla (Ca-CASHT-la) feature vividly colored and well-preserved frescos showing, among many other scenes, nearly life-size jaguar and eagle warriors engaged in battle. The ruins were discovered in September 1975 when a group of men from the nearby village of San Miguel del Milagro, hoping to confirm suspicions of the presence of the ruins, dug a tunnel and came across a mural.

The much older ruins at Xochitécatl (So-chi-TEH-catl) two km away include an exceptionally wide pyramid as well as a circular pyramid. A German archaeologist confirmed the presence of the ruins in 1930, but it wasn't until 1992 that excavation of the site began. That job took two years, and Xochitécatl was opened to the public soon after. The two archaeological sites, 35 km northwest of Puebla and 20 km southwest of Tlaxcala, are among Mexico's most interesting. Both are easy to tour

and have explanatory signs in English and Spanish.

History
Cacaxtla was the capital of a group of Olmeca-Xicallanca or Putún Maya, who first came to central Mexico as early as 400 AD. After the decline of Cholula (which they may have helped bring about) around 600 AD, the Putún Maya became the chief power in southern Tlaxcala and the Puebla valley. Cacaxtla peaked from 650 to 900 AD before being abandoned by the year 1000 in the face of possibly Chichimec newcomers.

Two km west of Cacaxtla, atop a higher hill, the ruins of Xochitécatl predate Christ by a millennium. Just who first occupied the area is a matter of dispute, but experts agree that whereas Cacaxtla primarily served as living quarters for the ruling class, Xochitécatl was chiefly used for gory ceremonies to honor Quecholli, the fertility god. That isn't to say Cacaxtla didn't hold similar ceremonies; the skeletal remains of more than 200 mutilated children found there attest to Cacaxtla's bloody past.

Cacaxtla
From the car park it's 200 meters' walk to the Cacaxtla ticket office, museum, shop and restaurant. The site is open Tuesday to Sunday from 10 am to 4.30 pm. Entry is US$2 (free on Sunday and holidays). Save your ticket, as it will get you into the Xochitécatl ruins as well, and vice versa.

From the ticket office it's 300 meters more to the main attraction – a natural platform 200 meters long and 25 meters high called the Gran Basamento (Great Base), which is now under a huge metal roof. Here stood Cacaxtla's main religious and civil buildings and the residences of its ruling priestly classes. In front at the top of the entry stairs is an open space called the Plaza Norte. From here you follow a clockwise path around the ruins till you reach the murals.

Murals Archaeologists have yet to determine the identity of the muralists. Many of the symbols found in the murals are clearly from the Mexican highlands. Yet a Mayan influence appears in all of them, and the Maya lived in Yucatán. The appearance of Mayan style and Mexican-highlands symbols in a mural is unique to Cacaxtla and the subject of much speculation.

Before reaching the first mural you come to an altar before which is a small square pit. Within it were found the remains of 218 mutilated children. Their cries presumably were meant to please the rain god Tláloc, who may have rewarded the people with rain.

Just beyond the altar you come upon the Templo de Venus, which contains two anthropomorphic figures in blue – a man and a woman, wearing short jaguar skins. The figures signify the dual nature of Venus.

In the Templo Rojo (named for the amount of red paint used), nearly opposite the Templo de Venus, four murals appear. One shows a group of figures relating to the underworld, while another displays a natural motif of crops and water creatures (one, a frog walking on water, is quite intriguing).

Facing the north side of the Plaza Norte is the long Mural de la Batalla (Battle Mural), dating from just before 750 AD. It shows two groups of people, one wearing jaguar skins and the other bird feathers, engaged in a battle. The Olmeca-Xicallanca (the jaguar-warriors, with round shields) are clearly repelling invading Huastecs (the bird-warriors, with green stone ornaments and deformed skulls).

At the end of the Mural de la Batalla, turn left and climb some steps to see the second main group of murals, to your right behind a fence. The two major murals, also from about 750 AD, show a figure in bird costume with black-painted body (who may be the Olmeca-Xicallanca priest-governor) and a figure in jaguar costume.

Xochitécatl

To enter the Xochitécatl car park you must show your ticket from Cacaxtla to a guard at the entrance of the car park, or buy a ticket from him. From the car park follow a path around to a circular pyramid, the Pirámide en Espiral, atop which there's a cross put there by people from a neighboring village long before they knew the hill contained a pyramid. From this pyramid the path leads you to three other pyramids – one low in stature (Volcanos Basamento), the next mid-size (the Pirámide de la Serpiente), and the last quite large (the Pirámide de las Flores).

The site is open Tuesday to Sunday from 10 am to 4.30 pm. Entry is US$2 (free on Sunday and holidays).

Pirámide en Espiral Because of its outline and the materials used, archaeologists believe this circular pyramid was built between 1000 and 800 BC. Its form and location atop a high hill suggest it may have been used as an astronomical observation post or as a temple to Ehecatl, the wind god.

Volcanos Basamento Only the base of this pyramid remains, and it is made of materials from two periods. In areas it is possible to see the original stone. Later, cut square stones were placed over the original stones and then stuccoed over. The colored stones used to build Tlaxcala's municipal palace appear to have come from this site.

Pirámide de la Serpiente This structure gets it name from a large piece of carved stone that has part of the head of a snake at one end. The most interesting feature of this pyramid is the huge pot found at its center. It is carved from a single boulder that was hauled from another region and then cut at its present site. Scientists surmise it was used to hold water.

Pirámide de las Flores Experts speculate that rituals honoring the fertility god were held here. Inside the 'Pyramid of Flowers' were found several sculptures and the remains of 30 sacrificed infants. Near the pyramid's base – the fourth widest in Latin America – is a pool carved from a massive rock. It is thought the infants were washed in the pool before being killed.

Getting There & Away

The Cacaxtla site is 1.5 km uphill from a back road between San Martín Texmelucan (near highway 190D) and highway 119, which is the secondary road between Puebla and Tlaxcala. A sign 1.5 km west of the village of Nativitas points to Cacaxtla and to the nearby village of San Miguel del Milagro. Some local buses go right to the site, while others only stop at its driveway. By car, turn west off highway 119 at the 'Cacaxtla' sign just north of Zacatelco. From there it's 7.5 km to the Cacaxtla turn-off. From Cacaxtla to Xochitécatl, take a taxi (US$3), or hike the two km.

By public transport from Tlaxcala, take a 'Texoloc-Tlaxcala-Nativitas' colectivo from Porfirio Díaz at Guerrero, or an Auto-buses Tepetitla 'Nativitas' bus from the bus station. From the Puebla bus station, take a 'Zacatelco-San Martín' bus. These leave every 10 minutes; tickets are sold at the Flecha Azul desk. Or get a bus from Tlax-cala or Puebla to Zacatelco, then a minibus to San Miguel del Milagro, which will drop you 300 meters from the site.

LA MALINCHE

This dormant 4450-meter volcano, named after Cortés' Indian interpreter and lover, is 30 km southeast of Tlaxcala and 30 km northeast of Puebla. Its long, sweeping slopes dominate the skyline north of Puebla.

The main route to the summit is from highway 136. Turn south on the road to Centro Vacacional Malintzi, a state-run resort 15 km from the highway that is only open to Mexico's top athletes. The road becomes impassable at 3000 meters. Then it's one km by footpath, through trees initially, on to a ridge leading to the top. La Malinche is snow-capped only a few weeks each year.

HUAMANTLA

pop 59,099; alt 2500m; ☎ 247

This town dates from 1534 and is a national historic monument. Two of the most notable buildings are the 16th century **Ex-Convento San Francisco** and the 18th century baroque **Iglesia de San Luis**. The state of Tlaxcala breeds many of Mexico's fighting bulls, and Huamantla boasts a **Museo Taurino** (Bullfight Museum) that will interest aficionados. During the **fiesta** (first two weeks of August) people cover the town's streets with beautifully arranged flowers. A 'running of the bulls' like that in Pamplona, Spain – but actually much more dangerous, because there is nothing to hide behind and because Huamantla's bulls charge from two directions – is held on the Sunday following the feast of the Assumption (August 15). A quieter attraction is the **Museo Nacional del Títere** (National Puppet Museum), with exhibits on puppetry. Huamantla's history of puppet-making and puppet shows dates to 1850. The museum exhibits locally made puppets and some from other countries.

There are three worthy hotels in the area: *El Centenario* (☎ 2-06-00) at Juárez 209 Nte has singles/doubles for US$10/12; the *Hotel Mesón del Portal* (☎ 2-26-26) at Parque Juárez 9 charges US$13 for one or two people; and the *Hotel Cuamanco* (☎ 2-22-09) at km 146 on the Mexico City-Veracruz road charges US$13/16.

PUEBLA

pop 1.2 million; alt 2162m; ☎ 22

Few Mexican cities preserve the Spanish imprint as faithfully as Puebla. There are more than 70 churches and a thousand other colonial buildings in the central area alone – many adorned with the hand-painted tiles for which the city is famous. Located on the Veracruz-Mexico City road, and set in a broad valley with Popocatépetl and Iztaccíhuatl rising to the west, Puebla has always played a main role in national affairs.

Strongly Catholic, criollo and conservative, its people (Poblanos) maintained Spanish affinities longer than most other Mexicans. In the 19th century their patriotism was regarded as suspect and today Puebla's Spanish-descended families have a reputation among other Mexicans for

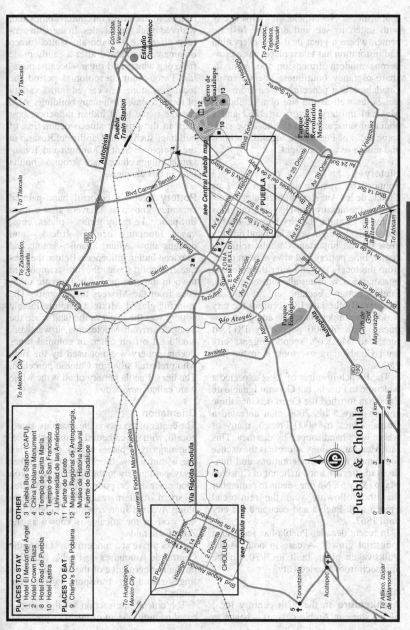

PLACES TO STAY
1 Hotel El Mesón del Angel
2 Hotel Crown Plaza
8 Hotel Real de Puebla
10 Hotel Lastra

PLACES TO EAT
9 Charlie's China Poblana

OTHER
3 China Poblana Monument
4 Templo de Santa María
6 Templo de San Francisco
7 Universidad de las Américas
11 Fuerte de Loreto
12 Museo Regional de Antropología,
   Museo de Historia Natural
13 Fuerte de Guadalupe

Puebla Bus Station (CAPU)

see Central Puebla map

PUEBLA

see Cholula map

CHOLULA

Puebla & Cholula

snobbishness. Nevertheless it's a lively city with much to see and do. The historic center, where a great deal of conservation and restoration has taken place, has a prosperous modern dimension too, with its share of fancy boutiques. The Cerro de Guadalupe is a peaceful retreat from city noises, as well as the site of a celebrated Mexican military victory in 1862 and a clutch of museums. On the negative side, some areas of Puebla are squalid, polluted and unsafe to walk at night.

History
Founded by Spanish settlers in 1531 as Ciudad de los Angeles, with the aim of surpassing the nearby pre-Hispanic religious center of Cholula, the city became Puebla de los Angeles eight years later and quickly grew into an important Catholic religious center. Fine pottery had always been made from the local clay, and after the colonists introduced new materials and techniques, Puebla pottery became an art and an industry. By the late 18th century the city was also an important textile and glass producer. With 50,000 people by 1811, it remained Mexico's second-biggest city until Guadalajara overtook it in the late 1800s.

The French invaders of 1862 expected a welcome in Puebla, but General Ignacio de Zaragoza fortified the Cerro de Guadalupe and on May 5 his 2000 men defeated a frontal attack by 6000 French, many of whom were handicapped by diarrhea. This rare Mexican military success is the excuse for annual national celebrations and hundreds of streets named in honor of Cinco de Mayo (May 5). No one seems to remember that the following year the reinforced French took Puebla and occupied the city until 1867.

In recent decades Puebla has seen huge industrial growth. A case in point is the Volkswagen plant, built in 1970, on the approach from Mexico City.

Arts
Architecture In the 17th century local tiles – some in Arabic designs – began to be used to fine effect on church domes and, with red brick, on façades. In the 18th century *alfeñique* – elaborate white stucco ornamentation named after a candy made from egg whites and sugar – became popular. Throughout the colonial period the local gray stone was carved into a variety of forms to embellish many buildings. Also notable is the local Indian influence, best seen in the prolific stucco decoration of buildings such as the Capilla del Rosario in the Templo de Santo Domingo and Tonantzintla village church (see Around Cholula later in this chapter).

Pottery Puebla's colorful hand-painted ceramics, known as Talavera after a town in Spain, take many forms – plates, cups, vases, fountains, *azulejos* (tiles) – and designs show Asian, Spanish-Arabic and Mexican Indian influences. Before the conquest, Cholula was the most important town in the area, and it had artistic influence from the Mixtecs to the south. The colorful glazed Mixteca-Cholula-Puebla pottery was the finest in the land when the Spanish arrived; Moctezuma, it was said, would eat off no other. In colonial times Puebla pottery was not used by the rich, who preferred silver or Chinese porcelain. The finest Puebla pottery of all is the white ware called *majolica*.

Orientation
The center of the city is the spacious, shady zócalo, with the cathedral on its south side. The majority of places to stay, eat and visit are within a few blocks of here. Farther away, particularly to the north or west, you soon enter dirtier, poorer streets. The area of smart, modern restaurants and shops along Avenida Juárez, which is about two km west of the zócalo, is known as the Zona Esmeralda.

Buses arrive at a modern bus station, the Central de Autobuses de Puebla (CAPU), on the northern edge of the city. (See Getting Around for transport to/from the center.)

The crucial intersection for the complicated naming system of Puebla's grid-plan

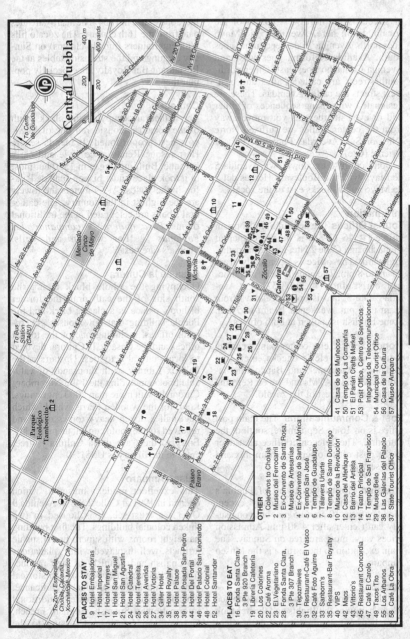

Central Puebla

PLACES TO STAY
9 Hotel Embajadoras
11 Hotel Imperial
17 Hotel Virreyes
18 Hotel San Miguel
21 Hotel San Agustín
24 Hotel Catedral
25 Hotel Teresita
26 Hotel Avenida
27 Hotel Victoria
34 Gilfer Hotel
35 Hotel Royalty
38 Hotel Palace
39 Hotel Posada San Pedro
44 Hotel Del Portal
46 Hotel Palacio San Leonardo
48 Hotel Colonial
52 Hotel Santander

PLACES TO EAT
16 Fonda Santa Clara,
   3 Pte 920 Branch
19 Librería Cafetería
20 Los Colorines
22 Café Aroma
23 El Vegetariano
28 Fonda Santa Clara,
   3 Pte 307 Branch
30 Tepoznieves
31 Restaurant-Café El Vasco
32 Café Foto Aguirre
33 Sanborn's
35 Restaurant-Bar Royalty
40 VIPS
42 Macs
43 Vittorio's
45 Restaurant Concordia
47 Café El Carolo
49 Tacos Tito
55 Los Arbanos
58 Café La Obra

OTHER
1 Colectivos to Cholula
2 Museo del Ferrocarril
3 Ex-Convento de Santa Rosa,
   Museo de Artesanías
4 Ex-Convento de Santa Mónica
5 Templo San José
6 Templo de Guadalupe
7 Talavera Uriarte
8 Templo de Santo Domingo
10 Museo de la Revolución
12 Casa del Alfeñique
13 Barrio del Artista
14 Teatro Principal
15 Templo de San Francisco
29 Museo Bello
36 Las Galerías del Palacio
37 State Tourist Office
41 Casa de los Muñecos
50 Templo de La Compañía
51 El Parián Crafts Market
53 Post Office, Centro de Servicios
   Integrados de Telecomunicaciones
54 Municipal Tourist Office
56 Casa de la Cultura
57 Museo Amparo

of streets is the northwest corner of the zócalo. From here, Avenida 5 de Mayo goes north, Avenida 16 de Septiembre goes south, Avenida Reforma goes west and Avenida Camacho goes east. Other north-south streets are called Calles and east-west streets are called Avenidas. These are designated with rising sequences of either odd or even numbers as you move away from the center. Calles are suffixed Norte (Nte) or Sur, Avenidas Poniente (Pte) or Oriente (Ote).

Don't confuse the downtown Avenida 5 de Mayo with the Boulevard Héroes del 5 de Mayo a few blocks east of the zócalo.

Information

Tourist Offices The helpful State Tourism Office (☎ 46-12-85) is on the corner of Camacho and Calle 2 Nte, facing the cathedral yard. The office is open daily from 10 am to 8 pm. The equally helpful municipal tourist office (☎ 32-03-57) is at Avenida 5 Ote 3, and is open weekdays from 9 am to 8 pm, weekends 10 am to 7 pm. Some English is spoken at both offices.

Money Several city-center banks change money and traveler's checks, including Banamex, Bancomer and Banco Internacional. All have ATMs and are on Reforma within a block west of the zócalo.

Post & Communications The main post office is on 16 de Septiembre, south of the cathedral. The Telecomm office next door to the post office offers telegram, fax and telex services.

Museum Hours Nearly all of Puebla's many museums are open daily except Monday from 10 am to 5 pm, but you usually can't enter after 4.30 pm. Admission prices vary; most are free on Sunday. The main exception to these rules is the Museo Amparo.

Zócalo

Puebla's central plaza was a marketplace where hangings, bullfights and theater took place before it acquired its current garden-

like appearance in 1854. The nearby arcades date from the 16th century. The zócalo fills with entertainers (mostly clowns) on Sunday evening and the streetside tables at the Restaurant-Bar Royalty are especially popular then.

Cathedral

The cathedral occupying the block south of the zócalo is considered one of Mexico's best proportioned. It blends severe Herreresque Renaissance style and early baroque. Building began in 1550 but most of it took place under bishop Juan de Palafox in the 1640s. At 69 meters the towers are the highest in the country. The cathedral's bells are celebrated in the traditional rhyme *Para mujeres y campanas, las Poblanas* – 'For women and bells, Puebla's (are best).'

Casa de la Cultura

Occupying the whole block facing the south side of the cathedral, the former bishop's palace is a classic brick-and-tile Puebla building that now houses government offices, including one of the tourist offices and the Casa de la Cultura, devoted to local cultural activities. Upstairs is the Palafox Library, with thousands of valuable books, including the 1493 Nuremberg Chronicle with more than 2000 engravings. Look for the wooden Ferris wheel, which held half a dozen heavy tomes open and revolved so one could consult them quickly. Entry to the Casa de la Cultura is free; entry to the library is US$1.30.

Museo Amparo

This excellent modern museum, which opened in 1991 at Calle 2 Sur at Avenida 9 Ote, is a must-see. It is housed in two linked colonial buildings. The first building has eight rooms with superb pre-Hispanic artifacts, well displayed with explanations (in English and Spanish) of their production techniques, regional and historical context and anthropological significance. An audiovisual system offers additional information in Spanish, English, French, German and Japanese. Crossing to the second building, you enter a series of rooms rich with the finest art and furnishings from the colonial period. The contrast between the pre-Hispanic and European styles shows the enormity of the clash of civilizations that commenced with the Conquest.

The museum is open daily except Tuesday from 10 am to 6 pm, and entry is US$2.25 (free on Monday). Rental of the headphones for the audiovisual system costs another US$1. The museum has a library, a cafeteria and a very good bookstore.

Museo Bello

This house at Avenida 3 Pte 302 is filled with the diverse art and crafts collection of 19th century industrialist José Luis Bello and his son Mariano. There is exquisite French, English, Japanese and Chinese porcelain, and a large collection of Pueblan Talavera. Other items include nuns' spiked flagellation chains and a door of glass columns, each with a different musical pitch. Admission costs US$1.50 (free Saturday). Tours are available in Spanish and English.

Las Galerías del Palacio

Las Galerías del Palacio displays contemporary art from throughout Mexico and features exhibits emphasizing Mexican culture. At the time of writing, three exhibits were displayed: one on traditional bread-making methods used in Mexico, another on signature stamps used by the Spanish, and a third on a local artist's watercolors of Puebla churches. The galleries, located near the State Tourism Office, are open daily from 9 am to 9 pm; admission is free.

Casa de los Muñecos

The tiles on the House of the Puppets on 2 Nte, near the zócalo's northeast corner, caricature the city fathers who took the house's owner to court because his home was taller than theirs. Inside is the Museo Universitario (US$1), telling the story of education in Puebla.

Templo de la Compañía

This Jesuit church with a 1767 Churrigueresque façade, on the corner of Camacho and 4 Sur, is also called Espíritu Santo. Beneath the altar is a tomb said to be that of a 17th century Asian princess who was sold into slavery in Mexico and later freed. She is supposed to have originated the colorful China Poblana costume of shawl, frilled blouse, embroidered skirt and gold and silver adornments – a kind of peasant chic fashionable in the 19th century. But *china* also meant maidservant and the style may have come from Spanish peasant costumes. Next door, the 16th century Edificio Carolino, formerly a Jesuit college, is now the main building of Puebla University.

Casa del Alfeñique

This house, on the corner of Calle 6 Nte and Avenida 4 Ote, is an outstanding example of the 18th century decorative style alfeñique. Inside is the Museo del Estado with 18th and 19th century Puebla paraphernalia such as China Poblana gear, carriages and furniture. The entry fee is US$1.50.

Teatro Principal & Barrio del Artista

The theater on Calle 6 Nte between Avenidas 6 and 8 Ote dates from 1756, which makes it one of the oldest in the Americas – sort of. It went up in flames in 1902 and was rebuilt in the 1930s. You can go inside between 10 am and 5 pm if it's not in use. Nearby, the pedestrian-only Calle 8 Nte, between Avenidas 4 and 6 Ote, is the Barrio del Artista, with open studios where you can meet artists and buy their work.

Templo de San Francisco

The north doorway of San Francisco, just east of Boulevard Héroes del 5 de Mayo on Avenida 14 Ote (Xonaca), is a good example of 16th century plateresque; the tower and fine brick-and-tile façade were added in the 18th century. In a glass case in the church's north chapel is the body of San Sebastián de Aparicio, a Spaniard who came to Mexico in 1533 and planned many of the country's roads before becoming a monk. His body attracts a stream of worshippers. The chapel contains many paintings of his life, and his statue stands outside the church.

Museo de la Revolución

This house at Avenida 6 Ote 206 was the scene of the first battle of the 1910 revolution. Betrayed only two days before a planned uprising against Porfirio Díaz's dictatorship, the Serdán family (Aquiles, Máximo, Carmen and Natalia) and 17 others fought 500 soldiers until only Aquiles, their leader, and Carmen were left alive. Aquiles, hidden under the floorboards, might have survived if the damp hadn't provoked a cough that gave him away. The house retains its bullet holes and other memorabilia, including a room dedicated to women of the revolution. Entry is US$1.50.

Templo de Santo Domingo

Santo Domingo, 2½ blocks north of the zócalo on Avenida 5 de Mayo, is a fine church, but its Capilla del Rosario (Rosary Chapel), south of the main altar, is a gem. Built between 1680 and 1720, it has a sumptuous baroque proliferation of gilded plaster and carved stone with angels and cherubim popping out from behind every leaf. See if you can spot the heavenly orchestra.

Ex-Convento de Santa Rosa & Museo de Artesanías

This 17th century ex-nunnery houses an extensive collection of Puebla state handicrafts. You must do an English or Spanish tour with a guide, who may try to rush you through the fine displays of Indian costumes, pottery, onyx, glass and metal work. *Mole poblano* is said to have been created in the kitchen of the ex-convent (see Puebla Specialties in the Places to Eat section). Enter from Avenida 14 Pte between Calles 3 and 5 Nte (US$1.50).

Ex-Convento de Santa Mónica

Another nunnery-museum, Santa Mónica has a lovely tiled courtyard, a collection of religious art, and old nuns' cells where you can see instruments of self-flagellation. It's at Avenida 18 Pte 101 near the corner of Avenida 5 de Mayo (US$1).

Museo del Ferrocarril

A dozen vintage locomotives from the majestic to the quaint repose outside the old station, facing the junction of 11 Nte and Avenida 12 Pte (free).

Cerro de Guadalupe

The hilltop park stretching one km east of 2 Nte, two km northeast of the zócalo, contains the historic forts of Loreto and Guadalupe and the Centro Cívico 5 de Mayo, a group of museums and exhibitions. Good views, relatively fresh air and eucalyptus woods add to the appeal. Take a 'Loreto' bus (US$0.30) from the corner of Avenidas 5 de Mayo and 10 Pte to get there.

The **Fuerte de Loreto** at the west end of the hilltop was one of the Mexican defense points on May 5, 1862, during the victory over the invading French. Today it houses the Museo de la Intervención, with displays of uniforms and documents relating to the French occupation of Mexico (US$2).

A short walk east of the fort, beyond the domed auditorium, are the **Museo Regional de Antropología** (US$2), tracing human history in the state, the **Museo de Historia Natural** (US$2) and the pyramid-shaped **Planetario de Puebla**. At the east end of the hilltop is the **Fuerte de Guadalupe** (US$3), which also played a part in the battle of May 5, 1862.

Africam Safari Park

One of the best places in Mexico to see wildlife is in this park 16 km southeast of Puebla, on the road to Presa Valsequillo. The animals – among them rhinos, bears and tigers – are free to roam in spacious 'natural' settings, and you can view them up close from within your car, a taxi or an Africam bus. On occasion lions and tigers approach the vehicles that cruise through their habitats, and monkeys like to mount the roofs of buses. Africam is great fun.

Estrella Roja runs direct buses from CAPU daily for US$2.50, US$2 for children; Africam buses will return you to CAPU for US$1.50. It's best to arrive at the park in the morning, when the animals are most active. Entry fees are a bargain at US$5, US$4.50 for children. The park is open every day of the year. Ring Africam for further details (☎ 35-09-75).

Places to Stay – budget

Some of Puebla's cheapest budget hotels bear a strong resemblance to jails. A good example is the *Hotel Santander* (☎ 46-31-75) on Avenida 5 Pte west of the cathedral, where the cheapest cells cost US$11 and have clanging steel doors and no windows. They do have hot water and TVs.

An even lower bottom-end place is the *Hotel Avenida* (☎ 32-21-04) at Avenida 5 Pte 141, 1½ blocks west of the center. It's an old building with singles/doubles facing a courtyard or the street for US$5/6. It's about as clean as a hotel can be with flaking plaster and missing tiles.

A huge step up in quality but not price is the *Hotel Teresita* (☎ 32-70-72) at Avenida 3 Pte 309, 1½ blocks west of the zócalo. The hotel has new carpet, retiled baths and good beds. It may be the best of the budgets for US$10/12, and US$13 for two beds.

The *Hotel Victoria* (☎ 32-89-92), across the street at 3 Pte 306, is gloomy and faded, but friendly enough and clean. Rooms with private bath are US$9/10. The *Hotel Catedral* (☎ 32-23-68) two doors down from the Victoria offers depressing rooms, but it has an econo community room with six good beds and clean shared bath with hot water for a very amenable US$4.

A block west at Avenida 3 Pte 531, the *Hotel San Agustín* (32-50-89) is a better deal than the Victoria – cleaner, with better beds – but pricier at US$13 for a room.

Hotel Virreyes (☎ 42-49-80) at Avenida 3 Pte 912 has large, clean, wood-beamed rooms along two wide balconies above a courtyard car park. It's a bit run-down, but is not a bad deal for US$13 for a single or double, US$15 for two beds.

The Virreyes also offers rooms with public bath for US$7/9.

North of the center, rooms at the *Hotel Embajadoras* (☎ 32-26-37), on 5 de Mayo between 6 and 8 Ote, are US$4/5 with shared bath, US$6/7 with private bath. The rooms are on three floors and are large and pretty clean, but are also dark, bare and very worn. The building surrounds a covered courtyard.

Places to Stay – middle

The *Hotel Imperial* (☎ 42-49-80), at Avenida 4 Ote 212, is a total dump; nevertheless, rates are US$13/22.

West of the zócalo, The *Hotel San Miguel* (☎ 42-48-60) at Avenida 3 Pte 721, has clean, respectably sized rooms with private bath and TV for US$23/26.

Some of the pricier mid-range places have lots of charm. *Hotel Colonial* (☎ 46-47-09) at 4 Sur 105 on the corner of 3 Ote, a block east of the zócalo, has lovely rooms for US$26/28. Once part of a Jesuit monastery, it maintains a hearty colonial atmosphere despite being modernized. Most of the 70 rooms are big and tiled, with TVs and phones. Upstairs exterior rooms are best. The hotel has an old glass-domed dining room with a carved stone fountain and several attractive sitting areas. It's often full, so you'd be wise to reserve a room. (The hotel's only elevator is slow, tiny and bellboy-operated; getting to your room quickly usually means having to climb stairs.)

The 54-room *Hotel Royalty* (☎ 42-47-40) is another friendly, well-kept colonial-style place, located on the zócalo at Portal Hidalgo 8. The smallish rooms are comfortable and colorful, with carpet and TV and cost a reasonable US$25/32.

The *Hotel Palace* (☎ 42-40-30) at Avenida 2 Ote 13 is yet another pleasant and centrally located mid-range place. It asks US$25 for a single or double, US$33 for two beds. A better deal is the 92-room *Gilfer Hotel* (☎ 46-06-11) one block off the zócalo at Avenida 2 Ote 11, which has comfortable modern rooms with TV, phone and a safe for US$24/30.

The outwardly colonial *Hotel Del Portal* (☎ 46-02-11) at Camacho 205 has a modern interior. The Portal's rooms are comparable to the Colonial's but cost considerably more (US$32/41).

Places to Stay – top end
The *Hotel Posada San Pedro* (☎ 46-50-77), in a colonial building at Avenida 2 Ote 202, has a small pool and two restaurants but the rooms, while pleasant, are not any nicer than the Royalty's and cost much more – US$42/54. The central *Hotel Palacio San Leonardo* (☎ 46-05-55), at Avenida 2 Ote 211, has an elegant lobby with a colored glass ceiling, but likewise charges way too much for its rooms – US$51/55.

The 52-room *Hotel Lastra* (☎ 35-97-55) at Calzada de los Fuertes 2633, two km northeast of the zócalo on the Cerro de Guadalupe, offers a peaceful location, good views, easy parking and a pleasing garden. Singles and doubles go for US$40 Monday through Thursday, US$48 Friday through Sunday. They are comfortable, sizable and come in various shapes. It's a long but pleasant walk to the city center.

There are three top hotels outside the city center, all of which offer rooms starting at US$75. They're all suitably luxurious, but you miss out on the charm of central Puebla. The best of these is the 190-room *Hotel El Mesón del Angel* (☎ 24-30-00) at Hermanos Serdán 807, six km northwest of the center, just off the Mexico City autopista. There are two pools, tennis courts and several restaurants and bars. The other two are the 400-room *Hotel Crown Plaza* (☎ 48-60-55), three km nearer the center at Hermanos Serdán 141, and the *Hotel Real de Puebla* (☎ 48-96-00) at Avenida 5 Pte 2522 in the Zona Esmeralda.

Places to Eat
Specialties A super place to try Poblano food is the *Fonda Santa Clara*, which has two branches, both on Avenida 3 Pte. Both have the same menu, which is available in English and Spanish. The one at No 307, which is closed on Monday, is nearer to the zócalo and usually busier, but the food at No 920, which closes on Tuesday, is equally good and the atmosphere more festive. The Santa Clara's delicious chicken mole costs US$6, and its enchiladas US$5. Also quite tasty is the *mixiotes* – a stew of sliced lamb – served with guacamole (US$7). Their soups, from US$2 to US$3, are excellent.

Vegetarian *El Vegetariano* at Avenida 3 Pte 525, open from 7.30 am to 9 pm, has a long menu of meatless dishes such as chiles rellenos, Nepalese rellenos (stuffed cactus ears) and enchiladas Suizas, all of which come with salad, soup and a drink for around US$4.50, or à la carte for about US$3.

Cheap Eats & Snacks A pan árabe taco (see Puebla Originals sidebar) costs around US$1 – try one at *Tacos Tito*, which has several branches in the blocks around the zócalo, or at *Los Arbanos* on Avenida 7 Ote. *Tepoznieves*, on 3 Pte at 3 Sur, is Puebla's top traditional Mexican ice cream restaurant – it has lovely tables and chairs at which to enjoy their many cold and inexpensive selections.

Zócalo Area The zócalo's culinary highlight is *Vittorio's*, on the east side at Portal Morelos (2 Sur) 106. This Italian-run restaurant bills itself 'La Casa de la Pizza Increíble' in memory of a 20-sq-meter monster pizza it baked as a stunt back in 1981. The pizzas are still good, but not cheap at US$3 to US$7 for an individual size, and US$8 to US$17 for a grande (three- or four-person). Spaghetti bolognese is US$4 and fresh salads around US$3. A few doors down is *Macs*, a popular cafeteria with good food, and nearly every item is available in a 'junior' size for about half the regular price.

Other places around the zócalo have lots of atmosphere, but they tend to be expensive. The *Restaurant-Café El Vasco* is in Portal Juárez on the west side. It's the kind of place where couples and old friends meet for a chat, with a varied menu of good food. Antojitos go for US$2 to US$6, fish

Puebla Originals

Mole poblano, found on almost every menu in Puebla and imitated throughout Mexico, is a spicy chocolate sauce usually served over turkey (pavo or guajolote) or chicken – a real taste sensation if well prepared. Supposedly invented by Sor (Sister) Andrea de la Asunción of the Convento de Santa Rosa for a visit by the viceroy, it traditionally contains fresh chile, chipotle (a fermented chili concoction), pepper, peanuts, almonds, cinnamon, aniseed, tomato, onion, garlic and, of course, chocolate.

A seasonal Puebla dish, available in July, August and September, is *chiles en nogada*, said to have been created in 1821 to honor Agustín de Iturbide, the first ruler of independent Mexico. Its colors are those of the national flag: large green chilies stuffed with meat and fruit are covered with a creamy white walnut sauce and sprinkled with red pomegranate seeds.

In April and May you can try *gusanos de maguey* and in March *escamoles* – respectively maguey worms and their eggs, prepared with avocados or hen eggs.

A *pan árabe* taco is Puebla's improvement on the taco – it's bigger, because it's made using pita bread. Another substantial Poblano snack is the *cemita*, a lightly toasted bread roll with cheese, chili, chicken, ham, onion, lettuce . . . sort of a super torta. *Camotes* are a local sticky sweet – sticks of fruit-flavored jelly. ∎

for US$3 to US$7, chicken US$4 to US$5, and beef for US$3 to US$6. On the north side, the smart *Restaurant-Bar Royalty* has outdoor tables where you can watch the world go by, but the view doesn't come cheap – even a café con leche will cost you US$1. Fish and meat dishes run to US$10.

Places off the zócalo are more reasonably priced, such as the *Café Foto Aguirre* on Avenida 5 de Mayo. It's a busy but clean and orderly place, popular with locals. Set breakfasts, with juice, coffee and eggs, cost around US$2.50, and the comida corrida

runs US$3. There's a *Sanborns* at Avenida 2 Ote 6 and a *VIPS* café and bookstore in a beautiful 19th century cast-iron building on the corner of Avenida 2 Ote and 2 Nte. Just east of VIPS on Avenida 2 Ote are some good cheapies like the popular *Restaurant Concordia*, with a range of four-course comidas corridas for around US$3. *Café El Carolo*, on Camacho half a block east of the zócalo, serves fruit salad, yogurt and other healthy stuff cheap, and a comida corrida for only US$2.50.

Café Aroma at 3 Pte 520, across the street from El Vegetariano, offers 25 different coffee drinks from 9 am to 8.45 pm. It has only six tables and they are usually occupied – a testament to Aroma's success with *the bean*. Typical price: US$1.50 per cup. Other offerings include sodas, sandwiches and hot dogs. *Los Colorines* on the corner of Reforma and 7 Nte is quite popular and its bilingual menu offers eggs and hotcakes for US$2.75 to US$5, Mexican plates ranging from US$2.75 to US$6, and sandwiches for US$2.75 to US$3.50.

Zona Esmeralda The upscale stretch of Juárez has lots of swish international-style restaurants – including German, Italian and Chinese. For a splash-out meal in gaudy surroundings go to *Charlie's China Poblana* at Juárez 1918. Now part of the Carlos Anderson chain, this venerable establishment serves meals from 1 pm to midnight, and the bar remains open much later. Salads cost US$3 and main courses around US$7 – a full meal could easily run to US$15. Pasta is *not* one of their strengths.

Entertainment

The *Librería Cafetería*, on the corner of Reforma and 7 Nte, is a bookstore-cum-café that fills up in the evenings with an arty/student crowd. There's live music most nights from 9 pm to 1 am. Coffee, cake, beer and booze are the most popular items here.

The bar at *Charlie's China Poblana* restaurant has a reputation as a pick-up spot. At night mariachis lurk around the

Callejón del Sapo, a pedestrian street between Avenidas 5 and 7 Ote, just east of 4 Sur.

For late-night live rock and roll in the Zona Esmeralda, try *Corcores* on Juárez two blocks east of Charlie's China Poblana. For live rock/blues on Sunday afternoon near the zócalo, the place to be is the *Café La Obra* on Avenida 3 Ote near 6 Sur.

For cultural events check with the tourist offices and the Casa de la Cultura.

Things to Buy

Quite a few shops along Avenida 18 Pte, west of the Ex-Convento de Santa Mónica, display and sell the pretty Puebla ceramics. The big pieces are very expensive and difficult for a traveler to carry, but you could buy a small hand-painted Talavera tile for US$5, or a plate for around US$10. Few of these places make pottery on site, but one that still does is Talavera Uriarte, with a factory and showroom at Avenida 4 Pte 911. The showroom is open daily; you can enter the factory on weekdays till 3 pm.

The city is also a good place to look for crafts from elsewhere in the state, like Indian textiles, Tecali onyx, and pottery from Acatlán de Osorio, Amozoc or Izúcar de Matamoros. A shop near the tourist office at Avenida 5 Ote 3 sells good examples of these crafts. It stays open weekdays till 8 pm.

El Parián crafts market, between 6 and 8 Nte and Avenidas 2 and 4 Ote, has local Talavera, onyx and trees of life, as well as the sorts of leather, jewelry and textiles that you find in other cities. Much of the work is crappy souvenirs, but there is some good stuff and prices are generally reasonable. There are lots of antique shops on and near Callejón del Sapo, between Avenidas 5 and 7 Ote just east of 4 Sur, with a wonderful variety of old books, furniture, bric-a-brac and junk. It's great for browsing, but most of these shops close for a long lunch break.

The three smart shopping areas are the streets just north of the zócalo, the Zona Esmeralda, and the Plaza Dorada beside Boulevard Héroes del 5 de Mayo.

Getting There & Away

Air The only flights into Aeropuerto Hermanos Serdán, which is 22 km west of Puebla on the Cholula-Huejotzingo road, are to/from Guadalajara and Tijuana by Aero California (☎ 30-48-55). Most people fly to Mexico City and travel by bus to Puebla.

Bus Puebla's bus station, the Central de Autobuses de Puebla (CAPU), is four km north of the zócalo and 1.5 km off the autopista, by the corner of Boulevards Norte and Carmen Serdán. It has a left-luggage facility, phone office, Banca Serfin branch (with ATM), restaurant and various shops.

Buses to/from Puebla use Mexico City's Terminal Oriente (TAPO). The 130-km trip takes about two hours. Three bus lines have frequent services: ADO, a 1st-class service, has directo buses leaving every 20 minutes (US$5); AU, a 2nd-class service, has directo buses leaving every 12 minutes (US$4.25); Estrella Roja has frequent 2nd-class buses (US$4.25). Estrella Roja also runs buses to the Mexico City airport hourly from 3 am to 8 pm, for US$8.

There is daily bus service from Puebla to just about everywhere in the south and east of Mexico, including:

Acapulco – 510 km, seven hours; one deluxe (US$26, 10 pm) and five 1st-class (US$24) by Estrella Blanca
Córdoba – 170 km, three hours; 11 ADO (US$12) and 25 AU (US$7.25)
Cuernavaca – 175 km, three hours; four deluxe (US$5.50) and 14 1st-class (US$5) by Autobuses Oro; frequent 2nd-class by Estrella Blanca (US$4.50)
Jalapa – 185 km, 3¼ hours; two ADO GL deluxe (US$8), seven ADO (US$7), and 13 AU (US$6)
Mérida – 1390 km, 22 hours; one ADO only, at 9.05 pm (US$70)
Oaxaca – 320 km, 4½ hours; two ADO GL deluxe (US$17), one UNO deluxe (US$20, 6 pm), five ADO (US$13) and three AU directos (US$11)
Tampico – 730 km, 14 hours; three ADO (US$20) and one 1st-class Estrella Blanca (US$20)

Tuxtla Gutiérrez – 870 km, 14½ hours; one UNO deluxe (US$52, 10.45 pm), one ADO (US$38, 10.40 pm) and one 1st-class Cristóbal Colón (US$38, 1.45 pm)

Veracruz – 300 km, five hours; five ADO-GL deluxe (US$12), seven ADO (US$11), and 13 AU (US$10)

Villahermosa – 690 km, 12 hours; one UNO deluxe (US$47), one ADO-GL deluxe (US$33), and two ADO (US$28)

Train Trains to/from Mexico City are absurdly slow (between five and 12 hours) but the train ride to Oaxaca is scenic. The best train is the daily El Oaxaqueño from Mexico City to Oaxaca, which is scheduled to leave Puebla at 11.50 pm and reach Oaxaca at 9.25 am, but is usually an hour or so late out of Puebla and two or three hours late reaching Oaxaca. It therefore passes through the dramatic Sierra Madre de Oaxaca in daylight. The Puebla-Oaxaca fare is US$8.75 in primera preferente and US$5 in segunda clase. Sleeper cars are not available. Check in the morning – or the day before – to find out when tickets are sold. The Oaxaqueño's reverse trip from Oaxaca to Puebla is in darkness.

The station is in the north of Puebla, 200 meters north of the corner of 9 Nte and Avenida 80 Pte. Ruta 1 'Estación Nueva' colectivos take 20 minutes to reach the station from 9 Sur at Avenida 5 Pte in the city center. In the reverse direction, board the colectivo about 200 meters straight ahead from the station entrance and get off at Paseo Bravo. A taxi between the train station and the zócalo will cost about US$3.

Car & Motorcycle Puebla is 136 km from Mexico City by a fast autopista, highway 150D (tolls total about US$8). East of Puebla, the 150D continues to Córdoba (negotiating a cloudy, winding 22-km descent from the 2385-meter Cumbres de Maltrata en route) and Veracruz.

Getting Around

Most hotels and places of interest are within walking distance of the zócalo. From the bus station you can take a taxi (US$3 ticket from the kiosk), or leave the bus station

and walk left along Boulevard Norte to its hectic junction with Carmen Serdán. Here you have two options: either go straight over to the far side of the junction and get a 'Blvd 5 de Mayo/Plaza Dorada' bus or colectivo east along Norte to Héroes del 5 de Mayo, where you can get off on the corner of Mendoza, three blocks east of the zócalo; or turn right and get a 'Paseo Bravo Directo' colectivo south down Carmen Serdán to Paseo Bravo, a park beside Calle 11 Sur five blocks west of the zócalo. Either way the ride takes 15 to 20 minutes.

To get from the city center to the bus station, catch any 'CAPU' colectivo from 9 Sur or 9 Norte, four blocks west of the zócalo. All city buses and colectivos cost US$0.50.

CHOLULA
pop 78,177; alt 2170m; ☎ *22*

Ten km west of Puebla stands the largest pyramid ever built, Pirámide Tepanapa – the Great Pyramid of Cholula. At 425 sq meters and 60 meters high it's even larger in volume than Egypt's Pyramid of Cheops. But because it's now overgrown and topped by a church, it's difficult even to recognize the huge grassy mound as a pyramid. The town of Cholula is fairly unimpressive, but the University of the Americas, with many foreign students, adds a cosmopolitan touch, and there's a hearty nightlife. The nearby villages of Tonantzintla and Acatepec have splendid churches.

History
Between 1 and 600 AD Cholula grew into one of central Mexico's largest cities, and an important religious center, while powerful Teotihuacán flourished 100 km to the northwest. The Great Pyramid was built over several times. Around 600 AD Cholula fell under the sway of the Olmeca-Xicallanca who built nearby Cacaxtla. Sometime between 900 and 1300 Toltecs and/or Chichimecs took it over. Later it fell under Aztec dominance. There was also artistic influence from the Mixtecs to the south.

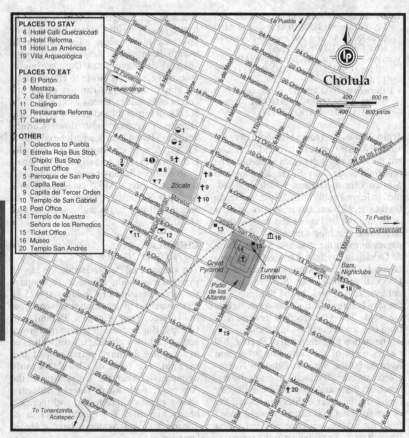

Cholula

PLACES TO STAY
6 Hotel Calli Quetzalcóatl
13 Hotel Reforma
18 Hotel Las Américas
19 Villa Arqueológica

PLACES TO EAT
3 El Portón
6 Mostaza
7 Café Enamorada
11 Chialingo
13 Restaurante Reforma
17 Caesar's

OTHER
1 Colectivos to Puebla
2 Estrella Roja Bus Stop,
   'Chipilo' Bus Stop
4 Tourist Office
5 Parroquia de San Pedro
5 Capilla Real
9 Capilla del Tercer Orden
10 Templo de San Gabriel
12 Post Office
14 Templo de Nuestra
   Señora de los Remedios
15 Ticket Office
16 Museo
20 Templo San Andrés

In 1519 Cholula had a population of
100,000, although the Great Pyramid was
already overgrown. Cortés, having made
friends with the nearby Tlaxcalans, traveled here at Moctezuma's request. Aztec
warriors set an ambush for him but unfortunately for them, the Tlaxcalans tipped off
Cortés about the plot and the Spanish
struck first. Within one day, they killed
6000 Cholulans before the city was looted
by the Tlaxcalans. Cortés vowed to build a
church here for each day of the year, or one
on top of every pagan temple, depending
which legend you prefer. Today there are

39 – far from 365 but still a lot for a small
town.

The Spanish developed the nearby town
of Puebla to overshadow the old pagan
center, and Cholula never regained its importance, especially after a severe plague
that took place in the 1540s decimated the
indigenous population.

Orientation & Information
Arriving buses and colectivos drop you two
or three blocks north of the zócalo. Two
long blocks to the east of there, the pyramid with its domed church on top is a clear

landmark. There is a tourist office (☎ 47-33-93) on Calle 4 half a block northwest of the zócalo. No English is spoken there but maps are available. The office is open weekdays from 9 am to 6.30 pm and closed weekends. Bancomer, Comermex and Banamex, on the zócalo, change money and have ATMs. Casa de Cambio Azteca is half a block south on 2 Sur; the post office is three blocks south at Alemán 314.

Zona Arqueológica

The **Great Pyramid**, probably originally dedicated to Quetzalcóatl, is topped by the church of **Nuestra Señora de los Remedios**. It's a classic symbol of conquest, but possibly an inadvertent one as the church may have been built before the Spanish knew the mound contained a pagan temple. You can climb to the church by a path from the pyramid's northwest corner (no charge).

The Zona Arqueológica comprises the excavated areas around the pyramid, and the tunnels underneath it. Entry to the zone is via the tunnel on the north side, open daily from 9 am to 5 pm. Entry costs US$2 (free Sundays and holidays), plus US$4.50 for a video camera. The small **museum**, across the road from the ticket office and down some steps, has the best introduction to the site – a large cutaway model of the pyramid mound showing the various superimposed structures. Museum admission is included with your site ticket, and the museum is open every day of the year. The nearby bookstore may have a useful small guide booklet.

Several pyramids were built on top of each other in various reconstructions. Over eight km of **tunnels** have been dug beneath the pyramid by archaeologists, to penetrate each stage. The tourist access tunnel is only a few hundred meters long, but from it you can see earlier layers of the building. Guides at the tunnel entrance will suggest you hire one of them (US$4/5 in Spanish/English for a one-hour tour; longer tours for US$10/12 and up). You don't need a guide to follow the tunnel through to the structures on the south and west sides of the pyramid, but they can be useful in pointing out and explaining various features in and around the site as nothing is labeled.

The access tunnel emerges on the east side of the pyramid, from where you can take a path around to the **Patio de los Altares**, or Great Plaza, on the south side. This was the main approach to the pyramid and it's ringed by platforms and unique diagonal stairways. Three large stone slabs on its east, north and west sides are carved in the Veracruz interlocking-scroll design. At its south end is an Aztec-style altar in a pit dating from shortly before the Spanish conquest. Human bones indicate this was possibly a sacrificial site. On the west side of the mound is a reconstructed section of the latest pyramid, with two earlier layers exposed to view.

Zócalo

The **Ex-Convento de San Gabriel**, along the east side of Cholula's wide zócalo, includes three fine churches. On the left, as you face the ex-convento, is the Arabic-style **Capilla Real**, dating from 1540, unique in Mexico with 49 domes. In the middle is the 17th century **Capilla del Tercer Orden**, and on the right the **Templo de San Gabriel**, founded in 1530 on the site of a pyramid. To the east, on 4 Pte, stands the **Parroquia de San Pedro** (1640).

Special Events

Cholula's fireworks-makers are renowned for their fabulous shows. Of the many festivals, one of the most important ones is the Festival de la Virgen de los Remedios and regional feria in the first week of September, with daily traditional dances on the Great Pyramid.

Places to Stay

Cholula is an easy daytrip from Puebla but there are options if you fancy staying. The best value in town is the *Hotel Reforma* (☎ 47-01-49) at the corner of Morelos and 4 Sur, midway between the zócalo and the pyramid. All 13 of the Reforma's rooms are nice, and price varies with size and features (all have private bath with hot water): US$6 to US$10 for one person, US$9 to US$11 for two. There's a pay phone beside the front office.

In the same price range, the *Hotel Las Américas* (☎ 47-09-91) at 14 Ote 6, three blocks east of the pyramid, offers comfortable singles/doubles with TV and private bath for US$9/11. There's a restaurant, a pleasant courtyard garden and a pool (filled only during the summer).

Stepping up in price and comfort, the *Hotel Calli Quetzalcóatl* (☎ 47-15-55) on the zócalo at Portal Guerrero 11 has modern rooms, a dining room and a bar. The building surrounds a lovely courtyard with a fountain. Singles/doubles cost US$20/24.

The nicest place in town is the 50-room *Villa Arqueológica* (☎ 47-19-66) at 2 Pte 601, south of the pyramid and across a couple of fields. A Club Med property, it has tennis courts, a pool and rooms at US$50, suites to US$65.

Places to Eat

Café Enamorada, at the southern corner of the Portal Guerrero on the zócalo, is about the most popular place in town, with live music most nights and sandwiches for US$2 to US$3, salads at US$3, and tostadas, quesadillas and tacos for about US$2.50.

Up a few doors, in the Hotel Calli Quetzalcóatl, is the *Mostaza*. This restaurant is open-roofed, cheerful and upscale – in quality more than price: breakfasts about US$3, sandwiches US$3, and fish and meat dishes around US$6.

El Portón on Hidalgo at Calle 5, two blocks west of the zócalo, is popular for its daily set menu, which typically includes a choice of four kinds of soup, an entree (chicken, beef or pasta) and dessert – all for under US$3. A few short blocks away, the *Chialingo* at 7 Pte and 3 Sur is a much finer place, with handsome walls decorated with antique tools, firearms and branding irons in a dining room overlooking a lovely courtyard. Salads are around US$2.50,

chicken dishes for US$5, seafood to US$10.

Southeast of the zócalo, the *Restaurante Reforma* next to the Hotel Reforma offers a nice bar and simple, comfortable tables in a small room with posters of Marilyn Monroe on one wall opposite another wall covered with photos of the town's many churches. The comida corrida runs US$2.50. Continuing on Hidalgo past the Great Pyramid you'll reach *Caesar's*, a festive two-story bar-restaurant that serves up delicious pizza, pastas, burgers and antojitos. Few items on the menu cost more than $4.

Entertainment

The nightclubs are in the dusty streets within several blocks of the intersection of 14 Pte and 5 de Mayo. They look like nothing during the day, but after about 10 pm from Thursday to Saturday, there are bright lights and loud music at *Faces*, *Keops* and *Milagro*, among others. The cover price in the better establishments is about US$5.

Getting There & Away

Frequent colectivos to Cholula leave from the corner of 6 Pte and 15 Nte in Puebla. They cost US$0.50 and take 20 minutes.

Estrella Roja has frequent buses between Mexico City's Terminal Oriente (TAPO) and Puebla that stop in Cholula on the corner of 3 Nte and 6 Pte (US$3).

AROUND CHOLULA
Tonantzintla & Acatepec

The interior of the small **Templo de Santa María** in Tonantzintla is among the most exuberant in Mexico. Under the dome, the surface is covered with colorful stucco saints, devils, flowers, fruit, birds and more – a great example of Indian artisanship applied to Christian themes. Tonantzintla holds a procession and traditional dances for the Festival of the Assumption on August 15.

The **Templo de San Francisco** in Acatepec, 1.5 km southeast of Tonantzintla, dates from about 1730. The brilliant exterior is beautifully decorated with blue, green and yellow Puebla tiles set in red brick on an ornate Churrigueresque façade.

Both of these small churches are open daily from 10 am to 1 pm and 3 to 5 pm.

Getting There & Away Autobuses Puebla-Cholula runs 'Chipilo' buses from Puebla bus station to Tonantzintla and Acatepec. In Cholula you can pick them up on the corner of 6 Pte and 3 Nte. Between the two villages you can wait for the next bus or walk.

Huejotzingo
pop 47,308; alt 2280m; ☎ *227*

Huejotzingo ('weh-hot-ZIN-goh'), 14 km northwest of Cholula on highway 150, is known for its cider and sarapes. The fine 16th century plateresque-style monastery has been restored as a museum, with exhibits on the Spanish missions and monastic life (open Tuesday to Sunday from 10 am to 5 pm; US$2, free Sunday). The fortified church is stark but imposing, with Gothic ribbing on its ceiling. There are old frescos and excellent carved stonework. On Shrove Tuesday, masked Carnaval dancers re-enact a battle between French and Mexicans. Estrella Roja buses serve Huejotzingo from Puebla, Cholula and Mexico City.

SIERRA NORTE DE PUEBLA
The Sierra Norte de Puebla covers much of the remote northern arm of Puebla state. The mountains rise to over 2500 meters before falling away to the gulf coastal plain. Although much of the land is deforested, it's beautiful with pine forests at higher altitudes and semitropical vegetation lower down. The main town is Teziutlán, but smaller Cuetzalán is considerably more attractive and nestled in a countryside that affords lovely strolling. Sierra Norte handicrafts – among them rebozos, quechquémitls and baskets – are sold in markets at Cuetzalán, Zacapoaxtla, Teziutlán, Tlatlauquitepec and elsewhere, as well as in Puebla and Mexico City.

The area has a large Indian population, mostly Nahua and Totonac. The ancestors of these Nahua are thought to have reached the Sierra Norte in the 14th century, from the Valle de México and southern and central Puebla. For more on the Nahua see the sidebar; for the Totonacs see the Central Gulf Coast chapter, which also covers some places in the low-lying far north of Puebla state.

Cuetzalán
pop 39,850; alt 1000m; ☎ *223*

The colonial town of Cuetzalán, in the center of a lush coffee-growing region, is famed for a Sunday market that fills the town's zócalo and attracts scores of Indians in traditional dress. Handicrafts include embroidered blouses and quechquémitls, but more likely you'll come across flowers, poultry and vegetables for sale.

Orientation & Information The main road into town from the south passes a tiny bus depot before ending 100 meters later at the zócalo. The center is on a hillside, and from the zócalo most hotels and restaurants are uphill. There's a tourist office (☎ 1-00-04) on Hidalgo west of the zócalo (look for large blue letters 'SEP' above a door; the office is two doors down). It's open Sunday to Thursday from 9 am to 4 pm, Friday and Saturday from 9.30 am to 8 pm. No English is spoken but maps of the town are available.

Things to See & Do Except for the Sunday market and a **regional museum** on the zócalo opposite the Posada Jackeline, there are few tourist attractions in town. However, there are several worthwhile ones nearby. Four and five km northeast of town are two lovely waterfalls called **Las Brisas**. To reach them you must first reach the village of San Andrés at the end of a dirt road and then hike dirt trails used by farmers who are quickly replacing the region's rain forest with coffee plants. The turnoff for San Andrés is the dirt road just west of the bus depot. Large pickups act as colectivos from here to San Andrés three km away; you can hop on one for US$0.30 (they pass by every 30 minutes or so).

The Nahua

Puebla state has about 400,000 of Mexico's most numerous Indian people, the Nahua – more than any other state. Another 200,000 Nahua live in western parts of Veracruz state adjoining Puebla. The Nahua language (Nahuatl) was spoken by the Aztecs and, like the Aztecs, the Nahua were probably of Chichimec origin. Traditional Nahua women's dress consists of a black wool enredo (waist sash) and embroidered blouse and quechquémitl (shoulder cape). The Nahua are Christian but often also believe in a pantheon of supernatural beings, including *tonos*, people's animal 'doubles,' and witches who can become blood-sucking birds and cause illness. ■

Or simply walk along this road, keeping to the right when it forks, until you come to San Andrés and its church with a striking green-tile dome. There, at least one boy will offer to take you to the falls for US$2. You should accept the offer, as there are many trails in the forest you will soon enter and no signs to the falls. If the weather is warm, you might want to wear a bathing suit under your clothes as the natural pools under the falls are enticing.

Special Events For several days around October 4 Cuetzalán holds lively celebrations of the festival of San Francisco de Assisi, combined with the Feria del Café y del Huipil. A traditional dance festival in mid-July attracts groups from all over the area.

Places to Stay The best value in town is the *Posada Jackeline* (☎ 1-03-54) on the south (uphill) side of the zócalo. Large, clean rooms with plenty of hot water go for US$8 per person.

The best place in town is the *Hotel Posada Cuetzalán* (☎ 1-01-54) on Zaragoza, 100 meters up from the zócalo. The hotel's 39 rooms – each cozy with white stucco walls, lots of lightly stained wood, a TV and a phone – surround two lovely courtyards. Singles/doubles cost US$22/26. The hotel also has a restaurant.

Places to Eat Cuetzalán has a couple of good places to eat. The *Restaurant Yoloxochitl*, opposite the Posada Jackeline, has lots of charm, a lovely view and OK food. Salads and antojitos go for US$2, meat dishes are US$2.50. A hearty breakfast of scrambled eggs and ham, black beans and tortillas, two cups of hot chocolate *and* a tasty chicken sandwich costs US$4.

El Zargo Pizza on Morelos 30 meters up from the zócalo does very good pizza and its toasted sandwiches are a treat. The *Bar El Calate* on the east side of the zócalo is a great place to try regional alcoholic drinks made from coffee, limes and berries.

Getting There & Away From Puebla, there are two 1st-class ADO buses daily (at 8.15 and 10.15 am; four hours; US$7) and several 2nd-class buses. From Cuetzalán to Puebla, there are two ADO Thursday to Sunday (at 4.30 and 6 pm; US$7) and many 2nd-class buses; get your return tickets early. There are also buses to Cuetzalán from Mexico City's Terminal Oriente (TAPO).

Yohualichán

Eight km from Cuetzalán by cobblestone road, this pre-Hispanic site has niche pyramids similar to those at El Tajín. The site is adjacent to the Yohualichán town plaza, and is open from Wednesday to Sunday from 10 am to 5 pm. Admission costs US$1. To get there, catch any of the colectivos taking the northwest road out of Cuetzalán and get off when it stops beside the blue sign with an image of a pyramid on it. Colectivos pass every 30 minutes and cost US$0.40.

SOUTHERN PUEBLA

The main route from Puebla to Oaxaca is the modern toll highway 135D, which turns south off the 150D, 83 km east of Puebla. Two older roads go through the southeast of the state of Puebla toward Oaxaca.

Highway 150

Heading east from Puebla, this road starts parallel to the 150D autopista, but it's a lot slower and more congested. Second-class buses stop at the towns en route. **Amozoc**, 16 km from Puebla, produces pottery and many of the fancy silver decorations worn by charros. **Tepeaca**, 40 km from Puebla, has a big Friday market, mainly for everyday goods, and a 16th century Franciscan monastery. The village of **Tecali**, 11 km southwest of Tepeaca, is a center for the carving of onyx from the nearby quarries.

Tehuacán

pop 190,416; alt 1640m; ☎ *238*

Modern Tehuacán, on highway 150, 115 km southeast of Puebla, is a pretty town with a fine zócalo. It's famed for its mineral water (mostly Peñafiel), sold in bottles all over Mexico; tours of the impressive **Peñafiel** plant, located 100 meters north of the Casas Cantarranas hotel (see below), are offered at 4.15 and 6 pm daily except Friday. The high, dry Tehuacán valley was the site of some of the earliest agriculture in Mexico. By 7000 to 5000 BC people were planting avocados, chilies, cotton and squashes, and around 5000 BC they were cultivating the first tiny forms of maize. Pottery, the sign of a truly settled existence, appeared about 2000 BC. The **Museo del Valle de Tehuacán**, three blocks northwest of the zócalo, explains some of the archaeological discoveries, and exhibits tiny preserved cobs of maize that were among the first to be cultivated.

Orientation & Information The main road into town coming from Puebla, Avenida Independencia, passes by the ADO bus station before reaching the north side of the Parque Juárez – the zócalo. The main north-south road is Avenida Reforma. The city's most popular restaurants are located around the zócalo, as is the Palacio Municipal, which has a tourist office (☎ 3-15-14, ext 36) in the southwest corner; English is spoken and maps are available. The office is open weekdays from 9 am to 6 pm, occasionally on Saturday and Sunday.

Places to Stay The best deal in town is to be had on the top (fifth) floor at the *Bogh Suites Hotel* (☎ 2-34-74) on the northeast side of the zócalo. Regular rates at the hotel – which has small but attractive rooms with TV, phone and fan – are a reasonable US$23/26 for a single/double. But because the elevator doesn't reach the top floor, rooms there go for US$18 for a single or double; some, such as room 24, have a lovely view of the plaza.

The *Hotel Monroy* at Reforma 7 offers very spacious basic but clean rooms for US$11/13. Some taxi drivers recommend the *Hotel Plaza Iberia* (☎ 3-15-00) for economy lodging, however the rooms (US$12/13) in the once-elegant colonial hotel are in dire need of new beds and paint.

The top accommodations in town are at the *Casas Cantarranas* (☎ 3-49-22) at Avenida de las Américas 2457. This 550-room resort with a large, blue-tile pool and superb rooms is new and, at the time of writing, bargain-priced (US$30/40); a similar hotel in Mexico City would cost three times as much.

Getting There & Away ADO, at Independencia 119, has frequent 1st-class buses to/from Puebla (US$4), and several per day to/from Mexico City and Veracruz. AU offers 2nd-class service to/from here. Buses to/from Oaxaca go via Huajuapan de León or Teotitlán del Camino.

Highway 190

This road swings southwest from Puebla to **Atlixco**, 31 km away, a town known for its mineral springs, avocados and near-perfect climate. The Atlixcáyotl festival, held during the last weekend in September, has traditional costumes, dances and music. Another 36 km brings you to **Izúcar de Matamoros**, which also has therapeutic balnearios but is best known for ceramic handicrafts. **Acatlán de Osorio** also a center for artistic handmade pottery.

South of Mexico City

Heading south from Mexico City, highway 95 and highway 95D (the toll road) climb to more than 3000 meters from the Valle de México into refreshing pine forests, then descend to Cuernavaca, capital of Morelos state and longtime popular retreat from Mexico City. On the way, highway 115D branches southeast to Tepoztlán, nestled beneath high cliffs, and to balnearios at Oaxtepec and Cuautla. South of Cuernavaca, highway 95 detours to the remarkable silver town of Taxco in the state of Guerrero.

Morelos is one of Mexico's smallest and most densely populated states. Valleys at different elevations have a variety of micro-climates, and many fruits, vegetables and grains have been cultivated since pre-Hispanic times. Archaeological sites at Cuernavaca, Tepoztlán and Xochicalco show signs of the agricultural Tlahuica civilization and the Aztecs who subjugated them. In the colonial era, most of the state was controlled by a few families, including descendants of Cortés. Their palaces and haciendas can still be seen, along with churches and monasteries from as early as the 16th century. Unsurprisingly, the campesinos of Morelos became fervent supporters of the Mexican Revolution, and local lad Emiliano Zapata is the state's hero.

A branch of highway 95D goes to Iguala in mountainous Guerrero state, and continues as highway 95 (no autopista pretensions) to Chilpancingo and Acapulco (see the Central Pacific Coast chapter). The high-speed toll road (95D) takes a more direct route to Chilpancingo. On this exorbitantly expensive privatized road you can drive the 400 km between Mexico City and Acapulco in three hours – the fluctuating tolls can total more than US$75. The alternative sections of free road are consequently heavily used, slow and dangerous. Driving at night in Guerrero is inadvisable because cars are sometimes stopped and robbed. The route from Iguala to Ixtapa via highways 51 and 134 is said to be particularly risky.

TEPOZTLÁN
pop 26,513; alt 1701m; ☎ 739

Just off highway 95D, 70 km from Mexico City, Tepoztlán (Place of Copper) sits in a valley surrounded by high, jagged cliffs. It's a magical place, the legendary birthplace, more than 1200 years ago, of Quetzalcóatl, the omnipotent serpent god of the Aztecs. The town retains Indian traditions, with many older people still speaking Nahuatl, and younger people now learning it in secondary school. Now something of a hippie venue, Tepoztlán attracts writers, artists and astrologers, as well as many more conventional weekend visitors from Mexico City.

Orientation & Information

Everything here is easily accessible by walking, except the Pyramid of Tepozteco on the cliff-top to the north. Street names change in the center of town, eg, Avenida 5 de Mayo becomes Avenida Tepozteco north of the plaza, and the east-west streets change names as they cross this axis.

Post and telegraph offices are on the north side of the main plaza. Long-distance and local telephone calls can be made from pay phones around town.

Ex-Convento Dominico de la Natividad

This monastery and the attached church were built by Dominican priests between 1560 and 1588 and are the chief feature of the town. The church is still in use, and schoolchildren play in the grounds, part of which were a capilla abierta. The plateresque church façade has Dominican seals interspersed with indigenous symbols, floral designs and various figures including the sun, moon and stars, animals, angels and the Virgin Mary. The church is open daily from 7 am to 8 pm.

The monastery section is no longer in everyday use, but is being restored as a museum. It is quiet and impressive, with remnants of murals from centuries past on the walls. The rear terrace on the upper floor offers a grand view of the Tepoztlán valley. The monastery is open Tuesday through Sunday from 10 am to 5 pm (free). Information is available in Spanish only.

Museo Arqueológico Carlos Pellicer

The museum at González 2 (behind the Dominican church) has a small but interesting collection of pieces from many parts of Mexico, which were donated to the people of Tepoztlán by the Tabascan poet Carlos Pellicer Cámara. Pellicer had a great love for Mexico's pre-Hispanic art;

the objects on display here are lively and vibrant, with an emphasis on human figures but also including some animals. Unfortunately it's not well lit, and the labels give only general information, in Spanish. The museum is open Tuesday through Sunday from 10 am to 6 pm; a donation of US$0.50 is requested.

Pyramid of Tepozteco

The 10-meter-high Pyramid of Tepozteco was built on a cliff 400 meters above Tepoztlán. It honors Tepoztécatl, the Aztec god of the harvest, fertility and pulque. The pyramid is visible at the top of the cliffs to

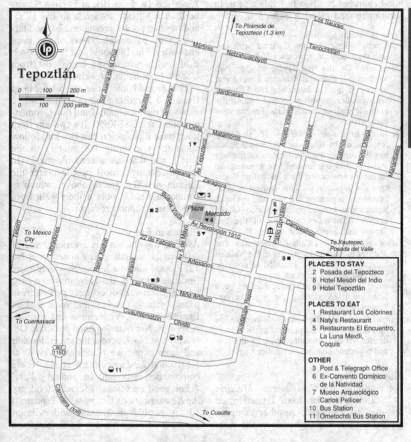

Tepoztlán

0   100   200 m
0   100   200 yards

To Pirámide de
Tepozteco (1.3 km)

To Mexico City

To Cuernavaca

To Yautepec,
Posada del Valle

To Cuautla

PLACES TO STAY
2 Posada del Tepozteco
8 Hotel Mesón del Indio
9 Hotel Tepoztlán

PLACES TO EAT
1 Restaurant Los Colorines
4 Naty's Restaurant
5 Restaurants El Encuentro,
   La Luna Mextli,
   Coquis

OTHER
3 Post & Telegraph Office
6 Ex-Convento Dominico
   de la Natividad
7 Museo Arqueológico
   Carlos Pellicer
10 Bus Station
11 Ometochtli Bus Station

the north. It's accessible by a steep path beginning at the end of Avenida Tepozteco; the 1.3-km walk takes one to 1½ hours. At the top you're rewarded with a panorama of Tepoztlán and the valley. Admission is US$1.50. The pyramid site is open daily from 9 am to 4.30 pm. It's best to climb early, when the air is clear and before it gets hot. Hiking boots or at least good tennis shoes are recommended.

Special Events

Tepoztlán is a festive place, with many Christian festivals superimposed on pagan celebrations. Each of the seven neighborhood churches has two festivals a year, in addition to the following larger festivals:

Feria de Santa Catarina – Celebrated in the nearby village of Santa Catarina, with various regional dances; January 16

Carnaval – On the five days preceding Ash Wednesday, Carnaval features the colorful dances of the Huehuenches and Chinelos with feather headdresses and beautifully embroidered costumes; late February or early March

Fiesta del Brinco del Chinelo – The three-day 'Festival of the Hop,' during Semana Santa, has dancers in bright costumes of feathers and silk jumping around like gymnasts to amuse the spectators; the week before Easter

El Reto del Tepozteco – This festival is celebrated on Tepozteco hill near the pyramid, with copious consumption of pulque (locally known as *ponche*) in honor of the god Tepoztécatl; September 7

Fiesta del Templo – A Catholic celebration that features theater performances in the Nahuatl language. It was first intended to coincide with, and perhaps supplant, the pagan Tepoztécatl festival, but the pulque drinkers get a jump on it by starting the night before; September 8

Festival Cultural de Tepoztlán – A more recent innovation, this event presents music, dance, theater, art and artesanías, with local artists and big-name visitors; November 1 to 10

Places to Stay

For camping, try *Campamento Meztitla* (☎ 5-00-68), two km from Tepoztlán, on the road to Yautepec. Another camping ground is three km farther down the same

road. About the cheapest place in town is the *Hotel Mesón del Indio* (☎ 5-02-38), at Revolución 44; its sign is barely larger than a loaf of bread. The hotel is a pleasant little place with eight rooms beside a garden, each with private bath and hot water, costing US$12/13 for singles/doubles.

The better hotels cater to the weekend crowd from Mexico City, and are expensive. The *Hotel Tepoztlán* (☎ 5-05-22) at Las Industrias 6 is a health-resort-style hotel with 36 rooms, two suites, a pool, restaurant and bar. Rooms cost US$35/50 on Saturday (with Sunday breakfast), US$30/40 on other days. The *Posada del Tepozteco* (☎ 5-00-10), at Paraíso 3, was built as a hillside hacienda in the 1930s and has two pools, a restaurant/bar and terraces with panoramic views of the town and valley. The 18 rooms cost from US$42; suites with private spa baths cost from US$60. Continental breakfast is included.

The *Posada del Valle* (☎ 5-05-21) at Camino a Meztitla 5 has a pool, majestic views of the mountains, and quiet, romantic rooms for US$40/50. It's two km from town (take Revolución east two km, follow signs the remaining 100 meters to the hotel), and that has a certain appeal. (In this price range, most people prefer the Posada del Tepozteco, above, which is comparable but is only a short walk from Tepoztlán's popular zócalo.)

Places to Eat

Avenida Revolución has a varied string of restaurants, including *El Encuentro* at No 12, located above a hippie/New Age store (incense burning, tie-dyes, massage oils, etc). El Encuentro offers tasty pizzas, fresh pastas, salads, chicken and meat dishes. English, French, Vietnamese and Spanish is spoken. Not quite so good but quite OK is *Naty's* at No 7, across the street. Fancier and more expensive places like *Coquis* at No 10 and *La Luna Mextli* at No 16 are combination restaurant, bar and art gallery.

For good traditional Mexican food, try the *Restaurant Los Colorines* at Tepozteco 13. A popular restaurant with vibrant decor, it offers a variety of dishes from

US$2 to US$5. The chicken mole is delicious, as is the tortilla soup. Many people swear by the enchiladas, which are made with blue corn tortillas.

Things to Buy

On weekends, Tepoztlán's market stalls sell a melange of handicrafts, including sarapes, embroidery, weaving, carvings, baskets and pottery. There's some good stuff. Shops in the adjacent streets also have interesting wares (some from Bali and India) at upscale prices. A local craft product is miniature houses and villages carved from the cork-like spines of the local *pochote* tree; the cute little buildings against a rough background are reminiscent of Tepoztlán itself, with its backdrop of rugged cliffs.

Getting There & Away

Buses to Mexico City (Terminal Sur) depart from Avenida 5 de Mayo 35 at the southern entrance to town (it's not really a bus station, but there's a waiting room and ticket office). Autos Pullman de Morelos has frequent buses during the day, more on weekends (70 km, 1¼ hours; US$3). Autobuses México-Zacatepec, at the same office, runs buses to Yautepec (18 km, 30 minutes; US$1) and Cuautla (25 minutes; US$2) eight times daily. If you need to leave Tepoztlán after-hours, go to the caseta (tollbooth) on the autopista outside town, where lots of buses pass going to or from the capital. This is also the place to catch a bus to Oaxtepec (15 minutes; US$1). Ometochtli buses to Cuernavaca go every 15 minutes from 5 am to 9 pm (23 km, 30 minutes; US$1). Their terminal is located on the road south of town on the way to the autopista.

OAXTEPEC

pop 4500; alt 1330m; ☎ 735

The attraction here is the 200,000-sq-meter Centro Vacacional Oaxtepec ('wahs-teh-PEC'), a balneario sponsored by the Mexican Social Security Institute, with 25 pools for diving and swimming and the benefits of soaking in sulfur springs. The giant park can handle 42,000 bathers at once. There are restaurants, a theater, picnic and sports areas, a supermarket, movies and a funicular taking you to the top of a hill for a bird's-eye view of the center. The balneario is open daily from 8 am to 6 pm, and a day ticket is US$3 for adults, half that for children and seniors. Be warned: the water is cool and most of the pools contain noisy children until closing.

Places to Stay

If you want to stay longer than a day, there are campgrounds (US$4 per adult), four-person rooms in the *Hotel Económico* (US$18 for the room), six-person rooms in the *Hotel Familiar* (US$30 for the room) and four-person cabins (US$40 per cabin). Reservation offices are in Mexico City (☎ 5-639-42-00) or the center itself (☎ 6-01-01).

Getting There & Away

Oaxtepec is just north of highway 115D, 100 km south of Mexico City. Frequent buses go from the capital's Terminal Sur by Cristóbal Colón, Autos Pullman de Morelos and Estrella Roja (1½ hours; US$3.50). Oaxtepec bus station is beside the entrance to the springs complex. There are also buses to/from Tepoztlán, Cuernavaca and Cuautla.

CUAUTLA

pop 142,250; alt 1290m; ☎ 735

The balnearios at Cuautla ('KWOUT-la') and its pleasant year-round climate have been attractions as far back as the time of Moctezuma, who reputedly enjoyed soaking in the sun and sulfur springs. These days, however, the city is uninspiring and spread out, though the center is pleasant enough.

José María Morelos y Pavón, one of Mexico's first leaders in the independence struggle, used Cuautla as a base, but the royalist army besieged the city from February 19 to May 2, 1812 (both dates are now street names in Cuautla). Morelos and his army were forced to evacuate when their food gave out. A century later, Cuautla was a center of support for the revolutionary army of Emiliano Zapata. In 1919 Zapata was assassinated by treacherous federalists at Chinameca, 31 km south of Cuautla. Now, every April 10, the Agrarian Reform Minister lays a wreath at Zapata's statue in Cuautla, and makes a speech quoting Zapata's principles of land reform. In Anenecuilco, about 10 km south of Cuautla, the ruins of the simple, two-room adobe cottage where Zapata was born is now a museum featuring photographs of the rebel leader. Outside the museum is a mural by Roberto Rodríguez running the full length of one of the garden walls. It depicts Zapata exploding with the force of a volcano into the center of Mexican history, sundering with both hands the chains that bound his countrymen.

Orientation

Cuautla spreads north to south roughly parallel to the Río Cuautla. The main avenue into town, Avenida Insurgentes, changes its name to Batalla 19 de Febrero, then to Galeana, then Los Bravos, then Guerrero (in the pedestrian area past the main plaza) and then Zemano.

Emiliano Zapata fought for the transfer of lands to the peasants with the cry '¡Tierra y Libertad!'

The zócalo has arcades with restaurants on the northern side, a church on the eastern side, the Palacio Municipal on the western side and the Hotel Colón on the southern side. Bus lines have separate terminals, in the blocks east of the plaza.

Information

The tourist office (☎ 2-52-21) is three blocks north of the plaza, in the 16th century Ex-Convento de San Diego. This building was the terminal of the Ferrocarril Escénica (Scenic Train), which no longer operates. The tourist office is behind the first door on the platform (open weekdays from 10 am to 6 pm; weekends from 10 am to 3 pm). The staff speak Spanish only.

Things to See

The **Museo José María Morelos**, in the same building as the tourist office, is open Tuesday through Sunday from 9 am to 2 pm, and 4 to 6 pm. The museum displays a few of the hero's personal items; there's not much to see but it's free. Morelos' residence, on the plaza, houses the **Museo Histórico del Oriente de Morelos**, with some ethnographic exhibits (masks and costumes) and early photos of Cuautla and Zapata.

Balnearios

The best-known balneario in Cuautla is **Agua Hedionda**, on the east side of the river. Its cool waters smell faintly of sulfur and fill two big swimming pools. The complex is open daily from 7 am to 6.30 pm; admission is US$6. You can get there on an 'Agua Hedionda' combi (US$0.50).

Other balnearios in town include **El Almeal**, **Agua Linda** and **Las Tazas**.

Places to Stay

One of the best reasons to stop in Cuautla is the comfortable, budget-priced youth hostel, the *Villa Deportiva Juvenil* (☎ 2-02-18). It's around behind the swimming pool of the Balneario Agua Linda, in the Unidad Deportiva sports center on the east side of the bridge where Niños Héroes crosses the river. A bed in one of the segregated dorms

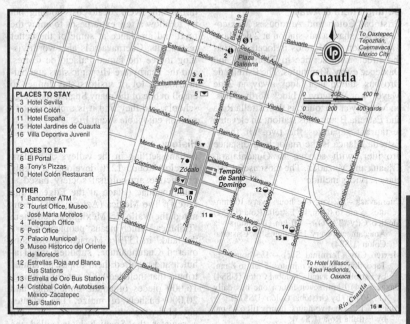

PLACES TO STAY
3 Hotel Sevilla
10 Hotel Colón
11 Hotel España
15 Hotel Jardines de Cuautla
16 Villa Deportiva Juvenil

PLACES TO EAT
6 El Portal
8 Tony's Pizzas
10 Hotel Colón Restaurant

OTHER
1 Bancomer ATM
2 Tourist Office, Museo
   José María Morelos
4 Telegraph Office
5 Post Office
7 Palacio Municipal
9 Museo Histórico del Oriente
   de Morelos
12 Estrellas Roja and Blanca
   Bus Stations
13 Estrella de Oro Bus Station
14 Cristóbal Colón, Autobuses
   México-Zacatepec
   Bus Station

costs US$3.50 with bedding included. The clean, communal washrooms have hot water. The hostel is open from 7 am to 11 pm, there's no age limit and a hostel card is not required.

Cheap hotels include the *Hotel Colón* (☎ 2-29-90), on the main plaza, where OK rooms with private bath cost US$8/9 for a single/double. The *Hotel España* (☎ 2-21-86), half a block east at 2 de Mayo 22, has 27 very nice rooms with private bath, hot water and parking. Rates are a bargain US$9/10. *Hotel Jardines de Cuautla* (☎ 2-00-88), opposite the Cristóbal Colón bus terminal at 2 de Mayo 94, has updated rooms with private bath, parking, a garden and two tiny swimming pools for US$11/18.

Hotel Sevilla (☎ 2-52-00), at Conspiradores 9, is an excellent mid-range place, with updated rooms with phone, TV and secure parking for US$13/16, or US$21 with two beds. If your only reason for visiting Cuautla is the Agua Hedionda, the

Hotel Villasor (☎ 2-65-21), a stone's throw from the balneario, is the place to stay. Clean, comfortable rooms with TV, fan and phone go for US$20/26, US$3 more Friday and Saturday nights. The hotel has an inviting pool.

Places to Eat

The places around the plaza are the most fun, especially the tables under the arcades. Most have fixed-price breakfasts and lunches for less than US$4. The restaurant at the *Hotel Colón* is very popular and open late.

On the west side of the plaza, *Tony's Pizzas* offers delicious *chicas* from US$4 on up and *familiar* size with the works for US$9. It also offers burgers, sandwiches and spaghetti. On the north side, *El Portal* specializes in charcoal-grilled meats (US$3.50 for hefty burgers).

North of the main plaza, Galeana has many little restaurants, cafés, fruit-juice stalls and ice-cream shops.

Getting There & Away

Cristóbal Colón and Autobuses México-Zacatepec share a bus station at 2 de Mayo 97. Pullman de Morelos is located across the street, with service to Tepoztlán and Oaxtepec every 30 minutes. The Estrella de Oro bus station is a block away, at 2 de Mayo 74 at Mongoy. A block north of this, on Mongoy at Vázquez, is the Estrella Roja and Estrella Blanca bus station; an elevated restaurant separates the two. Of these, Estrella Blanca is the major long-distance provider, with service to Guadalajara, Tijuana and Mazatlán. The most useful 1st-class services include:

Cuernavaca – 42 km, one hour; every 10 minutes, 5 am to 6 pm, by Estrella Roja (US$2)
Mexico City (TAPO) – 70 km, 1½ hours via Amecameca; every 15 minutes by Cristóbal Colón (US$4)
Mexico City (Terminal Sur) – 1½ hours via Tepoztlán; every 20 minutes, 5 am to 8 pm, by Estrella Roja and Cristóbal Colón (US$4)
Oaxaca – 410 km, seven hours; one bus daily (11.30 pm) by Cristóbal Colón (US$12)
Puebla – 125 km, two hours; hourly till 6.45 pm by Estrella Roja (US$3)

CUERNAVACA

pop 316,760; alt 1480m; ☎ *73*

With a mild climate, once described as 'eternal spring,' Cuernavaca ('kwehr-nah-VAH-kah') has been a retreat from Mexico City since colonial times. It has attracted the wealthy and fashionable from Mexico and abroad, many of whom stayed on to become temporary or semipermanent residents. A number of their residences have become attractions in themselves, now housing museums, galleries, expensive restaurants and hotels. As the local population grows and more and more visitors come, especially on weekends, Cuernavaca is unfortunately losing some of its charm and acquiring the problems that people from the capital try to escape – crowds, traffic, smog and crime.

Much of the city's elegance is hidden behind high walls and in colonial courtyards, and is largely inaccessible to the casual visitor on a tight budget. A stroll through the lively zócalo costs nothing, but try to allow a few extra pesos to enjoy the food and ambiance at some of the better restaurants. Cuernavaca is also worth visiting to see the famed Palacio de Cortés, and the nearby pre-Hispanic sites and balnearios. A lot of visitors stay longer to enroll in one of the many Spanish-language schools, and they find it is a pleasant city with an enjoyable social life.

History

Indians settling in the valleys of modern Morelos around 1220 developed a highly productive agricultural society based at Cuauhnáhuac (Place at the Edge of the Forest). The Mexica (Aztecs), who dominated the Valle de México, called them 'Tlahuica,' which means 'people who work the land.' In 1379, a Mexica warlord conquered Cuauhnáhuac, subdued the Tlahuica and required them to pay an annual tribute that included 8000 sets of clothing, 16,000 pieces of amate bark paper and 20,000 bushels of maize. The tributes payable by the subject states were set out in a register the Spanish later called the *Códice Mendocino* in which Cuauhnáhuac was represented by a three-branched tree; this symbol now appears on the city's coat of arms.

The successor to the Mexican lord married the daughter of the Cuauhnáhuac leader, and from this marriage was born Moctezuma I, the great Aztec king. The Tlahuica prospered under the Aztec empire, themselves dominating small states to the south and trading extensively with other regions. Their city was also a center for religious ceremonies and learning, and archaeological remains show they had a considerable knowledge of astronomy.

When the Spanish arrived, the Tlahuica were fiercely loyal to the Aztec empire, savagely resisting the advance of the conquistadors. In April 1521 they were finally overcome, and Cortés torched the city. Destroying the city pyramid, Cortés used the stones to build a fortress-palace on the pyramid's base. He also had built from the rubble the Catedral de la Asunción, another

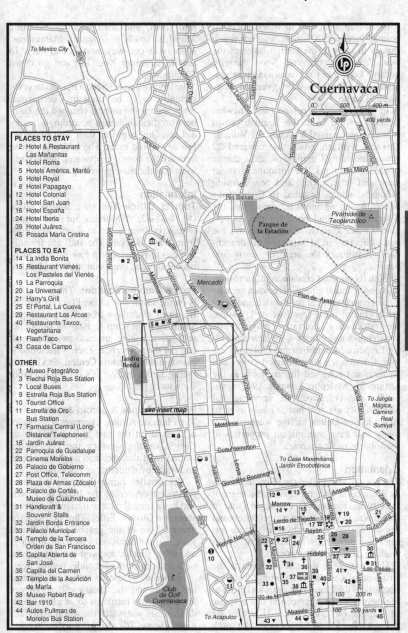

Cuernavaca

PLACES TO STAY
2 Hotel & Restaurant
    Las Mañanitas
4 Hotel Roma
5 Hotels América, Marilú
6 Hotel Royal
8 Hotel Papagayo
12 Hotel Colonial
13 Hotel San Juan
16 Hotel España
24 Hotel Iberia
39 Hotel Juárez
45 Posada María Cristina

PLACES TO EAT
14 La India Bonita
15 Restaurant Vienés,
    Los Pasteles del Vienés
19 La Parroquia
20 La Universal
21 Harry's Grill
25 El Portal, La Cueva
29 Restaurant Los Arcos
40 Restaurants Taxco,
    Vegetariana
41 Flash Taco
43 Casa de Campo

OTHER
1 Museo Fotográfico
3 Flecha Roja Bus Station
7 Local Buses
9 Estrella Roja Bus Station
10 Tourist Office
11 Estrella de Oro
    Bus Station
17 Farmacia Central (Long-
    Distance Telephones)
18 Jardín Juárez
22 Parroquia de Guadalupe
23 Cinema Morelos
26 Palacio de Gobierno
27 Post Office, Telecomm
28 Plaza de Armas (Zócalo)
30 Palacio de Cortés,
    Museo de Cuauhnáhuac
31 Handicraft &
    Souvenir Stalls
32 Jardín Borda Entrance
33 Palacio Municipal
34 Templo de la Tercera
    Orden de San Francisco
35 Capilla Abierta de
    San José
36 Capilla del Carmen
37 Templo de la Asunción
    de María
38 Museo Robert Brady
42 Bar 1910
44 Autos Pullman de
    Morelos Bus Station

AROUND MEXICO CITY

fortress-like structure in a walled compound; in the 1520s there was not much reason to trust in the benign favor of the new Catholic 'converts.' Soon the city became known as Cuernavaca, a more pronounceable (to the Spanish) version of its original name.

In 1529 Cortés received his somewhat belated reward from the Spanish crown when he was named Marqués del Valle de Oaxaca, with an estate that covered 22 towns, including Cuernavaca, and a charge of 23,000 Indians. He introduced sugar cane and other crops, and new farming methods, which resulted in Cuernavaca becoming an agricultural center for the Spanish, as it had been for the Aztecs. Cortés made Cuernavaca his home for the rest of his stay in Mexico, and his descendants dominated the area for nearly 300 years.

With its pleasant climate, rural surroundings and colonial elite, Cuernavaca became a refuge and a retreat for the rich and powerful. One of these was José de la Borda, the 18th century Taxco silver magnate. His lavish home and garden were later a retreat for Emperor Maximilian and Empress Carlota. Cuernavaca also attracted artists and writers, and achieved literary fame as the setting for Malcolm Lowry's 1947 novel *Under the Volcano*. The very rich of Mexico City are now just as likely to go to Acapulco or Dallas for the weekend, but many still have magnificent properties in the suburbs of Cuernavaca.

Orientation

The zócalo, also called the Plaza de Armas or Plaza de la Constitución, is the heart of the city and the best place to begin a tour of Cuernavaca. Most of the budget hotels and important sites are nearby. The various bus lines use different terminals, most within walking distance of the zócalo.

Highway 95D, the toll road, skirts the east side of Cuernavaca; coming from the north, take the Cuernavaca exit and cross to highway 95 (the intersection has a statue of Zapata on horseback). Highway 95 becomes Boulevard Zapata as you go south

into town, and then becomes Avenida Morelos; south of Avenida Matamoros, Morelos is one-way, northbound only. To reach the center, veer left and go down Matamoros.

In 1995 officials issued a new address for virtually every building in Cuernavaca. Since then some owners changed the numbers on their buildings accordingly; many did not. Others posted their new addresses beside the old ones. The addresses given here are the ones that appeared most prominently at the time of writing.

Information

Tourist Office The state tourist office (☎ 14-38-72) at Morelos Sur 187 is open weekdays from 9 am to 8 pm, weekends from 9 am to 6 pm. The staff are friendly and can provide facts in English and Spanish on sites and events throughout Morelos.

Post & Communications The post office is on the south side of the Plaza de Armas. It's open weekdays from 8 am to 7 pm, Saturday from 9 am to 1 pm. It offers fax service, and there are card pay phones in front of the post office. There's a telephone caseta at the Farmacia Central, on Galeana facing Jardín Juárez; it's open daily from 7 am to 10 pm.

Plaza de Armas & Jardín Juárez

The Plaza de Armas, Cuernavaca's zócalo, is flanked on the east by the Palacio de Cortés, on the west by the Palacio del Gobierno of the state and on the northeast and south by a number of restaurants.

The smaller Jardín Juárez adjoins the northwest corner of the Plaza de Armas and has a central gazebo designed by tower specialist Gustave Eiffel. The booths on the ground floor of the gazebo sell fruit and juice. Various stalls sell ice cream, hot dogs and other snacks, and you can enjoy them on a wrought-iron seat under nearby trees.

Numerous sidewalk restaurants around the jardín and the zócalo will serve you anything from breakfast to an after-dinner drink while you watch the world go by. It's quite a scene. It's also the only main plaza in Mexico *without* a church, chapel, convent or cathedral overlooking it.

Palacio de Cortés & Museo de Cuauhnáhuac

Cortés' imposing medieval-style fortress stands at the southeastern end of the Plaza de Armas. Construction of this two-story stone palace was accomplished between 1522 and 1532, on the base of the pyramid that Cortés destroyed. Cortés resided here until he returned to Spain in 1540. The palace remained with Cortés' family for most of the next century, but by the 18th century it was being used as a prison, and during the days of Porfirio Díaz in the late 19th century it was used as government offices.

Today the palace houses the Museo de Cuauhnáhuac, with two floors of exhibits highlighting the history and cultures of Mexico. On the ground floor, exhibits focus on pre-Hispanic cultures, including the local Tlahuica and their relationship with the Aztec empire. The base of the original pyramid can still be seen at various places around the museum's ground floor.

Upstairs, exhibits cover events from the Spanish conquest to the present. On the balcony is a fascinating mural by Diego Rivera. It was commissioned in the mid-1920s as a gift to the people of Cuernavaca by Dwight Morrow, the US ambassador to Mexico. Reading from right to left, the giant mural shows scenes from the conquest to the 1910 Revolution, emphasizing the cruelty, oppression and violence that have characterized Mexican history.

The museum is open Tuesday through Sunday from 10 am to 5 pm. Admission is US$2 (free on Sunday).

Jardín Borda

These gardens were built in 1783 for Manuel de la Borda, as an addition to the stately residence built by his father, José de la Borda, the Taxco silver magnate. From 1866, the house was the summer residence of Emperor Maximilian and Empress Carlota, who entertained their courtiers in the gardens. Today the site is one of Cuernavaca's main draws – although it isn't what it used to be in many ways.

From the entrance on Morelos, you can tour the house and gardens to get an idea of how Mexico's aristocracy lived. In typical colonial style, the buildings are arranged around courtyards. In one wing, the **Museo de Sitio** has exhibits on daily life during the empire period, and original documents with the signatures of Morelos, Juárez and Maximilian. Several romantic paintings show scenes of the garden in Maximilian's time, with ladies and gentlemen rowing on the pond. One of the most famous paintings depicts Maximilian in the garden with La India Bonita, the 'pretty Indian' who was to become his lover. Another part of the house has a gallery for temporary exhibitions.

The gardens are formally laid out on a series of terraces, with paths, steps and fountains, and they originally featured a botanical collection with hundreds of varieties of fruit trees and ornamental plants. The vegetation is still exuberant, with large trees and semitropical shrubs, though there is no longer a wide range of species, and the pretty pond you see in the painting now looks more like a dirty concrete swimming pool. Also, because of a water shortage in the city the fountains have been turned off, which greatly diminishes the aesthetic appeal of the gardens. You can hire a little boat and go rowing for US$1.50 an hour. The house and garden are open Tuesday through Sunday from 10 am to 5.30 pm; admission is US$1 (free on Wednesday).

Beside the house is the Parroquia de Guadalupe church, also built by José de la Borda, and dedicated in December 1784. The schedule of masses is posted behind the iron gate; the church's hours otherwise vary.

Recinto de la Catedral

Cuernavaca's cathedral stands in a large high-walled compound *(recinto)* on the corner of Morelos and Hidalgo (the entrance gate is on Hidalgo). Like the Palacio de Cortés, the cathedral was built on a grand scale and in a fortress-like style, as a defense against the natives and to impress and intimidate them. Franciscans started work under Cortés in 1526, using Indian labor and stones from the rubble of Cuauhnáhuac; it was one of the earliest Christian missions in Mexico. The first part to be built was the **Capilla Abierta de San José**, the open chapel on the west side of the cathedral.

The cathedral itself, the **Templo de la Asunción de María**, is plain and solid, with an unembellished façade. The side door, which faces north to the compound's entrance, shows a mixture of indigenous and European features – the skull and crossbones above it is a symbol of the Franciscan order. Inside are frescos that were discovered early this century. They are said to show the persecution of Christian missionaries in Japan, though it's difficult to decipher them. Cuernavaca *was* a center for Franciscan missionary activities in Asia, and the frescos were supposedly painted in the 17th century by a Japanese convert to Christianity.

The cathedral compound also holds two smaller churches, one on either side of the Hidalgo entrance. On the right as you enter is the **Templo de la Tercera Orden de San Francisco**, commenced in 1723, with its exterior carved in 18th century baroque style by Indian artisans, and its interior with ornate, gilded decorations. Left as you enter is the 19th century **Capilla del Carmen**, where believers seek cures for illness.

Museo Robert Brady

Robert Brady (1928-86), an American artist and collector, lived in Cuernavaca for 24 years. His home, the Casa de la Torre, was originally part of the monastery within the Recinto de la Catedral, and he had it extensively renovated and decorated. Brady was from a wealthy family and he traveled widely, acquiring paintings, carvings, textiles, antiques and decorative and folk arts from around the world. There are several paintings by well-known Mexican artists, including Tamayo, Kahlo

and Covarrubias, but the main attraction is the sheer size and diversity of the collection, and the way it is arranged with delightful combinations and contrasts of styles, periods and places. One wall displays masks from Mexico, Bali and Central Africa. New Guinea carvings stand next to a Mexican table on a Persian carpet. Cushions are covered in embroidered fabrics from Asia, America and the Middle East.

The museum (☎ 18-85-54) is open Thursday through Saturday from 10 am to 6 pm. All visitors must be accompanied by one of the guides; they're very informative and some speak English. It's a good idea to call first to check the hours (they can be flexible) and to ensure there's an English-speaking guide available, if you'd prefer. The museum is a short walk from the zócalo, at Netzahualcóyotl 4. Admission is US$2.50.

Palacio Municipal

The 1883 Palacio Municipal is on Avenida Morelos, just south of the Jardín Borda. A collection of large and colorful paintings is displayed around the courtyard, upstairs and down. They depict the history of the region, particularly pre-Hispanic history, in a somewhat romantic light and definitely not in chronological order. The building is open weekdays from 8 am to 6 pm, and you can enter for free to see the paintings. Temporary exhibitions by visiting artists are often held in the courtyard.

Salto de San Antón

For a pleasant walk less than a km from the city center, follow the small streets west of the Jardín Borda to the *salto*, a 40-meter waterfall. A walkway is built into the cliff face so you can walk right behind the falls. It's a picturesque place, with many trees, and the village of San Antón, above the falls, is a traditional center for pottery.

Casa Maximiliano & Jardín Etnobotánico

In Cuernavaca's suburbs, 1.5 km southeast of the center, this 1866 house was once a

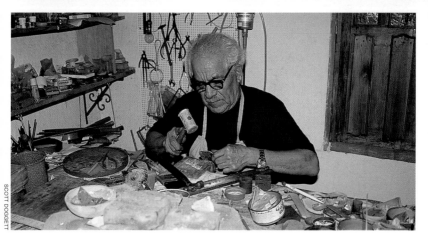

Top Left: Telamones (atlantes) atop Pyramid B, Tula
Top Right: Stone warrior at Tula
Center: Detail, Teotihuacán
Bottom: Silversmith Don Tomás at work, Taxco

Top Left: Church-topped Great Pyramid of Cholula
Top Right: Processional cross, Cuetzalán
Bottom: Taxco

rural retreat for the Emperor Maximilian, where he would meet his Indian lover. It was called La Casa del Olvido (The House of Forgetfulness), because Maximilian 'forgot' to include a room for his wife there. He did remember to include a small house in the back for his lover; it is now the **Museo de la Herbolaria**, a museum of traditional herbal medicine. Around the museum, the Jardín Etnobotánico has a vast collection of herbs and medicinal plants from around the world, all labeled with their botanical names. The site is open daily from 9 am to 5 pm; the museum (free) closes at 3 pm. The address is Matamoros 14 in Colonia Acapantzingo; it's 200 meters south of Tamayo.

Pirámide de Teopanzolco

This small archaeological site is on Calle Río Balsas in the colonia Vista Hermosa. The pyramid is actually two pyramids, one inside the other; this was a typical Tlahuica Indian method of expanding pyramids.

The older (inside) pyramid was built over 800 years ago; the outside one was under construction when Cortés arrived and was never completed. The name Teopanzolco means 'Place of the Ancient Temple,' and may relate to an ancient construction to the west of the current pyramid, where artifacts dating from around 7000 BC have been found, as well as others with an Olmec influence.

Several other smaller platform structures surround the pyramid. The rectangular platform west of the double pyramid is notable because human remains, mixed with ceramic pieces, were found there. They are believed to be products of human sacrifice in which decapitation and dismemberment were practiced.

The site is open daily from 10 am to 5 pm (US$2; free on Sunday). It's over one km from the center, and quite a walk as you have to go around the north side of the old train station. Try a local bus on Ruta 9.

Other Things to See & Do

If you're going to be in Cuernavaca for a while, there are quite a few other sights.

Those out in the suburbs can be difficult to reach – see the Getting Around section.

The great Mexican muralist David Alfaro Siqueiros had his workshop *(taller)* in Cuernavaca from 1964 until his death in 1974. The **Taller Alfaro Siqueiros**, at Venus 52 in Fraccionamiento Jardines de Cuernavaca, is open Tuesday through Sunday from 10 am to 5 pm (US$1). On display are four murals left unfinished at the artist's death, a photographic display of his major works, and other mementos of his life.

The **Hacienda de San Antonio Atlacomulco** was built in the 17th century by Martín Cortés, who succeeded Hernán Cortés as Marqués del Valle de Oaxaca. The hacienda was nationalized in 1833 and, after various changes, it became an aguardiente factory in 1852. During the revolution, Emiliano Zapata took it over and used it as a base for his troops. After the revolution the estate deteriorated, but in 1980 it was renovated to become the Hotel Hacienda de Cortés. It's about four km southeast of the center, in Atlacomulco.

Another notable residence converted to a hotel is **Sumiya**, former house of Baroness Barbara Hutton, heiress to the Woolworth fortune. Built in Japanese style at great expense, it uses fittings, tiles and even boulders imported from Japan, and has a kabuki theater, meditation garden and wooden bridges between the rooms. The estate is now incorporated into the Camino Real Sumiya hotel (see Places to Stay). A splurge meal at the Sumiya Restaurant is the best excuse to look at the place.

The **Museo Fotográfico de Cuernavaca** has a few early photos and maps of the city. It's in a cute little 1897 building called the Castellito, at Güemes 1, one km north of the zócalo. It's free and open from 9 am to 2 pm and 4 to 6 pm weekdays, and 10 am to 2 pm weekends.

Jungla Mágica (☎ 15-87-76) at Bajada de Chapultepec 27 is a children's park with a jungle theme and a popular bird show, and boating and picnicking facilities where you can swim with dolphins. Despite the steep price (US$14), the park draws large crowds and reservations are recommended. It's open Thursday to Sunday from 10 am to 6 pm. To get there, take a 'Ruta 17' bus, tell the driver you're going to 'La Luna,' which is a roundabout; walk two blocks along Chapultepec and you'll come to the entrance of the park.

Language Courses

Many foreigners come to Cuernavaca to study Spanish. The best schools offer small-group or individual instruction, at all levels from beginner to advanced, with four to five hours per day of intensive instruction plus a couple of hours' conversation practice. Classes begin each Monday, and most schools recommend a minimum enrollment of four weeks, though you can study for as many weeks as you want.

Tuition fees vary from US$600 to US$1000 for four weeks, usually payable in advance. You may get a discount outside the peak months of January, February, July and August; some schools offer discounts if you stay more than four weeks. Most schools also charge a nonrefundable one-time enrollment fee of US$60 to US$100.

The schools can arrange for students to live with a Mexican family to experience 'total immersion' in the language. The host families charge about US$18 per day with shared room and bath, or about US$25 per day with private room and bath; price includes three meals daily. The schools can often help with hotel reservations too. For free brochures from the schools, write or call them at:

CALE – Center of Art and Languages
Apdo Postal 1777, Cuernavaca, Morelos, Mexico 62000; former students cite CALE's limited staff size and personalized approach to learning as its best assets (☎ 13-06-03, fax 13-73-52)

Cemanahuac Educational Community
Apdo Postal 5-21, Cuernavaca, Morelos, Mexico 62051; a strong emphasis is placed on both language acquisition and cultural awareness (☎ 12-64-19, fax 12-54-18)

Center for Bilingual Multicultural Studies
Apdo Postal 1520, Cuernavaca, Morelos, Mexico 62170; the center, affiliated with the Universidad Autónoma del Estado de Morelos, is a fully accredited school (☎ 17-10-87, fax 17-05-33)

Cetlalic Alternative Language School
Apdo Postal 1-201, Cuernavaca, Morelos, Mexico 62000; equal weight is placed on language, cultural awareness and social responsibility (☎ 12-67-18, fax 12-67-18)

Cuauhnáhuac Instituto Colectivo de Lengua y Cultura
Apdo Postal 5-26, Cuernavaca, Morelos, Mexico 62051; the school is dedicated to meeting the specific language needs of its clients, from students needing university language credits to members of the business and medical communities with special needs (☎ 12-36-73, fax 18-26-93)

Cuernavaca Language School
Apdo Postal 4-254, Cuernavaca, Morelos, Mexico 62430; the school claims that its focus on the rapid acquisition of communication skills, coupled with its long history of teaching Spanish, makes it ideal for students to learn as much as possible in a short period of time (☎ 15-27-81, fax 17-51-51)

Encuentros Comunicación y Cultura
Apdo Postal 2-71, Cuernavaca, Morelos, Mexico 62158; taking into consideration the specific interests and needs of their students, Encuentros arranges meetings with local professionals, as well as visits to local organizations and institutions (☎/fax 12-50-88)

Experiencia – Centro de Intercambio Bilingüe y Cultural
Apdo Postal 596, Cuernavaca, Morelos, Mexico 62050; a defining feature of Experiencia is its *intercambio* program, whereby two-hour conversational exchanges between Mexican and international students are organized by the school twice each week (☎/fax 18-52-09)

IDEL – Instituto de Idiomas y Culturas Latino-americanas
Apdo Postal 12771-1, Cuernavaca, Morelos, Mexico 62001; IDEL complements language study with excursions to places of historical interest in and around Cuernavaca, video presentations, cultural events and parties (☎/fax 13-01-57)

IDEAL – Instituto de Estudios de América Latina
Apdo Postal 2-65, Cuernavaca, Morelos, Mexico 62158; IDEAL was founded with the philosophy that in order to learn a language, total immersion in a relaxed environment is the best method – 'spaces' rather than formal classrooms are used for instruction (☎ 11-75-51, fax 11-75-51)

Instituto de Idioma y Cultura en Cuernavaca
Apdo Postal 2-42, Cuernavaca, Morelos, Mexico 62158; the school places great importance on creating a family-like atmosphere and assigns a different teacher to each class each week so students are exposed to different voices and personalities (☎ 17-04-55, fax 17-57-10)

Instituto Tecnológico Estudios Superiores de Monterrey
ITSM Morelos, International Programs 9051-C, Siempre Viva Road, Suite MX21-178, San Diego, CA, USA 92173; as a university campus, it offers students whose Spanish is good enough the opportunity to take a variety of courses, not only language courses (☎ 26-01-21, fax 26-10-24)

Prolingua Instituto Español Xochicalco
Apdo Postal 1-888, Cuernavaca, Morelos, Mexico 62000; Prolingua offers grammar, vocabulary, conversational and cultural classes, allowing each student the opportunity to take specific classes to improve areas of weakness (☎/fax 18-98-39)

Spanish Language Institute
Apdo Postal 2-3, Cuernavaca, Morelos, Mexico 62191; this popular school promises classes of no more than five students and offers a variety of cultural courses, including Mexican customs and traditions, psychology of the Latin American and Latin American literature (☎ 11-00-63, fax 17-52-94)

Tlahuica Spanish Language Learning Center
Apdo Postal 2-135, Cuernavaca, Morelos, Mexico 62158; this school, which is smaller and more personal than others, is located in the grounds of a tennis resort and its athletic facilities are available to students at no extra charge (☎ 80-07-73, fax 80-10-36)

Universal Centro de Lingua y Comunicación
Apdo Postal 1-1826, Cuernavaca, Morelos, Mexico 62000; Universal mixes language study with visits to local communities as well as visits from local politicians, community leaders and scholars (☎ 18-29-04, fax 18-29-10)

Universidad Autónoma del Estado de Morelos
Apdo Postal 20, Cuernavaca, Morelos, Mexico 62350; teachers at the university's Centro de Lengua Arte e Historia para Extranjeros organize innovative activities designed to encourage students to practice their Spanish while learning about Mexican culture (☎ 16-16-26, fax 22-35-13)

Special Events

These are among the festivals and special events you can see in Cuernavaca:

Carnaval In the five days before Ash Wednesday, this colorful week-long celebration of Mardi Gras includes street performances by the Chinelo dancers of Tepoztlán, and parades, art exhibits and more; late February or early March

Feria de la Primavera Cuernavaca's Spring Fair includes cultural and artistic events, concerts and a beautiful exhibit of the city's spring flowers; March 21 to April 10

San Isidro Labrador On the day of Saint Isidro the Farmer, local farmers adorn their mules and oxen with flowers and bring them to town for a blessing; May 15

Día de la Virgen de Guadalupe The day of the Virgen de Guadalupe is celebrated in Cuernavaca, as it is everywhere in Mexico, on December 12.

Places to Stay

Accommodations in Cuernavaca don't offer great value for the money. The cheap places tend to be depressingly basic, the mid-range ones are lacking in charm and the top-end hotels are wonderful but very expensive. On weekends and holidays the town fills up with visitors from the capital, so phone ahead or try to secure your room early in the day.

Places to Stay – budget

The cheapest accommodations are on Aragón y León between Morelos and Matamoros – a section of street worked by a handful of prostitutes – and charge US$5 a night for basic, worn rooms: the *América* (cold water), the *Marilú* (hot water), the *San Juan* (undergoing upgrades, may be OK). The *Hotel Colonial* charges US$12/13 for a clean single/double with fan, hot water and a shower with a shower curtain.

Round the corner, at Matamoros 17, the *Hotel Roma* (☎ 18-87-78) offers small rooms with grungy bathrooms for US$9. Only four of the hotel's 40 rooms have fans, and hot water is limited to certain hours. The *Hotel Royal* (☎ 18-64-80), at Matamoros 11, has clean rooms with hot water around a central car park at US$10/12, or with TV for US$3 more.

AROUND MEXICO CITY

The *Hotel Juárez* (☎ 14-02-19) at Netzahualcóyotl 17 is the best of the budgets. Centrally located but quiet, with a large garden and swimming pool, the Juárez offers 13 simple but light, spacious and airy rooms with 24-hour hot water for US$10/13. Get there early if you want a parking space (there's only one!).

Places to Stay – middle

The *Hotel Iberia* (☎ 12-60-40) at Rayón 9, has long been patronized by travelers and foreign students. Its small, basic rooms are set around a small, tiled car park. At US$10/18 it's a tad pricey, but it is located only a short walk to the zócalo.

The colonial *Hotel España* (☎ 18-67-44), at the corner of Rayón and Morelos, is nicer than the Iberia because it has toilet seats, shower curtains and better ventilation, but in other cities its fairly worn rooms (US$12/14) would cost less.

The *Hotel Papagayo* (☎ 14-17-11) at Motolinía 13, is the most pleasant place in this price range, with 77 modern rooms around a large garden with two swimming pools, children's play equipment and plenty of parking. Rates are US$18/27.

Places to Stay – top end

Las Mañanitas (☎ 14-14-66) at Linares 107 is one of the finest hotels in Mexico. Prices run from US$120 for standard rooms up to US$250 for gorgeous garden suites. Renowned for its large private garden where peacocks stroll around while guests enjoy the pool, this hotel has been included in several listings of the world's best hotels. Its restaurant is also justly famous.

Occupying the former home of Baroness Barbara Hutton, the *Camino Real Sumiya* (☎ 20-91-99) is an exquisite hotel in Fraccionamiento Sumiya on the southern outskirts of town. The surrounding gardens have established trees, fountains and ponds, and the elegant Japanese style of the place is unique in Mexico. Prices start at US$145 a room; suites run to US$350.

The *Posada María Cristina* (☎ 18-69-84) at Leyva 20 is not as luxurious as the

Sumiya but it's one of Cuernavaca's longtime favorites, with tastefully appointed rooms in a nicely restored colonial building with lovely, hillside gardens and an inviting swimming pool. Room rates start at US$70, and private cabañas are available for US$95.

Places to Eat

Budget For a simple healthy snack or breakfast of yogurt with fruit, escamochas (a kind of fruit salad), corn on the cob, ice cream, or fresh fruit/vegetable juice, you could patronize one of the booths at the *Jardín Juárez* gazebo, then eat your treat on one of the park's many benches.

Heading south down Galeana from the Jardín Juárez, *El Portal* has budget-priced burgers, chicken and fries, and *La Cueva* has a slightly more expensive menu with seafood and Mexican standards.

Another block down Galeana is the popular *Restaurant Taxco*, with a choice of comidas corridas from US$3.50 to US$6. Next door is the small, simple *Restaurant Vegetariana*, with a delicious four-course comida corrida of salad, vegetable soup, a hot main dish with brown rice, tea and dessert for US$3.

There are numerous cheap eateries uphill and away from the plazas on Rayón. A few places have hamburgers, others serve tacos, ice cream or fruit juices – there's even a Chinese restaurant.

Middle On the east side of Jardín Juárez, *La Parroquia*, open every day from 7.30 am to 11.30 pm, is one of Cuernavaca's favorite restaurants. It serves delicious meals, is open long hours and has a good view of the plaza, but you pay for the location – main meat dishes, for example, cost around US$7.50. Its extensive menu of meals, coffees and desserts includes some Middle Eastern specialties.

Nearby, *La Universal* occupies a strategic position on the corner of the two plazas, with tables under an awning facing the Plaza de Armas. It's open from 9 am to midnight and is a popular place to be seen, but it's quite expensive.

On the south side of the Plaza de Armas, the umbrella-covered tables of the *Restaurant Los Arcos* are a pleasant place for a meal or just to hang out, sip coffee or a soda and watch the action on the plaza. Their varied bilingual menu has something for everyone and is not too expensive. It's open every day from 8 am to 11 pm.

La India Bonita, northwest of Jardín Juárez at Morrow 106, is a lovely courtyard restaurant with tasty, traditional Mexican food. The house specialties are: chicken mole, with that great mole sauce that is a combination of chocolate, chilies and about 70 other ingredients (US$8); charcoal-grilled filet mignon (US$9); and a special Mexican plate with seven different selections (US$7). Hours are Tuesday through Saturday 8.30 am to 7.30 pm, and Sunday 8.30 am to 6.30 pm.

Restaurant Vienés, at Tejada 4, offers a delicious variety of traditional European dishes, like the 'farmer's plate' (smoked pork ribs, roast veal, frankfurter, potatoes and sauerkraut), knackwurst with sauerkraut and German fried potatoes, or stuffed roast meatloaf served with potatoes, vegetables and salad. Main courses are around US$8. It's open every day except Tuesday, from 1 to 10 pm. The same owners run *Los Pasteles del Vienés*, next door, which serves the best cakes, cookies, cream puffs and chocolate-rum truffles you've tasted since the last time you were in Vienna. Their superb coffee comes with free refills.

Harry's Grill, at Gutenberg 5, is one of the Carlos Anderson chain of bar/restaurants where rock music shakes the posters lining every inch of wall space. All the Anderson restaurants are popular with gringos, and this one is no exception. Main courses cost around US$5 to US$9. The grill is open from 1 pm to midnight, but the bar stays open later.

Top End As a haven for the rich, Cuernavaca boasts a number of sumptuous restaurants. There are Lebanese, Japanese, Chinese, Italian, Spanish and seafood places, but if you can afford an indulgence,

try the *Restaurant Las Mañanitas* (☎ 14-14-66), at the hotel of the same name at Linares 107. One of Mexico's best and most famous restaurants, it has tables inside the mansion or on the garden terrace where you can see peacocks and flamingos strolling through an emerald-green garden and swans gliding around on a pond. The menu features meals from around the world, and you should bring at least US$20 in cash per person (no credit cards). It's open daily from 1 to 5 pm and from 7 to 10.30 pm; reservations are recommended.

The *Casa de Campo*, at Abasolo 101, serves excellent food in a classic colonial courtyard with lots of greenery and tinkling fountains. Expect to pay US$5 for a salad, US$4 for soup, US$8 for pasta and US$10 for a main course.

Entertainment

Hanging around the central plazas is always a popular activity in Cuernavaca, especially on Sunday and Thursday from 6 pm on, when open-air concerts are often held.

The better discos are usually open only on Friday and Saturday nights; *Barba Azul*, at Prado 10, Colonia San Jeronimo, and *Kaova*, near the corner of Motolinía and Morelos, are two of the best. *1910* (☎ 14-35-30), which took its name from the first year of the Mexican Revolution, was so popular at the time of writing you needed to make a reservation well in advance to get in.

For live salsa dance music, try the very cool *Rúmbale* at Bajada Chapultepec 50B, or *Sammaná*, at Domingo Diez 1522, open Thursday, Friday and Saturday nights. *Flash Taco*, a 'video antojitos bar' opposite the Palacio de Cortés, has 43 monitors tuned to soccer during the day and rock and roll at night.

Some of Cuernavaca's better hotels have live music in their bars nightly; you could try the bars at the *Hotel Villa Bejar*, Domingo Diez 2350, or the *Villa del Conquistador*, Paseo del Conquistador 134. These places are mostly way out in the posh suburbs – get a taxi.

The bar at *Harry's Grill* is a fun place to meet people. For quieter drinks in elegant surroundings, the garden bar at the *Hotel Las Mañanitas* is hard to beat; it's open every day from noon to midnight.

The *Cinema Morelos*, on the corner of Morelos and Rayón, is the state theater of Morelos, hosting a variety of cultural offerings, including quality film series, plays and dance performances.

Things to Buy

Cuernavaca has no distinctive handicrafts, but if you want an onyx ashtray, a leather belt or some second-rate silver, try the stalls just south of the Palacio de Cortés.

Getting There & Away

Bus Quite a few bus companies serve Cuernavaca. There are four separate terminals, operated by the main lines:

Autos Pullman de Morelos (APM) – corner of Abasolo and Netzahualcóyotl

Estrella de Oro (EDO) – Avenida Morelos Sur 900

Estrella Roja (ER) – corner of Galeana and Cuauhtémotzin

Flecha Roja (FR) – Avenida Morelos 503, between Arista and Victoria

You might want to get a local bus to/from the Estrella de Oro terminal, which is 1.5 km south, but the others are within walking distance of the zócalo. Many local buses and those to nearby towns go from the southern corner of the city market. Daily first-class buses from Cuernavaca include:

Acapulco – 315 km, 3½ hours; seven EDO (US$14) and seven FR (directos US$13, deluxe US$14)

Chilpancingo – 180 km, three hours; seven EDO and seven FR (US$9)

Cuautla – 42 km, one hour; every 20 minutes, 5 am to 10 pm, by ER (US$2)

Grutas de Cacahuamilpa – 80 km, 2½ hours; hourly FR 6 am to 6 pm (US$2)

Iguala – 90 km, 1½ hours; seven EDO and seven FR (US$4)

Izúcar de Matamoros – 100 km, two hours; hourly ER 5 am to 8 pm (US$3)

Mexico City (Terminal Sur) – 85 km, one hour; every 15 minutes, 5 am to 9.30 pm, by PDM (ordinario US$3.50, deluxe US$4); every 30 minutes, 6.30 am to 10 pm, by FR (US$3.50); five by EDO (US$3.50)

Mexico City Airport – 100 km, 1¼ hours; five by PDM except on Sunday when there are 11 (US$7)

Puebla – 175 km, three hours; hourly, 5 am to 8 pm, by ER (US$5)

Taxco – 80 km, one hour; 10 per day by FR and three by EDO (US$3)

Tepoztlán – 23 km, 30 minutes; every 15 minutes till 10 pm from the local bus terminal at the city market (US$1)

Car & Motorcycle Cuernavaca is 85 km south of Mexico City, a 1½-hour drive on highway 95 and a one-hour trip on the toll road (highway 95D). Both roads continue south to Acapulco: highway 95 goes through Taxco; highway 95D is more direct and much faster, but the tolls will total at least US$30.

Getting Around

You can walk to most places of interest in central Cuernavaca, but getting to places in the suburbs on the cheap can be tough; the local buses cost only US$0.50, but the system is hard to figure out. However, they usually have the colonia they're going to marked on their windshield. Taxis will go to most places in town for US$2.

AROUND CUERNAVACA

Many places can be visited on day trips from Cuernavaca – or on the way north to Mexico City, or south to Taxco (thus avoiding some stretches of the toll road).

Parque Nacional Lagunas de Zempoala

Only 25 km northwest of Cuernavaca, by winding roads, is a group of seven lakes high in the hills. Some of them are stocked with fish for anglers, and the surrounding forest offers some pleasant walks and camping.

Xochicalco

Atop a desolate plateau 15 km southwest of Cuernavaca as the crow flies, but about 38 km by road, is the ancient ceremonial center of Xochicalco ('so-chee-CAL-co'), one of the most important archaeological sites in central Mexico. In Nahuatl, the language of the Aztecs, Xochicalco means 'Place of the House of Flowers,' which it probably was for Toltecs in the 7th century.

Today it is a collection of white stone ruins covering approximately 10 sq km, many yet to be excavated. They represent the various cultures – Toltec, Olmec, Zapotec, Mixtec and Aztec – for which Xochicalco was a commercial, cultural or religious center. When Teotihuacán began to weaken around 650 to 700 AD, Xochicalco began to rise in importance, achieving its maximum splendor between 650 and 850 AD with far-reaching commercial and cultural relations. Around the year 650 a congress of spiritual leaders met in Xochicalco, representing the Zapotec, Mayan and Gulf Coast peoples, to correlate their respective calendars.

The most famous monument here is the Pirámide de Quetzalcóatl (Pyramid of the Plumed Serpent); from its well-preserved bas-reliefs archaeologists have surmised that astronomer-priests met here at the beginning and end of each 52-year cycle of the pre-Hispanic calendar. Xochicalco remained an important center until around 1200, when its excessive growth caused a fall similar to that of Teotihuacán. Signs at the site are in English and Spanish, but information appearing beside displays at an impressive new museum 200 meters from the ruins is in Spanish only.

Getting There & Away Flecha Roja and Autos Pullman de Morelos run hourly buses to within four km of the site, from where you can walk (uphill) or catch a taxi (US$2). The site is open every day from 10 am to 5 pm (admission is US$2; free on Sunday).

Laguna de Tequisquitengo

This lake, 37 km south of Cuernavaca, is a popular location for water sports, particularly water-skiing. There are hotels, restaurants and other facilities around the lakeshore. In the area are several of the state of Morelos' famous balnearios – often natural springs that have been used as bathing and therapeutic places for hundreds of years – including the relaxing Las Estacas (☎ 734-2-14-44) in Tlaltizapán and El Rollo (☎ 734-2-19-88) in Tlaquiltenango, which has several large slides and is geared for family fun. There are also old Franciscan monasteries at Tlaquiltenango and Tlaltizapán. Check with the Cuernavaca tourist office for more information.

Zoofari

More than 150 animal species inhabit this drive-through zoo, many wandering freely in large fenced areas, but quite a few in miserable cages as well. It's a good chance to see the difference between an emu and an ostrich, and children will enjoy seeing the giraffes and zebras from the windows of a car or Zoofari bus. Zoofari (☎ 73-20-97-23) is open every day from 9 am to 5 pm. It's 55 km from Cuernavaca on highway 95 (the non-toll road) to Taxco. Admission is US$4.50 for adults, US$3.50 for kids.

TAXCO

pop 95,135; alt 1800m; ☎ *762*

The old silver-mining town of Taxco ('TASS-co'), 170 km southwest of Mexico City, is a gorgeous colonial antique, and one of the most picturesque and pleasant places in Mexico. Clinging to a steep hillside, its narrow, cobblestoned streets twist and turn between well-worn buildings, open unexpectedly onto pretty plazas and reveal delightful vistas at every corner. Unlike many Mexican towns from the colonial era, it has not surrounded itself with industrial suburbs, and even the traffic in Taxco has a certain charm. Rather than the daily tides of commuting cars, a fleet of VW taxis and combis beetle through the labyrinth like ants on an anthill. And few

AROUND MEXICO CITY

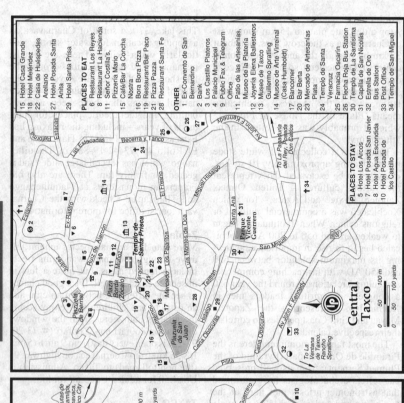

PLACES TO STAY
15 Hotel Casa Grande
18 Hotel Meléndez
22 Casa de Huéspedes Arellano
27 Hotel Posada Santa Anita
29 Hotel Santa Prisca

PLACES TO EAT
6 Restaurant Los Reyes
8 Restaurant La Hacienda
11 Señor Costilla's,
   Pizzería Mario
15 Café/Bar La Concha Nostra
16 Bora Bora Pizza
19 Restaurant/Bar Paco
21 Pizza Pazza
28 Restaurant Santa Fe

OTHER
1 Ex-Convento de San Bernardino
2 Bank
3 Los Castillo Plateros
4 Palacio Municipal
9 Public Fax & Telegram Office
11 Patio de las Artesanías, Museo de la Platería
12 Joyería Elena Ballesteros
13 Museo de Taxco
14 Museo de Arte Virreinal (Casa Humboldt)
17 Bancomer
20 Bar Berta
23 Mercado de Artesanías Plata
24 Templo de Santa Veracruz
25 Farmacia Oscarín
26 Flecha Roja Bus Station
30 Templo de La Santísima
31 Capilla de San Nicolás
32 Estrella de Oro Bus Station
33 Post Office
34 Templo de San Miguel

PLACES TO STAY
5 Hotel Los Arcos
7 Hotel Posada San Javier
8 Hotel Agua Escondida
10 Hotel Posada de los Castillo

Central Taxco

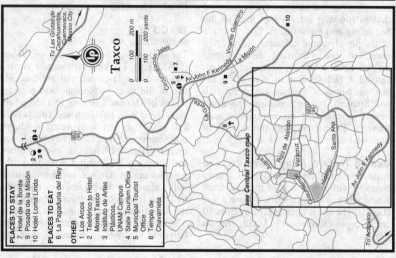

PLACES TO STAY
7 Hotel de la Borda
9 Posada de la Misión
10 Hotel Loma Linda

PLACES TO EAT
6 La Pagaduría del Rey

OTHER
1 Los Arcos
2 Teleférico to Hotel Monte Taxco
3 Instituto de Artes Plásticos,
   UNAM Campus
4 State Tourism Office
5 Municipal Tourist Office
8 Templo de Chavarrieta

Taxco

streetscapes are defaced with rows of parked cars, because there's simply no room for them.

The federal government has declared the city a national historical monument, and local laws preserve Taxco's colonial-style architecture and heritage. Old buildings are preserved and restored wherever possible, and any new buildings must conform to the old in scale, style and materials – have a look at the colonial Pemex station.

Though Taxco's silver mines are almost exhausted, handmade silver jewelry is one of the town's main industries. There are hundreds of silver shops, and visiting them is an excellent reason to wander the streets. Taxco's hotels and restaurants are priced fairly, and they are generally so appealing that they are good value.

History

Taxco was called Tlachco (literally, 'place where ball is played') by the Aztecs, who dominated the region from 1440 until the Spanish arrived. In 1529 the colonial city was founded by Captain Rodrigo de Castañeda, acting under a mandate from Hernán Cortés. Among the town's first Spanish residents were three miners – Juan de Cabra, Juan Salcedo and Diego de Nava – and the carpenter Pedro Muriel. In 1531 they established the first Spanish mine on the North American continent.

The Spaniards came searching for tin, which they found in small quantities, but by 1534 they had discovered tremendous lodes of silver. That year the Hacienda del Chorrillo was built, complete with water wheel, smelter and aqueduct. The old arches (Los Arcos) standing over the highway at the northern end of Taxco are all that remains of the aqueduct. The water wheel and smelter have long since vanished, but the hacienda has gone through several metamorphoses and is now part of an art school.

The prospectors quickly emptied the first veins of silver from the hacienda and left Taxco. Further quantities of silver were not discovered until two centuries later, in 1743. Don José de la Borda, who had arrived in 1716 from France at the age of 16 to work with his miner brother, accidentally uncovered one of the area's richest veins. According to a Taxco legend, Borda was riding near where the church of Santa Prisca now stands when his horse stumbled, dislodged a stone and exposed the silver.

Borda went on to make three fortunes, and lose two. He introduced new techniques of draining and repairing mines, and he reportedly treated his Indian workers much better than those working in other colonial mines. A devout man, his two children both joined the clergy, and the church of Santa Prisca was his gift to Taxco. He is remembered for the saying *'Dios da a Borda, Borda da a Dios'* ('God gives to Borda, Borda gives to God').

His success attracted many more prospectors and miners, and new veins of silver were found, and emptied. With most of the silver gone, Taxco became a quiet town with a dwindling population and economy. In 1929 an American professor and architect named William (Guillermo) Spratling arrived and, at the suggestion of then US Ambassador Dwight Morrow, set up a small silver workshop as a way to rejuvenate the town. (Another version has it that Spratling was writing a book in Taxco and resorted to the silver business because his publisher went broke. A third has it that Spratling had a notion to design and create jewelry that synthesized pre-Columbian motifs with Art Deco modernism, and acted on that notion.) The workshop became a factory and Spratling's apprentices began establishing their own shops. Today there are more than 300 silver shops in Taxco.

Orientation

Taxco's twisting streets may make you feel like a mouse in a maze, and even maps of the town look confusing at first, but you'll learn your way around – in any case it's a nice place to get lost. Plaza Borda, also called the zócalo, is the heart of the town, and its church, Santa Prisca, is a good landmark.

Highway 95 is called Avenida John F Kennedy as it winds its way around the eastern side of central Taxco. Both bus stations are on Kennedy. Calle La Garita branches west from Kennedy opposite the Pemex station, and it becomes the main thoroughfare through the middle of town. It follows a convoluted route, more or less southwest (one-way only), to the Plaza Borda, changing its name to Calle Juárez on the way. Past the plaza, this main artery becomes Cuauhtémoc, and goes down to the Plazuela de San Juan. Most of the essentials are along this La Garita-Juárez-Cuauhtémoc route, or pretty close to it. It's actually quite easy to follow and a standard route for the combis. Several side roads go east back to Kennedy, which is two-way and therefore the only way a vehicle can get back to the north end of town. The basic combi route is a counterclockwise loop going north on Kennedy and south through the center of town, but there are several variants on this.

Information

Tourist Offices The Secretaría de Fomento Turístico (☎ 2-22-74) has an office in the Centro de Convenciones de Taxco, on Kennedy at the north end of town, where the old aqueduct crosses the highway. But the Tourist Information Office (☎ 2-07-98) two km farther south along Kennedy has a friendlier staff, and there's always someone there who speaks English. The office is open daily from 8 am to 7 pm.

Money There are several banks with ATMs around the town's main plazas.

Post & Communications The post office is at Kennedy 34, at the south end of town. It's open weekdays from 8.30 am to 7 pm, and Saturday from 9 am to 1 pm.

Telephone cards are sold at hotels, banks and stores. There are card phones near Plaza Borda and in hotel lobbies. The Telecomm office (telegram, telegraph and fax), on the south side of Plazuela de Bernal, is open weekdays from 9 am to 3 pm.

Museum Hours All of Taxco's museums are open Tuesday through Sunday from 9 am to 2 pm, and 4 to 6 pm.

Templo de Santa Prisca

On Plaza Borda, this church of rose-colored stone is a treasure of baroque architecture, its Churrigueresque façade decorated with elaborately sculpted figures. Over the doorway, the bas-relief depicts Christ's baptism. Inside, the intricately sculpted altarpieces covered with gold are equally fine examples of Churrigueresque art.

The local Catholic hierarchy allowed Don José de la Borda to donate this church to Taxco on the condition that he mortgage his personal mansion and other assets to guarantee its completion. It was designed by Spanish architects Diego Durán and Juan Caballero and constructed between 1748 and 1758, and it almost bankrupted Borda.

Other Churches

Other colonial churches and chapels in Taxco include La Santísima, San Nicolás, San Miguel Arcángel, Santa Veracruz, Chavarrieta and the Ex-Convento de San Bernardino. Uphill from the Plaza Borda are the churches of Ojeda and Guadalupe. The square in front of the Guadalupe affords a fine view over the town.

Museo de Taxco Guillermo Spratling

This three-story museum of archaeology and history is at Delgado 1, directly behind the Templo de Santa Prisca. Pre-Hispanic art exhibits on the two upper floors include jade statuettes, Olmec ceramics and other interesting pieces, mostly from the private collection of William Spratling. The ground floor is devoted to temporary exhibits. Admission is US$2.

Museo de Arte Virreinal

On Ruiz de Alarcón, a couple of blocks down the hill from the Plazuela de Bernal, is one of the oldest colonial homes in Taxco. It is commonly known as **Casa Humboldt**, though the German explorer and naturalist Baron von Friedrich Heinrich Alexander von Humboldt stayed here for only one night in 1803. The restored building now houses a museum of colonial religious art, with a small but well-displayed collection, with informative labels in English and Spanish. An interesting exhibit describes some of the restoration work on the Templo de Santa Prisca, when some fabulous material was found in the basement. Admission is US$2.

Museo de la Platería

The small museum of silverwork exhibits some superb examples of the silversmith's art, and outlines (in Spanish) its development in Taxco. Included are some classic designs by William Spratling, and prize-winning pieces from national and international competitions. Notice the very colorful, sculptural combinations of silver with semiprecious minerals such as jade, lapis lazuli, turquoise, malachite, agate and obsidian – a feature of much of the silverwork for sale in the town, and a link with pre-Hispanic stone-carving traditions.

The museum is at Plaza Borda 1, downstairs from the Patio de las Artesanías (enter from the sidewalk as if you were going to the Señor Costilla's restaurant, turn left instead of right on the patio and go down the stairs). Admission is US$1.

Rancho Spratling

Although William Spratling died in 1967, his former workshop continues to produce some of the finest silver in Mexico – employing the same hand-crafted methods and classic designs that have made Spratling pieces collectibles. Purchased by longtime friend Alberto Ulrich, the former Spratling ranch has been pridefully maintained, and a new generation of artisans here adhere to Spratling's standards under the guidance of maestro Don Tomás, who was one of Spratling's principal workers for many years. A perfectionist and workaholic, Tomás may spend two weeks on a single silver pitcher. Now in his 70s, the maestro told us that he has always had one woman in mind every time he has begun work on a piece of jewelry – his beautiful

friend, Carmela Urbina, who died of tuberculosis in 1943 at the age of 17. Her image has been his inspiration for more than 50 years! The death of Urbina remains a very painful subject for Tomás and one we hope readers will not bring up. The story is mentioned here only because it's so romantic!

Visitors are encouraged to enter the workshop and see how fine silver is crafted. Also on the premises is a museum, focusing on Spratling's life, and a showroom. The ranch (☎ 2-00-26) is located 20 minutes by car south of Taxco on highway 95. The cheapest way to get there from Taxco is by combi; take one marked either 'Campusano' or 'Iguala' and tell the driver to stop at Rancho Spratling, as it is not an official stop. The ride costs US$1. Catch any combi heading north to return to Taxco. There is no cost to visit the ranch. Hours are Monday through Saturday, 8 am to 1 pm and 2 to 5 pm.

Teleférico & Monte Taxco

From the northern end of Taxco, near Los Arcos, a Swiss-made cable car ascends 173 meters to the luxurious Monte Taxco resort hotel. The view of Taxco and the surrounding mountains from the cable car and resort is fantastic. The cable car runs daily from 7.30 am to 7 pm and costs US$3.50 round-trip (children half-price). To find it, walk uphill from Los Arcos and turn right into the gate of the Instituto de Artes Plásticos; you can see the cable-car terminal from the gate.

Special Events

Try to time your visit to Taxco during one of its annual festivals, but be sure to reserve a hotel room in advance. During Semana Santa, in particular, visitors pour into the city to see the processions and events.

Fiestas de Santa Prisca & San Sebastián The festivals of Taxco's two patron saints are celebrated on January 18 (Santa Prisca) and January 20 (San Sebastián). Mass is celebrated in the Templo de Santa Prisca while people parade by the entrance with their pets and farm animals in tow for an annual blessing. Game booths are set up outside the church's gates and dancers entertain the many who come for the mass.

Palm Sunday Christ's triumphant entry into Jerusalem on a donkey is re-enacted in the streets of Taxco on the Sunday before Easter.

Maundy Thursday On the Thursday before Easter, the institution of the Eucharist is commemorated with beautiful presentations and street processions of hooded penitents. Some of the penitents, bearing crosses, flagellate themselves with thorns as the procession winds through town.

Día de San Miguel Regional dance groups perform in the front court of the exquisite 18th century Capilla de San Miguel Arcángel on September 29.

Día del Jumil El Día del Jumil is celebrated on the first Monday after the Day of the Dead (which is on November 1 and 2). See the sidebar for details of this unusual festival.

Feria de la Plata The week-long national silver fair is held during the last week in November or the first week in December (check with the tourist office for exact dates). Silverwork competitions are held in various categories (statuary, jewelry, etc) and some of Mexico's best silverwork is on display. Other festivities include organ recitals in Santa Prisca, rodeos, burro races, concerts and dances.

Las Posadas From December 16 to 24, nightly candlelit processions pass through the streets of Taxco singing from door to door, going from one church to another each night, and finally arriving at Santa Prisca on Christmas Eve. Children are dressed up to resemble various Biblical characters, and at the end of the processions they attack piñatas.

Places to Stay – budget

The least expensive hotels in Taxco have water-everywhere bathrooms – no shower curtains – and no toilet seats. Otherwise, the budget places listed here are quite OK, with plenty of hot water and decent beds in clean or cleanish rooms.

The *Hotel Casa Grande* (☎ 2-11-08) is on Plazuela de San Juan, through the archway and upstairs. It has 12 clean, basic rooms arranged around an inner courtyard; the roof-top rooms are the most pleasant, with plenty of windows and cross-ventilation, opening onto a rooftop terrace. On one side is a laundry where you can wash clothes. Singles/doubles are US$9/13.

The *Casa de Huéspedes Arellano* (☎ 2-02-15) at Calle los Pajaritos 23 offers 10 simple but clean rooms in a central location, tucked away in a back street across from the Mercado de Artesanías Plata. It's a family-run place with terraces for sitting and a place on the roof for washing clothes. Rooms go for US$9/15. To find it, walk down the alley on the south side of Santa Prisca until you reach a staircase going down to your right. Follow it down past the stalls until you see a flight of stairs down to your left; walk down these and the Casa de Huéspedes is 30 steps down, on the left.

The *Hotel Posada Santa Anita* (☎ 2-07-52), at Avenida Kennedy 106, is a basic place with small, somewhat dark but quiet rooms at US$9 per person. It's nearly one km from the center of town, but it's close to the 2nd-class bus station and has plenty of parking.

Places to Stay – middle

One of the most attractive places to stay in Taxco at any price is the *Hotel Posada San Javier* (☎ 2-31-77), at Calle Ex-Rastro 4, a block down the hill from the Palacio Municipal. Though centrally located, it's quiet and peaceful, with a private parking area and a lovely, large enclosed garden with a big swimming pool. The high-ceilinged rooms are clean, spacious, comfortable and pleasant, and many have private terraces. Rooms start at US$20/22 and junior suites range from US$22/26.

The *Hotel Los Arcos* (☎ 2-18-36), at Ruiz de Alarcón 2, has 26 clean and spacious rooms at US$15/22. In 1620 the building was a monastery, and it retains a pleasant courtyard, sitting areas, a rooftop terrace and lots of character. Across the road, the *Hotel Posada de los Castillo* (☎ 2-13-96), at Juan Ruiz de Alarcón 3, is another place with colonial charm and even better prices – US$13/18.

The *Hotel Meléndez* (☎ 2-00-06) at Cuauhtémoc 6 is an older place, but it has many pleasant terrace sitting areas, a nice off-street restaurant and a good location between the Plazuela de San Juan and the

---

El Día del Jumil

Jumiles are small beetles, about one cm long, which migrate annually to the Cerro de Huixteco (the hill behind Taxco) to reproduce. They begin to arrive around September; the last ones are gone by about January or February. During this time, the jumiles are a great delicacy for the people of Taxco, who eat them alone or mixed in salsa with tomatoes, garlic, onion and chilies, or even *alive*, rolled into tortillas. (You can buy live jumiles in the market during this time; the Restaurant Santa Fe serves *salsa de jumil* prepared in the traditional way.)

Traditionally, the entire population of the town climbs the Cerro de Huixteco on this day (first Monday after the Day of the Dead, usually the first week of November), collecting jumiles, bringing picnics and sharing food and fellowship. Many families come early and camp on the hill over the preceding weekend. The celebration is said to represent the jumiles giving energy and life to the people of Taxco for another year. ■

Plaza Borda. There are lots of plants as well. Singles/doubles are US$18/24.

Right on the zócalo, the *Hotel Agua Escondida* (☎ 2-07-26), at Spratling 4, has attractive terraces, large and small swimming pools and a basement car park. The comfy, airy rooms cost US$25/28.

On the south side of the Plazuela de San Juan, the colonial-style *Hotel Santa Prisca* (☎ 2-09-80) at Cena Obscuras 1 is an elegant place with a quiet interior patio, a bright, comfortable sitting room with a library of books in English, and a pleasant restaurant where breakfast is served daily. Rooms, most with private terraces, are US$19, or US$24 with breakfast.

On the highway near town, the motel-style *Hotel Loma Linda* (☎ 2-02-06) at Avenida Kennedy 52 is perched on the ledge of a vast but polluted chasm. There's a swimming pool and a restaurant. Rooms are US$19/23.

Places to Stay – top end

The four-star *Hotel de la Borda* (☎ 2-00-25) at Cerro del Pedregal 2 is a 120-room, modern, mission-style hotel with a pool and large, clean rooms from US$45. Some rooms offer panoramic views of the city. However, reaching this place on foot becomes an increasingly tedious exercise, and combis don't travel its long and steep driveway.

Also away from the center is the new *Posada Don Carlos* (☎ 2-00-75), at Calle del Consuelo 8, which has nine rooms, six

of which have superb views of Taxco. Four of these six go for US$50 per room, and two (slightly smaller than the others) go for US$40. All of the rooms are tastefully appointed and have terraces. Although the hill to the Don Carlos is a tough walk, any combi with 'Bermeja' scrawled on the windshield will take you nearly to the doorstep for US$0.30 (or take a taxi for US$1.50); just tell the combi driver 'Posada Don Carlos' so he'll drop you near it.

The *Posada de la Misión* (☎ 2-00-63) at Avenida Kennedy 32 is a luxurious place whose 120 large rooms have private terraces with views of Taxco. Overlooking the large pool is a mosaic mural designed by Juan O'Gorman. A standard room is US$40; a junior suite is US$50.

Way up on top of the mountain overlooking Taxco, the five-star *Hotel Monte Taxco* (☎ 2-13-00) is probably the most luxurious place to stay in Taxco. It can be reached by car, taxi or cable car. The rates of US$100 for standard rooms, or US$150 for suites, do not include use of the hotel's tennis courts, gym, steam baths or pool. Horseback riding and golf also cost extra. There are also restaurants, bars and a disco.

Places to Eat

The *Restaurant Santa Fe* at Hidalgo 2, a few doors downhill from the Plazuela de San Juan, is often recommended by locals, and it does indeed serve good food at fair prices. Main courses are US$5 or less, set breakfasts cost US$4.50 or less, and the US$3.50 comida corrida includes four courses.

Overlooking the Plaza Borda, the open-air *Restaurant/Bar Paco* is great for people-watching, and is open daily from 1 to 11 pm. One of the house specialties is ensalada Popeye (a spinach salad with mushrooms, bacon and nuts) for US$4. There's a wide selection of soups, meat dishes (US$5 to US$9) and chicken (US$4 to US$5). The food and the atmosphere are both very enjoyable.

Señor Costilla's, upstairs in the Patio de las Artesanías and overlooking the Plaza Borda, is one of the Carlos Anderson chain and resembles the gringo-style Carlos 'n Charlie's restaurants that have sprung up all over Mexico, with loud rock music and prodigious decorations. The prices and portions are pretty big by Mexican standards. It's open for meals daily from 1 pm to midnight.

In the same building, up the stairs on the left from Señor Costilla's, is the *Pizzería Mario*, an open-air restaurant with a few tiny tables on a terrace and one of the best views in Taxco. It's worth eating here just to see it, and the pizza, spaghetti and garlic bread are swell as well.

Bora Bora Pizza has a complimentary address – Delicias 4. It's just off Calle Cuauhtémoc not far from the Plaza Borda, and it serves the best pizza in Taxco. (Some wrongfully prefer *Pizza Pazza* beside the cathedral, which makes thin crust and goes lighter on the toppings.) Prices at the Bora Bora range from US$2.50 to US$4.50 for a small, up to US$5 to US$9 for a maxi; they also serve spaghetti, cheese fondue and desserts, dishing it up daily from 1 pm to midnight.

Restaurant La Hacienda, just off the Plaza Borda, can be reached through the lobby of the Hotel Agua Escondida. Their specialty, cecina hacienda, is a large, delicious Mexican meal of tender beefsteak served with sausage, rice, beans, guacamole, cheese, *chicharrones* (crisp pork rinds) and a *chalupita* (a tiny tostada). They also serve breakfast (under US$4), a large comida corrida (US$6) and dinner until 10 pm.

Opposite the Palacio Municipal, the *Restaurant Los Reyes* at Juárez 9 is a quieter place for a meal, away from the Plaza Borda. It's an upstairs restaurant, with colorful tablecloths and some tables out on a terrace; it's open daily from 8 am to 10 pm.

The top two restaurants in Taxco are on hills overlooking the city center and are most easily reached by taxi. *La Ventana de Taxco* specializes in Italian food; its Piccata Ventana (veal sautéed in a lemon, butter and parsley sauce) is superb; expect to spend about US$25 here for dinner. *La Pagaduria del Rey* is equally fancy but less expensive, with salads up to US$4, seafood to US$10, chicken US$6, and Mexican plates for around US$7. La Pagaduria is a great place simply to sip a drink and admire the view.

Things to Buy

Silver With more than 300 shops selling silverwork, the selection is mind-boggling. Look at some of the best places first, to see what's available, then try to focus on the things you're really interested in, and shop around for them. If you are careful and willing to bargain a bit, you can buy wonderful pieces at reasonable prices.

Most shops are either *menudeo* and *mayoreo* (retail and wholesale); to get the wholesale price you will have to buy maybe 10 pieces of a kind.

The price of a piece is principally determined by its weight; the creative work serves mainly to make it salable, though items with exceptional artisanship can command a premium. If you're serious about buying silver, find out the current pesos-per-gram rate when you're in Taxco and weigh any piece before you agree on a price. All the silver shops have scales, mostly electronic devices that should be accurate. If a piece costs less than the going price per gram, it's not real silver. Don't buy anything that doesn't have the Mexican government '.925' stamp and spread-eagle hallmark (sometimes only one of these symbols appears), which certify that the piece is 92.5% sterling silver. If a piece is too small or delicate to stamp, a reputable shop will supply a certificate as to its purity. Anyone who is discovered selling forged .925 pieces is sent to prison.

The shops in and around the Plaza Borda tend to have higher prices than shops farther from the center, but they also tend to have more interesting work. The shops on Avenida Kennedy are often branches of downtown businesses, set up for the tourist buses that can't make it through the narrow streets.

Several shops are in the Patio de las Artesanías building on the corner of Plaza Borda, on your left as you face Santa Prisca. Pineda's, on the corner of Calle Muñoz and the plaza, is a famous shop; a couple of doors down Muñoz, at No 4, the Joyería Elena Ballesteros is another. Los Castillo Plateros, on Plazuela de Bernal, display not only jewelry, but also statues, vases, tableware and other unusual items. For quantity rather than quality, see the stalls in the Mercado de Artesanías Plata, with vast quantities of rings, chains and pendants. The work is not as well displayed here, but you can often spot something special.

Other Crafts It's easy to overlook them among the silver, but there are other things to buy in Taxco. Finely painted wood and papier-mâché trays, platters and boxes are sold on the street, along with bark paintings and wood carvings. Quite a few shops sell semiprecious stones, fossils and mineral crystals, and some have a good selection of masks, puppets and semi-antique carvings.

Getting There & Away
Taxco has two long-distance bus terminals, both on Avenida Kennedy. The Flecha Roja (also known as Estrella Blanca) terminal, at Kennedy 104, also serves as the terminal for Cuauhtémoc and other 2nd-class bus lines. The Estrella de Oro terminal is at Kennedy 126, at the south end of town. Combis pass these terminals every few minutes and will take you up the hill to

the Plaza Borda for US$0.50 (get one marked 'Zócalo'). Book early for buses out of Taxco as it can be hard to get a seat. Long-distance services (directos unless otherwise stated) include:

Acapulco – 266 km, 4½ to five hours; four daily (US$9) by Cuauhtémoc; four daily (1st-class US$9, deluxe US$13) by Estrella de Oro
Chilpancingo – 130 km, three hours; four daily (1st-class US$5) by Estrella de Oro; four daily (US$5) by Cuauhtémoc
Cuernavaca – 80 km, 1½ hours; hourly directos (US$3.50) and more frequent ordinarios (US$3) by Flecha Roja; 13 daily by Cuauhtémoc (US$4); two daily (US$3) by Estrella de Oro
Grutas de Cacahuamilpa – 30 km, 45 minutes; take an hourly Toluca bus and get off at the 'Grutas' crossroads, or an hourly combi from in front of the Flecha Roja terminal (US$1.50)
Iguala – 35 km, one hour; every 15 minutes from 5 am to 9 pm (US$1.50) by Cuauhtémoc
Ixtapan de la Sal – 68 km, two hours; every hour (US$3) by Flecha Roja
Mexico City (Terminal Sur) – 170 km, three hours; 12 per day (US$6) by Flecha Roja; four daily (1st-class US$7, deluxe US$8) by Estrella de Oro; Futura has three 1st-class to Mexico City for US$7
Toluca – 145 km, three hours; three daily (US$5) by Cuauhtémoc

Getting Around
Apart from walking, combis and taxis are the most popular ways of getting around the steep, winding streets of Taxco.

Combi Combis (white Volkswagen minibuses) are frequent and cheap (US$0.50) and operate from 7 am to 8 pm. The 'Zócalo' combi departs from Plaza Borda, goes down Cuauhtémoc to the Plazuela de San Juan, then heads down the hill on Hidalgo, turns right at San Miguel, left at Avenida Kennedy and follows it northwards until La Garita, where it turns left and goes back to the zócalo. The 'Arcos/Zócalo' combi follows basically the same route except that it continues past La Garita to Los Arcos, where it does a U-turn and heads back to La Garita. Combis marked 'PM' for Pedro Martín' go to the south end of town, past the Estrella de Oro bus station. There are other combis.

Taxi Taxis are plentiful in Taxco and cost from US$1.50 to US$2 for trips around town. You can telephone for a taxi (☎ 2-03-01).

AROUND TAXCO
Las Grutas de Cacahuamilpa

The caverns of Cacahuamilpa are a beautiful natural wonder of stalactites, stalagmites and twisted rock formations, with huge chambers up to 82 meters high. The caves, 30 km northeast of Taxco, are protected as a national park and well worth visiting.

You must tour the caves with a group and a guide, who will lead the way through two km of an illuminated walkway. Many of the formations are named for some fanciful resemblance – 'the elephant,' 'the champagne bottle,' 'Dante's head,' 'the tortillas' and so on – and the lighting is used to enhance these resemblances. Much of the guide's commentary focuses on these and can be quite amusing, but the geological information is minimal. When you reach the end of the guided part, you return to the entrance at your own pace, but you can't enjoy it much as most of the cave lights are turned off. The entire tour takes two hours.

As you leave the caves, a path goes down the steep valley to Río Dos Bocas, where two rivers emerge from the caves. The walk down and back takes 30 minutes if you do it slowly, and it's very pretty.

Cave tours depart from the visitors' center at the entrance every hour on the hour from 10 am to 5 pm; the cost is US$2.50 (US$2 for children ages five to 12). They *might* be able to arrange an English-speaking tour guide if there is a big group of foreigners. There are restaurants, snacks and souvenir shops at the visitors' center.

Getting There & Away From Taxco, hourly combis depart from in front of the Flecha Roja bus terminal and go right to the visitors' center at the caves (30 km, 45 minutes; US$2). Alternatively, you can take any bus heading for Toluca or Ixtapan de la Sal, get off at the 'Grutas' crossroads and walk one km down the road to the entrance, on your right. The last combis leave the site at 5 pm on weekdays, 6 pm on weekends; after this you might be able to catch a bus to Taxco at the crossroads, but don't count on it.

Tehuilotepec

In the village of Tehuilotepec (or simply 'Tehui'), five km north of Taxco on highway 95 to Cuernavaca, is a mining museum, the **Museo de la Minería**, in a historic house built by José de la Borda. The museum, which doesn't have regular hours, is right on the town plaza, where there is also an old colonial church. Take a 'Tehui' combi from in front of the Flecha Roja terminal in Taxco (US$1).

Ixcateopan

The village of Ixcateopan, southwest of Taxco, was the birthplace of Cuauhtémoc, the final Aztec emperor, who was defeated and later executed by Cortés. After the emperor's death his remains were returned to his native village; they are entombed in the church on the town plaza. A historical museum, the **Museo de la Mexicanidad**, is also on the plaza. Marble is quarried nearby and, being the most common stone in the area, was often used in construction; Ixcateopan is one of the few towns in the world with marble streets.

Getting There & Away A combi marked 'Ixcateopan' departs Taxco from in front of the Seguro Social where Calle San Miguel meets the highway, approximately every hour from around 7 am to 5 pm (26 km, one or two hours; US$2).

IGUALA
pop 116,591; alt 720m; ☎ 733

Iguala is an industrial city on highway 95 about 35 km south of Taxco and 190 km south of Mexico City. The city is of interest for its past rather than its present.

On February 24, 1821, at the height of Mexico's struggle for independence, Agustín Iturbide, an officer in the Spanish army, and rebel leader Vicente Guerrero met here and issued the historic Plan de Iguala, an unusual declaration of independence. The declaration was the result of Iturbide's defection from the Spanish crown and offer to make peace with Guerrero.

Iturbide and Guerrero recognized the need for conservative support in Mexico for a new government to succeed. They also wanted to appease liberal factions clamoring for an independent republic. Consequently, rather than berate Spain in the declaration, they stated that Spain was the most generous of nations but, after 300 years as a colony, it was time for Mexico to become a nation in its own right. Spain ultimately agreed to the plan, Mexico's first flag was sewn and raised in Iguala and a provisional junta was installed in Mexico City as a prelude to an independent congress.

Iguala's only interesting sight is the block-like **Monumento a la Bandera** (Monument to the Flag) on the main plaza. Built in 1942, it features the sculpted figures of Mexico's independence heroes: Morelos, Guerrero and Hidalgo. Tamarind trees planted around the plaza in 1832 in honor of the Plan de Iguala established tamarind as the city's fruit. Try an *agua de tamarindo* at any of the juice stands near the plaza.

Every year, from February 17 to 28, Iguala hosts the Feria de la Bandera, a colorful celebration with rodeos, horse racing, a parade and exhibits from local farms and businesses.

West of Mexico City

The main road west of the capital, highway 15D, goes to Toluca, which has a pleasant center, an interesting museum and several art galleries. There are ruins nearby, and some of the surrounding villages are known for their handicrafts. The country-side to the east, south and west of Toluca is scenic, with pine forests, rivers and a huge volcano. Valle de Bravo, a lakeside resort 70 km west of Toluca, is a chic weekend getaway. The road heading south toward Taxco (highway 55D/55) passes a number of popular places, including the spa at Ixtapan de la Sal, 80 km south of Toluca.

TOLUCA
pop 564,287; alt 2660m; ☎ *17*

Toluca, 67 km west of Mexico City, is 400 meters higher than the capital and the extra altitude is noticeable. The eastern outskirts are an industrial area, but the colonial-era city center has attractive plazas and lively arcades. Its cultural sites include a good number of museums and art galleries.

Toluca was an Indian settlement from at least the 13th century; the Spanish founded the city in the 16th century after defeating the Aztecs and Matlazincas who lived in the valley. It became part of the Marquesado del Valle de Oaxaca, Hernán Cortés' personal estates in Mexico. Since 1830 it has been capital of the state of México, which surrounds the Distrito Federal on three sides like an upside down U.

Orientation
The main road from Mexico City becomes Paseo Tollocan, a dual carriageway, as it approaches Toluca. On reaching the east side of the city proper, Paseo Tollocan bears southwest and becomes a ring road around the south side of the city center. The bus station and the large Mercado Juárez are two km southeast of the city center, just off Paseo Tollocan.

The vast Plaza de los Mártires, with the Palacio de Gobierno and the cathedral, is the center of town, but most of the life is in the block to the south that is surrounded by arched colonnades on its east, south and west sides. These portales are lined with shops and restaurants and thronged with people most of the day. The block itself, and the street to the east, is a pedestrian precinct. The pleasant Parque Alameda is three blocks to the west along Hidalgo.

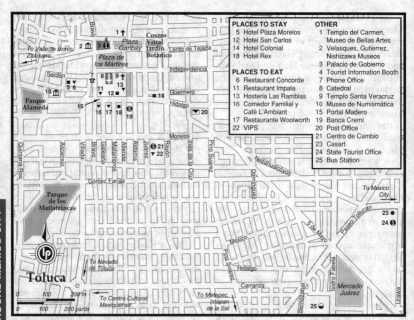

PLACES TO STAY	OTHER
5 Hotel Plaza Morelos	1 Templo del Carmen,
12 Hotel San Carlos	Museo de Bellas Artes
14 Hotel Colonial	2 Velasques, Gutierrez,
18 Hotel Rex	Nishizawa Museos
	3 Palacio de Gobierno
PLACES TO EAT	4 Tourist Information Booth
6 Restaurant Concorde	7 Phone Office
11 Restaurant Impala	8 Catedral
13 Hosteria Las Ramblas	9 Templo Santa Veracruz
16 Comedor Familial y	10 Museo de Numismática
Café L'Ambiant	15 Portal Madero
17 Restaurante Woolworth	19 Banca Cremi
22 VIPS	20 Post Office
	21 Centro de Cambio
	23 Casart
	24 State Tourist Office
	25 Bus Station

Information

Tourist Offices The state tourist office (☎ 12-60-48) is in the Edificio de Servicios Administrativos, office 110, at the corner of Urawa and Paseo Tollocan; good maps of Toluca and the state of México are available, and English is spoken. It's closed Sunday. There is also an information booth in the Palacio de Gobierno; some English is spoken.

Money There are many banks near the Portal Madero, but at the time of writing only one was willing to change money or traveler's checks – Banca Cremi on Allende. There's a Centro de Cambio next to the VIPS restaurant on Juárez.

Post & Communications The main post office is on the corner of Hidalgo and de la Cruz, 500 meters east of Portal Madero. There are pay phones all around the portales, and a phone office at the north end of the underground car park, west of the

cathedral. It's open from 7.30 am to 8.45 pm daily for long-distance phone calls and faxes.

City Center

The 19th century **Portal Madero** (Madero Arcade), running 250 meters along Avenida Hidalgo, is lively and bustling, as is the arcade on the pedestrian street to the east. A block north, the big, open expanse of the **Plaza de los Mártires** may induce agoraphobia, but it's surrounded by fine old government buildings; the 19th century **Catedral** and the 18th-century **Templo Santa Veracruz** are on its south side.

Immediately northeast of the Plaza de los Mártires is the fountained **Plaza Garibay**, at the east end of which stands the unique **Cosmo Vitral Jardín Botánico** (Cosmic Glass Botanic Garden). Built in 1909 as a market, and until 1975 the site of the weekly *tianguis* (Indian market), this now houses 3500 sq meters of lovely botanical garden, lit since 1980 through 48 stained-glass panels by the Tolucan artist Leopoldo Flores. It's open Tuesday through Sunday from 9 am to 5 pm, for US$2. On the north side of Plaza Garibay is the 18th century **Templo del Carmen**.

Mercado Juárez & Casart

The Juárez Market, on Fabela behind the bus station, is open daily. On Friday villagers from all around swarm in to buy and sell fruit, flowers, pots, clothes and plastic goods. The market is huge, colorful and chaotic, but it's not a great place to buy local handicrafts. There are baskets, blankets and big earthenware bowls, but mostly they are everyday domestic requirements rather than the finely made decorative objects produced in the surrounding villages.

You can see quality local arts and crafts in more peaceful surroundings at Casart (Casa de Artesanía), the state crafts store on Paseo Tollocan. There's a big range and the quality is often better than you find in the villages where the crafts are made. Prices are fixed and higher than you can get with some haggling in the markets, but you can gauge prices and quality here first. It seems that much of the best work is now being sold to bigger retail outlets rather than in village workshops and markets.

Centro Cultural Mexiquense

The impressive State of México Cultural Center, eight km west of the city center, comprises three very good museums and a library. The **Museo de Culturas Populares** has superb examples of the traditional arts and crafts of México state, with some astounding trees of life, whimsical Day of the Dead figures and a fine display of charro equipment – saddles, sombreros, swords, pistols, ropes and spurs. The **Museo de Antropología e Historia** has fine displays from prehistoric times to the 20th century, with a good collection of pre-Hispanic artifacts. The **Museo de Arte Moderno** traces the development of Mexican art from the late 19th century Academia de San Carlos to the Nueva Plástica, and includes paintings by Tamayo, Orozco

and many others. The museums are open daily except Monday from 10 am to 6 pm (free). Buses marked 'Hípico' or 'Centro Cultural' go there every 20 minutes from the corner of Independencia and Juárez.

Other Museums

The ex-convent buildings adjacent to the Plaza Garibay house Toluca's **Museo de Bellas Artes**, with paintings from the colonial period to the early 20th century. On Bravo, opposite the Palacio de Gobierno, are museums devoted to the work of José María Velasco, Felipe Gutiérrez and Luis Nishizawa. The latter was an artist of Mexican-Japanese parentage whose work shows influences from both cultures. The state tourist office can provide details about the Museo de Estampa (stamps), Museo de Numismática (currency) and the Museo de Ciencias Naturales (natural sciences).

Places to Stay

The *Hotel San Carlos* (☎ 14-94-22) on Hidalgo at Portal Madero 210 and the *Hotel Rex* (☎ 15-93-00), a few meters away at Matamoros Sur 101, are both basic but acceptable, with private bath and TV. The San Carlos is the better deal, with good-sized, clean singles/doubles for US$6/8. The Rex costs US$9/11.

For true colonial ambiance, try the *Hotel Colonial* (☎ 15-97-00) at Hidalgo Oriente 103, just east of Juárez, with well-maintained, comfortable rooms around an interior courtyard for US$19/22. Guests can use a nearby car park.

The *Hotel Plaza Morelos* (☎ 15-92-00) at Serdán 115 is an OK place. An agreeable lobby leads to comfortable, if not huge, rooms with TV and phone for US$25/30. There's parking, a pleasant stairwell-lounge and a decent restaurant too.

Places to Eat

In the city center, one of the best and most atmospheric places is the *Hostería Las Ramblas* at Portal 20 de Noviembre 105 (the pedestrian mall). Antojitos, served only from 6 pm, are about US$2. Sandwiches are under US$3. Meat courses are

US$3 to US$4. An order of papaya is US$1.50. A pitcher of strong sangría (they top theirs off with vodka) is US$4.

The popular *Restaurant Impala* in the Portal Madero offers a good comida corrida for US$2.50. On the other side of the road, at Hidalgo Pte 229, the cheerful *Comedor Familial y Café L'Ambiant* also has a US$2.50 comida corrida. The à la carte menu has enchiladas, egg dishes and ensalada de verduras each for around US$2, and meats from US$3 to US$4. The upscale Franco-Mexican *Restaurant Concorde* on Serdán next door to the Hotel Plaza Morelos offers fish dishes for US$9 and a host of steaks from US$8.

There's the popular *Restaurante Woolworth* opposite the Hotel San Carlos that offers large set breakfasts for about US$3 and salads for US$4. The comida corrida goes for US$2.50. There's a terribly popular *VIPS* inside the Grand Plaza shopping mall, looking oh-so American and offering US and Mexican food at US prices: burgers US$4, antojitos US$2.50 to US$5, entrées from US$4.50, breakfasts from US$4 to US$6.

Getting There & Away

Toluca's bus station is at Berriozábal 101, two km southeast of the center. In Mexico City, Toluca buses use the Terminal Poniente. The all-round best service between the two cities is by the 1st-class TMT line, which runs buses every five minutes in both directions from 6 am to 10 pm; the trip takes 80 minutes. There are frequent departures from Toluca to Chalma, Cuernavaca, Guadalajara, Malinalco, Morelia, Pátzcuaro, Querétaro, Taxco and Uruapan.

Getting Around

Taxis from the bus station or market to the city center cost about US$2. The city bus system is difficult to decipher; ask at your hotel for the bus route to your destination. 'Centro' buses go from outside the bus station to the town center; 'Terminal' buses go from Juárez (just south of Lerdo de Tejada) in the center to the bus station.

AROUND TOLUCA
Calixtlahuaca

This Aztec site is two km west of highway 55, eight km north of Toluca. It's partly excavated and restored, with some unusual features such as a circular pyramid, which supported a temple to Quetzalcóatl, and the Calmecac, believed to have been a school for the children of priests and nobles. Entry is US$1.50 (free Sunday, closed Monday). A bus goes to within a short walk of the site.

Metepec
pop 177,969; alt 2610m; ☎ *72*

Virtually a suburb of Toluca, seven km to the south on highway 55, Metepec is the center for producing elaborate and symbolic pottery *árboles de vida* (trees of life) and 'Metepec suns' (earthenware discs brightly painted with sun and moon faces). Unfortunately it is not a center for selling these wonderful creations. The potters' workshops *(alfarerías)* are spread out all over town, and many seem to specialize in large pieces and Disney characters rather than traditional styles. There is only a limited selection of small, well-detailed pieces that a traveler might feasibly carry. The triangular building beside the bus stop has a map that may be of some help locating the workshops. Frequent 2nd-class buses go from Toluca bus station.

NEVADO DE TOLUCA

The extinct volcano Nevado de Toluca (or Xinantécatl), 4583 meters high, lies across the horizon south of Toluca. A road runs 48 km up to its crater, with the two lakes, El Sol and La Luna. The earlier you reach the summit, the better the chance of clear views; expect to see clouds after noon. The summit area is *nevado* (snowy) from November to March, and sometimes OK for cross-country skiing. Buses on highway 134, the Toluca-Tejupilco road, will stop at the turnoff, and on weekends it should be possible to hitch a lift for the 27 km up to the crater. Buses on highway 10 to Sultepec will get you eight km closer to the top.

There's an attendant, a boom gate and a café (lunch on weekends) six km by rough road from the crater, or 1.5 km by a very scenic walking track.

Places to Stay & Eat
You can stay at the *Posada Familiar* near the entry gate (US$4.50) or the *Albergue Ejidal* (US$3.50) one km farther up. Food is available at both, but only on Saturdays and Sundays, and you should bring a sleeping bag.

VALLE DE BRAVO
pop 47,520; alt 1800m; ☎ *726*
About 70 km west of Toluca, this was a quiet colonial-era village in the hills until the 1940s, when it became a base for construction of a dam and hydroelectric station. The new lake gave the town a waterside location and it was soon a popular weekend and holiday spot for the wealthy. Sailing on the lake is the main activity, while water-skiing, horse riding and hang-gliding are also popular. You can walk and camp in the hills around town, which attract monarch butterflies from December to March. A tourist office is located near the waterfront. A map of the town and useful information appear in the free local newspaper.

Places to Stay & Eat
Most of the town's budget hotels – such as the *Hotel Mary* and *Hotel Blanquita* – are dives but cost at least US$10, more on weekends.

The *Posada Casa Vieja* (☎ 2-03-38) at Juárez 101 is a lovely exception. Fifteen bright, cheerful and clean rooms that have good beds and plenty of hot water go for US$9 Sunday to Thursday, US$20 Friday and Saturday; this century-old ex-hacienda is a great find.

The *Hotel ISSEMYM* (☎ 2-00-04) at Independencia 404 is a holiday center for state workers, but it accepts other guests and is good value at US$28/32 for a single/double. It has parking, a big pool and other recreational facilities.

There are scores of restaurants, cafés and food stalls. For ambiance, have a drink and/or a light meal at the floating restaurant-bars *La Balsa Avadaro* and *Los Pericos*.

Getting There & Away
There are many direct and de paso buses to Toluca (US$3) and Mexico City's Terminal Poniente (US$4) from the Valle de Bravo terminal, the last one leaving at 7 pm. Likewise, there are many buses from Toluca; the direct buses make the journey in just under two hours. If you're driving between Toluca and Valle de Bravo, the southern route via highway 134 is quicker and more scenic.

TENANGO DEL VALLE & TEOTENANGO
Tenango, 25 km south of Toluca on highway 55, is overlooked from the west by the large, well-restored hilltop ruins of Teotenango, a Matlazinca ceremonial center dating from the 9th century. The archeological site, with several pyramids, plazas and a ball court, is quite extensive, and affords great views. It's open daily except Monday (US$2). The road to Teotenango climbs up the north side of the hill – from Toluca, pass the toll road and turn right into town. Turn right again to find the road. There is a museum where the road makes its final turn up to the hilltop. Buses run from Toluca bus station to Tenango every 10 minutes; you'll have a 20- to 30-minute walk up to the site.

TENANCINGO
pop 62,742; alt 2020m; ☎ *714*
This pleasant colonial town, 50 km from Toluca on highway 55, is famous for its brightly colored rebozos and fruit liqueurs. There's a market on Sunday. You can stay in the budget-priced *Hotel Jardín* on the plaza, and explore the attractions in the surrounding area, including the nearby **El Salto** waterfall, the ex-convent of **Santo Desierto del Carmen**, 12 km southeast in the national park of the same name, and the Malinalco ruins (see the entry below).

MALINALCO
pop 20,157; alt 1740m; ☎ *714*

One of the few reasonably well-preserved Aztec temples stands on a hillside above beautiful but little-visited Malinalco, 20 km east of Tenancingo. The site is one km uphill west of the town center by a good dirt road.

The Aztecs conquered this area in 1476 and were still building a ritual center here when they were themselves conquered by the Spanish. The Temple of Eagle and Jaguar Warriors, where sons of Aztec nobles were initiated into the Jaguar and Eagle orders of warriors, survived because it is hewn from the mountainside itself. It is recognizable by its reconstructed thatched roof. Its entrance is carved in the form of a fanged serpent or earth god – you walk over its tongue to enter the temple. The site is open daily except Monday from 10 am to 4.30 pm; admission is US$2. The 300-plus steps to the site, combined with the altitude, are too much for some people.

Places to Stay & Eat
Avenidas Guerrero and Hidalgo flank Malinalco's main square, and it is on these streets not far from the stairs leading to the ruins that you'll find three lovely but inexpensive restaurants and a cheap place to spend the night. Heading west away from the zócalo on Guerrero are the open-sided *La Playa* restaurant in a tropical setting, the *Restaurante Copil* in a semi-elegant brick-and-stone-walled room, and *Los Pericos* restaurant-bar with tables under palapas and ringed by tropical plants. A block to the north, on Hidalgo, the *Hotel Santa Monica* (☎ 7-00-31) has 13 very basic rooms with hot water but no fans for US$6 per person.

Getting There & Away
You can reach Malinalco by bus or colectivo from Tenancingo, by bus from the Toluca bus station or from Mexico City's Terminal Poniente. By car from Toluca you can turn off highway 55, 12 km south of Tenango, and they reach Malinalco via Joquicingo.

CHALMA
One of Mexico's most important shrines is in the village of Chalma, 12 km east of Malinalco. In 1533 an image of Christ, El Señor de Chalma, 'miraculously' appeared in a cave to replace one of the local gods, Oxtéotl, and proceeded to stamp out dangerous beasts locally and do other wondrous things. The Señor now resides in Chalma's 17th century church. The biggest of many annual pilgrimages here is for Pentecost (May 3) when thousands of people from Mexico City and elsewhere camp, hold a market and perform traditional dances.

Getting There & Away
Líneas Unidas del Sur has 2nd-class buses from Toluca (US$2). There are also four buses a day (morning and early afternoon) from Cuernavaca's Flecha Roja bus station, and a number of companies run 2nd-class buses from Mexico City's Terminal Poniente.

IXTAPAN DE LA SAL
pop 24,892; alt 1880m; ☎ *714*

The spa town of Ixtapan features a kind of giant curative water fun park, the **Ixtapan Vacation Center Aquatic Park**, combining thermal water pools with waterfalls, lakes, water slides, a wave pool and a miniature railway. It's unashamedly a tourist town, but it's worth a stop if you want to take the waters or give your kids a fun day. The spa is open from 10 am to 6 pm and costs US$6 for adults, U$3.50 for kids. The water slide section shuts down slightly earlier and costs US$1 extra on weekends and holidays.

Orientation
Highway 55 is called Boulevard San Román as it circles the west side of town. Avenida Juárez cuts across the arc from north to south, from balneario to bus station.

Places to Stay & Eat
Most of the city's hotels are located on or near Juárez, with a good range of lodging. *Hotel San Francisco* (☎ 3-22-50) on Juárez

near Aldama was only two months old at the time of writing and offered basic rooms with hot water and new everything for only US$6 per person, but the hotel's video bar is loud and remains open late. A much quieter option is the *Casa de Huéspedes María Alejandra* (☎ 3-04-23) at Juárez 55, which has perfectly acceptable rooms with firm beds and hot water for US$9/17.

The next three Juárez places all have pools and similar rooms – standard size, comfortable, with TV, good beds, hot water, no phone: *Hotel Casa Blanca* (☎ 3-00-36) is the most charming of the lot and charges US$25/28; the sprawling *Hotel Avenida* (☎ 3-10-39) asks US$28 for rooms; the *Hotel Belisana* (☎ 3-00-13) is more pleasant than the Avenida and asks US$21 per person.

The one resort in town, the *Hotel Ixtapan* (☎ 3-00-21) at the north end of Juárez, has rooms with all the modern conveniences for US$95/120 including meals (tennis and golf fees are extra).

A so-so lunch with lousy service at the Hotel Ixtapan runs US$15. Restaurants at the north end of Juárez offer set meals for US$4, and the food gets cheaper as you go south. The *Restaurant Los Soles*, just south of Aldama, is the best of the mid-range places, and it uses purified water for its ice; tasty antojitos cost US$3, soups US$2.50, a club sandwich with fries is US$3.50.

Getting There & Away

From the Tres Estrellas de Oro bus station on the south end of Juárez there are regular buses to Toluca, Taxco, Cuernavaca, Mexico City (Terminal Poniente) and Tenancingo (all for US$3 to US$4). Going north, a toll highway, 55D, parallels part of highway 55, bypassing Tenango and Tenancingo. Going south to Taxco, you could pass on the Grutas de la Estrella, but the Grutas de Cacahuamilpa are a must (see Around Taxco, in the South of Mexico City section).

EL DIABLITO

EL CORAZON

LA MANO

LA PERA

EL VIOLONCELLO

EL MUNDO

Baja California

Baja California's native peoples left memorable murals in caves and on canyon walls, but permanent European settlement failed to reach the world's longest peninsula until the Jesuit missions of the 17th and 18th centuries, which collapsed as Indians fell prey to European diseases.

Mainland ranchers, miners and fishermen settled when foreigners built port facilities and acquired huge land grants in the 19th century. During US Prohibition, Baja became a popular south-of-the-border destination for gamblers, drinkers and other 'sinners.' It still attracts more than 50 million visitors annually for duty-free shopping, sumptuous seafood and activities such as horseback riding, diving, snorkeling, windsurfing, clamming, fishing, sailing, kayaking, cycling, surfing, hiking and whale-watching.

La Frontera & the Desierto del Colorado

La Frontera, the northernmost part of the state of Baja California, corresponds roughly to the colonial Dominican mission

---

HIGHLIGHTS

- Tijuana – world's most-visited border town; historically, notorious for lowlife partying but now an impressive locus of commerce, education and cultural activities

- Reserva de la Biosfera El Vizcaíno – biosphere reserve; includes major gray whale breeding sites at Laguna Ojo de Liebre and Laguna San Ignacio and pre-Hispanic rock art in the dissected volcanic plateau of the Sierra de San Francisco; a UNESCO World Heritage Site

- Loreto – first capital of the Californias; notable for two restored missions, its own and that of nearby San Francisco Javier; also known for recreational opportunities such as kayaking on the Gulf of California and mountain biking in the Sierra de la Giganta

- Los Cabos – an uneasy mixture of gaudily inappropriate overdevelopment (Cabo San Lucas and vicinity), suitably unpretentious tropical retreats (San José del Cabo and the East Cape), artists' colonies (Todos Santos) and biological wonders (Sierra de la Laguna, probably the best hiking and backpacking area on the peninsula)

Central Tijuana pp 284-285
Mexicali pp 296-297
Ensenada pp 290-291
Central Mexicali p 299
USA
Baja California
Sonora
Baja California Sur
Loreto p 308
La Paz pp 312-313
Central La Paz p 315
San José del Cabo pp 320-321
Central Cabo San Lucas p 324

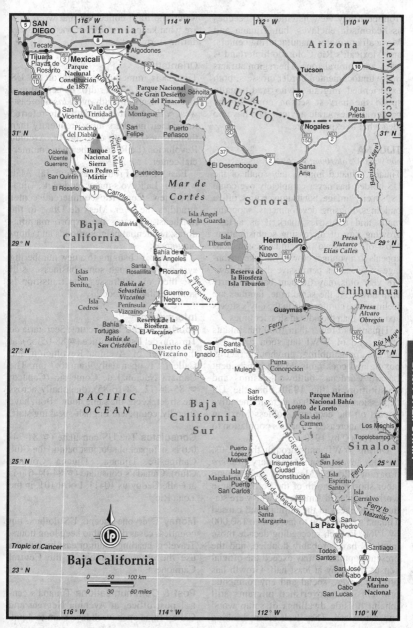

Baja California

frontier. Many view its cities and beaches as hedonistic enclaves, but Tijuana and Mexicali are major manufacturing centers, and Mexicali's Río Colorado hinterland is a key agricultural zone. The region attracts many undocumented border crossers, both experienced migrants who traditionally spend the harvest season north of the border and desperate novices who have no idea what to expect there.

TIJUANA
pop 966,097; alt 100m; ☎ *66*

Tijuana, situated immediately south of the US border, has never completely overcome its 'sin city' image, but its universities, office buildings, housing developments, shopping malls and industries mark it as a fast-growing city of increasing sophistication. Most of 'La Revo' (Avenida Revolución) appeals to a younger crowd who take advantage of Mexico's permissive drinking laws (18 year olds may frequent bars) to party until dawn. At the same time, families are feeling more comfortable in the city's streets and shops than they did in sleazier times.

Tijuana had fewer than 1000 inhabitants at the end of WWI but soon drew US tourists for gambling, greyhound racing, boxing and cockfights. Mexican president Lázaro Cárdenas outlawed casinos and prostitution in the 1930s, but the US depression probably had a greater negative impact on the economy. Jobless Mexican returnees increased Tijuana's population to about 16,500 by 1940.

During WWII and through the 1950s, the US government's temporary *bracero* program allowed Mexicans to alleviate labor shortages north of the border. These workers replaced Americans who were stationed overseas in the military and caused Tijuana's population to increase to 180,000 by 1960. In each succeeding decade those numbers have probably doubled, and the present population may exceed the official census figure by at least half. Growth has brought severe social and environmental problems – impoverished migrants still inhabit hillside dwellings of scrap wood and cardboard. They lack clean drinking water and trash collection, and worn tires are what keep the soil from washing away during storms.

Orientation

Tijuana is immediately south of the US border post of San Ysidro. Its central grid consists of north-south *avenidas* and east-west *calles* (most of the latter are referred to by their numbers more frequently than their names). South of Calle 1a, Avenida Revolución (La Revo) is the main commercial center.

East of the Frontón Palacio Jai Alai, which is La Revo's major landmark, Tijuana's 'new' Zona Río commercial center straddles the river. Mesa de Otay, to the northeast, contains the airport, maquiladoras, residential neighborhoods and shopping areas.

The city is changing to a new numbering system, and though some businesses still use their old addresses, the transition is going relatively smoothly.

Information

Tourist Offices The Secture (Secretaría de Turismo del Estado) office (☎ 88-05-55), at the corner of Avenida Revolución and Calle 1a, is open daily 9 am to 7 pm. The Cámara Nacional de Comercio (Canaco; ☎ 85-84-72, 88-16-85), diagonally across the street, keeps the same hours. Both have friendly, competent English-speaking staff.

Consulates The US consulate (☎ 81-74-00) is at Tapachula 96, just behind the Club Campestre Tijuana (Tijuana Country Club). Canada's consulate (☎ 84-04-61) is at Calle Gedovius 10411, Local 101, in the Zona Río.

Money Everyone accepts US dollars, but countless casas de cambio keep long hours. Travelers heading south or east by bus can use the casa de cambio at the Central Camionera.

Post & Communications Tijuana's central post office, at Avenida Negrete and Calle 11a, is open weekdays 8 am to 4 pm.

Public telephones and long-distance offices are common, including several *cabinas (casetas)* and a public fax at the Central Camionera.

Travel Agencies Travel agencies are numerous, but Viajes Honold's (☎ 88-11-11), on Revolución near Calle 2a, is one of the longest established.

Bookstores The book department in Sanborn's, at the corner of Revolución and Calle 8a, has a large selection of US and Mexican newspapers and magazines. Librería El Día (☎ 84-09-08), Boulevard Sánchez Taboada 10050 in the Zona Río, specializes in Mexican history and culture, with a small selection in English.

Medical Services The Red Cross (☎ 132) has moved to Vía Oriente in the Zona Río. Tijuana's Hospital General (☎ 84-09-22) is north of the river on Avenida Padre Kino, northwest of the junction with Avenida Rodríguez, but Tijuana has many other medical facilities catering to visitors from north of the border.

Dangers & Annoyances Coyotes and *polleros* – smugglers of humans – and their clients congregate along the river west of the San Ysidro crossing. After dark, avoid this area and Colonia Libertad, east of the crossing.

La Revo
South of Calle 1a, Avenida Revolución is Tijuana's tourist heart. Every visitor braves at least a brief stroll up this raucous avenue of futuristic discos, fine restaurants, seedy bars with bellowing hawkers, brash taxi drivers, tacky souvenir shops and street photographers with zebra-striped burros.

Frontón Palacio Jai Alai
Fast-moving jai alai matches at the Frontón (☎ 85-25-24), on Revolución between Calles 7a and 8a, resemble a hybrid of tennis and handball. Frontón staff explain details to neophyte bettors,

and the bilingual narration is also helpful. General admission costs US$2; it's open most evenings and some afternoons, but closed Wednesdays.

Vinícola LA Cetto
The LA Cetto winery (☎ 85-30-31) offers tours and tasting from 10 am to 5.30 pm Tuesday to Sunday, for a modest charge. It's at Cañón Johnson 8151, southwest of Avenida Constitución.

Centro Cultural Tijuana (Cecut)
Mexico's federal government built this modern landmark, a cultural center at Paseo de los Héroes and Avenida Independencia in the Zona Río, to reinforce the Mexican identity of its border populations. It is a facility of which any comparably sized city north of the border would be proud. Cecut houses the **Museo de las Identidades Mexicanas** (Museum of Mexican Identities), an art gallery, a theater and the globular **Cine Planetario** (colloquially known as La Bola – 'The Ball').

Museum admission costs US$1; most programs at the Cine Planetario cost about US$4.50; prices for theater programs vary; admission to the art gallery is free. Cecut (☎ 84-11-11) is open weekdays 11 am to 8 pm, weekends 11 am to 9 pm.

Places to Stay – budget
Hotel del Prado (☎ 88-23-29), at Calle 5a No 8163, between Revolución and Constitución, is clean and comfortable for US$10 single or double. Perhaps downtown's best budget hotel is *Hotel Lafayette* (☎ 85-39-40), at Avenida Revolución 926, above Café La Especial, but it's often full, especially on weekends. Rates are US$16/22 singles/doubles.

Centrally located *Hotel Arreola* (☎ 85-26-18), at Revolución 1080, has carpeted rooms with TV and telephone for US$20/26. *Motel Plaza Hermosa* (☎ 85-33-53), Avenida Constitución 1821, is a good value at US$20/26 weekdays, US$25/30 weekends, with secure parking.

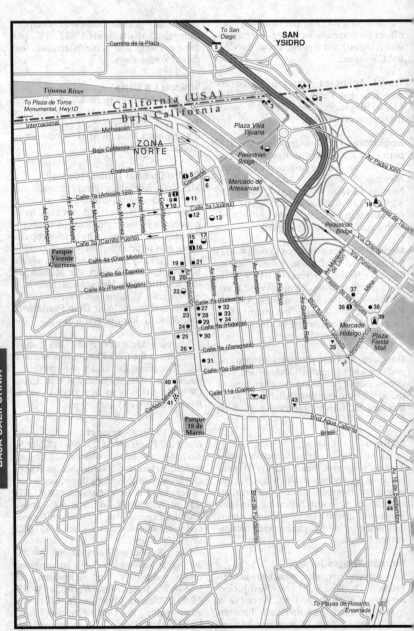

BAJA CALIFORNIA

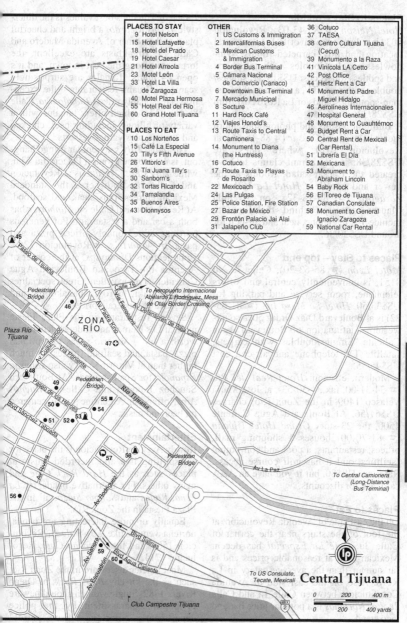

PLACES TO STAY
9   Hotel Nelson
15 Hotel Lafayette
18 Hotel del Prado
19 Hotel Caesar
21 Hotel Arreola
23 Motel León
33 Hotel La Villa
    de Zaragoza
40 Motel Plaza Hermosa
55 Hotel Real del Río
60 Grand Hotel Tijuana

PLACES TO EAT
10 Los Norteños
15 Café La Especial
20 Tilly's Fifth Avenue
26 Vittorio's
28 Tía Juana Tilly's
30 Sanborn's
32 Tortas Ricardo
34 Tamalandia
35 Buenos Aires
43 Dionnysos

OTHER
1   US Customs & Immigration
2   Intercalifornias Buses
3   Mexican Customs
    & Immigration
4   Border Bus Terminal
5   Cámara Nacional
    de Comercio (Canaco)
6   Downtown Bus Terminal
7   Mercado Municipal
8   Secture
11 Hard Rock Café
12 Viajes Honold's
13 Route Taxis to Central
    Camionera
14 Monument to Diana
    (the Huntress)
16 Cotuco
17 Route Taxis to Playas
    de Rosarito
22 Mexicoach
24 Las Pulgas
25 Police Station, Fire Station
27 Bazar de México
29 Frontón Palacio Jai Alai
31 Jalapeño Club

36 Cotuco
37 TAESA
38 Centro Cultural Tijuana
    (Cecut)
39 Monumento a la Raza
41 Vinícola LA Cetto
42 Post Office
44 Hertz Rent a Car
45 Monument to Padre
    Miguel Hidalgo
46 Aerolíneas Internacionales
47 Hospital General
48 Monument to Cuauhtémoc
49 Budget Rent a Car
50 Central Rent de Mexicali
    (Car Rental)
51 Librería El Día
52 Mexicana
53 Monument to
    Abraham Lincoln
54 Baby Rock
56 El Toreo de Tijuana
57 Canadian Consulate
58 Monument to General
    Ignacio Zaragoza
59 National Car Rental

To Aeropuerto Internacional
Abelardo L Rodríguez, Mesa
de Otay Border Crossing

Calle 16

Av Padre Kino

Vía Ferrocarril

Av Defensores de Baja California

Paseo de Tijuana

Pedestrian
Bridge

ZONA
RÍO

Plaza Río
Tijuana

Vía Oriente

Vía Poniente

Av Cuauhtémoc

Río Tijuana

Paseo de los Héroes

Blvd Sánchez Taboada

Pedestrian
Bridge

Av Rueda

Pedestrian
Bridge

Av La Paz

To Central Camionera
(Long-Distance
Bus Terminal)

Av Rodríguez

Blvd Salinas

Av Sonora

Blvd Agua Caliente

Av Escuadrón

To US Consulate,
Tecate, Mexicali   **Central Tijuana**

Club Campestre Tijuana

0   200   400 m
0   200   400 yards

BAJA CALIFORNIA

Places to Stay – middle

Hotel Nelson (☎ 85-43-03), Revolución 503, is a long-time favorite for its central location and tidy, carpeted rooms. Windowless singles/doubles with telephone and spotless toilets cost US$19/22; singles/doubles with color TV, a view and the less-than-soothing sounds of La Revo cost from US$28/32.

Bullfight posters and photographs adorn the walls of *Hotel Caesar* (☎ 88-16-66), at Revolución 1079, where rates are US$28/38; its restaurant claims to have created the Caesar salad. Rooms at the newer and excellent *Hotel La Villa de Zaragoza* (☎ 85-18-32), on Avenida Madero directly behind the Frontón, include TV, telephone, heat and air-con for around US$30/36.

Places to Stay – top end

Motel León (☎ 85-63-20), Calle 7a No 8151, is conveniently central and offers telephone, room service and parking for US$33/50. *Hotel La Mesa Inn* (☎ 81-65-22) is at Boulevard Díaz Ordaz 50, a southwestern continuation of Boulevard Agua Caliente. Singles/doubles with carpets, satellite TV, telephone and air-con cost US$45/55.

Modern, efficient *Hotel Real del Río* (☎ 34-31-00, fax 34-30-53), at José María Velasco 1409 in the Zona Río, charges US$51/56. At Boulevard Agua Caliente 4500, the 23-story *Grand Hotel Tijuana* (☎ 81-70-00) houses a shopping mall, offices, restaurants, a pool and convention facilities, and it has golf course access. Rates are US$80, but if you have an AAA card, ask for discounts.

Places to Eat

On the east side of Avenida Revolución, at the foot of the stairs near the corner of Calle 3a, *Café La Especial* has decent Mexican food at reasonable prices and is far quieter than the average eatery in La Revo. Also on the east side of Avenida Constitución, between Calle 1a and Calle 2a, *Los Norteños* is a popular juice bar and taco stand.

One of Tijuana's best values is the diner-style *Tortas Ricardo*, a bright and cheerful place at the corner of Avenida Madero and Calle 7a. Breakfasts are excellent, the tortas are among the best in town, and it's open 24 hours. Tamales are surprisingly scarce in Tijuana restaurants – the exception is reasonably priced *Tamalandia*, Calle 8a No 8374, which offers tamales with a variety of fillings, including beef, chicken and shrimp, plus varied desserts.

Tía Juana Tilly's, a popular gringo hangout, is next to the Frontón Palacio Jai Alai, while *Tilly's Fifth Avenue* is at Revolución and Calle 5a. Both serve the standard Mexican entrees, plus steak and seafood. At Revolución and Calle 8a, *Sanborn's* has both a bar and a restaurant. For generous portions of reasonably priced pizza and pasta, try *Vittorio's*, at Revolución 1269. Unpretentious *Dionnysos*, at the corner of Avenida Pío Pico and Boulevard Agua Caliente, serves excellent Greek specialties like souvlaki, gyros, spanakopita and moussaka at moderate prices.

Several restaurants in the Plaza Fiesta mall, at Los Héroes and Independencia, are worth a try – *Saverio's* has exceptional pizza, pasta, and seafood (prices are much higher than at Vittorio's). Try also *Taberna Española* for Spanish tapas. At Boulevard Sánchez Taboada and Calle 9a, *Buenos Aires* offers an Argentine menu centered on beef and pasta.

Entertainment

Rowdy Avenida Revolución is the place for ear-splitting live and recorded music at places such as the *Hard Rock Café* and many others. For alternative bands, try *La Peña*, *Ranas* and *Sótano Suizo*, all in the Plaza Fiesta in the Zona Río.

Equally or more interesting are banda/norteña venues like *Las Pulgas*, Revolución 1501, and the *Jalapeño Club*, Revolución 1714.

Most fancier discos are in the Zona Río, such as the kitschy *Baby Rock*, at Diego Rivera 1482. Single women should beware of possible harassment by the police department's notorious 'disco patrol,' which reportedly lurks nearby at closing time; for the unsavory details, see Luis Alberto Urrea's *Across the Wire*.

Spectator Sports
From May to September, Sunday bullfights take place at two bullrings: El Toreo de Tijuana, on Boulevard Agua Caliente northwest of Club Campestre Tijuana, and the oceanfront Plaza de Toros Monumental. Call ☎ 85-22-10 or ☎ 85-15-72 for reservations at either bullring (☎ 619-232-5049 in San Diego). Tickets cost from US$19 to US$45.

Things to Buy
Jewelry, wrought-iron furniture, baskets, silver, blown glass, pottery and leather goods are available in stores on Avenidas Revolución and Constitución; at the municipal market on Niños Héroes between Calles 1a and 2a; at the sprawling Mercado de Artesanías, at Comercio (Calle 1a) and Ocampo; and at the new Bazar de México (which has a particularly good selection of handcrafted furniture), at the corner of Revolución and Calle 7a. Auto body and upholstery shops along Ocampo offer real bargains.

Getting There & Away
Air Aeroméxico (☎ 85-22-30, 82-41-69 at the airport) and its commuter subsidiary Aerolitoral have moved to Local A 12-1 in the Plaza Río Tijuana, at Paseo de los Héroes and Avenida Independencia. Besides serving many mainland Mexican destinations, they have daily nonstops to La Paz as well as flights to Tucson and Phoenix, both via Hermosillo.

Aero California (☎ 84-21-00), also in the Plaza Río Tijuana, flies daily to La Paz and serves many mainland destinations from Mexico City northward. Mexicana (☎ 34-65-66, 82-41-83 at the airport), Avenida Diego Rivera 1511, in the Zona Río, flies daily to Los Angeles (but not *from* Los Angeles) and also serves many mainland Mexican cities.

TAESA (☎ /fax 34-15-03, 83-55-93 at the airport), Paseo de los Héroes 9288, flies to mainland Mexican destinations, with Sunday connections to Chicago via Mexico City. Aerolíneas Internacionales (☎ 83-61-31), a recent start-up, Avenida Cuauhtémoc 1209, Local 105, in the Zona Río, flies to mainland destinations from Hermosillo to Mexico City.

Bus Only ABC (local buses; ☎ 86-90-10) and the US-based Greyhound use the handy downtown terminal, at Avenida Madero and Comercio (Calle 1a). From the Plaza Viva Tijuana, near the border, ABC and Autotransportes Aragón go to Ensenada.

Both ABC and Greyhound also use the Central Camionera (☎ 26-17-01), about five km southeast of downtown. From Calle 2a, east of Constitución, take any 'Buena Vista,' 'Centro' or 'Central Camionera' bus, or a quicker and more convenient gold-and-white 'Mesa de Otay' route taxi from Avenida Madero between Calles 2a and 3a (both US$0.50).

The USA Between 5.30 and 12.30 am, Greyhound (☎ 619-239-3266, in USA 800-231-2222), 120 West Broadway in San Diego, stops at San Ysidro (☎ 619-428-1194), 799 East San Ysidro Boulevard, en route to Tijuana's downtown terminal (US$5) and the Central Camionera (US$7). Intercalifornias, on the east side of the road just south of the San Ysidro border crossing, goes to Los Angeles (US$18) and US California's Central Valley.

Mexicoach runs frequent buses (US$1) from its San Ysidro terminal (☎ 619-428-9517), 4570 Camino de la Plaza, to its new Tijuana terminal (☎ 85-14-70) on Avenida Revolución between Calle 6a and Calle 7a.

Elsewhere in Mexico Elite and Crucero offer 1st-class buses with air-con and toilets to mainland Mexico. Autotransportes del Pacífico, Norte de Sonora and ABC operate mostly 2nd-class buses to mainland Mexico's Pacific Coast and around Baja California. ABC's Servicio Plus resembles Elite and Crucero.

Frequent services leave downtown for Ensenada (1½ hours, US$5.50), Rosarito (US$1 for route taxis from Madero between Calles 3a and 4a) and Tecate (US$1.25).

From the Central Camionera (☎ 21-29-82), there are services to Ensenada (US$5.50), Tecate (US$1.25), Mexicali (four hours, US$7), San Felipe (six hours, US$15), La Paz (24 hours, US$48), Guerrero Negro (12 hours, US$23) and Loreto (18 hours, US$35). Elite and Crucero express buses to Guadalajara/Mexico City (US$74/85) take 35 and 42 hours, respectively. Autotransportes del Pacífico and Norte de Sonora are cheaper but also less comfortable. All lines stop at major mainland destinations.

From Plaza Viva Tijuana near the border, ABC (☎ 83-56-81) and Autotransportes Aragón offer inexpensive Ensenada buses. Aragón leaves hourly between 8 am and 9 pm for US$5/7.50 one way/roundtrip.

Trolley San Diego's popular light-rail trolley (☎ 619-233-3004) runs from downtown San Diego to San Ysidro every 15 minutes from about 5 am to midnight (US$1.75). From San Diego's Lindbergh Field airport, city bus No 2 goes directly to the Plaza America trolley stop, across from the Amtrak depot.

Car & Motorcycle The San Ysidro border crossing, a 10-minute walk from downtown Tijuana, is open 24 hours, but motorists may find the Otay Mesa crossing (open 6 am to 10 pm) much less congested. For rentals, agencies in San Diego are cheaper, but try Central Rent de Mexicali (☎ 84-22-57), Paseo de los Héroes 10001, Zona Río.

Getting Around
To/From the Airport Sharing can reduce the cost of a taxi (about US$10 if hailed on the street) to busy Aeropuerto Internacional Abelardo L Rodríguez (☎ 83-20-21) on Mesa de Otay, east of downtown. Alternatively, take any 'Aeropuerto' bus from the street just past the San Ysidro border taxi stand (about US$0.30); from down-

town, catch it on Calle 5a between Constitución and Niños Héroes.

Bus & Taxi For about US$0.30, local buses go everywhere, but slightly higher route taxis are much quicker. From Avenida Madero between Calles 2a and 3a, gold-and-white 'Mesa de Otay' route taxis go frequently to the Central Camionera (US$0.50). Tijuana taxis lack meters, but most rides cost about US$5 or less. However, beware of the occasional unscrupulous taxi driver.

AROUND TIJUANA
Playas de Rosarito
pop 37,121
South of Tijuana, the valley of Rosarito marks the original boundary between mainland California and Baja California. Recently declared a separate municipality, the town of Playas de Rosarito (21 km from Tijuana) dates from 1885, but the Hotel Rosarito (now the landmark Rosarito Beach Hotel) and its long, sandy beach pioneered local tourism in the late 1920s. The town's main street – the noisy commercial strip of Boulevard Juárez (a segment of the Transpeninsular, highway 1) – has many good restaurants and moderately priced accommodations.

The amphitheater at the beachfront **Parque Municipal Abelardo L Rodríguez** contains Juan Zuñiga Padilla's impressive 1987 mural *Tierra y Libertad* (Land and Liberty).

Route taxis for Playas de Rosarito leave from Madero between Calles 3a and 4a in downtown Tijuana (US$1).

Tecate
pop 47,005; alt 500m
About 55 km east of Tijuana by highway 2, the east-west route linking Tijuana and Mexicali, Tecate resembles a mainland Mexican village more than a border town but hosts several popular tourist events, such as bicycle races. Its landmark brewery, open for tours by reservation only, produces two of Mexico's best-known beers, Tecate and Carta Blanca, but maquiladoras drive

BAJA CALIFORNIA
Top: Land's End, Cabo San Lucas
Middle Left: Cueva de las Flechas,
Sierra de San Francisco
Middle Right: *Tierra y Libertad*, mural by Juan
Zuñiga Padilla, Playas de Rosarito
Bottom Left: Setting sail in Cabo San Lucas
Bottom Right: Swimming hole

WAYNE BERNHARDSON

RODNEY ADAMO

WAYNE BERNHARDSON

WAYNE BERNHARDSON

RICK GERHARTER

BAJA CALIFORNIA

Top Left: Volcanic plug
Middle Left: Rancher
Bottom Left: Only the brave sit out of shade in the Desierto Central

Top Right: Desert road, Bahía Concepción
Bottom Right: The grand mountainscape of the Sierra de San Francisco

the local economy. The border crossing, open 6 am to midnight daily, is less congested than either Tijuana or Mesa de Otay.

ENSENADA
pop 192,550; ☎ *61*

Aging Americans stroll the streets with shopping lists of pharmaceuticals (which are generally much cheaper in Ensenada than in the US), but this major fishing and commercial port 110 km south of Tijuana is also Baja California state's biggest party town. Outdoor activities such as fishing and surfing are popular, and Ensenada is the locus of Baja's wine industry. US visitors sometimes make the city a reluctant host for spontaneous Fourth of July celebrations, when guests from the north should scrupulously avoid offensive behavior.

In colonial times, Ensenada de Todos los Santos occasionally sheltered Acapulco-bound galleons returning from Manila, but the first permanent settlement was established in 1804. The discovery of gold in 1870 at Real del Castillo, 35 km inland, brought a short-lived boom. Ensenada was capital of Baja territory from 1882 to 1915, but the capital shifted to Mexicali during the revolution. After the revolution the city catered to 'sin' industries until the federal government outlawed gambling in the 1930s.

Orientation
Hotels and restaurants line the waterfront Boulevard Costero, also known as Boulevard Cárdenas. Avenida López Mateos (Calle 1a) parallels Boulevard Costero for a short distance one block inland (north), beyond which is the party district – Avenidas Gastelum and Ruiz.

North of town, highway 3 heads northeast to Tecate; at the eastern edge of town it leads east toward Ojos Negros and Parque Nacional Constitución de 1857 before continuing south to the Valle de Trinidad and San Felipe.

Information
Immigration Open daily 8 am to 8 pm, the Delegación de Servicios Migratorios

(☎ 74-10-64) has moved to Azueta 101, across the street from its old location.

Tourist Offices Ensenada's Comité de Turismo y Convenciones (Cotuco; ☎ 78-24-11), at Boulevard Costero and Gastelum (Azueta), carries maps, brochures and current hotel information. Hours are Monday to Saturday 9 am to 7 pm, Sunday 9 am to 2 pm.

Secture (☎ 72-30-22), at Boulevard Costero 1477, near Las Rocas, is open weekdays 9 am to 7 pm, weekends 9 am to 3 pm.

Money Most banks and casas de cambio are on Avenidas Ruiz and Juárez. Only banks provide cash advances, but there are numerous ATMs throughout Ensenada. Servicio La Comercial, on Uribe just north of Gastelum (Azueta), charges 1.5% for cashing traveler's checks.

Post & Communications The main post office, at López Mateos and Riviera, is open weekdays 8 am to 7 pm, weekends 9 am to 1 pm. Pay phones are widespread, and the bus terminal's Computel Ensenada office allows calls to be paid for by credit card.

Wineries
Bodegas de Santo Tomás (☎ 78-33-33), Miramar 666, holds tours and tastings daily at 11 am and 1 and 3 pm (US$2). Cavas Valmar (☎ 78-64-05), at the north end of Avenida Miramar, offers free tours and tastings by appointment.

Riviera del Pacífico
Opened in the early 1930s as Hotel Playa Ensenada, this extravagant, Spanish-style, former casino on Boulevard Costero features an impressive three-dimensional mural of the Californias, emphasizing mission sites. Now a cultural center (Centro Social, Cívico y Cultural de Ensenada), it offers retrospective film cycles, art exhibitions, a renovated museum and the atmospheric Bar Andaluz.

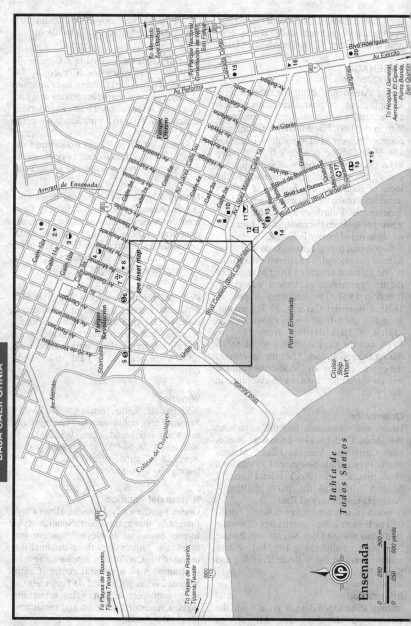

To Mercado
Los Globos

To Parque Nacional
Constitución de 1857,
San Felipe

Calzada Cortez 3

15

16

Av Reforma

Blvd Rodríguez
20
Av Ejército

To Hospital General,
Aeropuerto El Ciprés,
Punta Banda,
San Quintín

Parque
Obrero

Av Gastélum
Av Granada
Av Riveroll
Av Floresta
Av Macheros
Av Alvarado

Av Ciprés

Av Guadalupe
Av Juárez / Calle 5a
Av Iturbide
Av Obregón
Av Moctezuma
Av Ryerson
Av Castillo
Av Blancarte
Av Miranda
Av Floresta
Av Gastélum
Av Ruiz

Calle 1a
Calle 2a
Calle 3a
Calle 4a
Calle 6a

Calle 8a

Av Ramón
Av López Mateos (Calle 1a)

Del Mar
Blvd de Bucaneros
Las Rocas
Las Dunas Ondinas
Medusas Cabañas

17
18
19

Arroyo de Ensenada

Blvd Las Dunas
Blvd Costero (Blvd Cárdenas)

9
10
11
12
13
14

1

2
3

4

8

5
6

7

sea inset map

Blvd Costero (Blvd Cárdenas)

Port of Ensenada

Parque
Revolución

Staircase
Uribe
Blvd Azueta

Av 20 de Noviembre
Av Aleman

To Playas de Rosarito,
Tijuana, Tecate

Colinas de Chapultepec

To Playas de Rosarito,
Tijuana, Tecate

Cruise
Ship
Wharf

Bahía de
Todos Santos

To Playas de Rosarito,
Tijuana, Tecate

1D

Ensenada

0   250   500 m
0   250   500 yards

LP

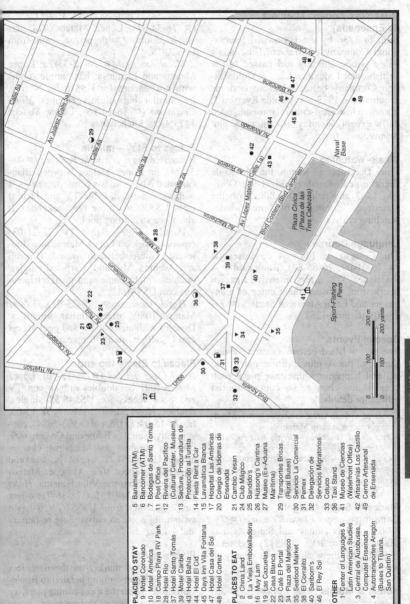

BAJA CALIFORNIA

PLACES TO STAY

9 Motel Coronado
10 Motel América
18 Campo Playa RV Park
28 Hotel Río
37 Hotel Santo Tomás
39 Motel Caribe
43 Hotel Bahía
44 Hotel El Cid
45 Days Inn Villa Fontana
47 Hotel Casa del Sol
48 Hotel Cortez

PLACES TO EAT

2 China Land
8 La Vieja Embotelladora
16 Muy Lam
19 Las Cazuelas
22 Casa Blanca
23 Café El Portal
34 Plaza del Marisco
35 Seafood Market
38 El Corralito
40 Sanborn's
46 El Rey Sol

OTHER

1 Center of Languages &
  Latin American Studies
3 Central de Autobuses,
  Computel Ensenada
4 Autotransportes Aragón
  (Buses to Tijuana,
  San Quintín)
5 Banamex (ATM)
6 Bancomer (ATM)
7 Bodegas de Santo Tomás
11 Post Office
12 Riviera del Pacífico
   (Cultural Center, Museum)
13 Secture, Procuraduría de
   Protección al Turista
14 Fiesta Rent a Car
15 Lavamática Blanca
17 Hospital Las Américas
20 Colegio de Idiomas de
   Ensenada
21 Cambio Yesan
25 Club Mágico
26 Bandido's
27 Hussong's Cantina
27 Museo (Ex-Aduana
   Marítima)
29 Transportes Brisas
   (Rural Buses)
30 Servicio La Comercial
31 Pemex
32 Delegación de
   Servicios Migratorios
33 Cotuco
36 Taxi Stand
41 Museo de Ciencias
   (Waterfront Office)
42 Artesanías Los Castillo
49 Centro Artesanal
   de Ensenada

Museo (ex-Aduana Marítima de Ensenada)
Built in 1886 by the US-owned International Company of Mexico, Ensenada's oldest public building had passed to the British-owned Mexican Land & Colonization Company before Mexican customs acquired it in 1922. At Avenida Ryerson 1, it's now a historical-cultural museum, open daily except Monday 10 am to 5 pm. Admission is free.

Whale-Watching
From December to March, the Museo de Ciencias de Ensenada (☎ 78-71-92), Obregón 1463 and behind Sanborn's on the waterfront, arranges offshore whale-watching cruises.

Language Courses
The Colegio de Idiomas de Ensenada (☎ 76-01-09, 76-65-87), Boulevard J A Rodríguez 377, offers intensive Spanish instruction, as does the Center of Languages and Latin American Studies (☎ 77-18-40), Riveroll 1287.

Special Events
The events listed below constitute a tiny sample of the 70-plus sporting, tourist and cultural happenings that take place each year. Dates change, so contact tourist offices for details.

Carnaval – Mardi Gras; sometime between mid-February and early March
Fiesta de la Vendimia – Wine harvest; mid-August
Fiestas Patrias – Mexican independence days; mid-September
Desfile Navideño Club Amigos de Ensenada – Christmas parade; mid-December

Places to Stay – budget
Camping *Campo Playa RV Park* (☎ 78-37-68), at Las Dunas and Sanginés, has shady sites for RVs (US$12) and tents (US$10), but there's loud music nearby on weekends.

Hotels & Motels *Hotel Río* (☎ 78-37-33) is one of several dubious cheapies on Avenida Miramar northeast of López Mateos;

rooms cost as little as US$7. *Motel Caribe* (☎ 78-34-81), López Mateos 628, has singles/doubles with private bath from US$10/15.

Motel América (☎ 76-13-33), at López Mateos and Espinosa, has simple rooms with kitchenettes for US$18/20. Nearby, the similar but slightly cheaper *Motel Coronado* (☎ 76-14-16), López Mateos 1275, lacks kitchenettes.

Places to Stay – middle
Renovated *Days Inn Villa Fontana* (☎ 78-34-34), on López Mateos between Blancarte and Alvarado, has comfortable rooms with view, air-con, cable TV and Jacuzzi from US$30/36 (more on weekends). It also has a swimming pool.

Popular *Hotel Bahía* (☎ 78-21-03) covers a block on López Mateos and Boulevard Costero, between Avenida Riveroll and Avenida Alvarado. Carpeted singles/doubles with balconies and small refrigerators cost US$31/42.

Hotel Cortez (☎ 78-23-07), López Mateos 1089, offers similar amenities. Doubles with air-con, TV and pool access cost US$40; it often fills up early.

Places to Stay – top end
Hotel Casa del Sol (☎ 78-15-70), López Mateos 1001, has doubles with air-con, TV and pool access for US$48/58 singles/doubles. *Hotel Santo Tomás* (☎ 78-15-03, fax 78-15-04; in USA 800-303-2684), conveniently central at Boulevard Costero 609, between Miramar and Macheros, charges around US$50/54 on weekdays; weekend rates rise by about 10%. At López Mateos 993, across from the Villa Fontana, *Hotel El Cid* (☎ 78-24-01, fax 78-36-71) offers singles/doubles from US$52/72. It has a swimming pool, an outstanding restaurant and a disco.

Places to Eat
At the seafood market on the nameless waterfront street running parallel to Boulevard Costero near the sport-fishing piers, try the deep-fried fish or shrimp tacos. *Plaza del Marisco*, on Boulevard Costero across

WAYNE BERNHARDSON

Beautiful views and blind curves – Baja roads are a challenge.

from the Pemex station, is a similar cluster of seafood taco stands of good quality.

Modest *El Corralito* (☎ 78-23-70), alongside the Motel Caribe annex at López Mateos 627, is a good breakfast spot, as is *Casa Blanca* (☎ 74-03-16), Ruiz 254, which also offers decent fixed-price lunches for about US$2. The sidewalk *Café El Portal*, Ruiz 153, lures caffeine junkies with satisfying cappuccinos, mochas, lattes and desserts, but it opens surprisingly late.

Las Cazuelas, at Sanginés near the corner of Boulevard Costero, has a pricey seafood menu, but antojitos are more reasonable. *Muy Lam*, at Avenida Ejército and Diamante, and *China Land*, Avenida Riveroll 1149, are Ensenada's favorite Chinese restaurants.

Most meals are expensive at *El Rey Sol*, a venerable Franco-Mexican institution at López Mateos and Blancarte, but selective diners can find good values. At Avenida Miramar and Calle 7a, cavernous *La Vieja Embotelladora*, modernized for upscale dining with huge wine casks and other features intact, has good food, particularly lobster, and great atmosphere.

Entertainment

At Ruiz 113, historic *Hussong's* is the best known cantina in the Californias, but the mariachi music is stereotypical. Instead, check out the norteña at *Bandido's*, at the corner of Avenida Ruiz and Calle 2a. Directly across Calle 2a, bands at *Club Mágico* rely on three chords and an attitude.

Things to Buy

Galería de Pérez Meillon, in the Centro Artesanal de Ensenada, Boulevard Costero 1094, Local 39, sells pottery and other crafts from Baja California's Paipai, Kumiai and Cucapah peoples, as well as from mainland Mexico's Tarahumara. Artesanías Los Castillo, López Mateos 815, sells Taxco silver.

Getting There & Away

Air Aerocedros (☎ 76-60-76), at Aeropuerto El Ciprés, south of town, flies to Isla Cedros, near the border of Baja California Sur, Tuesday and Friday at 9 am (US$65); book at least a week in advance. Cheaper, more frequent flights leave for Isla Cedros from Guerrero Negro (see the Desierto Central & Llano de Magdalena section).

Bus Ensenada's Central de Autobuses (☎ 78-65-50) is at Avenida Riveroll 1075. Elite/Tres Estrellas de Oro (☎ 78-67-70) and Norte de Sonora (☎ 78-66-77) serve

BAJA CALIFORNIA

mainland Mexican destinations as far as Guadalajara (US$77) and Mexico City (US$88). Norte de Sonora's 2nd-class fares are about 15% cheaper.

ABC (☎ 78-66-80) serves La Paz (23 hours, US$43), San Felipe (five hours, US$10), Tecate (1½ hours, US$6) and Tijuana (1½ hours, US$5). Autotransportes Aragón (☎ 74-04-86), Riveroll 861, goes hourly to Tijuana (US$5).

AROUND ENSENADA
Guadalupe
pop 1220

North of Ensenada on highway 3, some Dominican mission ruins remain at the village of Guadalupe. Turn-of-the-century Russian immigrants settled here; their history is now documented by the **Museo Comunitario de Guadalupe**. The **Fiesta de la Vendimia** (wine-harvest festival) takes place in August; the Domecq and Cetto wineries are open for tours.

PARQUE NACIONAL CONSTITUCIÓN DE 1857

From Ojos Negros, east of Ensenada at km 39 on highway 3, a 43-km dirt road climbs to the Sierra de Juárez and Parque Nacional Constitución de 1857, highlight of which is the marshy, pine-sheltered **Laguna Hanson**. At 1200 meters, the lake abounds with migratory birds in autumn, as well as catfish, bluegill and large-mouth bass.

Camping is pleasant, but livestock have contaminated the water, so bring your own. Firewood is scarce along the lake, abundant in the hills. Only pit toilets are available. Nearby granite outcrops offer stupendous views but tiring ascents through dense brush and massive rock falls – beware of ticks and rattlesnakes. Technical climbers will find short but challenging routes.

The park is also accessible by a steeper road east of km 55, 16 km southeast of the Ojos Negros junction. There's no public transport, but many ranchers have pickup trucks, and you can get a ride with them.

PARQUE NACIONAL SIERRA SAN PEDRO MÁRTIR

In the Sierra San Pedro Mártir, east of San Telmo and west of San Felipe, Baja's most notable national park comprises 630 sq km of coniferous forests, granite peaks exceeding 3000 meters and deep canyons cutting into its steep eastern scarp. The elusive desert bighorn sheep inhabits some remote areas of the park. Snow falls in winter, but the area also gets summer thunderstorms.

Camping areas and hiking trails are numerous, but maintenance is limited; carry a compass and a topographic map, along with cold- and wet-weather supplies, canteens and water purification tablets. Below about 1800 meters, beware of rattlesnakes.

The **Observatorio Astronómico Nacional**, Mexico's national observatory, is two km from the parking area at the end of the San Telmo road. It's open Saturday only, 11 am to 1 pm.

Picacho del Diablo

Few climbers who attempt Picacho del Diablo (Devil's Peak), the peninsula's highest point, reach the 3095-meter summit, because route-finding is so difficult. The second edition of Walt Peterson's *Baja Adventure Book* includes a good map and describes possible routes.

Places to Stay

The *Rancho Meling*, 44 km southeast of San Telmo, is a Baja institution offering accommodations (US$65/115 singles/doubles with full board), horseback riding and backcountry trips. For details, contact Rancho Meling (☎ 61-76-98-85) at Apartado Postal 1326, Ensenada, México, or PO Box 189003, No 73, Coronado, CA 92178, USA.

Getting There & Away

From San Telmo de Abajo, south of km 140 on the Transpeninsular (highway 1), a graded dirt road climbs through San Telmo past Rancho Meling to the park entrance, about 80 km east. The road is passable to most passenger vehicles, but you do have to cross a river along the way, and snow-melt can raise it to hazardous levels.

MEXICALI
pop 505,016 (officially); ☎ 65

European settlement came late to the Río Colorado lowlands, but the Mexicali area grew rapidly – in more than one sense – as irrigation allowed early 20th century farmers to take advantage of rich alluvial lowlands and a long, productive agricultural season. Many visitors pass through Mexicali en route to San Felipe or mainland Mexico; the state capital does not pander to tourists, but a new Centro Cívico-Comercial (Civic and Commercial Center) features government offices, a medical school, a bullring, cinemas, a bus station, hospitals and restaurants. Mexicali is also the northwestern terminus of Mexico's antiquated passenger rail system.

Orientation

Mexicali is on the east bank of the Río Nuevo, opposite Calexico, California. Most of the historic center's main streets parallel the border. Avenida Madero passes through the central business district of modest restaurants, shops, bars and budget hotels. The broad diagonal Calzada López Mateos heads southeast through newer industrial and commercial areas before dividing into highway 5 (to San Felipe) and highway 2 (to Sonora).

Information

Tourist Offices In the Plaza Baja California mall, on Avenida Calafia opposite the Plaza de Toros in the Centro Cívico-Comercial, Secture (☎ 55-49-50) is open weekdays 8 am to 7 pm, Saturday 9 am to 3 pm, Sunday 9 am to 1 pm. The private Comité de Turismo y Convenciones (Cotuco; ☎ 57-23-76) is at Calzada López Mateos and Calle Camelias, about three km southeast of the border. It's open weekdays 8 am to 7 pm.

Money Casas de cambio are abundant and keep long hours, while banks offer ex-change services weekday mornings only. Several banks in Mexicali and Calexico have 24-hour ATMs.

Post & Communications The post office is on Avenida Madero near Morelos. Both cabinas (mostly in pharmacies but also to be found in other small businesses) and pay phones are common.

Bookstores Librería Universitaria, near the Universidad Autónoma on Calzada Juárez, has a good selection of books on Mexican history, archaeology, anthropology and literature. It also carries the Guías Urbanas series of Mexican city maps.

Medical Services The Hospital Civil (☎ 56-11-28) is at Calle del Hospital and Avenida de la Libertad, near the Centro Cívico. Near the border are many clinics, laboratories and hospitals. Locally trained dentists offer quality work at very good prices.

Things to See

The country's largest Chinatown, **La Chinesca**, is centered around Avenida Juárez and Altamirano, south of Calzada López Mateos. La Chinesca is a good place to hear *banda* groups rehearse in the late afternoon.

Most of Mexicali's historic buildings are northeast of López Mateos. The **Catedral de la Virgen de Guadalupe**, at Avenida Reforma and Morelos, is the city's major religious landmark. Now the rectory of the Universidad Autónoma, the former **Palacio de Gobierno** (Government Palace, built between 1919 and 1922) interrupts Avenida Obregón just east of Calle E. To the north, at Avenida Reforma and Calle F, the ex-headquarters of the **Colorado River Land Company** dates from 1924. At Avenida Zaragoza and Calle E, two blocks southwest of the rectory, the former brewery, **Cervecería Mexicali** (opened in 1923) now sits vacant.

The modest eight-room **Museo Regional de la Universidad Autónoma de**

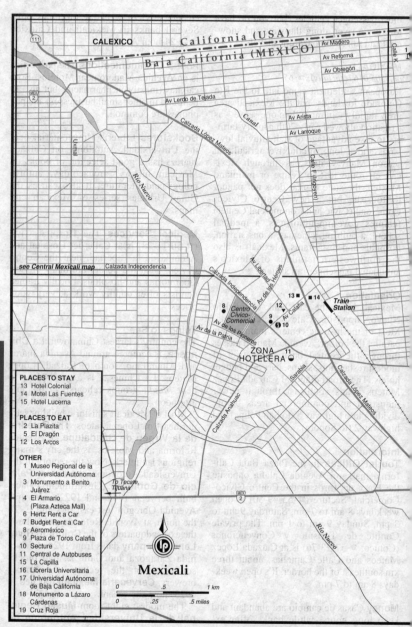

CALEXICO
California (USA)
Baja California (MEXICO)

Av Madero
Av Reforma
Av Obregón

Av Lerdo de Tejada

Calzada López Mateos

Canal

Av Arista
Av Larroque

Calle F (Indoven)

Río Nuevo

Uxmal

see Central Mexicali map   Calzada Independencia

Calzada Independencia

Av Libertad
Av de los Héroes

13 14   Train Station

12
8   Centro Cívico-Comercial
9 10   Av Calafia
Av de los Pioneros
Av de la Patria

ZONA HOTELERA   11

Sarabia

Calzada Anáhuac

Calzada López Mateos

PLACES TO STAY
13 Hotel Colonial
14 Motel Las Fuentes
15 Hotel Lucerna

PLACES TO EAT
2 La Plazita
5 El Dragón
12 Los Arcos

OTHER
1 Museo Regional de la
   Universidad Autónoma
3 Monumento a Benito
   Juárez
4 El Armario
   (Plaza Azteca Mall)
6 Hertz Rent a Car
7 Budget Rent a Car
8 Aeroméxico
9 Plaza de Toros Calafia
10 Secture
11 Central de Autobuses
15 La Capilla
16 Librería Universitaria
17 Universidad Autónoma
    de Baja California
18 Monumento a Lázaro
    Cárdenas
19 Cruz Roja

To Tecate,
Tijuana

Río Nuevo

Mexicali

0   .5   1 km
0   .25   .5 miles

Baja California (☎ 52-57-15), at Avenida Reforma and Calle L, features exhibits on geology, paleontology, human evolution, colonial history and photography. It's open Tuesday to Friday 9 am to 6 pm, Saturday 10 am to 4 pm.

On the east side of López Mateos, just north of Compresora, the ultramodern **Teatro del Estado** (State Theater; ☎ 54-64-18) seats 1100 spectators. The Instituto de Cultura de Baja California presents film cycles at the Teatro's Café Literario.

Special Events

From mid-October to early November, the **Fiesta del Sol** (Festival of the Sun) commemorates the city's founding in 1903. Events include concerts, art exhibits, a crafts exposition, theatrical performances and parades. It also features local industrial and agricultural products.

Places to Stay – budget

Central Mexicali's best bargain is family-oriented *Hotel México* (☎ 54-06-09), Lerdo de Tejada 476, between Altamirano and Morelos, with singles from US$10. Amenities like air-con, TV, private bath and parking are higher. The respectable *Hotel Plaza* (☎ 52-97-57), Madero 366, charges a reasonable US$15/18 for singles/doubles.

Places to Stay – middle

Greatly improved *Hotel Casa Grande* (☎ 53-66-51), Colón 612, has air-con, TV and a swimming pool for US$24/26 singles/doubles. Near the train station, *Motel Las Fuentes* (☎ 57-15-25), López Mateos 1655, charges US$18/26 with TV. Convenient to the border at Melgar 205, the landmark *Hotel del Norte* (☎ 52-81-01) has 52 rooms, some with color TV and air-con, for US$23/33 with breakfast.

Places to Stay – top end

Highly regarded *Hotel Colonial* (☎ 56-53-12), López Mateos 1048, charges US$60, single or double. Popular *Hotel Lucerna* (☎ 66-10-00), about five km from downtown at Calzada Juárez 2151, has rooms for US$70/75.

BAJA CALIFORNIA

Places to Eat

One good, inexpensive breakfast choice is *Petunia 2*, on Avenida Madero between Altamirano and Morelos. Part of Hotel del Norte, *Restaurant del Norte* is a coffee shop offering mediocre but cheap specials. *El Sarape*, Bravo 140, is a raucous spot with live music.

Moderately priced *La Plazita*, in a pleasant atmosphere at Calzada Sierra 377, is a tremendous value for Mexican and international dishes. *La Villa del Seri*, a pricier restaurant at Reforma and Calle D, specializes in Sonoran beef but also has excellent seafood and antojitos. *Cenaduría Selecta* is an institution at Arista 1510 (at Calle G). It specializes in antojitos-recent improvements have raised prices.

Opened in 1928 at Avenida Juárez 8, near Azueta, the inexpensive *Alley 19* is Mexicali's oldest continuously operating Chinese restaurant. *El Dragón* (☎ 66-20-20), at Calzada Juárez 1830, occupies a huge pagoda. It is more expensive but highly regarded.

Mandolino (☎ 52-95-44), Reforma 1070, has excellent Italian food. Mexicali's most popular seafood restaurant is *Los Arcos* (☎ 56-09-03), at Calafia 454, near the Plaza de Toros in the Centro Cívico-Comercial.

Entertainment

La Capilla (☎ 66-11-00), at Hotel Lucerna, Calzada Juárez 2151, is a music and dance club especially popular with university students; hours are 8 pm to 2 am. Nationally known musicians often play at *Los Cristales*, Calzada López Mateos 570, open 6 pm to 3 am.

Spectator Sports

Starting in October, Las Águilas, Mexicali's professional baseball team, hosts other teams from the Liga Mexicana del Pacífico at El Nido de Las Águilas (Eagles' Nest), in the Sports City Complex on Calzada Cuauhtémoc about five km east of the border post. Weeknight games begin at 7 pm, Sunday games at 1 pm. Ticket prices range from US$1 to US$6; a taxi to the ballpark costs around US$6.

Things to Buy

Shops selling cheap leather goods and kitsch souvenirs fill Calle Melgar and Avenida Reforma near the border. For a more sophisticated selection, try El Armario, Calzada Sierra 1700, Suite 1-A, in the Plaza Azteca shopping center.

Getting There & Away

Air Mexicana (☎ 53-54-01, 52-93-91 at the airport), Avenida Madero 833, flies daily to Guadalajara, Mexico City and intermediate points. Aeroméxico (☎ 57-25-51) is at Pasaje Alamos 1008-D, in the Centro Cívico-Comercial; its subsidiary Aerolitoral flies three times daily to Hermosillo, connecting to many mainland Mexican destinations and to Tucson, Arizona.

Bus Long-distance bus companies leave from the Central de Autobuses (☎ 57-24-50), on Calzada Independencia near López Mateos. Autotransportes del Pacífico (☎ 57-24-61) and Norte de Sonora (☎ 57-24-22) serve mainland Mexican destinations such as Mazatlán (US$65 in 1st-class), Guadalajara (US$75) and Mexico City (US$85). When you cross the state line into Sonora, some 70 km east of Mexicali, you enter a new time zone; put your watch forward one hour.

Tres Estrellas (☎ 57-24-10) and ABC (☎ 57-24-20) destinations within Baja California include Tijuana (four hours, US$7), Ensenada (3½ hours, US$11), Guerrero Negro (16 hours, US$30), Loreto (US$42) and La Paz (30 hours, US$55). ABC buses to San Felipe (two hours, US$7) depart at 8 am, noon, and 4 and 8 pm.

From a stop on the south side of Calzada López Mateos near Melgar, Transportes Golden State (☎ 53-61-59) serves Palm Springs (US$22), Los Angeles (US$27) and intermediates at 8 am and 2.30 and 8 pm. The Calexico stop is at Church's Fried Chicken, 344 Imperial Avenue.

In Calexico, Greyhound (☎ 760-357-1895) is at 121 East First St, directly across from the border. There are five departures daily from the Los Angeles terminal

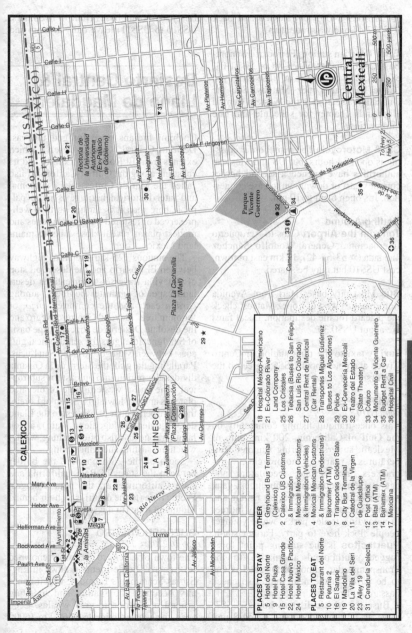

CALEXICO

California (USA)
Baja California (MEXICO)

Calexico

La Chinesca

Rectoría de la Universidad Autónoma de Baja California (Ex-Palacio de Gobierno)

Parque Vicente Guerrero

Plaza La Cachanilla (Mall)

Plaza del Mariachi (Plaza Constitución)

Central Mexicali

To Tijuana

To Hwy 2; Hwy 5

PLACES TO STAY
5   Hotel del Norte
9   Hotel Plaza
15 Hotel Casa Grande
22 Hotel Nuevo Pacífico
24 Hotel México

PLACES TO EAT
5   Restaurant del Norte
10 Petunia 2
16 El Sarape
19 Mandolino
20 La Villa del Seri
23 Alley 19
31 Cenaduría Selecta

OTHER
1   Greyhound Bus Terminal (Calexico)
2   Calexico US Customs & Immigration
3   Mexicali Mexican Customs & Immigration (Vehicles)
4   Mexicali Mexican Customs & Immigration (Pedestrians)
6   Bancomer (ATM)
7   Transportes Golden State
8   City Bus Terminal
11 Catedral de la Virgen de Guadalupe
12 Post Office
13 Bital (ATM)
14 Banamex (ATM)
17 Mexicana
18 Hospital México-Americano
21 Ex-Colorado River Land Company
25 Los Cristales
26 Tebacsa (Buses to San Felipe, San Luis Río Colorado)
27 Central Rent de Mexicali (Car Rental)
28 Transportes Miguel Gutiérrez (Buses to Los Algodones)
29 Police
30 Ex-Cervecería Mexicali
32 Teatro del Estado (State Theater)
33 Cotuco
34 Monumento a Vicente Guerrero
35 Budget Rent a Car
36 Hospital Civil

BAJA CALIFORNIA

(☎ 213-629-8400) to Calexico and back (US$27/47 one way/roundtrip).

Train The train station (Ferrocarril Sonora-Baja California; ☎ 57-23-86 or 57-21-01, ext 213, 222 or 223) is at Ulíses Irigoyen (Calle F) near López Mateos. See the Guadalajara section in the Western Central Highlands chapter for schedule and fare information.

Car & Motorcycle The main border crossing is open 24 hours, but US and Mexican authorities have opened a second border complex east of downtown to ease congestion. It's open 6 am to 10 pm.

Getting Around
To/From the Airport Cabs to Aeropuerto Internacional General Rodolfo Sánchez Taboada (☎ 53-67-42), 12 km east of town, cost US$10 but may be shared.

Bus Most city buses start from Avenida Reforma, just west of López Mateos; check the placard for the destination. Local fares are about US$0.30.

Taxi A taxi to the train station or Centro Cívico averages about US$5; agree on the fare first.

SAN FELIPE
pop 11,310

This once-tranquil fishing community on the Gulf of California, 200 km south of Mexicali, suffers blistering summer temperatures, roaring motorcycles, firecrackers, real estate speculators and aggressive restaurateurs who almost yank patrons off the sidewalk. Sport fishing and warm winters have attracted many retirees to sprawling trailer parks, while younger people flock here to party. Farther south, **Puertecitos** is the starting point for a rugged southbound alternative to the Transpeninsular, although the road is due to be paved in the near future, so check passability first.

Buses to Mexicali (two hours, US$7) leave at 7.30 am, noon and 4 and 8 pm;

Ensenada-bound buses (four to five hours, US$10 to US$11) leave daily at 8 am and 6 pm.

Desierto Central & Llano de Magdalena

Cochimí Indians once foraged the vast Desierto Central (Central Desert), which extends from El Rosario to Loreto, and its coastline along the Gulf of California (also called the Mar de Cortés). Baja's colonial and later historical heritage is more palpable here than it is farther north – well-preserved or restored mission churches and modest plazas reveal close links to mainland Mexico.

The sinuous 125-km stretch of highway between El Rosario and the desert pit stop of Cataviña traverses a surrealistic desert landscape of granite boulders among *cardón* cacti and the contorted *cirio*, or 'boojum tree.' Beyond Guerrero Negro and the desolate Desierto de Vizcaíno, the oasis of San Ignacio augurs the semitropical gulf coast between Mulegé and Cabo San Lucas. Paralleling the gulf, the Sierra de la Giganta divides the region into an eastern subtropical zone and a western zone of elevated plateaus and dry lowlands. South of Loreto, the Transpeninsular turns west to the Llano de Magdalena (Magdalena Plain), a rich farming zone that also offers fishing, whale-watching, surfing and windsurfing.

South of the 28th parallel, the border between the states of Baja California and Baja California Sur, the hour changes; Pacific time (to the north) is an hour behind Mountain time (to the south).

GUERRERO NEGRO
pop 10,220; ☎ *115*

The town of Guerrero Negro is renowned for Laguna Ojo de Liebre (known in English as Scammon's Lagoon), which annually becomes the mating and breeding ground of California gray whales. Each year, the whales migrate 9660 km (6000 miles) from the Bering Sea to the lagoon, where they stay from early January through March. The lagoon is south of the town's evaporative saltworks (the largest of its kind in the world), about 24 km from the junction of highway 1.

The town comprises two distinct sectors: a disorderly strip along Boulevard Zapata, west of the Transpeninsular and an orderly company town run by Exportadora de Sal (ESSA). Nearly all accommodations, restaurants and other services are along Boulevard Zapata.

Places to Stay

The whale-watching season can strain local accommodations; reservations are advisable from January to March.

Barren *Malarrimo Trailer Park* (☎ 7-02-50), at the eastern entrance to town, charges US$5 (tents) to US$10 (RVs). Hot water is plentiful and toilets are clean, but check electrical outlets. Clean and tidy *Motel Las Ballenas* (☎ 7-01-16) has hot water and color TV in every room, for US$12/16 singles/doubles. It's just north of upgraded *Hotel El Morro* (☎ 7-04-14),

Pass the Salt, Please

Despite having survived and recovered from the brutality of commercial whaling, the California gray whale faces contemporary challenges in Baja California. At present it has become an innocent bystander in a tug of war between Mexican government agencies with dramatically different visions of Laguna San Ignacio (see the Around San Ignacio section).

The point of contention is Exportadora de Sal's proposed 520-sq-km, US$100 million saltworks, which it would like to establish at the 470-sq-km lagoon. (Those statistics deceptively understate the scale of the project, since ancillary works would directly affect 2100 sq km and indirectly impact up to 15,000 sq km of El Vizcaíno Biosphere Reserve). The Guerrero Negro-based Exportadora, a state-owned enterprise with a large minority holding (49%) by the Japanese multinational Mitsubishi Corporation, plans a 1.6-km canal to pump water continuously from Laguna San Ignacio to clay-lined evaporation beds, producing six million tons of salt yearly – a figure that would double the company's current production. A 25-km conveyor belt would shift the salt to a two-km pier near Punta Abreojos, northwest of the lagoon.

Mexico's powerful Secretaría de Comercio y Fomento Industrial (SECOFI; the Secretariat of Commerce and Industrial Development) backs the project, but the resolute Instituto Nacional de Ecología (INE; National Ecology Institute) vigorously objects to the project's potential impact on the gray whale, the endangered peninsular pronghorn antelope and the mangrove wetlands that serve as incubators for fish and shellfish. The impact on the whales, though, is the biggest, literally and figuratively, and most controversial issue.

One problem is that nobody really knows how much disruption the whales can tolerate during courtship and during the birth and raising of their young. Exportadora claims that whale numbers have doubled in its three decades of operations at Ojo de Liebre, but conservationists are skeptical of the company's data. In addition, less than half of the narrower and shallower Laguna San Ignacio is suitable for whales. It might also suffer more from turbulence caused by pumping, which could reduce salinity and temperature in areas frequented by newborn calves. While gray whales have adapted to some human activities at Ojo de Liebre, studies have shown that noises like oil drilling seriously disturb them.

For these reasons, Exportadora's project is on hold until the Universidad Autónoma de Baja California Sur completes a new environmental impact assessment. If the new assessment upholds Exportadora's contentions, however, there will be increased pressure on the project's opponents to accede to development. Meanwhile, organizations such as the US-based Natural Resources Defense Council (NRDC) and the Mexican branch of the Worldwide Fund for Nature (WWF-México) have made stopping the project their number one environmental priority in Mexico. ∎

BAJA CALIFORNIA

on the north side of Boulevard Zapata, which has clean, pleasant rooms for US$19/21. *Cabañas Don Miguelito* (☎ 7-02-50), part of the Malarrimo complex, has detached units for US$22/25.

Places to Eat

Guerrero Negro's many taco stands keep erratic hours. *Cocina Económica Letty*, a good breakfast choice on the south side of Boulevard Zapata, has moderately priced antojitos and seafood. Specializing in seafood, both as antojitos and as sophisticated international dishes, *Malarrimo* (see above) is no longer cheap, but portions are generous.

Getting There & Away

Air The Aeroméxico subsidiary airline Aerolitoral (☎ 7-17-33), on the north side of Boulevard Zapata near the Pemex station, flies daily except Sunday to Hermosillo, connecting to mainland Mexican cities and Phoenix, Arizona. It leaves from the new airfield two km north of the state border, just west of the Transpeninsular.

Aerolíneas California Pacífico (☎ 7-10-00) flies DC-3s of dubious safety to nearby Isla Cedros (US$25). Flights are often booked early, so it's best to book at least a day in advance and to arrive by 8 am for the 10 am (Mountain time) flights, which run daily except Sunday. The airline's offices are on the north side of Boulevard Zapata, but flights leave from the airfield near the ESSA sector; at the airstrip, look for the yellow shed with blue trim and doors. Aerocedros (☎ 7-09-62), also on the north side of Boulevard Zapata, flies Tuesday and Friday at 1 pm to Cedros (US$34) and Ensenada (US$63).

Bus The bus station is on the south side of Boulevard Zapata. Northbound fares include Ensenada (US$19) and Tijuana (US$23); southbound fares include Mulegé (five hours, US$9), Loreto (seven hours, US$15) and La Paz (12 hours, US$25).

AROUND GUERRERO NEGRO
Reserva de la Biosfera El Vizcaíno

Sprawling from Laguna San Ignacio, Guerrero Negro and Isla Cedros across to the Gulf of California, this 25,000-sq-km reserve is Latin America's largest single protected area. Guerrero Negro travel agencies arrange whale-watching trips for about US$30, while a bit farther south, *pangueros* (boatmen) from Ejido Benito Juárez take visitors for whale-watching excursions on Laguna Ojo de Liebre's shallow waters for about US$15 adults, US$10 children.

Eight km south of Guerrero Negro, an excellent graded road leads 25 km west to Ojo de Liebre, where the US$3 parking fee includes the right to camp; the ejido runs a simple but very good restaurant.

Whales are not usually present until after January 1.

ISLA CEDROS
pop 1465

Isla Cedros is not a touristy destination – it has few services, and you can't even get a margarita – but this mountainous northward extension of Península Vizcaíno supports unusual flora, marine mammals such as elephant seals and sea lions, and the endangered Cedros mule deer. The hiking is good here, but water is scarce.

Most of the island's inhabitants live in the port of Cedros on the eastern shore, but a fair number live at Punta Morro Redondo, the transshipment point for salt barged over from Guerrero Negro.

Places to Stay & Eat

The basic *Casa de Huéspedes Elsa García*, uphill from the port's dusty triangular plaza, has clean singles or doubles for US$10. *Restaurant El Marino* has good, reasonably priced antojitos, fish and shrimp. A friendly taco stand up the main drag from El Marino serves only carne asada.

Getting There & Away

Taxis charge about US$5 per person to Cedros' airfield at Punta Morro Redondo, eight km south of town, but even the police stop to offer lifts!

Aerolíneas California Pacífico flights to Guerrero Negro (US$25) ostensibly leave at 1 pm (Pacific time), but to be on the safe side you should arrive at the airport at least an hour early. Purchase tickets at Licores La Panga, up the hill from Cedros' plaza. Tickets for Ensenada (US$63) are available at the Sociedad Cooperativa de Producción Pesquera, in Cedros village.

AROUND ISLA CEDROS
Islas San Benito
This tiny archipelago consists of three small islands 30 nautical miles west of Cedros. The largest supports a winter camp of abalone divers and their families and a winter colony of northern elephant seals. The seals start to arrive in December but are most numerous in January and February.

Budget travelers can catch a free lift from Cedros with the daily supply ship *Tito I*. To do so, visit the Sociedad de Producción Pesquera before 1 pm; with the chief's approval, the secretary issues a letter for you to present to the captain that evening for the next morning's voyage. If you are prone to seasickness, avoid eating; the four-hour voyage out is generally rougher than the one back.

Bring camping equipment, food and water if you hope to spend more than an hour ashore. Avoid getting too close to the elephant seals - frightened bulls can accidentally crush or injure newborn pups.

SAN IGNACIO
pop 761; alt 200m; ☎ 115
Jesuits located Misión San Ignacio de Kadakaamán in this soothing oasis in 1728, planting dense groves of date palms and citrus trees, but it was Dominicans who supervised construction of the striking church (finished in 1786) that still dominates the cool, laurel-shaded plaza. With lava-block walls nearly 1.2 meters thick, this is one of Baja's most beautiful churches.

The lush village of San Ignacio proper is about 1.6 km south of the Transpeninsular

Misión San Ignacio de Kadakaamán

and is a welcome sight after the scrub brush and dense cacti of the Desierto de Vizcaíno. Most services are around the plaza, including public telephones, but there is no bank.

Places to Stay & Eat
Just south of Hotel La Pinta, on the west side of the road into town, palm-shaded *El Padrino RV Park* (☎ 4-00-89) has more than 25 sites, some with full hookups. Fees are US$7 for camping, US$9 for large RVs.

At Venustiano Carranza 22, southeast of the plaza, *Motel La Posada* (☎ 4-03-13) has spartan doubles with hot shower for about US$20. The pseudocolonial *Hotel La Pinta* (☎ /fax 4-03-00), on the main road just before entering San Ignacio, appeals to more affluent travelers, with singles/doubles at US$55.

Specializing in local beef, Hotel La Pinta's restaurant serves typical antojitos at upscale prices. *Tota*, a few blocks east of the plaza, serves good, reasonably priced antojitos and seafood dishes. *Flojos*, at El Padrino RV Park, prepares good, fresh seafood; its lobster is cheaper than Tota's.

Getting There & Away
At least five buses daily in each direction pick up passengers at the San Lino terminal on the Transpeninsular.

BAJA CALIFORNIA

AROUND SAN IGNACIO
San Francisco de la Sierra

At km 118 on the Transpeninsular, 43 km northwest of San Ignacio, a graded but poorly consolidated road climbs east to San Francisco de la Sierra, gateway to the Desierto Central's most spectacular pre-Columbian rock art. **Cueva del Ratón**, about 2.5 km before San Francisco, is the most accessible site, but independent visitors *must* obtain permission from the Instituto Nacional de Historia y Antropología (INAH) office in San Ignacio to visit it,

and a local guide must open the locked gate. The INAH office is open 8 am to 6 pm Monday through Saturday. Oscar Fischer, at Motel La Posada, arranges moderately priced day trips to Cueva del Ratón, which has representations of *monos* (human figures), *borregos* (bighorn sheep) and deer.

In the dramatic Cañón San Pablo, **Cueva Pintada**, **Cueva de Las Flechas** and other sites are better preserved. Cueva Pintada's rock overhang is the most impressive. The awesome mule-back

---

The Rock Art of the Desierto Central

When Jesuit missionaries inquired as to who created the giant rock paintings of the Sierra de San Francisco and about the meaning of those paintings, the Cochimí Indians responded with a bewilderment that was, in all likelihood, utterly feigned. The Cochimí claimed ignorance of both symbols and techniques, but it was not unusual, when missionaries came calling, to deny knowledge of the profound religious beliefs which those missionaries wanted to eradicate.

At sites such as Cueva Pintada, Cochimí painters and their predecessors decorated high rock overhangs with vivid red and black representations of *monos* (human figures), *borregos* (bighorn sheep), pumas and deer, as well as of more abstract designs. It is speculated that the painters built scaffolds of palm logs to reach the ceilings. Postcontact motifs do include Christian crosses, but these are few and small in contrast to the dazzling pre-Hispanic figures surrounding them.

Cueva de las Flechas, across Cañón San Pablo, has similar paintings, but the uncommon feature of arrows through some of the figures is the subject of serious speculation. One interpretation is that these paintings depict a period of warfare. Similar opinions suggest that they record a raid or an instance of trespass on tribal territory or perhaps constitute a warning against such trespass. One researcher, however, has hypothesized that the arrows represent a shaman's metaphor for death in the course of a vision quest; if that is the case, it is no wonder that the Cochimí would claim ignorance of the paintings and their significance in the face of a missionary presence unrelentingly hostile to such beliefs.

Such speculation is impossible to prove since the Cochimí no longer exist, but over the past two years the Instituto Nacional de Historia y Antropología (INAH) has undertaken the largest systematic archaeological survey of a hunter-gatherer people yet attempted in Mexico. Results reveal that, besides well-known features such as rock art sites and grinding stones, the Cochimí left evidence of permanent dwellings. In recognition of its cultural importance, the Sierra de San Francisco has been declared a UNESCO World Heritage Site. It is already part of the Reserva de la Biosfera El Vizcaíno, which includes the major gray whale calving areas of Laguna San Ignacio and Laguna Ojo de Liebre.

Unfortunately that means more publicity than protection. The sierra will remain an INAH-protected archaeological zone, which means that foreigners need entry permits to conduct research – not everyone has been scrupulous in that regard. INAH has already instituted regulations for tourists (see Around San Ignacio) and will impose a modest admission fee to guarantee basic infrastructure and provide services such as an interpretive guidebook to the paintings. It will also be challenged to provide area residents with a stake in the management of the sites, without which the project is unlikely to be successful. ■

descent of Cañón San Pablo requires at least two days, preferably three. Visitors must refrain from touching the paintings, smoking at sites and employing flash photography (400 ASA film suffices even in dim light).

Entrance to Cueva del Ratón requires a modest tip to the guide. Visitors to Cañón San Pablo must hire a guide with mule through INAH for US$12 per day, plus a mule for each person for US$7 per day and additional pack animals for supplies (US$6 per day each). You must also feed the guide. The best season for visiting is early spring, when the days are fairly long but temperatures are not yet unpleasantly hot. Backpacking is permitted, but you must still hire a guide and mule.

Laguna San Ignacio
Along with Laguna Ojo de Liebre and Bahía Magdalena, Laguna San Ignacio is one of the Pacific Coast's major winter whale-watching sites, with three-hour excursions costing around US$25 per person. Kuyima, a cooperative based in the village of San Ignacio, can arrange transport and accommodations, but most vehicles can make the 61-km drive to La Fridera in about two hours.

In other seasons the area offers outstanding bird-watching in the stunted mangroves and at Isla Pelícanos, where ospreys and cormorants nest (landing on the island is prohibited). Laguna San Ignacio has attracted controversy because ESSA plans to develop an even larger saltworks here than at Guerrero Negro. (See the sidebar, Pass the Salt, Please.)

SANTA ROSALÍA
pop 10,451; ☎ 115
Imported timber frames the clapboard houses lining the main streets of Santa Rosalía, a copper town built by the French-owned Compañía del Boleo in the 1880s. The French also assembled a prefabricated church here that was designed by Alexandre Gustave Eiffel (the same!) for Paris' 1889 World's Fair. And they bequeathed a bakery that sells Baja's best baguettes.

Orientation & Information
Central Santa Rosalía nestles in the canyon of its namesake arroyo, west of the Transpeninsular, but French administrators built their houses on the northern Mesa Francia, now home to municipal authorities and the historic Hotel Francés. Santa Rosalía's narrow avenidas run east-west, while its short calles run north-south; one-way traffic is the rule. Plaza Benito Juárez, four blocks west of the highway, is the town center.

Money Travelers bound for Mulegé, which has no banks, should change US cash or traveler's checks here, where Banamex also has an ATM.

Post & Communications The post office is at Avenida Constitución and Calle 2. Hotel del Real, on the exit road from town, also has long-distance cabinas.

Iglesia Santa Bárbara
Designed and erected in Paris, disassembled and stored in Brussels, intended for West Africa, Gustave Eiffel's prefab church was finally shipped here when a Compañía del Boleo director chanced upon it 1895. It was reassembled by 1897. It has attractive stained-glass windows.

Places to Stay & Eat
Just south of town, *Las Palmas RV Park* (☎ 2-01-09) has grassy sites with hot showers and clean toilets from about US$6 (tents) to US$10 (RVs).

Travelers have recommended the 'very quaint' *Hotel Blanco y Negro* (☎ 2-00-80), up a spiral staircase on the second floor of a small building at Avenida Sarabia 1, with clean, basic singles/doubles with hot water for about US$7 with shared bath, US$9 with private bath. Family-run *Motel San Victor* (☎ 2-01-16), Avenida Progreso 36, has a dozen tidy rooms with ceiling fans, air-con and tiled baths for US$13 singles/doubles. Historic *Hotel Francés* (☎ 2-08-29), on Mesa Francia, offers an atmospheric bar, views of the rusting copper works and air-con singles/doubles for US$26/29.

Taco stands are numerous along Avenida Obregón, while *Cenaduría Gaby*, on Calle 4 just north of Obregón, serves reasonably priced antojitos. South of downtown, the waterfront *Restaurant Selene* serves sumptuous seafood at upscale prices.

The Panadería El Boleo, on Obregón between Calles 3 and 4, is an obligatory stop for Mexican and French-style baked goods. Baguettes usually sell out early.

Getting There & Away

Bus At least six buses daily in each direction stop at the terminal, which is south of town on the west side of the Transpeninsular. Northbound fares include San Ignacio (1½ hours, US$2.50), Guerrero Negro (five hours, US$7.50), Ensenada (16 hours, US$25) and Tijuana (18 hours, US$28); southbound fares include Mulegé (1½ hours, US$3), Loreto (three hours, US$5.50), Ciudad Constitución (six hours, US$10) and La Paz (nine hours, US$17).

Ferry Sematur passenger/auto ferries sail to Guaymas on Sunday and Wednesday at 8 am, arriving at 3 pm; the return ferry to Santa Rosalía sails at 8 am Tuesday and Friday, arriving at 3 pm. Strong winter winds may cause delays.

Ticket windows at the terminal (☎ 2-00-13), right along the highway, are open Tuesday and Friday 8 am to 1 pm and 3 to 6 pm, Sunday and Wednesday 6 to 7.30 am, and Thursday and Saturday 8 am to 3 pm. See the accompanying chart for schedules and vehicle fares. Make reservations at least three days in advance and, even if you have reservations, arrive early at the ticket office. Passenger fares are US$14 in *salón* (numbered seats) and US$27 in *turista* (two- to four-bunk cabins with shared bath). Vehicle rates vary with vehicle length:

Vehicle	Length	Rate
Car	Up to 5 meters	US$133
	5.01 to 6.5 meters	US$174
	With trailer up to 9 meters	US$240
	9.01 to 17 meters	US$453
Motorcycle		US$20

Before shipping any vehicle to the mainland, officials require a vehicle permit (see the Car & Motorcycle section of the introductory Getting There & Away chapter for details on bringing a car into Mexico). Vehicle permits are no longer obtainable in Santa Rosalía, so get them in Tijuana, Mexicali, Ensenada or La Paz.

MULEGÉ
pop 3169; ☎ *115*

Beyond Santa Rosalía, the Transpeninsular hugs the eastern scarp of the Sierra de la Giganta before winding through the Sierra Azteca and dropping into the subtropical oasis of Mulegé, a popular divers' destination. Straddling the palm-lined Arroyo de Santa Rosalía (Río Mulegé), three km inland from the gulf, the village of Mulegé has an 18th century mission.

Information

Most services, including the post office, are on or near Jardín Corona, the town plaza. Mulegé has no bank, but merchants change cash dollars or accept them for payment. For long-distance phones and fax, visit the grocery store on Zaragoza at Avenida Martínez or dial an international operator from the pay phones on the plaza.

Things to See

Across the highway, near the south bank of the arroyo, the hilltop **Misión Santa Rosalía de Mulegé** was founded in 1705, completed in 1766, and abandoned in 1828. A short path climbs to a scenic overlook of the palm-lined arroyo.

Desperately needing major restoration, the former territorial prison is now the **Museo Mulegé**, overlooking the town. Its eclectic artifacts include cotton gins, antique diving equipment and firearms.

Diving

Owners Miguel and Claudia Quintana of Mulegé Divers (☎ 3-00-59), on Avenida General Francisco Martínez, specialize in diving instruction and excursions (Claudia is American). They also sell fins and masks, fishing equipment and other supplies, T-shirts, and Baja books and maps. The shop, open daily except Sunday 9 am to 1 pm and 3 to 6 pm, is also a ready source of information.

Places to Stay

Friendly *Huerta Saucedo RV Park* (☎ 3-03-00), south of town on the gulf side of the highway, rents RV spaces for about US$10 to US$12 (half that without hookups).

The *Canett Casa de Huéspedes*, on Madero, isn't bad for US$4, but the church bells next door start ringing at 6 am. *Casa de Huéspedes Manuelita* (☎ 3-01-75), on Moctezuma across from Lavamática Claudia, and *Casa de Huéspedes Nachita*, half a block northwest, are comparable.

Family-oriented *Hotel Suites Rosita* (☎ 3-02-70), on Madero east of the plaza, has air-con rooms with kitchenettes for US$16. Poet Alán Gorosave once inhabited shady *Hotel Las Casitas* (☎ 3-00-19), on Madero near General Martínez, where the rooms all have hot showers and air-con for US$20. *Hotel Hacienda* (☎ 3-00-21), an ongoing construction project at Madero 3, has twin-bedded rooms with fridge, air-con and hot shower for US$35.

Places to Eat

Dany's is the closest the humble taco will ever get to haute cuisine, with various fillings and a cornucopia of tasty condiments at reasonable prices; it's at the intersection of Romero Rubio and Madero. Try *Las Casitas*, in its namesake hotel, for antojitos and a few seafood dishes, or *Los Equipales*, on General Martínez just west of Zaragoza, for outstanding meals that are a good value for the money. *El Candil*, near the plaza, has filling meat and seafood dishes at moderate prices; its bar is a popular meeting place.

Getting There & Away

Half a dozen buses pass daily in each direction at the Y-junction ('La Y Griega') on the Transpeninsular at the western edge of town.

LORETO

pop 8299; ☎ *113*

In 1697 Jesuit Juan María Salvatierra established the Californias' first permanent European settlement at this modest port of cobbled streets some 135 km south of Mulegé, between the Transpeninsular and the gulf. Though aggressive tourist development in nearby Nopoló has threatened to siphon off Loreto's water or turn it into Cabo San Lucas Norte, local pressure recently forced Mexico's federal government to establish Parque Marino Nacional Bahía de Loreto, protecting 2065 sq km of shoreline, ocean and offshore islands. Fishing, diving, snorkeling and kayaking are popular in this area.

Orientation

Loreto has an irregular street plan. Most hotels and services are near the landmark mission church on Salvatierra, while the attractive *malecón* (waterfront boulevard) is ideal for sunset strolls. The Plaza Cívica is just north of Salvatierra, between Madero and Davis.

Information

Tourist Office Loreto's Departamento de Turismo Municipal (☎ 5-04-11), on the west side of the Plaza Cívica, is open weekdays 8.30 am to 3 pm. Helpful English-speaking staff are usually on duty, and it has a good selection of brochures and flyers.

Money Bancomer, at Salvatierra and Madero, changes US cash and traveler's checks weekday mornings but sometimes runs short of cash.

Post & Communications The post office is on Deportiva, north of Salvatierra. Several businesses along Salvatierra have long-distance cabinas, but they add a surcharge for international collect calls.

Things to See

Above the entrance to **Misión Nuestra Señora de Loreto**, the inscription 'Cabeza y Madre de Las Misiones de Baja

BAJA CALIFORNIA

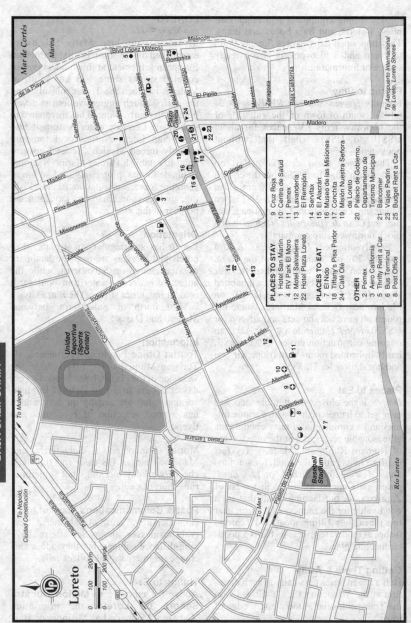

Loreto

0   100   200m
0   100   200 yards

To Nopoló,
Ciudad Constitución

To Mulegé

To Mex 1

PLACES TO STAY
1 Hotel San Martín
4 RV Park El Moro
12 Motel Salvatierra
22 Hotel Plaza Loreto

PLACES TO EAT
7 El Nido
18 Tiffany's Pisa Parlor
24 Café Olé

OTHER
2 Pemex
3 Aero California
5 Thrifty Rent a Car
6 Bus Terminal
8 Post Office
9 Cruz Roja
10 Centro de Salud
11 Pemex
13 Lavandería
14 El Remojón
15 Servitax
16 El Alacrán
17 Museo de las Misiones
19 Misión Nuestra Señora de Loreto
20 Palacio de Gobierno, Departamento de Turismo Municipal
21 Bancomer
23 Viajes Pedrín
25 Budget Rent a Car

To Aeropuerto Internacional
de Loreto, Loreto Shores

y Alta California' (Head and Mother of the Missions of Lower and Upper California) aptly describes the mission's role in the history of the Californias.

Alongside the church, INAH's revamped **Museo de las Misiones** (☎ 5-04-41) chronicles the settlement of Baja California, paying more attention to the indigenous heritage than it once did. It's open weekdays 9 am to 4 pm; admission costs US$1.25.

Places to Stay

At Rosendo Robles 8, half a block from the beach, friendly *RV Park El Moro* has 20 sites with full hookups for US$6 to US$10, depending on vehicle size. It has clean baths and hot showers as well.

Basic *Hotel San Martín* (☎ 5-00-42), at Juárez 4, charges only US$9 single or double but is often full. *Motel Salvatierra* (☎ 5-00-21), Salvatierra 123, has clean but worn rooms with air-con and hot shower for US$13/18 singles/doubles. The central and very attractive *Hotel Plaza Loreto* (☎ 5-02-80), Avenida Hidalgo 2, charges US$35/43.

Places to Eat

Inexpensive *Café Olé*, Madero 14, serves good breakfasts and antojitos. *Tiffany's Pisa Parlor*, at Avenida Hidalgo and Pino Suárez, has high prices but also high-quality food and is tobacco-free. *El Nido*, across from the bus station on Salvatierra, is the local branch of the Baja steakhouse chain.

Things to Buy

For varied handicrafts, try El Alacrán, at Salvatierra and Misioneros. High-priced Conchita, at Salvatierra and Pino Suárez, sells jewelry and selected Baja books, as well as a suspect line of products made from black coral or endangered species like sea turtles; these products are banned in the US.

Getting There & Away

Air Aero California (☎ 5-05-00), on Juárez between Misioneros and Zapata, flies twice

Misión Nuestra Señora de Loreto

daily to Los Angeles. Aerolitoral, represented by Viajes Pedrín (☎ 5-02-04), on the south side of Avenida Hidalgo at Madero, flies daily to and from La Paz.

Bus Loreto's bus station (☎ 5-07-67) is near the convergence of Salvatierra, Paseo de Ugarte and Paseo Tamaral. Northbound buses leave at 2 pm (Santa Rosalía, US$5.50), 3 pm (Tijuana, US$35), 5 pm (Santa Rosalía), 9 pm (Mexicali, US$40), 11 pm (Guerrero Negro, US$15) and 1 am (Tijuana). Southbound buses for La Paz (US$10) and intermediate stops leave at midnight, 8 am and 1, 2 and 11 pm.

Getting Around

To/From the Airport Taxis to Aeropuerto Internacional de Loreto (☎ 5-04-54),

BAJA CALIFORNIA

reached by a lateral off the highway south of the Río Loreto, cost US$5 for one person, US$2 for each additional passenger.

AROUND LORETO
Misión San Francisco Javier
Two km south of Loreto on the Transpeninsular is the junction for the spectacular 35-km mountain road to beautifully preserved San Francisco Javier de Viggé-Biaundó (founded 1699). Every December 3, pilgrims celebrate the saint's fiesta here. Restaurant Palapa San Javier serves simple meals, cold sodas and beer and offers simple accommodations.

CIUDAD CONSTITUCIÓN
pop 35,447; alt 50m; ☎ 113
Conveniently close to whale-watching sites, Ciudad Constitución, 215 km northwest of La Paz, has grown dramatically with the growth of commercial agriculture. Most services are within a block or two of the north-south Transpeninsular, commonly known as Boulevard Olachea. The post office is on Galeana, west of Olachea; for phone service, try the cabinas on the east side of Olachea between Matamoros and Francisco J Mina. For information on whale-watching, refer to Around Ciudad Constitución.

Places to Stay
At the north end of town, near the junction of the highway to Puerto López Mateos, Austrian-run *Manfred's RV Trailer Park* (☎ 2-11-03) has spacious, shady pull-through sites for US$12 for one person, US$14 for two. It gives a break to cyclists and motorcyclists (US$6 per site) and car campers (US$9 per site).

Hotel Casino (☎ 2-04-55), on Guadalupe Victoria east of Hotel Maribel, has spartan rooms for US$13. *Hotel Conchita* (☎ 2-02-66), Olachea 180, has similar rates – about US$12/19 singles/doubles with TV, slightly cheaper without. *Hotel Maribel* (☎ 2-01-55), Guadalupe Victoria 156, near Boulevard Olachea, is comfortable enough at US$14 upstairs, US$19 downstairs.

Places to Eat
Constitución's many taco stands and the *Mercado Central*, on Avenida Juárez between Hidalgo and Bravo, have the cheapest eats. *Super Pollo*, at the north end of Olachea, specializes in grilled chicken. Next door, *Estrella del Mar* and *Rincón Jarocho*, on the east side of Olachea, are seafood restaurants. Another seafood choice is *Mariscos El Delfín*, at Olachea and Zapata.

Getting There & Away
Long-distance buses stop at the terminal at Avenida Juárez and Pino Suárez, one block east of Olachea, but there are also buses to Puerto San Carlos, Puerto López Mateos, La Purísima and San Isidro.

AROUND CIUDAD CONSTITUCIÓN
Puerto López Mateos
pop 2391
Shielded from the open Pacific by the offshore barrier of Isla Magdalena, Puerto Adolfo López Mateos is one of Baja's best whale-watching sites. Whales are visible from the shore near Playa El Faro, where tidy free camping is possible. Three-hour *panga* (skiff) excursions cost US$45 per hour for up to six people and are easy to arrange.

Places to Stay & Eat Free camping, with pit toilets only (bring water), is possible at Playa Soledad. The only other accommodations in Puerto López Mateos are at the small and simple but new and tidy *Posada Ballena López*, for US$10/15 singles/doubles.

Besides a couple of so-so taco stands, López Mateos has several decent restaurants. *El Palomar*, directly opposite the plaza, serves good and moderately priced seafood specialties in a homey environment; across the street, *Cabaña Brisa* is also pretty good.

Getting There & Away Puerto López Mateos is 32 km west of Ciudad Insurgentes by a good paved road. Autotransportes Águila provides twice-daily buses from Ciudad Constitución (US$2) at 11.30 am and 7 pm; return service to Constitución leaves at 6.30 am and 12.30 pm.

Puerto San Carlos
pop 3644; ☎ *113*

On Bahía Magdalena, 58 km west of Ciudad Constitución, Puerto San Carlos is a deep-water port from which Llano de Magdalena produce is shipped. From January through March, pangueros take up to five or six passengers for whale-watching excursions for US$35 per hour.

Places to Stay & Eat Free camping is possible north of town on the shabby public beach, but the whale-watching season strains regular accommodations. *Motel Las Brisas* (☎ 6-01-52), on Madero, has basic but clean rooms from US$11/13 for singles/doubles and *Hotel Palmar* (☎ 6-00-35), on Puerto Morelos, charges US$13/16. *Hotel Alcatraz* (☎ 6-00-17) has singles/doubles with TV for US$30/40; its *Restaurant Bar El Patio* is the town's best eatery.

There is an inexpensive stand at Calle Puerto La Paz and Calle Puerto Madero, around the corner from Las Brisas, that has tremendous shrimp tacos.

Getting There & Away From a small house on Calle Puerto Morelos, Autotransportes Águilar runs two buses daily, at 7.30 am and 1.45 pm, to Ciudad Constitución (US$3) and La Paz (US$10). This is the only public transportation to and from Puerto San Carlos.

La Paz & Los Cabos

The southernmost part of the peninsula gets more visitors than any other area except the border region.

LA PAZ
pop 154,314; ☎ *112*

Hernán Cortés established Baja's first European outpost near La Paz, but permanent settlement waited until 1811. US troops occupied the city during the Mexican-American War (1846-48). In 1853 the quixotic American adventurer William Walker proclaimed a 'Republic of Lower California,' but he left soon after under Mexican pressure.

After Walker's fiasco La Paz settled down. It had a rich pearl industry but that pretty nearly disappeared during the revolution of 1910-20. Today the capital of Baja California Sur is a peaceful place with beautiful beaches, a palm-lined malecón, a handful of colonial buildings and spectacular sunsets over the bay. It is also a popular winter resort, whose port of Pichilingue receives ferries from the mainland ports of Topolobampo and Mazatlán.

Orientation

Approaching La Paz from the southwest, the Transpeninsular becomes Calzada (Calle) Abasolo as it runs parallel to the bay. Four blocks east of 5 de Febrero, Abasolo becomes Paseo Obregón, leading along the palm-lined malecón toward Península Pichilingue.

La Paz's grid makes basic orientation easy, but the center's crooked streets and alleys change names almost every block. Four blocks southeast of the tourist pier, Jardín Velasco (Plaza Constitución) is the city's heart.

Information

Immigration Servicios Migratorios (☎ 5-34-93), on the second floor of the Edificio Milhe at Paseo Obregón 2140 between Allende and Juárez, is open weekdays 8 am to 8 pm.

Tourist Office The well-organized, English-speaking staff at the Coordinación Estatal de Turismo (☎ 2-59-39), on the waterfront at Paseo Obregón and 16 de Septiembre, distribute a variety of leaflets and keep a current list of hotel rates. The office is open weekdays 8 am to 8 pm, Saturdays 9 am to 1 pm.

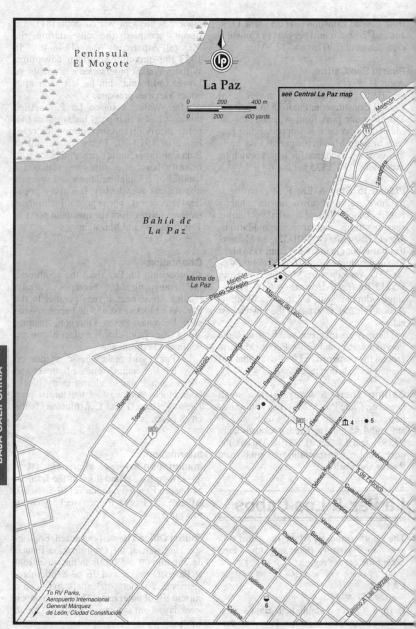

Península
El Mogote

La Paz

0   200   400 m
0   200   400 yards

see Central La Paz map

Bahía de
La Paz

Marina de
La Paz

Malecón
Paseo Obregón

Malecón

Zaragoza

Bravo

Márquez de León

Atasso

Domínguez

Madero

Revolución

Aquiles Serdán

Ramírez

Paseo

Altamirano

Rangel

Topete

Navarro

5 de Febrero

Cuauhtémoc

Gómez Farías

Sonora

Veracruz

Puebla

Sinaloa

Nayarit

Oaxaca

Jalisco

Colima

Camino A Las Garzas

1

2

3

4   5

6

To RV Parks,
Aeropuerto Internacional
General Márquez
de León, Ciudad Constitución

BAJA CALIFORNIA

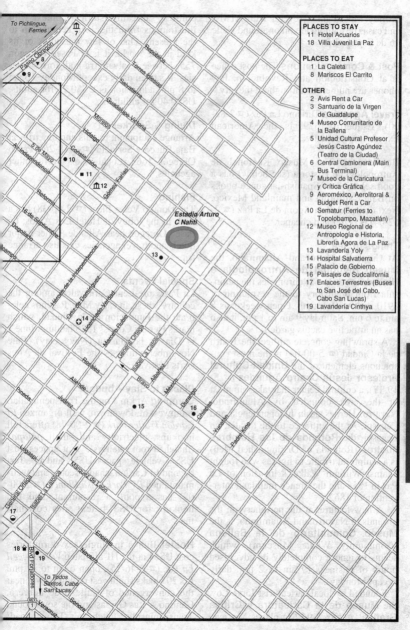

PLACES TO STAY
11 Hotel Acuarios
18 Villa Juvenil La Paz

PLACES TO EAT
1 La Caleta
8 Mariscos El Carrito

OTHER
2 Avis Rent a Car
3 Santuario de la Virgen
de Guadalupe
4 Museo Comunitario de
la Ballena
5 Unidad Cultural Profesor
Jesús Castro Agúndez
(Teatro de la Ciudad)
6 Central Camionera (Main
Bus Terminal)
7 Museo de la Caricatura
y Crítica Gráfica
9 Aeroméxico, Aerolitoral &
Budget Rent a Car
10 Sematur (Ferries to
Topolobampo, Mazatlán)
12 Museo Regional de
Antropología e Historia,
Librería Agora de La Paz
13 Lavandería Yoly
14 Hospital Salvatierra
15 Palacio de Gobierno
16 Paisajes de Sudcalifornia
17 Enlaces Terrestres (Buses
to San José del Cabo,
Cabo San Lucas)
19 Lavandería Cinthya

Money Most banks (several with ATMs) and casas de cambio are on or around Calle 16 de Septiembre.

Post & Communications The post office is at Constitución and Revolución. Pay phones are numerous throughout the city.

Travel Agencies Turismo La Paz (☎ 2-83-00), Esquerro 1679, is the American Express representative.

Bookstores The Museo Regional de Antropología e Historia (see below) has a good selection of Spanish-language books on Baja California and mainland Mexico. Next door, Librería Agora de La Paz (☎ 2-62-04) is better and cheaper.

Things to See

At Cinco de Mayo and Altamirano, the **Museo Regional de Antropología e Historia** (☎ 2-01-62) chronicles the peninsula from prehistory to the revolution of 1910 and its aftermath. Open weekdays 8 am to 6 pm, Saturday 9 am to 1 pm, it also has an attractive cactus garden.

A sprawling concrete edifice, the Teatro de la Ciudad (☎ 5-00-04) is the most conspicuous element of the **Unidad Cultural Profesor Jesús Castro Agúndez** (☎ 5-19-17), a cultural center that takes up most of the area bounded by Altamirano, Navarro, Héroes de la Independencia and Legaspi. At the entrance to the theater, on Legaspi, the **Rotonda de los Hombres Ilustres** (Rotunda of Distinguished Men) is a sculptural tribute to figures who fought against William Walker's invasion of La Paz in 1853 and the French mainland intervention of 1862.

A new feature, at the periphery on the grounds at Navarro and Altamirano, is the **Museo Comunitario de la Ballena** (Community Whale Museum), which seems to ignore completely its advertised hours of business (9 am to 2 pm, daily except Monday).

Founded by local caricaturist Jorge Loy, the **Museo de la Caricatura y Crítica Gráfica** (☎ /fax 2-96-61) places Mexican political satire in historical context with illustrations from the 19th century up to the present. One of few museums of its kind in the world, it is at Paseo Obregón 755, between Salvatierra and Torres Iglesias. It's open daily except Monday 10 am to 8 pm; admission is US$0.75 for adults, US$0.40 for children.

Diving & Snorkeling

Arrange equipment rentals and day trips at Baja Buceo y Servicio (☎ 2-18-26), Paseo Obregón 1663, Local 2, or several other agencies.

Fishing

The Dorado Vélez Fleet (☎ 2-00-38) has a desk in the lobby of Hotel Los Arcos, on Paseo Obregón near Allende. Other major hotels and travel agencies can also arrange trips.

Special Events

La Paz's pre-Lent Carnaval is among the country's best. In early May, Paceños celebrate the Fundación de la Ciudad, which marks Hernán Cortés' 1535 landing. June 1 is Día de la Marina (Navy Day). Late November witnesses the Festival de Artes (Arts Festival).

Places to Stay – budget

Camping At km 4 on the Transpeninsular, southwest of downtown, well-organized *El Cardón Trailer Park* (☎ 2-00-78) offers full hookups, electricity and small *palapas* (thatched-roof shelters). Tent spaces cost US$6, vehicle spaces US$8 and up. Just beyond El Cardón, shady, secure and well-maintained *RV Park Casa Blanca* (☎ 2-00-09) has a pool, a restaurant, and full hookups for US$14; tent sites cost half that.

Hostel Bunks in single-sex dormitories cost US$4 at the HI-affiliated *Villa Juvenil La Paz* (☎ 2-46-15), open 6 am to 11 pm. It's 20 blocks southwest of downtown, near the convergence of Calle 5 de Febrero, Camino A Las Garzas and the southbound Transpeninsular; catch any 'Universidad'

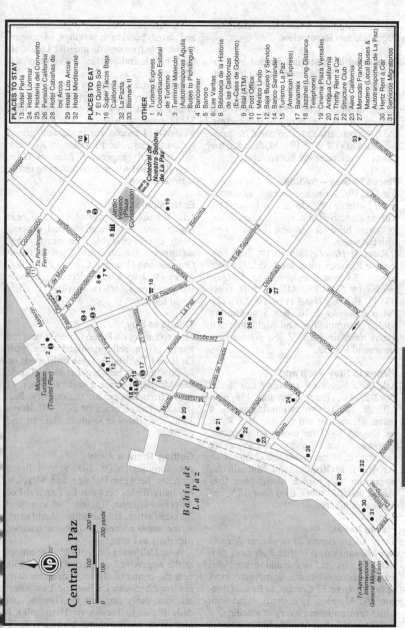

Central La Paz

0   100   200 m
0   100   200 yards

Muelle Turístico (Tourist Pier)

Bahía de La Paz

To Pichilingue Ferries

Catedral de Nuestra Señora de La Paz

Jardín Velasco (Plaza Constitución)

To Aeropuerto Internacional General Márquez de León

PLACES TO STAY
13 Hotel Perla
24 Hotel Lorimar
25 Hostería del Convento
26 Pensión California
28 Hotel Cabañas de los Arcos
29 Hotel Los Arcos
32 Hotel Mediterrané

PLACES TO EAT
7   El Quinto Sol
16 Super Tacos Baja California
32 La Pazta
33 Bismark II

OTHER
1   Turismo Express
2   Coordinación Estatal de Turismo
3   Terminal Malecón (Autotransportes Águila Buses to Pichilingue)
4   Bancomer
5   Banoro
6   Las Varitas
8   Biblioteca de la Historia de las Californias (Ex-Casa de Gobierno)
9   Bital (ATM)
10 Post Office
11 México Lindo
12 Baja Buceo y Servicio
14 Banco Santander
15 Turismo La Paz
17 Banamex (American Express)
18 Jazahel (Long-Distance Telephone)
19 Cinema Plaza Versalles
20 Antigua California
21 Thrifty Rent a Car
22 Structure Club
23 Aero California
27 Mercado Francisco Madero (Local Buses & Autotransportes de La Paz)
30 Hertz Rent a Car
31 Servicios Migratorios

bus from Mercado Francisco Madero, at Degollado and Revolución.

Pensiones & Hosterías Shaded by tropical plants, its walls lined with quirky art, *Pensión California* (☎ 2-28-96), Degollado 209, is a budget favorite at US$7/11 for singles/doubles with ceiling fans and showers. Rates are identical at the clean and basic but dark and dilapidated *Hostería del Convento* (☎ 2-35-08), Madero 85; the toilets are tolerable but not spotless.

Places to Stay – middle
For US$19/23 singles/doubles, expanded *Hotel Lorimar* (☎ 5-38-22), at Bravo 110, with an attractive patio, is a popular choice. Its rooms have air-con and tiled showers with hot water.

Rates at *Hotel Acuarios* (☎ 2-92-66), Ignacio Ramírez 1665, are US$25/27 with air-con, TV and telephone. *Hotel Mediterrané* (☎ 5-11-95), Allende 36B, costs US$44. Historic *Hotel Perla* (☎ 2-07-77), Paseo Obregón 1570, has a swimming pool, restaurant, bar and nightclub. All rooms have air-con, TV and private bath for around US$50.

Places to Stay – top end
Ask for a bay view at *Hotel Los Arcos* (☎ 2-27-44), Paseo Obregón 498 near Allende. It has two swimming pools, a sauna, a restaurant and a coffee shop. Rates are about US$83 for rooms with air-con, telephone, color TV and shower. Prices are comparable at nearby *Hotel Cabañas de los Arcos*, at Rosales and Mutualismo, where the lush garden rooms have fireplaces, thatched roofs, tiled floors, TV, air-con and minibars.

Places to Eat
Super Tacos Baja California, at Arreola and Mutualismo, is higher than most taco stands, but its quality fish and shrimp, plus exceptional condiments, justify the extra peso. *Mariscos El Carrito*, at Paseo Obregón and Morelos, is a shady stand with tables for taco-lovers weary of standing.

El Quinto Sol, at Avenida Independencia and Domínguez, has tasty vegetarian meals and large breakfast servings of yogurt (plain, with fruit or with muesli). Licuados, fresh breads and pastries are some of the other specialties.

Popular *La Caleta*, on the malecón at Pineda, serves reasonably priced meals and drinks. *La Pazta* (☎ 5-11-95), in the Hotel Mediterrané, at Allende 36B, just southwest of the malecón, has moderately priced Italian specials, but drinks are small, weak and relatively expensive. *Bismark II*, at Degollado and Altamirano, offers generous seafood platters.

Entertainment
Las Varitas, Independencia 111, near Domínguez, has live music and dancing (with cover charge). The current hot nightspot is the *Structure Club*, at Paseo Obregón and Ocampo. *Cinema Plaza Versalles* (☎ 2-95-55), on Revolución near Independencia, offers first-run international films.

Things to Buy
México Lindo, on Paseo Obregón near the tourist office, sells mainland items, post cards and T-shirts. Antigua California, on Paseo Obregón between Lerdo de Tejada and Muelle, features a wide selection of crafts from throughout the country. Paisajes de Sudcalifornia (☎ 3-37-00), Bravo 1890, specializes in southern Baja art and crafts.

Getting There & Away
Air Aeroméxico (☎ 2-00-91), at Paseo Obregón between Hidalgo and Morelos, has daily flights between La Paz and Los Angeles, Tijuana, Tucson and mainland Mexican cities. Its subsidiary Aerolitoral, at the same address and phone number, flies daily to Loreto.

Aero California (☎ 5-10-23) has offices at the airport and at Paseo Obregón 550, near the corner of Bravo; it operates daily nonstops between La Paz and Los Angeles, one daily nonstop to Tijuana, and daily flights to Tucson via Hermosillo. It also flies to mainland Mexican destinations, including Los Mochis (for the Barranca del Cobre railway), Mazatlán and Mexico City.

Bus ABC (☎ 2-30-63) and Autotransportes Águila (☎ 2-42-70) use the Central Camionera at Jalisco and Héroes de la Independencia. Northbound ABC buses go to Ciudad Constitución (three hours, US$5.50), Ensenada (22 hours, US$43), Guerrero Negro (12 hours, US$25), Loreto (5½ hours, US$10), Mulegé (eight hours, US$13), San Ignacio (10 hours, US$20) and Tijuana (24 hours, US$48).

Frequent southbound ABC buses serve San José del Cabo (two hours, US$8) and intermediates via the Transpeninsular. Autotransportes Águila takes highway 19 to Todos Santos (US$3) and Cabo San Lucas (US$6) at least five times daily.

Buses by Autotransportes de La Paz (☎ 2-21-57) leave the Mercado Francisco Madero, at Revolución and Degollado, for Todos Santos, Cabo San Lucas and San José del Cabo five times daily.

Car & Motorcycle Rental rates start around US$45 per day with 300 km free; taxes and insurance are extra. The least expensive agency is probably Félix (☎ 1-62-54, ext 13, ext 112, fax 1-63-69), at the Hotel Marina, at km 2.5 on the Pichilingue road, highway 11. Budget (☎ 2-10-97) is on Paseo Obregón between Morelos and Hidalgo.

Ferry Ferries to Mazatlán and Topolobampo leave from Pichilingue, 23 km north of La Paz, but the Sematur offices (☎ 5-38-33) are at Prieto and 5 de Mayo in La Paz. Before shipping any vehicle to the mainland, officials require a vehicle permit (see the Car & Motorcycle section of the introductory Getting There & Away chapter for details on bringing a car into Mexico). Vehicle permits are obtainable at Pichilingue weekdays 8 am to 3 pm, weekends 9 am to 1 pm, but it's probably safer to get one in Tijuana, Mexicali or Ensenada. Confirm tickets by 2 pm the day before departure; at 3 pm that day, unconfirmed cabins are sold on a first-come, first-served basis.

Weather permitting (high winds often delay winter sailings), the ferry to Mazatlán departs at 3 pm daily except Saturday, arriving at 9 am the following day; the return schedule is identical. Approximate passenger fares are US$21 in salón (numbered seats), US$41 in turista (two- to four-bunk cabins with shared bath), US$61 in *cabina* (two bunks with private bath), and US$81 in *especial* (suite).

The Topolobampo ferry sails at 8 pm daily except Tuesday, arriving at 6 am; the return ferry leaves at 9 am daily except Monday, arriving in La Paz at 6 pm. Passenger fares are US$13 in salón, US$27 in turista, US$41 in cabina and US$54 in especial.

Vehicle rates vary with vehicle length:

Vehicle Length	Fare to Topolobampo	Fare to Mazatlán
Car		
Up to 5 meters	US$190	US$116
5.01 to 6.5 meters	US$247	US$151
With trailer up to 9 meters	US$342	US$209
9.01 to 17 meters	US$646	US$393
Motorcycle	US$25	US$15

Yacht Between November and March, the Marina de La Paz, southwest of central La Paz, can be a good place to hitch a lift on a yacht to mainland Mexico.

Getting Around
To/From the Airport The government-regulated Transporte Terrestre minivan service (☎ 5-32-74, 5-62-29) charges US$7 per person to or from the airport. Private taxis cost about US$13 but may be shared.

To/From the Ferry Terminal From the Terminal Malecón (☎ 2-78-98), at Paseo Obregón and Avenida Independencia, Autotransportes Águila goes to Pichilingue (US$1) hourly between 7 am and 6 pm.

Bus Most local buses leave from Mercado Francisco Madero, which is at Degollado and Revolución.

AROUND LA PAZ
Beaches
On Península Pichilingue, the beaches nearest to La Paz are **Playa Palmira** (with the Hotel Palmira and a marina) and **Playa Coromuel** and **Playa Caimancito** (both with restaurant-bars, toilets and palapas). **Playa Tesoro**, the next beach north, also has a restaurant.

Camping is possible at **Playa Pichilingue**, 100 meters north of the ferry terminal, and it has a restaurant and bar, toilets and shade. The road is paved to **Playa Balandra** and **Playa Tecolote** (where windsurf rentals are available). Balandra is problematic for camping because of insects in the mangroves, and Tecolote lacks potable water. **Playa Coyote**, on the gulf, is more isolated. Particularly stealthy thieves break into campers' vehicles in all these areas, especially the more remote ones.

LOS BARRILES
pop 590; ☎ *112*
South of La Paz, the Transpeninsular brushes the gulf at Los Barriles, Baja's windsurfing capital. Brisk westerlies, averaging 20 to 25 knots, descend the 1800-meter cordillera.

Several fairly good dirt roads follow the coast south. Beyond Cabo Pulmo and Bahía Los Frailes, they are rough but passable for vehicles with good clearance and a short wheelbase. However, south of the junction with the road to the village of Palo Escopeta and San José del Cabo's international airport, the road is impassable for RVs and difficult for most other vehicles, rendered so by the rains of November 1993. Pedestrians, mountain bikers, burros and mules will do just fine.

Places to Stay & Eat
Crowded *Martín Verdugo's Trailer Park* charges US$8 for a small vehicle or US$10 for a larger one, with hot showers, full hookups, laundry and a sizable paperback book exchange. Camping costs US$5. Well-organized, Chilean-run *Juanito's Garden* charges US$10 with full hookups.

Other than camping, Los Barriles lacks inexpensive accommodations. *Casa Miramar* (☎ 5-36-36), at km 109, is a B&B catering mostly to windsurfers. Rates are US$40/60 singles/doubles, but there is also a bunk room for US$25 per person. *Hotel Playa del Sol* (☎ 1-00-44) offers clean, comfortable singles/doubles for US$70/100, including meals. The room rates are comparable at *Hotel Palmas de Cortez* (☎ 1-00-44).

Popular with gringos, *Tío Pablo* has a good pizza menu and massive portions of Mexican specialties like chicken fajitas, but the margaritas are weak. Despite the raucous decor and satellite TV, it's fairly sedate.

RESERVA DE LA BIOSFERA SIERRA DE LA LAGUNA
Even travelers who deplore the ugly coastal development around Los Cabos will enjoy the Sierra de La Laguna, an ecological treasure. Several foothill villages provide access to these unique interior mountains.

Tranquil **Santiago**, 10 km south of the junction for La Rivera and 2.5 km west of the Transpeninsular, once witnessed a bloody Pericú Indian revolt against the Jesuits. Its modest *Hotel Palomar* has singles/doubles amid pleasant grounds for about US$20/25, with cheaper tent sites, but the place is more notable for its moderately priced seafood than for its accommodations. The English-speaking owner is a good source of information.

Cañón San Dionisio, about 25 km west of Santiago, is the northernmost of three major east-west walking routes across the sierra; the others are **Cañón San Bernardo**, west of Miraflores, and **Cañón San Pedro**, west of Caduaño. San Dionisio offers scenic hiking in an ecologically unique area where cacti, palms, oaks, aspens and pines grow side by side. The trail requires scrambling over large granite boulders; if rainfall has been sufficient, there are pools suitable for swimming.

The best guide for hiking these routes is Walt Peterson's *Baja Adventure Book*.

SAN JOSÉ DEL CABO
pop 21,737; ☎ 114

Attacks by terrorist developers have not yet succeeded in transforming San José del Cabo, a quaint town of narrow streets, Spanish-style buildings and shady plazas, into a major tourist resort. Grandiose plans for a yacht marina at the outlet of the ecologically sensitive Arroyo San José fizzled because of local opposition, and, having maintained its open space, San José remains a far more pleasant destination than congested, overdeveloped Cabo San Lucas.

The Fiesta de San José, on March 19, celebrates the town's patron saint.

Orientation
San José del Cabo consists of San José proper, about 1.5 km inland, and a *zona hotelera* of tacky beachfront hotels, condominiums and time-shares. Linking the two areas, just south of shady Plaza Mijares, Boulevard José Antonio Mijares is a *gringolandia* of restaurants and souvenir shops (but tasteful and tranquil in comparison to Cabo San Lucas).

Information
Tourist Office The staff at the Dirección General de Turismo Municipal (☎ 2-04-46), on Plaza Mijares, could be more helpful, but the supply of printed matter is increasing. Hours are weekdays 8 am to 3 pm.

Money The casa de cambio at Aeropuerto Internacional Los Cabos offers very poor rates, so avoid changing money until you get to town, where several casas de cambio keep long hours.

Banks pay better rates, but keep shorter hours. Bancomer, at the corner of Zaragoza and Morelos, and Banca Serfin, at Zaragoza and Degollado, both cash traveler's checks and have ATMs; Bancomer has longer lines, but Serfin will not cash more than US$200.

Post & Communications The post office is at Boulevard Mijares and Valerio González. Direct and collect calls to the USA

are fairly simple from the cabinas on Doblado across from the hospital, but pay phones are more common than in the past.

Things to See
Between raids on Spanish galleons, 18th century pirates took refuge at the freshwater **Arroyo San José**, now a protected wildlife area replenished by a subterranean spring. From the corner of Juárez a newly constructed, palm-lined pedestrian trail along the estuary parallels Boulevard Mijares all the way to the zona hotelera – a delightful alternative to the busy boulevard. Among the common bird species along the trail are coots, pelicans, herons, egrets, plovers and many others.

Off to a good start, San José's new cultural center, **Los Cabos Centro Cultural**, features small but meaningful exhibits on pre-Columbian peoples, their rock art and subsistence, and the natural history of whales, plus a collection of historical photographs that could use more narration. At the east end of Paseo San José alongside the estuary, it's open daily except Monday 9 am to 5 pm; admission is US$0.75.

Beaches
Playa del Nuevo Sol and its eastward extension, **Playa de California**, are at the south end of Boulevard Mijares. **Pueblo La Playa** is a small fishing community about 2.5 km east of the junction of Juárez and Boulevard Mijares.

Fishing
In San José proper, Deportiva Piscis (☎ 2-03-02), on Castro near Ibarra, arranges fishing excursions and also sells and rents tackle. Fishermen at Pueblo La Playa arrange similar trips; ask them in the late afternoon as they cut up the day's catch on the beach.

Surfing
The best source of surfing information is Killer Hook Surf Shop (☎ 2-24-30), on Hidalgo between Zaragoza and Doblado, which also rents fishing gear and mountain bikes.

BAJA CALIFORNIA

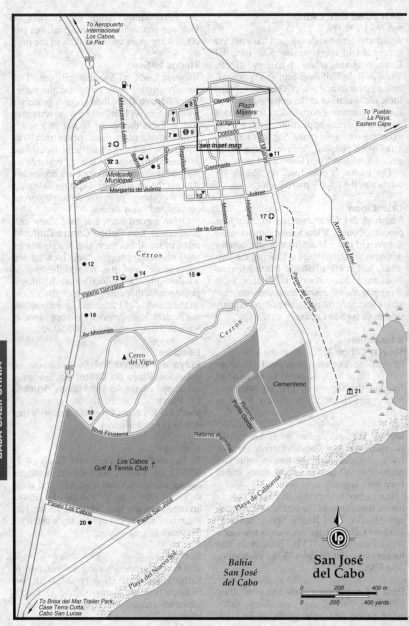

To Aeropuerto
Internacional
Los Cabos,
La Paz

To Pueblo
La Playa,
Eastern Cape

Plaza
Mijares

Obregón

Zaragoza

Doblado

Guerrero

see inset map

Marqués de León

Ibarra

Green

Degollado

Castro

Mercado
Municipal

Margarita de Juárez

Coronado

Juárez

Morelos

Hidalgo

de la Cruz

Cerros

Valerio González

Av Misiones

Cerros

Cerro
del Vigía

Cementerio

Blvd Mijares

Arroyo San José

Paseo del Estero

Blvd Finisterra

Retorno Palmilla

Retorno Punta Gaviota

Los Cabos
Golf & Tennis Club

Paseo Los Cabos

Paseo San José

Playa de California

Playa del Nuevo Sol

To Brisa del Mar Trailer Park,
Case Terra Cotta,
Cabo San Lucas

Bahía
San José
del Cabo

San José
del Cabo

0   200   400 m
0   200   400 yards

BAJA CALIFORNIA

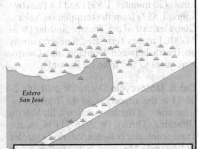

Estero
San José

PLACES TO STAY
7 Posada Terranova
8 San José Inn
19 Howard Johnson Plaza
   Suite Resort
26 Posada Señor Mañana
32 Hotel Ceci
38 Hotel Tropicana

PLACES TO EAT
6 Barra La Navidad
10 El Paraje (The Tree House)
23 Kokopelli's
1 Jazmín's
27 Damiana
29 Café Fiesta

OTHER
1 Pemex
2 Hospital Municipal
3 Telephone Office
4 Enlaces Terrestres
   (Buses to La Paz)
5 Deportiva Piscis
9 Banca Serfín (ATM)

11 Eclipse
12 Dollar Rent a Car
13 Bus Terminal
14 Lavamática San José
15 Lavandería Vera
16 Post Office
17 Cruz Roja
18 Thrifty Rent a Car
20 Mexicana
21 Los Cabos Centro
   Cultural
22 Galería de Arte
   Da Vinci
25 Iglesia San José
28 Copal
30 Casa de Cambio
31 Bancomer (ATM)
33 Antigua Los Cabos
34 Killer Hook Surf Shop
35 Dirección General de
   Turismo Municipal
36 Palacio Municipal
37 Thrifty Rent a Car
39 La Mina

Places to Stay – budget & middle

Camping Free camping is possible at Pueblo La Playa. The best paying site, also at Pueblo La Playa, is Swedish-run *El Delfín RV Park* (☎ 2-11-99), which is too small for RVs but excellent for tents (US$9). It also has cozy twin-bedded cabañas for US$26/32. singles/doubles.

Hostel & Hotels Though urgently in need of a plasterer and a painter, the friendly *San José Inn* (☎ 2-24-64), on Obregón between Degollado and Guerrero, has spacious singles/doubles with private baths, ceiling fans and hot water for US$10/13; it also offers (unofficial) hostel accommodations for as little as US$5 per person. Comparably priced *Hotel Ceci* (☎ 2-00-51), Zaragoza 22, has 20 clean, redecorated rooms with private showers and air-con, but it gets crowded in high season.

Woodsy, casual *Posada Señor Mañana* (☎ 2-04-62), Obregón 1 just north of Plaza Mijares, may be San José's best value, starting at US$25/30, though some rooms are higher. Inviting *Posada Terranova* (☎ 2-05-34), on Degollado between Doblado and Zaragoza, has singles/doubles for US$40/45, plus a good restaurant.

Places to Stay – top end

Probably the best hotel in San José proper, the inconspicuous *Hotel Tropicana* (☎ 2-09-09), on Boulevard Mijares, has doubles with satellite TV for US$65. At the *Howard Johnson Plaza Suite Resort* (☎ 2-09-09), on Boulevard Finisterra overlooking Los Cabos Golf and Tennis Club, rates start at US$90.

Places to Eat

The very clean *Mercado Municipal*, on Ibarra between Coronado and Castro, has numerous stalls offering simple and inexpensive but good and filling meals.

Kokopelli's, on Obregón near Morelos, serves superb breakfast burritos in pleasant surroundings but may change hands. *Café Fiesta*, on the east side of Plaza Mijares, has good breakfasts, light meals and desserts and pleasant outdoor seating, but prices are on the high side.

Jazmín's, on Morelos between Obregón and Zaragoza, offers a wide variety of tasty breakfasts, plus lunches and dinners at midrange prices, with excellent but unobtrusive service and, incongruously, a paperback book exchange. *Barra La Navidad*, a bit out of the way on Degollado near Obregón, has outstanding beef but also prepares vegetarian brochettes; it has outdoor seating.

In a restored 18th century house on Plaza Mijares, *Damiana* is a romantic seafood restaurant. *El Paraje* (also known as *The Tree House*), in an attractive adobe structure with a palapa roof at the corner of Guerrero and Margarita de Juárez, serves outstanding fish, fowl, meat and antojitos; it provides outside seating for warm nights or to flee the live entertainment from local Neil Diamond wannabes.

Entertainment

Noisy nightlife doesn't dominate San José the way it does Cabo San Lucas, but clubs like *Eclipse*, on Boulevard Mijares north of Coronado, satisfy most partygoers. *La Playita*, part of its namesake hotel in Pueblo La Playa, offers live jazz several nights a week.

Things to Buy

Antigua Los Cabos, in a mission-style building on Zaragoza between Morelos and Hidalgo, offers a nicely displayed selection of handcrafted household items like sturdy glassware, plates, mugs and wall hangings. Copal, on the west side of Plaza Mijares, has an interesting assortment of crafts, especially masks.

Galería de Arte Da Vinci, an attractive space at Morelos 11, displays and sells works by local, national and international artists. La Mina, on Boulevard Mijares between Doblado and Coronado, sells gold and silver jewelry in an imaginative setting.

Getting There & Away

Air Mexicana (☎ 2-15-30, 2-06-06 at the airport), the only airline with offices in town, is on Paseo Los Cabos at the Plaza Los Cabos mall. It flies daily to Los Angeles and Mexico City, less frequently to Denver. All other airlines have their offices at the airport, which serves both San José and Cabo San Lucas.

Alaska Airlines (☎ 2-10-15) flies daily to San Diego, San Francisco and Phoenix, less frequently to Los Angeles and San José (California, USA). Aero California (☎ 2-09-43, fax 2-09-42) flies at least daily to Los Angeles, Phoenix and Denver.

Continental Airlines (☎ 2-38-40) flies daily between Houston and Los Cabos, while America West (☎ 2-28-80) serves Phoenix daily. Aeroméxico (☎ 2-03-41) flies daily to San Diego and many mainland Mexican destinations, with international connections via Mexico City.

Bus Frequent buses leave for Cabo San Lucas (30 minutes, US$1) and La Paz (two hours, US$7) from the terminal on Valerio González east of the Transpeninsular (☎ 2-11-00). Enlaces Terrestres, a new company on Ibarra between Doblado and Castro, runs buses to and from La Paz only.

Car & Motorcycle Dollar (☎ 2-01-00, 2-06-71 at the airport) is on the Transpeninsular north of the intersection with Valerio González. Thrifty (☎ 2-16-71) is on the Transpeninsular between Valerio González and Avenida Misiones, with another office at Doblado and Mijares.

Getting Around

To/From the Airport The official, government-run company Aeroterrestre (☎ 2-05-55) runs bright yellow taxis and minibuses to Aeropuerto Internacional Los Cabos, 10 km north of San José, for about US$12, divisible by the number of passengers. Local buses from the station to the airport junction cost less than US$1, but taking one means a half-hour walk to the terminal.

LOS CABOS CORRIDOR

West of San José, all the way to Cabo San Lucas, a string of tacky luxury resorts blights the once scenic coastline. Around km 27, near *Hotel Palmilla*, are choice surfing beaches at **Punta Mirador** and at **km 28** of the Transpeninsular. Experienced surfers claim that summer reef and point breaks at km 28 (popularly known as Zipper's) match Hawaii's best.

CABO SAN LUCAS
pop 28,483; ☎ 114
By reputation Cabo San Lucas, 220 km south of La Paz, is a resort of international stature, but its quintessential experience might be to stagger out of a bar at 3 am, pass out on the beach, and be crushed or smothered at daybreak by a rampaging developer's bulldozer. Cabo's most sinister bottom-feeders are avaricious, unscrupulous developers and time-share sellers who have metamorphosed a placid fishing village into a depressing jumble of exorbitantly priced hotels, pretentious restaurants, rowdy bars and tacky souvenir stands – an achievement comparable to turning Cinderella into her stepsisters. Its status as a North American tourist enclave and retirement retreat has engendered resentment among Mexicans.

Orientation
Northwest of Calle Cárdenas, central Cabo has a fairly regular grid, while southeast of Cárdenas, Boulevard Marina curves along the western harbor toward Land's End. Few places have street addresses; so refer to the map to locate them.

Information
Immigration Servicios Migratorios (☎ 3-01-35) is at the corner of Cárdenas and Gómez Farías.

Tourist Office Cabo's Fondo Mixto de Promoción Turística (☎ 3-41-80), on Madero between Hidalgo and Guerrero, is open weekdays 9 am to 2 pm and 4 to 7 pm, Saturdays, 9 am to 1 pm.

US Consulate The US Consulate (☎ 3-35-36) is on the west side of Boulevard Marina, just south of Plaza Las Glorias.

Money Several downtown banks cash traveler's checks and have ATMs. Baja Money Exchange, whose most central office is on Plaza Náutica, on Boulevard Marina near Guerrero, changes at slightly lower rates than the banks but keeps longer hours. (Beware of usurious commissions on cash advances.)

Post & Communications The post office is on the south side of Cárdenas, near 16 de Noviembre, northeast of downtown. Long-distance cabinas have sprung up in many shops and pharmacies, and pay phones are abundant.

Dangers & Annoyances Beware time-share sellers on Boulevard Marina, though they distribute town maps and happily provide information (along with their sales pitch).

Beaches
For sunbathing and calm waters **Playa Médano**, in front of the Hacienda Beach Resort, on the Bahía de Cabo San Lucas, is ideal. **Playa Solmar**, on the Pacific, has a reputation for unpredictable, dangerous breakers. Nearly unspoiled **Playa del Amor**, near Land's End, is accessible by boat or a class-three scramble over the rocks (at least at high tide) from Hotel Solmar.

Diving
Among the best diving areas are Roca Pelícano, the sea lion colony off Land's End, and the reef off Playa Chileno, east of town. Some divers have complained of poor visibility near Land's End due to raw sewage from tourist hotels, though residents report that this situation has abated – ask dive shops about current conditions.

At most shops, two-tank dives cost around US$75, introductory courses around US$100 and full-certification courses from US$350 to US$400. Rental equipment is readily available at shops like Amigos del Mar (☎ 3-05-05), across from the sportfishing dock at the southern end of Boulevard Marina, and Cabo Acuadeportes

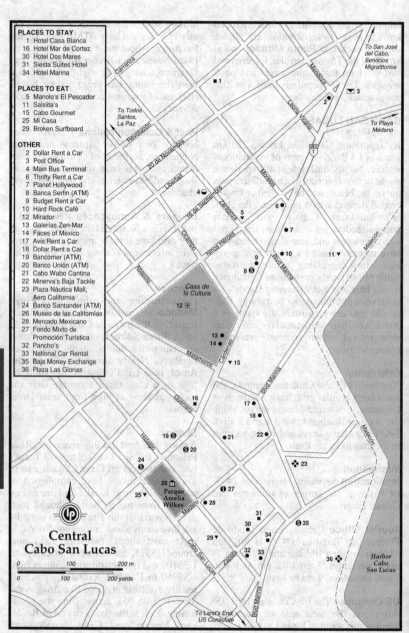

PLACES TO STAY
1 Hotel Casa Blanca
16 Hotel Mar de Cortez
30 Hotel Dos Mares
31 Siesta Suites Hotel
34 Hotel Marina

PLACES TO EAT
5 Manolo's El Pescador
11 Salsiita's
15 Cabo Gourmet
25 Mi Casa
29 Broken Surfboard

OTHER
2 Dollar Rent a Car
3 Post Office
4 Main Bus Terminal
7 Thrifty Rent a Car
7 Planet Hollywood
8 Banca Serfín (ATM)
9 Budget Rent a Car
10 Hard Rock Café
12 Mirador
13 Galerías Zen-Mar
14 Faces of Mexico
17 Avis Rent a Car
18 Dollar Rent a Car
19 Bancomer (ATM)
20 Banco Unión (ATM)
21 Cabo Wabo Cantina
22 Minerva's Baja Tackle
23 Plaza Náutica Mall,
   Aero California
24 Banco Santander (ATM)
26 Museo de las Californias
28 Mercado Mexicano
27 Fondo Mixto de
   Promoción Turística
32 Pancho's
33 National Car Rental
35 Baja Money Exchange
36 Plaza Las Glorias

Central Cabo San Lucas

0   100   200 m
0   100   200 yards

To San José
del Cabo,
Servicios
Migrattorios

To Playa
Médano

To Todos
Santos,
La Paz

Carranza
Mendoza
Leona Vicario
Revolución
20 de Noviembre
Libertad
16 de Septiembre
Zaragoza
Morelos
Niños Héroes
Ocampo
Abasolo
Matamoros
Cárdenas
Blvd Marina
Guerrero
Hidalgo
Madero
Zapata
Cabo San Lucas
Malecón

Casa de
la Cultura

Parque
Amelia
Wilkes

Harbor
Cabo
San Lucas

To Land's End,
US Consulate

BAJA CALIFORNIA

(☎ 3-01-17), in front of the Hacienda Beach Resort.

Fishing

Minerva's Baja Tackle (☎ 3-12-82), at Madero and Boulevard Marina, charters fishing boats and rents gear. Panga rates start around US$25 to US$30 per hour, with a four- to six-hour minimum for three people; 28-foot cruisers, for up to four passengers, cost US$275 to US$350 per hour. Sportfisher 31-footers can take five or six for US$400 to US$500 per hour.

Boat Trips

Trips to El Arco (the natural arch at Land's End), the sea-lion colony, and Playa del Amor on the yacht *Trinidad* (☎ 3-14-17) cost about US$15 to US$30 per hour. Dos Mares (☎ 3-32-66) sails glass-bottomed boats every 20 minutes from 9 am to 4 pm and will drop off and pick up passengers on Playa del Amor (US$6).

From the Plaza Las Glorias dock, *Pez Gato I* and *Pez Gato II* (☎ 3-24-58) offer two-hour sunset sailings on catamarans, which segregate their clientele into 'booze cruises' and 'romantic cruises'; prices are US$30 for adults, US$15 for children. The semisubmersible *Nautilus VII* offers similarly priced one-hour tours to view whales, dolphins and sea turtles; make reservations (☎ 3-30-33) at Boulevard Marina 39F or by calling Baja Tourist & Travel Services (☎ 3-19-34).

Special Events

Cabo San Lucas is a popular staging ground for fishing tournaments in October and November. One local celebration is Día de San Lucas, honoring the town's patron saint, on October 18.

Places to Stay – budget & middle

Except for camping and RV parks, even mid-range accommodations are scarce. Many visitors may prefer to stay in San José del Cabo, which is cheaper and close enough for day trips.

Camping Tents and RVs are welcome at *Surf Camp Club Cabo* (☎ 3-33-48), down a narrow dirt road east of town, toward San José del Cabo. Rates are US$10 per site; a cabaña and two kitchenette apartments are available for US$39, single or double.

About three km east of Cabo on the Transpeninsular, spacious but shadeless *Cabo Cielo* (☎ 3-07-21) has full hookups, spotless baths and excellent hot showers for US$10.

Hotels For US$17/20 singles/doubles, *Hotel Casa Blanca* (☎ 3-02-60), on Revolución near Morelos, has clean but run-down rooms with hot showers and ceiling fans. *Hotel Marina* (☎ 3-14-99), Boulevard Marina near Guerrero, has modest poolside rooms with air-con for US$30/50. The comparable *Hotel Dos Mares* (☎ 3-03-30), on Zapata between Hidalgo and Guerrero, charges US$35/40.

Pseudocolonial *Hotel Mar de Cortez* (☎ 3-14-32), at Cárdenas and Guerrero, has a pool and an outdoor bar/restaurant. Newer air-con rooms cost US$48/53 in high season, but older rooms are a good value for US$36/41. Off-season rates (June to October) are about 25% lower.

Siesta Suites Hotel (☎ /fax 3-27-73), on Zapata between Hidalgo and Guerrero, has kitchenette apartments for US$55 a double, plus US$10 for each additional person.

Places to Stay – top end

The *Hacienda Beach Resort* (☎ 3-01-22), on Paseo de la Marina near Playa Médano, has fountains, tropical gardens, tennis and paddle-tennis courts, a swimming pool and a putting green. Garden patio rooms start at US$150, but beach cabañas cost US$250.

All rooms face the Pacific at *Hotel Solmar* (☎ 3-00-22), a secluded beachfront resort near Land's End that has tennis courts, a pool and horseback riding. Singles and doubles start at US$156 in low season (June to October).

Places to Eat

Broken Surfboard, on Hidalgo between Madero and Zapata, serves up inexpensive burritos, burgers, fish with rice, salads, tortillas and beans and so forth. *Cabo Gourmet*, on Cárdenas between Matamoros and Ocampo, offers takeout sandwiches, cold cuts and cheeses.

Highly regarded *Salsitas*, in the Plaza Bonita mall on Boulevard Marina just south of Cárdenas, serves Mexican specialties. For fine and reasonably priced seafood, try the modest but friendly *Manolo's El Pescador*, at the corner of Zaragoza and Niños Héroes.

Near the eastern entrance to town, on Paseo del Pescador just south of Cárdenas and across from the Pemex station, popular *La Golondrina* is expensive but offers large portions. *El Rey Sol*, two blocks south of La Golondrina, serves appealing Mexican food and seafood; prices are moderate by Cabo standards.

Faro Viejo Trailer Park Restaurant, at Matamoros and Rosario Morales, northwest of Central Cabo San Lucas, lures the wealthy from their beachfront hotels for barbecued ribs, steaks and seafood. *Mi Casa*, on Calle Cabo San Lucas across from Parque Amelia Wilkes, has a pleasant, homey environment and excellent seafood. *Romeo y Julieta*, west of the point where Boulevard Marina turns east toward Land's End, is a local institution for pizza and pasta.

Entertainment
Gold records and rock photos line the walls of *Cabo Wabo Cantina*, on Guerrero between Madero and Cárdenas, which features live music from late at night to early in the morning. Barhoppers will reportedly find Mexico's largest selection of tequilas at *Pancho's*, on Hidalgo between Zapata and Boulevard Marina. The megatransnational bar scene has clobbered Cabo hard with the arrival of *Planet Hollywood* and the *Hard Rock Café*, both on Lázaro Cárdenas near Boulevard Marina.

Things to Buy
Cabo's most comprehensive shopping area, located at Madero and Hidalgo, is the sprawling Mercado Mexicano, containing dozens of stalls with crafts from all around the country. Faces of Mexico, on Cárdenas between Matamoros and Ocampo, has a good selection of crafts, including spectacular masks. Galerías Zen-Mar (☎ 3-06-61), almost next door, offers Zapotec Indian weavings, bracelets and masks, as well as traditional crafts from other mainland Indian peoples.

Getting There & Away
Air The closest airport is north of San José del Cabo; for flight information, see the San José del Cabo Getting There & Away section. Aero California's main office (☎ 3-37-00, fax 3-08-27) has moved to the Plaza Náutica mall, on Boulevard Marina near Madero.

Bus From the main terminal at Zaragoza and 16 de Septiembre (☎ 3-04-00), buses leave for San José del Cabo (30 minutes, US$1) and La Paz via Todos Santos (US$6) or San José del Cabo (US$8). Autotransportes de La Paz has a separate terminal at the junction of México 19 and the Cabo bypass, north of downtown, as does Enlaces Terrestres. These buses go to La Paz only.

Car & Motorcycle Numerous rental agencies have booths along Boulevard Marina and elsewhere in town.

Getting Around
To/From the Airport The government-regulated airport minibus (☎ 3-12-20, US$10 per person) leaves Plaza Las Glorias at 9 and 11 am, noon, and 1 and 3 pm. For US$20, shared taxis (☎ 3-00-90) can be a cheaper alternative for large groups.

Taxi Taxis are plentiful but not cheap; fares within town average about US$3 to US$5.

TODOS SANTOS
pop 3765; ☎ 114

Created in 1734 but nearly destroyed by the Pericú rebellion, Misión Santa Rosa de Todos los Santos limped along until its abandonment in 1840. In the late 19th century Todos Santos became a prosperous sugar town with several brick *trapiches* (mills), but depleted aquifers have nearly eliminated this thirsty industry. In recent years Todos Santos has seen a North American invasion, including artists from Santa Fe and Taos and organic farmers whose produce gets premium prices north of the border.

Orientation
Todos Santos has a regular grid, but residents rely more on landmarks than street names for directions. The plaza is surrounded by Márquez de León, Centenario, Legaspi and Avenida Hidalgo.

Information
Tourist Office Todos Santos' de facto tourist office is El Tecolote, an English-language bookstore that distributes a very detailed (some might say cluttered) town map and a sketch map of nearby beach areas. It's in a cluster of shops at the corner of Juárez and Avenida Hidalgo.

Money Change cash weekday mornings only at Banoro, at the corner of Juárez and Obregón, which now has an ATM. For traveler's checks, try Baja Money Exchange, at Heróico Colegio Militar and Hidalgo.

Post & Communications The post office is on Heróico Colegio Militar between Hidalgo and Márquez de León. The Message Center (☎ 5-02-88, fax 5-00-03), adjacent to El Tecolote at Juárez and Hidalgo, provides phone, fax and message services

Things to See
Scattered around town are several former trapiches, including **Molino El Progreso**, at what was formerly El Molino restaurant, and **Molino de los Santana**, on Juárez opposite the hospital. The restored **Teatro Cine General Manuel Márquez de León** is on the north side of the plaza.

Murals at the **Centro Cultural Todo-santeño**, a former schoolhouse on Juárez

across from Bancomer, date from 1933. They contain nationalist and revolutionary motifs such as missionaries and Indians, Spanish conquistadors, Emiliano Zapata, rural labor and industry, athletics and 'emancipation of the rural spirit.'

Special Events
Todos Santos' late January Festival de Artes (Arts Festival) lasts two days. At other times it's possible to visit local artists in their homes/studios. A tour of historic homes takes place in late February.

Places to Stay
Hotel Miramar (☎ 5-03-41), at the corner of Verduzco and Pedrajo southwest of the town center, is a bargain at US$8/11 singles/doubles. Remodeled *Motel Guluarte* (☎ 5-00-06), at Juárez and Morelos, now has a swimming pool; doubles cost about US$18.

Distinctive *Hotel California* (☎ 5-00-02), on Juárez between Márquez de León and Morelos, has a pool and clean rooms, each with private bath and ceiling fan, for about US$35/42. *Hostería Las Casitas* (☎ 5-02-55), a Canadian-run B&B on Calle Rangel between Obregón and Hidalgo, charges US$30 to US$50 per double with a superb breakfast and also offers inexpensive tent sites; its fine restaurant is open to the public.

Places to Eat
Taco stands along Heróico Colegio Militar between Márquez de León and Degollado offer fish, chicken, shrimp or beef at bargain prices. Family-run *Casa de Margarita*, on Pedrajo between Progreso and Villarino, has gained a devoted following for fine, reasonably priced antojitos and seafood; it has also taken over the Sunday champagne brunch from the now defunct El Molino Trailer Park restaurant.

The coffee-conscious can consume their cappuccinos with savory pastries or enticing fruit salads at *Caffé Todos Santos*, located on Centenario between Topete and Obregón. Moderately priced *Las Fuentes*, in a bougainvillea-shaded patio with three

BAJA CALIFORNIA

refreshing fountains on Degollado at Heróico Colegio Militar, has antojitos (try the chicken with mole sauce) and seafood specialties.

Prices are high at *Café Santa Fe*, which attracts patrons from La Paz and Cabo San Lucas to its plaza location for Italian dining, but it's worth a splurge.

Things to Buy

Galería de Todos Santos, at Topete and Legaspi, features imaginative artwork by Mexican and North American artists. Galería Santa Fe, alongside its namesake restaurant on the south side of the plaza, is well worth a visit, as is the Stewart Gallery, which is on Obregón between Legaspí and Centenario.

Getting There & Away

At least six buses go daily to La Paz (1½ hours, US$3) and also to Cabo San Lucas (1½ hours, US$3) from the bus station at Heróico Colegio Militar and Zaragoza.

Northwest Mexico

This chapter covers the northwestern state of Sonora, Los Mochis and Culiacán in the north of Sinaloa state, and the spectacular Barranca del Cobre (Copper Canyon) railway from Los Mochis to Chihuahua.

Many travelers pass through Sonora, a large state known for its beef, agriculture (principally wheat and cotton) and the great Desierto Sonorense (Sonora Desert) which covers much of the state. Highway 15, Mexico's principal Pacific coast highway, begins at the border town of Nogales, Sonora, opposite Nogales, Arizona, about 1½ hours' drive south of Tucson. This is one of the most convenient border crossings between western Mexico and the USA. From Nogales, highway 15/15D heads south through the Desierto Sonorense for about four hours' drive to Hermosillo and then cuts over to the coast at Guaymas, about 1½ hours south of Hermosillo. From Guaymas the highway parallels the beautiful Pacific coast for about 1000 km, finally turning inland at Tepic and heading on to Guadalajara and Mexico City. There are regular toll booths along highway 15 (including two between Nogales and Hermosillo, each charging US$4.25 per car).

It can be dangerous to travel on Sinaloa highways after dark – see Dangers & Annoyances in the Facts for the Visitor chapter.

Not to be missed, the Barranca del Cobre railway (the Chihuahua al Pacífico) between Los Mochis and Chihuahua traverses Copper Canyon, justifiably referred to as the 'Grand Canyon of Mexico.' Los Mochis is near Topolobampo, where the ferry from La Paz in Baja California reaches the mainland.

NOGALES
pop 250,000; alt 1170m; ☎ 631

Like its border-city cousins Tijuana, Ciudad Juárez, Nuevo Laredo and Matamoros, Nogales is a major transit point for goods

and people traveling between the USA and Mexico. On the northern side of the border in Arizona is its smaller US counterpart, also named Nogales. (The name means

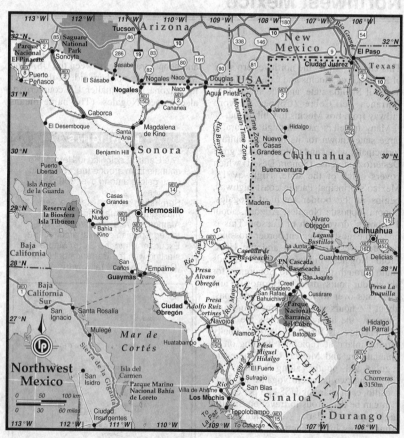

'walnuts,' a reference to the many walnut trees that once flourished here.)

Nogales presents an easier introduction to Mexico than Tijuana. Nogales has everything Tijuana has – curio shops overflowing with Mexican handicrafts, trinkets and souvenirs, Mexican restaurants, cheap bars and plenty of liquor stores – but all on a much smaller scale.

On the Arizona side, the small Pimería Alta Historical Society Museum (no phone) at 136 N Grand Ave at the intersection with Crawford, one block from the border crossing, has interesting exhibits on the history of Nogales. It's open Friday from 10 am to 5 pm, Saturday from 10 am to 4 pm, Sunday from 1 to 4 pm; admission is free but you are welcome to make a donation.

Orientation

The commercial section of Nogales is only a few blocks in width, being hemmed in on either side by hills. The main commercial street is Obregón, two blocks west of the border crossing, which eventually runs south into Mexico's highway 15. Almost everything is within walking distance of the border crossing; it's virtually impossible to get lost here.

Information

Immigration If you'll be heading farther south into Mexico, pick up a Mexican tourist card at the Migración office (see the Tourist Office section; it's in the same building), or at the customs and immigration desk in the Nogales (Mexico) bus station, open every day from 6 am to 10 pm. If you're staying within 21 km of the border you don't need a tourist card, but 21 km south of the border there's a checkpoint and if you don't have the proper paperwork, you'll be turned back. See the Facts for the Visitor chapter for more information on crossing the border between Mexico and the USA.

Tourist Office The Secretaría de Fomento al Turismo (☎ 2-06-66) is in the large, modern, white building at the border crossing, just west of the big white arches. The office is staffed weekdays from 8 am to 3 pm, but you can get access daily to its small selection of brochures, including a simple map of the Mexican side of Nogales.

Money There are plenty of casas de cambio, where you can change US dollars to pesos or vice versa, on both sides of the border crossing (no commission charged). On the Mexican side of Nogales, dollars and pesos are used interchangeably.

Post & Communications The post office on the Mexican side, on the corner of Juárez and Campillo, is open weekdays from 8 am to 7 pm, Saturday 8 am to noon. Next door, the Telecomm office is open the same hours, with telegram, telex and fax. Telephone casetas for long-distance calls are everywhere in the small Nogales shopping district.

Places to Stay

The *Hotel San Carlos* (☎ 2-13-46, fax 2-15-57) at Juárez 22 is very clean, with helpful staff; rooms have bathroom, air-con, TV and telephone. Singles/doubles are US$18/19 with one double bed, US$22

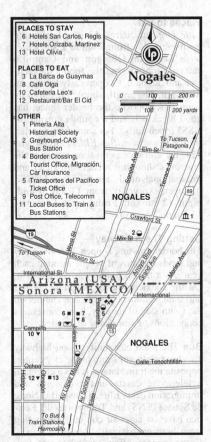

PLACES TO STAY
6   Hotels San Carlos, Regis
7   Hotels Orizaba, Martinez
13 Hotel Olivia

PLACES TO EAT
3   La Barca de Guaymas
8   Café Olga
10 Cafetería Leo's
12 Restaurant/Bar El Cid

OTHER
1   Pimería Alta
    Historical Society
2   Greyhound-CAS
    Bus Station
4   Border Crossing,
    Tourist Office, Migración,
    Car Insurance
5   Transportes del Pacífico
    Ticket Office
9   Post Office, Telecomm
11 Local Buses to Train &
    Bus Stations

Nogales

with two beds. The *Hotel Regis* (☎ 2-51-81) at Juárez 34 is a similar standard and has free coffee in the lobby; singles/doubles are US$19. Across the street, the very basic *Hotel Orizaba* (☎ 2-54-80) at Juárez 29 has rooms at US$10, some with private bath, some without. The *Hotel Olivia* (☎ 2-22-00/67, fax 2-46-95) at Obregón 125 is a good hotel with parking and a restaurant; the 51 clean rooms with air-con and other facilities cost US$18/20, or US$22 with two beds. If you just want to clean up before crossing the border, the *Hotel Martinez* at Juárez 33 will rent you a shower for US$1.30.

Places to Eat

Café Olga at Juárez 43 is a basic café open every day from 7 am to 2 am. *Cafeteria Leo's* on Obregón and Campillo caters to tourists, but the food's inexpensive and not bad; it's open daily from 8 am to 10 pm. The small, simple *La Barca de Guaymas*, opposite the border fence, has good breakfasts and a comida corrida for US$3 (open daily). For something fancier, try the *Restaurant/Bar El Cid* at Obregón 124; the entrance is up some stairs at the rear of a shopping arcade. Mexican and international meals are US$7 to US$17; it's open every day from 11 am to midnight (2 am on Friday and Saturday, 11 pm on Sunday).

Getting There & Away

The border crossing is open 24 hours a day and sends millions of people through each year. As a transit point, you can't beat it. On the Mexico side of Nogales, the bus and train stations, opposite one another on the south side of the city, have convenient connections to other parts of Mexico.

Bus The main bus station is on highway 15, about eight km south of the city center, opposite the train station. It has a cafeteria, a telephone caseta and a customs and immigration desk. Elite, Transportes Norte de Sonora (TNS) and Transportes del Pacífico have 1st-class air-con buses operating from here on basically the same routes. Each company offers around two to four buses daily to each destination, except to Hermosillo and Guaymas which are served every 30 minutes between 4 am and 11 pm. There's also Transportes Caballero Azteca, which has six daily buses to Chihuahua. Tufesa has its own station 400 meters nearer Nogales on the main road, and goes to Los Mochis (9 am), Ciudad Obregón (seven daily) and Culiacán (six daily), all stopping at Hermosillo. Tickets are available from the bus stations, though Transportes del Pacífico also has a ticket office in the town center on Pesqueira, open daily.

Bus distances, trip times and fares include:

Chihuahua – 962 km, 12 hours (US$26)
Guadalajara – 1692 km, 25 hours (US$56 to US$65)
Guaymas – 416 km, five hours (US$10 to US$12)
Hermosillo – 282 km, 3½ hours (US$7.25 to US$8)
Los Mochis – 765 km, 10 hours (US$19 to US$22)
Mazatlán – 1186 km, 16 hours (US$39 to US$45)
Mexico City (Terminal Norte) – 2227 km, 33 hours (US$71 to US$83)
Tepic – 1476 km, 21 hours (US$48 to US$55)

The USA The CAS bus coming from the Greyhound bus station in Tucson arrives in Nogales, Arizona, at the Greyhound bus station on Terrace Ave, a block from the border crossing; the station has luggage lockers. Nogales-Tucson buses depart at the same time in each direction daily: hourly on the hour from 9 am to 9 pm, except at 8 pm. The cost is US$6.50 for the 1½-hour ride. Shuttle minibuses (US$7) also leave regularly for Tucson from the car park just north of the Nogales bus station.

You can't take a bus or taxi through the border crossing into Mexico – you must either walk or drive. If you have a lot to carry, men and boys with handcarts will help carry your luggage across for a small tip.

Train The train station (☎ 3-10-91) is opposite the bus station, about eight km south of the city center on highway 15. Schedules for the primera especial Estrella del Pacífico and the segunda clase 'Burro' trains to Guadalajara are given in the Guadalajara section of the Western Central Highlands chapter. The ticket office sells Estrella del Pacífico tickets every day from 8 to 11 am and from 2 to 3.30 pm. Tickets for the 'Burro' are sold in the 90 minutes before departure.

Car & Motorcycle Approaching Nogales from Tucson, the left lanes go to central Nogales; the right lanes, which go to a vehicular border crossing outside the city (favored by trucks), are the quickest way to enter Mexico, but the crossing is only open from 6 am to 10 pm. Outside these hours you'll have to come through the city, where the border crossing is open 24 hours a day. As you approach Nogales you'll see plenty of signs for Mexican auto insurance, which you'll need if you're bringing a vehicle into Mexico. There's also an office for Mexican car insurance in the tourist office, open daily from 8 am to 8 pm (8 am to noon on Sunday).

Temporary vehicle import procedures are dealt with at the Aguazarca inspection site at the 21 km point on the highway south of Nogales. See the Car & Motorcycle section of the Getting There & Away chapter for more on bringing a vehicle into Mexico and on simplified procedures for those who are only visiting Sonora.

Getting Around
For the bus or train station, take a city bus marked 'Central' or 'Central Camionera'; they depart frequently from a corner on Avenida López Mateos two blocks south of the crossing (US$0.30). A taxi costs around US$4. Everything else you'll need in Nogales is within easy walking distance of the border crossing.

OTHER BORDER CROSSINGS
The Nogales border crossing is the quickest and easiest route when crossing the border in this region. There are other border crossings between Sonora and Arizona, however. West of Nogales, **San Luis Río Colorado** on the banks of the Río Colorado (Colorado River), 42 km southwest of Yuma, Arizona, has a 24-hour border crossing. **Sonoita**, opposite Lukeville, Arizona, and immediately south of the picturesque Organ Pipe Cactus National Monument on the Arizona side of the border, has another 24-hour crossing. About 130 km east of Nogales, **Agua Prieta** opposite Douglas, Arizona, also has a 24-hour crossing. All are on Mexican highway 2, with frequent bus connections on the Mexican side (though possibly not on the USA side between San Luis Río Colorado and Yuma).

El Sásabe, opposite Sasabe, Arizona, about 60 km west of Nogales, is out in the middle of nowhere, with no bus connections on either side of the border and nowhere to get your Mexican car insurance if you're driving down from the north. The border crossing is open daily from 8 am to 10 pm but you're probably better off crossing somewhere else. About 90 km east of Nogales, **Naco**, opposite Naco, Arizona, is another small place in the middle of nowhere.

AROUND NORTHERN SONORA
On the northeast coast of the Gulf of California, **Puerto Peñasco** is a popular place for residents of Arizona and southern California to bring trailers (caravans) and RVs, making tourism an even more profitable industry than the shrimping and fishing for

WAYNE BERNHARDSON

which this small town is also known. About 1½ hours' drive south of the Sonoita border crossing, this is the nearest beach if you live in southern Arizona. There are around 14 hotels, 10 trailer parks and plenty of restaurants. English is widely spoken and local businesses are as keen to take US dollars as pesos.

Between Puerto Peñasco and the border, the **Reserva de la Biosfera El Pinacate y Gran Desierto de Altar** is a large biosphere reserve with several extinct volcanic craters, a large lava flow, cinder cones, a cinder mine and vast sand dunes. Visitors must register at the park entrance, reached by going down a 10-km gravel road heading south from a turnoff about 10 km east of Los Vidrios, on highway 2 due north of Puerto Peñasco.

The small town of **Cananea**, on highway 2 about halfway between Santa Ana and Agua Prieta, is a mining town which is not of much note today, but it is significant in Mexican history because the miners' revolt that broke out here on June 1, 1906, near the end of the rule of Porfirio Díaz, helped to precipitate the Mexican Revolution. Displays in the small town museum tell the story of the strike.

HERMOSILLO
pop 750,000; alt 238m; ☎ *62*

Founded in 1700 by Juan Bautista Escalante for the resettlement of Pima Indians, Hermosillo ('ehrr-mo-SEE-yo') is the large, bustling, multi-industry capital of the state of Sonora, on highway 15 about 280 km south of Nogales. Like many cities in Mexico, Hermosillo industrialized quickly – in the early 1980s it was little more than an agricultural and administrative center of 45,000 people. Many travelers pass through Hermosillo heading north or south. Smack in the middle of the great Sonora Desert, Hermosillo gets very hot in summer; the rest of the year it's quite pleasant.

Orientation
Highway 15 enters Hermosillo from the northeast and becomes Boulevard Francisco Eusebio Kino, a wide street lined with orange and laurel trees. Boulevard Kino continues west through the city, curves southwest and becomes Boulevard Rodríguez, then Boulevard Rosales as it passes through the city center, then Boulevard Agustín de Vildosola before becoming highway 15 again south of the city. The major business and administrative sections of town lie on either side of Boulevard Rosales and along Boulevard Encinas, which transects the center from northeast to southwest. The Periférico, once a beltway around Hermosillo, has become practically an inner loop due to the city's rapid expansion.

Information
Tourist Office The Secretaría de Fomento al Turismo (☎ 17-29-64, in Mexico 800-62555, in the USA 800-476-6672; fax 17-00-60) is on the 3rd floor of the north wing of the giant Centro de Gobierno building, which straddles Comonfort just south of Paseo Canal, on the south side of the city center. It's open weekdays from 8 am to 3 pm, though someone's usually there till 8 pm and on Saturday morning. Staff hand out an adequate free city map; a better city map is sold for US$2 at the bookstore of the Hotel San Alberto, on Boulevard Rosales opposite the post office.

The tourist office has information on all Sonora and has links with the Arizona office of tourism in Phoenix.

Money Banks and casas de cambio are scattered along Boulevards Rosales and Encinas. The banks are open weekdays from 9 am to around 1 pm; the casas de cambio are open longer hours. The American Express agent, Hermex Travel (☎ 13-44-15, 17-17-18) on the corner of Boulevard Rosales and Monterrey, is open weekdays from 8.30 am to 1 pm and 3 to 6 pm, Saturday 9 am to 1 pm.

Post & Communications The main post office is on the corner of Boulevard Rosales and Avenida Serdán. It's open weekdays from 8 am to 7 pm, Saturday 8 am to

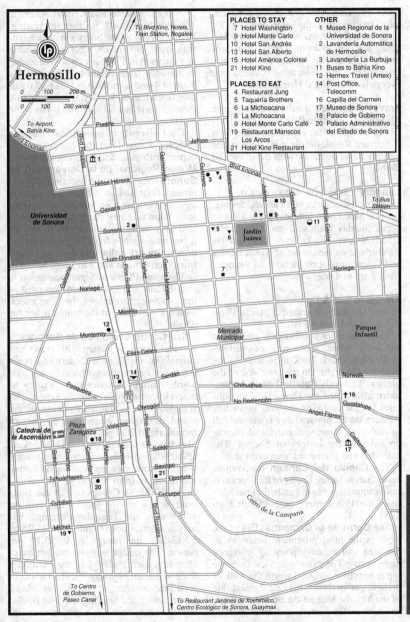

Hermosillo

0   100   200 m
0   100   200 yards

To Blvd Kino, Hotels,
Train Station, Nogales

To Airport,
Bahía Kino

To Bus
Station

Universidad
de Sonora

Jardín
Juárez

Parque
Infantil

Mercado
Municipal

Catedral de
la Ascensión

Plaza
Zaragoza

Cerro de la Campana

To Centro
de Gobierno,
Paseo Canal

To Restaurant Jardines de Xochimilco,
Centro Ecológico de Sonora, Guaymas

Streets and places labelled on map:
Blvd Encinas, Blvd Rosales, Puebla, Jalisco, Blvd Encinas, Garmendia, Guerrero, Matamoros, Juárez, González, Jesús García, Niños Héroes, Oaxaca, Sonora, Luis Donaldo Colosio, Pino Suárez, Yáñez, García Morales, Noriega, Morella, Monterrey, Elías Calles, Serdán, Chihuahua, No Reelección, Norwalk, Guadalupe, Ángel Flores, California, Pesqueira, Obregón, Velazco, Salido, Bavispe, Oposura, Gucurpe, Gabanilla, Tehuántepec, Cubillas, Michel, Brasil, Ocampo, Allende, Moreno, Comonfort

PLACES TO STAY
7 Hotel Washington
9 Hotel Monte Carlo
10 Hotel San Andrés
13 Hotel San Alberto
15 Hotel América Colonial
21 Hotel Kino

PLACES TO EAT
4 Restaurant Jung
5 Taquería Brothers
6 La Michoacana
8 La Michoacana
9 Hotel Monte Carlo Café
19 Restaurant Mariscos
   Los Arcos
21 Hotel Kino Restaurant

OTHER
1 Museo Regional de la
   Universidad de Sonora
2 Lavandería Automática
   de Hermosillo
3 Lavandería La Burbuja
11 Buses to Bahía Kino
12 Hermex Travel (Amex)
14 Post Office,
   Telecomm
16 Capilla del Carmen
17 Museo de Sonora
18 Palacio de Gobierno
20 Palacio Administrativo
   del Estado de Sonora

NORTHWEST MEXICO

noon. The Telecomm office, with telegram, telex and fax, is in the same building; it's open weekdays from 8 am to 7 pm, Saturday 8.30 am to 4 pm, Sunday (for giros and telegrams only) 9 am to 12.30 pm. Payphones and telephone casetas are everywhere in central Hermosillo.

Travel Agencies Hermex Travel (see Money) and Turismo Palo Verde (☎ 13-47-01, 13-18-45), at the Hotel San Alberto on Boulevard Rosales at Avenida Serdán, are helpful travel agencies with details on all flights.

Laundry Lavandería Automática de Hermosillo, on the corner of Yañez and Sonora, is open Monday to Saturday from 8 am to 8 pm, Sunday 8 am to 2 pm, and charges US$1.30 per 3½-kg load. Lavandería La Burbuja on the corner of Niños Héroes and Guerrero is open Monday to Saturday from 9 am to 4 pm.

Things to See & Do

Hermosillo has two principal plazas: Plaza Zaragoza and Jardín Juárez.

Plaza Zaragoza is especially pleasant at sundown when thousands of yellow-headed blackbirds flock in to roost in the trees for the night. On the west side of the plaza is the lovely **Catedral de la Ascensión**, also called the Catedral Metropolitana. On the east side, the grey-and-white **Palacio de Gobierno** has a courtyard full of colorful, dramatic murals depicting episodes in the history of Sonora. The cathedral and palace are open every day.

The **Capilla del Carmen** on Avenida Jesús García facing Calle No Reelección is not as impressive as the cathedral but it's a fine little 19th century chapel, built from 1837 to 1842.

The **Cerro de la Campana** (Hill of the Bell) is the most prominent landmark in the area and an easy point of reference night or day. The panoramic view from the top is beautiful and well worth the walk or drive to get up there. Hugging the east side of the hill, the **Museo de Sonora** has fine exhibits on the history and anthropology of Sonora, Mexico and Central America. The building itself is also interesting, having served as the Sonora state penitentiary from 1907 to 1979 before reopening as a museum in 1985. It's open Wednesday to Saturday from 10 am to 5 pm, Sunday 9 am to 4 pm; admission is US$1.30 (children free), free on Sunday. It's easy to walk there, or local bus No 8 will drop you at the entrance.

The University of Sonora has a fine arts complex across from the campus on the corner of Rosales and Encinas; inside, the **Museo Regional de la Universidad de Sonora** has a history section on the ground floor and an archaeology section upstairs. Both are open Monday to Saturday from 9 am to 1 pm; the history section is also open weekday afternoons from 4 to 6 pm; admission is free. Also upstairs, the **university art gallery** is open weekdays from 9 am to noon and 3 to 7 pm, Saturday and Sunday 10 am to 5 pm; admission is free. Events and exhibits are presented at the university throughout the year; check with the university or the tourist office for details.

The **Centro Ecológico de Sonora** is a zoo and botanical garden with plants and animals of the Sonora Desert and other ecosystems of northwest Mexico. It's well worth visiting – there's more variety of desert life than you'd probably expect. The zoo also contains animals from around the world. It's open Wednesday to Sunday from 8 am to 7.30 pm (5 pm December to March); admission is US$1.30 (kids US$0.90). Also here is an observatory, with telescope viewing sessions on Friday and Saturday from 7.30 to 11 pm; admission is US$1.30. Groups (which can comprise as few as two people) can visit on Wednesday and Thursday evenings, but only with prior notice (call ☎ 50-12-25 or 50-12-25); the charge is US$0.70 per person. The center is about five km south of central Hermosillo, past the Periférico Sur and just off highway 15. The Luis Orcí local bus, departing from the west side of Jardín Juárez and heading south on Boulevard Rosales, stops at a gate about 500 meters from the entrance – ask the driver where to get off as there are no signs.

Hermosillo has some impressively large government buildings, including the huge, brown **Centro de Gobierno** complex, just south of Paseo Canal on the south side of the city center, and the **Palacio Administrativo del Estado de Sonora** (see its courtyard) on Avenida Tehuántepec between Comonfort and Allende.

Hermosillo boasts a couple of enjoyable **recreation parks** with miniature golf, boats, bathing pools and much else to do for both children and adults: Mundo Divertido at Colosio 653 is open daily from noon to 9 pm (11 pm Friday to Sunday); La Sauceda on Boulevard Serna, east of Cerro de la Campana, is open on Thursday and Friday from 9 am to 5 pm, Saturday and Sunday 9 am to 8 pm.

Special Events
The city's major annual event, the Exposición Ganadera (the Sonora state fair) is held in the Unión Gándara each year for 10 days from the end of April. La Vendimia, or the Fiesta de la Uva (Festival of the Grape), is held on a weekend in late June.

Places to Stay
If you spend a night here in summer, you must have a room with air-con that works. Some hotels advertise air-con, but actually provide somewhat cool air that blows with barely more force than a whisper. Check the room before you accept it.

Places to Stay – budget
The *Hotel Washington* (☎ 13-11-83, fax 13-65-02) at Dr Noriega 68, between Guerrero and Matamoros, has clean, simple air-con rooms for US$10. The *Hotel Monte Carlo* (☎ 12-33-54, fax 12-08-53), on the corner of Juárez and Sonora on the northeast corner of Jardín Juárez, is a reasonably priced older hotel with clean air-con rooms with TV; singles/doubles are US$15/17. The *Hotel América Colonial* (☎ 12-24-48) at Juárez 171 Sur, between Avenida Serdán and Chihuahua, is a basic hotel with rooms that are a bit dark and bare but most do have TV and (noisy) air-con; singles/doubles/triples are US$11/12/14.

Places to Stay – middle
The *Hotel Kino* (☎ 13-31-31, fax 13-38-52) at Pino Suárez 151 Sur, conveniently situated near Boulevard Rosales, has a small indoor swimming pool, parking, a pleasant restaurant, and cool air-con throughout; singles/doubles cost from US$19/23. The *Hotel San Alberto* (☎ 13-18-40, fax 12-63-14) on the corner of Boulevard Rosales and Avenida Serdán has a swimming pool, parking, bar, travel agency, bookstore and 80 air-con rooms at US$24/27, breakfast included. The *Hotel San Andrés* (☎ 17-30-99, fax 17-31-39) at Oaxaca 14 near Juárez, a block from Jardín Juárez, has parking and 80 refurbished rooms around a pleasant courtyard; rooms have air-con and tea/coffee-making facilities and cost US$30 with one bed, US$32 to US$35 with two beds.

Places to Stay – top end
Many of Hermosillo's better hotels and motels are strung along Boulevard Kino in the northeast corner of the city. These include the *Fiesta Americana* (☎ 50-60-00, 59-60-11, fax 59-60-60) at No 369 and the *Araiza Inn* (☎ 10-27-17, fax 10-45-41) at No 353, as well as the *Señorial, Bugambilia, Gándara, Holiday Inn* and others.

Places to Eat
Some of the cheapest food in Hermosillo can be bought from the hot-dog carts on many street corners. The hot dogs, for US$0.60, are surprisingly good, especially when piled high with guacamole, refried beans, chiles, relish and/or mustard; those at the university are said to be especially tasty. Another street-cart treat is the pico de gallo – chunks of orange, apple, pineapple, cucumber, jícama, watermelon and coconut – refreshing on a hot day.

For a cool fruit salad, yogurt with fruit, ice cream, fruit or vegetable juice or other cold drinks, check out the many branches of *La Michoacana* and *La Flor de*

Michoacán. The two bordering Jardín Juárez, open till 10 pm, are convenient for getting snacks to take out on the plaza.

There are cheap food stalls in the *Mercado Municipal*, on Calle Matamoros between Avenidas Calles and Monterrey. *Taquería Brothers* is a simple stall on the corner of Sonora and Guerrero serving great tacos for US$0.50 each.

Restaurant Jung is a clean, cheerful air-con vegetarian restaurant and health food store on Niños Héroes, near Boulevard Encinas, with a big comida corrida buffet (US$6) from 12.30 to 4 pm. Earlier, there's a breakfast buffet (US$3.75); it's open Monday to Saturday from 8 am to 8 pm. The simple air-con restaurant at the *Hotel Kino* has reasonable meals, including a comida corrida for US$4; it's open Monday to Saturday from 7 am to 10.30 pm, Sunday 8 am to 4 pm. The *Hotel Monte Carlo* has a cheap café open Monday to Saturday from 7 am to 10 pm.

Probably the best known restaurant in the city is the *Jardines de Xochimilco* (☎ 50-40-89), a pleasant place where mariachis play and you can eat the beef for which Sonora is famous. The dinner special for two (US$18) is a memorable feast. It's in Villa de Seris, an old part of town just south of the center. Come in a taxi at night, as the neighborhood is not the best; anyone can direct you to it in the daytime. It's open daily from 11 am to 9.30 pm; reservations are advised in the evening. The *Restaurant Mariscos Los Arcos* (☎ 13-22-20), Michel 43, is noted for its seafood. It's open daily, and most meals are US$7.75.

Things to Buy

If you always wanted to buy a pair of cowboy boots and a 10-gallon hat, you'll probably find what you want in Hermosillo – the city has one of the best selections of cowboy gear in Mexico. Seri Indian ironwood carvings, another distinctive product of the region, are sold in front of the post office and at other places around town.

Getting There & Away

Air The airport (☎ 61-00-08, 61-01-23) is about 10 km from central Hermosillo, on the road to Bahía Kino. Daily direct flights (all with connections to other centers) include: Aero California to Guadalajara and Los Angeles; Aeroméxico to Ciudad Obregón, Chihuahua, Guadalajara, Los Mochis, Mexico City, Tijuana and Tucson; Mexicana to Mexicali and Mexico City; and TAESA to Mexico City.

Bus The Central de Autobuses is on Boulevard Encinas, about two km southeast of the city center, and has services by Transportes del Pacífico, Elite, Futura, TNS and others. Other companies have their own terminals close by – Transportes Baldomero Corral (TBC) is next door, and Tufesa and Autobuses de Guaymas are opposite. First-class buses include:

Guadalajara – 1410 km, 21 hours; hourly buses, 24 hours, by Elite and Transportes del Pacífico (US$55), all via highway 15/15D (via Guaymas, Los Mochis, Mazatlán, Tepic etc)
Guaymas – 134 km, 1¾ hours; every half hour, 24 hours, by Transportes del Pacífico, every hour by TNS (US$3.75); hourly 5 am to 6 pm by Autobuses de Guaymas (US$3.25)
Mexico City (Terminal Norte) – 1945 km, 29 hours; 14 by Transportes del Pacífico (US$79), every three hours by TNS (US$76)
Nogales – 282 km, four hours; frequent services by most operators (US$8); Tufesa charges only US$4.50
Tijuana – 892 km, 13 hours; hourly by TNS (US$30); 12 by Transportes del Pacífico

Buses to Bahía Kino depart not from the main bus station, but from another one in the center; see the Bahía Kino section that follows.

Train The train station (☎ 14-34-61) is just off Boulevard Eusebio Kino about four km northeast of the center. The primera especial Estrella del Pacífico and the segunda clase 'Burro' trains stop here; see their schedules in the Guadalajara section of the Western Central Highlands chapter.

Getting Around

Local buses operate every day from 5.30 am to 10 pm; the cost is US$0.30. To get to the Central de Autobuses, take any bus marked 'Central' from Calle Juárez on the east side of Jardín Juárez. Buses heading south on Boulevard Rosales depart from Matamoros on the west side of Jardín Juárez and turn west along Dr Noriega.

BAHÍA KINO
(KINO NUEVO & KINO VIEJO)
☎ 624

Named for Father Eusebio Kino, a Jesuit missionary who established a small mission here for Seri Indians in the late 17th century, the bayfront town of Kino, 110 km west of Hermosillo, is divided into old and new parts that are as different as night and day.

Kino Viejo, the old quarter on your left as you drive into Kino, is a dusty, run-down fishing village. Kino Nuevo, on your right, is basically a single beachfront road stretching for about eight km north along the beach, lined with the holiday homes and retreats of wealthy gringos and Mexi-cans. It's a fine beach with soft sand and safe swimming. From around November to March the 'snowbirds' drift down in their trailers from colder climes. The rest of the time it's not crowded – but it's always a popular day outing for families from Hermosillo escaping the city, especially in summer. The beach has many palapas providing welcome shade.

The **Museo de los Seris**, about half-way along the beachfront road in Kino Nuevo, has fascinating exhibits about the Seri Indians, the traditionally nomadic indigenous tribe of this area. It's open Wednesday to Sunday from 8 am to 5 pm; admission is free, and there's a Seri artesanías shop next door. Seri ironwood carvings are sold in both Kinos.

Places to Stay & Eat

Kino Nuevo Most people come to Kino for the day from Hermosillo, but there are several places to stay. Prices tend to be considerably higher than in Hermosillo. There are plenty of palapas all along the beach – you could easily string up a hammock and camp out under these for free.

The Seris

The Seris are the smallest Indian tribe in Sonora, but one of the most recognized due to their distinctive handicrafts. Traditionally a nomadic tribe living by hunting, gathering and fishing – not agriculture, as was prevalent among many other tribes of Mexico – the tribe's area ranges along the Gulf of California from roughly the areas of El Desemboque in the north to Bahía Kino in the south, and inland to the area around Hermosillo.

The Seris are one of the few indigenous tribes that do not work for outsiders, preferring to live by fishing, hunting and handicrafts. Their most famous handicrafts are their ironwood carvings of animals, humans and other figures; other important traditional handicrafts, including pottery and basketry, are no longer as important. The old-time Seris were one of very few tribes in the world that were nomadic and also made pottery.

Though the Seris are no longer strictly nomadic, they still often move from place to place in groups; sometimes you can see them camped at Bahía Kino, or traveling up and down the coast. You will also see Seris in Hermosillo, where some sell ironwood carvings outside the post office. Many, though, live far from modern civilization – the large Isla Tiburón belongs to them, and they live in many other inconspicuous places up and down the Sonora coast, still maintaining many of their old traditions and living between the desert and the sea.

A visit to the Museo de los Seris in Kino Nuevo is a rewarding experience – it has illuminating exhibits on many aspects of Seri culture, including their distinctive clothing, traditional houses with frames of *ocotillo* cactus, musical instruments and traditional handicrafts, nomadic social structure, nature-based religion and more. ■

At the far (north) end of Kino Nuevo, at the end of the bus line, the clean, attractive and well-equipped *Kino Bay RV Park* (☎ 2-02-16, fax 2-00-83) has trailer or tent spaces at US$15 per day (reducing for stays over eight days) and motel rooms at US$35 per day (US$40 at weekends). The *Parador Bellavista* (☎ 2-01-39), right on the beach, has camping spaces at US$10 for tents, US$15 for trailers, and two rooms with fridge, air-con and private bath for US$25. The *Posada Santa Gemma* (☎ 2-00-26, fax in Hermosillo 62-14-55-79), also on the beach, is a little more expensive for camping, trailers and bungalows, but prices seem to be negotiable. The beachfront *Restaurant & Hotel Saro* (☎ 2-00-07) has 16 rooms with fridge, TV and air-con for US$35. The 50-room *Hotel Posada del Mar* (☎ 2-01-55, fax in Hermosillo 62-18-12-37) is the luxury place to stay in Kino, with singles/doubles from US$26/32.

Various places to eat – all specializing in fresh seafood, of course – are found along the beachfront road and in some of the hotels. The *Restaurant Palapa* has a good reputation (open daily).

Kino Viejo The *Islandia Marina* (☎ /fax 2-00-81), right on the beach in Kino Viejo, is a trailer park with spaces at US$5 for tents and US$12 for trailers, plus eight free-standing self-contained bungalows at US$22 for up to four people; you must provide your own bed linen and dishes. A block away, the pricey, air-con *Restaurant Marlin* is a popular place open from 1 to 10 pm every day except Monday. Other small eateries – open-air places serving fresh barbecued fish or tacos – are dotted around Kino Viejo.

Getting There & Away

Bus Buses to Bahía Kino depart from the AMH & TCH bus terminal (☎ 62-12-25-56) in central Hermosillo, on Sonora between González and Jesús García, 1½ blocks east of Jardín Juárez. Second-class buses depart at 5.40, 6.30, 7.30, 8.30, 9.30 and 11.30 am, and 12.30, 1.30, 3.30 and

5.30 pm; the cost is US$3 for the dusty, bumpy two-hour trip.

The return buses from Kino to Hermosillo run on a similar schedule, with the last bus departing from Kino Nuevo at 5.30 pm and Kino Viejo at 6 pm. If you come at a busy time – on a Sunday, for example, when lots of families are there – and you want to get the last bus of the day – catch it at the first stop, on the north end of Kino Nuevo, while it still has space. Fortunately it's an easy hitch back to Hermosillo, if the bus is too crowded.

Car & Motorcycle If you're driving, you can make the trip from Hermosillo to Bahía Kino in about an hour. From central Hermosillo, head northwest out of town on Boulevard Encinas and just keep going.

GUAYMAS
pop 170,000; ☎ 622

Founded in 1769 by the Spaniards at the site of Yaqui and Guaymas Indian villages on the shores of a sparkling blue bay, Guaymas is Sonora's main port, with significant fishing and commerce as its main economic activities; there's little tourism in town, but enjoy the view of the fishing boats, town and surrounding hills from the El Pescador statue by the park. The tourist resort town of San Carlos, on Bahía San Carlos, is 20 km northwest. A ferry connects Guaymas with Santa Rosalía, Baja California.

Orientation & Information

Highway 15 becomes Boulevard García López as it passes along the northern edge of Guaymas. Central Guaymas and the port area are along Avenida Serdán, the town's main drag; everything you'll need is on or near this avenue, including banks and casas de cambio. There's no longer a tourist office in town.

The post office on Avenida 10 between Calles 19 and 20 is open weekdays from 8 am to 7 pm, Saturday 8 am to noon. Next door is the Telecomm office, with telegram, telex and fax; it's open weekdays from 8 am to 5 pm, Saturday 9 am to noon, and Sunday (for telegraph only) 9 am to noon.

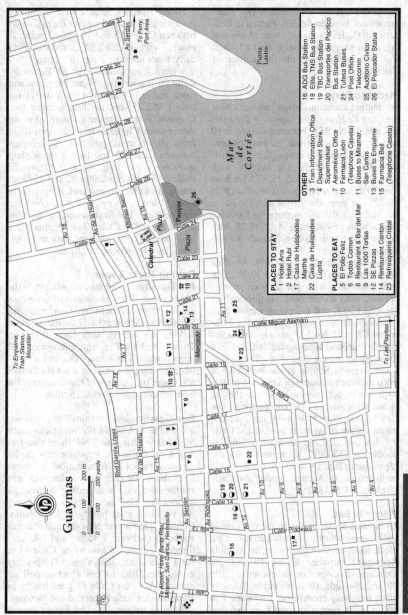

Guaymas

0   100   200 m
0   100   200 yards

PLACES TO STAY
1   Hotel Ana
2   Hotel Rubí
17 Casa de Huéspedes
    Martha
22 Casa de Huéspedes
    Lupita

PLACES TO EAT
5   El Pollo Feliz
6   Todos Comen
8   Restaurant & Bar del Mar
9   Las 1000 Tortas
12 SE Pizzas
14 Restaurant Canton
23 Refresquería Cristal

OTHER
3   Train Information Office
4   Department Store,
    Supermarket
7   Aeroméxico Office
10 Farmacia León
    (Telephone Caseta)
11 Buses to Miramar,
    San Carlos
15 Farmacia Bell
    (Telephone Caseta)
16 ADG Bus Station
18 Elite, TNS Bus Station
19 TBC Bus Station
20 Transportes del Pacifico
    Bus Station
21 Tufesa Buses
24 Post Office,
    Telecomm
25 Auditorio Civico
26 El Pescador Statue

To Empalme,
Train Station,
Mazatlán

To Airport, Hotel Santa Rita
Miramar, San Carlos, Hermosillo

Mar
de
Cortés

Punta
Lastre

To Las Playitas

NORTHWEST MEXICO

Telephone casetas are found in two pharmacies on Avenida Serdán: Farmacia Bell, between Calles 21 and 22, with phone and fax, open every day from 8 am to 10 pm; and Farmacia León, on the corner of Calle 19.

Places to Stay

For budget accommodation you can't beat the *Casa de Huéspedes Lupita* (☎ 2-84-09) at Calle 15 No 125, between Avenidas 10 and 12, 1½ blocks from the bus stations. Clean rooms opening onto a pleasant courtyard cost US$4/6.50 for singles with shared/private bath, US$5.25/7.75 for doubles. The *Casa de Huéspedes Martha* (☎ 2-83-32), on Avenida 9 by Calle 13, has a similar friendly atmosphere and twelve rooms with private bath at US$5.25 with fan or US$9 with air-con. There's an off-street parking area.

The *Hotel Rubí* (☎ 4-01-69), Avenida Serdán between Calles 29 and 30, is clean and pleasant, with 20 air-con rooms opening onto a courtyard; singles/doubles are US$12/15, and there's an inexpensive restaurant. *Hotel Ana* (☎ 2-30-48, fax 2-68-66) at Calle 25 No 135 has air-con rooms with TV around a courtyard at US$12/14 for singles/doubles.

On Avenida Serdán at the west end of town there are a couple of US-style motels with not much personality but they're clean, with air-con, TV and parking. The *Hotel Santa Rita* (☎ 4-14-64, fax 2-81-00) on the corner of Avenida Serdán and Calle 9 (also called Calle Mesa) has singles/doubles at US$15/17; in the next block, the *Motel Santa Rita* (☎ 4-19-19, fax 4-16-17) on the corner of Avenida Serdán and Calle 10 charges US$18/20.

Places to Eat

As in most Mexican towns, the market has stalls where you can sit down to eat; it's a block south of Avenida Serdán, on Avenida Rodríguez between Calles 19 and 20. *Refresquería Cristal* on the corner of Calle 20 and Avenida 10 is a simple, friendly place for cheap breakfasts, snacks and fish dishes, open every day from 8 am to 6 pm.

Along Avenida Serdán there are many restaurants. The small air-con *Todos Comen* between Calles 15 and 16 has economical meals, with a US$2.50 comida corrida daily from noon to 3 pm; it's open every day from 7 am to midnight. *SE Pizzas* by Calle 20 has an all-you-can-eat pizza and pasta buffet (11 am to 11 pm daily) for only US$2.25, and the beer's cheap too. Opposite is *Restaurant Canton*, offering inexpensive Chinese fare; it's open daily from 10 am to 10 pm. *Las 1000 Tortas* between Calles 17 and 18 is a snack shop open every day from 8 am to 11 pm. *El Pollo Feliz* between Calles 12 and 13, with char-grilled chicken and beef, is open daily from 11 am to 11 pm; call ☎ 4-17-81 for free delivery. The *Restaurant/Bar del Mar* on the corner of Calle 17 is a higher-class seafood restaurant, pleasant, dark and cool, open daily from noon to 11 pm.

Getting There & Away

Air The small Guaymas airport (☎ 1-10-11) is about 10 km northwest of Guaymas on the highway between Guaymas and San Carlos. Aeroméxico is the main airline serving this airport, with direct flights to Tucson and La Paz, and connections to other centers. The Aeroméxico office (☎ 2-01-23) is on the corner of Avenida Serdán and Calle 16; a couple of travel agents also have offices along Avenida Serdán.

Bus Guaymas has four small bus stations, all on or near Avenida 12, two blocks south of Serdán. Elite and TNS share one terminal on Calle 14; opposite this is the Transportes del Pacífico station. All these lines have far-ranging northbound and southbound routes departing hourly, 24 hours a day. TBC, next door to Transportes del Pacífico, goes hourly to Hermosillo, Ciudad Obregón and Navojoa, and also has six buses (between 1.45 pm and 1.45 am) direct to Alamos. Close by on Calle 14 is the Tufesa office, and its buses (10 per day to Nogales, four to Los Mochis) pull up outside. ADG on Calle 12 goes hourly to Hermosillo, Ciudad Obregón and Navojoa. All operators run 1st-class buses, though

Pacífico also has 2nd-class buses. Distances, trip times and fares include:

Alamos – 247 km, four hours; TBC only (US$6.50)

Guadalajara – 1276 km, 20 hours (US$44 to US$56), via Navojoa (194 km, three hours, US$4.50 to US$5.75), Los Mochis (349 km, five hours, US$8.25 to US$10), Mazatlán (770 km, 11 hours, US$28 to US$35) and Tepic (1060 km, 16 hours, US$36 to US$46)

Hermosillo – 134 km, 1¾ hours (US$3 to US$4)

Mexico City (Terminal Norte) – 1811 km, 28 hours (US$64 to US$83)

Nogales – 416 km, five hours (US$10 to US$12)

Tijuana – 1026 km, 15 hours (US$31 to US$40)

Train The information office of Ferrocarriles Nacionales de México on Avenida Serdán near Calle 30, at the east end of town, is open Monday to Saturday from 8 am to noon and 2 to 4.30 pm. The train station is at Empalme (☎ 3-10-65), about 10 km east of Guaymas, where you buy the tickets. The primera especial Estrella del Pacífico and segunda clase 'Burro' trains stop at Empalme; see their schedules in the Guadalajara section of the Western Central Highlands chapter.

Ferry The ferry *(transbordador)* terminal (☎ 2-23-24) is on Avenida Serdán at the east end of town. Reservations can be made by telephone up to two weeks in advance, but you can only buy your ticket the day before departure, or on the same day two hours before departure. The office is open Monday to Saturday from 8 am to 3 pm, opening at 6 am on Tuesday and Friday for ticket sales for the morning departure. See the Santa Rosalía section of the Baja California chapter for schedule and fare information.

Getting Around

To/From the Airport From Avenida Serdán, catch one of the buses heading to Itson or San José, or take a taxi for US$5.25.

Bus Local buses run along Avenida Serdán frequently every day from 6 am to 9 pm;

the cost is US$0.30. Several of the eastbound buses stop at the ferry terminal; ask for 'Transbordador.'

Buses to Empalme (for the train station) go from Calle 20 beside the market, every eight minutes from 5.30 am to 11 pm; the cost is US$0.20 for the 15-minute ride. At Empalme you must switch to an 'Estación' bus which will get you to the station in about five minutes. A taxi between Guaymas and Empalme costs US$5.25.

AROUND GUAYMAS
☎ 622

Miramar
Miramar, about five km west of Guaymas, is the closest good beach to town, but it's not a tourist destination like San Carlos. 'Miramar' buses head west on Avenida Serdán (starting from between Calles 19 and 20) every 30 minutes from 6 am to about 8.30 pm.

San Carlos
San Carlos, on the Bahía San Carlos about 20 km northwest of Guaymas, is situated on a beautiful desert-and-bay landscape, but from around October to April it's full of *norteamericanos* and trailer homes, and the accommodation is overpriced; the rest of the year it's pretty quiet. Part of the movie *Catch-22* was filmed on the beach near the Club Méditerranée; only a few rusty pieces of the set remain. There's a tourist office (☎ 6-12-12) at Bellamar Local 2.

The *Teta Kawi Trailer Park* (☎ 6-02-20, fax 6-02-48), 8.5 km west of the highway 15 San Carlos exit, has tent/trailer spaces at US$10/18 and a hotel with rooms costing from US$55 to US$75.

The most economical hotel in San Carlos is *Posada del Desierto* (☎ /fax 6-04-67), overlooking the marina, with seven basic air-con studio apartments with kitchen. Four small apartments for up to three people cost US$25 and three larger apartments for up to five people cost US$28 or US$31, both with reductions by the week and month. The *Motel Creston* (☎ 6-00-20) at km 10 on the main road into San

1 Local Buses to Alamos, Huatabampo
2 TBC Bus Station
3 ADG Bus Station
4 Transportes del Pacífico Bus Station
5 Elite Bus Station
6 Transportes Norte de Sonora Bus Station

Navojoa
Bus Stations

Plaza

To Ciudad
Obregón,
Guaymas

Mercado

To Los
Mochis

0   100   200 m
0   100   200 yards

Carlos has a swimming pool and 24 air-con rooms at US$34.

Opposite the Motel Creston, Gary's (☎ 6-00-49, fax 6-00-24) conducts boat trips for sightseeing, fishing, scuba diving, snorkeling, whale-watching (November to March) and a Margarita sunset cruise. Scuba and snorkeling gear is available for rent.

Buses to San Carlos from Guaymas run west along Avenida Serdán (starting from between Calles 19 and 20) every 10 minutes from 6 am to 8 pm; the cost is US$0.40.

CIUDAD OBREGÓN & NAVOJOA

Heading southeast from Guaymas, highway 15D passes through Ciudad Obregón (125 km from Guaymas), a modern agricultural center with nothing of interest to the tourist, and Navojoa (194 km from Guaymas), a similarly mundane place. From Navojoa a side road leaves highway 15 and heads east 53 km into the foothills of the Sierra Madre Occidental to the picturesque town of Alamos.

Navojoa has five bus stations, all within six blocks of each other. Second-class buses to Alamos depart from the station on the corner of Guerrero and Rincón hourly every day from 6.30 am to 6.30 pm. The 55-minute trip costs US$0.90. TBC has six 1st-class buses to Alamos departing from its own station on the corner of Guerrero and No Reelección between 4.45 pm and 4.45 am (US$1.30). Navojoa is a stop on the Pacific coast train route; see the schedule for the primera especial Estrella del Pacífico and segunda clase 'Burro' trains in the Guadalajara section of the Western Central Highlands chapter.

ALAMOS

pop 8000; alt 432m; ☎ 642

This small, quiet town in the foothills of the Sierra Madre Occidental, 53 km east of Navojoa, has been declared a national historic monument. Its beautifully restored Spanish colonial architecture has a Moorish influence, brought by 17th century architects from Andalucía in southern Spain. The façades of colonial mansions line narrow cobblestoned streets, concealing courtyards lush with bougainvillea; several of the old mansions have been converted to hotels and restaurants.

Alamos is also becoming known for its natural surroundings. On the border of two large ecosystem areas – the great Desierto Sonorense to the north and the lush tropical jungles of Sinaloa to the south – Alamos attracts nature-lovers to its 450 species of birds and animals (including some endangered and endemic species) and over 1000 species of plants. Horseback riding, hunting, fishing, hiking, swimming and dining in opulent colonial mansions are also popular activities.

From mid-October to mid-April, when the air is cool and fresh, norteamericanos arrive to live in their winter homes and the town hums with foreign visitors. Mexican tourists come in the scorching hot summer months of July and August, when school is out. At other times you may find scarcely another visitor.

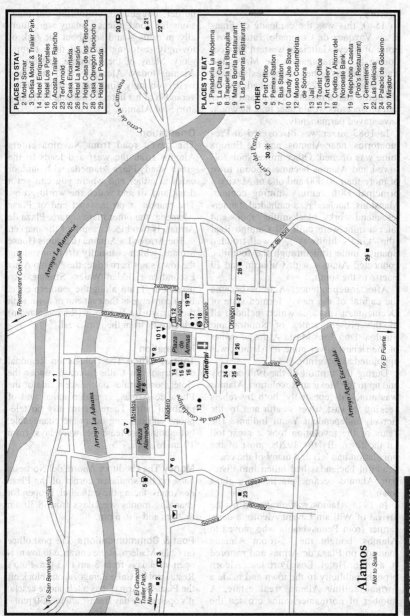

PLACES TO STAY
2 Motel Somar
3 Dolisa Motel & Trailer Park
14 Hotel Enriquez
16 Hotel Los Portales
20 Acosta Trailer Rancho
23 Teri Arnold
25 Casa Encantada
26 Hotel La Mansión
27 Hotel Casa de los Tesoros
28 Casa Obregón Dieciocho
29 Hotel La Posada

PLACES TO EAT
1 Panadería La Moderna
6 La Cita Café
8 Taquería La Blanquita
9 María Bonita Restaurant
11 Las Palmeras Restaurant

OTHER
4 Post Office
5 Pemex Station
7 Bus Station
10 Candy Joe Store
12 Museo Costumbrista de Sonora
13 Jail
15 Tourist Office
17 Art Gallery
18 Credito y Ahorra del Noroeste Bank
19 Telephone Caseta (Polo's Restaurant)
21 Cementerio
22 Las Delicias
24 Palacio de Gobierno
30 Mirador

Alamos
Not to Scale

History

In 1540, this was the campsite of Francisco Vázquez de Coronado, future governor of Nueva Galicia in western Mexico, during his wars against the Mayo and Yaqui Indians (the Yaqui resisted all invaders until 1928). If he had known about the vast amounts of gold and silver that prospectors would later find, he would have stayed permanently.

In 1683 silver was discovered at Promontorios, near Alamos, and the Europa mine was opened. Other mines soon followed and Alamos became a boom town of more than 30,000 and one of Mexico's principal 18th century mining centers. Mansions, haciendas, a cathedral, tanneries, metal works, blacksmiths' shops and later a mint were built. El Camino Real (the 'king's highway'), a well-trodden Spanish mule trail through the foothills, connected Alamos with Culiacán and El Fuerte to the south.

After independence, Alamos became the capital of the newly formed state of Occidente, a vast area which included all of the present states of Sonora and Sinaloa. Don José María Almada, owner of the richest silver mine in Alamos, was appointed as governor.

During the turmoil of the 19th century and up to the Mexican Revolution, Alamos was attacked repeatedly, both by rebels seeking its vast silver wealth and by the fiercely independent Yaqui Indians. The years of the revolution took a great toll on the town. By the 1920s, most of the population had left and many of the once-beautiful haciendas had fallen into disrepair. Alamos became practically a ghost town.

In 1948 Alamos was awakened by the arrival of William Levant Alcorn, a dairy farmer from Pennsylvania who moved to Alamos, bought the 15-room Almada mansion on Plaza de Armas and restored it as the Hotel Los Portales. Alcorn brought publicity to the town and made a fortune selling Alamos real estate. A number of norteamericanos crossed the border, bought the crumbling old mansions for good prices – many were literally in ruins – and set about the task of lovingly restoring them to their former glory. Many of these people still live in Alamos today. Alcorn is also alive and well; you may find him sitting on the verandah of his hotel recounting intriguing stories of Alamos.

Orientation

The paved road from Navojoa enters Alamos from the west and leads to the green, shady Plaza Alameda, with outdoor cafés at either end where you can get a drink and sit and watch the world go by. The market is on the east end of Plaza Alameda; the other main square, Plaza de Armas, is two blocks south of the market.

The Arroyo La Aduana (Customs House Stream, which is usually dry) runs along the town's northern edge; the Arroyo Agua Escondida (Hidden Waters Stream, also usually dry) runs along the southern edge. Both converge at the east end of town with the Arroyo La Barranca (Ravine Stream) which runs from the northwest.

Information

Tourist Office The Delegación Regional de Turismo at Calle Juárez 6, under the Hotel Los Portales on the west side of the Plaza de Armas, is underfunded and of minimal help. There's currently no telephone and opening hours are changeable, but should at least be weekdays from 10 am to 3 pm.

Money The Crédito y Ahorra del Noroeste bank on the southeast corner of the Plaza de Armas, facing the cathedral, is open for changing money weekdays from 8.30 am to 2 pm and 4 to 6 pm.

Post & Communications The post office on Calle Madero, at the entrance to town, is open weekdays from 8 am to 3 pm. Polo's Restaurant on Calle Zaragoza, one block off the Plaza de Armas, has a telephone caseta; it's open every day from 7 am to 9.30 pm.

Mexican Jumping Beans

Mexican jumping beans, or *brincadores*, are not really beans, and it's not really the 'beans' themselves that jump – it's the larvae of a small moth, the *Carpocapsa saltitans*. The moth lays its eggs on the flower of a shrub called the *Sebastiana palmieri* or *Sebastiana pavoniana*, of the spurge family. When the egg hatches, the caterpillar burrows into the plant's developing seed pod, which continues to grow and closes up leaving no sign that a caterpillar is inside. The larva eats the seed in the pod and builds itself a tiny web. By yanking the web, the caterpillar makes the 'bean' jump.

The brincadores only jump at certain times of year, and they can only be found in one small part of the world – an area of about 650 sq km in southern Sonora and northern Sinaloa. Alamos is known as the 'jumping bean capital,' and the beans play a significant role in the economy of the town.

Twenty days after the first rain of the season, sometime in June, the seed pods with the caterpillars inside start jumping. People from Alamos and other small towns in the region take to the hills to gather the beans, searching them out by their sound as they rustle in dry leaves on the ground. The hotter the weather, the more the jumping beans jump. They keep on jumping for about three to six months; the larva then spins a cocoon inside the seed, mutates and eventually emerges as a moth.

If you're in Alamos at the right time of year, you can go into the hills and find some brincadores yourself, or simply buy them from vendors in front of the cathedral. José Trinidad ('Trini'), a popular tour guide and owner of the Candy Joe store on the north side of the plaza, has been dubbed the 'jumping bean king.' He sells brincadores (about 40) in a small bag for US$2, or by the liter (about 1200 brincadores) for US$30. He can send them internationally; write (in English or Spanish) to José Trinidad Hurtado S, Apartado Postal 9, Alamos, Sonora 85760, Mexico. The brincadores are sent out from around July to September. If you get some jumping beans and they don't jump very much, close your hand around them to warm them up.

Interestingly, though Mexican jumping beans are sold as a curiosity in other parts of the world including the USA, Europe and the Far East, you almost never see them sold in other parts of Mexico. ∎

Books Books about Alamos are available at the gift shop of the Hotel Casa de los Tesoros, Las Delicias (the former home of local author, Ida Luisa Franklin) and elsewhere. *A Brief History of Alamos* is an excellent short history of the town. *The Stately Homes of Alamos* by Leila Gillette tells stories of many of the town's old homes.

Laundry The town laundry is at the Dolisa Motel & Trailer Park, on Calle Madero at the entrance to town.

Things to See & Do

The **Catedral** is the tallest building in Alamos and also one of its oldest, constructed from 1786 to 1804 on the site of a 1630 adobe Jesuit mission. Legend relates that every family in Alamos contributed to the construction of the church – every high-ranking Spanish lady of the town contributed a plate from her finest set of china, to be placed at the base of the pilasters in the church tower. There is also a three-tiered belfry. Inside, the altar rail, lamps, censers and candelabra were fashioned from silver, but were all ordered to be melted down in 1866 by General Ángel Martínez after he booted French imperialist troops out of Alamos. Subterranean passageways between the church and several of the mansions – probably built as escape routes for the safety of the rich families in time of attack – were blocked off in the 1950s.

The **Museo Costumbrista de Sonora**, on the east side of the Plaza de Armas, is a fine little museum open Wednesday to

Sunday (entry US$0.40). Less than one km east of the town center, opposite the cemetery, **Las Delicias** was the home of Ida Luisa Franklin. It's a charming restored mansion full of antiques and interesting stories; the US$0.40 admission includes a guided tour. It's open every day from 7 am to 6 pm.

There are a couple of good **vantage points** for a view over the town. One is the Mirador (lookout), on top of a small hill on the south side of town. The other is outside the jail, on a small hill just west of the cathedral. The jail is closer to the center, but the view is better from the Mirador.

A **tianguis** (Indian market) is held every Sunday from around 6 am to 2 pm beside the Arroyo La Aduana, near Matamoros.

Organized Tours

The Home & Garden Tour sponsored by Friends of the Library leaves on Saturday at 10 am from in front of the museum on the Plaza de Armas, culminating in refreshments back at the library; the cost is US$8. The tour is given from around mid-October to mid-May; at other times, Alamos' tour guides can take you to some of the homes.

Alamos has four professional tour guides who can take you around to the sights and tell you the stories of the town. Ask at the tourist office; the cost is around US$5 per person for a two-hour tour.

Special Events

The biggest yearly fiesta is that of the Virgen de Concepción, the town's patron saint, on December 8. On the night of November 1 everyone goes to the cemetery for the Día de los Muertos. The cemetery is cleaned up, and people bring candles, flowers and food and walk around visiting the graves in an almost festive atmosphere.

Places to Stay – budget

Camping The *Dolisa Motel & Trailer Park* (☎ /fax 8-01-31) at the entrance to town has 42 spaces with full hookups, and charges US$13 for trailers and from US$6 for tents. The *Acosta Trailer Rancho* (☎ 8-02-46), once a fruit farm, is about a km east

of the town center and has 30 sites with full hookups, barbecue areas, plenty of shady trees and two swimming pools; follow the signs across town. Prices start at US$8 for trailers and US$5 for tents. Another possibility is the *El Caracol Trailer Resort*, 13 km west of Alamos on the road to Navojoa; the Navojoa-Alamos bus stops at the gate.

Hotels The *Hotel Enríquez* (☎ 8-06-19), on the west side of Plaza de Armas, is a 250-year-old building with a central courtyard; basic rooms with shared bath are US$6.50 per person. At the entrance to town, *Motel Somar* (☎ 8-01-95), Madero 110, has 30 reasonably-sized rooms with singles/doubles with private shower/WC from US$12/13 to US$18/19.

Places to Stay – middle & top end

The *Dolisa Motel & Trailer Park* (see Camping above) has pleasant rooms with air-con, some with fireplace, at US$21/24 for singles/doubles and a suite with kitchen for US$26.

All other places in this category are restored Spanish colonial buildings. The least impressive (but still a fine place) is the *Hotel Los Portales* (☎ 8-02-01) on the west side of the Plaza de Armas. It's the restored mansion of the Almada family, with a courtyard surrounded by stone arches and cool, comfortable rooms with fireplaces; singles/doubles are US$28/39.

The *Hotel La Mansión* at Obregón 2, a block behind the cathedral, was built in 1685 for one of the region's first major mining families, the Salidos. The 12 rooms have fireplaces, stone floors, fans and air-con. Rooms start at US$46/58, or US$58/69 from November 1 to March 31. For bookings, contact the similarly luxurious *Casa Encantada* (☎ 8-04-82, fax 8-02-21), close by at Juárez 20. This nine-room mansion has a beautiful courtyard with a tiny swimming pool; its prices are about 40% higher but include breakfast.

Formerly an 18th-century convent, the *Hotel Casa de los Tesoros* (☎ 8-00-10, fax 8-04-00) at Obregón 10 is now a 14-room hotel with a swimming pool, cozy bar and courtyard restaurant with entertainment. The rooms all have air-con and fireplaces and cost US$59/65, or US$73/82 from mid-October to mid-May. Breakfast is included.

South of town, across the dry stream bed, the *Hotel La Posada* (☎ 8-00-45) at Calle 2 de Abril, Prolongación Sur, in the Barrio El Perico, is a restored former hospital. It has a restaurant, bar and some rooms with private kitchens and sleeping lofts; all rooms have air-con and fireplace and cost US$45 to US$52.

Some North American residents have turned their colonial-era homes into B&Bs, providing a more personal environment. *Casa Obregón Dieciocho*, Obregón 18, has a beautiful garden filled with art objects. *Teri Arnold* (☎ 8-01-42), Galeana 46, is less central but has a small swimming pool. Rooms in both places are around US$45 or US$55, with reductions for longer stays.

Places to Eat

Some of the cheapest food can be had at the food stalls in the market. Outside the market building, the simple *Taquería La Blanquita* is open every day from around 6 am to 10.30 pm. The *María Bonita* restaurant is opposite the southeast corner of the market, open daily from 9 am to 9 pm.

Good 'home cooking' is served by Doña Celsa at *Las Palmeras Restaurant*, on the north side of the Plaza de Armas, every day from around 7 am to 10 pm. The food is tasty and the prices are good too – this is a favorite among expatriate residents. *La Cita Café*, Madero 37, opposite the gas station, is a simple inexpensive restaurant, open daily from 6.30 am to 9.30 pm.

Try the very popular place at the top of Matamoros, across the stream bed and about a 10-minute walk from the town center. There's no sign; everyone calls it simply '*Con Julia*' ('with Julia') or '*Allá con Julia*' ('over there with Julia') after the friendly cook who runs it. Cheap but delicious tortas, tostadas, tacos, carne asada and hamburgers are served every evening from around 6 to 11 pm or later. To find it,

walk north of town to a fork on Matamoros, take the left fork, then go 200 meters; it's in a white house on the right with tables set up under arches out front.

The restaurant-bars at Alamos' beautifully restored colonial hotels provide an elegant atmosphere for a fine meal. The bar-and-grill restaurant at the *Hotel La Mansión* is open for lunch and dinner every day, but only from October to April. At the *Hotel Casa de los Tesoros* you can dine in the air-con restaurant, on the courtyard or in the cozy bar. It's open every day from 7 am to 9.30 pm with Indian dances on Saturday nights in winter; there is live dinner music (starting 6.30 pm) all other evenings in winter, Saturday only in summer. The *Top o' the Park* restaurant at the El Caracol trailer park, open Tuesday to Sunday from noon to 9 pm, has also won rave reviews.

There are several bakeries in town but one of the best is the *Panadería La Moderna*, on Macías just across the dry stream bed on the north edge of town. The best time to come is at about 1 pm, when the baked goods emerge from the outdoor oven.

Getting There & Away

Access to Alamos is via a paved road coming 53 km up into the foothills from Navojoa – see the Ciudad Obregón & Navojoa section for bus information. Alamos' bus station is on the north side of the Plaza Alameda. There's a taxi stand on the east end of the Plaza Alameda, opposite the market.

AROUND ALAMOS

El Chalotón, El Chalotóna park about two km east of town, is a popular place to swim in the summer. About 10 km east of town, the **Arroyo de Cuchujaqui** is a delightful swimming hole, and people go there for fishing, camping and bird-watching. If you have no car you'll have to go by taxi or walk; taxis charge about US$20 roundtrip, and will pick you up at an appointed time. The **Presa El Mocuzari** reservoir is also good for swimming, camping and fishing, with abundant largemouth bass, bluegill and catfish. Take the turnoff on the

Navojoa-Alamos road, about 20 km west of Alamos; the reservoir is about 12 km from the turnoff.

A few small historic towns near Alamos make interesting day excursions. Check out **Minas Nuevas**, about nine km from Alamos on the Navojoa-Alamos road; the bus to Navojoa will drop you there for about US$0.30. Other historic towns near Alamos include **La Aduana** and **Promontorios**. You can visit all these places on your own, or the tourist office can arrange for a guide to take you.

LOS MOCHIS
pop 181,000; ☎ *68*

Many travelers pass through Los Mochis, as it's the western terminus of the famous Barranca del Cobre (Chihuahua al Pacífico) railway. Topolobampo, 24 km southwest of the city, is the terminus of a ferry from La Paz, connecting Baja California to the mainland. The city is unremarkable otherwise, but it does have everything travelers may need.

Orientation
The streets are laid out on a grid. Gabriel Leyva, the main street through the city, runs southwest from highway 15D directly into the center of town, changing names from Calzada López Mateos to Leyva as it enters the city center. Boulevard Castro is another major artery. Some blocks in the center are split by smaller streets (not shown on our map) that run parallel to the main streets.

Information
Tourist Office The Coordinación de Turismo (☎ /fax 12-66-40) on the ground floor of the large government building on Allende near the corner of Cuauhtémoc is open weekdays from 9 am to 3 pm and 5.30 to 7 pm. They have a brochure in English about Sinaloa state, and an excellent free map of the state and its main cities.

Money Banks are dotted around the center, open weekdays from 9 am to 1 pm; a branch of Bancomer is on the corner of Leyva and Juárez. A few doors down is Servicio de Cambio, open Monday to Saturday from 8.30 am to 6.30 pm, with another branch (open daily) on Obregón; though there are plenty more casas de cambio in the center, these offered the best rates at the time of research. The American Express agent is Viajes Araceli (☎ 12-20-84, 12-41-39) at Obregón 471A Pte between Leyva and Ángel Flores, open weekdays from 8.30 am to 1.30 pm and 3 to 6 pm, Saturday 8.30 am to 1 pm.

Post & Communications The post office, on Ordoñez between Zaragoza and Prieto, is open weekdays from 8 am to 7 pm, Saturday 8 am to 1 pm. Payphones are plentiful in the downtown area. A telephone caseta with fax is on Leyva between Obregón and Hidalgo, open every day from 8 am to 10 pm, with discounts in the evenings; another on the corner of Allende and Hidalgo is open daily from 8 am to 9 pm, Sunday 8 am to 6 pm. There's also one in the Transportes del Pacífico bus station, on Morelos between Leyva and Zaragoza.

Laundry Lavamatic 2000 at Allende 218 Sur, between Juárez and Independencia, is open Monday to Saturday from 7 am to 7 pm, Sunday 7 am to 1 pm.

Places to Stay – budget
Camping The *Los Mochis-Copper Canyon RV Park* (☎ 12-68-17), on Calzada López Mateos one km west of highway 15D, has 140 spaces with full hookups at US$11 per space. You can reserve and pay at the RV office (☎ 12-00-21) on Obregón beside the Hotel Santa Anita.

Hotels Los Mochis has few hotels in the budget range, which makes *Hotel Arcos* (☎ 12-32-53), on Allende by Obregón, all the better. It's a little shabby, but friendly and clean; singles/doubles with shared bath are US$5.25/6.50. The *Hotel Hidalgo* (☎ 18-34-53) upstairs at Hidalgo 260 Pte between Zaragoza and Prieto has small, basic singles/doubles with private bath at US$12/15.

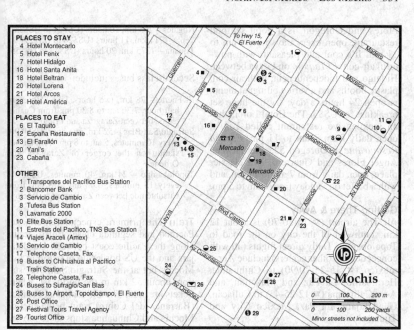

PLACES TO STAY
4 Hotel Montecarlo
5 Hotel Fenix
7 Hotel Hidalgo
16 Hotel Santa Anita
18 Hotel Beltran
20 Hotel Lorena
21 Hotel Arcos
28 Hotel América

PLACES TO EAT
6 El Taquito
12 España Restaurante
13 El Farallón
20 Yani's
23 Cabaña

OTHER
1 Transportes del Pacífico Bus Station
2 Bancomer Bank
3 Servicio de Cambio
8 Tufesa Bus Station
9 Lavamatic 2000
10 Elite Bus Station
11 Estrellas del Pacífico, TNS Bus Station
14 Viajes Araceli (Amex)
15 Servicio de Cambio
17 Telephone Caseta, Fax
19 Buses to Chihuahua al Pacífico
    Train Station
22 Telephone Caseta, Fax
24 Buses to Sufragio/San Blas
25 Buses to Airport, Topolobampo, El Fuerte
26 Post Office
27 Festival Tours Travel Agency
29 Tourist Office

Los Mochis

0   100   200 m
0   100   200 yards
Minor streets not included

Places to Stay – middle

There are plenty of hotels in the middle
price range. The following are all clean,
with air-con, and cable TV in the rooms.
The *Hotel Montecarlo* (☎ 12-18-18, 12-13-
44), on the corner of Independencia and
Ángel Flores, has rooms around a sunny
courtyard, and a bar; singles/doubles are
US$15/16. The *Hotel América* (☎ 12-13-
55/56, fax 12-59-83), at Allende 655 Sur
between Castro and Cuauhtémoc, has
rooms at US$18/21; rooms facing the rear
are quieter. Both have enclosed parking at
the back where you can leave a vehicle
while you visit the Barranca del Cobre.

Also good are the *Hotel Lorena* (☎ 12-
02-39, 12-09-58, fax 12-45-17), Obregón
186 Pte on the corner of Prieto, charging
US$16/19, and the *Hotel Fenix* (☎ 12-26-
23/25, fax 5-89-48), Ángel Flores 365 Sur
between Independencia and Hidalgo,
charging US$16/20. The *Hotel Beltran*
(☎ 12-06-88; fax 12-07-10), at Hidalgo
281 Pte on the corner of Zaragoza, is more

worn around the edges; normal singles/
doubles are US$18/21, though it also has
'económico' rooms for US$12/15 that
aren't advertised on the board.

Places to Stay – top end

The *Hotel Santa Anita* (☎ 18-70-46/31, fax
12-00-46, hotelsbal@tsi.com.mx), on the
corner of Leyva and Hidalgo, has an
English-speaking staff, air-con, restaurant,
travel agent, parking and singles/doubles
at US$75/90. A bus for hotel guests only
(US$4 per person) departs daily at 5.15 am
for the Barranca del Cobre train station;
you can store a vehicle here while you visit
the canyon.

Places to Eat

There are plenty of places for an inexpensive taco or quesadilla; the air-con *Cabaña*
on the corner of Allende and Obregón,
open every day from 7 am to 1 am (2 am
on Friday and Saturday), is clean and
good. *El Farallón* on the corner of Ángel

Flores and Obregón, is a good seafood restaurant, open every day from 8 am to 11 pm. It's cool and pleasant, with powerful air-con. *El Taquito* on Leyva between Hidalgo and Independencia, with air-con, plastic booths and a varied bilingual menu, is open 24 hours a day; try the huge set breakfast for US$3. The Hotel Lorena has an inexpensive restaurant called *Yani's*, open daily from 7 am to 11 pm. *España Restaurante* at Obregón 525 Pte between Ángel Flores and Guerrero, is a classier place, open daily from 7 am to 11 pm, and with a buffet on Sunday from 8 am to 5 pm.

Getting There & Away

Air The airport (☎ 15-30-70) is about 12 km southwest of the city on the road to Topolobampo. Daily direct flights (all with connections to other centers) include Aeroméxico (☎ 15-25-70/90) to Chihuahua, Hermosillo, La Paz and Mazatlán, and Aero California (☎ 12-25-43) to Culiacán, Guadalajara, La Paz, Mexico City and Tijuana.

Bus Los Mochis is on highway 15D; several major bus lines offer hourly buses heading both north and south, 24 hours a day. Each 1st-class bus line has its own terminal: Elite is on the corner of Juárez and Degollado; Estrellas del Pacífico is a couple of doors up, as is TNS which also has 2nd-class buses; Transportes del Pacífico is on Morelos between Zaragoza and Leyva; Tufesa is on Allende between Juárez and Independencia. All bus companies serve the same places, except Tufesa only goes north and has fewer routes.

Distances, times and fares include:

Guadalajara – 927 km, 15 hours (US$32 to US$41)
Guaymas – 349 km, five hours (US$9 to US$11)
Hermosillo – 483 km, six hours (US$13 to US$14)
Mazatlán – 421 km, six hours (US$14 to US$18)
Mexico City (Terminal Norte) – 1462 km, 23 hours (US$58 to US$68)
Navojoa – 155 km, two hours (US$4.50 to US$5.50)
Nogales – 765 km, 10 hours (US$21 to US$23)
Tepic – 711 km, 11 hours (US$26 to US$29)
Tijuana – 1375 km, 20 hours (US$47 to US$55)

Second-class buses include:

El Fuerte – 78 km, two hours, US$2.50; every half hour, 7.30 am to 8.30 pm, from Cuauhtémoc between Zaragoza and Prieto
Sufragio/San Blas – 52 km, one hour, US$0.90; every 10 minutes, 5 am to 8 pm, from the bus station on the corner of Zaragoza and Ordoñez
Topolobampo – 24 km, 40 minutes, US$0.60; every 15 minutes, 5.45 am to 8 pm, from Cuauhtémoc between Zaragoza and Prieto

Train The primera especial Estrella del Pacífico and segunda clase 'Burro' trains along the Pacific coast between Guadalajara and the US border do not stop in Los Mochis but at the Sufragio/San Blas station, about 52 km to the northeast, where tickets are sold. The Chihuahua al Pacífico (Barranca del Cobre) train between Los Mochis and Chihuahua stops there too but the connections between it and the Pacific coast trains are inconvenient (and often late). See the Guadalajara section of the Western Central Highlands chapter for schedules of the Pacific coast trains. Information and schedules for the Chihuahua al Pacífico are given in the Barranca del Cobre section.

Ferry The Festival Tours travel agency (☎ 18-39-86, fax 18-39-90) at Allende 655 by the Hotel América sells tickets for the ferry from Topolobampo to La Paz. It's open weekdays from 9 am to 7 pm, Saturday 10 am to 1 pm. See the La Paz section of the Baja California chapter for the ferry schedule and fares.

Getting Around

Nearly everything in Los Mochis is within walking distance of the center.

Buses to the airport depart from Cuauhtémoc between Zaragoza and Prieto, approximately hourly between 6.30 am and 5.45 pm; the fare is US$0.70.

The Chihuahua al Pacífico train station is at the southeastern edge of Los Mochis, several km from the center. 'Castro-Estación' buses to the station depart every five minutes between 5.30 am and 8 pm from Zaragoza between Hidalgo and Obregón. The trip takes 15 minutes and costs US$0.30. You can take the bus to get the segunda clase train for the Barranca del Cobre, but for the primera especial train (and if arriving by either train) you'll need to fork out US$5.25 for a taxi.

TOPOLOBAMPO

Topolobampo, 24 km south of Los Mochis, is the terminus for ferries to La Paz, in Baja California. There are plenty of places to eat in Topolobampo, and good beaches nearby, but there's nowhere to stay in town.

Ferry tickets are sold at the Festival Tours travel agency in Los Mochis (see the Los Mochis Getting There & Away section); it can sell tickets up to 15 days in advance, but at the Topolobampo ferry terminal (☎ 686-2-01-41, fax 686-2-00-35) you can only buy them on the day of departure.

EL FUERTE

pop 30,000; alt 180m

Founded in 1564 by the Spanish conqueror Francisco de Ibarra, El Fuerte (The Fort) is a picturesque Spanish colonial town notable for its colonial ambience and Spanish architecture; the Palacio Municipal, the plaza, the church, the museum and the Hotel Posada del Hidalgo are its most notable features.

El Fuerte was an important Spanish settlement throughout the colonial period; for more than three centuries it was a major farming and commercial center and trading post on El Camino Real, the Spanish mule trail between Guadalajara to the southeast, the mines of Alamos to the north and the Sierra Madre Occidental to the northeast. In 1824 El Fuerte became the capital of the state of Sinaloa, a title it retained for several years.

The rich silver-mining Almada family of Alamos had strong connections in El Fuerte. In 1890 Rafael Almada built an opulent mansion, now the *Hotel Posada del Hidalgo*, in the center of El Fuerte in the street behind the church. The hotel is worth seeing, even if you just stop by; it has beautiful interior gardens, a swimming pool, a restaurant/bar and 39 rooms, with singles/doubles at US$75/90. Reservations can be made at Viajes Flamingo (☎ 68-12-16-13, 68-12-19-29, fax 68-18-33-93) at the Hotel Santa Anita in Los Mochis. There are several budget places to stay near the bus station.

See the Los Mochis section for details on getting to El Fuerte by bus, and the Barranca del Cobre section for details on getting there by train.

CULIACÁN

pop 800,000; ☎ 67

The present capital of the state of Sinaloa, Culiacán, is equidistant from Los Mochis and Mazatlán – about 210 km (a three-hour drive) from either place. Primarily a commercial, administrative and agricultural center, the city has little to attract tourists. If you do spend time in Culiacán you could check out the 17th century cathedral, the Palacio Municipal, the Museo Regional de Sinaloa in the Centro Cívico Constitución, and the Malecón walkway along the Río Tamazula and Río Humaya.

BARRANCA DEL COBRE (COPPER CANYON)

The Barranca del Cobre is a natural wonder that actually consists of not one but 20 canyons. Together they are four times larger than Arizona's Grand Canyon and equally spectacular. The route of the famous Ferrocarril Chihuahua al Pacífico between Los Mochis and Chihuahua, known in English as the Copper Canyon Railway, includes several stops in the Barranca del Cobre.

Ferrocarril Chihuahua al Pacífico

The Copper Canyon Railway is among Mexico's most scenic rail journeys. A considerable feat of engineering, it has 39 bridges and 86 tunnels along 655 km of railway line connecting the mountainous,

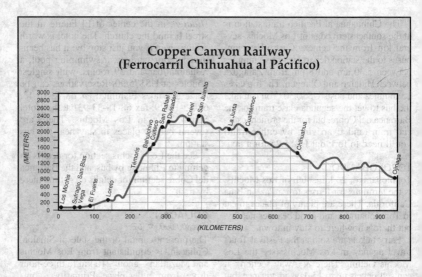

Copper Canyon Railway
(Ferrocarríl Chihuahua al Pácifico)

arid interior of northern Mexico to the Pacific coast. It was opened in 1961 after taking many decades to build. The major link between Chihuahua and the coast, the line is used heavily by passengers and freight; the beauty of the landscape it traverses has made it one of the country's prime tourist excursions as well.

The Chihuahua al Pacífico railway operates two trains: the primera especial train, which is faster, cleaner, more comfortable and has air-con and heating, and the segunda clase which is more crowded and dirtier, but much cheaper. It takes about 13 hours to make the trip on the primera especial train, and at least three hours longer on the segunda clase train, which stops frequently along the way. If you're heading toward Los Mochis from Chihuahua, take the primera train, as the segunda, running later, passes much of the best scenery (between Creel and Loreto) after dark. Heading the other direction, you should be able to see the best views on either train, unless the segunda clase is excessively delayed. If you're traveling only between Creel and Chihuahua you may prefer to take the bus, as the schedule is more convenient.

The majority of the good views are on the right side of the carriage heading inland, on the left side going to the coast. The segunda clase train has windows that open – although they can let in dust and smoke, they're better for taking photographs. In the primera train passengers often congregate in the vestibules between cars (where the windows open) to take photos. Pricey food and drinks are sold on the train.

Things to See along the Way Departing from Los Mochis as the sun rises, the train passes through flat, grey farmland and gradually begins to climb through fog-shrouded hills, speckled with dark pillars of cacti.

About three hours from Los Mochis the train passes over the long Río Fuerte bridge and through the first of the 86 tunnels. It cuts through small canyons and hugs the sides of cliffs as it climbs higher and higher through the mountains of the Sierra Tarahumara, a sub-range of the Sierra Madre Occidental. The trip becomes an exciting sequence of dramatic geological images – craggy cliffs, sheer canyon walls and the river bed far below. Seven hours out of Los

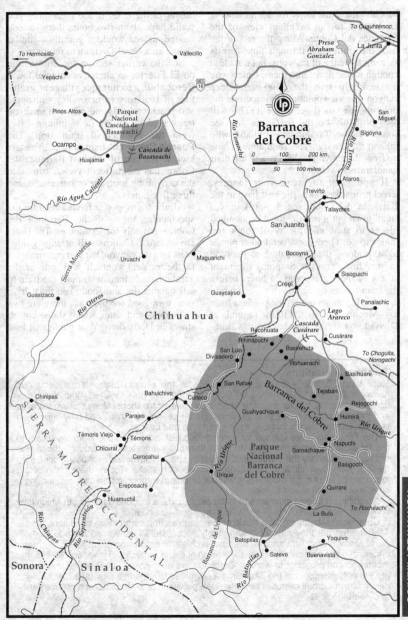

Mochis, the train stops for 15 minutes at Divisadero for an excellent view of the Barranca del Cobre. Along the rest of the trip, the train runs through pine forests skirting the edge of canyons, but not close enough to see down into them. Unless you make a trip into the 2300-meter-deep canyon, the viewpoint at Divisadero is the only chance you'll get to see it. This will also probably be the first time you see some of the Tarahumara Indians who inhabit the canyon. The Tarahumara come up from the canyon to display and sell their handicrafts to visitors.

If you want to break your journey, Creel probably makes the best base in the Barranca del Cobre region – it's only a small town but it has the most economical places to stay, and plenty of tours and things to do. There are several other places to stay along the Chihuahua al Pacífico railway line, however. Stopping overnight at any of them gives you 24 hours before the train passes by again – time enough to explore. If you set out on the primera from Los Mochis, and switch to the segunda at Divisadero (storing your bags with a store-holder or the hotel in the meantime) you could have about two hours there to look around, as you would if you did a similar switch on a Creel-Divisadero return trip.

See the earlier section for information on **El Fuerte**, an attractive colonial town. **Cerocahui**, a picturesque village at an altitude of 1630 meters, in a valley with apple and peach orchards and pine and madrone trees, is about 16 km (a 35-minute drive) from the Bahuichivo train stop. The **Posada Barrancas** train stop, 2220 meters high at the rim of the vast Barranca del Cobre, has magnificent views, trips into the canyon by foot, car or horseback, and three fine hotels.

All the trains stop at **Divisadero** for the spectacular view of the Barranca del Cobre – but only for 15 minutes. The Hotel Divisadero Barrancas will arrange guided tours into the canyon, but you can arrange a far better deal yourself with one of the Tarahumara Indians who meet the train to sell handicrafts and food. You must have your own food for the tour; there are two restaurants and some snack stalls, but no stores in Divisadero. Your guide will lead

---

Tarahumara Indians

More than 50,000 Tarahumara Indians live in the Sierra Tarahumara's numerous canyons, including the Barranca del Cobre (Copper Canyon). Isolated within this formidable topography, the Tarahumara retain many of their traditions. Many still live in caves and log cabins (a few of these dwellings can be seen near Creel) and they subsist on very basic agriculture consisting mainly of maize and beans.

The Tarahumara are famous for running long distances. Running is so significant to the Tarahumara that in their own language they call themselves 'Rarámuri' – those who run fast. Traditionally the Tarahumara hunted by chasing down and exhausting deer, then driving them over cliffs to be impaled on wooden sticks. Today they run grueling footraces of 160 km (or more – and without stopping) through rough canyons, kicking a small wooden ball ahead of them.

A tradition of quite a different sort is the *tesquinada*, a raucous gathering in which they consume copious amounts of *tesquino*, a potent maize beer.

Catholic missionaries have made some progress improving living conditions for the Tarahumara, but they haven't been entirely successful in converting them to Catholicism. Many of the Tarahumara attend church services, but continue to worship their ancestral gods, particularly Raiénari, the sun god and protector of men, and Mechá, the moon god and protector of women. Sorcerers are as important as Catholic priests and are the only members of the Tarahumara permitted to consume peyote, a hallucinogen derived from a small cactus. They often take peyote in order to perform a bizarre dance to cure the sick. ■

you down 1820 meters to the Río Urique. Carry enough water for the descent and be prepared for a change in climate from cool – Divisadero is over 2460 meters high – to warm and humid near the river. Fall (autumn) is the best time to come because flash floods and suffocatingly high temperatures are a problem in summer.

Places to Stay

Cerocahui The *Hotel Misión*, opposite the Misión de Cerocahui church founded in 1690 by the Jesuit Padre Juan María de Salvatierra, has 36 comfortable rooms at US$114/179 for singles/doubles, including three meals a day. A variety of short and long excursions depart from the hotel by foot, vehicle and horseback. Reservations are made at the Hotel Santa Anita in Los Mochis (see the Los Mochis section). A hotel bus provides free transport to/from the train.

Five km north of Cerocahui village, you can camp at the *Rancho del Oro* campground on the banks of the Arroyo del Ranchito, a tranquil spot with a pleasant beach and swimming, good bird-watching (over 100 species), burial caves and archaeological sites a short walk away, and interesting excursions. Tents can be rented if you don't have your own. Hot showers are available at the nearby *Hotel Paraíso del Oso*, which can also provide meals and other services. The campground is 12 km from the Bahuichivo train station; there's a bus service.

Posada Barrancas Heading toward Chihuahua, this station comes after San Rafael – it's about five km southwest of Divisadero. For budget accommodation at a farmhouse, five minutes from the station, ask locally for *Casa de Armando Díaz*. Perched on the rim of the canyon with exceptional views from the private terraces of all the rooms, the *Posada Barrancas Mirador* has 32 luxury rooms and suites at US$114/179 for singles/doubles, including three meals a day. Right at the train stop and just a five-minute walk from the viewpoint, the *Rancho Posada* has 36 rooms at US$35/66 for singles/doubles, with

breakfast included and a restaurant serving other meals. Reservations for both can be made at the Hotel Santa Anita in Los Mochis (see the Los Mochis section). The *Mansión Tarahumara* (☎ in Chihuahua 14-15-47-21, fax 14-16-54-44) is also known as El Castillo because it looks like a medieval stone castle; from May to September singles/doubles are US$85/108, rising to US$100/133 from October to May; meals and one walking tour are included.

Divisadero At the train stop, the *Hotel Divisadero Barrancas* (☎ in Chihuahua 14-10-33-30, 14-15-11-99, fax 14-15-65-75) has 52 rooms, all with that same magnificent view. Singles/doubles are US$95/139, with a surcharge at peak times; the price includes two walking tours and three meals a day. About a 20-minute walk along the rim to the southwest is *Rancho de Lencho*, run by the Mancinas family. They provide beds for US$4 per person and meals for US$2.75; two of the family, Rosalva and Loli, work at the stalls by the station.

Getting There & Away

Tickets Primera especial tickets are available from the train stations, from travel agencies or by mail in advance.

The train station in Chihuahua (☎ 14-15-77-56) sells primera especial tickets every day from 6 am to 2 pm; in Los Mochis the train station (☎ 68-12-08-53) sells primera especial tickets weekdays from 5 am to 1 pm, Saturday, Sunday and holidays from 5 to 9 am. Tickets for the segunda clase trains are sold an hour before the train departs.

The Viajes Flamingo travel agency (☎ 68-12-16-13, fax 68-18-33-93) at the Hotel Santa Anita on the corner of Leyva and Hidalgo in Los Mochis specializes in the Barranca del Cobre, and will sell primera especial tickets for the same price as sold at train stations, though there's a surcharge if you want them to mail them to you. You can be pretty sure of getting a ticket a day or two in advance, though you should allow a few days longer than this

Copper Canyon Railway – Los Mochis to Chihuahua

| | Primera Especial Train No 73 | | Segunda Clase Train No 75 | |
| | | Fare from | | Fare from |
Station	Departs	Los Mochis	Departs	Los Mochis
Los Mochis	6.00 am	–	7.00 am	–
Sufragio/San Blas	6.43 am	US$ 7.25	7.55 am	US$0.80
El Fuerte	7.30 am	US$ 7.25	8.40 am	US$1.30
Loreto	8.10 am	US$ 9.25	9.30 am	US$2.00
Témoris	11.11 am	US$15.25	12.40 pm	US$3.25
Bahuichivo	12.12 pm	US$18.25	1.50 pm	US$3.75
Cuiteco	12.24 pm	US$18.75	2.05 pm	US$3.75
San Rafael	1.15 pm	US$20.25	3.00 pm	US$4.00
Posada Barrancas	1.30 pm	US$21.00	3.15 pm	US$4.25
Divisadero	1.50 pm	US$21.50	3.35 pm	US$4.25
Creel	3.14 pm	US$25.00	5.10 pm	US$5.25
San Juanito	4.51 pm	US$27.50	5.55 pm	US$5.50
La Junta	5.25 pm	US$33.50	7.35 pm	US$6.75
Cuauhtémoc	6.25 pm	US$36.50	8.50 pm	US$7.50
Chihuahua	8.50 pm	US$46.00	11.25 pm	US$9.25

Copper Canyon Railway – Chihuahua to Los Mochis

| | Primera Especial Train No 74 | | Segunda Clase Train No 76 | |
| | | Fare from | | Fare from |
Station	Departs	Chihuahua	Departs	Chihuahua
Chihuahua	7.00 am	–	8.00 am	–
Cuauhtémoc	9.15 am	US$ 9.50	10.25 am	US$2.15
La Junta	10.05 am	US$13.00	11.25 am	US$2.80
San Juanito	11.19 am	US$18.75	1.15 pm	US$3.75
Creel	12.26 pm	US$21.00	2.00 pm	US$4.25
Divisadero	2.00 pm	US$25.00	3.45 pm	US$5.25
Posada Barrancas	2.15 pm	US$25.25	4.00 pm	US$5.25
San Rafael	2.30 pm	US$26.00	4.15 pm	US$5.50
Cuiteco	3.20 pm	US$27.75	5.14 pm	US$5.50
Bahuichivo	3.32 pm	US$28.25	5.25 pm	US$5.75
Témoris	4.30 pm	US$31.00	6.35 pm	US$6.25
Loreto	5.30 pm	US$36.75	7.50 pm	US$7.50
El Fuerte	6.20 pm	US$40.25	8.50 pm	US$8.25
Sufragio/San Blas	6.59 pm	US$43.25	9.25 pm	US$8.75
Los Mochis	7.50 pm	US$46.00	10.25 pm	US$9.25

for travel in Semana Santa, July or August or at Christmas (they recommend making reservations at least one month in advance for these times, but that's extremely pessimistic). Even if they say the train is sold out, there are always plenty of tickets available at the station, including on the morning of departure. It isn't uncommon to see a supposedly full train during Semana Santa departing with scores of empty seats. For a same-day primera especial ticket,

queue up before 5 am. If you're still in the combined primera/segunda queue as the primera train is about to depart, go to the train and ask the conductor if you can pay on board.

Primera especial tickets can be purchased in advance by mail in the USA from Mexico by Train, PO Box 2782, Laredo, TX 78044 USA (☎/fax 956-725-3659, ☎ 800-321-1699); the cost is very much higher if you do this (US$85 one way,

US$150 return), but you are assured of getting a seat.

Schedule The primera especial runs every day; the segunda clase train runs from Chihuahua to Los Mochis only on Monday, Wednesday and Friday, and then makes the return trip on Tuesday, Thursday and Saurday.

Check departure times carefully, as the train crosses a time zone boundary at the border of Sinaloa and Chihuahua states. Previously schedules were all given in Central (Chihuahua) time, an hour ahead of Mountain (Sinaloa) time. Now, the Sinaloa train stops (Los Mochis, Sufragio/San Blas, El Fuerte and Loreto) are usually given in Mountain (Sinaloa) time. We're doing the same in the chart in this section – we're using the time the train actually leaves each stop according to the appropriate time zone. Beware the old system, though, which may still be used (eg, in Creel station), and may fool you into turning up at Los Mochis station one hour too late.

At the time of research the Ferrocarríl Chihuahua al Pacífico was due to be privatized though a buyer was yet to be found. When this happens, fares and schedules may change, so this is another reason to doublecheck before making plans. Currently, children aged five to 11 pay just over half fare; children under five years ride free. Trains tend to run late; cargo trains en route cause delays. The segunda clase train is virtually never on time, often arriving at the end of the line around 1 am.

CREEL
pop 3000; alt 2338; ☎ *145*
Creel, a pleasant small town surrounded by pine forests and interesting rock formations, is many travelers' favorite stop on the Copper Canyon Railway. You can stock up on maps and staples and catch a bus to Batopilas, a village 140 km away deep in the heart of the canyon and Tarahumara country. Creel is also convenient for a number of other interesting day tours and hikes.

This is also a regional center for the Tarahumara Indians, and you will see many of them in traditional dress here.

Its high elevation means Creel can be very cold, even snowy, especially in winter. In summer the cool air and the smell of pine from the town's lumber mill are a welcome relief from the heat of the tropical coastal lowlands or the deserts of northern Mexico.

Orientation
Creel is a very small town, so it's virtually impossible to get lost. Most things you need, including many hotels and restaurants, are on López Mateos, the town's main street. This leads from the town plaza, where there are two churches, the post office, a bank, and the Artesanías Misíon shop. The train station is one block north of the plaza. Across the tracks are a couple more hotels and restaurants and the bus station for buses to Chihuahua.

Information
Creel has no formal tourist office but information about local attractions is available from the tour operators, the Artesanías Misíon shop and from most of the places to stay.

Money Banca Serfin on the plaza changes money; it's open weekdays from 9 am to 1.30 pm. The store right by the Motel Cascada Inn also changes US dollars cash and traveler's checks.

Post & Communications The post office in the Presidencia Municipal on the plaza is open Monday to Saturday from 9 am to 4 pm. There are several telephone casetas, including one in the papelería (paper shop) beside the Farmacia Cristo Rey on López Mateos, half a block south of the plaza; it's open daily from 9 am to 8 pm (6 pm on Sunday).

Books & Maps A large map of Creel is posted on the outside wall of the Artesanías Misíon shop on the north side of the plaza. Maps of the surrounding area are sold at the paper shop on López Mateos

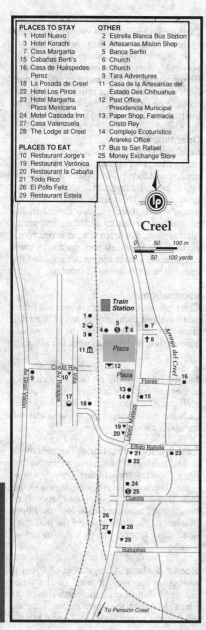

PLACES TO STAY
1   Hotel Nuevo
3   Hotel Korachi
7   Casa Margarita
15 Cabañas Berti's
16 Casa de Huéspedes
    Perez
18 La Posada de Creel
22 Hotel Los Pinos
23 Hotel Margarita
    Plaza Mexicana
24 Motel Cascada Inn
27 Casa Valenzuela
28 The Lodge at Creel

PLACES TO EAT
10 Restaurant Jorge's
19 Restaurant Verónica
20 Restaurant la Cabaña
21 Todo Rico
26 El Pollo Feliz
29 Restaurant Estela

OTHER
2   Estrella Blanca Bus Station
4   Artesanías Misíon Shop
5   Banca Serfin
6   Church
8   Church
9   Tara Adventures
11 Casa de la Artesanías del
    Estado Des Chihuahua
12 Post Office,
    Presidencia Municipal
13 Paper Shop, Farmacia
    Cristo Rey
14 Complejo Ecoturístico
    Arareko Office
17 Bus to San Rafael
25 Money Exchange Store

Creel

0   50   100 m
0   50   100 yards

and elsewhere. Better maps, including the topographical maps *San Jacinto No G 13-1, Chihuahua* and *San José Guacayvo G13-A21* (US$4.50 each; recommended) can be bought at the Artesanías Misíon shop. This shop also sells a number of books about the Barranca del Cobre and the Tarahumara, such as *The Tarahumara of Mexico: Their Environment and Material Culture* by Campbell W Pennington (1997) and *National Parks of Northern Mexico* by Richard Fisher.

Laundry The public lavandería at The Lodge at Creel, López Mateos 61, is open Monday to Saturday from 10 am to 6 pm.

Museum
The Casa de las Artesanías del Estado De Chihuahua overlooks the plaza and contains exhibits on Tarahumara culture and crafts. It is open Tuesday to Saturday from 9 am to 1 pm and 3 to 7 pm, Sunday 9 am to 1 pm; admission costs US$0.40.

Complejo Ecoturístico Arareko
An excellent local hike (or drive) is to the Complejo Ecoturístico Arareko, an area of Tarahumara communal land (ejido) with over 200 sq km of pine forest with waterfalls, hot springs, caves and other rock formations, deep canyons, farmlands, Tarahumara villages, Lago Arareco and more. Their office on López Mateos beside the Farmacia Cristo Rey, half a block south of the plaza, rents bicycles, and boats for excursions on Lago Arareco.

To get there from Creel, head south on López Mateos and veer left, passing the town cemetery on your left. About 1.5 km south of town there's a gate where an entrance fee is charged (US$1.30, children US$0.70) and you're given a map and printed information about the ejido. Continue straight ahead; caves and farmlands will appear on both sides of the road before you eventually arrive at the small Tarahumara village of San Ignacio, where there's a 400-year-old mission church. You can enter the ejido on foot or by car. Lago Arareco is seven km south of Creel on the road to Cusárare; the ejido offers camping, a hostel and a hotel near the lake (see Places to Stay).

Trips & Organized Tours

Most of Creel's hotels offer tours of the surrounding area, with trips to canyons, rivers, hot springs, Lago Arareco and other places. There's also Tara Adventures (☎/fax 6-02-24), at the corner of Cristo Rey and Avenida Gran Visión, which offers tours, trekking, camping, maps, mountain bike rental and other services.

All tours require a minimum number of people, usually four or five; the easiest place to get a group together is often at the Casa Margarita, but any hotel will organize a tour if there are four or five people wanting to go. Most hotels don't require that you be a guest in order to go on a tour. Expect to pay about US$8 per person for a half-day tour, but shop around – the pricier hotels tend to have more expensive tours. The drivers hanging around the plaza might give you a better price. If you have your own transport you can do many of these excursions on your own. Popular trips include (one or more destinations may be combined on the same organized tour):

Lago Arareco – An easy seven-km hike or drive from town along the road to Cusárare; hitchhiking is also relatively easy. A few caves inhabited by Tarahumaras can be seen along the way. At the lake there's an old log cabin that was used as a set for the filming of a Mexican movie, *El Refugio del Lobo* (Refuge of the Wolf).

Valle de los Monjes – The Valley of the Monks is nine km away and is considered a day trip by horse. Tour operators can either rent horses or tell you where to get them.

Cascada Cusárare – The 30-meter-high Cusárare waterfall is 22 km south of Creel near the Tarahumara village of Cusárare. As you get near the town, look for a small roadside shrine and km marker on the right side of the road. Just past that is a small sign marking the road to the 'Cascada – Waterfall Hotel.' Follow that road to the right for three km, crossing the river three or four times. When the road ends, follow the trail to the top of the waterfall. The trail winds around to the bottom of the falls. Hitchhiking to the 'hotel'

road is usually easy. The four to five-hour tour involves going 22 km by car, stopping at Lago Arareco on the way, then 2.5 km by foot to the waterfall.

Recohuata Hot Springs – The seven-hour trip begins with a 1½-hour truck ride and then a hike down 607 meters into the canyon to the hot springs (US$0.90 entry charge to springs).

Cascada de Basaseachi – Basaseachi Falls, 140 km northwest of Creel, is a 298 meter high dramatic waterfall (the highest in Mexico), especially spectacular in the rainy season. It takes all day to visit the falls – a bumpy three-hour drive, then three hours walking down, half an hour at the waterfall, three hours walking up again, and a bumpy three-hour return ride – but if you're up for it, it's worth it.

Río Urique – The seven-hour tour to this river, at the bottom of the spectacular Urique Canyon, passes several indigenous villages.

Río Oteros – The Río Oteros walk is considered a day hike; ask before you go.

Campos Menonitas – An eight-hour excursion to the Mennonite country includes a tour of a Mennonite cheese factory (see the Central North Mexico chapter for more on the Mennonites).

La Bufa – The nine-hour tour to La Bufa, a canyon 1750 meters deep with a cool river at the bottom, takes you up and down through five spectacular canyons until you reach La Bufa, 105 km from Creel. Batopilas is two hours farther along the same road; if you don't have two days to spare to visit Batopilas, this tour to La Bufa (US$17 per person with Casa Margarita) lets you experience some of that spectacular scenery in one day, with plenty of stops along the way.

Batopilas – See farther on in this chapter. Offered as one-day (12 hours) or two-day excursions by hotels.

Tour Guides For all of these trips as well as for more extensive trips into the canyons, you could hire your own guide. Expect to pay around US$8 per day; inquire at the office of the Complejo Ecoturístico Arareko, on López Mateos.

Places to Stay

Camping & Cabins The *Complejo Ecoturístico Arareko* (☎ /fax 6-01-26) has a campground on the northeast shore of Lago

Arareco, seven km south of town, with barbecue pits, picnic areas and bathrooms, but no electricity. The cost is US$2.75 per person. They also operate two lodges. The *Albergue de Batosárachi* one km south of Lago Arareco has three rustic cabins with bunk beds or individual rooms, and hot showers; you can cook in the communal kitchen or arrange to have meals prepared. The cost is US$13 per person. The *Cabaña de Segórachi* on the south shore of Lago Arareco, is more luxurious, with the use of a rowboat and other amenities included; the cost is US$19 per person. If you stay at their lodges they'll pick you up at the train or bus station if you give advance notice.

The Lodge at Creel (☎ 6-00-71, in Mexico 800-90475, in the USA 888-879-4071; fax 6-02-00) at López Mateos 61, 500 meters south of the plaza, is a plush Best Western place. Spacious, comfortable self-contained wooden cabins with two beds, cable TV, private kitchen and bath are US$64, breakfast included. West of the rail tracks, by the bus station, is *Hotel Nuevo* (☎ 6-00-22, fax 6-00-22) with pleasant two-bed cabins for US$51, as well as ordinary singles/doubles for US$23/39.

Guesthouses & Hotels The most popular place to stay in Creel is the *Casa Margarita* (☎ /fax 6-00-45) at López Mateos 11, on the northeast corner of the plaza between the two churches, with a variety of accommodations and prices. A bed in the cramped dorm room is US$4, or US$2.75 if you use your own bedding or have a mattress on the floor. Singles/doubles with private bath are US$13/16, or there are larger rooms that work out about US$7.75 per person. All of these prices include both breakfast and dinner. Margarita's is a great place to meet other travelers, as everyone gathers at the table to eat together – often in shifts, since the place is so popular.

The same family runs the comfortable *Hotel Margarita Plaza Mexicana* (☎ /fax 6-02-45), on Calle Elfido Batista, a block from López Mateos. It has a restaurant, bar and 26 big rooms around a pleasant courtyard; singles/doubles are US$26/30,

including breakfast and three-course dinner. Non-guests can come for the set dinner (US$25; call ahead).

Pensión Creel is linked with The Lodge at Creel (see Camping & Cabins), which can make reservations and provide free transport – it's about a 20-minute walk south of the train station otherwise, down López Mateos. There are 11 rooms (some with bunk beds) around a stone courtyard, and a communal sitting room and kitchen. The cost is US$10 per person with breakfast included.

Casa de Huéspedes Perez (☎ 6-00-47), Oscar Flores, is a convenient, friendly place with kitchen facilities; simple rooms with one to three beds are US$5.25 per person. Round the corner is *Cabañas Berti's* (☎ 6-00-86), López Mateos 31, with 12 rooms, all with private bath, starting at US$10/12 for singles/doubles. *Hotel Los Pinos* (☎ 6-00-44), also on López Mateos, has 30 tidy, new-looking rooms with bath and heater at US$9/13 for one/two people. *Casa Valenzuela* at López Mateos 68 has basic small rooms with shared or private bath at US$5.25 per person.

Across the train tracks from the plaza, beside the Estrella Blanca bus station, the *Hotel Korachi* (☎ 6-02-07) has simple rooms with bath at US$11/16 for singles/doubles. A block south, *La Posada de Creel* (☎ /fax 6-01-42) has rooms with shared bath at US$4.25 per person, or rooms with private bath (one to four people) at US$16.

The *Motel Cascada Inn* (☎ 6-02-53, fax 6-01-51) at López Mateos 49 has a covered swimming pool, parking spaces, steakhouse, bar and disco. Its 32 rooms (at US$42/45 for one/two people) each have bathroom, cable TV and two double beds – one soft and one harder.

Places to Eat

There are plenty of restaurants on López Mateos in the few blocks south of the plaza – stroll along and take your pick. *Restaurant Verónica* and *Restaurant Estela* are recommended by locals. Various places have a comida corrida – it's US$1.60 in

Todo Rico and US$2 in *Restaurant la Cabaña*. *Restaurant Laura* on López Mateos has a vegetarian plate for US$2.50; *El Pollo Feliz* specializes in chicken. *Restaurant Jorge's* on Calle Cristo Rey is a tiny place with good food.

Things to Buy

Many places around Creel sell Tarahumara handicrafts, including baskets, colorful dolls, wood carvings, violins, flutes, archery sets, pottery, clothing and more. Prices are very reasonable. The best place to buy them is at the Artesanías Misíon shop on the north side of the plaza; not only is the quality some of the best you'll find, but all the money earned at the shop goes to support the Catholic mission hospital which provides free medical care for the Tarahumara. The shop is open Monday to Saturday from 9.30 am to 1 pm and 3 to 6 pm, Sunday 9.30 am to 1 pm.

Getting There & Away

Bus The Estrella Blanca bus station, across the train tracks from the plaza, has buses to Chihuahua (256 km, 4½ hours; US$10), passing through San Juanito (30 km, one hour; US$2), La Junta (102 km, 2½ hours; US$4.75) and Cuauhtémoc (170 km, three hours; US$7) on the way. Departures are at 7, 8.15 and 10.30 am, at noon, and at 2, 4 and 5.30 pm.

A bus to Batopilas (140 km, seven hours; US$9) departs from outside the Hotel Los Pinos on López Mateos, two blocks south of the plaza. The bus leaves Creel at 7 am on Tuesday, Thursday and Saturday, leaving Batopilas for the return trip at 6 am on Monday, Wednesday and Friday. The road from Creel is paved initially, but the second half is bumpy and rough.

Daily at 4 pm a bus goes to San Rafael, via Divisadero; it departs from Francisco Villa, on the west side of the tracks. The road to Divisadero is newly paved.

Train See the Barranca del Cobre section for schedules and information about the Chihuahua al Pacífico train – you can buy tickets on board.

BATOPILAS
pop 600; alt 495m

Batopilas, a serene 19th century silver-mining village 140 km south of Creel, deep in the heart of the canyon country, is a great starting point for treks into the canyons. Even the journey to get there is a thrilling descent into the canyons, from an altitude of 2338 meters at Creel to 495 meters at Batopilas, with dramatic descents and climbs through several canyons along the way. Batopilas' climate is distinctly warmer and more tropical than Creel's; you descend from a vegetation zone of cool pine forest to a semitropical zone where mangoes, bananas and other tropical fruits are grown. Batopilas has a few small hotels and guesthouses where you can rent rooms. Prices are modest; *Batopilas* charges only US$4/6 for rooms with bath.

Central North Mexico

This chapter includes the entire state of Durango, much of the state of Chihuahua and a tiny part of the state of Coahuila. It covers a long-used travel route between the USA and central Mexico. The route is along the high plains, parallel to the Sierra Madre Occidental, through flat or undulating country with occasional rocky ranges jutting from the plains. The mostly dry, sparsely populated range land is intersected by rivers that flow intermittently from the sierra. The irrigated areas are verdant oases where fruit, cotton and other crops are grown, and where most of the towns have been established.

CIUDAD JUÁREZ & EL PASO (Texas)
Juárez: pop 1 million; alt 1145m; ☎ 16
El Paso: pop 583,421; alt 1165m; ☎ 915

For many short-term visitors, the main attractions of Juárez are cheap dental work, 'bargain' shopping and under-21 drinking. It's a grimy, noisy, booming border town, inextricably linked with El Paso.

The two cities are a study in the unequal relationships 'across the line,' but they stand on a travel route that was being used long before the conquistador Cabeza de Vaca found El Paso del Norte in the 16th century. Modern travelers use the same crossroads, and most find that the ambiance improves as they leave the border.

The area can be insufferably hot in summer, and freezing and windy in winter, but between these extremes it is often warm, dry, sunny and very pleasant. A bustling nightlife in both cities, including a large number of gay and lesbian bars, draws festive people from miles around.

History
For Indians, Spanish explorers and traders, the main north-south travel route followed the course of the Rio Grande (Río Bravo del Norte to Mexicans), which breaks through the low but rugged range of

---

HIGHLIGHTS

- The Paquimé Ruins, a restored complex of adobe structures that once was a major Indian trading settlement
- Chihuahua's Mexican Revolution Museum, housed in Pancho Villa's headquarters – a must-see for history buffs
- Durango's lively Plaza de Armas for people-watching and the rugged countryside outside the city, filming site of many Westerns
- Vivacious Parral, with its quaint narrow streets, several good and cheap places to eat and stay, and a rich history
- Pancho Villa's hacienda at Canutillo, in a dusty Western setting that evokes images of the days long gone

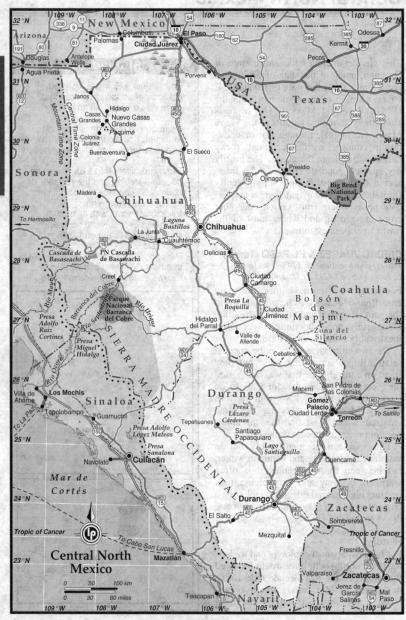

Central North Mexico

mountains at El Paso. In 1848, following the Mexican-American War, the river became the border between the US state of Texas and the Mexican state of Chihuahua.

In the 1860s, the river changed course, shifting southward so that an additional couple of sq km came to be on the US side. The resulting border dispute was the subject of international arbitration in 1911, but wasn't resolved until 1963, when a treaty was signed that provided for engineering works to move the channel of the Rio Grande and transfer some of the land to Mexico. This land is now the Parque Chamizal in Ciudad Juárez.

In the turbulent years of the Mexican Revolution (from 1910), Juárez had a strategic importance beyond its small size. Pancho Villa stormed the town on May 10, 1911, enabling Francisco Madero's faction to force the resignation of the dictator Porfirio Díaz. After Victoriano Huerta's coup against Madero, Villa escaped to refuge in El Paso. In March 1913, he rode back across the Rio Grande with just eight followers to begin the reconquest of Mexico. Within months, he had recruited and equipped an army of thousands, El División del Norte, and, in November, conquered Juárez for a second time – this time by loading his troops onto a train, deceiving the defenders into thinking it was one of their own, and steaming into the middle of town in a modern version of the Trojan horse tactic. Juárez was a vital strategic asset situated at the northern end of the railway that Villa employed to transport captured goods and cattle from other parts of Mexico, which were then smuggled into the USA and traded for munitions and supplies.

Today Juárez is a major center for maquiladoras, which employ thousands of people and have attracted many new arrivals, making Juárez one of Mexico's largest cities.

Orientation

Ciudad Juárez and El Paso sprawl over a wide area on both sides of the Rio Grande, but most places of interest to travelers are concentrated in the central areas of the two cities – in El Paso, around Stanton and Santa Fe Sts, which pass over separate bridges and continue as Avenidas Lerdo and Juárez on the Mexican side of the border. You can walk across either bridge, but by car you must take Stanton St going south and Lerdo going north. Avenida Juárez, lined with shops, bars, restaurants and seedy hotels, is the most important tourist street in Ciudad Juárez and the one to follow if you're heading for the center of town. About five km east of the Santa Fe St/Avenida Juárez bridge, the Cordova Rd bridge (called the 'Bridge of the Americas') leads to a less congested part of Juárez, and to a bypass road that in turn leads directly to the main highway south to Chihuahua. Even farther east, the Zaragoza toll bridge entirely avoids both El Paso and Juárez. Remember to reset your watch when entering Juárez; time here is always an hour ahead of El Paso.

Information

Immigration If you don't intend to venture beyond Ciudad Juárez and you're staying less than 72 hours, you won't need a tourist card. Those moving deeper into Mexico can get one from a Mexican immigration office (at the foot of the Stanton St bridge and on the Cordova Rd bridge), or from the Mexican consulate. To enter the USA, you must show proof of US or Canadian citizenship or residency, or have a passport with a US visa.

Tourist Offices The Juárez tourist office (☎ 16-20-38) is located beside the southern end of the Cordova Rd bridge. There is usually someone there who speaks English. The office is open weekdays from 8 am to 8 pm, weekends until 3 pm.

The El Paso visitor's center (☎ 544-0062), at the intersection of Santa Fe and Main, is open daily from 8 am to 4 pm. They have lots of brochures on El Paso, but not much on Juárez. This office is the starting point for the El Paso-Juárez trolley (see Getting Around in this section).

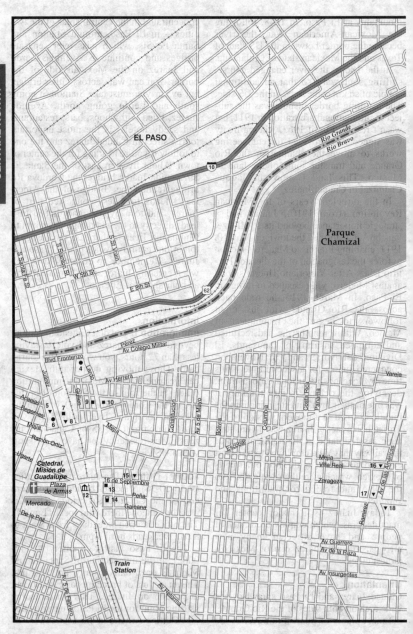

EL PASO

Río Grande
Río Bravo

10

62

Parque
Chamizal

Pérez
Av Colegio Militar

Blvd Fronterizo

4

Lerdo

Av Herrera

Juárez

Corona

9

10

Varela

5

7

6

8

Mejía

Constitución

Av 5 de Mayo

Bolivia

Escobar

Costa Rica

Panamá

Columbia

Abrahia
Segorbias

Ramón Ortiz

Ugarte

Catedral,
Misión de
Guadalupe

Plaza
de Armas

Mercado

De la Paz

16 de Septiembre

15

16

Mejía
Villa Real

Zaragoza

Av de las Américas

13

12

14

Peña

Galeana

17

18

Ramírez

Av Guerrero
Av de la Raza

Train
Station

Av Insurgentes

R. 5 de Febrero

Av Reforma

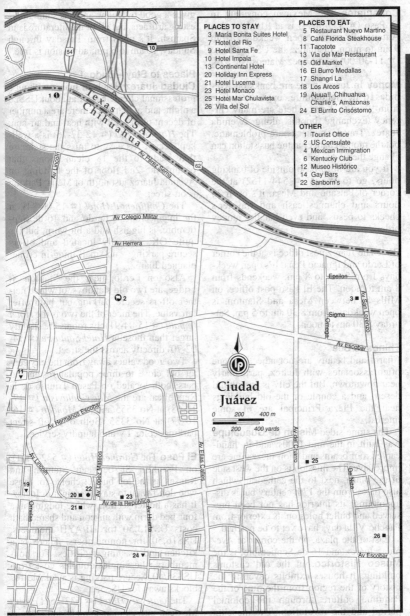

PLACES TO STAY
3   María Bonita Suites Hotel
7   Hotel del Rio
9   Hotel Santa Fe
10 Hotel Impala
13 Continental Hotel
20 Holiday Inn Express
21 Hotel Lucerna
23 Hotel Monaco
25 Hotel Mar Chulavista
26 Villa del Sol

PLACES TO EAT
5   Restaurant Nuevo Martino
8   Café Florida Steakhouse
11 Tacotote
13 Via del Mar Restaurant
15 Old Market
16 El Burro Medallas
17 Shangri La
18 Los Arcos
19 Ajuua!!, Chihuahua
    Charlie's, Amazonas
24 El Burrito Crisóstomo

OTHER
1   Tourist Office
2   US Consulate
4   Mexican Immigration
6   Kentucky Club
12 Museo Histórico
14 Gay Bars
22 Sanborn's

Ciudad Juárez

0   200   400 m
0   200   400 yards

Consulates The Mexican consulate in El Paso (☎ 533-3644) is at 910 East San Antonio St and is open weekdays from 9 am to noon. In Juárez, the US consulate (☎ 11-30-00) is at López Mateos Nte 924.

Money In Juárez there are banks on Avenida 16 de Septiembre, open weekdays from 9 am to 1 pm. There are many currency exchange booths along Avenida Juárez. Traveler's checks are problematic, but the moneychanger at the bus station can change them.

If you are in El Paso outside of banking hours, go to Valuta (☎ 544-1152) at the corner of Paisano and Mesa; it's open 24 hours and changes cash and traveler's checks to pesos, and even handles money orders.

Post The Juárez post office is at the corner of Lerdo and Ignacio Peña. It's open weekdays from 8 am to 8 pm, weekends from 8 am to noon. The El Paso post office, on Mills St between Mesa and Stanton, is open weekdays from 8.30 am to 5 pm, Saturday 8.30 am to noon.

Things to See

Charm and beauty are not adjectives one often associates with Juárez, particularly near downtown. But the city is no cultural desert, and a couple of the old buildings near the Plaza Principal are of some interest.

The stone-sided **Misión de Guadalupe** was built in the mid-1600s, and its hand-carved roof beams and choir mezzanine are impressive. The mission is on the west side of the plaza, next to the cathedral, which also dates from the 17th century but is disappointing; its interior has not been preserved and bullet holes on its exterior from Pancho Villa days have yet to be patched.

East of the plaza, on the corner of Avenidas Juárez and 16 de Septiembre, is **Museo Histórico**, in the old customs building. It houses exhibits covering the history of the region from the time of the Paquimé culture through the colonial period and the revolution. The museum

gives a good overview and has some interesting artifacts, but all of the literature is in Spanish. It's open from Tuesday through Sunday, 10 am to 6 pm; admission is free.

Places to Stay – budget

Ciudad Juárez Hotels in Juárez without a professional clientele start at about US$20 a night, and at that price there are a number of decent places, all with heat and air-con. The *Hotel del Río* (☎ 12-37-76) is a well-kept secret. It's easy to miss the staircase that leads to the 18 clean rooms that occupy the 2nd floor of the building on Avenida Juárez just north of Mejía. Parking is on-street.

The *Continental Hotel* (☎ 15-00-84), at the intersection of Lerdo and 16 de Septiembre, is biggish and a bit worn, but it's quite OK, centrally located and offers secure parking – no small thing in crime-plagued Juárez.

Also on Lerdo, near the Stanton St bridge, are two old standbys, of which neither offers secure parking but both offer fair value. The nicer of the two is the *Hotel Impala* (☎ 15-04-91). Its rooms are slightly larger than those at *Hotel Santa Fe* (☎ 14-02-70) directly across the street.

Two good values away from the city center but close to three popular restaurant/bars, both located on Paseo Triunfo de la República, are the *Mar Chulavista* (☎ 17-14-68) at No 3555 and the *Monaco* (☎ 16-16-77) at No 3335. Both offer off-street parking, color TV and laundry service.

El Paso The *Gardner Hotel* (☎ 532-3661), on Franklin St between Stanton and Kansas, is the top budget choice for those who don't want to stay overnight in Juárez. It has a hostel section, where lodging in a four-bed dorm with air-con and shared bath costs US$13.50 for HI/AYH members, US$16.50 for nonmembers. There is a kitchen and washing facilities. For nonmembers, the singles/doubles cost from US$35/40. Secure parking is available 1½ blocks away for US$5.

The *Gateway Hotel* (☎ 532-2611), with Mexican guests, management and style, is centrally located at 104 Stanton St near the San Antonio St corner, but is not nearly as nice as the Gardner. It has air-con singles and doubles from US$25, and provides secure parking a block away for US$1.50.

Travelers with wheels can look for a motel on the outskirts of town. There are plenty of budget places on N Mesa St – try the *Mesa Inn Hotel* (☎ 532-7911) at No 4151; a former Sheraton, it costs US$27 for singles or doubles and has an inviting pool.

Places to Stay – middle
Ciudad Juárez The middle-weight champion of Juárez is the *María Bonita Suites Hotel* (☎ 27-03-03) on Avenida San Lorenzo just north of Hermanos Escobar. Starting at US$40 a night, every suite is cheerful and tastefully done and contains a large bedroom, private bathroom with beauty bench, a fully equipped kitchen and a sitting area with a large, comfy couch. For US$60, a master suite comes with a king bed and two doubles, a Jacuzzi tub and enough space to throw a party. A gym, pool, hot tub, bar and restaurant round out the facilities. Secure parking is provided.

Rooms at the *Villa del Sol* (17-24-24) on Pérez Serna just south of Paseo Triunfo de la República go for US$38 for a single, US$41 for a double, and are very acceptable. The hotel has a nice pool and lounge and secure parking.

El Paso There is a big selection of mid-range places, with several of the major US chains represented. One of the more popular places in this price bracket is *El Paso City Centre Travelodge* (☎ 544-3333) at 409 E Missouri St. It's centrally located, has a restaurant and lounge, and costs US$45 for singles and doubles. Many motels on the edge of town offer air-con rooms and pools for around US$35.

Places to Stay – top end
Ciudad Juárez *Hotel Lucerna* (☎ 91-16-29) at Avenidas López Mateos and Triunfo de la República is the classiest hotel in town. Little expense was spared on its pool-side restaurant, its gardens or its lounge. Service is excellent. Rooms start at US$58. Directly across the street is a *Holiday Inn Express*, which is new and has all the amenities of a Holiday Inn and larger rooms than the Lucerna. But, with rates starting at US$84, it's not exactly the best value in town.

El Paso The *Camino Real Paso del Norte* (☎ 534-3000) at 101 S El Paso St is the only five-star option in El Paso. The 1912 hotel was recently renovated, and the main bar has retained a superb Tiffany glass dome and ornate decor on a grand scale. Standard rooms start at US$120.

Places to Eat
Ciudad Juárez Juárez is famous for its burritos, and some of the most authentic can be found at *El Burrito Crisóstomo* burrito stand, which is named after the owner's donkey and is located at the corner of Guerrero and Huerta. Two burritos there cost US$1.50. *El Burro Medallas* on Mejía at Américas also serves up banner burritos.

For tacos, try a *Tacotote* ('huge taco'). There are several around town (one is at the corner of Américas and Hermanos Escobar). All use sirloin in their tacos and, unlike the burrito stands mentioned above, Tacototes are enclosed, sit-down restaurants.

Juárez has some excellent fish, meat and Chinese restaurants (many Chinese settled in the area after building the USA's Transcontinental Railroad), and the best of the bunch are named here. Satisfying meals at each can be had for as little as US$6.

For marlin tacos and choice cuts of fish, *Los Arcos* at the corner of Américas and Triunfo de la República is a fine catch. At *Via del Mar*, at the intersection of Lerdo and 16 de Septiembre, try the pescado entero normandi – if black bass stuffed with shrimp and oysters and smothered in white salsa sounds good to you.

Carnivores can take delight in *Restaurant Nuevo Martino* on Juárez, a short walk from the border, and at *Café Florida Steakhouse* at the corner of Mejía and Juárez.

The *Shangri La* on Américas, 50 meters north of 16 de Septiembre, serves excellent Chinese cuisine. A meal at the Shangri La consisting of egg rolls, barbecue pork ribs, cabbage soup, Szechwan shrimp, steam rice and a bowl of mint ice cream costs US$9.

El Paso Bargain eating places can be found downtown along San Antonio east of Stanton. One of them, *The Tap* bar and restaurant, looks more like the former than the latter, but serves tasty Mexican meals ranging from US$3.75 to US$7.50.

Leo's, on Mills just east of Stanton, offers good Mexican food and hamburgers; prices range from US$1.99 to US$8.75. There are several fast-food restaurants on Mills between Stanton and El Paso.

For vegetarian fare, *Aladdin's Family Restaurant* on Stanton between Franklin and Missouri offers several delicious meatless Arabic dishes for under US$7.

Entertainment

Ciudad Juárez The bars and discotheques on Avenida Juárez tend to be grimy and unspectacular – the *Kentucky Club* being the greatest exception – while those near the intersection of Ornelas and Triunfo de la República – *Chihuahua Charlie's*, *Ajuua!!* and *Amazonas* – are impressive. Juárez has many gay and lesbian bars, with many located near Calle Peña at Lerdo, including the *Ritz* and *Club Olímpico*.

El Paso The city is hopping on Friday and Saturday nights, and the downtown area has seen a fivefold increase in the number of its bars in recent years. *The Basement* at 127 Pioneer Plaza and *The Realm* on Stanton near Mills are packed on weekends. The most popular watering hole is *The Old Plantation* at 301 S Ochoa. Although predominantly gay, the multilevel ultramodern bar/disco has become a hit with straights too. *U-Got-It*, 50 meters to the north, is a lively lesbian bar.

Things to Buy

Juárez boasts some quality crafts amid its sea of junk, but at prices much higher than elsewhere in Mexico. Unless this is your last chance to buy a knickknack for Aunt Tilly or a bottle of mezcal for Uncle Bob, don't waste your time shopping in Juárez. The old Juárez market, east of the center on Avenida 16 de Septiembre, has a big collection of souvenir stalls, where you can be overwhelmed by tacky possibilities.

The best place to go for quality goods is *Sanborn's*, adjacent to the Holiday Inn Express. There you will find beautifully carved figurines, wonderful ceramics, exquisite gold and silver jewelry, and breathtaking pottery – all Mexican in style and reasonably priced.

Getting There & Away

Air The Juárez airport (Aeropuerto Internacional Abraham González) is just east of highway 45, about 15 km south of the center of town. There are direct flights to Mexico City, Aguascalientes, Mazatlán and Chicago. Flights to other major cities go via Chihuahua or Mexico City. El Paso is also an important airline hub, with flights to/from many US cities and some European and Asian capitals.

Bus The Juárez bus station (Central de Autobuses) is big and a long way from town. For information on getting there, see the Getting Around section. Mexican buses are generally cleaner and more comfortable than Greyhounds. Main destinations are:

Chihuahua – 398 km, 4½ hours; many 1st-class (US$12) and 2nd-class (US$8)
Mexico City (Terminal Norte) – 1900 km, 26 hours; seven 1st-class (US$64), several 2nd-class (US$53)
Nuevo Casas Grandes – 315 km, four hours; six 1st-class (US$8), frequent 2nd-class (US$5)

Direct buses also go to Durango (US$34), Mazatlán (US$59), Monterrey (US$42), San Luis Potosí (US$63), Saltillo (US$35), Tijuana (US$65) and Zacatecas (US$44).

Mexican buses going direct to US cities (eg, Albuquerque, US$20; Los Angeles, US$35; Denver, US$40) are generally cheaper than the Greyhounds from El Paso.

The El Paso Greyhound station (☎ 542-1355) is at 200 W San Antonio St, just south of the Civic Center Plaza. There are several buses a day to Los Angeles (15 hours, US$35), Chicago (34 hours, US$95), New York (50 hours, US$99), Miami (43 hours, US$99) and other major US cities.

Train You can walk to Juárez's train station from the Mexican side of the Stanton St bridge. Just keep walking straight along Lerdo for about 11 blocks (its name changes to Gabriel). The station (Ferrocarriles Nacionales) is at the corner of Gabriel and Insurgentes. Note: In Mexico, buses are cleaner and far more comfortable than trains.

Trains depart Juárez for Mexico City twice daily (US$45.75/25.75 for primera/segunda clase) via Chihuahua (US$8.50/5), Torreón, Zacatecas, Aguascalientes and Querétaro. For more information, see Getting There & Away in the Mexico City chapter. There are no passenger trains to Nuevo Casas Grandes. Tickets are sold daily from 9 am to noon.

El Paso's Amtrak station (☎ 545-2247) is at 700 San Francisco, three blocks west of the Civic Center Plaza. Trains run three times a week on many routes, eg, Los Angeles (14 hours, US$167), Miami (51 hours, US$239), Chicago (45 hours, US$200) and New York (63 hours, US$259).

Car & Motorcycle For liability and vehicle insurance while in Mexico, try these companies in El Paso: Insurance Consultants International (☎ 591-8279), at 1155 Larry Mahan Drive; Sanborn's (☎ 779-3538), at 440 Raynolds St; or AAA (☎ 778-9521), at 1210 Airway Blvd.

In Juárez, follow the signs to the Aeropuerto to reach highway 45, which goes south to Chihuahua. It's a good road, but it comes with a US$5 toll. The good road to Nuevo Casas Grandes branches west at a traffic circle just south of town. On either road you will come to at least one checkpoint. If your papers are not in order or you don't have a vehicle permit, you will be turned around.

Getting Around

Local buses to the Juárez bus station leave from the corner of Guerrero and Corona. Catch a Ruta 1A bus marked 'Lomas' or 'Granjera' on the southeast corner of the intersection; it runs direct to the station, located 10 km from downtown on Boulevard Oscar Flores, for less than a dollar. From the bus station, local buses marked 'Centro' will drop you near the cathedral.

You can bypass central Juárez altogether if you take one of the direct buses between the El Paso and Juárez bus stations; they leave hourly and take 45 minutes (US$7).

The El Paso-Juárez trolley starts and ends at the El Paso visitor's center (☎ 544-0062), making a one hour loop through Juárez with 11 stops en route, all at places for eating, drinking or shopping. You can get off at any of them and catch a later trolley to return to El Paso. The 'trolley' is actually a bus done up like one of El Paso's old street-cars. Cost is US$11, US$8.50 for kids.

OTHER BORDER CROSSINGS

Though El Paso-Juárez is the most important and frequently used route between Central North Mexico and the USA, there are some alternative crossing points.

Columbus (New Mexico)
General Rodrigo M Quevedo

The small town of General Rodrigo M Quevedo (also called Palomas) is about 150 km west of Juárez, and the border is open 24 hours a day. Motorists can obtain a vehicle permit in one of the trailers beside the border checkpoint. There are a motel and a cheapish hotel, and 2nd-class bus connections to Juárez and Nuevo Casas Grandes.

Columbus has a campground and a motel, but no public transport connections into the USA. It's known as the site of the only foreign invasion of the continental USA – Pancho Villa sacked the town in 1916 (see the sidebar on Villa in this chapter). A museum in Columbus has some exhibits about the attack.

Presidio (Texas)-Ojinaga

This border crossing is 209 km northeast of Chihuahua, and little used by travelers. Still, there are a few daily buses between Chihuahua and Ojinaga, and one 2nd-class train. From Presidio, Greyhound offers daily service to San Antonio, Houston and Dallas; there's no depot, just a bus stop on the corner of O'Riley and Anderson. Both Presidio and Ojinaga have some cheap places to stay and eat.

NUEVO CASAS GRANDES & CASAS GRANDES

Nuevo Casas Grandes: pop 45,685; alt 1463m; ☎ *169*
Casas Grandes: pop 6300; alt 1463m; ☎ *169*

Nuevo Casas Grandes is a four-hour bus trip southwest of Ciudad Juárez, and you could make it to here for a quiet first night in Mexico. It's a peaceful, prosperous, country town serving the surrounding farmlands. The substantial brick houses around the town, which look like they should be in the US Midwest, belong to local Mennonites. The main reason to visit is to see the ruins of Paquimé, adjacent to the nearby village of Casas Grandes.

Orientation & Information

Most of the facilities useful to visitors are within a few blocks of 5 de Mayo and Constitución (the street with railway tracks down the middle). There are banks (ATMs at Banamex and Bancomer), a casa de cambio (next to the Hotel California) and a post office.

Paquimé Ruins & Museum

The 'Casas Grandes' (big houses) are a complex of adobe structures, partially excavated and restored so the networks of crumbled walls now resemble roofless mazes. The area is known as Paquimé, as were the people who lived here. The Paquimé civilization was the major Indian trading settlement in northern Mexico between 900 and 1340 AD. Agriculture flourished, with irrigated maize crops and poultry kept in adobe cages for protection against the extremes of heat and cold.

The Paquimé structures are similar to Pueblo houses of the US Southwest, with distinctive T-shaped door openings designed to slow invaders. Timber beams set into the walls supported roofs and upper floors, some of which have been reconstructed. The largest dwellings had up to three levels.

As the city grew, it was influenced through trade with southern Indian civilizations, particularly the Toltecs. Paquimé acquired some Toltec features, such as a ball court, of which there are remnants. At its peak, the local population is estimated to have been around 10,000.

Despite fortifications, Paquimé was invaded, perhaps by Apaches, in 1340. The city was sacked, burned and abandoned, and its great structures were left alone for more than 600 years. The site was partially excavated in the late 1950s, and exposure to the elements led to erosion of the walls. They have benn now dutifully restored, and some of the unique interior water systems and hidden cisterns have been rebuilt.

The Paquimé were great potters and produced earthenware with striking red, brown or black geometric designs over a cream background. Other pieces were made from black clay. Fine examples can be seen in a new and impressive museum near the ruins. Admission to the Museo de las Culturas de Norte and the ruins is free. Hours are Tuesday to Saturday, 10 am to 5 pm. A restaurant and gift shop are also in the museum.

To reach the site, take a bus from the center of Nuevo Casas Grandes to Casas Grandes; they run every half-hour during the day, and are marked 'Casas Grandes/Col Juárez.' The eight-km journey takes about 15 minutes. You will be let off at the main plaza of Casas Grandes, which is quite picturesque, and from there signs will direct you to the 15 minute walk to the ruins.

Places to Stay

In Nuevo Casas Grandes, most budget travelers stay at the dingy *Hotel Juárez* (☎ 4-02-33) on Obregón just south of 5 de Mayo and close to the bus stops. It costs

US$6/7.50 for singles/doubles, 10% less if you ask owner Mario Pérez for a discount. There's no heating and only fans in the summer, but for one or two nights it's tolerable, and Mario is friendly and speaks very good English.

The *Hotel California* (☎ 4-08-34) at Constitución 209 has clean, air-con rooms with private bath at US$17/19.

Two mid-range motels are on Juárez as you come into town from the north. Both have well-maintained air-con rooms with TV and hot water. The *Motel Piñón* (☎ 4-06-55) costs US$22/25 and has a restaurant and pool (summer only). A block closer to town, the *Motel Paquimé* (☎ 4-13-20) charges US$14/23.

Top honors go to *Motel Hacienda* (☎ 4-10-46) on Juárez 1.5 km farther north of town, with a garden courtyard, swimming pool and restaurant. Comfortable air-con rooms cost US$34/39.

Places to Eat
Nuevo Casas Grandes has a number of good, reasonably priced restaurants. The restaurants at *Motel Piñón*, *Denni's* and *Constantino* are all on Avenida Juárez, and serve good food in pleasant surroundings, but none of them are all that cheap. The best budget eatery is *Café de la Esquina*, convenient to the bus depot at the intersection of 5 de Mayo and Obregón.

Getting There & Away
Daily buses run to/from Ciudad Juárez (315 km, four hours; US$8) and Chihuahua (352 km, 4½ hours; US$10). Other buses go daily to Madera, La Junta, Cuauhtémoc and Creel. The road south, via Zaragoza and Gomez Farías, is very scenic. Passenger train service to Nuevo Casas Grandes has been discontinued.

AROUND NUEVO CASAS GRANDES
Trips in the areas west and south of Nuevo Casas Grandes take in some interesting little towns, cool forests and several archaeological sites. Most can be reached by bus, but to see the ancient rock carvings in the rugged **Arroyo los Monos** you will need a vehicle with good clearance.

A good day trip could include the Mormon village of **Colonia Juárez**, the **Hacienda de San Diego** (a 1904 mansion owned by the Terrazas family, who controlled most of Chihuahua state until the revolution), and the mountain-flanked village of **Mata Ortiz**. This village is a center for the production of pottery, using materials, techniques and decorative styles like those used by the ancient Paquimé culture. Juan Quezada is the most famous of Mata Ortiz's 300 potters, the best of whom can command US$1000 per pot and have an international clientele. Although few visitors stay overnight in Mata Ortiz, there is at least one charming and inexpensive hotel in town.

Getting There & Away
Several direct buses run between Mata Ortiz and Nuevo Casas Grandes daily; cost is US$1.50. Passenger train service to Mata Ortiz has been discontinued.

MADERA
pop 34,608; alt 2092m; ☎ 157

In the sierra south of Nuevo Casas Grandes, Madera retains some forest despite a hearty timber industry. The surrounding area has a number of archaeological sites, as well as some natural attractions. About 66 km west of the town, **Cueva Grande** sits behind a cascading waterfall; inside the cave are some ancient Indian dwellings.

More of these cliff dwellings can be seen at **Complejo Anasazi**, about 40 km west of Madera; a strenuous four-km canyon climb is required. In the same area is the **Puente Colgante** (suspension bridge) over the Río Huápoca, and some **thermal springs**. Several lakes and dams west and north of town offer so-so fishing, and camping is permitted beside the lake just past the 8 km road sign west of Madera; bathrooms and tap water are available.

Places to Stay
For budget lodging, try the *Hotel María* (☎ 2-03-23) at Calle 5a and 5 de Mayo,

with singles and doubles for US$10.25. Much more expensive (and much nicer) is the *Motel Real del Bosque* (☎ 2-05-38) on the highway coming in from Chihuahua, with singles and doubles for US$25.

Getting There & Away

There are several buses daily to Madera from Nuevo Casas Grandes, Cuauhtémoc and Chihuahua. The winding, cliff road linking Madera and Nuevo Casas Grandes should not be driven at night. There is no passenger train service to Madera. Getting to the places of interest north and west of

town is easiest with your own wheels, but your hotel can help with transport.

CHIHUAHUA
pop 627,187; alt 1455m; ☎ 14

Chihuahua, capital city of the state of Chihuahua (Mexico's largest state), is attractive and prosperous, with some fine colonial buildings in the center and a sprawl of newer suburbs and industries around the edges. Most travelers stay here as an overnight stop on a journey to the north or south, or at the start or finish of a trip on the Copper Canyon Railway.

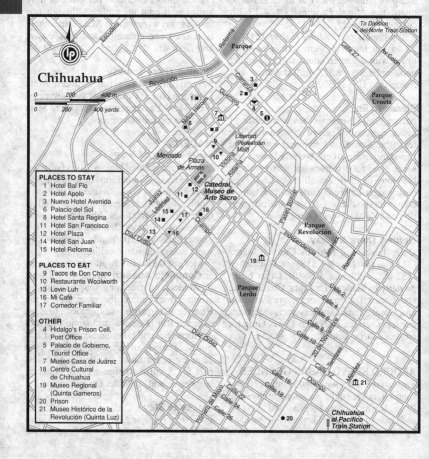

Chihuahua

PLACES TO STAY
1 Hotel Bal Flo
2 Hotel Apolo
3 Nuevo Hotel Avenida
6 Palacio del Sol
8 Hotel Santa Regina
11 Hotel San Francisco
12 Hotel Plaza
14 Hotel San Juan
15 Hotel Reforma

PLACES TO EAT
9 Tacos de Don Chano
10 Restaurante Woolworth
13 Lovin Luh
16 Mi Café
17 Comedor Familiar

OTHER
4 Hidalgo's Prison Cell,
   Post Office
5 Palacio de Gobierno,
   Tourist Office
7 Museo Casa de Juárez
18 Centro Cultural
   de Chihuahua
19 Museo Regional
   (Quinta Gameros)
20 Prison
21 Museo Histórico de la
   Revolución (Quinta Luz)

To Division del Norte Train Station

Parque Urueta

Parque Revolución

Parque Lerdo

Chihuahua al Pacífico Train Station

Chihuahua's main attraction is its museum of the Mexican Revolution located in Pancho Villa's old house, Quinta Luz, but there are other points of interest. The market is visited early morning by Mennonites and colorfully attired Tarahumara Indians. Lots of men wear cowboy hats and boots, reminding you that this is cattle country, as it has been since the days of the great haciendas.

History

Chihuahua, in the language of the indigenous Nahua people, means 'dry and sandy zone.' The first Spanish settlers were miners seeking silver. Franciscan and Jesuit missionaries Christianized the agrarian people of the area, but brutal treatment by the Spaniards led to rebellions by even the most tranquil tribes.

The city of Chihuahua gradually grew in size to administer the surrounding territory and to serve as a commercial center for cattle and mining interests. In the War of Independence, rebel leader Miguel Hidalgo fled here, only to be betrayed, imprisoned by the Spaniards and shot. President Benito Juárez made Chihuahua his headquarters for a while when forced to flee northward by the French troops of Emperor Maximilian. The city also served as a major garrison for cavalry guarding vulnerable settlements from the incessant raids of the Apaches, until the tribe was subdued by the legendary Mexican Indian fighter, Colonel Joaquín Terrazas.

The Porfirio Díaz regime brought railways to Chihuahua and helped consolidate the wealth of the huge cattle fiefdoms – one of which, the Terrazas family, controlled estates the size of Belgium.

After Pancho Villa's forces took Chihuahua in 1913 during the Mexican Revolution, Villa established his headquarters here, had schools built and arranged other civic works. Because of his association with the area, he is a local hero. His former headquarters is a major attraction, and there is a statue of him at the intersection of Avenidas Universidad and División del Norte.

Orientation

Most areas of interest in Chihuahua are within a dozen or so blocks of the central Plaza de Armas – sometimes this means a longish walk, but taxis are expensive and the local bus system is difficult to decipher. The bus station is a long way out of town.

Information

Tourist Office On the ground floor of the Palacio de Gobierno (see below), the state tourist office (☎ 10-10-77) is conveniently located and has a helpful, English-speaking staff. The office is open weekdays 9 am to 7 pm and weekends 10 am to 2 pm.

Money Most of the larger banks are around the Plaza de Armas; Banamex is two blocks northwest on Independencia. Banks tend to be open weekdays from 9 am to 1 pm and 4 to 6 pm. Outside these times, you'll find casas de cambio in the streets behind the cathedral, but their rates are not very competitive.

Post The main post office is on Juárez between Guerrero and Carranza (in the building above Hidalgo's cell). It's open weekdays 8 am to 7 pm, Saturday 9 am to 1 pm.

Catedral

Chihuahua's cathedral, towering magnificently over the Plaza de Armas, has a marvelous baroque façade. Although construction began in 1717, frequent raids by Indians postponed its completion until 1789. The interior is simpler, in Doric style, but with 16 Corinthian columns. On the south side is the entrance to the **Museo de Arte Sacro**, which houses religious paintings and objects from the colonial period.

Museo Histórico de la Revolución Mexicana (Quinta Luz)

The museum of the Mexican Revolution is housed in the mansion and former headquarters of Pancho Villa and is a must-see for history buffs. After his assassination in 1923, a number of Villa's 'wives' filed

Pancho Villa: Bandit-Turned-Revolutionary

Although best known as a hero of the Mexican Revolution, for much of his adult life Francisco 'Pancho' Villa was a murderous thief more given to robbing and womanizing than any noble cause. Born Doroteo Arango on June 5, 1878, in the village of Río Grande in rural Durango, the future revolutionary legend lived the rather unremarkable childhood of a typical peasant boy who later found work on a farm. That peaceful life took an abrupt turn on September 22, 1894, when 16-year-old Doroteo took the law into his own hands.

Accounts of what happened that day vary, but the popular version involves an alleged affront to the honor of his 12-year-old sister, Martina. According to this account, Doroteo was returning from work in the fields when he came upon the landowner attempting to abduct Martina. Doroteo ran to a cousin's house, took a pistol down from a wall, then ran down the landowner and shot him. Fearing reprisal, Doroteo took to the hills and abandoned his baptismal name, calling

JAMES LYON

himself Francisco Villa. 'Pancho,' as his associates called him, spent the next 16 years as a bandit and cattle thief, variously riding with three vicious gangs.

Although the life of Pancho Villa The Revolutionary is well documented, his years as a bandit are obscured by contradictory claims, half-truths and outright lies. According to one story, Villa was once captured by three bounty hunters and would have been executed had he not killed a guard and escaped from prison. Another tale has Villa taking his new name from a bandido who was slain in a shootout – an action Villa supposedly took to demonstrate his authority over the dead man's gang. The tales abound, but one thing is certain: although an outlaw and ever the bully, Villa detested alcohol, and the sight of excessive drinking made his blood boil. In his *Memorias*, Villa gleefully recalled how he once stole a magnificent horse from a man who was preoccupied with getting drunk in a cantina.

Long after his outlaw years, Pancho Villa became uncharacteristically mum whenever the subject of his criminal past came up. When he did admit to banditry, he described his deeds in the loftiest terms, often referring to himself as the Mexican Robin Hood. But unlike the legendary English outlaw famed for robbing the rich and giving to the poor, Villa and the gangs he rode with killed many innocent people. For instance, José Solís, who rode with Villa as part of the Ignacio Parra gang, once killed an old man because he wouldn't sell him some bread.

By 1909, at age 31, Villa had bought a house in Chihuahua and was running a peaceful, if not entirely legitimate, business trading in horses and meat from dubious sources. That spring, Chihuahua's revolutionary governor Abraham González began recruiting men to break dictator Porfirio Díaz's grip on Mexico, and among the people he lobbied was Villa. González knew about Villa's past, but he also knew that he needed men like Villa – natural leaders who knew how to fight – if he ever hoped to depose Díaz. Thus, González encouraged Villa to return to marauding, but this time for a noble cause: agrarian reform. The idea appealed to Villa, and a year later he joined the revolution.

Villa had no trouble finding men to fight beside him against federal troops. There was much poverty, and rich Mexicans and Americans seemed to own all the land in Mexico. Villa's knowledge of the sierra and bandit tactics greatly aided him in battle; federal troops, who had been taught only to march in perfect step and fire in volleys, knew nothing about how to deal with these mobs of men who, armed with hand bombs and rifles, attacked one minute then disappeared the next. Villa's guerrilla tactics – lightning strikes, ambushes and night attacks – confounded them. When rebels under Villa's leadership took Ciudad Juárez in May 1911, Díaz resigned. Francisco Madero, a wealthy liberal from the state of Coahuila, was elected president in November 1911.

But Madero was unable to create a stable government or contain the various factions fighting for power throughout the country. The basic divide thwarting any revolutionary gains was between liberals such as Madero, who sought gradual reform and more radical leaders such as Emiliano Zapata, who was fighting for quick and uncompromising change. Rival forces of varied political complexions pushed Mexico toward chaos, and in early 1913 Madero was toppled from power by one of his own commanders, General Victoriano Huerta.

Huerta did nothing for Mexico except foment greater strife. Pancho Villa fled across the US border to El Paso. But within a couple of months he was back in Mexico, one of four revolutionary leaders opposed to Huerta – the others were Zapata, Venustiano Carranza and Alvaro Obregón. Villa quickly raised an army of thousands, the División del Norte, and by the end of 1913 he had taken Ciudad Juárez (again) and Chihuahua. His victory at Zacatecas the following year is reckoned one of his most brilliant. Terror reigned in the countryside as Huerta's troops fought and pillaged, but Huerta was finally defeated and forced to resign in July 1914. With his defeat, the four revolutionary forces split into two camps, with Carranza and Obregón on one side and Villa and Zapata on the other. The latter pair, however, never formed a serious alliance and the war became increasingly anarchic. Villa never fully recovered from defeat by Obregón in the big battle of Celaya (1915), and Carranza eventually emerged the victor, becoming president in 1917.

But before their fighting days were over, Villa's soldiers would go down in history as the only force ever to invade the United States (Hawaii was not yet a state when the Japanese attacked Pearl Harbor 25 years later). Angered by troop support provided to Obregón by the US government in the battle of Celaya, and by the refusal of American merchants to sell them contraband despite cash advances for goods, in 1916 the Villistas ravaged the town of Columbus, New Mexico, and killed 18 Americans. The attack resulted in the United States sending 12,000 soldiers into Mexico to pursue the invaders, but the slow-moving columns never did catch Villa's men.

In July 1920, after 10 years of revolutionary fighting and 26 years of marauding, Villa signed a peace treaty with Adolfo de la Huerta, who had been chosen provisional president two months earlier. Under the terms of the accord, Villa pledged to lay down his arms and retire to a hacienda called Canutillo, 80 km south of Hidalgo del Parral, for which the Huerta government paid 636,000 pesos. In addition, Villa was given 35,926 pesos to cover wages owed to his troops. He also received money to buy farm tools, pay a security guard and help the widows and orphans of the División del Norte.

For the next three years, Villa led a relatively quiet life. He bought a hotel in Parral and regularly attended cockfights. He installed one of his many 'wives,' Soledad Seañez, in a Parral apartment, and kept another at Canutillo. Then, one day while leaving Parral in his big Dodge touring car, a volley of shots rang out from a two-story house. Five out of the seven passengers in the car were killed, including the legendary revolutionary. An eight-man assassin team fired the fatal shots, but just who ordered the killings remains a mystery. Villa was 45 at the time of his death. ■

claim for his estate. Government investigations determined that Luz Corral de Villa was the generalissimo's legal spouse; the mansion was awarded to her and became known as Quinta Luz.

When Luz died in 1981, the government acquired the estate and made it a museum. Inside are rooms with their original furnishings, a veritable arsenal of weaponry, and some exceptional photographs of the revolution and its principals. Unfortunately, the accompanying explanations are only in Spanish. Parked in a courtyard is the black Dodge Villa was driving when he was murdered in 1923. It's been restored, except for the bullet holes.

You can walk to the museum from the city center or take a red city bus designated 'Avaloz y Juárez,' running south on Ocampo. Get off at the corner of Méndez, cross the road and walk downhill on Méndez for two blocks. Quinta Luz will be on your right, with the entrance in Calle 10a. It's open daily from 9 am to 1 pm and 3 to 7 pm. Admission is US$1.

Museo Regional (Quinta Gameros)

Manuel Gameros started building this mansion in 1907 and promised it to his fiancée as a wedding present. By the time it was finished four years later, she had fallen in love with the architect and decided to marry him instead. The story goes that Gameros insisted on giving her the mansion anyway as a wedding present. It's a gorgeous building with striking art nouveau decoration – the woodcarvings in the dining room are particularly exuberant. Upstairs, one room has Paquimé artifacts and another is made to resemble the inside of a Paquimé house – interesting, but out of place. Quinta Gameros is open Tuesday through Sunday from 9 am to 2 pm and 4 to 7 pm. Admission is US$1.50, half that for students and children.

Palacio de Gobierno

This handsome, 19th century building is on Aldama between Carranza and Guerrero, facing the Plaza Hidalgo. The classic courtyard is surrounded by colonnades of arches, and the walls are covered with murals by Aaron Piña Morales showing the history of Chihuahua; if you can't follow them, the tourist office has a leaflet that helps. On one side of the courtyard is a small room with an eternal flame, which marks the place where Hidalgo was shot.

Hidalgo's Prison Cell

The cell in which Hidalgo was held prior to his execution is beneath the post office (a later construction) on Juárez behind the Palacio – look for the dirty eagle's head with the inscription 'Libertad' to find the entrance. There are a number of historic letters on display, and the cell contains Hidalgo's crucifix, pistol and other personal effects. Despite modern lighting, it still has a real dungeon ambiance and is quite moving if you have some imagination and a sense of history. It's open Tuesday through Friday from 10 am to 1 pm and 4 to 7 pm, weekends from 10 am to 1 pm. Admission is US$1.

Museo Casa de Juárez

Home and office of Benito Juárez during the period of French occupation, this museum exhibits documents and artifacts of the great reformer. It's open weekdays from 9 am to 3 pm and 4 to 6 pm, and weekends from 10 am to 4 pm. Admission is US$1.

Centro Cultural de Chihuahua

This small center has a permanent exhibition of local archaeological artifacts, and often interesting temporary exhibits as well. On Aldama near Ocampo, it's open Tuesday through Sunday from 10 am to 2 pm and 4 to 7 pm. Admission is free.

Places to Stay – budget

The *Hotel San Juan* (☎ 10-00-35) at Victoria 823 is an older-style hotel with a courtyard and singles/doubles with heating and private bath for US$4.50/5.75. Another old place with style is the *Hotel Reforma* (☎ 10-68-46) at Victoria 814, with clean, spacious rooms and private bath for US$7.50/10.25. *Hotel Plaza* (☎ 15-58-34), directly behind the cathedral on Calle 4, is run-down but cheap at US$4.50/5.50.

Places to Stay – middle

The *Hotel Bal Flo* (☎ 16-03-00), at the intersection of Niños Héroes and Calle 5a 702, has secure parking and air-con rooms with bath for US$14.25/16.75. The *Hotel Santa Regina* (☎ 15-38-89) at Calle 3a 107 is a better choice if you want a modern place near the center. It's clean, has parking and is quite OK at US$18/21.

Chihuahua's first hotel, the *Hotel Apolo* (☎ 16-11-00), opposite the post office, has parking, a great-looking lobby and nice rooms for US$16/17. The *Nuevo Hotel Avenida* (☎ 15-28-91), across the street from the Apolo, is modern and offers rooms for US$16.75/21.50.

For vehicled visitors there are a number of motels on the main roads into town. One, the *Hotel Marrod* (☎ 19-46-11) on the main road north, offers air-con rooms with breakfast for US$21.50/24.

Places to Stay – top end

The *San Francisco* (☎ 16-75-50) at Victoria 504 is nearest the plaza and costs US$60/64. The high-rise, deluxe *Palacio del Sol* (☎ 16-60-00) on the corner of Niños Héroes and Independencia is quite central and costs US$64/67. For more luxuries and higher prices you have to go farther from the center, where the *Hotel Casa Grande* (☎ 19-66-33) at Avenida Tecnológico 4702 has enough room for tennis courts and swimming pools.

Places to Eat

The *Hotel San Juan* and *Hotel Reforma* serve good, cheap food in their restaurants – the San Juan has a more earthy atmosphere and is more popular. *Comedor Familiar* at Victoria 830 serves a good breakfast, while *Mi Café* at Victoria 807 is more modern and more expensive but not a bad value. For vegetarian, try *Lovin Luh* at the intersection of Victoria and Díaz Ordaz for very good, very cheap Chinese food. Across the street is a blue-and-yellow stand

where whole grilled chickens with tortillas and two kinds of salsa sell for US$4.50.

Restaurante Woolworth, on the Libertad pedestrian mall, is ultra-clean, very popular and quite filling for under US$7. Across the way, *Tacos de Don Chano* serves them up hot and delicious for US$2 apiece. The *Rincón Mexicana*, on Cuauhtémoc just south of Talaver, is one of the city's top Mexican restaurants and charges about US$9 per meal.

Getting There & Away

Air Chihuahua's airport has three flights a day to Mexico City and daily flights to Los Angeles and to major cities in northern Mexico.

Bus The bus station has restaurants, luggage storage, a moneychanger (weekdays 9 am to 9 pm, weekends 9 am to 5 pm) and a telephone office. Chihuahua is a major center for buses in every direction. The destinations mostly likely to be of interest to travelers are:

Ciudad Juárez – 398 km, 4½ hours; several 1st-(US$12) and frequent 2nd-class (US$8)
Creel – 256 km, 4½ hours; hourly 1st-class (US$10.25)
Cuauhtémoc – 104 km, 1½ hours; several 1st-class (US$11)
Durango – 700 km, nine hours; several 1st-class (US$20.75)
Hidalgo del Parral – 301 km, three hours; several 2nd-class (US$7.75)
Mexico City (Terminal Norte) – 1500 km, 21 hours; many 1st-class (US$52) and some deluxe
Nuevo Casas Grandes – 352 km, 4½ hours; many 1st-class (US$10)
Zacatecas – 853 km, 12½ hours; several 1st-class (US$30)

Other buses go to Acapulco, Aguascalientes, Guaymas, Hermosillo, Mazatlán, Ojinaga, Mexicali, Monterrey, Nogales, Nuevo Laredo, Saltillo, San Luis Potosí, Tampico, Torreón and Tijuana.

Train El División del Norte (train No 8) from Ciudad Juárez to Mexico City departs the Ferrocarriles Nacionales de México

CENTRAL NORTH

station on the north side of Chihuahua at 3.15 am. The northbound train No 7 leaves at 1.20 am. See the Mexico City Getting There & Away section for more on this train.

Chihuahua is also the northeastern terminus of the Chihuahua al Pacífico line for Barranca del Cobre (Copper Canyon) trains. These trains use the Chihuahua al Pacífico station, near the intersection of Calles Méndez and 24. The air-con primera especial *vistatren*, No 74, departs daily at 7 am for the 13½ hour run down through the canyon country to Los Mochis, near the Pacific. The vistatren from the coast, No 73, arrives in Chihuahua at 8.50 pm. Fare is US$46 in either direction. There is also a far less comfortable segunda clase train (No 76) that leaves Chihuahua three times a week at 8 am and takes about two hours longer (US$9.25); it may be delayed and it doesn't reach the most scenic area till after dark. For more information on the train and stops along the way, see the Barranca del Cobre (Copper Canyon) section in the Northwest Mexico chapter.

Note that you enter a different time zone when you cross the Chihuahua-Sinaloa state border; Sinaloa is one hour behind Chihuahua.

Getting Around

Airport buses collect passengers from the better city hotels; contact the nearest one even if you're not staying there.

The bus station is way out to the east of town along Avenida Pacheco. To get there, catch a city bus marked 'Aeropuerto' or 'Central Camionera' from the corner of Avenidas Victoria and Ocampo.

For the Ferrocarriles Nacionales de México station, take a 'Granjas Colón' or 'Villa Colón' bus running from the center and ask the driver to let you know when you're there. For the Chihuahua al Pacífico station, take a 'Villa Juárez,' 'Santa Rosa' or 'Avelos' bus and get out at the prison – it looks like a medieval castle – then walk behind the prison to the station.

There are local buses going throughout the city, but most places of interest to visitors are within walking distance of the center. Taxis are unmetered so you have to bargain.

AROUND CHIHUAHUA
Cuauhtémoc
pop 120,228; alt 2010m; ☎ 158

West of Chihuahua, this is a center for the Mennonite population of northern Mexico. There are several decent places to stay in Cuauhtémoc, including the *Hotel Linda-vista* (☎ 2-02-53), on the corner of California and Calle 18a, for US$7.50/9 for a single/double; the *Hotel San Francisco* (☎ 2-31-52), on Calle 18a near Morelos, for US$4.75/6; and the very comfortable *Motel Tarahumara Inn* (☎ 1-19-19), on the corner of Calle 5a and Allende, with rooms going for US$25.

Cuauhtémoc is 1½ hours by bus or 3½ hours by train from Chihuahua. You'll need a car or tour operator to see the nearby villages where the Mennonites actually live.

The Mennonites

Founded by the Dutchman Menno Simonis in the 16th century, the Mennonite sect takes no oaths of loyalty other than to God, and eschews military service. Persecuted for their beliefs, the sect's members moved from Germany to Russia to Canada, and thousands settled in the tolerant, post-revolutionary Mexico of the 1920s.

In villages around Cuauhtémoc, you might encounter Mennonite men in baggy overalls and women in black dresses driving horse-drawn buggies and speaking their own dialect of old German. Traditionally, they lead a spartan existence, speak little Spanish, and marry only among themselves, though some of the prosperous communities seem these days to be using tractors and driving cars. Their best known product is Mennonite cheese *(queso Menonito)*, which is sold in many shops and sometimes peddled on the street. ■

La Junta
pop 75,000; alt 2010m; ☎ 158

The next town west of Cuauhtémoc, La Junta has little to offer the tourist. However, it *is* a stop for trains running between Chihuahua and Los Mochis. By car, one can head west from La Junta to the spectacular Cascada de Basaseachi and Hermosillo (see the Northwest Mexico chapter). The *Hotel Viajero* (no phone), on 16 de Septiembre a half block from the train station, has basic but clean rooms for US$6.50/10.25.

HIDALGO DEL PARRAL
pop 98,372; alt 1652m; ☎ 152

Founded as a mining settlement in 1631, the town took the 'Hidalgo' tag later and is still commonly called just 'Parral.' In the 16th century, enslaved Indians mined the rich veins of silver, copper and lead. During the French intervention (1861-67), a fort on Parral's Cerro de la Cruz (Hill of the Cross) was occupied by French troops under orders from Emperor Maximilian.

Parral is now most famous as the place where Pancho Villa was murdered on July 20, 1923 (see the Pancho Villa sidebar in this chapter). A hero to the campesinos of the state of Chihuahua, Villa was buried in Parral, with 30,000 attending his funeral. In 1976, his body (and Parral's major tourist attraction) was moved to Mexico City. The building from which Villa was shot is now a library, with a small collection of Villa photos, guns and memorabilia upstairs.

Parral has churches from the 16th and 17th centuries, some quaint narrow streets and plazas, and a couple of old mansions and theaters. It's a pleasant enough town and quite prosperous, as well as the most interesting place to break a journey between Chihuahua and Durango.

Orientation
With its narrow, winding one-way streets, Parral can be confusing at first. A tourist map is available from the better hotels, and most of the places of interest are roughly in a line north of the riverbed.

Places to Stay & Eat
The *Hotel Acosta* (☎ 2-00-16) at Barbachano 3, near Plaza Principal, is the best value in town at US$12/14 for a single/double; ask for a 3rd-floor room and be sure to check out the view from the roof (the management doesn't mind if you take a chair and bottle of wine up there). The cheapest decent place is the *Hotel Fuentes* at Maclovia 79; its clean and spacious rooms go for US$6.50/7. The *Motel El Camino Real* (☎ 3-02-02) offers comfortable rooms for US$23.50/28.50, has a pool and is near the bus station on Avenida Independencia.

The restaurant in the *Hotel Adriana* on Calle Colegio has tasty Mexican food, a pleasant ambiance and low prices. Decked out in pastels and sided by tall windows offering sweeping city vistas, *J Cuissine Bar & Grill* opposite the Motel El Camino Real is Parral's hippest restaurant. But with most meals topping US$7, J Cuissine certainly is not for everyone. The restaurant beside the *Hotel Turista* near Plaza Independencia whips up an excellent traditional Mexican breakfast for US$5.

Getting There & Away
The bus station on the southeast outskirts of town is most easily reached by taxi ($3). There are regular buses to Chihuahua (three hours; US$7.75), Durango (3½ hours; US$12.75), and Valle de Allende (one hour; US$4.50).

AROUND HIDALGO DEL PARRAL
The road east to Ciudad Jiménez goes through dry, undulating country, but just south of this road, the village of **Valle de Allende** is lush with trees and surrounded by green farmland. The stream through the valley is fed by mineral springs that start near **Ojo de Talamantes**, a few km west, where there's a small bathing area. It's not very deep, but it's a cool and pretty place for a picnic, walking or camping; it costs US$1.

Canutillo, 80 km south of Parral on the road to Durango, is where Pancho Villa spent the last three years of his life (see the

Pancho Villa sidebar in this chapter). His former hacienda, which is attached to a 200-year-old church, is now a museum. The two front rooms contain photographs of the revolutionary, his guns, etc. Unfortunately, the roofs of the remaining rooms, including Villa's bedroom, long ago collapsed, and the floors have given way to weeds.

TORREÓN, GÓMEZ PALACIO & CIUDAD LERDO

Torreón: pop 507,800; alt 1150m; ☎ 17
Gómez Palacio: pop 256,983; alt 1140m; ☎ 17
Ciudad Lerdo: pop 105,372; alt 1155m; ☎ 17

Of these three contiguous cities, Torreón is actually in the state of Coahuila while the others are in Durango. Torreón was established in 1887 as a railway town, and continues as a center for transport, as well as mining, smelting and other industries. On the other side of the Río Nazas, in Durango state, Lerdo dates from 1827 and has lots of trees and gardens, while Gómez Palacio, founded in 1899, is something of a commercial center. Some of the surrounding land has been irrigated and grows wheat and cotton. The whole district, including the three towns, is known as La Laguna.

The 1910 battle for Torreón was Pancho Villa's first big victory in the Mexican Revolution, and it gave him control of the railways that radiate from the city. There were two more battles for Torreón in the ensuing struggles.

Torreón has few tourists, though it has an attractive central plaza and a couple of decent museums. The Christ statue overlooking Torreón, flanked by TV antennas, is the second-largest in the Americas, behind the one in Rio de Janeiro.

Information

There's a state tourist office (☎ 12-38-29) in Torreón, on Matamoros between Vicario and Corona, open weekdays 9 am to 2 pm and 4 to 7 pm, Saturday 9 am to 2 pm. Some members of the staff speak English.

Museo Regional de la Laguna

This museum has a small but interesting collection of pre-Hispanic artifacts from the region and a selection of pieces from other parts of the country. It's on Avenida Juárez a couple of km east of Torreón's main plaza, and is open Tuesday through Sunday from 9 am to 2 pm and 5 to 7 pm; admission is free.

Museo Casa del Cerro

This museum, located in a beautifully restored 1904 Torreón residence, houses a fine collection of regional photos taken during the first three decades of the 20th century. For gun buffs, there is also an array of hundred-year-old Winchester rifles and Colt pistols. The museum, open Monday through Saturday 9 am to 5 pm and Sunday 9 am to 2 pm, is located a short walk uphill from the corner of Avenida Central and Calle Industria.

Places to Stay & Eat

All the following places are in Torreón.

The *Hotel Galicia* (☎ 16-11-11), on the north side of Torreón's main plaza at Morelos 1360, is the city's cheapest place to stay at US$7 for a single or double, but it has a substantial cockroach population and could use a good scrubbing. A major step up in price and quality is the *Hotel del Paso* (☎ 16-03-03), on the corner of Morelos and Fuentes, which offers rooms for US$15/17. Better still, for US$2 more, is the *Hotel Calvete* (☎ 16-15-30), on the corner of Juárez and Reforma, which offers large, clean rooms with firm beds, color TV, air-con, heating and private phone.

Restaurante El Pastor, on Morelos between Juárez and Hidalgo, serves up tasty tacos for US$0.80 apiece. The ever-popular *Restaurante Woolworth*, on Carrillo between Hidalgo and Revolución, offers a good selection of meals, with few more than US$7 and most under US$5. One block north on Carrillo, *La Copa de Leche* is a popular diner offering burritos, tacos and tostadas for about US$3; sandwiches are not their forte. For good Mexican meals costing about US$5 and served in a large, cheerful room with a youthful ambiance, try the *Alameda Restaurant & Bar* at the intersection of Guerra and Juárez.

Getting There & Away

There are bus stations in both Torreón and Gómez Palacio, and long-distance buses will stop at both or will transfer you to the other without charge. The Torreón bus station is east of town on Juárez six blocks east of Reforma. Taxis are the best way to get into downtown, with the trip costing less than US$3. There are regular connections to Chihuahua (467 km, six hours; US$17), Durango (257 km, four hours; US$9), Mazatlán, Mexico City, Saltillo and Zacatecas. For details of the train connections to the north and south, see the Mexico City chapter. The tolls on the pay highway to Durango total nearly US$20, as do the tolls from Torreón to Saltillo; most vehicles take the slightly slower, free road.

AROUND TORREÓN

The deserts north of La Laguna are starkly beautiful, with strange geological formations around **Dinamita**, and many semiprecious stones for gem hunters. It's easiest to get around with your own transport, but the tourist office in Gómez Palacio can arrange tours, and rental cars are available.

To reach the dusty old mining town of **Mapimí** from Gómez Palacio, go about 35 km north on highway 49 to Bermejillo, then 35 km west on highway 30. The town looks unchanged since Benito Juárez stayed here in the mid-19th century – the house where he stayed, near the northwest corner of the plaza, is now a small museum (closed Mondays). East of town is the turnoff to the abandoned **Mina Ojuela**, now a ruined ghost town. The spectacular 300-meter-long suspension bridge was built in 1892 and carried ore trains from the mine; its engineer later designed a better-known suspension bridge in San Francisco.

At Ceballos, 87 km north of Gómez Palacio, a rough road goes east to the **Zona del Silencio**, so called because conditions here are said to prevent propagation of radio waves. Peppered with meteorites, it is also believed to be a UFO landing area. The surrounding **Bolsón de Mapimí** desert is a 'reserva de la biosfera' (biosphere reserve) dedicated to the study of the plants and animals of this very arid area, including a very rare land-based tortoise. This is a remote area with rough roads.

DURANGO

pop 464,213; alt 1912m; ☎ *18*

Don't be too put off by the modernization on the outskirts of the city – proceed directly to Durango's delightful Plaza de Armas, where you'll discover fine colonial architecture. The city was founded in 1523 by conquistador Don Francisco de Ibarra and named after the Spanish city of his birth. Just north of the city, Cerro del Mercado is one of the world's richest iron ore deposits and was the basis of Durango's early importance, along with gold and silver from the Sierra Madre.

Other industries of the area include farming and grazing, timber and paper. Durango is also in the movie business, with a number of locations outside the city, especially for Westerns. Many of the restaurants have movie or cowboy decor, and lots of shops sell cowboy boots, belts and hats. It's a fun town, and very friendly.

Orientation

Durango is a good town to walk around in, and most of the interesting places to see and stay are within a few blocks of the plaza. For some greenery, go to the extensive Parque Guadiana on the west side of town.

Information

Tourist Offices The local tourist office (☎ 11-11-07) is located at the corner of Felipe Pescador and Cuauhtémoc. The staff are helpful and speak some English. The office is open daily, except Thursday, from 8 am to 4 pm. The state tourist office (☎ 11-21-39) at Hidalgo No 408 Sur has no English speakers and little printed information in English.

Money For currency exchange you will find a Bancomer at the northwest corner of the Plaza de Armas. It's open weekdays from 9 am to 1.30 pm, but come early to avoid a long wait. There are other banks nearby (with ATMs), and a casa de cambio next to the Hotel Roma that has longer hours and quicker service, but lower rates.

Post & Communications The post office is on 20 de Noviembre at Roncai, about 1.5 km east of the plaza. Hours are weekdays 8 am to 8 pm, and Saturday 8 am to 4 pm.

There are pay phones in the plaza and elsewhere around town, and a telephone caseta just north of the plaza on Martínez.

Walking Tour

The **Plaza de Armas** is attractive, especially on Sunday, when musicians perform on the bandstand and locals promenade. On the north side is the **Catedral**, with its imposing baroque façade, constructed from 1695 to 1750. Walk west on 20 de Noviembre and on your right you will see the elegant 19th century **Teatro Ricardo Castro**, which houses temporary exhibitions and serves more as a cinema than a theater.

Turn south on Martínez, past the **Teatro Victoria**, to another plaza. On its north side is the **Palacio de Gobierno**, built on the estate of a Spanish mine owner and expropriated by the government after the War of Independence. Inside are colorful murals depicting the history of the state. On the plaza's east side is the **Universidad Juárez**. From there, walk east on 5 de Febrero to the **Casa del Conde de Suchil**, the 17th century home of the Spanish governor of Durango, the Conde de Suchil. Two blocks farther east is the **Mercado de Gómez Palacio**, a good place for a snack and a rest.

Special Events

On July 8, Feria Nacional, the celebration of Durango's founding, is one of the most exciting festivals in Mexico. The fiesta brings some of the country's most famous musicians, bands and dancers to the city, along with local industrial, agricultural and artistic exhibits. All hotels are booked in advance, so make a reservation.

Places to Stay – budget

The best value in town is the *Hotel Posada Durán* (☎ 11-24-12), next to the cathedral

on 20 de Noviembre; the Duran has a handsome courtyard and spacious singles/doubles for US$10/12. On the other side of the cathedral, *Hotel Plaza Catedral* (☎ 13-24-80) is another attractive colonial hotel with rooms surrounding a courtyard, for US$14/15.50. Also acceptable and attractive, though with slightly smaller rooms, is the *Hotel Roma* (☎ 12-01-22) at 20 de Noviembre 705; rates are US$12.25/16.

Hotel Ana Isabel, on 5 de Febrero a stone's throw east of León de la Peña, has lovely, newer rooms in a cheerful setting for US$14.75 for one or two people. The *Hotel Gallo* (☎ 11-52-90), on 5 de Febrero at Progreso, isn't going to win any contests for charm but it's centrally located and for US$5 per room, it's a deal.

Durango's cheapest digs can be found at the *Villa Deportiva Juvenil* (☎ 8-70-71). This youth hostel, on Colegio Militar, 400 meters south of the intersection of Pescador and Colegio Militar on the east side of the street, offers clean dorm beds for US$2.50 a night – even less for HI members.

Places to Stay – middle

The *Posada San Jorge* (☎ 13-32-57), on Constitución two blocks north of the plaza, was undergoing major upgrades in 1997, with Jacuzzi tubs being added to elegant rooms in a handsome colonial building. If the rates remain at US$20/22 (as the owner said they would), this inn would win the mid-range title by a knockout.

The *Hotel Casablanca* (☎ 11-35-99), only two blocks from the plaza at 20 de Noviembre 811, has large, well-appointed rooms with air-con and private bath for US$27/30.

Places to Stay – top end

The *Hotel Gobernador* (☎ 13-19-19), one km east of the Plaza de Armas at 20 de Noviembre 257, is a modern building with colonial-style rooms, a swimming pool and an elegant restaurant. It's the best hotel in town, with air-con singles or doubles with phones, TV and the works for US$70 and up.

CENTRAL NORTH

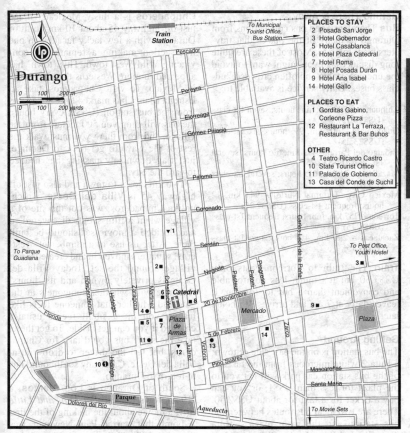

PLACES TO STAY
2 Posada San Jorge
3 Hotel Gobernador
5 Hotel Casablanca
6 Hotel Plaza Catedral
7 Hotel Roma
8 Hotel Posada Durán
9 Hotel Ana Isabel
14 Hotel Gallo

PLACES TO EAT
1 Gorditas Gabino,
   Corleone Pizza
12 Restaurant La Terraza,
   Restaurant & Bar Buhos

OTHER
4 Teatro Ricardo Castro
10 State Tourist Office
11 Palacio de Gobierno
13 Casa del Conde de Suchil

Places to Eat

The best place to eat cheaply is at the market on 20 de Noviembre, four blocks east of the plaza. On Constitución, three blocks north of the plaza, *Gorditas Gabino* offers a variety of tasty gorditas for US$1 apiece. Next door, the hugely popular *Corleone Pizza* serves excellent pizzas from US$2.50 for a small with cheese to US$10 for a large pizza pie with all the toppings.

For eating with ambiance, try the very popular *Restaurant La Terraza*, upstairs at 5 de Febrero overlooking the plaza. Break-fast costs about US$2, sandwiches from US$2.50 to US$4, and traditional dinners generally from US$3 to US$7.50 (a large, delicious ham-and-cheese burrito costs only $2). The restaurant is open late, as is the *Restaurant & Bar Buhos* two doors down, which is slightly more expensive but has entertainment most evenings.

If you like ice cream, don't ignore the many ice cream shops around the plaza and on 20 de Noviembre just east of it. Many flavors are available, and you can get several big scoops for US$1.

Getting There & Away

Bus There are good bus connections from Durango to many of the places that travelers want to go to. Most of these are quite long distances, so you might want to avoid the uncomfortable and often crowded 2nd-class buses. Daily service is available to:

Chihuahua – 700 km, nine hours; seven 1st-class (US$20.75)
Guadalajara – 609 km, 9½ hours; six 1st-class (US$23.25)
Hidalgo del Parral – 412 km, 6½ hours; several 1st-class (US$12.75)
Mazatlán – 318 km, 6½ hours; several 1st-class (US$10.75)
Mexico City (Terminal Norte) – 941 km, 12 hours; frequent 1st-class (US$32.25)
Torreón – 257 km, four hours; frequent 1st-class (US$8.75)
Zacatecas – 290 km, 4½ hours; two 1st-class (US$9.75)

Train The train to Torreón costs only US$3.50 but it's much less comfortable and convenient than a bus to Torreón. It leaves daily at 7 am and arrives 4½ hours later.

Getting Around

The bus station is on the east side of town; a Ruta 2 white microbus from the far side of the bus station car park will get you to the plaza for less than US$1, or you can buy a ticket for a taxi for about US$2.50. There are two local bus routes between the bus station and the main plaza – Ruta Amarillo and Ruta Azules. Buses marked 'Central Camionera' go to the bus station; those marked 'Centro' go to the main plaza. They are slow and crowded but cost less than US$1.

AROUND DURANGO
Movie Locations

The clear light and stark countryside make Durango a popular location for Hollywood movies. Around 120 have been shot in the area – mostly Westerns, including John Wayne vehicles such as *Chisum*, *Big Jake* and *The War Wagon*. If you're into movies, you might enjoy visiting the sets.

Chupaderos is a dusty Mexican village just off highway 45 about 10 km north of Durango with a few tacky façades on one intersection making a remarkably convincing Wild West town. This 'town' has appeared in more Westerns than any other in Mexico. To visit Chupaderos, take an Estrella Blanca bus marked for Chupaderos from the bus station (US$2; every hour); the bus will drop you 500 meters from the village, and from there you must walk the rest of the way. To get back to Durango, just flag down any passing bus headed toward the city.

Two km closer to town and also just off highway 45 is **Villa del Oeste**, which, unlike Chupaderos, was not the site of a village when a film scout 'discovered' it and decided a movie set should be built there. After its use in a number of Westerns, squatters moved in and created a real village around the set. Today Villa del Oeste is privately owned and its 'hours' fluctuate with whether someone's at the gate and whether that someone feels like letting you in; a small fee is usually charged if you can get inside. To get there, take the same bus you'd take for Chupaderos, but tell the driver to drop you at Villa del Oeste. Catch any southbound bus to return to Durango.

South of Durango is **Los Alamos**, a '1940s town' where *Fat Man and Little Boy*, a movie about the making of the first A-bomb that starred Paul Newman, was filmed in 1989. Today it is the most intact of the sets, but many of the buildings are marked with graffiti, and the four-km drive from the main road to the set is unpaved and deeply rutted. The highlight of the trip is the area's canyons. To get to the movie set, take Boulevard Arrieta south of town and stay on it for about 30 km. Watch for a sign on the right announcing the turnoff for the set. Buses are not an option.

West of Durango

The road west of Durango to Mazatlán, on the coast, is particularly scenic, with a number of natural attractions on the way.

In the area around **El Salto**, you can trek to waterfalls, canyons and forests. The spectacular stretch of road about 160 km from Durango is called **El Espinazo del Diablo** (The Devil's Backbone). You enter a new time zone when you cross the Durango-Sinaloa state border; Sinaloa is one hour behind Durango.

EL SOL

LA SANDIA

EL GALLO

EL BANDOLON

EL CAMARON

LA ESTRELLA

Northeast Mexico

This chapter covers the state of Nuevo León and most of the states of Tamaulipas and Coahuila – a huge area, stretching nearly 1000 km from north to south and 500 km from east to west. Many travelers enter Mexico at one of the five main border crossings from the USA, and take one of the several routes heading south to the Bajío region, central Mexico or the Gulf Coast. But most travelers pass through the region as quickly as they can to what is seen as the 'real' Mexico. This is not surprising, as northeast Mexico does not have impressive pre-Hispanic ruins, charming colonial towns, or pretty palm-fringed beaches. What it does have is a geography unlike anywhere else in Mexico, and an emerging culture that is unique in the world.

Geographically, the deserts of northeast Mexico are the southern extension of the Great Plains of the USA and Canada, impressive for their stark, rugged beauty and sheer expanse. The Rio Grande, often called the Río Bravo del Norte in Mexico, is vital for irrigation in this arid region, and it has been developed as a resource by joint Mexican-US projects. In fact, it may have been over-developed, and attention is now being paid to environmental quality along

---

HIGHLIGHTS

- The prosperous state capital of Monterrey, home to some of Mexico's finest modern architecture
- The high-sierra city of Saltillo, with its pleasant climate and some lovely colonial buildings
- The tranquil town of Parras – an oasis in the Coahuilan desert and home to the Americas' oldest winery
- Matamoros' Playa Bagdad, a wide stretch of clean sand with a number of seaside restaurants serving up cheap seafood

JAMES LYON

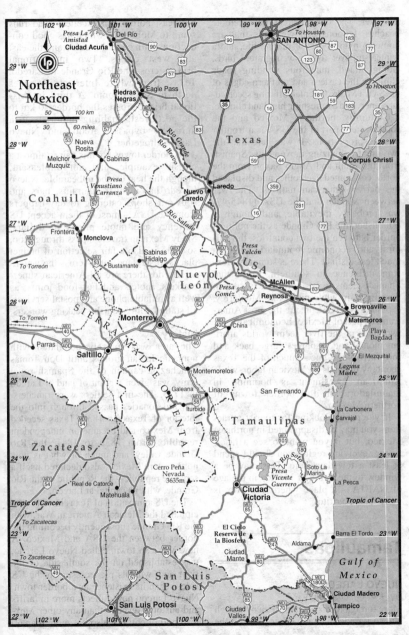

the river. The coastal areas have remote beaches, lagoons and wetlands that are home to many types of marine life, and a winter stopover for many migratory birds. Going inland, numerous winding roads climb to the eastern and northern edges of the Sierra Madre Oriental, offering spectacular scenery and a refreshing highland climate.

Culturally, northeast Mexico and the southwestern part of the USA is a frontier of epic proportions. It was here that the two great colonizing movements, Spanish from the south and Anglo-Saxon from the north, confronted each other and displaced the native American nations. The war between Mexico and the USA (1845-47) was probably inevitable, and though it established the Rio Grande as the political border between the two countries, the cultural and economic boundaries remain much less distinct. There is so much Mexican influence in southern Texas that Spanish seems to be more widely spoken than English, while cities like Monterrey, capital of Nuevo León, are the most Americanized part of Mexico. Economically, the two sides of the river seem worlds apart, but money and resources surge back and forth across the line – much of the Texas economy depends on Mexican labor, while American investment is booming in maquiladoras in the border towns of northern Mexico.

If you're just looking for tourist attractions you may be disappointed in northeast Mexico, but if you want to see a fascinating, evolving region you should spend at least a few days here. This may be a window to the future of Mexico in the age of NAFTA – a place where Tex-Mex is more than a burrito.

Tamaulipas

NUEVO LAREDO
pop 450,000; alt 438m; ☎ *87*
More foreign tourists enter Mexico through Nuevo Laredo than any other town on the

northeast border. An excellent road runs south to Monterrey, which has good connections with central Mexico and the east and west coasts. Two international bridges cross the Rio Grande to Laredo, Texas, from where Interstate 35 goes north to San Antonio. A third international bridge crosses the border 20 km to the northwest, enabling motorists in a hurry to bypass Laredo and Nuevo Laredo altogether.

As border towns go, this pair is almost a classic example, and not unpleasant, though the heat can be unbearable. Nuevo Laredo has many restaurants, bars and souvenir shops catering to day-trippers from the USA – most of them accept US currency and quote prices in dollars. Many Mexican travelers pass through too, so there is also a fair selection of budget places to stay and eat. 'Across the water,' in Laredo, there are all-American supermarkets, motels and fast-food joints, as well as reliable phone and postal services, all staffed with Spanish-speaking workers.

History
The area was sparsely populated with nomadic Indian groups until Don Tomás Sánchez, a captain of the Spanish royal army, was given a grant of land at Laredo in 1775. The first settlers were ranchers, and missionaries passed through into the interior of Texas. In 1836, Texas seceded from Mexico and became an independent republic. From 1839 to 1841, the Rio Grande valley, and much of what is now northeastern Mexico, also declared itself a separate republic – the Republic of the Rio Grande, with its capital at Laredo.

The US annexation of Texas in 1845 precipitated the Mexican-American War, with the Rio Grande subsequently becoming the border between the USA and Mexico. A new Mexican town, called Nuevo Laredo, was established on the south side of the river and, with its predecessor on the US side, began its existence as a border town. Nuevo Laredo now collects more in tariffs and customs revenue than any other Mexican port of entry. It also has more than 60

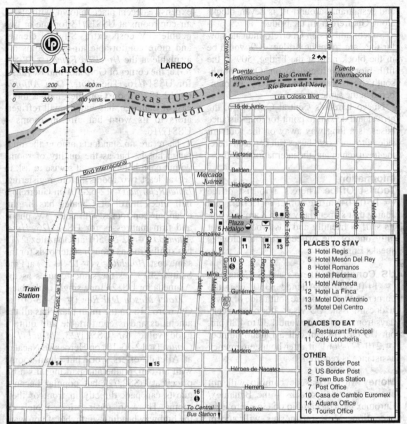

Nuevo Laredo

LAREDO

0   200   400 m
0   200   400 yards

Texas (USA)

Nuevo León

Convent Ave

San Dario Ave

Puente Internacional #1

Rio Grande
Río Bravo del Norte

Puente Internacional #2

Luis Colosio Blvd

15 de Junio

Blvd Internacional

Mercado Juárez

Bravo
Victoria
Belden
Hidalgo
Pino Suárez
Mier
Plaza Hidalgo
González
Canales
Mina
Gutiérrez
Arteaga
Independencia
Madero
Hérbes de Nacatez
Herrera
Bolivar

Mendoza
Riva Palacio
Aldama
Obregón
Allende
Morelos
Juárez
Matamoros
Guerrero
Ocampo
Galeana
Reynosa
Camargo
Lerdo de Tejada
Serdán
Valle
Carranza
Degollado
Méndez

Av López de Lara

Train Station

To Central Bus Station

PLACES TO STAY
3 Hotel Regis
5 Hotel Mesón Del Rey
8 Hotel Romanos
9 Hotel Reforma
11 Hotel Alameda
12 Hotel La Finca
13 Motel Don Antonio
15 Motel Del Centro

PLACES TO EAT
4 Restaurant Principal
11 Café Lonchería

OTHER
1 US Border Post
2 US Border Post
6 Town Bus Station
7 Post Office
10 Casa de Cambio Euromex
14 Aduana Office
16 Tourist Office

NORTHEAST MEXICO

maquiladoras producing goods for the US market.

Orientation

There are two international bridges carrying vehicles and pedestrians between the two Laredos. Puente Internacional No 1 is the one to use if you're heading into Mexico. It has an immigration office at its southern end where you can get your tourist card, but you have to go to the *aduana* (customs) office in town to get a vehicle permit. This bridge brings you into Mexico at the north end of Guerrero,

Nuevo Laredo's main street, which stretches for two km (one way going south). Heading north, signs direct traffic around the western side of the city, via Avenida López de Lara, to Puente Internacional No 1.

Puente Internacional No 2 is for those who don't need a tourist card, and is often used by heavy vehicles.

The city center area spreads along either side of Guerrero for the first km from Puente Internacional No 1. Its main plaza, with a kiosk in the middle, the Palacio de Gobierno on the east side, and a few hotels and restaurants around it, is seven blocks along Guerrero from the bridge.

Street numbers on Guerrero indicate how far they are from the bridge: 109 would be in the block nearest the bridge, 509 in the fifth block south and so on. Other north-south streets, parallel to Guerrero, are numbered in the same way.

Nuevo Laredo's Central Camionera, the arrival and departure point for long-distance buses, is a long way away on the southern side of town. Local buses run between there, the town center and the international bridges.

Information

Tourist Office There's a tourist office (☎ 12-01-04) at the corner of Herrera and Juárez that's open daily from 8 am to 8 pm. Its staff is friendly and has brochures, but only one of the office's four employees speaks English.

US Consulate There's a US Consulate (☎ 14-05-12) at Allende 3330, near the corner of Nayarit, on the south side of town. It doesn't issue US visas. It's open weekdays from 8 am to noon and 1.30 to 4.30 pm, but US citizens can call a Laredo number (☎ 210-727-9661) if after-hours emergency assistance is required.

Money Most casas de cambio will not change traveler's checks – the Banamex/Euromex casa de cambio on Guerrero is an exception. Most businesses will accept them if you want to make a purchase, and the main Mexican banks should change them. Businesses also accept cash dollars, but the exchange rate can be low.

Post The post office is on Camargo, behind the government offices east of the plaza.

Special Events

Nuevo Laredo holds an agricultural, live-stock, industrial and cultural fair during the second week of September.

Places to Stay

Hotel Romanos (☎ 12-23-91) at Dr Mier No 2434 just east of the plaza is the least expensive decent place in town, with clean, air-con rooms at US$12/13 for one or two people; TV costs extra. Slightly cleaner and more comfortable air-con rooms are available at the *Hotel La Finca* (☎ 12-88-83) at the corner of González and Reynosa, for US$14/16. The *Motel Don Antonio* (☎ 12-18-76), on González half a block east of Camargo, has added small refrigerators to its worn but air-con rooms – US$12/16.

There are no standouts among the mid-range hotels, but as the quality of rooms within each hotel varies, it's wise to ask to see at least two rooms before registering. *Hotel Reforma* (☎ 12-62-50) on Guerrero a half block north of Canales has bright, clean, air-con rooms with color TV, phone and firm mattresses for US$22/26. *Hotel Alameda* (☎ 12-50-50) at González 2715 has similar rooms though softer beds for the same cost. *Hotel Regis* (☎ 12-90-35) at Pino Suárez 3013 has the same features as the Alameda for US$23 for a single or double.

Hotel Mesón Del Rey (☎ 12-63-60) at Guerrero 718 on the main plaza has all the amenities and is comfortable and quite a good value for US$21/23. *Motel Del Centro* (☎ 12-13-10) on Héroes de Nacataz at Allende offers worn but clean rooms with air-con, phone and parking; it's a bit pricey at US$23/29 but popular because guests can park directly in front of their rooms. There are nicer, pricier motels on the highway heading south, but if you want this sort of lodging, you'd do better in Laredo on the US side.

Places to Eat

There are lots of eating possibilities, though the places on Guerrero for the first few blocks south of the bridge can be overpriced tourist joints. The side streets have cheaper restaurants less geared to the tourist trade, and the tourist eateries offer better value as you go farther south. One of the first attractive-looking places is the *Restaurant Principal* at Guerrero 624, with a substantial Mexican menu with antojitos around US$4 and meat dishes from US$3.50; *cabrito* (roast kid) costs about US$7.

On the south side of the plaza, on the corner of Ocampo and González, is a small, cozy, family-run place, fairly clean and not too expensive. It is the *Café Lonchería*, and the menu includes fish (US$3 to US$5) and soups and breakfasts (about US$2.50), and it's open from 7 am to midnight. The north side of the plaza has some small, plain cafés with standard Mexican fare and a place selling pizzas for US$2.75 and up.

Two places very popular with locals lie a km or so down Guerrero from the international bridge. At Guerrero 2114, between Venezuela and Lincoln, *El Rancho* is a not-so-poor person's taco-and-beer hall, offering a long list of different types of tacos. The *Río Mar*, at Guerrero 2403, is packed at night with people gobbling mouth-watering seafood dishes starting at around US$4.

Spectator Sports
Nuevo Laredo's horse and greyhound racing venue, the *Hipódromo-Galgódromo*, is closed and doesn't appear likely to reopen. However, gamblers can place off-track bets, and watch US and Mexican sports on satellite TV, at the *Turf Club*, at the intersection of Bravo and Ocampo.

Two or three bullfights are held each month at the Plaza de Toros, on Avenida Monterrey No 4101 near Anáhuac. Admission ranges from US$6 to US$8. For dates and times, call ☎ 12-71-92 in Mexico or 888-240-8460 from the USA.

Things to Buy
If you're just setting out, the less you buy the better. But if you're on the way home, it's worth browsing around some of the shops and markets for the odd souvenir. There's a crafts market on the east side of Guerrero half a block north of the main plaza, another one on the west side of Guerrero half a block south of Hidalgo, and the small Mercado Juárez on the west side of Guerrero, between Hidalgo and Belden. There are also lots of individual shops along this northern section of Guerrero. There's a great deal of overpriced junk, but some quality work is available. Prices are a bit higher than in places farther south, but not outrageously so, and with a bit of bargaining and cash payment, you may get 10% to 20% off the asking price.

Getting There & Away
Air Nuevo Laredo airport is off the Monterrey road, 14 km south of town. Mexicana has direct flights to/from Mexico City and Guadalajara. The Mexicana office (☎ 18-12-70) is at Héroes de Nacataz 2335.

Bus Nuevo Laredo's bus station is three km from the international bridge, on Ocampo between 15 de Septiembre and Anáhuac on the southern side of town. It has a left-luggage section and restaurant, and 1st- and 2nd-class buses to every city in the northern half of Mexico. The main companies providing 1st-class services here are Futura and Omnibus de México. For longer trips, 2nd-class buses are slow and not recommended. Daily service from Nuevo Laredo includes:

Ciudad Victoria – 510 km, seven hours; three 1st-class (US$26), many 2nd-class (US$19)

Matehuala – 549 km, eight hours; one Futura at 11 am (US$21), many 2nd-class (US$17)

Mexico City (Terminal Norte) – 1158 km, 15 hours; one deluxe (US$59), frequent 1st-class (US$44) and 2nd-class (US$38)

Monterrey – 224 km, three hours; frequent 1st-class (US$9)

Reynosa – 251 km, four hours; many 1st-class (US$8.50)

Saltillo – 310 km, 4½ hours; many 1st-class (US$12)

San Luis Potosí – 740 km, 10½ hours; hourly departures (US$36, US$27, US$22.50)

Tampico – 755 km, 11 hours; two Futura daily (US$28)

Zacatecas – 683 km, nine hours; two Futura daily (US$26), several 2nd-class (US$22)

There are also buses to Aguascalientes, Durango, Guadalajara and Querétaro. At the Futura desk you can buy tickets directly to major cities in Texas.

Laredo, Texas There are buses from the Greyhound terminal in Laredo direct to cities in Mexico, including San Luis Potosí,

Querétaro and Mexico City, but these are more expensive than services from Nuevo Laredo. You can sometimes use these buses to go between Laredo and Nuevo Laredo bus stations, but you have to ask the driver – it's less hassle and often quicker just to walk over the international bridge.

Train The Nuevo Laredo train station (☎ 12-21-29) is on Avenida López de Lara (also called Avenida Mexico, its old name), at the western end of Mina. The level of service gets worse every year, and for speed, comfort and convenience, trains fall a long way behind the buses. Only one passenger train serves Nuevo Laredo, leaving the station nightly at 6.55 pm for Monterrey (five hours, US$6.50 for 1st-class, US$3.75 for 2nd), Saltillo, San Luis Potosí, San Miguel de Allende, Querétaro and Mexico City (24 hours, US$30, US$17). Tickets go on sale at 6 pm.

For trains from Mexico City to Nuevo Laredo, see Getting There & Away in the Mexico City chapter.

Car & Motorcycle For a vehicle permit you have to go to the customs office. To get there, go about 14 blocks south on Guerrero, turn right at Héroes de Nacataz and then go about nine blocks west to the corner of López de Lara, where you'll see the agency on the right. The office is always open and should issue a permit without hassle if your papers are in order (see the Getting There & Away chapter). Don't forget to cancel the permit when you leave the country to avoid a fine.

The route via Monterrey is the most direct way to central Mexico, the Pacific Coast and/or the Gulf Coast. An excellent toll road, highway 85D, goes south to Monterrey. It's fast but expensive (tolls total US$15). The alternative free road is longer, rougher and slower. Highway 2 is a rural road that follows the Rio Grande to Reynosa and Matamoros. To the USA, the bridge toll is US$1.40.

Getting Around
Frequent city buses (US$0.40) make getting around Nuevo Laredo simple enough.

The easiest place to catch them is on the east side of the plaza, where all the buses seem to pass. Bus No 51 goes from there to the bus station, but you may be able to get one from closer to the bridge. For the train station from the city center, catch a blue-and-white 'Arteaga González' bus. From the bus station there are local buses into town. A taxi from the bus station to the bridge will cost about US$2.75.

REYNOSA
pop 350,000; alt 90m; ☎ 89

Reynosa was founded in 1749 as Villa de Nuestra Señora de Guadalupe de Reynosa, 20 km from its present location. Flooding forced the move to the present site in 1802. Reynosa was one of the first towns to rise up in the independence movement of 1810, but there is little of historical interest today.

Today, Reynosa is one of northeast Mexico's most important industrial towns, with oil refineries, petrochemical plants, cotton mills, distilleries and maquiladoras. Pipelines from here carry natural gas to Monterrey and into the USA. It's also the center of a big cattle-raising, cotton, sugar cane and maize-growing area.

As a commercial border crossing, Reynosa is busier than Matamoros but less important than Nuevo Laredo. It has good road connections into Mexico and Texas, but most travelers will probably find one of the other crossings more direct and convenient. Across the Rio Grande, on the US side, is the small settlement of Hidalgo, with the bigger town of McAllen nine km away. The tourist trade is geared to short-term Texan visitors, with restaurants, nightclubs, bars and even bawdier diversions. Some handicrafts are available in the tourist markets, but the quality is generally low, while the prices are not.

Orientation
Reynosa's central streets are laid out on a grid pattern, between the Rio Grande and the Anzalduas Canal. The main plaza is on a rise a few blocks southwest of the international bridge, with a modern church, town hall, banks and hotels.

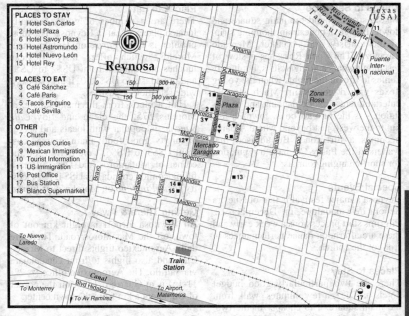

PLACES TO STAY
1   Hotel San Carlos
2   Hotel Plaza
6   Hotel Savoy Plaza
13 Hotel Astromundo
14 Hotel Nuevo León
15 Hotel Rey

PLACES TO EAT
3   Café Sánchez
4   Café Paris
5   Tacos Pinguino
12 Café Sevilla

OTHER
7   Church
8   Campos Curios
9   Mexican Immigration
10 Tourist Information
11 US Immigration
16 Post Office
17 Bus Station
18 Blanco Supermarket

Reynosa

Texas (USA)
Tamaulipas
Rio Grande
Rio Bravo del Norte
Puente Inter-nacional
Zona Rosa

To Nuevo Laredo
To Monterrey
To Av Ramírez
To Airport, Matamoros

Train Station
Canal
Blvd Hidalgo

NORTHEAST MEXICO

Between the bridge and the center lies the Zona Rosa, with restaurants, bars and nightclubs. Reynosa's industries have expanded so much on the south side of town that the 'central' area has more or less become the northern edge. If you're driving in from Mexico, follow the signs to the Puente Internacional, then go to the town center if you want to. Avoid the maze of streets in the industrial zone south of the canal.

Information

Immigration US immigration is at the north end of the international bridge. Mexican immigration is at the south end, and there's another immigration post in the Reynosa bus station. Get a tourist card stamped at either post if you're proceeding beyond Reynosa deeper into Mexico.

Tourist Office There's a so-called tourist information office at the south end of the bridge, opposite the immigration office, but its staff are unhelpful and given to fabricating information; the office doesn't even have a sign indicating what it is. However, the owner and staff of Campos Curios (☎ 22-44-20), located just around the corner from the immigration office, speak English and enjoy assisting tourists. Campos Curios is open daily from 9 am to 8 pm.

Money The customs building has a Bancomer that changes traveler's checks. You can also change traveler's checks at Banamex, on Guerrero between Hidalgo and Juárez. The main banks have ATMs, some of which will dispense US dollars as well as pesos, and there are several casas de cambio. Some shops also will change money.

Post The post office is on the corner of Díaz and Colón.

Things to See & Do

Take a stroll around the main square and down Hidalgo, a pedestrian shopping strip, to the touristy crafts market, Mercado Zaragoza. The Zona Rosa has a slew of restaurants, bars and nightclubs, but it only comes to life on the nights when the young Texas crowd comes in. Much sleazier entertainment – exotic dancing and prostitution – is the rule at 'boys' town,' a few km to the west, just beyond where Aldama becomes a dirt road. Be advised that waiters at the Pussy Cat have a reputation for short-changing tourists.

Special Events

Reynosa's major festival is that of Nuestra Señora de Guadalupe, on December 12. Pilgrims start processions a week early and there are afternoon dance performances in front of the church.

Places to Stay

There are two particularly good budget hotels on Díaz, a few minutes' walk from the main square. The cheaper of the two, the *Hotel Nuevo León* (☎ 22-13-10) between Méndez and Madero, has sizable, clean singles/doubles with fan and private bathroom at US$9/11; some rooms are much better than others. The *Hotel Rey* (☎ 22-29-80), two doors down, has clean, bright rooms with air-con and TV at US$15/17. It may not have a vacant room if you arrive late.

On the west side of the main square, the somewhat run-down *Hotel Plaza* (☎ 22-00-39) has OK rooms for US$7/8. Nearby, the *Hotel San Carlos* (☎ 22-12-80) is a step toward the luxury bracket, with clean, bright, air-con rooms with phone and TV for US$24/27. It has its own restaurant and parking. Just south of the plaza, at Juárez 860, the pleasant *Hotel Savoy Plaza* (☎ 22-00-67) has air-con rooms for US$25/27.

The top downtown place is the *Hotel Astromundo* (☎ 22-56-25) on Juárez between Guerrero and Méndez. It has clean, spacious rooms with TV, plus a swimming pool, parking facilities and a restaurant. Room rates are US$27/30.

Places to Eat

There are a number of good, centrally located places to eat in Reynosa. The most popular is *Café Paris*, on Hidalgo near Morelos, which offers tasty Mexican lunches and dinners from US$2 to US$4 and breakfasts to US$2.50. It also stocks a wide selection of pastries.

Half a block from the main square, at Morelos 575, the clean and tidy *Café Sánchez* is popular with locals and serves up pretty good food; main courses cost from US$3 to US$5. *Café Sevilla*, on the corner of Matamoros and Díaz, offers a filling comida corrida for US$4. For tacos, try *Tacos Pinguino* on Morelos near Juárez.

Getting There & Away

Air Reynosa airport is eight km out of town, off the Matamoros road. There are daily Aeroméxico flights direct to Mexico City, and also flights to/from Guadalajara via Saltillo. The Aeroméxico office (☎ 22-11-15) is at Guerrero 1510, on the corner of Gil, about a km from the town center.

Bus Both 1st- and 2nd-class buses run to almost anywhere you'd want to go in Mexico, but avoid 2nd-class buses on long trips because they're very slow. The Central de Autobuses is on the southeastern corner of the central grid, next to the Blanco supermarket. First-class lines serving Reynosa are Transportes del Norte, ADO, Ómnibus de México, Tres Estrellas de Oro, Futura, Transportes Frontera and Blanca. Daily service from Reynosa includes:

Aguascalientes – 808 km, 11½ hours; 10 1st-class (US$28)
Ciudad Victoria – 330 km, five hours; several 1st- (US$10) and 2nd-class (US$8)
Durango – 793 km, 11½ hours; one 1st-class (US$31)
Guadalajara – 990 km, 12 hours; four 1st-class (US$36)
Matamoros – 104 km, two hours; many 1st- (US$4) and 2nd-class (US$3)
Mexico City (Terminal Norte) – 970 km, 13 hours; six 1st-class (US$39)
Monterrey – 220 km, 2½ hours; frequent 1st-class (US$8.50)

Querétaro – 805 km, 12½ hours; one 1st-class (US$30)

Saltillo – 305 km, 3½ hours; one 1st-class bus (US$10.75)

San Luis Potosí – 737 km, 9½ hours; eight 1st-class (US$23)

Tampico – 580 km, nine hours; many 1st- (US$17) and 2nd-class (US$15)

Torreón – 536 km, seven hours; one 1st-class (US$21)

Tuxpan – 770 km, 13 hours; one 1st-class (US$23)

Zacatecas – 678 km, 7½ hours; one 1st-class (US$23.50)

First-class buses also serve Chihuahua, Ciudad Juárez, Veracruz and Villahermosa, with 2nd-class buses serving mainly local destinations. Some bus lines run direct to major US cities.

McAllen, Texas The nearest Texas transport center, McAllen, is nine km from the border. Valley Transit Company (☎ 210-686-5479) runs buses both ways between the McAllen and Reynosa bus stations for US$2 one way, every 30 minutes between 5 am and 7.30 pm. There are three later services, with the last leaving the Reynosa depot at 10.05 pm.

Coming from McAllen, if you don't want to go all the way to the Reynosa bus station, you can get off at the Greyhound office on the US side and walk over the bridge into Reynosa. Leaving Mexico, you can walk over the bridge and pick up the buses at the same Greyhound office.

Train The Reynosa train station is at the southern end of Hidalgo, six blocks from the main square. There's one slow train daily to Matamoros (scheduled departure time is 2.40 pm) and one to Monterrey (scheduled departure time is 11.25 am). Journey time is about 2½ hours to Matamoros and 5½ hours to Monterrey. Primera clase fare to Monterrey is US$6.

Car & Motorcycle There's an aduana (customs) office on Avenida Miguel Alemán that can issue temporary car import permits; to get there, simply turn left after clearing immigration and look for the office on the south side of the street half a block away.

Going west to Monterrey (225 km), the toll highway 40D is excellent and patrolled by Green Angels; the tolls total US$15. Highways 97 and 180, going south to Tampico, are two-lane surfaced roads, but not too busy. Highway 101 branches off the 180 to Ciudad Victoria and the scenic climb to San Luis Potosí. If you want to follow the Rio Grande upstream to Nuevo Laredo or downstream to Matamoros, highway 2 is not in bad shape, but it is quicker and safer to travel on the US side. Side roads cross to lakes like the Presa Falcón (Falcon Dam) and to a number of obscure border crossings.

Getting Around
Battered yellow microbuses rattle around Reynosa, providing cheap but jarring transport. From the international bridge to the bus station, catch one of the Valley Transit Company coaches coming from McAllen with 'Reynosa' on the front; the service is free. You can also catch the '17 Obrera' bus from Madero, which travels Canales, Aldama, Bravo and Colón; it's a slower, less comfortable way to go, and costs US$0.50. From the bus station to the center, turn left out of the main entrance, walk to the end of the block, turn left again, and catch a '17 Obrera' on the next corner (Colón at Rubio).

MATAMOROS
pop 600,000; ☎ 88
First settled during the Spanish colonization of Tamaulipas in 1686, with the name Los Esteros Hermosas (The Beautiful Estuaries), it was renamed in 1793 after Father Mariano Matamoros. In 1846, Matamoros was the first Mexican city to be taken by US forces in the Mexican-American War, and Zachary Taylor then used it as a base for his attack on Monterrey. During the US Civil War, when sea routes to the Confederacy were blockaded, Matamoros transshipped cotton out of Confederate Texas, and supplies and war material into it.

NORTHEAST MEXICO

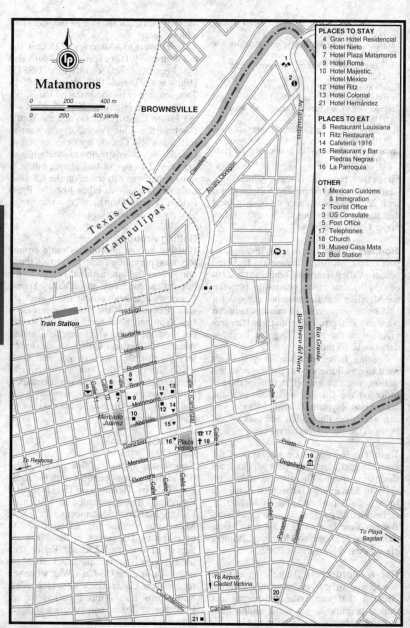

Matamoros

BROWNSVILLE

Texas (USA)
Tamaulipas

Rio Bravo del Norte

Rio Grande

Train Station

To Reynosa

Mercado Juárez

Plaza Hidalgo

To Airport,
Ciudad Victoria

To Playa Bagdad

PLACES TO STAY
4 Gran Hotel Residencial
6 Hotel Nieto
7 Hotel Plaza Matamoros
9 Hotel Roma
10 Hotel Majestic,
   Hotel México
12 Hotel Ritz
13 Hotel Colonial
21 Hotel Hernández

PLACES TO EAT
8 Restaurant Louisiana
11 Ritz Restaurant
14 Cafetería 1916
15 Restaurant y Bar
   Piedras Negras
16 La Parroquia

OTHER
1 Mexican Customs
   & Immigration
2 Tourist Office
3 US Consulate
5 Post Office
17 Telephones
18 Church
19 Museo Casa Mata
20 Bus Station

Streets/places labeled: Av. Tamaulipas, Cavieles, Álvaro Obregón, Hidalgo, Iturbide, Herrera, Bustamente, Bravo, Matamoros, Abasolo, González, Morelos, Guerrero, Cuauhtémoc, Canales, Prieto, Degollado, Calle 5 Carranza, Calle 1, Calle 6, Calle 8, Calle 7, Calle 9, Calle 11

Today, Matamoros is no historical monument, but there is more evidence of the past than in most border towns, and the town center, with its church and plaza, looks typically Mexican. South of the central area is a broad circle of newer industrial zones. Apart from its maquiladoras, Matamoros is a commercial center for a large agricultural hinterland – tanneries, cotton mills and distilleries are among its main industries.

Orientation

Matamoros lies across the Rio Grande from Brownsville, Texas. The river, which forms the international boundary, is spanned by a bridge with US border controls at the north end and Mexican border controls to the south. The Rio Grande is a disappointing trickle at this point, as most of its water has been siphoned off upstream for irrigation.

From the southern end of the bridge, Obregón winds around toward the town's central grid, 1.5 km to the southwest. The cheap lodging is around Abasolo, a pedestrian street a block north of Plaza Hidalgo. Nearby are two markets with tourist-oriented crafts.

Information

Immigration The Mexican border post waves most pedestrians through on the assumption that they're just there for a day's shopping or eating, but some cars will get the red light to be checked. If you're proceeding farther south into Mexico than the border zone, get a tourist card and have it stamped before you leave Matamoros.

Tourist Offices An informal tourist office (☎ 12-17-35) is in a shack on the right-hand side at the beginning of Obregón. What it lacks in written material it makes up for with the helpfulness of its staff, who are mostly bilingual taxi drivers. They offer transport and guided tours for a price, but are happy to answer questions for nothing. Someone's usually there daily from 8 am to noon, and 2 to 5 pm. If you need maps, brochures and printed giveaways, you may do better at the Brownsville Chamber of Commerce (☎ 210-542-4341), on the east

side about 200 meters north of the bridge; open weekdays 8 am to 5 pm, closed weekends. You might also try the Brownsville Visitors Bureau (☎ 210-546-3721), located near the intersection of US highway 77/83 and Ruben Torres Sr. Blvd; it's open Monday through Saturday 8 am to 5 pm, Sunday 9 am to 4 pm.

US Consulate The US Consulate (☎ 12-44-02), at Calle 1 No 232, can issue visas but usually takes more than a day to do so. It's open weekdays from 8 to 10 am and 1 to 4 pm, but does not issue visas on Wednesdays.

Money Matamoros has several banks (with ATMs) on Plaza Hidalgo and Calle 6, which will change cash or traveler's checks. Often you get a better rate for cash dollars in the casas de cambio dotted around the central area. Casa de Cambio Astorga, on Calle 7 between Bravo and Matamoros, will change traveler's checks.

In Brownsville, there are casas de cambio on International Boulevard, the road running straight ahead from the north end of the international bridge. Some of them are open 24 hours a day.

Post & Communications There is a post office at Calle 11 and Bravo. There are plenty of pay phones around. There is a telecommunications office at the bus station, at Canales and Guatemala.

Museo Casa Mata

This old fort, on the corner of Guatemala and Santos Degollado, was the scene of fighting in the Mexican-American War. It now contains some memorabilia of the Mexican Revolution, a few Indian artifacts and some ill-assorted miscellany. Entry is free. To reach it from Plaza Hidalgo, head east on Morelos as far as Calle 1, turn right, go five blocks to Santos Degollado, then two blocks to the left.

Playa Bagdad

Matamoros' beach was formerly known as Playa Lauro Villar but it has adopted the name of Bagdad, from a town at the mouth of the Rio Grande that prospered during the US Civil War but later succumbed to floods, hurricanes and military attacks. It's 37 km east of Matamoros on highway 2, and has a wide stretch of clean sand and a few beachside seafood restaurants. There are some mid-range motels along the road approaching the beach. 'Playa' buses go from the corner of Abasolo and Calle 11 in downtown Matamoros.

Places to Stay

There is one decent budget hotel near the bus station, with others to be found on or near Abasolo near the center of town. Budget rooms are basic, but cheap enough at around US$7 a double. Mid-range lodging, with air-con and parking, starts at around US$20, and there's not much in between these levels.

One of the better deals in town is the *Hotel Hernández* (13-35-58) on Calle 6, 50 meters south of Canales. The hotel is five short blocks from the bus station, twice that to the main plaza. The popular Hernández is a four-story hotel set around a narrow courtyard containing palm trees. The rooms are clean and have new air-con units and firm beds. Singles/doubles go for US$18/20.

The *Hotel México* (☎ 12-08-56) at Abasolo 87, between Calles 8 and 9, charges US$5.50/11 for cleanish rooms with bathroom and ceiling fan. Nearby, the *Hotel Majestic* (☎ 13-36-80) at Abasolo 89 is not quite as clean but has more character and some classic 1950s furnishings. It's a family-run place that charges US$6.50/8 for rooms with private bath. Both are often filled, and neither is as pleasant as the Hernández.

One block north of Abasolo, on the corner of Matamoros and Calle 6, the *Hotel Colonial* (☎ 14-64-18) is friendly and has lots of cleanish rooms with minimum comforts for US$5/7. Check the room before you decide – some need maintenance and others are noisy, but it's not a bad place to stay.

Moving up the scale a little, the *Hotel Nieto* (☎ 13-08-57), at Calle 10 No 1508, is like stepping back in time. It's an ordinary-looking 1960s-style hotel, with original wall paneling, carpet and paintings, and air-con, TV and parking, charging US$20/23. Its rooms are worn but spacious and quite tolerable. The *Hotel Roma* (☎ 16-05-73), on Calle 9 between Matamoros and Bravo, is central, modern, clean and friendly. It charges US$24/28 for smallish rooms with cable TV, telephone and carpeting. The *Hotel Ritz* (☎ 12-11-90), on Matamoros between Calles 6 and 7, is a lot classier with bigger rooms and fax and laundry services for US$26/32.

Top places include the *Hotel Plaza Matamoros* (☎ 16-16-96), on the corner of Calle 9 and Bravo, which is tasteful and comfortable but pricey for US$42/49. For slightly more money, a better bargain is the *Gran Hotel Residencial* (☎ 13-94-40) at Álvaro Obregón 249, with pleasant gardens and a swimming pool. The 120 air-con rooms with cable TV go for US$49/52.

Places to Eat

Near the plaza, the clean, classy and cool *La Parroquia*, on González between Calles 6 and 7, is popular from morning to evening with a wide selection of breakfasts from US$1.30 to US$2.50 and dinners from US$2 to US$4; their chicken mole (US$3) is delicious. In the same price range is the *Ritz Restaurant*, opposite the *Hotel Ritz*. Popular meals at this tasteful and stylish restaurant, with cozy booths and lots of scrubbed tile, include grilled chicken (US$3) and filet mignon (US$4.50).

The *Cafetería 1916*, on Calle 6 between Matamoros and Abasolo, is slightly less atmospheric but quite popular with local residents. It's a tad pricier than the restaurants listed above, with antojitos starting at US$2.50, but it's still very reasonable.

Farther up the scale is the *Restaurant y Bar Piedras Negras* at 175 Calle 6 half a block north of the main square. Favored by better-off Mexicans and a few gringos, a meal at this restaurant – perhaps the best in town – could well set you back US$8 or more. The *Restaurant Louisiana*, on Bravo between Calles 8 and 9, has a somewhat elegant atmosphere and offers meals ranging from US$4.50 to US$9. These include: Rib-eye steak with mushrooms (US$9), Louisiana frog legs (US$8) and shish kabob (US$9).

Things to Buy

The 'new market,' or Mercado Juárez, is the larger of Matamoros' two markets, occupying a block between Abasolo, Matamoros, and Calles 9 and 10. A lot of the stuff is second-rate but there's plenty of variety, including blankets, hats, pottery, leather and glass, so you may find something appealing. Prices are 20% to 30% higher than the cheapest markets farther south, but you can bargain them down a bit.

The second market is in an arcade with entrances on Bravo and Calle 9. Called Pasaje Juárez, its range of goods is more limited, and it has a slightly more aggressive sales style. There are a few interesting but expensive folk-art shops along Obregón.

Getting There & Away

Air Matamoros has an airport (☎ 12-00-01) 17 km out of town on the road to Ciudad Victoria. There are direct daily flights with Aeroméxico to/from Mexico City. The Aeroméxico office (☎ 12-51-60) in Matamoros is at Obregón 21. Aero California (☎ 12-19-43), at Abasolo 1308, offers service to Matamoros from Los Angeles and Tucson.

Bus Both 1st- and 2nd-class buses run from the bus station on Canales, near the corner of Guatemala. The bus station has a telephone caseta, a casa de cambio and a 24-hour restaurant. It also has a left-luggage service (US$0.20 per hour).

A number of big companies provide 1st-class bus service to/from Matamoros, including ADO, Transportes del Norte, Ómnibus de México, Transportes Frontera and Tres Estrellas de Oro. Smaller companies providing both 1st- and 2nd-class service to local destinations include Transportes Monterrey-Cadereyta-Reynosa

and Autotransportes Mante. Daily service from Matamoros includes:

Ciudad Victoria – 320 km, 4½ hours; many 1st- (US$10) and 2nd-class (US$9)
Mexico City (Terminal Norte) – 1010 km, 15 hours; one deluxe (US$51), several 1st- (US$38) and 2nd-class (US$34)
Monterrey – 324 km, 4½ hours; three 1st-class (US$11.50)
Reynosa – 102 km, two hours; many 1st-class (US$3.50)
Saltillo – 410 km, 5½ hours; one 1st-class (US$14)
Tampico – 570 km, eight hours; many 1st-class (US$18)
Torreón – 640 km, 8½ hours; one 1st-class (US$25)
Tuxpan – 760 km, 12 hours; one 1st-class (US$25)

Buses go to many more distant destinations including Chihuahua, Culiacán, Durango, Guadalajara, Guaymas, Hermosillo, Los Mochis, Mazatlán, Mexicali, Querétaro, San Luis Potosí, Tijuana and Veracruz.

Brownsville, Texas You can get buses from the Brownsville bus station direct to several cities inside Mexico, but they cost more than from Matamoros, and they may take up to two hours to get over the international bridge, through customs and immigration. It's quicker to walk across the bridge and take a maxi-taxi to the Matamoros bus station. Going into the USA, it's also better to get local transport to the bridge and walk across.

The Brownsville bus station (☎ 210-546-7171) is at 1165 Saint Charles on the corner of 12th St. Facing the USA from the north end of the international bridge, walk left (west) on Elizabeth, then two blocks south on 12th. There are buses to all the major cities in Texas, and connections to other US cities.

Train There's one train a day in each direction between Matamoros and Monterrey, via Reynosa. Though cheap, it's neither quick nor reliable. The 9.20 am departure from Matamoros is scheduled to take about two hours to Reynosa and seven hours to

Monterrey, but may take longer (primera clase fare to Monterrey is US$8).

Car & Motorcycle Driving across the bridge to/from Brownsville costs US$1.40. The main routes into Mexico from Matamoros are highway 180 south to Tampico and the Gulf Coast, and highway 101 southwest to Ciudad Victoria and into the Bajío region. These are both two-lane roads, not very busy, in fair condition and free of heavy tolls. Officials at various checkpoints will want to see your tourist card and vehicle permit; if your papers are not in order you will be sent back to Matamoros. You can also go west to Monterrey via Reynosa.

Getting Around

Matamoros is served by small buses called maxi-taxis, which charge US$0.70 to anywhere in town. You can stop them on almost any street corner. They usually have their destinations painted on the front windscreen: the town center is 'Centro'; the bus station 'Central de Autobuses'; and the international bridge 'Puente Internacional.' From the international bridge, walk south until you see a row of yellow maxi-taxis; read the scrawl on their windscreens to find one going to the town center or the bus station.

Taxis from the border to the center or to the bus station cost about US$5.

SOUTH OF MATAMOROS

Most of the 500-km highway to Tampico is 30 to 40 km inland from the coast, crossing several rivers but passing mainly through coastal lowlands where sugar cane is the main crop. For the first 183 km the route follows highway 101 toward Ciudad Victoria, then turns off along highway 180. There are budget and mid-range hotels in San Fernando (137 km from Matamoros), Soto La Marina (269 km) and Aldama (381 km).

The landscape is fairly unspectacular, but there are some more scenic stretches where the outliers of the Sierra Madre Oriental come close to the coast. Side roads go

east to the coast at various points. Most of the coast is lagoons that are separated from the Gulf of Mexico by narrow sand spits. The longest of the lagoons is the Laguna Madre, which extends hundreds of km up the coasts of Tamaulipas and Texas. The lagoons, sand dunes and coastal wetlands support a unique ecosystem, with many bird species and excellent fishing. If you're interested in exploring this part of the coast of the Gulf of Mexico in detail, read Donald Schueler's *Adventuring along the Gulf of Mexico* (Sierra Club Books, San Francisco, CA), which gives full coverage of the ecology and wildlife.

El Mezquital
pop 600

This is a small fishing village, with a lighthouse and beach, on the long thin spit of land that divides the Laguna Madre from the Gulf of Mexico. A road crosses marshland to reach El Mezquital, about 60 km off the highway, just south of Matamoros airport. Minibuses wait at the turnoff.

La Carbonera
pop 2446; ☎ 127

This is a small, nondescript fishing village facing the lagoon. You might be able to get a boat out to the lagoon barrier island, where porpoises can sometimes be seen. Food is available, but there are no rooms for rent. A road leads here from San Fernando (about 50 km). The only beach is at Carvajal, eight km south of La Carbonera, and it's polluted.

La Pesca
pop 1226; ☎ 132

Forty-eight km east from Soto La Marina is the fishing village of La Pesca, which has five hotels (two budget, three mid-range), a camping area and restaurants, and plans to develop itself into a major resort. It has a long, wide beach – Playa La Pesca – with shady palapas and seaside restaurants. There is good fishing in the estuary of the Río Soto La Marina, and in the Laguna de Morales. A fishing tournament for sea bass and other species takes place in November.

Other attractions include hunting, as well as surfing on the beaches that face the Gulf of Mexico. However, this beach and the others in northeast Mexico do not compare favorably to those farther south.

Barra El Tordo
pop 641; ☎ 127

A 44-km road goes east then north from Aldama, through the eastern fringes of the Sierra de Tamaulipas, to Barra El Tordo. It's another fishing village with a beach and good sport fishing and is well known for its oyster harvest. Turtles spawn on the beaches between here and Altamira. There are four hotels (two budget, two mid-range), two restaurants and a campground.

CIUDAD VICTORIA
pop 243,960; alt 333m; ☎ 131

About 40 km north of the Tropic of Cancer, the capital of Tamaulipas state is a clean and pleasant city with just enough altitude to moderate the steamy heat of the coastal plains or the Rio Grande valley. It's around 320 km south of Matamoros and Reynosa, well served by buses in every direction, and a good spot to break a journey between central Mexico and the Texas border.

Orientation

Five highways converge at Ciudad Victoria, and a ring road allows through traffic to move between them without entering the city itself. The center is laid out in a grid pattern with one-way streets and a few pedestrian precincts. The north-south streets have both numbers (Calle 7, Calle 8, etc) and names (Calle Díaz, Calle Tijerina, etc).

Information

The tourist office (☎ 2-11-11) is on the south side of town on the corner of Rosales and 5 de Mayo. It's open daily from 8.30 am to 3.30 pm and 6 to 8 pm. The staff are friendly but speak little English.

Things to See

Ciudad Victoria has no compelling tourist attractions, but there is the **Museo de Antropología e Historia**, run by the University of Tamaulipas. It has a collection of mammoth bones, Indian artifacts, colonial memorabilia and revolutionary photos. The museum is on Calle Colón just north of the Plaza Hidalgo, and is supposedly open daily from 9 am to 1 pm and 2 to 7 pm, but hours seem to be irregular.

Ciudad Victoria also has some interesting public buildings, like the **Palacio de Gobierno** and the **Teatro Juárez**, both with large murals. There are several parks and a public swimming pool. The Sierra Madre forms an impressive backdrop to the city, and highway 101, which climbs the slopes to San Luis Potosí, is incredibly scenic. Forty km northeast of Ciudad Victoria, **Presa Vicente Guerrero** is a huge reservoir that attracts Mexicans and US citizens for bass fishing. The Reserva de la Biosfera El Cielo is 100 km south and more easily reached from Ciudad Mante (see the South of Ciudad Victoria section).

Places to Stay & Eat

The *Hostal De Escandón* (☎ 2-90-04), on Tijerina between Hidalgo and Juárez, is the best budget deal in town. All of the rooms are small, and some come with bunk beds, but the mattresses are firm, the rooms very clean and secure, and the staff friendly and helpful. The centrally located hotel offers singles/doubles, with color TV, phones and fans, for US$7.50/9. And the inexpensive restaurant is OK.

Next best in the budget category is the *Hotel Los Monteros* (☎ 2-03-00), on Plaza Hidalgo. The hotel resides in a lovely old colonial-style building, and its rooms (from US$8 to US$15 for a single or double) are spacious, cleanish and comfortable, but a little mildewy. The *Hotel San Bernabe* (no phone), on the corner of Calle Colón and Matamoros, is the cheapest place downtown, with worn singles and doubles for US$6.50 and a significant cockroach problem.

The *Hotel Sierra Gorda* (☎ 2-20-10), on the south side of Plaza Hidalgo, has an attractive colonial-looking lobby, and rooms with air-con, TV and phone for

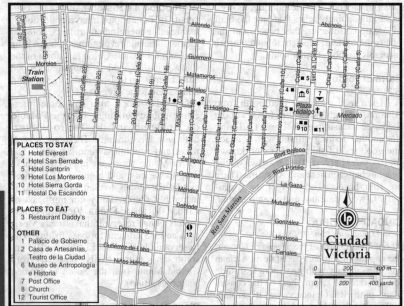

PLACES TO STAY
3 Hotel Everest
4 Hotel San Bernabe
5 Hotel Santorín
9 Hotel Los Monteros
10 Hotel Sierra Gorda
11 Hostal De Escandón

PLACES TO EAT
3 Restaurant Daddy's

OTHER
1 Palacio de Gobierno
2 Casa de Artesanías,
   Teatro de la Ciudad
6 Museo de Antropología
   e Historia
7 Post Office
8 Church
12 Tourist Office

US$31/41. The *Hotel Everest* (☎ 2-40-50), on the west side of the same plaza, is a modern place with all the usual comforts and a VCR for US$35/40. The *Hotel Santorín* (☎ 2-80-66), at Calle Colón 349, is another modern place with exactly the same prices and comparable rooms. The Everest is maybe the better and more popular of the two.

Restaurant Daddy's, in the Hotel Everest, looks like a 1960s American cafeteria, but the food is OK and reasonably priced with most meals about US$5 with beverage. The restaurant in the *Hotel Los Monteros* has a lot more Mexican charm, slightly higher prices and good meals.

Getting There & Away

Air Ciudad Victoria has an airport, east of town off the Soto La Marina road. There are flights to Matamoros, Mexico City and Poza Rica with Aero California (☎ 5-18-51) and/or Aeromar (☎ 6-91-91).

Bus The bus station is near the ring road on the east side of town, and has a left-luggage service (US$2.50 per day), a post office and a telecommunications center. Daily service from Ciudad Victoria includes:

Ciudad Valles – 234 km, 3½ hours; three 1st-class (US$7.50)
Matamoros – 320 km, 4½ hours; two deluxe (US$17.25) and many 1st-class (US$10)
Mexico City (Terminal Norte) – 690 km, 11 hours; one deluxe (US$27.75) and three 1st-class (US$39)
Monterrey – 285 km, four hours; two 1st-class (US$10)
Reynosa – 330 km, five hours; one deluxe (US$19) and many 1st-class (US$10.50)
San Luis Potosí – 357 km, 5½ hours; hourly 1st-class (US$11.75)
Soto La Marina – 124 km, two hours; 2nd-class only (US$3.75)
Tampico – 245 km, 3½ hours; many 1st-class (US$7.75)

Train From the old train station at the west side of town, slow segunda clase trains depart for Monterrey at 3 pm and for Tampico at 2 pm.

Car & Motorcycle From Ciudad Victoria, you can go southeast to Tampico for the Huasteca or the Gulf Coast, or take one of the steep but scenic roads to the Sierra. For San Luis Potosí, take highway 101 to the southwest – a lovely route. For Mexico City, highway 85 south, via Ciudad Mante and Ciudad Valles, is the most direct.

SOUTH OF CIUDAD VICTORIA
Balcón de Montezuma
Although this site has been known by archaeologists for a number of years, it was not until late 1988 that any excavations were done. Very little is known about these ruins, but they are generally thought to have been a Huastec settlement. The site is made up of numerous circles set around two open spaces which were probably public plazas. While not as imposing as other pre-Hispanic ruins, this is one of the dwindling number of sites which can still be seen in an undeveloped state.

Balcón de Montezuma is not easily accessible – first you need to get to Ejido de Alta Cumbre, a tiny hamlet some 25 km south of Ciudad Victoria on highway 101. If you don't have a car, take a bus bound for Jaumave, Tula or San Luis Potosí and ask the driver to let you off. Go down the gravel road on the left of the highway and through a metal gate with the words 'Alta Cumbre.' Follow this track through the village, going down the hill to the right, and after a few hundred meters there's a faded 'Zona Arqueológica' sign. From there it's about four km down a 4WD track to the ruins.

Ciudad Mante
pop 116,451; alt 190m; ☎ 123
Ciudad Mante is a center for processing the sugar and cotton grown in the area. There are some cheap to mid-range hotels, motels and restaurants, and it's a quiet, clean place to stop for a night.

Reserva de la Biosfera El Cielo
A reserve of 1440 sq km, El Cielo covers a range of altitudes on the slopes of the Sierra, and is a transition zone between tropical, semi-desert and temperate ecosystems. It marks the northern limit for quite a number of tropical species of plant and animal.

The best access point for the reserve is the village of Gómez Farías, 14 km up a side road going west from the highway about 40 km north of Ciudad Mante. There's a sign on the left as you get to the plaza, and an office behind it that may have some information on weekdays. The reserve starts about two km down the rough track next to the sign.

Nuevo León

It was the search for silver (not found) and slaves, and the desire of missionaries to proselytize, which first brought the Spanish to this sparsely inhabited region. In 1579, Luis de Carvajal was commissioned to found Nuevo León. He set up abortive settlements in Monterrey and Monclova, and it was not until 1596 and 1644 respectively that the Spanish established themselves permanently at those sites. They used Indians from Tlaxcala and other areas to the south to help settle these new northern regions. In the late 17th century, Nuevo León and Coahuila were the starting points for Spanish expansion into Texas.

Slowly, ranching became viable around the small new towns, despite raids by hostile Chichimecs that continued into the 18th century. Nuevo León had an estimated 1.5 million sheep by 1710. Huge empty areas were taken over by a few powerful landowners who came to dominate the region. As the 19th century progressed and the railways arrived, ranching continued to expand, and industry developed, especially in Monterrey. By 1900, Nuevo León had 328,000 inhabitants.

MONTERREY
pop 3 million; alt 538m; ☎ *8*

Monterrey, capital of Nuevo León, is Mexico's third-biggest city and its second-biggest industrial center. It's perhaps the most Americanized city in Mexico, and parts of it, with leafy suburbs, 7-Eleven stores and giant air-con malls, look just like suburbs in Texas or California. Industry and commerce drive Monterrey, and its pursuit of profit also seems more American than Mexican.

The central city area has been ambitiously remodeled, with a series of linked plazas and gardens, a pedestrian precinct on the west side and a historical zone on the east. Jagged mountains, including the distinctive saddle-shaped Cerro de la Silla (1288 meters), make a dramatic backdrop for the city, and provide opportunities for some worthwhile side trips; the surrounding country offers caves, canyons, lakes and waterfalls.

Most travelers bypass Monterrey in their haste to get to/from the 'real' Mexico, but the city is a fascinating mixture of old and new, industry and style, tradition and efficiency. There's a lot to see too, particularly if you like modern art and architecture. For budget travelers, Monterrey's disadvantage is that lodging is expensive and the cheaper places are mainly in a seedy area near the bus station, which is a 20-minute ride from the city center. The smog and the weather can be bad too, but you are just as likely to find fresh breezes, blue skies and clear, dry desert air.

History
There were three attempts to found a city here, the first in 1577. The second, in 1592, was by Luis de Carvajal and the third, in 1596, was by Diego de Montemayor. He christened his 34-person settlement Ciudad Metropolitana de Nuestra Señora de Monterrey, after the Conde de Monterrey who was viceroy of Mexico at the time.

Monterrey struggled as an outpost, but it slowly became the core of a sheep-ranching area that was often raided by Chichimec Indians. Its importance grew with the colonization of Tamaulipas in the mid-18th century, since it was on the trade route to the new settlements. In 1777, when Monterrey had about 4000 inhabitants, it became the seat of the new bishopric of Linares.

In 1824, Monterrey became the capital of the state of Nuevo León in newly independent Mexico. In the Mexican-American War, Monterrey was occupied by Zachary Taylor's troops after three days of fierce fighting. The city was occupied again in the 1860s by French troops, who were driven out by Benito Juárez's forces in 1866.

Monterrey's location close to the USA gave it advantages in trade and smuggling: in the US Civil War it was a staging post for cotton exports by the blockaded Confederates. Railway lines came in 1881, and tax exemptions for industry during the Porfiriato (1876-1910) attracted Mexican, US, British and French investment. Monterrey began to emerge as an industrial center in the 1860s and by the early 20th century was one of Mexico's biggest cities; its population grew from 27,000 in 1853 to about 80,000 in 1910.

The city was the site of the first heavy industry in Latin America – the iron and steel works of the Compañía Fundidora de Fierro y Acero de Monterrey. In 1890, José Schneider founded the Cervecería Cuauhtémoc, which became Mexico's biggest brewery as well as manufacturer of glass, cartons and bottle caps. Other industries produced furniture, clothes, cigarettes, soap, cement and bricks. Two intermarried families, the Garzas and the Sadas, came to dominate business and built a huge empire – the Monterrey Group – that owned many of the city's biggest companies.

After the 1940s, electricity enabled scores of new industries to develop. Little planning went into the city's growth, and the environment and the poor were mainly left to fend for themselves, but education was promoted by the Garza and Sada families, and today Monterrey has four

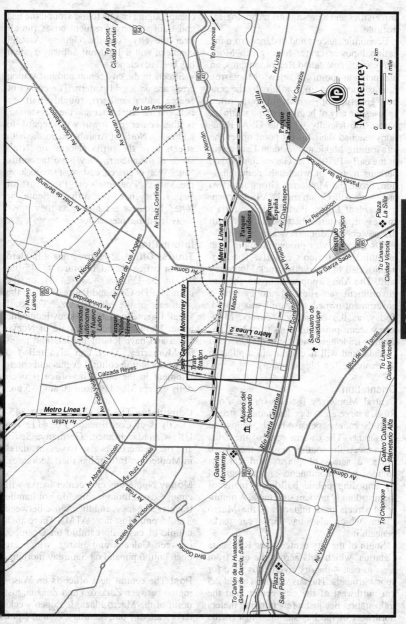

Monterrey

To Airport,
Ciudad Aleman

To Reynosa

Av Las Americas

Av Livas

Av Cavazos

Rio La silla

Parque
La Pastora

Av Lopez Mateos

Av Galvan Lopez

Av Aleman

Paseo de las Americas

Av Diaz de Berlanga

Av Ruiz Cortines

Parque
España

Parque
Chapultepec

Av Revolucion

Plaza
La Silla

Av Nogalar Sur

Av Ciudad de los Angeles

Parque
Fundidora

Av Gomez

Metro Linea 1

Av Pirelo

Av Garza Sada

Instituto
Tecnológico

To Linares,
Ciudad Victoria

To Nuevo
Laredo

Universidad
Autonoma
de Nuevo Leon

Parque
Niños
Heroes

Av Universidad

see Central Monterrey map

Av Colon

Madero

Av Constitucion

Santuario de
Guadalupe

Metro Linea 2

To Linares,
Ciudad Victoria

Calzada Reyes

Train
Station

Blvd de las Torres

Metro Linea 1

Av Aztlan

Av Fidel Velasquez

Museo del
Obispado

Rio Santa Catarina

Av Abraham Lincoln

Av Ruiz Cortines

Av Frias

Galerias
Monterrey

Centro Cultural
Planetario Alfa

Av Gomez Morin

To Chipinque

Paseo de la Victoria

Blvd Gomez

To Cañon de la Huasteca,
Grutas de García, Saltillo

Plaza
San Pedro

Av Vasconcelos

NORTHEAST MEXICO

0   1   2 km
0   .5   1 mile

universities and a prestigious technological institute.

Economic success and distance from the national power center have given Monterrey's citizens, called Regiomontanos, an independent point of view. Monterrey resents 'meddling' in its affairs by the central government, which in turn often accuses the city of being too capitalistic or, worse, too friendly with the USA. Relations reached their lowest point under the left-leaning Mexican President Echeverría in the early 1970s. The Garzas and Sadas, perhaps in fear of wholesale nationalization, broke the Monterrey Group into two parts – the Alfa Group and the VISA Group.

President López Portillo, Echeverría's successor, fostered better relations with the powers of Monterrey, and in the late 1970s the city was producing more than one-third of Mexico's exports. The economic crisis of the 1980s struck Monterrey hard. The Alfa Group went broke, the city government ran short of money, and a government-owned steel mill was closed. Today, as the economy recovers, Monterrey seems poised to profit from NAFTA, the free-trade agreement with the USA and Canada, and will likely remain a pillar in the evolving Tex-Mex economy.

Orientation

Central Monterrey focuses on the Zona Rosa, a large area of pedestrianized streets with the more expensive hotels, shops and restaurants. The eastern edge of the Zona Rosa meets the southern end of the Macro Plaza, a series of plazas and gardens studded with monuments and surrounded by imposing public buildings, many of them strikingly modern structures. A number of streets pass underneath the Macro Plaza, which also has large car parks beneath it.

South of the city center is the Río Santa Catarina, which cuts across the city from west to east – the dry riverbed is used for sports grounds. The bus station is about 2.5 km northwest of the city center, and the train station lies just a few hundred meters northwest of the bus station. Most of the cheap lodging can be found around the bus and train stations. Frequent buses run all over the city (see the Getting Around chapter), and a light-rail subway system has been developed.

Streets in the city center and bus station areas are on a grid pattern. The corner of Juárez and Aramberri, roughly halfway between the city center and the bus station, is the center of town with regard to addresses. North of Aramberri, north-south streets have the suffix 'Norte' or 'Nte'; south of Aramberri, they have the suffix 'Sur.' West of Juárez, east-west streets have the suffix 'Poniente' or 'Pte'; east of Juárez, they have the suffix 'Oriente' or 'Ote.' Numbers get higher as they move away from the intersection.

Information

Tourist Office Monterrey has a modern tourist office called Infotur (☎ 345-08-70, in the USA 800-235-2438), on the corner of Dr Coss and Padre Mier, to the southeast of the Macro Plaza. The staff speak fluent English, are knowledgeable about Monterrey and the state of Nuevo León and have lots of leaflets and maps of Monterrey. They can also tell you about upcoming cultural events and entertainment in the city. The office is open daily except Monday from 10 am to 5 pm.

Consulates The US Consulate (☎ 345-21-20) is at Constitución Pte 411. The UK, Canada, France, Germany, Spain and the Netherlands also have consulates in Monterrey; Infotur has their addresses.

Money Numerous city-center banks will change cash, though some do not handle traveler's checks, and they close between 3 and 5 pm. Most have ATMs. There are a couple of casas de cambio on Ocampo, between Galeana and Juárez, which are open until 6 pm and on Saturday morning.

Post The central post office is on Washington between Zaragoza and Zuazua, just north of the Macro Plaza. It's open weekdays 9 am to 7 pm, Saturday 9 am to 1 pm.

Macro Plaza

A city block wide and a km long, this great swath of urban open space is a controversial piece of redevelopment. Carved out in the 1980s by the demolition of several entire city blocks, many regard it as a grandiose monument to Monterrey's ambition. The initially desolate space has been softened by greenery and offers well-planned vistas of the surrounding mountains. Enclosed by the best of the city's old and new architecture, the area offers respite from the urban bustle and helps manage traffic problems with underpasses and extensive underground car parks.

Though the overall size of the Macro Plaza could have been overwhelming, it actually comprises a series of smaller spaces at a human scale, which have various styles and functions. These spaces are interspersed with buildings, monuments, sculptures, fountains, trees and gardens – there are no vast expanses of unrelieved pavement. At the very southern end, nearest the Río Santa Catarina, the **Monumento Homenaje al Sol** is a tall sculpture on a traffic island that faces the **Palacio Municipal**, a modern building raised up on concrete legs.

This occupies the south side of **Plaza Zaragoza**, a semi-formal space often busy with people walking through, having lunch or listening to music from the covered bandstand. On the east side of Plaza Zaragoza is the **Museo de Arte Contemporáneo** (MARCO), with its gigantic black dove sculpture, and the baroque-façaded **Catedral**, built between 1600 and 1750 (the bell tower was added in 1851). Facing it across the plaza is the old city hall, which now houses the **Museo Metropolitano de Monterrey**. North of the old city hall, new and old buildings flank the end of **Calle Morelos**, a bustling pedestrian mall.

The centerpiece of Plaza Zaragoza is the stunning **Faro del Comercio** (Beacon of Commerce), a tall, flat, orange concrete slab designed by the architect Luis Barragán in the love-it-or-hate-it-but-you-can't-ignore-it style. If you're lucky you'll see green laser beams from the top sweep over the city at night. It couldn't be in greater contrast to the adjacent cathedral. On the north side of Plaza Zaragoza is a modern subway station.

Across Padre Mier is the **Fuente de la Vida** (Fountain of Life) with a Neptune-like character riding a chariot in the middle. North of this, the modern **Teatro de la Ciudad** and **Congreso del Estado** buildings face each other from the east and west sides of the **Esplanada Cultural** plaza. Farther north again, the **Biblioteca Central** (State Library) and the **Tribunal Superior de Justica** (Supreme Court) stand on either side of the **Parque Hundido** (Sunken Garden), a favorite spot for couples.

North again and down some steps, you come to the **Esplanada de los Héroes** (Esplanade of the Heroes), also called the Plaza Cinco de Mayo, with statues of national heroes in each corner. It's the most formal and traditional of the spaces in the Macro Plaza and looks like a standard Plaza de Armas with the 1908 neoclassical **Palacio de Gobierno** on its north side. From the steps of the palacio you can look back down the length of the Macro Plaza to the south side of the river and up the hills beyond. Behind the palacio, a small park faces the 1930s **post office** and federal government building, providing yet another architectural contrast.

Zona Rosa

This is the area of top hotels, restaurants and shops just west of Plaza Zaragoza, bounded roughly by Morelos to the north, Zaragoza to the east, Hidalgo to the south, and Carranza to the west. Two of the streets are pedestrian-only and it's usually a bustling place where it's a pleasure to walk around, window-shop or find somewhere to eat or drink.

Barrio Antiguo

This is the old neighborhood, east of the Macro Plaza, in the blocks between Dr Coss to the west, Gómez to the east, Padre Mier to the north and Constitución to the south. It's nice to stroll around and see

NORTHEAST MEXICO

PLACES TO STAY

1   Hotel Nogales
4   Hotel Son Mar
7   Fastos Hotel
8   Hotel Posada
9   Hotel Amado Nervo
10 Hotel Virreyes
12 Hotel Jandal
13 Hotel Patricia
14 Hotel Quinta Avenida
16 Gran Hotel Yamallel
21 Hotel Río
26 Ambassador Camino Real
27 Hotel Royalty
29 Santa Rosa Suites Hotel
30 Hotel Colonial
31 Radisson Ancira Sierra
    Plaza Hotel
33 Hotel Monterrey
36 Holiday Inn Crowne Plaza

PLACES TO EAT

6   El Pastor Restaurant
7   Fastory Restaurant
14 Restaurant York
17 Los Cabritos

20 La Cabaña
22 Restaurante Vegetariano
    Superbom
25 Restaurant Puntada
28 Mi Tierra
32 El Monasterio

OTHER

2   Cervecería Cuauhtémoc,
    Museums
3   Bus Station
5   Museo del Vidrio,
    Kristaluxus Factory
11 Arco de la Independencia
15 Casa de la Cultura
18 Post Office
19 Iglesia de la Purísima
23 Fuente de la Vida
24 Tourist Office
34 Museo Metropolitano
    de Monterrey
35 Faro del Comercio
37 Monumento Homenaje
    al Sol
38 Museo de Arte
    Contemporáneo (MARCO)

Metro Línea 2

Universidad

Metro Línea 1

Central Monterrey

0   100   200 m
0   100   200 yards

some of Monterrey's more traditional architecture.

Museo de Arte Contemporáneo
Just east of Plaza Zaragoza, at the south end of the Macro Plaza, MARCO has temporary exhibitions of work by artists from Nuevo León and elsewhere. Unless it's being prepared for the next exhibition, it's open Tuesday to Sunday from 11 am to 7 pm, or on Wednesday and Sunday to 9 pm. Admission is US$2 (but it's free on Wednesday).

Museo Metropolitano de Monterrey
In the old Palacio Municipal, this museum is upstairs around a 16th-century courtyard. Unusually for Mexico, its earliest exhibits are from the colonial period, with no reference to pre-Hispanic cultures at all. There is an interesting section on the work of sculptor, early resident and local hero Alberto del Campo, commemorating the 400th anniversary of Monterrey. It's open Tuesday through Sunday from 10 am to 5 pm (free).

Alameda
Occupying several blocks a km northwest of the city center, this park is bounded by Pino Suárez, Aramberri, Villagrán and Washington. It is a venue for occasional Sunday morning concerts for children.

Cervecería Cuauhtémoc
In the gardens of the old Cuauhtémoc brewery, this complex has an art gallery, a sports museum, a baseball hall of fame, brewery tours and ... free beer! Brought to you by the maker of Bohemia, Tecate, and Carta Blanca beer, it's a km north of the bus station at Avenida Universidad 2202.

The art gallery, **Museo de Monterrey**, in a converted industrial building, features some excellent visiting exhibitions from artists such as Picasso, Siqueiros, Miró and Moore.

The **Salon de la Fama** (Hall of Fame) has photos, memorabilia, and facts and figures on Mexican baseball. It features many Mexican players who made the big leagues

in the USA, and some Americans whose careers made more headway south of the border. The **Museo Deportivo de Monterrey** covers a variety of sports in which Mexicans have excelled, including boxing, diving, shooting and rodeo. Some fine charro equipment – saddles, bridles, etc – is on display.

You should make an appointment to visit the brewery and **Museo de la Cervecería** (☎ 328-60-60), but tours are usually Tuesday through Friday at 11 am, noon and 3 pm. There is a very pleasant little garden facing the art gallery, a nice place to sit even if you don't partake of the free beer. There's also a café upstairs, among old brewing vats, where tasty sweet pastries are served. The complex is open Tuesday through Saturday from 9.30 am to 9 pm, and Sunday from 9 am to 5 pm (free).

Casa de la Cultura
This is housed in a curious, Gothic-style ex-train station. The gallery downstairs has temporary exhibitions of work by local artists: upstairs is the Teatro Estación, with small productions. It's in an unattractive location, on Colón, near the corner of Escobedo – open daily except Monday from 10 am to 6 pm (free).

Museo del Vidrio
This specialized but interesting museum (☎ 329-10-00 ext 1105) shows the history of glass in Mexico (ground floor), the manufacture and use of glass (1st floor), and glass as an artistic and sculptural medium (2nd floor). It's on the corner of Zaragoza and Magallanes, two blocks north of Colón, and is open daily except Thursday from 10 am to 7 pm (free). Call ahead to schedule a tour in English.

Kristaluxus Crystal Factory
You can watch artisans turning lead crystal into jugs, glasses, etc, at the factory of Kristaluxus (☎ 351-63-96, 351-91-00 ext 96), in the north of town at JM Vigil 400, between Zuazua and E Carranza, Colonia del Norte. Tours are available at 10.30 am Monday through Saturday (call first) and

there's a showroom where you can buy the products.

Parque Niños Héroes

A number of sporting, recreational and cultural facilities are in this large park, entered from Avenida Reyes about five km north of the city center. Most impressive is the permanent collection of painting and sculpture at **Pinacoteca de Nuevo León**, which shows the outstanding work of the state's artists since colonial times. Their images of the desert landscape are particularly striking. A building next door shows temporary exhibitions, and also has some excellent work. These galleries are open daily except Monday from 10 am to 5 pm (free).

The **Museo del Automóvil** has a small collection of old cars, mainly of US origin, from the 1920s, '30s and '40s. It's next to the Pinacoteca, with the same hours (free).

At the **Museo de la Fauna y Ciencias Naturales**, you can see life-sized dioramas with stuffed wildlife in its 'natural' habitat, from Saharan Africa to the Arctic, with good labels and descriptions in Spanish. Kids will like it, and it's not *too* tacky, except for the moose's head hanging on the wall with its body and legs painted behind. It's open Tuesday through Friday from 9 am to 7 pm, and on weekends from 10 am to 5.30 pm (US$1).

Iglesia de La Purísima

About a km west of the city center, near a park on the corner of Hidalgo and Peña, this church was designed by Enrique de la Mora and built in 1946. It's an engaging example of once-modern architecture. The main body of the church is supported by parabolic arches, and a squat rectangular school building has been added to the back. The statues on the sides of the church are of the 12 apostles, each with an air-con unit beside him.

Museo del Obispado

The former bishop's palace *(obispado)*, on a hill 2.5 km west of the Zona Rosa along Matamoros, gives fine views over the city and surrounding mountains, smog permitting. Built in 1786-87, it served as a fort during the US attack on Monterrey in 1846, weathered the French intervention of the 1860s and conflicts between local Constitutionalists and the forces of Pancho Villa in the revolution years. It was also a yellow-fever hospital before becoming what it is now – a small historical museum with various colonial and revolutionary relics. It's open daily except Monday from 10 am to 5 pm and costs US$2 – don't feel too bad if you miss it.

Santuario de Guadalupe

This church is the strange pyramid you can see from the south end of the Macro Plaza. It looks like it was made from a gigantic piece of folded cardboard.

Instituto Tecnológico

The Technological Institute, in the southeast part of the city on Avenida Garza Sada between Pernambuco and Octavio Paz, is one of Mexico's best-regarded higher-education schools. It has some surprising architecture, like the building that appears to have been sliced apart, leaving the two halves toppling away from each other.

Parque La Pastora

Five km east of the center, off Avenida Cavazos, this park has an open-air zoo, woodlands and rental-boat rides (admission is US$1). Beside the park is the **Bosque Mágico**, a fun park that's open every day.

Colonia del Valle & Chipinque

Colonia del Valle, six km southwest of the center, is one of Monterrey's most exclusive suburbs, with big houses on lovely tree-lined streets. The wealthiest people live farther south, high up on the slopes of the Mesa de Chipinque, which rises to 835 meters above the city. Colonia del Valle has a mall and other areas of classy shops and restaurants in the streets off Calzada del Valle.

The Mesa de Chipinque, several km up the hill from Colonia del Valle, offers woodland walks, fine views of the city and the luxury Hotel Chipinque, where there are horses for hire. You need a taxi or your own vehicle to get there, since buses don't run beyond Colonia del Valle. It's open from 7 am to 7 pm. Vehicle entry is US$1.50.

Centro Cultural Alfa

This cultural complex (☎ 356-56-96), sponsored by the Alfa industrial group, is in Colonia del Valle at Roberto Garza Sada 1000, and is well worth the trip. The main building, which looks like a water tank tipping over, has floors devoted to computers, astronomy, physics, Mexican antiquities and temporary exhibitions. The scientific displays have lots of educational hands-on exhibits, and everything is well lit and carefully labeled (in Spanish only). In the center of the building is the planetarium, which also functions as an Omnimax cinema.

Outside is the Jardín Cientifico, with more educational stuff, the Jardín Prehispánico, with replicas of some of the great archaeological finds, and an aviary. El Universo, a superb glass mural, was created by Rufino Tamayo for the headquarters of the Alfa group, but was considered so beautiful that a special building was constructed to display it to a wider audience. It's in the large building called the Pabellón (Pavilion), which resembles a covered wagon.

The complex is open Tuesday through Friday from 3 to 9 pm, Saturday from 2 to 9 pm and Sunday from noon to 9 pm. Admission is US$4. Special buses go every hour from the Alameda, at the intersection of Washington and Villagrán, and every half-hour on Sunday. The last bus departs from the planetarium at 9 pm.

Organized Tours

Gray Line Tours (☎ 369-64-72) runs sightseeing and shopping tours to places in and around the city. Destinations covered depend on the day of the week but include the Macro Plaza, Cuauhtémoc brewery complex, Kristaluxus crystal factory, Galerías Monterrey shopping mall, and various craft shops. Tours outside the city include Centro Cultural Alfa, Grutas de García and Cola de Caballo. A basic morning city tour covers two or three destinations and costs between US$6 and US$9. Call first or ask the tourist office where the tour goes on a particular day. Also, Trolley Tours operates several trolley cars that make a loop around downtown every half-hour; cost is US$1.30.

Special Events

Monterrey's festivals include:

Feria de Primavera – There are many festivities during the spring fair, which begins on Palm Sunday (the Sunday before Easter).

Aniversario de Independencia – Monterrey's biggest celebrations, for Mexico's independence anniversary, are held on September 15 and 16, with a big parade on the 16th.

Nuestra Señora de Guadalupe – Celebrations of the Día de Nuestra Señora de Guadalupe, December 12, begin as early as the last week of November at two churches, an old one at Tepeyac and Jalisco and a newer one at Castelar and Jalisco, one block away. The festivities include the offering of a magnificent floral arrangement to the Virgin by the people. On December 12 and the days leading up to it, thousands of pilgrims head for the Santuario de Guadalupe. The festival is also celebrated in a big way in Abasolo, a village 25 km from Monterrey off the Monclova road, where there are pilgrimages, a fair, a parade of floats and horse riders, and folk-dancing.

Places to Stay

Nearly all of the cheaper hotels are within a few blocks of the bus and train stations. A room away from the noisy street is a definite plus. There's also mid-range lodging around the bus station and in the Zona Rosa, while the top-end places are nearly all in the Zona Rosa.

Places to Stay – budget

Some of the best budget accommodations can be found on Nervo, in the two blocks running south of the enormous bus station. The first place you come to, at Nervo 1138, is the Hotel Posada (☎ 372-72-48), which

Top: Shopfront, Chihuahua
Center: Children near Creel

Bottom Left: Cascada Cusárare, south of Creel
Bottom Right: Tarahumara woman, Divisadero

Top Left: A roadside cross near Durango
Top Right: Indian children enjoy the cool tiles of a doorway, Saltillo
Bottom: Sisal harvesting, Tamaulipas

SCOTT DOGGETT

has clean rooms with fans, TV and plenty of hot water. Prices are US$13 for a single or double (TV is extra). Some rooms are better than others, and several rooms on the upper floors have sweeping views.

A block farther down at Nervo 1110, the *Hotel Amado Nervo* (☎ 375-46-32) has some good rooms with TV and firm beds for US$11/12 for a single/double. The *Hotel Virreyes* (☎ 374-66-10), at Nervo 902, is an excellent value with larger but slightly tattier rooms with air-con for US$7.50 for one or two people.

If you arrive at the train station late at night, the best budget hotel in the area is the newer *Hotel Nogales* (☎ 375-21-73) at the north end of the train station's parking lot. The hotel offers clean, standard rooms with air-con for US$13 for one or two people.

Places to Stay – middle

The mid-range in Monterrey starts at around US$15 for a single. There are no great bargains in this range, but the comfort is a quantum leap up from the budget choices.

Bus Station Area The *Hotel Patricia* (☎ 375-07-50), at Madero Ote 123 between Juárez and Guerrero, has secure parking and fine singles/doubles with air-con for US$23/26. The *Hotel 5a Avenida* (Quinta Avenida) (☎ 375-65-65), at Madero Ote 234 between Guerrero and Galeana, has secure parking and is much less expensive (US$14/16) but the rooms are small and the beds pretty worn.

The *Hotel Jandal* (☎ 372-31-72), at Cuauhtémoc Nte 825 on the corner of Salazar, is the best bargain in the US$20/23 range, with some very spacious, spotless, air-con singles/doubles with TV; there's parking and a restaurant. Request room 201 or one of comparable size.

The *Fastos Hotel* (☎ 372-32-50), over the road from the bus station at Colón Pte 956, on the corner of Villagrán, is classy and comfortable. The hotel's 'económico' rooms, with air-con, TV and phone, are worth considering if there are three or four

of you. They cost US$24/26/30/34 for one to four people.

East of the bus station, the *Hotel Son Mar* (☎ 375-44-00), at Universidad Nte 1211 near Colón, also has its own restaurant and parking, and newly remodeled rooms, but is on the expensive side at US$30 for a single or double. A comparable hotel downtown can be had for a few more dollars.

City Center The very central location of the *Hotel Colonial* (☎ 343-67-91), at Hidalgo Ote 475, makes it a tempting splurge. It has air-con, phone and TV, but smallish rooms at US$33 for one or two people. The *Hotel Royalty* (☎ 340-28-00) offers much larger rooms and bathrooms, air-con and heater, and walk-in closet for US$4 more. It's also located on a quieter street, as the Colonial is situated near two noisy nightclubs.

Other Areas Between the bus station and the city center is the towering *Gran Hotel Yamallel* (☎ 375-35-00), at Zaragoza Nte 912. Modern in style, it offers parking, phone, TV and a view over the city from the upper floors. Singles and doubles cost US$21. The rooms are dark and worn – not nearly as nice as those at the Jandal.

Places to Stay – top end

Downtown Monterrey has plenty of places for more than US$50. They mostly cater to business travelers and may give discounts on weekends. At all of them you can expect restaurants and bars, and carpeted rooms with air-con, heater, TV and phone. For atmosphere, none rivals the *Radisson Ancira Sierra Plaza Hotel* (☎ 345-75-75), on the corner of Escobedo and Plaza Hidalgo. It's been around since 1912, and it's said that Pancho Villa once rode into the lobby, which now has shops, a piano player, a restaurant and hovering waiters. Big rooms and plenty of old-fashioned elegance go for US$93.

The 200-room *Hotel Monterrey* (☎ 380-60-00), fronting the Plaza Zaragoza at Morelos Ote 574, has an electric band in its lobby bar and is one of the more popular top-end places. It charges US$90 for a room.

The enormous *Hotel Río* (☎ 344-90-40) at Padre Mier Pte 194 occupies a whole block between Morelos and Padre Mier. It has a swimming pool, and its 400 rooms cost from US$88 on weekends and from US$113 weekdays.

The *Ambassador Camino Real* (☎ 342-20-40), on the corner of Hidalgo and E Carranza, has 239 rooms at US$83 on weekends and US$110 weekdays. The *Holiday Inn Crowne Plaza* (☎ 344-93-00), at Constitución Ote 300, is a 390-room place with elevators that glide up and down above a cavernous restaurant/lounge where a band plays in the evenings. It is the most expensive place in town with singles and doubles going for US$85 on weekends, US$135 weekdays.

Places to Eat

Monterrey abounds in *norteño* ('northern-style') ranch cooking, of which cabrito is perhaps the best-known dish: whole young goats are split open, flattened on racks and roasted before charcoal or wood fires. The best cabrito is tender and juicy, and tastes like spring lamb. It is not particularly cheap. Good steak, on the other hand, is very reasonable in Monterrey – a big, tender T-bone can cost as little as US$4.50. Delicious sweets are another local specialty – try a *gloria*, made with milk, sugar and pecan nuts.

City Center Every block of the Zona Rosa seems to have at least one restaurant or café. There's a wide range of prices and types of food, but real value for the money is hard to come by at either end of the scale. The cheapest places are the *comedores* (basic cookshops) in the markets.

At Hidalgo Ote 123, *Restaurant Puntada* has a long menu of Mexican items with nothing above US$3, and is always packed. More expensive but with a pleasant atmosphere is *La Cabaña*, on Matamoros between Pino Suárez and Cuauhtémoc. It's a kind of large but comfortable log cabin

where you can drink beer or eat soup, seafood, meat, or chicken enchiladas with mole sauce; the most expensive item on the menu is around US$5.30.

The ever-popular *Mi Tierra*, on Morelos a half block west of Escobedo, serves up tasty tacos (five for US$2.50), flautas (five for US$1.80), and quesadillas (five for US$1.60); all meals come with stir-fried potatoes, a salad and beans. This is a fun place for people-watching.

Vegetarians will find a haven at *Restaurante Vegetariano Superbom*, upstairs on the corner of Padre Mier and Galeana. It does an excellent buffet lunch for US$3, but closes at 5 pm and on weekends. Other vegetarian restaurants are on Escobedo, half a block north of Padre Mier, and on the corner of Ocampo and Cuauhtémoc.

For good international fare in a bizarre setting, try *El Monasterio* on Escobedo between Morelos and Plaza Hidalgo. You are served by waitresses dressed as nuns as you sit in the cloisters and contemplate the wall paintings of smiling nuns preparing and serving food. Generous entrees go for US$3 to US$5. Breakfast costs as little as US$2.50.

Bus Station Area Although a little on the expensive side, *El Pastor* at Madero Pte 1067 on the corner of Alvárez specializes in cabrito. They do a variety of different parts of the animal, usually char-grilled, at prices between US$6.50 and US$8. El Pastor is open from 11 am to 11 pm.

Fastory Restaurant, in the Fastos Hotel on Colón opposite the bus station, is a tidy modern place, open 24 hours, with Mexican and Western food. Spaghetti bolognese (no trimmings) costs US$2.75, enchiladas US$3 and breakfasts up to US$3. The *Restaurant York*, in Hotel Quinta Avenida, is not as expensive as it looks, with main courses from around US$3.25 and an all-you-can-eat buffet lunch for US$3.

Other Areas Near the Alameda, *Los Cabritos*, on the corner of Aramberri and Villagrán, is another place specializing in cabrito. It's slightly more expensive than El

Pastor. Also popular in this part of town, but not cheap, is the *Café Lisboa*, on Aramberri on the north side of the park.

Entertainment

Monterrey has numerous cinemas and an active cultural life including theater, concerts and art exhibitions. The tourist office can tell you what's on, and posters listing events are placed in strategic spots around town. You might also come across some street theater in the Zona Rosa.

Monterrey's affluent younger set supports an active nightlife. The fashionable spots are always changing, so you might check at the tourist office for the current favorite. Places near the city center include: *Fonda San Miguel* (☎ 342-09-02) at Morelos Ote 940, with live music on Thursday, Friday and Saturday; and *La Casa de Pancho Villa* (☎ 343-0345) at Padre Mier Pte 837, with Latin American music every night. There are more places in the expensive southwestern suburbs, like *Kao's* (☎ 357-34-12) at Eugenio Garza Sada 4502, *Black Jack* (☎ 333-77-64) at Insurgentes 3987 in Vista Hermosa, and one of the popular *Señor Frog's* nightclubs (☎ 363-23-38) at Plaza Fiesta San Agustín, in San Pedro Garza García. For all these places you should be elegantly dressed (no grunge here), bring plenty of cash for drinks and taxis, and not arrive before 10 or 11 pm.

Spectator Sports

There are Western-style rodeos every Sunday, and occasional charreadas in which charros appear in all their finery to demonstrate their skills. Two better-known charreada venues are in Guadalupe, on the eastern edge of the city, and Cryco, 35 km south by highway 85. Bullfights are held at 4 pm at one of three sites (they rotate): the *Plaza de Toros*, at Alfonso Reyes 2401; *Cortijo San Felipe*, on San Pedro; and the *Plaza de Toros Cuauhtémoc*, on Guadalupe. September and October is the main bullfight season. The professional soccer season is from August to May, and the professional baseball season from March to August.

Things to Buy

Lead crystal is a Monterrey specialty but it's expensive, heavy and fragile and about the last thing a traveler would want to carry. If you're returning to the USA by car you could consider it (see Kristaluxus Crystal Factory in this section). There are lots of leather goods, which are cheaper and more portable. Don't forget some of the delicious sweets made locally with sugar, milk, nuts and fruit.

Interesting shops with quality handicrafts from different parts of Mexico are *Carápan*, at Hidalgo Ote 305, and *Tikal*, at Río Guadalquivir 319 in Colonia del Valle. There are no bargains, but some items are reasonably priced given their quality.

The two main downtown markets, Mercado Colón and Mercado Juárez, are big, bustling places selling everyday items. The richer Regiomontanos, of which there are many, prefer to shop at one of the big aircon malls like Plaza la Silla, south of town on Eugenio Garza Sada; Plaza San Pedro, southwest in the suburb of San Pedro; or Galerías Monterrey, to the west of town near the intersection of Pablo González and José E González.

Getting There & Away

Air Aeroméxico (☎ 343-55-60) is at Cuauhtémoc 812 Sur near Padre Mier. The main Mexicana office (☎ 380-73-00) is at Hidalgo Pte 922, but there are several other offices. Aeromonterrey (☎ 380-73-00), a regional airline, is at Calzada San Pedro 500 in the Garza García district. Continental Airlines (☎ 333-26-82) is at Insurgentes 2500, in the Galerías Monterrey. American Airlines (☎ 340-30-31) is at Zaragoza Sur 1300. Aero California (☎ 345-97-00) is at Ocampo 145 Ote.

There are direct flights, usually at least daily, to all major cities in Mexico, including Mexico City, Guadalajara, Puebla, Tampico, Torreón and Veracruz, and connections to just about anywhere else. Direct flights also go to Chicago, Dallas, Houston, Los Angeles, Miami and New York City. Connections to other international destinations are best made through Houston.

Bus Monterrey's enormous bus station (Central de Autobuses) occupies three blocks along Colón between Villagrán and Rayón. It's like a small city in itself, with ticket desks strung out along its whole length, restaurants, pay phones and a 24-hour left-luggage service (US$2). First-class lines that sevice Monterrey include Anáhuac (☎ 375-64-80) and Ómnibus de México (☎ 375-71-21). Sistema Estrella de Oro (☎ 318-37-88) provides deluxe service. Second-class services go to most places listed below and are slightly cheaper than the 1st-class fares shown, but can be a lot slower. Daily service from Monterrey includes:

Aguascalientes – 588 km, eight hours; three 1st-class (US$21)
Chihuahua – 783 km, 11 hours; two 1st-class (US$29)
Ciudad Acuña – 492 km, seven hours; four 1st-class (US$21) and two 2nd-class (US$18)
Ciudad Valles – 520 km, eight hours; many 1st- (US$21) and 2nd-class (US$17)
Ciudad Victoria – 285 km, four hours; many 1st- (US$10) and 2nd-class (US$7)
Durango – 573 km, nine hours; five 1st-class (US$23)
Guadalajara – 778 km, 11 hours; two 1st-class (US$36)
Matamoros – 324 km, six hours; many 1st-class (US$11)
Matehuala – 325 km, five hours; one 1st-class (US$11)
Mexico City (Terminal Norte) – 934 km, 11 or 12 hours; many 1st- (US$34) and 2nd-class (US$29)
Nuevo Laredo – 224 km, three hours; many 1st- (US$9) and 2nd-class (US$7)
Querétaro – 719 km, 10 hours; one 1st-class (US$26)
Reynosa – 220 km, 2½ hours; six 1st-class (US$8.25)
Saltillo – 85 km, 1½ hours; many 1st- (US$4.50) and 2nd-class (US$4)
San Luis Potosí – 517 km, seven hours; many 1st- (US$18) and 2nd-class (US$16)
Tampico – 530 km, 7½ hours; many 1st-class (US$19)
Torreón – 316 km, five hours; many 1st- (US$13) and 2nd-class (US$11)
Zacatecas – 458 km, 6½ hours; several 1st- (US$16) and 2nd-class (U$13)

Train Monterrey's train station (☎ 375-46-04) is about half a km west of the bus station along Colón, then three blocks north on Nieto. Tickets and information for primera clase and coche dormitorio travel are only available from 8.30 am to 12.30 pm, and from 4 to 8 pm. Other tickets are sold in the hour before scheduled departure. Trains are always slower than buses and often delayed. Service on the railways is not good.

There are two trains daily to Mexico City. For timetable details, see the Mexico City Getting There & Away section. El Regiomontano has primera preferente seats, a dining car, and, on Friday, Saturday and Sunday, a coche dormitorio. El Regiomontano leaves Monterrey at 7.50 pm, reaching Mexico City about 11 am; it also stops at Saltillo and San Luis Potosí. A primera preferente ticket to Mexico City costs US$22; a camarín costs US$47/78 for one/two people.

The Águila Azteca has no sleeping cars. It departs Monterrey at 11.30 pm, calls at Saltillo, San Luis Potosí, San Miguel de Allende and Querétaro, and is due in Mexico City at 7 pm. Fares on this train are US$23 for primera preferente and US$13 for segunda clase.

Only the northbound Águila Azteca from Mexico City continues past Monterrey to Nuevo Laredo; it is scheduled to leave Monterrey at 2.20 am and takes about six hours to reach Nuevo Laredo (US$4.75 primera, US$3.25 segunda). El Tamaulipeco departs Monterrey at 10.30 am for Reynosa (four or five hours, US$6 in primera) and Matamoros (seven or eight hours, US$8).

There are also daily slow trains between Monterrey and Tampico (El Tampico; departs 8 am, takes 11 hours) via Ciudad Victoria and other points, and between Monterrey, Torreón and Durango (El Torreón; departs 8.10 am).

Car & Motorcycle Going to/from the US border there's an excellent toll road, highway 85D, to Nuevo Laredo (US$14) and another, highway 40D, to Reynosa (US$6.50).

A number of ring roads bypass Monterrey, notably between highway 85D from the north and highway 40 going west to Saltillo. Take the toll bypass and you won't see Monterrey at all. For any destination in northwest Mexico, head for Saltillo then go west via Torreón or southwest via Zacatecas.

The quickest route south to Mexico City (934 km) is via Saltillo and highway 57 to San Luis Potosí and Querétaro. It has heavy traffic but is mostly divided highway, except for a two-lane stretch most of the way from Saltillo to San Luis Potosí. Alternative routes south start on highway 85 through Linares and Ciudad Victoria.

Rental There is enough to see within a day's drive of Monterrey to make car rental worth considering. Big companies like Avis (☎ 369-08-34), Hertz (☎ 369-08-22) and Dollar (☎ 369-08-97) have branches at the airport and usually in town as well. You may get a cheaper deal with one of the smaller local outfits like Max (☎ 342-63-75) at Hidalgo Pte 480, Excellent (☎ 345-77-00) at Hidalgo 1612, or Renee (☎ 342-06-04) at Hidalgo Ote 418. Infotur has a long list of them.

Getting Around
To/From the Airport The Monterrey airport is off the road to Ciudad Alemán (highway 54), northeast of the city, about 15 km from the city center. There is no shuttle service to the airport. A taxi costs about US$1.30.

Bus Buses (US$1.50) go frequently to most everywhere in Monterrey, but often by circuitous routes. A good idea is to ask at the front desk of your hotel before you go out. Many of the buses are privately owned and supplied by the large factories for their workers. These routes might be useful:

Bus station to center – Bus 18, from the corner of Nervo and Reforma, goes to the edge of the Zona Rosa, then doglegs around it. For Macro Plaza, the best place to get off is the corner of Juárez and 15 de Mayo. For the Zona Rosa, get off on Pino Suárez on the corners of Padre Mier, Hidalgo or Ocampo.

Center to bus station – No 39 (orange) can be picked up on Juárez at the corner with Padre Mier. It takes you to Colón. No 17-Pío X, going north from the corner of Cuauhtémoc and Padre Mier, also goes to Colón.

Bus station to Obispado, La Purísima and the city center – No 1 from the corner of Nervo and Reforma goes within a few blocks of the Obispado, passes La Purísima church, then goes along Ocampo to Zaragoza.

Center to Obispado – No 4 from five stops on Padre Mier goes west along Padre Mier. For the Obispado, get off when it turns left at Degollado, walk up the hill, turn left at the top of the steps, then take the first right (a 10-minute walk).

Center or bus station to Cuauhtémoc brewery – No 1 ('San Nicolás-Tecnológico') goes up Juárez from the city center and passes the corner of Cuauhtémoc and Colón (near the bus station) on its way up Universidad to the brewery. No 17 ('Universidad') goes north up Cuauhtémoc from Padre Mier to Colón, then on up Universidad to the brewery.

Cuauhtémoc Brewery to bus station and city center – No 18 goes south along Universidad, then right along Colón and left down Nervo before heading toward the city center.

Center to Colonia del Valle/Garza García – 'San Pedro,' from the corner of Hidalgo and Cuauhtémoc, goes to the big traffic circle in Colonia del Valle (where Gómez Morin, Vasconcelos and Calzada del Valle meet), then heads west along Vasconcelos.

Center to Instituto Tecnológico – Take No 1 from the corner of Hidalgo and Pino Suárez.

Metro The first line of Monterrey's Metro opened in 1991. It runs east to west in the north of the city, primarily going to outlying residential areas. Fares are about US$0.50. A second line opened three years later and runs from near the Cuauhtémoc brewery, past the bus station, and down to the Zona Rosa and the Macro Plaza. The two lines cross at the intersection of Colón and Cuauhtémoc, where the giant overhead Cuauhtémoc metro station is located.

AROUND MONTERREY
A number of sights near Monterrey are easily accessible in your own vehicle, and

somewhat less accessible by bus. You might consider taking a tour to some of them, or renting a car between a few people.

Grutas de García

An illuminated, 2.5-km route leads through 16 chambers in this cave system high in the Sierra del Fraile, reached by a 700-meter ascent by funicular railway. The caves were formed about 50 million years ago and discovered by the parish priest in 1843. There are lots of stalactites and stalagmites, as well as petrified seashells. Each chamber has a different name such as 'The Eagle's Nest,' 'Chamber of Clouds' and 'The Eighth Wonder.'

On Sunday a Transportes Monterrey-Saltillo bus leaves Monterrey bus station at 9, 10 and 11 am and at noon, returning in the afternoon (US$4 for the round trip). On other days the same line runs buses every half-hour to Villa de García, nine km from the caves. To get there by car from Monterrey, take highway 40 toward Saltillo. After about 25 km a sign points the way to the caves; turn right and go another 18 km to the bottom of the funicular. This is a popular weekend outing, but the caves and funicular are open every day from 9 am to 5 pm. Entry is US$3.50 and includes the funicular ride.

Cañón de la Huasteca

On the western edge of Monterrey, 16 km from the center, this canyon is 300 meters deep and has some dramatic rock formations. There is a town at one end of it and a playground in the middle, which reduces its attraction as a wilderness area. Reach the mouth of the canyon by taking a 'Santa Catarina/Huasteca' bus from the corner of Hidalgo and Pino Suárez, or Cuauhtémoc and Madero, in the center of Monterrey. The same bus brings you back to the city center. It's open daily from 8 am to 6 pm; entry is US$1.50 for a vehicle, US$0.40 for a person.

The town of **Santa Catarina**, at the north end of the canyon, celebrates the festival of the Virgen de San Juan de Los Lagos with dances and fireworks from August 10 to 15.

Cascada Cola de Caballo

'Horsetail Falls,' a 25 meter waterfall, is six km up a rough road from El Cercado, a village 35 km south of the center of Monterrey by highway 85. It has its share of hawkers and food stalls, but it's quite pretty and attracts a lot of picnickers. Walk up the valley beyond the falls to see the vegetation that flourishes on the slopes of the sierra. The waterfall is on private land and open Tuesday through Sunday from 9 am to 5 pm; entry is US$1. Horses and donkeys can be hired for the last km to the falls (US$3). Autobuses Monterrey-Villa de Santiago-El Cercado go to El Cercado from the Monterrey bus station.

On the way to El Cercado you pass close to the **Presa Rodrigo Gómez**, known as La Boca – an artificial lake where Regiomontanos go swimming, sailing and water-skiing.

If you have your own vehicle, you can drive 33 km up a rough road from El Cercado to the **Laguna de Sánchez**, a mountain lake surrounded by pine forests.

NORTH OF MONTERREY

On the toll road to Nuevo Laredo, highway 85D, you'll see nothing but cacti, cattle and the occasional eagle. On the free road you pass the town of **Sabinas Hidalgo**, about halfway there; it has a few motels and restaurants. Forty km west of Sabinas Hidalgo are the **Grutas de Bustamente**, a series of underground chambers three km long. At the time of writing, the caves were closed but were being developed for visitors.

SOUTH OF MONTERREY

You can go southwest from Monterrey to Saltillo (95 km) by the excellent highway 40 (the main route toward Mexico City).

Going southeast on highway 85 toward Ciudad Victoria, you follow the edge of the sierra through Mexico's most important citrus-growing area, centered on the towns of Allende, Montemorelos, Hualahuises and Linares. There are hotels in Montemorelos and Linares.

A new park, the **Bioparque Estrella**, has a large variety of large animals from Africa, Asia and the Americas, and is a nice place to spend a day. Before reaching Montemorelos, take the turnoff for Reyones and go nine km; the entrance to the park is just past the nine km sign, to the left. The park is open Friday, Saturday and Sunday only, from 8 am to 5 pm (to 3 pm November to March). Cost is US$4.

Sierra Madre Oriental

From Linares a scenic road (highway 58) heads west up into the Sierra Madre to the towns of Iturbide (44 km) and, with an eight-km northward detour, Galeana (72 km), climbing 1000 meters from the valley. Highway 58 continues west down to the Altiplano Central, where it meets highway 57 between Saltillo and Matehuala, 98 km from Linares. It's superb up on the Sierra, with clear air, sparkling streams and unspoiled landscapes.

Iturbide This area has several caves, canyons and waterfalls. There's a hotel where you can hire horses to reach some of them. Nine km east of Iturbide, a giant bas-relief, *Los Altares*, by Nuevo León sculptor Federico Cantú, is cut into the cliff beside the road; it's dedicated to road builders.

Galeana High on a wheat-producing plateau, Galeana is a center for hand-loomed wool shawls and blankets. The town celebrates the festival of San Pablo with fireworks and processions from January 20 to 25. On the plaza, the *Hotel Magdalena* is OK for US$7/9; the *Hotel Jardín* is not much better at US$13/15. Nine km north (turn right at the Río San Lucas junction) is a 15-meter-high natural bridge called the **Puente de Dios**, over which a local road passes. For the best view, park on the flat area to the left just before the bridge. The 3635-meter peak of **Cerro Potosí**, one of the highest in the Sierra Madre Oriental, is 35 km west of Galeana.

Coahuila

The state of Coahuila is large, mostly desert and sparsely populated. The border crossings into Coahuila from Texas are less frequently used than those farther southeast in Tamaulipas, because the road connections into Mexico and the USA are not as convenient for most travelers. The state capital, Saltillo, is definitely worth a visit, and the remoteness and the harsh, arid landscapes will appeal to some. For information about the west of the state, including the city of Torreón and the Zona del Silencio, see the Central North Mexico chapter.

The Spanish came to Coahuila in search of silver, slaves and souls, but stayed to establish sheep and cattle ranches that became viable despite Indian attacks. A few big landowners came to dominate the area. In southeast Coahuila, one holding of 890 sq km was bought from the crown for US$33 in 1731, and grew to 58,700 sq km by 1771, becoming the Marquesado de Aguaya, protected by a private cavalry. The population remained sparse though; in 1800, Coahuila still had fewer than 7000 people.

After 1821, in the early years of independence, Coahuila and Texas were one state of the new Mexican republic, but Texas was lost after the Mexican-American War. As the 19th century progressed, ranching grew in importance, helped by the arrival of railways. By 1900, Coahuila had 297,000 inhabitants. In the 20th century, a steel foundry was established in Monclova, using coal mined near Sabinas, giving Coahuila a major industrial center.

BORDER CROSSINGS
Ciudad Acuña
pop 75,000; alt 1250m; ☎ 877

Ciudad Acuña, across from the US town of Del Rio, is a fairly busy border crossing, open 24 hours a day. The **Presa de la Amistad** (Friendship Dam) is about 20 km upriver from Ciudad Acuña. A joint

Mexican-US water management project, this artificial lake offers good fishing and boating facilities. From Ciudad Acuña to Saltillo it's an eight-hour bus ride on good, two-lane roads.

Piedras Negras
pop 170,000; alt 1450m; ☎ *878*

The border crossing between Piedras Negras and the US town of Eagle Pass is a major commercial route. Piedras Negras attracts quite a few short-term visitors from Texas. There's a crafts shop in the old San Bernardino mission that features work from all over Mexico, and the casa de cultura has occasional displays of Mexican art, music and dance.

Highway 57 goes southeast to Allende, Sabinas and Monclova and continues to Saltillo, about eight hours away by bus. Not recommended is the train (segunda clase only) which leaves Piedras Negras at 9.15 am and is supposed to arrive in Saltillo at 6.55 pm.

MONCLOVA
pop 275,000; alt 1200m; ☎ *86*

The Altos Hornos iron and steel works are one of the largest in Mexico. The city also has a number of 17th and 18th century buildings, and its Pape library and museum have a surprisingly good collection of Mexican and European artists. Highway 57 runs south to Saltillo, about 190 km away, or 2½ hours by bus; 25 km south of Monclova, highway 53 branches southeast to Monterrey (there are no fuel stations on this highway).

SALTILLO
pop 1 million; alt 1599m; ☎ *84*

Set high in the arid Sierra Madre Oriental, Saltillo was founded in 1577 and is the oldest city in the northeast. It's on the main road and rail routes between the northeast border and central and western Mexico and is a pleasant place to break a journey. Like Monterrey, it has excellent transport links with the rest of Mexico.

In the late 17th century, Saltillo was capital of an area that included Coahuila, Nuevo León, Tamaulipas, Texas and 'all the land to the north which reaches toward the pole.' These days it has a quiet, central area with a small-town feel and some lovely colonial buildings, but there are extensive new suburbs and major industries on the city's outskirts. It's quite a prosperous city, and its pleasant climate and relaxed pace of life make it a popular place to stay.

History
The first mission here was established in 1591 as a center for the education and religious conversion of the local Indian populations. Indians from Tlaxcala were brought to help the Spanish stabilize the area, and they set up a colony beside the Spanish one at Saltillo. The Tlaxcalans' skill on the treadle-loom and the abundance of wool in the area led to the development of a unique type of sarape, for which Saltillo became famous in the 18th and 19th centuries.

Capital of the state of Coahuila & Texas after Mexican independence, it was occupied by US troops under Zachary Taylor in 1846 during the Mexican-American War. At Buenavista, 10 km south of Saltillo, the 20,000-strong army of General Santa Anna was repulsed by Taylor's men in 1847 in the decisive battle for control of the northeast during that war.

President Benito Juárez came to Saltillo during his flight from the invading French forces in 1864, and the city was occupied again by foreign troops before being freed in 1866. During the Porfiriato, agriculture and ranching prospered in the area, and the coming of the railway helped trade and the first industries in the city, but Monterrey was by this time quickly overtaking Saltillo in size and importance.

Saltillo's industrial development started with the processing of local primary products, including wheat and wool, and it is still a commercial and communications center for a large livestock and agricultural area. In recent decades it has expanded to include big automobile and petrochemical plants. Saltillo is still the capital of

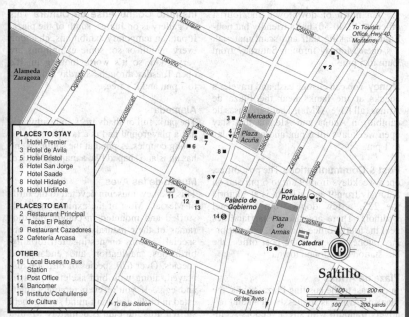

PLACES TO STAY
1 Hotel Premier
3 Hotel de Avila
5 Hotel Bristol
6 Hotel San Jorge
7 Hotel Saade
8 Hotel Hidalgo
13 Hotel Urdiñola

PLACES TO EAT
2 Restaurant Principal
4 Tacos El Pastor
9 Restaurant Cazadores
12 Cafetería Arcasa

OTHER
10 Local Buses to Bus
    Station
11 Post Office
14 Bancomer
15 Instituto Coahuilense
    de Cultura

Saltillo

To Tourist Office, Hwy 40, Monterrey

Mercado
Plaza Acuña
Los Portales
Palacio de Gobierno
Plaza de Armas
Catedral

To Bus Station
To Museo de las Aves

0   100   200 m
0   100   200 yards

NORTHEAST MEXICO

Coahuila, but it has been outgrown by the modern city of Torreón in the southwest of the state.

Orientation

Saltillo spreads out over a large area, but most of the tourist attractions are located in the blocks around the two central plazas. Periférico Echeverría, a ring road, enables through traffic to bypass the inner-city area.

The Plaza de Armas is quite large and austere and is surrounded by fine colonial buildings, including the cathedral on the southeast side. Two main streets, Hidalgo and Juárez, meet at the plaza, at the western corner of the cathedral. This junction is a dividing point for Saltillo's street addresses; with your back to the main façade of the cathedral, up the hill on Hidalgo (to the left) is Sur (south), downhill to the right is Norte (or Nte, north), behind you is Oriente (or Ote, east), and in front of you is Poniente (or Pte, west). It's only approximate, however, as the street grid is not exactly north-south.

Two blocks away is the Plaza Acuña, with the market building on its north side. It's smaller, less formal and usually more lively than the Plaza de Armas. The Alameda Zaragoza is a large, shady public park, reached by going down Victoria from the west side of the Palacio de Gobierno.

The bus station is in the southwest side of town, on Periférico Echeverría Sur at Calle Libertad – a 15-minute bus ride away. The train station is a 20-minute walk west of the center; from the west side of the Alameda, turn left on E Carranza and walk three long blocks to the station on your right. The station is on E Carranza one block south of Ramos Arizpe.

Information

Tourist Office Inconveniently located on the corner of Dr Coss and Allende, about

1.5 km north of downtown, the tourist office (☎ 12-40-50) has a friendly but non-English-speaking staff and scant material. It's open Monday through Saturday from 9 am to 5 pm.

Money You can change cash and traveler's checks at the banks near the Plaza de Armas (all have ATMs). There are casas de cambio on Acuña and Aldama that stay open weekdays till 6 pm, and on Saturday to 1 pm.

Post & Communications The post office, open weekdays from 9 am to 6 pm and on Saturday from 9 am to 1 pm, is at Victoria Pte 223, a few doors from the Hotel Urdiñola. There are also postal facilities near the tourist office and at the bus station. Pay phones appear at the post office, the bus station and around town.

Plaza de Armas
In contrast to the bustling Plaza Acuña, the Plaza de Armas is spotlessly clean and relatively tranquil, with street vendors seemingly banished.

Catedral Built between 1746 and 1801, the cathedral of Santiago dominates the plaza and has one of Mexico's finest Churrigueresque façades, with columns of elaborately carved pale gray stone. It's particularly splendid when lit up at night. Inside, the transepts are full of gilt ornamentation – look for the human figure perched on a ledge at the top of the dome. You can sometimes go up the smaller of the two towers if you ask the man in the religious goods shop underneath.

Palacio de Gobierno Facing the plaza is the state government headquarters. You are free to wander into this elegant building, which has a fountain in its inner courtyard.

Los Portales This is the colonnade under the arches on the northeast side of the plaza. It harbors a few café-restaurants and a video-games parlor.

Instituto Coahuilense de Cultura This art gallery is on Juarez, south of the plaza. It puts on temporary exhibitions, changing every month or so; some exhibitions are very good, so it's worth looking in. It's open Tuesday through Saturday from 9 am to 7 pm, and it's free.

Alameda
The park, full of shady trees and pathways, has a playground and is a favorite spot for young couples. A pond at the southern end has an island shaped like a map of Mexico.

Museo de las Aves
This is a new museum devoted to the birds of Mexico. Most of the exhibits are birds stuffed and mounted in convincing dioramas of their natural habitat. There are special sections on nesting, territoriality, birdsongs, navigation and endangered species. Over 670 species of bird are displayed, along with bird skeletons, fossils and eggs. If you're even remotely interested in birds, and don't mind seeing them stuffed, this museum is definitely worth a visit. It's between Hidalgo and Allende, a few blocks south of the plaza, and is open Tuesday through Saturday from 10 am to 6 pm, Sunday 11 am to 6 pm. Entry is US$1 for adults, half that for children and US$2 for families; it's free on Wednesdays.

Plaza México
Also known as the Fortín de Carlota (Carlota's Fortress), this spot in the south of the city offers the best views over Saltillo and the surrounding country. It's a 10-minute bus ride from the city center (see Getting Around later in this section).

Special Events
Saltillo has some interesting festivals:

Día del Santo Cristo de la Capilla – On August 6, the Day of the Holy Christ of the Chapel, dance groups from different parts of Coahuila come to Saltillo to honor a holy image.
Feria Anual – The city holds its annual fair in mid-August.

Feria de San Nicolás Tolentino – On September 10 in Ramos Arizpe, about 10 km north of Saltillo on the Monterrey road, there are dances starting before dawn, and a parade at about 5 pm.

Places to Stay – budget

The *Hotel Hidalgo* (☎ 14-98-53) at Padre Flores 217 is very basic with shared bathrooms, but cheap at around US$7 a room. The *Hotel De Avila* (another sign calls it Hotel Jardín; ☎ 12-59-16), at Padre Flores 211 in the northwest corner of Plaza Acuña, is not much better, with singles/doubles at US$8/9.

A vast improvement is the *Hotel Saade* (☎ 12-91-20) on Aldama between Acuña and Padre Flores, with a range of rooms from US$13 up to US$16/19 with TV and phone. The *Hotel Bristol* (☎ 10-43-37), on Aldama Pte 405, is a step down in cleanliness, with rooms at US$8/10.25. The *Hotel Premier* (☎ 12-10-50) at Allende Nte 566 is clean and comfortable enough, with singles/doubles for US$13/13.50.

There are two cheap hotels over the road from the bus station. The *Hotel Central* is decent enough, with rooms for US$6/7.50. The *Hotel Siesta* is similar but less grungy, at US$8.50/9.50 (add US$0.50 for TV).

Places to Stay – middle

A place that offers lots of character and good value is the *Hotel Urdiñola* (☎ 14-09-40) at Victoria Pte 207. There's a sparkling white lobby with a wide stairway that sweeps up to a stained-glass window. Rooms face a long courtyard with trees and a fountain. For big, clean rooms with TV, you pay US$17 for one person, US$20 for two. The hotel also has a pleasant, inexpensive restaurant, helpful staff and car parking just up the street.

The top downtown establishment is the *Hotel San Jorge* (☎ 12-22-22) at Acuña Nte 240. It's modern and well maintained, with a restaurant, rooftop swimming pool, and clean, comfortable rooms with all the modern conveniences for US$25/28.

Across from the bus station, the *Hotel Saltillo* (☎ 17-22-00) offers OK rooms with color TV and phone for US$16/18. *Motel Huizache* (☎ 16-10-00), 1.5 km north of the city center at Carranza 1746 – where highway 40 to Torreón meets highway 57 going north to Monclova – has a pool and offers spacious rooms with kitchenettes, air-con and heating for US$35/39.

Places to Stay – top end

There are several excellent motels on the highways near Saltillo. The *Best Western Eurotel Plaza* (☎ 15-10-00) is at Carranza 4100, just south of the Carranza monument; it costs US$45/49. Even classier is the *Camino Real Motor Inn* (☎ 30-00-00), six km out of town on highway 57 to San Luis Potosí, from US$69 for a single or double.

Places to Eat

Saltillo is short on upscale restaurants but has some good snack places and fast-food joints.

Cafetería Arcasa, on Victoria next door to Hotel Urdiñola, does reasonable Mexican and Western food. A comida corrida costs around US$3. For breakfast, egg dishes start at U$2, and a meat dish for dinner will run about US$5. There's a selection of newspapers to help you pass the time. *Restaurant Principal*, at Allende Nte 710 four blocks down the hill from Plaza Acuña, specializes in cabrito, with various goat bits from US$3 to US$7. If neither of these places grabs you, try the more expensive restaurants in the hotels Urdiñola or San Jorge.

For tacos, try *Tacos El Pastor*, on Plaza Acuña on the corner of Aldama and Padre Flores. Delicious tacos al pastor are US$2 for four, tacos de lengua (beef tongue) cost US$2.50 for four. *Restaurant Cazadores* at 155 Padre Flores, near Victoria, serves up a filling traditional Mexican breakfast for about US$3.

Things to Buy

Saltillo used to be so famous for its sarapes that a certain type was known as a 'Saltillo' even if it was made elsewhere in Mexico. The technique involves leaving out color fixatives in the dyeing process so that the different bands of color *lloran* ('weep,' or blend) into each other. The finest sarapes have silk or gold and silver threads woven into them. Nowadays the local workshops have stopped making classic all-wool sarapes and seem to be obsessed with jarring combinations of bright colors. But you can still get ponchos and blankets in more 'natural' colors, some of which are pure wool.

Shops where you can see these and other handicrafts include the Silver & Sarape Factory, on the corner of Victoria and Acuña, and the Sarape Shop on Hidalgo, a couple of blocks up the hill from the cathedral. In the latter you can watch people at work on treadle looms. The Mercado Juárez, next to Plaza Acuña, has a selection of sarapes, leatherwork and other souvenirs.

Getting There & Away

Air Aeroméxico (☎ 14-10-11), at Allende Nte 815, has flights between Mexico City and Saltillo.

Bus Saltillo's modern bus station is on the periférico at Calle Libertad. It has postal facilities and phones. First-class lines have ticket desks to the right end of the booking hall as you enter; 2nd-class is to the left.

Lots of buses serve Saltillo but few start their journeys here. This means that on some buses, 2nd-class ones in particular, you often can't buy a ticket until the bus has arrived and they know how much room there is for new passengers. It also means that, on 2nd-class buses, you may have to stand for a while. Try to buy your tickets early and board the bus first or, better still, take a 1st-class bus. The 1st-class lines include Transportes del Norte, Ómnibus de México and Tres Estrellas de Oro. Anáhuac and Transportes Frontera have 1st- and 2nd-class buses, while Línea Verde has 2nd-class buses only. Daily destinations include:

Aguascalientes – 503 km, 6½ hours; one 1st-class buses (US$18) and several 2nd-class (US$15) buses
Durango – 488 km, seven hours; several 1st-class (US$19)

Guadalajara – 693 km, nine hours; several 1st- (US$25) and 2nd-class (US$22); try to get a bus on a direct route and avoid ones that go via Aguascalientes
Matamoros – 410 km, seven hours; five 1st-class (US$14)
Matehuala – 261 km, four hours; two 1st- (US$8.50) and several 2nd-class (US$8)
Mazatlán – 807 km, 13 hours; one 1st-class (US$33)
Mexico City (Terminal Norte) – 870 km, 12 hours; six 1st- (US$30) and several 2nd-class (US$26)
Monterrey – 85 km, 1½ hours; frequent 1st-class (US$4)
Nuevo Laredo – 310 km, 4½ hours; one 1st-class (US$12)
Parras – 160 km, 2½ hours; numerous 2nd-class only (US$4)
Reynosa – 305 km, 3½ hours; two 1st-class (US$11)
San Luis Potosí – 455 km, five hours; two 1st-class (US$13)
Torreón – 231 km, 3½ hours; hourly de paso buses (US$10)
Zacatecas – 373 km, five hours; several 1st- (US$13) and 2nd-class (US$11)

Buses also go to Chihuahua, Ciudad Acuña, Ciudad Juárez, Ciudad Victoria, Monclova, Querétaro and Tepic.

Train The Saltillo train station (☎ 12-88-79) is on E Carranza, one block south of Ramos Arizpe. El Regiomontano (train No 71) leaves in the evening for San Luis Potosí (5¾ hours) and Mexico City (12 hours). In the other direction, El Regiomontano (No 72) leaves for Monterrey at 5.44 am (2½ hours). Train No 2 leaves at 2.35 am for San Luis Potosí (7½ hours) and Mexico City (16½ hours). Train No 1 leaves at 11.55 pm for Monterrey and Nuevo Laredo (7½ hours). See the Mexico City Getting There & Away section for more details.

The station is open for ticket sales from 8 am to 2 pm. Two trains run daily to Mexico City, both primera especial; the fare is US$20.

Car & Motorcycle Saltillo is a junction of major roads in each direction. Highway 40 going northeast to Monterrey is a good four-lane road, and there are no tolls until you reach the Monterrey bypass. Going west to Torreón (277 km), highway 40D is an overpriced toll road (nearly US$20) and most of it is two-lane. The alternative route, highway 40, is free and quite OK. Highway 57 goes north to Monclova and Piedras Negras and south to Mexico City (852 km). Outside Saltillo, it climbs to over 2000 meters, then descends gradually along the Altiplano Central to Matehuala (260 km) and San Luis Potosí (455 km) through barren but often scenic country. To the southwest, highway 54 crosses high, dry plains toward Zacatecas (363 km) and Guadalajara (680 km).

Getting Around

The airport is 12 km northeast of town on highway 40; take a Ramos Arizpe bus (less than US$1) or a taxi. To reach the city center from the bus station, go outside and turn right; minibus Nos 9 and 10 go to the center for US$1. Get off at the cathedral or the main downtown bus stop on the corner of Allende and Treviño. To reach the bus depot from downtown, catch a No 9 on the corner of Aldama and Hidalgo.

From the train station, go out to the big road, E Carranza, turn left and walk three blocks, then turn right on Madero for one block to the Alameda. Cross the park to Victoria and walk up the hill three or four blocks to the center of town.

PARRAS

pop 50,000; alt 1580m; ☎ 842

This town, 160 km west of Saltillo off the Torreón road, is an oasis in the Coahuilan desert. Underground streams carrying water from the Sierra come to the surface here as springs, supplying water to irrigate the grapevines for which the area is famous and giving the town its full name – Parras de la Fuente. Parras was the birthplace of revolutionary leader Francisco Madero, and an obelisk on Calle Arizpe honors him.

Information

The Parras tourist office (☎ 2-02-59) is on the roadside two km north of town. Open

weekdays from 9 am to 1 pm and 3 to 6 pm, and Saturday from 9 am to 1 pm, it has a helpful staff but has maps of such poor quality they're virtually useless.

Things to See & Do

The first winery in the Americas was established in Parras in 1597, a year before the town itself was founded. The winery, now called **Casa Madero**, is about four km north of town in San Lorenzo on the road going to the main highway. It's open every day from 9 am to 5 pm. Tours are conducted in Spanish only; you can buy wine and brandy on site.

The town has an old aqueduct, some colonial buildings, and three *estanques* (large pools where water from the springs is stored) that are great for swimming. The **Iglesia del Santo Madero**, on the southern edge of town, sits on the plug of an extinct volcano. It's a good little climb, and there's an expansive view from the top.

Special Events

The week-long grape fair, the Feria de la Uva, in mid-August, includes religious celebrations on Assumption Day and traditional dances by descendants of early Tlaxcalan settlers.

Places to Stay

The best value for the money by far is the *Hotel Posada Santa Isabel* (☎ 2-05-72) at Madero 514, with comfortable rooms around a quiet garden for US$18/20 for one/two people.

The *Hotel La Siesta* (☎ 2-03-74), on Acuña near Madero, is runner-up with basic but clean rooms at US$8/13.

Hotel Parras (☎ 2-06-44), at the corner of Arizpe and Reforma, has some clean rooms with firm beds (ask for No 6); rates are US$5/6.50.

At the other end of the spectrum is the *Hotel Rincón del Montero* (☎ 17-58-35), a few km north of town. It's a resort with golf, tennis, swimming and horse riding, and charges from US$44 for one or two people.

Places to Eat

Sweets made of sugar, nuts and milk are a local specialty; get some at one of the *dulcerías* (sweet shops) before you leave.

There are quite a few cafés and restaurants with more substantial fare. *Restaurant Rincón del Recuerdo*, on Cayuso opposite the parish church, has a very nice atmosphere and good food, and is not too expensive. The restaurants *El Tiburón* and *Chávez Cocina Economica* on Reforma just north of Madero serve decent and inexpensive Mexican food and hamburgers.

Getting There & Away

Parras is easy to reach by car; at La Paila, halfway between Saltillo and Torreón, turn off the highway and go 27 km south. Only 2nd-class buses go to Parras; there are numerous buses daily from Saltillo (2½ hours, US$4) and from Torreón (US$4). A 1st-class bus might drop you at La Paila, from where you can catch a local bus.

Stretching from Mazatlán to Acapulco, the Central Pacific Coast contains some of Mexico's principal beach resorts – Mazatlán, Puerto Vallarta, Zihuatanejo-Ixtapa and Acapulco – and some lesser-known but beautiful spots.

Coastal highways make travel easy up and down the coast, with frequent buses and easy driving, while several other highways connect the coast to the mountainous interior of the country. Due to the high volume of tourists, both national and international, air services to this region are also frequent and convenient.

MAZATLÁN
pop 600,000; ☎ *69*

Situated just 13 km south of the Tropic of Cancer, Mazatlán is Mexico's principal Pacific Coast fishing, shrimp and commercial port, as well as one of its prime Pacific resorts. Affectionately known as the 'Pearl of the Pacific,' Mazatlán is famous for its beaches and its sport fishing, with over 7000 billfish (sailfish and marlin) tagged and released each year. Another of the city's distinctions is that El Faro, high on a peak at the south end of the city, is the second-highest lighthouse in the world; you can climb up to it for a magnificent 360-degree view of the city and coast. The sunset is especially beautiful in Mazatlán, as the sun sets behind three offshore islands which gradually change color and fade into silhouettes, finally disappearing into the starry night.

In pre-Hispanic times Mazatlán was populated by Totorames, who lived by hunting, gathering, fishing and agriculture. Though a group of 25 Spaniards led by Nuño de Guzmán officially founded a settlement here on Easter Sunday in 1531, almost three centuries elapsed before a permanent colony was established, in the early 1820s. During this time the Spanish referred to the area as 'Islas de Mazatlán'

due to its many estuaries and lagoons, punctuated by hills.

Orientation
Mazatlán has both 'old' and 'new' sections. The original city occupies a wide peninsula

HIGHLIGHTS

- International beach resorts – particularly Acapulco and Puerto Vallarta
- Small beach resorts with local character – Playa Azul, San Blas, Cuyutlán and El Paraíso
- Delicious seafood all along the coast
- La Quebrada cliff divers in Acapulco
- Huichol crafts in Nayarit state
- Bird-watching in San Blas & Mexcaltitán

at the south end of town; the newer tourist-oriented zone arcs northward, with a 17-km boulevard passing fine beaches, hotels, restaurants, nightspots and other attractions.

Old Mazatlán is concentrated on a wide peninsula at the southern end of the city, bound on the west by the Pacific Ocean and on the east by the Bahía Dársena. At the south end of the peninsula are El Faro (the lighthouse), Mazatlán's sport fishing fleet, the terminal for ferries to La Paz, and Isla de la Piedra, which is not really an island but a long peninsula with a popular beach. On the east side are the shrimp, fishing and commercial docks, and the train station. The center of the 'old' city is the cathedral, on the Plaza Principal.

A beachside boulevard (that changes names frequently) runs along the Pacific side of the peninsula past Olas Altas, Mazatlán's first 'tourist' beach back in the 1950s, around some rocky outcrops, and north around the wide arc of Playa del Norte to the Zona Dorada (Golden Zone), which begins at the traffic circle at Punta Camarón and heads a few blocks north. The Zona Dorada and the large hotels stretching north along the beaches comprise the city's major tourist zone.

Information

Tourist Office The Coordinación General de Turismo (☎ 16-51-60/65, fax 16-51-66; turismo@red2000.com.mx) offers helpful information, but it's inconveniently north of the Zona Dorada. It's on the 4th floor of the large Banrural building (which, confusingly, is marked 'Banco Nacional de Comercio Exteriors') on Avenida Camarón Sábalo, open weekdays from 8.30 am to 3 pm and 5 to 7.30 pm, and on Saturday morning for phone inquiries only. It gives out an excellent free map of the city. Two free bilingual tourist newspapers, *Pacific Pearl* and *The Sun*, are available at the tourist office and at many hotels and tourist establishments.

Consulates Foreign consulates in Mazatlán are usually open weekdays from 9 am to 1 pm. They include:

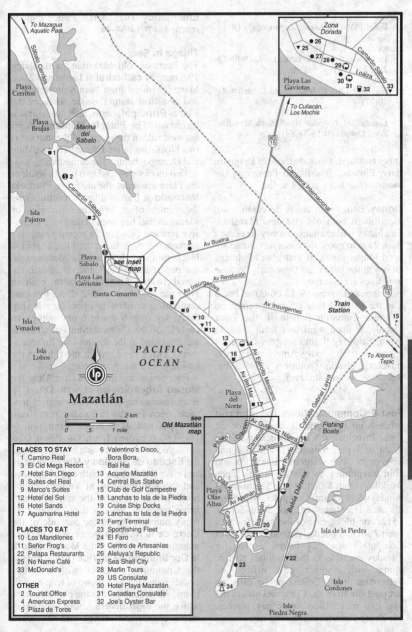

To Mazagua
Aquatic Park

Zona
Dorada

Camarón Sábalo

Playa Las
Gaviotas

To Culiacán,
Los Mochis

MEX
15

Carretera Internacional

Sábalo Cerritos

Playa
Cerritos

Playa
Brujas

Marina
del
Sábalo

Camarón Sábalo

Isla
Pajaros

Playa
Sábalo

Playa Las
Gaviotas

Punta Camarón

Isla
Venados

Isla
Lobos

PACIFIC
OCEAN

Mazatlán

0   1   2 km
0   .5   1 mile

Av Buelna

Av Revolución

Av Insurgentes

Av Insurgentes

Train
Station

MEX
15

To Airport,
Tepic

Calzada Gabriel Leyva

Av Ejército Mexicano

Av Del Mar

Playa
del
Norte

see
Old Mazatlán
map

Paseo

Cruañas

Carrasco

Av Gutiérrez Nájera

Zaragoza

Aquiles Serdán

Olas Altas

Av del Puerto

Bahía Dársena

Fishing
Boats

Cruise Ship Docks

Playa Olas
Altas

Av Alemán

Centenario Av E

Barragán

Isla de la Piedra

Isla
Cordones

Isla
Piedra Negra

CENTRAL PACIFIC COAST

PLACES TO STAY
1 Camino Real
3 El Cid Mega Resort
7 Hotel San Diego
8 Suites del Real
9 Marco's Suites
12 Hotel del Sol
16 Hotel Sands
17 Aguamarina Hotel

PLACES TO EAT
10 Los Mandilones
11 Señor Frog's
22 Palapa Restaurants
25 No Name Café
33 McDonald's

OTHER
2 Tourist Office
4 American Express
5 Plaza de Toros

6 Valentino's Disco,
    Bora Bora,
    Bali Hai
13 Acuario Mazatlán
14 Central Bus Station
15 Club de Golf Campestre
18 Lanchas to Isla de la Piedra
19 Cruise Ship Docks
20 Lanchas to Isla de la Piedra
21 Ferry Terminal
23 Sportfishing Fleet
24 El Faro
25 Centro de Artesanías
26 Aleluya's Republic
27 Sea Shell City
28 Marlin Tours
29 US Consulate
30 Hotel Playa Mazatlán
31 Canadian Consulate
32 Joe's Oyster Bar

Canada
   Hotel Playa Mazatlán, Zona Dorada (☎ 13-76-20)
France
   Jacarandas 6, Colonia Loma Linda (☎ 85-12-28, 82-85-52)
Germany
   Jacarandas 10, Colonia Loma Linda (☎ 81-20-77)
USA
   Loaiza 202, opposite Hotel Playa Mazatlán, Zona Dorada (☎ 16-58-89)

Other consulates include those of Belgium, Italy, Finland, Brazil and Paraguay; the tourist office has a complete list.

Money Banks and casas de cambio are plentiful in both old and new Mazatlán. The banks will exchange money weekdays from 9 am to noon; the casas de cambio are open longer hours. If you plan to change money at the banks, get there early because long lines are common.

American Express (☎ 13-06-00) at Local 4 in the Plaza Balboa shopping center, on Avenida Camarón Sábalo in the Zona Dorada, is open weekdays from 9 am to 6 pm, Saturday 9 am to 1 pm. It doesn't exchange cash – only American Express traveler's checks (counters close 5 pm weekdays, noon Saturday).

Post & Communications The main post office is on Juárez on the east side of the Plaza Principal; it's open weekdays from 8 am to 7 pm, Saturday 9 am to 1 pm. Telecomm, with telegraph, telex, fax and coin telephones, is next door; it's open weekdays from 8 am to 8 pm, Saturday and holidays 8 to 11 am. Computel, with long-distance telephone and fax, is at Serdán 1512, one block east of the cathedral; it's open 7 am to 9 pm daily; another branch of Computel (open 24 hours, except for Tuesday night) is in the main bus station, along with another post office and Telecomm office. Collect phone calls are not possible from the Computel offices but you can make them from pay phones, which are plentiful around the city.

Emergency The Tourist Police can be reached at ☎ 14-84-44.

Things to See
The heart of 'old Mazatlán' is the large 19th century **cathedral** at Juárez and 21 de Marzo, with its high twin yellow towers and beautiful statues inside. It faces the **Plaza Principal**, with lush trees and a bandstand. The **Palacio Municipal** is on the west side of the plaza and the **market** is two blocks north on Juárez between Valle and Ocampo, behind the cathedral.

Two blocks west and two blocks south of the Plaza Principal, the attractive **Plazuela Machado** at Carnaval and Constitución is the center of a large historic area of Mazatlán that has been undergoing a massive renewal program in recent years. It's surrounded by historic buildings. Half a block south of the Plazuela Machado on the pedestrian street Carnaval, the three-tiered **Teatro Angela Peralta**, built in 1865 and reopened in 1992 after a five-year restoration project, is open for viewing every day from 9 am to 6 pm; admission costs US$0.40. Cultural events of all kinds are presented at the theater (see Entertainment); check the kiosk at the front of the building for announcements.

Four blocks toward Playa Olas Altas, the **Museo Arqueológico** at Sixto Osuna 76 is an interesting little archaeological museum, open Tuesday to Sunday from 10 am to 1 pm and 4 to 7 pm; admission is US$0.80 (children free). On Paseo Olas Altas you'll notice a couple of monuments: the **Escudo de Sinaloa y Mazatlán** (state and city shield) at the south end of the cove and the **Monumento al Venado** at the north end, a tribute to the city's Nahuatl name, meaning 'place of deer.' Around the rocky outcropping on the sea side of the **Cerro de la Nevería** are a couple of other monuments, including the **Monumento a la Continuidad de la Vida** (Monument to the Continuity of Life), with a human couple being led by a group of leaping dolphins. Also along here is the platform from which the **high divers** (*clavadistas*) leap into a chasm and plunge into the ocean

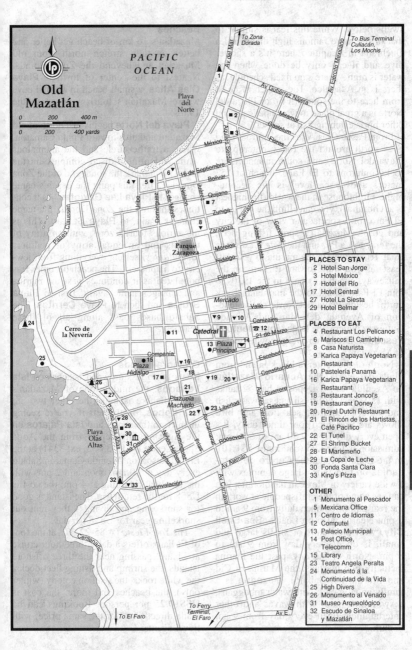

PLACES TO STAY
2 Hotel San Jorge
3 Hotel México
7 Hotel del Río
17 Hotel Central
27 Hotel La Siesta
29 Hotel Belmar

PLACES TO EAT
4 Restaurant Los Pelícanos
6 Mariscos El Camichin
8 Casa Naturista
9 Karica Papaya Vegetarian Restaurant
10 Pastelería Panamá
16 Karica Papaya Vegetarian Restaurant
18 Restaurant Joncol's
19 Restaurant Doney
20 Royal Dutch Restaurant
21 El Rincón de los Hartistas, Café Pacífico
22 El Tunel
27 El Shrimp Bucket
28 El Marismeño
29 La Copa de Leche
30 Fonda Santa Clara
33 King's Pizza

OTHER
1 Monumento al Pescador
5 Mexicana Office
11 Centro de Idiomas
12 Computel
13 Palacio Municipal
14 Post Office, Telecomm
15 Library
23 Teatro Angela Peralta
24 Monumento a la Continuidad de la Vida
25 High Divers
26 Monumento al Venado
31 Museo Arqueológico
32 Escudo de Sinaloa y Mazatlán

swells below. While this feat is similar to that of the more famous high divers at La Quebrada in Acapulco, here it's a shorter dive and it can only be done when the water is high – there's no fixed schedule, as there is in Acapulco. The stretch of coast from here to the southern tip of Playa del Norte is a great place to watch pelicans and other birds catching fish at sunset.

From Paseo Olas Altas the seafront road goes north around the rocky outcrops to Playa del Norte, and south around more rocky outcrops to **El Faro**, which at 157 meters above sea level is the second-highest lighthouse in the world (the highest is at Gibraltar); you can climb the hill up to El Faro for a spectacular view of the city and coast. Mazatlán's sport fishing fleet, the ferry to La Paz and the *Yate Fiesta* (see Boat Trips) dock in the marina to your left (east) as you walk toward El Faro on the causeway, which was built in the 1930s to join El Faro island to the mainland. Back north, beside Playa del Norte at the junction of Avenida del Mar and Avenida Gutiérrez Najera, the large **Monumento al Pescador** is another well-known symbol of Mazatlán.

North of the center, a block inland from Playa del Norte, the **Acuario Mazatlán** on Avenida de los Deportes has 52 tanks with 150 species of fresh and saltwater fish and other creatures; sea lion and bird shows are presented four times daily. It's open every day from 9.30 am to 6.30 pm; admission is US$3.25 (children US$1.10). In the Zona Dorada, the **Centro de Artesanías** on Loaiza is a large complex with a wide variety of Mexican handicrafts; you can see some of the craftspeople at work in the rear patio. It's open daily from 9 am to 6 pm. Nearby, also on Loaiza, **Sea Shell City**, with thousands of shells large and small, is open every day from 9 am to 8 pm. North of the city, past the marina (actually two marinas: the Marina El Cid and Marina del Sábalo), **Mazagua** is a family aquatic park with water toboggans, a swimming pool with waves and other entertainment open every day from 9 am to dark.

Beaches

Mazatlán's 16 km of beach get better and better as they stretch north from old Mazatlán and beyond the Zona Dorada. Nearest to the center of town is **Playa Olas Altas**, a small beach in a small cove where Mazatlán's tourism began in the 1950s.

Playa del Norte begins just north of old Mazatlán and arcs toward Punta Camarón, where a traffic circle and the anomalous white Valentino's disco complex on the rocky point mark the south end of the Zona Dorada. After this point the beach's name changes to **Playa Las Gaviotas**. As it continues through the Zona Dorada the name changes again, to **Playa Sábalo**. This is the serious tourist zone, with an army of tourists and an equal army of peddlers (*ambulantes*) selling everything from jewelry to hammocks. The beach becomes less populated as it continues past the marina and changes name again, first to **Playa Brujas** and then to **Playa Cerritos**. The Sábalo buses pass along all of these beaches.

Offshore Islands

Boats go to less crowded beaches on **Isla Venados**, the middle one of Mazatlán's three offshore islands (the other two are **Isla Lobos**, on the left if you're seeing them from the shore, and **Isla Pájaros** on the right). Boats depart from the Aqua Sport Centre (☎ 13-33-33, ext 3341) at the El Cid Resort on Avenida Camarón Sábalo every day at 10 am, noon and 2 pm, with the last boat returning at 4 pm; the cost is US$8 for the return trip. The island is good for snorkeling and diving – they rent out snorkeling gear for US$8 per day.

The *Yate Fiesta* (☎ 85-22-37), at the foot of El Faro, offers a daily three-hour cruise at 11 am, passing near the three offshore islands, the shrimp and fishing fleet docks, the white rocks, the sea lion colony (winter only), the beaches and more; the cost is US$10.25 per person. Bookings can be made directly or (for the same price) with travel agents.

Isla de la Piedra

The island beach most visited by locals, Isla de la Piedra (Stone Island), is actually a long, thin peninsula whose tip is opposite El Faro, at the south end of the city. To get there, take a small boat across to the island from one of two docks – there's one near the intersection of Calzada Leyva, Avenida del Puerto, Avenida Zaragoza and Calzada Gutiérrez Najera, and another at the extreme south end of the city, a block or two east of the ferry terminal. The boats operate every day, departing every 10 minutes from around 6 am to midnight for the five-minute ride to the island; the each-way cost is US$0.40, or US$0.70 after 8 pm.

When you land, walk through the village to the far side of the island and a long, pale sandy beach bordered by coconut groves (or a taxi will take you for US$0.50). The beach has several palapa restaurants, three of which hold dances on Sunday afternoon. Camping out or budget accommodation is offered at Lety's and Carmelita's, and Victor's is recommended for food. Continue south (toward El Faro) to reach another beach at **Isla Chivos**.

Water Sports

The Aqua Sport Centre (☎ 13-33-33, ext 3341) at the El Cid Resort is the place to go for water sports, including scuba diving, water-skiing, jet skis, Hobie cats, parasailing, the 'banana,' boogie boards and more. Jet skis, sailboats and boogie boards can also be hired at the Camino Real Hotel, north of El Cid. Surfing is popular at Punta Camarón and Playa Olas Altas; local surfers also head down the coast to San Blas for the 'world's longest wave.'

Sport Fishing

Mazatlán is famous for its sport fishing – especially for marlin, swordfish, sailfish, tuna and dorado (dolphinfish). The operator most often recommended is the Bill Heimpel Star Fleet (☎ 82-38-78, 82-26-65; fax 82-51-55), with over 35 years experience and a fleet of 15 boats in the marina next to their office at the foot of El Faro; many other sport fishing operators also have offices along here. It's a good idea to make fishing reservations as far in advance as you can in the winter high season.

Golf & Tennis

There's golf at the Club de Golf Campestre (☎ /fax 80-15-70), east of town on highway 15, the Estrella del Mar Golf Club (☎ 82-33-00), south of the airport by the coast, and the El Cid Resort (☎ 13-33-33), north of the center. There are tennis courts at the Racquet Club Gaviotas (☎ 13-59-39) in the Zona Dorada, at the El Cid Resort and at almost any of the large hotels north of the center.

Walks

Mazatlán has many great places for walking. Besides 16 km of beautiful beaches, with a broad Malecón along the entire stretch of Playa del Norte offering a fine view of the three offshore islands, there are also the seafront road around the rocky outcrops on the north and south sides of the Olas Altas cove, the climb up the hill to El Faro and, to the southeast, the long, deserted beach of Isla de la Piedra.

Language Courses

The Centro de Idiomas (☎ 82-20-53, fax 85-56-06) at Domínguez 1908 offers Spanish courses with a maximum of six students per class. You can begin any Monday and study for as many weeks as you like; registration is every Saturday morning from 9 am to noon. The weekly cost is US$110/140 for two/four hours of instruction each weekday, with discounts if you sign up for four weeks. Homestays can be arranged with a Mexican family; the cost is US$130/150 per week for a shared/individual room, including three meals a day (30 days advance notice required).

Organized Tours

Marlin Tours (☎ 13-53-01) offers a three-hour city tour (US$12); a high-country tour to the foothill villages of Concordia and Copala (US$31); a jungle tour to Teacapan, south of the city (US$41); and a tour to Rosario and Agua Caliente villages

(US$31). Travel agents can arrange these and other tours. Check the tours desk in Sea Shell City for discounted tours.

Special Events

Celebrated with music, dancing, parades, other events and general reveling for the entire week leading up to Ash Wednesday in February or March, Carnaval (Mardi Gras) is celebrated in Mexico most flamboyantly in Mazatlán and Veracruz. The entire city goes on a week-long partying spree, with people pouring in from around the country for the festivities. Be sure to reserve a hotel room in advance, as the city fills up. On the morning of Ash Wednesday the party ends abruptly, and people go to church to receive ash marks on their foreheads for the first day of Lent. A Torneo de Pesca (fishing tournament) for sailfish, marlin and dorado is held in May and November. On December 12 the day of the Virgen de Guadalupe is celebrated at the cathedral, with children brought there in costumes.

Places to Stay – budget

Camping Mazatlán has a number of trailer parks on or near the beaches at the north end of town ('s/n' means there is no street number in the address). They have between 26 and 236 spaces; in ascending order of size they are:

Maravillas Trailer Park
    Calzada Sábalo Cerritos s/n (☎ 14-04-00)
San Bartolo Trailer Park
    Calle del Pulpo s/n (☎ 13-57-65)
Las Palmas Trailer Park
    Avenida Camarón Sábalo 333 (☎ 83-53-11, 13-64-24), 66 spaces
Mar Rosa Trailer Park
    Avenida Camarón Sábalo 702 (☎ 13-61-87)
La Posta Trailer Park
    Avenida Buelna 7 (☎ 83-53-10)
Holiday Trailer Park
    Calzada Sábalo Cerritos 999 (☎ 13-25-78)
Las Canoas Trailer Park
    Calzada Sábalo Cerritos s/n (☎ 14-16-16)
Playa Escondida Bungalows & Trailer Park
    Calzada Sábalo Cerritos 999 (☎ 82-02-85, ☎ /fax 88-00-77), 236 spaces, 19 beachfront bungalows

Camping is also possible on Isla de la Piedra – see the Boat Trips section.

Hotels – Old Mazatlán The *Hotel del Río* (☎ 82-46-54), at Juárez 2410 on the corner of Quijano, has 30 rooms at US$6.50/7.75 for singles/doubles, US$9 for a family room. It's clean and friendly, and a very good deal. The *Hotel San Jorge* (☎ 81-36-95) on Serdán on the corner of Gastelum, also a block from the beach, is old but clean, with 17 singles/doubles at US$11/14.

The *Hotel Central* (☎ 82-18-66), Domínguez 2 Sur near Ángel Flores, four blocks from Playa Olas Altas and four blocks from the cathedral, has 67 well-kept rooms with air-con and TV at US$14 for singles/doubles. If you're at the end of your economic rope, the 17-room *Hotel México* (☎ 81-38-06) at México 201 on the corner of Serdán, a block from the beach, is very basic, but clean; the cost is US$5.25.

The hotels on Playa Olas Altas are some of the most charming in town – old, but refurbished, well maintained and recalling a simpler era. The area itself is rather run-down but full of character. The *Hotel Belmar* (☎ 85-11-11/12, fax 81-34-28) at Olas Altas 166 Sur, a formerly grand but now somewhat faded hotel, is a good deal. It has a swimming pool, bar, parking and 150 rooms, 60 with private balconies overlooking Olas Altas beach, some with TV and air-con. Singles/doubles are US$11/13, or US$13/16 with sea view. The *Hotel La Siesta* (☎ 81-26-40, fax 13-74-76) at Olas Altas 11, above El Shrimp Bucket restaurant, has a courtyard full of tropical plants and the Bucket's tables. The 51 rooms are large and clean, with air-con, and some have balconies and TV; singles/doubles are US$15/17, or US$18/21 with sea view.

Places to Stay – middle

There are some decent mid-range choices on Avenida del Mar, opposite Playa del Norte, with frequent buses heading north and south. The *Hotel del Sol* (☎ 85-11-03, fax 85-26-03) at Avenida del Mar 800, near the aquarium, is a good value. There's a swimming pool, parking and 21 rooms with air-con at US$15; rooms with kitchen and cable TV cost US$27. The *Hotel San Diego* (☎ 83-57-03) at Avenida del Mar and Buelna, on the traffic circle near Valentino's Disco at the south end of the Zona Dorada, has 62 rooms with air-con and TV at US$18/23. It's a noisy but convenient location, and the hotel offers parking. The *Hotel Sands* (☎ 82-00-00, 800-69808; fax 82-10-25) at Avenida del Mar 1910 has a swimming pool, restaurant/bar, parking and 87 rooms (some with a sea view) with balcony, air-con, fan, satellite color TV and refrigerator; singles/doubles are US$20/26, rising to US$34 in July, August and from mid-December to Easter.

Marco's Suites (☎ 83-59-98) at Avenida del Mar 1234, has 12 rooms with kitchen and air-con at US$15/23 for two/four people (parking available). *Suites del Real* (☎ 83-19-55, 83-18-44) at Avenida del Mar 1020, is well run and charges US$32/42 for standard/kitchenette rooms with two beds, TV and air-con. Both places have pools and reduced rates for long stays.

Places to Stay – top end
Air/hotel packages may make room rates cheaper; travel agents should have information on all of Mazatlán's big luxury hotels.

The *Aguamarina Hotel* (☎ 81-70-80, fax 82-46-24) at Avenida del Mar 110, remodeled in 1994, is a good place, with a swimming pool, restaurant/bar, parking, travel agency and 125 rooms with air-con, cable TV and phone for US$60.

Mazatlán has many luxurious top-end hotels on the beaches north of town. Most imposing is the 1000-room *El Cid Mega Resort* (☎ 13-33-33, in the USA 800-525-1925; fax 14-31-11) at Avenida Camarón Sábalo; rates start at US$100 per night, or US$129 in winter and July and August. Another good choice is the *Camino Real* (☎ 13-11-11, fax 14-03-11) at Punta del Sábalo s/n, with 169 rooms at US$110/120 with marina/ocean view.

Places to Eat
Pastelería Panamá at Juárez 1702 on the corner of Canizales, diagonally opposite the rear of the cathedral, is a popular air-con restaurant, café and bakery open every day from 7 am to 10.30 pm; several other branches are found around town. *Restaurant Joncol's* at Ángel Flores 608, two blocks west of the Plaza Principal, is a simple air-con family restaurant with economical meals, including a comida corrida for US$3; it's open every day from 7 am to 10.30 pm. Across the street is *Karica Papaya Vegetarian Restaurant*, serving breakfasts and a set lunch (US$3). It's open daily and may soon start serving dinners. Another branch is on Valle, near the market.

Restaurant Doney, Escobedo 610 at 5 de Mayo, is an air-con restaurant with colorful wall displays; tasty traditional Mexican food is served every day from 8 am to 10.30 pm. The *Casa Naturista* at Zaragoza 807 Pte is a wholegrain bakery and health food store, open Monday to Saturday from 8 am to 8 pm, Sunday from 8 am to 1 pm.

For seafood, the *Restaurant Los Pelícanos*, on the corner of Paseo Claussen and Uribe, is a small open-air thatched-roof place with some of the cheapest and tastiest seafood in Mazatlán: shrimp for US$3.25, breaded fish fillet for US$3.75, ceviche for US$1.30 to US$3.25, or charcoal broiled fish (pescado zarandeado) for US$5 or US$6. It has a great view of the entire arc of Playa del Norte, catches any sea breezes coming by, and is altogether a delightful place, open every day from 10 am to 6 pm. *Mariscos El Camichin*, another seafood restaurant nearby at Paseo Claussen 97 on the corner of Nelson, is a popular open-air patio restaurant with a jolly crowd eating delicious seafood under cool shady trees; it's open every day from 10 am to 10 pm, with live music from 2 pm on.

The Plazuela Machado is a peaceful place to enjoy a meal or snack. Run by Mirla and Rosa, *El Rincón de los Hartistas* at Constitución 517 serves tacos and other simple Mexican fare at sidewalk tables after 7 pm and is a popular gathering spot for artists and cultural types. Next door, the *Café Pacífico* has sidewalk tables for enjoying a beer on the plaza; it's open daily but doesn't serve food on Sunday. *El Tunel*, opposite the Teatro Angela Peralta, is good for inexpensive Mexican food, or try a *raspado* (flavored shaved ice). It's open from about 6 pm (closed Wednesday). Nearby, the *Royal Dutch Restaurant* on Constitución serves Dutch and European food in a relaxing courtyard; American breakfast costs US$2.25. It's open daily from 8 am to 9 pm and has its own bakery.

Olas Altas also has several good restaurants. The sole cheap choice is *King's Pizza* for no-frills Italian food; spaghetti with sauce is only US$1.40, and it's open daily from 11 am to 10 pm. *El Shrimp Bucket* at Olas Altas 11 is one of Mazatlán's best known restaurants. Opened in 1963, it was the first of what has become an international chain of Carlos Anderson restaurants. It's air-con, with tables inside and out in the hotel's tropical courtyard, and is open every day from 6 am to 11 pm, with a marimba band in high season (not Mondays). *La Copa de Leche* and *Fonda Santa Clara* are popular open-air restaurant/bars with sidewalk and interior tables, open daily from 7 am to 11 pm. *El Marismeño* is another possibility for seafood.

North of the center, *Señor Frog's* on Avenida del Mar is a Mazatlán landmark that's almost always packed with Americans. Part of the Carlos Anderson chain, it advertises 'lousy food and warm beer,' but actually the food is good (just overpriced) and the beer only warm when they can't cool the bottles fast enough to keep up with demand. It's air-con and open every day from noon until 1 am or later (food finishes at midnight). About 300 meters north is *Los Mandilones*, with ocean views from the 1st-floor terrace and low prices – breakfast US$1.50, three-course menus for US$3.25 and beer for US$0.70. It's open daily from 7.30 am to 11 pm.

In the Zona Dorada, the *No Name Café* at Loaiza 417, at the entrance to the Centro de Artesanías, boasts 'the best damn ribs you'll ever eat' (US$10) and other delicious food in a pleasant ambience with an air-con sports bar and a tropical patio; it's open every day from 8 am to 2 am. Homesick gringos (or their children) might like to know there's a *McDonald's* by the traffic circle at the south end of the Zona Dorada, open every day from 8 am to 11 pm.

Entertainment

Cultural Events & Cinema Cultural events of all kinds – concerts, opera (Mazatlán has its own opera company), theater and more – are presented at the Teatro Angela Peralta near the Plazuela Machado; a kiosk on the walkway in front of the theater announces current and upcoming cultural events here and at other venues around the city. Also at the theater, the Cine Club sponsors quality films every Saturday at 5 or 6 pm; admission is free.

Mazatlán has several cinemas; check the local daily newspapers *El Sol del Pacífico* and *El Noroeste* for movie listings and other events. Films are often shown in English, with Spanish subtitles.

If you get a chance, try to hear a rousing traditional Banda Sinaloense – a loud, boisterous multipiece brass band unique to the state of Sinaloa and particularly Mazatlán.

Bars & Discos Mazatlán has several discos, most of them in the Zona Dorada. The best known and most obvious is *Valentino's*, in the very out-of-place, whitewashed fairytale castle on the rocky outcropping at the traffic circle at the south end of the Zona Dorada. In the same complex is *Bora Bora*, a popular beachfront bar with a sandy volleyball court, two swimming pools and a beachside dance floor, while the *Bali Hai* is a lively bar with big-screen videos.

About 500 meters north, *Joe's Oyster Bar* at the Hotel Los Sábalos is a pleasant beachfront bar with a fine view of the offshore islands. Farther north, *El Caracól* at the El Cid Resort on Avenida Camarón Sábalo is another popular disco. The beachside restaurant/bar at the *Hotel Playa Mazatlán* is popular with the 30s-and-up age group for dancing under the stars. *Aleluya's Republic* on Avenida Camarón

Sábalo is another popular dining and dancing spot, as is *Señor Frog's* on Avenida del Mar (see Places to Eat). On Sunday afternoon there's live music and dancing at several palapas on the beach at Isla de la Piedra (see Boat Trips), patronized mostly by locals.

Fiesta Mexicana A Fiesta Mexicana, with a Mexican buffet, open bar, folkloric floorshow and live music for dancing is held every Tuesday, Thursday and Saturday night from 7 to 10.30 pm at the Hotel Playa Mazatlán at Loaiza 202 in the Zona Dorada; phone for reservations (☎ 13-53-20) or reserve through travel agents. The cost is US$23. There's a similar fiesta at the El Cid Resort on Wednesday.

Spectator Sports

At the bullring on Avenida Buelna, inland from the Zona Dorada traffic circle, bullfights are held on Sunday at 4 pm from Christmas to Easter; the Sábalo-Cocos bus will drop you there. Tickets are sold at the Bora Bora shop (open daily; ☎ 84-16-66) beside Valentino's disco on the traffic circle. Charreadas are held at the Lienzo charro ring in Colonia Juárez; ☎ 83-35-10 or 86-47-11 for information.

Getting There & Away

Air The Mazatlán international airport is 20 km south of the city. Airlines serving this airport, and their direct flights (all with connections to other places), include:

Aero California
   Hotel El Cid, Local 30 & 31, Avenida Camarón Sábalo (☎ 13-20-42) – La Paz, Mexico City
Aeroméxico
   Avenida Camarón Sábalo 310, Local 1 & 2 (☎ 14-11-11, 14-16-21, airport 82-34-44) – Ciudad Juárez, Durango, Guadalajara, La Paz, León, Los Mochis, Mexico City, Tijuana, Torreón
Alaska Airlines
   Airport (☎ 85-27-30) – Los Angeles, San Francisco
Delta
   Airport (☎ 82-13-49, 82-41-55) – Los Angeles

Mexicana
   Paseo Claussen 101B (☎ 82-77-22, airport 82-28-88) – Denver, Mexico City, Puerto Vallarta

Bus The main bus station (Central de Autobuses) is just off Avenida Ejército Mexicano on Avenida de los Deportes, about three blocks inland from the beach, and ringed by inexpensive hotels. The station has a cafeteria and left-luggage area, a post office, a Telecomm office with telegram, telex and fax, and a 24-hour Computel office with telephone and fax. First- and 2nd-class bus lines operate from separate halls in the main terminal; buses to small towns nearby (Concordia, Copala, Rosario, etc) operate from a smaller terminal behind the main terminal.

Daily buses from the 1st-class hall go north and south along the coast on highway 15/15D, and inland over the mountains (and across a time zone boundary) to Durango. They include:

Durango – 319 km, seven hours; five each by Transportes Chihuahuenses-Transportes del Norte and Elite (US$13), three by Autobuses Interstatales de México (US$9.25)
Guadalajara – 506 km, eight hours; at least hourly round the clock (US$22)
Mexico City (Terminal Norte) – 1041 km, 17 hours; nine by Transportes del Pacífico, four/ five daily by other operators (US$49)
Puerto Vallarta – 459 km, seven hours; at 9.45 pm by Elite (US$19), or take a bus to Tepic, from where buses depart frequently for Puerto Vallarta
Tepic – 290 km, 4½ to five hours; at least hourly round the clock (US$11)
Tijuana – 1796 km, 25 hours; 13 by Transportes del Pacífico (US$68), two daily by other operators

Buses from the 2nd-class hall go to all the places listed above, as well as to Santiago Ixcuintla at 6.15 am and 4 pm (235 km, four hours, US$5.25). Four buses to Santiago Ixcuintla (6.15, 7.15 and 11.15 am, 4.15 pm; US$7.75) depart from Transporte Rapido's separate terminal, on Avenida Ejército Mexicano by the main terminal.

To get to San Blas (290 km), take a Tepic-bound bus to 'Crucero San Blas' then wait for one of the hourly buses coming from Tepic.

Train The train station (☎ 84-67-10) is on the eastern outskirts of the city; tickets go on sale an hour before each departure. See the schedule in the Guadalajara section of the Western Central Highlands chapter.

Car & Motorcycle Car-rental agencies include Aga (☎ 14-44-05, 13-40-77), Budget (☎ 13-20-00), Hertz (☎ 13-60-60, airport 85-08-45), National (☎ 13-60-00, 13-61-00) and Price (☎ 86-66-16). As always, it pays to shop around for the best rates.

Boat Ferries operate between Mazatlán and La Paz, Baja California. The ferry (transbordador) terminal (☎ 81-70-20/21, 800-69696) is at the south end of town; the office is open every day from 8 am to 3 pm. Tickets are sold the morning of departure, or several days in advance. See the La Paz section in the Baja California chapter for schedule and fare details.

Getting Around
To/From the Airport Colectivo vans and a bus operate from the airport to town, but not from town to the airport. Taxis are more expensive – about US$11 each way.

Bus Local buses operate every day from around 5.30 am to 10.30 pm; the cost is US$0.30. A good network of frequent buses provides convenient service to anywhere around the city you'd want to go. Routes include:

Sábalo-Centro – from the market to the beach via Juárez, then north on Avenida del Mar to the Zona Dorada and farther north on Avenida Camarón Sábalo

Playa Sur – south along Avenida Ejército Mexicano near the bus station and through the city, passing the market, then the ferry terminal and El Faro

Villa Galaxia – same route as the Playa Sur bus, but doesn't continue past the market

Insurgentes – south along Avenida Ejército Mexicano and through the city to the market, continuing on to the train station

Cerritos-Juárez – shuttles between the train station and the city center

To get into the center of Mazatlán from the bus terminal, go to Avenida Ejército Mexicano and catch an Insurgentes, Villa Galaxia, Playa Sur or any other bus going to your right if the bus terminal is behind you. Alternatively, you can walk 500 meters from the bus station to the beach and take a Sábalo-Centro bus heading south (left) to the center.

Car & Motorcycle Various companies in the Zona Dorada and elsewhere hire small motorcycles for getting around town – keep an eye out for the bikes lined up beside the road. You need a driver's license to hire one; any type of license will do.

Pulmonías & Taxis Mazatlán has a special type of taxi called a *pulmonía*, which is a small open-air vehicle similar to a golf cart. The word 'pulmonía' literally means 'pneumonia.' There are also taxis marked 'eco-taxi'; like pulmonías they tend to be slightly cheaper than normal taxis. Both types are plentiful around town. Be sure to agree on the price for the ride before you climb in; it never hurts to bargain. A late night ride from the Zona Dorada to Playa Olas Altas should cost about US$3.

AROUND MAZATLÁN
Several small, picturesque colonial towns in the Sierra Madre foothills make pleasant day trips from Mazatlán. **Concordia**, founded in 1565, has an 18th century church with a baroque façade and elaborately decorated columns, and hot mineral springs nearby; the village is known for its manufacture of high-quality pottery and handcarved furniture. It's about a 45-minute drive east of Mazatlán; head southeast on highway 15 for 20 km to Villa Unión, turn inland on highway 40 (the highway to Durango) and go another 20 km to reach Concordia. **Copala**, 40 km past Concordia on highway 40, and also founded in 1565, was one of Mexico's first mining towns. It still has its colonial church

(built in 1748), colonial houses and cobble-stoned streets.

Rosario, 76 km southeast of Mazatlán on highway 15, is another colonial mining town, founded in 1655. Its most famous feature is the gold-leaf altar in its church, Nuestra Señora del Rosario. **Cosalá**, a beautiful colonial mining village in the mountains north of Mazatlán, was founded in 1550 and has a 17th century church, a historical and mining museum in a colonial mansion on the plaza, and two simple but clean hotels. Attractions nearby include **Vado Hondo**, a balneario (bathing resort) with a large natural swimming pool and three waterfalls, 15 km from the town; **La Gruta México**, a large cave 18 km from the town; and the **Presa El Comedero** reservoir, 20 km from the town, with hired rowboats for fishing. To get to Cosalá, go north on highway 15 for 113 km to the turnoff (opposite the turnoff for La Cruz de Alota on the coast) and then go about 45 km up into the mountains.

Buses to all these places depart from the small bus terminal at the rear of the main bus station in Mazatlán. Alternatively, there are tours (see Organized Tours in the Mazatlán section).

SANTIAGO IXCUINTLA
pop 19,000; ☎ *323*

This town is mainly of interest as the jumping-off point for Mexcaltitán (see section following). It is not a tourist town but it does have the **Centro Huichol** (☎ 5-11-71), a handicrafts center where Huichol Indians make their distinctive arts and crafts, at Calle 20 de Noviembre 10 Pte on the outskirts of town toward Mexcaltitán. You can stop there to see them at work or buy their products – prices are good. About 60 Huichols work there from October to June, but in summer most go to the mountains to plant crops. The center is open every day from 9 am to 7 pm. A block from the bus station on the road to the church you'll see some striking mosaic murals. There are a couple of hotels near the market.

Getting There & Away

Turn off highway 15, 63 km northwest of Tepic, to get to Santiago Ixcuintla; the town is eight km west of the turnoff. Buses to Santiago leave frequently from Tepic and Mazatlán. Santiago Ixcuintla has two 2nd-class bus stations, Transportes del Pacífico and Transportes Norte de Sonora (TNS), half a block apart. Daily services from these stations include:

La Batanga – 37 km, one hour; six by Transportes del Pacífico (US$1.40)
San Blas – 62 km, 1¼ hours; at 5.45 and 8.30 am and 2.30 pm by Transportes del Pacífico (US$2.75)
Tepic – 70 km, one hour; every half-hour, 5.30 am to 8.30 pm, by TNS (US$2.75)

MEXCALTITÁN
pop 2000; ☎ *323*

A small, ancient island village, Mexcaltitán is far from the tourist trail but a fascinating place to visit. Tourism has scarcely touched the island, though it does have a few facilities and a captivating small museum. To get there you must take a *lancha* (motorized wooden boat) through a large mangrove lagoon full of fish, shrimp and many aquatic birds.

Mexcaltitán is sometimes called the 'Venice of Mexico' because the streets occasionally become flooded when the water level of the lagoon rises after heavy rains near the end of the rainy season, around September to November. At that time the high cement sidewalks turn the dirt streets into canals and all travel is done in canoes. If the water level rises very high, families may sleep in canoes tied to the posts in their houses, too!

Be sure to bring plenty of insect repellent, as the lagoon is a breeding ground for mosquitoes.

History

Mexcaltitán has a long, enthralling history. It is believed that this small island, originally called Aztlán, was the homeland of the Aztec people. From here (around 1116) they departed on a generations-long pilgrimage, eventually ending at Tenochtitlán (modern Mexico City) around 1325, when the wandering Aztecs found the symbol that signified they had come to their 'promised land' – an eagle with a serpent in its claws, perched upon a cactus. Today this symbol of Mexico appears on the national flag.

Orientation & Information

The island is a small oval, about 350 meters from east to west, 400 meters from north to south, and about one km around the perimeter. At the center of the island is a plaza with a gazebo in the center, a church on the east side, the museum on the north side and a restaurant on the west side. The hotel is a block behind the museum.

All the telephones on the island go through one operator, who has a switchboard in the sitting room of her house. From outside the island, phone the switchboard (☎ 2-02-11) and ask for the extension you want.

Things to See & Do

The **Museo Aztlán del Origen** on the north side of the plaza is small but enchanting. Among the exhibits are ancient objects and a fascinating long scroll, the Codice Ruturini, telling the story of the peregrinations of the Aztec people, with notes in Spanish. The museum is open daily from 9 am to 1 pm and 3 to 6 pm; admission is US$0.50.

You can easily arrange for **boat trips** on the lagoon for bird-watching, fishing and sightseeing – every family has one or more boats.

There's a **billiards hall** next to the church.

Special Events

Semana Santa is celebrated in a big way. On Good Friday a statue of Christ is put on a cross in the church, then taken down and carried through the streets.

The Fiesta de San Pedro Apóstol, patron saint of fishermen, is celebrated on June 29 with statues of St Peter and St Paul

taken out into the lagoon in decorated lanchas for the blessing of the waters. Festivities start around June 20 and lead up to the big day.

On the Día de Independencia, September 16, Miguel Hidalgo's Cry of Independence is re-enacted at the church on the plaza, with fiestas and celebrations.

Places to Stay & Eat

Mexcaltitán has one hotel and a few restaurants. The *Hotel Ruta Azteca* (☎ 2-02-11, ext 128) at Venecia 5 is a simple place with eight rooms. Rooms with one double bed are US$9, with two beds US$13, with three beds US$17, and with four beds (and aircon) US$23.

The island's restaurants specialize in seafood. The *Restaurant El Camarón* on the plaza, opposite the church, is open daily from around 9 am to 10 pm. The more attractive *Restaurant Alberca*, by the water and accessed by a rickety wooden walkway, has a great view of the lagoon and catches any breezes coming by. It's open every day from around 8 am to 9 pm and concentrates on shrimp dishes. Also by the water is *La Camichina*, open daily from 10 am to 7 pm.

Getting There & Away

Getting to Mexcaltitán involves first getting to Santiago Ixcuintla (see the section earlier). From there, take a bus from the bus station or a colectivo taxi from the market, to La Batanga, a small wharf from where lanchas depart for Mexcaltitán.

Colectivo lanchas between La Batanga and Mexcaltitán are coordinated with the Santiago Ixcuintla bus arrivals and departures; there are six lanchas in each direction between 6 am and 6 pm. The boat journey takes 15 minutes and costs US$0.50 per person. If you miss the colectivo lancha you can hire a whole lancha for US$4.

There is another way to reach Mexcaltitán that does not involve going through Santiago Ixcuintla, but through Tuxpan instead. However this route is less well made, isolated and dangerous.

SAN BLAS
pop 10,000; ☎ 328

The small fishing village of San Blas, 70 km northwest of Tepic, was an important Spanish port from the late 16th to the 19th century. The Spanish built a fortress here to protect their *naos* (trading galleons) from marauding British and French pirates. Today's visitors come to enjoy isolated beaches, exotic birds, a thick tropical jungle, estuaries and a navigable river.

San Blas has the amenities of a small beach resort town – hotels, restaurants and grocery stores – yet it retains the character of a typical Mexican village. One suspects that the real reason the village hasn't been developed as a major resort is due to the proliferation of *jejenes* (sandflies), tiny gnat-like insects with huge appetites for human flesh that leave you with an indomitable itch. Abundant mosquitoes compete with the jejenes for your last drop of blood. During daylight hours they're not too active, but around sunset they appear from nowhere to attack. Be sure to bring plenty of insect repellent and to accept a hotel room only if it has good window screens with no holes or tears.

Orientation
San Blas sits on a tongue of land bound on the west and southwest by El Pozo estuary, on the east by the San Cristóbal estuary, and on the south by Playa El Borrego and the Pacific Ocean. The only road into and out of the village is the 36-km paved road coming in from highway 15. Near San Blas, a coast road heads out around the Bahía Matanchén to Santa Cruz village and on to Puerto Vallarta.

Just west of the bridge over the San Cristóbal estuary, the road passes the Cerro de la Contaduría and the ruins of the old Spanish fortress. At the Pemex station, the road splits into three branches with the center one, Juárez, becoming the main street of San Blas and leading to the village's small zócalo. Calle Batallón de San Blas runs along the western side of the zócalo and leads south to the beach; this could be considered the village's other main street. Everything in the village is within walking distance.

Information
Tourist Office The small Delegación Municipal de Turismo (☎ 5-04-20) at Juárez 65, half a block from the zócalo, has free maps and information about the town. It's open weekdays from 9 am to 2 pm and 5 to 9 pm.

Money The Banamex bank on Juárez, about a block east of the zócalo, is open weekdays from 8.30 am to 1.30 pm but changes money only from 8 am to 11 am. It also has an ATM. Opposite is an Agencia de Cambio, open daily from 8 am to 2 pm and 4 to 8 pm.

Post & Communications The post office, on Sonora on the corner of Echeverría, is open weekdays from 8 am to 1 pm and 3 to 5 pm, Saturday and holidays from 8 am to

WAYNE BERNHARDSON

noon. Next door, Telecomm, with telegraph, telex and fax, is open weekdays from 8 am to 2 pm.

A telephone caseta with fax at the south end of the zócalo, opposite the church, is open daily from 8.15 am to 10 pm.

Travel Agency There's no official travel agency in San Blas, but Federico Rodríguez at the Posada Portolá (see Hotels) reserves and sells air tickets and provides current information on the Mazatlán-La Paz ferry.

Things to See & Do

Climb the **Cerro de la Contaduría** to see the ruins of the 18th century church and fortress (US$0.90); there's a fine view from the top.

San Blas' main attractions are its natural wonders – the surrounding beaches and jungles. The nearest beach is **Playa El Borrego** at the end of Teniente Azueta.

The best beaches are southeast of the village around the Bahía de Matanchén, starting with **Playa Las Islitas**, seven km from San Blas. A paved road that bears south from the road to highway 15 passes the dirt road to Playa Las Islitas and continues past the Oceanography School and through the village of Aticama, eight km along the beach from Playa Las Islitas. Between Playa Las Islitas and Aticama the beach is wonderfully isolated; it's very popular with surfers, who claim that the world's longest wave sweeps ashore here. Farther on, **Playa Los Cocos** and **Playa Miramar**, also popular for

surfing, have palapas under which you can lounge and drink the milk of a fresh coconut.

Boat Trips

A boat trip through the jungle to the freshwater spring of **La Tovara** is one of the highlights of a visit to San Blas. Small boats (maximum of 10 passengers) depart from the embarcadero (jetty) to your left as you cross the bridge into town. Boats go up the San Cristóbal estuary to the spring, passing thick jungle vegetation and mangroves; you'll see exotic birds, turtles, and perhaps a few crocodiles. Bring your swimsuit to swim at La Tovara; there's a restaurant there too. The price is fixed at US$17 for one to four people, US$4 for each extra person, and the trip takes three hours. A shorter boat trip to La Tovara can be made from Matanchén village farther up the river; this takes two hours and costs US$14 for one to four people, US$2.75 for each extra person. For an extra US$10 or so an excursion to visit the Cocodrilario (crocodile farm) can be added to either trip.

A 4½- to five-hour bird-watching trip up the Estuario San Juan to the **Santuario de Aves** (Bird Sanctuary), leaving from the same embarcadero by the bridge, costs US$45 for one to four people, US$13 for each extra person. Other boat trips from San Blas include a trip to **Piedra Blanca** to visit the statue of the Virgin, to **Estero Casa Blanca** to gather clams, to **Isla del Rey**, which is just across from San Blas, and to **Playa del Rey**, a 20-km beach on

Red macaw

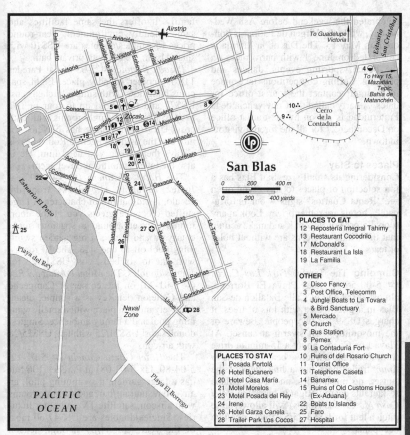

San Blas

0   200   400 m
0   200   400 yards

PLACES TO EAT
12 Repostería Integral Tahimy
13 Restaurant Cocodrilo
17 McDonald's
18 Restaurant La Isla
19 La Familia

OTHER
2 Disco Fancy
3 Post Office, Telecomm
4 Jungle Boats to La Tovara
   & Bird Sanctuary
5 Mercado
6 Church
7 Bus Station
8 Pemex
9 La Contaduría Fort
10 Ruins of del Rosario Church
11 Tourist Office
13 Telephone Caseta
14 Banamex
15 Ruins of Old Customs House
   (Ex-Aduana)
22 Boats to Islands
25 Faro
27 Hospital

PLACES TO STAY
1 Posada Portolá
16 Hotel Bucanero
20 Hotel Casa María
23 Motel Posada del Rey
24 Irene
26 Hotel Garza Canela
28 Trailer Park Los Cocos

the other side of Isla del Rey. Unfortunately it's not advisable for a woman to go to Playa del Rey alone.

You can make an interesting trip farther afield to **Isla Isabel**, also called Isla María Isabelita, four hours northwest of San Blas by boat. The island is a bird-watcher's paradise, with colonies of many species, and there's a volcanic crater lake on the island. Isla Isabel is only about 1.5 km long and one km wide, with no facilities, so you must be prepared for self-sufficient camping. Permission is required to visit the island; the boatmen can arrange it.

Special Events

Every year on January 31 the anniversary of the death of Father José María Mercado is commemorated with a parade, a demonstration march by Mexican marines and fireworks in the zócalo. Mercado lived in San Blas in the early 19th century and helped Miguel Hidalgo with the independence movement by sending him a set of old Spanish cannons from the village.

On February 3, festivities for San Blas, the town's patron saint, are an extension of those begun on January 31, with dance and musical presentations. Carnaval is celebrated the weekend before Ash Wednesday, while the Virgen de Fátima is honored on May 13. The Día de la Marina is celebrated on June 1 with burro races on the beach, sporting events, dances and partying. Surfing competitions take place in summer; contact the tourist office for dates. A party called the Convivencia de la Fraternidad is put on by the tourist office on December 27 for all the foreign visitors in town.

Places to Stay

Considering its small size, San Blas has a fair selection of places to stay – you often see 'Renta Cuartos' signs – but unfortunately, hotels are rather pricey. Look at any room before you accept it and make certain that the window screens are without holes or tears.

Camping The *Trailer Park Los Cocos* (☎ 5-00-55) is near Playa El Borrego, almost at the end of Calle Batallón de San Blas in a grassy area with lots of trees; it charges US$9 for two people. Beware of the mosquitoes that swarm at sunset. At Playa Los Cocos, about a 15-minute drive from town, the attractive beachfront *Playa Amor* trailer park has a fine view of the sunset, no mosquitoes, and a few palapa restaurants nearby. Right in town, the *Hotel Casa María* (see Hotels) will allow you to pitch a tent for US$3.25/5.25 with one/two occupants.

Hotels *Irene* (☎ 5-03-99) at Batallón de San Blas 122 has 10 simple singles/doubles for only US$6.50/7.75; there's no sign outside: it's immediately north of the Posada Azul Hotel.

Motel Morelos (☎ 5-06-32), Batallón de San Blas, is a simple, family-run guesthouse with five rooms (more are being built) round a courtyard and a friendly, homey ambience where all the guests are treated like family – you can cook here and wash your clothes. Rooms with shower/ WC cost US$10 for one/two people, or US$13 in summer. Across the road at No 108 is *Hotel Casa María*, run by the same

family. It offers the same facilities and same friendly environment; year-round prices for singles/doubles are US$10 with shared bath, US$13 with private bath.

Posada Portolá (☎ 5-03-86) at Paredes 118 is another friendly place. Eight spacious bungalows with simple kitchens cost US$22 and they hold up to four or five people; two small single rooms with bath costs US$16. The place has bicycles for hire and the owner, Federico Rodríguez, is always there when you need him. He is also the town's unofficial travel agent.

The *Hotel Bucanero* (☎ 5-01-01), at Juárez 75 about 1½ blocks from the zócalo, is old but full of character. A large stuffed crocodile greets you at the door; rooms are set around a spacious inner courtyard and there's a big garden swimming pool off to one side. The 30 rooms, with one to six beds, cost US$18/23 for singles/doubles. The *Motel Posada del Rey* (☎ 5-01-23) on the corner of Campeche and Callejón del Rey is a simple, clean, relatively modern place with a small swimming pool and a family ambience. Singles/ doubles cost US$21/25 with fan, US$25/28 with air-con.

The *Hotel Garza Canela* (☎ 5-01-12, 5-04-80, fax 5-03-08) at Paredes 106 Sur has a large garden, a swimming pool, an air-con restaurant/bar, and 42 large rooms with air-con, satellite TV and other luxuries. Singles/doubles are US$47/60 most of the year, US$54/69 in high season from December 15 to April 15, with breakfast included. They also have some more expensive suites with kitchens.

Places to Eat

McDonald's (no relation to the burger chain), Juárez 36, half a block southwest of the zócalo, is a favorite among travelers for its good food at good prices. Filling meals are US$3.25 to US$4.50; it's open daily from 7 am to 10 pm. Another favorite is the *Restaurant La Isla* on the corner of Paredes and Mercado, a seafood restaurant with good food, reasonable prices and nautical decor featuring millions of shells. It's open from 2 to 10 pm every day except Monday.

Huichol Indian ceremonial dress, Puerto Vallarta

Top: Manzanillo
Middle Left: Acapulco

Middle Right: Roadside palms and cross
Bottom: La Quebrada diver, Acapulco

The restaurant/video bar *La Familia*, at Batallón de San Blas 62, is another pleasant family restaurant with moderate prices, open every day from 8 am to 10 pm.

There are also a couple of good eating places on the zócalo; *Restaurant Cocodrilo* attracts a lot of gringos and is open daily from 5 to 10.30 pm. The *Repostería Integral Tahimy* on Juárez, near the southwest corner of the zócalo, is a wholemeal bakery open every day from 2 to 9 pm.

There's a good selection of places to eat on the beaches, too, with seafood the speciality – of course.

Entertainment

Considering the small size of the town, San Blas has quite an array of places to go to in the evening. For dancing there's the *Disco Laffite* on Juárez in the Hotel Bucanero; *Mike's Place* over McDonald's restaurant, also on Juárez; and *Disco Fancy* on Canalizo, a block back from the zócalo and bus station. Pleasant bars include *El Mirador*, upstairs at the Motel Posada del Rey, and *El Coco Loco*, by the Trailer Park Los Cocos near Playa El Borrego. *Restaurant Cocodrilo* on the zócalo has a rear bar (open 6 pm to 2 am) where dummies' legs dangle from the ceiling.

Getting There & Away

The bus station is on the corner of Sinaloa and Canalizo, at the northeast corner of the zócalo. Buses depart for Tepic (1½ hours, US$2.75, hourly from 6 am to 7 pm), Puerto Vallarta (3½ hours, US$7.25, at 7 and 10 am), Guadalajara (six hours, US$12, at 9 am) and Mazatlán (five hours, US$11, at 5 pm).

Getting Around

Bicycles can be rented from Motel Morelos (US$2.75 per day) and Posada Portolá (US$6.50 per day), whether or not you're a guest at these places.

To Santa Cruz, the village at the far end of Bahía de Matanchén, buses depart hourly from the bus station; there are also small buses leaving from the corner of Sinaloa and Paredes at 8.20 and 10.30 am,

12.30 and 2.30 pm. The buses serve all the villages and beaches on Bahía de Matanchén, including Matanchén, Playa Las Islitas, Aticama, Playa Los Cocos and Playa Miramar. You can also take a taxi.

TEPIC
pop 200,000; alt 900m; ☎ 32

Tepic is the bustling capital of the small state of Nayarit. It's the crossroads for highways 15/15D and 200, the two Pacific Coast highways; from here highway 15/15D turns inland toward Guadalajara and Mexico City. Local time is one hour behind Puerto Vallarta and Guadalajara in the neighboring state of Jalisco.

Many travelers pass through the outskirts of Tepic by car, bus or train without stopping off. But it doesn't take long to visit the city and there are a few things of interest, including a large neo-Gothic cathedral and several museums. Huichol Indians, who live in the mountains of Nayarit, can often be seen in town wearing colorful traditional clothing. Huichol artwork (reasonably priced) is sold in shops and in front of the cathedral, and displayed in museums. The climate in Tepic is noticeably cooler than on the coast.

Orientation

The Plaza Principal, with the large cathedral at the east end, is the heart of the city. Running south from the cathedral, Avenida México is the city's main street. Six blocks south of Plaza Principal is another plaza, Plaza Constituyentes. Along Avenida México between these two plazas are banks, the tourist office, restaurants, the state museum and other places of interest. The bus and train stations are on the eastern and southeastern outskirts of the city. Peripheral roads make it possible to drive or bus through Tepic without entering the city center.

Information

Tourist Offices The Secretaría de Turismo (☎ 14-80-71 to 75, fax 14-10-17) at the Ex-Convento de la Cruz at the foot of Avenida México, is open weekdays from 9 am to

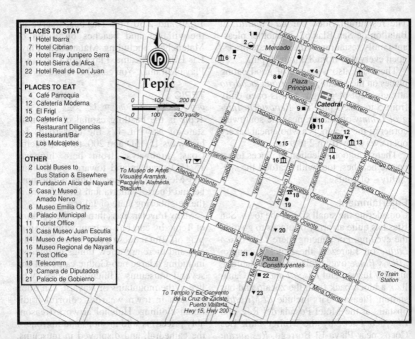

PLACES TO STAY
1 Hotel Ibarra
7 Hotel Cibrian
9 Hotel Fray Junipero Serra
10 Hotel Sierra de Alica
22 Hotel Real de Don Juan

PLACES TO EAT
4 Café Parroquia
12 Cafetería Moderna
15 El Frigl
20 Cafetería y
     Restaurant Diligencias
23 Restaurant/Bar
     Los Molcajetes

OTHER
2 Local Buses to
    Bus Station & Elsewhere
3 Fundación Alica de Nayarit
5 Casa y Museo
    Amado Nervo
6 Museo Emilia Ortiz
8 Palacio Municipal
11 Tourist Office
13 Casa Museo Juan Escutia
14 Museo de Artes Populares
16 Museo Regional de Nayarit
17 Post Office
18 Telecomm
19 Camara de Diputados
21 Palacio de Gobierno

Tepic

8 pm. More convenient is the tourist information office (☎ 12-19-05) at Avenida México 178 Nte, with free maps and information on Tepic and the state of Nayarit; it's open weekdays from 9 am to 7.30 pm. If you're interested in the area and you can read Spanish, ask for the paperback *Estado de Nayarit Guía Turística*, a guidebook about Nayarit (US$4).

Money Banks and casas de cambio line Avenida México Nte between the two plazas.

Post & Communications The post office, on Durango between Allende and Morelos, is open weekdays from 8 am to 7 pm, Saturday 8.30 am to noon. Telecomm, with telegram, telex and fax, is at Avenida México 50 Nte, on the corner of Morelos; it's open weekdays from 8 am to 7 pm, Saturday 8 am to 4 pm. Long-distance telephone and fax services are available at the Cafetería Moderna at Hidalgo 61-4 Ote.

Post and Telecomm offices, and pay phones, are also found in the bus station.

Things to See
The large **cathedral** on the Plaza Principal opposite the Palacio Municipal was dedicated in 1750; the towers were completed in 1885.

The 18th century **Templo y Ex-Convento de la Cruz de Zacate** is at the end of Avenida México on the corner of Calzada del Ejército, about two km south of the cathedral. It was here in 1767 that Father Junípero Serra organized his expedition that established the chain of Spanish missions in the Californias; you can visit the room where he stayed. Outside the adjacent church there's a cross of age-old plants growing from the ground, which is said to have appeared miraculously and to have lived on untended.

There are **murals** inside the Palacio de Gobierno and in the Camara de Diputados on Avenida México. In the southwest section of the city is the large **Parque Paseo de la Loma**.

Cultural events are held at the **Fundación Alica de Nayarit** at Veracruz 256 Nte, half a block north of the Plaza Principal; stop by any time to see a schedule of events and view antique furnishings and other exhibits. It's open weekdays from 9 am to 2 pm and 4 to 7 pm, Saturday 9 am to 2 pm.

Museums All of Tepic's museums have free admission. The **Museo Regional de Nayarit** at Avenida México 91, with a variety of interesting exhibits, is worth a visit; it's open weekdays from 9 am to 7 pm, Saturday 9 am to 3 pm. The **Casa y Museo Amado Nervo** at Zacatecas 284 Nte celebrates the life of the poet Amado Nervo, who was born in this house in 1870. It's open weekdays from 10 am to 2 pm and 4 to 8 pm, Saturday 10 am to 1 pm.

Casa Museo Juan Escutia at Hidalgo 71 Ote was the home of Juan Escutia, one of Mexico's illustrious 'Niños Héroes,' who died in 1847 at age 17 defending Mexico City's Castillo de Chapultepec from US forces. It's open Tuesday to Friday from 9 am to 2 pm and 4 to 7 pm, Saturday from 10 am to 2 pm.

Opposite, the **Museo de Artes Populares** at Hidalgo 60 Ote is also called the Casa de los Cuatro Pueblos. Contemporary popular arts of Nayarit's Huichol, Cora, Nahuatl and Tepehuano peoples are displayed and sold here, including clothing, yarn art, weaving, musical instruments, ceramics, beadwork and more. It's open weekdays from 9 am to 2 pm and 4 to 7 pm, Saturday and Sunday 9 am to 2 pm.

The **Museo de Artes Visuales Aramara** at Allende 329 Pte is another museum of visual arts. It's open weekdays from 9 am to 2 pm and 4 to 7 pm, Saturday 9 am to 2 pm. The **Museo Emilia Ortiz**, at Lerdo de Tejada 192 Pte, honors the painter Emilia Ortiz and her work; it's open Tuesday to Saturday, 10 am to 7 pm.

Special Events

The Feria de la Mexicanidad, which is held from mid-November to early December,

celebrates Mexican culture with all kinds of events.

Places to Stay

Camping About five km south of the Plaza Principal, the *Trailer Park Los Piños* (☎ 13-12-32) offers bungalows (US$13) and spaces for trailers and tents.

Hotels The *Hotel Ibarra* (☎ /fax 12-36-34, 12-32-97) at Durango 297 Nte is a fine place to stay, with 54 clean, bright rooms, a restaurant and enclosed parking. Singles/doubles are US$12/14. The *Hotel Cibrian* (☎ 12-86-98/99) at Nervo 163 Pte is another good, clean hotel, charging US$10/12.

In the block south of the cathedral, the *Hotel Sierra de Alica* (☎ 12-03-25, fax 12-13-09) at Avenida México 180 Nte has 60 rooms at US$13/16. Right on the Plaza Principal, the *Hotel Fray Junípero Serra* (☎ 12-25-25, 2-22-11, fax 2-20-51) is luxurious but more expensive, with rooms at US$29. Overlooking Plaza Constituyentes is *Hotel Real de Don Juan* (☎ /fax 16-18-80/88) Avenida México 105 Sur, an older-style hotel with more character; rooms are US$34.

Two cheaper hotels are behind the bus station; neither is luxurious, but both are clean and acceptable, and all rooms have private bath. The *Hotel Tepic* (☎ 14-76-15) at Dr Martinez 438 has 85 small, clean singles/doubles at US$6.50/7.25; add US$1.30 for TV. In the next block, the *Hotel Nayar* (☎ 13-23-22) at Dr Martinez 430 has 47 large rooms at US$6.50/7.25. Frequent local buses provide easy transport to the center of town.

Places to Eat

A popular gathering spot with good food at good prices is the *Cafetería y Restaurant Diligencias* at Avenida México 29 Sur, open Monday to Saturday from 7 am to 10 pm, Sunday 5 to 10 pm.

On the north side of the Plaza Principal, the *Café Parroquia*, upstairs under the arches, is worth a visit for drinks and light meals; it's open Monday to Saturday from

9 am to 9 pm, Sunday 3 to 9 pm. The *Cafetería Moderna* at Hidalgo 61-4 Ote, another simple place, is open Monday to Saturday from 7 am to 9.30 pm, Sunday 7 am to 2 pm.

For good traditional Mexican food in a fancier atmosphere, yet still reasonably priced, try the *Restaurant/Bar Los Molcajetes* at Avenida México 133 Sur, open Monday to Saturday from 1 pm to 12.30 am. *El Frigal* is an inexpensive vegetarian restaurant in a courtyard at Veracruz 112, at the corner of Zapata. It's open daily from 8.30 am to 9 pm.

There are several cheap places to eat in or near the bus station, particularly the *Restaurant Tepic*, Dr Martinez 438, with a comida corrida for US$1.80.

Getting There & Away
Air Tepic's airport is in Pantanal, about a 25-minute drive from Tepic, going toward Guadalajara. Aero California and Aeroméxico offer direct flights to Mexico City and Tijuana, and Aeroméxico has direct flights to Guadalajara, all with connections to other centers.

Bus The bus station is on the southeastern outskirts of town; local buses marked 'Central' and 'Centro' make frequent connections between the bus station and the city center. The bus station has a cafeteria, left-luggage office, shops, post office, tourist information, telephone caseta and a Telecomm office with fax, telegram and telex. The main bus companies are Autotransportes Transpacíficos, Elite, Futura and Ómnibus de México (all 1st-class), Transportes del Pacífico (1st- and 2nd-class), and TNS (2nd-class). Buses include:

Guadalajara – 216 km, 3½ hours; hourly or half-hourly 1st-class (US$12) and 2nd-class (US$10)

Ixtlán del Río – 88 km, 1½ hours; take Guadalajara buses which are not 'por autopista' (US$2.75 or US$3.50)

Mazatlán – 290 km, four to five hours; hourly 1st-class (US$12) and 2nd-class (US$10)

Mexico City (Terminal Norte) – 751 km, 12 hours; fairly frequent 1st-class (US$35 or US$36), hourly 2nd-class (US$32)

Puerto Vallarta – 169 km, 3½ hours, only by Transportes del Pacífico: 1st-class (US$9) at 2 pm, half-hourly 2nd-class (US$7.75) between 4 am and 8 pm

San Blas – 70 km, 1½ hours; hourly, 6 am to 7 pm, by TNS (US$2.75)

Santiago Ixcuintla – 70 km, 1½ hours; half-hourly, 5.30 am to 8 pm, by TNS (US$2.75)

Train The train station (☎ 13-48-13/61) is on the eastern outskirts of town; local 'Estación' buses will take you there. Tickets are sold at the station every day from 11 am to 6 pm. See the Guadalajara section of the Western Central Highlands chapter for schedules.

Getting Around
Local buses operate from around 5 am to 8.30 or 9 pm; the cost is US$0.20. Otherwise there are plenty of taxis; a ride in town costs US$1.30.

AROUND TEPIC
About 10 km southwest of town is the Cerro de San Juan ecological reserve, a good place for bird-watching.

Laguna Santa María del Oro
This idyllic lake surrounded by steep forested mountains is in a volcanic crater thought to be 100 to 200 meters deep. The clear, clean water takes on colors ranging from turquoise to slate. You can make a very pleasant walk around the lake on a footpath in about 1½ hours, seeing numerous birds and butterflies along the way. You can also climb to an abandoned gold mine or row on the lake, or swim. A few small restaurants serve fresh lake fish.

The good *Koala Bungalows* (☎ 32-14-05-09), owned and operated by Englishman Chris French, has bungalows, camping spaces for trailers or tents, and a restaurant.

To get to the lake, take the Santa María del Oro turnoff about 40 km from Tepic along the Guadalajara road; from the turnoff it's about 10 km to the village, then another eight km from the village to the lake. Buses to the village depart from the bus station in Tepic, then you can take another bus (or a taxi) to the lake.

Volcán Ceboruco

This extinct volcano, with several old craters, interesting plants and volcanic forms, has several short, interesting walks at the top. The 15-km cobblestoned road up the volcano passes lava fields and fumaroles (steam vents), with plenty of vegetation growing on the slopes. The road begins at the village of Jala, seven km off the highway from Tepic to Guadalajara; the turnoff is 76 km from Tepic, 12 km before you reach Ixtlán del Río.

Ixtlán del Río

The small town of Ixtlán del Río, 1½ hours (88 km) from Tepic on the road to Guadalajara, is unremarkable in itself, but Carlos Castaneda fans will remember that this is where Don Juan took Carlos in the book *Journey to Ixtlán*. You may see an occasional soul paying a pilgrimage to the place, watching the plaza for crows. Outside Ixtlán is an archaeological site, **Los Toriles**, with an impressive round stone temple, the Templo a Quetzalcóatl. Any bus between Tepic and Guadalajara will drop you at Ixtlán.

Mirador del Águila

This lookout point on highway 15, about 11 km northwest of Tepic, offers a wide view over a lush jungle canyon; it's known for bird-watching in the early morning and late afternoon.

PUERTO VALLARTA
pop 150,000; ☎ *322*

Puerto Vallarta brackets the Río Cuale between green palm-covered mountains and the sparkling blue Bahía de las Banderas (Bay of Flags). It's in Jalisco state, one hour ahead of neighboring Nayarit.

Formerly a quaint seaside village, Vallarta has been transformed into a world-famous resort city with 2.5 million visitors annually (one million foreigners, 1.5 million Mexicans). They're accommodated in 14,000 hotel rooms and 3000 condominiums, with more being built all the time. Some of the most beautiful beaches, secluded and romantic just a few years ago, are now dominated by giant luxury megaresorts. Tourism – Vallarta's only industry – has made it a bilingual city, with English almost as commonly spoken as Spanish. Despite all this, the cobblestoned streets, lined with old-fashioned white adobe buildings with red tile roofs, still make Vallarta one of Mexico's most picturesque coastal cities.

Vallarta's attractions suit all tastes and pockets, with idyllic white-sand beaches, water sports and cruises, horseback rides and tours, shopping, art galleries, abundant restaurants and an active nightlife.

History

Puerto Vallarta's history is not very long; the first recorded settlement here was in 1851, when the Sánchez family came and made their home by the mouth of the Río Cuale, which now divides the city. Farmers and fisherfolk followed. By 1918, enough people lived around the Río Cuale to give the settlement a name on the map. The name Vallarta was chosen in honor of Ignacio Luis Vallarta, a former governor of the state of Jalisco. It was called Puerto (port) because farmers had been shipping their harvests by boat from a small port area north of the Río Cuale.

Tourists began to visit Vallarta in 1954 when Mexicana airlines started a promotional campaign and initiated the first flights here, landing on a dirt airstrip in Emiliano Zapata, an area which is now the center of Vallarta. But it was not until a decade later, when John Huston chose the nearby deserted cove of Mismaloya for the shooting of the film version of Tennessee Williams' play *The Night of the Iguana*, that the town was put on the international tourist map.

During that film's shooting, the paparazzi of Hollywood descended to report on every development of the romance between Richard Burton and Elizabeth Taylor.

Burton's co-star Ava Gardner also raised more than a few eyebrows, and Puerto Vallarta suddenly became world-famous with an aura of steamy tropical romance. Tour groups began arriving not long after the film crew left and they've been coming ever since.

Orientation

The town center is around the Río Cuale, with the small Isla Cuale in the middle of the river and two bridges allowing easy passage between the two sides of town. To the north of the city are the airport (10 km) and two recent developments: Marina Vallarta, a large yachting marina about one km south of the airport, and Nuevo Vallarta, farther north around the bay, about 25 km from the city center. Also north of the city are a host of giant luxury hotels fanning out along the shore, and some fine beaches. To the south of the city are more resorts and some of the most beautiful beaches in the area.

The heart of the city center is the Plaza Principal, also called Plaza de Armas, sitting by the sea between Morelos and Juárez, the city's two principal thoroughfares. The crown-topped cathedral, called the Templo de Guadalupe, towers a block behind the plaza, while on the sea side of the plaza is an amphitheater with arches that have become a symbol of the town. The wide seaside walkway known as the Malecón, stretching about 10 blocks north from the plaza, is lined with bars, restaurants, nightclubs and boutiques.

South of the river are bus stations, hotels, restaurants and the only two beaches in the city center: Playa Olas Altas (poorly named, because it doesn't really have 'big waves') and Playa de los Muertos (Beach of the Dead), taking its strange name from a fierce fight there sometime in the distant past.

City traffic has been reduced dramatically by the opening of the *libramiento* or bypass road on the inland side of the city center, diverting traffic away from the center.

Information

Tourist Office The Delegación de Turismo (☎ 2-02-42, 3-07-66, fax 2-02-43), in the municipal building on the northeast corner of the Plaza Principal, has free maps, bilingual tourist literature and friendly bilingual staff. It's open weekdays from 9 am to 2 pm and 2.30 to 5 pm.

Consulates The US consulate (☎ 2-00-69, fax 3-00-74) is upstairs at Zaragoza 160 on the Plaza Principal. It's open weekdays from 10 am to 2 pm. One floor below is the Canadian consulate (☎ 2-53-98, fax 2-35-17), open weekdays from 9 am to 5 pm.

Money Most businesses in Vallarta accept US dollars cash as readily as they accept

---

Bahía de las Banderas

The Bahía de las Banderas ('Bay of Flags') is the seventh-largest bay in the world, with an area of about 34 km by 52 km, a 161-km shoreline and a probable depth of around 1800 meters, though depth-measuring instruments have never found the bottom. Supposedly the bay was formed by the sunken crater of a giant, extinct volcano. If you fly over the bay you might actually see the perimeter of this crater.

The bay is teeming with life, but it has the unusual distinction of being virtually shark-free. This is because dolphins inhabiting the bay bear their young all year round. To protect their colony they mount a patrol at the bay's entrance to keep sharks out.

Pilot and gray whales also bear their young in the bay, but only around February and March. If you're out in a boat you will probably see dolphins, and whales in season. The bay's giant manta rays – with four-meter 'wingspans' – mate in April; during that month they often jump above the water's surface, which you might actually witness from the Malecón. ■

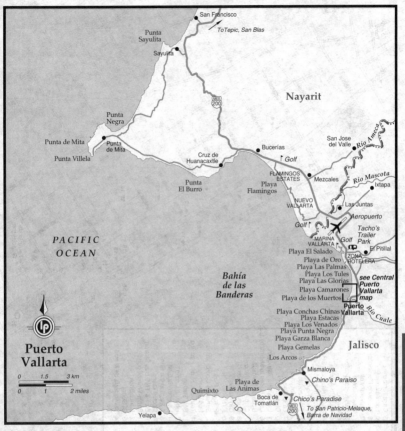

Puerto Vallarta

pesos, though the rate of exchange they give is usually less favorable than the banks, which offer the best rate. Several banks are found around the Plaza Principal; they are open weekdays from 9 am to around 3 pm (times vary) but often have long queues. Banamex, on the south side of the plaza, has a separate currency exchange office, open weekdays from 9 am to 3 pm.

A great number of casas de cambio are found around Vallarta; their rates differ slightly so it may pay to shop around. Though their rates are less favorable than those given by banks, the difference may be only a few cents and the longer opening hours and faster service may make it worthwhile to change money there. Most are open daily from around 9 am to 7.30 pm, sometimes with a lunch break from 2 to 4 pm. Look for them on Insurgentes, Vallarta, the Malecón and many other streets.

American Express (☎ 3-29-55) is north of the Río Cuale at Morelos 660. It's open weekdays from 9 am to 6 pm, Saturday 9 am to 1 pm.

Post & Communications The post office, Juárez 628, is open weekdays from 8 am to 7.30 pm, Saturday from 9 am to 1 pm.

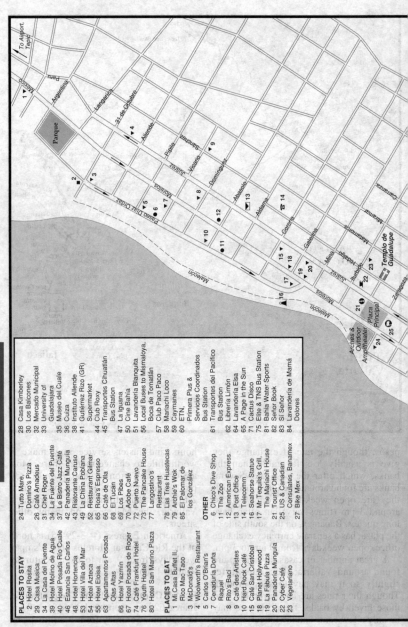

PLACES TO STAY
2 Hotel Rosita
29 Casa Musica
39 La Casa del Puente
40 Hotel Molino de Agua
46 Hotel Posada Río Cuale
48 Estancia San Carlos
53 Hotel Hortencia
54 Hotel Villa del Mar
55 Hotel Azteca
63 Hotel Eloisa
     Apartamentos Posada
     Olas Altas
66 Hotel Yazmin
67 Hotel Posada de Roger
76 Café Frankfurt Hotel
     Youth Hostel
80 Hotel San Marino Plaza

PLACES TO EAT
1 Mi Casa Buffet II,
     Rico Mac Taco
3 McDonald's
4 Woolworth's Restaurant
5 Carlos O'Brian's
7 Cenaduría Doña
     Raquel
8 Rito's Baci
9 Café des Artistes
10 Hard Rock Café
15 Café San Cristóbal
18 Planet Hollywood
19 La Fabula Pizza
20 Panadería Munguía
23 Cyber Café
     Vegetariano

24 Tutto Mare,
     Domino's Pizza
26 Café Amadeus
31 Chef Roger
34 La Fuente del Puente
37 Le Bistro Jazz Café
42 Panadería Munguía
43 Ristorante Caruso
49 La China Poblana
52 Restaurant Gilmar
65 Rosa's Espresso
66 Café de Olla
68 El Tucan
69 Los Pibes
70 Adobe Café
72 Puerto Nuevo
73 The Pancake House
77 Langostino's
     Restaurant
78 Las Tres Huastecas
79 Archie's Wok
85 El Palomar de
     los González

OTHER
6 Chico's Dive Shop
11 The Zoo
12 American Express
13 Post Office
14 Telecomm
16 Seahorse Statue
17 Mr Tequila's Grill,
     The Mariachi House
21 Tourist Office
25 US & Canadian
     Consulates, Banamex
27 Bike Mex

28 Casa Kimberley
30 Los Balcones
32 Mercado Municipal
33 University of
     Guadalajara
35 Museo del Cuale
36 Cuiza
38 Instituto Allende
41 Gutiérrez Rizo (GR)
     Supermarket
44 Club Roxy
45 Transportes Cihuatlán
     Bus Station
47 La Iguana
50 Cine Bahia
51 Lavandería Blanquita
56 Local Buses to Mismaloya,
     Boca de Tomatlán
57 Club Paco Paco
58 Mariachi Loco
59 Caymanes
60 ETN,
     Primera Plus &
     Servicios Coordinados
     Bus Station
61 Transportes del Pacifico
     Bus Station
62 Librería Limón
64 Lavandería Elsa
65 A Page in the Sun
71 Cactus Disco
75 Elite & TNS Bus Station
81 Bahia Water Sports
82 Señor Book
83 Si Señor
84 Lavandería de Mamá
     Dolores

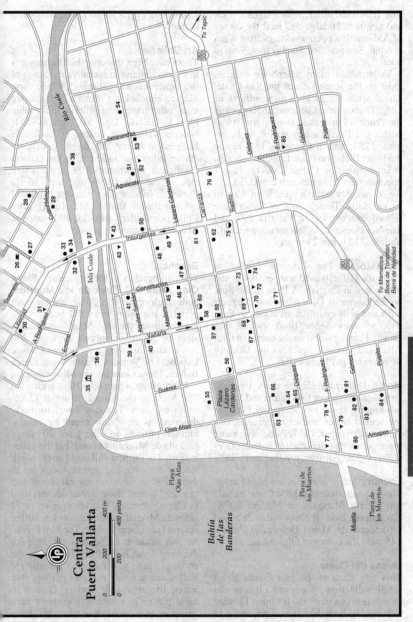

Central
Puerto Vallarta

CENTRAL PACIFIC COAST

The Telecomm office, with telegram, telex and fax, is at Hidalgo 582 near the corner of Aldama. It's open weekdays from 8 am to 6 pm, Saturday and Sunday from 9 am to noon.

Vallarta has many telephone casetas, most on the south side of the Río Cuale. Those with fax include three offices of Larga Distancia: at Cárdenas 267, opposite the Primera Plus bus station; at the Transportes del Pacífico bus station at Insurgentes 282; and at Cárdenas 181, beside the Hotel Eloisa on Plaza Lázaro Cárdenas.

Send email at Cyber Cafe on Juárez opposite the tourist office. It costs US$2.75 for 30 minutes and it's open from 9 am to 11 pm daily. There's another Cyber Cafe (eltorito@acnet.net) at Vallarta 290, and The Net House (cafe@the-net-house.com), Vallarta 232 (open 24 hours).

Bookstores The Librería Limón at Carranza 310 sells used and new books and magazines in English. A Page in the Sun, on the corner of Olas Altas and Diéguez, buys and sells quality used books in English, as does Señor Book (which has Lonely Planet guides) on the corner of Olas Altas and Gómez. See also the Grocery Stores entry in Places to Eat.

Media *Vallarta Today*, a daily English-language newspaper for visitors and Vallarta's English-speaking community, is free at the tourist office and elsewhere, as is a similar newspaper, *PV Tribune*. The same places often also sell *Puerto Vallarta Lifestyles*, a glossy quarterly magazine (US$2).

Laundry Many laundries are round town. Those found south of the Río Cuale include Lavandería Blanquita at Madero 407A, Lavandería Elsa at Olas Altas 385 and Lavandería de Mamá Dolores at Púlpito 145, near the corner of Olas Altas.

Museo del Cuale
This tiny museum on Isla Cuale, has a small collection of ancient objects and changing art exhibitions. It's open Tuesday to Saturday from 10 am to 3 pm and 4 to 7 pm, Sunday 10 am to 2 pm; admission is free.

Art Galleries
These have been sprouting like mushrooms in Puerto Vallarta in recent years. Some of the better known galleries include Arte Mágico Huichol at Corona 179 (there are many other interesting galleries in the same block), Galería Uno at Morelos 561, Galería Vallarta at Juárez 263, Galería Indígena at Juárez 270, the Sergio Bustamante gallery at Juárez 275, the Galería Pacífico at Insurgentes 109 on the south side of the Río Cuale and the Galería Pyrámide (which has a pleasant courtyard cafe) at Basilio Badillo 272. The Huichol Collection Gallery, Morelos 490, supports a Huichol community project.

Beaches
The two beaches in the city center, **Playa Olas Altas** and **Playa de los Muertos**, both south of the Río Cuale, are the most popular, but many beautiful beaches are found outside the city. Southward, accessible by minibuses plying highway 200 (the coastal highway) are Conchas Chinas, Estacas, Los Venados, Punta Negra, Garza Blanca, Playa Gemelas and Mismaloya.

Mismaloya, where John Huston directed *The Night of the Iguana*, is about 12 km south of town. The tiny cove, formerly deserted, is now dominated by condominium projects and the giant 303-room La Jolla de Mismaloya hotel, but the buildings used in the film still stand on the south side of the cove and you can walk up to them. For an adventurous excursion you can head inland along a riverside dirt road to Chino's Paraíso, two km upriver, or El Edén de Mismaloya, about five km farther upriver (see Places to Eat). The film *Predator* was made at El Edén, accounting for the burned-out hull of a helicopter at the entrance; here you can also take jungle walks, see a small zoo and explore two waterfalls just a little upriver. Getting to these places is a hike if you don't have transport; you can hitch or take a taxi from

Mismaloya. The walk back is downhill all the way and makes a pleasant stroll.

About four km past Mismaloya, **Boca de Tomatlán** is a peaceful, less commercialized seaside village in a small cove where the Río de Tomatlán meets the sea – a jungly place with quiet water, a beach and a number of restaurants.

Farther around the south side of the bay are the more isolated beaches of Las Ánimas, Quimixto and Yelapa, accessible only by boat. **Playa de las Ánimas** (Beach of the Spirits), a lovely beach with a small fishing village and some palapa restaurants offering fresh seafood, is said to be the most beautiful beach on the bay. **Quimixto**, not far from Las Ánimas, has a waterfall you can reach with a half-hour hike, or you can hire a pony on the beach to take you up.

Yelapa, farthest from town, is probably the most popular cruise destination; this picturesque cove is crowded with tourists, restaurants and parasailing operators. The charming village at Yelapa has a sizeable colony of US residents; you can find a place to stay if you ask around. Take a hike upriver to see the waterfalls.

Still more beaches are found around the north side of the bay. Nearest Vallarta are the beaches in the Zona Hotelera: Camarones, Las Glorias, Los Tules, Las Palmas, Playa de Oro and, past the Marina, El Salado. Nuevo Vallarta also has beaches. Farther on around the bay are Playa Flamingos, Bucerías, Destiladeras, Punta del Burro, Paraíso Escondido, El Anclote and Punta de Mita, at the northern boundary of the bay.

Water Sports
Snorkeling, scuba diving, deep-sea fishing, water-skiing, jet-skiing, windsurfing, sailing, parasailing, riding the 'banana' and just plain swimming are all popular in Vallarta. Most can be arranged on the beaches in front of any of the large hotels. The tourist office can help connect you with operators.

The most spectacular spots for snorkeling and diving are **Los Arcos**, a protected ecological zone on an island rock formation just north of Mismaloya, and the **Islas Marietas** at the entrance to the bay, with impressive reefs, underwater caves, tunnels, walls and opportunities to see dolphins, whales and giant manta rays.

Vallarta has a number of diving and snorkeling operators. Chico's Dive Shop (☎ 2-18-95, 2-54-39), on the Malecón at Paseo Díaz Ordaz 772, open daily from 8 am to 10 pm, is the biggest outfit. It offers several good diving and snorkeling trips as well as diving instruction; a two-tank diving trip costs around US$80. Bahia Water Sports (☎ 3-24-94), Olas Altas 477A, is a good smaller operator.

Deep-sea fishing is popular all year, with a major international sailfish tournament each November. Prime catches are sailfish, marlin, tuna, red snapper and sea bass. The tourist office can recommend fishing operators for the type of trip you have in mind.

See the Getting Around section for information on hiring private yachts and lanchas for snorkeling and fishing trips.

Horseback Riding
Expect to pay around US$10 per hour for horseback riding. The Rancho Amigo-Marco Polo (☎ 4-73-42), a small, personal and friendly horseback riding enterprise, operates 3½- to four-hour rides up into the hills through isolated terrain that you can't get to any other way. Two larger operators are Rancho El Charro (☎ 4-01-14) and Rancho Ojo de Agua (☎ 4-06-07). Horsemen offer beach rides north of the Río Cuale.

Golf & Tennis
These are both popular sports in Puerto Vallarta. Golf courses north of the city include the exclusive Marina Vallarta Golf Club (☎ 1-05-45) and the less exotic Los Flamingos Golf Club (☎ (329) 7-15-15). Another golf course is in Nuevo Vallarta.

A favorite with tennis players is the John Newcombe Tennis Club (☎ 4-43-60 ext 500) in the Zona Hotelera, also north of the city. Most of the large luxury hotels also have courts; phone them to reserve a court.

Los Tules (☎ 4-54-25), the Sheraton Buganvilias (☎ 3-04-04), the Hotel Krystal (☎ 4-02-02) and the Marriott Hotel (☎ 1-00-04) all have courts available, and there are plenty of others.

Cruises

A host of cruises are available in Vallarta, with daytime, sunset and evening cruises, some including snorkeling stops at Los Arcos (see Water Sports). The most popular are probably the cruises to Yelapa and Las Ánimas beaches. The tourist office or any travel agency can tell you what cruises are operating, details of where they go, what they offer (many include meals, an open bar, live music and dancing) and current prices.

If you just want to visit the beaches, a cheaper way to get there is by water taxi (see Getting Around).

Language Courses

The University of Guadalajara's Foreign Student Study Center (☎ 3-20-82, fax 3-29-82; cipv@clxvta.udg.mx), Libertad and Miramar, specializes in teaching Spanish and can arrange lodging with a Mexican family. A beginners' class begins every Monday, minimum enrollment one week. Classes are semi-intensive (two hours per day, 10 hours per week) or intensive (four hours per day, 20 hours per week); the cost is US$16 per hour for instruction, plus a one-time US$30 registration fee. Intermediate and advanced courses are also offered. Instituto Allende (☎/fax 2-00-76), Isla Cuale, also has a range of Spanish classes starting every Monday; it's a little cheaper. University credits are given in both places.

Organized Tours

The tourist office and travel agents can set you up with city tours, jungle tours, bicycle tours and horseback riding tours.

Bike Mex Mountain Bike Adventures (☎ 3-16-80), Guerrero 361, offers mountain bike tours with experienced bilingual guides, tailored to your level of fitness and experience. Prices start at US$36.

The Friendship Club (☎ 2-51-28) offers two-hour tours of some of Puerto Vallarta's luxurious private homes, usually departing at 11 am on Thursday and Friday from the Plaza Principal. Or you can take a tour of Casa Kimberley, the house that Richard Burton bought for Elizabeth Taylor back in the 1960s, still with its original furnishings. It's at Zaragoza 445, in 'gringo gulch' (☎ 2-13-36), and is open weekdays 9 am to 6 pm, weekends 9 am to 4 pm; tours take 20 to 60 minutes, cost US$5 and include refreshments.

Special Events

The Regatta Marina del Rey-Puerto Vallarta, held during February in odd-numbered years, is a boat race beginning at Marina del Rey, near San Diego, California, and ending here with festivities.

The busiest holiday in Puerto Vallarta is Semana Santa, when hotels fill up and hundreds (or thousands) of excess visitors camp out on the beaches and party. It's a wild time.

The Fiestas de Mayo, a city-wide fair with cultural and sporting events, popular music concerts, carnival rides, art exhibits and more, is held throughout May.

A big international Torneo de Pesca is held each year in November; dates vary according to the phase of the moon, which must be right for fishing. The tourist office can provide exact dates.

The Día de Santa Cecilia (November 22) honors the patron saint of mariachis with all the city's mariachis forming a musical procession to the Templo de Guadalupe in the early evening. They come playing and singing, enter the church and sing homage to their saint, then go out into the plaza and continue to play. During the entire day one or another group of mariachis stays in church making music.

All Mexico celebrates December 12 as the day of the country's patron saint, the Virgen de Guadalupe, but in Puerto Vallarta the celebrations are more drawn out. Pilgrimages and processions go to the cathedral day and night from November 30 until the big bash on December 12.

Places to Stay

Vallarta has a good selection of cheap accommodation. Most hotel prices are higher during Vallarta's high season, roughly from December to April. For accommodation at the very busiest times – Semana Santa or between Christmas and New Year – be sure to reserve in advance.

Places to Stay – budget

Camping Closest in is the *Puerto Vallarta Trailer Park* (☎ 4-24-24) at Francia 134 in Colonia Versailles, in the Zona Hotelera, a few km north of the city. It has plenty of shady trees and 60 spaces with full hook-ups at about US$12 per space. A few km farther north, *Tacho's Trailer Park* (☎ 4-21-63) has a swimming pool and 120 spaces; the cost is US$14 per space, with monthly discounts.

Hostel & Hotels The cheapest places to stay are south of the Río Cuale, particularly along Madero to the west of Insurgentes. All are basic but clean, with fan and private bath. There is a *Youth Hostel* (☎ 2-21-08), Aguacate 302A, which at US$5.50 per dorm bed isn't cheaper than staying in a hotel, though there are kitchen facilities and a 10% discount with student ID.

The *Hotel Villa del Mar* (☎ 2-07-85) at Madero 440, on the corner of Jacarandas, has 49 rooms, many featuring private balconies with chairs and flowering plants; up on the roof are sitting areas with a view of the town. Singles/doubles are US$8.25/10.25, and studio apartments with fully equipped kitchens are US$13/16, or US$300/350 by the month. Prices reduce from May 1 to November 30. In the same block are several other good-value places charging only US$6/8.50 for singles/doubles; they are more basic but perfectly acceptable.

The 46-room *Hotel Azteca* (☎ 2-27-50) at Madero 473 has clean, pleasant singles/doubles at US$7.25/9 all year round, US$12 for rooms with kitchenettes. The *Hotel Hortencia* (☎ 2-24-84) at Madero 336 has 18 rooms at US$12/15.

Timeshares

Attending a timeshare presentation is one way to get a greatly discounted (perhaps even free) cruise, dinner, jeep rental or horse ride. This involves putting up with a 90-minute salespitch (with a free breakfast) about the benefits of investing in one of Puerto Vallarta's burgeoning timeshare condominium projects, and then touring the project. You'll see many timeshare hawkers along Puerto Vallarta's main streets.

Generally you must be more than 25 years of age, in possession of a major credit card and employed; many hawkers also require that you be married, and that both husband and wife attend the presentation. The hawker will pay the taxi fare from your hotel to the project. You are under no obligation to buy or sign anything.

Travelers give mixed reports about the presentations. Some say it's a painless enough way to get a cheap jeep, tour or cruise. Others are still angry days later, after fending off the 'hard sell.' ■

The *Hotel Yazmín* (☎ 2-00-87), at Basilio Badillo 168, has rooms at US$14/16 all year round. The hotel is a favorite, clean and friendly, with courtyard gardens and a good, inexpensive restaurant next door. It is an excellent deal and just a block from Playa de los Muertos, the most popular beach in Vallarta.

Nearby, the *Apartamentos Posada Olas Altas*, Olas Altas 356, seems an anomaly in this district of fancier places. It has six apartments, with kitchens, that are quite basic and perhaps only a true beach bum would like them. However, the price is right at US$154 for a month, with shorter stays possible. There's no sign and access is via stairs on Badillo. Get information at the unnamed torta place on Badillo by the casa de cambio.

Places to Stay – middle

The *Café Frankfurt Hotel* (☎ 2-34-03) at Badillo 300 is an older hotel with a friendly family atmosphere and a garden. Regular rooms with cable TV are US$17, cabañas are US$23; one-bedroom apartments with kitchen are US$26, two-bedroom apartments are US$39. All room prices include accommodation for one child, and all are cheaper by the month. It has enclosed parking.

The *Hotel Posada de Roger* (☎ 2-08-36, 2-06-39, fax 3-04-82), at Badillo 237, is famous for its friendly atmosphere, cleanliness and security, and has a pleasant courtyard swimming pool plus a convivial restaurant/bar, El Tucan. Singles/doubles with air-con and cable TV are US$25/32, or US$30/39 from mid-December to Easter.

The *Casa Corazón* (☎/fax 2-13-71; in the USA ☎ 505-523-4666, 505-522-4684) at Amapas 326 is an attractive B&B guesthouse with spacious terraces overlooking Playa de los Muertos. Low-season rates are US$30 or US$45 for singles, US$40 or US$45 for doubles, rising to US$55/60 at peak periods. All prices include breakfast and they have a beachside restaurant, Looney Tunes, down the hill.

The *Hotel Eloisa* (☎ 2-64-65, fax 2-02-86) at Cárdenas 179, half a block from Playa Olas Altas, has a rooftop terrace with a children's pool and 76 bright, clean rooms with air-con and cable TV; they're a good value at US$17/21, rising slightly from November to Easter.

Beside the beach at the north end of town, the *Hotel Rosita* (☎/fax 2-10-33) at Paseo Díaz Ordaz 901 is a popular older hotel with a beachside swimming pool, restaurant and bar. Singles/doubles start at US$21/27 for regular rooms, higher for suites, but cheaper in the low season. You have to pay more for rooms with sea view or air-con.

The *Hotel Posada Río Cuale* (☎/fax 2-04-50, 2-09-14), at Serdán 242 on the corner of Vallarta, is a pleasant hotel with a swimming pool, a poolside restaurant/bar, and 21 rooms with air-con. Singles/doubles are US$20/25 most of the year, rising to US$40/45 from December 1 to April 30.

A good deal for mid-range apartments is the *Estancia San Carlos* (☎/fax 2-53-27) at Constitución 210, with a courtyard swimming pool, covered parking and 24 clean, modern apartments with fully equipped kitchen, air-con, TV and private balcony. One-bedroom apartments are US$47, two-bedroom apartments are US$59, with discounts by the month.

One of Vallarta's hidden treasures is the tiny *La Casa del Puente* (☎ 2-07-49), tucked behind the Restaurant La Fuente del Puente beside the Río Cuale, with just a one-bedroom apartment and a two-bedroom apartment; each costs US$41 in low season, US$76 from December 15 until the week after Easter. Molly Muir, the owner, is a wonderful hostess and impromptu tour guide. Dick Baker at *Casa Musica* (☎ 2-17-58), Cuauhtémoc 460, offers a comparable deal.

Places to Stay – top end

Puerto Vallarta has many beautiful places to stay at the upper end of the market. From mid-April to mid-December, low-season discounts bring even some of the finest places down to a more affordable level.

One of Vallarta's best centrally located hotels is the *Hotel Molino de Agua* (☎ 2-19-07/57, fax 2-60-56) at Vallarta 130, facing the beach on the south side of the Río Cuale. Though it's in the city center, it's remarkably quiet and peaceful, with 65 cabins, rooms and suites set among tropical gardens covering two city blocks. Prices from November 30 to April 15 start at US$82 for cabins, higher for beachfront suites, with low-season discounts.

Top-end hotels line the beach at Playa de los Muertos. Typically they are high-rises with air-con, beachfront swimming pools and restaurants. For example, the *Hotel San Marino Plaza* (☎ 2-30-50, 2-15-55, fax 2-24-31) at Rodolfo Gómez 111 has 162 rooms at US$62, rising to US$78 from mid-December to Easter.

Many giant five-star and Grand Tourism-category hotels, often with hundreds of rooms, line the beaches both to the north and south of town. Some of the most attractive are on the beaches south of town, including the *Camino Real* and *Presidente Inter-Continental*. In the Zona Hotelera are the *Sheraton Buganvilias, Qualton, Plaza Las Glorias, Krystal Vallarta, Continental Plaza, Fiesta Americana* and *Holiday Inn*. Farther north, in Marina Vallarta, are the *Marriott Casa Magna, Paradisus, Bel-Air, Westin Regina, Vidafel* and *Velas Vallarta*. Still farther north in Nuevo Vallarta are the *Sierra Radisson, Diamond Resorts* and *Jack Tar Village*. Travel agents can connect you with any of these places; they all do big business in foreign package tours.

Several elegant guesthouses provide a comfortable 'gay-friendly' ambience, including the *Casa de los Arcos* (☎ 2-59-90), a luxurious mountainside villa overlooking the south part of town, and the *Casa Panorámica* (☎ 2-36-56, in the USA 800-745-7805) at km 1 on the highway to Mismaloya.

Places to Eat
Cafés & Coffee Houses *Café Amadeus* at Miramar 271 is a relaxing and friendly retreat, open Monday to Saturday from 8 am to 10 pm. *Rosa's Espresso* on the corner of Olas Altas and Diéguez shares space with A Page in the Sun, which has good-quality used books in English; it's open daily from 8 am to 11 pm. North of the river, the *Café San Cristóbal* at Corona 272, 1½ blocks from the Malecón, is another good coffee house and roastery, open Monday to Saturday from 8 am to 10 pm.

Bakeries The *Panadería Munguía* at Juárez 467 is a good bakery, with everything from sweets to healthy wholegrain baked goods, open daily from 7 am (9 am on Sunday) to 9.30 pm. A smaller branch is on the corner of Insurgentes and Serdán on the south side of the Río Cuale.

Restaurants – south of the Río Cuale
There are some small, cheap, family-run restaurants along Madero. One is *Restaurant Gilmar*, Madero 418, providing good,

tasty food at very low prices: the comida corrida for US$2 includes three courses and a drink. It's open daily from 8 am to 11 pm. *Restaurant/Bar La China Poblana*, Insurgentes 222, has typical Mexican food and an upstairs dining terrace, open daily from 7 am to 2 am. There are several places offering broiled chicken nearby, including a good take-away place on Serdán between Constitución and Insurgentes.

Many other restaurants south of the river are a step up in class; this being the city's main hotel district, most are heavily patronized by tourists.

The attractive *Ristorante Caruso* at Insurgentes 109, overlooking the Río Cuale, serves up pasta, salad and garlic bread for US$4.50 (closed Sunday lunch).

Two restaurants on Badillo each claim to serve the best breakfast in town: *El Tucan*, connected to the Hotel Posada de Roger on the corner of Vallarta and Badillo, and *The Pancake House*, a block away at Badillo 289. Each has been nominated in letters from travelers as winning 'hands down' so you'd best decide for yourself. Both are great places for breakfast, with about 20 varieties of pancakes and waffles, plus treats like eggs Benedict, cheese blintzes and omelettes; eggs with hash browns, toast, butter and coffee come to around US$3 at either place. In El Tucan, try the filling French toast (US$2.25); it's open daily from 8 am to 2 pm for breakfast and (except Sunday) 6 to 11 pm for dinner. The Pancake house is open daily from 8 am to 2 pm.

This block of Badillo has several other good restaurants. *Los Pibes* at No 261, is an Argentine restaurant serving excellent steaks (from US$12); it's open daily from 2 pm to midnight. Opposite is the pricey, stylish, air-con *Adobe Café* at No 252, open from 6 to 11 pm every day except Tuesday. The popular *Puerto Nuevo* at No 284 offers good seafood and other meals daily from noon to 12.30 am.

The *Café de Olla* at Badillo 168, beside the Hotel Yazmín, is a good find – a small, busy, very pleasant restaurant with good traditional Mexican food (from US$3.25) and an 'Old Mexico' atmosphere, open from noon to 11 pm daily except Tuesday.

One of Vallarta's best known restaurants is *Archie's Wok* at Francisca Rodríguez 130, half a block from the Playa de los Muertos pier. It was created by the former personal chef of film director John Huston. Archie's features wok specialities from many parts of Asia, with vegetarian or meat selections like gingery stir-fried vegetables (US$4.75) or fish sautéed in coconut milk and Thai red chili sauce (US$8.75). It's open from 2 to 11 pm daily except Sunday.

In the same neighborhood, *Las Tres Huastecas*, on the corner of Olas Altas and Francisca Rodríguez, is a cheerful spot, with good food and moderate prices, open every day from 7 am to 10 pm.

El Palomar de los González (☎ 2-07-95) at Aguacate 425 is a hillside restaurant with good food and an exceptional view over the city and bay, especially at sunset – a great place for a special night out, open nightly (with live music) from 6 to 11 pm. Another elegant, peaceful spot is the garden restaurant of the *Hotel Molino de Agua*, on Vallarta just south of the Río Cuale, open daily from 7.30 am to 10.30 pm.

There are a number of beachside restaurants. A good one is *Langostino's Restaurant* on Playa Los Muertos, open everyday from 7 am to 11 pm. Also known as the Sand Bar, it's atmospheric and inexpensive, with good seafood, ribs and breakfasts.

Restaurants – north of the Río Cuale

As in most Mexican towns, one of the cheapest places to eat is at the *Mercado Municipal* – but in Vallarta the market is relatively clean and pleasant. It's on the north side of the Río Cuale beside the inland bridge, and the upstairs floor has a number of simple restaurant stalls serving typical Mexican market foods – you can eat well here for US$2. It's open every day from around 7 am to 9.30 pm.

Equally economical is *Mi Casa Buffet II*, Mexico 1121 between Uruguay and Chile,

where an all-you-can-eat buffet of soup, salad, rice, two main courses and fruit costs just US$2.25; lunch is from 1 to 4.30 pm and dinner is from 6.30 to 9 pm; breakfast, from 9 am to noon, is the same price. A couple of doors north is *Rico Mac Taco*, a taco place open 24 hours that attracts some interesting characters.

An all-you-can-eat buffet for vegetarians is provided by *Vegetariano*, Iturbide 270, up the steps from Hidalgo. It's a small place, open Monday to Saturday from noon to 6 pm; the buffet costs US$4. *La Fabula Pizza*, Morelos 484 overlooking the seahorse statue, has an all-you-can-eat pasta/pizza buffet for US$2.75, weekdays from noon to 4 pm.

Just off the Malecón, *Rito's Baci* at Domínguez 181 is a tiny Italian restaurant with excellent food, open every day from 1 to 11.30 pm. Phone for free delivery within the city (☎ 2-64-48). *Tutto Mare*, by the sea on the south side of the arches near the plaza, is a large air-con restaurant also with good Italian food (above US$4.50).

The Malecón is lined with boutiques and restaurant/bars. Many have upstairs terraces with fine views of the bay. Prices are considerably higher than in other parts of the city. The *Hard Rock Café* and *Carlos O'Brian's* both serve expensive food but are nonetheless popular with visitors for their festive atmosphere in the evening; *Planet Hollywood*, on the corner of Morelos and Galeana, is similar. Various other places along the Malecón also have music and dancing.

Half a block off the Malecón, the *Cenaduría Doña Raquel* at Vicario 131, serving inexpensive but delicious traditional Mexican food, is open nightly except Monday from 6 to 11.30 pm.

La Fuente del Puente on Insurgentes, just north of the bridge, is a pleasant open-air restaurant/bar with a traditional Mexican quartet every evening except Sunday. It's open Monday to Saturday from 8 am to 10.30 pm, Sunday 9 am to 4 pm. The air-con *Woolworth's Restaurant* at Juárez and 31 de Octubre has good-value set meals for US$2.25, including a drink, with breakfast from 7 to 11 am and lunch from 1 to 4 pm; it's open daily to 6 pm.

Chef Roger (☎ 2-59-00) at Agustín Rodríguez 267, near the market, is an expensive but high quality Swiss restaurant, open Monday to Saturday from 6.30 to 11 pm. *Café des Artistes*, Sánchez 740, has a fine ambience to match its good French cuisine; breakfast/brunch is from 8 am to 3 pm, dinner is from 6.30 to 11.30 pm.

At the other end of the culinary spectrum, a few US fast-food chains have made it to Vallarta, including *McDonald's*, on the corner of Paseo Díaz Ordaz and 31 de Octubre, and *Domino's Pizza*, beside Tutto Mare on the south side of the Malecón. Both are air-con and open every day.

Restaurants – elsewhere The Isla Cuale has a couple of atmospheric but expensive places to enjoy, including *Le Bistro Jazz Café*. Stop by for a drink and the scenery.

Mismaloya has two well-known restaurants: *Chino's Paraíso*, two km upriver from the beach, and *El Edén de Mismaloya*, about five km farther upriver. Both are beautiful (but expensive) open-air restaurants with tables under palapas at spots where you can swim and stretch out in the sun on the boulders, and maybe see some meter-long iguanas doing the same. Both are open daily from around 11 am to 6 pm.

Grocery Stores In the center of town, the giant air-con Gutiérrez Rizo (GR) supermarket on the corner of Constitución and Serdán on the south side of the river, has local merchandise as well as items imported from the USA, including magazines and paperbacks in English. It's open every day from 6.30 am to 11 pm.

Entertainment
Dancing and drinking are Puerto Vallarta's main forms of nighttime entertainment. At night a lot of people just stroll down the Malecón, where you can choose from romantic open-air restaurant/bars to riotous reveling. Entertainment is often presented in the amphitheater by the sea opposite the Plaza Principal. The softly lit Isla Cuale makes a beautiful, quiet, romantic haven for walking in the evening.

Bars & Discos The *Hard Rock Café* along the Malecón has live rock music and dancing every night except Wednesday from around 10 pm to 2 am. The *Zoo* is another place with music and dancing (open 9 pm to 5 am). Or there's *Carlos O'Brian's*, a favorite drinking hole for fun-seeking, rabble-rousing gringos, with dancing into the wee hours. *Planet Hollywood*, on the corner of Morelos and Galeana, also has dancing.

On the south side of the river, *Sí Señor*, a bar/concert hall on Rodolfo Gómez near the corner of Olas Altas, has live rock, jazz, blues or soul bands every night from 10 pm to 2 am (opens 6 pm). *Club Roxy* at Vallarta 217, between Madero and Cárdenas, also has live music (closed Sunday). *Caymanes* on Vallarta is a cheap bar with a pool table, and live music on the weekends.

For jazz fans, the classy *Le Bistro Jazz Café* on the Isla Cuale has over 1000 jazz CDs and a pleasant tropical atmosphere. *Cuiza*, also on Isla Cuale, has live jazz from 8.30 to 11.30 pm (closed Tuesday).

Discos in Vallarta appear and disappear with some regularity. Still popular are *Cactus*, on the south side of the river on the corner of Vallarta and Francisca Rodríguez, and *Christine*, at the Hotel Krystal about seven km north of the city.

Many of the large resort hotels offer evening entertainment. The *Camino Real* south of town gives a free concert, with free drinks and hors d'oeuvres, on the first Thursday of every month.

Puerto Vallarta has a relaxed, congenial gay scene. *Club Paco Paco* at Vallarta 278 is a gay bar where you can get all the latest scoop on gay accommodations and activities; it's open every day from 3 pm to 6 am. *Los Balcones*, upstairs at Juárez 182 near the corner of Libertad, has a dance floor and lots of little balconies; it's open every night from around 9.30 pm. The 'Blue Chairs' at the south end of Playa de los Muertos, beside the Looney Tunes restaurant, is a popular gay beach hangout.

Mariachis Traditional Mexican mariachi music can be enjoyed at several places around town. On the Malecón near the seahorse statue, the upstairs *Mr Tequila's Grill & the Mariachi House* has live mariachi music nightly from 8 to 11.30 pm. After hours, the *Mariachi Loco* restaurant/bar on the corner of Cárdenas and Vallarta has mariachis and other entertainment every night from 10 pm to 1 am (free, but US$5.25 minimum consumption); it's open from 7 pm to 6 am.

Fiestas Mexicanas *La Iguana* at Cárdenas 311 is an old Vallarta favorite, presenting a Fiesta Mexicana with traditional Mexican folkloric dances, mariachis, *ranchero* rope tricks, a piñata, bloodless cockfights, a Mexican buffet, an open bar and a dance band for dancing under the stars every Thursday and Sunday evening from 7 to 11.15 pm. This is said to be the original of what has become a much-copied tourist show; the entry charge is US$25 per person. Other Fiesta Mexicana nights are held at some of the giant luxury hotels around the area, including the *Hotel Krystal, Westin Regina* and *Sheraton Buganvilias*. A weekly schedule is published in the *Vallarta Today* newspaper, or ask at the tourist office.

Cinemas Vallarta has several cinemas, including the *Cine Bahía* on Insurgentes near Madero, the *Cine Vallarta* on Uruguay opposite the Conasupo supermarket on Avenida México a few blocks north of the center, and the *Cine Luz Maria* nearby at Avenida México 227. Often the films are shown in English with Spanish subtitles.

The Chess Club gets together most evenings at around 7 or 8 pm in the lobby of the Hotel Cecattur on the corner of Hidalgo and Guerrero.

Spectator Sports
Bullfights are held every Wednesday from September to May, starting at 5 pm, in the bullring across from the marina.

Things to Buy
Shops and boutiques in Puerto Vallarta sell just about every type of handicraft made in Mexico, but prices are higher here than elsewhere. Try the Mercado Municipal for anything from Taxco silver, sarapes and huarache sandals to wool wall-hangings and blown glass. The market has over 150 shops and stalls; it's open Monday to Saturday from 9 am to 8 pm, Sunday 9 am to 2 pm. Many other shops line Agustín Rodríguez, facing the market.

Getting There & Away
Air Puerto Vallarta's international airport, on highway 200 about 10 km north of the city, is served by a number of national and international airlines. The following list includes details of direct flight destinations, all with connections to other places:

Aeroméxico
   Plaza Genovesa, Locales 2 & 3 (☎ 4-27-77) – Aguascalientes, Guadalajara, León, Los Angeles, Mexico City, San Diego (California)
Alaska Airlines
   Airport (☎ 1-13-50) – Los Angeles, San Francisco, Seattle
American Airlines
   Airport (☎ 1-19-27) – Dallas
Continental
   Airport (☎ 1-10-25) – Houston
Delta
   Airport (☎ 1-10-32) – Los Angeles
Mexicana
   Centro Comercial Villa Vallarta, Local G-18 (☎ 4-89-00, 4-61-65) – Chicago, Guadalajara, Los Angeles, Los Cabos, Mazatlán, Mexico City, San Francisco
TAESA
   Opposite airport (☎ 1-15-21/31) – Mexico City, New York

Bus Intercity bus lines have individual terminals on the south side of the Río Cuale. They include Elite and TNS (☎ 3-11-17, 2-66-66) on the corner of Badillo and Insurgentes, ETN, Primera Plus & Servicios Coordinados/Costalegre (☎ 3-16-16, 2-69-86) on Cárdenas between Constitución and Vallarta, Transportes del Pacífico (☎ 2-06-15) at Insurgentes 282, and Transportes Cihuatlán & Autocamiones del Pacífico

CENTRAL PACIFIC COAST

(☎ 2-34-36) on the corner of Madero and Constitución. Buses depart from the individual terminals or from Plaza Lázaro Cárdenas at Playa Olas Altas. Daily buses include:

Barra de Navidad – 225 km, 3½ hours 1st-class (US$10), five hours 2nd-class (US$8.25); same buses as to Manzanillo
Guadalajara – 344 km, five hours: eight deluxe buses by ETN (US$24); 19 1st-class between 6 am and 1.30 am by Elite (US$18), seven by Primera Plus (US$20) and nine by Transportes del Pacífico (US$18), which also has six slower 2nd-class buses (US$16)
Manzanillo – 285 km, five hours in 1st-class, 6½ hours in 2nd-class: two 1st-class (US$13) and seven 2nd-class (US$10) by Transportes Cihuatlán; five 2nd-class by Servicios Coordinados/Costalegre (US$10); two 1st-class by Elite (US$11); and 1st-class at 8 am by Primera Plus (US$13)
Mazatlán – 459 km, eight hours; four 1st-class by Elite (US$19); 2nd-class at 3 pm by TNS (US$18)
Mexico City (Terminal Norte) – 880 km, 13 to 15 hours: deluxe bus at 6.30 pm by ETN (US$56); four 1st-class by Elite (US$42) and one at 6 pm by Transportes del Pacífico (US$42)
San Blas – 175 km, three hours; 2nd-class at 12.30 and 3 pm by TNS (US$7.25)
San Patricio-Melaque – 220 km, 3½ hours 1st-class (US$10), five hours 2nd-class (US$8); same buses as to Manzanillo
Tepic – 169 km, three to four hours (US$7.75); 2nd-class every half-hour from 4.15 am to 8 pm, and at 10.30 pm, by Transportes del Pacífico
Zihuatanejo – 720 km, 15 hours; 1st-class at 6.35 am and 11.45 pm by Elite (US$28), continuing on to Acapulco (18 hours, US$37)

Car & Motorcycle
Rental agencies in Puerto Vallarta include:

Alfa	☎ 2-56-78
Amigo	☎ 4-68-80
Ansa	☎ 2-65-45
Auto Rentas (Guadalajara)	☎ 2-42-56, 2-61-01
Avis	☎ 1-11-12
Clover	☎ 4-49-10
De Alba	☎ 2-35-76
Dollar	☎ 2-42-56
Hertz	☎ 2-00-24
Marina	☎ 4-77-87
National	☎ 2-05-15
Quick	☎ 2-00-06, 2-35-05

To hire a vehicle you must be at least 25 years of age, have a valid driver's license (a foreign one will do) and a major credit card. If you don't have a credit card you'll have to pay a large cash deposit. It pays to shop around as rates vary widely.

Jeeps are the most popular vehicles. Discounts on jeeps are frequently offered in Puerto Vallarta as an inducement to attend timeshare presentations.

Motorcycles can be hired from Moto Gallo (☎ 2-16-72) at Badillo 324.

Getting Around
To/From the Airport Colectivo vans operate from the airport to town, but not from town to the airport. The cheapest way to get to the airport is on a local bus, which costs US$0.30; the 'Aeropuerto,' 'Juntas' and 'Ixtapa' buses stop outside the airport entrance. A taxi from the city center costs around US$4.

Bus Local buses operate every five minutes from 5 am to 11 pm on most routes and cost US$0.30. Plaza Lázaro Cárdenas at Playa Olas Altas is a major departure hub.

Northbound buses marked 'Hoteles,' 'Aeropuerto,' 'Ixtapa,' 'Pitillal' and 'Juntas' pass through the city heading north to the airport, the Zona Hotelera and Marina Vallarta; the 'Hoteles,' 'Pitillal' and 'Ixtapa' routes can take you to any of the large hotels north of the city.

Southbound 'Boca de Tomatlán' buses pass along the southern coastal highway through Mismaloya to Boca de Tomatlán. They operate every 10 minutes from 6 am to 9 pm and cost US$0.40.

Taxi Taxi prices are regulated by zones; the cost for a ride is determined by how many zones you cross; around town is US$1.30, to the airport US$4, to Mismaloya US$6, and to Nuevo Vallarta US$10.

Boat In addition to taxis on land, Vallarta also has a water taxi departing from Los Muertos Pier and heading south around the bay with stops at Las Ánimas (25 minutes), Quimixto (30 minutes) and Yelapa (45 minutes); the cost is US$13 return for any destination. The boat goes twice a day, at 10.30 and 11 am, and returns mid-afternoon. A water taxi also goes to Yelapa from the beach just north of Chico's dive shop; it departs around 11.30 am.

Cheaper water taxis to the same places depart from Boca de Tomatlán and Mismaloya, both south of town and reachable by local bus. A water taxi to Las Ánimas (15 minutes), Quimixto (20 minutes) and Yelapa (30 minutes) leaves Boca de Tomatlán daily at 10 am and 1 pm, more frequently if enough people want to make the trip; the cost is US$5.25 one way for any destination (double for return). From Mismaloya to these destinations only one water taxi departs, at around 9.30 or 10 am.

Private yachts and lanchas can be hired from the south side of the Playa de los Muertos pier. They'll take you to any secluded beach around the bay; most have gear aboard for snorkeling and fishing. The cost is US$25 per hour for the boat, which holds seven to 10 people. Lanchas can also be hired privately at Mismaloya and Boca de Tomatlán, but they are expensive.

CHAMELA

Chamela, 165 km south of Puerto Vallarta, is little more than a scattering of small settlements along the 11-km shore of the Bahía de Chamela. Much of this shore consists of fine, untouched beaches – perfect escapes, though tourism is slowly creeping in to alter the landscape.

From Chamela's Super Mercado, a km-long road leads to the beachfront *Villa Polinesia & Camping Club* (☎ in Guadalajara 3-285-52-47), with 12 villas, 35 Polynesian-style huts, and shaded trailer spaces with full hookups. The appropriately named *Motel Trailer Park* is just north of the turnoff to the Villa Polinesia.

SAN PATRICIO-MELAQUE
pop 8000; ☎ *335*

Known to locals as Melaque, the small beach resort town of San Patricio-Melaque on the lovely Bahía de Navidad is 60 km southeast of Chamela, just after highway 80 from Guadalajara merges with highway 200. Although it is a little larger than its twin resort town of Barra de Navidad a couple of km along the beach to the southeast, it rarely appears on maps.

Two haciendas owned by foreigners, those of San Patricio (on the east side) and Melaque (on the west), used to stand side by side here, with the dividing line between them running where Calle López Mateos is today. Settlements gradually grew around the two haciendas, and eventually merged into one town, preserving the names of the original towns.

In addition to being a popular beach resort for Mexican families when school is out, and a watering hole for yachties from November to May, the town is famous for its week-long St Patrick's Day celebrations (Fiesta de San Patricio) in March.

The crumbling walls of the once proud Casa Grande Hotel & Resort are a reminder of the earthquake in October 1995 that damaged the town.

Orientation
Everything in Melaque is within walking distance. Most of the hotels, restaurants and public services are concentrated on or near Gómez Farías, running beside the beach, and López Mateos, the street coming in from the highway. Building numbers on Gómez Farías and some other streets are not consecutive, so refer to the map for locations. Barra de Navidad is accessible from Melaque via highway 200 (five km) or by walking down the beach (two km).

Information
Information is provided by the tourist office in Barra de Navidad.

Money The Casa de Cambio Melaque at Local 11 in the Pasaje Comercial Melaque,

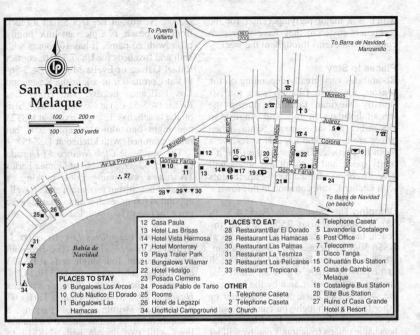

San Patricio-
Melaque

0   100   200 m
0   100   200 yards

To Puerto
Vallarta

To Barra de Navidad,
Manzanillo

To Barra de Navidad
(on beach)

Bahía de
Navidad

PLACES TO STAY
9   Bungalows Los Arcos
10 Club Náutico El Dorado
11 Bungalows Las
    Hamacas
12 Casa Paula
13 Hotel Las Brisas
14 Hotel Vista Hermosa
17 Hotel Monterrey
19 Playa Trailer Park
21 Bungalows Villamar
22 Hotel Hidalgo
23 Posada Clemens
24 Posada Pablo de Tarso
25 Rooms
26 Hotel de Legazpi
34 Unofficial Campground

PLACES TO EAT
28 Restaurant/Bar El Dorado
29 Restaurant Las Hamacas
30 Restaurant Las Palmas
31 Restaurant La Tesmiza
32 Restaurant Los Pelícanos
33 Restaurant Tropicana

OTHER
1   Telephone Caseta
2   Telephone Caseta
3   Church
4   Telephone Caseta
5   Lavandería Costalegre
6   Post Office
7   Telecomm
8   Disco Tanga
15 Cihuatlán Bus Station
16 Casa de Cambio
    Melaque
18 Costalegre Bus Station
20 Elite Bus Station
27 Ruins of Casa Grande
    Hotel & Resort

on Gómez Farías opposite the main bus
station, changes cash and traveler's checks
Monday to Saturday from 9 am to 2 pm
and 4 to 7 pm, Sunday 9 am to 2 pm. There
are no banks in either San Patricio-
Melaque or Barra de Navidad; the closest
banks are in Cihuatlán, about 15 km away.

Post & Communications The post office
is on Orozco near the corner of Corona. It's
open weekdays from 8 am to 3 pm and Saturday from 8 am to noon. Telecomm, with
fax and telegram, is at Juárez 100, on the
corner of Moreno. It's open weekdays from
9 am to 3 pm.

There are several telephone casetas with
fax, including on Corona near the corner of
Hidalgo, on the north and west sides of the
plaza, and by the bus station.

Laundry The Lavandería Costalegre,
Juárez 63, is open Monday to Saturday
from 9 am to 1 pm and 2 to 6 pm and
charges US$0.70 per kg.

Things to See & Do
This is a peaceful little beach town with not
a lot to do – swimming, lazing or walking
on the beach, watching the pelicans fishing
at sunset down at the west end of the bay,
or walking down the beach to Barra de
Navidad are the main activities here. It's a
great place to simply relax and take life
easy.

Fiesta de San Patricio
St Patrick's Day is celebrated in a big way
in this town, with week-long festivities
leading up to March 17 – parties all day,
domino competitions, bull races through
the town every afternoon, and a fiesta with
fireworks every night in the plaza. The 17th
begins with a mass and the blessing of the
fleet. It's held in Los Pelícanos restaurant,

which is a major partying center for the foreigners in town; they have their own contests and events throughout the week.

Places to Stay

Room rates vary greatly depending on the season; the town fills up with tourists (mostly Mexican families) during the school holidays in July and August, in December and at Semana Santa, when prices are higher and it's best to reserve a room in advance. The rest of the time it's pretty quiet, and many of the hotels will give discounts. Bungalows – apartments with kitchens – are common in this town.

Camping The *Playa Trailer Park* (☎ 5-50-65) at Gómez Farías 250, right on the beach, has 45 spaces with full hookups at US$6.50/8.50 for one/two people in a tent, US$8.50 in a trailer, US$0.70 for each extra person. There's also an unofficial campground on a flat area by the beach at the west end of town; it has no water or other facilities, though you can buy water from a truck that comes by. Most of the beachside palapa restaurants nearby will let you have a free shower.

Hotels *Casa Paula* (☎ 5-50-93) at Vallarta 6 is a simple place with just four rooms, each with two double beds; price for two/three/four people is only US$6.50/9/11.

Posada Clemens (☎ 5-51-79) at Gómez Farías 70 on the corner of Guzmán has 14 clean, simple singles/doubles at US$12/14 in winter, US$9/12 in summer. The *Hotel Hidalgo* (☎ 5-50-45) at Hidalgo 7 is a better value, with 13 simple rooms at US$5.25/7.75 and a communal kitchen area. The *Hotel Monterrey* (☎ 5-50-04) at Gómez Farías 27, on the beach opposite the bus station, has a swimming pool, restaurant, parking and 20 rooms with singles/doubles at US$12/22.

The *Hotel de Legazpi* (☎ 5-53-97) on Avenida Las Palmas, on the beach at the west end of town, has a swimming pool and 16 large, bright rooms, some with a sea view and balcony; singles/doubles are US$19/26 in low season, US$41 in high

season. Nearby, at Legazpi 5 half a block from the beach, is a pleasant little family place with no name. It has 10 rooms with bath and two beds for US$7.75/10; contact Rafael Gálvez or Evelia Moreno (☎ 5-56-81) at Corona 95, or ask at the Restaurant Los Pelícanos nearby. The *Hotel Las Brisas* (☎ 5-51-08) at Gómez Farías 9, also on the beach, has 32 triple rooms at US$23 and eight bungalows (sleeping six, but rather cramped) with kitchen at US$45.

The beachside *Club Náutico El Dorado* (☎ /fax 5-52-39, 5-57-66) at Gómez Farías 1A has a swimming pool, parking, a pleasant beachfront restaurant and 56 well-appointed rooms, each with two large beds; price for one to four people is US$34.

Bungalows *Bungalows Los Arcos* (☎ 5-51-84) at Gómez Farías 2 has two-bedroom bungalows with four single beds at US$23 and single/double rooms for US$10/14.

Beside the beach, *Bungalows Las Hamacas* (☎ 5-51-13) at Gómez Farías 97 has a small swimming pool, parking, a cheap beachfront restaurant and 26 bungalows with two double beds (US$13 to US$26 for one to four people); larger bungalows are available. Also on the beach, the *Hotel Vista Hermosa* (☎ 5-50-02) at Gómez Farías 23 opposite the bus station has a swimming pool, parking and 26 bungalows at US$46 for five people, US$67 for eight, plus 21 regular rooms, overpriced at US$26/32; it's free for children under 10.

Bungalows Villamar (☎/fax 5-50-05) at Hidalgo 1 is a pleasant place with five spacious garden bungalows, a children's pool and a raised terrace overlooking the beach. A studio bungalow is US$13, two-bedroom bungalows are US$16, with discounts for weekly or monthly stays. It's popular with North American visitors (English spoken).

The *Posada Pablo de Tarso* (☎ 5-51-17) at Gómez Farías 408 is an attractive place with a large beachside pool and terrace. Prices are low for what you get: 12 big bungalows (with kitchen) sleeping two to six people for US$27 to US$48, and 14 suites (no kitchen) sleeping one to four people for US$12 to US$34.

Places to Eat

A row of pleasant palm-thatched palapa restaurants stretches along the beach at the west end of town. The most popular gringo hangout – especially with yachties – is the *Restaurant Los Pelícanos* (open daily from 9 am to 9 pm). It's run by a gregarious but volatile American woman, Phil Garcia.

Other palapa restaurants along this stretch include the *Restaurant Tropicana* and the *Restaurant La Tesmiza*. A fancier beachside restaurant/bar is the *Restaurant/Bar El Dorado* at the Club Nautico El Dorado, with a great view of the bay. It's open every day from 7 am to 11 pm. Close by (with the same view) are two cheaper places, *Las Palmas* and *Las Hamacas*. You can get a simple snack or meal at many places around the plaza.

Entertainment

Disco Tanga on Gómez Farías is the only one in town; it's open from 10 pm to 3 am every night in high season, Friday to Sunday night in low season. The beachside *Restaurant/Bar El Dorado* at the Hotel Club Naútico has live music and dancing on weekend evenings.

Getting There & Away

Air See the following Barra de Navidad Getting There & Away section for details of air services. The travel agent for flight arrangements is found in that town.

Bus Melaque has three bus stations. The Costalegre and Cihuatlán stations are side by side on the corner of Gómez Farías and Carranza. Both have 1st-class Primera Plus and 2nd-class buses, and serve similar routes with the same prices, though departure times vary. Buses departing daily from these stations go to:

Barra de Navidad – five km, 10 minutes; every 15 minutes, 6 am to 9 pm (US$0.20) or southbound long-distance buses
Guadalajara – 294 km; 10 1st-class (five hours, US$14) and 22 2nd-class (6½ hours, US$12)
Manzanillo – 65 km; 11 1st-class (one hour, US$3); at least hourly 2nd-class, 5.30 am to 9.30 pm (1½ hours, US$2.50)

Puerto Vallarta – 220 km; four 1st-class (3½ hours, US$10) and 17 2nd-class (five hours, US$8.25)

The 1st-class Elite bus station is on Gómez Farías, one block east of the other bus stations. Two buses go daily to Puerto Vallarta (3½ hours, US$10); the one at 5.30 pm continues up the coast all the way to Tijuana (US$85). A bus heads south at 10.30 am for Acapulco (US$29), via Manzanillo (1¼ hours, US$3.25) and Zihuatanejo (US$20).

Taxi A taxi between San Patricio-Melaque and Barra de Navidad costs US$2.75.

BARRA DE NAVIDAD

pop 3000; ☎ 335

The beach resort town of Barra de Navidad is around the bay from San Patricio-Melaque – a two-km walk along the beach, or five km by road. The waves are bigger here than in Melaque – locals from Melaque often come over here for surfing, especially in January when the waves are best. The town is squeezed onto a sandbar between the Bahía de Navidad and the Laguna de Navidad. Like San Patricio-Melaque, it suffered earthquake damage in October 1995 – some of it still visible.

Orientation

Legazpi, the main street, runs beside the beach. Veracruz, the town's other major street and the route to the highway, runs parallel to Legazpi before merging with it at the south end of town, which terminates in a fingerlike sandbar.

Information

Tourist Office The Delegación Regional de Turismo (☎/fax 5-51-00, 5-51-59) is at Jalisco 67, open weekdays from 9 am to 6 pm.

Money There are no banks in Barra de Navidad or San Patricio-Melaque; for banks you must go to Cihuatlán, about 15 km away. You can change money at Vinos y Licores Licorín on Legazpi near the southwest corner of the plaza, open every day

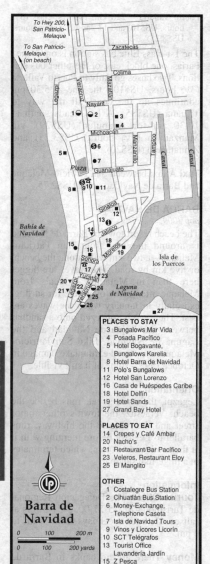

Barra de Navidad

0   100   200 m
0   100   200 yards

PLACES TO STAY
3   Bungalows Mar Vida
4   Posada Pacífico
5   Hotel Bogavante,
    Bungalows Karelia
8   Hotel Barra de Navidad
11 Polo's Bungalows
12 Hotel San Lorenzo
16 Casa de Huéspedes Caribe
18 Hotel Delfín
19 Hotel Sands
27 Grand Bay Hotel

PLACES TO EAT
14 Crepes y Café Ambar
20 Nacho's
21 Restaurant/Bar Pacífico
23 Veleros, Restaurant Eloy
25 El Manglito

OTHER
1   Costalegre Bus Station
2   Cihuatlán Bus Station
6   Money-Exchange,
    Telephone Caseta
7   Isla de Navidad Tours
9   Vinos y Licores Licorín
10 SCT Telégrafos
13 Tourist Office
    Lavandería Jardín
15 Z Pesca
17 Mini-Market,
    Telephone Caseta
22 Parrot Head Inc
24 Cooperativa Boats
26 Colectivo Boats (to Colimilla,
    Grand Bay Hotel)

from 8.30 am to 11 pm, and at Veracruz 212, between Michoacán and Guanajuato.

Post & Communications The post office is inconveniently out of the way on Nueva España, six blocks north and four blocks east of the bus stations; it's open weekdays from 8 am to 2 pm and 4 to 6 pm, Saturday 9 am to 1 pm. The telegraph office, SCT Telégrafos, is on the corner of Veracruz and Guanajuato, on the southeast corner of the plaza. It's open weekdays from 9 am to at least 2 pm.

The mini-market on the corner of Legazpi and Sonora has a telephone caseta, open Monday to Saturday from 11 am to 10 pm, Sunday 11 am to 6 pm. There's another caseta at Veracruz 212.

Travel Agency Isla de Navidad Tours (☎ 5-56-65/66, fax 5-56-67) at Veracruz 204A, opposite the plaza, can make flight arrangements. It's open Monday to Saturday from 10 am to 8 pm.

Laundry Lavandería Jardín at Jalisco 71 opens weekdays from 9 am to 2 pm and 4 to 7 pm, Saturday from 9 am to noon.

Activities
The beach, of course, is Barra de Navidad's prime attraction. Boating on the lagoon is also popular. The local boat operators' cooperative, the Sociedad Cooperativa de Servicios Turísticos Miguel López de Legazpi, at Veracruz 40, is open every day from 6 am to 6 pm, with a price list posted on the wall. Tours are anything from half-hour trips around the lagoon (US$10 for up to eight people) to all-day jungle trips to Tenacatita (US$103). They also offer deep-sea fishing, snorkeling and diving trips, and rides on the 'banana.'

For serious fishing trips, Z Pesca (☎ 5-64-64, fax 5-64-65), Legazpi 213, has better boats and equipment; a six-hour trip costs from US$123. Parrot Head Inc (☎ 5-63-24), run by a Texan known as Butch, offers boat excursions and scuba diving. Find him in El Manglito Restaurant, or in his office opposite.

Tours may be taken to the village of Colimilla across the lagoon. Or you can go halfway down the block where colectivo boats to Colimilla operate every day from 6.30 am to 7.30 pm; the cost is US$0.40 per person each way.

Fishing Tournaments

National and international fishing tournaments are held annually for marlin, sailfish, tuna and dorado, with prizes that include boats and cars.

The most important, the Torneo Internacional de Pesca de Marlin, Pez Vela y Dorado por Equipos, is held for three days around the 3rd week in January. The second most important is the Torneo Internacional de Marlin Club de Pesca Barra de Navidad, held for two days during late May or early June, with another two-day tournament in mid-August. The final tournament of the year is held before Independence Day on September 15 and 16.

Places to Stay – budget

The *Casa de Huéspedes Caribe* (☎ 5-52-37) at Sonora 15 offers one of the best budget deals in town. It has a rooftop terrace and 17 rooms with new bathrooms; singles/doubles are US$5.75/10, or US$6.50/12 in winter. Also good is *Posada Pacífico* (☎ 5-53-59) at Mazatlán 136, on the corner of Michoacán; 25 large, clean rooms are US$7.75/10, or US$9.75/12 in winter. There are also four bungalows (with kitchen) for US$17 for one/two people. If these places are full, try the *Hotel San Lorenzo* (☎ 5-51-39) at Sinaloa 7 near the corner of Mazatlán; its 24 rooms cost from US$10/12.

Places to Stay – middle & top

Barra de Navidad has a number of good mid-range places to stay. One of the best is the *Hotel Delfín* (☎ 5-50-68, fax 5-60-20) at Morelos 23, with 22 large, clean and pleasant rooms looking out onto wide walkways; from most rooms you can view the lagoon and the swimming pool below. It has an exercise and weight room and an outdoor restaurant with a breakfast buffet from US$3. Singles/doubles are US$14/21,

or US$17/25 from December to Easter. The *Hotel Sands* (☎/fax 5-50-18) at Morelos 24 beside the lagoon has a swimming pool, a poolside restaurant/bar and 43 rooms at US$28 (cheaper from June to mid-November), with more expensive suites and bungalows.

On Legazpi several good hotels are right on the beach, including the *Hotel Bogavante* (☎ 5-53-84, fax 5-61-20) with regular rooms at US$18/24, bungalows with kitchen starting at US$35. Next door, the less attractive *Bungalows Karelia* has bungalows at US$23. The *Hotel Barra de Navidad* (☎ 5-51-22, fax 5-53-03) at Legazpi 250, with a restaurant/bar and a beachside swimming pool, has 60 rooms with air-con and cable TV at US$32/39.

Polo's Bungalows (☎ 5-64-10), Veracruz 174, opened in 1995. Nine compact bungalows with kitchen are US$19 for one/two people. The *Bungalows Mar Vida* (☎ 5-59-11, fax 5-53-49) at Mazatlán 168 is a fine little guesthouse with a swimming pool; five studio apartments have air-con and cable TV and cost US$35.

The luxurious new *Grand Bay Hotel* (☎ 5-63-90), on an island in the lagoon, is very expensive but use of its golf course is included. Take a colectivo boat over (US$0.30, every 10 minutes).

Places to Eat

There are plenty of restaurants to choose from. Several are on terraces overlooking the beach, with a beautiful view of the sunset. Several more are beside the lagoon, and still others are on Calle Veracruz, in the center of town.

Beside the beach, *Nacho's* on Legazpi just south of Yucatán has good food; it's open daily from 8 am to 10 pm. Next door, at Legazpi 206, the *Restaurant/Bar Pacífico* offers a comida corrida for US$2.75; in low season it closes evenings and on Monday. Beside the lagoon, *Veleros* on Veracruz is a good restaurant/bar with a fine view, open every day from noon to 10 pm. Nearby, also overlooking the lagoon, are the *Restaurante Eloy* and *El Manglito*.

One of the most enjoyable restaurants in town is *Crepes y Café Ambar*, upstairs on the corner of Veracruz and Jalisco. It's a clean '50% vegetarian' restaurant topped by a high palapa roof, with good music and probably the best coffee in town. It's open daily from 8 am to 3 pm and 5 to 11 pm, but only from November to Easter.

Entertainment
The Hotel Sands has the *El Galeón* disco. It also has a poolside bar open from November to Easter; the two-for-one happy hour, from 4 to 6 pm, is popular, especially since it includes the use of their lagoonside pool.

Getting There & Away
Air Barra de Navidad and Melaque are served by the Playa de Oro international airport, 25 km southeast on highway 200. To get there take a taxi (half an hour, US$14), or a bus 15 km to Cihuatlán and a cheaper taxi from there. Daily direct flights include Aeroméxico to Guadalajara, Mexicana to Mexico City and Aero California to Tijuana and Los Angeles.

Bus See the entry for San Patricio-Melaque – just about every bus that stops there also stops here, and vice versa (15 minutes before or after). The Cihuatlán bus station is at Veracruz 228; virtually opposite is the Costalegre bus station.

Melaque In addition to the northbound long-distance buses, you can take one of two local buses to Melaque (every 15 minutes, 6 am to 9 pm; US$0.20), each stopping at one of the bus stations (buses stopping on the southward side of the road loop round Legazpi and back to Melaque).

A taxi between Barra de Navidad and San Patricio-Melaque costs US$2.75.

MANZANILLO
pop 93,000; ☎ *333*
Manzanillo is a major port and industrial city, with a tangle of train tracks, shipping piers and traffic surrounded by stagnant marshes that locals call lagoons. Surprisingly, away from the center and out around the Bahía de Manzanillo and Bahía de Santiago there are beaches – but you have to search for them. There's also deep-sea fishing, and good bird-watching in the lagoons and around the golf course.

Orientation
Manzanillo extends for 16 km from northwest to southeast. The resort hotels and finest beaches begin on Playa Azul across the Bahía de Manzanillo from Playa San Pedrito, the closest beach to the center (about one km away). Farther around the bay is the Santiago Peninsula, a rocky outcrop occupied by Las Hadas Resort and the beaches of La Audiencia, Santiago, Olas Altas and Miramar. Just west of Miramar is the Laguna Juluapan.

Central Manzanillo is bound by the Bahía de Manzanillo to the north, the Pacific Ocean to the west, and the Laguna de Cuyutlán to the southeast and south. Avenida Morelos, the principal avenue, runs along the northern edge of the city beside the sea, west from Avenida Niños Héroes, which leads to highway 200. The city center begins at the zócalo (also known as Jardín Obregón) on Avenida Morelos, and continues southward with the major street, Avenida México, crossed from west to east by a number of streets that change names on either side of it.

Information
Tourist Offices The helpful tourist office (☎ 3-22-77/64, fax 3-14-26) is around the bay in Playa Azul at Boulevard Miguel de la Madrid 4960, between the Fiesta Mexicana and Marbella hotels. It's open weekdays from 8.30 am to 3 pm and 6 to 8 pm, and on weekends in high season. In the center of Manzanillo, basic tourist information is available from the tourist police (☎ 2-10-02) and (in high season) from the Presidencia Municipal building.

Money Many banks are scattered around the city's center. Bital on Avenida México

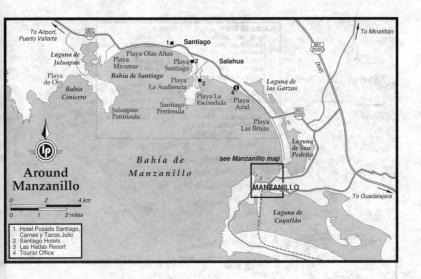

Around Manzanillo

0	2	4 km
0	1	2 miles

1 Hotel Posada Santiago,
  Carnes y Tacos Julio
2 Santiago Hotels
3 Las Hadas Resort
4 Tourist Office

is open weekdays from 8 am to 7 pm and Saturday from 9 am to 2.30 pm.

Post & Communications The post office is south of the zócalo at Galindo 30. It's open weekdays from 8 am to 7 pm, Saturday 9 am to 1 pm.

The Telecomm office, with telegram, telex and fax, is in the Presidencia Municipal building on the southeast corner of the zócalo. It's open weekdays from 8 am to 6 pm, Saturday 9 am to 12.30 pm.

There are pay phones in the zócalo and on Avenida México. Computel, with long-distance telephone and fax, has offices at Avenida Morelos 144, between the zócalo and the train station, and at Avenida México 302, between Guerrero and Cuauhtémoc. Both offices are open daily from 7 am to 10 pm.

Beaches
The closest beach to town, **Playa San Pedrito**, about one km east of the zócalo, is too close to the port. The next closest beach, **Playa Las Brisas**, caters to a few hotels and has plenty of space. **Playa Azul** stretches northwest from Las Brisas

and curves around to Las Hadas Resort and the best beaches in the area: **La Audiencia, Santiago, Olas Altas** and **Miramar**.

Getting to these beaches from the town center is easy: take any 'Santiago,' 'Las Brisas' or 'Miramar' bus from the train station. The 'Miramar' bus to Playa Miramar takes 40 minutes; it stops en route at Las Brisas, Playa Azul, Santiago, La Audiencia and Olas Altas. Miramar and Olas Altas have good waves for surfing or bodysurfing. Boards can be rented at Miramar. Playa La Audiencia, on a quiet cove at the west side of the Santiago Peninsula, has more tranquil water and is popular for water-skiing. The 'Las Hadas' bus takes a scenic, circular route down the Santiago Peninsula – there's a magnificent view of the beaches either side if you get off 30 meters up from the Hotel Risco la Audiencia.

Water Sports
Snorkeling, diving, windsurfing, water-skiing, sailing and deep-sea fishing are all popular water sports around the bay. Underworld Scuba (☎ /fax 3-06-42), Plaza Pacífico on the Santiago Peninsula, charges US$80

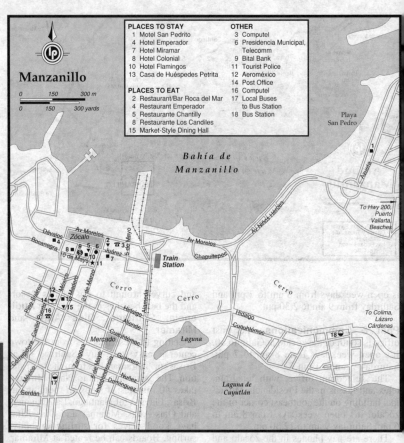

PLACES TO STAY
1 Motel San Pedrito
4 Hotel Emperador
7 Hotel Miramar
8 Hotel Colonial
10 Hotel Flamingos
13 Casa de Huéspedes Petrita

PLACES TO EAT
2 Restaurant/Bar Roca del Mar
4 Restaurant Emperador
5 Restaurante Chantilly
8 Restaurante Los Candiles
15 Market-Style Dining Hall

OTHER
3 Computel
6 Presidencia Municipal, Telecomm
9 Bital Bank
11 Tourist Police
12 Aeroméxico
14 Post Office
16 Computel
17 Local Buses to Bus Station
18 Bus Station

for two beach or boat dives including equipment: feed eels and octopuses by hand in Playa La Audiencia, or view the cargo ship, which sank in 1959 and sits nine meters under water near Playa Miramar.

Special Events
In early February a sailing tournament coming from San Diego, California, in even-numbered years, and from Puerto Vallarta in odd-numbered years, ends with celebrations at the Las Hadas Resort.

The Fiestas de Mayo, held from May 1 to 10, celebrate Manzanillo's anniversary with sporting competitions and other events. The Fiesta de Nuestra Señora de Guadalupe is held from December 1 to 12 in honor of Mexico's patron saint.

Manzanillo calls itself the 'World Capital of Sailfish'; in 1957 it was the site of a world record when 336 sailfish were caught during a three-day fishing tournament. The sailfish *(pez vela)* season is from November to March, with marlin, red snapper, sea bass and tuna also plentiful. The biggest international tournament is held in November, with a smaller national tournament in February.

Places to Stay

The best places to stay in central Manzanillo are within a block or two of the zócalo. This area is safe and clean. A few blocks south in the town center there are a number of places to stay, but the area is comparatively dirty and squalid. Around the bay, where the better beaches are, hotels tend to be more expensive; Playa Santiago, half an hour away by bus, is an exception.

Places to Stay – budget & middle

Camping The only trailer park is *La Marmota* (☎ 2-32-90) on the road to Minatitlán, but the tourist office says it's not clean.

Hotels – center A few doors from the southeast corner of the zócalo, the *Hotel Miramar* (☎ 2-10-08) at Juárez 122 has clean singles/doubles at US$6.50/10. Half a block south of the zócalo, the *Hotel Flamingos* (☎ 2-10-37) at Madero 72 charges US$6.50/9; rooms are nicely furnished for a budget place. Half a block from the southwest corner of the zócalo, the clean but very basic *Hotel Emperador* (☎ 2-23-74), at Dávalos 69, has singles/doubles (one bed) for US$6.50/7.75; two-bed doubles are US$9. Top-floor rooms are a little brighter than the rest. The hotel's restaurant has good food and is one of the cheapest in town.

In the center, the *Casa de Huéspedes Petrita* (☎ 2-01-87) at Allende 20 is very basic (no hot water) but clean and economical. Rooms with one double bed and shared bath are US$4.50; rooms with two double beds and private bath are US$9.75 for two/three people, US$11 for four people.

Rather less faded than the others is the *Hotel Colonial* (☎/fax 2-10-80, 2-12-30) at Bocanegra 100 on the corner of Avenida México, a block south of the zócalo; it has a restaurant, parking and 38 rooms at US$16/17 with air-con and TV.

Motel San Pedrito (☎ 2-05-35, fax 2-22-24), Teniente Azueta 3, by Playa San Pedrito, has a swimming pool and enclosed parking; rooms are US$10/16. From the center, walk 10 minutes along the newly built Malecón walkway, or take a bus.

Hotels – Playa Santiago A 10- or 15-minute walk (or five-minute ride) from highway 200 and Santiago town, on a fine stretch of beach on the bluff at Playa Santiago, are four reasonably priced beachfront hotels. All have swimming pools and two (the Marlyn and Playa de Santiago) have restaurant/bars.

Cheapest of the lot is the *Hotel Anita* (☎ 3-01-61) with 36 big if slightly faded rooms at US$6.50/10. Next door, the *Hotel Marlyn* (☎ 3-01-07) has regular rooms at US$19/26 for singles/doubles, and bungalows (sleeping six) with kitchen for US$58, all with private balconies overlooking the sea. Next door to that, the attractive *Hotel Brillamar* (☎ 4-11-88) has rooms with air-con and TV at US$26, plus a variety of bungalows with kitchen. Last is the *Hotel Playa de Santiago* (☎ 3-00-55, 3-02-70, fax 3-03-44) with 61 rooms with private sea-view balcony for US$34; two children under 10 can share the room free with their parents. Charging this price, the place could do with some renovations.

In Santiago on the main road is *Hotel Posada Santiago* (☎ 3-00-14), Boulevard Costero; it's a simple place that doesn't provide hot water. Singles/doubles cost US$6.50/7.75. There are good places to eat close by.

Places to Stay – top end

Most of Manzanillo's top-end accommodations are on or near the beaches outside the city center. Many are situated along the beach side of the main road along Playa Azul. The best known of the top-end hotels is *Las Hadas Resort* (☎ 4-00-00, fax 4-19-50), a white Arabian-style resort on the Santiago peninsula where the film *10*, featuring Bo Derek, was made. Rates for the 220 rooms are upwards of US$135 a night – 25% higher from Christmas to Easter.

A couple of newer top-end places perhaps surpass even Las Hadas. The *Club Maeva* (☎ 5-05-95/96, fax 5-03-95) at Playa Miramar has 514 villas and rooms and is great for active types. The nightly cost of US$90 per person (US$135 in winter) includes all you can eat and drink, water sports and good entertainment. A similar deal is given by the *Sierra Radisson Plaza* (☎ 3-20-00, fax 3-22-72) on the Santiago Peninsula near Las Hadas, where the whole package costs US$103/170 in a single/double room.

More moderately priced, the *Hotel Villas La Audiencia* (☎ 3-08-61, 3-06-83, fax 3-26-53) on the Santiago peninsula is a good value in the top-end range, especially for families. All the villas are equipped with kitchen, air-con and satellite TV, and there's a swimming pool and restaurant/bar. Villas with one/two/three bedrooms cost US$79/103/110. Also more moderately priced and closer to town is the *Hotel La Posada* (☎ /fax 3-18-99), at Lázaro Cárdenas 201 on Playa Azul, a friendly beachfront lodge with a swimming pool. The hotel is in a good position for snorkeling and windsurfing. Singles/doubles are US$45/56 most of the year, US$75/84 from December 16 to April 30, breakfast included.

Places to Eat

There are a number of good places to eat around the zócalo. The *Restaurant/Bar Roca del Mar* on the east side of the zócalo has a pleasant atmosphere and is good for all meals. Among its specialities is a seafood comida corrida with seafood soup, rice, fish or shrimp, and dessert for US$4.50. It's open daily from 7 am to 10 pm. On the south side of the zócalo, the *Restaurante Chantilly* is a popular restaurant open from 7 am to 10 pm every day except Saturday.

Restaurant Emperador, on the ground floor of the Hotel Emperador at Dávalos 69, half a block west of the zócalo, is simple and small but has good food at some of the most economical prices in Manzanillo, with a comida corrida, meat or seafood meals for US$1.70, breakfast or enchiladas for just US$0.90. It's open every day from 8 am to 10 pm.

Also good is *Los Candiles* at the Hotel Colonial, a block south of the zócalo on the corner of Avenida México and Bocanegra. It has a patio section and comida corrida costs US$4; opening times are Monday to Saturday from 8 am to 11 pm.

A market-style dining hall on the corner of Madero and Cuauhtémoc is open daily from around 7 am to 8 pm, with a number of stalls to choose from.

Many more restaurants are spread out around the bay. *Colima Bay Café* on the highway at Playa Azul is a fun place with good food. At Santiago, on the main boulevard about 300 meters west of the Jardín, is *Carnes y Tacos Julio*, serving excellent inexpensive meat choices daily from noon to 1 am. The similarly-named place a few doors down is also good, and across the road 100 meters to the west is *Juanito's*, popular with gringos.

Entertainment

If you're here on a Sunday evening, stop by the zócalo, where everyone from toddlers to grandparents are out enjoying an ice cream, the company and the balmy night air. This tradition, which has disappeared in many parts of Mexico, is still alive and well in Manzanillo. Sometimes a band plays in the gazebo to entertain the crowd.

The nightlife for tourists in Manzanillo is mostly spread out around the bay. *Vog*, on the highway at Playa Azul, is a popular disco with a US$5.75 cover charge. Beside it, the *Bar de Felix* has no cover charge and many people like it better for dancing. *Teto's Bar* near the Hotel Fiesta Mexicana on Playa Azul is another popular dancing spot with live music. Also on Playa Azul, *Colima Bay Café*, one of the Carlos Anderson chain, puts on a good time for tourists.

The luxurious *Club Maeva* on Playa Miramar has the *Disco Boom Boom* (cover charge US$6.50/10 for women/men) and the *Tropical Hut*. They also present theme entertainment several nights weekly: sometimes entry is free (eg, the Tropical Latin night), other times (eg, Saturday's Mexican Fiesta night, Tuesday's Best of Broadway night) entry costs US$16 which includes a theme buffet and open bar. Events last from 8 to 11.30 pm; phone for reservations (☎ 5-05-96 ext 4).

Getting There & Away

Air The Playa de Oro international airport is 35 km northwest of the city on highway 200. Aeroméxico has daily direct flights to Guadalajara, while Mexicana has daily (except Tuesday in low season) direct flights to Mexico City, both with connections to many other places.

The Aeroméxico office (☎ 2-12-67, 2-17-11) is at Local 107, in the Centro Comercial on Avenida Carrillo Puerto between Allende and Cuauhtémoc; it's open weekdays from 9 am to 2 pm and 4 to 7 pm, Saturday 9 am to 2 pm. Mexicana (☎ 3-23-23) only has an office at the airport, but its tickets are sold and serviced at the Aeroméxico office in town, as are those of Aero California which has direct daily flights to Los Angeles and Tijuana, via Tepic.

Bus The bus terminal is about 1.5 km east of the center. Ticket offices, luggage-storage, a telephone caseta and small restaurants are in a row of huts along the north side. Daily destinations include:

Armería – 45 km, 45 minutes (US$1.40); every 15 minutes, 5 am to 10.30 pm, by Sociedad Cooperativa de Autotransportes Colima, Armería, Cuyutlán, Manzanillo; seven by Autotransportes del Sur de Jalisco

Barra de Navidad – 60 km, one hour; at least hourly 2nd-class, 5.30 am to 9.30 pm, by Costalegre and Autocamiones Cihuatlán (US$2.50)

Colima – 101 km, 1½ to two hours; 2nd-class every 30 minutes, 5 am to 10 pm, by Sociedad Cooperativa de Autotransportes Colima, Armería, Cuyutlán, Manzanillo (US$2.75); and nearly all buses to Guadalajara (1¼ to 1½ hours, 1st-class US$4)

Guadalajara – 325 km, 4½ hours (2nd-class US$11, 1st-class US$12 to US$14); 16 by Autobuses de Jalisco; 11 by Costalegre; 12 by Autocamiones Cihuatlan; seven by Autotransportes Sur de Jalisco

Lázaro Cárdenas – 313 km, seven hours; 1st-class 5 am and noon by Elite (US$13); five 2nd-class by Autotransportes Sur de Jalisco (US$11)

Mexico City (Terminal Norte) – 843 km, 12 hours; 'via corta' (short route) or via Morelia; 1st-class 7.30 pm and 9 pm by Elite (US$34); 1st-class 7 pm and 9.30 pm and 2nd-class 3.45 pm and 6.15 pm by Costalegre (US$35); 2nd-class 2.30 pm and 5 pm by Autobuses de Occidente (US$29)

Puerto Vallarta – 285 km, five to six hours; 1st-class 8 am and noon (US$13) and 10 2nd-class (US$10) by Autocamiones Cihuatlan; three 1st-class (US$11) by Elite; three 2nd-class by Costalegre (US$10)

San Patricio-Melaque – 65 km, one to 1½ hours; same as to Barra de Navidad

ETN (☎ 4-10-40) has its own bus terminal near Santiago at km 13.5 on Boulevard Costera; its deluxe buses go to Mexico City, Guadalajara and Colima.

Train The train station is on Avenida Morelos, two blocks east of the zócalo. The ticket office (☎ 2-28-50; 2-19-92 from 9 am to 2 pm) is open daily for ticket sales from 9.30 pm. There's only one departure, the segunda clase Train 91, which leaves at 11.10 pm for Guadalajara (supposedly 7½ hours, US$5) via Colima (two hours, US$1.10). Train 92 departs Guadalajara at 8 pm, arriving in Manzanillo about 5.30 am.

Getting Around

To/From the Airport Transportes Turísticos Benito Juárez (☎ 4-15-55) operates a door-to-door van to/from the airport. The cost is US$18 for private service or US$6.50 per person for colectivo service. A taxi from the center to the airport costs about US$13.

Bus Local buses heading around the bay to San Pedrito, Salahua, Santiago, Miramar and all the beaches along the way depart from Avenida México in front of the train station or from the main bus station every 10 minutes from about 6 am to 11 pm. The fare ranges from US$0.30 to US$0.50, depending on how far you go.

The 'Campos,' 'Rocío' and 'Torres' local bus routes connect the center with the bus station, stopping on the corner of Avenida Madero and Domínguez and at the market along the way. They operate daily from 6 am to 9.30 pm (US$0.30).

Taxi Taxis are plentiful around Manzanillo. From the center of town it's US$0.80 to the bus station, US$3.25 to Playa Azul, US$4.50 to Playa Santiago, US$6.50 to Playa Miramar and US$13 to the airport. Agree on the price before you get into the cab.

CUYUTLÁN & PARAÍSO
pop Cuyutlán 1900; Paraíso 200; ☎ *332*

The small black-sand beach resort towns of Cuyutlán and Paraíso are southeast of Manzanillo. Cuyutlán, the more developed of the two, is near the southeastern end of the Laguna de Cuyutlán, about 40 km from Manzanillo and 12 km from the inland town of Armería. Paraíso is some six km farther southeast.

Both towns have a few hotels and restaurants that are popular with Mexican families and seldom visited by norteamericanos. Beachfront accommodation consequently costs much less here.

In Cuyutlán most of the hotels and places to eat are clustered near the beach. If you arrive in town by bus you'll be let off on Hidalgo, on one side of the zócalo.

Walk four blocks toward the sea on Hidalgo and you'll be right in the middle of the hotel and restaurant area beside the beach.

Aside from its long stretch of relatively isolated beach, Cuyutlán is known for its 'green wave' in April and May, caused by little green phosphorescent critters. There's also a turtle farm, on the beach about three km toward Paraíso; it's open daily and entry costs US$0.70.

Paraíso is a small fishing village, with a black-sand beach and a number of hotels and *enramadas* (simple thatched-roof seafood restaurants).

Information

Neither Cuyutlán or Paraíso has a post office or bank; for these you'll have to go into Armería (see Getting There & Away). Both towns do have telephone casetas, however. Cuyutlán's caseta is on Hidalgo, in the shop on the corner one block past the zócalo, heading away from the beach. In Paraíso it's in the restaurant opposite the beach and by the bus stop.

Places to Stay – Cuyutlán

At Christmas and Semana Santa, all the hotels fill up with Mexican families on holiday. If you come at these times you should reserve in advance. Most of the hotels require that you take three meals a day included in the price at these times; the cost for room and meals will be around US$20 per person.

Camping You can camp on the beach to the right of the hotels. A couple of simple thatch-roofed restaurants nearby have signs posted out front saying they rent showers and baths or '*cuartos con baño*' – simple rooms that may be only partitions in large halls behind the restaurants. These are the cheapest rooms in town.

Hotels As you come to the beach on Hidalgo you'll reach the corner of Veracruz, the beachside road. On this corner are two of Cuyutlán's best budget hotels, with other hotels a block or two either side. The *Hotel Morelos* (☎ 6-40-13), on this corner at Hidalgo 185, has 48 clean, pleasant rooms with private bath and ceiling fan at US$5.25 per person. Opposite this, the *Hotel Fénix* (☎/fax 6-40-82) is another good place, with 15 rooms also at US$5.25 per person; English is spoken. To your right is the *Hotel Tlaquepaque* (☎ 6-40-11) at Veracruz 30, with simple singles/doubles/triples at US$6.50 per person.

Also pleasant is the *Hotel El Bucanero* (☎ 6-40-05), on the beachfront behind the Hotel Fénix; the cost is US$4/5.25 per person for interior/sea-view rooms. Opposite this, also right on the beach, the large *Hotel Ceballos* (☎ 6-40-04) at Veracruz 10 is more expensive but not really much better. To the left of this at Veracruz 46, the *Hotel San Rafael* (☎ 6-40-15) has a swimming pool and a beachfront restaurant/bar; singles/doubles are US$7.75/13, or US$10/19 with sea view.

Places to Stay – Paraíso

Of the hotels, the fancy one is the *Hotel Paraíso* (cellular ☎ 7-18-25; in Colima ☎ 331-2-10-32, fax 331-2-24-07), with a swimming pool, pleasant terraces, a seafood restaurant and 60 rooms at US$18 for up to two adults and two children.

The other hotels can be reached via the resort's caseta (☎ 2-00-25). *Posada & Enramada Valencia*, new in 1993, has eight rooms with one/two beds at US$9/13. Or there's the very basic *Enramada Los Equipales* with 12 rooms at US$5.25 each. A couple of similar places are nearby. Otherwise you could camp on the beach, or probably string up a hammock under one of the enramadas.

Places to Eat

Cuyutlán Several of the hotels have good seafood restaurants. The *El Bucanero* and the *Siete Mares*, attached respectively to the Hotel El Bucanero and the Hotel San Rafael, are attractive beachfront restaurant/bars. On the corner of Hidalgo and Veracruz, also sharing with hotels, are two of the town's most economical restaurants:

the *Restaurante Morelos* and the *Restaurante Fénix*. Both offer good-value meals at about US$2.50 for breakfast or dinner, US$2.75 for a comida corrida. For a simple snack, stands on the beach sell seafood and cold drinks. Or you can grab a snack at one of the restaurants near the plaza.

Paraíso All the beachfront enramadas serve basically the same food at the same price. The classiest of the hotel restaurants is poolside at the *Hotel Paraíso*, open daily from 8 am to 6 pm. Some enramadas stay open later, until around 9 pm.

Getting There & Away

Cuyutlán and Paraíso are connected to the rest of the world through Armería, a dusty town on highway 200 about 50 km southeast of Manzanillo and 45 km southwest of Colima. From Armería to Cuyutlán it is 15 km down a paved road passing through orchards and coconut plantations to the coast; a similar road runs eight km southwest from Armería to Paraíso.

To reach either place by bus involves going first to Armería and changing buses there. The Sociedad Cooperativo de Autotransportes Colima Manzanillo bus line, with an office and bus stop on Armería's main street, operates 2nd-class buses to Manzanillo every 15 minutes from 5.30 am to 11 pm (US$1.40, 45 minutes) and to Colima every half-hour from 5.40 am to 11.40 pm (US$1.40, 45 minutes). Its buses leave every 15 minutes for Tecoman (US$0.50, 15 minutes), where you can connect with buses going southeast on highway 200 (to Lázaro Cárdenas etc). A couple of doors away, Flecha Amarilla has 2nd-class buses to Mexico City and Guadalajara.

Buses to Cuyutlán and Paraíso depart from Armería's market, a block or two northwest of the long-distance bus offices; they cross Netzahualcóyotl (the main street) beside the Restaurant El Frontera. To Cuyutlán they depart every half-hour from 6.30 am to 8 pm (US$0.50, 20 minutes). To Paraíso they go every 45 minutes from 6 am to 7.30 pm (US$0.40, 15 minutes).

Between Cuyutlán and Paraíso, there are taxis but no buses; to go by bus from one to the other, you must return to Armería and change buses there. By taxi, Armería to Cuyutlán is US$4, Armería to Paraíso is US$2, and Cuyutlán to Paraíso is US$3.

LÁZARO CÁRDENAS
pop 135,000; ☎ 753
Lázaro Cárdenas is the largest city on the coast of Michoacán, one of Mexico's most beautiful states. The city is named after the reform-minded leader who served as governor of Michoacán from 1928 to 1932, and as president of Mexico from 1934 to 1940. In the late 1960s he encouraged President Díaz Ordaz to begin constructing a huge US$500-million Sicartsa iron and steel works and US$40-million port in the village of Melchor Ocampo. The project didn't get under way until after his death in 1970, during the administration of President Luis Echeverría (1970-76).

Echeverría renamed the village Lázaro Cárdenas and erected what became a slum city around the project, which by then was slated to cost over US$1 billion. The resulting plant produced steel wire, which Mexico really didn't need, and was run with coal imported from Colombia. The plant cost much more than it could ever earn and greatly contributed to a 450% increase in Mexico's foreign debt, which was more than US$19 billion by 1976.

Today the plant continues to run, supposedly with injections of British capital, but more emphasis seems to have been placed on the city's burgeoning port facilities. While not as much of an eyesore as it was in the past, the city has nothing of real interest to travelers. Reasons to stop here are to stock up on food and water, change buses, and head for Playa Azul, a beach resort 24 km to the west.

Getting There & Away
Air Lázaro Cárdenas has an airport served by a variety of obscure airlines; Aeromar flies to Mexico City and Aerocuahonte flies to Uruapan, Morelia and Guadalajara.

Tickets are sold at Chinameca Viajes (see Train).

Bus While the town itself is not of much interest to travelers, Lázaro Cárdenas is a terminus for some bus routes, so you may need to change buses here if you're traveling in this part of the country.

Lázaro has several bus terminals, all within a few blocks of each other. The Galeana and Parhikuni bus lines (☎ 2-02-62, 2-30-06), with services northwest to Manzanillo and inland to Uruapan, Morelia and Mexico City, share a terminal at Avenida Lázaro Cárdenas 1810, on the corner of Calle Constitución de 1814. Opposite is the terminal (☎ 7-18-50) shared by Autobuses de Jalisco, Sur de Jalisco and Autobuses de Occidente; the same destinations are serviced, plus Guadalajara. Avenida Lázaro Cárdenas is the city's main street and there are many hotels, restaurants and shops around these bus stations.

The Estrella Blanca terminal (☎ 2-11-71), used by the Elite and Cuauhtémoc bus lines, has buses southeast to Zihuatanejo, Acapulco, and then inland from Acapulco to Mexico City, with other daily services heading up the coast to Mazatlán and Tijuana. Its terminal is two blocks behind the Galeana terminal, on Calle Francisco Villa, between Corregidora and Calle Constitución de 1814. Tres Estrellas de Oro (☎ 2-02-75), with buses to Mexico City and Acapulco, is at Corregidora 318, two blocks from Estrella Blanca and four blocks from Galeana.

Daily services from Lázaro Cárdenas include:

Acapulco – 340 km, six hours. Estrella de Oro, hourly 2nd-class 4.50 am to 4.50 pm (US$6.75), hourly 1st-class 5.50 am to 9.50 am and at 9 pm (US$11); Estrella Blanca, hourly 2nd-class from 11.15 am to 4.15 pm (US$7.50), seven 1st-class (US$9)

Manzanillo – 313 km, seven hours, 2nd-class; 4.15, 5.30 and 11.30 am, from Galeana terminal (US$11); 2.30 pm by Sur de Jalisco (US$11)

Mexico City (Terminal Sur or Terminal Poniente) – 711 km; Estrella de Oro, hourly

1st-class 5.50 am to 9.50 am and at 9 pm (US$25); Autobuses de Occidente, 2nd-class at 3 pm (13 hours, US$22); Estrella Blanca, 1st-class at 8 pm and 9.45 pm (10 hours, US$25 and US$31); Galeana terminal, two 2nd-class via Uruapan and Morelia

Morelia – 406 km, seven hours; 23 daily, 1st- and 2nd-class, from Galeana terminal (US$14 and US$15); 7.30 pm by Autobuses de Occidente; 11.30 pm by Estrella Blanca

Uruapan – 280 km, six hours; same buses as to Morelia (US$9 to US$12)

Zihuatanejo – 100 km, two hours; same buses as to Acapulco (US$2.25 to US$3.75)

Combis to Playa Azul, via La Mira, go along Avenida Lázaro Cárdenas every 10 minutes from 6 am to 9 pm. They stop outside the Jalisco/Occidente bus terminal. The 24-km trip takes about half an hour and costs US$0.80.

Train If you're heading inland toward the mountains of Michoacán, the train from Lázaro Cárdenas to Uruapan makes a pleasant alternative to the bus. It takes six hours to reach Uruapan, the same as the bus, but it does not have to negotiate as many curves as the highway, making for a smoother trip. The train departs Lázaro Cárdenas every day at noon, arriving in Uruapan at around 6.15 pm. Primera clase seats cost US$7.25. The same train continues on from Uruapan to Pátzcuaro, Morelia, Toluca and Mexico City. See the schedule in the Mexico City Getting There & Away section.

In Lázaro Cárdenas the train station is on the outskirts of town, several km from the center. Tickets are sold at the station (☎ 2-28-36) every day from 9 am to noon. They are also sold in town at Chinameca Viajes (☎ 7-08-74, fax 2-49-44) at Mina 178, in the Sol del Pacífico Hotel, two blocks from the Estrella Blanca bus station. This helpful travel agency is open weekdays from 8 am to 8 pm, Saturday 8 am to 7 pm.

The '44 Estación' local combi route, stopping on Avenida Lázaro Cárdenas outside the Galeana bus terminal, connects the bus and train stations (US$0.40); a taxi would cost US$2.

PLAYA AZUL
pop 3200; ☎ *753*

Playa Azul is a small beach resort town backed by lagoons formed by a tributary of the Río Balsas. Although it mostly attracts Mexican families, foreign travelers also enjoy its beautiful beach and surfable waves. A strong undertow, however, can make swimming in the seas here dangerous; also beware of stingrays lying on the sand. Swimming is better at Barra de Pichi, on the coast a km or two east of Playa Azul, where there's a large lagoon with boat trips for seeing the plants, animals and birds.

Orientation & Information

Playa Azul is so small and everything is so close that there's little need for street names, since everyone knows where everything is – but basically there are four streets in town, all running parallel to the beach. The beachside street, usually referred to as the Malecón, is officially named Zapata. The second street inland is Carranza; the third one is Madero; and the fourth is Independencia.

A Pemex station *(la gasolinera)* on the corner of Independencia marks the beginning of town as you enter from the highway. This is a major landmark in the town, with buses and combis arriving and departing from here. The beach is three blocks straight ahead. A few blocks east (left as you face the sea) is a large plaza. Almost everything you need in the town is found somewhere between the plaza and the gasolinera. A long row of enramadas stretches along the beach.

The post office, on Madero at the northwest corner of the plaza, is open weekdays from 9 am to 4 pm. Telecomm is in the same building (different entrance). A telephone caseta is on Carranza.

Activities

Pools provide a safer alternative to swimming in the sea. The Balneario Playa Azul, on the Malecón behind the Hotel Playa Azul, has a large swimming pool, a big waterslide and a restaurant/bar. It's open every day from 10 am to 6 pm; admission is US$1.30 per person, but it's free to guests of the Hotel Playa Azul or its trailer park.

Both the Hotel Playa Azul and the Hotel María Teresa Jericó also have courtyard swimming pools with poolside restaurants (see Places to Eat).

There are swimming and boat trips at Barra de Pichi, one or two km down the beach.

Places to Stay

Camping If you have a hammock, you can string it up at one of the enramadas along the beach; ask permission from the family running the restaurant, who probably won't mind, especially if you eat there once or twice. If you don't have your own hammock they may let you use one of theirs. There are public toilets and showers at a couple of the enramadas, and on the road running between the Pemex station and the beach.

The *Hotel Playa Azul* has a small trailer park with full hookups in the rear; the cost of US$7.75 per space includes free use of the balneario and the hotel's swimming pool.

Hotels & Bungalows *Hotel Costa de Oro* (☎ 6-00-86) on Madero, near the plaza, has some parking and 18 clean rooms for US$6.50/9 (may be negotiable).

The *Bungalows de la Curva* (☎ 6-00-58) on Independencia, one block toward the beach from the Pemex station at the entrance to town, has a small swimming pool. Singles/doubles without kitchen are US$10, rooms with kitchen for two or three people are US$19. Next door, the *Hotel Delfín* (☎ 6-00-07) on Carranza is a pleasant place with 25 clean rooms around a small swimming pool courtyard with a restaurant; singles/doubles are US$12. Light sleepers in both places may be disturbed by nighttime crowing from the chicken farm, opposite on Madero.

Bungalows Delfín is on the west side of the plaza, and has 10 bungalows at only US$7.75/13/16 for two/four/five people. *Hotel María Isabel* (☎ 6-00-30/16), on Madero on the far side of the plaza, has a swimming pool and 30 large, clean rooms at US$9/11 for singles/doubles.

The large, 73-room *Hotel Playa Azul* (☎ 6-00-24/88, fax 6-00-92) on Carranza is the town's most upmarket hotel, with 'económica' rooms for US$21; rooms around the attractive pool start at US$28. Another fine hotel, and better value, is the *Hotel María Teresa Jericó* (☎ 6-00-05, 6-01-30, fax 6-00-55) at Independencia 626, on the inland side of the plaza. It has a swimming pool and poolside restaurant/bar, parking, and 42 clean, comfortable rooms, all with air-con and TV; singles/doubles are US$19 the first night, with a 10% discount for subsequent nights.

Places to Eat

Two small family restaurants, the *Restaurant Galdy* and the *Restaurant Familiar Martita*, both on the market street near Madero, around the corner from the Hotel Playa Azul, are often recommended by locals – both serve good food at very economical prices and are open every day from around 7 am to 11 pm. Galdy has good comida corridas for US$1.70.

The poolside restaurant/bar at the *Hotel Playa Azul* is a favorite with travelers; if you come here to eat or drink, you can swim in the pool for free. It's open every day from 7 am to 11 pm. The same applies with the pool at the *Hotel María Teresa Jericó*, but here you must spend at least US$10 per person in its restaurant/bar. The small poolside restaurant at the *Hotel Delfín* is also recommended by travelers – it has a limited but cheap menu.

Enramadas line the beachfront. All charge the same prices and serve basically the same selection of fresh seafood.

Getting There & Away

Combis run about every 10 minutes from 6 am to 9 pm from Lázaro Cárdenas (see under that listing). They enter Playa Azul and go down Carranza, dropping you off anywhere along the way. In Playa Azul, catch the combis on Carranza or when they loop back on Independencia. The fare to Lázaro Cárdenas (30 minutes) is US$0.80.

Intercity buses do not pass through Playa Azul; they will drop you off at the highway junction in La Mira, seven km away.

A taxi from Lázaro Cárdenas to Playa Azul costs about US$11.

ZIHUATANEJO & IXTAPA

pop Zihuatanejo 80,000; Ixtapa 12,000; ☎ *755*

Not so long ago, Zihuatanejo ('see-wah-tah-NAY-ho') was a small fishing village and nearby Ixtapa ('iks-STAP-pah') was a coconut plantation. Then in 1970 Fonatur, the Mexican government tourism development organization that built Cancún, decided that the Pacific Coast needed a Cancún-like resort to bring more tourist dollars into Mexico.

Using market studies of American tourists, Fonatur chose Ixtapa, 210 km northwest of Acapulco, for its new resort complex. Proximity to the USA, an average temperature of 27°C, tropical vegetation and, most importantly, the quality of the beaches, were its criteria. Fonatur bought the coconut plantation, laid out streets, built reservoirs, strung electrical lines and invited the world's best known hotel chains to begin construction.

Today, Ixtapa is a string of impressive resort hotels spread out along the Bahía del Palmar; the Club Méditerranée and some fine beaches are farther west beyond Punta Ixtapa. The luxurious hotels, restaurants and shops of Ixtapa are expensive, and many travelers cringe at Ixtapa's artificial glitz created for the gringos.

Zihuatanejo, on the other hand, eight km away, though quite touristy, retains an easy-going coastal town ambience, and its setting on a small, beautiful bay with a number of fine beaches makes it a pleasant place to visit. Small-scale fishing is an important part of the town's economy; if you walk down on the beach near the pier in the early morning you can join the pelicans in greeting the returning fishermen and see the morning's catch.

Orientation

Though Zihuatanejo's suburbs are growing considerably, spreading around the Bahía de Zihuatanejo and climbing the hills behind the town, in the city's center everything is compressed within a few square blocks. It's difficult to get lost; there are only a few streets and their names are clearly marked. Ixtapa, eight km away, is easily reached by frequent local buses or by taxi.

Information

Tourist Offices In Zihuatanejo the municipal Dirección de Turismo (☎/fax 4-83-01), on Alvarez just east of the basketball court, is open Monday to Saturday from 9 am to 3 pm and 6 to 8.30 pm and Sunday from 9 am to 6 pm. Free maps and brochures are available.

'Las Gatas' Were Not Cats . . . & Other Tales of Zihuatanejo

Several places around Zihuatanejo and Ixtapa have names rooted in the distant past. The name 'Zihuatanejo' comes from the Nahuatl word 'Zihuatlán,' meaning 'place of women' (it was occupied solely by women); the Spanish added the suffix '-ejo,' meaning 'small.' 'Ixtapa,' also from the Nahuatl dialect, means 'white place'; it was so named not only for its white sands but also for the white guano left by the sea birds on the rocky islands just offshore.

The beaches around the Bahía de Zihuatanejo also have historical names. Playa Madera (Wood Beach) got its name from the timber that was sent from here to various parts of the world; at one time there was also a shipyard here. The name of Playa La Ropa (Beach of the Clothes) commemorates an occasion when a Spanish galleon coming from the Philippines was wrecked in front of the bay, and its cargo of fine silks was washed up on this beach. Playa Las Gatas (Beach of the Cats) was not actually named for cats, but for the nurse sharks that inhabited the waters here in ancient times – harmless sharks without teeth, called 'cats' because of their whiskers. ∎

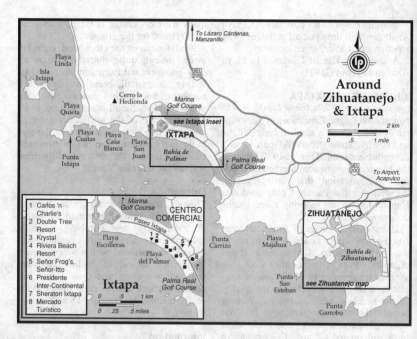

Around Zihuatanejo & Ixtapa

In Ixtapa the state-run Sefotur tourist information office (☎ /fax 3-19-67), officially called the Sub-Secretaría de Fomento Turístico de la Costa Grande de Guerrero, is at Seco la Puerta 2, near the tourist police station and opposite the Hotel Presidente Inter-Continental. It's open weekdays from 9 am to 7 pm and usually Saturday morning.

Zihuatanejo and Ixtapa both have many sidewalk kiosks and small offices with tourist information. While their real purpose is to promote time-share schemes in Ixtapa, they can provide free maps and answer any questions you may have. (They'll encourage you to go for a free breakfast or cocktail at some new development in Ixtapa.)

Money Zihuatanejo and Ixtapa both have a number of banks and casas de cambio where you can change US dollars and traveler's checks. The banks give the best rate of exchange; Banamex on Galeana in Zihuatanejo is open weekdays from 9 am to 3 pm. The casas de cambio give a slightly less favorable rate but they're open longer, more convenient hours. In Zihuatanejo the Casa de Cambio Ballesteros on Galeana near the corner of Bravo is open daily from 8 am to 9 pm.

American Express (☎ 3-08-53, fax 3-12-06), in Ixtapa at the Hotel Krystal Ixtapa, is open Monday to Saturday from 9 am to 2 pm and 4 to 6 pm.

Post & Communications The post office in Zihuatanejo, situated in the northwest section of the town center, is open weekdays from 8 am to 7 pm, Saturday 9 am to 1 pm. Since it has been moved to this slightly inconvenient location, several other places in town, all of them near post boxes which are serviced daily, have started selling stamps. Among them is the Byblos bookstore at Galeana 2, with a post box outside. In Ixtapa you can mail letters from any big hotel.

The Zihuatanejo Telecomm office, with pay phones, telegram, telex and fax, is in the same building as the post office; it's open weekdays from 9 am to 6 pm, Saturday and Sunday 9 am to noon.

Long-distance telephone and fax are available at a number of telephone casetas in Zihuatanejo, including two places on the corner of Galeana and Ascencio.

Laundry Lavandería Super Clean, in Zihuatanejo at González 11 on the corner of Galeana, offers free delivery within Zihuatanejo (☎ 4-23-47); a three-kg service wash costs US$2.75. It's open Monday to Saturday from 8 am to 8 pm. Around the corner on Cuauhtémoc near the corner of González, the Tintorería y Lavandería Aldan does laundry and dry cleaning.

Museo Arqueológico de la Costa Grande

At the north end of Paseo del Pescador in Zihuatanejo, this museum houses exhibits on the culture and archaeology of the Guerrero coast, plus changing exhibitions. It is open Tuesday to Sunday from 10 am to 6 pm; admission is US$0.50.

Beaches

Waves are gentle at all of the beaches on the Bahía de Zihuatanejo. If you want big ocean waves you'll have to go over to Ixtapa, which takes only a few minutes on the local bus.

On the Bahía de Zihuatanejo, **Playa Municipal**, right in front of town, is the least appealing for swimming. Standing on this beach you can see several other beaches spread around the bay, starting with Playa Madera just past the rocky point on your left, then the long, white stretch of Playa La Ropa past that, and finally, directly across the bay, Playa Las Gatas.

Playa Madera was formerly isolated from Playa Municipal by a couple of rocky points, but now a lighted walkway around the rocky sections has made it an easy five-minute walk from town.

Walk over the hill along the coast road for about another 20 minutes or so from Playa Madera and you reach the broad, two-km expanse of **Playa La Ropa**, bordered by palm trees and seafood restaurants. It's a pleasant walk, with the road rising up onto cliffs offering a fine view over the bay. About the most beautiful beach on the bay, La Ropa is great for swimming, parasailing, water-skiing, jet-skiing and the 'banana.' You can also hire sailboards or sailboats.

Opposite Zihuatanejo, **Playa Las Gatas** is a protected beach, crowded with sunbeds and restaurants. It's good for snorkeling (there's some coral growth) and as a swimming spot for children, but beware of sea urchins. According to legend, Calzontzin, a Tarascan chief, built a stone barrier here in pre-Hispanic times to keep the waves down and prevent sea creatures from entering, making it a sort of private swimming pool. Shacks on the beach hire snorkeling gear for around US$4 per day.

Boats to Playa Las Gatas depart from the Zihuatanejo pier every 20 minutes (if there are enough passengers) from 8 am to about 5 pm. Tickets (US$1 each way) are sold at the ticket booth at the foot of the pier; return tickets (US$2) are valid only on the day of purchase. Or you can reach Playa Las Gatas by walking around the bay from Playa La Ropa; a road takes you half the way, then there's 10 minutes of scrambling up and down rocks before you reach Playa Las Gatas.

Between Zihuatanejo and Ixtapa, **Playa Majahua** is accessible via a new road that serves a new hotel zone there, similar to Ixtapa. The beach faces the open sea, so it has large waves and similar conditions to Ixtapa.

Ixtapa's big hotels line **Playa del Palmar**, a long, broad stretch of white sand. Be very careful if you swim here: the large waves crash straight down and there's a powerful undertow. The west end of this beach, just before the entrance to the lagoon, is called **Playa Escolleras** by the locals and it's a favorite spot for surfing. Farther west, past the marina, are three small beaches that are among the most beautiful in the area: **Playa San Juan, Playa Casa Blanca** and **Playa Cuatas**.

To the west, past Punta Ixtapa, are **Playa Quieta** and **Playa Linda**. From Playa Linda boats run every 40 minutes (if there are enough passengers) to **Isla Ixtapa**, which is just offshore and has four beaches, all with calm water – they're excellent for snorkeling. The roundtrip boat ride (five minutes each way) costs US$2; the boats operate every day from 8 am to about 5 pm.

A boat also goes to Isla Ixtapa from the Zihuatanejo pier. It departs once a day (if there are eight people or more) at 11 or 11.30 am, departing the island at around 4 pm. The trip (US$6.25 roundtrip) takes about an hour each way. The ticket office is at the foot of the pier.

Snorkeling & Scuba Diving

Snorkeling is good at Playa Las Gatas and even better on Isla Ixtapa. There is an abundance of species here due to a convergence of currents, and there is sometimes great visibility, up to 35 meters. Whales and manta rays might be seen in the summer.

Snorkel gear can be rented at either place for around US$4 per day. The same beaches also have dive operators, who will take you for a dive for around US$45/70 for one/two tanks, or give you scuba lessons in the quiet water. The most professional dive outfit in Zihuatanejo is the NAUI-affiliated Zihuatanejo Scuba Center (☎/fax 4-21-47, divemexico@mail.com) at Cuauhtémoc 3, opposite Banamex. They offer morning and afternoon dives every day; stop by to look at their underwater photos and pose any questions you may have about diving in the area.

Sport Fishing

Sport fishing is also popular. Sailfish are caught here all year round; seasonal fish include blue or black marlin from March to May, roosterfish in September-October, wahoo in October, mahi mahi or dorado in November-December, and Spanish mackerel in December. Three fishermen's cooperatives are based near Zihuatanejo pier: the Sociedad Cooperativa de Lanchas de

PLACES TO STAY
5 Hotel Lari's
8 Casa de Huéspedes Miriam
9 Hotel Imelda
13 Hotel Posada Coral
14 Villa Juvenil Zihuatanejo
18 Hotel Casa Aurora
19 Hotel Amueblados Valle
23 Hotel Casa Bravo
33 Hotel Raúl Tres Marías Centro
37 Hotel Amueblados Isabel
39 Posada Citlali
41 Hotel Raúl Tres Marias
50 Hotel Avila & Casa de Huéspedes La Playa
53 Bungalows Pacíficos
54 Bungalows Sotelo
55 Bungalows Allec, Bungalows Ley
56 Hotel Brisas del Mar
57 Hotel Palacios
59 La Casa Que Canta
61 Hotel Sotavento-Catalina
62 Trailer Park Los Cabañas
63 Hotel Villa Mexicana
64 Trailer Park La Ropa
65 Villa del Sol
70 Owen's Beach Bungalows

PLACES TO EAT
10 Los Braceros
11 Tamales y Atoles Any
16 Cafetería Nueva Zelanda
20 Il Paccolo & Don Juliano
21 Fonda Economica Susy
22 Pollos Locos
25 Paul's
26 Restaurant Deli
34 Garrobo's
35 Restaurant El Patio
38 Panificadora El Buen Gusto
40 Casa Puntarenas
44 La Sirena Gorda
45 Casa Elvira
49 Mariscos Los Paisanos
66 Restaurant/Bar Tata's
66 La Perla
67 Rossy's
69 Oliverio, Chez Arnoldo's

OTHER
1 Post Office, Telecomm
2 Local Buses to Ixtapa
3 Cinemas Vicente Guerrero
4 Estrella de Oro Bus Station
6 Lavandería Super Clean
7 Tintorería y Lavandería Aldan
12 Mercado Municipal de las Artesanías
15 Mercado Turístico La Marina
17 Plata de Taxco
27 Byblos Bookshop
29 Casa de Cambio Ballesteros
29 Telephone Casetas
30 D'Latino
31 Hertz
32 Mexicana
34 Aeroméxico
36 Zihuatanejo Scuba Center
42 Ticket Office for Boats to Playa Las Gatas, Isla Ixtapa
43 Harbor Master
47 Basketball Court
48 Tourist Office
51 Museo Arqueológico de la Costa Grande
52 Plaza Olof Palme
58 Puerto Mío, Tristar Trimaran
60 Mirador
68 Las Gatas Pier

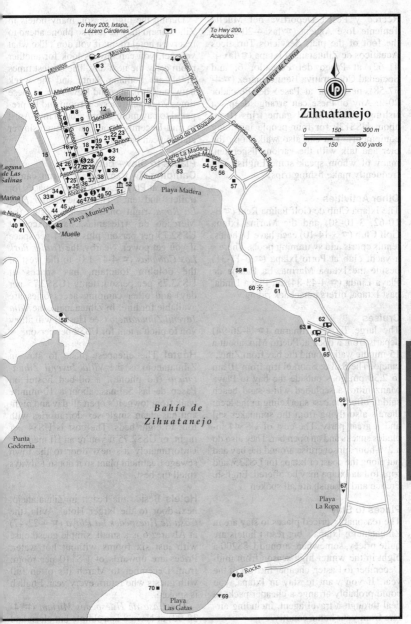

Zihuatanejo

0   150   300 m
0   150   300 yards

To Hwy 200, Ixtapa,
Lázaro Cárdenas

To Hwy 200,
Acapulco

Morelos
Morelos

Paseo del Pinar
Canal Agua de Correa

Cerro de Mayo
Altamirano
Cuauhtémoc
Nava
Guerrero
Juárez
Mercado
González
Ejido
Galeana
Bravo
Paseo de la Boquita
Camino a Playa La Ropa

Cerro La Madera
Cerro de López Mateos

Ascencio
Alvarez
Pescador

Laguna
de Las
Salinas

Marina

a Noria

Playa Municipal

Muelle

Playa Madera

Playa
La Ropa

Bahía de
Zihuatanejo

Punta
Godornia

Rocks

Playa
La Gatas

Playa
Las Gatas

CENTRAL PACIFIC COAST

Recreo y Pesca Deportiva del Muelle Teniente José Azueta (☎/fax 4-20-56) at the foot of the pier; Servicios Turísticos Acuáticos de Zihuatanejo Ixtapa (☎/fax 4-41-62) at Paseo del Pescador 6; and Sociedad Cooperativa Benito Juárez (☎ 4-37-58), next door at Paseo del Pescador 20-2. Any of these can arrange deep-sea fishing trips or small game trips (from about US$120 for four people including equipment). You can also walk along the pier and talk with the various fishermen, many of whom speak some English and frequently make fishing trips.

Other Activities

The Ixtapa Club de Golf Palma Real (☎ 3-10-62, 3-10-30) and the Marina Ixtapa Golf Club (☎ 3-14-10) each have 18 holes, tennis courts and swimming pools. There's a yacht club at Porto Ixtapa (☎ 3-11-31) beside the Ixtapa Marina. La Palapa de Playa Linda (☎ 4-43-84) on Playa Linda, past Ixtapa, offers horseback riding.

Cruises

The large *Tristar* trimaran (☎ 4-26-94) departs from a dock at Puerto Mio, about a 15-minute walk around the bay from Zihuatanejo. The Sail & Snorkel trip from 10 am to 2.30 pm goes outside the bay to Playa Manzanillo, a secluded white-sand beach said to offer the best snorkeling in the area; there's also flying from the spinnaker sail and a great party. The cost of US$44 includes snacks and an open bar. They also do a 2½-hour sunset cruise around the bay and out along the coast of Ixtapa for US$35, and trips to Isla Ixtapa may be offered. English, French and Spanish are all spoken.

Places to Stay

The reasonably priced places to stay are in Zihuatanejo; Ixtapa's big resort hotels are quite pricey, somewhere around US$200 a night in the winter high season from mid-December to Easter, cheaper the rest of the year. If you want to stay in Ixtapa, you could probably arrange a cheaper package deal through a travel agent, including air-fare from your home country.

During the high season many hotels in Zihuatanejo may be full, so phone ahead to reserve a hotel room; if you don't like what you get, you can always look for another room early the next day. The busiest times of all are Semana Santa and the week between Christmas and New Year; at these times you must reserve a room and be prepared to pay more. From around mid-April to mid-December, tourism is much slower and you can bargain.

Places to Stay – budget

Camping Two small family-run camp-grounds at Playa La Ropa offer spaces for trailers and tents. The basic *Trailer Park La Ropa*, right on the beach beside the Mercado de Artesanías, has spaces at US$2.75 per person, plus US$4 per space if you get power. Nearby, the *Trailer Park Los Cabañas* (☎ 4-47-18), to the west of the dolphin fountain, has spaces at US$3.75 per person; tents (US$2.75 per day) and other camping accessories are available for hire. In Zihuatanejo, the *Villa Juvenil Zihuatanejo* (see Hostel) will allow you to pitch a tent for US$2 per person.

Hostel The cheapest place to stay in Zihuatanejo is the *Villa Juvenil Zihuatanejo* (no phone), a 60-bed hostel on Paseo de las Salinas, about a 10-minute walk from town. It's open all day and night and has clean single-sex dormitories with four to eight beds. The cost is US$4 per night, or US$2.75 if you're an HI member. Unfortunately it's next door to the town sewage treatment plant so it doesn't always smell the best.

Hotels Beside the beach in Zihuatanejo, next door to the larger Hotel Avila, the *Casa de Huéspedes La Playa* (☎ 4-22-47) at Alvarez 6 is a small, simple guesthouse with just six rooms without hot water. Prices are upwards of US$10 per room; from December to March it's often full with guests who return every year. English is spoken.

The *Casa de Huéspedes Miriam* (☎ 4-38-90) at Nava 8 is a simple but clean and quiet guesthouse with rooms at only US$5.25 per person. *Hotel Lari's* (☎ 4-37-67) at Altamirano 4 is a similar place, with off-street parking and singles/doubles at US$7.75/13. *Hotel Posada Coral* (☎ 4-54-77), on Los Mangos at Las Palmas, near the market, has clean rooms with tiled bathrooms for US$7.75/12.

The *Hotel Casa Aurora* (☎ 4-30-46) at Bravo 27 has 14 rooms at US$7.75/16 per person in low/high seasons, US$19 with air-con; ask for one of the upstairs rooms. The *Hotel Casa Bravo* (☎ 4-25-48) at Bravo 11 has six clean, pleasant rooms with TV at US$10/17, but traffic outside can be noisy.

Posada Citlali (☎ 4-20-43) at Guerrero 3 is very pleasant, with terrace sitting areas and rooms around a courtyard filled with trees and plants. The rooms are comfortable and clean and cost US$13/20 most of the year, US$16/22 December to April.

The *Hotel Raúl Tres Marias* (☎ 4-21-91, 4-25-91) at La Noria 4, Colonia Lázaro Cárdenas, is just across the water from town, over a small footbridge. This is many budget travelers' favorite place to stay in Zihuatanejo; many of its 25 rooms open onto large terraces with flowers and views over town and the bay. Rooms with cold-water bath are US$10/16 most of the year, US$12/22 from December to April.

Places to Stay – middle

The *Hotel Imelda* (☎ 4-76-62, fax 4-31-99) at González 11 has a small swimming pool and enclosed parking. Compact clean rooms with one double bed and fan are US$19; rooms with two beds, TV and air-con are much bigger and cost US$27. *Hotel Raúl Tres Marías Centro* (☎/fax 4-67-06), Alvarez 52, has 17 simple but clean singles/doubles with air-con at US$23/27.

The *Hotel Avila* (☎/fax 4-20-10) at Alvarez 8, right on the beach, has terraces overlooking the sea, private parking and large, well-equipped rooms with air-con, fan and TV. Rooms are US$32/39, or US$39/45 with sea view; add US$6.50 in high season.

The *Hotel Amueblados Valle* (☎ 4-20-84, ☎/fax 4-32-20) at Guerrero 14 is a good deal, with five large, airy one-bedroom apartments with everything you need, including fully equipped kitchens, at US$22/25 in low/high season and three two-bedroom apartments at US$40/50 in low/high season. If they're full (which they often are in high season), try the *Hotel Amueblados Isabel* (☎ 4-36-61, fax 4-26-69) at Ascencio 11, with fully equipped two/three-bedroom apartments at US$43/48, US$10 higher in July and August and at Christmas and Easter. Or ask Luis Valle at the Hotel Amueblados Valle about other apartments in town, which may be cheaper, especially for longer stays.

Playa Madera Playa Madera, only a five-minute walk from the center of Zihuatanejo, has several good places to stay, most of them bungalows with fully equipped kitchens, all with large terraces offering fine views of the bay. Closest to town, *Bungalows Pacíficos* (☎ /fax 4-21-12) on Eva S de López Mateos, Cerro de la Madera, has six attractive bungalows with fully equipped kitchens at US$50. Anita Hahner, the Swiss owner, is a gracious and helpful hostess who speaks English, Spanish and German, and can help you find anything from good restaurants to good bird-watching spots.

At Eva S de López Mateos 3, the *Bungalows Sotelo* (☎ 4-35-45) has one/two/three-bedroom bungalows that cost US$26/52/77 most of the year. Next door, *Bungalows Allec* (☎ 4-20-02) has one/two-bedroom bungalows at US$19/39. Next door again, *Bungalows Ley* (☎ 4-45-63, 4-40-87) has six one/two-bedroom bungalows with fan or air-con; prices start at US$25 and rise in high season (June to August and November to April).

Most rooms at the *Hotel Brisas del Mar* (☎/fax 4-21-42) on Eva S de López Mateos don't have kitchens but it's a pleasant hotel with a large swimming pool, terraces, a beachfront restaurant and doubles at US$32/41 with street/sea view (cheaper in summer). The *Hotel Palacios* (☎ 4-20-55) on Adelita, also with a beachfront terrace and small swimming pool, has singles/

doubles for US$23/34, slightly higher with air-con and in high season. The price includes breakfast.

Playa Las Gatas Playa Las Gatas has just one place to stay, *Owen's Beach Club Bungalows* (☎ 4-83-07), with six free-standing bungalows around peaceful grounds with only the sound of the surf and the sea breezes rustling through the palms – a very Polynesian feel. The bungalows, all made of natural materials, cost US$50/65 for three/four people (kids free). It's operated by Owen, an ex-New Yorker who has been living on this beach since 1969 'and loving every minute of it'; he's written a useful guide to Zihuatanejo and Ixtapa.

Places to Stay – top end
Most of the top-end places to stay are giant resorts in Ixtapa, but Playa La Ropa also has some good top-end hotels. A favorite, the *Hotel Sotavento-Catalina* (☎ 4-20-32/34, fax 4-29-75), on the hill overlooking Playa La Ropa, has one of Zihuatanejo's most beautiful settings; its white terraces are visible from all around the bay. Singles/doubles cost from US$44/47 up to US$106/112, depending on size, view and facilities (rates drop in low season); there's no charge for children under 12 staying with their parents. Nearby, *La Casa Que Canta* (☎ 4-65-29, fax 4-79-00), also visible from all around the bay, is much more expensive; its thatched awnings and rustic adobe-style walls are eye-catching but rather pretentious in a luxury hotel.

Villa del Sol (☎ 4-22-39, in the USA and Canada 888-389-2645; fax 4-27-58) on Playa La Ropa is a 36-room luxury resort where low-season rates are US$176 per double. During winter high season the price is US$305 including breakfast and dinner, and children under 14 aren't permitted. Also on Playa La Ropa, the *Hotel Villa Mexicana* (☎/fax 4-36-36, 4-37-76) has rooms from US$65.

Other top-end hotels, all in Ixtapa, include the *Sheraton Ixtapa, Riviera Beach Resort, Westin Ixtapa, Double Tree Resort, Krystal, Qualton Club, Stouffer Presidente* and *Continental Plaza*, among others. *Presidente Inter-Continental* and *Club Méditerranée* have all-inclusive rates. Travel agents can arrange packages at any of Ixtapa's big top-end hotels.

Places to Eat
Seafood in Zihuatanejo is fresh and delicious. *Casa Elvira* at Paseo del Pescador 8, open every day from 7 am to noon and 1 to 10 pm, specializes in seafood and has some of the best food in town, as does the pricier *Garrobo's* across the street at Alvarez 52, open daily from 2 to 10.30 pm. On Paseo del Pescador near the basketball court, *Mariscos Los Paisanos* and *Restaurant/Bar Tata's* have tables inside or right on the beach, with fine views of the bay. Mariscos Los Paisanos has good fresh seafood and is open daily from 9 am to 9 pm, while Tata's is open daily from 8 am to 10 or 11 pm, with a good selection of breakfasts.

La Sirena Gorda, on Paseo del Pescador near the foot of the pier, is a casual open-air place popular for all meals from breakfast to a late-night snack; it's open from 7 am to 10 pm daily except Wednesday. *Fonda Economica Susy* on Bravo serves some of the cheapest food in town; the comida corrida is US$1.60 and it's open Monday to Saturday from 8 am to 6 pm.

Tamales y Atoles Any, at Ejido 35 on the corner of Guerrero, has excellent traditional Mexican food. It's reasonably priced and open from 8 am to 11 pm or midnight every day; phone for free delivery (☎ 4-73-73).

Paul's, named after its Swiss owner/chef, serves expensive but delicious food, Monday to Saturday from 2 to 10 pm. It's currently on Cinco de Mayo between Ascencio and Bravo but may move in 1998 – check with the tourist office.

On Cinco de Mayo, beside the Catholic church on the corner of Ascencio, the *Restaurant El Patio* is a popular patio restaurant, open only in high season. For Italian food there's *Ristorante-Bar-Pizzeria Don Juliano* and *Il Piccolo*, next door to each other at Bravo 22 near the corner of Guerrero. Don Juliano is open daily from 3 to

11 pm (closed Tuesday in low season), Il Piccolo daily from 4.30 pm to midnight. Both serve meals from about US$3.

Restaurant Deli, Cuauhtémoc 12B, serving Mexican and international fare, has tables on the sidewalk, inside and on the rear garden patio; it's open Monday to Saturday from 8 am to 11 pm. The new US owner plans to introduce barbecues and live jazz music. *Cafetería Nueva Zelanda* at Cuauhtémoc 23, stretching through the block to Galeana on the other side, is a clean, popular café open every day from 7 am to 10 or 11 pm; English and Spanish are spoken and you can get anything they have 'to go' *(para llevar)*.

Pollos Locos at Bravo 15 is a simple open-air place serving wood-grilled chicken and other meats; it's open every day from 1 to 11 pm. *Los Braceros* at Ejido 21 has a sidewalk grill where you can see the meat being cooked – their menu features a variety of meat and vegetable combinations and other tasty meat dishes. It's open daily from 6 pm to 1 am.

Casa Puntarenas on La Noria, across the water from town over a small footbridge, is a simple family-run patio restaurant open for breakfast daily from 8.30 to 11 am and for dinner from 6 to 9 pm. The atmosphere is relaxed and enjoyable, and its reputation for serving large portions of good, inexpensive food draws a steady crowd; it's open only from December to March.

A good bakery is the *Panificadora El Buen Gusto* at Guerrero 8A, open Monday to Saturday from 7.30 am to 10 pm.

Playa La Ropa & Playa Las Gatas Both beaches have plenty of beachside restaurants specializing in seafood. On Playa La Ropa, *Rossy's* and *La Perla* are popular and good. On Playa Las Gatas, *Restaurante Oliverio* prepares good seafood; *Chez Arnoldo's* is better but pricier. *Owen* (see Places to Stay) has opened a nicely-situated restaurant – reserve ahead in the evening.

Ixtapa Ixtapa has plenty of restaurants to choose from, in addition to all the big hotel restaurants. *Carlos 'n Charlie's, Señor Frog's* and *Señor-Itto* are all popular for a good meal and a good time; the latter two are side by side in the Centro Comercial, opposite the Presidente Inter-Continental, Carlos 'n Charlie's is farther west, by the Hotel Posada Real. Between the two locations is *Montmartre*, serving up tasty French cuisine.

Entertainment

Many bars have a happy hour; *Tata's* (5 to 7 pm) and *Los Paisanos* (5 to 8 pm), side by side on the beach on Zihuatanejo's Playa Municipal, attract a jolly sunset crowd. The bar of the Hotel Sotavento-Catalina, Playa La Ropa, is a great place to watch the sunset (happy hour till 8 pm).

Zihuatanejo has a new disco, *D'Latino*, open from 10 pm to 4 am. There's a cover charge of US$2.75 on Friday to Sunday, other times entry is free (closed Monday).

Most of the nightlife is in Ixtapa. All the big hotels have bars and nightclubs, and most also have discos. Perhaps the best disco is *Christine* at the Hotel Krystal. The *Sanca Bar* at the Sheraton is popular for dancing, with Mexican music. Also popular in Ixtapa are *Carlos 'n Charlie's* and *Señor Frog's*, lively restaurant/bars with dancing, both in the Carlos Anderson chain. Behind Señor Frog's is *Los Mandiles*, a restaurant/bar with an upstairs disco. The new *Skyfuss* disco is nearby.

Several of Ixtapa's big hotels hold Fiestas Mexicanas in the evening, with a Mexican buffet and open bar, and entertainment including traditional Mexican dancing, mariachis, rope and cockfighting demonstrations, as well as door prizes and dancing; the total price is around US$35. The Sheraton has fiestas on Wednesday night from 7 to 10.30 pm all year round; in the high season several other hotels also have fiestas, including the Dorado Pacífico (on Thursday). Reservations can be made directly or through travel agents.

Things to Buy

Mexican handicrafts, including ceramics, wood carvings, huaraches, shells and shell crafts, silver from Taxco and masks from around the state of Guerrero, are available. In Ixtapa there's the Tourist Market opposite the Sheraton. In Zihuatanejo the Mercado Turístico La Marina on Cinco de Mayo has the most stalls. A few stalls are in the Mercado Municipal de las Artesanías on González near Juárez. Many artesanías shops are in the block west of the basketball court, such as El Jumil, Paseo del Pescador 9. It specializes in authentic Guerrero masks; Guerrero is known for its variety of interesting masks and there are some museum quality ones here, many costing around US$12.

Several shops around Zihuatanejo sell silver from Taxco; Plata de Taxco on the corner of Cuauhtémoc and Bravo has a large selection of quality items. Beach clothing is sold at a great many shops around Zihuatanejo. Large Pacific shells are sold at shops on Zihuatanejo's Playa Municipal.

Getting There & Away

Air The Ixtapa/Zihuatanejo international airport is 19 km from Zihuatanejo, about two km off highway 200 heading toward Acapulco. Airlines serving this airport, and their direct flights, are listed below; all have connections to other centers.

Aeroméxico
     Alvarez 34, corner Cinco de Mayo, Zihuatanejo (☎ 4-20-18/19/22); Airport (☎ 4-22-37, 4-26-34) – Guadalajara, Mexico City, León/El Bajío, and twice a week to/from Dallas
Alaska
     Airport (☎ 4-84-57); four times a week to Los Angeles or San Francisco (November to April only)
Continental
     Airport (☎ 4-42-19); Houston thrice-weekly
Mexicana
     Guerrero 15 near the corner of Bravo, Zihuatanejo (☎ 4-22-08/9, 3-22-10); Hotel Dorado Pacífico, Ixtapa (☎ 3-22-08/9); Airport (☎ 4-22-27) – Mexico City

Bus Estrella Blanca (☎ 4-34-77) has a large bus terminal, the Central de Autobuses, on highway 200 about two km out of Zihuatanejo, heading toward Acapulco. It includes 1st-class Elite, Futura, Plus and Cuauhtémoc buses. Elite has a daily 10 am bus going up the coast to Mazatlán (US$48), and another at noon going up the coast all the way to Tijuana (US$101). Estrella de Oro (☎ 4-21-75) has its own small terminal, closer to town at Paseo del Palmar 54.

Daily buses include:

Acapulco – 239 km, four hours; Estrella Blanca, hourly 1st-class, 4 am to 6 pm (US$6 or US$7.75); slow 2nd-class half-hourly, 3.45 am to 11 pm (five hours, US$5.25); Estrella de Oro, three 1st-class (US$9) and nine 2nd-class (US$5.50)

Lázaro Cárdenas – 100 km, two hours; Estrella Blanca, 11 1st-class, 1 am to 7.30 pm (US$3); hourly 2nd-class, 6 am to 11 pm (US$2.75); Estrella de Oro, 1st-class at 11.30 am (US$3.75), 2nd-class every two hours, 6 am to 6 pm (US$2.25)

Mexico City (Terminal Sur) – 640 km, nine to 10 hours; Estrella Blanca, 1st-class at 5 am, 6.30 pm and 9 pm (US$22); Futura at 6 am, 12.30, 10 and 11 pm (US$27); Estrella de Oro, 1st-class at 8 am, noon and 8 pm (US$22), 'Plus' service at 10 pm (US$26), deluxe Diamante service at 9.15 pm (US$35)

Car & Motorcycle Car-rental companies include Hertz at Bravo 9, Zihuatanejo (☎ 4-22-55), and at the airport (☎ 4-25-90); and National at the Hotel Double Tree (☎ 3-00-03) and the Centro Comercial Patios (☎ 3-10-32), Ixtapa. There's also Dollar (☎ 3-18-58, 4-23-14), Quick (☎ 3-18-30) and several others.

Motorbikes can be hired in Zihuatanejo at Renta de Motos Michelle (☎ 3-16-30), Galeana 4 near Ascencio, and in Ixtapa at Moto Rent (☎ 3-16-30) in the Centro Comercial Patios. At either place you must have current ID and a credit card or pay a deposit; a driver's license is not needed.

Getting Around

To/From the Airport Trans-Ixtapa (☎ 3-11-65, 4-36-80) offers transport from the airport for US$3.25 per person, but not in the other direction. A taxi from Zihuatanejo/Ixtapa to the airport costs US$5.25/7.75.

Bus Local buses run frequently between Zihuatanejo and Ixtapa, departing every 15 minutes from around 6 am to 10 pm; the cost is US$0.30. for the 15-minute ride. In Zihuatanejo the buses depart from the corner of Juárez and Morelos. In Ixtapa the bus stops all along the main street, in front of all the large hotels. Some of these buses, marked 'Zihuatanejo-Ixtapa-Playa Linda,' continue on through Ixtapa to Playa Linda (US$0.50), stopping near Playa Quieta on the way. They operate only from around 7 am to 6 pm, going hourly during the middle of the day but more frequently in the morning and late afternoon. The 'Correa' route goes from Zihuatanejo to the Central de Autobuses, departing from the same bus stop as the buses to Ixtapa, every day from around 6 am to 9.30 pm; the cost is US$0.20.

Taxi There are plenty of taxis in both Ixtapa and Zihuatanejo. Zihuatanejo to Ixtapa costs US$2.75 during the day and US$4 at night, but always agree on the price before setting off.

AROUND ZIHUATANEJO & IXTAPA
Troncones
☎ 755

About a 25-minute drive northwest of Zihuatanejo, Playa Troncones is a beach on the open sea with a number of beachfront seafood restaurants, a popular outing for Zihuatanejo families. Troncones Point, with a left-hand break, attracts surfers. Activities include fishing, sea kayaking, surfing, horseback riding, hiking, bird and sea turtle watching (the sea turtles lay their eggs here in the sand on moonlit nights) and plenty more.

The *Burro Borracho* is a beachfront restaurant/bar with three duplex bungalows (six units), all with relaxing hammocks on beachfront terraces. Singles/doubles are US$50/60 (reducing by 40% in low season); fax 4-32-96 for reservations. Also here are camping sites with full hookups at US$10 to US$15 per space. A couple of other B&Bs are close by.

Dewey and Karolyn, a friendly, easy-going American couple from Seattle, operate the *Casa de la Tortuga* (cell ☎ 7-07-32, fax 3-24-17), a pleasant guesthouse with doubles for US$75 (one big bed, private bath) or US$50 (two beds, shared bath), including breakfast; prices are 50% lower from May 2 to November 30.

Getting There & Away To get to Troncones, head northwest from Zihuatanejo on highway 200, as if going to Lázaro Cárdenas; after about 40 km you'll come to the village of Buena Vista. The turnoff to Troncones is about six km farther on; it's marked by signs for the Casa de la Tortuga and many restaurants, including the Burro Borracho, La Gaviota and Costa Brava. Troncones is three km from the turnoff; when the road meets the sea, the Burro Borracho is about 1.5 km to your left, the Casa de la Tortuga about 1.5 km to your right. Buses will let you off at the highway turnoff, but there are no buses all the way to Troncones. A taxi from Zihuatanejo costs about US$13 (negotiable).

Barra de Potosí
About a 40-minute drive from Zihuatanejo, Barra de Potosí is a popular area with a long, sandy, open sea beach, beautiful but dangerous for swimming, and another beach on a large (eight-sq-km) lagoon with good swimming and a number of seafood restaurants. There are places to stay.

Getting There & Away To get there, drive on highway 200 heading toward Acapulco; turn off at the town of Los Achotes, about 25 km from Zihuatanejo, and head for the sea, about another 10 km. You can take a local bus to Los Achotes from the bus stop on Ejido in the block east of the market in Zihuatanejo; take the bus heading to Petatlán, tell the driver you're going to Barra de Potosí and you'll be let off where you can meet a minibus going the rest of the way. The cost is about US$1 if you go by bus; a taxi from Zihuatanejo costs about US$17 (negotiable).

ACAPULCO

pop 1.5 million; ☎ 74

Acapulco is the granddaddy of Mexican coastal resort cities. Tourism is the city's No 1 industry, and has been for decades. The name Acapulco evokes images of white-sand beaches, high-rise hotels, glittery nightlife and the divers at La Quebrada gracefully swan-diving into a narrow chasm with the surf rising and falling inside.

Acapulco is a fast-growing city of dual personalities. Around the curve of the Bahía de Acapulco stretches an arc of beautiful beaches, luxury hotels, discos, shopping plazas and restaurants with trilingual menus (many French Canadians come here). Just inland is a none-too-glamorous commercial center with filthy streets, crowded sidewalks, congested traffic and long lines of loud, fuming buses choking passersby.

Hurricane Pauline

On October 7 to 9, 1997, shortly before this book went to press, Hurricane Pauline caused great damage and loss of life all along the Pacific Coast. Worst hit was Acapulco, where many people died and hundreds of residents of nearby hill communities were left temporarily without homes. Puerto Vallarta, Manzanillo, Ixtapa and Zihuatanejo were largely bypassed by the storm.

Within days of the storm, Mexican tourism officials announced that Acapulco's tourism infrastructure was quickly recovering. Transportation facilities and beachfront hotels and resorts, which suffered minimal damage, should be running at full capacity by the time readers of this book arrive in Acapulco. However, as detailed information on damage was unavailable in the aftermath of the hurricane, it should be expected that some hotels, restaurants and other services referred to in this chapter may no longer be open. See the Oaxaca chapter for information on effects of the hurricane in that region. ■

Throughout the year you can expect average daytime temperatures of 27°C to 33°C and nighttime temperatures of 21°C to 27°C. Afternoon showers are common from June to September, but quite rare the rest of the year.

Orientation

Acapulco is on a narrow coastal plain along the 11-km shore of the Bahía de Acapulco. Reached by highway 200 from the east and west and by highway 95 and 95D from the north, it is 400 km south of Mexico City and 240 km southeast of Zihuatanejo and Ixtapa.

For tourism purposes, Acapulco is divided into three parts: 'Acapulco Naútico (Nautical Acapulco, formerly known as Acapulco Tradicionál) in the west (old) part of the city; 'Acapulco Dorado' (Golden Acapulco) heading around the bay east from Playa Hornos; and 'Acapulco Diamante' (Diamond Acapulco), a new luxury tourist resort stretching from the peninsula on the southern tip of Puerto Marqués – a bay about 18 km southeast of Acapulco proper – and continuing about 10 km down Playa Revolcadero to the international airport. Pie de la Cuesta, a lagoon and beach area about 10 km west of Acapulco, is another attractive area where tourism is more low key (see the Around Acapulco section following).

At the western end of the Bahía de Acapulco, the Peninsula de las Playas juts south from central Acapulco. Just south of the peninsula is the popular Isla de la Roqueta and, nearby, the so-called 'underwater shrine,' a submerged bronze statue of the Virgen de Guadalupe. From Playa Caleta on the southern edge of the peninsula, Avenida López Mateos climbs west and then north to Playa La Angosta and La Quebrada before curling east back toward the city center.

Playa Caleta also marks the beginning of Avenida Costera Miguel Alemán. Known alternatively as simply 'La Costera' or as 'Miguel Alemán,' it's Acapulco's principal bayside avenue. From Playa Caleta, La

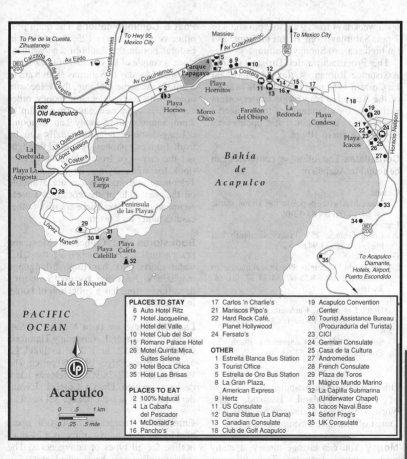

Acapulco

PACIFIC
OCEAN

0   .5   1 km
0 .25 .5 mile

PLACES TO STAY
6   Auto Hotel Ritz
7   Hotel Jacqueline,
    Hotel del Valle
10 Hotel Club del Sol
15 Romano Palace Hotel
26 Motel Quinta Mica,
    Suites Selene
30 Hotel Boca Chica
35 Hotel Las Brisas

PLACES TO EAT
2   100% Natural
4   La Cabaña
    del Pescador
14 McDonald's
16 Pancho's

17 Carlos 'n Charlie's
21 Mariscos Pipo's
22 Hard Rock Café,
    Planet Hollywood
24 Fersato's

OTHER
1   Estrella Blanca Bus Station
3   Tourist Office
5   Estrella de Oro Bus Station
8   La Gran Plaza,
    American Express
9   Hertz
11 US Consulate
12 Diana Statue (La Diana)
13 Canadian Consulate
18 Club de Golf Acapulco

19 Acapulco Convention
    Center
20 Tourist Assistance Bureau
    (Procuraduría del Turista)
23 CICI
24 German Consulate
25 Casa de la Cultura
27 Andromedas
28 French Consulate
29 Plaza de Toros
31 Mágico Mundo Marino
32 La Capilla Submarina
    (Underwater Chapel)
33 Icacos Naval Base
34 Señor Frog's
35 UK Consulate

CENTRAL PACIFIC COAST

Costera cuts north/northwest across the Peninsula de las Playas and then hugs the shore all the way around the bay to the Icacos naval base at the east end of the city. Most of Acapulco's major hotels, restaurants, discos and other points of interest are along or just off La Costera. After passing the naval base, La Costera becomes La Carretera Escénica (The Scenic Highway) for nine km, at which point it intersects highway 200 on the left and the road to Puerto Marqués on the right. The airport is 2.5 km straight ahead.

As in most Spanish colonial cities, the heart of the old central district is the cathedral and the adjacent zócalo.

Information

Tourist Offices The Secretaría de Fomento Turístico del Estado de Guerrero (☎ 86-91-67, 86-91-68, fax 86-45-50), east of Old Acapulco in a white office building on the ocean side at La Costera 187, hands out free city maps and plenty of printed information on Acapulco and the state of Guerrero, and answers any questions. It's open weekdays from 9 am to 2 pm and 4 to 7 pm, Saturday from 10 am to 2 pm, and (in high season) Sunday morning.

The Procuraduría del Turista (Tourist Assistance Bureau; ☎ /fax 84-44-16), at La Costera 4455 near the sidewalk in front of the Acapulco convention center, offers assistance for all manner of tourist needs, problems or complaints. It's open every day from 8 am to 10 pm.

Consulates The following consulates can be found in Acapulco:

Canada
    Plaza Marbella, opposite the Diana statue
    (☎ 84-13-05, fax 84-13-06)
France
    Costa Grande 235, Fraccionamiento Las
    Playas (☎ 82-33-94)
Germany
    Antón de Alaminos 26, Fraccionamiento
    Costa Azul (☎ 84-18-60, 84-74-37, fax 84-
    38-10)
UK
    Hotel Las Brisas, Carretera Escénica 5255
    (☎ 84-66-05, 84-15-80, fax 84-14-95)
USA
    Suite 14, Hotel Continental Plaza, La
    Costera 121 (☎ /fax 84-03-00)

Other consulates in Acapulco include those of Austria, Finland, Holland, Italy, Norway, Panama, Spain and Sweden. The tourist offices have a complete list.

Money You can change money at many places around Acapulco. The numerous banks give the best rates; they are open weekdays from 9 am to around 3 or 5 pm. The casas de cambio pay a slightly lower rate but are open longer hours and are less crowded than the banks; shop around as rates vary. There are many casas de cambio all along La Costera. Hotels will also change money, but their rates are usually not good.

American Express (☎ 69-11-00, fax 69-11-88) at La Costera 1628, in La Gran Plaza, changes Amex traveler's checks at the same rates as the banks, with no crowds and with convenient hours: Monday to Saturday from 10 am to 7 pm.

Post & Communications The main post office is at La Costera 125, in the Palacio Federal beside the Sanborn's department store, a couple of blocks east of the zócalo. It's open Monday to Saturday from 8 am to 8 pm. In the same building, the Telecomm office, with telex, telegram, money order and fax, is open weekdays from 8 am to 7 pm, Saturday and Sunday 9 am to noon.

Long-distance telephone calls can be made from pay phones – plentiful throughout the city – or from telephone casetas (look for signs saying 'larga distancia'). Telephone and fax services are available on the west side of the zócalo at Caseta Alameda on La Paz. There are many other casetas along La Costera.

Bookstores The Comercial Mexicana branch on La Costera opposite the CICI water-sports park has English-language magazines. Near the zócalo, Sanborn's department store has a collection of books in English.

Laundry These are open Monday to Saturday. In the center, Lavandería y Tintorería Coral, Juárez 12, next door to hotel La Mama Hélène, charges US$0.60 per kg. The Lavandería (☎ 82-28-90) on Iglesias has a delivery service. On La Costera, Lavandería del Sol is at the Club del Sol hotel.

Emergency Locatel (☎ 81-11-00), operated by the state tourist office, is a 24-hour hotline for all types of emergencies. The tourist police can be reached at ☎ 80-02-10.

Fuerte de San Diego
This five-sided fort was built in 1616 atop a hill just east of the zócalo to protect the naos (galleons) that conducted trade between the Philippines and Mexico from marauding Dutch and English pirates. It must have done some good because this trade route lasted until the early 19th century. Apparently it was also strong enough to forestall independence leader Morelos' takeover of the city in 1812 for four months. The fort had to be rebuilt after a

A Long & Illustrious History

The name 'Acapulco' is derived from ancient Nahuatl words meaning 'where the reeds stood' or 'place of giant reeds.' Archaeological finds show that when the Spaniards arrived, Indians had been living around the Bahía de Acapulco and the nearby bay of Puerto Marqués for about 2000 years, and had progressed from a hunting and gathering society to an agricultural one.

Spanish sailors discovered the Bay of Acapulco in 1512. Port and shipbuilding facilities were later established here because of the bay's substantial natural harbor.

In 1523 Hernán Cortés, Juan Rodríguez Villafuerte and merchant Juan de Sala joined forces to finance an overland trade route between Acapulco and Mexico City. This route, known as the 'Camino de Asia,' was the principal trade route between Mexico City and the Pacific; the 'Camino de Europa,' continuing on from Mexico City to Veracruz on the Gulf Coast, formed a link between Asia and Spain.

Acapulco became the only port in the New World authorized to receive naos (Spanish trading galleons) from the Philippines and China. During the annual Acapulco Fair, lasting three to eight weeks after the galleons arrived from Manila in spring, traders converged on Acapulco from Mexico City, Manila and Peru.

By the 17th century, trade with Asia was flourishing and Dutch and English pirate ships abounded in the Pacific and along the coastlines of Mexico and Baja California. To ward off the pirates, Fuerte de San Diego was built atop a low hill overlooking the bay. It was not until the end of the 18th century that Spain permitted its American colonies to engage in free trade, ending the monopoly of the naos and the Manila-Acapulco route for trade with Asia. The naos continued trading until the early 19th century.

Upon gaining independence, Mexico severed most of its trade links with Spain and its colonies, and Acapulco declined as a port city. It became relatively isolated from the rest of the world until a paved road was built in 1927 linking it with Mexico City. As Mexico City grew larger, its citizens began flocking to the Pacific Coast for vacations. A new international airport was built, and by the 1950s Acapulco was a booming resort. ■

1776 earthquake damaged most of Acapulco. It remains basically unchanged today, having been restored to top condition. The fort is now the home of the **Museo Histórico de Acapulco**, a museum with interesting historical exhibits. It's open Tuesday to Sunday from 10.30 am to 4.40 pm; admission is US$1.80 (free on Sunday and holidays, and free every day for children and students).

La Quebrada Divers

The famous clavadistas de La Quebrada have been amazing visitors to Acapulco ever since 1934, diving with graceful finesse from heights of 25 to 45 meters into a narrow chasm with the ocean swells rising and falling inside. Understandably, the divers pray at a small shrine before leaping over the edge. (So did Elvis Presley in the film *Fun in Acapulco*.) Diving times are daily at 12.45, 7.30, 8.30, 9.30 and 10.30 pm, with at least three divers leaping

each time; admission is US$1.30 (children under eight free). To get to La Quebrada you can either walk up the hill from the zócalo on Calle La Quebrada, or take a taxi. La Quebrada is also an excellent place to come and watch the sunset.

You can also get a great view of the divers from the restaurant/bar of the Plaza Las Glorias hotel, but it costs US$8.50 to enter the bar while the diving's going on (the price includes two drinks).

Parque Papagayo

This large amusement park is a large park full of tropical trees and provides access to Playas Hornos and Hornitos. Its attractions, for both kids and adults, include a roller-skating rink, a lake with paddle boats, a children's train, mechanical rides and a hill that affords an excellent view. To get up you can take a chair lift *(telesilla)* for US$0.40; toboggan back down for US$0.70. The chair lift and toboggan are open daily

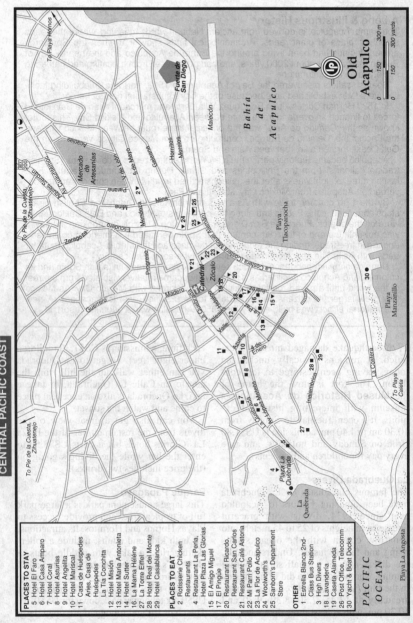

PLACES TO STAY
5 Hotel El Faro
6 Hotel Casa Amparo
7 Hotel Coral
8 Hotel Asturias
9 Hotel Angelita
10 Hotel Mariscal
11 Casa de Huéspedes
   Aries, Casa de
   Huéspedes
   La Tía Conchita
12 Hotel Misión
13 Hotel Maria Antonieta
14 Hotel Sutter
16 La Mama Hélène
27 La Torre Eiffel
28 Hotel Real del Monte
29 Hotel Casablanca

PLACES TO EAT
2 Rotisserie Chicken
   Restaurants
4 Restaurant La Perla,
   Hotel Plaza Las Glorias
15 El Amigo Miguel
17 El Pingüe
20 Restaurant Ricardo,
   Restaurant San Carlos
21 Restaurant Café Astoria
22 Mi Parri Pollo
23 La Flor de Acapulco
24 Woolworth's
25 Sanborn's Department
   Store

OTHER
1 Estrella Blanca 2nd-
   Class Bus Station
3 High Divers
18 Lavandería
19 Caseta Alameda
26 Post Office, Telecomm
30 Yacht & Boat Docks

from 1 to 8 pm. The park is open weekdays from 6 am to 8 pm, with no admission charge (donation requested). The mechanical rides section is open weekdays from 4 to 10 pm (11 pm on Friday and Saturday).

CICI

The Centro Internacional de Convivencia Infantil (all it's ever called is CICI) is a family water-sports park on La Costera on the east side of Acapulco. Shows with dolphins and seals are held several times daily; there's also a 30-meter-high water toboggan, a pool with artificial waves and a small tidepool aquarium. It's open every day from 10 am to 6 pm; admission is US$6.50 (US$5.75 for children aged two to 10), plus you'll need to rent a locker (US$0.70) and an inflatable ring (US$1.30) to use the toboggan. Any local bus marked 'CICI,' 'Base' or 'Puerto Marqués' will take you there.

Centro de Convenciones

Also called the Centro Internacional Acapulco (☎ 84-71-52), Acapulco's convention center is a large complex on the north side of La Costera, not far from CICI. The center has a permanent craft gallery (Galería de Artesanías), temporary special exhibitions, a large plaza, theaters and concert halls. A Fiesta Mexicana is held several evenings each week (see Entertainment). Phone the center to ask about current offerings, or stop by the information kiosk in front of the center.

Casa de la Cultura

This complex of buildings (☎ 84-23-90, 84-38-14 for schedules), set around a garden at La Costera 4834, just east of CICI, houses an archaeological museum, an innovative art gallery and a handicrafts shop. All are open Monday to Saturday. Also here are an open-air theater and an indoor auditorium.

Mágico Mundo Marino

This aquarium stands on a small point of land between Playas Caleta and Caletilla. Highlights include a sea lion show, the feeding of sharks and piranhas, swimming pools, water toboggans and an oceanographic museum. It's open every day from 9 am to 7 pm; admission is US$3.25 (US$2 for children aged three to 12).

Isla de la Roqueta

In addition to a popular beach and snorkeling and diving possibilities, Isla de la Roqueta has a zoo that features telescopes and children's games. The zoo is open daily except Tuesday from 10 am to 5 pm; admission is US$0.40.

From Playas Caleta and Caletilla boats make the eight-minute trip every 30 minutes (US$2 return). Or a less-direct glass-bottomed boat departs from the same beaches for Isla de la Roqueta via La Capilla Submarina (The Underwater Chapel), a submerged bronze statue of the Virgen de Guadalupe. The roundtrip fare is US$3.25; the trip takes 45 minutes, unless you alight on the island and take a later boat back.

Beaches

Visiting Acapulco's beaches tops most visitors' lists of things to do here. The beaches heading east around the bay from the zócalo – **Playas Hornos, Hornitos, Condesa** and **Icacos** – are the most popular. The high-rise hotel district begins on Playa Hornitos, at the eastern side of Parque Papagayo, and heads east from there. City buses constantly ply La Costera, the beachside avenue, making it easy to get up and down this long arc of beaches.

Playas **Caleta** and **Caletilla** are two small, protected beaches beside one another in a cove on the south side of the Peninsula de las Playas. They're especially popular among families with small children, as the water is very calm. All buses marked 'Caleta' heading down La Costera go there. An aquarium on a tiny point of land separates the two beaches, and regular boats go from there to Isla de la Roqueta.

Playa La Angosta is another beach in a tiny, protected cove on the west side of the peninsula. From the zócalo it takes about 20 minutes to walk there. Or you can take any 'Caleta' bus and get off near the Hotel Avenida, on La Costera, just one short block west of the beach.

Water Sports

Just about everything that can be done on, under and above the water is done in Acapulco. On the Bahía de Acapulco, water-skiing, jet-skiing, boating, the 'banana' and parasailing are all popular activities. The smaller Playas Caleta and Caletilla have all of these plus sailboats, fishing boats, motor boats, pedal boats, canoes, snorkel gear, black inner tubes and bicycles for hire.

Scuba-diving trips and/or instruction can be arranged through several diving operators. These include Aqua Mundo (☎ 82-10-41) and Divers de México (☎ 82-13-98, 83-60-20), both at La Costera 100, and Mantarraya (☎ /fax 82-41-76) at Gran Via Tropical 2, in front of Playa Caleta.

Deep-sea fishing is another possibility; ask on the beaches or at travel agencies, or just stroll along the Malecón near the zócalo and see which boats look likely. Barracuda's Fleet (☎ 83-85-43, 82-52-56) charges anything from US$100 to US$250 for a five hour trip, depending on the size of the boat. Aqua Munda and Mantarraya also do fishing trips.

If you want a fast, white-knuckle boat ride on the Río Papagayo, contact Shotover Jet (☎ 84-11-54) at the Hotel Continental Plaza, La Costera 121.

Other Activities

Acapulco has three 18-hole golf courses. The Club de Golf Acapulco (☎ 84-65-83) is on La Costera; in Acapulco Diamante (near the airport) there is Tres Vidas (☎ 62-10-00) and another at the Acapulco Princess Hotel (☎ 69-10-00). There's a nine-hole course at the Vidafel Mayan Palace Hotel (☎ 62-00-20). For tennis, try the Club de Tenis Hyatt (☎ 84-12-25), the Villa Vera Racquet Club (☎ 84-03-33) or the Acapulco Princess Hotel. Acapulco also has gymnasiums, squash courts and facilities for other sports. The tourist office has information on sports in Acapulco.

Cruises

Various boats and yachts offer cruises, departing from the Malecón near the zócalo. Cruises are available day and night; they range from multilevel boats with blaring salsa music and open bars to yachts offering quiet sunset cruises around the bay. All take basically the same route – they leave from the Malecón, go around the Peninsula de las Playas to Isla de la Roqueta, pass by to see the cliff divers at La Quebrada, cross over to Puerto Marqués, and then come back around the Bahía de Acapulco. The *Hawaiano* (☎ 82-21-99, 82-07-85), the *Fiesta* and *Bonanza* (☎ 83-18-03, fax 83-25-31), and the large *Aca Tiki* catamaran (☎ 84-61-40) are all popular; you can make reservations by calling them directly, or through any travel agency and at most hotels.

Special Events

Probably the busiest time of the year for tourism in Acapulco is Semana Santa, when the city fills up with tourists and there's lots of action in the discos, on the beaches and all over town. A Tianguis Turístico held for one week in April features promotions relating to the tourist industry. Following the tianguis, the Festivales de Acapulco, held for one week in May, features Mexican and international music at many venues around Acapulco.

The festival for Mexico's patron saint, the Virgen de Guadalupe, is celebrated all night on December 11 and all the following day, with street processions accompanied by small marching bands, fireworks and folk dances, all converging on the cathedral in the zócalo, where children dressed in costumes congregate. It's a lesser version of the Mexico City festival. Expo-Acapulco, an industrial and commercial exposition that encourages investment in Acapulco, takes place December 20 to January 7. Film festivals are in June and December.

Places to Stay

Acapulco has a great number of hotels in all categories and over 30,000 hotel rooms, but its tourism is seasonal. High season is from the middle of December until the end of Easter, with another flurry of activity during the July and August school holidays; the rest of the year, tourism is much slower. Most hotels raise their rates during these times, when they can be as much as double the low-season price, though some do this for only part of the season. At other times of year you can often bargain for a better rate, especially if you plan to stay a while. If you come to Acapulco at Semana Santa or Christmas and New Year, be sure to have hotel reservations or you may do a lot of searching for a room.

Places to Stay – budget

Most of Acapulco's budget hotels are concentrated around the zócalo area and on Calle La Quebrada, the street going up the hill from behind the cathedral to La Quebrada, where the divers do their stuff. All places have hot water, unless noted. There are many more hotels in this area, if all the ones listed here are full.

On Calle La Quebrada, *Hotel Angelita* (☎ 83-57-34) at No 37 is clean and popular, with singles/doubles at US$6.50/12 most of the year, US$7.75/13 in winter. Next door, the *Hotel Mariscal* (☎ 82-00-15) at No 35 has rooms at US$5.25/7.75 (US$10 per person in high season). The *Hotel Asturias* (☎ 83-65-48) at No 45 is a popular place, very clean and well tended, with pleasant rooms on a courtyard with a small swimming pool; the cost is US$8.50/16 (US$10/19 in high season). Also with a small swimming pool is *Hotel Coral* (☎ 82-07-56), at No 56, with rooms at US$6.50 per person, or US$9 in winter. Similarly priced, without hot water but with a pool, is *Hotel Casa Amparo* (☎ 82-21-72) at No 69. If you're at the end of your economic rope, check out the *Casa de Huéspedes Aries* (☎ 83-24-01) at No 30 and the *Casa de Huéspedes La Tía Conchita* (☎ 82-18-82) next door at No 32; both have tiny rooms (no hot water) at only US$3.25 per person all year round.

Up the hill at the top of Calle La Quebrada is the Plaza La Quebrada, overlooking the sea. The large attended parking lot here is a safe place to park, but it gets very busy and loud in the evening, when the cliff divers perform. The hotels here are somewhat cooler than places down the hill in town, since they catch the sea breezes. Perched on a hill above the plaza, *La Torre Eiffel* (☎ 82-16-83) at Inalámbrica 110 has a small swimming pool and large balconies with sitting areas set up for a view of the sea. Its bright rooms cost US$5.25 per person most of the year, US$7.75 per person in high season; bargain for a good rate here. Right on the plaza at Calle La Quebrada 83, the *Hotel El Faro* (☎ 82-13-65) has large rooms with balconies at US$6.50/13, rising by 20% in winter.

A good place near the zócalo is *Hotel María Antonieta* (☎ 82-50-24) at Azueta 17, with reasonably quiet rooms at US$6.50 per person and a kitchen you can use. Opposite, the *Hotel Sutter* (☎ 82-02-09), Azueta 10, charges US$6.50/10, but is noisier and has no hot water. Nearby, *La Mama Hélène* (☎ 82-23-96, fax 83-86-97), Juárez 12, is reasonable value in high season, as rooms without hot water are US$10/16 year round. English and French are spoken, and there's a courtyard, with aquariums, where breakfast (US$2.75) is served.

Places to Stay – middle

In the zócalo area, the *Hotel Misión* (☎ 82-36-43, fax 82-20-76) at Valle 12 is a relaxing colonial-style place offering stylish rooms with tiles and heavy Spanish furniture. Rooms are set around a lovely, shady courtyard where breakfast is served for US$2.75; rooms are US$10/21, rising by 50% in high season.

On the east side of Parque Papagayo, near La Costera and the popular Playa Hornitos, the *Hotel Jacqueline* (☎ 85-93-38) has 10 air-con rooms at US$19 (higher at busy times) around a pleasant little garden. Next door, the *Hotel del Valle* (☎ 85-83-36/88) has a small swimming pool, kitchens (US$5.75 surcharge per day), and rooms at US$23/26 with fan/air-con. Both are on Espinosa, though the nearest street sign indicates Morin (that actually starts a block north).

Also half a block from Playa Hornitos, on Avenida Wilfrido Massieu, the *Auto Hotel Ritz* (☎ 85-80-23, fax 85-56-47) is an attractive six-story hotel with indoor parking. Air-con rooms have large private balconies overlooking the swimming pool; it closed during 1997 for extensive renovations.

Near CICI and Playa Icacos are a number of hotels, including two with large apartments with swimming pool, parking, air-con and fully equipped kitchens: *Suites Selene* (☎ /fax 84-29-77) at Colón 175, one door from the beach, has attractive one/ two-bedroom apartments at US$30/60, and rooms for US$24 (higher during holidays); *Motel Quinta Mica* (☎ 84-01-21/22) at Colón 115 has simpler apartments at US$32, though the price rises with demand (and on weekends). The Comercial Mexicana supermarket nearby is convenient for groceries.

The high-rise hotels along La Costera tend to be expensive. One of the more economical ones is the *Romano Palace Hotel*

(☎ 84-77-30, fax 84-13-50) at La Costera 130, whose luxurious rooms have private balconies and floor-to-ceiling windows with a great view of Acapulco; ask for an upper-story room for the best view (there are 22 floors). Rooms cost US$45 for one to four people most of the year, US$74 during holidays.

Also on La Costera, the *Club del Sol* (☎ 85-66-00, fax 85-66-95) at La Costera and Reyes Católicos is a large hotel with four swimming pools, a gym, squash, volleyball and aerobics and sauna facilities. The rooms, all with air-con, kitchenette and private balcony, are US$38 most of the year, US$60 from July 15 to August 30 and December 15 to Easter.

Overlooking Playa Caletilla, the *Hotel Boca Chica* (☎ 83-63-88, fax 83-95-13; bchica@mpsnet.com.mx) on Privada de Caletilla, is a lovely place with a 'natural swimming pool' beside the sea, gardens with a view toward Isla de la Roqueta, and air-con rooms with fine views. Singles/ doubles are US$35/48, rising annually in December.

Also with magnificent views, high on a hill on the Peninsula de las Playas, are the

ERIN REID

fancy *Hotel Real del Monte* and *Hotel Casablanca Tropical* (☎ 82-12-12, fax 82-12-14), linked hotels at Cerro de la Pinzona 80. Rooms are good value at US$27 (higher at Easter and Christmas), and there's a swimming pool.

Places to Stay – top end

If you want to spend a lot of money, there's plenty of opportunity for it in Acapulco, with its numerous deluxe, 'grand tourism' and 'special category' hotels. The super-luxury special category hotels include the *Las Brisas, Acapulco Princess, Pierre Marqués, Camino Real* and the *Hyatt Regency Acapulco*. Grand tourism hotels include the *Acapulco Plaza, Sheraton Acapulco Resort, Villa Vera, Fiesta Americana Condesa* and *Vidafel Mayan Palace*. Many of the luxury hotels are found in the new Acapulco Diamante development, east of Puerto Marqués, and on the beachfront along La Costera; the high-rise hotel zone begins at the east end of Parque Papagayo and runs east around the bay. Travel agents should have literature on all these hotels.

Places to Eat

Near the Zócalo On the east side of the zócalo, *La Flor de Acapulco* has an indoor dining room and sidewalk tables out on the plaza, good for people-watching. It's open daily from 8 am to 1 am. Around the corner on the Carranza pedestrian street, with sidewalk tables under a large shady tree, is *Mi Parri Pollo*, open 8 am to midnight. Hidden away at the back of the plaza east of the cathedral, the *Restaurant Café Astoria* has outdoor tables in a pleasant, shady, quietish spot. It's open every day from 8 am to 11 pm, with a comida corrida (US$3.25) from 1.30 to 4 pm. On the west side of the zócalo there's a place specializing in German food.

A couple of blocks east of the zócalo on Avenida Escadero, the *Woolworth's* department store has an air-con restaurant open daily from 7 am to 10 pm, offering good-value set breakfasts, lunches and dinners. Nearby, *Sanborn's* department

store also has a restaurant, but it's much more expensive.

Coming out of the zócalo on the west side, Calle Juárez has about a dozen restaurants. *Restaurant Ricardo* at Juárez 9 is popular with the locals and open daily from 7 am to midnight; the comida corrida is US$2. A couple of doors nearer the zócalo, the *Restaurant San Carlos*, with an open-air patio, a nicer ambience and similar prices, is open daily from 7.30 am until 10.30 pm. In the next block west, *El Pingüe* at Juárez 10 is an attractive patio restaurant with one of the best breakfast deals in Acapulco. For just US$1.70 you get eggs with ham or bacon, toast, fruit or juice, and coffee; and there are trashy US magazines to read. Perfect! It's open daily from 8 am to around 10 pm.

There are many other restaurants west of the zócalo, many specializing in seafood. On the corner of Juárez and Azueta, the open-air *El Amigo Miguel* is one of the most patronized; it's open daily from 10.30 am to 9.30 pm. Several other seafood restaurants are nearby. For rotisserie roasted chicken, eat-in or takeout, go to 5 de Mayo, where there are four places side by side.

La Costera There are dozens of restaurants as you head east down La Costera toward the big high-rise hotels. *Fersato's*, on La Costera opposite the Casa de la Cultura, near CICI, is a long-standing family establishment with delicious Mexican food; comida corrida is US$3.25 and it's open every day from 7.30 am to midnight. One block west of CICI, side by side, are the famous (and much more expensive) 'theme' restaurants, *Hard Rock Café* and *Planet Hollywood*; both are open daily from noon to 2 am. Another block west, *Mariscos Pipo's* is known for its good seafood; try a combination seafood plate for US$6 (small) or US$6.50 (large). It's open every day from 1 to 9.30 pm.

For cheaper fare near La Costera, try the small *La Cabaña del Pescador* on Morin, where a comida corrida costs US$1.70. It's open daily from 8 am to 7 pm.

Back along La Costera, the open-air *Pancho's* at No 109 is reasonably priced and serves Mexican and international food, especially grilled and barbecued meats. Daily hours are 6 am to 10.30 pm. Carlos Anderson's *Carlos 'n Charlie's* at No 999, opposite Las Torres Gemelas, has a fascinating collection of old photos on one wall, rowdy music and a quirky bilingual menu. It's not cheap, but it puts on a good time for the tourists. It's open daily from 6 pm to midnight or later. Anderson's *Señor Frog's*, on the Carretera Escénica on the east side of the Bahía de Acapulco, has a great view.

Restaurants in the *100% Natural* chain are found throughout Acapulco; there are several spread out along La Costera (at Nos 200 and No 248), serving mostly vegetarian fare. Several US chain restaurants are also found on La Costera, including *Denny's*, *Bob's Big Boy* (both open 24 hours), *Shakey's Pizza*, *Domino's Pizza*, *Pizza Hut*, *Kentucky Fried Chicken* and *McDonald's*.

Playa Caletilla There are many open-air seafood restaurants under the big trees lining the rear of Playa Caletilla; they all have similar inexpensive menus.

La Quebrada You can splurge at the *Restaurant La Perla* (☎ 83-11-55) in the Plaza Las Glorias Hotel on the Plaza La Quebrada. The nightly buffet (US$22 per person), on candlelit terraces under the stars, is open from 7 pm to midnight. It's overpriced, but the great view of the divers makes the evening.

Grocery Stores The large Comercial Mexicana, Gigante and Bodega combination supermarkets and discount department stores are along La Costera between the zócalo and Parque Papagayo.

Entertainment

Discos, Clubs & Bars Acapulco's active nightlife rivals its beaches as the main attraction. Much of the nightlife revolves around discos and nightclubs, with new ones continually opening up to challenge the old. Most of the discos open around 10 pm and have a cover charge of US$11 or more, sometimes with an open bar. 'Single girls' sometimes get in free.

A popular new place on La Costera, *Andromedas*, is a nautical theme techno-pop disco (closed Monday). Close by on La Costera are *Salon Q*, with Latin rhythms and live music, and a smaller disco, *Atrium*. Also here is *Baby'O*; it has a laser light show and is supposedly one of the best discos in Acapulco, attracting a younger crowd. About 400 meters south on La Costera is the *News* disco and concert hall, billing itself as 'one of the largest and most spectacular discos in the world.'

Extravaganzza and the *Palladium* are both popular places in the Las Brisas area in the southeast part of the city; Palladium attracts the younger crowd of the two. *Fantasy*, also in the Las Brisas area, has a laser light show and disco dancing.

Disco Beach is also popular, and right on Playa Condesa. *Nina's* at La Costera 41 and *Cat's* at Juan de la Cosa 32, just off La Costera, specialize in live Latin music. *B&B* at Gran Via Tropical 5 in the Caleta area features hits of the 1950s to 1980s.

Don't forget the *Hard Rock Café*; the Acapulco branch of the famous chain, at La Costera 37 just west of CICI, is open every day from noon until 2 am, with live music six nights a week (the rest day varies) from 11 pm to 1.30 am. Its neighbor, *Planet Hollywood*, has dancing from about 11 pm (or movie shows if it's a quiet night).

Acapulco has an active gay scene and several predominantly gay bars and clubs. Transvestite shows are one feature of the scene, such as those in *Tequila's Le Club* opposite Gigante.

If you don't feel up to a disco, most of the big hotels along La Costera have bars with entertainment, be it quiet piano music or live bands.

Other Entertainment Apart from the disco scene there are plenty of other things to do around Acapulco in the evening. At the Centro de Convenciones there's a Fiesta Mexicana every Monday,

Wednesday and Friday night from 7 to 10 pm, featuring regional dances from many parts of Mexico, mariachis, the famous Papantla voladores and a rope performer; there's also a sumptuous Mexican buffet. The cost per person is US$18, or US$30 including an open bar; call ☎ 84-71-52 for reservations.

Other theaters at the Centro de Convenciones present plays, concerts, dance and other cultural performances, as does the Casa de la Cultura (☎ 84-23-90, 84-38-14); phone or stop by for current schedules.

Acapulco has several cinemas – there's one on the zócalo, a couple on La Costera, and several more around town. Current cinema listings are found in the *Novedades* and *Sol de Acapulco* newspapers.

Evening cruises are another possibility, and there are the spectacular cliff divers at La Quebrada. Or it's pleasant to sit at one of the sidewalk restaurants on the zócalo, feel the warm night air, and watch the activity in the plaza.

Spectator Sports

Bullfights are held at the *Plaza de Toros* southeast of La Quebrada and northwest of Playas Caleta and Caletilla on Sunday at 5.30 pm; tickets are sold at the bullring from 4.30 pm, and at travel agencies. The traditional bullfighting season is from December to April (Christmas to Easter) but sometimes it ends earlier; travel agencies or the bullring ticket office (☎ 82-11-82, 83-95-61) will have details. The 'Caleta' bus passes near the bullring.

Things to Buy

Acapulco's main craft market, the 400-stall Mercado de Artesanías, is a few blocks east of the zócalo between Avenida Cuauhtémoc and Vicente de León. Paved and pleasant, it's a good place to get better deals on everything that you see in the hotel shops – sarapes, hammocks, silver jewelry, huaraches, clothing and T-shirts. Bargaining is definitely the rule. It's open every day from 9 am to 8 pm. On La Costera, Artesanías markets are in front of Parque Papagayo and by the Diana Statue.

Getting There & Away

Air Acapulco has a busy international airport, with direct flights to/from the USA, including Oakland, Chicago and New York with TAESA, Los Angeles with Delta, and Houston with Continental. Most other flights connect through either Mexico City or Guadalajara, both short hops from Acapulco. Airlines serving Acapulco include:

Aeroméxico
  La Costera 286, beside Cine Playa Hornos (☎ 85-16-00/25)
Continental Airlines
  Airport (☎ 66-90-63)
Delta Airlines
  Airport (☎ 66-94-84)
Mexicana
  Torre Acapulco, La Costera 1252 (☎ 84-68-90/37)
TAESA
  Hotel Imperial, La Costera 251 (☎ 86-56-00/01)

Bus Acapulco has two major long-distance bus stations. The Estrella de Oro terminal (☎ 85-93-60, 85-87-05) is on the corner of Avenidas Cuauhtémoc and Wilfrido Massieu. The Base-Cine Río-Caleta local bus (see Getting Around) passes by this terminal; you can catch it opposite the Sanborn's department store on La Costera, two blocks east of the zócalo. The Estrella Blanca terminal (☎ 69-20-28/30) is at Avenida Ejido 47; any local bus marked 'Ejido' departing from opposite the Sanborn's department store will get you there. Estrella Blanca tickets are also sold at its agency at Gran Plaza 1616, La Costera, and at Zocalo Travel Agency, La Costera 207, near the zócalo.

Both companies offer frequent services to Mexico City with various levels of luxury; journey durations depend on whether they use the new, faster autopista (highway 95D) or the old federal highway 95. Both lines have buses to the Terminal Sur and Terminal Norte in Mexico City.

Destinations served daily include:

Chilpancingo – 132 km, 1½ to two hours (US$3.75 to US$4.50); regular 1st-class by both companies, also every 20 minutes from 5 am to 8 pm (US$3) from Estrella Blanca's 2nd-class terminal at Avenida Cuauhtémoc 101

Cuernavaca – 315 km, four to five hours; eight 1st-class by Estrella Blanca and Futura (US$13 to US$15, four to five hours); by Estrella de Oro, 1st-class 'Plus' service at 10.30 am, 3.40 and 8 pm (US$15, four hours)

Iguala – 231 km, three hours; hourly 3.40 am to 11.55 pm (US$8) by Estrella Blanca; five between 8 am and 6.40 pm by Estrella de Oro (US$6.50)

Mexico City (Terminal Sur or Terminal Norte) – 400 km, five to 6½ hours; Estrella Blanca runs 1st-class buses ('primera,' 'primera especial' and 'Futura' classes, five to 6½ hours, US$15 to US$19), and deluxe 'ejecutivo' buses (US$26, five hours), with departures hourly from midnight to 6.35 pm; Estrella de Oro has 16 1st-class 'Primera,' 'Plus' and 'Crucero' buses (US$15 to US$19, five to six hours) and four deluxe 'Diamante' class (US$26, five hours)

Puerto Escondido – 400 km, 6½ to 7½ hours (US$8.50 to US$10); five by Estrella Blanca (morning buses are slower and cheaper)

Taxco – 266 km, 4½ to five hours (US$10); five by Estrella Blanca, four by Estrella de Oro

Zihuatanejo – 239 km, four hours; hourly 1st-class 4.30 am to 6.30 pm, and at 9, 11.15 pm and 12.55 am, by Estrella Blanca (US$6 or US$7.75); 2nd-class (US$5.50) at 10.50 am and 3 pm and 1st-class (US$9) at 6.20 pm, by Estrella de Oro

Car & Motorcycle Many car-rental companies hire jeeps as well as cars; several have offices at the airport as well as in town, and/or offer free delivery to you. As always, it's a good idea to shop around to compare prices. Hertz (☎ 85-89-47) is at La Costera 1945, with Budget (☎ 81-05-92) and Quick (☎ 86-34-20) opposite. Other rental companies include:

Alamo	☎ 84-23-67, 84-33-05
Autos Hernández	☎ 85-86-99, 86-34-20
Avis	☎ 62-00-85
Bet Mer	☎ 66-95-09
Dollar	☎ 84-30-66
Economovil	☎ 84-18-19, 66-90-02
Flash	☎ 85-66-22
National	☎ 84-82-34
Saad	☎ 84-34-45, 84-53-25
Sands	☎ 84-38-32

Motorcycles can be rented beside the Acapulco Plaza Hotel on La Costera.

Getting Around

To/From the Airport Acapulco's airport is 23 km southeast of the zócalo, beyond the junction for Puerto Marqués. If you arrive by air, buy a ticket for transport into town from one of the colectivo desks before you leave the terminal; they all cost the same – US$5 per person for a lift directly to your hotel. Taxis from the airport cost between US$19 (Diamante area) and US$30 (center and west).

Leaving Acapulco, phone Transportación de Pasajeros (☎ 62-10-95), Transportación Turística (☎ 82-93-75, 86-49-32) or Movil Aca (☎ 66-92-98/99) 24 hours in advance to reserve your transport back to the airport. They'll pick you up 90 minutes before your departure for domestic flights, two hours ahead for international flights; the cost is US$5. Taxis from the center to the airport cost about US$10 if hailed in the street; 'hotel rates' are higher.

Bus Acapulco has a good city bus system, with buses going every few minutes to most places you'd want to go. They operate every day from 5 am to 11 pm and cost US$0.30. From the zócalo area, the bus stop opposite Sanborn's department store on La Costera, two blocks east of the zócalo, is a good place to catch buses – it's the beginning of several bus routes so you can usually get a seat. The most useful city routes include:

Base-Caleta – from the Icacos Naval Base at the southeast end of Acapulco, along La Costera, past the zócalo to Playa Caleta

Base-Cine Río-Caleta – from the Icacos Naval Base, cuts inland from La Costera on Avenida Wilfrido Massieu to Avenida Cuauhtémoc, heads down Cuauhtémoc through the business district, turning back to

La Costera just before reaching the zócalo, continuing west to Caleta

Puerto Marqués-Centro – from opposite Sanborn's, along La Costera to Puerto Marqués

Zócalo-Playa Pie de la Cuesta – from opposite Sanborn's, to Pie de la Cuesta. Buses marked 'Playa' or 'Luces' go all the way down the Pie de la Cuesta beach road; those marked 'San Isidro' stop only at the entrance to Pie de la Cuesta

Taxi Taxis are plentiful in Acapulco and taxi drivers are happy to take gringos for a ride, especially for fares higher than the official rates. Always agree on the fare before you climb into the cab; it never hurts to bargain with taxi drivers.

AROUND ACAPULCO
Pie de la Cuesta
☎ 74

About 10 km northwest of Acapulco, Pie de la Cuesta is a narrow peninsula two km long stretching between the ocean and the large, freshwater Laguna de Coyuca. Compared to Acapulco, it's quieter, cleaner, closer to nature and much more peaceful. However, swimming in the ocean at Pie de la Cuesta can be dangerous due to a riptide and the shape of the waves; each year a number of people are killed in the surf. Laguna de Coyuca, three times as large as the Bahía de Acapulco, is better for swimming; in the lagoon are the islands of Montosa, Presido and a bird sanctuary called Pájaros.

Pie de la Cuesta has many beachside restaurants, specializing in seafood, and it's a great place for watching the sunset. There's no nightlife, so if you're looking for excitement you may be better off staying in Acapulco. Water-skiing is popular on the Laguna de Coyuca; several water-ski clubs provide the wherewithall (around US$32 per hour), and perhaps canoes, jet skis and other equipment too. Boat trips on the lagoon are another popular activity; you can cross to the place where Sylvester Stallone filmed *Rambo*. Negotiate a price for your own boat any time, or take a colectivo (US$4 per person)

departing at specific hours. You can also ride a horse on the beach.

Places to Stay For accommodations, Pie de la Cuesta is a good alternative to Acapulco. Since there's only one road, you can easily check out the 15 or so hotels along the two-km stretch between the beach and the lagoon. Every place has private parking.

Camping Pie de la Cuesta has two clean, pleasant trailer parks at the far end of the road from the highway, near the end of the bus line coming from Acapulco: the *Trailer Park Quinta Dora* (☎ 60-11-38) and the *Acapulco Trailer Park & Mini-Super* (☎ 60-00-10, fax 60-24-57). Both have full hookups and are good for both tents and trailers. Take a look at both parks and ask for prices before you choose your spot; they're only about a two-minute walk from each other but most campers have a distinct preference for one or the other. Each place has camping areas on both the beach and lagoon sides of the road. The cost is around US$10 for trailers and US$6 for tents.

Hotels & Guesthouses Accommodation is mostly small-scale, family-run, and by the beach. Hot water is a rarity. Places are listed in order from east to west.

The *Hotel & Restaurant Rocío* (☎ 60-10-08) has doubles at US$16/19 with one/two beds and hot water. Félix López, the resident bartender, chef, guitarist and songster, provides music and good times. *Quinta Karla* (☎ 60-12-55) has a swimming pool and rooms at US$7.75/18 in low/high season.

The *Villa Nirvana* (☎ 60-16-31) provides a garden with a beachside swimming pool. Singles/doubles are US$16/19 from May to October, US$19/26 from November to April, and there's a four-person apartment. Nearby, the *Hotel Quinta Blanca* (no phone) has a big swimming pool and 24 large rooms at US$10/13, or US$16/19 in high season.

The *Hotel Sunset – Puesta del Sol* (☎ 60-04-12), about 50 meters from the coast road down a narrow lane, is an excellent choice by the beach. There's a lovely shaded

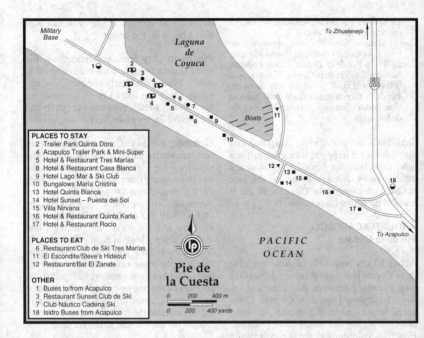

PLACES TO STAY
2   Trailer Park Quinta Dora
4   Acapulco Trailer Park & Mini-Super
5   Hotel & Restaurant Tres Marías
8   Hotel & Restaurant Casa Blanca
9   Hotel Lago Mar & Ski Club
10 Bungalows María Cristina
13 Hotel Quinta Blanca
14 Hotel Sunset – Puesta del Sol
15 Villa Nirvana
16 Hotel & Restaurant Quinta Karla
17 Hotel & Restaurant Rocío

PLACES TO EAT
6   Restaurant/Club de Ski Tres Marías
11 El Escondite/Steve's Hideout
12 Restaurant/Bar El Zanate

OTHER
1   Buses to/from Acapulco
3   Restaurant Sunset Club de Ski
7   Club Náutico Cadena Ski
18 Isidro Buses from Acapulco

garden, a swimming pool, tennis court and restaurant/bar. Regular rooms are US$16/19 in low/high season, large four-bed rooms with kitchen are US$32/45.

Bungalows María Cristina (☎ 60-02-62), run by a friendly family who speak English and Spanish, is a clean, well-tended, relaxing place with a barbecue and hammocks overlooking the beach. Prices are comparable to Villa Nirvana, though larger upstairs rooms with kitchens and sea views for up to five people cost US$32/45 in summer/winter.

Hotel Lago Mar (no phone) is on the lagoon side and has hot water, a swimming pool, and a ski club. Its big rooms have a bit of style, with tiled floors and bathrooms; prices are US$19 for up to three people, or US$32 in high season.

The *Hotel & Restaurant Casa Blanca* (☎ 60-03-24) is another clean, well-tended place on the beachfront, with a homey atmosphere; rates are US$7.75/13, or slightly more in the high season.

Hotel & Restaurant Tres Marías (☎ 60-01-78) has a swimming pool and good doubles for US$36 year round, so it's a reasonable value in high season.

Places to Eat Restaurants are known for their fresh seafood. There are plenty of open-air places right beside the beach, though some close early evening. Nearly all the hotels and guesthouses in town have restaurants, as do some of the water-ski clubs. The *Tres Marías* is known to have some of the best food in the area.

The *Restaurant El Zanate* beside the road is a small, simple place with meals for only US$1.60. Opposite this, on the shore of the lagoon, is *El Escondite/Steve's Hideout*. This attractive place is built on stilts over the water and offers a fine view.

Getting There & Away To get there from Acapulco, take a 'Playa Pie de la Cuesta' bus on La Costera opposite the post office (the one next to Sanborn's, near the zócalo), on the bay side of the street. Buses go every 15 minutes from 6 am until around 8 pm; the cost is US$0.30 for the 35-minute ride. Be sure to find out what time the last bus leaves Pie de la Cuesta for the return trip, unless you intend to stay the night. A taxi costs about US$8 one way.

Other Destinations

About 18 km southeast of Acapulco, **Puerto Marqués** is a cove much smaller than the Bahía de Acapulco. You get a magnificent view of the Bahía de Acapulco as the Carretera Escénica climbs south out of the city. The calm water at Puerto Marqués makes it a good place for water-skiing and sailing. Buses marked 'Puerto Marqués' depart from Acapulco's La Costera every 10 minutes from 5 am to 9 pm and cost US$0.30.

Past Puerto Marqués and heading out toward the airport, **Playa Revolcadero** is the long, straight beach of the new Acapulco Diamante luxury tourism developments. The waves are large and surfing is popular here, especially in summer, but a strong undertow makes swimming dangerous. Horseback riding on the beach is another popular activity.

During Semana Santa, the Passion of Christ is acted out in the town of **Treinta**, 30km northeast of Acapulco; the Acapulco tourist office will have details.

CHILPANCINGO

pop 136,200; alt 1360 meters; ☎ *747*

Chilpancingo is capital of the state of Guerrero as well as a university city and agricultural center. It's located on highways 95 and 95D, about 130 km due north of Acapulco and 270 km south of Mexico City. It's a rather nondescript place between two much more interesting destinations, Acapulco and Taxco.

Murals in the former **Palacio Municipal** showing the 1813 Congress of Chilpancingo are the only remaining signs of the city's important place in Mexico's history. In the spring of 1813, rebel leader José Maria Morelos y Pavón encircled Mexico City with his guerrilla army and then called for a congress to meet in Chilpancingo. The congress issued a Declaration of Independence and began to lay down the principles of a new constitution. Their achievements, however, were short-lived because Spanish troops broke the circle around Mexico City and recaptured most of Guerrero, including Chilpancingo. Morelos was tried for treason and executed by a firing squad.

LA SIRENA

EL PARAGUAS

LA LUNA

LA ROSA

LA ESCALERA

LA MUERTE

Western Central Highlands

West of Mexico City lies an upland area of great geographical and cultural variety encompassing the inland parts of the states of Jalisco, Michoacán and Colima. (These states' narrow Pacific coastal plains are covered in the Central Pacific Coast chapter.) This region is off the really major tourist routes but has many attractive destinations, among them the country's vibrant, second largest city Guadalajara, capital of Jalisco; the fine capital of Michoacán, Morelia, and the spectacular El Rosario monarch butterfly sanctuary to its east; the lovely colonial town of Pátzcuaro in the Michoacán highlands inhabited by Tarascan (Purépecha) Indians; and the volcano Paricutín, which rose in 1943 from the lush Michoacán country around Uruapan. Beyond these lie hundreds of kilometers of backcountry ripe for exploration.

History

The Western Central Highlands were remote from Mexico's major pre-Hispanic empires, though a fairly advanced agricultural village society flourished in parts of the region as early as 200 BC. The major pre-Hispanic civilization here was developed by the Tarascans of northern Michoacán in the 14th to 16th centuries AD, with its capital at Tzintzuntzan near Pátzcuaro. The zenith of the Tarascan empire coincided with the Aztec empire but the Tarascans always managed to fend off Aztec attacks. West of the Tarascans – and occasionally at war with them – was the Chimalhuacán confederation of four Indian kingdoms, in parts of what are now Jalisco, Colima and Nayarit states. To the north were Chichimecs, whom the Aztecs regarded as barbarians.

Colima, the leading Chimalhuacán kingdom, was conquered by the Spanish in 1523, but the region as a whole was not brought under Spanish control until the 1529-36 campaigns of Nuño de Guzmán,

HIGHLIGHTS

- Guadalajara, often called the country's most Mexican city, birthplace of mariachi music, charreadas and tequila
- The smoldering Volcán Paricutín, which swallowed two villages and makes for an unforgettable hike
- The beautiful highland town of Pátzcuaro, heart of Purépecha Indian country
- Lovely Ajijic, a friendly little town with cobbled streets and prettily painted houses on the shore of Lago de Chapala
- El Rosario monarch butterfly sanctuary, home to millions of migratory butterflies from November to March

Zacatecas   San Luís Potosí

Nayarit

Jalisco   Guanajuato

Guadalajara p 515
Guadalajara City Center pp 518-519
Around Guadalajara p 536

Colima p 572
Around Colima p 578

Uruapan p 562

Morelia p 541

Pátzcuaro p 550
Lago de Pátzcuaro p 559

Michoacán

OTHER MAPS
Michoacán p 539

Guerrero

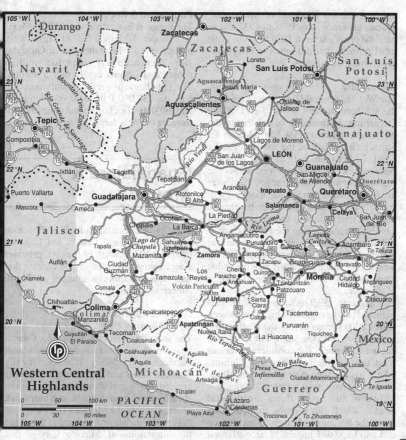

Western Central Highlands

0	50	100 km
0	30	60 miles

PACIFIC OCEAN

who tortured, killed and enslaved Indians from Michoacán to Sinaloa in his pursuit of riches, territory and glory. Guzmán was appointed governor of most of what he had conquered, but eventually his misdeeds caught up with him and in 1538 he was sent back to Spain. These territories came to be called Nueva Galicia and retained some autonomy from the rest of Nueva España until 1786.

An Indian rebellion in Jalisco in 1540 set that area aflame in what is known as the Mixtón War; it was ended the next year by an army led by the Spanish viceroy. Guadalajara was established in its present location in 1542, after three earlier settlements were abandoned in the face of Indian attacks.

Although the region was slower to develop than mineral-rich areas such as Zacatecas or Guanajuato, it did develop. Ranching and agriculture grew, and Guadalajara, always one of Mexico's biggest cities, became the 'capital of the west.' The church helped by fostering small industries and handicraft traditions in its effort to ease the poverty of the Indians.

In the 1920s Michoacán and Jalisco were the hotbeds of the Cristero rebellion by Catholics against government antichurch policies. Lázaro Cárdenas of Michoacán, as state governor from 1928 to 1932 and as national president from 1934 to 1940, instituted reforms that did much to allay antigovernment sentiments.

Geography

The Western Central Highlands reach from the southern outliers of the Sierra Madre Occidental, in the north of Jalisco, to the western extremities of the Sierra Madre del Sur, which rise behind the southern Pacific coast. In between, part of the Cordillera Neovolcánica sweeps east-west across the region. Between these ranges lie lesser hills and basins. Among the most rugged, sparsely populated expanses are the remote northern spur of Jalisco and the rather inaccessible ranges backing the Pacific coast.

Jalisco is Mexico's sixth largest state, at 80,836 sq km. Guadalajara lies toward the west end of an agriculturally rich basin that stretches down from the northeast portion of the state.

Michoacán (59,928 sq km) has the real highlands of the region – a big, green sweep above 2000 meters across the north of the state, strewn with the stumps of living and extinct volcanoes. The cordillera continues west into southern Jalisco and Colima, where sits the Volcán de Fuego de Colima, one of Mexico's most active volcanoes.

Two of the major rivers are the Río Lerma, which flows down from the east along the border of Michoacán and Jalisco and into Lago de Chapala, Mexico's largest lake, south of Guadalajara, and the Río Balsas, which carries almost all the runoff from the southern side of the Cordillera Neovolcánica.

Climate

Warm and dry most of the year, the region has a distinct rainy season from June to September, when some 200 mm of rain falls each month in most areas. At lower altitudes, such as Uruapan and around Colima city, temperature and humidity rise and tropical plants abound. Winter nights can get chilly at higher altitudes such as Pátzcuaro.

Population & People

The region is home to about 10% of Mexico's people. Well over half of Jalisco's six million or so inhabitants live in Guadalajara. Michoacán has about four million people and Colima barely half a million. The population is predominantly mestizo, with the 130,000 Purépecha of Michoacán and 60,000 Huichol in northern Jalisco forming the only large Indian groups.

Guadalajara & Around

The city of Guadalajara itself is the major attraction of inland Jalisco, but Lago de Chapala, 40 km south of the city, provides a nice change, with an idyllic climate that has attracted quite a number of North American expatriates.

GUADALAJARA

pop 5 million; alt 1540m; ☎ *3*

The second largest city in Mexico, Guadalajara has a reputation as the nation's most Mexican city. Many characteristically Mexican things and Tapatío traditions were created here, including mariachi music, tequila, the broad-rimmed sombrero hat, charreadas and the Mexican Hat Dance.

Part of Guadalajara's appeal is that it has the attractions of Mexico City – fine museums and galleries, beautiful historic buildings, nightlife, culture, good places to stay and eat – without the capital's problems. Guadalajara is western Mexico's biggest industrial center but it's also a modern, orderly city where traffic flows fairly freely and pollution is not trapped by mountains. Also, it is probably Mexico's most musical city, with many venues and a wide range of musical styles to be heard.

Excursions to the suburbs of Tlaquepaque and Tonalá, renowned for their arts and crafts, and farther afield to Lago de Chapala, Mexico's largest lake, are popular. You'll never get bored in this city.

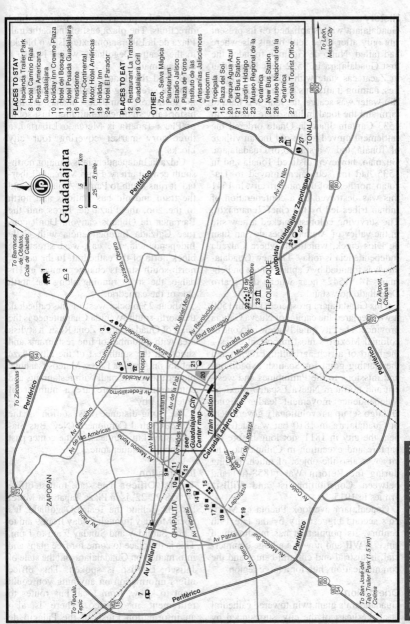

PLACES TO STAY
7 Hacienda Trailer Park
8 Hotel Camino Real
9 Fiesta Americana Guadalajara
10 Holiday Inn Crowne Plaza
11 Hotel del Bosque
13 Hotel Posada Guadalajara
16 Presidente Inter-Continental
17 Motor Hotel Américas
18 Holiday Inn
24 Hotel El Parador

PLACES TO EAT
12 Restaurant La Trattoria
19 Guadalajara Grill

OTHER
1 Zoo, Selva Magica
2 Planetarium
3 Estadio Jalisco
4 Plaza de Toros
5 Instituto de las Artesanías Jaliscienses
6 Telecomm
14 Tropigala
15 Plaza del Sol
20 Parque Agua Azul
21 Old Bus Station
22 16 de Septiembre
23 Jardín Hidalgo
23 Museo Regional de la Cerámica
25 New Bus Station
26 Museo Nacional de la Cerámica
27 Tonalá Tourist Office

Guadalajara

History

Guadalajara was established on its present site only after three settlements elsewhere had failed. Nuño de Guzmán founded the first Guadalajara in 1532 near Nochistlán in Zacatecas state with 63 Spanish families, naming it after his home city in Spain. But water was scarce, the land was hard to farm and the local Indians were hostile. In 1533 Captain Juan de Oñate ordered the settlement moved to the old Indian village of Tonalá, today a suburb of Guadalajara. Guzmán, however, disliked Tonalá and in 1535 had the settlement moved to Tlacotán, northeast of the modern city. In 1541 this was destroyed by a confederation of Indian tribes led by the chief Tenamaxtli. The surviving colonists picked a new site in the valley of Atemajac beside San Juan de Dios creek, which ran where Calzada Independencia is today. The new Guadalajara was founded by Captain Oñate on February 14, 1542, near where the Teatro Degollado now stands.

This Guadalajara prospered, and in 1560 it was declared the capital of Nueva Galicia province. The city quickly grew into one of colonial Mexico's most important cities – the heart of a rich agricultural region and the starting point for Spanish expeditions and missions to the Philippines and western and northern Nueva España. Mexican independence movement leader Miguel Hidalgo set up a revolutionary government in Guadalajara in 1810 but was defeated near the city in 1811, not long before his capture and execution in Chihuahua. The city was also the object of much fighting during the Reform War (1858-61) and between Constitutionalist and Villista armies in 1915.

Guadalajara overtook Puebla as Mexico's second biggest city by the late 19th century. Its population has mushroomed since WWII and now it's a huge commercial, industrial and cultural center and the communications hub for a large region.

Orientation

Guadalajara's giant twin-towered cathedral is at the heart of the city, surrounded by four lovely plazas in the four cardinal directions. The plaza east of the cathedral, Plaza de la Liberación, extends two blocks to the Teatro Degollado, which is also a city landmark.

Behind the Teatro Degollado is Plaza Tapatía, stretching half a kilometer east to the Instituto Cultural de Cabañas, another historically significant building. Just south of Plaza Tapatía is Mercado Libertad, a three-story market covering four city blocks.

Calzada Independencia is a major north-south central artery. From Mercado Libertad, it runs south to Parque Agua Azul and the train and old bus stations and north to the zoo, the Plaza de Toros and the Barranca de Oblatos canyon. Don't confuse Calzada Independencia with Calle Independencia, the east-west street one block north of the cathedral. In the center, north-south streets change names at Hidalgo, the street running along the north side of the cathedral.

About 25 blocks west of the cathedral, the north-south Avenida Chapultepec is the heart of Guadalajara's Zona Rosa, a stylish area with a number of fine restaurants and shops. In the southwest of the city, Plaza del Sol on Avenida López Mateos is a huge modern shopping mall with restaurants and entertainment. There are a number of hotels nearby.

The long-distance bus station is the Nueva Central Camionera (New Bus Station), nine km southeast of the center past the suburb Tlaquepaque.

Information

Tourist Offices The state tourist office (☎ 658-22-22) is in Plaza Tapatía at Morelos 102, behind the Teatro Degollado. It's open Monday through Friday from 9 am to 8 pm, Saturday and Sunday 9 am to 1 pm. This is the place to come for free maps and information on Guadalajara and the state of Jalisco. English is spoken. This office offers information on anything you could want to know, from local bus routes to retirement in Mexico. There is also an information kiosk in the Palacio de

Gobierno, facing the Plaza de Armas just south of the cathedral, open Monday through Friday from 9 am to 3 pm and 6 to 8 pm, Saturday from 9 am to 1 pm.

Consulates More than 30 countries have consular offices in Guadalajara. The tourist office has a complete list, or you can contact the Consular Association (☎ 616-06-29) for information. Consulates include:

Canada
    Hotel Fiesta Americana, Local 30, Aceves 225 (☎ 616-56-42)
France
    López Mateos Nte 484 (☎ 616-55-16)
Germany
    Corona 202 at Madero (☎ 613-96-23)
Guatemala
    Mango 1440 (☎ 811-15-03)
Netherlands
    Calzada Lázaro Cárdenas 601, 6th Floor, Zona Industrial (☎ 669-55-15)
UK and Northern Ireland
    Miguel Ángel de Quevedo 601 (☎ 616-06-29)
USA
    Progreso 175 (☎ 825-27-00)

Money Banks are plentiful in Guadalajara and are open for currency exchange and other services Monday through Friday from 9 am to at least 1.30 pm. Many banks have ATMs. In addition some casas de cambio on López Cotilla in the three blocks between Corona and Molina offer competitive exchange rates and are open on Saturday.

The American Express office (☎ 630-02-00) is at Vallarta 2440, opposite Plaza Vallarta, and will change or issue traveler's checks Monday through Friday from 9 am to 2.30 pm and 4 to 6 pm, Saturday 9 am to 1 pm. Canadians, be advised that Banamex is one of the few banks in Guadalajara that will change traveler's checks issued in Canadian dollars.

Post & Communications The main post office is on Carranza, between Manuel and Calle Independencia. It's open Monday through Friday from 8 am to 7 pm, Saturday from 9 am to 1 pm.

The Telecomm office, with telegram, telex and fax services, is in the Palacio Federal on Alcalde at Calle Hospital, opposite the Santuario church nine blocks north of the center. It's open Monday through Friday from 9 am to 7 pm, Saturday 9 am to noon. There's a post office branch there too.

Telmex, the main telephone caseta, is at Guerra 84 near the corner of Juárez. It's open daily from 7 am to 8.30 pm.

Computel, with long-distance telephone and fax services, has several offices around the city. There's one on Corona opposite the Hotel Fénix. Another is at 16 de Septiembre 599. Computel also has offices at the train and bus stations.

Bookstores A fair selection of books and magazines in English is available in the gift shops of most major hotels and at many of the larger bookstores. Sandi Bookstore (☎ 121-42-10), Tepayac No 718, has a good travel section. Also, many of the newsstands in central Guadalajara sell English-language periodicals.

Newspapers & Magazines *The Guadalajara Colony Reporter* is a daily English-language newspaper covering Guadalajara and has lots of information about cultural events in the city. The Spanish-language *Siglo 21* also covers Guadalajara on a daily basis. Both newspapers can be found at most any newsstand around town.

Let's Enjoy, a free monthly bilingual magazine, contains features on Jalisco's people and places and can often be found at the tourist office. *Tentaciones* is a weekly newspaper insert containing information on cultural activities in Guadalajara for the coming week. The insert appears in Friday's edition of *Siglo 21* and is *the* place to look for movie listings and information on exhibits and the club scene.

Mexico Retirement & Travel Assistance (MRTA) publishes the book *Guadalajara – A Great Place to Visit or Retire* and the newsletter *MRTA Guadalajara/Chapala Update*. They are often available at the tourist office. MRTA editor John Bryant

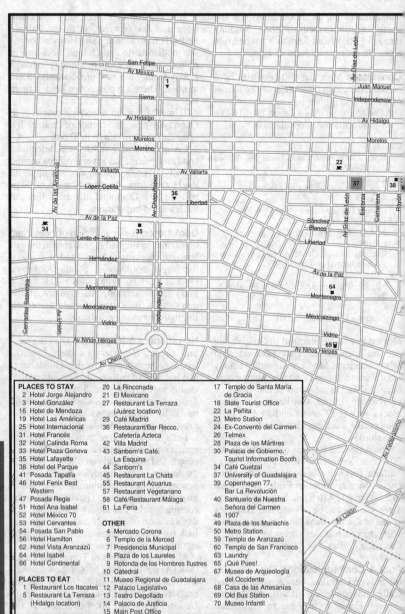

PLACES TO STAY
2   Hotel Jorge Alejandro
3   Hotel González
16   Hotel de Mendoza
19   Hotel Las Américas
25   Hotel Internacional
31   Hotel Francés
32   Hotel Calinda Roma
33   Hotel Plaza Genova
35   Hotel Lafayette
38   Hotel del Parque
41   Posada Tapatía
46   Hotel Fenix Best
      Western
47   Posada Regis
51   Hotel Ana Isabel
52   Hotel México 70
53   Hotel Cervantes
54   Posada San Pablo
56   Hotel Hamilton
62   Hotel Vista Aranzazú
64   Hotel Isabel
66   Hotel Continental

PLACES TO EAT
1   Restaurant Los Itacates
5   Restaurant La Terraza
      (Hidalgo location)
20   La Rinconada
21   El Mexicano
27   Restaurant La Terraza
      (Juárez location)
29   Café Madrid
36   Restaurant/Bar Recco,
      Cafetería Azteca
42   Villa Madrid
43   Sanborn's Café,
      La Esquina
44   Sanborn's
45   Restaurant La Chata
55   Restaurant Acuarius
57   Restaurant Vegetariano
58   Café/Restaurant Málaga
61   La Feria

OTHER
4   Mercado Corona
6   Templo de la Merced
7   Presidencia Municipal
8   Plaza de los Laureles
9   Rotonda de los Hombres Ilustres
10   Catedral
11   Museo Regional de Guadalajara
12   Palacio Legislativo
13   Teatro Degollado
14   Palacio de Justicia
15   Main Post Office
17   Templo de Santa María
      de Gracia
18   State Tourist Office
22   La Peñita
23   Metro Station
24   Ex-Convento del Carmen
26   Telmex
28   Plaza de los Mártires
30   Palacio de Gobierno,
      Tourist Information Booth
34   Café Quetzal
37   University of Guadalajara
39   Copenhagen 77,
      Bar La Revolución
40   Santuario de Nuestra
      Señora del Carmen
48   1907
49   Plaza de los Mariachis
50   Metro Station
59   Templo de Aranzazú
60   Templo de San Francisco
63   Laundry
65   ¡Qué Pues!
67   Museo de Arqueología
      del Occidente
68   Casa de las Artesanías
69   Old Bus Station
70   Museo Infantil

To Zapopan
Garibaldi
Reforma
To Zoo, Selva Mágica,
Estadio Jalisco,
Barra de Oblatos,
Cola de Caballo
Parque
Morelos
Santa Mónica
Medellín
Ortega
Ocampo
Av Federalismo
Mezquitán
M Bárcenas
San Felipe
Loza
Av Alcalde
Juan Manuel
Independencia
Hidalgo
Morelos
Santo Degollado
Reforma
Vicente Guerrero
Ibor
Suárez
Belén
Humbolt
Arsquilla
Calzada Independencia Norte
2 ■
3 ■
8
4 ▼
5 ▼
6 †
7 ●
9 ■
10 ■
11 ●
12 ●
14 ●
15 ▼
16 ■
17 †
19 ■
Plaza de la
Liberación
13 ■
18 ❶
▼ 20
▼ 21
Plaza Tapatía
Instituto
Cultural de
Cabañas
arque
M 23
24 ●
26 ☎
27 ●
25 ■
28
Plaza de
Armas
30 ■
31 ■
29 ▼
32 ■
33 ■
evolución
40 ▼
41 ■
42 ▼
46 ■
Av Juárez
López Cotilla
Madere
Sánchez
Blanco
Guerrero
Ocampo
Galeana
Colón
Av 16 de Septiembre
43 ▼
44 ▼
45 ▼
Av Corona
47 ●
48 ■
Maestranza
Molina
Huerto
Av Javier Mina
Obregón
49 ■
M 50
Mercado
Libertad
To Hotel
Azteca
51 ■
52 ■
53 ■
54 ■
55 ▼
56 ■
57 ▼
58 ▼
59 †
60 †
61 ▼
62 ■
Gigantes
Verdía
Aldama
63 ●
Farías
Medrano
Av Revolución
Torres
Cabañas
Gutierro
Libertad
Leandro Valle
Nueva Galicia
66 ■
Av de la Paz
Montenegro
González
Mexicalzingo
Vidrio
Av Niños Héroes
B de Hidalgo
Maturino
Av Federalismo
Av Colón
Calzada de Aguila
Av 16 de Septiembre
Calzada Independencia Sur
Dr Michel
Estadio
Los Angeles
69 ●
Av 5 de Febrero
Curiel
Calzada Gallo
67 �🏛
68 ●
Parque
Agua Azul
70 🏛
Circunvalación Santa Eduwiges
Train
Station

Guadalajara
City Center

0   150   300 m
0   150   300 yards

can be reached on ☎ 641-11-52 most days. The MRTA mailing address is PO Box 2190-23, Pahrump, NV 89041-2190, USA.

Laundry There's a laundry at Aldama 125 open Monday through Friday from 9 am to 7.30 pm. Drop your stuff off and return for it two hours later; it'll be waiting, clean and folded, in the same sack you brought it in. Two pairs of jeans, three shirts and five pairs of underwear run about US$3.50.

Catedral

Guadalajara's twin-towered cathedral, surrounded on all four sides by plazas, is its most famous symbol and most conspicuous landmark. Begun in 1558 and consecrated in 1618, it's almost as old as the city. Up close you can see that it's a stylistic hodge-podge. The exterior decorations, some of which were completed long after the consecration, are in Churrigueresque, baroque, neoclassical and other styles. The towers date from 1848; they're much higher than the originals, which were destroyed in an earthquake. The interior includes 11 richly decorated altars given to Guadalajara by King Fernando VII of Spain (1784-1833), Gothic vaults and Tuscany-style pillars. In the sacristy, which you can ask an attendant to open for you, is *La Asunción de la Virgen* (The Assumption of the Virgin), painted by Spanish artist Bartolomé Murillo in 1650.

Plaza de los Laureles & Presidencia Municipal

The Plaza de los Laureles is the square directly in front of the cathedral. As its name suggests, it's planted with laurels. On its north side is the Presidencia Municipal (City Hall), which was built between 1949 and 1952 but appears much older. Above its interior stairway there is a mural by Gabriel Flores depicting the founding of Guadalajara.

Plaza de Armas & Palacio de Gobierno

The Plaza de Armas, on the south side of the cathedral, with the Palacio de Gobierno

to its east, is a nice place to sit and imagine how the city was in colonial times. Free concerts of Jaliscan music are generally held here on Thursday and Sunday at 6.30 pm.

The Palacio de Gobierno was finished in 1774 and, like the cathedral, was built in a combination of styles – in this case, a mix of simple, neoclassical features and riotous Churrigueresque decorations. Its most interesting artistic feature is the huge 1937 portrait of Miguel Hidalgo painted by José Clemente Orozco in a mural over the interior stairway. In it, an angry Hidalgo, father of Mexico's movement for independence from Spain, brandishes a torch with one fist raised high and the struggling masses at his feet. In this mural Orozco also comments on the pressing issues of his time: communism, fascism and religion. Another Orozco mural in the upstairs Congreso (Congress Hall) depicts Hidalgo, Benito Juárez and other figures important in Mexican history. The murals can be viewed daily from 9 am to 9 pm.

Rotonda de los Hombres Ilustres & Museo Regional de Guadalajara

The plaza on the north side of the cathedral is ringed by bronze sculptures of 12 of Jalisco's favorite characters – a poet, a composer, a writer, an architect, a university reformer and others. Six of them are buried beneath the Rotonda de los Hombres Ilustres (Rotunda of Illustrious Men), the round pillared monument in the center of the plaza.

Facing the east side of this plaza, the Regional Museum of Guadalajara occupies the former seminary of San José, a late 17th century baroque building with two stories of arcades and an inner court. This must-see museum has an eclectic collection covering the history and prehistory of western Mexico. Displays in the ground-floor archaeological section include the skeleton of a woolly mammoth. Upstairs, there are painting galleries, a history gallery covering life in Jalisco since the Spanish conquest and an ethnography section with displays about Indian life in Jalisco and the *charro*, or Mexican cowboy.

The museum is open Tuesday through Saturday from 9 am to 6.45 pm; however, many of the rooms close at 2.45 pm. On Sunday the entire museum closes at 2.45 pm. Admission is US$2 for adults and US$1 for children under 13. Sunday is free.

Plaza de la Liberación & Teatro Degollado

East of the cathedral on the former site of several colonial buildings is the Plaza de la Liberación, with the impressive Teatro Degollado at its far end. Begun in 1856 and inaugurated 30 years later, the neoclassical-style theater has been reconstructed many times. Over the columns on its front is a frieze depicting Apollo and the Nine Muses. The five-tiered theater's interior is decorated with red velvet and gold and is crowned by a Gerardo Suárez mural based on the fourth canto of Dante's *Divine Comedy*.

Frequent performances are staged in the theater (see Entertainment). It can be visited free Monday through Saturday from 10 am to 1 pm.

On the north side of the Plaza de la Liberación is the **Palacio Legislativo** (State Congress), with massive stone columns in its interior courtyard.

Palacio de Justicia & Templo de Santa María de Gracia

Across Hidalgo from the Teatro Degollado, the Palacio de Justicia (State Courthouse) was built in 1588 as part of the Convento de Santa María, Guadalajara's first nunnery. A 1965 mural by Guillermo Chávez, depicting Benito Juárez and other legendary Mexican lawmakers, graces the interior stairway.

Also near the theater, at the corner of Hidalgo and Carranza, is the Templo de Santa María de Gracia, which served as the city's first cathedral (from 1549 to 1618).

Plaza Tapatía

Behind the Teatro Degollado, Plaza Tapatía is a modern square and pedestrian mall of shops, restaurants, street performers, fountains and the tourist office. It stretches half a km east to the Instituto Cultural de Cabañas. Calzada Independencia passes underneath it at about its midpoint.

Instituto Cultural de Cabañas

This huge neoclassical gem at the east end of Plaza Tapatía was built between 1805 and 1810 by Spanish architect Manuel Tolsá. Called the Hospicio Cabañas after its founder Bishop Don Juan Cruz Ruiz de Cabañas, it served mainly as an orphanage for over 150 years until 1980, often housing up to 3000 children at a time. It has also served as an insane asylum, a military barracks and a jail. It was in this building that Miguel Hidalgo signed a proclamation against slavery in 1811.

Between 1936 and 1939 José Clemente Orozco painted murals in the main chapel. They are widely regarded as his finest works. Most notable is *El Hombre de Fuego* (The Man of Fire) in the dome – interpretations of this work vary. Fifty-three other frescoes cover the walls and ceiling of the chapel. A small book in English and Spanish, *The Murals of Orozco in the Cabañas Cultural Institute*, on sale at the main entrance, gives information on the artist and the murals.

The Instituto Cultural Cabañas is a cultural institute housing a museum, theater and school. All 23 courts and the chapel that Tolsá designed are intact; tours in English and Spanish are available. The museum features a permanent exhibition of more than 100 Orozco drawings and paintings, plus temporary exhibitions of painting, sculpture and engraving. The institute also hosts dance festivals, theater performances and concerts.

The Instituto is open Tuesday through Saturday from 10.15 am to 5.45 pm, Sunday 10.15 am to 2.45 pm. Admission is US$1.25, except on Sunday when it's free.

Plaza de los Mariachis

The Plaza de los Mariachis, near the intersection of Mina and Calzada Independencia Sur, is known throughout Mexico for the mariachi bands that play here (mainly after 10 pm). Several restaurants have tables out on the plaza and the mariachis come around and offer music to the customers – for US$5 and up per song.

Colonial Churches

Besides the cathedral and the Templo de Santa María de Gracia, there are 13 other churches in central Guadalajara, some quite impressive. The baroque **Templo de La Merced**, near the cathedral on the corner of Hidalgo and Loza, was built in 1650; inside are several fine large paintings, crystal chandeliers and lots of gold decoration.

The **Santuario de Nuestra Señora del Carmen**, facing the small plaza on the corner of Juárez and 8 de Julio, is another lovely church, with lots of gold decoration, old paintings, and murals in the dome.

On the corner of 16 de Septiembre and Blanco, the **Templo de Aranzazú**, built from 1749 to 1752, has three ornate Churrigueresque golden altars. Beside it is the older, less showy **Templo de San Francisco**, built two centuries earlier.

Parque Agua Azul

About 20 blocks south of the center, near the south end of Calzada Independencia Sur, Parque Agua Azul is a large verdant park offering pleasant relief from the city hubbub, with an orchid house, a butterfly house, an aviary and a children's wading pool and playground. It's open daily from 7 am to 6.30 pm; admission is US$0.75 for adults, US$0.25 for children. Bus No 60 or 62 heading south on Calzada Independencia will bring you there from the city center.

The **Casa de las Artesanías de Jalisco** on the north side of the park, which has its own separate entrance on González Gallo, features handicrafts and arts from all over Jalisco. Everything is for sale; prices are high but the quality can't be beaten. It's open Monday through Friday 10 am to 6 pm, Saturday 11 am to 3 pm and Sunday 11 am to 2 pm. Admission is free.

The collection of the **Museo de Arqueología del Occidente de México**, on Calzada Independencia Sur opposite the entrance to the park, includes some pre-Hispanic figurines and artifacts from

---

Mariachis

In many minds no image captures the spirit of Mexico better than that of proud-faced *mariachis*, in matching garb and broad-rimmed sombreros, belting out traditional Mexican ballads before a festive crowd. But the origin of the word 'mariachi' is something of a mystery.

Some historians contend that 'mariachi' is a corruption of the French word *mariage* (marriage) and that the name stems from the time of the French intervention in 1861-67. Mariachi bands were said to have played at wedding ceremonies during that period, hence the name.

Others say that the word was in use before the French arrived, and they suggest it arose from festivals honoring the Virgin Mary at which musicians performed. They note that the mariachi is indigenous to the region south of Guadalajara and say the word probably derived from the name María with the Náhuatl diminutive '-chi' tacked on.

Still others point out that in the 1870s a Mexican poet designated as *mariache* the stage upon which dancers and musicians performed *jarabes*. A 'jarabe' consisted of an ensemble that played and sang while a couple – a man attired as a Mexican cowboy in chaps and a wide-rimmed hat and a woman in a handwoven shawl and full, brightly colored skirt – danced beside them.

Today's mariachi bands are of two types. The original version consists of musicians who play only string instruments and who limit their repertoire to traditional Jalisco melodies. The modern, more commercial mariachi band's main instrument is the trumpet, and they have quite a broad repertoire. Both types can be heard in Guadalajara's Plaza de los Mariachis. ∎

Jalisco and the states of Nayarit and Colima.

On the east side of the park at its south end is the **Museo Infantil** (Children's Museum), reached through an entrance on Dr Michel near the corner of González Gallo. It features exhibits on geography, space and prehistoric animals, with several interactive exhibits. It's open Tuesday through Friday 9 am to 1 pm and 3 to 7 pm (free).

Universidad de Guadalajara
West of the center, where Juárez meets Federalismo, is another shady park, **Parque Revolución**. Three blocks farther west at Juárez 975 is one of the main buildings of the University of Guadalajara. Inside, the **Paraninfo** (theater hall) contains large, powerful murals by Orozco on the stage backdrop and dome.

Zoológico Guadalajara, Selva Mágica & Planetario
The zoo, the Selva Mágica amusement park and the planetarium are near one another just off Calzada Independencia Norte on the northern outskirts of the city. Bus Nos 60 and 62 (marked 'Zoológico') heading north on Calzada Independencia will drop you at the entrance monument. From there, it's a 10-minute walk to the actual entrances.

The Zoológico Guadalajara is a large, older zoo. At one end is a view of **Barranca de Oblatos** canyon. Other features are two pyramid-shaped aviaries, a snake house, a children's petting zoo and a train that will take you around the zoo if you don't feel like walking. The zoo is open Wednesday through Sunday from 10 am to 5 pm; admission is US$2 (US$1 for children).

Beside the zoo is Selva Mágica, a children's amusement park with mechanical rides, a dolphin and seal show and a trained bird show. It's open Tuesday through Sunday from 10 am to 7 pm; entrance is US$2 for adults or children. If you pay to visit the zoo, you can enter Selva Mágica free. There is an additional fee for the animal shows.

About a five-minute walk from the zoo (turn left after 200 meters) is the planetarium, the Centro de Ciencia y Tecnología. It has exhibits on astronomy, space, airplanes, the body and other science-related topics. Planetarium shows are held hourly from 10.30 am. It's open Tuesday through Sunday from 9 am to 7.30 pm; admission is US$0.50 (free for children under 12), plus an extra US$0.75 for the planetarium show.

Barranca de Oblatos & Cascada Cola de Caballo
You can see the 670-meter-deep Barranca de Oblatos canyon from the zoo. Otherwise, you can take bus No 60 north on Calzada Independencia to **Parque Mirador**, a little past the entrance to the zoo, for a view. The park is always open. This canyon rivals Barranca del Cobre (Copper Canyon) in northwestern Mexico for the title of 'Mexico's Grand Canyon,' though Copper Canyon is more spectacular.

The long waterfall Cola de Caballo (Horse Tail) is in Barranca de Oblatos canyon. It flows all year but is most impressive during the rainy season. For a view of the falls take the Ixcatan bus from the Glorieta de la Normal, on Alcalde about 10 blocks north of the cathedral, and get off at Parque Dr Atl.

Zapopan
pop 924,983; alt 1560m; ☎ *3*
About eight km from downtown, on the northwestern edge of Guadalajara, Zapopan was an Indian village before the Spanish arrived and an important maize-producing village in colonial times. Its main attractions are its basilica and the Huichol museum.

The Zapopan tourist office (☎ 636-97-97, ext 116) is upstairs in the Casa de la Cultura, a block north of the basilica, at Vicente Guerrero 233. Staff give out maps of Zapopan and leaflets, in Spanish, detailing places of interest in and around the suburb. Hours are Monday through Friday from 9 am to 7 pm and Saturday 9 am to 1 pm.

The large **Basílica de Zapopan**, built in 1730, is home to Nuestra Señora de Zapopan, a tiny statue visited by pilgrims from near and far. On October 12, during Guadalajara's Fiestas de Octubre, the statue, which has been visiting other churches in Jalisco before reaching Guadalajara, is taken from Guadalajara's cathedral and returned to its home in Zapopan amid throngs of people and much merrymaking. The statue receives a new car each year for the procession, but the engine is never turned on; instead, the car is hauled along by ropes.

To the right of the basilica entrance the small **Museo Huichol** is a museum of Huichol Indian art with many colorful yarn paintings and other crafts. Most of the items on display are for sale. Hours are Monday through Friday from 9 am to 1 pm and 4 to 7 pm, weekends from 10 am to 1 pm (free).

Bus Nos 275, 275A and 275B heading north on 16 de Septiembre stop beside the basilica; the trip takes 20 minutes.

Tlaquepaque
pop 449,495; alt 1570m; ☎ 3

About seven km southeast of downtown Guadalajara, Tlaquepaque ('tlah-keh-PAH-keh') also used to be a separate village, with an initial population of potters swelled by Guadalajara gentry who built mansions here in the 19th century. More recently Tlaquepaque's many artisans decided to capitalize on their talents by cleaning up the central plaza, and renaming many of the shops (formerly large country homes) 'galleries' to attract tourists. Fortunately, the throngs of crafts-hungry gringos who have descended on the place have not yet spoiled the refurbishment of central Tlaquepaque.

Many flowers, small benches and monuments grace the plaza. The shops are full of ceramics, papier-mâché animals, bronze figures, handmade glassware, embroidered clothing and more, including items from elsewhere. Many shops are closed on Sunday. The Tlaquepaque tourist office (☎ 659-02-43) is next to the post office at Prieto 80. Hours are Monday through Friday 9 am to 3 pm, closed weekends.

Visit the **Museo Regional de la Cerámica y los Artes Populares de Jalisco** at Independencia 237 to get an idea of the best handicrafts available in Tlaquepaque. It's open Tuesday through Saturday from 10 am to 4 pm, Sunday 10 am to 1 pm (free). Also visit the glass factory opposite the museum. There are some good restaurants, many attached to Tlaquepaque's 'galleries,' serving up tasty Mexican food to live music – see the Places to Eat section.

To get to Tlaquepaque, take local bus Nos 275, 275A or 275B heading south on 16 de Septiembre. The trip takes about 30 minutes. After turning off Avenida Revolución, watch for a brick pedestrian bridge then a small traffic circle. Get off here and on the left is Independencia, which will take you to the heart of Tlaquepaque.

Tonalá
pop 271,969; alt 1660m; ☎ 3

The suburb of Tonalá, beyond Tlaquepaque, about 13 km southeast of the center, is the poorer, less touristic relative of Tlaquepaque. The shops here call themselves factories, not galleries – an accurate description considering that many of them manufacture the glassware and ceramics found in Tlaquepaque and in other parts of Guadalajara as well. On Thursday and Sunday most of the town becomes a street market that takes hours to explore. The best crafts are to be found in the factories, but you can pick up some bargains at the market. Tonalá has several old churches of interest and holds a charreada after 4 pm every Saturday.

The Tonalá tourist office (☎ 683-17-40) is at Tonaltecas 140, in the Casa de Artesanos. Staff give out maps and information in Spanish. Hours are Monday through Friday 9 am to 3 pm, weekends 9 am to 1 pm.

The **Museo Nacional de la Cerámica**, at Constitución 110, houses an eclectic array of pots from all over Mexico. It's open Tuesday through Sunday from 10 am to 5 pm (free).

Bus No 275, 275A or 275B heading south on 16 de Septiembre will take you to Tonalá, passing through Tlaquepaque on the way. The trip takes 45 minutes. As you enter Tonalá, get off on the corner of Avenidas Tonalá and Tonaltecas. It's three blocks from there to the tourist office and about six blocks to the Plaza Principal.

Courses

The Universidad de Guadalajara is the second largest university in Mexico, with over 180,000 students. Its Foreign Student Study Center offers 10 levels of intensive five-week Spanish-language courses. It also offers courses in history, culture, politics, economics, literature and other subjects, all taught in Spanish, which can be taken in addition to or independently from the language courses. Workshops in folkloric dance, guitar and singing, Mexican cuisine and so forth are also offered, as are special cultural events and excursions to other parts of Mexico.

Registration and tuition fees amount to US$585 for each five-week session of four hours per day Monday through Friday. Lodging and three meals daily are arranged with local Mexican families at a cost of US$490 for the session. The workshops and excursions are an optional expense.

For more specific information and an application form, write to Universidad de Guadalajara, Centro de Estudios para Extranjeros (☎ 616-43-99, fax 616-40-13), Tomás V Gómez 125, Apartado Postal 1-1362, Guadalajara, Jalisco 44100, Mexico.

In the USA, the University of Arizona (☎ 520-621-47-29) offers a summer program in Guadalajara. Write to Guadalajara Summer School, University of Arizona, PO Box 40966, Tucson, AZ 85717.

Organized Tours

Panoramex (☎ 810-51-09), at Federalismo Sur 944, offers numerous tours with English-, French- and Spanish-speaking guides.

Tour No 1 (Monday through Saturday) visits some of the main sights of Guadalajara and Tlaquepaque; the cost is US$15.

Tour No 2 (Tuesday, Thursday, Saturday and Sunday), visits Chapala and Ajijic; the cost is US$20.

Tour No 3 (Monday, Wednesday, Friday) visits the city of Tequila and includes agave fields, a tequila processing plant and so on; the cost is US$20.

During holidays (Easter and the second half of December) there are free guided city walking tours (two and three hours) organized by the tourist office.

Special Events

Several major festivals are celebrated in Guadalajara and nearby towns. They include:

Feria de Tonalá – Annual handicrafts fair in Tonalá, specializing in ceramics; Semana Santa

Fiestas de Tlaquepaque – Tlaquepaque's annual fiesta and handicrafts fair; mid-June to the first week of July

Fiestas de Octubre – Beginning with a parade on the first Sunday in October, the October Fiestas, lasting all month, are Guadalajara's principal annual fair. There's free entertainment daily from noon to 10 pm in the fairgrounds at the Benito Juárez auditorium plus, around the city, livestock shows, art and other exhibitions and sporting and cultural events. On October 12 a religious element enters the festivities with a procession from the cathedral to Zapopan carrying the miniature statue of the Virgin of Zapopan (see Zapopan earlier in this chapter).

Places to Stay – budget

Camping Guadalajara has two trailer parks, both offering full hookups and spaces for tents, trailers and motor homes.

San José del Tajo trailer park (☎ 686-17-38) is 15 km southwest of the city center at km 15 on Avenida López Mateos (highway 54/80), the start of the Colima road. Facilities include pool, tennis court, laundry and 200 sites; cost is US$15 per site, a little cheaper for tents. English is spoken.

Hacienda Trailer Park (☎ 627-17-24) is at Circunvalación Poniente 66, Ciudad Granja, 10 km west of the city center, between Avenida Vallarta and the Periférico. Facilities include pool, billiards, laundry, barbecue, plenty of trees and 98 sites. Cost is US$13 for two people.

Central District The *Hotel Hamilton* (☎ 614-67-26) at Madero 381 offers simple but clean and generally quiet rooms with private bath and 24-hour hot water at US$6/7 for a single/double, US$8 for two people with two single beds. Some rooms have TV. If you stay five or more nights and pay in advance, the rate is slightly lower. You can make local calls free of charge at the reception desk. This place is very popular with foreign travelers.

The *Posada Regis* (☎ 614-86-33) at Corona 171 is in the upstairs of a converted 19th century French-style mansion with high ceilings and ornate details. The 19 original rooms with bath, phone and 24-hour hot water open onto a covered patio; they cost US$13/17. There are also four rooms without carpeting up on the roof for US$6/8.50. Discounts are given for stays of a few days or more.

Another good value is the *Posada Tapatía* (☎ 614-91-46) at López Cotilla 619, which has a bright, cheerful decor (quite the opposite adjectives describe the manager). The 12 rooms with high ceilings and large bathrooms open onto a covered central courtyard with lots of plants. Your cost: US$8/12.

The *Hotel Las Américas* (☎ 613-96-22) at Hidalgo 76 near Plaza Tapatía, is a great value. The 49 rooms are clean and fairly modern, with TV, phone, carpeting, 24-hour hot water and large windows. The price of US$10/11 (US$12 for a double with two beds) is cheap for what you get. Beware: The streetside rooms are noisy.

The *Posada San Pablo* (☎ 614-28-11) at Madero 429 is a friendly, family-run hotel. It has three rooms with private bath and seven without, all ringing an open courtyard. Hot water is available from 6 am to noon, other times upon request. Without-bath rates are US$8/9 and US$12 for a double with two beds. Rooms with private bath cost US$9/10 and US$12.

Hotel González (☎ 614-56-81) at González Ortega 77 is a basic, friendly hotel

with 24 rooms at US$5.50/6.50 and US$8 for a double with two beds. The rooms are arranged around an interior courtyard full of clotheslines that you are welcome to use. There's 24-hour hot water. Rooms here can be stifling on hot days.

Near Mercado Libertad Several other popular budget hotels are found along Mina, opposite Mercado Libertad and near the Plaza de los Mariachis. This part of town is not quite as pleasant or safe as the center. The hotels are large and can be noisy.

The best of this bunch is the *Hotel Ana Isabel* (☎ 617-79-20), at Mina 164, opposite the Mercado Libertad. It has 50 clean rooms lined up along three floors of walkways draped with plants. Each has a TV, private bath and ceiling fan; cost is US$9/10. Hot water is always available.

The *Hotel México 70* (☎ 617-99-78) at Mina 230 has 80 clean rooms with private bath, at US$7/8. The rooms have two or more beds, 24-hour hot water, a TV, a writing table and decent mattresses.

The *Hotel Azteca* (☎ 617-74-65) at Mina 311 has 70 fairly clean rooms on five floors around an interior well. There's a restaurant and parking too. All the rooms have a bath and ceiling fan. Cost is US$11 for a single or double; add US$2 for a TV.

Places to Stay – middle
Central District The *Hotel Jorge Alejandro* (☎ 613-19-14) at Hidalgo 656 is a former convent and, fittingly, management has posted a large blue cross on the wall behind every bed in this clean 28-room, two-story hotel. There's plenty of hot water, and every room has a TV, fan and private bath. Rates are US$16/20.

Another of the center's attractive midrange hotels is the *Hotel del Parque* (☎ 825-28-00) at Juárez 845 near the Parque Revolución. It has a pleasant restaurant and lobby bar with sidewalk café tables, and 81 rooms in two price categories: US$27/33 for 'plus' rooms (with bathtub, TV, minibar, phone and alarm clock), and US$22/27 for 'superior' rooms (shower,

TV and phone). The rooms at the Alejandro are nicer than the Parque's superior rooms, but the plus rooms are tops – much nicer than the rooms at the comparably priced Hotel Internacional.

The *Hotel Internacional* (☎ 613-03-30) at Moreno 570 has 112 carpeted rooms, some with TV, all at US$27/33. This place is overpriced, and its thin walls and doors allow unwanted noise to enter rooms.

The *Hotel Continental* (☎ 614-11-17) at Corona 450 has parking and 124 fairly clean, comfortable, old-fashioned rooms. They have carpeting and telephone and cost US$18/24.

More expensive but also more luxurious is the historic *Hotel Francés* (☎ 613-11-90), the oldest hotel in Guadalajara, at Maestranza 35. It was founded in 1610 as an inn, with rooms upstairs and horses kept in the arched stone courtyard, which is now an elegant lobby bar. It has 52 good rooms of varying sizes at US$30 for a single or double and eight suites at US$38. All of the rooms have tiled floors, satellite TV and fan; some have bathtub and shower. The exterior rooms all have French doors that open onto small wrought-iron balconies.

By contrast, a new but also lovely place is the *Hotel Cervantes* (☎ 613-68-46) at Sánchez 442, which has 100 elegant rooms with all the amenities on five floors. There's even a phone beside each bathtub, underground parking and a second-floor pool. Rates are a very agreeable US$33/40.

Nueva Central Camionera The *Hotel El Parador* (☎ 600-09-10), at the new bus terminal, has two swimming pools and 377 basic but clean rooms with color TV at US$22 for a single or double. Its restaurant is OK if you have time to kill at the bus station.

West of the Center Avenida López Mateos is Guadalajara's 'motel row.' A good place is the *Hotel del Bosque* (☎ 621-46-50) at López Mateos Sur 265. It has an interior garden, swimming pool, restaurant and bar, and all 74 rooms have satellite TV.

Singles and doubles are US$30 with one twin bed and one single, and US$37 with two twin beds, more carpet and more space.

The *Hotel Posada Guadalajara* (☎ 121-20-22) at López Mateos Sur 1280 has a popular bar and restaurant and 170 lovely, modern rooms on six floors. All rooms flank an open courtyard, which has a swimming pool in the center. Rates are a very fair US$33/40.

The *Motor Hotel Américas* (☎ 631-44-15) at López Mateos Sur 2400, opposite the Plaza del Sol mall, is a four-star motel with swimming pool, air-conditioning and other amenities; its 101 rooms cost US$28/34, US$39 with kitchen. There are plenty of other motels near the Plaza del Sol. Bus No 258 heading west on San Felipe will bring you here from the center.

Another fine motel, cheaper and closer to the center, is the *Motel Isabel* (☎ 826-26-30) at Guadalupe Montenegro 1572, one block from Avenida de la Paz and eight blocks toward the center from Avenida Chapultepec. It has 50 rooms with phone and firm beds, and a pool, restaurant, bar and inside parking. The cost is US$23/27.

Places to Stay – top end

The *Hotel de Mendoza* (☎ 613-46-46), at Carranza 16 on the north side of the Teatro Degollado, was built as the convent to the church of Santa María de Gracia, which is still standing at one of its sides. The convent has been refurbished, and today is a four-star hotel with 104 modern rooms and all the amenities – satellite TV, air-conditioning, restaurant, bar, pool and parking. Some rooms have bathtubs and private balconies. Singles/doubles cost US$56/60.

The modern *Hotel Plaza Génova* (☎ 613-75-00) at Juárez 123 offers air-con rooms with phone, satellite TV, and minibar for US$50 for a single or double, including American breakfast. This Best Western hotel has a car rental agency and a travel agency in the lobby, and a gym and sauna baths.

Hotel Fénix Best Western (☎ 614-57-14) at Corona 160 charges US$63 for big, bright, pleasant rooms (exterior ones have balconies) for one or two people.

Other fine, centrally located hotels include the *Hotel Calinda Roma* (☎ 614-86-50), Juárez 170, with 172 rooms at US$42/53 and a rooftop pool; and the *Hotel Vista Aranzazú* (☎ 613-32-32), Revolución 110, which has a pool and 500 very comfortable rooms in two towers. The rooms have Cinemax, phone, minibar and air-conditioning at US$70 for a single or double.

The lovely *Hotel Lafayette* (☎ 615-02-52) at Avenida de la Paz 2055 in the Zona Rosa, just west of Avenida Chapultepec, has a pool, an attractive café and 181 attractive rooms with carpeting, color TV and air-conditioning at US$49/54.

Several upscale hotel chains offer accommodations in Guadalajara. They include the *Camino Real* (☎ 121-80-00) at Vallarta 5005 (US$95/105); the *Holiday Inn Crowne Plaza* (☎ 634-10-34) at López Mateos Sur 2500 (US$86 per room); the *Holiday Inn* (☎ 122-20-20) at López Mateos at Héroes (US$110 per room); and the *Fiesta Americana Guadalajara* (☎ 825-34-34) at Aceves 225 (US$100/111).

Places to Eat

Central District For quality Mexican food, try the *Restaurant La Chata* at Corona 126. The specialty of the house is the platillo Jalisciense – a quarter chicken, potatoes, a sope, an enchilada and a flauta, all for US$4.50. Enchiladas and chiles rellenos go for US$4. The mole sauce and pozole are excellent. La Chata has been in business for over 50 years, and when you taste the food you'll see why. It's open daily from 8 am to midnight.

Another Guadalajara favorite is the *Café Madrid* at Juárez 264, near the corner of Corona. The Madrid serves good, cheap food and excellent coffee in an air-con atmosphere from 8 am to 10 pm every day. Wearing cropped white coats and black bow ties (an odd contrast with the linoleum floor and steel and plastic tables), the waiters offer brisk, efficient service.

La Feria at Corona 291 is a new, huge restaurant-bar in a former mansion. This place is hip with Guadalajara's yuppies. The sound system is state of the art, the three levels are filled with comfortable leather chairs and matching leather-covered tables. The food is decent, and no menu item tops US$10. Mariachis play most nights after 9 pm, which is when La Feria is most popular.

There are two good restaurants near the tourist office. *La Rinconada* is an elegant place serving Mexican and US breakfasts for about US$4, salads and soups US$3, chicken US$6 and beef dishes US$6 to US$9. Nearby, *El Mexicano* is a good place to fill up on inexpensive Mexican food. The walls of the festive, gym-size eatery are lined with photos of revolutionary figures and murals depicting village life. The cooking oil is applied with a heavy hand, but the food is quite tasty and the prices right on: breakfasts US$2 or less, comida corrida US$2.50, meat plates about US$3.50, antojitos under US$3. There's also live music most nights from 6 to 10 pm.

The *Restaurant La Terraza*, on an upstairs terrace at Hidalgo 436 just off the Plaza de los Laureles, is another popular spot. It serves economical meals, with meat and chicken around US$3, burgers US$2. It's open daily from 11 am to 10 pm. A second La Terraza has opened at Juárez 442 near Ocampo. The crowd is similarly festive, but the menu is limited to antojitos.

There's a *Sanborn's Café* at Juárez 305 on the corner of 16 de Septiembre, and a *Sanborn's* restaurant on the opposite corner. The spacious and popular *Café/Restaurant Málaga*, 2½ blocks south at 16 de Septiembre 210, is a good, reasonably priced place with all main dishes under US$6, various salads and enchiladas around US$3, and breakfasts starting at US$1.50. A piano player is often at work here during the afternoon. Hours are 7 am to 10 pm daily.

Located directly above *Sanborn's Café* is a super place for eating and people-watching, *La Esquina*. It offers a large selection of dishes from the US and

Mexico: tortilla soup (US$2), chef's salad (US$4.50), hamburger with Oaxaca cheese (US$4), sirloin steak (US$7), pork tacos (US$4), mushroom omelet (US$4) and much more. There's also a drink menu.

The *Mercado Libertad* has scores of food stalls, serving maybe the cheapest eats you'll find in town. But sensitive stomachs beware: the hygiene here is not ideal.

All the fancy hotels have classy restaurants. The ones at the *Hotel Francés*, the *Hotel de Mendoza* and the *Hotel Fénix* are quite successful.

Vegetarian The *Villa Madrid* at López Cotilla 223 is not an exclusively vegetarian restaurant, but its tasty meals are good values and include vegetarian options like soy burger, salad and fries (US$2) and salads with cottage cheese or soya (US$4). Nothing on the menu tops US$4.50. The chicken burritos with mole sauce and the yogurt with fruit are superb. It's open daily from noon to 9 pm. Warning: The burgers will come with lots of mayonnaise unless you specify otherwise.

The friendly *Restaurant Acuarius* at Sánchez 416 is a popular vegetarian restaurant and health food store, especially at lunchtime when the excellent, filling comida corrida is served (US$3). They also serve soya-based meals, yogurt with fruit and similar vegetarian fare; it's open daily except Sunday, from 9.30 am to 8 pm.

Restaurant Vegetariano at Sánchez 370B, one block east of the Acuarius, has a bakery with wholemeal breads, even croissants; its comida corrida runs US$2.50. Hours are Monday through Saturday from 8 am to 6 pm.

Near Avenida Chapultepec Just a 10-minute bus ride from the city center, Guadalajara's Zona Rosa is a much quieter district, with some fine restaurants worth the trip to reach them. Catch the 'Par Vial' bus heading west on Calle Independencia and get off at Avenidas Chapultepec and Vallarta, 2.5 km from the cathedral.

Restaurant Los Itacates at Chapultepec Nte 110, 4½ blocks north of Vallarta, is a

pleasant restaurant specializing in traditional food at surprisingly low prices. A quarter pollo adobado with two cheese enchiladas, potatoes, rice and tortillas is only US$3. There are tacos with 19 fillings to choose from at US$0.75 each. The ample breakfast buffet for US$3, served every day from 8.30 am to noon, is a good deal. The restaurant is open daily from 8 am to 11 pm except Sunday, when it closes at 7 pm.

Restaurant/Bar Recco at Libertad 1981, just east of Chapultepec two blocks south of Vallarta, is a more elegant place specializing in European food, with main courses from US$6 to US$10. It's open every day from 1 to 11.45 pm (10 pm on Sunday).

A few doors down from the Recco, at the corner of Libertad and Chapultepec, the *Cafetería Azteca* serves up sandwiches, burgers, tacos and meat dishes for US$4 or less, indoors and outdoors. This is a breezy place that lends itself to long chats and letter writing. It's open daily from 8 am to 11.30 pm.

Near Avenida López Mateos About 20 blocks west of Avenida Chapultepec, López Mateos is another large avenue with a number of better restaurants. Bus No 258 from Calle San Felipe in the city center runs along López Mateos to, or near, all these restaurants (a 30-minute trip).

Restaurant La Trattoria at Niños Héroes 3051, a block east of López Mateos, is one of the top Italian restaurants in Guadalajara, and not overly pricey. A salad bar visit accompanies all meals, which range from US$4 for pastas to US$6 to US$8 for meat and seafood meals. La Trattoria is open every day from 1 pm to midnight.

The *Guadalajara Grill*, López Mateos Sur 3711, at Conchita about a kilometer south of the Plaza del Sol, is a large, fun place with a lively atmosphere, good music and dancing in the bar. Steak, shrimp and red snapper are US$7, chicken US$5. The Grill is open Monday through Saturday from 1.30 pm to midnight and to 5 pm Sunday.

Tlaquepaque Besides the central, atmospheric but noisy *El Parián*, there are a number of pleasant restaurant/bars. Several have lively mariachi bands in the afternoon and evening. *El Patio* at Independencia 186 has dining in a fine garden patio. Seafood and meat dishes go for around US$6, quesadillas for US$2. *Casa Fuerte* at Independencia 224 has a restaurant with live music – folk and Latin American – on Friday, Saturday and Sunday afternoons. *Restaurant Abajeño* at Juárez 231 has garden dining and mariachis. The *No Name Restaurant* at Madero 80 also has dining in a garden patio; be sure to ask for a menu. *Mariscos Progreso* at Progreso 80 specializes in seafood, which is served under the trees.

Entertainment

Guadalajara has something going on to fit any taste, from classic films to some of the best mariachi music in Mexico. Above all, the city is in love with music of all kinds, and live performers can be heard any night of the week.

Stop by the tourist office to view their weekly schedule of events; the bilingual staff will help you find something to suit your fancy. The Spanish-language daily *Siglo 21*, available at newsstands, lists nightly social activities; its Friday edition contains the glossy insert *Tentaciones*, which includes a calendar of events for the upcoming week. The *Occidental* and *Informador*, also Spanish-language dailies, have entertainment listings as well.

Cultural performances are often held at the *Teatro Degollado* (☎ 658-3812) and the *Instituto Cultural de Cabañas* (☎ 617-43-22), both downtown, and at the *Ex-Convento del Carmen* (☎ 614-71-84) at Juárez 638.

Free concerts of typical Jaliscan music are held in the Plaza de Armas most Thursdays and Sundays at 6.30 pm.

Cinemas Several cinemas show international films. Check *Tentaciones* or the local newspapers. Some of the best places to catch them are:

Alianza Francesa – López Cotilla 1199 (☎ 825-55-95)
Cine Charles Chaplin – López Mateos Norte 873 (☎ 641-54-07)
Cine Cinematógrafo (Nos 1, 2 and 3) – Vallarta 1102 (☎ 825-05-14); México 2222 (☎ 630-12-08); and Patria 600 (☎ 629-47-80)
Cine-Teatro Cabañas – in the Instituto Cultural de Cabañas (☎ 617-43-22)
Premier 1 y 2 – Parra 2233, on the corner of Avenida Las Américas (☎ 825-05-14)

Ballet Folklórico Sunday from 10 am to noon the Ballet Folklórico of the University of Guadalajara stages a grand performance at the Teatro Degollado. Tickets range from US$3 in the gallery to US$11 in the *lunetas* (stalls); buy them at the theater ticket office, open daily from 10 am to 1 pm and 4 to 7 pm. On a Wednesday night you might check out the Ballet Folklórico of the Instituto Cultural de Cabañas, performing at 8.30 pm. Tickets are US$3.

Music If you head west out of the center along Juárez and stay on it as it becomes Vallarta, you'll come across half a dozen music spots within three km of the cathedral. There's another cluster of nightlife venues on López Mateos south of Vallarta, around the Plaza del Sol. (The westward 'Par Vial' bus on Calle Independencia travels all the way along Vallarta to Avenida Chapultepec and the Zona Rosa. Bus No 258 west on San Felipe goes out to Plaza del Sol. Also, bus No 706 travels along Revolución to Plaza del Sol.)

Copenhagen 77, on the west side of Parque Revolución at the corner of López Cotilla, about 700 meters west of the center, serves up 'gourmet jazz' in its restaurant Monday through Saturday after 9.30 pm. They also serve good paella.

Next door, the *Bar La Revolución* is *the* place to be Friday and Saturday from 9.30 pm to 1 am for excellent rock and roll. This is especially true when the English-singing band Spiders is performing. If you like the music of Tracy Chapman, Eric Clapton or Jimi Hendrix, you'll enjoy Spiders. Check *Siglo 21* to see where they're playing.

Cover charge at the Revolución, the Spiders' usual weekend venue, is US$4.

About 500 meters farther west at Vallarta 1110 is *La Peñita*, a pleasant café-restaurant that generally presents Latin American music (often folk) Tuesday through Sunday from 9 to 11 pm. The cover charge varies with each group, but it usually runs US$4. It's an enjoyable place. It's also open as a restaurant from 11.30 am daily. Call to find out what music is booked (☎ 825-58-53).

The tourist office often recommends the club *Yesterday's* at Inglaterra 2630. Be advised that the soft-rock band that plays there is only slightly more alive than the stuffy crowd that frequents the place, and that the US classics the band plays are sung in Spanish. A much livelier place is the bar *1907* on Madero near Maestranza, where every night a DJ spins a good mix of popular American and Mexican music to a usually festive crowd.

¡Qué Pues! at Niños Héroes at Díaz de Leon has live rock and roll Tuesday nights. The rest of the week it's just a bar showing rock videos from the US.

On Wednesday nights, *La Ruta Vallarta* is the happening event for the twenty-something crowd. It involves three discotheques – *El Preludio* at Vallarta 1920, *Lado B* at Vallarta 2451 and, the most popular, *La Marcha* at Vallarta 2648. For US$11, you get a bracelet that allows you to enter all three clubs and drink as much as you want for no additional fee. Your bracelet also allows you to ride in a horse-drawn carriage from one club to the next. Most Ruta Vallarta participants are dressed to the nines, especially the women.

At Avenida Unión 236, *Café Quetzal* is a relaxed café presenting a variety of live music Tuesday through Saturday. The cover charge is usually US$4.

Other popular music venues include the Instituto Cultural Mexicano Norteamericano de Jalisco (☎ 825-58-38) at Díaz de León 300; the Centro Cultural Centenario (☎ 658-17-58) at Cruz Verde 272; and the Peña Cuicacalli (☎ 825-46-90) at Niños Héroes 1988 near Avenida Chapultepec.

Most of the fancy hotels offer live music. In the center, the attractive lobby piano bar of the Hotel Francés, at Maestranza 35 near the Plaza de la Liberación, is quite popular with gringos.

To hear mariachi music in its birthplace, head for the Plaza de los Mariachis (see Plaza de los Mariachis earlier in the Guadalajara section).

Discos & Dance Halls For dancing, especially after the other clubs shut down around 1 am, head to the *Tropigala* at López Mateos Sur 2011. There's live popular Mexican music at this large, very hip, multilevel club Wednesday through Saturday usually until 3 am. Cover charge varies but it's generally around US$4; keep your receipt as you'll need it to exit.

For salsa, try the *Copacabana* at López Mateos Sur 5290 near Las Águilas. This club is open Wednesday through Saturday from 8 pm until 3 am; it doesn't really get hopping before 11 pm. Cover is about US$4. Women get to drink for free on Wednesday.

The *Coco & Coco* dance hall next door to the Hotel Fénix is a popular downtown place with salsa and other música tropical to get the feet moving. Cover charges range from nothing for women from Monday through Wednesday to US$4 for everyone on Saturday.

Spectator Sports
Rodeos, Bullfights & Cockfights Charreadas are held most Sundays at noon in the rodeo ring behind Parque Agua Azul. Charros and charras come from all over Jalisco and Mexico to show off their skills.

The bullfighting season is September to March, but bullfights are not held every Sunday. There will be a couple for sure during the October fiestas; the rest of the season they may be sporadic. Check with the tourist office. When bullfights are held, they're on Sunday at 4 pm in the Plaza de Toros at the northern end of Calzada Independencia; bus No 60 heading north on Calzada Independencia will take you there.

WESTERN CENTRAL HIGHLANDS

Cockfights are held at the palenque (cockfighting arena) near Parque Agua Azul in October and at the palenques in Tlaquepaque and Zapopan during fairs there.

Soccer Fútbol is one of Guadalajara's favorite sports. The city usually has four teams playing in the national primera división: Guadalajara (las Chivas), the second most popular team in the country after América of Mexico City, Atlas (los Zorros), Universidad de Guadalajara (los Leones Negros) and Universidad Autónoma de Guadalajara (los Tecos). They play at stadiums around the city during the season from August/September to May. The tourist office keeps abreast of the matches, or you can call the main Estadio Jalisco (☎ 637-05-63). Take bus No 60 heading north on Calzada Independencia to reach that stadium.

Things to Buy

Handicrafts from Jalisco, Michoacán and other Mexican states are available in Guadalajara. (See the earlier Tlaquepaque and Tonalá sections for information on these two craft-making suburbs.) The Casa de las Artesanías, 20 blocks south of the center, has a good selection. It's on the north side of Parque Agua Azul at González Gallo. Prices are high but the quality is good. It's open Tuesday through Friday from 10 am to 6 pm, Saturday 11 am to 4 pm, Sunday 11 am to 3 pm. Bus No 60 heading south on Calzada Independencia or No 52 on 16 de Septiembre will drop you at the entrance to the park.

Mercado Libertad, right in the center, is a general market with three floors of shops covering an area equal to four city blocks. It's open daily. On Sunday you can check out the huge El Baratillo market stretching for blocks in every direction, beginning about 15 blocks east of Mercado Libertad. Take the 'Par Vial' bus east along Hidalgo.

There are several good department stores. About seven km southwest of the center, Plaza del Sol on López Mateos Sur offers some exclusive shopping in air-con comfort. Take bus Nos 258 or 258A west on San Felipe to get to Plaza del Sol.

Getting There & Away

Air Guadalajara's Aeropuerto Internacional Miguel Hidalgo (☎ 688-57-66) is 17 km south of downtown, just off the highway to Chapala. It is served by many airlines, with direct flights to and from about a dozen North American cities and over 20 Mexican cities, and one-stop connections to many others. There is a tourist office located in the terminal.

There are many travel agencies in Guadalajara where you can book flights. Look in the phone directory yellow pages under 'Agencias de Viajes.' Airlines appear under 'Aviación – Lineas de.' They include:

Aero California
    López Cotilla 1423 (☎ 826-19-62)
Aeroméxico, Aerolitoral & Aeromar
    Corona 196, corner of Madero (☎ 688-50-98)
American Airlines
    Vallarta 2440 (☎ 616-40-90)
Continental
    Hotel Presidente Inter-Continental, Avenida Moctezuma 3415 (☎ 647-45-04)
Delta
    López Cotilla 1701 (☎ 630-31-30)
Mexicana
    Otero 2353 (☎ 112-00-11)
TAESA
    López Cotilla 1531 (☎ 616-89-89)
United Airlines
    Vallarta 2440 (☎ 616-79-93)

Bus Guadalajara has two bus stations. The long-distance bus station (the Nueva Central Camionera), is a huge modern terminal with seven separate buildings (*módulos*). It's nine km southeast of the center past Tlaquepaque.

Each módulo is the base for a number of bus lines and has an information kiosk that can tell you where to find buses to a particular destination. Each módulo also has places to eat, pay phones, a telephone caseta, an area for leaving luggage and fax service.

There are buses, often frequent, to just about everywhere in western, central and northern Mexico. Distances, travel times and typical 1st-class prices include:

Barra de Navidad – 291 km, six hours (US$15)
Colima – 220 km, 2½ to three hours (US$10)
Guanajuato – 300 km, five hours (US$13)
Mazatlán – 506 km, eight hours (US$22)
Mexico City (Terminal Norte) – 535 km, seven to eight hours (US$27)
Morelia – 278 km, five hours (US$15)
Puerto Vallarta – 344 km, five hours (US$20)
Querétaro – 348 km, five hours (US$15)
San Miguel de Allende – 380 km, six hours (US$15)
Tepic – 216 km, 3½ hours (US$12)
Uruapan – 305 km, five hours (US$11)
Zacatecas – 320 km, five hours (US$15)

Bus tickets can be bought in the center at the Agencia de Viajes MaCull, López Cotilla 163, near the corner of Degollado. It's open Monday through Friday from 9 am to 2 pm and 4 to 7 pm, Saturday 9 am to 2 pm.

Guadalajara's other bus station is called the Vieja Central Camionera (old bus station) and is about 1.5 km south of the cathedral, near Parque Agua Azul. It occupies the block bounded by Avenida 5 de Febrero, Los Ángeles and Dr Michel (which is the southward continuation of Avenida Corona). The old bus station serves as the terminal for destinations nearer Guadalajara. There are sets of ticket booths on both the Los Ángeles and 5 de Febrero sides. Primera Plus buses go every half-hour, from 6 am to 9.40 pm, to Chapala (40 km, 45 minutes, US$2), Ajijic (47 km, 55 minutes, US$2) and Jocotepec (68 km, one hour, US$2). Rojo de Los Altos buses go every 15 or 20 minutes, from 6 am to 9 pm, to Tequila (50 km, 1¾ hours, US$2.50).

Train The Estación del Ferrocarril (☎ 650-08-26) is at the southern end of Calzada Independencia Sur, about 20 blocks from the center. Tickets for the Estrella del Pacífico and El Tapatío trains can be bought in advance at the station.

El Tapatío to Mexico City (train No 6, 11½ hours) departs Guadalajara daily at 9 pm. This is one of Mexico's better trains and has coches dormitorios (sleeper cars)

on Friday, Saturday and Sunday and primera preferente cars daily; fares are US$14.25/31 in primera preferente/one-person camarín. Tickets for El Tapatío are sold from 9 am to 9 pm. The corresponding train No 5 leaves Mexico City daily at 8.30 pm.

The Estrella del Pacífico (train No 1, also known as Servicio Estrella) departs Guadalajara daily at 9.30 am for Mexicali. This train also pulls carriages bound for Nogales, which are separated at Benjamín Hill, north of Hermosillo in Sonora state. The Estrella del Pacífico has primera seats only. Tickets are sold from 8 am to 1 pm. Its schedule (with fares from Guadalajara) is:

departs		cost
Guadalajara	9.30 am	–
Tepic	1.35 pm	US$7
Mazatlán	6.30 pm	US$15
Culiacán	9.44 pm	US$21
Sufragio	12.45 am	US$26
Navojoa	2.10 am	US$30
Ciudad Obregón	3.57 am	US$32
Empalme (Guaymas)	5.40 am	US$35
Hermosillo	7.45 am	US$38
Caborca	12.20 pm	US$44
Puerto Peñasco	2.10 pm	US$49
arrives		
Nogales	12.30 pm	US$45
Mexicali	5.55 pm	US$55

Times from Mexicali for the southbound Estrella del Pacífico (train No 2) are:

departs	
Mexicali	9.00 am
Puerto Peñasco	1.20 pm
Caborca	3.17 pm
Nogales	3.00 pm
Hermosillo	7.45 pm
Empalme (Guaymas)	9.40 pm
Ciudad Obregón	11.24 pm
Navojoa	12.28 am
Sufragio	2.15 am
Culiacán	5.26 am
Mazatlán	8.15 am
Tepic	1.30 pm
arrives	
Guadalajara	7.30 pm

A segunda clase train (known as El Burro) following the same route departs Guadalajara daily at noon, but it's slower (about

35 hours to Nogales, 44 hours to Mexicali), more crowded and dirtier. Fares are just US$25 to Nogales, US$31 to Mexicali, but it's worth spending the extra money on the Estrella del Pacífico.

Segunda clase train No 92 leaves Guadalajara daily at 8 pm, supposedly reaching Colima (US$4) at 1 am and Manzanillo (US$5) at 4 am.

Car & Motorcycle Guadalajara is 535 km northwest of Mexico City and 345 km east of Puerto Vallarta. Highways 15, 15D, 23, 54, 54D, 70, 80, 80D and 90 all converge here, combining temporarily to form the Periférico, a ring road around the city.

Guadalajara has many car-rental agencies, which are listed in the telephone yellow pages under 'Automóviles – Renta de.' Several of the large US companies are represented, and they tend to be pricey. At National, for example, a VW Beetle with 300 free km, insurance and taxes costs US$53 per day. You may get a better deal from a local company. Agencies include:

Auto Rent de Guadalajara
    Federalismo Sur 542A (☎ 826-20-14)
    Airport (☎ 689-04-32)
Budget
    Niños Héroes 934 (☎ 613-00-27)
Hertz
    Niños Héroes 9 (☎ 614-61-62)
    Airport (☎ 688-56-33)
National
    Hotel Fiesta Americana, Aceves 225 (☎ 825-48-48)
Quick Rent A Car
    Niños Héroes 954 (☎ 614-22-47)

Getting Around

To/From the Airport Bus No 176 travels Corona and passes in front of Hotel Vista Aranzazú as it makes its way toward the airport. The cost is US$0.50. The bus passes every 20 minutes. Tell the driver you're going to the *aeropuerto,* and he'll drop you two blocks from the airport, which is visible from the bus stop. For US$1 more, you can take a shuttle bus direct to the airport from downtown. It travels hourly between the airport and

Avenida Alemania at Tolsá. The shuttle's route is: Tolsá to Calzada Independencia (in front of Parque Agua Azul) to Dr Michel and then to the airport. The cost of a taxi to the airport is US$10.

To/From the Bus & Train Stations To reach the city center from the Nueva Central Camionera, you can take any 'Centro' or No 644 city bus from the loop road within the station (immediately outside your módulo). These are not very frequent so it's often quicker to walk out of the station between módulo 1 and the Hotel El Parador and take any bus No 275, 275A or 275B going to the right (north) along the road outside. These run every 15 minutes from 5.30 am to 10.30 pm, and bring you into the center along Avenida 16 de Septiembre. For a taxi into town, buy a ticket from the taxi taquilla in any of the módulos. Taxi fares are regulated by zones – to the center (zona 3), it's US$5 in daytime and US$6 at night, for up to four people.

From the city to the Nueva Central Camionera, you can take bus Nos 275, 275A and 275B southward on 16 de Septiembre, anywhere between the cathedral and Avenida Revolución. They run frequently but tend to be crowded and can take half an hour or more to get there. Bus No 644B heading east from the corner of Corona and Revolución is less frequent but takes a more direct route. A taxi should cost US$5 to US$6.

Bus Nos 60 and 174 south on Calzada Independencia will take you from the city center to the Vieja Central Camionera and to within two blocks of the train station. No 616 and other buses run between the two bus stations.

Bus & Combi Guadalajara has a good city bus system. On the major routes, buses go every five minutes or so, from 5.30 am to 10.30 pm daily; they cost US$0.50. A few routes are served by combis. The tourist office has a list of the 140 bus routes in Guadalajara, and can help you figure out how to get anywhere you want to go.

Metro Two subway lines crisscross the city. Stops are marked around town by a red and blue 'T' symbol. Línea 1 runs north-south for 15 km below Federalismo, a few blocks west of the center, and Avenida Colón, going all the way from the Periférico Norte to the Periférico Sur. You can catch it at Parque Revolución, on the corner of Avenida Juárez. Línea 2 runs east-west for 10 km below Avenida Juárez and makes getting to the Zona Rosa much easier. Stops include Mercado Libertad/San Juan de Dios, the University of Guadalajara, Avenida Chapultepec and Avenida López Mateos. The Metro operates daily from 6 am to 11 pm; the fare is US$0.50.

Taxi Taxis are plentiful in the center. They are supposed to charge fixed rates, according to distance. Typical fares from the center are US$3 to the train station, the Vieja Central Camionera or Parque Agua Azul; US$4 to the Plaza del Sol, Tlaquepaque, the zoo or Zapopan; US$5 to the Nueva Central Camionera; US$7 to Tonalá; and US$10 to the airport. Clarify the fare before you get into the taxi.

LAGO DE CHAPALA

Mexico's largest lake, 40 km south of Guadalajara, is picturesque and ringed by hills, but it does need attention. Large areas of its surface are now clogged by water hyacinth, a fast-growing plant nourished by the fertilizers and soil washed into the lake. In addition, the lake is shrinking. Guadalajara's water needs exceed the flow of water into the lake, which itself is reduced because water is pumped out of the main river feeding the lake, the Río Lerma, to supply Mexico City. Also, the Lerma, still the lake's main source, brings large amounts of industrial pollution into the lake. Still, the near-perfect climate and lovely countryside in the small northern lakeside towns of Chapala, Ajijic and Jocotepec has attracted an estimated 5000 full-time residents from North America. Most are retirees who are enjoying a higher standard of living in Mexico than they could in the US or Canada.

Getting There & Away

Chapala, Ajijic and Jocotepec are easy to reach by bus from Guadalajara (see Guadalajara Getting There & Away). There are also Chapala-Ajijic buses every 30 minutes (a 20-minute trip, US$0.50), and Chapala-Ajijic-Jocotepec buses half-hourly (50 minutes, US$0.75), from 7 am to 10 pm.

The scenic road along the south shore of the lake is an attractive alternative route to Michoacán if you're driving.

Chapala

pop 15,000; alt 1560m; ☎ *376*

The largest of the settlements toward the western end of the lake, Chapala took off as a resort when President Porfirio Díaz vacationed here every year from 1904 to 1909. DH Lawrence wrote most of *The Plumed Serpent* in the house at Zaragoza 307 – San Francisco church at the lake end of Avenida Madero, the main street, figures in the book's final pages. Today Chapala is a small, laid-back place that only gets busy on weekends and holidays.

Orientation & Information From the bus station it's a 10-minute walk down Avenida Madero to the lake. Hidalgo heads west off Madero 200 meters before the lake to become the road to Ajijic. All services can be found on Madero or Hidalgo. There's a tourist office at Serdán 26, on the first street to the left off Hidalgo. Libros de Chapala, opposite the plaza three blocks down Madero from the bus station, has many North American magazines, plus some newspapers and books. The market is on the opposite (east) side of the same plaza.

Things to See & Do On the waterfront at the foot of Avenida Madero are a small park and a few craft stalls, some selling attractive, inexpensive weavings from Jocotepec. There's a covered crafts market, the **Mercado de Artesanías**, about 400 meters east along Paseo Corona from the end of Madero. The large lakeside **Parque La Cristiania**, entered from Calle Cristiania off Corona, has a big swimming pool, a playground and nice picnic lawns.

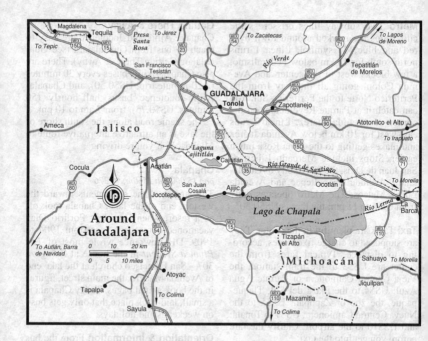

From the *embarcadero* (jetty) at the foot of Madero you can take a boat to the **Isla de los Alacranes** (Scorpion Island), six km east, which has some restaurants; or to **Isla de Mezcala**, also called Isla El Presidio, about 15 km east, which has ruins of a fort and other buildings constructed by Mexican independence fighters who heroically held out there from 1812 to 1816, repulsing several Spanish attempts to dislodge them, and finally winning a full pardon from their enemies. An Alacranes trip, with 30 minutes on the island, costs US$18 per boat.

Places to Stay *Casa de Huéspedes Las Palmitas* (☎ 5-30-70) at Juárez 531, just south of the east side of the market, has 15 clean singles/doubles with private bath, cable TV and 24-hour hot water for US$9/10, doubles with two beds for US$13.

The long-established *Gran Hotel Nido* (☎ 5-21-16) at Madero 202 near the waterfront offers fairly pleasant, clean, sizable singles/doubles for US$16/21 (US$2 more with TV). It has a moderately clean pool.

The best place in town is the *Villa Montecarlo* (☎ 5-22-16) at Hidalgo 296, one km west of the center. Its peacock-speckled grounds reach the lake and a thermal swimming pool. Each room has a private balcony and costs US$32.

Places to Eat Chapala's specialty is pescado blanco (whitefish), the same little creature found around Lago de Pátzcuaro. Today it's as likely to come from fish farms as from Lago de Chapala, which suffers from overfishing and pollution. A restaurant portion costs around US$7 or more.

The *Café Paris* and the *Restaurant Superior*, a couple of doors apart on the east side of Madero just north of Hidalgo, are both clean, popular places doing a good range of decent food at reasonable prices. The Paris has a four-course comida for

US$3. The *Gran Hotel Nido* has a slightly more expensive restaurant adorned with photos of old Chapala. There are also waterfront restaurants in both directions from the embarcadero and a couple of cheaper places behind the market.

Ajijic
pop 10,000; alt 1555m; ☎ *376*

Ajijic ('ah-hee-HEEK'), about seven km west of Chapala along the lakeside, is a beautiful, friendly little town of cobbled streets and prettily painted houses, home to a sizable colony of Mexican and North American artists. It's fairly sleepy except during the nine-day Fiesta de San Andrés at the end of November, and over Easter, when a well-known reenactment of Christ's trial and crucifixion is staged over three days.

Buses will drop you on the highway at the top of Colón, the main street, which leads six blocks to the lake. The chapel on the north side of the plaza, two blocks down, dates from at least the 18th century. There are a handful of galleries and some upmarket crafts shops on and off Colón.

Places to Stay & Eat *Pal Trailer Park* (☎ 6-00-40), two km east of central Ajijic on the Ajijic-Chapala highway, has a pool, laundry and 110 sites with full hookups. Cost is US$12 a night for one or two people.

Apartments Suite Plaza Ajijic (☎ 6-03-83), at Colón 33 on the plaza, has sizable two-room suites with kitchen at US$25/27 for a single/double.

Less attractive but also less pricey is the *Hotel Mariana* (☎ 6-22-21) at Guadalupe Victoria 10. The 30 rooms are spacious and clean, and the price (US$12/15) includes breakfast and cable TV. Visit the rooftop terrace for a nice view of the lake.

La Nueva Posada (☎ 6-14-44) at Donato Guerra 9, three blocks east of Colón by the lake, is a lovely hotel run by a friendly Canadian family. It has 16 large, artistically decorated rooms, five with great lake views; these cost US$45/50 – those without a lake view cost US$41/45. The price

includes breakfast. There's also an inviting pool and an excellent restaurant that spills out into a fine lakeside garden. Most meat or fish dishes are US$8 to US$9, but there are cheaper daily specials.

Trattoria di Giovanni, on the highway 1½ blocks east of Colón, is a popular restaurant with some of the best food in town. Chicken and seafood go for US$4 to US$8, pasta US$3 to US$4 and pizzas US$3 to US$4 for a small and US$5 to US$8 for a large. There are happy hours and, often, live music in the evenings (closed Tuesday).

The main cluster of cheaper cafés and restaurants is around the plaza on Colón.

San Juan Cosalá
At San Juan Cosalá, 10 km west of Ajijic toward Jocotepec, there's a thermal water spa in an attractive lakeside setting, with its own natural geyser and several swimming pools. You can visit for the day or stay in the *Motel Balneario San Juan Cosalá* (☎ 1-02-22) right on the spot for US$32/40.

Jocotepec
pop 12,000; alt 1540m; ☎ *376*

Jocotepec ('ho-co-teh-PEC'), 21 km west of Chapala and a kilometer from the lake, is far less gringo-influenced than Chapala or Ajijic. It's a pleasant town but there's nothing special to see or do except look for the handsome blankets, sarapes and wall hangings that are woven here and sold along Calle Hidalgo. The main festival is the two-week Fiesta del Señor del Monte in early January.

TEQUILA
pop 33,010; alt 1180m; ☎ *374*

The town of Tequila, 50 km northwest of Guadalajara, has been home to the liquor of the same name since the 17th century. Fields of agave, the cactus-like plant from which tequila is distilled, surround the town. You can almost get drunk just breathing the heavily scented air that drifts from the town's distilleries. The two largest distilleries – Sauza and Cuervo – offer public tours of their operations and, of course, free samples.

Tequila

In ancient times, the *agave tequilana weber* (blue agave) was used by Indians as a source of food, cloth and paper. The plant was even used in torture. The needlelike tips of its long leaves were customarily thrust into human flesh as penance to the gods. Today, the blue agave is more widely known as the fount of Mexico's national drink – tequila.

To ensure quality control, by law the blue agave can only be grown in the state of Jalisco and in parts of Nayarit, Michoacán, Guanajuato and Tamaulipas states. It is here, and nowhere else in Mexico, that conditions are right for the blue agave to produce a good-tasting tequila. At any given moment more than 100 million tequila agaves are in cultivation within this designated territory.

In some ways the production of tequila has changed little since Indians living near Guadalajara invented it hundreds of years ago. The blue agaves are still planted and harvested by hand, and the heavy, pineapple-resembling hearts, from which the alcohol is derived, are still removed from the fields on the backs of mules.

When planted, the agave heart is no bigger than an onion. Its blue-gray, swordlike leaves give the plant the appearance of a cactus, although botanists agree it has more in common genetically with the lily. By the time the agave is ready for harvesting, eight to 12 years after planting, its heart is the size of a beach ball and can weigh 50 kg.

The harvested agave heart *(piña)* is chopped to bits, fed into ovens and cooked for up to three days. After cooking, the softened plants are shredded and juiced. The juice, called *aguamiel* (honey water) for its golden, syrupy appearance, is then pumped into vats, where it is typically mixed with sugar cane and yeast before being allowed to ferment. By law, the mixture can contain no less than 51% agave. A bottle of tequila made from 100% agave will bear a label stating so.

There are four varieties of tequila. Which is best is a matter of personal opinion. White (or silver) tequila is not aged, and no colors or flavors are added. The gold variety is unaged but color and flavor, usually caramel, are added. *Tequila reposado* (rested tequila) has been aged at least two months in oak barrels and coloring and flavoring agents usually have been added. *Añejo* (aged) tequila has spent at least one year in oak barrels, and coloring and flavoring agents usually have been added. ∎

Tequila is easy to reach from Guadalajara. Buses depart every 15 or 20 minutes from the old bus station (see Guadalajara Getting There & Away for details).

Inland Michoacán

Michoacán is a beautiful state with a number of fascinating destinations along the Cordillera Neovolcánica, the volcanic range that gives it both fertile soils and a striking mountainous landscape. In a 200-km stretch of the cordillera across the northern part of Michoacán are found the spectacular El Rosario monarch butterfly sanctuary; the handsome state capital Morelia; the beautiful colonial town of Pátzcuaro, set near scenic Lago de Pátzcuaro in Purépecha Indian country, with several interesting villages, archaeological sites, islands and other lakes nearby; the town of Uruapan, with a fine miniature tropical national park within city boundaries; and the famous volcano Paricutín a short distance beyond Uruapan.

The name Michoacán is an Aztec word meaning 'Place of the Masters of Fish' – an apt description of the Lago de Pátzcuaro area, although nowadays the traditional 'butterfly' nets are used on the lake as much to catch tourists' pesos as fish.

The more tropical coastal areas of Michoacán, reached by spectacular highway 37 down through the hills from Uruapan, are covered in the Central Pacific Coast chapter.

MORELIA
pop 577,570; alt 1920m; ☎ 43

Morelia, the capital of Michoacán, lies in the northeastern part of the state, 315 km west of Mexico City and 367 km southeast of Guadalajara. It's a lively city with a university, an active cultural scene and a number of language schools offering Spanish courses – a good place for an extended visit, as many foreigners have discovered.

Morelia was officially founded in 1541, although a Franciscan monastery had been in the area since 1537. Nueva España's first viceroy, Antonio de Mendoza, named it Valladolid after the Spanish city of that name and encouraged families of Spanish nobility to move here. The families remained and maintained Valladolid as a very Spanish city, at least architecturally, until 1828.

By that time, Nueva España had become the independent republic of Mexico. The state legislature changed the city's name to Morelia to honor one of its native sons, José María Morelos y Pavón, a key figure in Mexico's independence movement.

Today, with its downtown streets lined by colonial buildings, Morelia looks nearly

as Spanish as it did before independence. City ordinances now require that all new construction in the center be done colonial-style with arches, baroque façades and carved pink-stone walls.

Orientation

Almost everything of interest is within walking distance of the zócalo, also called the Plaza Central, Plaza de los Mártires and Plaza de Armas. The large cathedral in the middle of the zócalo is a major landmark.

Avenida Madero, along the north side of the zócalo, is the major downtown avenue; to the west it's Madero Poniente, to the east Madero Oriente. Nine blocks east of the zócalo on Madero, the Fuente Tarasca (Tarascan Fountain) is another main landmark, marking a major intersection; it's here that you will enter Morelia city center if you're driving in from Mexico City.

Information

Tourist Offices The helpful Galería de Turismo (☎ 13-26-54) is a block west of the zócalo on the corner of Madero Poniente and Nigromante, on an outside corner of the Palacio Clavijero. It has free maps and leaflets in Spanish and English about Morelia and Michoacán, plus a monthly calendar of films and cultural events in the city. Hours are Monday through Friday from 8 am to 8 pm, and Saturday and Sunday 8 am to 3 pm.

The Dirección de Promoción y Desarrollo Turístico (☎ 13-26-54), in the courtyard of the Palacio Clavijero, also has information. Hours are Monday through Friday from 9 am to 3 pm and 6 to 8 pm.

Money Banks are plentiful in the zócalo area, particularly on and around Madero. They give the best rates for changing money but generally are only open Monday through Friday from 9 am to 1.30 pm.

There are many money brokers in Morelia. Among them are: Casa de Cambio Michoacán at Valladolid 22, Casa de Cambio Majapara at Pino Suárez 166, and Casa de Cambio Troca-Mex at Nigromante 132. All change US dollars and traveler's

checks and are open Monday through Friday from 9 am to 6 pm and Saturday from 9 am to 1 pm.

Post & Communications The main post office and the Telecomm office, which has telegram, telex and fax services, are in the Palacio Federal at Madero Oriente 369. The post office is open Monday through Friday from 8 am to 7 pm, weekends 9 am to 1 pm. Telex and fax hours are Monday through Friday 9 am to 8 pm, Saturday to 1 pm.

Computel has telephone casetas, with fax service too, at the bus station. It advertises 24-hour service.

Laundry Lavandería American Klean, at Corregidora 787 on the corner of Bravo, is open Monday through Saturday from 9 am to 7 pm, Sunday to 2 pm.

Catedral

The cathedral dominating the zócalo took more than a century to build, from 1640 to 1744. Architecturally, it is a combination of Herreresque, baroque and neoclassical styles. Its twin 70-meter-high towers, for instance, have classical Herreresque bases, baroque midsections and multicolumned neoclassical tops. Inside, much of the baroque relief work was replaced in the 19th century with more balanced and calculated neoclassical pieces. Fortunately, one of the cathedral's interior highlights was preserved: a sculpture of the Señor de la Sacristía made from dried maize and topped with a gold crown from the 16th century Spanish king, Felipe II. There's also a very large pipe organ with 4600 pipes.

Museo Regional Michoacano & Palacio de Justicia

Just off the zócalo at Allende 305 and Abasolo is the Michoacán Regional Museum. Housed in the late 18th century baroque palace of Isidro Huarte, the museum displays a great variety of pre-Hispanic artifacts, colonial art and relics, contemporary paintings by local artists and exhibits on

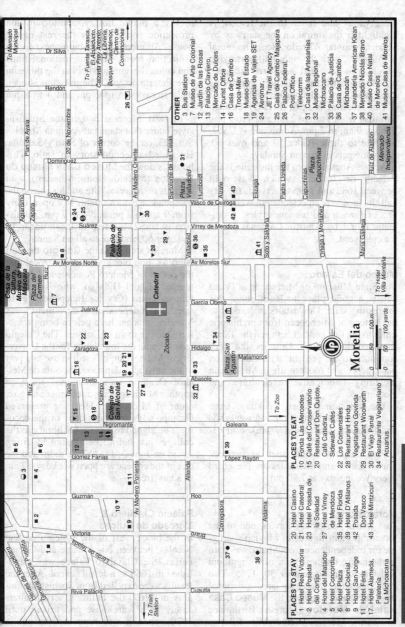

OTHER
3 Bus Station
7 Museo de Arte Colonial
12 Jardín de las Rosas
13 Palacio Clavijero,
  Mercado de Dulces
14 Tourist Office
16 Casa de Cambio
18 Troca-Mex
19 Museo del Estado
24 Agencia de Viajes SET
  Aeromar,
  JET Travel Agency
25 Casa de Cambio Majapara
26 Palacio Federal,
  Post Office,
  Telecomm
31 Casa de las Artesanías
32 Museo Regional
  Michoacano
33 Palacio de Justicia
36 Casa de Cambio
  Michoacán
37 Lavandería American Klean
38 Mercado Nicolás Bravo
40 Museo Casa Natal
  de Morelos
41 Museo Casa de Morelos

PLACES TO STAY
1 Hotel Real Victoria
2 Hotel Posada
  del Cortijo
4 Hotel del Matador
5 Hotel Virrey
  de Mendoza
6 Hotel Plaza
8 Hotel Colonial
9 Hotel San Jorge
11 Hotel Fénix
17 Hotel Alameda,
  Paletería
  La Michoacana
20 Hotel Casino
21 Hotel Catedral
23 Hotel Posada de
  la Soledad
27 Hotel Virrey
  de Mendoza
35 Hotel Florida
39 Hotel D'Atilanos
42 Posada
  Don Vasco
43 Hotel Mintzicuri

PLACES TO EAT
10 Fonda Las Mercedes
15 Café del Conservatorio
20 Restaurant Don Quijote,
  Café Catedral,
  Sidewalk Cafés
22 Los Comensales
28 Restaurant Hindu
  Vegetariano Govinda
29 Restaurant Woolworth
30 El Viejo Panal
34 Restaurante Vegetariano
  Acuarius

Morelia

0   50   100 m.
0   50   100 yards

the geology and fauna of the region. A highlight is the mural on the stairway by Mexican painter Alfredo Alce. The mural is in halves, with the right half portraying people who have had a positive influence on Mexico and the left half portraying those who have had a negative influence.

The museum is open Tuesday through Saturday from 9 am to 2 pm and 4 to 7 pm, Sunday 9 am to 2 pm. Admission is US$2, but free to those under 13 and over 60. Everyone gets in free on Sunday.

Across Abasolo from the museum is the Palacio de Justicia, which was built between 1682 and 1695 to serve as the city hall. Its façade is an eclectic but well-done mix of French and baroque styles. A dramatic mural by Agustín Cárdenas graces the courtyard.

Museo del Estado

The State Museum of Michoacán at Prieto 176 is a good place to learn about this interesting state. Downstairs is devoted to the history of Michoacán from prehistoric times to the first contact between the Tarascans and the Spanish. Upstairs, the story continues to the present, with exhibits on many aspects of modern life in Michoacán including handicrafts, agriculture and clothing.

The museum is open weekdays from 9 am to 2 pm and 4 to 8 pm (on weekends and holidays it closes at 7 pm). Entry is free.

Free cultural events such as regional music, dance and artesanías are presented every Wednesday at 7.30 pm.

Morelos Sites

José María Morelos y Pavón, one of the most important figures in Mexico's struggle for independence from Spain, was born in the house on the corner of Corregidora and Obeso on September 30, 1765. Two centuries later, it was declared a national monument and made into the **Museo Casa Natal de Morelos** (Morelos Birthplace Museum). Morelos memorabilia fill two

rooms; a public library, auditorium and projection room occupy the rest of the house. An eternal torch burns next to the projection room. Free international films and cultural events are held at the museum (see Entertainment). The museum is open daily from 9 am to 2 pm and 4 to 8 pm (free).

In 1801 Morelos bought the Spanish-style house that stands at Avenida Morelos Sur 323, on the corner of Soto y Saldaña. He added a second story in 1806. This house is now the **Museo Casa Museo de Morelos** (Morelos House Museum), with exhibits on Morelos' life and his role in the independence movement. It's open daily from 9 am to 2 pm and 4 to 7 pm. Admission is US$2, but free to those under 13 and over 60, and free to all on Sunday.

Morelos studied at the **Colegio de San Nicolás**, one block west of the zócalo on the corner of Madero Poniente and Nigromante. Miguel Hidalgo, who issued the famous Grito (Cry for Independence) to start the independence movement, was Morelos' teacher here before being transferred to the town of Dolores. The Colegio later became the foundation for the University of Michoacán; it is still in use as a part of the university. Upstairs, the Sala de Melchor Ocampo is a memorial room to another Mexican hero, a reformer and governor of Michoacán. Here are preserved Ocampo's library and a copy of the document he signed to donate his library to the college, just before being shot by firing squad on June 3, 1861. This room and the rest of the college are open weekdays, 7 am to 8 pm (free).

Palacio Clavijero & Mercado de Dulces

In the block west of the Colegio de San Nicolás, between Nigromante and Gómez Farías, the Clavijero Palace was established in 1660 as a Jesuit school. After the Jesuits were expelled from Spanish dominions in 1767, the building served alternately as a warehouse and prison until 1970, when it was renovated as public offices, including the state tourist office and public library.

Be sure to visit the arcade on the western side of the palace to taste some of the goodies on sale in the Mercado de Dulces (Market of Sweets). It's open daily from 9 am to 10 pm. Michoacán handicrafts are also sold in the arcade, but you can find better wares at the Casa de las Artesanías.

Museo de Arte Colonial
The Museum of Colonial Art, Juárez 240 at Eduardo Ruiz, three blocks north of the cathedral, contains 18th century religious paintings, crucifixes and models of galleons. It's open Tuesday through Sunday from 10 am to 2 pm and 5 to 8 pm (free).

Casa de la Cultura & Museo de la Máscara
A block away, across the Plaza del Carmen at Avenida Morelos Norte 485, the Casa de la Cultura hosts dance and music performances, films and art exhibitions. Stop by for a free monthly brochure describing cultural events in the city.

The mask museum has masks from around Mexico, all associated with particular dances. It's open daily from 10 am to 9 pm (free).

Casa de las Artesanías
The House of Handicrafts occupies the Ex-Convento de San Francisco, attached to the Templo de San Francisco on the Plaza de Valladolid, three blocks east of the zócalo. Arts and handicrafts from all over Michoacán are displayed and sold; they're expensive but some of the best you'll see anywhere in the state. There's also a small selection of cassettes of regional music. Hours are daily from 9 am to 8 pm.

Upstairs, small shops represent many of Michoacán's towns, with craftspeople demonstrating how the specialties of their areas are made: guitars from Paracho, copperware from Santa Clara del Cobre, lacquerware, weaving and much more. The shops are open daily from 10 am to 8 pm.

Fuente Tarasca, El Acueducto & Bosque Cuauhtémoc
The Tarascan Fountain at the end of Madero Oriente, nine blocks east of the zócalo, consists of a sculpture of Tarascan women in bare native dress, holding aloft a basket of fruits. It's a 1960s replacement of the fountain that mysteriously disappeared in 1940. The fountain is strangely beautiful at night.

The aqueduct beginning at the Tarascan Fountain extends southeast along Avenida Acueducto. Although it looks older, the aqueduct was built between 1785 and 1788 to meet the city's growing water needs. With 253 arches stretching two km, it is an impressive sight, especially at night when spotlights illuminate the fountain and arches .

The Bosque Cuauhtémoc, or Cuauhtémoc Forest, is a large park stretching south from Avenida Acueducto. In the park at Acueducto 18, a couple of blocks from the Tarascan Fountain, is an interesting **Museo de Arte Contemporáneo** with changing exhibitions of modern art. It's open Tuesday through Sunday from 10 am to 2 pm and 4 to 8 pm. Admission is free.

On Plaza Morelos, about 100 meters northeast of Bosque Cuauhtémoc between Avenida Acueducto and the cobbled Calzada Fray Antonio de San Miguel, stands the **Estatua Ecuestre al Patriota Morelos**, a statue of Morelos on horseback trotting to battle. It was sculpted by the Italian Giuseppe Ingillieri between 1910 and 1913.

Centro de Convenciones
The Convention Center complex, about 1.5 km south of the Bosque Cuauhtémoc on Calzada Ventura Puente, has several places of interest in extensive park-like grounds. You can reach it on the red route ('Ruta Roja') combi heading east on Santiago Tapia or 20 de Noviembre.

The **Planetario de Morelia**, with 164 projectors and a cupola 20 meters in diameter, presents one-hour programs on Friday and Saturday at 5 and 7 pm, and Sunday at 6.30 pm. On Sunday at 5 pm there's a separate family program (minimum age five). Admission is US$2.

The **Orquidario**, or orchid house, is open Monday through Friday from 10 am to 6 pm, weekends 10 am to 3 pm and 4 to 6 pm. Admission is a 'donation' of about US$1; you decide how much. The large, modern **Teatro Morelos** is also in the complex.

Parque Zoológico Benito Juárez

The zoo is three km south of the zócalo on Calzada Juárez, which is an extension of Nigromante and Galeana. It's a pleasant zoo with many animals, a lake with rowboats for hire, a small train, picnic areas and a playground. It's open daily from 10 am to 6 pm.

The maroon combi route (called 'Ruta Guinda'), heading south on Nigromante from the stop on the east side of the Palacio Clavijero, will drop you at the zoo entrance.

Markets

Three markets are within 10 blocks of the zócalo: Mercado Nicolás Bravo on Bravo between Corregidora and Guerrero; Mercado Independencia on the corner of Vicente Santa María and Ana María Gallaga; and Mercado Municipal Revolución on the corner of Revolución and Plan de Ayala.

Language Courses

There are several Spanish-language schools. Most central is the Centro Cultural de Lenguas (☎/fax 12-05-89) at Madero Oriente 560. Courses here run from two to four weeks, four hours daily with three hours of classroom work and an hour spent on workshops related to Mexican history, literature and culture. The instruction costs US$150 per week, less if you're there many weeks; class size is two to six students. One-to-one tuition is US$10 per hour. Living with Mexican families is encouraged (cost is US$16 per day) and organized by the school.

The Baden-Powell Institute (☎/fax 12-40-70) at Alzate 565, three blocks south of

Madero Oriente, is a small school offering courses in Spanish language and Mexican politics, cooking, culture, guitar playing and folk dancing – mostly on a one-to-one basis, though group classes can be arranged. One-to-one classes cost US$10 per hour, US$9 after 80 hours. Lodging with a Mexican family is US$15 per day, with three meals.

Centro Mexicano Internacional (☎ 12-45-96, fax 13-98-98) in a large colonial building at Calzada Fray Antonio 173, offers courses in Spanish language, Mexican culture and so forth for US$245 for the first week, US$195 thereafter. Classes run for four hours daily in groups of five students or less. Family living costs US$12 a day double occupancy, US$15 a day single occupancy.

Organized Tours

The Dirección de Operación y Desarrollo Turístico (☎ 13-26-54) in the Palacio Clavijero offers free walking tours of the historical city center weekends at 11 am.

Agencia de Viajes SET (☎ 13-19-08) on Madero opposite the zócalo, between the Hotel Valladolid and Hotel Casino, arranges guided three-hour city tours, on foot or by van (US$6 per person). There are also day tours for US$20 or more to Uruapan; to Los Azufres, a forest reserve in a volcanic area about 100 km east of Morelia with pine forests, lakes, geysers and a hot sulfur pool; and, from November to March, to El Rosario monarch butterfly sanctuary (see the Santuario de Mariposas El Rosario section for how to get there independently).

Special Events

Morelia's many annual festivals include:

Feria de Morelia – Morelia's major fair, with exhibits of handicrafts, agriculture and livestock from around Michoacán, plus regional dances, bullfights and fiestas. The *Feria de Órgano*, an international organ festival during the first two weeks of May, is part of the celebrations. The anniversary of the founding of Morelia in 1541 is celebrated on May 18 with fireworks, displays of historical photos and more; April 29 to May 20

Festival Internacional de Música – International Music Festival; final week of July and first week of August

Cumpleaños de Morelos (Morelos' Birthday) – This is celebrated with a parade, fireworks and more; September 30

Día de la Virgen de Guadalupe – The Day of the Virgen de Guadalupe is celebrated on December 12 at the Templo de San Diego; in the preceding weeks, typical Mexican foods are sold on the pedestrian street Calzada Fray Antonio de San Miguel

Feria Navideña – Christmas Fair, with traditional Christmas items, foods and handicrafts from Michoacán; from approximately December 1 to January 6

Places to Stay – budget

The cheapest place to stay in Morelia is *Las Villas* (☎ 13-31-77), a hostel in the IMJUDE sports complex on the corner of Oaxaca and Chiapas, a 20-minute walk southwest of the zócalo. The hostel is clean, with four beds (two bunks) and a locker in each room, and separate men's and women's areas. Cost is US$4 per person. The complex houses a popular pool, a gym and several athletic fields. There's no age limit and an HI card is not required. Open 7 am to 11 pm.

Two blocks from the zócalo, the *Hotel Colonial* (☎ 12-18-97) at 20 de Noviembre 15, is a colonial-style hotel with 25 rooms at US$6/8 without TV; add US$3 with it. Street-facing rooms are large, with high beamed ceilings and small balconies, but they catch a lot of traffic noise. The interior rooms are quieter.

The *Hotel Posada del Cortijo* (☎ 12-96-42) at Eduardo Ruiz 673 faces a bus station and shares a wall with a porno theater, but most of its 16 rooms are decent. They're clean with firm beds, shower curtains and lots of hot water. Cost is US$10/12. Farther up the street, at No 53, the once-proud *Hotel El Carmen* has gone to pot.

The *Hotel Concordia* (☎ 12-30-53) at Gómez Farías 328 asks US$12/13 for decent singles/doubles. The rooms facing the street are best, with little balconies and a whole wall of windows, though the interior rooms are quieter. The *Hotel Plaza* 50

meters away, on the corner of Eduardo Ruiz and Gómez Farías, has comparable rooms but is louder and pricier.

The *Hotel Fénix* (☎ 12-05-12) at Madero Poniente 537 offers singles/doubles for US$6/10 with splash-everywhere showers (no shower curtains) and no toilet seats, but the rooms are clean and well maintained and the mattresses are firm. There's no shortage of hot water. It's a good find given its price and central location. There's parking for two vehicles.

The *Hotel del Matador* (☎ 12-46-49), at Eduardo Ruiz 531 opposite the bus station, has 57 worn rooms with carpet displaying stains in every shape and color. Singles/doubles run US$13/14.

The *Posada Don Vasco* (☎ 12-14-84) at Vasco de Quiroga 232 is a colonial-style hotel with rooms ringing a courtyard that has sitting areas and plants. The rooms are varied; some are quite pleasant. All have carpet, phone and private bath (hot water 6.30 am to 2 pm). Price is US$10/13 – a real bargain if you get one of the better rooms (ask to see two or three). The hotel's restaurant is popular and cheap.

Opposite the Don Vasco, *Hotel Mintzicuri* (☎ 12-06-64) at Vasco de Quiroga 227 has 37 small, clean rooms around a courtyard. All have carpet and a phone, and there is parking. Cost is US$10/13. Turkish baths are available next door.

Four blocks west of the zócalo, the *Hotel San Jorge* (☎ 12-46-10) at Madero Poniente 719 has some rooms that are large and clean and have shower curtains, toilet seats and ample windows opening onto an interior walkway; others have splash-everywhere showers and no toilet seats. Ask to see a room before registering. The rates are US$7/9.

Places to Stay – middle

For a little more silver, the *Hotel D'Atilanos* (☎ 12-01-21) at Corregidora 465 is a well-kept colonial-style hotel with 27 large, comfy rooms, all with color TV and phone, arranged around a lovely covered courtyard. This place has 'diary entry' written all over it. The singles/doubles cost US$14/21.

The *Hotel Florida* (☎ 12-18-19) at Morelos Sur 161 is equally priced but offers loud, depressing rooms. It's mentioned here only because one can't help but notice the hotel's sign looming over the zócalo and wonder about the place.

On the north side of the zócalo, the Best Western *Hotel Casino* (☎ 13-10-03) at Portal Hidalgo 229 has 48 cozy rooms, all with carpet, phone and color TV. Those facing the street have balconies overlooking the zócalo; the interior rooms open onto a covered courtyard with a popular restaurant on the ground floor. You pay US$23/27.

In the same block, the *Hotel Catedral* (☎ 13-07-83) at Zaragoza 37, opposite the cathedral, is another attractive colonial-style hotel with cushy rooms around a covered courtyard. The regular rate is US$30, single or double. The rooms facing the cathedral are quite lovely.

The *Hotel Real Victoria* (☎ 13-23-00) at Guadalupe Victoria 245 is a modern hotel with 110 clean, pleasant rooms, all with TV and carpet, at US$23/30. There's enclosed parking, and a popular restaurant at the center of a covered courtyard.

Places to Stay – top end

On the northwest corner of the zócalo, the *Hotel Virrey de Mendoza* (☎ 12-49-40) at Portal Matamoros 16 is the converted mansion of Antonio de Mendoza, the first viceroy of Mexico. The 55 rooms are elegantly furnished with antiques and crystal chandeliers. Standard rooms cost US$62, and suites range from US$70 to US$180.

Another upscale option is the *Hotel de la Soledad* (☎ 12-18-88) at Zaragoza 90, on the corner of Ocampo. Built around 1700, it has been a carriage house, a convent and a private mansion. It has 49 standard rooms at US$40, plus nine suites.

The *Hotel Alameda* (☎ 12-20-23) at Madero Poniente 313 is an attractive, modern, 116-room hotel. Rooms in the older section are US$40 for a single or double, US$55 in the newer section. There's a popular restaurant and bar, too.

For a room with a sweeping view of Morelia, try the *Hotel Villa Montaña*

(☎ 14-02-31) at Patzimba 201, two km from the zócalo. The hotel has 40 courtly rooms with all the modern conveniences and an inviting swimming pool. The restaurant is mediocre. Rooms go for US$120 to US$220.

Places to Eat

Morelia has many fine and reasonably priced restaurants. A wise choice is *Fonda Las Mercedes* at Guzmán 47, which occupies a handsome colonial building. Most of its tables reside in a cozy covered courtyard decked with stately potted palms. The house specialty is *sabana Mercedes* – grilled, thinly sliced fillet of beef lightly covered with fresh parsley, garlic and olive oil; one delicious serving covers an entire dinner plate (veggies and a baked potato arrive separately). Other offerings: pastas (US$4), chicken (US$5), beef (US$7), seafood (up to US$9). A fruit crêpe is a must-eat dessert.

Equally popular and also quite nice is *Los Comensales*, 1½ blocks north of the zócalo. The restaurant has tables in several rooms of a lovely colonial building and is a good place to escape street noise. There's lots of seafood with that Pátzcuaro favorite, pescado blanco, at US$7, or paella, steaks and other meat dishes from US$4 to US$7. Antojitos go for US$1.50 to US$4. Hours are 8 am to 10 pm daily.

Along Madero, opposite the zócalo, is a row of restaurants and sidewalk cafés, open daily from around 8 am to 10 pm. The *Café Catedral* is a popular spot, as is the *Restaurant Don Quijote*, the restaurant of the Hotel Casino, with tables both inside and out on the sidewalk. The outside tables are perfect for coffee and people-watching. Breakfasts here run to US$4, the menú del día costs US$4, and beers go for US$1.25.

Half a block off the zócalo, at Madero Poniente 327, the *Paletería La Michoacana* makes delicious fruit drinks and ice cream. It's open daily from 8 am to 9 pm. Another choice café/juice bar is *El Viejo Panal* on the south side of Madero Oriente, just east of the cathedral. It's clean with attentive service and a homey touch to food presentation. A tasty set breakfast costs US$2.50, antojitos US$1 to US$2.50, meat dishes less than US$4.

A peaceful place to have coffee is the *Café del Conservatorio* at Santiago Tapia 363. Covered tables face a handsome plaza with lovely plants and mature shade trees. Classical music plays as you nibble on a pastry or from a cheese plate and sip wine, coffee or juice. Open weekdays 8 am to 10 pm, weekends noon to 10 pm.

The *Restaurante Woolworth* is a pleasant enough and clean cafeteria in a former church on Virrey de Mendoza, half a block south of Madero. Breakfasts start at US$2. It's open Monday through Saturday from 8 am to 9 pm, Sunday 9 am to 8 pm.

For real cheap eats, there are several basic restaurants near the bus station, open daily from 7 am to midnight. A comida corrida at one of these costs as little as US$1.50. There's also a row of eating stalls with tables under the covered arches running around three sides of the Plaza San Agustín, one block south of the zócalo; they're open daily from around 3 pm until around 1 am.

Vegetarian On the east side of the zócalo at Morelos Sur 39, *Restaurant Hindú Vegetariano Govinda* is a quiet place offering a variety of breakfasts, vegetarian burgers and comida corrida combos for around US$2.50. It's open Monday through Saturday from 9 am to noon for breakfast, and 2 to 5 pm for dinner; closed Sunday.

South of the zócalo at Hidalgo 75, *Restaurante Vegetariano Acuarius* is open daily from 9 am to 5 pm, serving breakfasts for US$3 and a good comida corrida for US$4. It's in a pleasant covered courtyard.

Entertainment

Being a university town as well as the capital of one of Mexico's most interesting states, Morelia has a lively cultural life. Stop by the tourist office and the Casa de la Cultura for their free monthly calendars listing films and cultural events around Morelia.

Morelia's two daily newspapers *El Sol de Morelia* and *La Voz de Michoacán* have cultural sections with events notices and theater and cinema ads. There are several cinemas around the center.

There are regular band concerts in both the zócalo (Sunday) and the Jardín de las Rosas on the corner of Gómez Farías and Santiago Tapia, and there are frequent organ recitals in the cathedral.

International film series are presented by various cinema clubs, with admission often free. Venues are the *Museo Regional Michoacano*, the *Casa Natal de Morelos* (both several times a week), the *Casa de la Cultura* and *La Librería* (see below for this last).

The Casa Natal de Morelos also presents free talks and other cultural events at its Viernes Culturales, on Friday at 7 pm.

Regional dances, music, stories and exhibitions from the state of Michoacán are presented most Wednesdays at 7.30 pm at the *Museo del Estado*.

La Librería, a bookstore and coffeehouse at Calzada Fray Antonio de San Miguel 284, two blocks east of the Fuente Tarasca, has a pleasant college atmosphere, a cinema club showing international films most Saturdays at 7.30 pm and live music most Sundays at 7.30 pm. There's rarely a fee; just have a coffee or tea from the café.

One of the many traditional regional dances, the Danza de los Viejitos (Dance of the Old Men), is presented most Fridays and Saturdays at 9 pm at the Hotel Alameda. The costumed dancers, wearing comical masks of grinning *viejitos* with long gray hair, hooked noses, rosy cheeks and no teeth, enter hobbling on skinny canes. Their dance gets more and more animated, with wooden sandals clacking on the floor, until finally they hobble off again, looking as if they can barely make it to the door. Admission is free.

Getting There & Away

Air The Francisco J Múgica airport is 27 km from Morelia, on the Morelia-Zinapécuaro highway. There are plenty of connections to other Mexican and some

North American cities. Maruata Viajes (☎ 17-12-10) next to the Hotel Alameda is a central agency for air and ETN bus tickets.

Mexicana (☎ 24-38-28), in the lobby of the Gran Hotel, Centro de Convenciones, has daily flights to/from San Francisco, Chicago, Los Angeles, Guadalajara and Zacatecas. Aeromar (☎ 13-68-86), on the corner of Pino Suárez and 20 de Noviembre, and TAESA (☎ 13-40-50), on Plaza de Rebollones, have daily flights to/from Mexico City. TAESA also serves Tijuana and Zacatecas. Aero Sudpacífico (☎ 15-33-89) flies most days to Uruapan, Lázaro Cárdenas, Mexico City and Guadalajara. Aerolitoral (☎ 13-68-33) has daily direct flights to/from Guadalajara.

Bus Morelia's Central Camionera is conveniently located just a few blocks northwest of the zócalo, on Eduardo Ruiz between Gómez Farías and Guzmán. In the bus station are a 24-hour Computel telephone caseta with fax service, several cafeterias, and places to store your luggage. Daily departures include:

Angangueo – 175 km, four hours; one 2nd-class bus at 2.50 pm by Autobuses de Occidente via Zitácuaro (US$7); or get off at Zitácuaro then take a local bus to Angangueo

Guadalajara – 278 km, five hours; eight deluxe buses by ETN (US$20) and eight by Primera Plus (US$10); 12 1st-class by Autobuses de Jalisco (US$12) and seven by Servicios Coordinados (US$12); frequent 2nd-class buses

Guanajuato – 176 km, four hours; eight 2nd-class Flecha Amarilla (US$7)

Lázaro Cárdenas – 406 km, seven hours; nine 1st-class by Parhikuni (US$14)

León – 197 km, 3½ to four hours; 17 deluxe buses by Primera Plus (US$9); five 1st-class by Servicios Coordinados (US$8); 2nd-class buses every 20 minutes by Flecha Amarilla (US$9)

Mexico City (Terminal Poniente or Terminal Norte) – 304 km, four hours; 25 deluxe buses by ETN (US$22) and nine 1st-class by Primera Plus (US$15); 2nd-class buses hourly by Herradura de Plata (US$12) and every 20 minutes by Autobuses de Occidente (US$11)

Pátzcuaro – 62 km, one hour; one 1st-class by Parhikuni (US$3) at 2.30 pm; 2nd-class buses every 10 minutes by Galeana (US$2.50) and every 30 minutes by Flecha Amarilla (US$2.50)

Querétaro – 259 km, three to four hours; a few deluxe and 1st-class buses by Primera Plus, Elite and Servicios Coordinados (US$6 to US$8); 2nd-class Mexico City-bound buses every 30 minutes by Flecha Amarilla (US$5.50)

Uruapan – 125 km, two hours; five deluxe by Primera Plus (US$6), two by ETN (US$7); one 1st-class every 15 minutes by Parhikuni, two daily by Elite (US$5) and one by Servicios Coordinados (US$7); 11 2nd-class by Flecha Amarilla (US$6)

Zitácuaro – 150 km, 2½ to three hours; 13 2nd-class buses by Vía 2000 (US$6) and one every 20 minutes by Autobuses de Occidente (US$6), others by Transportes Frontera and Autobuses México-Toluca-Zinacantepec (US$6)

Train The Estación del Ferrocarril (☎ 16-39-65) is on Avenida Periodismo, on the southwest edge of the city, a 15-minute combi ride from the center (see Getting Around).

El Purépecha (train No 31 westbound, No 32 eastbound) leaves at 5.20 am for Pátzcuaro, Uruapan and Lázaro Cárdenas and at 10.40 pm for Mexico City (see the Mexico City Getting There & Away section for more information). The ticket office is open Monday through Saturday from 5 to 6 am and 9 to 11 pm.

Getting Around

A Zinapécuaro bus will get you to/from the airport; a taxi costs US$12. There are several airport taxi services, reachable at ☎ 15-63-53, 15-06-46, 13-10-43, 16-75-00 or 16-37-78.

Around town, the local combis (white VW vans) operate from 6 am to 9 pm and cost US$0.50. Their routes are designated by the color of their stripe: Ruta Roja, red; Ruta Amarilla, yellow; Ruta Guinda, maroon; Ruta Azul, blue; and Ruta Verde, green. A few routes operate until 10 pm.

Red combis run along Eduardo Ruiz. Green combis go to the train station; catch them heading south on García Obeso. Local buses marked 'Indeco' or 'Magisterio' run between the station and the center.

Taxis are plentiful in the city center; the average taxi ride costs around US$1.50. They usually charge a little more money to go to the train station or to Centro de Convenciones.

SANTUARIO DE MARIPOSAS EL ROSARIO

In the easternmost part of Michoacán, near the border of México state, is the El Rosario monarch butterfly (mariposa monarca) sanctuary. Many millions of monarch butterflies come here every year to breed, arriving from the US and Canada around the end of October or start of November and departing around the beginning of March for their long migration back. When they are present, there are so many butterflies in the sanctuary that they cover the trees, turning them a flaming orange; it's a great sight.

The sanctuary is open daily from 9 am to 6 pm during the season the butterflies are present. The entry fee of US$2 includes a guide who takes you through the sanctuary, explaining the butterflies' life cycle and patterns. You can stay in the sanctuary as long as you like, but it only takes two hours to tour it. It's a good idea to get there early – that's when the butterflies are up in the trees. As the day warms up, they begin to flutter around. They end up coming down onto the ground where it's more humid, and there are so many you can't avoid crushing some as you walk.

Angangueo
pop 9699; alt 2980m; ☎ 715

The starting point for visits to the sanctuary is the pretty mountain village of Angangueo, a former mining town 25 km north of Zitácuaro, which is a regional commercial center on highway 15 from Mexico City to Morelia.

In Angangueo you can enjoy strolling around, seeing the two churches and the Monument to the Miner, with a good view over the town.

Places to Stay & Eat

Angangueo has several places to stay (none with a phone), including the *Hotel Parakata* at Matamoros 7, with a small sign on the main road about a kilometer before the village center; singles/doubles with private bath cost US$12/15. On the main street between Matamoros and the two churches are the *Casa Huéspedes El Paso de la Monarca* and the *Casa Huéspedes Juárez*. The Monarca has rooms set in a tiered garden with views of the hills; cost with private bath is US$10/12. Rooms at the Juárez are centered on a rose-filled courtyard; cost is US$10/13. *Hotel Albergue Don Bruno* on Morelos, 300 meters before Matamoros as you come into town, is more expensive, with rooms at US$18/20.

The *Restaurant La Margarita* beside the Hotel Albergue Don Bruno is a good place to eat, and there's quite an acceptable restaurant at the Hotel Parakata.

Getting There & Away

An Autobuses de Occidente bus leaves Morelia at 2.50 pm for Angangueo (175 km, four hours, US$7). The same line has buses to Zitácuaro every 30 minutes (US$6). And plenty of local buses make the 45-minute uphill trip from there to Angangueo (US$3). You can reach Angangueo from Mexico City's Terminal Poniente on buses of the México-Toluca-Zinacántepec y Ramales line or the Autobuses de Occidente line (both 2nd-class). The 200-km trip takes four hours and costs US$7. There are about seven buses daily.

Camionetas, or vans, depart from the main road in Angangueo for the rugged nine-km, one-hour trip to the monarch sanctuary. It's another 15 minutes on foot from the parking place to the sanctuary. You have to hire the whole van, so the more people sharing the cost, the better.

WESTERN CENTRAL HIGHLANDS

The fee for the 10-person van is about US$35 (be sure to bargain) for the round trip, including waiting while you visit the sanctuary. You'll have the best chance of finding other travelers to share the ride on weekends.

If you walk from Angangueo to the sanctuary, it's a steep uphill journey that takes around three hours. The track to the sanctuary is the continuation of Calle Matamoros so the Hotel Parakata is a useful starting point. After about an hour, you come to a statue of the Virgin of Guadalupe; turn left here then stay on the middle

track until you reach the sanctuary's entrance, where there are usually stalls and people milling about.

PÁTZCUARO
pop 75,176; alt 2175m; ☎ *434*

Pátzcuaro is a lovely highland town with some stately colonial architecture in the heart of Purépecha Indian country. The center of town lies 3.5 km from the southeast shore of Lago de Pátzcuaro, almost equidistant between Morelia and Uruapan (both are about 60 km away on the good highway 14). Mexican tourists come in

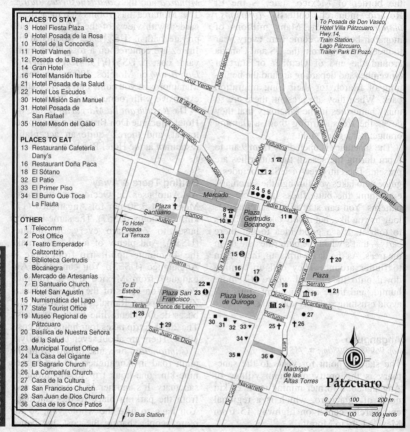

PLACES TO STAY
3 Hotel Fiesta Plaza
9 Hotel Posada de la Rosa
10 Hotel de la Concordia
11 Hotel Valmen
12 Posada de la Basílica
14 Gran Hotel
16 Hotel Mansión Iturbe
21 Hotel Posada de la Salud
22 Hotel Los Escudos
30 Hotel Misión San Manuel
31 Hotel Posada de San Rafael
35 Hotel Mesón del Gallo

PLACES TO EAT
13 Restaurante Cafetería Dany's
16 Restaurant Doña Paca
18 El Sótano
32 El Patio
33 El Primer Piso
34 El Burro Que Toca La Flauta

OTHER
1 Telecomm
2 Post Office
4 Teatro Emperador Caltzontzin
5 Biblioteca Gertrudis Bocanegra
6 Mercado de Artesanías
7 El Santuario Church
8 Hotel San Agustín
15 Numismática del Lago
17 State Tourist Office
19 Museo Regional de Pátzcuaro
20 Basílica de Nuestra Señora de la Salud
23 Municipal Tourist Office
24 La Casa del Gigante
25 El Sagrario Church
26 La Compañía Church
27 Casa de la Cultura
28 San Francisco Church
29 San Juan de Dios Church
36 Casa de los Once Patios

To Posada de Don Vasco, Hotel Villa Pátzcuaro, Hwy 14, Train Station, Lago Pátzcuaro, Trailer Park El Pozo

Pátzcuaro

To Bus Station

large numbers over Christmas and New Year, for Semana Santa and for the area's famous Day of the Dead celebrations on November 1 and 2. It can get quite chilly in this mountainous area in winter – bring at least a warm sweater.

History

Pátzcuaro was the capital of the Tarascan people from about 1325 to 1400. Then, on the death of King Tariácuri, the Tarascan state became a three-part league comprising Pátzcuaro and, on the east side of the lake, Tzintzuntzan and Ihuatzio. First Ihuatzio dominated, then Tzintzuntzan. The league repulsed Aztec attacks. The Spanish first came to the area in 1522, when they received a friendly reception. Then they returned in 1529 under Nuño de Guzmán, a conquistador of legendary cruelty.

Guzmán's inhumanity to the Indians was so severe that the Catholic church and the colonial government sent Vasco de Quiroga, a respected judge and churchman from Mexico City, to clean up the mess Guzmán left. Quiroga, who arrived in 1536, established a bishopric (based initially at Tzintzuntzan, then, from 1540, at Pátzcuaro) and pioneered village cooperatives based on the humanistic ideas of Sir Thomas More's *Utopia*. To avoid Indian dependence on Spanish mining lords and landowners, Quiroga successfully encouraged education and agricultural self-sufficiency in the villages around Lago de Pátzcuaro, with all villagers contributing equally to the community. He also helped each village develop its own craft specialty. The Utopian communities declined after his death in 1565 but the craft traditions continue to this day. Not surprisingly, Tata Vascu, as the Indians called him, is much venerated for his work. Streets, plazas, restaurants and hotels all over Michoacán are named after him.

Orientation

Pátzcuaro has a handsome core of lovely colonial buildings and some less attractive outlying areas stretching as far as the lake, 3.5 km to the north. Central Pátzcuaro focuses on the fine Plaza Vasco de Quiroga. There is also the smaller but busier Plaza Gertrudis Bocanegra one block north with the town market on its west side. The center is fairly flat, with just a few gentle hills.

Calle Ahumada heads north from Plaza Vasco de Quiroga to the Morelia-Uruapan highway three km away, changing its name first to Avenida Lázaro Cárdenas then to Avenida de las Américas along the way (these last two names are sometimes used interchangeably). Lago de Pátzcuaro is half a km north of the highway.

The bus station is on a ring road on the southwest side of town, one km from the center.

Information

Tourist Offices The municipal tourist office (☎ 2-02-15) is on the west side of Plaza Vasco de Quiroga at Portal Hidalgo 1. English, French and Spanish are spoken at this office, which is open Monday through Friday from 10 am to 2.30 pm and 4.30 to 7 pm, and weekends from 10 am to 2.30 pm.

The state tourist office (☎ 2-12-14) is in the Palacio de Huitzimengari on the north side of the Plaza Vasco de Quiroga. Only Spanish is spoken at this office, which can provide information and maps on the state of Michoacán. Hours are Monday through Saturday 9 am to 3 pm and 4 to 7 pm, weekends from 9 am to 2 pm.

Money You can change cash dollars or traveler's checks at several banks on the two main plazas. Some will only change money between 10 am and noon. Bancomer at Mendoza 23 will change money during regular business hours and has an ATM. There is a Banamex ATM directly across the street, but the bank itself is located on the west side of Plaza Gertrudis Bocanegra. Numismática del Lago at Iturbe 30 changes cash dollars Monday through Wednesday from 10 am to 2 pm and 4 to 7 pm, and Friday through Sunday from 10 am to 1 pm.

Post & Communications The post office is at Obregón 13, half a block north of Plaza Gertrudis Bocanegra. It's open Monday through Friday from 8 am to 7 pm, Saturday from 9 am to 1 pm.

The Telecomm office at Títere 15 offers telegram and fax services Monday through Friday from 9 am to 1 pm and 3 to 5 pm, Saturday from 9 am to 2 pm. Aeroflash on Iturbe also offers public fax service.

Plaza Vasco de Quiroga

Pátzcuaro's wide, peaceful main plaza is one of the loveliest in Mexico. A tall statue of Bishop Vasco de Quiroga gazes benignly down from the central fountain. The plaza is ringed by trees and flanked by numerous arched 17th century mansions now used as hotels, restaurants and shops, all in pleasing proportion to the dimensions of the plaza.

One of the finest buildings is **La Casa del Gigante** at Portal Matamoros 40 on the east side of the plaza. Built in 1663, it takes its name from a giant statue of a man in the interior courtyard. Today it's a private home and not open to the public.

Another old mansion, the **Palacio de Huitzimengari** on the north side of the plaza, which is said to have belonged to the last Tarascan emperor, now houses a tourist office and a few unexceptional craft stalls as well as a Purépecha cultural organiztion.

Casa de los Once Patios

The House of the 11 Courtyards, 1½ blocks southeast of Plaza Vasco de Quiroga on the cobbled Calle de la Madrigal de las Altas Torres, is a fine rambling building built as a Dominican convent in the 1740s. Earlier, one of Mexico's first hospitals, founded by Vasco de Quiroga, had stood on the site. Today the house is a warren of small artesanías shops, each specializing in a particular regional craft. Copperware from Santa Clara del Cobre, straw goods from Tzintzuntzan, musical instruments from Paracho, as well as gold-leaf-decorated lacquerware, handpainted ceramics and attractive textiles, can all be

found. The shops are open daily from 10 am to 7 pm.

Around Plaza Gertrudis Bocanegra

Pátzcuaro's second main plaza is named after a local heroine who was shot by firing squad in the town in 1818 for her support of the independence movement. Her statue adorns the center of the plaza.

The plaza bustles with the activity of the town's market, stretching away from its west side. The busiest market days are Sunday, Monday and Friday. You can find everything from fruit, vegetables and fresh lake fish to herbal medicines, crafts and clothing, including the region's distinctive striped shawls, sarapes and *peruanas* (a kind of sarape-shawl worn by women).

The **Biblioteca Gertrudis Bocanegra** (Gertrudis Bocanegra Library) occupies the 16th century former San Agustín church on the north side of the plaza. A large, colorful Juan O'Gorman mural covering the rear wall depicts the history of Michoacán from pre-Hispanic times to the 1910 revolution. A good selection of books in English at the back is testimony to the large number of gringos passing through. The library is open Monday through Friday from 9 am to 2 pm and 4 to 7 pm, Saturday 9 am to 2 pm.

A small **Mercado de Artesanías** stands next to the library. Crafts sold here include grotesque Tocuaro masks, carved wooden forks and knives from Zirahuén and pottery. The prices are very favorable.

On the other (west) side of the library, the **Teatro Emperador Caltzontzin** was a convent until it was converted to a theater in 1936. Movies and cultural events are presented here. Murals in the main upstairs hall colorfully remind moviegoers of various epochs in Michoacán's history, including the meeting of Tarascan King Tangahxuan II and the Spanish conquistador Cristóbal de Olid near Pátzcuaro in 1522.

Basílica de Nuestra Señora de la Salud

Two blocks east of the south end of Plaza Gertrudis Bocanegra, the basilica was intended by Vasco de Quiroga to be the centerpiece of his Michoacán community, a cathedral big enough for 30,000 worshippers, but the existing basilica, finished in the 19th century, is only the central nave of the original design. Quiroga's tomb, the Mausoleo de Don Vasco, is just to the left inside the main west doors.

Behind the altar at the east end stands a much-revered figure of the Virgin, Nuestra Señora de la Salud (Our Lady of Health). The image was made in the 16th century, on Quiroga's request, by Tarascan Indians from a corncob and honey paste called *tatzingue*. Soon the Indians began to receive miraculous healings, and Quiroga had the words 'Salus Infirmorum' (Healer of the Sick) inscribed at the figure's feet. Ever since, pilgrims to Pátzcuaro have come from all over Mexico to ask this Virgin for a miracle. Many make their way on their knees across the plaza, into the church and along its nave. You can walk up the stairs behind the image to see the many small tin representations of hands, feet, legs and so on that pilgrims have offered to the Virgin.

Museo Regional de Pátzcuaro & Museo de Artes Populares

One block south of the basilica on the corner of Enseñanza and Alcantarillas, the Pátzcuaro Regional Museum is in the former Colegio de San Nicolás Obispo, a college founded in the 16th century by Vasco de Quiroga. This comprehensive museum of Michoacán arts and crafts includes delicate white lace rebozos from

---

The Purépecha, the Tarascans & the Day of the Dead

The territory inhabited by Michoacán's 130,000 Purépecha Indians extends from around Lago de Pátzcuaro to west of Uruapan. The Purépecha are direct descendants of the Tarascans, who developed western Mexico's most advanced pre-Hispanic civilization, but their early origins are obscure and the Purépecha language has no established links to any other. The Tarascans emerged around Lago de Pátzcuaro about the 14th century. They may have originated as semi-barbaric Chichimecs from farther north, but neither does their language have any established links with any other tongue (although linguists have suggested connections with various languages including Zuni, spoken in the US southwest, and Quechua, spoken in Peru). The Spanish supposedly began calling them Tarascos because the Indians often used a word that sounded like that.

The old Tarascans were noted potters and metalsmiths, and many Purépecha villages still specialize in some of those handicrafts. The modern Purépecha also maintain some of the country's most vital and ancient religious traditions. Día de los Muertos (Day of the Dead) remembrances around Lago de Pátzcuaro are particularly famous.

The Día de los Muertos attracts visitors to the Pátzcuaro region from all over Mexico and beyond. The local Purépecha villagers' celebrations have a magical quality and pre-Hispanic undertones. They build special altars of flowers (mainly of marigolds, which have had ceremonial importance since before Spanish times) in graveyards, and women hold candlelit vigils there from midnight on the night of November 1-2. Best known – to the point where sightseers almost overwhelm the place – are the events on Isla Janitzio, including traditional dances and a parade of decorated canoes late in the evening on November 1. The tradition arises from a story about Mintzita and Itzihuapa, a pair of royal Purépecha lovers who are at the heart of a sunken treasure legend. It involves, as so many stories do, the cruelty of the conquistador Nuño de Guzmán. It is said that the royal lovers make their way to the graveyard of the island church on this night.

There are also picturesque ceremonies in many other villages including Tzintzuntzan, Ihuatzio, Jarácuaro and Tzurumútaro. The Pátzcuaro tourist offices can provide details. Many more events – including craft markets, traditional dances, exhibitions and concerts – are held in Pátzcuaro and nearby villages around the time of the Día de los Muertos. In Jarácuaro local dance groups and musicians stage a traditional contest of their skills in the village square on the evening of November 1. ■

Aranza, handpainted ceramics from Santa Fe de la Laguna and copperware from Santa Clara del Cobre. One room is set up as a typical Michoacán kitchen with a tremendous brick oven.

The museum is open Tuesday through Friday from 9 am to 7 pm, weekends from 9 am to 3 pm. Admission is US$2.

Opposite the museum on Alcantarillas is a large building constructed in the 16th century as a Jesuit college. The building was recently restored and is now a **Museo de Artes Populares**. Attached to it is the 16th century Iglesia de la Compañía.

Other Churches
If you like old churches, Pátzcuaro has several others of interest, including El Sagrario, San Juan de Dios, San Francisco and El Santuario. All are shown on the map.

El Estribo
El Estribo, a lookout point on a hill four km west of the town center, offers a magnificent view of the entire Lago de Pátzcuaro area. It takes up to an hour to walk there. It takes only a few minutes to get there in a vehicle. Either way, you can reach it by taking Ponce de León from the southwest corner of Plaza Vasco de Quiroga and following the signs.

Special Events
Aside from the famous local events for the Day of the Dead (see sidebar), Pátzcuaro stages some interesting events at other times too.

Pastorelas These dramatizations of the journey of the shepherds to see the infant Jesus are staged in Plaza Vasco de Quiroga on several evenings around Christmas. *Pastorelas indígenas*, on the same theme but including mask dances, enact the struggle of angels against the devils that are trying to hinder the shepherds. They are held in eight villages around Lago de Pátzcuaro on different days between December 26 and February 2. Rodeos and other events accompany them. The tourist offices can provide details.

Semana Santa The week leading up to Easter is full of events in Pátzcuaro and the villages around the lake, including: Palm Sunday processions in several places; *Viacrucis* processions, enacting Christ's journey to Calvary and the crucifixion itself, on Good Friday morning; candlelit processions in silence on Good Friday evening; and a ceremonial burning of Judas on Easter Sunday evening in Plaza Vasco de Quiroga. There are many local variations; the tourist offices can provide details.

Nuestra Señora de la Salud The high point of a two-week feria in honor of the Virgin of Health in the first half of December is a colorful procession to the basilica on December 8. Traditional dances, including Los Reboceros, Los Moros, Los Viejitos and Los Panaderos, are performed.

Places to Stay – budget
Camping The *Hotel Villa Pátzcuaro* (☎ 2-07-67) at Avenida de las Américas 506, 2.5 km north of the town center on the road to the lake, has a small trailer park in pleasant grounds. Two people with a vehicle pay about US$9 for a space with full hookups. There's a lawn area for tents, a small kitchen with a fireplace and showers. Campers can use the hotel's swimming pool.

Nearer to town on the same road, the *Posada de Don Vasco* (☎ 2-02-27) has a trailer park with 25 spaces with full hookups, costing US$10 a space, plus room for tents. It's only open during the busy tourist periods, however. Guests can use the hotel's facilities.

Trailer Park El Pozo (☎ 2-09-37) is on the lakeside, just off the Pátzcuaro-Morelia highway, one km east of its junction with Avenida de las Américas. Watch for the sign pointing across the train tracks to the site, which has 20 places with full hookups, hot showers and a dock. Cost is US$5 if you use a tent, twice that if you use a trailer.

Hotels On the west side of the Plaza Gertrudis Bocanegra at Portal Juárez 29, the *Hotel Posada de la Rosa* (☎ 2-08-11) is the cheapest decent place in town. Its rooms, along an upstairs patio, all have two beds and lots of hot water. Cost per single/double with private bath is US$6/9.

Two doors down, the *Hotel de la Concordia* (☎ 2-00-03) offers nicer rooms, 30-channel TV, parking, private bath and hot water for US$18/22. It also offers four spacious rooms overlooking the plaza with a clean shared bathroom; at US$7/11, these rooms are an excellent bargain.

Hotel Valmen (☎ 2-11-61) at Padre Lloreda 34, near Plaza Gertrudis Bocanegra, is pretty worn but it's OK for many people given its price of US$5 per room. All of its 16 rooms have private bath. Most are around a covered patio and have large exterior windows. Look before registering.

Hotel Posada de la Salud (☎ 2-00-58) at Serrato 9, half a block behind the basilica, is a well-kept little place with 15 clean, pleasant rooms at US$11/16 looking onto a grassy courtyard.

Three long blocks west of the plazas, *Hotel Posada La Terraza* (☎ 2-10-27) at Juárez 46 is a family-run hotel with 11 rooms. There's a long front garden and an upstairs enclosed terrace with a bit of a view. The rooms, all with private bath and 24-hour hot water, are US$6 a person. A couple of rooms sleep up to seven people.

Places to Stay – middle

Several of the 17th century mansions around Plaza Vasco de Quiroga have been turned into elegant colonial-style hotels, all with restaurants. One of the most attractive is the *Hotel Los Escudos* (☎ 2-01-38) at Portal Hidalgo 73, on the west side of the plaza. Most of the 30 rooms have colonial paintings on the walls, and all have carpeting, private bath and satellite TV; some have fireplaces. They're set around two patios full of plants and cost US$25 for one or two people and one bed, US$32 for two people and two beds. The restaurant's food is mediocre.

On the north side of the plaza, *Mansión Iturbe* (☎ 2-03-68) at Portal Morelos 59 retains all of its colonial elegance, with 14 tastefully decorated, wood-beamed, carpeted rooms. Antique lovers will marvel at all the original furniture. Rooms go for US$45 or US$55, and because each is different (some have deep bathtubs, others private balconies and so on), it's smart to see several before checking in (English and Spanish are spoken). Price includes breakfast, newspaper and two hours' bicycle use, plus there's a free coffee station all night long. The hotel also has two good restaurants and an art gallery, and live music every Friday night.

On the south side of the plaza, *Hotel Misión San Manuel* (☎ 2-13-13) at Portal Aldama 12 is a former monastery building with 42 rooms. Some have a fireplace, all have carpeting, painted tile bathrooms and beamed ceilings. Cost is US$25 for a single or double (US$35 for a two-bed double).

At Portal Aldama 18, the *Hotel Posada de San Rafael* (☎ 2-07-70) has 103 smaller, more basic rooms, with carpeting but no fireplaces. They cost US$20/23 in the *sección remodelada* (which means they have TV and newer carpets and mattresses), and US$18/20 elsewhere.

One block south of Plaza Vasco de Quiroga, *Hotel Mesón del Gallo* (☎ 2-14-74), at Dr Coss 20, is less historic and less maintained than all of the hotels on the plaza, but it has a swimming pool, a pleasant restaurant, a lawn and garden area and a bar. The 20 singles/doubles cost US$20/23.

The *Gran Hotel* (☎ 2-04-43) at Plaza Gertrudis Bocanegra 6 is quite popular at US$18 for one or two people. Its rooms are smallish but clean and nicely furnished.

The *Hotel Fiesta Plaza* (☎ 2-25-15) at Plaza Gertrudis Bocanegra 24 is a modern place in colonial style with 60 pleasant, medium-size rooms on three floors around two courtyards. Singles/doubles, with TV, cost US$25/28.

Away from the plazas, *Posada de la Basílica* (☎ 2-11-08), opposite the basilica at Arciga 6, has very cheerful and sizable rooms around an open courtyard that overlooks the red-tile roofs of the town.

Singles/doubles are a very reasonable US$18/25. Wood for the fireplaces is provided. Room 13, with two balconies, is tops. The Basílica's restaurant is a charming place to have breakfast.

The pleasant *Hotel Villa Pátzcuaro* (☎ 2-07-67) at Avenida de las Américas 506 is set back from the road to the lake, about 2.5 km from the center of town. The 12 cozy rooms all have fireplaces, and there's a swimming pool. Singles/doubles are US$15/21. It's most convenient if you have a vehicle, but local buses to the lake or town pass by every few minutes.

Places to Stay – top end

The *Posada de Don Vasco* (☎ 2-02-27), about 2.5 km north of the center at Avenida de las Américas 450, is the most expensive place in town at US$75 for a single or double. It has 101 comfortable though not huge rooms (those in the newer blocks at the back are bigger and brighter), plus a tennis court, swimming pool, games room with tenpin bowling, restaurant, bar and so on.

Places to Eat

While you're in Pátzcuaro, you might want to try some of the area's typical foods. Most famous is the pescado blanco (whitefish). This small fish is traditionally caught on Lago de Pátzcuaro by fishermen in canoes with 'butterfly' nets but is equally likely to come from fish farms nowadays. Other specialties include *corundas,* tamales with a pork, bean and cream filling, and *sopa Tarasca,* a tomato-based soup with cream and bits of crisp tortilla and dried chili.

The best dinners in town can be found at the following restaurants: *El Patio* at Plaza Vasco de Quiroga 19; *El Sótano* at Cuesta Vasco de Quiroga 2; *El Primer Piso* at Plaza Vasco Quiroga 29; and, at Dr Coss 4, *El Burro Que Toca La Flauta,* which translates literally as 'The donkey that plays the flute.' Which of these is tops is a matter of personal taste, the meal ordered, the mood at the moment – but you aren't likely to be disappointed by any of them.

El Patio specializes in regional food at reasonable prices – soups around US$2, chicken US$3 to US$4, beef US$5, fish US$4 to US$7 – and its sopa Tarasca is very tasty. The reddish-brown sauce on the Patio's *pollo en mole* (chicken with mole sauce) is divine, and the chicken breast served to one of our authors was the size of an airplane wing. Well, almost.

El Sótano specializes in crêpes (there are 10 to choose from), and it does them right. The environment is somewhat elegant, and the back room is even somewhat intimate. But the prices are decent: soups and typical plates are US$1 to US$3, meat dishes around US$4, fish up to US$7 (the meager whitefish is pricey everywhere). The stone walls and beamed ceilings make a good escape from the plaza noise.

El Primer Piso is located on the second floor of a very old building and its four intimate dining balconies are a favorite of romantics and people-watchers. The *pollo en nogada* (chicken covered with a spicy Indian sauce containing three varieties of peppers) is very good. Soups run about US$2.50, salads just a bit more, pastas US$5, chicken and beef dishes US$4 to US$6. It's quite all right to occupy a balcony table and order only a café au lait and a dessert (they're excellent).

El Burro Que Toca La Flauta is located in a beautifully restored 500-year-old exhacienda owned by an American and run by him and his Mexican sweetheart. The restaurant occupies a proudly maintained courtyard ringed by tall walls decorated with orchids and flora paintings. In the center of the restaurant, amid custom-made tables, are three gorgeous Indian fireplaces called *cocuchas* that are fired up daily. The food is very tasty. Pasta is the specialty and runs US$4 to US$5. El Burro also makes bagels and scones that sell like hotcakes. The restaurant is also open for breakfast – an excellent way to start the day.

All of the mansions-turned-hotels on Plaza Vasco de Quiroga have restaurants. One of the most popular of these is in the *Hotel Los Escudos*, but the food leaves a lot to be desired. *Restaurant Doña Paca* in the Mansión Iturbe hotel is a pleasant place to sip coffee and savor a slice of cake.

Restaurante Cafetería Dany's at Mendoza 30, less than a block north of Plaza Vasco de Quiroga, appears in many guidebooks because it's cheap, but the food certainly is nothing special. The restaurant at the Gran Hotel has good, reasonably priced food but closes early.

In the evenings you can feast on plates of chicken, vegetables and tortillas for US$3 at the food stalls outside the market on Plaza Gertrudis Bocanegra. At the stall nearest to the plaza, under a red tarp at the time this was written, is a woman who has been filling plates with chicken dinners for 20 years. She works so fast over her *comal* (the large pan she cooks with) that she's probably the most videotaped person in all Michoacán. Her food is as appealing as her smile.

For a meal with a view, try the restaurant at the *Posada de la Basílica*, which is only open for breakfast and lunch. It has attractive tablecloths and heavy Michoacán ceramic plates. Breakfasts are US$3 to US$4, lunches about US$4.

A cheap place to try local fish is beside the main jetty on the lake, where the boats depart for Isla Janitzio. A row of fish stands all charge the same – US$5 for pescado blanco, US$3 for mojarra (perch) and US$2.50 for a cupful of *charales* (tiny fish that are eaten whole). You can choose your fish, and they'll fry it up on the spot. Be forewarned: all of Pátzcuaro's wastewater pours untreated into the lake (which, incidentally, won't exist in 50 years at its current rate of shrinkage).

Entertainment

There are two popular weekly musical performances held at Pátzcuaro hotels. The better of them takes place Saturdays between 9 and 11 pm in the restaurant in the back of the Hotel Fiesta Plaza. Twelve guitarists and a bass player – fourth-place finishers in a national contest that drew 300 such groups – perform traditional Mexican songs to a mostly local audience. There is no charge. Good music and strong drinks

also are to be had Friday night at the Hotel Mansión Iturbe. There is a cover charge to non-guests of US$7.

Less formal and in some ways more fun are performances by local musicians held most Friday and Saturday nights at the pizza-café *Charandas'n* a few doors west of the Mansión Iturbe. The music ranges from Mexican love ballads to American blues. There's no cover charge. The tequila at the Charandas'n is home-grown and quite good.

Teatro Emperador Caltzontzin on Plaza Gertrudis Bocanegra hosts occasional performances of theater, music and dance in addition to the usual fare of cinema in small-town Mexico (such as F-grade kung fu movies).

Things to Buy

Good places to find Michoacán crafts include the Casa de los Once Patios and the main market and the Mercado de Artesanías, both on Plaza Gertrudis Bocanegra. (See the earlier sections on those places.) One useful buy for cool Pátzcuaro nights can be a woolly poncho, available for US$25. Attractive tablecloths in bright check patterns cost around US$20.

On Friday mornings a ceramics market, with pottery from different villages, is held in Plaza San Francisco, one block west of Plaza Vasco de Quiroga.

Getting There & Away

Bus Pátzcuaro's Central Camionera is on the southwest edge of town, on the ring road variously called Avenida Circunvalación or El Libramiento. It has a cafeteria, a *guarda equipaje* where you can store your luggage, and a telephone caseta. Buses from Pátzcuaro (2nd-class unless otherwise stated) include:

Erongarícuaro – 18 km, 30 minutes; every 20 minutes, 7 am to 8 pm, by Autobuses de Occidente (US$1)

Guadalajara – 347 km, six hours; one 1st-class by Vía 2000 at 12.15 pm and one by Primera Plus at 11.45 pm (US$11)

Lázaro Cárdenas – 342 km, seven hours; about half-hourly, 6 am to 6.30 pm, by Galeana (US$11)

Mexico City (Terminal Poniente) – 370 km, 5 hours; 18 daily by Herradura de Plata (1st-class US$17, 2nd-class US$14); hourly by Flecha Amarilla

Morelia – 62 km, one hour; one 1st-class bus by Parhikuni (US$3); 2nd-class every 15 minutes, 5.30 am to 8.30 pm, by Galeana (US$2.50)

Quiroga – 22 km, 30 minutes; every 15 minutes, 5.50 am to 8.45 pm, by Galeana (US$1)

Santa Clara del Cobre – 20 km, 30 minutes; every 30 minutes, 5.45 am to 8.25 pm, by Galeana (US$1)

Tzintzuntzan – 15 km, 20 minutes; same buses as to Quiroga (US$1)

Uruapan – 62 km, one hour; buses every 15 minutes by Galeana (US$2.50)

Train The Estación del Ferrocarril (☎ 2-08-03) is three km north of city center, on the road to the lake. The main train is El Purépecha, running between Mexico City and Lázaro Cárdenas. It leaves Pátzcuaro at 6.45 am westbound (train No 31) and 9.15 pm eastbound (No 32). (See the Mexico City Getting There & Away section for more details.)

Getting Around

Centro buses and *colectivos* (minibuses), from the yard to your right when you walk out of the bus station, will take you to Plaza Gertrudis Bocanegra. Returning to the bus station, catch a Central vehicle from Plaza Gertrudis Bocanegra – colectivos stop on the north side of the plaza, buses on the west side. For the train station and the jetty where boats leave for Isla Janitzio, Lago buses and colectivos go from the northeast corner of Plaza Gertrudis Bocanegra. Returning to town from the station or jetty, you'll be dropped at Plaza Gertrudis Bocanegra. Buses cost US$0.50, colectivos slightly more. They run from about 6 am to 10 pm.

AROUND PÁTZCUARO

There are many interesting day trips from Pátzcuaro. All of the following places can be reached or nearly reached by public transport. Details of bus services to most of them appear in the Pátzcuaro section.

Isla Janitzio

Janitzio, the largest island in Lago de Pátzcuaro, is heavily devoted to tourism and on weekends and holidays it gets overrun by Mexican day-trippers. The 20-minute launch trip from Pátzcuaro offers distant views of villages along the shore while fishermen occasionally demonstrate the use of their famous butterfly-shaped fishing nets from conveniently placed canoes. They then paddle alongside your launch holding out trays for your coins.

You can see the island in an hour. It has plenty of fish restaurants and cheap souvenir shops, a few kids begging and a 40-meter-high statue of independence hero Jose María Morelos on its highest point. Inside the statue is a set of murals depicting Morelos' life; for US$0.50 you can climb up inside all the way to his raised fist, from which there's a panoramic view. Janitzio certainly is no must-see, and the polluted lake looks much prettier from afar.

Getting There & Away Launches to Janitzio go daily from around 7 am to 6 pm from two jetties on the lakeside 3.5 km north of central Pátzcuaro. They leave whenever they fill up, which is usually about every 30 minutes. From the main jetty, about half a km past the train station on Avenida de las Américas, launches cost US$3 for the round trip. Keep your ticket for the return trip.

Buses and colectivos marked 'Lago' run frequently to the lakeside from Plaza Gertrudis Bocanegra.

Ihuatzio
pop 500; alt 2035m; ☎ *434*

Ihuatzio, 14 km from Pátzcuaro near the eastern shore of the lake, was capital of the Tarascan league after Pátzcuaro but before Tzintzuntzan. Buses run to this village from Plaza Gertrudis Bocanegra. There's a large archaeological site, only partly excavated, a short walk from the village. The main feature is an open cere-

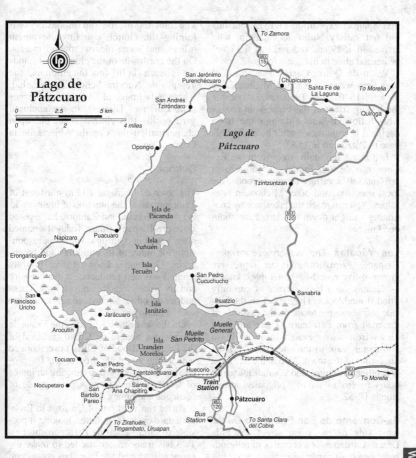

Lago de Pátzcuaro

To Zamora

San Jerónimo Purenchécuaro

Chupícuaro

Santa Fe de La Laguna

To Morelia

San Andrés Tziróndaro

Quiroga

Lago de Pátzcuaro

Opongio

Tzintzuntzan

Isla de Pacanda

Napizaro

Puacuaro

Isla Yunúen

Erongarícuaro

Isla Tecuén

San Pedro Cucuchucho

Sanabría

San Francisco Uricho

Isla Janitzío

Ihuatzio

Arocutín

Jarácuaro

Isla Uranden Morelos

Muelle San Pedrito

Muelle General

Tocuaro

San Pedro Pareo

Tzentzénguaro

Huecorio

Tzurumútaro

To Morelia

Nocupetaro

San Bartolo Pareo

Santa Ana Chapitiro

Train Station

Pátzcuaro

To Zirahuén, Tingambato, Uruapan

Bus Station

To Santa Clara del Cobre

monial space 200 meters long with two pyramids at its west end. The unexcavated areas include walled causeways and a round-based building thought to have been an observatory. It is open daily, from 10 am to 3 pm. The ruins are more memorable than those at Tzintzuntzan, especially at sunset, mainly because they appear in a more natural setting.

Tzintzuntzan
pop 12,394; alt 2050m; ☎ 435

The interesting little town of Tzintzuntzan ('tseen-TSOON-tsahn') is 15 km from Pátzcuaro near the northeastern corner of Lago de Pátzcuaro. It has impressive buildings from both the pre-Hispanic Tarascan empire and the early Spanish missionary period, and there are modern handicrafts on sale.

Tzintzuntzan is a Purépecha name meaning Place of Hummingbirds. It was the capital of the Tarascan league at the time of invasions by the Aztecs (which were repulsed) in the late 15th century and when the Spanish invaded in the 1520s. The Purépecha chief came to peaceable terms with Cristóbal de Olid, the leader of the first Spanish expedition in 1522, but this did not satisfy Nuño de Guzmán, who arrived in 1529 and ordered that the chief be burned alive in his quest for gold.

Vasco de Quiroga established his first base here when he reached Michoacán in the mid-1530s, and Tzintzuntzan became the headquarters of the Franciscan monks who followed him, although the town declined in importance after he shifted his base to Pátzcuaro in 1540.

Just along the main street from the Ex-Convento de San Francisco, some local artisans sell a variety of straw goods, the local specialty, and other Michoacán artesanías. You can reach the lakeshore by continuing straight down this street for about one km.

Las Yácatas The centerpiece of pre-Hispanic Tzintzuntzan is an impressive group of five round-based temples, known as yácatas, on a large terrace of carefully fitted stone blocks. They stand on the hillside just above the town, on the east side of the road from Pátzcuaro. There are good views from this elevated location. It's a 700-meter walk to the site entrance from the center of the town. Also at the site are a few other structures and a small museum; hours are from 9 am to 6 pm daily, admission is US$2.

Ex-Convento de San Francisco On the west side of the main street, Avenida Lázaro Cárdenas, is a complex of religious buildings built partly with stones from Las Yácatas, which the Spanish wrecked. Here Franciscan monks began the Spanish missionary effort in Michoacán in the 16th century. The olive trees in the churchyard are said to have been brought from Spain and planted by Vasco de Quiroga.

Straight ahead as you walk into the churchyard is the still-functioning Templo de San Francisco, built for the monks' own use. Inside, halfway along its north side, is the Capilla del Señor del Rescate (Chapel of the Saviour), with a much-revered painting of Christ. This painting is the focus of a weeklong festival in February.

The cloister of the old monastery adjoining the church contains the parish offices and some old, weathered murals. On the north side of the churchyard stands the church built for the Indians, the Templo de Nuestra Señora de la Salud, with a holy image of El Cristo de Goznes (The Christ of Hinges). In the enclosed yard beside this church is an old open chapel called the Capilla Abierta de la Concepción.

Quiroga
pop 23,825; alt 2074m; ☎ 435

The town of Quiroga, 10 km northeast of Tzintzuntzan at the junction of highway 15 between Morelia and Zamora, has existed since pre-Hispanic times. Today it's named after Vasco de Quiroga, who was responsible for many of its buildings and handicrafts. Quiroga is known for its brightly painted wooden products, its leatherwork and its wool sweaters and sarapes. These and many other Michoacán artesanías are sold in the town.

On the first Sunday in July, the Fiesta de la Preciosa Sangre de Cristo (Festival of the Precious Blood of Christ) is celebrated with a long torchlight procession. The procession is led by a group carrying an image of Christ crafted from a paste made of corncobs and honey.

Buses run west out of Quiroga to Erongarícuaro every 90 minutes, making it possible to circle Lago de Pátzcuaro by bus. Two bus transfers are needed to make the entire trip around the lake (bus routes end at Quiroga, Erongarícuaro and Pátzcuaro).

Erongarícuaro
pop 13,368; alt 2080m; ☎ 434

On the southwest edge of Lago de Pátzcuaro, a pretty 16-km trip from Pátzcuaro, Erongarícuaro (often just called 'Eronga') is one of the oldest settlements on the lake. It's just a peaceful little town where you can enjoy strolling along streets still lined with old Spanish-style houses. Top attractions are the plaza, the church a block away, and the old seminary attached to the church. However, be sure to check out

Muebles Finos, an American-run factory that produces quite unusual furniture. They make a Day-of-the-Dead chair resembling a human skeleton that's a true work of art.

On January 6, the Fiesta de los Reyes Magos (Festival of the Three Kings) is celebrated with festive music and dances.

Tocuaro
pop 1000; alt 2035m; ☎ *434*

Some of Mexico's finest mask makers live in this sleepy, one-bus-stop town 10 km from Pátzcuaro, although you wouldn't know it from advertising. Indeed, although many families in Tocuaro are involved in mask making, none have shops or even small signs outside their homes indicating as much. (Such signs invite unwanted attention by officials seeking 'taxes.') And since there are no street signs in Tocuaro, locating the town's mask makers is a bit of an adventure.

To find Tocuaro's most famous mask maker, Juan Orta Castillo, walk up the street that runs from the bus stop and the church; when you're about halfway to the church, knock on a door on the left side of the street and politely repeat his name. If you're at his home, you'll be invited in and shown masks for sale; if not, you'll be directed to his home. If you're lucky, you will see Orta at work. He has won Mexico's National Mask Maker competition several times.

Tocuaro's other highly regarded mask makers include Gustavo Horta, Felipe Terra and Felipe Anciola. If you're in the market for a mask, don't hesitate to knock on doors and ask if masks are made there; the word for mask in Spanish is *máscara*.

Santa Clara del Cobre
pop 32,000; alt 2180m; ☎ *434*

Santa Clara del Cobre (also called Villa Escalante), 20 km south of Pátzcuaro, was a copper-mining center from 1553 onwards. Though the mines are closed, the town still specializes in copperware, with over 50 workshops making copper goods. There's a copper museum too, next to the main plaza.

A week-long Feria del Cobre (Copper Fair) is held each August; exact dates vary.

Zirahuén
pop 7000; alt 2240m; ☎ *434*

Smaller but much deeper than Lago de Pátzcuaro, the blue lake beside the colonial town of Zirahuén, 20 km from Pátzcuaro off the road to Uruapan, makes a peaceful spot for a day trip or for camping. Few buses go to Zirahuén; as an option, you could take an Uruapan bus, get off at the Zirahuén turnoff and walk the remaining five km.

Tingambato
pop 11,045; alt 1980m; ☎ *459*

At Tingambato, a village about 40 km from Pátzcuaro on the road to Uruapan, are ruins of a ceremonial site that existed from about 450 to 900 AD. They show Teotihuacán influence and date from well before the Tarascan empire. The ruins include a ball court (rare in western Mexico), temple pyramids and an underground tomb where a skeleton and 32 skulls were found. A blue sign with a white pyramid points to the site from the highway, about one km away.

URUAPAN
pop 250,717; alt 1620m; ☎ *452*

When the Spanish monk Fray Juan de San Miguel arrived here in 1533, he was so impressed with the Río Cupatitzio and the lush vegetation surrounding it that he named the area Uruapan ('oo-roo-AH-pahn'), which translates roughly as 'Eternal Spring.' Uruapan is 500 meters lower in altitude than Pátzcuaro, and much warmer. The vegetation becomes noticeably more tropical on the 62-km trip between the two cities.

Fray Juan had a large market square, hospital and chapel built, and arranged streets in an orderly checkerboard pattern. Under Spanish rule Uruapan quickly grew into a productive agricultural center, and today it's renowned for its high-quality avocados and fruit. Its craftspeople are famed for their handpainted cedar lacquerware, particularly trays and boxes.

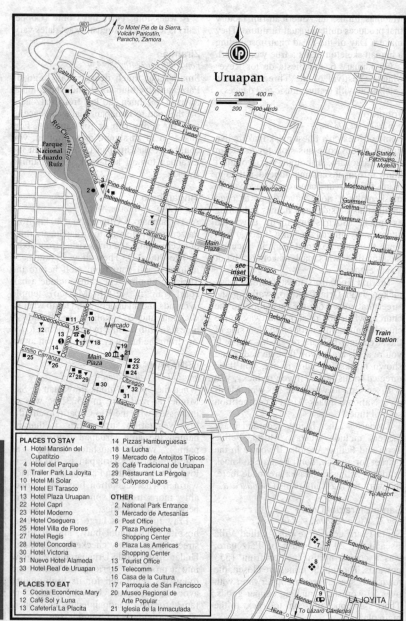

Uruapan

| 0 | 200 | 400 m |
| 0 | 200 | 400 yards |

To Motel Pie de la Sierra,
Volcán Paricutín,
Paracho, Zamora

To Bus Station,
Pátzcuaro,
Morelia

Parque
Nacional
Eduardo
Ruiz

Train
Station

To Airport

To Lázaro Cárdenas

LA JOYITA

PLACES TO STAY
1 Hotel Mansión del
    Cupatitzio
4 Hotel del Parque
9 Trailer Park La Joyita
10 Hotel Mi Solar
11 Hotel El Tarasco
13 Hotel Plaza Uruapan
22 Hotel Capri
23 Hotel Moderno
24 Hotel Oseguera
25 Hotel Villa de Flores
27 Hotel Regis
28 Hotel Concordia
30 Hotel Victoria
31 Nuevo Hotel Alameda
33 Hotel Real de Uruapan

PLACES TO EAT
5 Cocina Económica Mary
12 Café Sol y Luna
13 Cafetería La Placita

14 Pizzas Hamburguesas
18 La Lucha
19 Mercado de Antojitos Típicos
26 Café Tradicional de Uruapan
29 Restaurant La Pérgola
32 Calypsso Jugos

OTHER
2 National Park Entrance
3 Mercado de Artesanías
6 Post Office
7 Plaza Purépecha
    Shopping Center
8 Plaza Las Américas
    Shopping Center
13 Tourist Office
15 Telecomm
16 Casa de la Cultura
17 Parroquia de San Francisco
20 Museo Regional de
    Arte Popular
21 Iglesia de la Inmaculada

Uruapan is a larger, less tidy place than Pátzcuaro, with far less colonial ambiance, but is still attractive with its red-tile roofs in a lush hillside setting. A pleasant miniature national park, the Parque Nacional Eduardo Ruiz, lies within the city, only 15 minutes' walk from the center. Uruapan is also the best base for visiting the remarkable volcano Paricutín, 35 km west.

Orientation

The city slopes down from north to south, with the Río Cupatitzio running down its west side. Most of the streets are still arranged in the grid pattern laid down in the 1530s. Apart from the bus station in the northeast of town and the train station in the east, everything of interest to travelers is within walking distance of the 300-meter-long main plaza. This is actually three joined plazas named, from east to west, El Jardín Morelos, La Pérgola Municipal and El Jardín de los Mártires de Uruapan. A colonial church stands at each end of the north side of the plaza.

Most streets change their names at this central plaza. The busy street along the south side of the plaza is called Emilio Carranza to the west and Obregón to the east. Farther east, it changes again to Sarabia, which intersects Paseo Lázaro Cárdenas, the main road south to the coast.

Information

Tourist Office The Delegación de Turismo (☎ 3-61-72) is in the basement of the Hotel Plaza Uruapan, in the far right corner. The staff give out a map of Uruapan and brochures about Michoacán in English and Spanish. Only one staff member speaks English. The office is open Monday through Saturday from 9 am to 2 pm and 4 to 7.30 pm, and Sunday from 9 am to 2 pm.

Money There are several banks near the central plaza, especially on Cupatitzio in the first two blocks south of the plaza. Most are open Monday through Friday from 9 am to 2 pm but have shorter hours for foreign exchange. Centro Cambiario de Divisas Hispanimex, at Portal Matamoros 19 near the east end of the plaza, and Compra y Venta de Dólares, on Cupatitzio 1½ blocks south of the plaza, will change cash or traveler's checks Monday through Friday from 9 am to 2 pm and 4 to 7 pm, and until 2 pm on Saturday.

Post & Communications The main post office is at Reforma 13 just west of 5 de Febrero, three blocks south of the central plaza. It's open Monday through Friday from 8 am to 7 pm, Saturday from 9 am to 1 pm.

The Telecomm office is on Ocampo, half a block north of the west end of the central plaza. It has a pay phone and fax service. It's open Monday through Friday from 9 am to 8 pm, Saturday from 9 am to noon.

Museo Regional de Arte Popular

For a quick overview of Michoacán crafts, visit the Museo Regional de Arte Popular, adjoining the Iglesia de la Inmaculada on the northeast corner of the central plaza. The museum building, erected in 1533, was the first hospital in the Americas. The carving around the door facing the plaza, and around the windows, is similar to the Moorish-style work on the church at Angahuan near Paricutín volcano. The museum is open Tuesday through Sunday from 9.30 am to 1.30 pm and from 3.30 to 6 pm (free).

Parque Nacional Eduardo Ruiz

This lovely tropical park is only 600 meters west of the central plaza. It begins at the gushing headwaters of the Río Cupatitzio and follows the lushly vegetated banks for a kilometer or so downstream. It's a shady place with waterfalls, bridges, a trout farm, a playground and paved paths for easy strolling. Boys dive into one or two of the river's deeper pools and ask for coins afterwards.

The main entrance is on Calzada La Quinta at the end of Independencia. If you don't want to walk there, take a 'Parque' bus up Independencia from Ocampo. The park is open daily from 8 am to 6 pm (admission is US$0.50). Maps and leaflets on its history are on sale at the ticket kiosk.

Special Events

Uruapan's festivals include:

Semana Santa – Palm Sunday is marked by a procession through the city streets. Figures and crosses woven from palm fronds are sold after the procession. There's also a ceramics contest, and a week-long exhibition/market of Michoacán handicrafts fills up the central plaza. Prices get lower as the week goes on.

Día de San Francisco – St Francis, the patron saint of Uruapan, is honored with colorful festivities and the Canácuas dance by women; October 4.

Festival de Coros y Danzas – The Choir & Dance Festival is a contest of Purépecha dance and musical groups; three days around October 24 (not held every year).

Feria del Aguacate – The Avocado Fair is a big event, with bullfights, cockfights and concerts and agricultural, industrial and handicraft exhibitions; two weeks in November (exact dates vary).

Places to Stay – budget

Camping *Trailer Park La Joyita* (☎ 3-03-64) is at Estocolmo 22, 1½ blocks east of Paseo Lázaro Cárdenas at the southern end of town. It has full hookups for 10 trailers, a lawn area for tents, a barbecue and 24-hour hot water in the showers. Cost for two people and a vehicle is US$7. Buses marked 'FOVISSSTE' operate frequently between here and Calle Cupatitzio, 1½ blocks south of the central plaza.

Hotels The *Hotel del Parque* (☎ 4-38-45) at Independencia 124, 6½ blocks west of the central plaza and half a block from the Parque Nacional Eduardo Ruiz, is easily the most pleasant of Uruapan's cheapies. Singles/doubles are US$7/10. The rooms are clean with tile floors, Japanese-design bedspreads, private bath and 24-hour hot water. There's a rear patio area and enclosed parking. The owner speaks English.

Runner-up is the *Hotel Mi Solar* (☎ 4-09-12) at Delgado 10, two blocks north of the plaza, with 20 slightly worn rooms

around two open courtyards. They have private bathrooms and cost US$7/9.

On the east side of the plaza is a trio of other cheapies, the best of which is the *Hotel Capri* (no phone), Portal Santos Degollado 12. It has 24-hour hot water and its rooms, at US$5 (US$6 for two beds), are bigger and brighter than those at the *Hotel Moderno* (☎ 4-02-12) or the *Hotel Oseguera* (☎ 3-98-56) down the block. The Moderno charges US$7 per room (US$14 for two beds), and the Oseguera US$7/9. All three hotels are very worn, need new beds and have spray-everywhere showers.

Places to Stay – middle

Uruapan has several attractive places in this range. *Hotel Villa de Flores* (☎ 4-28-00) at Emilio Carranza 15, 1½ blocks west of the central plaza, is a well-kept colonial-style hotel. Its 27 comfortable rooms, with private bath but no phones, open onto pleasant courtyards. Singles/doubles are US$12/18. The two-bed rooms on the rear courtyard are newer and brighter than the other, equally priced rooms.

On the south side of the plaza, *Hotel Regis* (☎ 3-58-44) at Portal Carrillo 12 has 40 brightly decorated, mostly well-lit rooms with fans, phones and TV for US$18/22, plus its own restaurant and parking. Next door, the *Hotel Concordia* (☎ 3-04-00) is a comfortable, modern hotel with 63 large, spotless rooms, all with TV and carpeting. It also has parking, a restaurant, and laundry service. Singles/doubles are US$22/30.

Half a block south of the central plaza, *Nuevo Hotel Alameda* (☎ 3-41-00) at 5 de Febrero 11 is another good mid-range hotel, better than Concordia, with clean, comfortable rooms that have TV and phones for US$15/18. There's parking as well.

Hotel El Tarasco (☎ 4-15-00), half a block north of the plaza at Independencia 2, is a step up in quality, with 65 large and bright rooms at US$30/38, plus a restaurant and a swimming pool. There are good views from some of the upper floors.

Near the central plaza are two other hotels worth considering – the *Hotel Real de Uruapan* (☎ 3-44-33) at Bravo 110, and the *Hotel Victoria* (☎ 4-25-00) at Cupatitzio 11. The Hotel Real has 70 rooms in nine stories, some with sweeping views, all very comfortable with carpet, TV and phone. There are junior suites with sitting areas, bathtubs and large TVs. Prices run US$25/30 and US$40 for a junior suite. The four-story, 80-room Hotel Victoria has nicer rooms than the Hotel Real, but can't match the Real's upper-story vistas. Prices at the Victoria are US$25/35 and US$30/40 for a junior suite.

The hacienda-style *Hotel Mansión del Cupatitzio* (☎ 3-21-00), at the north end of the Parque Nacional Eduardo Ruiz on Calzada Fray Juan de San Miguel, is one of the best hotels in Uruapan. Its restaurant overlooks the Rodilla del Diablo pool where the Río Cupatitzio begins. The hotel has a swimming pool, lovely grounds, laundry service and so forth. Rates are US$33/43.

If you have wheels, you might like the *Motel Pie de la Sierra* (☎ 4-25-10), four km north of the center on highway 37 toward Paracho. Located at the foot of the mountains, which is what the name means, it has large, well-kept grounds, a swimming pool and games room, and a pleasant restaurant. There are 72 attractive rooms with fireplace, color TV, private terraces and mountain views. Rates are US$25/33.

Places to Stay – top end

Hotel Plaza Uruapan (☎ 3-37-00) at Ocampo 64 on the west side of the main plaza charges US$40/50. There's a big difference between the interior rooms with no view and some of the exterior ones, which have great views through floor-to-ceiling windows.

Places to Eat

One of the best places to eat in town is the tiny, cheap *Cocina Económica Mary* at Independencia 57, 3½ blocks west of the central plaza. Open Monday through Saturday from 8.30 am to 5.30 pm, this family-run place serves a delicious US$3 home-style comida corrida of sopa followed by your choice of several main courses – which can range from bístek ranchero to fish to cactus-ear salad – plus a soda or glass of fresh juice. You can also get a breakfast of huevos a la Mexicana and café con leche for US$2.50.

The popular *Pizzas Hamburguesas* at Emilio Carranza 8, a few steps west of the central plaza, does tasty pizzas with generous toppings from 8 am to 10.30 pm daily. The chica size at US$3 is plenty for one person. There are burgers, tacos, quesadillas, burritos and other snacks too; of these, the burgers and burritos are particularly good.

Calypsso Jugos at Obregón 2A, just off the southeast corner of the central plaza, is an inexpensive juice and licuado bar also offering snacks such as tortas or yogurt with fruit. It serves a US$2.50 breakfast of fruit or juice, eggs and coffee from 7 am.

The classier *Cafetería La Placita*, beneath the Hotel Plaza Uruapan on the west side of the plaza, serves up good food off two long menus. There are antojitos for under US$4. Fruit salad is (US$1.50), yogurt with granola (US$1) and various egg dishes (US$3). Nothing on the dinner menu tops US$10. It's open daily from 7 am to 11 pm.

The *Restaurant La Pérgola* at Portal Carrillo 4 on the south side of the plaza, open daily from 8 am to 11.30 pm, is popular, but its comida corrida is ordinary.

Uruapan also has a couple of excellent cafés for enjoying good, strong coffee amid carved wooden furniture. One is *La Lucha*, half a block north of the central plaza on the small street García Ortiz. It's open daily from 9 am to 2 pm and 4 to 9 pm. The other is the *Café Tradicional de Uruapan* at Emilio Carranza 5B, half a block west of the central plaza. It's more expensive but has a large selection of coffees. Hours are 8.30 am to 2 pm and 4 to 10 pm daily. They also serve breakfasts and desserts.

The *Mercado de Antojitos Típicos*, on Corregidora one short block north of the plaza, is a cheap place to sample local food. Forty food stalls serve Michoacán dishes every day from around 6 am to midnight. Pick a stall that looks popular.

Several hotel restaurants are praiseworthy. The *Hotel Concordia*, the *Hotel Regis* and the *Hotel El Tarasco* serve ample four-course comidas corridas for around US$4. The restaurant on the ninth floor of the *Hotel Real de Uruapan* has decent food, sweeping vistas and live music nightly. Breakfast and chicken dishes run to US$3, typical plates around US$4 and seafood and beef dishes US$5 to US$6.

Entertainment

Uruapan doesn't yet rival New York City for nightlife, but you might find one or two things to do after dark besides lingering over coffee at a café or going to church.

The Casa de la Cultura on García Ortiz, half a block north of the plaza, hosts exhibitions, occasional concerts and so on.

The Hotel Plaza Uruapan has a bar and disco and live entertainment on weekends. Several of the other better-class hotels near the central plaza also have bars.

Café Sol y Luna at Independencia 15A bills itself as an art-café and is quite popular with the twentysomething crowd. This newer place displays photos and paintings by local artists. Jazz, blues and rock are often played here at night.

Check with the tourist office to see what's cooking during your stay in Uruapan.

Things to Buy

Local crafts such as lacquered trays and boxes can be bought at the Mercado de Artesanías opposite the entrance to the Parque Nacional Eduardo Ruiz. A few shops nearby on Independencia sell the same sort of thing. But by far the best selection of handicrafts – high quality and from all over Mexico – is sold in the artesanías shop in the Hotel Mansión del Cupatitzio. The town market, which stretches more than half a kilometer up Constitución from the central plaza to Calzada Juárez, is worth a browse too.

Getting There & Away

Air Aeromar (☎ 3-50-50 at the airport) flies daily to/from Mexico City via Morelia. Aerocuahonte flies twice daily, Monday through Saturday, to/from Lázaro Cárdenas, and once or twice a day (except Sunday) to/from Guadalajara. A helpful travel agency for booking flights is Viajes Tzitzi (☎ 3-34-19) in an office located beside the entrance of the Hotel Plaza Uruapan; you can also purchase ETN and Primera Plus bus tickets here.

Bus The Central Camionera is three km northeast of central Uruapan on the highway to Pátzcuaro and Morelia. It has a post office, telegraph and fax office, telephone caseta, a guardería for leaving luggage, cafeterias and a few shops. Daily buses run all over central and northern Mexico, including:

Colima – 400 km, six hours; one 1st-class by La Linea, 11.15 am, US$12; one 2nd-class by Autobuses de Occidente, 9.30 pm, US$11

Guadalajara – 305 km, five hours, via La Barca; five deluxe buses each by ETN (US$15) and Primera Plus (US$11), and four by La Línea Plus (US$11); six 1st-class each by La Línea and Servicios Coordinados (US$10); for the more scenic route around the south side of Lake Chapala, you need to change to local buses at Zamora

Lázaro Cárdenas – 280 km, six hours; nine buses by Parhikuni (US$12 deluxe, US$10 1st-class); two deluxe buses by La Línea Plus (US$12); hourly 2nd-class buses by Galeana (US$10)

Mexico City (Terminal Poniente or Terminal Norte) – 430 km, six hours; seven deluxe buses by ETN (US$26); four 1st-class by Primera Plus (US$21) and 11 by Vía 2000 (US$19 or US$21); five 2nd-class by Autobuses de Occidente (US$19)

Morelia – 125 km, two hours; buses every 20 minutes until 11 pm by Parhikuni (US$6 deluxe, US$5.50 1st-class); two deluxe by ETN (US$7) and seven by Primera Plus (US$6); 2nd-class every 20 minutes with Galeana Ruta Paraíso (US$4)

Pátzcuaro – 62 km, one hour; 2nd-class buses every 15 minutes with Galeana Ruta Paraíso (US$2.50)

Train The train station (☎ 4-09-81) is two km east of the center on Paseo Lázaro Cárdenas at the east end of Calle Américas.

El Purépecha, running between Mexico City and Lázaro Cárdenas, departs Uruapan southbound (train No 31) at 9 am and eastbound (No 32) at 6.15 pm. Tickets for this train are sold from 8 am to 7 pm. (See the Mexico City Getting There & Away section for more details.)

Getting Around
To/From the Airport The airport is on Avenida Latinoamericana about eight km southeast of the city center, a 15-minute drive. A taxi costs about US$3.

Bus Local buses marked 'Centro' run from the door of the bus station to the central plaza. If you want a taxi, buy a ticket from the taquilla in the station. On the return trip catch a Central Camionera or Central bus on the south side of the central plaza.

From the train station, take a Centro bus west along Calle Américas to the plaza. Heading from the center of town to the station, a Quinta bus from outside La Pérgola restaurant on the central plaza will drop you on Paseo Lázaro Cárdenas three short blocks south of the station.

The local buses run every day from around 6 am to 9 pm. They cost US$0.50.

AROUND URUAPAN
Cascada de Tzaráracua
Ten km south of Uruapan just off highway 37, the Río Cupatitzio falls 30 meters into two pools flanked by lush vegetation. Two km upstream there's another lovely waterfall, the smaller Tzararacuita. Tzaráracua buses depart from the middle of the south side of Uruapan's main plaza. They depart every half-hour on weekends and holidays (which are when the falls attract crowds). Other days these buses go only every couple of hours, so it's better to take an Autotransportes Galeana bus heading for Nueva Italia from the Uruapan bus station; these depart every 20 minutes and will drop you at Tzaráracua. The buses stop at a car park. From there, it's a steep descent of about one km to the main falls.

Paracho
pop 30,751; alt 2220m; ☎ 452
Paracho, 40 km north of Uruapan on highway 37, is a small Purépecha town famous for its handmade guitars. It's worth visiting if you want to buy an instrument or watch some of the country's best guitar makers at work. The local artisans are also known for their high-quality violins, cellos and other woodcrafts, including furniture. The liveliest time to come is during the annual Feria Nacional de la Guitarra (National Guitar Fair), a big weeklong splurge of music, dance, exhibitions, markets and cockfights in early August.

Many buses leaving from Uruapan to Zamora will stop in Paracho. Autotransportes Galeana has 2nd-class buses leaving every 15 minutes for the one-hour trip (US$1.50).

Volcán Paricutín
On the afternoon of February 20, 1943, a Purépecha farmer, Dionisio Pulido, was plowing his cornfield 35 km west of Uruapan when the ground began to shake and swell and to emit steam, sparks and hot ash. The farmer tried at first to cover the moving earth, but when that proved impossible, he fled. A volcano started to rise from the spot. Within a year it had risen 410 meters above the surrounding land and its lava had engulfed the Purépecha villages of San Salvador Paricutín and San Juan Parangaricutiro. The villagers had plenty of time to flee as the lava flow was so gradual.

The volcano continued to spit lava and fire until 1952. Today its large, black cone stands mute, emitting gentle wisps of steam. Near the edge of the 20-sq-km lava field, the top of San Juan's church protrudes eerily from the sea of solidified, black lava. It's the only visible trace of the two buried villages.

Visiting the Area An excursion to Paricutín from Uruapan makes a fine day trip,

SCOTT DOGGETT

San Juan's church emerges from a sea of solidified lava

although litter and graffiti at the church take some of the fun out of it. The volcano is not a particularly high mountain – the much bigger Tancítaro towers to its south – but it's certainly memorable and fairly easy to access.

If you want to do it in one day from Uruapan, as most people do, start early. First you have to reach the Purépecha village of Angahuan, 32 km from Uruapan on the road to Los Reyes, which branches west off highway 37 about 15 km north of Uruapan. Galeana 2nd-class buses leave the Uruapan bus station for Angahuan every 30 minutes from 5 am to 7 pm. On the 45-minute ride to Angahuan (US$1) you pass the now-forested stumps of a dozen or so older volcanoes. There are buses back from Angahuan to Uruapan up until at least 7 pm.

At the Angahuan bus stop, guides with ponies will offer to take you one km to the Centro Turístico de Angahuan, a small,

low-key accommodation place, often just called 'Las Cabañas.' Here there is a lookout point with good views of the lava field, the protruding San Juan church tower and the volcano itself. There's also a good restaurant here and a small exhibition on the volcano and its history. If you don't want to ride into town, gently fend the guides off. To reach Las Cabañas on foot, walk into the village center, turn right at the main plaza, then left after 200 meters at a building with a TV satellite dish, opposite a shoe shop. From here the track leads straight to Las Cabañas, about a 15-minute walk.

San Juan church is a 45-minute walk down a path that begins near the entrance to Las Cabañas. The path is wide, gray with volcanic ash, and at times flanked by barbed-wire fences. Getting to the church and back does not require a guide or a horse. There is no cost to visit the church or the volcano.

Reaching the Cone A much more exciting option is to go to the top of the volcano. You can do this on foot or by pony, but either way you should hire a guide.

There are two routes to the crater. The more direct begins behind the restaurant at Las Cabañas, to the left of the viewing area. The path is narrow and winds for 500 meters through a pine forest that can be disorienting. At times the path forks and unless you know which fork to take you can become lost. Detailed directions are impractical as such paths, created by wood gatherers, frequently appear and disappear.

After the first 500 meters you'll cross a dirt road and pick up the trail at the other side. Within 30 meters you should pass through a gate and soon afterward the path begins to slope upward considerably. The trail weaves through thickets where lovely purple and yellow wildflowers bloom much of the year. After about 30 minutes of hiking, the woods give way to a barren lava field. From here to the crater the path, which consists solely of jagged black rock, is marked in spots with splashes of paint.

About 150 meters from the summit, the rock gives way to a sandy ash and you'll see steam rising from fumaroles on knolls to the left of the cone. A narrow 40-meter-long trail links the main trail to the knolls, which are worth visiting. They are covered with bright yellow rock that is quite striking amid the surrounding black lava. On the knolls you will at times feel steam rising from the crevices around you.

The lip of the crater has two high points. Beneath the one on the right as you face the caldera, on the outside of the cone, is a dust slide. It's fun to descend it at a fast, high-stepping walk. At the end of the dust slide, your guide can lead you back through the lava field to the viewing area you set out from, or you can follow a flat, dusty horse trail back to the entrance of Las Cabañas. The latter option is considerably longer, but the trail brings you near the San Juan church, which is worth seeing. Most people need 2½ hours to reach the summit and another three hours

for the return trip using this route. If you negotiate well, a guide costs about US$20 for one person, US$35 for two.

Another option is to go by horse or on foot entirely via the horse trail, which starts beside the entrance to Las Cabañas and skirts the southeastern edge of the lava field that engulfs San Juan church. The trail initially is wide and gray and cuts across earth otherwise covered with pine needles. From the church to the base of the cone, the pine needles disappear and the trail follows a road past some farms. The trail will narrow and pass through brush before reaching an open, sandy area 15 minutes' walk from the foot of the volcano. There the horses are tied up under a shade tree while their riders make the final, 20-minute ascent on foot. The ride takes about two hours each way. Renting a pony and guide to the cone costs around US$30 for one person, US$50 for two.

Angahuan Angahuan itself is worth a stop on your way through. It's a typical Purépecha village with characteristic wooden houses, dusty streets, little electricity and loudspeakers booming out announcements in the Purépecha language. On the main plaza is the 16th century Iglesia de Santiago Apostol, with some fine carving around its door, done by a Moorish stonemason who accompanied the early Spanish missionaries here. Around to the right of the church, a couple of doors back from the plaza, there's an interesting wooden door, carved with the story of Paricutín.

Festival days in Angahuan are the Fiesta de San Isidro Labrador on May 15, with a weaving contest, and the Fiesta de Santiago Apostol on July 25, with handicraft displays, music, contests and games.

Places to Stay & Eat Las Cabañas has eight clean cabins of various sizes, each with a living room and fireplace, plus a trailer park and campsite, and a restaurant with decent regional food. The smallest cabaña, for two people, costs US$7 a night and the bathroom is communal; a six-person cabaña is US$30; others sleep up to

24 people. You can make reservations at the tourist office in Uruapan.

Guides may be able to offer you lodging in a house at about US$5 per person.

ZAMORA

pop 160,023; alt 1560m; ☎ 351

Zamora, about 115 km northwest of Uruapan and 190 km southeast of Guadalajara, is the center for a rich agricultural region known for its strawberries. It's a pleasant town to stroll around in. It was founded in 1574 and has a curious unfinished cathedral, the **Catedral Inconclusa**. Fifteen km southeast of Zamora, a short distance off highway 15 at Tangancícuaro, is the clear, spring-fed, tree-shaded **Lago de Camécuaro**, a lovely spot for drivers to stop and picnic. If you need to spend the night in Zamora, there's a range of hotels to choose from. The bus station is on the outskirts of town. Primera Plus runs three 1st-class buses a day from Uruapan (2½ hours, US$6) and Galeana has 2nd-class service every 15 minutes.

Inland Colima

The tiny (5191 sq km) state of Colima ranges from tall volcanoes on its northern fringes to lagoons near the Pacific coast. The climate is equally diverse with heat along the coast and cooler temperatures in the highlands. This section deals with the upland three-quarters of the state; the narrow coastal plain, with the beach resorts of Manzanillo, Cuyutlán and Paraíso, is discussed in the Central Pacific Coast chapter.

Colima, the state capital, is a small and little-visited but pleasant and interesting semitropical city. Overlooking it from the north are two spectacular volcanoes – the active, constantly steaming Volcán de Fuego de Colima (3960 meters) and the extinct snowcapped Volcán Nevado de Colima (4330 meters). Both can be reached relatively easily if you have a taste for adventure and a not-too-tight budget.

Colima state's main agricultural products are coconuts, limes, bananas and mangos. Its biggest industry is mining – one of Mexico's richest iron deposits is near Minatitlán.

History

Pre-hispanic Colima was remote from the major ancient cultures of Mexico. Seaborne contacts with more distant places may have been more important, and there's even a legend that one king of Colima, Ix, had regular treasure-bearing visitors from China.

Colima produced some remarkable pottery, which has been found in over 250 sites, mainly tombs, dating from about 200 BC to 800 AD. The pottery includes a variety of figures, often quite comical and expressive of emotion and movement. Best known are the rotund figures of hairless dogs, known as Tepezcuintles. In some ancient Mexican cultures dogs were buried with their owners. It was believed that they were able to carry the dead to paradise. The dogs also had a more mundane function: they were a part of the indigenous diet.

Archaeologists believe the makers of the pottery lived in villages spread around the state. The type of grave in which much of the pottery was found, the shaft tomb, occurs not only in the western Mexican states of Colima, Michoacán, Jalisco and Nayarit, but in Panama and South America as well, which suggests seaborne contacts with places much farther south.

When the Spanish reached Mexico, Colima was the leading force in the Chimalhuacán Indian confederation that dominated Colima and parts of Jalisco and Nayarit. Two Spanish expeditions were defeated by the Colimans before Gonzalo de Sandoval, one of Cortés' lieutenants, conquered them in 1523. That same year he founded the town of Colima – the third Spanish town in Nueva España, after Veracruz and Mexico City. The town was moved to its present site, from its unhealthy original lowland location near Tecomán, in 1527.

COLIMA
pop 120,749; alt 550m; ☎ 331

Colima lives at the mercy of the forces of nature. Volcán de Fuego de Colima, clearly visible 30 km to the north (along with the taller but extinct Nevado de Colima), has had nine major eruptions in the past four centuries. Of even greater concern, the city has been hit by a series of earthquakes over the centuries – the most recent major one was in 1941. These natural events are why Colima, even though it was the first Spanish city in western Mexico, has few colonial buildings.

Today Colima is a pleasant, small city graced by palm trees, lying on a fertile plain ringed by mountains. Few tourists come here, but there are a number of interesting things to see and do in town and farther out, in the surrounding farmland. Though only 45 km from the coast, Colima is at a higher elevation and, consequently, is cooler and less humid. The rainy months are July through September.

Orientation
Central Colima spreads around three plazas, with the Plaza Principal (also known as the Jardín Libertad) at the center of things. The Jardín Quintero lies directly behind the cathedral, and three blocks farther east is the Jardín Núñez. Street names change at the Plaza Principal.

The shiny modern main bus terminal is about two km east of the center, on the Guadalajara-Manzanillo road.

Information
Tourist Office The state tourist office (☎ 2-43-80) is at Portal Hidalgo 20 on the west side of the Plaza Principal. Look for the big 'Turismo' sign over the door. The office is open Monday through Friday from 8.30 am to 3 pm and 5.30 to 9 pm, weekends from 9 am to 1 pm. It has free maps, brochures and information on the city and state of Colima.

Money There are numerous banks around the center where you can change money. They are open Monday through Friday from 9 am to 1 pm. Banamex, on Hidalgo a block east of the cathedral, has an ATM.

Majapara Casa de Cambio at the southwest corner of Jardín Núñez is open longer hours: Monday through Saturday from 9 am to 2 pm and 4.30 to 7 pm. There are other money changers nearby.

Post & Communications The post office is at Madero 247 at the northeast corner of Jardín Núñez. It's open weekdays from 8 am to 7 pm. Saturday it closes at noon. The Telecomm office, with telegram, telex and fax services, is one door to the left of the post office. It's open weekdays from 9 am to 8 pm, Saturday from 9 am to 1 pm.

Several coin and card pay phones can be found beside the Plaza Principal and Jardín Núñez. There are also three Computel offices with telephone casetas and fax service: at Morelos 236, facing Jardín Núñez, at Medellín 55 near the corner of Hidalgo and at the bus station. All are open daily from 7 am to 10 pm.

Laundry Lavandería Victoria at Victoria 131 between Ocampo and De la Vega charges US$2 for 3 kg of laundry if you do it yourself, and US$3 if you drop it off to be washed. It's open Monday through Saturday from 7 am to 2 pm and 3 to 8 pm.

Around Plaza Principal
The **Catedral**, or Santa Iglesia, on the east side of the Plaza Principal, has been rebuilt several times since the Spanish first erected a cathedral here in 1527. The most recent reconstruction dates from just after the 1941 earthquake.

Next to the cathedral is the **Palacio de Gobierno**, built between 1884 and 1904. Local artist Jorge Chávez Carrillo painted the murals on the stairway to celebrate the 200th anniversary of the birth of independence hero Miguel Hidalgo, who was once parish priest of Colima. The murals depict Mexican history from the Spanish conquest to independence.

The **Museo de Historia de Colima**, on the south side of the plaza, is worth a visit to see both ceramic vessels and figurines

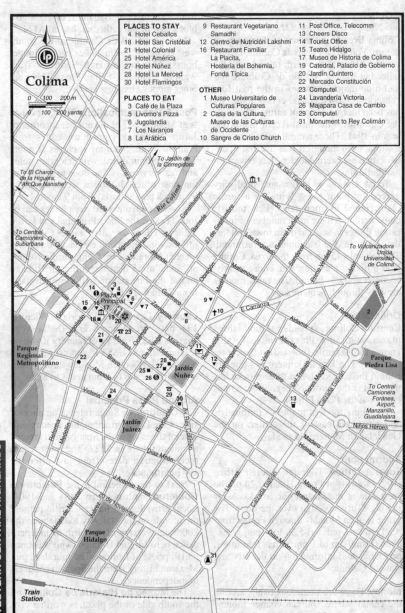

Colima

0   100   200 m

0   100   200 yards

PLACES TO STAY
4   Hotel Ceballos
18 Hotel San Cristóbal
21 Hotel Colonial
25 Hotel América
27 Hotel Núñez
28 Hotel La Merced
30 Hotel Flamingos

PLACES TO EAT
3   Café de la Plaza
5   Livorno's Pizza
6   Jugolandia
7   Los Naranjos
8   La Arábica

9   Restaurant Vegetariano
    Samadhi
12 Centro de Nutrición Lakshmi
16 Restaurant Familiar
    La Placita,
    Hostería del Bohemia,
    Fonda Típica

OTHER
1   Museo Universitario de
    Culturas Populares
2   Casa de la Cultura,
    Museo de las Culturas
    de Occidente
10 Sangre de Cristo Church

11 Post Office, Telecomm
13 Cheers Disco
14 Tourist Office
15 Teatro Hidalgo
17 Museo de Historia de Colima
19 Catedral, Palacio de Gobierno
20 Jardín Quintero
22 Mercado Constitución
23 Computel
24 Lavandería Victoria
26 Majapara Casa de Cambio
29 Computel
31 Monument to Rey Colimán

(mostly people and Tepezcuintle dogs) unearthed in Colima state. There are also permanent displays of masks, textiles, costumes, basketry and shellwork from the Colima coast plus temporary exhibits. The museum is open Tuesday through Sunday from 10 am to 2 pm and 4 to 8 pm (free). Next door is the **Sala de Exposiciones de la Universidad de Colima**, offering changing art exhibitions. It's open the same hours as the museum and is also free.

The **Teatro Hidalgo** on the corner of Degollado and Independencia, one block south of the Plaza Principal, was built in neoclassical style between 1871 and 1883 on a site originally donated to the city by Miguel Hidalgo. The theater was destroyed by the earthquakes of 1932 and 1941 and reconstruction was undertaken in 1942.

Casa de la Cultura & Museo de las Culturas de Occidente

This large, modern cultural center for the state of Colima is at the intersection of Calzada Galván and Ejército Nacional, a little over one km northeast of the center.

The chief attraction is the **Museo de las Culturas de Occidente** (Museum of Western Cultures), fronting Ejército Nacional. Here, in a well-lit building, are exhibited hundreds of pre-Hispanic ceramic vessels and figurines from Colima state, with explanations in Spanish. Most impressive are the human figures and Tepezcuintle dogs, but there's a wide variety of other figures including musical instruments, mammals, reptiles, fish and birds. Some of the species depicted still exist in the area, others have disappeared. The museum is open Tuesday through Sunday from 9 am to 7 pm (free).

The site's administrative building has a permanent exhibition of the renowned Colima modernistic painter Alfonso Michel (1897-1957). It also sometimes has high-quality temporary art exhibits. The **Teatro Casa de la Cultura** adjoins this building. There's a café on the ground floor of the **Edificio de Talleres** (Workshops Building) next door. Also on the site is the **Biblioteca Central del Estado**, the state library. Nearby, the Cine Teatro USI presents cultural film series.

Museo Universitario de Culturas Populares

The University Museum of Popular Cultures is in the Instituto Universitario de Bellas Artes (IUBA), on the corner of 27 de Septiembre and Gallardo, about 900 meters north of the Plaza Principal. It displays folk art from Colima and other states, with a particularly good section of costumes and masks used in traditional Colima dances. Other exhibits include textiles, ceramics, musical instruments and furniture. Hours are Monday through Saturday from 9 am to 2 pm and 4 to 7 pm, holidays 9 am to 2 pm (free).

Also at IUBA is the interesting **Taller de Reproducciones**, just inside the gate and to your right, where you can sometimes see the process of reproducing ancient Coliman ceramic figures. In the museum foyer is a shop with inexpensive handicrafts from Colima, including figurines that are manufactured in the Taller de Reproducciones.

Parks

The **Parque Regional Metropolitano** on Degollado, a few blocks southwest of the center, has a small zoo, a swimming pool, a café and an area of forest with an artificial lake and rowboats. You can rent bikes to ride in the forested area.

East of the center on Calzada Galván, **Parque Piedra Lisa** is named after its famous Sliding Stone, which is visible from the park entrance (near the traffic circle where Galván and Aldama meet). Legend says that visitors who slide on this stone will someday return to Colima, either to marry or to die.

Special Events

Many masked dances are enacted at fiestas in Colima state. The Museo Universitario de Culturas Populares has a good display of the costumes and plenty of information on the subject. The following festivals take place in or very near Colima city.

Ferias Charro-Taurinas San Felipe de Jesús –
This festival, celebrated in honor of the
Virgen de la Candelaria (whose day is February 2), takes place in Villa de Álvarez,
about five km north of the city center. Each
day of the festival except Tuesday and Friday, a large group rides from Colima's cathedral to Villa de Álvarez preceded by giant
mojigangos – figures of the village's mayor
and wife, followed by musical groups. When
they arrive at Villa de Álvarez the celebrations continue with food, music, rodeos and
bullfights; late January and early February.

Feria de Todos los Santos – Also called the Feria
de Colima, the Colima state fair includes
agricultural and handicraft exhibitions, cultural events and funfairs; late October and
early November.

Día de la Virgen de Guadalupe – Women and
children dress in costume to pay homage at
the Virgin's altar in the cathedral. In the
evenings the Jardín Quintero behind the
cathedral fills with busy food stalls; around
December 1 to 12.

Places to Stay – budget

The *Hotel San Cristóbal* (☎ 2-05-15) at
Reforma 98 is centrally located and offers
33 basic but clean rooms with fans, 24-
hour hot water and firm beds; 28 of the
rooms have private bathrooms. Rooms
without private bath have only one bed and
are US$6 per room. The remaining rates
are: one bed, US$7 per room; two beds,
US$9 per room.

Also centrally located is the *Hotel Colonial* (☎ 3-08-77) at Medellín 142, which
offers rooms of varying quality and with
different features; ask to see at least two
rooms before registering. In general, this
place is proudly maintained and its 46
rooms are clean and cool. The rates: one
person with shared bathroom, US$6; one
person with private bath, US$7; one person
with private bath and TV, US$8; one
person with king-size bed and private bath,
US$11; two people with private bath and
TV, US$10; two people with private bath,
king-size bed and TV, US$13.

Another very good budget place is the
Hotel La Merced (☎ 2-69-69) at Juárez 82.
All rooms in this small, well-maintained
hotel have private bath and fan, and most
are around an open courtyard. Singles are

US$10, doubles US$12 with one bed,
US$13 with two beds. The rooms are cool
and pleasant and have good showers.
Those with two beds are a very good size.

A couple of doors down is the *Hotel
Núñez* (☎ 2-70-30) at Juárez 88. It's old
and basic but tolerable for a night or two.
The 32 rooms around two courtyards have
no windows, so they tend to be stuffy, but
they have fans and TV and are kept clean.
Rooms with shared bathrooms (which are
OK) cost US$6; there are also rooms with
private bath at US$7, though these are
mostly beside the noisier first courtyard.

Hotel Flamingos (☎ 2-25-25) at Avenida
Rey Colimán 18 has 56 clean, modern
rooms with private bath and fan, and all
have full-wall windows and balconies.
Those on the upper floors offer a bit of a
view over the town; those on the side away
from the street are much quieter. There's a
restaurant on the ground floor. Rates are
US$11/13.

Places to Stay – middle

Hotel Ceballos (☎ 2-44-44), at Portal
Medellín 12 on the north side of the Plaza
Principal, is a stately building that dates
from 1880 and has been the home of three
state governors. Many of the 63 clean,
pleasant, high-ceilinged rooms have French
windows opening onto small balconies.
Most have air-con and cost US$30 for one
or two people. All of the rooms were
recently remodeled.

More modern is the *Hotel América* (☎ 2-
74-88) at Morelos 162, half a block west of
Jardín Núñez. Its 75 rooms have high
wood-beamed ceilings, are air-conditioned,
come with color TV and more. Facilities
include steam baths and a pool, and there's
also a laundry service. Cost is US$25 per
room.

Places to Eat

The best food in town is served at *"Ah Que
Nanishe"* (which translates to 'How Delicious!') at 5 de Mayo 267. This aptly
named restaurant specializes in Oaxacan
food and has menus in English and Spanish. Mole fans will be pleased to know

Nanishe offers negro (a black mole from Oaxaca made with chocolate and 50 spices including 10 different chili peppers), verde (made with a variety of vegetables) and colorado (sweet red mole made with only one chili). A large chicken breast smothered in mole sauce runs US$5, chiles rellenos US$4, tamales US$1.50 and antojitos US$1 to US$3.

For a simple meal there are many small restaurants around the Plaza Principal. Some offer cold drinks, ice cream and frozen juice bars; Nevería La Michoacán on one corner of the plaza has a good selection, and it's open daily from 8 am to 10 pm.

Restaurant Familiar La Placita on the south side of the Plaza Principal is a reasonable all-purpose eatery. It serves breakfasts from US$2, a four-course comida corrida for US$3, antojitos for under US$4 and chicken or beef main dishes around US$5. It's open daily from 7 am to 10 pm.

Café de la Plaza beside the Hotel Ceballos is a newer, pleasant place with tall, stately ceilings and a jukebox packed with popular Mexican and US music. Nothing is priced over US$4, and a large traditional American or Mexican breakfast runs US$3. The restaurant opens at 7.30 am daily.

Fonda Típíca at Degollado 67 occupies a breezy, second-story corner location overlooking the Plaza Principal, making it a good place to go on hot days. The food is pretty good and reasonably priced, with antojitos and sandwiches around US$2, meat dishes about US$3, and seafood taking the high road at up to US$6. Live music is often performed after 9 pm Friday and Saturday.

Jugolandia, just a few doors from the Plaza Principal at Madero 17, is an inexpensive place for fresh juices, tortas, burgers, yogurt and fruit salads. It's open every day from 7 am to 11 pm.

A clean, pleasant restaurant good for all meals is Los Naranjos at Barreda 34, half a block north of Jardín Quintero. Chicken and meat dishes cost between US$4 and US$8, or you could have three enchiladas for US$3. Overhead fans keep you cool,

and a pianist plays some of the time. It's open from 8 am to 11.30 pm daily.

Livorno's Pizza near the Plaza Principal puts together tasty pizza pies at fair prices; small ones cost about US$4, large ones US$9. Among their other offerings are cheese fondues (about US$4), spaghetti (about US$3), and soups, quesadillas and submarine sandwiches (all about US$3).

Just around the corner from "Ah Que Nanishe" on Jardín de San José is El Charco de la Higuera, which is a lovely place to have breakfast. El Charco faces a wall of handsome, potted plants and a garden that is just beyond them. The food is quite good and also reasonable. Breakfasts are under US$5, soups, antojitos and sandwiches are under US$4 and chicken and beef dishes are around US$5.

Vegetarians shouldn't miss the Restaurant Vegetariano Samadhi at Medina 125, two blocks north of Jardín Núñez. The restaurant occupies an arched courtyard with a large palm tree and other tropical plants. The menu is large and caters to non-vegetarians too. Choices include soy burgers with salad and French fries, mushroom or maize and bean crêpes with salad, a range of breakfasts and much more. Samadhi is open daily from 8 am to 10 pm, except Thursday when it closes at 5 pm.

Centro de Nutrición Lakshmi is also near Jardín Núñez, at Madero 265. It includes a wholegrain bakery, a section with health products and a restaurant serving soy burgers, yogurts and more. It's open Monday through Saturday from 8.30 am to 9 pm, Sunday from 6 to 9 pm.

La Arábica, at Guerrero 162, near the corner of Obregón, is a small coffeehouse where people come to chat at the tables in the front or in the shady patio out back. It's open Monday through Saturday from 8.30 am to 2 pm and 4 to 8.30 pm.

Entertainment

Colima is basically a quiet city but there are a few things you can do in the evening.

There are several cafés featuring live music in the evening. Most popular is the Café Colima, in the middle of the Jardín de la Corregidora, with música romántica on the patio most nights from around 9 pm to midnight.

The *Café Arte*, also called the Restaurante Dali, in the Edificio de Talleres at the Casa de la Cultura, also has live music – usually a singer-guitarist or two – most nights after 9 pm.

The disco for Colima's well-heeled is *Cheers*, at Zaragoza 528 on the corner of Calle del Trabajo. *La Mina* on Avenida Rey Colimán, just south of the Hotel Flamingos, is popular but less upscale.

Concerts, theater and other performing arts are staged at places such as the Teatro Hidalgo, the Teatro Casa de la Cultura and the Museo de Historia de Colima. Stop by these places to see their posted schedules.

Things to Buy
Tienda de Artesanías DIF, a block north of the Plaza Principal on the corner of Constitución and Zaragoza, has a good range of Colima handicrafts including attractive reproductions of Tepezcuintle dogs. Tepezcuintles and other artesanías are also sold at the Museo Universitario de Culturas Populares. The main market is the Mercado Constitución, on Calle Reforma three blocks south of the Plaza Principal.

Getting There & Away
Air Aeromar (☎ 3-13-40 at the airport) and Aero California (☎ 4-48-50) both fly daily to/from Mexico City, with onward connections. Aero California also has daily flights to/from Tijuana. Avitesa travel agency (☎ 2-19-84) on the corner of Constitución and Zaragoza, a block north of the Plaza Principal, can make flight arrangements, and English is sometimes spoken. They're open Monday through Friday from 8.30 am to 8.30 pm, Saturday 9 am to 2 pm.

Bus Colima has two bus stations. The main long-distance terminal is the Central Camionera Foránea, two km from the center at the meeting of Avenida Niños Héroes and the city's eastern bypass. At the station are pay phones, a telephone caseta, a pharmacy and various restaurants

and snack shops. Daily departures from here include:

Guadalajara – 220 km, 2½ hours; several deluxe buses by ETN (US$13); frequent 1st-class by La Línea, Primera Plus, Ómnibus de México, Servicios Coordinados and Tres Estrellas de Oro (US$9 or US$10); many 2nd-class buses by Sur de Jalisco (US$8)

Manzanillo – 101 km, 1½ hours; many deluxe buses by ETN (US$6); many 1st-class (US$4) by La Línea, Primera Plus, Servicios Coordinados and Tres Estrellas de Oro; 54 2nd-class buses via Tecomán and Armería (two hours) by Autotransportes del Sur de Jalisco (US$3)

Mexico City (Terminal Norte) – 740 km, 11 hours; a few deluxe buses by ETN (US$50); a few 1st-class by Tres Estrellas de Oro, Primera Plus, Servicios Coordinados, Elite and Ómnibus de México (US$32 to US$35); seven 2nd-class by Autobuses de Occidente

There are also many daily buses to Ciudad Guzmán and Morelia by various companies, one to Melaque by Tres Estrellas de Oro and three to Lázaro Cárdenas and one to Uruapan by Autobuses de Occidente.

The second bus station is the Central Camionera Suburbana, also known as the Terminal Suburbana, about 1.5 km southwest of the Plaza Principal on the Carretera a Coquimatlán. This is the station for buses to Comala and other places close to Colima and for 2nd-class line Autobuses Colima-Manzanillo, which goes to Manzanillo every 30 minutes (1½ hours, US$3), Tecomán every 15 minutes (US$2) and Armería every 30 minutes (US$2).

Train The Estación del Ferrocarril (☎ 2-92-50) is about 10 blocks south of the Jardín Quintero down Medellín. There's one daily segunda clase train in each direction. Train No 91, departing about 1.30 am, takes about seven hours to Guadalajara (US$4). Train No 92, departing about 2 am, takes two hours or so to Manzanillo (US$1.10).

Getting Around
To/From the Airport Colima's airport is near Cuauhtémoc, 12 km northeast of the

ROBERT FRERCK

SCOTT DOGGETT

Top: Traditional fishermen using butterfly nets to catch white fish, Lago de Pátzcuaro
Bottom: School children lunching in Guadalajara's principal plaza

ROBERT FRERCK

Top Left: Monarch butterflies at Santuario de Mariposas El Rosario, Michoacán
Top Right: Cutting the heart of an agave to make tequila, Jalisco
Bottom: Lago de Chapala

SUSAN KAYE

city center off the highway to Guadalajara. A taxi to/from the center is about US$9.

Bus & Taxi Local buses (US$0.50) run daily from 6 am to 9 pm. Ruta 4A buses from the main bus station will take you to the city center. To return to the bus station you can catch Ruta 4A on 5 de Mayo or Zaragoza. To reach the Central Camionera Suburbana, take a Ruta 2 or Ruta 4 bus west along Morelos.

Taxis are plentiful. The maximum fare within town is US$1.

AROUND COLIMA
Comala
pop 17,562; alt 600m; ☎ *331*

A picturesque town nine km north of Colima, Comala is known for its fine handicrafts, especially its hand-carved wood furniture. It is also a popular weekend outing from Colima. On Sunday there are markets for browsing.

You can see Comala furniture being made at the Sociedad Cooperativa Artesanías Pueblo Blanco, which is famous for colonial-style hand-carved furniture, wood paintings and ironwork. The center is one km south of town, just off the road from Colima: it's open Monday through Friday from 9 am to 6 pm, Saturday 9 am to 2 pm.

There's a simple but pretty church on the plaza, which has a fine white gazebo and trees blooming with brilliant yellow flowers. Under the arches along one side of the plaza are some attractive *centros botaneros*, which are bars where minors are allowed (but not served alcohol) and where each beverage is accompanied by a free snack. They're open from 11 am or noon to 6 pm. Many people come to Comala just to enjoy these restaurants. There are more restaurants on the Colima road at the edge of Comala.

Comala buses leave Colima's Central Camionera Suburbana about every 10 minutes; fare is US$0.50 for the 15-minute ride. In Comala, the buses back to Colima depart from the plaza.

Suchitlán
pop 7000; alt 1200m; ☎ *339*

The village of Suchitlán, eight km northeast of Comala, is famous for its animal masks and its witches. The masks are carved in the village and worn by the dancers in the traditional Danza de los Morenos, which takes place here during Semana Santa. The dance commemorates the legend that dancing animals enabled the Marys to rescue Christ's body by distracting the Roman guards. Masks and other crafts are sold in Suchitlán's Sunday Indian market. There are several restaurants in the village. There are buses to Suchitlán from the Central Camionera Suburbana in Colima.

San Antonio & La María

About 15 km north of Suchitlán the paved road ends at the Ex-Hacienda de San Antonio, a 19th century coffee farm that's been in the process of being converted into an elegant hotel for nearly two decades; it's rarely open to the public. It has large grounds crossed by a stone aqueduct and fine views of the Volcán de Fuego de Colima towering some seven km to the north.

A gravel road continues from San Antonio to La María, about 10 minutes' drive to the east. There's a lovely lake here, the Laguna La María, which is a popular weekend picnic and camping spot. You'll find a few rustic cabins with simple stoves costing US$25 to US$30 for four to six people. There's also a pool and restaurant. You should book the cabins at the Avitesa travel agency in Colima (see Getting There & Away – Air in the Colima section).

A few buses run daily from Colima's Central Camionera Suburbana to San Antonio; those saying 'La Becerrera' will go there. From San Antonio you must walk to La María if you don't have a vehicle.

Volcán de Fuego de Colima & Nevado de Colima

These two dramatic mountains overlook Colima from the north. The nearer, the

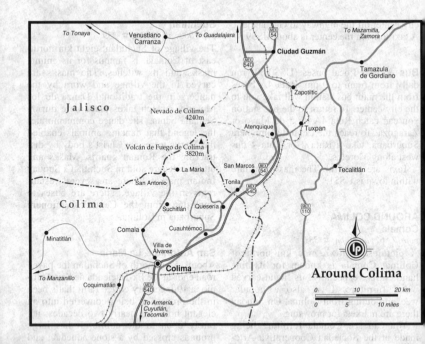

To Tonaya
Venustiano Carranza
To Guadalajara
MEX 54
Ciudad Guzmán
MEX 54D
To Mazamitla, Zamora
Tamazula de Gordiano
Zapotiltic
Jalisco
Nevado de Colima 4240m
Atenquique
Tuxpan
Volcán de Fuego de Colima 3820m
San Marcos
MEX 54
Tecalitlán
La María
Tonila
MEX 54D
San Antonio
MEX 110
Colima
Suchitlán
Quesería
Comala
Cuauhtémoc
Minatitlán
Villa de Alvarez
To Manzanillo
Colima
Coquimatlán
MEX 54D
To Armería, Cuyutlán, Tecomán

Around Colima

0   10   20 km
0   5   10 miles

steaming Volcán de Fuego (Fireworks Volcano, 3960 meters), is 30 km from the city as the crow flies. Most of Fuego, including its crater, and all of the more northerly and higher, but extinct, Volcán Nevado (Snowy Volcano, 4330 meters) are in Jalisco state. Either mountain would make a great trip from Colima – if you can get there. A 4WD vehicle with high ground clearance is definitely needed for Fuego.

Fuego is one of Mexico's most active volcanoes, having erupted 30 times in the past four centuries. There's a big eruption about every 70 years. A major eruption in 1913 spelled the end of one cycle of activity, but another began in the 1960s and is ongoing.

Ascending the Volcanoes Remnants of a pine forest cover most of Nevado, and alpine desert appears at the highest altitudes. Most of the year it's possible to get within four hours' walk of either summit

by vehicle. However, deadly gases and risk of explosions and avalanches make it unwise to visit Fuego's crater. The track up Nevado is rough but passable for most cars unless the weather has been particularly wet. The Fuego track is in poor condition and usually impassable even for 4WD vehicles after the July to September/October rains. It's also closed when the volcano is considered dangerous. Mitchell Ventura, a bilingual member of the Colima Fire Department, can advise on this. He can usually be reached at the department's non-emergency number, ☎ 331-4-59-44. Spanish speakers could obtain current information on the road from anyone answering at this number. The nearest you can get to the volcanoes by bus is some 25 to 30 km from Nevado's summit or about 33 km from Fuego's. Be advised that Nevado could have snow on its upper flanks between December and March; Fuego rarely has snow.

Ventura can lead groups that have their own truck or 4WD vehicle. Be advised that rental trucks are not available in Colima or even in much larger Guadalajara. However, Ventura said he might be able to procure a rental truck if given enough notice. He charges from US$50 to US$100 per group per day. The cost varies with the group's objectives and requirements (he has some camping equipment for rent).

For those driving themselves, the 32-km track to Fuego turns left (west) off highway 54 (the free road to Guadalajara) 58 km from Colima, a few kilometers before the mill town of Atenquique. A faster option is to take the toll road going toward Guadalajara and get off at the first exit past Atenquique (the exit is marked 'Tuxpan'). There's a gas station and a traffic circle there. From the traffic circle take the free road toward Colima (Colima Libre) for two km, passing through Atenquique. At the end of Atenquique, go uphill one km and, just beyond the lumber mill, look for a dirt road on the right-hand side that is usually marked by a 'Volcán de Fuego' sign. Once on the dirt road, stay on what seems to be the main route (there are two turnoffs that should not be taken). Expect bushes to brush against your vehicle, and expect to encounter deep potholes. Eighteen km along the dirt road, there's a large bump in the road to prevent most vehicles from proceeding; at this point you are 14 km from the base of the crater. There is little traffic on this road and no water or facilities; if you're fearful your vehicle won't make it, turn around.

Once at the base of the crater, non-climbers can take a 3½-km walk around it. Looking toward the top of the volcano, on the left-hand side are two knolls – growths that developed in the 1860s. Atop these knolls is scientific equipment that should not be disturbed. From the second knoll, it's a two-hour hike to the summit, but as mentioned earlier, this should not be attempted because of the dangers of a live crater. It's a good idea to pay careful attention to where you've been so you can locate your vehicle later.

To get to Nevado, take the free highway 54 almost to Ciudad Guzmán, some 83 km from Colima. Or, follow the toll route as far as Fuego, but at the traffic circle take the toll-free road toward Guadalajara (Guadalajara Libre). Shortly before you reach Ciudad Guzmán, turn left (west) toward Venustiano Carranza and Tonaya; at a fork after eight km, go right, then after another kilometer turn left along the dirt road to the village of Fresnito. From this turnoff it's another 30 km to the summit. In Fresnito, ask directions to La Joya, which is a climbers' cabin on the upper slopes of Nevado, or to Las Antenas, a TV transmitting station near La Joya where the track ends and the final four-hour ascent on foot begins. For non-Spanish speakers, simply saying 'La Joya' (pronounced 'la hoy-ya') to passersby will generally result in fingers being pointed in the right direction.

Also, a few days prior to leaving for the mountain, you may want to call Agustín Ibarra, a bus operator by profession and part-time guide who lives in Fresnito. Ibarra can provide transportation to Las Antenas for groups up to 10 people. Ibarra speaks broken English. People using his guide services can usually stay at his house the night prior to departure. Ibarra didn't have a phone at the time of writing but could usually be reached by calling a pay phone not far from his home; that number is ☎ 341-2-58-59.

Getting There & Away Those planning to walk up the volcanoes should plan on at least one night up there and take all supplies, including water, with them. This is particularly true for Nevado, which is at a higher elevation. The 2nd-class buses of Autotransportes del Sur de Jalisco run from Colima's main bus station to Atenquique six times daily (one hour, US$2) and to Ciudad Guzmán 17 times (1½ hours, US$3). There are a few other services too. Once in Ciudad Guzmán you can take a bus to Fresnito. If you hire Ibarra, he can pick you up at the Ciudad Guzmán bus station.

Tampumacchay

There are interesting shaft tombs from about 200 AD beside a hotel on the edge of a ravine here, near the town of Los Ortices about 15 km south of Colima. There is a small fee to enter the tombs. The hotel has a restaurant and a few clean, basic rooms at about US$20. Staff will guide you around the tombs. There are buses from Colima's Central Camionera Suburbana to Los Ortices, about 10 km south of Colima, but then you'll have to walk about five km to the hotel unless you happen upon a taxi.

Minatitlán

pop 8314; alt 740m; ☎ 333

Minatitlán is an iron-ore mining town 55 km west of Colima. It's on a scenic route through the mountains from Colima to the coast that drivers might consider as a long alternative to the main toll road or the main free road. Seven km south of Minatitlán, in the direction of Manzanillo, is a lovely waterfall with a natural swimming pool. The last half km to the waterfall, located at El Salto, is on a steep section of road better traveled on foot.

EL DIABLITO

EL CORAZON

LA MANO

LA PERA

EL VIOLONCELLO

EL MUNDO

Northern Central Highlands

Northwest from Mexico City stretches a fairly dry, temperate upland region comprising the southern part of the Altiplano Central. This was where the Spanish found most of the silver and other precious metals that were so central to their colonial ambitions in Mexico – and where they built some of the country's most magnificent cities from the great fortunes that silver brought them. The most spectacular of these are Guanajuato and Zacatecas, which along with Potosí in Bolivia were the major silver-producing centers of the Americas. San Miguel de Allende, Querétaro and San Luis Potosí also have a wealth of colonial architecture. Today most of these cities are still of moderate size and have lively arts and entertainment scenes.

This is a highly rewarding region to visit. The distances are not huge and the landscape between the cities is always impressive, with vistas to mountains near or far. The land becomes steadily more fertile as you move south from Zacatecas and San Luis Potosí to the area around Guanajuato and Querétaro known as the Bajío ('ba-HEE-o'), which has long been one of Mexico's major agricultural zones.

The Bajío is also known to Mexicans as La Cuna de la Independencia (the Cradle of Independence), for it was here that the movement for independence from Spain

HIGHLIGHTS

- Zacatecas, a desert city built on silver, with a dramatic setting, stupendous cathedral and fabulous museums

- The mountain ghost town of Real de Catorce, surrounded by magical semi-desert country

- The silver city of Guanajuato with superb mansions, colorful houses crammed onto steep slopes, crooked cobbled alleyways and a lively student atmosphere

- The beautiful colonial town of San Miguel de Allende, with vibrant fiestas, excellent shopping and a multitude of good restaurants

- The energizing hot springs channeled into balnearios around San Miguel de Allende

- Talavera pottery and tiles from the small, historic town of Dolores Hidalgo

NORTHERN CENTRAL HIGHLANDS

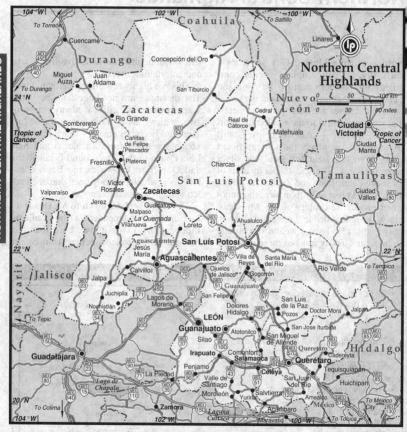

began in 1810. The town of Dolores Hidalgo, where the uprising started, and nearby places like San Miguel de Allende, Querétaro and Guanajuato are full of key sites from this historic movement.

Before the Spanish reached Mexico, the Northern Central Highlands were inhabited by fierce semi-nomadic tribes known to the Aztecs as the Chichimecs. They resisted Spanish conquest longer than all other Mexican peoples and were only finally pacified in the late 16th century by an offer of food and clothing in return for peace. The wealth subsequently amassed in the

region by the Spanish was at the cost of the lives of many of these people, who were used as virtual slave labor in the mines.

Mining is still important in the region, and there's industry as well – in León, Querétaro, Aguascalientes and elsewhere – but the industry doesn't detract from the region's historical, artistic and scenic attractions.

This chapter encompasses the states of Zacatecas, Aguascalientes, Guanajuato and Querétaro and most of San Luis Potosí state. Eastern San Luis Potosí state is covered in the Central Gulf Coast chapter.

Zacatecas

The state of Zacatecas is one of Mexico's larger in area (73,252 sq km) but smaller in population (1.3 million). It's a dry, rugged, cactus-strewn expanse on the fringe of Mexico's northern semi-deserts, with large tracts that are almost empty on the map. The fact that it has any significant population at all is largely due to the mineral wealth the Spanish discovered here, mainly around the capital city Zacatecas. Today there are still over 100 mines of various kinds in the state, and it remains Mexico's biggest silver producer.

ZACATECAS
pop 200,000; alt 2445m; ☎ 492

If you've come down from the north, welcome to the first of Mexico's justly fabled silver cities. If you've been visiting more southerly silver cities like Guanajuato, take the time if you can to journey a few hours farther north. Zacatecas is particularly beautiful and fascinating.

Some of Mexico's finest colonial buildings, including perhaps its most stunning cathedral, all built from the riches of the local silver mines, cluster along narrow, winding streets at the foot of a spectacular rock-topped hill called Cerro de la Bufa. Set amid dry, arid country, this historic city has much to detain you, from trips into an old silver mine to some excellent museums and the ascent of la Bufa itself by teleférico (cable car). A state capital and university city, Zacatecas is sophisticated for its size – and it's all the more to be appreciated for its off-center location and consequent lack of tourists.

History
Before the Spanish arrived, the area was inhabited by Zacateco Indians, one of the wild Chichimec tribes. Indians had mined local mineral deposits for centuries before the Spanish arrived; it's said that the silver rush here was started by an Indian giving a piece of the fabled metal to a conquistador.

The Spaniards founded a settlement and, in 1548, started mining operations, virtually enslaving many Indians in the process. Caravan after caravan of silver was sent off to Mexico City. While some treasure-laden wagons were raided by the Indians, enough silver reached its destination to create fabulously wealthy silver barons. Agriculture and ranching developed to serve the rapidly growing town.

In the first quarter of the 18th century, Zacatecas' mines were producing 20% of Nueva España's silver. At this time too the city became an important base for missionaries spreading Catholicism to as far away as northwestern Nueva España (the modern US Southwest).

In the 19th century political events diminished the flow of silver as various forces fought to control the city. Although silver production later improved under Porfirio Díaz, the revolution disrupted it. And it was here in 1914 that Pancho Villa, through brilliant tactics, defeated a stronghold of 12,000 soldiers loyal to the unpopular President Victoriano Huerta.

After the revolution, Zacatecas continued to thrive on silver. It remains a mining center to this day, with the 200-year-old El Bote mine still productive.

Orientation
The city center lies in a valley between Cerro de la Bufa, with its strange rocky cap, to the northeast and the smaller Cerro del Grillo to the northwest. Most places of interest and places to stay are within walking distance of each other. There are two key streets in the central area. One is Avenida Hidalgo, running roughly north-south, with the cathedral toward its north end. The other is Avenida Juárez, running roughly east-west across the south end of Avenida Hidalgo. If you get lost, just ask the way back to one of these two streets. Avenida Hidalgo becomes Avenida González Ortega south of its intersection with Avenida Juárez.

Information
Tourist Office The tourist office (☎ 4-03-93, 4-05-52) is opposite the cathedral at

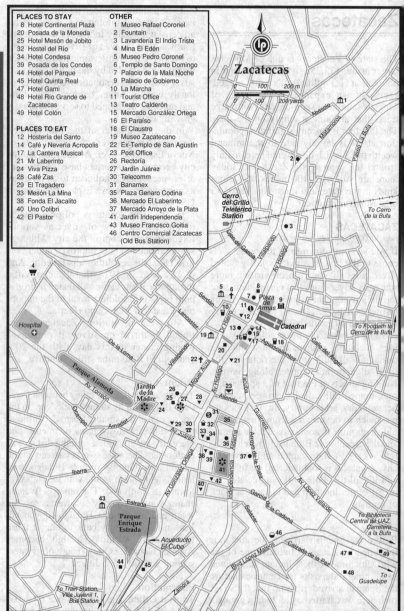

PLACES TO STAY
- 8 Hotel Continental Plaza
- 20 Posada de la Moneda
- 25 Hotel Mesón de Jobito
- 32 Hostel del Río
- 34 Hotel Condesa
- 39 Posada de los Condes
- 44 Hotel del Parque
- 45 Hotel Quinta Real
- 47 Hotel Gami
- 48 Hotel Río Grande de Zacatecas
- 49 Hotel Colón

PLACES TO EAT
- 12 Hostería del Santo
- 14 Café y Nevería Acropolis
- 17 La Cantera Musical
- 21 Mr Laberinto
- 24 Viva Pizza
- 28 Café Zas
- 29 El Tragadero
- 38 Mesón La Mina
- 38 Fonda El Jacalito
- 40 Uno Colibri
- 42 El Pastor

OTHER
- 1 Museo Rafael Coronel
- 2 Fountain
- 3 Lavandería El Indio Triste
- 4 Mina El Edén
- 5 Museo Pedro Coronel
- 6 Templo de Santo Domingo
- 7 Palacio de la Mala Noche
- 9 Palacio de Gobierno
- 10 La Marcha
- 11 Tourist Office
- 13 Teatro Calderón
- 15 Mercado González Ortega
- 16 El Paraíso
- 18 El Claustro
- 19 Museo Zacatecano
- 22 Ex-Templo de San Agustín
- 23 Post Office
- 26 Rectoría
- 27 Jardín Juárez
- 30 Telecomm
- 31 Banamex
- 35 Plaza Genaro Codina
- 36 Mercado El Laberinto
- 37 Mercado Arroyo de la Plata
- 41 Jardín Independencia
- 43 Museo Francisco Goitia
- 46 Centro Comercial Zacatecas (Old Bus Station)

Zacatecas

0   100   200 m
0   100   200 yards

Hidalgo 629, open daily from 9 am to 8.30 pm. Someone on duty may speak English. They have plenty of brochures, in Spanish, on Zacatecas city and state.

Money The best place to change traveler's checks is at Banco Promex at González Ortega 122, just beyond Juárez. Rates are good, service efficient and hours long – weekdays from 8 am to 7 pm and Saturday 10 am to 2 pm. There are several banks with ATMs and much the same exchange rates and opening times – weekdays from 9 am to 3 pm – on Hidalgo between the cathedral and Juárez. Banamex, toward the southern end, is the best of these for changing traveler's checks.

Post & Communications The post office is at Allende 111, just east of Hidalgo. Its hours are weekdays from 8 am to 7 pm and Saturday 9 am to 1 pm.

There are pay phones at the main entrance to the Mercado González Ortega on Hidalgo, and on Hidalgo near the corner of Callejón San Agustín. Telephone casetas are in the bus station and on Callejón de las Cuevas, off Hidalgo beside Café Zas. The Telecomm office on Hidalgo at Juárez offers public fax service. There's also a fax service in the bus station.

Laundry Lavandería El Indio Triste at Hidalgo 824, opposite the corner of Villalpando, does a service wash for US$1 per kg. Open hours are Monday to Saturday from 9 am to 9 pm and Sunday from 9 am to noon.

Catedral
Zacatecas' pink-stone cathedral is perhaps the ultimate expression of Mexican baroque. It was built chiefly between 1729 and 1752, just before baroque edged into its final Churrigueresque phase. And in this city of affluent silver barons, no expense was spared. The highlight is the stupendous main façade, which faces Hidalgo. It is a wall of amazingly detailed yet harmonious carvings. This façade has been interpreted as a giant symbol of the tabernacle, which is the receptacle for the wafer and

the wine that confer communion with God, the heart of Catholic worship. A tiny figure of an angel holding a tabernacle can be seen at the heart of the design, the keystone at the top of the round central window. Above this, at the center of the third tier, is Christ, and above Christ is God. The other main statues are the 12 apostles, while a smaller figure of the Virgin stands immediately above the center of the doorway.

The south and north façades, though simpler, are also very fine. The central sculpture on the southern façade is of La Virgen de los Zacatecas, the city's patroness. The north façade shows Christ crucified, attended by the Virgin Mary and St John.

The interior of the cathedral is disarmingly plain, though it was once adorned with elaborate gold and silver ornaments and festooned with tapestries and paintings. This wealth was plundered in the course of Zacatecas' turbulent history.

Plaza de Armas
This is the open space on the north side of the cathedral. The **Palacio de Gobierno** on the plaza's east side was built in the 18th century for a family of colonial gentry. It was acquired by the state in the 19th century. In the turret of its main staircase is a mural of the history of Zacatecas state, painted in 1970 by Antonio Rodríguez.

The lovely, white **Palacio de la Mala Noche** on the west side of the plaza was built in the late 18th century for the owner of the Mala Noche mine near Zacatecas. It houses state government offices.

Mercado González Ortega
South of the cathedral, between Hidalgo and Tacuba, is the impressive, iron-columned building from the 1880s that used to hold Zacatecas' main market. In the 1980s the upper level, entered from Hidalgo, was renovated into an upscale shopping center complete with restaurants.

Teatro Calderón
Also dating from the Porfiriato period, built in the 1890s, is the Teatro Calderón,

across Hidalgo from the southern end of the Mercado González Ortega. This lovely theater is as busy as ever staging plays, concerts, films and art exhibitions.

Templo de Santo Domingo

Santo Domingo Church dominates the Plazuela de Santo Domingo, reached from the Plaza de Armas by a narrow lane, Callejón de Veyna. Done in a more sober baroque style than the cathedral, it has some fine gilded altars and paintings and a graceful horseshoe staircase. Built by the Jesuits in the 1740s, the church was taken over by Dominican monks when the Jesuits were expelled in 1767.

Museo Pedro Coronel

The Pedro Coronel Museum is housed in a 17th century former Jesuit college beside Santo Domingo. Pedro Coronel (1923-85) was an affluent Zacatecan artist who bequeathed to his home town this collection of his own art and of artifacts from all over the world. Coronel amassed art from Asia and Africa and ancient Mexico, Rome, Greece and Egypt. The collection includes works by Hogarth, Goya, Picasso, Roualt, Chagall, Kandinsky and Miró as well. It all adds up to one of provincial Mexico's best art museums – open Monday, Tuesday, Wednesday, Friday and Saturday from 10 am to 2 pm and 4 to 7 pm, and Sunday from 10 am to 4.30 pm (US$1.30).

Calle Dr Hierro & Calle Auza

Dr Hierro, leading south from Plazuela de Santo Domingo, and its continuation Auza, are quiet, narrow streets. About 150 meters from Plazuela de Santo Domingo is the **Casa de Moneda**, which housed the Zacatecas mint (Mexico's second biggest), during the 19th century. It's now the **Museo Zacateno** and is largely devoted to Huichol art. Another 100 meters south is the **ex-Templo de San Agustín,** built as a church for Augustinian monks in the 17th century. During the anticlerical movement of the 19th century, the church was turned into a casino. Then, in 1882, it was

purchased by American Presbyterian missionaries who destroyed its 'too Catholic' main façade, replacing it with a blank white wall. In the 20th century the church returned to Catholic use, and its adjoining ex-monastery is now the seat of the Zacatecas bishopric. The church's finest feature is the plateresque carving over the north doorway of the conversion of St Augustine.

The street ends at **Jardín Juárez**, a tiny rectangle of a park. The Rectoría, or administrative headquarters, of the Universidad Autónoma de Zacatecas is housed in a neoclassical building on its west side.

Mina El Edén

El Edén mine, once one of Mexico's richest mines, is a 'must' for visitors to Zacatecas because of the dramatic insight it gives into the source of wealth in this region – and the terrible price paid for it. Digging for fabulous hoards of silver, gold, iron, copper and zinc, enslaved Indians, including many children, worked under horrific conditions. At one time up to five a day died from accidents or illness.

El Edén was worked from 1586 until the 1950s. Today the fourth of its seven levels is kept open for visitors. The lower levels are flooded. A miniature road train runs you a short distance deep inside the Cerro del Grillo, the hill in which the mine is located. Then guides – who may or may not speak a little English – lead you along floodlit walkways past deep shafts and over subterranean pools. It is easy to see why so many miners lost their lives to accidents and to diseases like silicosis and tuberculosis.

To reach the mine, walk west along Juárez and stay on it after its name changes to Torreón at the Alameda park. Turn right immediately after the big hospital above the park. You can take a Ruta 7 bus up Juárez from the corner of Hidalgo. Mine tours leave every 15 minutes daily from 11 am to 6.30 pm (US$1.60).

Teleférico

The most exhilarating ride in Zacatecas, and the easiest way to reach the Cerro de la

Bufa, is the teleférico that crosses high above the city from the Cerro del Grillo. Just walk to the left from the exit of El Edén mine and you'll reach the teleférico's Cerro del Grillo station after a couple of minutes. Alternatively, Ruta 7 buses coming from the bus station run up González Ortega, west along Juárez and Torreón and go right by El Edén on their way to the teleférico. You could also climb the steps of Callejón de García Rojas, which lead straight up to the teleférico from the north end of Villalpando. The Swiss-built teleférico operates every 15 minutes from 10 am to 6 pm daily, except when it's raining or when winds exceed 60 kph. The trip takes about seven minutes and costs US$0.70 one way.

Cerro de la Bufa

Cerro de la Bufa is the rock-topped hill that dominates Zacatecas from the northeast. The most appealing of the many explanations for its name is that *bufa* is an old Spanish word for wineskin, which is certainly what the rocky formation atop the hill looks like. The views from the top are superb and there's an interesting group of monuments, a chapel and a museum up there.

An exciting and convenient way to ascend la Bufa is by the teleférico from near the El Edén mine exit. More strenuously, you can walk up it (start by going up Calle del Ángel at the rear, east end of the cathedral). There's also a road, Carretera a la Bufa, which begins beside the university library on Avenida López Velarde. A taxi costs US$2.25. All three routes bring you out near the group of monuments, chapel and museum. Just above the teleférico station is a meteorological observatory.

The **Museo de la Toma de Zacatecas** commemorates the 1914 battle fought on the slopes of la Bufa in which the revolutionary División del Norte, led by Pancho Villa and Felipe Ángeles, defeated the forces of President Victoriano Huerta. The victory gave the revolutionaries control of Zacatecas, which was the gateway to Mexico City, in this war to depose the unpopular Huerta. The museum is open Tuesday to Sunday from 10 am to 4.30 pm (US$0.70).

La Capilla de la Virgen del Patrocinio, adjacent to the museum, is named after the patron saint of miners. Above the altar of this 18th century chapel is an image of the Virgin said to be capable of healing the sick. Thousands of pilgrims make their way here each year during the weeks either side of September 8, when the image is carried to the cathedral.

Just east of the museum and chapel stand three imposing equestrian **statues** of the victors of the battle of Zacatecas – Villa, Ángeles and Pánfilo Natera. A path behind the Villa and Natera statues leads to the rocky **summit of la Bufa**, where there are marvelous views on all sides, stretching over the city and away to mountain ranges far in the distance. The hill is topped by a metal cross that is illuminated at night.

A path along the foot of the rocky hilltop, starting to the right of the statues, leads to the **Mausoleo de los Hombres Ilustres de Zacatecas**, with the tombs of Zacatecan heroes from 1841 to the present day.

You can return to the city by the teleférico or by a footpath leading downhill from the statues.

Museo Rafael Coronel

The Rafael Coronel Museum, imaginatively housed in the ruins of the lovely 16th century ex-Convento de San Francisco in the north of the city, contains Mexican folk art collected by the Zacatecan artist Rafael Coronel, brother of Pedro Coronel and son-in-law of Diego Rivera. The highlight is the astonishing colorful display of over 2000 masks used in traditional dances and rituals. This is probably the biggest mask collection in the country. Also to be seen are pottery, puppets, pre-Hispanic objects and drawings and sketches by Rivera. To reach the museum follow Hidalgo about 800 meters north from the cathedral to a fountain where the street forks. Follow the right fork, Matamoros, for 400 meters, and the museum will be on the left. It's open Monday, Tuesday, and Thursday through

Museo Francisco Goitia

The Francisco Goitia Museum displays work by six major Zacatecan artists of the 20th century. Set in a fine former governor's mansion at Estrada 102, above the pleasant Parque Enrique Estrada south of the city's central area, it's well worth visiting. Francisco Goitia (1882-1960) himself did some particularly good paintings of Indians. There's also a very striking Goitia self-portrait in the museum. Other artists represented include Pedro and Rafael Coronel.

The museum's hours are Tuesday to Saturday from 10 am to 1.30 pm and 5 to 8 pm, Sunday from 10 am to 4.30 pm (US$1.30). To reach it, go south on González Ortega from the corner of Hidalgo and Juárez, till you come to the Parque Enrique Estrada on the right, crossed by part of a 19th century aqueduct named El Cubo. Make a sharp right turn onto the street along the edge of the park. Follow this street to the museum.

Organized Tours

A couple of companies run tours of city sights and to places of interest out of town, such as Guadalupe, La Quemada and Plateros. Tours last around four hours and cost US$13 per person in town, US$16 out of town.

Special Events

La Morisma Usually held on the last Friday, Saturday and Sunday in August, this festival features the most spectacular of the many mock battles staged at Mexican fiestas commemorating the triumph of the Christians over the Muslims (Moors) in old Spain. Rival 'armies' parade through the city streets in the mornings then, accompanied by bands of musicians, enact two battle sequences, around midday and in the afternoon, between Lomas de Bracho in the northeast of the city and Cerro de la Bufa. One sequence portrays a conflict between Emperor Charlemagne and Almirante Balám, king of Alexandria. The other deals with a 16th century Muslim rebellion led by Argel Osmán. The enactments develop over the festival's three days, both culminating in Christian victory on the Sunday. Church services and other ceremonies also form part of the celebrations.

Feria de Zacatecas Zacatecas stages its annual feria from about September 5 to 21. Renowned matadors come to fight the famous local bulls; charreadas, concerts, plays and agricultural and craft shows are staged; and on September 8 the image of La Virgen del Patrocinio is carried to the cathedral from its chapel on the Cerro de la Bufa.

Places to Stay – budget

Zacatecas' cheap lodgings are in extreme contrast to the stately beauty of its colonial architecture.

Hostel The *Villa Deportiva Juvenil 1* youth hostel (☎ 2-02-23, ext 7) is at Paseo de la Encantado s/n, about seven minutes' walk south of the train station and halfway between the bus station and the center. The hostel is in the far corner of the CREA sports grounds where there is a large swimming pool. Open 24 hours, it has 70 or so dorm beds in reasonably spacious, clean rooms at US$2 per person. Meals are available (US$1.50 each). From the bus station, take a Ruta 7 or 8 bus and after about seven minutes watch for an overpass before the intersection of Boulevard Nueva Celaya and Avenida 5 Señores where the bus turns right heading into the center. As you near the overpass, look for Calle Celaya, which leads left to the sports grounds and hostel from Boulevard Nueva Celaya.

Hotels The cheapest hotel worth considering is the *Hotel Río Grande de Zacatecas* (☎ 2-98-76) at Calzada de la Paz 513. This is a basic but clean place on a hillside about 1.25 km southeast of the cathedral. Smallish singles/doubles, with private bath, cost US$5.25/7.25 (US$9.25 for a twin).

Exterior rooms have great views of la Bufa but also traffic noise. Calzada de la Paz is a small street almost opposite the old bus station on Avenida López Mateos. The hotel is 250 meters down the street.

About 1.5 km southwest of the cathedral, near Parque Enrique Estrada and opposite the Quinta Real, is *Hotel del Parque* (☎ 2-04-79), at González Ortega 302-4. It is popular with travelers. The large rooms have private bath, cost US$7.75/9.25 and are clean enough but a bit short on natural light.

Back to southeast of the center at López Mateos 106 or López Velarde 508 – depending which entrance you use – the *Hotel Colón* (☎ 2-04-64) has medium-sized rooms, somewhat fusty, that cost US$10.75/12.25 with bathroom. The hotel is sandwiched between the two busy, noisy streets. *Hotel Gami* (☎ 2-80-05) across the road at López Mateos 309 has barer but reasonably clean rooms at US$8.50/9.75 (US$15 for a twin).

Places to Stay – middle
Hotel Condesa (☎ 2-11-60), centrally located at Juárez 5 near the corner of Hidalgo, is a good value. Agreeable singles/doubles with private bath start at US$11/13 (US$15 for twin beds). The best and slightly more expensive rooms are on the renovated top floor. The rooms are around a central well with a plastic roof. Nearly all have exterior windows – those facing northeast have fine views of La Bufa.

Posada de los Condes (☎ 2-10-93), across the street from the Condesa at Juárez 107, is a colonial monument over three centuries old, but a recent modernization has removed most evidence of its age from the interior. The rooms, though not big, are pleasant and well kept, with TV, phone and carpet. They cost US$17/20. The attached restaurant is good.

Around the corner and back toward the center at Hidalgo 170 and up several flights of stairs, *Hostel del Río* (☎ 2-78-33) has a handful of spacious, comfortable rooms with singles/doubles/triples at US$17/20/25.

Another fair choice is *Posada de la Moneda* (☎ 2-08-81), a block south of the cathedral at Hidalgo 413. The rooms range along wide corridors. They are pleasant with TV and bath and Huichol yarn paintings on the walls. Singles/doubles cost US$23/30.

Places to Stay – top end
Hotel Continental Plaza (☎ 2-61-83, fax 2-62-45) is superbly located in a modernized colonial building at Hidalgo 703 on the Plaza de Armas. The 115 air-con rooms and suites are attractively furnished and equipped with TV and mini-bars. There's a good restaurant. Rooms cost from US$81, single or double.

Hotel Mesón de Jobito (☎ 4-17-22, fax 4-35-00) centrally but peacefully situated at Jardín Juárez 143, is another lovely old building with 31 finely decorated rooms and suites from US$81 to US$120. It has a restaurant and bar.

The top place is the classy *Hotel Quinta Real* (☎ 2-91-04, fax 2-84-40), about 1.5 km south of the cathedral just off González Ortega. It's spectacularly constructed around Zacatecas' former main bullring, with the arches of the fine old El Cubo aqueduct running across the front of the hotel. Large, very comfortable rooms cost from around US$95.

Places to Eat
There are several good places on Hidalgo and Juárez. For expensive top-class meals, make your way to the restaurants of the Quinta Real, Continental Plaza or Mesón de Jobito hotels. Many places to eat have local specialties using such ingredients as nopal, pumpkin and pumpkin seeds. Locally produced wine is good. You might also like to try *aguamiel* (honey water), a nutritional drink made from a type of cactus. Early in the day, on and around Hidalgo, you'll see burros carrying pottery jugs containing the beverage.

There are two produce markets in the center. Mercado El Laberinto has its main entrance on Juárez. Close by, Mercado Arroyo de la Plata can be entered from the curved street Arroyo de la Plata. There are plenty of budget eateries in this vicinity.

Avenida Hidalgo *Café y Nevería Acrópolis*, on Hidalgo immediately south of the cathedral, is the most popular central meeting place, busy from 8.30 am to 10 pm with a range of customers. It's not especially cheap, but there's a wide choice of all sorts of cakes, snacks, meals and drinks. Egg dishes are from US$3.25, with more substantial meals from US$4. A big cappuccino costs US$1.60.

West off Hidalgo opposite the Café Acrópolis, on Callejón del Santero (also called Callejón Gómez Farías), is *Hostería El Santero*. It serves a good comida corrida with excellent salsas in an attractive small dining room. Evening fare includes tamales, pozole and more, all at reasonable prices. It's closed during the low season.

Below the Mercado González Ortega, at Tacuba 16, *La Cantera Musical* is a relaxed place with pretty decor, the kitchen in full view out front and waiters niftily dressed in ranchero gear. It's open from 8 am to 10.30 pm. Breakfasts are from US$1.70 to US$2.50, and typical Mexican dishes are from US$4.

Mr Laberinto, Hidalgo 342 half a block south of the Mercado González Ortega, is a popular restaurant serving tasty, well-presented food in bright, pleasant surroundings. Pollo a la naranja (grilled chicken with orange) is good at US$4.75. Meat dishes start at US$5.25.

Popular, clean, friendly *Café Zas*, toward the south end of Hidalgo at No 201, serves decent breakfasts at around US$2.75, antojitos from US$2.50 to US$3 and chicken or meat dishes from US$3 to US$6. It's open from 9 am to 10 pm.

Avenida Juárez The friendly *El Pastor* at Independencia 214 on the south side of Jardín Independencia, just off the east end of Juárez, is busy from 8 am to 9 pm serving up economical charcoal-roasted chicken dishes – with crisps and a bit of salad for US$2 with mole and rice for US$2.50. Around the corner at Rayon 311,

Uno Colibri is a simple, family-run Yucatán restaurant. Mexican handicrafts brighten the walls, and there's sometimes theater here. The comida corrida is only US$1.60. Closed Saturday!

Several eateries on Juárez between Jardín Independencia and Avenida Hidalgo offer adequate if unspectacular Mexican fare, with antojitos in the US$2.75 to US$4 range, chicken and meat dishes for US$4 to US$6, and breakfasts from US$3. These include *Mesón La Mina* at Juárez 15, *Restaurant Condesa* next door, and *Fonda El Jacalito*, the best of the three, across the street.

El Tragadero on Juárez a block west of Hidalgo is a good-value Mexican eatery. To order, you mark your choices on a list. Most items are priced between US$1.10 and US$3.50. Alambre con queso (slices of grilled meat with cheese) is a good choice at US$3.25. There's a tasty platillo vegetariano (US$3), and the beer is cheap. Nearby is *Viva Pizza*, on the east side of Jardín de la Madre. It has several rooms with folksy decor and serves reasonable pizzas. The 'vegetariana' at US$3.75 is a good size for one person. Ask for the homemade salsas.

Entertainment

The exotically situated disco in the *Mina El Edén* (☎ 2-30-02) functions Thursday to Saturday, 9 pm to 3 am. It's aimed as much at tourists (Mexican and foreign) as at locals, and entry costs around US$11, with drinks extra. Numbers are limited, so it's a good idea to reserve a table. Phone a little before 9 pm or go to the mine during the day and ask to speak with someone who knows about the disco.

Disco El Elefante Blanco next to the Cerro del Grillo teleférico station has a more local flavor, a young crowd and romantic views of the city. It's open Thursday to Saturday, 9 pm to 2 am.

El Paraíso, a smart bar in the southwest corner of the Mercado González Ortega on Hidalgo, is busy most nights. A beer is US$1.30, a cocktail US$2.25, and there's food too, such as botanas for US$3.50. The *Nueva Galicia* bar, across the little plaza outside El Paraíso, is similar. Less smart but cheaper, the video bar of *Mr Laberinto,* a restaurant down the street, is another popular haunt.

In the center there are at least three hot spots for dancing. Wear your best clothes! *El Claustro* on Aguascalientes, a small street east off the top of Tacuba, is the most popular. It's open Thursday through Saturday from 10 pm until late. Cover is US$4. *La Marcha,* Dr Hierro 409, has much the same hours and costs the same. *Cactus,* at the Juárez end of Hidalgo, is a video-and-billiards bar with a disco Thursday to Saturday from 11 pm. Cover is US$2.75.

Like Guanajuato, Zacatecas has a tradition of callejoneadas, but here musicians with horns rather than singers with guitars lead the street parties. (See Guanajuato – Entertainment for more on callejoneadas.) There doesn't seem to be a regular schedule but during fiestas and on some weekends, callejoneadas set off around 8 pm from the Alameda. You can join in for free. Ask for details at the tourist office.

Teatro Calderón is the top central venue for cultural events.

Things to Buy

Zacatecas is known for its fine leather and silver and colorful sarapes. Try the shops around Plaza Genaro Codina and other shops along Arroyo de la Plata and in the indoor market off this street. The Mercado González Ortega is more upmarket with silver jewelry, a shop specializing in local wines and another in charrería gear – boots, saddles, chaps, belts, sarapes and more. There's another excellent shop with the same gear on Villalpando, facing the Jardín de la Madre. Cazzorra, on Hidalgo just north of the Hotel Continental Plaza, sells locally produced crafts and wines.

Tour companies can take you to visit silversmithing workshops, or ask at the tourist office for details of how to do this independently.

Getting There & Away

Air Mexicana flies direct daily to/from Mexico City and Tijuana. They also have several direct flights weekly to/from Chicago and León and one to/from Denver. The Mexicana office (☎ 2-74-29) is at Avenida Hidalgo 406.

TAESA flies direct most days to/from Chicago, Oakland (California), Mexico City, Ciudad Juárez, Morelia and Tijuana. It also has flights to/from Guadalajara and Aguascalientes. Its office (☎ 2-00-50) is at Avenida Hidalgo 305-1.

Bus Zacatecas bus station is on the southwest edge of town, about three km from the center. Many buses from here are de paso. The station has a checkroom for baggage (open from 7 am to 10 pm), telephone casetas and a fax office. Daily departures include:

Aguascalientes – 130 km, two hours; 14 1st-class by Transportes Chihuahuenses (US$5); 2nd-class every half hour by Estrella Blanca (US$4.25)

Durango – 290 km, 4½ hours; 13 1st-class by Ómnibus de México (US$11); six 2nd-class by Estrella Blanca (US$9.25)

Fresnillo – 60 km, one to 1½ hours; hourly 1st-class by Futura (US$2); hourly 2nd-class by Estrella Blanca and Camiones de los Altos (US$1.90); 2nd-class every 10 minutes, 6 am to 9.30 pm, from Centro Comercial Zacatecas (Old Bus Station) on Avenida López Mateos (US$1.30)

Guadalajara – 320 km, five hours; 28 1st-class by Ómnibus de México and Transportes Chihuahuenses (US$14); hourly 2nd-class by Estrella Blanca/Rojo de los Altos (US$12)

Guanajuato – 310 km, five hours; take León bus and change there for Guanajuato

León – 260 km, four hours; five 1st-class by Transportes Chihuahuenses

Mexico City (Terminal Norte) – 651 km, eight to nine hours; 16 1st-class by Futura, Transportes Chihuahuenses and Ómnibus de México (US$26); four 2nd-class by Estrella Blanca (US$22)

Monterrey – 460 km, six hours; five 1st-class by Transportes del Norte (US$17); 10 2nd-class by Estrella Blanca/Rojo de los Altos (US$15)

San Luis Potosí – 190 km, three hours; 12 1st-class by Futura and Ómnibus de México (US$6.75); 15 2nd-class by Estrella Blanca (US$6.25)

There are also frequent buses to Torreón and several a day to Chihuahua, Ciudad Juárez, Saltillo and Nuevo Laredo.

Train The 'División del Norte' train between Mexico City and Ciudad Juárez stops at Zacatecas at 9.30 am northbound (train No 7) and 8 pm southbound (train No 8). Primera fares are US$32 to Ciudad Juárez, US$23 to Chihuahua and US$3.25 to Aguascalientes. See the Mexico City Train section for further details.

Zacatecas train station is on González Ortega, about 1.25 km south of Juárez. Tickets are on sale starting about one hour before a train's arrival.

Car & Motorcycle Budget (☎ 2-94-58) has a rental office next to the Hotel Colón on Avenida López Mateos. Numero Uno Autorentas (☎ 2-34-07) at Avenida López Mateos 201 offers discounts for guests of several hotels, including Hotel Condesa and Posada de los Condes.

Getting Around
Zacatecas airport is about 20 km north of the city. For airport transportation for about US$3.25 call ☎ 2-59-46. A taxi from the airport costs about US$12.

The Ruta 8 bus from the bus and rail stations runs directly to the cathedral. Heading back out to the bus and rail stations from the center, you can catch it going south on Villalpando. The Ruta 7 bus from the bus and rail stations runs to the intersection of González Ortega and Juárez in the center, then heads west along Juárez and winds around to the teleférico station on Cerro del Grillo. Heading out to the bus or train stations, pick it up south of the González Ortega and Juárez intersection. Bus fares are US$0.20. A taxi from the bus station to the center costs US$1.30.

GUADALUPE
This small town, about 10 km east of the Zacatecas city center, is home to one of Mexico's best collections of colonial art –

the **Museo y Templo de Guadalupe**. It's housed in a historic ex-monastery next to a still-working church, and is worth the trip if you have any interest in colonial history, art or architecture.

The monastery Convento de Guadalupe was established by Franciscan monks in the early 18th century as a Colegio Apostólica de Propaganda Fide (Apostolic College for the Propagation of the Faith). It was a base for missionary work in northern Nueva España and had a strong academic tradition and a renowned library. It was closed in the 1850s. The building now houses the Museo y Templo de Guadalupe with many works by Miguel Cabrera, Juan Correa, Antonio Torres and Cristóbal Villalpando. Visitors can also see part of its library and step into the choir on the upper floor of the monastery church (templo), with its fine carved and painted chairs. From the choir you can look down into the beautifully decorated 19th century Capilla de Nápoles on the church's north side. Museum hours are Tuesday to Sunday, 10 am to 4.30 pm (US$1.90). The ground level of the church, also with a view into the Capilla de Nápoles, can be visited free. There's some fine baroque carving on the church's exterior.

Next door to the Museo de Guadalupe is the embryonic **Museo Regional de Zacatecas**, with a small collection of old carriages and cars – free and worth a look.

The town holds its annual **feria** from December 3 to 13, focused on the Día de la Virgen de Guadalupe (December 12).

Getting There & Away
From Zacatecas, Transportes de Guadalupe buses run to Guadalupe every few minutes along López Mateos. There's a bus stop just beyond the old bus station, now called the Centro Comercial Zacatecas, on the corner of López Mateos and Callejón del Barro. The fare is US$0.20 for a 20-minute ride. Get off at a small plaza in the middle of Guadalupe where a 'Museo Convento' sign points to the right, along Madero. Walk about 250 meters along Madero to a

sizable plaza, called Jardín Juárez. The museums are on the left side of the plaza. To return to Zacatecas, you can pick up the bus where you disembarked.

FRESNILLO
pop 80,000; ☎ 493

Fresnillo is an unexciting town 60 km north of Zacatecas on the road to Torreón and Durango. The main reason to stop here is the Santuario de Plateros, one of Mexico's most-visited shrines, five km northeast of the town in the village of Plateros.

Orientation
Fresnillo bus station is on Ébano, about one km northeast of the center. If you need to go into town for a meal or a room, you'll find it's a higgledy-piggledy place with three main plazas. The most pleasant of the three is Jardín Madero with the colonial church of Nuestra Señora de la Purificación on its north side. Three blocks west, along Avenida Juárez, is the Jardín Obalisco with a theater on its north side. Between these two, Avenida Hidalgo heads two blocks south off Juárez to the Jardín Hidalgo.

Santuario de Plateros
A visit to Plateros gives quite an insight into Mexican Catholicism. The goal of the pilgrims who flock here every day of the year is El Santo Niño de Atocha. This quaint image of the infant Jesus, holding a staff and basket and wearing a colonial pilgrim's feathered hat, resides on the altar of the Santuario de Plateros, an 18th century church. The avenue leading up to the church is lined with stalls selling a vast array of gaudy religious imagery and other souvenirs. The Santo Niño is credited with all manner of wonders – a series of rooms to the right of the church entrance is lined with thousands of little retablos depicting his miracles.

Buses of the Fresnillo-Plateros line run from Fresnillo bus station to Plateros every 15 minutes from 6.50 am to 6.20 pm. Ruta 6 city buses also run to Plateros, from Calle Emiliano Zapata, 2½ blocks east of the

Jardín Madero. Fare is US$0.40 on either service.

Places to Stay & Eat
The fairly modern *Hotel Lirmar* (☎ 2-45-98) at Durango 400 on the corner of Ébano, just outside the bus station, has reasonable singles/doubles with private bath for US$10.50/13.

In town, the *Hotel Maya* (☎ 2-03-51) at Ensaye 9, one block south of Avenida Juárez and one block west of Avenida Hidalgo, has bright, fairly clean rooms with bathroom and TV for US$11/13. *Hotel Del Fresno* (☎ 2-11-20), at Avenida Hidalgo 411 facing Jardín Hidalgo, is more expensive with comfortable rooms at US$29/33. The pleasant *Hotel Casa Blanca* (☎ 2-12-88) at García Salinas 503, three blocks east of Jardín Hidalgo, costs US$21/28.

El Molinito is a bright, clean, busy restaurant on Jardín Hidalgo. It serves a good-value three-course comida corrida for US$2.75 and à la carte main courses for about the same price.

Getting There & Away
Fresnillo is served well by long-distance buses, though many are de paso. The bus station has a telephone caseta and luggage storage. There are frequent 1st- and 2nd-class buses to Durango (230 km, 3½ hours, from US$7.25), Torreón (330 km, five hours, US$11 to US$13) and Zacatecas (60 km, one to 1½ hours, US$1.30 to US$2), as well as many buses to Aguascalientes, Chihuahua, Mexico City, Guadalajara, San Luis Potosí and elsewhere.

Getting Around
Ruta 3 'Central-Centro' buses run between Ébano, outside the bus station, and the town center. Leaving town, you can pick them up on the south side of Jardín Madero.

JEREZ
pop 35,000; ☎ 494

A small country town 30 km southwest of Zacatecas, Jerez has some surprisingly fine

18th and 19th century buildings that testify to the wealth that silver brought to even the lesser towns of the Zacatecas region. Jerez holds a lively Easter feria with charreadas, cockfights and other activities. It starts on Good Friday and lasts about 10 days.

Information
There's a tourist office next to Teatro Hinojosa on Jardín Juárez, a short walk southwest of the central plaza, Jardín Páez, but it opens erratically. On the north side of Jardín Páez, Banco Promex changes traveler's checks and cash weekdays from 8 am to 7 pm and Sunday from 10 am to 2.30 pm. There's an ATM here, and others are at Bancomer and Banamex on Calle San Luis, which heads northeast from Jardín Páez. All banks are closed on Saturday. The post office and the Telecomm office, with a fax service, are side by side on Calle de la Bizarra Capital, which heads south from the southwest corner of Jardín Páez. There's a telephone caseta in the pharmacy at Obregón 20B, half a block north of Jardín Páez, and pay phones outside Banco Promex.

Things to See
Jardín Páez, the town's main square, is pleasant with a gazebo and plenty of trees, birds and seats. The 18th century **Parroquia de la Inmaculada Concepción** and the 19th century **Santuario de la Soledad** have fine stone carvings. To find them go one block south from the southeast corner of Jardín Páez, then one block east for the parroquia, or one block west for the santuario. Just past the santuario, on the north side of Jardín Hidalgo, is a beautiful little 19th century theater, **Teatro Hinojosa.**

Places to Stay & Eat
Hotel Plaza (☎ 5-20-63) on the south side of Jardín Páez has small, bare, clean singles/doubles with bathroom and TV for US$6.50/7.75. The 'hot' water may be a long time coming. The hotel's restaurant is OK – a quarter chicken with fries, beans, greens and tortillas is yours for US$1.90.

The *Hotel Del Jardín* (☎ 5-20-26), on the west side of the same plaza, has similar room prices to the Hotel Plaza.

Restaurant La Luz, a block west of Jardín Páez along Reseno, is a good little family-run eating place where you can get a good bistek with beans, salsa, tortillas and a beer for around US$3. On the east side of Jardín Páez, the little *El Jarro Café* is a central meeting place with excellent coffee and good cheap meals.

Things to Buy
Fine leatherwork can be found at shops like *Zapatería Lo Legalidad* on Del Refugio, half a block south of Jardín Páez, or *La Palma*, which specializes in charrería gear, one block east and half a block north of Jardín Páez.

The market is two blocks east of Jardín Páez on Calzada Suave Patria, the continuation of Calle San Luis.

Getting There & Away
The turnoff to Jerez is at Malpaso, on the Zacatecas-Guadalajara road 23 km south of Zacatecas. The Zacatecas-Jerez line runs 2nd-class buses from Zacatecas bus station to Jerez every 30 minutes from 5 am to 9 pm for US$1.90. There are also services by Ómnibus de México and Estrella Blanca/Rojo de los Altos. Jerez bus station is on the east side of town, about one km from the center along Calzada Suave Patria. 'Centro-Central' buses, from inside the bus station, run to/from the center for US$0.20. There are also several buses a day to/from Guadalajara (US$12) and Fresnillo (US$1.70).

LA QUEMADA
The ruins of La Quemada stand on a hill in a broad valley about 55 km south of Zacatecas, one km east of the Zacatecas-Guadalajara road. They're also known as Chicomostoc, because they were once thought to be the place of that name where the Aztecs halted during their legendary wanderings toward the Valle de México. The ruins' fine, rather isolated setting makes them well worth the trip from Zacatecas if you have time.

Crunch, Munch

November must be the high season for crickets in the La Quemada area. The approach road to the site, as I walked along it in that warm, dry month, was carpeted with the creatures – big, fat, juicy ones. Vehicles had inevitably squashed hundreds of them. And the presence of so many fresh corpses had brought thousands more crickets out from the undergrowth for a feast on this source of juicy, immobile nourishment. Many other crickets were in the mood to sate other bodily urges, and were climbing on the backs of the chomping cannibals to procreate. All this produced great heaving mounds of living and dead crickets dotted all the way along the road to the site, and it was impossible to avoid crunching them underfoot if I lifted my eyes from the road to take in the landscape or look for the ruins up on the hill. Happily these crickets were either not of the flying variety or were too sated to do anything but crawl.

For some reason the ruins site itself was cricket-free, and I was able to forget all about them as I climbed up level with the soaring eagles. There I cut red tuna – cactus fruit – to munch on while I surveyed the fine views from the top of this thousand-year-old settlement. ∎

John Noble

La Quemada was inhabited between about 300 and 1200 AD. Early in that period it was part of a regional trade network linked to Teotihuacán, but fortifications at the site suggest that La Quemada later tried to dominate trade in this part of Mexico. Traces of a big fire indicate that its final downfall was violent.

Some of the ruins can be seen up on the hill to the left as you approach from the Zacatecas-Guadalajara road. Of the main structures, the nearest to the site entrance is the Salón de las Columnas (Hall of the Columns), which was probably a ceremonial hall. A bit farther up the hill are a ball court, a steep offerings pyramid and an equally steep staircase leading toward the upper levels of the site. From the upper levels of the main hill a path leads westward to a spur hilltop with the remains of a cluster of buildings called the Citadel (la Ciudadela). A stone wall, thought to have been built for defensive purposes later in La Quemada's history, stretches across the slopes to the north.

The site is open daily from 10 am to 4.30 pm. Entrance is US$1.90, free on Sunday.

Getting There & Away

From Zacatecas bus station, take an Ómnibus de México or Rojo de los Altos bus heading to Villanueva. Each company has six or seven daily services. Some buses heading for Guadalajara may also stop at La Quemada. The fare is around US$2. Tell the conductor you want 'las ruinas' and you'll be dropped at the Restaurant Las Siete Cuevas at the start of the one-km paved road that approaches the site. When returning to Zacatecas, you may have to wait a while before a bus shows up.

Aguascalientes

The state of Aguascalientes, bordered on the south by Jalisco and surrounded on its other sides by Zacatecas, is one of Mexico's smallest. It was originally part of Zacatecas; according to history, a kiss planted on the lips of dictator Santa Anna by the attractive wife of a prominent local politician brought about the creation of a separate Aguascalientes state.

Aguascalientes is primarily agricultural, with maize, beans, chilies, fruits and grains grown on its fertile lands. Livestock is also important and the state's ranches raise famous bulls for bullfights all over Mexico as well as cattle for meat and hides. Industry is concentrated in and around the capital city, Aguascalientes.

AGUASCALIENTES

pop 550,000; alt 1800m; ☎ 49

Aguascalientes (Hot Waters), named for its hot springs, is a prosperous industrial city with just enough colonial legacies to justify a brief visit.

History

Some time before the Spanish invasion, indigenous people built a labyrinth of catacombs, which made the first Spaniards arriving here dub Aguascalientes La Ciudad Perforada – the perforated city. Archaeologists have no explanation for the tunnels, which are off-limits to visitors.

Pedro de Alvarado came to subdue the tribes in this region in 1522 but was driven back by Chichimec Indians. A small garrison was founded here in 1575 to protect silver convoys from Zacatecas to Mexico City. Eventually, as the Chichimecs were pacified, the region's hot springs at Ojo Caliente served as the basis for the growth of a town; a large tank beside the springs helped irrigate local farms where fruits, vegetables and grains were cultivated.

Today, more than half of the state's population lives in the city, where industry and textiles and trade from its ranches, vineyards and orchards provide jobs.

Orientation

Aguascalientes is flat and easy to get around. The center of town is Plaza de la Patria, formerly Plaza de Armas, with many hotels, restaurants, sites of interest and shops within a few blocks. Avenida López Mateos, the main east-west artery across the central part of the city, is a couple of blocks south of Plaza de la Patria. The bus and train stations, both on the outskirts of town, are served by frequent local buses.

Information

Tourist Office The Delegación de Turismo del Estado de Aguascalientes (☎ 15-11-55) is beside the Palacio de Gobierno on Plaza de la Patria. Open daily except holidays from 10 am to 8 pm, it gives out free city maps and information on the city and state of Aguascalientes, all in Spanish.

Money There are plenty of banks for money exchange and with ATMs around Plaza de la Patria. Open hours are generally weekdays from 9 am to 5 pm, 9 am to 1 pm for exchanging cash or traveler's checks. Bancomer, on 5 de Mayo just north of Plaza de la Patria, has a separate 'casa de cambio' with good rates, open weekdays from 9 am to 6 pm, Saturday and Sunday from 10 am to 2 pm. On holidays, you'll need a casa de cambio. Monrey has two branches in the center – one half a block east of the plaza on Montoro, another in the Centro Comercial, just short of the plaza.

Post & Communications The post office is at Hospitalidad 108, a couple of blocks northeast of Plaza de la Patria. It's open weekdays from 8 am to 7 pm, Saturday 9 am to 1 pm. The main Telecomm office, with fax service, is at Galeana 102, a block from Plaza de la Patria – open weekdays from 8 am to 6 pm, Saturday 9 am to noon.

There are several pay phones on Plaza de la Patria. The telephone caseta opposite the southeast corner of Plaza de la Patria, next door to the Hotel Señorial, is open Monday to Saturday from 8.30 am to 9 pm, Sunday 9.30 am to 8.30 pm.

Travel Agencies Viajes Gomzo (☎ 16-61-92), at Montoro 114, is especially helpful. Convenient for flight tickets is Wagons-Lits Viajes (☎ 15-59-73) on the corner of Plaza de la Patria and Madero.

Plaza de la Patria

The 18th century baroque **Catedral**, on the west side of the plaza, is more magnificent on the inside than the outside. Over the altar at the east end of the south aisle is a painting of the Virgin of Guadalupe by Miguel Cabrera. There are more Cabrera works in the cathedral's *pinacoteca* (picture gallery) – ask one of the priests to let you in. In 1997, the cathedral was undergoing heavy restoration.

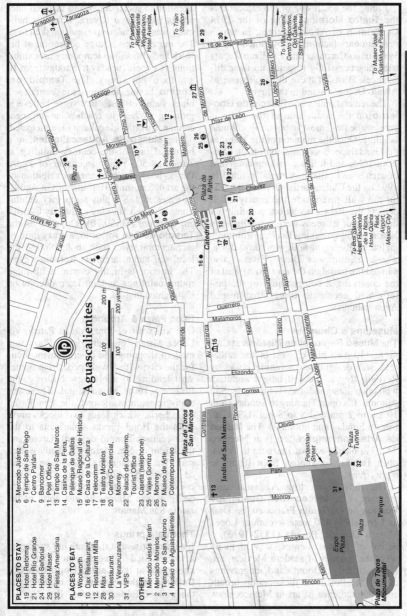

Aguascalientes

PLACES TO STAY
19 Hotel Reforma
21 Hotel Río Grande
24 Hotel Señorial
29 Hotel Maser
32 Fiesta Americana

PLACES TO EAT
8 Woolworth
10 Dax Restaurant
12 Restaurant Mitla
28 Max
30 Restaurant
La Veracruzana
31 VIPS

OTHER
1 Mercado Jesús Terán
2 Mercado Morelos
3 Templo de San Antonio
4 Museo de Aguascalientes
5 Mercado Juárez
6 Templo de San Diego
7 Centro Parián
9 Bancomer
11 Post Office
13 Templo de San Marcos
14 Casino de la Feria,
Palenque de Gallos
15 Museo Regional de Historia
16 Casa de la Cultura
17 Teatro Morelos
18 Teatro Morelos
20 Centro Comercial,
Monrey
22 Palacio de Gobierno,
Tourist Office
23 Caseta (telephone)
25 Viajes Gomzo
26 Monrey
27 Museo de Arte
Contemporaneo

200 m
200 yards

**To Paetilanía
Restaurante
Vegetariano,
Hotel Avenida,**

**To Train
Station**

**To Villa Juvenil,
Centro Deportivo,
Oriente,
San Luis Potosí**

**To Museo José
Guadalupe Posada**

**To Bus Station,
Hotel Hacienda
Los Morales,
Hotel Quinta
Real,
Airport,
Mexico City**

Facing the south side of the cathedral is the **Teatro Morelos**, scene of the 1914 Convention of Aguascalientes, in which revolutionary factions led by Pancho Villa, Venustiano Carranza and Emiliano Zapata tried unsuccessfully to patch up their differences. Busts of these three plus one of Álvaro Obregón stand in the foyer.

The red and pink stone **Palacio de Gobierno** on the south side of the plaza is Aguascalientes' most noteworthy colonial building. Once the mansion of the Marqués de Guadalupe, a colonial baron, it dates from 1665, and it has a striking courtyard of arches and pillars. A mural painted in 1992 by the Chilean artist Osvaldo Barra is on the wall just inside the courtyard. It depicts the 1914 convention, pointing out that some of its ideas were crystallized in Mexico's still-governing 1917 constitution – including the eight-hour workday. Barra, whose mentor was Diego Rivera, also painted the mural on the far (south) wall of the courtyard, a compendium of the historic and economic forces that forged Aguascalientes.

Museums & Churches

The **Museo Regional de Historia** at Carranza 110, two blocks west of the cathedral, was designed as a family home by Refugio Reyes, the self-taught architect who also designed the Templo de San Antonio. It's open Tuesday to Sunday from 10 am to 2 pm and 5 to 8 pm (US$1.30, free on Sunday and holidays). The **Museo de Arte Contemporáneo** is at Montoro 222, 1½ blocks east of Plaza de la Patria, open Tuesday to Sunday from 10 am to 6 pm (free).

The most interesting Aguascalientes museum is the **Museo José Guadalupe Posada** on the Jardín Francisco, on Díaz de León about 450 meters south of López Mateos Oriente. Posada (1852-1913), a native of Aguascalientes, was in many ways the founder of modern Mexican art. His satirical cartoons and engravings during the Porfiriato dictatorship broadened the audience of art in Mexico, drew

attention to social decay and inspired later artists like Diego Rivera. Posada's hallmark was the *calavera* (skull or skeleton). The museum has a large collection of his work and also shows temporary art exhibitions. It's open Tuesday to Sunday from 10 am to 6 pm (free). The **Templo del Encino** beside the museum contains a black statue of Jesus that some believe is growing. When it reaches an adjacent column, a worldwide calamity is anticipated.

The **Museo de Aguascalientes**, in a beautiful turn-of-the-century building at Zaragoza 505 near the corner of Pedro Parga, houses a permanent exhibition of the art of Saturnino Herrán, born in Aguascalientes in 1887, plus temporary exhibitions. It's open Tuesday to Sunday from 11 am to 6 pm (US$0.70). Opposite is the **Templo de San Antonio**, a crazy quilt of architectural styles built about 1900 by the local self-taught architect Refugio Reyes. The interior is highly ornate, with huge round paintings and intricate decoration highlighted in gold.

Expo Plaza & Around

One km west of Plaza de la Patria, via López Mateos or Nieto, Expo Plaza is a modern shopping and entertainment focus for the city, with a wide pedestrian boulevard leading to a big new bullring, the Plaza de Toros Monumental. There are many restaurants along Calle Pani/Paseo de la Feria, which leads two blocks north from the Hotel Fiesta Americana to the 18th century Templo de San Marcos and the Jardín de San Marcos, a shady walled park. The Palenque de Gallos in the Casino de la Feria building on Pani is the city's cockfighting arena. The old bullring, Plaza de Toros San Marcos, is just north of the Jardín San Marcos.

Thermal Springs

It's no surprise that there are hot springs in a town called Aguascalientes. The best known are at the **Centro Deportivo Ojo Caliente** on the eastern edge of the city at the end of López Mateos. Bus No 27, which you can pick up eastbound on Rivero y Gutiérrez, and No 12, which runs along López Mateos, go from the center to Ojo Caliente. Entrance is US$1.60 a day. The large pool, and some other smaller pools, have warmish water; the hot water is in private pools, which rent for US$7.25 or US$10.50 an hour for four or six people. In the large park-like grounds are tennis, volleyball and squash courts and a restaurant. Hours are 7 am to 7 pm daily. Returning to the city center, bus No 12 will take you along López Mateos to the corner of Chávez just south of Plaza de la Patria.

Special Events
Feria de San Marcos This is the biggest national fair in Mexico, attracting around a million visitors each year for exhibitions, bullfights, cockfights, rodeos, free concerts, an extravaganza of cultural events – including an international film festival – and a big national-scale parade taking place on the saint's day, April 25. The fair starts in mid-April and lasts 22 days. Programs of cultural events can be picked up at theaters and museums. Expo Plaza is the hub of things.

Places to Stay
Prices skyrocket during the Feria de San Marcos and places to stay are completely booked by early May for the feria's final weekend – local residents run a lucrative homestay service at this time. Ask around at the feria if you're stuck.

Places to Stay – budget
Hostel The *Villa Juvenil* youth hostel (no telephone) is about three km east of the center on the ring road Avenida Circunvalación, also called Avenida Convención at this point, on the corner of Jaime Nunó. The sign out front says 'Instituto Aguascalentense del Deporte.' The hostel has 72 beds in clean separate-sex rooms holding up to eight each; cost is US$4. In the park-like grounds are a cafeteria, swimming pool, gym and various ball courts. Bus No 20 from the bus station and No 36 from

Rivero y Gutiérrez in the city center will take you to the hostel.

Hotels There are a number of good budget hotels right in the center. One of the best is the *Hotel Maser* (☎ 15-35-62), Montoro 303 at 16 de Septiembre. It has 47 clean, pleasant rooms with private bath around a covered inner courtyard; there is enclosed parking in the rear. Singles/doubles are US$11/13.

The friendly *Hotel Señorial* (☎ 15-16-30, 15-14-73), at Colón 104 just off the southeast corner of Plaza de la Patria, has 32 reasonable rooms with TV. Some of the rooms have balconies. It's a good value at US$11/15.

A block west of the plaza at Nieto 118, on the corner of Galeana, *Hotel Reforma* (☎ 15-11-07) has sizable rooms on two floors around a plant-filled covered courtyard. It's aging and a bit dilapidated but decent and friendly. Room rates are US$9.25/10.50 with private bath.

Hotel Avenida (☎ 15-36-13) at Madero 486, about 750 meters east of Plaza de la Patria, has 48 pleasant rooms with cable TV and private bath for US$13/15. It also has a small restaurant.

Places to Stay – middle
Hotel Río Grande (☎ 16-16-66), Avenida Chávez 101 on the southwest corner of Plaza de la Patria, is the center's most luxurious option. It has 92 rooms with all modern conveniences for US$39/43. The hotel restaurant is reasonable. The elegant *Hotel Francia* on the northeast corner of Plaza de la Patria was closed due to bankruptcy at the time of research.

Places to Stay – top end
The 192-room *Fiesta Americana* (☎ 18-60-10, fax 18-51-18) on Expo Plaza has singles/doubles for US$85/91, more on weekends. *Hotel Hacienda de la Noria* (☎ 18-43-43, fax 18-52-44) in the southeast of the city at Héroes de Nacozari 1315, at the intersection with Avenida Circunvalación/ Convención, has 50 comfortable

suites with balconies or their own patios overlooking the gardens, plus a heated pool and restaurant. Suites are US$53.

Hotel Quinta Real (☎ 78-58-18, fax 78-56-16), on the southeast edge of the city at Avenida Aguascalientes Sur 601, is a luxury modern place in colonial style with rooms at about US$115.

Places to Eat

Right in the center on 5 de Mayo just short of Allende, *Woolworth* has good-value breakfasts (from US$2.25) and other meals (from US$3.25), plus decent coffee.

Equally convenient, the *Restaurant Mitla* at Madero 220 is large, clean and pleasant, with a varied menu. The four-course comida corrida is US$3.25, and meat, chicken or seafood dishes range from US$4.50 to US$6. It's open daily from 8 am to 11 pm. On Madero near the corner of Zaragoza, *Restaurante Vegetariano* has a lunch buffet (US$2.50) daily except Sunday. There's a good bakery nearby on Madero at Zaragoza.

The cool, modern *Dax Restaurant-Video Bar*, Allende 229 at Morelos, serves good food – antojitos US$2 to US$2.75, main meals US$3.25 to US$5.25. It's open daily from 8 am to 1 am. Across the road, the *Excelsior* café/bookstore in the Centro Parián is *the* place to read your newspaper and sip coffee.

There are several more eateries in the Dax price range on the pedestrian street Pani in the Expo Plaza area, and a branch of the reliable chain restaurant *VIPS* in the Expo Plaza building itself.

Two blocks east and a block south of Plaza de la Patria, *Restaurant La Vera-cruzana* on Hornedo at 16 de Septiembre is a small, simple, family-run restaurant with excellent home-style cooking at a good price: the four-course comida corrida is a bargain at US$2.25, and the frijoles are some of the best in Mexico! It's open Monday through Saturday from 8.30 am to 5 pm.

Max at López Mateos Oriente 322, 1½ blocks east and three blocks south of Plaza de la Patria, serves some of the best tacos in this or any other city, but only from 8 pm to 4 am. Max, its *simpático* owner, prefers these hours because, he says, people are more relaxed at night. Choose from the five or six fillings displayed on the counter: the tacos are US$0.40 – so tasty that it's very hard to resist when Max inquires: *'¿Otro taquito, señor?'*

Fresh produce is available in three markets a few blocks north of Plaza de la Patria: *Mercado Juárez*, *Mercado Jesús Terán* and *Mercado Morelos*.

Entertainment

The *Casa de la Cultura*, housed in a fine 17th century building on Carranza just west of Galeana, hosts art exhibitions, concerts, theater, dance and other cultural events. Stop in to look at their schedule.

The *Teatro Morelos* on Plaza de la Patria and *Teatro de Aguascalientes* on Chávez at Avenida Aguascalientes, in the south of the city, both stage a variety of cultural events.

Free concerts, dance and theater are presented some Sunday lunchtimes in the courtyard of the Museo José Guadalupe Posada. There's often live music in the Plaza de Toros de San Marcos, the old bullring.

Aguascalientes' top discos are *El Cabús* (☎ 73-00-06) in the fancy Hotel Las Trojes, about 15 minutes north of the center on the highway to Zacatecas, and *Meneos* (☎ 13-32-70) in the Centro Comercial El Dorado on Avenida Las Américas, about two km southwest of the center.

Getting There & Away

Air Jesús Terán airport is 22 km south from Aguascalientes on the road to Mexico City. Aeroméxico (☎ 16-13-55), at Madero 474, flies direct daily to/from Mexico City and Tijuana, and three times a week to/from Puerto Vallarta, Los Angeles and Houston. Aerolitoral (same office as Aeroméxico) flies daily to/from Monterrey, San Luis Potosí and San Antonio (Texas). Aero California (☎ 15-24-00), at Montoro 203, and TAESA (☎ 18-26-98), at Madero 447, also have flights.

Bus The bus station (Central Camionera) is about two km south of the center on

Avenida Circunvalación Sur, also called Avenida Convención, on the corner of Quinta Avenida. It has post and fax offices, pay phones, a cafeteria and luggage storage. Daily departures include:

Guadalajara – 250 km, 3½ to four hours; several deluxe by ETN (US$14) and Primera Plus (US$11); frequent 1st-class by Elite, Futura, Ómnibus de México and Estrella Blanca (US$11); seven 2nd-class de paso by Rojo de los Altos (US$8.75)

Guanajuato – 180 km, three hours; one 1st-class de paso by Ómnibus de México (US$8); three 2nd-class by Flecha Amarilla (US$6)

Mexico City (Terminal Norte) – 521 km, seven hours; 19 deluxe by ETN and Primera Plus (US$29 and US$23); 26 1st-class by Futura or Ómnibus de México (US$22); six 2nd-class by Flecha Amarilla (US$18)

San Luis Potosí – 168 km, three hours; 14 1st-class by Futura (US$7.75); hourly 2nd-class by Estrella Blanca

Zacatecas – 130 km, two hours; 13 1st-class by Ómnibus de México or Transportes Chihuahuenses (US$5); 2nd-class every half-hour, 6.30 am to 11 pm, by Rojo de los Altos (US$4.25)

There's also frequent service to Ciudad Juárez, León, Monterrey, Morelia and Torreón, and two buses daily to San Miguel de Allende.

Train The station is about two km east of the center, on Jardín del Ferrocarril, a few meters north of Avenida Alameda, the eastward continuation of Montoro. The ticket office is open daily from 6 to 9 am and 8 to 10.30 pm, plus Monday to Saturday noon to 2 pm.

The 'División del Norte' train between Mexico City and Ciudad Juárez stops at Aguascalientes at 6.30 am northbound (train No 7) and 10.30 pm southbound (train No 8). Primera fares are US$2 to Zacatecas and US$15 to Mexico City. See the Mexico City Train section for further details.

A slow 2nd-class train, No 13 northbound (departing 9.15 pm) and No 14 southbound (7.50 am), also operates on the Mexico City-Ciudad Juárez route.

Getting Around

Most places of interest are within easy walking distance of the center. City buses (US$0.20) run from 6 am to 10 pm.

Bus Nos 3, 4 and 19 run from the bus station to the city center. Get off at the first stop after the tunnel under Plaza de la Patria: this will be on 5 de Mayo or Rivero y Gutiérrez. From the city center to the bus station, take any 'Central' bus on Moctezuma opposite the north side of the cathedral, or around the corner on Galeana.

For the train station take Bus No 36 from Rivero y Gutiérrez, or any 'Estación' bus heading east along Montoro from Morelos. From the station to the center take any 'Centro' bus west along Avenida Alameda.

A taxi from the center to the bus or train station costs around US$1.10, to the airport about US$6.50.

San Luis Potosí

The state of San Luis Potosí ('poh-toh-SEE') has two of the most interesting destinations on the way south from Mexico's northeast border: the mountain ghost town of Real de Catorce and the city of San Luis Potosí itself, steeped in history and the first major colonial town reached on this route into Mexico.

The state is high (average altitude around 2000 meters) and dry, with little rainfall. The exception is its eastern corner, which drops into a tropical valley (see Tampico & the Huasteca in the Central Gulf Coast chapter for information about this area).

Before the Spanish conquest in 1521, western San Luis Potosí was inhabited by warlike hunters and collectors known as Guachichiles, the Aztec word for sparrows, after their widespread custom of wearing only loincloths and, sometimes, pointed headdresses resembling sparrows' crowns.

A couple of Christian missions entered the southwest of the state in the 1570s and 1580s, but it was the discovery of silver in the Cerro de San Pedro hills that really awakened Spanish interest in that region. San Luis Potosí city was founded near these deposits in 1592. Cattle ranchers moved into the area in the 1590s too. Indians from farther south – Tlaxcalans, Tarascans and Otomíes – were brought to work the mines and haciendas.

In the 18th century the area had a reputation for maltreatment of Indians. This was partly because a number of parishes were transferred from the hands of the Franciscans, who did their best to protect the Indians, to the control of the secular (non-monk) clergy. In 1767 there was an uprising sparked by the appalling conditions in the mines and the discontent over the expulsion of the Jesuits, who ran the best schools in Mexico and managed their estates relatively well.

Under Spanish reforms in 1786, San Luis Potosí city became capital of a huge area covering the modern states of San Luis Potosí, Tamaulipas, Nuevo León, Coahuila and Texas. But this lasted only until Mexican independence, and in 1824 the state of San Luis Potosí was formed with its present area.

Today it's a fairly rich state; its silver mines, mostly in the northern area, are some of the richest in the country, and gold, copper, zinc and other minerals are also extracted. Other major sources of wealth are agriculture (maize, beans, wheat and cotton), livestock and industry, which is mainly concentrated in the capital city.

SAN LUIS POTOSÍ
pop 700,000; alt 1860m; ☎ 48

The state capital is the first major colonial city on the way south from Mexico's northeastern border. San Luis has played important roles in Mexican history, first as a silver-producing center, later as host to governments-in-exile and revolutionaries. Today its main importance is as a regional capital and center of industry, including brewing, textiles and metal foundries. San Luis is scruffier and less spectacular than Zacatecas, which is on an alternate route south from the USA, but its colonial heart has been preserved from industry. It has a

university and a fairly active cultural life, and its plazas, churches, museums, markets, cafés and restaurants all make it well worth some of your time if you're passing this way.

History
Founded in 1592, 20 km west of the silver deposits in the Cerro de San Pedro hills, San Luis is named Potosí after the immensely rich Bolivian silver town of that name, which the Spanish hoped it would rival.

Yields from the mines started to decline in the 1620s, but the city was well enough established as a ranching center to remain the major city of northeastern Mexico until overtaken by Monterrey at the start of the 20th century.

It was known in the 19th century for its lavish houses and luxury goods imported from the USA and Europe. And San Luis was twice the seat of President Benito Juárez's government during the French intervention of the 1860s. In 1910 the dictatorial President Porfirio Díaz jailed Francisco Madero, his liberal opponent in that year's presidential election, in San Luis. Bailed out after the election, Madero here hatched his Plan de San Luis Potosí – a strategy to depose Díaz – and announced it in San Antonio, Texas, in October 1910. The plan declared the recent election illegal, named Madero provisional president and designated November 20 as the day for Mexico to rise in revolt.

Orientation
Central San Luis Potosí is a flat, compact area, stretching about 600 meters from the Alameda park in the east to Plaza de los Fundadores and Plaza San Francisco in the west. Within this triangle lie two more main plazas, Plaza del Carmen and the Plaza de Armas. Hotels and restaurants are mainly in this central area, with most cheaper lodgings close to the Alameda, near the train station. There's a new bus station on the eastern edge of the city, about 2.5 km from the center. The old bus station with most 2nd- and 3rd-class

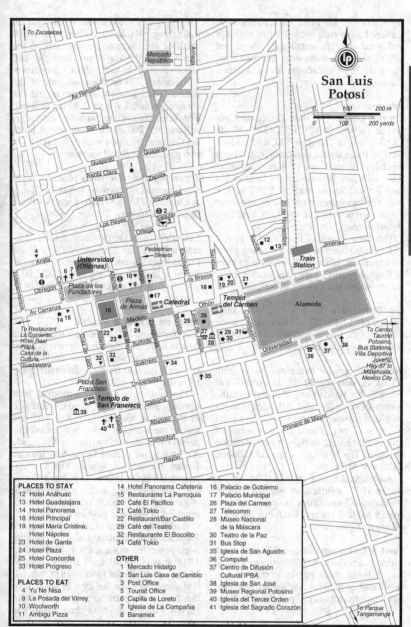

San Luis
Potosí

PLACES TO STAY
12 Hotel Anáhuac
13 Hotel Guadalajara
14 Hotel Panorama
18 Hotel Principal
19 Hotel María Cristina,
     Hotel Nápoles
23 Hotel de Gante
24 Hotel Plaza
25 Hotel Concordia
33 Hotel Progreso

PLACES TO EAT
4 Yu Ne Nisa
9 La Posada del Virrey
10 Woolworth
11 Ambigu Pizza

14 Hotel Panorama Cafetería
15 Restaurante La Parroquia
20 Café El Pacífico
21 Café Tokio
22 Restaurant/Bar Castillo
29 Café del Teatro
32 Restaurante El Bocolito
34 Café Tokio

OTHER
1 Mercado Hidalgo
2 San Luis Casa de Cambio
3 Post Office
5 Tourist Office
6 Capilla de Loreto
7 Iglesia de La Compañia
8 Banamex

16 Palacio de Gobierno
17 Palacio Municipal
26 Plaza del Carmen
27 Telecomm
28 Museo Nacional
     de la Máscara
30 Teatro de la Paz
31 Bus Stop
35 Iglesia de San Agustin
36 Computel
37 Centro de Difusión
     Cultural IPBA
38 Iglesia de San José
39 Museo Regional Potosino
40 Iglesia del Tercer Orden
41 Iglesia del Sagrado Corazón

service is 1.75 km in the same direction. A scattered zona rosa, with a bit of nightlife and some upscale restaurants, shops and offices, stretches some three km west from Plaza de los Fundadores along Avenida Carranza.

Information

Tourist Office The state Dirección General de Turismo (☎ 12-23-57, 12-99-39, fax 12-67-69) is at Obregón 520, half a block west of Plaza de los Fundadores. It's open weekdays from 8 am to 8 pm, Saturday 9 am to 1 pm. No one speaks English but they do sell tourist maps (US$0.70). Ask here for brochures with lots of ideas for getting off the beaten track in San Luis Potosí state.

The New Franklin Institute (☎ 11-65-47), at Justo Sierra 115, is a meeting place for expats and has a small library with titles in English. Justo Sierra runs south off Carranza, seven blocks west of Reforma.

US Consulate There's a US consular agency (☎ 12-15-28) at Mariel 103, south off Carranza, four blocks west of Reforma. It's open weekday mornings only.

Money There are numerous banks with ATMs around the Plaza de Armas and Plaza de los Fundadores. Banamex, on the corner of Obregón and Allende, changes cash and traveler's checks weekdays from 9 am to 2 pm. There are a number of money exchange offices near Mercado Hidalgo. Try San Luis Casa de Cambio, Salazar at Morelos.

American Express (☎ 17-60-04) at Carranza 1077, a little over one km west of Plaza de los Fundadores, is open weekdays from 9 am to 2 pm and 4 to 6 pm, Saturday 10 am to 1 pm.

Post & Communications The main post office is at Morelos 235 between Ortega and Salazar, three blocks north and one block east of the Plaza de Armas. It's open weekdays from 8 am to 7 pm, Saturday 9 am to 1 pm.

Pay phones are outside Woolworth on the Obregón/Hidalgo corner, one block north of the Plaza de Armas, and on the corner of 5 de Mayo and Iturbide, one block south of the same plaza. Computel at Universidad 700 on the south side of the Alameda has a telephone caseta and fax service, open daily from 7.30 am to 9 pm. The Telecomm office, with fax service, is at Escobedo 200 on the south side of Plaza del Carmen. It's open weekdays from 8 am to 6 pm, and weekend mornings.

Travel Agencies A handy place for flight arrangements is Solymar (☎ /fax 14-71-87) at Carranza 713, 400 meters west of Plaza de los Fundadores.

Laundry Lavandería Automática at Carranza 1093, 1.25 km west of Plaza de los Fundadores, is open daily from 9 am to 9 pm. A load of washing costs US$1.90 if you drop it off or US$1.50 if you do it yourself.

Plaza de Armas & Around

Also known as Jardín Hidalgo, the Plaza de Armas is the city's central square, popular for chatting and watching the world go by. It's fairly quiet as traffic is channeled away from it.

The three-nave baroque **Catedral**, built between 1660 and 1730, is on the east side of the plaza. Originally it had just one tower; the northern tower was added this century. The marble apostles on the façade are replicas of statues in the San Juan de Letrán Basilica in Rome. The interior, remodeled in the 19th century, has a Gothic feel, with sweeping arches carved in pink stone; the leaf motif on the arches is repeated in blue and gold on the ceiling.

Beside the cathedral, the 19th century **Palacio Municipal** is a stocky building with powerful stone arches. Finished in 1838, it was the home of Bishop Ignacio Montes de Oca from 1892 to 1915, when it was turned over to the city. In the rear of the building's patio is a stone fountain carved with the heads of three lions. The city's coat of arms in stained glass overlooks a double staircase.

The **Palacio de Gobierno**, built between 1798 and 1816, lines the west side of the plaza. Numerous important Mexicans have lodged here, including presidents Iturbide and Santa Anna, but its most illustrious occupant was Benito Juárez – first in 1863 when he was fleeing from invading French forces, then in 1867 when he confirmed the death sentence on French puppet emperor Maximilian. In the Sala Juárez, one of the upstairs rooms that Juárez occupied, are life-size models of Juárez and, kneeling before him, Princess Inés de Salm Salm, an American who had married into Maximilian's family and had come to San Luis in June 1867 to make one last plea for his life. The Sala Juárez is open Monday through Saturday from 9 am to 3 pm and 6 to 9 pm (free).

Plaza de los Fundadores & Around

The busy Founders' Plaza, also called Plaza Juárez, is where the city started. On the north side is a large building housing the offices of the **Universidad de San Luis Potosí**. It was probably on this site that Diego de la Magdalena, a Franciscan friar, started a small settlement of Guachichil Indians about 1585. The building, which has a lovely courtyard, was constructed in 1653 as a Jesuit college.

To the west is the **Iglesia de La Compañía**, also called del Sagrario, built by the Jesuits in 1675 with a baroque façade. A little farther west is the **Capilla de Loreto**, a Jesuit chapel from 1700 with unusual twisted pillars.

Plaza San Francisco & Around

Dominated by the red bulk of the Templo de San Francisco, this quiet square is one of the most beautiful in the city.

The interior of the 17th and 18th century **Templo de San Francisco** was remodeled this century but the sacristy (priest's dressing room), reached by a door to the right of the altar, is original and has a fine dome and carved pink stone. The Sala De Profundis,

through the arch at the south end of the sacristy, has more paintings and a stone fountain carved by Indians. A beautiful crystal ship hangs from the main dome.

The **Museo Regional Potosino** at Galeana 450, along the street to the west of Templo de San Francisco, was originally part of a Franciscan monastery founded in 1590. The ground floor has exhibits on pre-Hispanic Mexico, especially the Huastec Indians. Upstairs is the lavish Capilla de Aranzazú, an elaborate private chapel for the monks constructed in the mid-18th century. It is dedicated to the cult of the Virgin of Aranzazú: according to legend, a Spanish shepherd found a statue of the Virgin in a thorn bush and named it Aranzazú, a Basque word meaning 'Among thorns, you.' The museum is open Tuesday to Sunday from 10 am to 5 pm (free).

The small **Iglesia del Tercer Orden** and **Iglesia del Sagrado Corazón**, both formerly part of the Franciscan monastery, stand together at the south end of the plaza. Tercer Orden, on the right, was finished in 1694 and restored in 1959 and 1960. Sagrado Corazón dates from 1728 to 1731.

Plaza del Carmen

Plaza del Carmen is dominated by the **Templo del Carmen**, a Churrigueresque church built between 1749 and 1764 and the most spectacular building in San Luis. On the vividly carved stone façade, perching and hovering angels show the touch of Indian artisans. The Camarín de la Virgen, with a splendid golden altar, is to the left of the main altar inside. The entrance and roof of this chapel are a riot of small plaster figures.

The **Teatro de la Paz**, built between 1889 and 1894, is near the church. It contains a concert hall and exhibition gallery as well as a theater. Posters announce upcoming events; there's usually something on. The art gallery, Sala Germán Gedovius, is open Tuesday to Sunday from 10 am to 2 pm and 4 to 8 pm (free). Its entrance is to the right of the main theater entrance.

The **Museo Nacional de la Máscara** (National Mask Museum), in an attractive 19th century building on the south side of the plaza, has a big collection of ceremonial masks from many regions of Mexico, with explanations of the dances and rituals in which they are used. It's open Tuesday to Friday from 10 am to 2 pm and 4 to 6 pm, Saturday and Sunday 10 am to 2 pm (US$0.10).

Alameda & Around

The Alameda marks the eastern boundary of the downtown area. It used to be the vegetable garden of the monastery attached to the Templo del Carmen. Today it's a large, attractive park with shady paths.

Inside the **Iglesia de San José,** facing the south side of the Alameda, is the image of El Señor de los Trabajos, a Christ figure attracting pilgrims from near and far. Numerous retablos around the statue testify to miracles received in finding jobs, regaining health and so on.

The **Centro de Difusión Cultural IPBA** is a cultural center sponsored by the Instituto Potosino de Bellas Artes (Potosino Fine Arts Institute), in a large, modernistic building facing the south side of the Alameda. Inside are art galleries with changing exhibitions, and a theater. The galleries are open Tuesday to Saturday from 10 am to 2 pm and 5 to 8 pm, Sunday 10 am to 2 pm and 6 to 8 pm (free).

On Universidad, just over the railway bridge east of the Alameda, is the **Centro Taurino Potosino**, with the Plaza de Toros and, just along the street, a bullfighting museum with intricately decorated matador suits and capes, historical posters and photos, stuffed bulls' heads and more. The museum is only open when there's a bullfight.

Parque Tangamanga I

Two or three km southwest of the center, this large 3.3-sq-km park has a history museum, planetarium, outdoor theater, amusement park, two lakes, sports fields and acres of green open spaces. To get there, take a southbound 'Perimetral' bus,

or Bus No 25 or 26, from the west end of the Alameda.

Special Events

Among San Luis' many festivals are the following:

Semana Santa – Holy week is celebrated with concerts, exhibitions and other activities. On Good Friday morning Christ's passion is re-enacted in the barrio of San Juan de Guadalupe, followed by a silent procession through the city.

Festival de Arte Primavera Potosina – The Spring Arts Festival in the last two weeks of May (but not held every year), presents concerts, art exhibitions, theater, dance, films and more, with national and international artists. Check with the tourist office for dates.

Festival Nacional de Danza – This national festival of contemporary dance is held in the last two weeks of July.

Feria Nacional Potosina – The San Luis Potosí National Fair, normally in the last two weeks of August, includes concerts, bullfights, rodeos, cockfights and sports events, and livestock and agriculture shows.

San Luis Rey – On August 25, the Día de San Luis Rey de Francia (St Louis, King of France), the city's patron saint, various events are organized including a large parade with floats and *gigantes*, papier-mâché giants.

Places to Stay – budget

You'll enjoy San Luis Potosí more if you choose a hotel room in the pedestrianized center, away from the traffic fumes and in among the attractive architecture!

Hostel The *Villa Deportiva Juvenil* youth hostel (☎ 18-16-17) is on Avenida Diagonal Sur, around 700 meters west of the new bus station, just south of the big Glorieta Juárez intersection. From the bus station, turn left and walk to the glorieta. Turn left onto Avenida Diagonal Sur and across the road you'll see sports grounds where you'll find the hostel. Or take Bus No 10 from the new bus station.

Separate-sex dorms sleep four to a room at US$3 a person. There's an 11 pm curfew.

Hotels *Hotel Plaza* (☎ 12-46-31), Jardín Hidalgo 22, is in an 18th century building on the south side of the Plaza de Armas. The 32 singles/doubles have private bathrooms and cost US$9.75/10.50 or US$12/16 with color TV. The few at the front, overlooking the plaza, are the best. The others open onto two upstairs patios, but are dark, dilapidated and somewhat airless.

Hotel de Gante (☎ 12-14-92/93) at 5 de Mayo 140, half a block south of the Plaza de Armas, is much better. Large, bright, comfortable rooms with sizable bathrooms and color TV cost US$13/15.

Hotel Progreso (☎ /fax 12-03-66) nearby at Aldama 415 is another older place, with classic 1920s-looking statues of ladies that overlook the staircase and lobby. In its day it was probably an elegant place. The 51 rooms are larger than many and have high ceilings to add to the spacious feel. Some have been modernized, others haven't, but either way the price for most is US$9/9.75. There are a couple of superior modernized doubles/triples with TV for US$11/12.

Hotel Anáhuac (☎ 12-65-04/05, fax 14-49-04) at Xochitl 140, one block west and north of the train station, has 78 sizable, bright rooms for US$11/12, plus parking.

Hotel Guadalajara (☎ 12-46-12) at Jiménez 253, on the small plaza between the station and the Hotel Anáhuac, has enclosed parking and 33 clean, comfortable rooms with ample windows, color TV and fan. Cost is US$14.30 single, US$15 for a one-bed double, US$15.75 for two beds.

Hotel Principal (☎ 12-07-84) at Sarabia 145, three blocks west of the train station, has 18 reasonable rooms with private bath at US$6.50/9.25 for singles/doubles.

Places to Stay – middle

Hotel María Cristina (☎ 12-94-08, fax 12-88-23) and *Hotel Nápoles* (☎ 12-84-18, fax 12-22-60), side by side on Sarabia, a short block northwest of the Alameda, are almost twins in price – around US$23/26 for singles/doubles – and very similar in quality. Both have modern, comfortable, bright rooms with satellite color TV, carpeting and fans, parking and a restaurant.

Slightly more central and much the same price, *Hotel Concordia* (☎ 12-06-66, fax 12-69-79), on Othón at Morelos, is an older hotel but in a modern style; its 94 rooms all have color TV, carpeting and other amenities. Choose an exterior room if you can, as the interior ones can be a bit musty. Standard rooms cost US$22/25, suites from US$32. There's parking and an inexpensive restaurant.

Near the southwest corner of Plaza de los Fundadores, at Carranza 315, is the very comfortable 10-story *Hotel Panorama* (☎ 12-17-77, fax 12-45-91). All 126 rooms have floor-to-ceiling windows and most on the south side have private balconies overlooking the swimming pool. Singles/doubles are US$35/38. The hotel has a good 10th-floor restaurant, a piano bar, one of the city's best discos and a reasonable cafetería.

About 700 meters farther west at Carranza 890, *Hotel Real Plaza* (☎ 14-60-55, fax 14-66-39) is another semi-luxury hotel, with prices similar to the Panorama's.

Motel Sand's (☎ 18-24-13), charging US$22/24, is on highway 57 heading out of San Luis toward Mexico City, just beyond the new bus station.

Places to Stay – top end

On highway 57 to Mexico City about 500 meters out past the Glorieta Juárez intersection on the eastern edge of the city, *Hotel Real de Minas* (☎ 18-26-16, fax 18-69-15) has 178 rooms in landscaped grounds from US$45 to US$89. *Hotel María Dolores* (☎ 22-18-82, fax 22-06-02) is across the road. *Motel Cactus* (☎ 22-19-95), nearby on highway 57, charges US$61 a room and has a 24-hour restaurant.

Places to Eat

Center *Ambigu Pizza*, a bright little café at the northeast corner of the Plaza de Armas, serves up quick chicken and fries for US$2 to US$4 and respectable pizzas from US$2.75 to US$6.50. Just a few doors up Hidalgo and opposite, *Woolworth* is reliable and cheap.

La Posada del Virrey, also on Plaza de Armas, is a fancier restaurant in a former home of Spanish viceroys, built in 1736. It has an attractive covered courtyard with live music some lunchtimes. Breakfast specials are available and the comida corrida is US$3.75. Generous meat and seafood meals are US$3.50 to US$6.25. Cakes and desserts are good too. It's open daily from 7 am to midnight.

Restaurant/Bar Castillo at Madero 145, half a block west of the Plaza de Armas, is a cheaper spot for dining or just hanging out over coffee. There are no economical set breakfasts but the egg choices are generous, coming with beans and salad for US$2. Meat and chicken dishes are US$4.50 to US$5.25. It's open daily from 8 am to 11 pm.

Café Tokio on Guerrero at Zaragoza, two blocks south of the Plaza de Armas, is a large, clean restaurant good for all meals. (The original Café Tokio is near the Alameda – see below.) The comida corrida is US$3.75, antojitos US$3, meat and seafood meals US$3.75 to US$5.25. It's open daily from 7 am to 11 pm.

Restaurante La Parroquia at the southwest corner of Plaza de los Fundadores is also large and clean and is a popular choice. The four-course comida corrida is US$2.75, US$4.25 on Sundays. Many à la carte main dishes are US$2.75 to US$5.75. A huge buffet spread appears at breakfast (US$3.50) on Saturday and Sunday. It's open daily from 7 am to midnight.

Yu Ne Nisa is a small vegetarian restaurant in a covered patio behind the health food shop on Arista, one block north and half a block west of Plaza de los Fundadores. Open Monday to Saturday from 8.30 am to 8.30 pm, it offers a comida corrida for US$3, and sandwiches, quesadillas, gorditas and soyburgers from US$1.30 to US$2. Mouth-watering juices and smoothies too!

The friendly *Restaurante El Bocolito* at the northwest corner of Plaza San Francisco serves up huge platters of food with names like gringa, sarape and mula india, which are combinations of meats fried up with herbs, onion, chili, tomato and green pepper, often with melted cheese on top.

These cost around US$3.50. Tacos and cheap breakfasts (US$1.70 to US$2.25) are served too. It's open daily from 7.30 am to 10.30 pm and is a cooperative venture of the Casas José Martí, benefiting young Indian students.

Worth considering for a special dinner is the *Sky Room* restaurant on the 10th floor of the Hotel Panorama at Carranza 315. It serves an array of international dishes and its floor-to-ceiling windows offer a panoramic view of the city. There's dance music every night from 9 pm to 2 am; Sunday there's a pianist.

Plaza del Carmen & Alameda *Café del Teatro*, beside the Teatro de la Paz, is a quirky, inexpensive place, good for a coffee, a meal, a drink or all three. It becomes a venue for live music on weekends.

The large, air-con *Café Tokio* at Othón 415, facing the northwest corner of the Alameda, is the original branch of the central Café Tokio, with the same food, prices and hours. *Café El Pacífico* on Los Bravos at Constitución is in much the same mold.

Zona Rosa One of San Luis' most attractive eateries is *Restaurant La Corriente* at Carranza 700, 400 meters west of Plaza de los Fundadores. This fancy, plant-filled courtyard restaurant specializes in regional ranch-style food. A good four-course comida corrida – adaptable for vegetarians – is served for US$4.75 Monday to Saturday. À la carte main dishes are US$4.75 to US$6.50, antojitos (served from 7 pm only) are US$3.25. It's open daily from 8 am to midnight except Sunday when it closes at 6 pm. Sometimes there's music in the evenings.

Entertainment

San Luis has quite an active entertainment scene. Ask in the tourist office for what's going on and keep your eye out for posters. The Teatro de la Paz has something most nights and Sundays around noon; concerts, theater, exhibitions and other events are also presented at places

F STOPPELMAN

SCOTT DOGGETT

PETER PTSCHELINZEW

Top: Rodeo, Pachuca
Middle: Panco Villa's ex-hacienda at Canutillo, 80 km south of Parral
Bottom Left: Real de Catorce
Bottom Right: Guanajuato

Top Left: Voladores, El Tajín
Top Right: Hat Seller, Tlacotalpan
Middle: Coconuts for sale at roadside, north of Tampico
Bottom: Ices and juices, Veracruz

like the Centro de Difusión Cultural IPBA, the Teatro de la Ciudad in Parque Tangamanga I, and the Casa de la Cultura at Carranza 1815 about 2.5 km west of Plaza de los Fundadores. *Guiarte* schedules posted at some of these places give full listings of what's happening.

Café del Teatro, beside the Teatro de la Paz, has live blues, jazz or rock from 9 pm on Friday and Saturday, sometimes Thursday too (cover US$0.60). Two of the best discos are *La Jaula* in the Hotel Panorama (US$3.25), and *Sirocco*, usually open Thursday to Saturday nights and popular with students, in the Hotel María Dolores.

Things to Buy

Several handicraft shops are dotted around town. Probably best is *Fonart* next to the Templo de San Francisco, but most of its merchandise is from other parts of Mexico rather than San Luis. *La Casa del Artesano*, at Carranza 540, just before Reforma, stocks Potosino pottery, masks, woodwork and canework. The main area of shops is between the Plaza de Armas and the Mercado Hidalgo, four blocks north. Just a few blocks farther northeast is the larger, more interesting Mercado República.

Getting There & Away

Air The airport is 23 km north of the city on highway 57. Aeromar and United (☎ 17-79-36, 17-50-62) share an office at Carranza 1030. Aeromar flies to/from Mexico City several times daily. United has daily flights via México City to Chicago or New York. Aerolitoral (☎ 17-79-31, 18-73-71), at the airport, flies direct to/from Monterrey, Guadalajara and San Antonio (Texas) daily and Puerto Vallarta six days a week.

Bus San Luis Potosí is a major bus hub. The new bus station, Terminal Camionera, with all deluxe and 1st-class services plus 2nd-class Flecha Amarilla and Estrella Blanca services, is on highway 57, 2.5 km east of the center. It has coin pay phones inside, card pay phones out front, a tele-

phone caseta, luggage-storage (open 24 hours), an ATM and two restaurants. Some 700 meters nearer the center is the old bus station, on the corner of Avenida Diagonal Sur and José Guadalupe Torres, just south of the big Glorieta Juárez intersection. The old bus station has additional 2nd-class buses and also 3rd-class buses to local villages and small towns.

Daily departures include:

Guadalajara – 340 km, five hours; seven deluxe by ETN (US$19); 10 1st-class by Transportes del Norte (US$14); hourly 2nd-class by Estrella Blanca (US$13)

Guanajuato – 225 km, four hours; five 2nd-class by Flecha Amarilla (US$8)

Matehuala – 192 km, 2½ hours; hourly (roughly) 1st-class by Tamaulipas, and nine 1st-class by Transportes del Norte (US$6.75); hourly 2nd-class by Estrella Blanca/Aguilar los Altos (US$6)

Mexico City (Terminal Norte) – 417 km, five to six hours; 15 deluxe by ETN (US$22); many 1st-class by Primera Plus and others (US$16 to US$18); five 2nd-class by Flecha Amarilla (US$15)

Monterrey – 517 km, six to seven hours; 20 1st-class by Transportes Chihuahuenses and others (US$19); 12 2nd-class by Estrella Blanca (US$16)

Querétaro – 202 km, 2½ to three hours; deluxe by Turistar, Primera Plus and ETN (US$8.75 to US$11); frequent 1st-class by Futura and others (US$8); 16 2nd-class by Flecha Amarilla (US$7)

San Miguel de Allende – 180 km, four hours; six 2nd-class by Flecha Amarilla (US$6.75)

Zacatecas – 190 km, three hours; seven to 10 1st-class by Transportes Chihuahuenses, Futura and Ómnibus de México (US$6.75 to US$7.50); 15 2nd-class by Estrella Blanca (US$6.25)

There are also many buses to Aguascalientes, Ciudad Juárez, Ciudad Valles, Ciudad Victoria, Chihuahua, Dolores Hidalgo, León, Morelia, Nuevo Laredo, Saltillo, Tampico and Torreón.

Train The Estación del Ferrocarril is on the north side of the Alameda. The main trains are El Regiomontano, train Nos 71 and 72, all running between Mexico City and Monterrey with primera clase and, on weekends, coches dormitorios; and train Nos 1 and 2 between Mexico City and Nuevo Laredo, with primera and segunda clase seats. See Mexico City Getting There & Away for schedules and fares to the capital – but trains are often late, so check at the station.

Tickets for El Regiomontano are sold only between 10.30 am and 12.30 pm. Tickets for other trains go on sale one hour before departure. Fare to Monterrey on El Regiomontano (primera preferente/one-person camarín) is US$12/26. Fares on train Nos 1 and 2 (segunda/primera clase) are US$2.50/4.25 to San Miguel de Allende and US$11/20 to Nuevo Laredo.

Car & Motorcycle Car rental agencies include Budget (☎ 22-18-12) in the Hotel María Dolores, Dollar (☎ 22-14-11) or Hertz (☎ 14-26-00).

Getting Around

To/From the Airport Taxi Aéreo (☎ 12-21-22) runs a colectivo to/from the airport for US$7.75 per person, but for two or more people a taxi (about the same price) is cheaper for the half-hour trip.

Bus City buses run from 6.30 am to 10.30 pm; they cost US$0.20. To reach the center from the new bus station, walk out front and take any 'Centro' bus. No 10 is the most direct. A convenient place to get off is on the Alameda, outside the train station. Returning from the city to the new bus station, take a 'Central' bus southbound on Constitución on the west side of the Alameda. Many of these also stop outside the old bus station en route.

For places along Carranza, pick up a 'Morales' or 'Carranza' bus in front of the train station or anywhere on Carranza west of Reforma, 400 meters west of Plaza de los Fundadores.

SANTA MARÍA DEL RÍO
pop 10,000; ☎ 485

Forty-seven km south of San Luis Potosí, just off the highway to Mexico City, this small town is known for its excellent hand-made rebozos and inlaid woodwork. The rebozos are usually made of synthetic silk thread called *artisela*, in less garish colors than in many Mexican textile centers. You can see and buy them at the Escuela del Rebozo (Rebozo School) on the central Plaza Hidalgo, and in a few private workshops. A Rebozo Fair is held each year in the first half of August. There's a motel and restaurant, the *Puesta del Sol* (☎ 3-00-59), at the entrance to Santa María from the highway. Autobuses Rojos and Autobuses Potosinos run frequent buses to Santa María from the old bus station in San Luis Potosí for US$1.

GOGORRÓN

The Balneario de Gogorrón is the major hot springs resort in the San Luis area; its waters reach 42°C and are allegedly beneficial for rheumatism and arthritis. It's 56 km south of the city on the Villa de Reyes-San Felipe road, which branches southwest off highway 57. Facilities include four large swimming pools, two children's pools, private Roman baths, large green areas, basketball and volleyball courts and horseback riding. The resort is open daily from 9 am to 6 pm; cost for day use is US$2.75 (children US$2).

If you want to stay over, there are comfortable bungalows. Including three meals a day, the cost for two adults is US$59 in a smaller bungalow, US$76 in a large one. The bungalows have private Roman baths.

You can get more information and make reservations at the Gogorrón office (☎ 12-36-36, 12-15-50), in the same building as the tourist office at Obregón 520 in San Luis Potosí. It's open weekdays from 9 am to 2 pm and 4 to 7 pm, Saturday 9 am to 1 pm.

Getting There & Away

Gogorrón can easily be visited in a day from San Luis. From the new bus station, Autobuses Rojos runs half-hourly to Gogorrón for US$1.60, or you could take a Flecha Amarilla bus heading for San Felipe. It takes about an hour to reach Gogorrón and the bus will drop you off right at the gate.

MATEHUALA
pop 60,000; alt 1600m; ☎ 488

The only town of any size on highway 57 between Saltillo and San Luis Potosí, Matehuala ('ma-te-WAL-a') is an unremarkable but quite pleasant and prosperous place high on the Altiplano Central. It was founded in the 17th century and its central streets have a colonial air. Most travelers just use it to get to Real de Catorce.

Orientation
Central Matehuala lies between two plazas about 400 meters apart: the shady Plaza de Armas with a kiosk in the middle, and the bustling Placita del Rey to the north, with a large concrete church. Cheaper hotels and the town's restaurants are in this area; motels are on highway 57, which bypasses the town to the east. Between the center and highway 57 is the shady Parque Vicente Guerrero.

The bus station is just off the highway, about two km south of the center. To walk to the center from the bus station, turn left out of the entrance, then go straight along the road (5 de Mayo) for about 1.5 km until you reach the corner of Guerrero, where you turn left. Guerrero ends after a few blocks when it meets Morelos. The Plaza de Armas is a few meters to the left along Morelos.

Information
You'll find a few banks with ATMs on Hidalgo. Bancomer, open weekdays from 8.30 am to 2.30 pm and 4 to 5 pm, Saturday 10 am to 2 pm, will change cash or traveler's checks. There are also money exchange offices on this street – San Luis Divisa has reasonable rates and is open long hours. There are a couple of pay phones on Placita del Rey and a telephone caseta in Restaurant Domi on Morelos near the Plaza de Armas. Telecomm, for fax service, is on the corner of Jaime Nunó and Juárez.

Places to Stay
In Town The place with the most atmosphere, *Hotel Matehuala* (☎ 2-06-80) on the corner of Bustamante and Hidalgo, has

become run-down, but it's close to the departure point for buses to Real de Catorce. The dark, dingy rooms are on two levels, set around a large, covered courtyard. Singles/doubles cost US$7.75/9.25.

Hotel Alamo (☎ 2-00-17) on Guerrero is slightly brighter and even closer to the buses for Real de Catorce. Rooms cost US$6/7.75, or US$11 for a twin. The best budget place is the family-run *Hotel María Esther* (☎ 2-07-14) on Madero. It has singles/doubles with private bath, TV, parking and a restaurant at only US$8.50/10.25. The best rooms are off a little plant-filled patio out back.

NORTHERN CENTRAL HIGHLANDS

Matehuala map:
Nunó
Telecomm
Hotel María Esther
Madero
To Parque Vicente Guerrero
Constitución
Church
Placita del Rey
Reyes
Hidalgo
Morelos
Banca Serfin
Bancomer
San Luís Divisa
Bustamante
Hotel Matehuala
Restaurant Fontella
To Buses to Real de Catorce, Main Bus Station
Guerrero
Restaurant Domi
Hotel Alamo
Plaza de Armas
Restaurant Santa Fe
Insurgentes
Matehuala
Not to Scale

On the Highway Several '60s-style motels dot highway 57 as it passes Matehuala to the east. They include, from north to south, the *Hacienda* (☎ 2-00-65) where rooms are US$19/20; *Las Palmas* (☎ 2-00-02), with a camping area/trailer park at US$11 per person with full hookups, and very nice rooms around landscaped gardens with a pool from US$34/43; and the *El Dorado* (☎ 2-01-74) at US$18/22. The Hacienda and Las Palmas have restaurants.

Places to Eat

Restaurant Santa Fe, on the Plaza de Armas, is clean, friendly and reasonably priced, and serves generous portions of good plain food. Tasty tacos are US$0.70 and less; meat dishes are US$2.25 to US$4.75. A comida corrida is around US$2.50. It's also a good place for an inexpensive breakfast.

Nearby, at Morelos 618, the relaxed *Restaurant Fontella* does a reasonable four-course comida corrida plus coffee for US$2.75 and has good regional dishes.

Getting There & Away

Bus There are fairly frequent 1st- and 2nd-class buses north and south, but Matehuala is mid-route for most of them so you can usually only buy tickets when the bus arrives. Daily departures include:

Mexico City (Terminal Norte) – 609 km, eight hours; some 1st-class directo (US$24) and many 2nd-class de paso (US$21)

Monterrey – 325 km, five hours; 1st-class (US$12) and 2nd-class (US$11)

Saltillo – 261 km, four hours; 1st-class (US$11) and 2nd-class (US$8.75)

San Luis Potosí – 192 km, 2½ hours; 1st-class (US$6.75) and 2nd-class (US$6)

Americanos has 1st-class weekend service to San Antonio, Houston and Dallas.

Real de Catorce Buses for Real de Catorce leave at 6, 8 and 10 am, noon, and 2 and 6 pm from Guerrero, a little to the east of and across the street from the Hotel Alamo. The one-way fare is US$2.25 and the journey takes at least 1¼ hours. It's a good idea to buy your ticket an hour before

departure time. If you buy a roundtrip ticket, note the time stated for the return journey – you may have difficulty getting on a bus at a different time! Buses depart Real de Catorce for Matehuala at 8 am, noon, and 2, 4 and 6 pm.

Getting Around

Beige buses marked 'Centro' run from the bus station to the town center but aren't very frequent; buses marked 'Central' go the other way. It can be quicker to walk (25 minutes).

REAL DE CATORCE
pop 1000; alt 2756m

This is a place with a touch of magic in an offshoot of the Sierra Madre Oriental. Real de Catorce was a wealthy and important silver-mining town of 40,000 people until early this century. Thirty km west of Matehuala, reached by a road tunnel through former mine shafts, the town lies in a narrow valley at a high elevation, with spectacular views westward to the plain below.

A few years ago the town was almost deserted, its paved streets lined with decaying or boarded-up stone houses, its mint a ruin and only a few hundred people eking out an existence from old mine workings or from visiting pilgrims. Pilgrims still come to pay homage to the figure of Saint Francis of Assisi in the town's church, and the festival of San Francisco, on October 4, attracts between 100,000 and 200,000 people between September 25 and October 12. Recently, Real has begun to attract trendier residents – wealthy Mexicans and gringos looking for an unusual retreat – and a few Europeans setting up hotels and restaurants. Filmmakers use the town and the surrounding hills; some artists have settled here; and old buildings are being restored. One day the town may well become another Taxco or San Miguel de Allende.

The Huichol Indians, who live 400 km away on the Durango-Nayarit-Jalisco-Zacatecas borders, believe that their peyote and maize gods live here. Every May or June they make a pilgrimage to the hills around Catorce, known to them as Wírikuta, for rituals involving peyote. This hallucinogenic cactus has great cultural and religious significance, and its indiscriminate use by foreigners is regarded as obnoxious and offensive.

You can take a day trip to Real de Catorce from Matehuala, but it's worth staying a few days to explore the surrounding hills and soak up the atmosphere.

History

The name Real de Catorce literally means 'Royal of 14': the '14' probably comes from 14 soldiers killed by Indians in the area about 1700. The town was founded in the mid-18th century, and the church was built between 1783 and 1817.

The mines had their ups and downs. During the independence war years (1810 to 1821) some of the shafts were flooded and in 1821 and 1822 an Englishman, Robert Phillips, made a yearlong journey from London to Catorce bringing a 'steam machine' for pumping the water out of the mines.

Real de Catorce reached its peak in the late 19th century when it was producing an estimated US$3 million in silver a year. It had a theater and a bullring, and shops that sold imported European goods. A number of large houses from this period of opulence are still standing. The dictator Porfirio Díaz journeyed here from Mexico City in 1895 to inaugurate two mine pumps purchased from California. Díaz had to travel by train, then by mule-carriage and then on horseback to reach Catorce.

Just why Catorce was transformed into a ghost town within three decades is a bit of a mystery. Locals in the town will tell you that during the revolution years (1910 to 1920) *bandidos* took refuge here and scared away the other inhabitants. The official state tourist guidebook explains, perhaps more plausibly, that the price of silver slumped after 1900.

Orientation & Information

The bus from Matehuala drops you at the end of the 2.3-km Ogarrio tunnel, from where the town spreads out before you. If you drive yourself, leave your car in the dusty open space here – local kids will hassle you to watch it all day for a few pesos. A stony street, Lanza Gorta, leads straight ahead (west), through a row of souvenir stalls, to the church at the center. There's one telephone caseta in town, on the north side of the plaza near the church. To change cash or traveler's checks, head to Mini-Super San Francisco at Ramón Corona 6, near the corner of Allende off Plaza Hidalgo. It's open from 8 am to 8 pm daily.

Parroquia

The parish church is quite an impressive neoclassical building but it's the reputedly miraculous image of St Francis of Assisi on one of the side altars that is the attraction for thousands of Mexican pilgrims. A cult has grown up this century around the statue, whose help is sought in solving problems. Some believe it can cleanse them of their sins.

In a separate area in the back of the church are walls covered with retablos. These usually have a simple depiction of some life-threatening situation from which St Francis has rescued the victim, and include a brief description of the incident and some words of prayer and gratitude. Car accidents and medical operations are common themes. Retablos have become much sought after by collectors and are sometimes seen in antique or souvenir shops. Many of those on sale have been stolen from old churches, which must be very bad karma.

Casa de la Moneda

Opposite the façade of the church, the old mint is used for weekend art exhibitions. Coins were minted here for a few years in the 1860s. It is in bad repair – restoration is being considered.

Plaza Hidalgo

Farther west along Lanza Gorta, past the church and mint, you reach some steps going up from the right side of the street to this small plaza, which is terraced into the hillside. The plaza was constructed in 1888 with a fountain in the middle; the kiosk you see now replaced the fountain in 1927. Around the plaza are a few pleasant restaurants.

Palenque de Gallos & Plaza de Toros

A block or so northwest of the plaza lies a monument to the town's heyday – a cock-fighting ring built like a Roman amphitheater. It was restored in the 1970s and sometimes hosts theater or dance performances. It's normally locked – ask around for the key. Farther up the hill on Calle Zaragoza you reach the edge of the town. Here you'll find the Panteón (graveyard), which is worth a look, and the bullring (Plaza de Toros), which has recently been restored.

Museum

On Lanza Gorta, facing one of the sides of the church, is a small museum containing photos, documents and other miscellanea rescued from the crumbling town, including an ancient, rusting car, said to have been the first to reach Catorce. It's supposed to be open Friday and Saturday from 9 am to 4 pm.

Horseback Riding & Walking

Numerous trails lead out into the stunning countryside around Real de Catorce. Ask at Plaza Hidalgo about arranging to rent a horse (US$4 per hour plus the cost of a guide). Or seek out the enigmatic character with pigtails who operates out of the hotel El Real from December to July. Ask at Mini-Super San Francisco about jeeps from Real to Estación de Catorce on the edge of the desert (US$2 per person). From here you can head off to explore. Or, if you prefer, simply walk out from Real.

Places to Stay & Eat

Real de Catorce has cheap casas de huéspedes, which cater mainly to pilgrims, and some attractive mid-range places in restored buildings. The high season includes Semana Santa, July/August, early October

and Christmas/New Year. Reservations can be made through the one telephone caseta in town, ☎ 488-2-37-33.

On Lanza Gorta between the bus stop and the church, *Casa de Huéspedes La Providencia* has basic singles or doubles for US$6.50, US$13 for a twin and some new rooms with fine views down the valley for US$26 and US$32. The attached restaurant does a comida corrida for US$2.50.

At Lanza Gorta 11, one block after the church, *Mesón de Abundancia* is a newly renovated place run by a young Swiss/Mexican couple. Of the 10 rooms, three have great views – others, in the 19th century part of the building, are very quaint. All are large and decorated with local crafts. The price for singles/doubles is US$11/17. We breakfasted well here for US$2.

El Real, at Morelos 20, uphill from the Abundancia, is an old house restored to provide a few comfortable, tastefully decorated bedrooms at US$18 single or double, plus doubles at US$21. There's an attractive medium-priced restaurant serving Italian, vegetarian and Mexican food.

Farther up Morelos, on the corner of Constitución, *El Corral de Conde* has six very comfortable rooms in a tastefully restored old house. Doubles cost US$26, rooms with four beds US$39. Along from here at Constitución 21, *Hospedaje Familiar* is clean with OK budget rooms (shared bathroom) at US$5.25 for singles or one-bed doubles, US$11 for a twin.

On the far side of town, on Zaragoza, is the *Quinta La Puesta Del Sol*, with little old-world charm but a superb view down the valley to the west. Singles/doubles with private bath cost US$16/20, suites US$24.

There are a couple of excellent but not especially cheap places to eat on and near Plaza Hidalgo. *El Cactus Café* on the plaza (open evenings and weekends) and the more expensive *Eucalipto* (weekends only), up the small street northwest of the plaza, both do good Italian food.

More standard fare is available on Allende, south off the plaza. *Teresa's* is good for coffee and whatever food she's whipped up. *Restaurant San Francisco*, on Allende at Ramón Corona, offers a good comida corrida for US$2.

Getting There & Away
Bus See Matehuala.

Train Estación de Catorce is at the bottom of the hill, down a very rough road about 17 km west of town. Very slow segunda clase trains pass through here – strictly for campesinos, rail enthusiasts or those on rock-bottom budgets. A train leaves San Luis Potosí at 5.30 pm and takes 3½ to five hours (US$2.50). Jeeps from Real de Catorce sometimes meet the train. (If stuck, you can probably rent a room for a couple of dollars in Estación de Catorce.)

Car & Motorcycle From highway 57 north of Matehuala, turn off to Cedral, 20 km west on a mostly paved road. From Matehuala you can take a back road to Cedral and avoid going out onto the highway. After Cedral, turn south to reach Catorce on what must be one of the longest cobblestone streets in the world. It's a slow but spectacular drive, up a steep mountainside, past various abandoned buildings. The Ogarrio tunnel, part of the old mine, is only wide enough for one vehicle; men stationed at each end with telephones control traffic and collect a US$1 toll as you go in. You may have to wait up to 20 minutes for traffic in the opposite direction to pass. If it's really busy, you may have to leave your car at the tunnel entrance and continue to Catorce on a minibus.

Guanajuato

The state of Guanajuato has historically been one of Mexico's richest. After silver was found in Zacatecas, Spanish prospectors combed the rugged lands north of Mexico City and were rewarded by discoveries of silver, gold, iron, lead, zinc and tin. For two centuries 30% to 40% of the world's silver was mined in Guanajuato. Silver barons in Guanajuato city lived opulent lives at the expense of Indians who worked the mines, first as slave labor and then as wage slaves.

Eventually the well-heeled criollo class of Guanajuato and Querétaro states began to resent the dominance and arrogance of the Spanish-born in the colony. After the occupation of much of Spain by Napoleon Bonaparte's troops in 1808 and subsequent political confusion in Mexico, some provincial criollos began – while meeting as 'literary societies' – to draw up plans for rebellion.

The house of a member of one such group in Querétaro city was raided on September 13, 1810. Three days later a colleague, parish priest Miguel Hidalgo, declared independence in Dolores, Guanajuato. After Dolores, San Miguel de Allende was the first town to fall to the rebels, Celaya the second, Guanajuato the third. Guanajuato state is proud to have given birth to Mexico's most glorious moment and is visited almost as a place of pilgrimage by people from far and wide.

Today, Guanajuato state – in addition to the quaint colonial towns of Guanajuato and San Miguel de Allende, which are its major attractions – has some important industrial centers like León (famous for its shoes and other leather goods), Salamanca (with a big oil refinery), Celaya and Irapuato. It's also a fertile agricultural state, producing grains, vegetables and fruit – the strawberries grown around Irapuato are famous. And it's still an important source of silver, gold and fluorspar. The state is thriving under the leadership of the PAN governor, Vicente Fox Quesada, a possible presidential candidate for the year 2000. It has the lowest unemployment rate in Mexico, and an export rate three times the national average.

GUANAJUATO
pop 110,000; alt 2017m; ☎ 473
Guanajuato is a city crammed onto the steep slopes of a ravine, with underground

tunnels acting as streets. This impossible topography was settled in 1559 because the silver and gold mines found here were among the richest in the world. Many of the colonial structures built from this wealth remain intact, making Guanajuato a living monument to a prosperous, turbulent past.

But it's not only the past that resounds from Guanajuato's narrow cobbled streets. The University of Guanajuato, known for its arts programs, attracts over 15,000 students each year, giving the city a youthfulness, vibrancy and cultural life that are as interesting to the visitor as the colonial architecture and exotic setting. The city's choice of cultural events peaks during the Festival Internacional Cervantino, held in October each year.

History

One of the hemisphere's richest veins of silver was uncovered in 1558 at La Valenciana Mine, five km north of Guanajuato. For 250 years, the excavation of a location that is now the northern periphery of the city produced 20% of the world's silver. Colonial barons benefiting from this mineral treasure were infuriated when King Carlos III of Spain slashed their share of the wealth in 1765. The king's 1767 decree banishing Jesuits from Spanish dominions further alienated both the wealthy barons and the poor Indian miners, who held allegiance to the Jesuits.

This anger found a focus in the War of Independence. In 1810 the priest and rebel leader Miguel Hidalgo – whose Grito (Cry for Independence) in nearby Dolores set off Mexico's independence movement – took Guanajuato with the assistance of its citizens. It was the first military victory of the independence rebellion. When the Spaniards eventually retook the city they retaliated by conducting the infamous 'lottery of death,' in which names of Guanajuato citizens were drawn at random and the 'winners' were tortured and hanged.

Independence was eventually won, freeing the silver barons to amass further wealth. From this wealth arose the mansions, churches and theaters that ensure Guanajuato's place as one of Mexico's most handsome cities.

Orientation

Guanajuato's central area is quite compact, with only a few major streets. The main street, running roughly west-east, is called Juárez from the Mercado Hidalgo to the basilica on Plaza de la Paz, then Obregón from the basilica to the Jardín de la Unión, the city's main plaza, then Sopeña as it continues east.

Roughly parallel to Juárez and Obregón is another long street, running from the Alhóndiga to the university, and bearing the names 28 de Septiembre, Galarza, Positos and Lascuraín de Retana along the way. Hidalgo, also called Cantarranas, paralleling Sopeña, is another important street. Once you know these streets you can't get lost in the center. You can, however, have a great time getting lost among the city's *callejones* – the maze of narrow, crooked alleys winding up the hills from the center.

Another twist on getting around the city is that several of the major roadways are underground. These are only used by vehicular traffic, however. Many were created along the dried-up bed of the Río Guanajuato, which was diverted elsewhere after it flooded the city in 1905.

Information

Tourist Office The tourist office (☎ 2-15-74, 2-82-75, fax 2-42-51), in a courtyard at Plaza de la Paz 14 almost opposite the basilica, has a large 'Información Turística' sign. The friendly staff, mostly English-speaking, give out free city maps and brochures (in Spanish and English) about the city and state of Guanajuato. The office is open weekdays from 8.30 am to 7.30 pm, Saturday and Sunday from 10 am to 2 pm.

Money There are a number of banks with ATMs on Plaza de la Paz and Juárez, open weekdays from 9 am to 5 pm, though some will only change cash and traveler's checks

NORTHERN CENTRAL HIGHLANDS

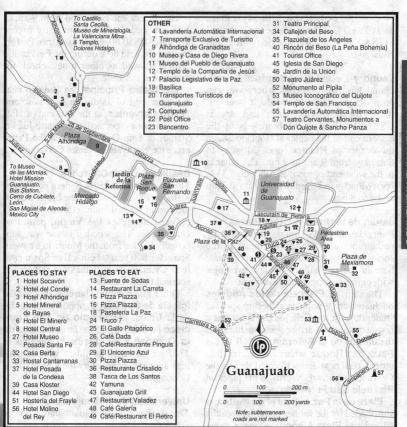

OTHER
4 Lavandería Automática Internacional
7 Transporte Exclusivo de Turismo
9 Alhóndiga de Granaditas
10 Museo y Casa de Diego Rivera
11 Museo del Pueblo de Guanajuato
12 Templo de la Compañía de Jesús
17 Palacio Legislativo de la Paz
19 Basílica
20 Transportes Turísticos de
    Guanajuato
21 Computel
22 Post Office
23 Bancentro
31 Teatro Principal
34 Callejón del Beso
35 Plazuela de los Ángeles
40 Rincón del Beso (La Peña Bohemia)
45 Iglesia de San Diego
50 Teatro Juárez
52 Monumento al Pípila
53 Museo Iconográfico del Quijote
54 Templo de San Francisco
55 Lavandería Automática Internacional
57 Teatro Cervantes, Monumentos a
    Don Quijote & Sancho Panza

Guanajuato

0   100   200 m
0   100   200 yards
Note: subterranean
roads are not marked

PLACES TO STAY
1 Hotel Socavón
2 Hotel del Conde
3 Hotel Alhóndiga
5 Hotel Mineral
   de Rayas
6 Hotel El Minero
8 Hotel Central
27 Hotel Museo
    Posada Santa Fé
32 Casa Berta
33 Hostal Cantarranas
37 Hotel Posada
    de la Condesa
39 Casa Kloster
44 Hotel San Diego
51 Hostería del Frayle
56 Hotel Molino
    del Rey

PLACES TO EAT
13 Fuente de Sodas
14 Restaurant La Carreta
15 Pizza Piazza
16 Pizza Piazza
18 Pastelería La Paz
24 Truco 7
25 El Gallo Pitagórico
26 Café Dada
28 Café/Restaurante Pinguis
29 El Unicornio Azul
30 Pizza Piazza
36 Restaurante Crisaldo
38 Tasca de Los Santos
42 Yamuna
47 Restaurant Valadez
48 Café Galería
49 Café/Restaurant El Retiro

from 9 am to 2 pm. Bancentro, opposite the state tourist office, is convenient and relatively quick. Intercambio Dólares at Juárez 33A, a casa de cambio with reasonable rates, is open weekdays from 9 am to 3 pm and 4.30 to 7 pm. The American Express agent is at Viajes Georama, Plaza de la Paz 34.

Post & Communications The main post office is at the eastern end of Lascuraín de Retana, opposite the Templo de la Compañía. It's open weekdays from 8 am to 7 pm, Saturday 8 am to 1 pm. There's another post office in the bus station.

There are pay phones in Pasaje de los Arcos, an alley off the south side of Obregón in the center. Computel, with a telephone caseta and fax service, is opposite the post office, a few doors farther south on Hidalgo. It's open Monday to Saturday from 8 am to 9 pm and Sunday from 10 am to 6 pm. The telephone caseta in the bus station is open 24 hours.

Travel Agencies You can purchase air tickets from agencies such as Viajes Frausto Guanajuato (☎ 2-35-80, fax 2-66-20) at Obregón 10, between the Jardín de la Unión and the basilica; Viajes Georama

(☎ 2-59-09, 2-51-01, fax 2-19-54) at Plaza de la Paz 34, in front of the basilica; and SITSA, in the Aeroméxico office at Hidalgo 6.

Laundry Lavandería Automática Internacional has two branches where you can drop off your laundry or do it yourself. (Cost for a service wash and dry is US$3.50 a load). One branch is at the eastern end of the center at Doblado 28, on the corner of Hidalgo, open Monday to Saturday from 9 am to 9 pm. The other is in the west end of town at Alhóndiga 35A, open Monday to Saturday from 9 am to 2 pm and 4 to 8 pm.

Jardín de la Unión & Other Plazas

Pretty Jardín de la Unión, surrounded by restaurants and shaded by trees, is the social heart of the city. People congregate here in the late afternoons and evenings, with guitarists serenading everyone.

The steps of **Plazuela de los Ángeles** on Juárez are a popular gathering spot for students, with the Callejón del Beso just a few steps away. Farther west on Juárez is the **Jardín de la Reforma**; just off this is **Plaza San Roque**, where *entremeses* (theatrical sketches) are performed during the Cervantino festival. Nearby is the pleasant **Plazuela San Fernando**.

Plaza de la Paz, in front of the basilica, is surrounded by the former homes of wealthy silver lords. **Plaza Alhóndiga**, on the corner of 28 de Septiembre and 5 de Mayo in front of the Alhóndiga, is quite bare.

Teatro Juárez & Other Theaters

Opposite the Jardín de la Unión stands the magnificent Teatro Juárez, built between 1873 and 1903. It was inaugurated by the dictator Porfirio Díaz, whose lavish yet refined tastes are reflected in the interior. The outside is festooned with columns, lampposts and statues; inside the impression is Moorish, with the bar and lobby gleaming with carved wood, stained glass and precious metals. The steps outside are a popular place to view the street theater down below.

The theater can be visited from 9 am to 1.45 pm and 5 to 7.45 pm daily except Monday (US$0.60, cameras extra). Performances are held here during the Cervantino festival as well as other times; check for the current schedule.

The **Teatro Principal**, on Hidalgo near the other end of Jardín de la Unión, and **Teatro Cervantes**, at the east end of Hidalgo, are not as spectacular as Teatro Juárez. Statues of Don Quijote and Sancho Panza grace the courtyard of Teatro Cervantes.

Basilica & Other Churches

The Basílica de Nuestra Señora de Guanajuato, on Plaza de la Paz, one block west of the Jardín de la Unión, contains a jewel-covered image of the Virgin, patron of Guanajuato. The wooden statue was supposedly hidden from the Moors in a cave in Spain for 800 years. Felipe II of Spain gave it to Guanajuato in thanks for riches that accrued to the Crown.

Other fine colonial churches include the **Iglesia de San Diego**, opposite the Jardín de la Unión, the **Templo de San Francisco** on Sopeña and the large **Templo de la Compañía de Jesús**, completed in 1747 for the Jesuit seminary whose buildings are now occupied by the University of Guanajuato.

Universidad de Guanajuato

The University of Guanajuato, whose green ramparts are visible above much of the city, is on Lascuraín de Retana one block up the hill from the basilica. It is considered one of Mexico's finest schools for music and theater. The buildings originally housed a large Jesuit seminary.

The university includes three art galleries – the Salas de Exposiciones Hermenegildo Bustos and Polivalente on the ground floor of the main building, and the Sala de Exposiciones El Atrio under the front courtyard of La Compañia church next door. On the fourth floor of the university building is the Museo de Historia Natural Alfredo Dugés, honoring one of the university's foremost naturalists. The extensive collection of preserved and stuffed animals, birds, reptiles and insects includes some freaks, such as a two-headed goat.

Museo del Pueblo de Guanajuato

Opposite the university at Positos 7, this art museum has a collection ranging from colonial to modern times. The museum occupies the former mansion of the Marqueses de San Juan de Rayas who owned the San Juan de Rayas mine. The private church in the courtyard contains a powerful mural by José Chávez Morado. The museum is open Monday to Saturday from 10 am to 7 pm, Sunday from 10 am to 3 pm (US$1.10).

Museo y Casa de Diego Rivera

The birthplace of Diego Rivera, today a museum honoring the painter, is at Positos 46 between the university and the Alhóndiga. Rivera and a twin brother were born in this house in 1886 (his twin died at the age of two). The family moved to Mexico City when he was six years old.

In conservative Guanajuato, where Catholic influence prevails, the Marxist Rivera was *persona non grata* for years. The city now honors its once blacklisted son with a small collection of his work in this house where he was born. The first floor contains the Rivera family's 19th century antiques and fine furniture. On the second and third floors are some 70 to 80 paintings and sketches by the master, including Indian and peasant portraits, a nude of Frida Kahlo and sketches for some of Rivera's memorable murals.

Hours are Tuesday to Saturday from 10 am to 6.30 pm, Sunday 10 am to 2.30 pm (US$1.10).

Alhóndiga de Granaditas

The Alhóndiga de Granaditas on 28 de Septiembre, site of the first major rebel victory in Mexico's War of Independence, is now a history and art museum.

A massive grain-and-seed storehouse built between 1798 and 1808, in 1810 the Alhóndiga became a fortress for Spanish troops and loyalist leaders. They barricaded themselves inside when 20,000 rebels led by Miguel Hidalgo attempted to take Guanajuato. It looked as if the outnumbered Spaniards would be able to hold out. Then, on September 28, 1810, a young Indian miner named Juan José de los Reyes Martínez (better known as El Pípila), under orders from Hidalgo, set the gates ablaze before succumbing to a hail of bullets. While the Spaniards choked on smoke, the rebels moved in and took the Alhóndiga, killing most of those inside.

The Spaniards later took their revenge: the heads of four leaders of the rebellion – Aldama, Allende, Jiménez and Hidalgo himself, who was executed in Chihuahua – were hung outside the Alhóndiga from 1811 to 1821. The long black hooks that held the metal cages in which the heads hung can still be seen at the top of the four outer corners of the building. The Alhóndiga was used as a prison for a century, beginning in 1864. It became a museum in 1967. Historical sections of the museum cover Guanajuato's pre-Hispanic past, its great flood of 1905 and modern times. There's also a fine art gallery that houses a permanent collection as well as temporary exhibits. Don't miss Chávez Morado's dramatic murals of Guanajuato's history on the staircases.

Open hours are Tuesday to Saturday from 10 am to 1.30 pm and 4 to 5.30 pm, Sunday from 10 am to 2.30 pm (US$1.90, free on Sunday).

Callejón del Beso

The narrowest of the many narrow alleys, or callejones, that climb the hills from Guanajuato's main streets is Callejón del Beso, where the balconies of the houses on either side of the alley practically touch. In Guanajuatan legend, lovers living on opposite sides used to exchange furtive kisses from these balconies. (*Beso* means kiss.) From the Plazuela de los Ángeles on Juárez, walk about 40 meters up Callejón del Patrocinio and you'll see Callejón del Beso taking off to your left.

Monumento al Pípila

The monument to El Pípila, with its torch raised high over the city, honors the hero who torched the Alhóndiga gates on September 28, 1810, enabling Hidalgo's forces to win the first victory of the independence movement. At the base of the statue is the inscription *'Aun hay otras Alhóndigas por incendiar.'* ('There are still other Alhóndigas to burn.')

It's worth going up to the statue for the magnificent view over the city; you can climb up inside the statue but the view is just as good from the terraces at its feet. Two routes from the center of town go up steep, picturesque lanes. One goes east on Sopeña from Jardín de la Unión, then turns right on Callejón de Calvario (you'll see the 'Al Pípila' sign). Another ascent, unmarked, goes uphill from the small plaza on Alonso. If the climb is too much for you, the 'Pípila-ISSSTE' bus heading west on Juárez will let you off right by the statue.

Museo Iconográfico del Quijote

This excellent museum at Doblado 1, on the tiny plaza in front of the Templo de San Francisco, holds an impressive collection of art relating to Don Quijote de la Mancha. Exhibits range from room-sized murals to a tiny painting on an eggshell, with dozens more paintings, statues, figurines and tapestries. There is even a collection of postage stamps from several countries honoring the famous hero of Spanish literature. The museum is open Tuesday through Saturday from 10 am to 6.30 pm, Sunday 10 am to 2.30 pm (free).

Ex-Hacienda San Gabriel de Barrera

Built at the end of the 17th century, this was the grand hacienda of Captain Gabriel de Barrera, whose family was descended from the first Count of Valencia of the famous La Valenciana mine. Opened as a museum in 1979, the hacienda has been magnificently restored with period European furniture and art; inside the chapel is an ornate gold-covered altar.

The large grounds, originally devoted to processing ore from La Valenciana, were converted in 1945 to beautiful terraced gardens with pavilions, pools, fountains and footpaths – a lovely and tranquil retreat from the city.

The museum, about two km west of the city center, is open daily from 9 am to 6 pm (US$0.70, extra for cameras). Frequent 'Marfil' buses heading west on Juárez will drop you at the Hotel Mission Guanajuato opposite the museum. Simply wend your way down past the hotel from the bus stop. Say you want to get off at Mission Guanajuato when you board the bus.

Museo de las Momias

The famous Museum of the Mummies, at the cemetery on the western outskirts of town, is a quintessential example of Mexico's obsession with death. Visitors from far and wide come to see scores of corpses disinterred from the public cemetery.

The first remains were dug up in 1865, when it was necessary to remove some bodies to make room for more. What the authorities uncovered were not skeletons but flesh mummified in grotesque forms and facial expressions. The mineral content of the soil and extremely dry atmospheric conditions had combined to preserve the bodies in this unique way.

Today 119 mummies are on display in the museum, including the first mummy to be discovered, the smallest mummy in the world, a pregnant mummy and plenty more. Since space is still tight in the cemetery, bodies whose relatives don't want to pay a fee to keep them there in perpetuity continue to be exhumed – and mummies are still being found. It takes only five or six years for a body to become mummified here, though only 1% or 2% of the bodies exhumed have turned into 'display quality' mummies. The others are cremated.

The museum is open daily from 9 am to 6 pm (US$2, extra for cameras). To get there take any 'Momias' or 'Panteón' bus heading west on Juárez.

Museo de Mineralogía

The Mineralogy Museum at the university's Escuela de Minas campus is among the world's foremost mineralogy museums. Over 20,000 specimens from around the world include some extremely rare minerals, some found only in the Guanajuato area. The museum overlooks the town a kilometer or two from the center on the road to La Valenciana. It's open weekdays from 9 am to 3 pm (free). Take a 'Presa-San Javier' bus heading west on Juárez and ask to get off at the Escuela de Minas.

Mina & Templo La Valenciana

For 250 years La Valenciana mine, which is on a hill overlooking Guanajuato about five km north of the center, produced 20% of the world's silver, in addition to quantities of gold.

Shut down after the revolution, the mine reopened in 1968 and is once again in operation, now cooperatively run. It can be visited any day from around 8 am to 7 pm (US$0.40). It still yields silver, gold, nickel and lead, and you can see the earth being extracted and miners descending an immense main shaft, nine meters wide and 500 meters deep.

Near the mine is the magnificent Templo La Valenciana, also called the Iglesia de San Cayetano. One legend says that the Spaniard who started the mine promised San Cayetano that if it made him rich, he would build a church to honor the saint. Another says that the silver baron of La Valenciana, Conde de Rul, tried to atone for exploiting the miners by building the ultimate in Churrigueresque churches.

Whatever the motive, ground was broken in 1765, and the church was completed in 1788. La Valenciana's façade is spectacular, and its interior is dazzling with ornate golden altars, filigree carvings and giant paintings. It's open daily except Monday from around 9 am to 7 pm.

To get to La Valenciana, take a Cristo Rey bus (every 15 minutes) from the bus stop on Alhóndiga just north of 28 de Septiembre. It will drop you 100 meters from the mine's entrance. Or, take a 'Valenciana' local bus departing every half-hour from the same bus stop. Get off at Templo La Valenciana; the mine is about 300 meters down the dirt road opposite the church.

Presa de la Olla

In the hills at the east end of the city are two small reservoirs, Presa de la Olla and Presa de San Renovato, with a green park between them and a lighthouse on the hill above. It's a popular family park on Sunday, when you can bring a picnic and hire small rowing boats. The rest of the week it's quiet and peaceful, though not especially scenic. Any eastbound 'Presa' bus, from the underground stop down the steps at the southwest corner of the Jardín de la Unión, will take you there.

Language Courses

Guanajuato is a university town and has an excellent atmosphere for studying Spanish.

The most flexible program is offered by the Instituto Falcón (☎ /fax 2-36-94, falcon@bajio.infonet.com.mx), Callejón de la Mora 158. Courses (maximum of six students per class) for beginners to advanced students are offered. There are cultural courses and weekend recreational trips too. Registration (US$75) is every Saturday morning. Fifty-five minutes of one-on-one instruction daily costs US$50 a week; two small-group sessions daily cost US$55 a week; five sessions daily cost US$100 a week. The institute can arrange accommodation with Mexican families; average daily cost with three meals is about US$20. You can write for more information to Instituto Falcón, Callejón de la Mora 158, 36000 Guanajuato, Gto, Mexico.

The Universidad de Guanajuato (☎ 2-00-06, 2-26-62 ext 8001, fax 2-72-53; montesa@quijote.ugto.mx) offers summer courses for foreigners in Spanish language and Mexican and Latin American culture. Cost is US$550 for a four-week period; classes begin in early June and early July with registration in February and May. The university can help you arrange to stay with Mexican families. The postal address is Centro de Idiomas, Universidad de Guanajuato, Lascuraín de Retana 5, 36000 Guanajuato, Gto, México.

The university also offers a range of semester courses in language and culture to foreigners. Semesters begin in January and July and last 19 weeks. Students must register in person and take a placement test the week before the semester begins. Cost is US$360 per semester.

Organized Tours

A few companies offer tours in Spanish of several of Guanajuato's major sights – their deals are identical. You can reach all the same places on local buses, but if your time is limited a tour may be useful.

Transporte Exclusivo de Turismo (☎ 2-59-68) has a kiosk on the corner of Juárez and 5 de Mayo while Transportes Turísticos de Guanajuato (☎ 2-17-91) has an office below the front courtyard of the basilica. 'Guanajuato Colonial' tours include the mummies, La Valenciana mine and church, the Pípila monument and the Panoramic Highway with a view over the town. Another tour goes to Cristo Rey. These trips go three times daily, last three to 3½ hours, and cost US$4. Other tours go farther and cost US$9.25. Night tours (five hours, US$9.25) take in Guanajuato's views and nightspots and the *callejoneadas* – see Entertainment.

Special Events

Fiestas de San Juan y Presa de la Olla

The Fiestas de San Juan are celebrated at the Presa de la Olla park from June 15 to 24. The 24th is the big bash for the saint's day itself, with dances, music, fireworks and picnics. On the first Monday in July, everyone comes back to the park for another big party celebrating the opening of the dam's floodgates.

Fiesta de la Virgen de Guanajuato

This festival, on August 8, commemorates the date when Felipe II gave the jeweled wooden Virgin now adorning the basilica to the people of Guanajuato.

Festival Internacional Cervantino

Guanajuato's arts festival is dedicated to the Spanish writer Miguel Cervantes, author of *Don Quijote*. In the 1950s the festival was entremeses (sketches) from Cervantes' work performed by students. It has grown to become one of the foremost arts extravaganzas in Latin America. Music, dance and theater groups converge on Guanajuato from around the world, performing work that nowadays may have nothing whatever to do with Cervantes. The festival lasts two to three weeks and is held in October. If your visit to Mexico coincides with it, don't miss it.

Tickets and hotels should be booked in advance. Tickets normally go on sale around September 6. In Guanajuato they're sold on the left side of the Teatro Juárez (not in the theater ticket office); in Mexico City they can be bought at the FIC office at Álvaro Obregón 273, Colonia Roma (☎ 5-533-41-21), or from Ticketmaster (☎ 5-325-90-00).

While some events are held in Teatro Juárez and other theaters, the most spectacular entremeses, with galloping horses and medieval costumes, are performed in the historic settings of Plazuela San Roque and Plaza Alhóndiga. Cervantino events are organized into morning, afternoon and evening sessions, for which tickets range from around US$3 to US$16.

Places to Stay

Except for budget rooms, expect prices to jump on long weekends (puentes), at Christmas, and during Semana Santa and the Festival Internacional Cervantino.

Places to Stay – budget

The top budget choice is *Casa Kloster* (☎ 2-00-88) at Alonso 32, a short block down an alley from the basilica. Birds and flowers grace the sunny courtyard, and the well-cared-for rooms with shared bath are clean and comfortable. Cost is US$6.50 per person, US$7.75 in the larger rooms. Many European and American travelers congregate here and it's a relaxed, friendly place. It fills up early in the day.

The friendly *Casa Berta* (☎ 2-13-16), at Tamboras 9, a few minutes east of the Jardín de la Unión, is a casa de huéspedes with four doubles at US$9.25 per person. There's an apartment too. There are no great vistas or relaxing patios but it has modern bathrooms, and it's homey, well-kept and centrally located. Walk up the street beside the Teatro Principal to Plaza de Mexiamora. Head straight uphill, turn first right, then left and follow the path to the door directly ahead.

Rock-bottom lodgings are available at *Hotel Posada de la Condesa* (☎ 2-14-62), at Plaza de la Paz 60, near the basilica. There are plenty of rooms, all with private bath and 24-hour hot water, but they're a bit tired and run down, though clean enough. Some are large and even have little balconies over the street, others are claustrophobic with no ventilation. Singles/doubles cost US$6.50/9.25.

In the area around the Mercado Hidalgo are several other cheap hotels, including the *Hotel Central*, *Hotel Juárez* and *Posada Hidalgo*, but none is as good as the Casa Kloster. The Hotel Central (☎ 2-00-80) is friendly enough and the rooms, at US$10.50/13, tolerable.

Places to Stay – middle

There are several medium-priced hotels around Plaza Alhóndiga and on Alhóndiga, the street heading north from the plaza. *Hotel Alhóndiga* (☎ 2-05-25) at Insurgencia 49, visible from the plaza, has clean, comfortable rooms with color TV, and some with small private balconies; there's also parking. Hot water is sporadic. Singles/doubles are US$18/22. Next door at Insurgencia 1, *Hotel del Conde* (☎ 2-14-65) is better, though its disco on weekend nights is a recipe for sleep deprivation. Spacious, bright rooms with private bath cost US$20.

Around the corner at Alhóndiga 7 is the *Hotel Mineral de Rayas* (☎ 2-19-67, 2-37-49). Some rooms are dark and damp and have seen better days; some have tiny balconies over a side street. We found it noisy here at night. Cost is US$16/19.

A little farther along Alhóndiga at 12A, *Hotel El Minero* (☎ 2-52-51) is a reasonable place with small, comfortable rooms, all with TV, and many with balconies over the street, at US$19/22.

Hotel Socavón (☎ 2-48-85, 2-66-66), Alhóndiga 41A, is an attractive, well-kept hostelry around a courtyard. All have copper washbasins, painted tiles in the bathrooms, color TV and plenty of windows; cost is US$17/21, US$22/26 at peak times. There's a restaurant/bar on the 2nd floor.

Near the Jardín de la Unión at Sopeña 3, *Hostería del Frayle* (☎ 2-11-79) is very attractive. All the rooms have high wood-beamed ceilings and color TV; though it's in the center of town, the building's thick adobe walls keep it quiet. Rooms here are US$34/42, suites US$42/54.

Hostal Cantarranas (☎ 2-52-41) a short hop southeast of the Jardín at Hidalgo 50, has eight pleasant, bright apartments with two to six beds. Each has an equipped kitchen and a sitting room. Prices start at singles/doubles US$21/26.

A few minutes farther south at Calle del Campanero, opposite the Teatro Cervantes, *Hotel Molino del Rey* (☎ 2-22-23) is a good choice for its quietish location. Set around a pretty patio, the 35 rooms with bath are US$19/24. Its restaurant prices are cheap.

Only a five-minute bus ride east of the center is the *Motel de las Embajadoras* (☎ 2-00-81) beside Parque Embajadoras on the corner of Embajadoras and Paseo Madero. It has an elegant but inexpensive restaurant/bar, plenty of parking and a lovely courtyard full of plants, trees and birds. Clean, comfortable rooms with color TV cost US$23/30. An 'Embajadoras' or 'Presa' bus heading east underneath the Jardín de la Unión (see Presa de la Olla) will take you there.

Places to Stay – top end

There are two old favorites right on Jardín de la Unión. *Hotel San Diego* (☎ 2-13-00/21, fax 2-56-26), Jardín de la Unión 1, has 52 elegant rooms and two suites, a second-floor restaurant overlooking the plaza and a large roof terrace. Rooms cost US$42 or US$74, single or double. At the other end of Jardín de la Unión, *Hotel Museo Posada Santa Fé* (☎ 2-00-84, fax 2-46-53) is a sumptuous hotel occupying an elegant 19th century mansion. The rooms cost US$49/55; suites are US$113. On the ground floor is a moderately expensive restaurant with some tables out on the plaza.

Hotel Mission Guanajuato (☎ 2-39-80, fax 2-74-60), in the west of the city beside the ex-Hacienda San Gabriel de Barrera at km 2.5 on the Camino Antigua a Marfil, has a restaurant, bar, swimming pool, tennis courts and 160 luxury rooms at US$65 and US$115.

Out in the suburb of Marfil, *La Casa De Espíritus Alegres* (The House of Good Spirits; ☎/fax 3-10-13), in a restored 18th century ex-hacienda, is an attractive B&B. Singles/doubles start at US$65/$70. In Marfil, ask for ex-Hacienda La Trinidad. Buses run to/from the center every 10 minutes.

Castillo Santa Cecilia (☎ 2-04-77/85, fax 2-01-53), on the road to La Valenciana mine at Carretera Valenciana km 1, is built of stone and resembles a castle. It is known both for its luxurious accommodations and excellent restaurant. Rooms are US$50/64. Suites start at US$73.

Places to Eat

There are a number of good, inexpensive restaurants around the Jardín de la Unión and the basilica. Two popular standbys are *Restaurant Valadez*, opposite the Teatro Juárez on the corner of the Jardín de la Unión, and the *Café/Restaurant El Retiro*, a few doors down at Sopeña 12. Both are open daily from 8 am to 11 pm, serving economical breakfasts for US$2.50 and a comida corrida for US$3.25. In between these two, with similar prices, and with outdoor tables across the street next to the Teatro Juárez, is the popular *Café Galería*.

Also at this end of the Jardín de la Unión, *Hotel San Diego* has an elegant upstairs restaurant with several balcony tables overlooking the plaza. It's rather expensive, but you can get a good breakfast special for US$2.25 to US$4.50. Close by on the north side of the Jardín, with tables outside, *El Gallo Pitagórico* has a prime location and tasty, not-too-expensive

Italian and Mexican food. We liked the spaghetti arrabiati, with a flavorsome salsa of tomatoes and dried chilies (US$3).

At the far end of the Jardín, *Café/Restaurante Pinguis* has no sign out front, but it's one of the most popular places in town for its good prices – there are sandwiches and tortas for US$1.60, and the comida corrida is only US$2.50. Breakfast dishes cost less than US$1.20. It's open daily from 8.30 am to 9.30 pm.

Pizza Piazza has a branch at Hidalgo 14, just off the Jardín de la Unión; another on the Plazuela de San Fernando; and another at Juárez 69A. All are open daily from 2 to 11 pm and have a relaxed student atmosphere and good pizza at good prices, around US$3.75 for the chica size (enough for one or two people) or US$5.25 mediana (two to four people).

One of our favorites near the basilica is *Truco 7*, at Truco 7. A small, intimate, artsy café/restaurant/gallery. It has great atmosphere and delicious food at reasonable prices. There are no breakfast specials but à la carte items are inexpensive. The comida corrida is US$2.25. Background music includes jazz, blues and classical. It's open daily from 8.30 am to 11 pm. A few doors east on Truco is the similarly laid-back, but less comfy, *Café Dada* with good coffee, snacks and meals, including a comida corrida at US$2.50.

On the plaza in front of the basilica, *Tasca de Los Santos* is a busy but pricey café/restaurant with a few outdoor tables. There are tapas (US$3.50) and lots of seafood and meat dishes at around US$6. Also near the basilica, *Pastelería La Paz* at Aguilar 53 is a large bakery and pastry shop, open daily from 7 am to 10 pm.

For delicious chicken try *Restaurant La Carreta* at Juárez 96, down toward the Mercado Hidalgo. Served with large portions of rice and salad, a quarter chicken costs US$1.70, a half chicken US$2.75, to take away or eat there. It's open daily from 8 am to 10 pm.

A few doors away at Juárez 120, *Fuente de Sodas* is good for a quick inexpensive juice, licuado, fruit salad or torta.

Vegetarian *El Unicornio Azul*, on Hidalgo near Truco, is a health food store with a bar where you can enjoy a snack such as a soy-burger (US$1.10) or yogurt with fruit (US$0.60). Open hours are 9 am to 9 pm Monday through Saturday, 9 am to 6 pm on Sundays and fiestas.

A few doors south of Casa Kloster, *Yamuna*, Alonso 10, is a Hindu vegetarian restaurant. It opens at 8 am for healthy breakfasts and a comida corrida of salad, dhal, rice, vegetables and yogurt (US$2.75) is served from 1 to 6 pm.

West of here, off Plazuela de los Ángeles at Callejón de Culixto 20, *Restaurante Crisalido* is a peaceful place serving a tasty comida corrida from 2 pm. The entire meal is a bit expensive at US$4.75 but you can skip the salad buffet and eat well for US$2.75. Breakfast is à la carte. It's open Monday to Saturday from 8 am to 6 pm.

For fresh produce and local sweets, head west on Juárez to the *Mercado Hidalgo*, an impressive structure from the Porfiriato.

Entertainment

Every evening, the *Jardín de la Unión* comes alive with students and others congregating there; the restaurants along one side of the plaza are popular for having a drink, people-watching and listening to the strolling musicians. The state band and other bands give free concerts in the gazebo some evenings from around 7 to 8 pm and on Sundays from around noon to 2 pm.

On Friday, Saturday and Sunday evenings around 8 or 8.30 pm, *callejoneadas* (or *estudiantinas*) depart from in front of San Diego church on the Jardín de la Unión. The callejoneada tradition is said to come from Spain. A group of professional songsters and musicians, dressed in traditional costumes, starts up in front of the church, a crowd gathers, then the whole mob winds through the ancient alleyways of the city, playing and singing heartily. On special occasions they take along a burro laden with wine – at other times wine is stashed midpoint on the route. Stories and jokes are told in between songs, though these are unintelligible unless you under-

stand Spanish well. It's good fun and one of Guanajuato's most enjoyable traditions. There's no cost except a small amount for the wine you drink. Tour companies and others try to sell you tickets for the callejoneadas, but you don't need them!

The *Rincón del Beso*, at Alonso 21A not far from the Jardín de la Unión, is also affectionately known as La Peña Bohemia since it used to be a rather bohemian club. Often it's deserted but occasionally it gets into full swing starting with live music at around 10.30 pm. On a good night, the whole club joins in singing, and they stay open as long as there are people there wanting to party. There's no cover charge, though the drinks are a bit expensive.

Guanajuato has three fine theaters, the *Teatro Juárez, Teatro Principal* and *Teatro Cervantes*, none far from the Jardín de la Unión. Check their posters to see what's on. International films are shown in several locations, including the Teatro Principal, Teatro Cervantes and *Museo y Casa de Diego Rivera*. The Museo y Casa de Diego Rivera and the Museo del Pueblo also have changing art exhibitions.

With its youthful population, Guanajuato has plenty of bars and discos. The *Guanajuato Grill* at Alonso 4 is a popular late-night restaurant/bar. *Bar Plaza* on the Jardín de la Unión has two-for-one beers most evenings. Some of the most popular discos are the *Galería* in the San Javier district, *Sancho's* in the Mineral de Cata district, and *Jav's* in Las Pastitas park in the west of the city. Cover is around US$4, and all are a short taxi ride from the city center.

Getting There & Away

Air Guanajuato is served by León airport, which is about 12 km before León on the Guanajuato-León road and about 40 km from Guanajuato. See the León section for flight information.

Bus Guanajuato's Central de Autobuses is on the southwestern outskirts of town. It has a post office, telephone caseta, restaurant and a luggage checkroom. Deluxe and

1st-class bus tickets can be bought in town at Viajes Frausto, Obregón 10. Daily departures include:

Dolores Hidalgo – 54 km, one hour; 2nd-class every 20 minutes, 6.20 am to 10.30 pm, by Flecha Amarilla (US$2)

Guadalajara – 300 km, five hours; three deluxe by ETN (US$18); six 1st-class by Primera Plus (US$14); 12 2nd-class by Flecha Amarilla (US$11)

León – 50 km, one hour; four deluxe by ETN (US$2.75); seven 1st-class by Primera Plus (US$2.25); 2nd-class every 10 minutes, 5.40 am to 10.30 pm, by Flecha Amarilla or Flecha de Oro (US$1.70)

Mexico City (Terminal Norte) – 380 km, 4½ hours; five deluxe by ETN (US$20); eight 1st-class by Primera Plus (US$16) and seven 1st-class by Futura and Ómnibus de México (US$15)

San Luis Potosí – 225 km, four hours; five 1st-class by Ómnibus de México (US$8.75); two 2nd-class by Flecha Amarilla (US$8)

San Miguel de Allende – 82 km, 1½ to two hours; four 1st-class by Primera Plus (US$4.50); eight 2nd-class by Flecha Amarilla (US$3.25)

There are also frequent 2nd-class Flecha Amarilla buses to Celaya and Morelia, plus four to Querétaro and Aguascalientes. For Morelia, it's quicker to take a deluxe ETN bus to Irapuato (three daily, US$2.50) and change there.

Getting Around

To/From the Airport A taxi from Guanajuato to León airport costs around US$13. A cheaper alternative is to take a bus to Silao, about 15 km before the airport, and a taxi from there (US$4 to US$5.25).

Bus & Taxi City buses operate from around 5 am to 10 pm; the fare is US$0.20. The tourist office is very helpful with bus information. The 'Central de Autobuses' buses run frequently between the bus station and city center up until midnight. From the center, you can catch them heading west on Juárez, or on the north side of the basilica.

Many of Guanajuato's principal sights are in the city center, within easy walking distance of each other, though there are plenty of steep slopes to negotiate. Shoes with a good grip are recommended.

Taxis are plentiful in the center. Cost for a ride within the center is about US$1.30; between the center and the bus station, it's around US$2, more if traffic is heavy.

AROUND GUANAJUATO
Cristo Rey

Cristo Rey (Christ the King) is a 20-meter bronze statue of Jesus erected in 1950 on the summit of the Cerro de Cubilete about 15 km west of Guanajuato, said to be the exact geographical center of Mexico. For religious Mexicans, there is a significance in having Jesus at the heart of their country, and the statue is a popular attraction for Mexicans visiting Guanajuato.

Tour companies offer 3½-hour trips to the statue (see Organized Tours above), but you can go on your own for only US$1 each way by an Autobuses Vasallo de Cristo bus from the bus station. They depart daily at 6, 7, 9, 10 and 11 am, 12.30, 2, 4 and 6 pm, with additional buses on weekends and holidays. From the bus station it is possible to see the statue up on the hill in the distance.

LEÓN
pop 1 million; alt 1854m; ☎ 47

The industrial city of León, 56 km west of Guanajuato, is a big bus interchange point and a likeable enough place if you need to stay a few hours or overnight. It's famous for its shoes, saddles and other leather goods; other products include steel, textiles and soap. In January/February, León hosts the Guanajuato State Fair with agricultural displays, rides, food and craft stalls, music and dancing. At this time, and a couple of other times during the year, 300 or so shoemakers display their wares in the Centro de Exposiciones (☎ 71-25-00).

There's a big map of the city center on a board in the Plaza Principal; city maps are available at reception in the Hotel Condesa.

Things to See & Do

The wide **Plaza Principal** is a pleasant, traffic-free space at the heart of the city, with one or two old buildings around it, such as the Casa Municipal and Parroquia del Sagrario on the west side. Beside the parroquia is a smaller plaza with the **Museo de la Ciudad de León** under one of its arcades, and a block north of here on the corner of Obregón and Hidalgo is the big twin-towered baroque **basilica**.

Take a look at some of the dozens of shoe shops around the center, or the main leather district on Hilario Medina out near the bus station – there's an enormous range of footwear and other leather goods at good prices. The central market is on the corner of Comonfort and Domínguez, two blocks south and west of the Plaza Principal.

Places to Stay & Eat

There are many economical hotels near the bus station on Calle La Luz (walk to the right from the station's main exit – La Luz is the first cross-street). In the center, pick from several. *Hotel Fundadores* (☎ 16-17-27) at Ortiz de Domínguez 220, 1½ blocks west of the Plaza Principal, has singles/doubles at US$7.75/9.25 (US$12 for a twin). *Hotel Rex* (☎ 14-24-15) on 5 de Febrero, one block south and half a block east of the Plaza Principal, has 120 bright rooms at US$16/20. The smart *Hotel León* (☎ 14-10-50) at Madero 113, half a block east of the Plaza Principal, has a stylish restaurant. The rooms cost US$26 or US$39, single or double. *Hotel Condesa* (☎ 13-11-20), at Portal Bravo 14 on the east side of the Plaza Principal, offers very comfortable rooms at US$30. Condesa's busy restaurant does a good four-course comida for just US$3.25 or light dishes from US$2 to US$3.25. More expensive top-end hotels are on Boulevard López Mateos.

Cafetería Rex on Pino Suárez, 1½ short blocks south of the Plaza Principal, does a cheap comida for US$2.75. *Refresquería El Pasaje* on Pasaje Orozco, the alley off the north side of the Plaza Principal, is popular for cheap tacos, tortas and other snacks.

Getting There & Away

Air León airport, also called Bajío airport, is about 12 km from town along the Mexico City road. Airlines serving it include Aerolitoral, Aeroméxico, American, Continental, Mexicana and TAESA. Aeroméxico has daily Los Angeles and Tijuana flights and Mexicana flies direct to/from Chicago five days a week. TAESA has direct flights to/from Oakland, California, on six days. Continental has flights to/from Houston, and American to/from Dallas/Fort Worth; both with onward connections. Domestic flights include daily direct services to/from Guadalajara, Mexico City, Monterrey, Tijuana and Zacatecas. Continental's (☎ 14-73-37) and American's (☎ 16-05-02) offices are at the airport.

Bus There's good service to/from just about everywhere in northern and western Mexico from the Central de Autobuses on Boulevard Hilario Medina, just north of Boulevard López Mateos toward the east edge of town. The bus station has a luggage checkroom and a money exchange office with good rates. Over 60 deluxe buses a day go to Mexico City and 29 to Guadalajara. To Guanajuato, 2nd-class Flecha Amarilla runs every 30 minutes from 5.20 am to 10.40 pm (one hour, US$1.70); there are also some better buses by ETN, Primera Plus and Servicios Coordinados. Primera Plus runs three daily afternoon 1st-class buses to San Miguel de Allende (2¼ hours, US$7).

Getting Around

Primera Plus/Flecha Amarilla operates four buses (US$1.30) daily between the bus station and the airport. 'Centro' buses (US$0.20) go to the city center from the bus station. To pick one up, cross the street from the bus station's main exit, walk left for about 150 meters and turn right onto López Mateos. To return to the bus station, catch a 'Central' bus east along López Mateos, two blocks north of the Plaza Principal. A taxi between the center and the bus station costs around US$2.

DOLORES HIDALGO
pop 40,000; alt 1955m; ☎ 468

This is where the Mexican independence movement began in earnest. At 5 am on September 16, 1810, Miguel Hidalgo, the parish priest, rang the bells to summon people to church earlier than usual and issued the Grito de Dolores, whose precise words have been lost to history but which boiled down to 'Long live Our Lady of Guadalupe! Death to bad government and the gachupines!' ('Gachupines' was the derisive name for Mexico's Spanish overlords, against whom a powder keg of resentment finally exploded in this small town.)

Hidalgo, Ignacio Allende and other conspirators had been alerted to the discovery of their plans for an uprising in Querétaro, so they decided to launch their rebellion immediately from Dolores. After the Grito they went to the lavish Spanish house on the plaza, today the Casa de Visitas, and took two prisoners – the local representative of the Spanish viceroy and the Spanish tax collector. They freed the prisoners that were in the town jail and, at the head of a growing band of criollos, mestizos and Indians, set off for San Miguel on a campaign that would bring their own deaths within a few months but that would ultimately lead to the independence of Mexico.

Today Hidalgo is Mexico's most revered hero, rivalled only by Benito Juárez in the number of streets, plazas and statues dedicated to him throughout the country. Dolores was renamed in his honor in 1824. Visiting Dolores Hidalgo has acquired pilgrimage status for Mexicans. If you're interested in the country's history, it's well worth a trip and is easily reached from Guanajuato or San Miguel de Allende.

Orientation
Everything of interest is within a couple of blocks of the Plaza Principal.

Information
Tourist Office The Delegación de Turismo is on the north side of the Plaza Principal in the Presidencia Municipal building to the left of the church. The staff can answer, in Spanish, any questions about the town. The office is open weekdays from 10 am to 3 pm and 5 to 7 pm, Saturday and Sunday from 10 am to 6 pm.

Money Cash and traveler's checks can be changed at Bancomer on the northwest corner of the Plaza Principal weekdays from 8.30 am to 5.30 pm, Saturday from 10 am to 2 pm. There's an ATM too. There are at least two casas de cambio, open daily, one on the northeast corner of the Plaza Principal, another on the corner of Jalisco and Puebla, a block southeast of the plaza.

Post & Communications The post office and Telecomm (with fax service) are in the same building at Puebla 22 on the corner of Veracruz, not far from the Plaza Principal. Both are open weekdays from 9 am to 4 pm, Saturday from 9 am to 1 pm.

There are card pay phones in the post office and outside the tourist office and the Flecha Amarilla bus station. You'll find a telephone caseta in the Restaurant Plaza on the south side of the Plaza Principal. There's another, with fax service, in front of the Flecha Amarilla bus station, open daily from 7 am to 11 pm.

Plaza Principal & Around
The **Parroquia de Nuestra Señora de Dolores**, the church where Hidalgo issued the Grito, is on the north side of the plaza. It has a fine 18th century Churrigueresque façade; inside, it's fairly plain. Some say that Hidalgo uttered his famous words from the pulpit, others that he spoke at the church door to the people gathered outside. The church is open daily from 6 am to 2 pm and from 4 to 8 pm.

To the left of the church is the **Presidencia Municipal**, which has two colorful murals on the theme of independence. The plaza contains a huge **statue of Hidalgo**

NORTHERN CENTRAL HIGHLANDS

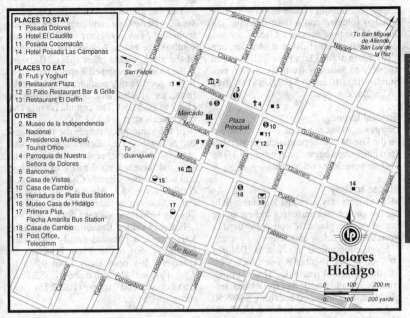

PLACES TO STAY
1 Posada Dolores
5 Hotel El Caudillo
11 Posada Cocomacán
14 Hotel Posada Las Campanas

PLACES TO EAT
8 Fruti y Yoghurt
9 Restaurant Plaza
12 El Patio Restaurant Bar & Grille
13 Restaurant El Delfin

OTHER
2 Museo de la Independencia Nacional
3 Presidencia Municipal, Tourist Office
4 Parroquia de Nuestra Señora de Dolores
6 Bancomer
7 Casa de Visitas
10 Casa de Cambio
15 Herradura de Plata Bus Station
16 Museo Casa de Hidalgo
17 Primera Plus, Flecha Amarilla Bus Station
18 Casa de Cambio
19 Post Office, Telecomm

Dolores Hidalgo

and a tree that, according to a plaque beneath it, is a sapling of the tree of the Noche Triste (Sad Night), under which Cortés is said to have wept when his men were driven out of Tenochtitlán in 1520.

The **Casa de Visitas** on the west side of the plaza was the residence of Don Nicolás Fernández del Rincón and Don Ignacio Díaz de la Cortina, the two representatives of Spanish rule in Dolores. On September 16, 1810, they became the first two prisoners of the independence movement. Today, this is where Mexican presidents and other dignitaries stay when they come to Dolores for ceremonies. It's open to visitors daily from 9.30 am to 2 pm and 4 to 6 pm (free).

Museo de la Independencia Nacional
Half a block west of the Plaza Principal at Zacatecas 6, this museum has few relics but plenty of information on the independence movement and its background. It charts the appalling decline in Nueva

España's Indian population between 1519 (an estimated 25 million) and 1605 (one million). It identifies 23 Indian rebellions before 1800 as well as several criollo conspiracies in the years leading up to 1810. There are vivid paintings, quotations and some details on the heroic last 10 months of Hidalgo's life. The museum is open every day but Thursday from 9 am to 5 pm (US$0.70, free on Sunday).

Museo Casa de Hidalgo
This is the house where Hidalgo lived and where he, Ignacio Allende and Juan de Aldama decided in the early hours of September 16, 1810, to launch the uprising. It is something of a national shrine. One large room is devoted to a big collection of memorials, wreaths and homages to Hidalgo. Other rooms contain replicas of Hidalgo's furniture and documents of the independence movement, including the order for Hidalgo's excommunication. Also on

display are ceramics made in the workshop Hidalgo founded and a door from the jail that held the prisoners he set free.

The house is on Hidalgo at Morelos, one block south of the Plaza Principal. It's open Tuesday to Saturday from 10 am to 6 pm, Sunday from 10 am to 5 pm (US$1.90, free on Sunday).

Special Events

Dolores is the scene of major celebrations on the Día de la Independencia, September 16. (Festivities begin September 15.) The Mexican president often officiates.

Places to Stay

Most visitors stay here just long enough to see the church and museums and eat an ice cream on the plaza. If you want to stay over, there are a few choices.

Most economical is *Posada Dolores* (☎ 2-06-42) at Yucatán 8, one block west of the Plaza Principal. This simple, friendly, clean casa de huéspedes has singles/doubles with shared bath for US$4/6.50 and rooms with private bath for US$7.75. *Hotel El Caudillo* (☎ 2-01-98, 2-04-65) at Querétaro 8, opposite the right side of the church, has 32 carpeted rooms that are clean enough, but small and stuffy, for US$9.75/12.50.

On the east side of the Plaza Principal is the fancier *Posada Cocomacán* (☎ 2-00-18). It has 50 rooms, all with private bath, windows for good ventilation and parquet floors. They cost US$14/16.

Hotel Posada Las Campanas (☎ 2-04-27, 2-14-24) at Guerrero 15, 2½ blocks east of the Plaza Principal, has 40 well-kept rooms, all with private bath, carpet and TV, for US$20/22.

Places to Eat

Dolores is famous not only for its historical attractions but also for its ice cream. On the southwest corner of the Plaza Principal you can get cones in a variety of unusual flavors including mole, chicharrón, avocado, maize, cheese, honey, shrimp, whisky, tequila and about 20 tropical fruit flavors.

You can grab a torta or a snack at many small eateries on and near the plaza, including *Fruti y Yoghurt* on Hidalgo just south of the plaza. Also on the south side of the plaza, on the other side of Hidalgo, is the recently revamped *Restaurant Plaza*. It is a good family restaurant with breakfasts, enchiladas and other antojitos at US$2 to US$3.50. The comida corrida and other meals start at US$3.50.

In the same price range, the restaurant/bar at the *Hotel El Caudillo* is cool and pleasant. À la carte breakfasts are inexpensive and there's a good range of antojitos and main dishes. *Posada Cocomacán* has a comida for US$3. Almost next door, *El Patio Restaurant Bar & Grille* does a Sunday buffet comida for US$5.

For seafood try *Restaurant El Delfín* at Veracruz 2, a pleasant family restaurant one block east of the Plaza Principal on Guerrero. It's open daily from 9 am to 7 pm. Fare includes fish dishes (US$2.75 to US$4), seafood soup (US$2.75) and shrimps (US$5.25).

Things to Buy

Ceramics, especially Talavera ware (including tiles), has been the special handicraft of Dolores ever since Padre Hidalgo founded the town's first ceramics workshop in the early 19th century. A number of shops sell these and other craft items. If you've got wheels, stop by the ceramics workshops along the approach roads to Dolores. The central market is also worth a look.

Getting There & Away

The bus station for Primera Plus (1st-class) and Flecha Amarilla (2nd-class) is on Hidalgo, 2½ blocks south of the Plaza Principal. Herradura de Plata (2nd-class) is on Chiapas at Chihuahua, around the corner and west one block. Daily departures include:

Guanajuato – 54 km, one hour; every 20 minutes, 5 am to 9 pm, by Flecha Amarilla (US$2)

Mexico City (Terminal Norte) – 325 km, five hours; every 20 or 40 minutes, 5.20 am to 11.40 pm, by Herradura de Plata or Flecha Amarilla (US$11)

Miguel Hidalgo

The balding head of the visionary priest Father Miguel Hidalgo y Costilla is familiar to anyone who has looked at Mexican murals or statues or at books about the country. He was, it seems, a genuine rebel idealist, who had already sacrificed his own career at least once before that fateful day in 1810. And he launched the independence movement clearly aware of the risks to his own life.

Born on May 8, 1753, son of a criollo hacienda manager in Guanajuato, he studied at the Colegio de San Nicolás in Valladolid (now Morelia), earned a bachelor's degree and, in 1778, was ordained a priest. He returned to teach at his old college and eventually became rector. But he was no orthodox cleric: Hidalgo questioned the virgin birth and the infallibility of the pope, read banned books, gambled, danced and had a mistress.

In 1800 he was brought before the Inquisition. Nothing was proved, but a few years later in 1804 he found himself transferred as priest to the hick town of Dolores.

Hidalgo's years in Dolores show that he was interested not only in the religious welfare of the local people but also in their economic and cultural welfare. Somewhat in the tradition of Don Vasco de Quiroga of Michoacán, founder of the Colegio de San Nicolás where Hidalgo had studied, he started new industries in the town such as tile-, ceramics- and pottery-making (all still practiced in the town today) plus silk production and vine-growing. He also started a band with local musicians.

When Hidalgo met Ignacio Allende from San Miguel, he got caught up in the criollo discontent with the Spanish stranglehold on Mexico. His standing among the mestizos and Indians of his parish was vital in broadening the base of the rebellion that followed.

On October 13, 1810, shortly after his Cry for Independence, he was formally excommunicated for 'heresy, apostasy and sedition.' He answered by proclaiming that he never would have been excommunicated had it not been for his call for the independence of Mexico and furthermore stated that the Spanish were not truly Catholic in any religious sense of the word, but only for political purposes, specifically to rape, pillage and exploit Mexico. A few days later, on October 19, Hidalgo dictated his first edict calling for the abolition of slavery in Mexico.

Hidalgo led his growing forces from Dolores to San Miguel, Celaya and Guanajuato, north to Zacatecas, south almost to Mexico City, and west to Guadalajara. But then, pushed northwards, their numbers dwindled and on July 30, 1811, having been captured by the Spanish, Hidalgo was shot by firing squad in Chihuahua. His head was returned to the city of Guanajuato, where his army had scored its first major victory. It hung in a cage for 10 years on an outer corner of the Alhóndiga de Granaditas, along with the heads of Allende, Aldama and Jiménez. Rather than intimidating the people, this lurid display kept the memory, the goal and the example of the heroic martyrs fresh in everyone's mind. ■

San Miguel de Allende – 43 km, one hour; every 20 to 40 minutes, 5 am to 8.40 pm, by Flecha Amarilla or Herradura de Plata (US$1.50).

There is also frequent service to Querétaro and León and about 12 Flecha Amarilla buses to San Luis Potosí (US$5.25).

SAN MIGUEL DE ALLENDE

pop 80,000; alt 1840m; ☎ 415

A charming colonial town in a beautiful setting, San Miguel has become known for its large colony of North Americans. Starting around the 1940s, when David Alfaro Siqueiros was giving mural-painting courses at the Escuela de Bellas Artes, the town began attracting artists of every persuasion from Mexico and the USA. Over the decades, many painters, sculptors, writers, poets, textile artists and all other creative types from Mexico as well as North America have come to San Miguel. Neal Cassady, the real-life hero of Jack Kerouac's novel *On the Road*, died here in February 1968, walking on the railroad tracks toward Celaya.

Once San Miguel was entrenched on the gringo circuit, it naturally lost some of its bohemian character. Today the town is home to several thousand foreigners. While many of them have retired here, others reside here during the winter months only. English is commonly spoken – you can easily visit San Miguel and speak no Spanish at all. There are ample tourist facilities but not many in the budget range.

The physical beauty of San Miguel stems from the hillside setting of its many lovely old buildings and cobbled streets, which afford vistas over the plains and distant hills. To protect its charm, the Mexican government has declared the entire town a national monument. San Miguel has a very agreeable climate and superbly clear light, which is one reason it still attracts artists.

San Miguel is well known as a place for foreigners to learn Spanish. Nearly all visitors find it easy to feel at home. For the Mexicans' part, they are inordinately addicted to the festivals that make the place even more colorful.

San Miguel's peak tourist period is from mid-December to the end of March, with a flurry from June to August.

History

The town, so the story goes, owes its founding to a few hot dogs. These hounds were dearly loved by a courageous barefoot Franciscan friar, Fray Juan de San Miguel, who started a mission in 1542 near an often-dry river five km from the present town. One day the dogs wandered off from the mission, to be found later reclining at the spring called El Chorro in the south of the present town. This site was so much better that the mission was moved.

San Miguel was then the most northerly Spanish settlement in central Mexico. Tarascan and Tlaxcalan Indians, allies of the Spanish, were brought to help pacify the local Otomí and Chichimecs. Even so, San Miguel barely survived the fierce Chichimec resistance until, in 1555, a Spanish garrison was established here to protect the new road from Mexico City to the silver center of Zacatecas. Then Spanish ranchers and crop growers settled in the area and San Miguel grew into a thriving commercial center known for its textiles, knives and horse tackle. It also became home to some of the wealthy Guanajuato silver barons.

San Miguel's favorite son, Ignacio Allende, was born here in 1779. He became a fervent believer in the need for Mexican independence and a leader of a Querétaro-based conspiracy that set December 8, 1810, as the date for an armed uprising. When the plan was discovered by the authorities in Querétaro on September 13, a messenger rushed to San Miguel and gave the news to Juan de Aldama, another conspirator. Aldama sped north to Dolores where, in the early hours of September 16, he found Allende at the house of the priest Miguel Hidalgo, also one of the coterie.

A few hours later Hidalgo proclaimed rebellion from his church. By the same evening, San Miguel was in rebel hands. Its local regiment had joined forces with the band of insurgent criollos, mestizos and Indians arriving from Dolores. San Miguel's Spanish population was locked up and Allende was only partly able to restrain the rebels from looting the town. After initial successes, Allende, Hidalgo and other rebel leaders were captured in 1811 in Chihuahua. Allende was executed almost immediately, Hidalgo four months later. It was not until 1821 that Mexico finally achieved independence.

In 1826 San Miguel was renamed San Miguel de Allende. It began to take on its current character with the founding of the

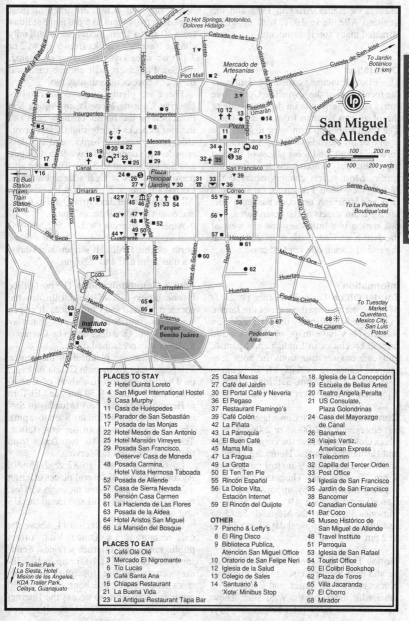

San Miguel
de Allende

PLACES TO STAY
2   Hotel Quinta Loreto
4   San Miguel International Hostel
5   Casa Murphy
11 Casa de Huéspedes
15 Parador de San Sebastián
17 Posada de las Monjas
22 Hotel Mesón de San Antonio
29 Hotel Mansión Virreyes
29 Posada San Francisco,
    'Deserve' Casa de Moneda
48 Posada Carmina,
    Hotel Vista Hermosa Taboada
52 Posada de Allende
57 Casa de Sierra Nevada
58 Pensión Casa Carmen
61 La Hacienda de Las Flores
63 Posada de la Aldea
64 Hotel Aristos San Miguel
66 La Mansión del Bosque

PLACES TO EAT
1   Café Olé Olé
3   Mercado El Nigromante
6   Tío Lucas
9   Café Santa Ana
16 Chiapas Restaurant
21 La Buena Vida
23 La Antigua Restaurant Tapa Bar

25 Casa Mexas
27 Café del Jardin
30 El Portal Café y Nevería
36 El Pegaso
37 Restaurant Flamingo's
39 Café Colón
42 La Piñata
43 La Parroquia
44 El Buen Café
45 Mama Mía
47 La Fragua
49 La Grotta
50 El Ten Ten Pie
55 Rincón Español
56 La Dolce Vita,
    Estación Internet
59 El Rincón del Quijote

OTHER
7   Pancho & Lefty's
8   El Ring Disco
9   Biblioteca Pública,
    Atención San Miguel Office
10 Oratorio de San Felipe Neri
12 Iglesia de la Salud
13 Colegio de Sales
14 'Santuario' &
    'Xote' Minibus Stop

18 Iglesia de La Concepción
19 Escuela de Bellas Artes
20 Teatro Angela Peralta
21 US Consulate,
    Plaza Golondrinas
24 Casa del Mayorazgo
    de Canal
26 Banamex
28 Viajes Vertiz,
    American Express
31 Telecomm
32 Capilla del Tercer Orden
33 Post Office
34 Iglesia de San Francisco
35 Jardín de San Francisco
38 Bancomer
40 Canadian Consulate
41 Bar Coco
46 Museo Histórico de
    San Miguel de Allende
48 Travel Institute
51 Parroquia
53 Iglesia de San Rafael
54 Tourist Office
60 El Colibrí Bookshop
62 Plaza de Toros
65 Villa Jacaranda
67 El Chorro
68 Mirador

To Trailer Park
La Siesta, Hotel
Misión de los Angeles,
KDA Trailer Park,
Celaya, Guanajuato

Escuela de Bellas Artes in 1938 and the Instituto Allende in 1951, both of which attracted many foreign students.

Orientation

The Plaza Principal, called the Jardín, is the focal point of the town. The Gothic-like spires of the parroquia on the south side of the plaza can be seen from far and wide. The town slopes up from west to east.

The central area is small with a straight-forward layout, and most places of interest are within easy walking distance from the Jardín. Most streets change names at the Jardín. Canal/San Francisco, on its north side, and Umarán/Correo, on the south side, are the main streets of the central area. The bus station is a little over one km west of the Jardín on Canal; the train station is at the end of Canal, one km farther on.

Information

Tourist Office The tourist office (☎ 2-17-47) is on the southeast corner of the Jardín, in a glassed-in office by the Iglesia de San Rafael. They have maps of the town and printed brochures in English and Spanish, and can answer questions in both languages. Hours are weekdays from 10 am to 2.45 pm and 5 to 7 pm, Saturday 10 am to 1 pm, and Sunday 10 am to noon.

Consulates The US Consulate (☎ 2-23-57; emergency ☎ 2-00-68 or 2-06-53) is in Plaza Golondrinas near the corner of Canal and Hernández Macías. Hours are Monday and Wednesday from 9 am to 1 pm and 4 to 7 pm, Tuesday and Thursday from 4 to 7 pm, other times by appointment. The Canadian consulate (☎ 2-30-25) is at Mesones 38, behind the Mesón de San José restaurant. It's open weekdays from 11 am to 2 pm.

Money There are several banks with ATMs on and near San Francisco in the couple of blocks east of the Jardín, and Banamex on the Jardín itself, on the west side. These have the best rates for changing money;

hours vary but a few are open at least weekdays from 9 am to 5 pm and Saturday from 10 am to 2 pm, though some will only change traveler's checks from 9 am to 2 or 3 pm on weekdays. Bancomer on Juárez, off San Francisco, will change cash and traveler's checks on Saturday too.

There are plenty of casas de cambio. Deserve Casa de Moneda, in Posada San Francisco on the Jardín, changes cash and traveler's checks at only slightly less favorable rates than the banks, and it's less crowded. It's open weekdays, 9 am to 7 pm, and Saturday 9 am to 5 pm. There are also reasonable rates at Deal's three branches, Correo 15, Juárez 27, and San Francisco 4. All are open weekdays from 9 am to 6 pm, and Saturday from 9 am to 2 pm.

American Express (☎ 2-18-56, 2-16-95) is at Viajes Vertiz, Hidalgo 1A, half a block north of the Jardín. It's open weekdays, 9 am to 2 pm and 4 to 6.30 pm.

Post & Communications The post office is one block east of the Jardín, on the corner of Correo and Corregidora. It's open weekdays from 8 am to 7 pm, Saturday 9 am to 1 pm. One door down on Correo is a Mexpost express mail office.

Pay phones are plentiful in the center. Telephone casetas include Caseta de Pepe, on Diez de Sollano just short of Correo (open daily, 8 am to 9.30 pm), and El Toro at Hernández Macías 58A (Monday to Saturday 8 am to 8 pm, Sunday 8 am to 2 pm). There's also a caseta in the bus station. Telecomm at Correo 16, two doors from the post office, has fax service.

La Conexión (☎ 2-16-87 & 2-15-99), Aldama 1, is one of several places offering a 24-hour fax and phone message service, mailboxes, express mail service to the US and more.

Estación Internet, Recreo 11, above the café-restaurant La Dolce Vita, offers public email and Internet services. Sending email costs US$1.10 for up to 10 minutes; computer use for other purposes costs US$6.50 for one hour, US$4 for 30 minutes. You can also access the Internet using your own laptop here. It's open weekdays from 9.30 am to 2 pm and 4 to 8 pm, Saturday from 9.30 am to 2 pm. Mail Boxes, next door to La Dolce Vita, will receive email messages.

Travel Agencies One place you can buy air tickets is Viajes Vertiz (☎ 2-18-56, 2-16-95), Hidalgo 1A.

Bookstores & Libraries The Biblioteca Pública (Public Library) at Insurgentes 25 also functions as an educational and cultural center with an emphasis on children's activities. Seek out its Quetzal room for an excellent collection of books in English and Spanish on Mexico – art, crafts, architecture, history, literature and more. There are English and Spanish sections for general reference books, novels and magazines. Used books in English are for sale at cheap prices. Open hours are weekdays from 10 am to 2 pm and 4 to 7 pm and Saturday from 10 am to 2 pm. An excellent café/restaurant is attached to the library.

Bookstores include El Colibrí at Diez de Sollano 30, 1½ blocks south of the plaza, with new books and magazines in English and Spanish, plus a few in French and German, and Lagundi, Umarán 17 at Hernández Macías.

Media & Notice Boards The expatriate community puts out a weekly English-language newspaper, *Atención San Miguel* (US$0.70); its office is in the Biblioteca Pública. It's full of what's on plus small ads offering rooms, apartments or houses to sell, rent or exchange; housesitter jobs; classes in yoga, Spanish, art or dance; and so on. You can buy it at the Biblioteca Pública and elsewhere. The same sorts of things are advertised on notice boards in the Biblioteca Pública, language schools, hotels, restaurants such as Casa Mexas at Canal 15, and, for information about what's on, the Escuela de Bellas Artes.

Laundry There are a number of laundromats, all charging around US$3 to wash and dry four kg; for half the price some will do a wash only. Lavanderías Automáticas ATL, at the bottom of Zacateros, is open weekdays from 8 am to 7 pm, Saturday 8 am to 2 pm. Lava Mágica, at Pila Seca 5, and Lavandería El Reloj, Reloj 34A, are both open Monday to Saturday from 8 am to 8 pm.

Parroquia
The pink 'cotton candy' pointed towers of the parish church dominate the Jardín. These strange soaring pinnacles were designed by an untutored local Indian, Zeferino Gutiérrez, in the late 19th century. He reputedly instructed the builders by scratching plans in the sand with a stick. Most of the rest of the church dates from the late 17th century. The crypt contains the remains of a 19th century Mexican president, Anastasio Bustamante. In the chapel to the left of the main altar is the much-revered image of the Cristo de la Conquista (Christ of the Conquest), made by Indians in Pátzcuaro from cornstalks and orchid bulbs, probably in the 16th century.

The church to the left of the parroquia, San Rafael, was founded in 1742 and has undergone Gothic-type alterations.

Museo Histórico de San Miguel de Allende
Near the parroquia on Cuna de Allende stands the house where Ignacio Allende was born, now a museum. Exhibits relate the interesting history of the San Miguel area, with special exhibits on Allende and the independence movement. An inscription in Latin on the façade says *'Hic natus ubique notus,'* which means 'Here born, everywhere known.' Another plaque points out that the more famous independence hero, Miguel Hidalgo, only joined the movement after being invited by Allende.

The museum is open Tuesday through Sunday from 10 am to 4 pm (free). It also hosts changing art exhibitions.

Casa del Mayorazgo de Canal
This house of the Canal family is one of the most imposing of San Miguel's old residences. The entrance (study the beautiful carved wooden doors) is at Canal 4, and it

stretches above the arcade on the west side of the Jardín. It's a neoclassical structure with some late baroque touches. Currently, it's closed to the public.

Iglesia de San Francisco

This church on the north side of the small Jardín de San Francisco, at San Francisco and Juárez, has an elaborate late 18th century Churrigueresque façade. An image of St Francis of Assisi is at the top.

Capilla del Tercer Orden

This chapel on the west side of the same garden was built in the early 18th century and, like the San Francisco church, was part of a Franciscan monastery complex. The main façade shows San Francisco (St Francis) and symbols of the Franciscan order.

Oratorio de San Felipe Neri

This multitowered and domed church, built in the early 18th century, stands on the corner of Insurgentes and Llamas. The pale pink main façade is baroque with an Indian influence. A passage to the right of this façade leads to the east wall, where an Indian-style doorway holds an image of Nuestra Señora de la Soledad (Our Lady of Solitude). You can see into the cloister from this side of the church.

Inside the church are 33 oil paintings showing scenes from the life of San Felipe Neri, the 16th century Florentine who founded the Oratorio Catholic order. In the east transept is a painting of the Virgin of Guadalupe by Miguel Cabrera. In the west transept is a lavishly decorated chapel, the Santa Casa de Loreto, built in 1735. It's a replica of a chapel in Loreto, Italy, legendary home of the Virgin Mary. If the chapel doors are open you can see tiles from Puebla, Valencia and China on the floor and walls, gilded cloth hangings and the tombs of chapel founder Conde Manuel de la Canal and his wife María de Hervas de Flores. Behind the altar, the camarín has six elaborately gilded baroque altars. In one is a reclining wax figure of San Columbano; it contains the saint's bones.

Iglesia de La Salud

This church, with a blue and yellow tiled dome and a big shell carved above its entrance, is just east of San Felipe Neri. The façade is early Churrigueresque. The church's paintings include one of San Javier by Miguel Cabrera.

Colegio de Sales

This was once a college, founded in the mid-18th century by the San Felipe Neri order. It's next door to La Salud, which also was once part of the same college. Many of the 1810 revolutionaries were educated here. The local Spaniards were locked up here when the rebels took San Miguel.

Iglesia de La Concepción

A couple of blocks west of the Jardín down Canal is the splendid church of La Concepción, with a fine altar and several magnificent old oil paintings. Painted on the interior doorway are a number of wise sayings to give pause to those entering the sanctuary. Construction of the church was begun in the mid-18th century; its dome, added in the late 19th century by the versatile Zeferino Gutiérrez, was possibly inspired by pictures of Les Invalides in Paris.

Escuela de Bellas Artes

This educational and cultural center, at Hernández Macías 75 near Canal, is housed in the beautiful former monastery of La Concepción church. It was converted into the Escuela de Bellas Artes (School of Fine Arts) in 1938. It's officially named the Centro Cultural Ignacio Ramírez, after a leading 19th century liberal thinker who lived in San Miguel. His nickname was El Nigromante (The Sorcerer).

One room in the cloister is devoted to an unfinished mural by Siqueiros, done in 1948 as part of a course in mural painting for US war veterans. Its subject – though you wouldn't guess it – is the life and work of Ignacio Allende. (There is a light switch to the right of the door just before you enter!)

Instituto Allende

This large building with several patios and

an old chapel at Ancha de San Antonio 4 was built in 1736 as the home of the Conde Manuel de la Canal. Later it was used as a Carmelite convent, eventually becoming an art and language school in 1951. Above the entrance is a carving of the Virgin of Loreto, patroness of the Canal family.

Mirador & Parque Juárez
One of the best views over the town and surrounding country is from the overlook up on Pedro Vargas, also known as the Salida a Querétaro, in the southeast of the town. If you take Callejón del Chorro, the track leading directly downhill from here, and turn left at the bottom, you reach El Chorro, the spring where the town was founded. Today it gushes out of a fountain built in 1960 and there are still public washing tubs here. Farther down the hill is the shady Parque Benito Juárez.

Botanical & Orchid Gardens
The large Jardín Botánico 'El Charco del Ingenio,' devoted mainly to cacti and other native plants of this semi-arid area, is on the hilltop about 1.5 km northeast of the town center. Though only a few years old, it's a lovely place for a walk – particularly in the early morning or late afternoon – though women alone should steer clear of its more secluded parts. Pathways range along the slope above a reservoir and above a deep canyon into which the reservoir flows. Open hours are 7 am to 6 pm (US$1). The garden is managed by CANTE, which is a nonprofit organization promoting conservation.

The direct approach to the garden is to walk uphill from the Mercado El Nigromante along Homobono and Cuesta de San José, then fork left up Montitlan past the Balcones housing development. Keep walking another few minutes along the track ahead at the top. If the gate here is shut, follow the fence around to the right to another entrance.

Alternatively, a two-km vehicle track leads north from the Gigante shopping center, which is 2.5 km east of the center on the Querétaro road. Gigante can be reached on 'Gigante' buses from the bus stop on the east side of Jardín de San Francisco. A taxi to the gardens from the center is US$1.60.

CANTE also administers **Los Pocitos**, an orchid garden with 2000 plants covering 230 species, at Santo Domingo 38.

Galleries
Galería San Miguel on the north side of the Jardín and Galería Atenea at Cuna de Allende 15 are two of the best and most established commercial galleries. The Escuela de Bellas Artes and Instituto Allende (see Courses) stage art exhibitions year-round. Many other galleries are advertised in *Atención San Miguel*.

Swimming
Several hotel pools are open to outsiders, including the clean pools of the Posada de la Aldea and the Hotel Aristos (US$2). Don't miss the balnearios in the surrounding countryside – see the Around San Miguel section.

Horseback Riding
Ask at the ice cream shop La Huerta, Correo 24, or contact Centro Ecuestre (☎ 2-30-87), three km out of town on the Dolores road, where lessons or riding cost around US$30 per hour.

Courses
San Miguel has an excellent atmosphere for developing your artistic inclinations. There are many easy-to-join courses that demand only enthusiasm. Language courses, group or private, are also numerous. Most courses run almost year-round with a mere three-week break in December. There are also numerous classes or sessions of a more spiritual nature, including meditation, yoga and tai chi. See *Atención San Miguel*.

Instituto Allende (☎ 2-01-90, fax 2-45-38; ferr@celaya.ugto.mx), in an old mansion on Ancha de San Antonio, offers courses in fine arts, crafts and Spanish. Art and craft courses can be joined at any time and usually involve about nine hours of attendance a week. The cost is US$211 a month, plus registration (US$13) and monthly insurance (US$11). Spanish courses begin about every four weeks and range from conversational (50 minutes a day, US$122 for four weeks) to total impact (six hours a day, US$443 for four weeks, maximum six students per class). Write to Instituto Allende, San Miguel de Allende 37700, Guanajuato, Mexico, for details.

The Academia Hispano Americana (☎ 2-03-49, fax 2-23-33) at Mesones 4 runs courses in Spanish language and Latin American culture at US$400 for a four-week session, or US$250 for two weeks. The cultural courses are taught in elementary Spanish. One-on-one language classes, for any period you like, are also available at US$10 an hour. The school can arrange for you to live in a private room with a Mexican family for about US$500 a month, meals included.

Centro Mexicana de Lengua y Cultura (☎ 2-07-63), Orizaba 15 off Ancha de San Antonio, and Universidad del Valle de México (☎ 2-60-49, fax 2-71-91; uvmsma@unisono.ciateq.mx), Zacateros 61, also offer Spanish language classes. The International Hostel at Organos 34 can arrange private tuition at economical rates.

The Escuela de Bellas Artes (☎ 2-02-89) is at Hernández Macías 75 on the corner of Canal in a beautiful ex-monastery. Courses in art, dance, crafts and music are usually given in Spanish and cost around US$100 a month; each class is nine hours a week. Registration is at the beginning of each month. Some classes are not held in July, and there are none in August.

Organized Tours

A House & Garden tour, visiting some of the lovely houses and gardens in San Miguel that are otherwise closed to the public, sets off by bus about noon every Sunday from the Biblioteca Pública. Tickets are on sale from 11 am. Cost is around US$15 for the two-hour tour, with three different houses visited each week.

The Travel Institute of San Miguel (☎ 2-00-78, fax 2-01-21), Cuna de Allende 11, conducts two-hour historical walking tours of central San Miguel for US$11, plus a variety of other tours. Stop by for a brochure.

Every Saturday at 10.30 am, three-hour minibus tours (US$11) set off from the Jardín to out-of-town destinations such as a monastery, ranch, hacienda or vineyard plus a workshop of a local artisan. Proceeds go to the Centro de Crecimiento, a school for handicapped children.

Special Events

Being so well endowed with churches and patron saints (it has six), San Miguel has a multitude of festivals every month. You'll probably learn of some by word of mouth – or the sound of fireworks – while you're there. Events include:

Blessing of the Animals – This happens in several churches, including the parroquia, on January 17.

Allende's Birthday – On January 21 various official events celebrate this occasion.

Cristo de la Conquista – This image in the parroquia is fêted on the first Friday in March, with scores of dancers in elaborate pre-Hispanic costumes and plumed headdresses in front of the parroquia.

Semana Santa – Two weekends before Easter pilgrims carry an image of the Señor de la Columna (Lord of the Column) from Atotonilco, 14 km north, to the church of San Juan de Dios in San Miguel on Saturday night or Sunday morning. During Semana Santa itself, the many activities include the lavish Procesión del Santo Entierro on Good Friday and the burning or exploding of images of Judas on Easter Day.

Fiesta de la Santa Cruz – This unusual, rather solemn festival has its roots in the 16th century; sensitivity is recommended if you want to observe it. It happens on the last weekend in May at Valle del Maíz, two km from the center of town. Oxen are dressed in lime necklaces and painted tortillas, and their yokes festooned with flowers and fruit. One beast carries two boxes of 'treasure' (bread and sugar) and is surrounded by characters in bizarre costumes on horses or donkeys. A mock battle between the 'Indians' and

'Federales' follows, with a wizard appearing to heal the 'wounded' and raise the 'dead.'

Corpus Christi – This movable feast in June features dances by children in front of the parroquia.

Chamber Music Festival – The Escuela de Bellas Artes sponsors an annual festival of chamber music (*música de cámara*), in the first two weeks of August.

San Miguel Arcángel – Celebrations honoring the town's chief patron saint are held on September 29 (or on the weekend after, if the 29th is a weekday). There are cockfights, bullfights and bull-running in the streets, but the hub of a general town party is provided by traditional dancers from several states who meet at Cruz del Cuarto, on the road to the train station. Wearing bells, feather headdresses, scarlet cloaks and masks, groups walk in procession to the parroquia carrying flower offerings called *xuchiles*, some playing armadillo-shell lutes. The roots of these events probably go back to pre-Hispanic times. Dances continue over a few days and include the Danza Guerrero in front of the parroquia, which represents the Spanish conquest of the Chichimecs.

San Miguel Music Festival – This largely classical music festival presents an almost daily program with Mexican and international performers throughout the second half of December. Most concerts are at the fine Teatro Angela Peralta, built in 1910, on the corner of Mesones and Hernández Macías.

Places to Stay

Some of the better-value places are often full; book ahead if you can, especially during the high seasons.

Many hotels give discounts for long-term guests. If you're planning to stay a while in San Miguel, there are houses, apartments and rooms to rent. Check the newspapers, notice boards and estate agents. Expect to pay from US$400 a month for a decent two-bedroom house. Housesitting is another possibility.

Places to Stay – budget

Camping *Lago Dorado KDA Trailer Park* (☎ 2-23-01, fax 2-36-86) beside the reservoir five km south of town, has a swimming pool, lounge, laundromat and 60 spaces with full hookups, plus 40 more spaces without hookups. Cost is US$7.75 per person, less for longer stays. From town, take the Celaya road, then after three km turn right at the Hotel Misión de los Ángeles and continue another two km toward the lake, crossing the train tracks.

Trailer Park La Siesta (☎ 2-02-07) is in the grounds of the Motel La Siesta, on the Celaya road two km south of town. It has 62 spaces with full hookups; amenities are minimal. Cost is US$8.50 for one or two people.

Hostel The friendly *San Miguel International Hostel* (☎ 2-06-74) at Organos 34 is in a pleasant colonial-style house (undergoing remodeling), with a gurgling fountain in a courtyard full of flowers and trees. Beds in separate-sex dorms are US$5.25 (US$4.75 with a hostel card); there are also a few singles/doubles with private bath at US$7.75/11.75. Free coffee, tea and continental breakfast are included; kitchen use costs US$1 extra per day, with staples like rice, beans, spaghetti and spices provided. There are laundry facilities and parking plus a splendid view from the rooftop.

Hotels Half a block south of the Jardín at Cuna de Allende 10, the *Posada de Allende* (☎ 2-06-98) looks a little old and worn. Its five rooms, all with private bath and some with balconies over the street, cost US$13/16 for singles/doubles.

There are two good choices on Mesones. The *Casa de Huéspedes* (☎ 2-13-78) at Mesones 27 is a clean, pleasant upstairs hostelry and has a rooftop terrace with a good view. All six rooms have private bath. Singles/doubles/triples cost US$7.75/13/20, slightly more with a kitchenette. Ask about discounts for longer stays. Many European travelers stay here.

Farther up the hill at Mesones 7, *Parador de San Sebastián* (☎ 2-70-84) is quiet and attractive. It has 24 rooms, all with fireplace and private bath, arranged around an arched courtyard full of plants. Singles/doubles are US$6.50/13.

Places to Stay – middle

San Miguel is brimming with good places in the middle range. Just off the Jardín at Cuna de Allende 7, *Posada Carmina* (☎ 2-04-58, fax 2-01-35) is a former colonial mansion with 12 large, attractive rooms with tiled bathrooms and color TV. Singles/doubles cost from US$30/37 to US$57/65. In the leafy courtyard there's a pleasant restaurant/bar. In the same block at No 11 is the similar but less elegant, and cheaper, *Hotel Vista Hermosa Taboada* (☎ 2-00-78, 2-04-37), whose 17 rooms with fireplace and carpet are US$18/26.

Half a block from the Jardín at Canal 19, *Hotel Mansión Virreyes* (☎ 2-08-51, fax 2-38-65) is another colonial place with 22 rooms around two courtyards and a restaurant/bar in the rear patio. Rooms are US$25/26 (US$28/39 on weekends).

Nearby, *Hotel Mesón de San Antonio* (☎ 2-05-80, 2-28-97) at Mesones 80 has nine rooms at US$22 single or double, and four townhouse-style suites at US$26, around an attractive courtyard with a lawn and small swimming pool.

The welcoming *Posada de las Monjas* (☎ 2-01-71), Canal 37, is a beautiful hotel in a former monastery. The 65 rooms are comfortable and nicely decorated, and the bathrooms all have slate floors and handpainted tiles. Rooms in the new section out back are in better condition than those in the old section. There are numerous terraces with lovely views, some overlooking the valley, plus a restaurant, bar, laundry and parking. The larger rooms with fireplaces and plenty of sun cost US$20/28 for singles/doubles. Smaller rooms go for US$19/23.

Hotel Quinta Loreto (☎ 2-00-42, fax 2-36-16) at Loreto 15 is a long-time favorite with North Americans. The 38 rooms, simple but pleasant and some with a small private patio, are set around large grounds with a swimming pool (out of action when we checked), tennis courts and plenty of parking space. The restaurant is good. Rooms are US$19/24 or US$24/29 with cable TV. Ask about discounts that are available for a stay of a week or longer. Reserve well ahead!

Posada San Francisco (☎/fax 2-00-72, 2-72-13) at Plaza Principal 2 (right on the Jardín) is another popular hotel, with rooms at US$36/41.

Opposite the Instituto Allende, on Ancha de San Antonio, is the attractive *Posada de la Aldea* (☎ 2-10-22, 2-12-96). Its 66 large rooms cost US$43 single or double.

Places to Stay – top end

All of these except Pensión Casa Carmen, La Mansión del Bosque and Casa Murphy have swimming pools.

Pensión Casa Carmen (☎ 2-08-44) at Correo 31 is an old colonial home whose 12 rooms, all with high-beamed ceilings, are set around a pleasant courtyard with a fountain, orange trees and flowers. The price of US$40/70 includes a delicious breakfast and lunch, served in a communal dining room. Reserve well in advance for the high seasons.

Another popular place is *La Mansión del Bosque* (☎ 2-02-77), Aldama 65 opposite Parque Benito Juárez. All 23 rooms are different and comfortable with good furniture and original art. Most have both tub and shower, and some also have fireplaces. During the low season, singles are US$39 or US$59, doubles US$69 or US$79, with breakfast and dinner. Winter and July/August rates are higher. Reserve well in advance. The address is Apdo Postal 206, San Miguel de Allende, Guanajuato 37700.

The very elegant *Casa de Sierra Nevada* (☎ 2-04-15, 2-18-95, fax 2-23-37), Hospicio 35, was converted from four colonial mansions. It has three rooms at US$184 and 17 suites from US$225 to US$345.

La Hacienda De Las Flores (☎ 2-18-08, 2-18-59), Hospicio 16, is a somewhat luxurious place with wonderful views from its upstairs rooms and verandahs. Rooms cost from US$70/75 to US$100/105 in the high season, US$55/60 to US$85/90 in the low season.

La Puertecita Boutique'otel (☎ 2-50-11, 2-22-50, fax 2-55-05) at Santo Domingo 75, about one km uphill from the post office, is another luxury place with rooms at US$168, suites from US$192 to US$215.

Behind the Instituto Allende is *Hotel Aristos San Miguel* (☎ 2-03-92, 2-35-10, fax 2-16-31), Ancha de San Antonio 30, with 56 rooms and four suites, all with outdoor terraces and around a large garden with tennis courts. Rooms cost US$58 for one or two people, suites US$75.

Casa Murphy (☎ 2-37-76, fax 2-21-88) at San Antonio Abad 22, off Canal, about 400 meters from the Jardín, is a luxury bed & breakfast in a colonial house with a pretty garden. Rooms cost US$65 for two people. There's also a casita with kitchen, cable TV, telephone, whirlpool bath and private patio at US$75 for two.

Places to Eat

The restaurant scene in San Miguel has exploded with yet more places to eat covering an array of international cuisines. Most are pretty good but be sure to find one that suits your pocket, as the bill can easily mount up.

Budget For quick cheap eats, there are some excellent bakeries such as *La Colmena Panadería* at Reloj 21 half a block north of the Jardín, *Genesis Tienda Naturista* at Reloj 34B, *Panadería La Espiga* at Insurgentes 19 near the International Hostel, and *La Buena Vida*, with a small attached café, in Plaza Golondrinas opposite the Bellas Artes. La Buena Vida is the pick of the bunch with a range of wholegrain breads, cakes and pastries to tempt your tastebuds.

The food stands on the east side of the Jardín offer cheap, tasty Mexican fare such as fried chicken with vegetables, tortillas, salsa and pickles for around US$2.50.

Northeast of the Jardín, there are a couple of good, basic, family-run chicken restaurants, with chickens turning on spits out front. One of them, *Restaurant Flamingo's*, Juárez 15, serves a good-value comida corrida (US$3.25) from 1 to 4 pm. It's open daily from around 9 am to 10 pm.

Close by, *Café Colón*, San Francisco 21, is a popular local haunt for all meals. *La Fragua*, Cuna de Allende 3, is a laid-back courtyard restaurant/bar with live music

nightly. The menú del día is only US$3. It's open daily from noon until at least midnight. On Cuna de Allende at Cuadrante, the little family-run *El Ten Ten Pie* serves up home-style cooking with excellent chili sauces. Try the cheese and mushroom tacos, US$1.60 for a small serving. The comida corrida is US$3.75.

El Buen Café, Jesús 23 at Cuadrante, does economical breakfasts and light meals; try the Cuban rice with beans and bananas (US$2.75). It's open Monday through Saturday from 9 am to 8 pm. North of here at Jesús and Umarán, the convivial *La Piñata* is popular for juices, salads and quesadillas. Between the two, *La Parroquia*, Jesús 11, is a popular spot for breakfast when its courtyard is sun-dappled and the birds are twittering. Breakfast is à la carte but not expensive, and your coffee cup is kept full! Main meals are US$2.75 to US$4.

Over at Canal 66, *Chiapas Restaurant* is a bright, hospitable place with good, economical food, around US$4 for a main meal. The entremeses Chiapaneco are suitable for vegetarians. It's open daily except Wednesday, 10 am to 10 pm.

Middle & Top End Several European-style places around the center do good coffee, cakes, snacks and light meals. They're open from around 9 or 10 am to 10 pm. They include *El Portal Café y Nevería* and the quite expensive *Café Del Jardín*, both on the Jardín. *La Dolce Vita*, Recreo 11, is another of this type – you can get a breakfast special here (US$2.75).

The friendly *El Pegaso* on Corregidora opposite the post office is good for all meals. Head there for an economical breakfast (fruit, eggs, bread and coffee for US$2.25) or try their fancy sandwiches such as smoked turkey (US$3) or smoked salmon with cream cheese (US$4.75). Main dishes start at US$4.75; some are Asian-inspired but there's also Mexican fare. Closed Sunday!

Rincón Español, Correo 29, has a comida corrida for US$4.50 and an evening menú for US$5.25. Their other dishes, Spanish specialties, are more expensive. It's open daily, noon to 10 or 11 pm.

Mama Mía at Umarán 8, in a pleasant, cool courtyard near the Jardín, has become a San Miguel institution, a favorite for its food and the live South American music performed nightly from around 8 pm to midnight. Many dishes are quite expensive (meats and seafoods around US$6.50, pastas US$3.25 to US$6) but their breakfasts (from US$1.20 to US$3) are a much better deal. They're open daily from 8 am to 12.30 am.

Also near the Jardín, *Posada Carmina* at Cuna de Allende 7 has a popular courtyard restaurant, particularly busy for Sunday lunch – menú del día US$4 to US$4.75. It's open from 8 am to 9.30 pm. Nearby, *La Grotta*, downstairs at Cuadrante 5, is a small, intimate Italian restaurant with tasty food but the bill quickly mounts up. It's more economical to share a medium pizza (US$6.50). The homemade desserts are delicious.

Casa Mexas at Canal 15 is also on the expensive side but it's a fun restaurant/bar with excellent Tex-Mex specialties and Texas-size portions. Meat is featured but there are a couple of vegetarian choices. In the back is a bar with a big-screen TV and, farther back, a billiards room. It's open daily from noon to 11 pm.

Tío Lucas at Mesones 103, with a covered patio, is known for its grilled fare (US$5.25 to US$10.25), but we like the excellent soups (US$2.25) and the salads (under US$3.25). It's open daily from noon – there's live blues or jazz at night.

Café Santa Ana, in a shady patio with a gurgling fountain, is attached to the Biblioteca Pública at Insurgentes 25. There's a Californian-type menu, and the tasty, moderately priced food is presented with flair. It's open weekdays from 9 am to 6 pm, Saturday 9 am to 2 pm.

A popular place with the foreign set and Mexicans alike, especially on Sunday, is the restaurant of the *Hotel Quinta Loreto* at Loreto 15. The ample comida corrida for US$4.75, served with soup, salad and spaghetti, features selections like roast beef

and orange chicken. Bread is homemade, and there are breakfast specials (US$2.25) too. The restaurant is open daily from 8 to 10.30 am and 1.30 to 5 pm.

The friendly, family-run *Café Olé Olé* at Loreto 66 is one of San Miguel's most popular eateries. It's brightly decorated with bullfighting memorabilia; the food is mainly char-grilled with prices starting at US$4.25 for chicken and beef. Open daily from 1 to 9 pm.

Vegetarian *El Rincón del Quijote*, at Hernández Macías 111, serves up classy food in a relaxed setting. There are travel magazines to read while you wait! The extensive menu includes typical vegetarian favorites and some Mexican specialties. The comida corrida is US$3.75, main meals around US$3.25.

Entertainment

San Miguel has a thriving entertainment scene. Keep an eye on the notice boards and *Atención San Miguel* to find out what's on. Some events are held in English.

Villa Jacaranda at Aldama 53 shows recent releases of North American movies on a big screen at 7.30 pm daily. Entry is US$4 and includes a drink and popcorn. Or try the back room of *Casa Mexas* at Canal 15; their satellite dish brings movies in English to a big-screen TV. If the movies are no good, you can always go in the back and play billiards.

Mama Mía restaurant at Umarán 8 has live South American music nightly from around 8 pm to late. There's also a wine bar at the front and a downstairs venue for live music – the action here starts around 10 pm on weekend nights in the low seasons with additional nights in the high seasons (no cover charge when we checked). *La Fragua*, Cuna de Allende 3, is another courtyard restaurant/bar with live music, generally mellow.

Rincón Español at Correo 29, one block from the Jardín, presents a flamenco dinner show Monday through Thursday at 8.30 pm, Friday and Saturday at 9.45 pm, and Sunday at 3 pm. *La Antigua Restaurant*

Tapa Bar at Canal 9 also has a flamenco show, on Friday and Saturday nights, starting at 8.45 pm.

Tío Lucas, Mesones 103, has live blues or jazz for diners most nights. *Los Arcángeles* at Canal 21 is a fancy restaurant with a pleasant courtyard where anyone can sit and enjoy live music most Friday and Saturday nights; the jazz was excellent when we stopped by.

Pancho & Lefty's, Mesones 99, attracts a young crowd with live rock music Monday, Wednesday and Saturday from around 10.30 pm to 3 am. There's usually a cover charge of about US$2.75 and 'two for one' drinks for much of the night. *Bar Coco*, Hernández Macías 85 at Umarán, is a laid-back place with guitar soloists or live blues or rock starting around 10.30 pm nightly. It offers 'two for one' beers from 6 to 8 pm. Snacks are available. *Char Rock*, upstairs at Correo and Diez de Sollano, blasts out '60s and '70s hits on Friday and Saturday nights.

San Miguel has several discos. Central and popular is *El Ring* at Hidalgo 25, open Wednesday through Sunday from 10 pm to 4 am (cover charge US$6.50 on Saturday, US$4 other nights). *Laberinto's* at Ancha de San Antonio 7 near the Instituto Allende is also popular.

On the more cultural side, the Escuela de Bellas Artes hosts a variety of events including art exhibitions, concerts, readings and theater; check its notice board for the current schedule.

For a great concert of birds in trees, be in the Jardín at sunset. The birds make a racket calling to one another from all the trees, while below them people are gathering to socialize, and are doing much the same.

Things to Buy

San Miguel has one of the biggest and best concentrations of craft shops in Mexico, selling folk art and handicrafts from all over the country. Prices are not low, but quality is high and the range of goods is mind-boggling. *Casa Maxwell* on Canal, a few doors down from the Jardín, is one place with a tremendous array; there are many, many more within a few blocks, especially on Canal, San Francisco and Zacateros. Local crafts include tinware, wrought iron, silver, brass, leather, glassware, pottery and textiles. Most of these crafts are traditions going back to the 18th century. There are also a couple of shops selling unique San Miguel women's fashions – check out *Mangos* at Hernández Macías 72. The *Mercado de Artesanías*, with a number of small handicraft stalls, is in an alleyway running between Colegio and Reloj. Its wares are of lower quality than those in San Miguel's smarter shops.

San Miguel has several regular markets. The daily *Mercado El Nigromante* is on Colegio, behind the Colegio de Sales; stalls with fruits, vegetables and assorted other goods stretch along Colegio. The biggest *market* takes place on Tuesday out of town beside the Gigante shopping center, 2.5 km southeast of the center on the Querétaro road. Take a 'Gigante' or 'Placita' bus (10 minutes) from the east side of the Jardín de San Francisco. *Espino's*, Codo 36, is a large supermarket. Fresh vegetables are sold daily on its doorsteps by an outside vendor.

Getting There & Away

Air The nearest airport is at León – see the León section. Otherwise you can fly to/from Mexico City.

Bus The Central de Autobuses is on Canal, about one km west of the center. ETN, Primera Plus and Pegasso Plus tickets can be bought at the Travel Institute, Cuna de Allende 11. Tickets for Primera Plus can also be bought at Transporte Turístico on Diez de Sollano just off Correo. Daily departures include:

Celaya – 52 km, 1¼ hours; 2nd-class every 15 minutes, 5 am to 8 pm, by Flecha Amarilla (US$1.60)

Dolores Hidalgo – 43 km, one hour; 2nd-class every 20 or 30 minutes, 6 am to 9 pm, by Flecha Amarilla or Herradura de Plata (US$1.50)

Guadalajara – 360 km, six hours; three 1st-class by Primera Plus (US$19)

Guanajuato – 82 km, one to 1½ hours; four 1st-class by Primera Plus (US$4.50) and one by

Ómnibus de México (US$4); 13 2nd-class by Flecha Amarilla and eight by Servicios Coordinados (US$3.25)

León – 138 km, 2¼ hours; a few 1st-class by Primera Plus; four 2nd-class by Flecha Amarilla (US$7)

Mexico City (Terminal Norte) – 280 km, 3¼ to four hours; three deluxe by ETN (US$17); four 1st-class by Primera Plus, three by Herradura de Plata and two by Pegasso Plus (US$12); 2nd-class semi-directo at least every 40 minutes, 5 am to 10 pm, by Servicios Coordinados, Herradura de Plata or Flecha Amarilla (US$9.25)

Querétaro – 60 km, one hour; three deluxe by ETN (US$4); frequent 2nd-class, 5 am to 9 pm, by Herradura de Plata and Flecha Amarilla (US$2.25)

Other services include a few Servicios Coordinados buses to San Luis Potosí (US$6.75) and Aguascalientes (US$7.50), Transportes del Norte buses to Monterrey (US$28) and weekend buses by Americanos to six cities in Texas.

Train The Estación del Ferrocarril (☎ 2-00-07) is at the end of Canal, about two km west of the center. Train Nos 1 and 2, between Mexico City and Nuevo Laredo, stop at San Miguel; see the Mexico City Train section for the schedule – although keep in mind that the trains are frequently late. Buy your ticket on the train. Primera fares are US$4.25 to San Luis Potosí, US$17 to Monterrey and US$24 to Nuevo Laredo.

Car & Motorcycle Gama (☎ 2-08-15), Hidalgo 3, rents VW sedans for US$24 a day plus US$0.20 per kilometer or an expensive US$50 a day with unlimited kilometers, both plus US$6.50 insurance and 15% tax. You should book at least a week ahead from December to March. Dollar (☎ 2-01-98) is out front of the Hotel Real de Minas on Ancha de San Antonio.

Getting Around
To/From the Airports American Express (☎ 2-18-56, 2-16-95) at Viajes Vertiz, Hidalgo 1A, offers combis, holding up to six people, to/from León and Mexico City

airports. Rates for the vehicle are US$70 to León (1½ hours) and US$160 to Mexico City (four hours). The Travel Institute (☎ 2-00-78 ext 4), Cuna de Allende 11, offers vans holding up to seven people for US$90 to León airport, or US$200 to Mexico City airport.

Bus Local buses run daily from 7 am to 9 pm and cost US$0.30. 'Central Estación' buses go every few minutes from the train and bus stations to the town center. Coming into town these go up Insurgentes, wind through the town a bit and terminate on the corner of Mesones and Colegio. Heading out from the center, you can pick one up on Canal.

Taxi A taxi between the center and the bus station costs US$1.30; to the train station it's US$2. Sometimes you have to bargain.

AROUND SAN MIGUEL
Hot Springs
There are several balnearios at hot springs near San Miguel, on or near the highway to Dolores Hidalgo. All have swimming pools with mineral waters (good for the skin) and pleasant surroundings. Entry for all but the Santa Verónica costs US$4 to US$4.75. You can reach any of them by taking any bus heading to Dolores Hidalgo from the Central de Autobuses in San Miguel. Or, from the bus stop on Puente de Umarán, off Colegio and opposite the Mercado El Nigromante, take a 'Santuario' minibus (half-hourly). This will stop out front, or within walking distance of, all the balnearios mentioned. See Taboada for an alternative bus that cuts the walk from the highway to this balneario from three to one km.

Returning to town, hail one of the buses that speed along the highway.

Taboada Most popular is Taboada, eight km north of San Miguel and then three km west along a signposted side-road. It has a large lawn area and three swimming pools – one Olympic-size with warm water, and two smaller ones that get quite hot. It's open daily except Tuesday from

8 am to 5 pm. There's a small kiosk and bar for drinks and snacks.

A taxi costs around US$5 one way. You can ask the driver to return for you at an appointed time. Minibuses to 'Xote,' hourly from the Puente de Umarán bus stop mentioned above, will get you most of the way to Taboada: get off where the bus turns off the Taboada side road and walk the remaining one km or so to the hot springs.

Santa Veronica This balneario is right beside the highway to Dolores Hidalgo, at the Taboada turnoff, eight km from San Miguel. It has a large Olympic-size swimming pool with water a bit cooler than at Taboada. It's open daily except Friday from 9 am to 5 pm (US$2.75).

Parador del Cortijo Nine km from San Miguel on the Dolores Hidalgo road, Parador del Cortijo (☎ 2-17-00, 2-07-58) is a hotel/restaurant with a thermal pool, sauna and whirlpool bath, offering a number of services, including facials and massages. They close the pool for cleaning on Monday or Tuesday; you can phone to find out which day. A sign for the center is clearly posted on the road.

La Gruta Only 100 meters beyond the Parador del Cortijo, on the same side of the highway, this balneario consists of three small pools into which the waters of a thermal spring have been channeled. The hottest is in a cave entered through a tunnel, lit by a single shaft of sunlight. You can have a shoulder massage from the hot water as it gushes from the roof. Outside there's an expensive restaurant and plenty of shade.

Escondido Place This, our favorite balneario, has two warm outdoor pools and three connected indoor pools, each progressively hotter. They all have pretty, stained-glass windows; the third indoor pool has a bricked dome with a hole in the middle and a jet of water gushes from high on a wall to pummel your body. The picturesque grounds have plenty of space for picnicking, and there's a small kiosk for drinks and snacks. Escondido Place is open daily from 8.30 am to 5.30 pm, and a sign for it too is clearly posted on the highway, just before the Parador del Cortijo. From here it's about one km down a dirt road. Or take a taxi for around US$5.25 one way.

Atotonilco
Turn off the Dolores Hidalgo highway at the Parador del Cortijo and go about one km, and you come to the hamlet of Atotonilco, dominated by its Santuario founded in 1740 as a spiritual retreat. Here Ignacio Allende was married in 1802. Eight years later he returned with Miguel Hidalgo and the band of independence rebels en route from Dolores to San Miguel to take the shrine's banner of the Virgin of Guadalupe as their flag.

Today a journey to Atotonilco is a goal of pilgrims and penitents from all over Mexico, and the starting point of an important and solemn procession two weekends before Easter, in which the image of the Señor de la Columna is carried to the church of San Juan de Dios in San Miguel. Inside, the sanctuary has six chapels and is vibrant with statues, folk murals and other paintings. Extensive restoration work has recently begun. Indian dances are held here on the third Sunday in July.

Pozos
A few years ago Pozos was more or less a ghost town. A couple of thousand people lived among abandoned houses and mine workings in what, 90 or so years ago, was a flourishing silver- and copper-mining center of about 50,000. Recently it has been targeted for development and there's now a plush place to stay, the *Hotel Casa Mexicana* (☎ 468-8-25-98, ext 116), at Ocampo 6 on the Jardín Principal, in a converted 100-year-old hacienda. Doubles with three meals are US$90. *Hidalgo B&B* (☎ 468-8-25-98, ext 119), Hidalgo 15, charges US$12 per person including breakfast. In Pozos, you can explore the underground tunnels of old mines, check out old ruins and chapels or tour the surrounding

area by horseback or mountain bike. There's also an art gallery and a couple of good restaurants. Some of the residents make a living from hand-carved replicas of pre-Hispanic musical instruments, including deerskin drums and rainmakers. These instruments, and pre-Hispanic dances, are featured in fiestas.

Pozos is about 35 minutes by car from San Miguel, 45 minutes from Querétaro. From San Miguel, take the Querétaro road, turn left off it after four km toward Dr Mora, follow that road for 35 km, crossing highway 57 on the way. Turn left at a crossroads from which Pozos is 14 km away. To get to Pozos from San Miguel by bus involves a trip of two or three hours on three different buses – first to Dolores Hidalgo, then to San Luis de la Paz and from there 11 km south to Pozos.

Querétaro

Querétaro is primarily an agricultural and livestock-raising state. Industry has developed around Querétaro city and certain other places, notably San Juan del Río. The state also turns out opals, mercury, zinc and lead. Many visitors never get past Querétaro city, with its fine colonial architecture, active cultural life and rich history, but there are other areas worth visiting, such as the pretty country town of Tequisquiapan, which is a nice place to relax.

QUERÉTARO
pop 500,000; alt 1762m; ☎ *42*

Querétaro's museums, monuments and colonial architecture are less spectacular than those of Guanajuato or Zacatecas, but it's a lively city. It's prettiest at night when many of its handsome buildings are floodlit, and wandering the streets and plazas is a real pleasure. It especially warrants a visit if you're interested in Mexico's history, in which it has played an important role. In 1996 the city officially took back its old name, Santiago de Querétaro, but it's generally still known as just Querétaro.

History
Founded in the 15th century by Otomí Indians, who were later absorbed into the Aztec empire, Querétaro was settled by the Spaniards in 1531. Franciscan monks used it as a base for missions not only to Mexico but also to what is now the southwestern US. In the early 19th century Querétaro became a center of intrigue among disaffected criollos plotting to free Mexico from Spanish rule. Conspirators, including Miguel Hidalgo, met secretly at the house of Doña Josefa Ortiz (La Corregidora), wife of a former *corregidor* (district administrator) of Querétaro.

When the conspiracy was discovered, the story goes, Doña Josefa was locked in a room in her house (now the Palacio de Gobierno) but managed to whisper through a keyhole to a co-conspirator, Ignacio Pérez, that their colleagues were in jeopardy. Pérez galloped off to inform another conspirator in San Miguel de Allende, who in turn carried the news to Dolores Hidalgo, where on September 16, 1810, Padre Hidalgo issued his famous Grito, a call to arms initiating the War of Independence.

In 1867 Emperor Maximilian surrendered to Benito Juárez's general Escobedo at Querétaro, after a siege lasting nearly 100 days. It was here that Maximilian was executed by firing squad.

In 1917 the Mexican constitution – still the basis of Mexico law – was drawn up by the Constitutionalist civil war faction in Querétaro. Mexico's ruling party, the PNR (ancestor of the PRI), was organized in Querétaro in 1929.

Orientation
The center is fairly compact, with many pedestrian plazas and streets, which makes for pleasant strolling. The heart of things is the Plaza Principal, also called Jardín Zenea. Running along its east side, by the Templo de San Francisco, is Corregidora, the main street of the downtown area.

Other important central plazas are Plaza de la Corregidora just off the northeast corner of the Plaza Principal, and Plaza de

NORTHERN CENTRAL HIGHLANDS

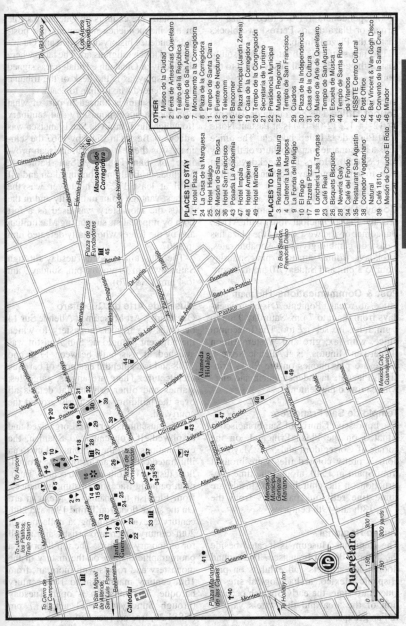

OTHER

1 Museo de la Ciudad
5 Feria de Artesanías Querétaro
7 Teatro de la República
8 Monumento a la Corregidora
9 Plaza de la Corregidora
13 Telecomm
15 Bancomer
16 Plaza Principal (Jardín Zenea)
19 Casa de la Corregidora
20 Templo de la Congregación
21 Secretaría de Turismo
22 Presidencia Municipal
27 Museo Regional;
   Templo de San Francisco
29 Cuadros
30 Plaza de la Independencia
31 Casa de la Cultura
33 Museo de Arte de Querétaro;
   Templo de San Agustín
37 Escuela de Música
40 Templo de Santa Rosa
   de Viterbos
41 ISSSTE Centro Cultural
42 Post Office
44 Bar Vincent & Van Gogh Disco
45 Convento de la Santa Cruz
46 Mirador

PLACES TO STAY

14 Hotel Plaza
24 La Casa de la Marquesa
25 Hotel Hidalgo
32 Mesón de Santa Rosa
36 Hotel San Francisco
43 Posada La Academia
47 Hotel Impala
48 Hotel Amberes
49 Hotel Mirabel

PLACES TO EAT

3 Restaurante Ibis Natura
4 Cafetería La Mariposa
10 La Fonda del Refugio
17 Pizzería Pizza
18 Lonchería Las Tortugas
23 Café Real
26 Bisquets Bisquets
28 Nevería Galy
34 Café del Fondo
35 Restaurant San Agustín
38 Comedor Vegetariano
   Natural
39 Café 1810;
   Mesón de Chucho El Roto

la Independencia (also called Plaza de Armas or Plaza de los Perros) two blocks east of the Plaza Principal.

The bus station is about five km southeast of the center – local buses link it to the center.

Information

Tourist Office The Secretaría de Turismo (☎ 12-14-12, 12-09-07) is at Pasteur Norte 4 off Plaza de la Independencia. The office sells a reasonable map/brochure of the city for US$0.70. Hours are weekdays from 9 am to 9 pm, Saturday and Sunday 9 am to 8 pm.

Money There are several banks on and near the Plaza Principal, most with ATMs. Bancomer on the west side of the plaza has a casa de cambio giving reasonable rates, weekdays from 9 am to 6 pm, Saturday 9 am to 3 pm, and Sunday 10 am to 2 pm.

Post & Communications The main post office, at Arteaga Poniente 7, is open weekdays from 8 am to 7 pm, Saturday 9 am to 1 pm. It has fax service too. The Telecomm office, with fax, giro and Western Union 'Dinero en Minutos,' is at Allende Norte 4. There are pay phones on the Plaza Principal, Plaza de la Independencia and elsewhere around the center.

Templo de San Francisco

The impressive Church of San Francisco is situated on the Plaza Principal, on the corner of Corregidora and 5 de Mayo. Its dome's pretty colored tiles were brought from Spain in 1540, around the time construction on the church began. Inside are some fine religious paintings from the 17th, 18th and 19th centuries.

Museo Regional

The Regional Museum is located beside the Templo de San Francisco. The ground floor holds artifacts and exhibits on pre-Hispanic Mexico, archaeological sites in Querétaro state, the early Spanish occupation of the area and the state's various Indian groups.

Upstairs are exhibits on Querétaro's role in the independence movement, the post-independence history of Mexico and Querétaro and much religious art. The table where the Treaty of Guadalupe Hidalgo was signed is on display, as is the desk of the tribunal that sentenced Maximilian to death.

The museum is housed in part of what was once a huge monastery and seminary (to which the Templo de San Francisco was attached). Begun in 1540, by 1567 the seminary was the seat of the Franciscan province of San Pedro y San Pablo de Michoacán. Building continued on and off until at least 1727. The tower was the highest vantage point in the city and in the 1860s the monastery was used as a fort both by imperialists supporting Maximilian and by the forces who finally defeated him in 1867.

The museum is open Tuesday through Saturday from 10 am to 5 pm, Sunday 9 am to 4 pm (US$1.70).

Museo de Arte de Querétaro

Querétaro's Art Museum at Allende Sur 14 occupies the former monastery to which the adjacent Templo de San Agustín was attached. It was built between 1731 and 1748 and is a splendid example of baroque architecture. There are angels, gargoyles, statues and other ornamental details all over the building, particularly around the courtyard.

The museum is very well organized and displayed. If you can read Spanish, the explanations with the exhibits add up to an illustrated course in art history. The ground-floor display of 16th and 17th century European painting traces interesting influences, from Flemish to Spanish to Mexican art. On the same floor you'll find 19th and 20th century Mexican painting, a collection of 20th century Querétaro artists, and a hall for temporary exhibits. The top floor has a photographic display on the history of the monastery and rooms with more art, from 16th century mannerism to 18th century baroque. The museum is open Tuesday through Sunday from 11 am to 7 pm (US$1.30, free on Tuesday).

Museo de la Ciudad
The new, 11-room City Museum on Guerrero at Hidalgo had not quite opened at the time of research but should be worth a visit.

Teatro de la República
One block north of the Plaza Principal, on the corner of Juárez and Peralta, this lovely old theater was where a tribunal met in 1867 to decide the fate of Emperor Maximilian. Mexico's constitution was signed here on January 31, 1917. The stage backdrop lists the names of its signatories and the states they represented. In 1929, politicians met in the theater to organize Mexico's ruling party, the PNR (now the PRI).

The theater is open to visitors Tuesday through Sunday from 10 am to 3 pm and 5 to 8 pm (free).

Casa de la Corregidora (Palacio de Gobierno)
The Casa de la Corregidora, Doña Josefa Ortiz's home, where she informed Ignacio Pérez of the plans to arrest the independence conspirators, stands on the north side of Plaza de la Independencia. Today the building is the Palacio de Gobierno, the state government building. It can be visited weekdays from 8 am to 9 pm, Saturday from 9 am to 2 pm.

The room where Doña Josefa was locked up is not marked, but it's the large room upstairs over the entrance to the building. A plaque to one side records her role in history. The room is now used as the governor's conference room.

Convento de la Santa Cruz
About 10 minutes' walk east of the center is one of the city's most interesting sights, the Convento de la Santa Cruz, on Plaza de los Fundadores. This monastery was built between 1654 and about 1815 on the site of a battle in which a miraculous appearance of Santiago (St James) had led Otomí Indians to surrender to the conquistadors and christianity. Emperor Maximilian had his headquarters here while under siege in Querétaro from March to May 1867. After his surrender and subsequent death sentence, he was jailed here while awaiting the firing squad. Today the monastery is used as a religious school.

A guide will provide insight into the Convento's history and artifacts, which include an ingenious water system and unique colonial ways of cooking and refrigeration. The guide will also relate several of the Convento's miracles, including the legendary growth of a tree from a walking stick stuck in the earth by a pious friar in 1697. The thorns of the tree form a cross.

The Convento is open weekdays from 9 am to 2 pm and 4 to 6 pm, Saturday and Sunday from 9 am to 4 pm. There's no admission fee, but your guide will request a donation to the convent at the end of your tour. Tours are given in English or Spanish.

Mirador & Mausoleo de la Corregidora
Walk east along Independencia past the Convento de la Santa Cruz then fork right along Ejército Republicano, and you come to a mirador with a view of 'Los Arcos,' Querétaro's emblematic 1.28-km aqueduct, which was built between 1726 and 1735 with 74 towering arches. It still brings water to the city from about 12 km away.

Across the street is the tomb of Doña Josefa Ortiz (La Corregidora) and her husband, Miguel Domínguez de Alemán. Behind the tomb is a shrine with pictures and documents relating to Doña Josefa's life.

Alameda Hidalgo
Three blocks south of the Plaza Principal on Corregidora, this large park, shady and green, is a popular place for picnics, jogging, roller skating, strolling and generally just taking it easy.

Other Central Sights
Plaza de la Corregidora is dominated by the **Monumento a la Corregidora**, a 1910 statue of Doña Josefa Ortiz bearing the flame of freedom.

One block west of the Plaza Principal along Madero is the **Fuente de Neptuno**

(Neptune Fountain), designed by the noted Mexican neoclassical architect Eduardo Tresguerras in 1797. The 17th century **Templo de Santa Clara**, adjacent, has an ornate baroque interior. On Madero at Ocampo is the rather plain 18th century **Catedral**. Hidalgo, parallel to Madero two blocks north, is lined with many fine mansions.

At the intersection of Arteaga and Montes stands the 18th century **Templo de Santa Rosa de Viterbos**, Querétaro's most splendid baroque church, with its pagoda-like bell tower, unusual exterior paintwork and curling buttresses, and lavishly gilt and marble interior. The church also boasts what some say is the earliest four-sided clock in the New World.

Other notable colonial churches include the **Templo de San Antonio** on Corregidora Norte at Peralta, with two large pipe organs, elaborate crystal chandeliers, red wallpaper and several oil paintings; and the **Templo de la Congregación** on Pasteur Norte at 16 de Septiembre, with beautiful stained glass windows and a splendid pipe organ.

Cerro de las Campanas

In the west of the city, a good 35-minute walk from the center, is the Cerro de las Campanas (Hill of the Bells), the site of Maximilian's execution. The emperor's family constructed a chapel on the spot. Today the area is a park, with a statue of Benito Juárez, a café and the Museo del Sitio (Siege) de Querétaro, all open Tuesday through Sunday (10 am to 2 pm and 3.30 to 6 pm for the museum, 6 am to 6 pm for the park). You can get there on a 'UAQ,' 'CU' or 'Universidad' bus going west on Avenida Zaragoza at the Alameda Hidalgo. Get off at the Ciudad Universitaria.

Organized Tours

Guided walking tours of the city center, in English or Spanish, leave the tourist office daily at 10.30 am and 6 pm. They cost US$1.30 a person and last around two hours.

Special Events

Querétaro's Feria Internacional in the first two weeks of December is one of Mexico's biggest state fairs. While it focuses on livestock, it also covers industry, commerce and artisanry and is the excuse for varied entertainment and fun.

Places to Stay – budget

Hotel San Francisco (☎ 12-08-58), Corregidora Sur 144, is a rambling three-story place with lots of smallish but decent rooms, all with private bath and TV, for US$6.50 a single, US$8.50 or US$9.25 a double.

Posada La Academia at Pino Suárez 52 has dark, cell-like rooms but they have TV and private bathroom and are kept clean. Cost is US$5.25/6.50 for singles/doubles, or US$7.75 for a twin-bed double.

Hotel Hidalgo (☎ 12-00-81), owned and managed by an Englishman, is just a few doors off the Plaza Principal at Madero 11 Poniente. Singles are US$8.50, doubles US$9.75 or US$11. All have private bathrooms. Some large rooms can hold up to seven people, at US$2 for each extra person. Some upper-floor rooms have small balconies overlooking the street. There's parking in the courtyard and an economical restaurant open from 8 am to 10 pm.

Hotel Plaza (☎ 12-11-38), at Juárez Norte 23 on the Plaza Principal, has 29 tidy and comfortable, if well-used, rooms. All have TV and either windows facing the interior courtyard or French doors opening on small balconies that face the plaza, offering plenty of light, air and noise. Singles cost from US$9.75 to US$13, doubles from US$13 to US$20.

Places to Stay – middle

Hotel Impala (☎ 12-25-70, fax 12-45-15) is a modern four-story hotel on the corner of Corregidora Sur and Zaragoza, opposite the Alameda Hidalgo. Its 108 rooms all have color TV and carpet. Some have a view of the park, but beware traffic noise – it's a very busy corner; the interior rooms are bright enough and quieter. Singles are US$15, doubles are US$17. The hotel has underground parking. Its official address is Colón 1.

Hotel Amberes (☎ 12-86-04, fax 12-41-51) at Corregidora Sur 188, also facing the Alameda, is similar but a bit smarter, with 140 singles/doubles at US$21/29 and a good restaurant.

Places to Stay – top end
Until recently Querétaro lacked any very stylish city-center lodgings. That gap has been well and truly filled by two places. The splendid *La Casa de la Marquesa* (☎ 12-00-92, fax 12-00-98) at Madero 41 is a magnificent 18th century baroque-cum-Mudéjar mansion transformed into a hotel full of lavish period furnishings, carved stone, tiles and frescoes (some original). Accommodations consist of 25 suites with names and styles such as Alhambra and Maximiliano y Carlota – each different but all with cable TV and air-con. They cost from US$140 to US$350 (including continental breakfast and welcome cocktail!). The cheaper ones are in a separate building, the Casa Azul, a couple of doors west on the corner of Madero and Allende. Children under 12 are not admitted.

Mesón de Santa Rosa (☎ 24-26-23, fax 12-55-22; starosa@sparc.ciateq.conacyt.mx), Pasteur Sur 17 on Plaza de la Independencia, is another recently converted colonial building. It's built around three patios, one with a heated swimming pool, one with a fountain, one with restaurant tables. There are 21 elegant and comfortable suites, each with a safe and satellite TV, costing from US$75 to US$98.

Hotel Mirabel (☎ 14-39-29, fax 14-35-85), at Constituyentes Oriente 2 facing the south side of the Alameda Hidalgo, has 171 modern rooms costing US$34/47. All rooms come with color TV and air-con, and some have a view over the park. There's a restaurant.

The *Holiday Inn* (☎ 16-02-02, fax 16-89-02), 2.5 km west of the center at Avenida 5 de Febrero 110, just north of Avenida Zaragoza, charges US$82 for one or two people. Rooms are air-con and have satellite TV, and there are also tennis courts and a swimming pool and a bar, cafeteria and restaurant.

Places to Eat
Café del Fondo at Pino Suárez 9 is a relaxed place with soothing background music from a creaky old sound system. You can get breakfast deals such as eggs, frijoles, bread roll, juice and coffee for US$1.10, or a four-course comida corrida with plenty of choice for US$1.60. It's open daily from 7.30 am to 10 pm and you can linger over a snack or coffee any time. One room has chess tables. Next door, *Restaurant San Agustín* has similar breakfast and comida deals.

Bisquets Bisquets facing Plaza de la Constitución, a block south of the Plaza Principal, is a small, friendly place with good food at good prices, open daily from 7 am to 11 pm. The comida corrida is US$2.50.

Vegetarians and natural food fans will like *Restaurante Ibis Natura* at Juárez Norte 47. It's open daily from 8 am to 9.30 pm. The comida corrida for US$2.50 is excellent value; so are the soyburgers with mushrooms and cheese at US$1.10. The little *Comedor Vegetariano Natura* at Vergara 7 is another good vegetarian restaurant. It's open Monday through Saturday from 8 am to 9 pm and does a four-course comida for US$2.50.

Plaza de la Corregidora, off the northeast corner of the Plaza Principal, and the pedestrian street 16 de Septiembre leading up to the east, have a number of sidewalk cafés and restaurant/bars. Those on the plaza include *El Regio*, *La Fonda del Refugio* and *Pizzeta Pizza*.

Nevería Galy at 5 de Mayo 8, off the Plaza Principal, is a Querétaro institution known for its homemade ice cream. Specialties include nieve de limón (lemon sorbet) with mineral water, or cola, or red wine. Opposite, *Lonchería las Tortugas* is popular for take-out food and has a spectacular array of bullfight photos.

A pleasant place for dessert and coffee is *Cafetería La Mariposa* at Peralta 7, one block north of the Plaza Principal. Enter through the ice cream and sweets shop to one side. It serves basic Mexican meals at good prices, and there's an Italian espresso machine in the back.

Café Real on the corner of Madero and Allende, in the Casa Azul of La Casa de la Marquesa, has a gurgling fountain and good food at reasonable prices. There are ham and cheese croissants, antojitos, salads, pasta and burgers, all for US$2 to US$3.25, as well as puntas de filete (beef fillet) for US$4.

The green and quiet Plaza de la Independencia has a handful of more expensive but popular restaurants with both indoor and outdoor tables. One, *Mesón de Chucho El Roto*, boasts 'alta cocina mexicana' (Mexican haute cuisine), with dishes such as camarones al molcajete (shrimps wrapped in bacon, cheese and nopalitos, with a tomato sauce) and medallones en salsa huitlacoche (beef medallions in a sauce made from a maize fungus that has been considered a delicacy since Aztec times). They also offer more conservative steak, seafood and chicken dishes. Main dishes are mostly in the US$4 to US$6.50 range. Next door, *Café 1810* is also good.

La Casa de la Marquesa and the *Mesón de Santa Rosa* (see Places to Stay) both have high-class restaurants.

Entertainment

Querétaro has cultural activities befitting a state capital and university city. You can pick up a calendar of events from the tourist office. Sit in the *Plaza Principal* any Sunday evening with local families enjoying concerts; the state band performs from around 6.30 to 8.30 pm, sometimes with dancers.

Other outdoor music can be enjoyed at the less central *Jardín de los Platitos*, on Juárez at Avenida Universidad. Mariachis, ranchera groups and others start tuning up every evening around dusk and go on until the wee hours, with people paying for their favorite tunes.

Cuadros, a café/bar/art gallery at 5 de Mayo Oriente 16, between the Plaza Principal and Plaza de la Independencia, has varied live music nightly except Monday till about 2 am. Thursday through Saturday there's a cover charge of US$2. *El Regio* bar on Plaza de la Corregidora also has live music and gets busy with a young crowd. The university *Escuela de Música* (Music School), on Independencia at Juárez Sur, has posters for rock and other concerts.

The *Casa de la Cultura* at 5 de Mayo 40 sponsors concerts, dance, theater, art exhibitions and other events, as does the ISSSTE Centro Cultural at Arteaga 70. Stop by during office hours to pick up their monthly schedules.

Galería Libertad at Libertad 56, on the south side of Plaza de la Independencia, hosts some excellent art exhibitions; it's open daily from 8 am to 8 pm. There are also usually exhibitions at the Universidad Autónoma de Querétaro's Escuela de Bellas Artes, on Hidalgo between Avenida Tecnológico and Régules.

Querétaro's discos *de moda* are currently *Van Gogh*, attached to the *Vincent* bar at Pasteur Sur 285; *JBJ* at Boulevard Bernardo Quintana 109, just east of the city's eastern ring road and south of the aqueduct; and *Freedom* at Constituyentes Oriente 119 in Colonia Carretas.

Things to Buy

Feria de Artesanías Querétaro, at Juárez Norte 49, is a large crafts shop with a wide range of goods. There are more craft shops and stalls on Libertad and 16 de Septiembre, east of Corregidora.

Getting There & Away

Air Aeromar (☎ 24-13-33) flies to/from Mexico City and Monterrey six days a week. Aerolitoral (☎ 24-27-88) flies to/from Guadalajara and Morelia.

Bus Querétaro is a hub for buses in many directions; the big, modern Central Camionera is five km southeast of the center on the south side of the Mexico City-León highway. There's one building for deluxe and 1st-class, another for 2nd-class. Both buildings have cafeterías, telephone casetas, coin-operated pay phones, shops and luggage guarderías. Daily departures include:

Guadalajara – 350 km, five to six hours; six deluxe by ETN (US$19); 14 1st-class by Primera Plus and others (US$13 to US$14); frequent 2nd-class by Flecha Amarilla and Oriente (US$13)

Guanajuato – 165 km, 2½ hours; two 1st-class by Ómnibus de México (US$5.75); four 2nd-class by Flecha Amarilla (US$5.25); or take one of the frequent buses to Irapuato from where buses leave for Guanajuato every few minutes

Mexico City Airport – 225 km, three hours; 11 1st-class by Aeroplus (US$9.75)

Mexico City (Terminal Norte) – 215 km, 2½ to three hours; 30 deluxe by ETN (US$12); 50 1st-class by Primera Plus (US$8.75); 2nd-class every 10 minutes by Flecha Amarilla and every 40 minutes by Herradura de Plata (US$6.50)

Morelia – 195 km, three to four hours; four 1st-class by Primera Plus (US$6.75); hourly 2nd-class by Flecha Amarilla (US$5.25)

San Luis Potosí – 202 km, 2½ hours; 20-odd 1st-class by Servicios Coordinados, Transportes del Norte or Primera Plus (US$7.25 to US$8); hourly 2nd-class by Flecha Amarilla (US$6.25)

San Miguel de Allende – 60 km, one hour; two deluxe by ETN (US$3.75); 2nd-class every 40 minutes by Herradura de Plata and Flecha Amarilla (US$2)

Tequisquiapan – 70 km, 1½ hours; 2nd-class every 30 minutes by Flecha Amarilla (US$1.30)

Train Querétaro is served by the División del Norte train between Mexico City and Ciudad Juárez and by Train Nos 1 and 2 between Mexico City and Nuevo Laredo. See the Mexico City Train section for information on schedules and fares.

The station (☎ 12-17-03) is on Avenida Héroes de Nacozari at Invierno, about one km north of the center. The ticket office is open daily from 9 am to 5 pm. Tickets for the División del Norte must be bought in advance.

Car & Motorcycle Tolls for cars on highway 57/57D from Mexico City total US$8.25. From Querétaro to Irapuato on highway 45D, it's US$7.

Getting Around

Once you have reached the city center, you can easily get to most sights on foot. The airport is an eight-km taxi ride northeast of the center.

City buses run from 6 am until 9 or 10 pm and cost US$0.30. They can be infuriatingly slow. At the bus station, they leave from an open lot that's a three- or four-minute walk down toward the main highway. Several routes go to the center including Nos 8 and 19, which both go to the Alameda Hidalgo then up Ocampo.

To get out to the bus station from the center, take city bus No 19 or 36 or any other saying 'Terminal de Autobuses' heading south on the east side of the Alameda Hidalgo. To the train station you can take No 110 going north on Allende at Madero.

TEQUISQUIAPAN
pop 22,500; alt 1880m; ☎ 427

This small town ('teh-kees-kee-AP-an') 70 km southeast of Querétaro is a quaint, pleasant retreat from Mexico City or Querétaro, popular with city dwellers on weekends. It has several very attractive places to stay with courtyards, gardens and pools. It used to be known for its thermal spring waters – Mexican presidents came here to ease their aches and tensions – but a couple of industries in the area have drained off the hot water. Nonetheless there are still some delightful cool-water pools. Another pleasure of the place is simply strolling the clean, low-rise colonial streets lined with brilliant purple bougainvillea. The town is also a thriving crafts center, with interesting goods in several shops, the main market and the Mercado de Artesanías. Tequisquiapan's name is sometimes playfully abbreviated to just TX, pronounced 'TEH-kees.'

Orientation & Information

The bus station is a vacant lot on the southwest outskirts of town, a 10-minute walk along Niños Héroes from the center. A local bus (US$0.30) to the Mercado will let you off on Carrizal, a two-minute walk northeast of the central Plaza Principal.

The tourist office (☎ 3-02-95) is at Morelos 7, a block south of the Plaza Principal. It has a brightly colored sign out front and helpful staff. It's normally open Wednesday through Sunday, 10 am to 5 pm, with free maps, brochures and information on Tequisquiapan and the state of Querétaro. The post office is next door.

Things to See & Do

The wide, pretty, traffic-free **Plaza Principal** is overlooked by the 19th century Templo de Santa María de la Asunción on its north side. Near the plaza are many artesanías shops. The main market, on Ezequiel Montes, and the **Mercado de Artesanías** (Crafts Market) on Carrizal, are just a couple of blocks away through little lanes. The large, verdant **Parque La Pila** is a short distance past the Mercado de Artesanías along Ezequiel Montes.

Balnearios The Hotel El Relox (see Places to Stay) has two excellent springfed swimming pools set in large, green, shady gardens. Non-guests can use these for US$11 a day, or take a private pool for the same per hour, or a hot pool for US$20 per hour.

The large, cool pool at the Hotel Neptuno (see Places to Stay) is not quite so pleasant but a good value at US$2 per person. It's open daily from around Semana Santa to October, and just Saturday and Sunday at other times, from 8 am to 6 pm.

Other Activities You can look for migratory birds at the **Santuario de Aves Migratorios La Palapa** by the dam at the north end of the lake just south of town – you'll see it on the right if you approach

Tequis from San Juan del Río. Other things you can do include horseback riding, tennis and golf (ask in your accommodations or the tourist office).

Special Events

The Feria Internacional del Queso y del Vino (International Wine & Cheese Fair), usually from about May 20 to June 1, is the big bash of the year, attracting people from far and wide for tastings, music, charreadas and other events.

Places to Stay – budget

Tequisquiapan has few good budget hotels, but an exception is the *Posada Mejia* (no telephone), run by a friendly and hospitable family at Prieto 17, on the corner of 16 de Septiembre. The 16 simple but clean rooms are set around a courtyard with trees and roses. Singles/doubles are US$7.75/14.50.

Places to Stay – middle

The friendly *Posada Los Arcos* (☎ 3-05-66) at Moctezuma 12, a couple of minutes northwest of the Plaza Principal, has nine very nice rooms with bath, around a garden courtyard, for US$11/20. Another fairly economical place nearby is the 11-room *Posada San Francisco* (☎ 3-02-31), Moctezuma 2 at Madero, with a large enclosed garden and swimming pool that are overlooked by a statue of a ruminating nymph. The San Francisco had just changed hands when we visited, so you should ask for current prices.

Hotel/Balneario Neptuno (☎ 3-02-24) is at Juárez Oriente 5, two blocks east of the Plaza Principal; singles/doubles are US$13/20. It has a large pool.

Posada del Virrey (☎ /fax 3-02-39), Prieto Norte 9 at 16 de Septiembre, one block west and two north of the Plaza Principal, is in a pretty building with a courtyard. It has 22 rooms and a pool at US$26 for a double (US$32 with breakfast).

On the Plaza Principal at Juárez 10, *Hotel La Plaza* (☎ 3-00-56, fax 3-02-89), with pool, restaurant, bar and parking, has

17 varied rooms and suites from US$24 to US$59.

Places to Stay – top end

Hotel Maridelfi (☎ 3-00-52, fax 3-10-78) on the Plaza Principal is a lovely, comfortable hotel around nice gardens. It's popular with Mexican families. Three meals a day are included for US$38 per person.

Hotel El Relox (☎ /fax 3-00-06, 3-00-66; relox@albec.com.mx) on Ezequiel Montes, 1½ blocks north of the Plaza Principal (though its official address is Morelos 8), has 110 singles/doubles with TV for US$43/52. The hotel is set in extensive gardens with pools (see Balnearios). Guests can also use a variety of thermal and cool private pools for US$6.50 to US$20 an hour per group. There's a restaurant and a gym too.

Places to Eat

There are many restaurants in all price categories around the center. The cheapest place for a meal or snack is the rear of the main market, where many clean little *fondas* (food stalls) have tables under awnings in the patio. They're open daily from around 8 am to 8 pm.

A nice place on the plaza is *K'puchinos*, with indoor and outdoor tables, where a good comida – for example spinach soup, spaghetti, main course, dessert and coffee – costs US$4.25 and is served in the evenings too. There's also medium-priced à la carte fare and a big choice of coffees. *La Casa de la Arrachera* next door does breakfasts for US$2.25 and comida for US$3.25.

The restaurant at the *Hotel Maridelfi* on the plaza is very good but a little expensive

with breakfast at US$4.75 and lunch at US$5.25.

Getting There & Away

Tequisquiapan is 20 km northeast up highway 120 from the larger town of San Juan del Río, which is on highway 57. Buses to/from Tequis are all 2nd-class. Flecha Azul runs every 30 minutes, 5.30 am to 7 pm, to Querétaro (70 km, 1½ hours, US$1.30); Flecha Amarilla goes every 40 minutes, 6 am to 8 pm, to/from Mexico City's Terminal Norte (184 km, 2¾ hours, US$6).

NORTHEAST QUERÉTARO

Those heading to/from northeast Mexico, or anyone with a hankering to get off the beaten track, might consider following highway 120 northeast from Tequisquiapan over the scenic Sierra Gorda to the lush Huasteca area (covered in the Central Gulf Coast chapter). This route climbs to over 2300 meters at Pinal de Amoles before descending rapidly to Jalpan at 760 meters. Along the way there's a botanic garden – the Invernadero Fernando Schmoll, with over 4400 varieties of cactus – in the town center at Cadereyta, 38 km from Tequis. Farther along, on and off highway 120, is a series of five beautiful mission churches. They were set up by Fray Junípero Serra in this remote region in the mid-18th century, at Jalpan, Concá, Landa de Matamoros, Tilaco and Tancoyol. Jalpan, 170 km from Tequis, has a good range of accommodations. The tourist offices in Querétaro and Tequis can give you plenty of information on this region.

Central Gulf Coast

The route from northeast to southeast Mexico lies along the hot coastal plain between the Gulf of Mexico and the country's central mountains. Veracruz – a holiday resort for Mexicans – is the most appealing of the coastal cities, with a festive atmosphere and one of the country's most riotous carnavales. A number of cities lie inland, in the foothills of the Sierra Madre; Jalapa, the capital of Veracruz state, and Córdoba are the most attractive.

This chapter covers the coast and hinterland from Ciudad Madero in the north to Coatzacoalcos in the south – just over 600 km as the crow flies but more than 800 km

by highway 180, which follows the curve of the coast. It's an area with a fascinating prehistory but only one major archaeological site – El Tajín, near Papantla, which shouldn't be missed as you travel through.

Southern Veracruz was the Olmec heartland, but there's little to see there now. The best collections of Olmec artifacts, including several of the mighty 'Olmec heads' of sculpted basalt, are in the Museo de Antropología in Jalapa, and at Parque-Museo La Venta in Villahermosa (see the Tabasco & Chiapas chapter). The Jalapa museum has by far the best archaeological collection from the Gulf Coast as a whole.

HIGHLIGHTS

- The tropical port of Veracruz, one of the country's most festive and historic cities
- Jalapa's superb Museum of Anthropology, home to seven huge Olmec heads and scores of other fantastic artifacts
- Catemaco, a quiet town that gently slopes down to a lake and is known throughout Mexico for its witch doctors
- The mystical jungle-ringed ruins of El Tajín, which have been extensively reconstructed
- Costa Esmeralda, home to numerous cozy hotels and restaurants that face a calming sea – a fine place to relax

TONY WHEELER

History

Olmec The first great center of Central America's earliest civilization, and Mexico's ancestral culture, the Olmec, prospered from about 1200 to 900 BC at San Lorenzo, in southern Veracruz state. After it fell, La Venta in neighboring Tabasco was the main Olmec center until around 600 BC when it, too, was violently destroyed. Olmec culture lingered – influenced gradually from elsewhere – for several centuries more at Tres Zapotes, in Veracruz.

Classic Veracruz After the Olmec decline, the centers of civilization on the Gulf Coast moved west and north. El Pital, the ruins of which were just discovered in the early 1990s, was a large city about 100 km northwest of Veracruz city. It existed from about 100 to 600 AD, had links with Teotihuacán, and may have held more than 20,000 people.

The Classic period (300 to 900 AD) saw the emergence in central and northern Veracruz of a number of power centers that were politically independent but shared religion and culture. Together they're known as the Classic Veracruz civilization. Their hallmark is the unique style of their carvings, with pairs of parallel lines curved and interwoven. The style often appears on three types of mysterious carved stone objects; these objects are probably connected with the civilization's important ritual ball game. They are the U-shaped *yugo*, probably representing a wooden or leather belt worn in the game; the long, paddle-like *palma*; and the flat *hacha*, shaped a little like an ax head. The last two objects, which are often carved in human or animal forms, are thought to represent items attached to the front of the belt. Hachas may also have been court markers.

The most important Classic Veracruz center, El Tajín, was at its height from about 600 to 900 AD and contains at least 11 ball courts. Other main centers were Las Higueras near Vega de Alatorre, by the coast south of Nautla, and El Zapotal near Ignacio de la Llave, south of Veracruz city.

Classic Veracruz sites show influences from the Mayan lands and from Teotihuacán; in turn, Veracruz cultures exported cotton, rubber, cacao and vanilla to central Mexico, influencing developments in Teotihuacán, Cholula and elsewhere.

Totonac, Huastec, Toltec & Aztec By 1200 AD, when El Tajín was abandoned, the Totonacs were establishing themselves from Tuxpan in the north to beyond Veracruz in the south. North of Tuxpan, the Huastec civilization, another web of small, probably independent states, flourished from 800 to 1200. It was Mexico's chief cotton producer. Also, the people built many ceremonial sites and developed great skill in stone carving.

During that time, the warlike Toltecs, who dominated much of central Mexico in the early Postclassic age, moved into the Gulf Coast area. They occupied the Huastec center Castillo de Teayo for some time between 900 and 1200. There's also Toltec influence at Zempoala, a Totonac site near Veracruz city. In the mid-15th century, the Aztecs subdued most of the Totonac and Huastec areas, exacting tribute of goods and sacrificial victims and maintaining garrisons to control revolts.

Colonial Era When Cortés arrived on the Gulf Coast in April 1519, he was able to make the Totonacs of Zempoala his first allies against the Aztecs – he told them to imprison five Aztec tribute collectors and vowed to protect them against reprisals. Cortés set up his first settlement, Villa Rica de la Vera Cruz (Rich Town of the True Cross), north of modern Veracruz city, and a second one at La Antigua, where he scuttled his ships before advancing to Tenochtitlán, the Aztec capital. In May 1520 he returned to Zempoala and defeated the rival Spanish expedition sent to arrest him.

All the Gulf Coast was in Spanish hands by 1523. Diseases, particularly recently introduced ones like smallpox, decimated the Indian population. Veracruz harbor became an essential link in trade and communication with Spain and was vital for anyone trying to rule Mexico, but the climate, tropical diseases and threat of pirate attacks inhibited the growth of Spanish settlements.

19th & 20th Centuries The population of Veracruz city actually shrank in the first half of the 19th century. Under dictator Porfirio Díaz, Mexico's first railway linked Veracruz to Mexico City in 1872, and some industries began to develop.

In 1901 oil was discovered in the Tampico area, which by the 1920s was producing a quarter of the world's oil. That proportion declined, but new oil fields were found in southern Veracruz, and by the 1980s the Gulf Coast had well over half of Mexico's reserves and refining capacity.

Geography & Climate
More than 40 rivers run from the inland mountains to the Central Gulf Coast, mostly passing through a well-watered, hilly landscape. In the north there is an undulating coastal plain, while in the southeast there are more low-lying areas, prone to flooding, with marshes and jungles that extend into Tabasco.

It's warm and humid most of the time: hotter along the coast, wetter in the foothills, hottest and wettest of all in the low-lying southeast. Two-thirds or more of the rain falls between June and September. The city of Veracruz receives about 1650 mm of rain a year. From April to October it has temperatures well over 30°C, falling into the teens at night only from December to February. Tuxpan and Tampico, on the north coast, are a bit drier, a little hotter in summer and a fraction cooler in winter. Coatzacoalcos in the southeast gets 3000 mm of rain a year.

Population & People
Veracruz, with about seven million people, is Mexico's third most populous state. Many Africans were shipped to the Gulf Coast in the 16th century, and their descendants, plus more recent immigrants from Cuba, contribute a visible African element to the population and culture. Of the

region's nearly half a million Indians, the most numerous are the 150,000 Totonacs and 150,000 Huastecs. (See the sidebars on The Huastecs, The Totonacs and Voladores in this chapter for more on these peoples.)

Tampico & the Huasteca

The fertile, often beautiful Huasteca ('wass-TEK-a') region is inland from Tampico, where the coastal plain meets the fringes of the Sierra Madre Oriental. Spread over southern Tamaulipas, eastern San Luis Potosí and northern Veracruz, the region is named after the Huastec people who have lived here for about 3000 years. If you're heading southeast, a couple of routes go through the Huasteca to the Central Gulf Coast. Going west from the coast to the Bajío region or Mexico City, there are four steep, winding routes that climb onto the Sierra – from Ciudad Valles, Xilitla, Tamazunchale and Huejutla.

TAMPICO-CIUDAD MADERO
pop 600,000; ☎ *12*

Sweaty, smelly, at times seedy but always jolly, Tampico, a few km upstream from the mouth of the Río Pánuco, detains few travelers. Somewhat faded since its 1920s heyday, it's still Mexico's busiest port, a tropical place where bars stay open late and where the city is beautifying its downtown after years of neglect. (But if tropical port atmosphere is what you're after, head on down to Veracruz city, which has it in spades.) Hotel prices are slightly inflated by the oil business, but reasonable-value lodging is available, as well as good seafood. Ciudad Madero, between Tampico and the coast, is the processing center for the country's oldest oil fields, and has a wide sandy beach.

History
In 1523 Cortés defeated the native Huastec Indians and founded a colony called San Estéban, now Pánuco, 30 km upriver from Tampico. In the next few years he prevailed not only over the rebellious Huastecs, but also over Spanish rivals including Nuño de Guzmán, who was named royal governor of the Pánuco area in 1527. De Guzmán concentrated on pillage and slaughter in western Mexico, and organized slave raids north of the Pánuco, but was eventually sent back to Spain.

In the 1530s a mission was established in Tampico, for the purpose of converting the Huastecs to Christianity. The town was destroyed by pirates in 1684 but was refounded in 1823 by families from Altamira, to the north. After 1901, when oil was discovered in the area, Tampico suddenly became the world's biggest oil port: rough, tough and booming. The oil and its profits were under foreign control until 1938, when the industry was nationalized by President Lázaro Cárdenas following a strike by Tampico oil workers.

Mexico's 1970s and '80s oil boom took place farther down the coast, but the Tampico-Ciudad Madero area remains important. Pipelines and barge fleets bring oil from fields north and south, onshore and offshore, to its refineries and harbor, and Ciudad Madero is the headquarters of the powerful oil workers' union, the STPRM.

Orientation
Tampico is in a marshy region near the mouth of the Río Pánuco, ringed by several lakes including Laguna del Chairel, which is used for recreation, and the unattractive Laguna del Carpintero, which isn't. You'll cross numerous smaller estuarine rivers as you approach the city from the north or the west. Going south, the spectacular Puente Tampico bridge crosses the Río Pánuco to Veracruz state.

Downtown Tampico centers on two plazas. One is the zócalo, or Plaza de Armas, with a 20th century cathedral on its north side and the Hotel Inglaterra on its south side. One block south and one east is the beautiful and popular Plaza de la Libertad. Hotels and restaurants of all

CENTRAL GULF COAST

PLACES TO STAY
3 Hotel Capri
4 Hotel Impala
5 Hotel Inglaterra
7 Hotel Mundo
8 Hotel La Paz
9 Hotel Jalisco
11 Hotel Plaza
12 Hotel Howard Johnson
13 Hotel Posada del Rey
16 Hotel Posada Don Francisco

PLACES TO EAT
2 Restaurant Super Cream
6 Cafetería Emir
15 VIPS Restaurant

OTHER
1 Tourist Office
10 Colectivos to Bus Station
14 Post Office

grades are within a few blocks of these two plazas. Down a gentle hill south of either plaza you come to a sleazy area containing the market, train station and riverside docks – it isn't very safe at night around here. Tampico's bus station is in the north of the city far from the downtown area. Colectivos will take you to the city center from there for US$0.50. The center of Ciudad Madero is a few km northeast of central Tampico, and its industrial zones extend east to Playa Miramar, on the Gulf of Mexico.

Addresses on east-west streets usually have the suffix Ote (east) or Pte (west), while those on north-south streets are Nte (north) or Sur (south). The dividing point is the junction of Colón and Carranza at the northwest corner of the zócalo.

Information
Tourist Office Tampico's tourist office (☎ 12-00-07) is on 20 de Noviembre, between Obregón and Altamira. The staff are helpful, speak some English and have brochures and maps. The office is open

weekdays from 8 am to 7 pm, and weekends from 9 am to 1 pm.

Money Banorte, Bancomer and other banks are on or around the central plazas. They change traveler's checks and have ATMs.

Post & Communications The main post office is across the street from Plaza de la Libertad to the north, at Madero 309. At the bus station, there's a post office in the 2nd-class hall, and pay phones and a telephone caseta in the 1st-class hall.

Museo de la Cultura Huasteca

The Museum of Huastec Culture, in Ciudad Madero's Instituto Tecnológico, has a small collection from the pre-Hispanic Huastec culture and a worthwhile book store. From central Tampico take a 'Boulevard A López Mateos' bus north on Alfaro, and ask for 'Tecnológico Madero.' The museum is open weekdays from 10 am to 5 pm and Saturday from 10 am to 3 pm; admission is free.

Playa Miramar

The 10-km-long Playa Miramar is about 15 km from downtown Tampico; to get there you pass central Ciudad Madero and several km of petrochemical installations. The beach is wide and reasonably clean, lined with some run-down restaurants and hotels; the exception is the *Hotel Moeva Miramar* (☎ 13-63-61), which has singles/doubles with air-con, TV and phone for US$35/40. The beach has lots of shady palapas and rental chairs, but it's deserted during the week. The water is lukewarm and not crystal-clear, but it's clean enough. From central Tampico, take a 'Playa' bus or colectivo.

Special Events

Semana Santa brings many activities to Playa Miramar, such as regattas, fishing and wind-surfing competitions, sand-sculpture contests, music, dancing and bonfires. The anniversary of Tampico's 1823 refounding is celebrated on April 12,

with a procession from Altamira that passes through Tampico's zócalo.

Places to Stay – budget

The *Hotel Capri* (☎ 12-26-80), at Juárez 202 Nte, is the best value in town with small, clean rooms with ceiling fans, private baths and hot water at US$6 for a single or double. Another cheapie is the *Hotel Señorial* (☎ 12-40-90), at Madero 1006 Ote, 400 meters east of the Plaza de la Libertad, with worn beds in tiny rooms for US$6.50. A much better option, but not quite the bargain to be had at the Capri, is the *Hotel Posada Don Francisco* (☎ 19-25-34), at Díaz Mirón 710 Ote. The inn is clean and well kept, and has air-con rooms from US$12/17.

Down among the foul smells, cheap cantinas and air of nocturnal danger near the markets are two inexpensive possibilities: the *Hotel La Paz* (☎ 14-11-19), at La Paz 307 Pte, with air-con rooms for US$9/10; and the *Hotel Jalisco* (☎ 12-27-92), at La Paz 120 Pte, without air-con but with secure parking for US$8/9. Female travelers who wish to avoid unsavory attention should stay clear of this area after 7 pm, when prostitutes and their clients appear in the neighborhood.

Places to Stay – middle

Mid-range hotels in Tampico are good values, with carpet, cable TV and phone in air-con rooms at fair prices. The *Hotel Posada del Rey* (☎ 14-11-55), at Madero 218 Ote, is one such place. It charges US$22/24 for singles/doubles; its strategic location, with rooms overlooking the handsome Plaza de la Libertad, make it a bargain. The *Hotel Plaza* (☎ 14-17-84), at Madero 204 Ote, has clean, comfortable, but smaller rooms with air-con for US$16/17. Between these two, and superior to both but considerably pricier, is a *Hotel Howard Johnson* (☎ 12-76-76), at Madero 210 Ote, with clean, tasteful, modern, air-con rooms for US$38/42.

If you must be in Tampico and there's nowhere else to stay, the *Hotel Impala* (☎ 12-09-90), at Díaz Mirón 220 Pte, 1½ blocks west of the zócalo, won't kill you with its worn rooms and very tacky carpet for US$24/28. For US$2 less, the *Hotel Mundo* (☎ 12-03-60), on Díaz Mirón between López de Lara and Aduana, offers spacious clean rooms with parking, color TV, air-con, phone and good beds; it also has a popular restaurant.

Places to Stay – top end
The top downtown place is the *Hotel Inglaterra* (☎ 19-28-57), on the zócalo at Díaz Mirón Ote 116, offering 120 air-con singles or doubles with all the modern conveniences at US$70; its own fancy but reasonably priced restaurant; and a small swimming pool. The hotel provides free shuttle service to and from the Tampico airport.

Out toward the airport, at Avenida Hidalgo 2000, the *Hotel Camino Real* (☎ 13-88-11) is Tampico's most luxurious hotel, with rooms and bungalows facing a tropical garden-courtyard and a large pool. Prices start at US$90 for one or two people.

Places to Eat
Tampico is no gourmet paradise, but the seafood can be good. A local specialty is *carne asada Tampiqueña*, which is beefsteak marinated in garlic, oil and oregano and usually served with guacamole, strips of chili and corn chips.

The best downtown restaurants are in the big hotels such as the Inglaterra, which serves up a delicious pepper steak (US$7) and an excellent fish fillet wrapped in banana leaf and boiled with achiote spice and orange sauce (US$9).

The *Restaurant Super Cream*, on the corner of Altamira and Olmos, has a pleasant atmosphere, friendly service and good food. Breakfasts range from US$1 for two biscuits with butter and jam to US$3 for a large omelet, a glass of juice and coffee. Burgers and Mexican food range from US$2 to US$3.

The *Cafetería Emir*, at Olmos 107 Sur, is popular with locals despite wobbly tables and loud music. Quesadillas and enchiladas cost about US$2.50, and meat and fish dishes from US$3.50 to US$5.

Equally popular and looking very American with its speedy service and its bright and cheery atmosphere is *VIPS*, at the corner of Aduana and Madero. VIPS offers a large selection of salads and American and Mexican dishes, with few items over US$5. VIPS is very 'in' with Tampico's yuppies.

Getting There & Away
Air Mexicana Airlines (☎ 13-96-00), whose city office is at Universidad 700-1, has flights daily to/from Mexico City, Monterrey, Veracruz, San Luis Potosí and McAllen, Texas. Aero Litoral (☎ 28-08-57), which has only one office (at the airport), flies to/from Monterrey, Veracruz and Villahermosa.

Bus The Tampico bus station is seven km from downtown, on Rosalio Bustamante. First-class service is handled on the right side of the bus station as you enter and is provided principally by ADO, Línea Azul (LA) and Futura; 2nd-class is on the left. The 1st-class side has left-luggage facilities and pay phones. There are connections to most main towns north of Mexico City and down the Gulf Coast. The main destinations and daily frequency of service include:

Matamoros – 570 km, eight hours; 13 Futura and three ADO buses (US$18) and many 2nd-class buses

Mexico City (Terminal Norte) – 515 km, 9½ hours; three deluxe overnight buses by UNO (US$31) and frequent 1st-class (US$21) and many 2nd-class (US$18) buses

Monterrey – 530 km, 7½ hours; three Futura (US$19) and many 2nd-class (US$17) buses

Nuevo Laredo – 755 km, 11 hours; three Futura (US$28) and eight 2nd-class (US$25) buses

Pachuca – 380 km, nine hours; one Futura (US$17) and a few 2nd-class buses

Poza Rica – 250 km, five hours; one deluxe UNO (US$12), 21 Futura (US$10) and frequent 2nd-class (US$8) buses

San Luis Potosí – 410 km, seven hours; five Futura and three LA (US$18) and several 2nd-class (US$14) buses

Tuxpan – 190 km, four hours; many 1st-class (US$7) and 2nd-class (US$6) buses

Veracruz – 490 km, 10 hours; one deluxe UNO (US$32), nine ADO (US$19) and many 2nd-class (US$17) buses

Long-distance 1st-class buses also go to Reynosa, Soto la Marina, Villahermosa and Jalapa, while towns in the Huasteca – such as Ciudad Valles, Tamazunchale and Huejutla – are mostly served by 2nd-class buses.

Train First-class trains go to Monterrey (via Ciudad Victoria) for US$6 (departing 7.45 am) and to San Luis Potosí for US$5 (departing 8 am).

Car & Motorcycle Highway 180 is in good condition for most of the 95-km stretch between Altamira and Aldama, north of Tampico. Heading south out of Tampico, the highway soars across the Puente Tampico (toll is US$3). Between the bridge and Tuxpan the road is good but night driving should be avoided.

Getting Around

To/From the Airport Tampico airport is 15 km north of downtown. Transporte Terrestre (☎ 28-45-88) runs colectivo combis from the airport to anywhere in Tampico-Ciudad Madero for about US$8 (the price varies with distance), but operates only a taxi service going *to* the airport (about US$20 from downtown). Transporte Terrestre dispatchers speak some English.

To/From the Bus Station & Beach The city's colectivo taxis are large, old US cars, usually bright yellow, with the destinations painted on the doors. They wait outside the bus station to take you to the city center (US$0.50). From the city center to the bus station, take a 'Perimetral' or 'Perimetral-CC' colectivo from Olmos, a block south of the zócalo (US$0.40). 'Playa' buses or colectivos north on Alfaro will reach Playa Miramar (US$5).

CIUDAD VALLES

pop 320,000; alt 80m; ☎ *138*

Ciudad Valles ('VAH-yes') lies on highway 85, the Pan-American, a little over halfway from Monterrey to Mexico City, at the junction of the highway from Tampico to San Luis Potosí. It's a convenient overnight stop for motorists. Cattle and coffee are among its most important commercial activities.

Orientation

The main plaza is about seven blocks west of highway 85; the Central de Autobuses is at the southern edge of town.

Museo Regional Huasteco

On the corner of Rotarios and Artes, the museum has a collection of Huastec artifacts, and is open on weekdays from 10 am to 6 pm.

Places to Stay

Two adequate places are the *Hotel Rex* (☎ 2-33-35) at Hidalgo 418, 3½ blocks from the plaza, and the *Hotel Piña* (☎ 2-01-83) at Juárez 210, a little closer to the plaza (Juárez is parallel to Hidalgo, one block north). Both are clean and unspectacular with moderately sized singles, but only the latter has rooms with air-con. Rates for both hotels range from US$9 to US$11 and US$10.50 to US$13, depending on whether you want TV.

Stepping up in price but a much better value is the *Hotel San Fernando* (☎ 2-22-80), on Mexico-Laredo 17 Nte. The San Fernando offers singles/doubles with air-con, TV and phone for US$18/19. The rooms are comfortable, spacious and clean.

One km north of the town along highway 85, the *Hotel Valles* (☎ 2-00-50) is a luxurious motel with large air-con rooms set amid a sprawling tropical garden for US$40/45. It has a big swimming pool and a 25-site campground/trailer park where full hook-ups cost around US$15.

There are three hotels across the street from the bus station, of which the *Hotel San Carlos* (☎ 1-21-42) is the best value.

The San Carlos offers clean, comfy rooms with air-con and TV for US$9/11.

Places to Eat

The *Pizza Bella Napoli*, next to the Hotel Piña at Juárez 210, does decent spaghetti (about US$3.50) and pizza (US$3 to US$4). For Mexican food, including comida corrida, try the *Restaurant Malibu* at Hidalgo 109, a few doors from the central plaza; most of the items are under US$3. Hotel Valles has a reasonably priced steakhouse, the *Restaurant Del Bosque*.

The Huastecs

The Huastec language is classified as one of the Mayance family, along with the languages of the Yucatán Maya – possibly stemming from a single tongue once spoken all down the Gulf Coast. The Huastec language may have split from the rest of the family in about 900 BC, when the Olmec culture arose in the intervening area. The central-Mexican feathered serpent god Quetzalcóatl was probably of Huastec origin.

The Huastecs' greatest period was roughly 800 to 1200 AD. Under a number of independent rulers, they built many ceremonial centers, practiced phallic fertility rites and expanded as far west as northeast Querétaro and Hidalgo. They developed great skill in potterymaking and in carving stone and shells. The two most interesting Huastec sites to visit are Tamuín and Castillo de Teayo (see the Around Tuxpan section), though neither is spectacular.

After the Spanish conquest, during the second half of the 16th century, slavery and imported diseases cut the Huastec population from an estimated one million to probably under 100,000. Rebellions began and continued into the 19th century. Today, about 150,000 Huastecs live in the Huasteca, mostly between Ciudad Valles and Tamazunchale, and east of Tantoyuca. Many of the women still wear quechquémitls, colorfully embroidered with traditional trees of life, animals, flowers and two-armed crosses. Huastecs still practice land fertility ceremonies, particularly dances. ■

Getting There & Away

Bus The bus station is on Contreras between Delgadillo and Davalos, off the highway to Mexico City. The principal 1st-class lines are Ómnibus de Oriente (ODO), Línea Azul (LA) and Transportes Frontera (TF). There are many 2nd-class services. Daily departures include:

Matamoros – 545 km, 10 hours; six ODO, six TF and three LA (US$18) and several 2nd-class (US$15) buses

Mexico City (Terminal Norte) – 465 km, 10 hours; five ODO, four TF and three LA (US$20) and hourly 2nd-class (US$13) buses

Monterrey – 520 km, eight hours; nine TF, 7 ODO and two LA (US$21) and numerous 2nd-class (US$17) buses

San Luis Potosí – 270 km, 4½ hours; dozens of 1st-class (US$13) and frequent 2nd-class (US$10) buses

Tampico – 140 km, 2½ hours; many 1st-class (US$5.50) and 2nd-class (US$4) buses

There are also buses to Pachuca, Ciudad Victoria and Tamazunchale.

Car & Motorcycle West to San Luis Potosí (270 km), highway 70 is spectacular as it rises across the Sierra Madre to the Altiplano Central. It's a twisting road, and you can get stuck behind slow trucks and buses, so don't count on doing it in a hurry. Highway 110, east to Tampico, is in worse condition but is straighter. Going south, highway 85 goes to Tamazunchale. You can continue past Tamazunchale to Huejutla, and circle the Huasteca back to Tampico.

TAMUÍN

The important Huastec ceremonial center of Tamuín flourished from about 700 to 1200 AD – the site of the ruins is not spectacular but it is one of the few Huastec sites worth visiting at all. It's seven km from the town of Tamuín and 30 km east of Ciudad Valles on highway 110. One km east of the town, turn south from the highway down a road marked 'San Vincente.' Continue for 5.5 km to a small sign indicating the 'zona arqueológica'; from there it's an 800-meter walk to the ruins. Frequent buses between

Tampico and Ciudad Valles go through Tamuín. The rest of the way you must walk or take a taxi.

The only cleared part of the 170,000-sq-meter site is a plaza with platforms made of river stones on all four sides. A low bench with two conical altars, extending from the east side of a small platform in the middle of the plaza, bears the remains of frescos (probably 8th or 9th century) that may represent priests of Quetzalcóatl.

TANCANHUITZ

The small town of Tancanhuitz, also called Ciudad Santos, is in the heart of the area inhabited by modern-day Huastecs. It's in a narrow, tree-covered valley 52 km south of Ciudad Valles, three km east of highway 85. A lively market takes place on Sunday. There are pre-Hispanic Huastec remains near **Tampamolón**, a few km east.

Tancanhuitz, and also Aquismón (see below), are centers for the festivals of San Miguel Arcángel on September 28 and 29 and the Virgen de Guadalupe on December 12. Huastec dances performed then include Las Varitas (The Little Twigs) and Zacamson (Small Music), which imitate the movements of wild creatures.

AQUISMÓN

The Huastec village of Aquismón, up a side road a few km west of highway 85, holds its market on Saturday. The Zacamson dance is a specialty around Aquismón. In its full version, it has more than 75 parts, danced at different times of the day and night. At festivals it is accompanied by much drinking of sugar-cane alcohol.

In the roadless country nearby are the 105-meter **Cascada de Tamul**, which is 300 meters wide when in flood, and the **Sótano de las Golondrinas** (Pit of the Swallows), a 300-meter-deep hole which is home to tens of thousands of swallows and parakeets, and a challenge for serious spelunkers.

XILITLA

On the slopes of the Sierra at 1000 meters, this small town has a 16th century church

and mission, a temperate climate and lots of rain. Two nearby attractions are the **Cueva del Saliter**, with stalactites, and the **Castillo de Sir Edward James**, the architectural folly of an eccentric English aristocrat. Xilitla is 21 km west of highway 85, up highway 120 – one of the least traveled routes between the Huasteca and the Sierra.

TAMAZUNCHALE

pop 65,000; alt 20m; ☎ 136

Quaint Tamazunchale, 95 km south of Ciudad Valles on highway 85, is in a low-lying area of tropical vegetation with exuberant bird life. The Sunday market is colorful, but has little in the way of Huastecan handicrafts. For Day of the Dead (November 2), the people spread carpets of confetti and marigold petals on the streets. There's no bus station as such, but buses pull in at various company offices on Avenida 20 de Noviembre.

The *Hotel González* (☎ 2-01-36) is the cheapest decent place in town with basic rooms with fan and TV for US$7.50/9.50 for a single/double. The *Hotel Mirador* (☎ 2-01-90) and the *Hotel Tropical* (☎ 2-00-41) both offer clean rooms for US$14/16, add a dollar for air-con; the Tropical has slightly nicer rooms. The best hotel in town is the *Hotel Tamazunchale* (☎ 2-04-96), which offers gorgeous rooms with all the modern conveniences for US$28/33. All of these hotels are located along highway 85 as it slows and passes through town.

Southeast of Tamazunchale, highway 85 climbs steeply to Ixmiquilpan, then continues to Pachuca and Mexico City. This is the most direct route from the Huasteca to Mexico City. It's another steep but scenic route up onto the Sierra Madre. You can encounter mist and fog – start early for the best chance of clear conditions.

HUEJUTLA

pop 50,000; alt 30m; ☎ 129

On the northern edge of Hidalgo state, but still in the semitropical lowlands, Huejutla has a fortress-monastery dating from the

16th century, when this area was frontier territory and subject to Indian attacks. The big Sunday market in the square attracts many Nahua Indians from outlying villages. For lodging try the *Hotel Oviedo* (☎ 6-05-90) at Morelos 12. It has clean rooms with refrigerator, air-con and TV for US$10. The *Hotel Fayad* (☎ 6-00-40), on Hidalgo at Morelos, also has air-con rooms for US$10, but they are more worn than those at the Oviedo.

SOUTH OF HUEJUTLA

Highway 105 mostly goes through lush, rolling farmland from Tampico, but south of Huejutla it climbs into the lovely Sierra Madre Oriental. It's a tortuous and sometimes foggy road to Pachuca. En route, there are old monasteries at **Molango** and **Zacualtipán**.

The highway then leaves the Sierra Madre and drops several hundred meters to **Metzquititlán** in the fertile Río Tulancingo Valley. The village of **Metztitlán**, 23 km northwest up the valley, has a fairly well-preserved monastery. It was the center of an Otomí Indian state that the Aztecs couldn't conquer. After another 100 km, and an 800-meter climb up from the Tulancingo valley, you reach **Atotonilco el Grande**, 34 km from Pachuca. (See the Around Mexico City chapter for information about places near Pachuca.)

Northern Veracruz

South of Tampico you enter the state of Veracruz, whose northern half is mostly rolling plains, lying between the coast and the southern end of the Sierra Madre Oriental. The Laguna de Tamiahua stretches 90 km along the coast, separated from the Gulf of Mexico by a series of sandbars and islands, with isolated though often polluted beaches and opportunities for fishing and birding. The major archaeological attraction is the site of El Tajín, usually reached from Papantla.

TUXPAN

pop 130,000; ☎ *783*

Tuxpan ('TOOKS-pahn') is a fishing town and minor oil port near the mouth of the Río Tuxpan, 300 km north of Veracruz and 190 km south of Tampico. The city itself has a wide river and pleasant parks, and an alluring beach is 12 km away. Though it's not an idyllic seaside resort, it is a more agreeable place to break a journey than Tampico.

Orientation

The downtown is on the north bank of the Río Tuxpan, spreading six blocks upstream from the high bridge that spans the river. The river-front road, Boulevard Heroles, passes under the bridge and runs 12 km east to the beach at Playa Norte. A block inland from Heroles is Avenida Juárez, with many hotels. Parque Reforma, at its west end, functions as a zócalo and is popular in the cool of the evening.

Information

There's a tourist office (☎ 4-01-77) in the Palacio Municipal, open daily, but its staff speak no English and are put off by questions in Spanish. There are pay phones in Parque Reforma, and a Banamex (with ATM) nearby. Banca Serfin and Bancomer, on Juárez, also have ATMs. The Hotel Plaza will change traveler's checks outside of business hours. The post office is at Morelos 12.

Museums

On the west side of Parque Reforma is a small **Museo Arqueológico** with Totonac and Huastec artifacts (open Tuesday through Saturday from 9 am to 7 pm; admission free).

The **Museo Histórico de la Amistad México-Cuba** (Mexican-Cuban Friendship Museum), on the south side of the river, commemorates Fidel Castro's 1956 stay in Tuxpan, when he planned and prepared for the Cuban revolution. It has a not-very-interesting collection of B&W photos and posters and a map of his Cuban campaign. Beside the museum stands a replica of the

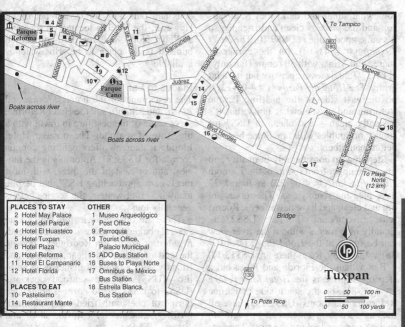

PLACES TO STAY
2 Hotel May Palace
3 Hotel del Parque
4 Hotel El Huasteco
5 Hotel Tuxpan
6 Hotel Plaza
8 Hotel Reforma
11 Hotel El Campanario
12 Hotel Florida

PLACES TO EAT
10 Pastelisimo
14 Restaurant Mante

OTHER
1 Museo Arqueológico
7 Post Office
9 Parroquia
13 Tourist Office,
   Palacio Municipal
15 ADO Bus Station
16 Buses to Playa Norte
17 Omnibus de México
   Bus Station
18 Estrella Blanca,
   Bus Station

Tuxpan

0   50   100 m
0   50   100 yards

CENTRAL GULF COAST

wooden *Granma*, in which Castro and 82 comrades sailed to Cuba to launch the revolution. The museum is open daily from 9 am to 5 pm; it's free but a donation is requested. To reach it, take one of the small boats across the river (US$0.40), walk several blocks to Obregón, then turn right. The museum is at the end of Obregón, just before you reach the river again.

Playa Norte

Tuxpan's beach is a wide strip of sand stretching 20 km north from the mouth of the Río Tuxpan, 12 km east of the town. Its beauty is lessened by a power station two km north of the river mouth, but the water and sand are fairly clean and, apart from holidays and weekends, it's almost empty. A line of palapas serve seafood and sell souvenirs. Local buses marked 'Playa' leave every 20 minutes from the south side of Heroles, and drop you at the south end of the beach (25 minutes; US$0.60). On

the way back they do a quick tour of downtown before leaving you on Heroles near the end of Rodríguez.

There's a scuba-diving operation – *Aqua Sports* (☎ 7-02-59) – on the road to Playa Norte a few km from downtown.

Special Events

A big fishing tournament brings hundreds of visitors to Tuxpan in late June or early July, and festivities for the Assumption on August 15 continue for a week with folk-dancing contests, bullfights and fireworks. The Totonac *voladores* (flyers; see the sidebar later in this chapter) usually perform.

Places to Stay

The *Hotel El Campanario* (☎ 4-08-55), at 5 de Febrero 9, has clean singles/doubles with private bath and fan for US$10/11, add US$1 for TV. Though rooms at *Hotel El Huasteco* (☎ 4-18-59) at Morelos 41 are somewhat small and dark, they're all air-con and the place is clean and friendly, so it's quite good value at US$9/10. The *Hotel Tuxpan* (☎ 4-41-10), on the corner of Juárez and Mina, with 30 rooms (fan only) at US$7/7.50, is less expensive but it's a bit grimy. The *Hotel del Parque* (☎ 4-08-12) is on the east side of the bustling Parque Reforma and is somewhat noisy, but it's basically clean – and cheap at US$7 for singles or doubles with fan. Some beds are better than others.

Stepping up considerably in quality and price, the upper front rooms of the 77-room *Hotel Florida* (☎ 4-02-22) at Juárez 23 have pleasing river views. The rooms are big and clean and have newer beds. Rooms with air-con and TV are US$23/26. Equally nice rooms without the river view can be found at the *Hotel Plaza* (☎ 4-07-38) at Juárez 39. Rates there are US$13/17.

Better than the Florida and Plaza but a step up in price is the *Hotel May Palace* (☎ 4-88-81), on the south side of Parque Reforma. The rooms (US$27/33) have all the modern conveniences; be sure to request one overlooking the river. The next most comfortable place in the town center is the *Hotel Reforma* (☎ 4-02-10) at Juárez 25 with singles/doubles with air-con, phone and TV offered at US$27/32. There's a pleasant covered courtyard with a fountain.

The fanciest digs in town are found 2½ km southeast of downtown, on the other side of the river. The standard rooms at the *Hotel Tajín* (☎ 4-22-60) go for US$25 for one or two people and are comfy enough but, because of the hotel's location, are not as desirable as those at the Florida, the May Palace or the Reforma. But the Tajín's spacious, two-story suites, which can accommodate up to five people comfortably, offer all the modern conveniences, sweeping river and city views and, in some cases, spas on wide balconies for a reasonable US$65.

At the opposite end of the luxury spectrum is the *Hotel Playa Azul* (no phone), which offers six worn rooms with worn beds and fans only for US$11 per room. However, the hotel is located on the sand at Playa Norte, and for hard-core beach bums it is *the* place to be. Hot water is available.

Places to Eat

The restaurants of the hotels *Florida* and *Plaza*, and *Antonio's* in the Hotel Reforma, serve some of the best fare in town, with a bias toward seafood. The popular Hotel Florida restaurant offers a filling comida corrida for US$3.50. Antonio's is the fanciest and priciest of the three, with most meals at or approaching US$7; but despite many hovering waiters, the service here is generally lousy.

There are other eateries on Juárez, and several bakeries toward the east end. *Restaurant Mante*, on Rodríguez opposite the end of Juárez, is cheap, popular and friendly with a range of dishes from antojitos (US$1.50) and seafood cocktails (US$2 to US$2.50) to *carne Tampiqueña* (strips of beef with fried bananas, small tortillas, guacamole, frijoles, salad and cheese; US$4).

Pastelísimo, east of Parque Cano, is clean and inviting for cakes and coffee. There is a pleasant cluster of places in the middle of Parque Reforma serving fresh fruit, juice and ice cream. The road to the beach passes several seafood restaurants and on the beach itself is a line of cheap palapa seafood joints, where you typically pay US$2 for fish soup, U$4 to US$5 for a fresh fish and US$4 for a large shrimp cocktail or octopus with rice.

Getting There & Away

Book 1st-class buses out of Tuxpan as far ahead as possible, as there's a limited number of seats for passengers boarding here. You might have to get a 2nd-class bus to Poza Rica, and a 1st-class one from there. The ADO (1st-class) station is on Rodríguez, half a block north of the river. Ómnibus de México (1st-class) is under the bridge on the north side of the river. The Estrella Blanca station, which offers both

1st- and 2nd-class service, is on the corner of Constitución and Alemán, two blocks east of the bridge; 'EB' below refers to the company's 1st-class buses. Daily departures include:

Jalapa – 350 km, 6½ hours; four ADO (US$11)
Matamoros – 760 km, 12 hours; one ADO and two EB buses (US$25); several 2nd-class buses
Mexico City (Terminal Norte) – 355 km, six hours; 11 ADO, six EB and four ODM (US$11)
Papantla – 90 km, 1¼ hours; eight ADO buses (US$25)
Poza Rica – 60 km, one hour; many ADO, EB and ODM buses (US$2); 2nd-class buses every 20 minutes
Tampico – 190 km, four hours; 19 ADO, three EB and two ODM buses (US$8.50); 2nd-class buses every 30 minutes
Veracruz – 300 km, six hours; 11 ADO (US$12)
Villahermosa – 780 km, 14 hours; four ADO (US$31)

AROUND TUXPAN
Tamiahua

Tamiahua, 43 km north from Tuxpan by paved road, is at the southern end of Laguna de Tamiahua. It has a few seafood shack-restaurants and you can rent boats for fishing or trips to the lagoon's barrier island. Ómnibus de México has several daily 1st-class buses from Tuxpan to Tamiahua for US$1.

Castillo de Teayo

This small town, 23 km up a bumpy road west off highway 180 (the turnoff is 44 km from Tuxpan, 15 km from Poza Rica), was from about 800 AD one of the southernmost points of the Huastec civilization. Beside its main plaza is a steep, 13-meter-high restored pyramid topped by a small temple. It's in Toltec style and was probably built during Toltec rule of the area some time between 900 and 1200.

Around the base of the pyramid are some stone sculptures found in the area, thought to be the work of both the Huastecs and the Aztecs. The Aztecs controlled the area briefly before the Spanish conquest.

POZA RICA
pop 179,000; alt 28m; ☎ *782*

The oil city of Poza Rica is at the junction of highway 180 and highway 130. You might find yourself changing buses here, though it's not a pleasant place to stay. If you're stuck here overnight, you might consider the *Auto Hotel* (☎ 2-16-00), 100 meters west of the 1st-class bus terminal, which has very OK rooms with air-con, TV and phones for US$10 for one or two people; or the *Hotel Farolino* (☎ 3-24-25), between the bus depot and the Auto Hotel, which has cleanish rooms with fan for US$6, add US$2 for air-con.

Getting There & Away

The main Poza Rica bus station, on Calle Puebla one km east of Cárdenas, has some 1st-class departures, but most are by ADO, which is in an adjoining building. Daily ADO service is provided to the following destinations:

Mexico City (Terminal Norte) – 260 km, five hours; 22 ADO (US$8.50)
Pachuca – 209 km, four hours; two ADO, at 12.45 am and 2 pm (US$6)
Tampico – 250 km, five hours; every 20 minutes (US$10)
Tuxpan – 60 km, one hour; also every 20 minutes (US$2)
Veracruz – 250 km, five hours; 18 ADO (US$9)

To Papantla there are ADO buses about every hour (25 km, 30 minutes; US$1) and 2nd-class buses (located on the lots directly behind the 1st-class depot) with Tranportes Papantla every 15 minutes (US$0.70). UNO provides deluxe service to Mexico City (US$14), Veracruz (US$14) and Tampico (US$15), one bus daily to each destination leaving the 1st-class terminal at 1 am.

El Tajín If you're in Poza Rica early enough, you can go directly to El Tajín on one of Transportes Papantla's hourly buses to Coyutla (US$1) and have plenty of time to explore the site. Buses to El Chote, Agua Dulce or San Andrés, by Autotransportes

Coatzintla and other 2nd-class companies, should also get you to El Tajín. Ask for 'Desviación El Tajín' (El Tajín turning).

POZA RICA TO PACHUCA

The 200-km Poza Rica-Pachuca road, highway 130, is the direct approach to Mexico City from the northern part of Veracruz state. It climbs into the Sierra Madre across the semitropical north of Puebla state into Hidalgo, a very scenic but often misty route. The area's population has a high proportion of Nahua and Totonac Indians.

Huauchinango, roughly halfway between Poza Rica and Pachuca, is the center of a flower-growing area. You'll also find embroidered textiles in the busy Saturday market. A week-long flower festival, including traditional dances, focuses on the third Friday in Lent. At **Xicotepec**, 22 km northeast of Huauchinango, *Mi Ranchito* is a fine budget place to stay. **Acaxochitlán**, 25 km west of Huauchinango, has a Sunday market; specialties include fruit wine and preserved fruit. The Nahua women here often wear richly embroidered blouses.

The traditional Nahua village of **Pahuatlán** is the source of many of the cloths woven with multicolored designs of animals and plants. It is reached from a turning north off highway 130 about 10 km past Acaxochitlán. A spectacular 27-km dirt road winds several hundred meters down to the village, which holds a sizable Sunday market. There's at least one hotel here. About half an hour's drive beyond Pahuatlán is **San Pablito**, an Otomí village, where colorfully embroidered blouses abound.

Highway 130 climbs steeply to Tulancingo, in the state of Hidalgo. (See the Around Mexico City chapter for details on the rest of this route to Pachuca.)

PAPANTLA

pop 125,000; alt 198m; ☎ *784*

Set on a hillside among the outliers of the southern Sierra Madre Oriental, Papantla is an interesting base for visiting El Tajín. It's a scruffy town, though the central zócalo is quite pleasant. And on Sunday evenings half the town is out and voladores perform beside the cathedral. Some Totonacs still wear traditional costume here – you see men sporting baggy white shirts and trousers and women in embroidered blouses and quechquémitls. The Corpus Christi festival, in late May and early June, is the big annual event, and a celebration of Totonac culture.

Orientation

Papantla lies on highway 180, which runs southeast from Poza Rica. The center of town is uphill from the main road. To get to the center from the ADO bus station, turn left as you go out, and walk a couple of hundred meters west along the main road until you reach Calle 20 de Noviembre. Turn left and go up 20 de Noviembre (it's steep) until you get to Enríquez, the downhill boundary of the zócalo. From the Transportes Papantla bus terminal, on the east side of 20 de Noviembre halfway down the hill, just turn left and walk uphill to the zócalo.

The Totonacs

Approximately 260,000 Totonacs survive in modern Mexico, mostly living between Tecolutla on the Veracruz coast and the southern Sierra Madre Oriental in northern Puebla. Roman Catholicism is superimposed on their more ancient beliefs, with traditional customs stronger in the mountain areas. The chief Totonac deities are their ancestors, the sun (which is also the maize god) and St John (also the lord of water and thunder). Venus and the moon are identified with Qotiti, the devil, who rules the kingdom of the dead beneath the earth. Some Totonacs believe that the world is flat, the sky is a dome and the sun travels beneath the earth at night. The Feast of the Holy Cross (May 3) coincides with ceremonies for fertility of the earth and the creation of new seeds. ■

Voladores

The voladores rite – a sort of slow-motion quadruple bungee jump – starts with five men in colorful costumes climbing to the top of a very tall pole. Four of them sit on the edges of a small, square, wooden frame atop the pole, arrange their ropes and then rotate the square to twist the ropes around the pole. The fifth man dances, bangs a drum and plays a whistle while standing on a tiny platform above them. Suddenly he stops and the others launch themselves backwards into thin air. Upside down, arms outstretched, they revolve gracefully round the pole and descend slowly to the ground as their ropes unwind.

This ancient ceremony is packed with symbolic meanings. One interpretation is that it's a fertility rite and the flyers are macaw-men who make invocations to the four corners of the universe before falling to the ground, bringing with them the sun and rain. It is also said that each flyer circles the pole 13 times, giving a total of 52 revolutions, which is not only the number of weeks in the modern year but was an important number in pre-Hispanic Mexico, which had two calendars – one corresponding to the 365-day solar year, the other to a ritual year of 260 days – with a day in one calendar coinciding with a day in the other calendar every 52 solar years.

JOHN NOBLE

While it's sad in a way to see a sacred rite turned into a show for tourists (the people who do it say they need the money) the dangerous feat is a spectacular sight. ■

Zócalo

The zócalo, officially called Parque Téllez, is on a slope with the cathedral high above its south side. Beneath the cathedral a 50-meter-long mural faces the square, depicting Totonac and Veracruz history. A serpent stretches along most of the mural, linking a pre-Hispanic stone carver, El Tajín's Pyramid of the Niches, voladores and an oil rig. Inside the Palacio Municipal are copies of carvings from the southern ball court at El Tajín.

Volador Monument

At the top of the hill, above the cathedral, towers a 1988 statue of a volador musician playing his pipe as preparation for the four flyers to launch themselves into space.

A red light adorns one of his fingers to warn off passing aircraft. Take the street heading uphill from the corner of the cathedral yard to reach the statue. Inscriptions around its base give an explanation of the voladores ritual.

Special Events

For the last week of May and the first couple days of June, Papantla is thronged for the parades, dances and other cultural events of the Corpus Christi. Voladores perform specially, maybe two or three times a day. The main procession is on the first Sunday. Dances you might catch are Los Negritos, Los Huehues (The Old Men) and Los Quetzalines.

Places to Stay

The *Hotel Tajín* (☎ 2-06-44) at Núñez 104 – a blue building a few meters uphill from the left end of the zócalo mural – has singles/doubles with air-con for US$17/23; rooms with two beds are from US$22/30. The rooms' views vary – those at the front have balconies overlooking the town – but all are clean, sizable and in good shape.

The cheaper *Hotel Pulido* (☎ 2-10-79) at Enríquez 205, 250 meters east from the downhill side of the zócalo, has smaller and dirtier rooms around a central parking area. It's quite friendly, though. Rooms cost US$8/9; US$11 for two beds.

The modern *Hotel Premier* (☎ 2-00-80), on the north side of the zócalo at Enríquez 103, has large, comfortable rooms with air-con for US$27/32, and mediocre suites for up to US$47. The rooms in back are much quieter at night.

Places to Eat

Papantla food is strictly Mexican, with an emphasis on meat in this cattle-raising area. The restaurant at the *Hotel Tajín* is adequate but not very cheap, with various beef filets at around US$5. There are a number of places on Enríquez, on the downhill side of the zócalo. The *Restaurant Sorrento* at Enríquez 105 is very ordinary and not overwhelmingly clean, but it has a cheap comida corrida for only US$2.

The fanciest place is the *Restaurante Enríquez*, in the Hotel Premier, with air-con, tablecloths, TV and black-tie waiters. Meat and fish dishes are US$5 and up, while set breakfasts run from US$2 to US$4. In between these two, in price and position, is the *Plaza Pardo*, which has some mediocre main courses from US$2.50 to US$3; their fried bananas with cream (US$1) are scrumptious. There are several shops around the plaza that sell delicious ice cream for US$0.75 a scoop.

Things to Buy

The Mercado Hidalgo, at the northwest corner of the zócalo, has Totonac costumes (some quite pretty), good baskets and vanilla. Papantla is Mexico's leading vanilla-growing center – you can buy it in extract form, in the original pods or in *figuras*, pods woven into shapes – of flowers or insects, for example. The Mercado Juárez, at the southwest corner opposite the cathedral, mainly sells food.

Getting There & Away

Few long-distance buses stop here and there's no service at all to/from Tampico (change at Tuxpan or Poza Rica). Try to book your bus out of Papantla as soon as you arrive, but even this is difficult as most buses are de paso. If desperate, consider going to Poza Rica and getting one of the much more frequent buses from there. ADO at Juárez 207 is the only 1st-class line serving Papantla. The 2nd-class alternative is Transportes Papantla (TP) on 20 de Noviembre, with slow, old vehicles. See the Orientation section earlier for directions to/from the terminals. Daily departures from Papantla include:

Jalapa – 260 km, 5½ hours; seven ADO (US$9) and eight TP (US$8) buses
Mexico City (Terminal Norte) – 290 km, 5½ hours; six ADO (US$10) buses
Poza Rica – 25 km, 30 minutes; 11 ADO buses (US$0.80); 2nd-class buses every 20 minutes by TP (US$0.70)
Tuxpan – 90 km, 1¼ hours; three ADO (US$26) buses
Veracruz – 230 km, five hours; six ADO (US$9) and eight TP (US$7) buses

El Tajín White microbuses go on the hour to El Tajín from 16 de Septiembre, the street on the uphill side of the cathedral (about 30 minutes; US$0.80). Alternatively, you can do the trip in two stages by getting a bus from the same stop to the village of El Chote, then any of the frequent buses going west (to the right) from El Chote to the El Tajín turnoff (Desviación El Tajín). Other buses from Papantla to El Chote leave from the TP terminal.

EL TAJÍN

Among verdant hills a few km from Papantla, is the site of El Tajín ('el ta-HEEN') – Totonac for thunder, lightning or

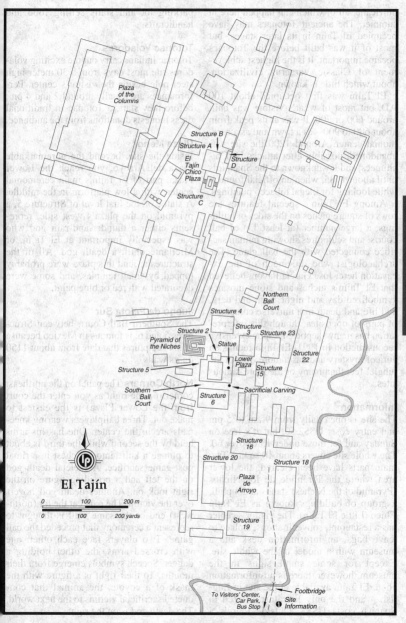

Plaza
of the
Columns

Structure B

Structure A

El Tajín
Chico
Plaza

Structure D

Structure C

Northern
Ball
Court

Structure 4

Structure 2

Structure 3

Structure 23

Pyramid of
the Niches

Statue

Structure 22

Structure 5

Lower
Plaza

Structure
15

Southern
Ball
Court

Structure 6

Sacrificial Carving

Structure 16

El Tajín

0   100   200 m
0   100   200 yards

Structure 20

Structure 18

Plaza
de
Arroyo

Structure 19

To Visitors' Center,
Car Park,
Bus Stop

Footbridge

Site
Information

hurricane, all of which can happen here in summer. The ancient Totonacs may have occupied El Tajín in its later stages, but most of it was built before the Totonacs became important. It is the highest achievement of Classic Veracruz civilization, about which little is known.

El Tajín was first occupied about 100 AD, but most of what's visible was built around 600 or 700. It was at its peak from about 600 to 900 – as a town and as a ceremonial center. Around 1200 the site was abandoned, possibly after attacks by Chichimecs, and lay unknown to the Spaniards until about 1785, when an official found it while looking for illegal tobacco plantings.

Among El Tajín's special features are rows of square niches on the sides of buildings, a large number (at least 11) of ball courts, and sculptures showing human sacrifice connected with the ball game. The archaeologist who did much of the excavation here, José García Payón, believed that El Tajín's niches and stone mosaics symbolized day and night, light and dark, and life and death in a universe composed of pairs of opposites, though this interpretation has many skeptics. Despite extensive reconstruction in 1991, El Tajín retains an aura of mystery and has a more 'lost in the jungle' feel than many of the more famous sites.

Information

The site is open daily from 9 am to 5 pm and entry costs US$2.50, but it's free on Sunday and for those under 13 or over 60. The whole site covers about 10 sq km. Two main parts have been cleared: the lower area where the Pirámide de los Nichos (Pyramid of the Niches) stands and, uphill, a group of buildings known as El Tajín Chico (Little El Tajín). The visitor's center has a restaurant, souvenir shops, a place to leave bags, an information desk and a museum with a model of the whole site. Except for some small signs in the museum, however, there is no information about El Tajín available at the site in English – and the only literature offered in Spanish costs US$3. Outside there's a

parking lot and stalls selling food and handicrafts.

Totonac Voladores

Totonac Indians carry out the exciting voladores rite most days from a 30 meter high steel pole beside the visitor's center. Performances are usually around 2 and 4 pm; before they start, a Totonac in traditional dress requests donations from the audience.

Plaza Menor

Inside the site, beyond the unremarkable Plaza del Arroyo, you reach the Lower Plaza, part of El Tajín's main ceremonial center, with a low platform in the middle. A statue on the first level of Structure 5, a pyramid on the plaza's west side, represents either a thunder-and-rain god who was especially important at El Tajín, or Mictlantecuhtli, a death god. All of the structures around this plaza were probably topped by small temples, and some were decorated with red or blue paint.

Juego de Pelota Sur

The Southern Ball Court, between Structures 5 and 6, is famous in Mexico because of six sculptures that date from about 1150 on its walls.

North Corners The panel on the northeast corner (on the right as you enter the court from the Lower Plaza) is the easiest to make out. Three ballplayers wearing knee-pads are in the center. One has his arms held by the second while the third is about to plunge a knife into his chest in a ritual post-game sacrifice. A skeletal death god on the left and a presiding figure on the right look on. Another death god hovers over the victim. The panel at the far (northwest) end of the same wall is thought to represent a ceremony that preceded the ball game. Two players face each other, one with crossed arms, the other holding a dagger. Speech symbols emerge from their mouths. To their right is a figure with the mask of a coyote, the animal that conducted sacrificial victims to the next world. The death god is on the right.

South Corners The southwest panel seems to show the initiation of a young man into a band of warriors associated with the eagle. A central figure lies on a table; to the left another holds a bell. Above is an eagle-masked figure, possibly a priest. On the southeast panel, a man offers spears or arrows to another, perhaps in the same ceremony.

Central Panels These are devoted to the ceremonial drinking of the cactus-beer pulque. In the northern central panel, a figure holding a drinking vessel signals to another leaning on a pulque container. Quetzalcóatl sits cross-legged beside Tláloc, the fanged god of water and lightning. On the south panel, Tláloc, squatting, passes a gourd to someone in a fish mask who appears to be in a pulque vat. On the left is the maguey plant, from which pulque is made. Maguey is not native to this part of Mexico, which points to influences from central Mexico (possibly Toltec) at this late stage of El Tajín.

Pirámide de los Nichos
The Pyramid of the Niches, 35 meters sq, is just off the Plaza Menor, by the northwest corner of Structure 5. The six lower levels, each surrounded by rows of small square niches, climb to a height of 18 meters. The wide staircase on the east side was a late addition, built over some of the niches. Archaeologists believe that there were originally 365 niches, suggesting that the building may have been used as a kind of calendar. The insides of the niches were painted red, and their frames blue. The only similar building known, probably an earlier site, is a seven-level niched pyramid at Yohualichán near Cuetzalán, 50 km southwest of El Tajín.

El Tajín Chico
The path north toward El Tajín Chico passes the Juego de Pelota Norte (Northern Ball Court), smaller and earlier than the southern one, but also with carvings on its sides. Many of the buildings of El Tajín Chico have geometric stone mosaic patterns known as Greco (Greek); similar patterns are found in decorations of Mitla (Oaxaca), a later site.

The main buildings, probably 9th century, are on the east and north sides of El Tajín Chico Plaza. Structure C, on the east side, with three levels and a staircase facing the plaza, was initially painted blue. Structure B, next to it, was probably home to priests or officials. Structure D, behind Structure B and off the plaza, has a large lozenge-design mosaic and a passage underneath it.

Structure A, on the plaza's north side, has a façade like a Mayan roofcomb, with a stairway leading up through an arch in the middle. This 'corbelled' arch, with the two sides jutting closer to each other until they are joined at the top by a single slab, is typical of Mayan architecture – yet another oddity in the confusing jigsaw puzzle of pre-Hispanic cultures.

Uphill to the northwest of El Tajín Chico Plaza is the as yet unreconstructed Plaza de las Columnas (Plaza of the Columns) – one of the site's most important structures. It originally had an open patio inside and adjoining buildings stretching over the hillside to cover an area of nearly 200 by 100 meters. Parts of the columns have been reassembled and are displayed in the museum at the visitor's center.

Getting There & Away
There are frequent buses to El Tajín from Papantla and Poza Rica – see the sections on those towns for details. To return, catch a local bus from the area next to the parking lot.

SOUTH OF PAPANTLA
Highway 180 runs near the coast for most of the 230 km from Papantla to Veracruz. Strong currents make for risky swimming here.

Tecolutla & the Costa Esmeralda
At Gutiérrez Zamora, 30 km east of Papantla, a side road goes to Tecolutla, 11 km northeast from highway 180 at the mouth of the Río Tecolutla. It's a minor

seaside resort with a palm-fringed beach and a few hotels. There are ADO and Transportes Papantla buses to/from Papantla.

The Costa Esmeralda (Emerald Coast) is the 20-km strip between La Guadalupe (20 km southeast of Gutiérrez Zamora) and Nautla. Numerous hotels, holiday homes, restaurants and at least three trailer parks line the strip between highway and beach. It's a popular summer spot, but very quiet for most of the year. **Nautla**, a small fishing town, has a handful of cheap but respectable hotels and a long beach where you can eat seafood.

Laguna Verde & Villa Rica

Mexico's controversial first nuclear power station is at Laguna Verde, about 80 km north of Veracruz city, on the coastal side of highway 180. The station generates 4% of Mexico's electricity. The first unit came into operation in 1989, the second in 1996, but government plans for a dozen or more follow-up reactors in the country have been abandoned in the face of public protest. The fishing village of Villa Rica, 69 km north of Veracruz, is where Cortés probably founded the first Spanish settlement in Mexico. There are traces of a fort and a church on the Cerro de la Cantera. The nearby Totonac tombs of **Quiahuiztlán** are well situated on a hill overlooking the coast.

Central Veracruz

Highway 180 follows the coast past the ruins of Zempoala to Cardel, where highway 140 branches west to Jalapa, the pleasant state capital surrounded by picturesque countryside. The bustling port city of Veracruz is 35 km south of Cardel. From Veracruz, highway 150D heads southwest to Córdoba, Fortín de las Flores and Orizaba, in the foothills of the Sierra Madre.

ZEMPOALA

The pre-Hispanic Totonac town of Zempoala holds a key place in the story of the Spanish Conquest. Its ruins stand 42 km

north of Veracruz and three km west of highway 180 in a modern town of the same name. The turnoff is by a Pemex station, eight km north of Cardel. Voladores perform at the ruins most weekends usually around noon and 2 pm.

The site is lovely, with lines of palms, and mountains in the background. Most of the buildings are faced with smooth, rounded river-bed stones. Their typical feature is battlement-like 'teeth' called *almenas*.

History

Zempoala became a major Totonac center after about 1200 AD, and may have been the leader of a 'federation' of southern Totonac states. It fell subject to the Aztecs in the mid-15th century, and many of the buildings are in Aztec style. The town had defensive walls, underground water and drainage pipes and, in May 1519 when the Spanish came, about 30,000 people. As Cortés approached the town, one of his

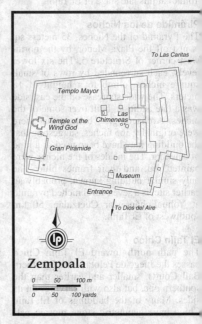

Zempoala

scouts reported back that its buildings were made of silver – but it was only white plaster or paint shining in the sun.

Zempoala's portly chief, Chicomacatl, known to history as 'the fat cacique' from a description by Bernal Díaz del Castillo, struck an alliance with Cortés for protection against the Aztecs. But his hospitality didn't stop the Spanish from smashing his gods' statues and lecturing the Zempoalans on the virtues of Christianity. Zempoalan carriers went with the Spaniards when they set off for Tenochtitlán in 1519. The following year, it was at Zempoala that Cortés defeated the Pánfilo de Narváez expedition, which had been sent by the governor of Cuba to arrest Cortés.

By the 17th century Zempoala had virtually ceased to exist. Its population, devastated by diseases, was down to eight families. Eventually the town was abandoned. The present town dates from 1832.

Zempoala Ruins

The main ruins are at the end of a short track to the right as you enter Zempoala, where a sign says 'Bienvenidos a Zempoala.' They're open daily from 9 am to 6 pm. Entrance is US$1.50 except on Sunday, when it's free.

Templo Mayor The Main Temple is an 11-meter-high, 13-platform pyramid. Initially it was plastered and painted. A wide staircase ascends to the remains of a three-room shrine on top. This was probably Pánfilo de Narváez's headquarters in 1520, which Cortés' men captured by setting fire to its thatched roof.

Las Chimeneas The Chimneys is where Cortés and his men lodged on their first visit to Zempoala. Its name comes from the hollow columns at the front, which were once filled with wood. A temple probably topped its seven platforms.

Western Structures The two main structures on the west side are known as the Gran Pirámide (Great Pyramid) and the Temple of the Wind God. Two stairways climb the Great Pyramid's three platforms in typically Toltec and Aztec style. It faces east and was probably devoted to the sun god. The round Temple of the Wind God, with a rectangular platform and ramps in front, is similar to Aztec temples to the wind god Ehecatl.

Other Structures Beyond the irrigation channel behind Las Chimeneas, you'll see a building called **Las Caritas** (The Little Heads) on your right. It once held large numbers of small pottery heads in niches. A large wind-god temple, known as **Dios del Aire**, is reached by going back down the site entrance road, straight on over the main road and then around the corner to the right.

Getting There & Away

Zempoala is most easily approached from Cardel, which is a stop for most buses on highway 180. From the Veracruz bus station the frequent buses to Cardel cost US$1.50 by 1st-class ADO or US$1.20 by 2nd-class AU buses. From the bus station at Cardel, you can take a bus marked 'Zempoala' to that town for US$0.75, or an orange-and-white taxi for US$3.50. Total journey time from Veracruz to Zempoala is about one hour.

AROUND ZEMPOALA

The main town in the area is **Cardel**, which most people only pass through on the way to the ruins (see above), but you can stay here – try the *Hotel Plaza* for about US$14/16 for a single/double. **Chachalacas** is on the coast a few km northeast from Cardel. There's a beach with seafood restaurants, and you can use the swimming pool at the upscale *Chachalacas Hotel*. North of the Zempoala turnoff, **Paso de Doña Juana** is on the coastal side of the highway and has a campground, trailer park and youth hostel.

JALAPA

pop 400,000; alt 1427m; ☎ *28*
Cool, clean and civilized, Jalapa (sometimes spelled Xalapa, always pronounced 'ha-LAP-a') is one of Mexico's colonial

CENTRAL GULF COAST

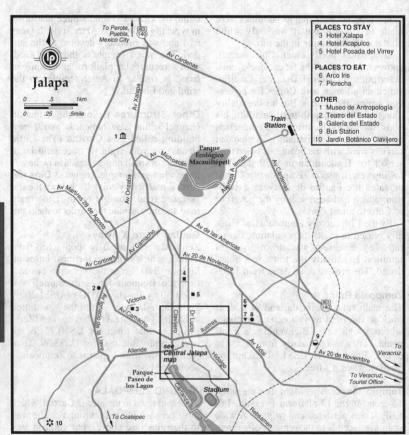

Jalapa

To Perote, Puebla, Mexico City

| 0 | .5 | 1km |
| 0 | .25 | .5mile |

Av Cárdenas
Av Xalapa
Av Michoacán
Av Orizaba
Av Martires 28 de Agosto
Av Camacho
Av Cortines
Av de las Americas
Av 20 de Noviembre
Alameda A Ieman
Av Cárdenas
Train Station
Parque Ecológico Macuiltépetl
Victoria
Av Ignacio de la Llave
Av Camacho
Clavijero
Dr. Lucio
Ilustres
Hidalgo
Allende
Av Vidal
Av 20 de Noviembre
To Veracruz
see Central Jalapa map
Parque Paseo de los Lagos
Carranza
Stadium
Rebsamen
To Coatepec
To Veracruz, Tourist Office

PLACES TO STAY
3 Hotel Xalapa
4 Hotel Acapulco
5 Hotel Posada del Virrey

PLACES TO EAT
6 Arco Iris
7 Picrecha

OTHER
1 Museo de Antropología
2 Teatro del Estado
8 Galería del Estado
9 Bus Station
10 Jardín Botánico Clavijero

gems. The capital of Veracruz state, this hill-country city has been home to the University of Veracruz since 1944. It enjoys a lively artistic and entertainment scene, a convivial café life and some good restaurants. Its pleasant setting, on the semitropical slope between the coast and the central highlands, offers fine parks and panoramas (though there is often mist and drizzle, and the traffic and the fumes can be vile). Many people come to Jalapa just to see its superb anthropology museum, but leave wishing they had allowed more time to get to know the place.

A pre-Hispanic town on this site became part of the Aztec empire around 1460, and Cortés and his men passed through in 1519. The Spanish town didn't take off until the annual trade fair of Spanish goods was first held here in 1720 (it ran until 1777). Today Jalapa is a commercial hub for the coffee and tobacco grown on the slopes, and is well known for its flowers.

Orientation
The city center is on a hillside with the plaza, Parque Juárez, more or less in the middle of things. Jalapa's cathedral is on

Enríquez, just east of the plaza. A little farther east on Enríquez and on Saragoza are many of the hotels and restaurants. The bus station is two km east of the center, and the must-see anthropology museum is a few km north.

Information

Tourist Office The state tourist office (☎ 12-85-00), in the sky-scraping Torre Animas building three km east of the center on the main road into town, has an English-speaking staff. The office is open weekdays from 9 am to 9 pm and is closed weekends.

Money Banca Serfin, Bancomer and Banamex are all on Enríquez. Bancomer won't change traveler's checks. They all have ATMs. Casa de Cambio Jalapa, at Gutiérrez Zamora 36, has slightly lower rates but is open longer hours – weekdays from 9 am to 1.30 pm and 4 to 6.30 pm.

Post & Communications The post office, open weekdays from 8 am to 7 pm and Saturday 9 am to 1 pm, is on Zamora at Leño. Next door is the telecommunications office, with fax, telex and telegram services. It's open weekdays from 8 am to

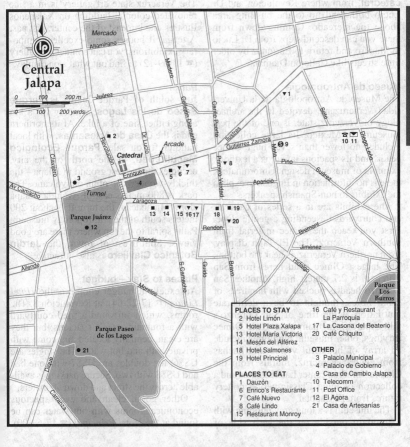

PLACES TO STAY
2 Hotel Limón
5 Hotel Plaza Xalapa
13 Hotel María Victoria
14 Mesón del Alférez
18 Hotel Salmones
19 Hotel Principal

PLACES TO EAT
1 Dauzón
6 Enrico's Restaurante
7 Café Nuevo
8 Café Lindo
15 Restaurant Monroy
16 Café y Restaurant La Parroquia
17 La Casona del Beaterio
20 Café Chiquito

OTHER
3 Palacio Municipal
4 Palacio de Gobierno
9 Casa de Cambio Jalapa
10 Telecomm
11 Post Office
12 El Agora
21 Casa de Artesanías

7 pm and Saturday 9 am to 1 pm. Pay phones are plentiful.

City Center

Parque Juárez is the central garden, with an elevated south side like a terrace overlooking the town below. The arcades of the **Palacio Municipal** are on its north side and the **Palacio de Gobierno**, the seat of the Veracruz state government, is on its east side. The Palacio de Gobierno has a fine **mural** by José Chávez Moreno depicting the history of justice; it's above the east stairway. Facing the Palacio de Gobierno across Enríquez is the 1772 **catedral**, from where Revolución and Dr Lucio both lead up to the bustling area above the mercado. Coming down from there you can descend steps from Dr Lucio to Madero and return to Enríquez by older little streets like Callejón Diamante.

Museo de Antropología

The Museo de Antropología de la Universidad Veracruzana, devoted to the archaeology of Veracruz state, is one of the best museums in Mexico. Its large collection includes no fewer than seven huge Olmec heads, and its spacious layout is a textbook example of museum design. Unfortunately, there is no information in English to explain the exhibits to non-Spanish speakers.

The exhibits are in a series of galleries and courtyards descending a gentle slope. First you reach the Olmec material from southern Veracruz. The El Tajín display, from northern Veracruz, is near the bottom. The largest Olmec head here, from San Lorenzo, is 2.7 meters high. Another San Lorenzo head is pocked with hundreds of small holes, thought to be a deliberate mutilation at the time of San Lorenzo's fall. Apart from many more fine Olmec carvings, other museum highlights include an array of beautiful yugos and hachas from central Veracruz, murals from the Classic Veracruz center Las Higueras and a collection of huge Classic-period pottery figures from El Zapotal.

The museum is a long gray building with a fountain outside on the west side of

Avenida Xalapa four km northwest of the city center. Take a 'Tesorería-Centro-SEP' or 'Museo' bus (US$0.50) west from the Restaurant Terraza Jardín on Enríquez. Buses marked 'Centro' will return you to the center. Buses can be infrequent or full, so a taxi may be worth the US$2 fare. The museum is open daily except Monday from 10 am to 5 pm; admission is US$1.50, US$1 more if you want to take photos (flash is not allowed). Admission to the museum, which has a book store and restaurant, is free on Sunday.

Galería del Estado

The Veracruz state art gallery is in a fine renovated colonial building on Xalapeños Ilustres one km east of the center, just past Arteaga. It houses some excellent temporary exhibitions; you can contact the gallery (☎ 18-09-12) to find out what's on display.

Parks

Just south of Parque Juárez is **Parque Paseo de los Lagos**, winding for a km along either side of a lake. At its northern end is the **Casa de Artesanías**, with local handicrafts on sale. **Parque Ecológico Macuiltépetl**, in the north of the city, occupies the highest ground in Jalapa – the thickly-wooded cap of an old volcano. The park is 800 meters east of Avenida Xalapa along Michoacán; the turnoff is about 200 meters south of the anthropology museum. Paths spiral to the top where there are good views. Southwest of town, the **Jardín Botánico Clavijero** is also attractive.

Places to Stay – budget

An excellent budget choice is the *Hotel Limón* (☎ 17-22-04), at Revolución 8. The rooms, which surround a tiled courtyard with a fountain, aren't spacious, but they are clean, centrally located and come with private bath and hot water. The singles are US$6; the doubles are US$7 with one bed and US$8 with two. Secure parking is available across the street and down 50 meters.

Other good, clean and even spacious economical rooms with hot water can be found at the *Hotel Principal* (☎ 17-64-00), at Zaragoza 28. Singles/doubles go for US$9/10. Beware of the noise in streetside rooms. Also an excellent value is the *Hotel Plaza Xalapa* (☎ 17-33-10), at Enríquez 4. This centrally located hotel offers cleanish, basic rooms for US$6/7. Avoid the rooms facing the street, or wear earplugs.

The large *Hotel Salmones* (☎ 17-54-31), at Zaragoza 24, has a small garden, a big lobby, a restaurant and worn rooms with carpet, phone and TV. Singles/doubles are US$12/14.

A km up the hill from the center, the *Hotel Acapulco* (☎ 18-24-58), on Julian Carrillo between Revolución and Lucio, has bare, basic but clean, well-kept rooms with private baths, for US$8/9.

Places to Stay – middle
The *Hotel Posada del Virrey* (☎ 18-61-00) at Lucio 142, about 300 meters uphill from the center, is a comfortable, modern hotel with TV in rooms, a bar and a restaurant. Moderately sized rooms are not a bad value at US$18/20 with two beds.

The No 1 downtown hotel is the 114-room *Hotel María Victoria* (☎ 18-60-11) at Zaragoza 6. Somewhat small but very clean rooms with phone, TV, air-con and heating are US$26/32. There are also a restaurant and a bar with entertainment. An interesting place with a bit of character is the *Mesón del Alférez* (☎ 18-01-13), also on Zaragoza, with a variety of rooms in a renovated building for US$22/25.

Places to Stay – top end
The top place in town is the modern, 200-room *Hotel Xalapa* (☎ 18-22-22), a km west of the center of the city on Victoria, 1½ blocks uphill from Avenida Camacho. The central part of the hotel is built around a swimming pool and there are bars, a restaurant and a good cafeteria. Rooms are air-con and cost US$34 for one or two people.

Places to Eat
The hippest places in town are located just a block from each other. *Café Lindo*, at Primero Verdad 21, has a bright, cheerful atmosphere, cozy chairs and an indoor fountain. College students can be seen flirting with each other at almost any hour, though the establishment is popular with people of all ages. Coffee drinks go for US$0.75 to US$1.80, juices US$0.50 to US$1.80, meat dishes from US$3 to US$3.50. A short walk south is the *Café Chiquito*, on Rendón at Bravo, which perhaps is nicer because jazz and *bamba* musicians play there most nights. The Chiquito offers a wide selection of coffee drinks and juices. An order of tacos, a popular choice here, sells for about US$2.50.

Another place to soak up the city's ambiance – and enjoy good, solid fare served by efficient waiters – is the *Café y Restaurant La Parroquia* at Zaragoza 18. Anyone and everyone meets, eats and drinks here between 7.30 am and 10.30 pm, and even if you squeeze breathlessly in at 10.25 pm, you'll still be served one of the set dinners – such as vegetable soup and chicken and chips for US$5 – without a quibble. There's a range of set breakfasts for US$4 or less; other snacks and meals range up to US$7.

Next door at Zaragoza 20, *La Casona del Beaterio* has an even more inviting ambiance in its pretty courtyard or in several rooms decorated with hundreds of photos of old Jalapa. The long menu of reliable choices includes yogurt with honey (US$2), spaghetti, crêpes, enchiladas (all under US$3), and meat dishes (US$4 to US$7). The five-course comida corrida is a bargain at US$3.

Also on Zaragoza, the clean *Restaurant Monroy* concentrates on antojitos and has a four-course comida corrida for US$2.50. The *Aries Restaurant* in the Hotel María Victoria farther along the street is open 24 hours. Good for late-night coffee or snacks is the *Café Nuevo* on Enríquez. It's open till 12.30 am, with antojitos from US$1 to US$2 and breakfasts from US$1.50 to US$2.50. A plate of sweet pastries comes with Nescafé con leche – you pay for what you eat. The place has been around for more than 60 years and is popular with older area residents.

Enrico's Restaurante, next door to the Hotel Plaza Xalapa, on Enríquez in the city center, is a large place with a calm ambiance that is popular with locals who aren't in a particular hurry. It's a good place to rest your feet and enjoy a cappuccino (US$0.80) or a glass of juice (US$1). Daily specials run about US$3. Meat dishes at Enrico's go for US$2 to US$7, breakfasts from US$2 to US$4.

There are plenty of good bakeries and cake shops, including several branches of *Dauzón*. The one on Xalapeños Ilustres between Mata and Soto has a café at the back where you can sample cakes, pies and strudels for US$0.75 to US$2, or down a full breakfast for around US$2.50.

A km east of the city center but well worth the walk for its candlelit, mildly Bohemian atmosphere and good Italian and Mexican food at reasonable prices is *Picrecha*, on the corner of Xalapeños Ilustres and Arteaga. For vegetarian fare, walk up Arteaga to *Arco Iris*.

Entertainment

El Ágora, an arts center under the Parque Juárez containing a cinema, theater and gallery, is the focus of Jalapa's busy arts scene. It's open daily except Monday from 8.30 am to 9 pm and has a bookstore and café. Look here, or on the notice board in the Café La Parroquia on Zaragoza, for news of what's happening around town. The *Teatro del Estado Ignacio de la Llave* (state theater), on the corner of Avenidas Camacho and Ignacio de la Llave, offers performances by the Orquesta Sinfónica de Jalapa and the Ballet Folklórico of the Universidad Veracruzana.

Getting There & Away

Bus Jalapa's gleaming, modern, well-organized bus station, two km east of the city center, is known as CAXA (Central de Autobuses de Xalapa). Deluxe service is offered by UNO, 1st-class service by ADO, and 2nd-class service by AU. Departures include:

Cardel – 72 km, 1½ hours; 20 ADO (US$2.50), and two AU (US$2) at 4.45 am and 7.15 pm
Mexico City (TAPO) – 315 km, five hours; five UNO (US$19.25), 19 ADO (US$11), and 20 AU (US$10)
Papantla – 260 km, 5½ hours; seven ADO (US$9)
Puebla – 185 km, 3¼ hours; eight ADO (US$7) and 15 AU (US$6)
Tampico – 525 km, 11 hours; one ADO at 10.30 pm (US$20)
Veracruz – 100 km, two hours; an ADO every 30 minutes from 5.30 am to 10 pm (US$4) and frequent AU (US$3.50)
Villahermosa – 575 km, nine hours; one UNO at 11.30 pm (US$34) and three ADO (US$20)

Other places served by ADO include Acayucan, Campeche, Catemaco, Córdoba, Fortín de las Flores, Mérida, Orizaba, Poza Rica, San Andrés Tuxtla and Santiago Tuxtla. AU also goes to Salina Cruz.

Car & Motorcycle Jalapa is 185 km from Puebla by highway 140, a rough road after Perote. The Jalapa-Veracruz road is better. From the northern Gulf Coast, it's easiest to follow highway 180 along the coast to Cardel, then turn inland; the inland road via Martínez de la Torre is scenic but slow.

Getting Around

For buses from the bus station to the city center, follow the signs to the taxi rank, then continue downhill to the big road, Avenida 20 de Noviembre. Turn right to the bus stop, from where any microbus or bus marked 'Centro' will take you within a short walk of Parque Juárez for US$0.25. Get a taxi ticket from the bus station to the center (US$1.75) or walk down to 20 de Noviembre and hail a taxi on the street. To return to the bus station, take a 'CAXA' bus east along Zaragoza.

AROUND JALAPA

The countryside around Jalapa is scenic, with mountains, caves and waterfalls. There are hot springs at **El Carrizal**, south of the Veracruz road 44 km from town. Spelunkers can check the **caves** at El Volcanillo and Acajete. **Hacienda Lencero,**

10 km from town, dates from the period of French rule and has a small museum.

Parque Nacional Cofre de Perote

The 4274-meter-high Cofre de Perote volcano is southwest of Jalapa. A dirt road (initially Calle Allende) from the town of Perote, 50 km west of Jalapa on highway 140, climbs 1900 meters in 24 km to just below the summit.

Coatepec & Xico

Coatepec, a colonial town 15 km south of Jalapa, is known for its coffee and orchids. The María Cristina orchid garden, on the main square, is open daily. Xico is another pretty colonial village, eight km south of Coatepec. Lodging and meals are available in both towns. The 40-meter Texolo waterfall is a pleasant two-km walk from Xico.

Buses go about every 15 minutes to Coatepec or Xico from Avenida Allende, about a km west of central Jalapa.

LA ANTIGUA

La Antigua is a km east of the coastal highway 150 and 23 km north of Veracruz. This riverside village, where Cortés is thought to have scuttled his ships, is the site of one of the Spanish settlements that preceded Veracruz. It boasts a house that was supposedly occupied by Cortés and the very early Ermita del Rosario church, probably dating from 1523. Small seafood restaurants here are popular with day-trippers from Veracruz.

VERACRUZ

pop 1.2 million; ☎ 29

Often referred to as Puerto Veracruz (to distinguish it from the state, of which it is *not* the capital), this is one of the most festive of Mexican cities, with a hedonistic, tropical port atmosphere, a zócalo that becomes a party every evening and one of the biggest carnavals between Rio de Janeiro and New Orleans. Its people, known as Jarochos, are good-humored and relaxed. Unfortunately, the seaside here is neither clean nor attractive, though people from Mexico City flood down here at

weekends and holiday times. At Christmas, Carnaval (the week before Ash Wednesday) and Semana Santa, the city and nearby beaches are jam-packed with visitors. You need to book accommodations and transport in advance for these times.

History

Veracruz was Mexico's main gateway to the outside world from the day Cortés landed here until the coming of the airplane. Invaders and pirates, incoming and exiled rulers, settlers, silver and slaves – all came and went to make the city a linchpin in Mexico's history. Before the Spanish,

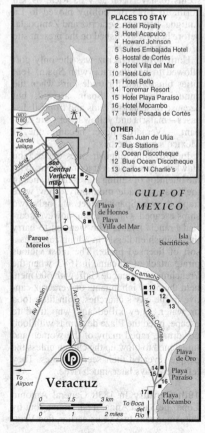

PLACES TO STAY
2 Hotel Royalty
3 Hotel Acapulco
4 Howard Johnson
5 Suites Embajada Hotel
6 Hostal de Cortés
8 Hotel Villa del Mar
10 Hotel Lois
11 Hotel Bello
14 Torremar Resort
15 Hotel Playa Paraíso
16 Hotel Mocambo
17 Hotel Posada de Cortés

OTHER
1 San Juan de Ulúa
7 Bus Stations
9 Ocean Discotheque
12 Blue Ocean Discotheque
13 Carlos 'N Charlie's

MEX 180

To Cardel, Jalapa

Juárez
Arista
Cuauhtémoc

see Central Veracruz map

Parque Morelos

GULF OF MEXICO

Playa de Hornos
Playa Villa del Mar

Isla Sacrificios

Blvd Camacho

Av Alemán
Av Díaz Mirón
Av Ruíz Cortines

Playa de Oro
Playa Paraíso
Playa Mocambo

To Airport

Veracruz

0   1.5   3 km
0   1   2 miles

To Boca del Río

the area was occupied by Totonacs, with influences from Toltecs and Aztecs (which can be seen at Zempoala 42 km to the north; see the previous Zempoala section).

The Spanish Cortés made his first landing here at an island two km offshore, where he found the remains of human sacrifices and which he named Isla de los Sacrificios. He anchored off another island, San Juan de Ulúa, on Good Friday, April 21, 1519, and here made his first contact with Moctezuma's envoys. The harbor here quickly became the Spaniards' most important anchorage, but Cortés' first settlement seems to have been at Villa Rica, 69 km north. In 1525 the colony moved to La Antigua, between Veracruz and Zempoala, before being established on the present site of Veracruz in 1598.

Until 1760 Veracruz was the only port allowed to handle trade with Spain. Tent cities blossomed for trade fairs when the annual fleet from Spain arrived, but because of seaborne raids and tropical diseases – malaria and yellow fever were rampant – Veracruz never became one of Mexico's biggest cities.

In 1567 nine English ships under John Hawkins sailed into Veracruz harbor, with the intention of selling slaves in defiance of the Spanish trade monopoly. They were trapped by a Spanish fleet and only two ships escaped. One of them, however, carried Francis Drake, who went on to harry the Spanish endlessly in a long career as a sort of licensed pirate. The most vicious pirate attack of all came in 1683, when the Frenchman Laurent de Gaff, with 600 men, held the 5000 inhabitants of Veracruz captive in the city's churches, with little food or water. They killed any who tried to escape, piled the Plaza de Armas with loot, got drunk, raped many of the women and threatened to blow up the church unless the people revealed their secret stashes. They left a few days later, much richer.

19th Century In 1838 General Antonio López de Santa Anna, fresh from a rout by the Americans two years earlier, fled Veracruz in his underwear under bombardment from a French fleet in the 'Pastry War' (an attack subsequent to various damage claims against Mexico, including that of a French pastry cook whose restaurant had been wrecked by unruly Mexican officers). But the general replied heroically, driving the invaders out and losing his left leg in the process.

When the 10,000-strong army of Winfield Scott attacked Veracruz in 1847 in the Mexican-American War, over 1000 Mexicans were killed in a week-long bombardment before the city surrendered.

In 1859, during Mexico's internal Reform War, Benito Juárez's Veracruz-based liberal government promulgated the reform laws that nationalized church property and put education into secular hands. In 1861 when Juárez, having won the war, announced that Mexico couldn't pay its foreign debts, a joint French-Spanish-British force occupied Veracruz. The British and Spanish planned only to take over the customs house and recover what Mexico owed them, but Napoleon III intended to conquer Mexico. Realizing this, the British and Spanish went home, while the French marched inland to begin their five-year intervention.

Mexico's first railway was built between Veracruz and Mexico City in 1872, and, under the dictatorship of Porfirio Díaz, investment poured into the city.

20th Century In 1914, during the civil war that followed Díaz's departure in the 1910-11 revolution, US troops occupied Veracruz to stop a delivery of German arms to the conservative dictator Victoriano Huerta. The Mexican casualties caused by the intervention alienated even Huerta's opponents. Later in the civil war, Veracruz was for a while the capital of the reformist Constitutionalist faction led by Venustiano Carranza.

Orientation
The center of the city's action is the Plaza de Armas, or zócalo, site of the cathedral and the Palacio Municipal. The harbor is

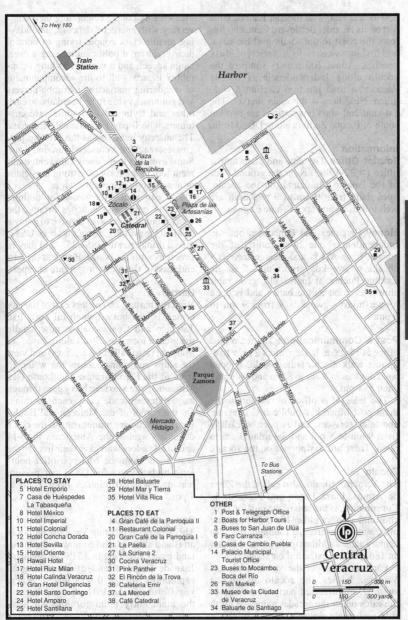

To Hwy 180

Train Station

Harbor

Viaducto

Morelos

Montesinos

Av Independencia

Constitución

Emparán

Juárez

Landero

Zaragoza

Lerdo

Molina

Serdán

Abasolo

Av 5 de Mayo

Av Herrera Necoxtan

Av Morelos

Canal

Madero

Calzada Reforma

Av Hidalgo

Av Bravo

Av Guerrero

Av Allende

Cortés

Soto

González Pages

Ocampo

Rayon

Mártires del 25 de Junio

21 de Noviembre

Primero de Mayo

Zapata

Doblado

Plaza de la República

Zócalo

Catedral

Plaza de las Artesanías

Parque Zamora

Mercado Hidalgo

Insurgentes

Arista

Av Figueroa

Blvd Camacho

Hernández

Av Xicoténcatl

J.M Pastor

Av 16 de Septiembre

Colina Pastas

Canterac

Av Zaragoza

Av Independencia

To Bus Stations

CENTRAL GULF COAST

Central Veracruz

| 0 | 150 | 300 m |
| 0 | 150 | 300 yards |

PLACES TO STAY
5 Hotel Emporio
7 Casa de Huéspedes La Tabasqueña
8 Hotel México
10 Hotel Imperial
11 Hotel Colonial
12 Hotel Concha Dorada
13 Hotel Sevilla
15 Hotel Oriente
16 Hawaii Hotel
17 Hotel Ruiz Milan
18 Hotel Calinda Veracruz
19 Gran Hotel Diligencias
22 Hotel Santo Domingo
24 Hotel Amparo
25 Hotel Santillana
28 Hotel Baluarte
29 Hotel Mar y Tierra
35 Hotel Villa Rica

PLACES TO EAT
4 Gran Café de la Parroquia II
11 Restaurant Colonial
20 Gran Café de la Parroquia I
21 La Paella
27 La Suriana 2
30 Cocina Veracruz
31 Pink Panther
32 El Rincón de la Trova
36 Cafetería Emir
37 La Merced
38 Café Catedral

OTHER
1 Post & Telegraph Office
2 Boats for Harbor Tours
3 Buses to San Juan de Ulúa
6 Faro Carranza
9 Casa de Cambio Puebla
14 Palacio Municipal, Tourist Office
23 Buses to Mocambo, Boca del Río
26 Fish Market
33 Museo de la Ciudad de Veracruz
34 Baluarte de Santiago

250 meters east, with the San Juan de Ulúa fort on its far side. Boulevard Camacho follows the coast to the south, past the naval and fishing vessels to a series of dirty beaches. About 700 meters south of the zócalo along Independencia is Parque Zamora, a road junction circling a wide green. Near here is the main market. The 1st- and 2nd-class bus stations are two km south of Parque Zamora along Díaz Mirón.

Information

Tourist Office The city and state tourist office (☎ 32-19-99) is on the ground floor of the Palacio Municipal, on the zócalo, open daily from 9 am to 9 pm. Staff are well informed and speak some English.

Money Banamex and Bancomer, both on Independencia one block north of the zócalo, have ATMs and change traveler's checks on weekday mornings. Casa de Cambio Puebla, at Juárez 112, gives rates almost as good as the banks and is open longer hours – weekdays from 9 am to 6 pm.

Post & Communications The main post office at Plaza de la República 213, a five-minute walk north of the zócalo, is open weekdays from 8 am to 8 pm and Saturday 9 am to 1 pm.

The telégrafos office next door to the main post office has public fax, telegram and telex services, and is open weekdays from 9 am to 8 pm and Saturday 9 am to noon. There are pay phones on the zócalo.

Zócalo

The Veracruz zócalo, also called the Plaza de Armas, Plaza Lerdo and Plaza de la Constitución, is the hub of the city for Jarochos and visitors alike. It's a fine-looking place with palm trees, a fountain, the 17th century Palacio Municipal on one side and an 18th century cathedral on another.

Each evening, as the sweat cools off Veracruz bodies, the zócalo becomes a swirling, multifaceted party. From one of the cafés under the arcades along the north side you might witness, in two blinks, a Mexico City couple celebrating their anniversary with energetic dancing, a holidaying middle-class couple trying to control their children, a politician making a campaign speech and a vendor hawking foam-rubber lizards – all to the accompaniment of wandering mariachis, marimba-players and guitarists vying to be heard above each other and trying to find some café customers who'll pay for personal serenades. The anarchy increases as the evening progresses, reaching a crescendo around 2 am. Some evenings there's scheduled entertainment too, in the form of visiting musicians or dancers on a temporary stage.

You can watch the show for nothing from the paths and benches around the zócalo, but it's not too expensive to enjoy a drink in the portales. A beer is about US$1; mixed drinks run to US$2.25 – and they're generous with the booze. Places at the east end, east of the plaza proper, are cheapest.

Harbor

Veracruz harbor, 250 meters east of the city center, is still busy, though oil ports like Tampico and Coatzacoalcos now handle the greater tonnages. Stroll along Paseo del Malecón (also called Insurgentes) and view the ships and cranes across the water. In front of the Faro Carranza lighthouse (see Museums), the Mexican Navy goes through an elaborate parade early each morning. On the corner of the Malecón and Boulevard Camacho are monuments to the city's defenders against the Americans in 1914 and to all sailors who gave their lives to the sea. Boats from the Malecón offer hour-long harbor tours for US$3 per person, leaving every 30 minutes from 7 am to 7 pm.

San Juan de Ulúa

This fortress protecting Veracruz harbor is an island although linked now to the mainland by a causeway. In 1518 the Spaniard Juan de Grijalva landed here during an exploratory voyage from Cuba. The next year Cortés also landed here, and it became the main entry point for Spanish newcomers to Mexico. The Franciscan chapel is thought to have been built in 1524 and the first fortifications in the 1530s, but what can be seen now mostly dates from 1552-1779.

The fortress has also acted as a prison, most notoriously under Porfirio Díaz who reserved three damp, stinking cells called El Purgatorio, La Gloria and El Infierno (Purgatory, Heaven and Hell) in the central part of the fortress, Fuerte San José (San José Fort), for political prisoners. Many inmates died of tuberculosis or yellow fever.

Today San Juan de Ulúa is an empty ruin of passageways, battlements, bridges and stairways, which you can wander around from Tuesday through Sunday between 9 am and 5 pm (entry US$2.25, except Sunday and holidays when it's free). Guided tours are available in Spanish and, sometimes, English.

To get there, take a 'San Juan de Ulúa' bus (US$0.50) from the east side of Plaza de la República. The last bus back to town leaves at 6 pm.

Museo Histórico de la Revolución
On Insurgentes, near the waterfront, stands the Faro Carranza, a yellow building housing a lighthouse, navy offices and the Museo Histórico de la Revolución. This small museum is devoted to the revolutionary hero Venustiano Carranza, whose government-in-exile was based in Veracruz for a time. The 1917 Mexican constitution was drafted here, and the museum has exhibits on Carranza's life, political struggles and assassination. The museum is open Tuesday through Saturday from 9 am to 4 pm. Entry is free, and there is an informative booklet available in English.

Baluarte de Santiago
Of the nine forts that once topped Veracruz's defensive wall, the Baluarte (Bastion) de Santiago on Canal at 16 de Septiembre is the only survivor. It was built in 1526. Inside, Las Joyas del Pescador is a small exhibit of pre-Hispanic gold jewelry. A fisherman found similar pieces in Veracruz harbor in 1976. Some of the exhibit's pieces are gorgeous, but it's a pricey visit at US$2. It's open daily from 10 am to 4.30 pm. You can walk around the outside of the fort at any time.

Museo de la Ciudad de Veracruz
The Veracruz City Museum, on Zaragoza at Morales, has fine displays on the city's early history (particularly slavery); exhibits on contemporary customs and Carnaval are not as good. Hours are Tuesday through Sunday from 9 am to 4 pm. Entry is US$0.75.

Beaches & Lagoons
Few people venture into the water at Playa de Hornos or Playa Villa del Mar, just south of the city center. Cleaner water and beaches are five km south of the city at **Costa de Oro** and seven km south at **Mocambo**. For swimming, you're better off paying US$2 to use the seaside pool at the Hotel Mocambo.

Farther south, the road goes to **Boca del Río**, with popular seafood restaurants. Over the bridge, the coast road continues to **Mandinga**, 21 km from Veracruz, where you can hire a boat to explore the lagoons.

Diving
The beaches near Veracruz may not be inviting, but there is good scuba diving on the reefs near the offshore islands, including at least one accessible wreck. Part of the area has been designated an underwater natural park. Two dive-boat operators are Curacao on Camacho in Boca del Río, and La Tienda SoBuca in Antón Lizardo. You can learn to scuba dive at the Tridente Diving School, at Boulevard Camacho 165A in Veracruz (☎ 31-79-34).

The Heroic City
Veracruz is now officially titled 'Four Times Heroic,' in reference to the final expulsion of the Spanish in 1825, the triumph over the French in the Pastry War and the resistance to the US in 1847 and 1914. ■

Carnaval

Veracruz breaks into a nine-day party before Ash Wednesday (February or March) each year. Starting the previous Tuesday, colorful parades wind through the city daily, beginning with one devoted to the 'burning of bad humor' and ending with the 'funeral of Juan Carnaval.' Other events include fireworks, dances, music (salsa and samba), handicrafts, folklore shows and children's parades. It's easy to pick up a program of events when you're there; the tourist office has scores.

Places to Stay

Hotel prices in Veracruz are fair, but in the peak times – mid-November to mid-January, Carnaval, Semana Santa and mid-June to early September – some places charge higher rates than shown here. The best area to stay is around the zócalo, where there are some budget hotels. Some of the seafront hotels can offer good value too. The cheapest places are near the bus stations, while expensive resort hotels are in the beach suburb of Mocambo, seven km south of the center.

Places to Stay – budget

The cheapest hotels in Veracruz don't always have hot water. It's a good idea to ask if *agua caliente* is available before checking in.

Zócalo On the corner of Lerdo, just east of the zócalo but with the entrance on Morelos, the *Hotel Sevilla* (☎ 32-42-46) has big rooms with ceiling fan, TV and private bath for US$9/12 for a single/double. They're pretty clean but can be noisy. Half a block up Morelos are the very basic *Casa de Huéspedes La Tabasqueña* (no phone), with airless rooms in cell-block style for US$15, and the *Hotel México* (☎ 32-05-60), with lots of brown tile and quiet, dark rooms with TV for US$9/15. *Hotel Concha Dorada* (☎ 31-29-96) at Lerdo 77 has clean, small, hot rooms with fan and private bath for US$11/12, or larger air-con ones with a balcony over the zócalo for US$19/21, or US$35 with two beds.

Other cheapies are grouped a couple of blocks southeast of the zócalo. The *Hotel Santo Domingo* (☎ 31-63-26) at Serdán 451 has small, sometimes grimy rooms with fan and private bath for US$11/15. The older *Hotel Amparo* (☎ 32-27-38) across the street at Serdán 482 is a basic but clean place with tiled floors and lime-green walls. The small rooms with fan and private bath are US$6/7. The slightly bigger, though worn, rooms in the nearby *Hotel Santillana* (☎ 32-31-16) at Landero y Cos 209 have the same color scheme and cost US$9/10. They're cleanish and have TV and fan.

City Seafront For a budget place directly across the street from the ocean, try the *Hotel Villa Rica* (☎ 32-48-54) at Boulevard Camacho 7, with small, tidy, fan-cooled rooms at US$10/12.

Bus Station Area The best deal is just over a km from the bus stations but worth the effort. It's the *Hotel Acapulco* (☎ 32-34-92) at Uribe 1327, just west of Díaz Mirón nine blocks north of the depots. Very clean, fairly bright, fan-cooled rooms of a reasonable size and with TV regularly cost US$8/9.

There are a few places close to the bus stations, all noisy. The *Hotel Rosa Mar* (☎ 37-07-47) at Lafragua 1100, opposite the 2nd-class bus station, is clean enough. Fan-cooled rooms with private bath cost US$6 a single, US$7 a double with one bed and US$18 a double with two beds.

Hotel Azteca (☎ 37-42-41), 22 de Marzo 218 at Orizaba, a block east from the 2nd-class bus station, is a green building with a small courtyard. Rooms with fan and private bath are US$9/11.

Places to Stay – middle

Zócalo Right on the zócalo there's a choice of four mid-range hotels. The 180-room *Hotel Colonial* (☎ 32-01-93), at Lerdo 117, has an indoor pool and tiled terraces on the 5th and 6th floors overlooking the square. Prices are US$17/26 for singles/doubles; interior rooms are dark but quiet and quite comfortable, while rooms at the back are lighter. Rooms at the front with balconies over the zócalo are noisier and pricier. All have air-con and TV, but they vary in value, so check out the room before you check in.

The *Gran Hotel Diligencias* (☎ 31-22-41), on the west side of the zócalo at Independencia 1115, has 134 cleanish, modern, air-con rooms for US$18 for one or two people; its strength is its central location.

Just off the zócalo at Lerdo 20, the *Hotel Oriente* (☎ 31-24-90) has clean but small air-con rooms for US$16/19. Outside rooms have balconies but also more noise.

By far the best of the four is the *Hotel Imperial* (☎ 32-30-31), which charges US$33 for a single or double with a sky-high ceiling, a marble-floored bathroom, and a king-size bed in a gorgeous frame (rates double during Carnaval). The lobby is elegant as well, with an old-fashioned elevator, towering columns and a stained-glass ceiling.

Southeast from the zócalo, on a quiet street facing the Baluarte de Santiago, the *Hotel Baluarte* (☎ 32-52-22), Canal 265 at 16 de Septiembre, is a superb value with its clean, modern, well-kept rooms. With TV and air-con, they go for US$19/21.

City Seafront The *Hawaii Hotel* (☎ 31-04-27), on Insurgentes six blocks from city center, has modern rooms with all the comforts but not nearly the elegance or central location of the Hotel Imperial. Still, it's a pretty good value with singles/doubles going for US$35/40. Next door is a less expensive place, the *Hotel Ruiz Milan* (☎ 32-27-72), with standard rooms with air-con, phone and secure parking for US$27/31; rooms on the upper floors have pleasing harbor views.

On the corner of Boulevard Camacho and Figueroa, the big and busy *Hotel Mar y Tierra* (☎ 31-38-66) has both an older front section and a preferable rear extension at US$23 for one or two people. All rooms have air-con, TV and carpet, but some are better than others so look before you sign. The *Hotel Royalty* (☎ 32-39-88) on the corner of Boulevard Camacho and Abasolo has clean, balconied but no-frills rooms for US$17/19 with fan, US$20/24 with air-con; there are particularly good views from the upper floors.

The *Hotel Villa del Mar* (☎ 31-33-66) at Boulevard Camacho 2707 opposite Playa Villa del Mar, 2.5 km south of the zócalo, is good value if you can get a room away from the noisy road. There's an open-air pool, and the rooms, all air-con, are in both a central block and garden bungalows. Few have a sea view owing to buildings on the other side of the road, but the location is pleasantly breezy. The rooms cost US$40 for singles or doubles. For a couple of dollars more, the *Howard Johnson* (☎ 31-00-11) at Boulevard Camacho 1263 is much better value and has a good restaurant.

An excellent option for a large group is the *Suites Embajada Hotel* (31-18-44) at the corner of Boulevard Camacho and Altamirano, which offers 11 sea-facing and nicely decorated suites with all the comforts, including a kitchenette. Rates range from US$80 for one to four people, US$92 for five or six people. There's an inviting swimming pool and spa.

On Ruiz Cortínes, between Calles 5 and 7, is the newer *Hotel Bello* (☎ 28-48-28). Though it's not on the seafront, half of the hotel's air-con rooms look out over the ocean; the other half face the Carnaval parade route. The rooms are a good value at US$30 a night for a single or double. The restaurant at the Bello is very good and reasonably priced.

Bus Station Area Hotel Impala (☎ 37-01-69), east of the bus station at Orizaba 650, has air-con, TV and phones at US$18 for a single or double. The *Hotel Central* (☎ 37-22-22), half a block north of the 1st-class bus station at Díaz Mirón 1612, is clean and very busy, with fan-cooled rooms at US$15/17, and US$8 more for air-con.

Mocambo A short walk from Playa Mocambo, the little *Hotel Posada de Cortés* (no phone) has junior suites (clean, pleasant, moderately sized, air-con rooms with one double bed) for US$24 and bungalows (larger rooms, which can hold four people) for US$30. A garden and pool are at the center of things. The hotel faces the inland side of Carretera Veracruz-Boca del Río; enter from the first street on the right a couple of hundred meters south of the traffic circle by the Hotel Mocambo.

Places to Stay – top end

Zócalo & Harbor The most central top-end place is the fully modernized *Hotel Calinda Veracruz* (☎ 31-22-33) on the corner of Independencia and Lerdo overlooking the zócalo, where well-decorated, air-con rooms, some with balconies, cost US$55/60 and up. There's a rooftop pool with a great view.

The *Hotel Emporio* (☎ 32-00-20) towers over the harbor on the corner of Insurgentes and Xicoténcatl. An outside elevator soars above three swimming pools to a roof garden. The 200 rooms and suites start from US$63/66 for 'standard' air-con singles/doubles that could be larger.

City Seafront The *Hostal de Cortés* (☎ 32-00-65), on the corner of Boulevard Camacho and Las Casas, facing Playa de Hornos, is the first top-end hotel on the way south down the coast. It's a modern place with 98 air-con rooms, some with sea-view balconies, and a pool. Singles and doubles are US$58, including breakfast.

On Boulevard Camacho at Avenida Ruiz Cortínes is the *Hotel Lois* (☎ 37-82-90), which was offering singles and doubles for a promotional price of US$40 (the price will no doubt be higher at the time you read this). The 108 rooms on nine floors come with air-con, TV, phone, minibar and bathtub, and those on the north side of the hotel have rooms looking down upon the Carnaval parade route.

Mocambo The *Hotel Mocambo* (☎ 22-02-05), on Carretera Veracruz-Mocambo seven km south of the city center, is a venerable luxury hotel, once the best in Veracruz – even now, only ever-so-slightly faded. It has terraced gardens, three sizable pools (two indoors) and more than 100 rooms. The rooms are all a good size, with air-con, TV and a variety of outlooks. Cost is US$60 for one or two people. Playa Mocambo is a minute's walk from the foot of the gardens.

The *Hotel Playa Paraíso* (☎ 21-86-00), at Ruiz Cortínes 3500, has 34 air-con rooms and suites from US$70. The eight-story *Torremar Resort* (☎ 21-34-66), at Ruiz Cortínes 4300, has scores of rooms at US$92 and junior suites at US$120. Both places have pools, gardens and a private beach.

Places to Eat

Veracruzana sauce, found on fish all over Mexico, is made from onions, garlic, tomatoes, olives, green peppers and spices. There is a risk of contracting cholera from uncooked seafood, including ceviche and oysters, so unfortunately these items are off the menus at most seafood restaurants.

Zócalo The cafés under the portales are more for drinks and atmosphere than for food. Stroll along the line and see which one grabs you. For a meal here, the air-con *Restaurant Colonial* beside the Hotel Colonial isn't a bad value, but expect to spend at least US$10 per person. The best food value on the zócalo is out of the limelight on the south side, at *La Paella*, where a meal of fish and salad will cost around US$4.50, paella US$5.50 and the comida corrida US$3 weekdays and US$4 on weekends.

Veracruz's quintessential eating experience is just off the zócalo at Independencia 105. It's the big, convivial *Gran Café de la Parroquia 1*, the city's favorite meeting place. It echoes with the clinking of spoons on glasses by customers needing a refill of the divine café con leche. The food is good but not as fancy as the energetic waiters in white after-dinner jackets and black tie might suggest: fish and meat range to US$8 (a large filet mignon smothered in mushroom sauce and served with a baked potato costs US$7); enchiladas and egg dishes go for US$2 to US$4; burgers and sandwiches cost US$3. The Parroquia is open from 6 am to midnight.

Cheaper places are west of the zócalo. *El Jarocho* on the corner of Emparán and Madero, is open from 8 am to 6.30 pm and is always crowded for its cheap lunch. The nearby *Cocina Veracruz* has cheap, basic, wholesome fare like egg dishes for US$1.50, fish for US$2 and a three-course comida corrida for only US$1.50. South of the zócalo, on and around Arista, are trendier places, such as the quaint *Callejón Héroes de Nacozari*, where you find quiet outdoor tables, and the *Pink Panther*, which has a set meal for US$3.

A few doors down from the Pink Panther is *El Rincón de la Trova*, a festive restaurant-bar with live music Friday and Saturday nights and a large selection of alcoholic drinks. The menu is limited to simple items, such as tostadas (US$2.50), empanadas (US$2) and tamales (US$1). The *Cafetería Emir*, at Independencia 1520, is a popular diner-like place with breakfasts from US$1.50 to US$2.50, and chicken or fish dishes for around US$4.50.

Harbor The *Gran Café de la Parroquia II*, even larger than the original near the zócalo, sits at Insurgentes 340 facing the harbor. The menu is the same and the atmosphere just as jovial as at Parroquia I. This is a good place to write letters or relax with a book while sipping coffee, as none of the Parroquia's waiters would ever pressure a patron to leave except long after closing time.

The top floor of the municipal fish market, on Landero y Cos, is packed with comedores doing bargain fish fillets or shrimps al mojo de ajo for US$3. These close in the early evening. Nearby, *La Suriana 2*, on the corner of Zaragoza and Arista, has a friendly family atmosphere and excellent seafood at budget prices – cocteles and soup at around US$3 and fish from US$3 to US$5.

Parque Zamora Area *La Merced*, on Rayón between Zaragoza and Clavijero, is Parque Zamora's jolly answer to the Cafés

de la Parroquia. A filling comida corrida of chicken soup, rice, bread, sweets and a drink is US$2.50 (US$3.50 on Sunday), fish and meat courses are mostly US$3.50 to US$5.50 and antojitos US$2.50. The nearby *Café Catedral*, at Ocampo 202, half a block west of Independencia, is a similar but more subdued place with comparable prices.

Down the Coast The restaurants at Mocambo beach tend to be pricey and nothing special. The coffee shop at the *Hotel Mocambo* has some atmosphere and does a good breakfast.

Enjoying a seafood meal in the river-mouth village of Boca del Río, 10 km south of Veracruz center, is an indispensable part of a visit to Veracruz for many Mexicans. And a long Sunday lunch is the favorite way to do it. *Pardiño's*, at Zamora 40 in the center of the village, is the best-known restaurant, but there are several more along the riverside.

Mandinga, about eight km farther down the coast from Boca del Río, is also known for its seafood (especially prawns) and has a clutch of small restaurants.

Entertainment

A café seat under the zócalo portales is a ringside ticket to the best entertainment in town, but if you hanker for something more formal, the tourist office has information on exhibitions, concerts and other cultural events. There are several cinemas, including two on Arista, and quite a few nightclubs and discos, mostly near the waterfront within two blocks of the Hotel Lois – *Carlos 'N Charlie's*, *Ocean*, *Underground*, *Club 21* and *Blue Ocean*, to name few. The discos show few signs of life before 11 pm.

Things to Buy

The Plaza de las Artesanías on the corner of Insurgentes and Landero y Cos, and the line of stalls across the street, are devoted more to seaside souvenirs than genuine artistry. Ordinary Jarochos shop for their daily needs at the Mercado Hidalgo, a block southwest of Parque Zamora

CENTRAL GULF COAST

between Cortés and Soto. There are a few higher-end shops on Independencia and the streets to its west.

Getting There & Away

Air Mexicana (☎ 32-22-42) flies four times daily to/from Mexico City (45 minutes; US$114). Its office is at 5 de Mayo 1266 at Serdán, in downtown. Aerocaribe (☎ 22-52-05) has direct flights daily to Mérida (two hours; US$113) and then on to Cancún (3¼ hours; US$143). Its office is at Costa Dorada 500, near Plaza Mocambo. Aeroméxico (☎ 35-01-42) has two flights daily to Mexico City (45 minutes; US$114) and one flight daily to Mérida (US$113) and Cancún (US$143) via Villahermosa. Aeroméxico's office is at García Auly 231.

Bus Veracruz is a major hub, with good services up and down the coast and inland along the Puebla-Mexico City corridor. The 1st- and 2nd-class depots are back-to-back between Díaz Mirón and Lafragua, two km south of Parque Zamora and 2.75 km south of the zócalo. The 1st-class side (almost exclusive to ADO) fronts Díaz Mirón on the corner with Xalapa. The 2nd-class side (AU buses) is at the rear, entered from Lafragua. There are also several deluxe UNO buses, with tickets sold at the 1st-class station.

Be advised that tickets for AU's ordinario buses are sold at a kiosk beside the 2nd-class platforms. Try to avoid the run-down buses of Transportes Los Tuxtlas (TLT) for all but short hops. Departures include:

Acayucan – 250 km, five hours; 15 ADO (US$8)
Catemaco – 165 km, three hours; five ADO starting with a 9.30 am departure (US$6), several directo AU and frequent TLT
Córdoba – 125 km, two hours; an ADO every 45 minutes starting at 6 am (US$5), six direct AU
Jalapa – 100 km, two hours; frequent ADO from 1.45 am to 11 pm (US$4) and 18 AU (US$3.50)
Mexico City (TAPO) – 430 km; five UNO (5 hours, US$27), 16 ADO (US$18) and six AU (US$17)

Oaxaca – 460 km, seven hours; ADO at 7.15 am and 10.30 pm (US$17); one AU directo (US$15)
Orizaba – 150 km, 2¼ hours; an ADO every 45 minutes starting at 6 am (US$6) and 16 directo AU (US$5)
Papantla – 230 km, five hours; one ADO at 2.30 pm (US$9) and 12 AU (US$7)
Poza Rica – 250 km, 5½ hours; 15 ADO (US$9)
Puebla – 300 km, five hours; seven ADO (US$12) and some directo AU (US$10)
San Andrés Tuxtla – 155 km, 2¾ hours; 32 ADO (US$5) and frequent TLT (US$4.50)
Santiago Tuxtla – 140 km, 2½ hours; 11 ADO (US$4.75) and frequent TLT (US$4.25)
Tampico – 490 km, 10 hours; one UNO (US$31) and 11 ADO (US$20)
Tuxpan – 300 km, six hours; eight ADO (US$12)
Villahermosa – 480 km, eight hours; one UNO at 11.45 pm (US$28) and 12 ADO (US$17)

Buses also go to Campeche, Cancún, Chetumal, Matamoros, Mérida and Salina Cruz.

Train El Jarocho (train No 54) leaves for Córdoba, Fortín de las Flores, Orizaba and Mexico City at 9.30 pm, with coche dormitorio, primera preferente and segunda clase accommodations. See the Mexico City Getting There & Away section for more information. Train No 52 at 8 am follows the same route but is segunda clase only (US$5.75 to Mexico City) and takes a scheduled 11 hours. Train No 102, also leaving in the morning, goes to Mexico City via Jalapa.

Incurable railway buffs could take a train to Tapachula, 885 km away on the Chiapas-Guatemala border. The daily service, segunda clase only, costs US$12, departs at 9 pm and takes at least 24 hours; in Chiapas, station staff say these trains can turn up at any time of day or night.

Veracruz station is at the north end of Plaza de la República, a five-minute walk from the zócalo. The ticket office is open daily from 6 to 10 am, and from 5 to 10 pm.

Car & Motorcycle From Veracruz, highway 180 runs north and south. Highway

140 goes northwest to Jalapa, and highway 150D goes south then west to Córdoba; both continue to Puebla.

Many car rental agencies have desks at the Veracruz airport, including: National (☎ 38-71-27), Autos Sobrevales (☎ 34-65-76) and Avis (☎ 34-96-23). Some have offices in hotels, including: Hertz (32-40-21) in the lobby of the Howard Johnson, Roca Rental (☎ 89-05-05) in the lobby of the Plaza Continental, and Powerfull Auto Rental (☎ 32-85-73) in the lobby of the Hostal de Cortés.

Getting Around
To/From the Airport The Veracruz airport (☎ 34-90-08) is 11 km southwest of town near highway 140. There is no bus service to/from town, leaving most passengers with two options: taking a taxi (US$8), or walking.

To/From the Bus Stations For the city center, take a bus marked 'Díaz Mirón y Madero' (US$0.40) from in front of the Hotel Central on Díaz Mirón, half a block north of the 1st-class bus station. The bus goes to Parque Zamora then up Madero. For the zócalo, get off on the corner of Madero and Lerdo and turn right. Returning to the depots, pick up the same bus going south on 5 de Mayo. From the booth outside the 1st-class depot a taxi ticket to the zócalo costs US$2.

Mocambo, Boca del Río & Mandinga A
bus marked 'Mocambo – Boca del Río' (US$0.80) leaves every few minutes from the corner of Zaragoza and Serdán near the zócalo; it goes to Parque Zamora then down the seafront Boulevard Camacho to Mocambo (15 minutes; get off at Expover exhibition hall on Calzada Mocambo and walk down the street left of the Hotel Mocambo to the beach) and Boca del Río (25 minutes).

AU ordinario 'Antón Lizardo' buses leave from the 2nd-class bus station every 20 minutes till 8.45 pm, stop at Boca del Río and Mandinga. The last one back to town leaves around 8 pm. The less frequent directo buses to Antón Lizardo stop at Boca del Río only.

CÓRDOBA
pop 180,000; alt 924m; ☎ *271*

Córdoba ('CORR-do-ba'), 125 km from Veracruz in the foothills of Mexico's central mountains, has a long colonial history and a pleasant center, and the verdant hill country around the town is enticing.

Córdoba was founded in 1618 by 30 Spanish families to stop escaped black slaves from attacking travelers between Mexico City and the coast. It's known as La Ciudad de los Treinta Caballeros (City of the 30 Knights). Today it's a commercial and processing center for sugar cane, tobacco and coffee from the nearby hillsides and fruit from the lowlands.

Orientation
Everything of interest is within a few blocks of the central Plaza de Armas. La Parroquia de la Inmaculada Concepción is at the plaza's southeast end, while its northeast side is lined by 18th century portales and a string of busy outdoor cafés. The new bus station is three km southeast of the plaza. Streets running northwest to southeast are Avenidas; Calles are at right angles to Avenidas. The market is bounded by Calles 7 and 9 and Avenidas 8 and 10. Shops are in the blocks south and east of the Plaza de Armas.

Information
There is a tourist office (☎ 2-25-81) in the northwest corner of the Palacio Municipal, which is open Monday through Saturday from 8.30 am to 3 pm and from 5 to 8 pm. One member of the staff speaks English. The office publishes a monthly schedule of local cultural activities. Its maps require magnifying glasses; larger maps are available at most of Córdoba's paper stores and copy centers (look for *papelería* and *copia* signs).

The post office is at 3 Avenida No 3, just northwest of the Plaza de Armas. The main banks are around the plaza and will change traveler's checks in the morning. There's a

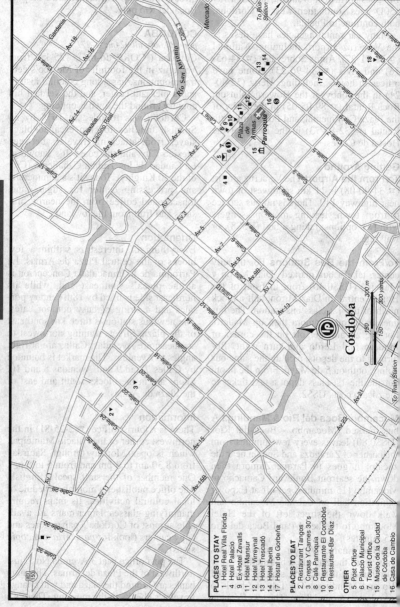

PLACES TO STAY
1 Hotel Real Villa Florida
3 Hotel Palacio
4 Ex-Hotel Zevalls
11 Hotel Mansur
12 Hotel Virreynal
13 Hotel Trescadó
14 Hotel Iberia
17 Hostal de Gorbeña

PLACES TO EAT
2 Restaurant Tangos
3 Crepas Y Carnes 30's
10 Café Parroquia
16 Restaurante El Cordobés
18 Restaurant-Bar Díaz

OTHER
5 Post Office
6 Palacio Municipal
7 Tourist Office
15 Museo de la Ciudad
de Córdoba
16 Casa de Cambio

casa de cambio on Avenida 3, just south-east of the plaza, open weekdays from 9 am to 2 pm and 4 to 7 pm, Saturday from 10 am to 1 pm.

Things to See

The **Ex-Hotel Zevallos** is not a hotel but the former home, built in 1687, of the Condes (Counts) of Zevallos. It's on the northeast side of the Plaza de Armas, behind the portales. Plaques in the court-yard record that Juan O'Donojú and Agus-tín de Iturbide met here after Mass on August 24, 1821, and agreed on terms for Mexico's independence. O'Donojú, the new viceroy, had concluded it was useless for Spain to try to cling to its colony; Itur-bide was the leader of the anti-imperial forces, a former royalist general who had changed sides. Contrary to the Plan de Iguala, in which Iturbide and Vicente Gue-rrero had proposed a European monarch as Mexican head of state, O'Donojú and Itur-bide agreed that a Mexican could hold that office. Iturbide went on to a brief reign as Emperor Agustín I. The historic building is not open to the public.

The **Museo de la Ciudad de Córdoba**, in a 17th century house at 303 Calle 3, has a small but well-displayed collection including a Classic Veracruz palma and some beautifully made personal orna-ments. The big, late 18th century church in the Plaza de Armas, **La Parroquia de la Inmaculada Concepción** is famous for its loud bells.

Special Events

On Good Friday, Córdoba marks Jesus' cru-cifixion with a procession of silence, in which thousands of residents walk behind an altar of the Virgin that is carried through the streets. Everyone holds a lit candle, no one utters a word, the church bells are eerily quiet. Few people are not moved by the sight of the procession, which traditionally starts at 8 pm and lasts about 90 minutes.

Places to Stay

The *Hostal de Gorbeña* (☎ 2-07-77), on Calle 11 between Avenidas 3 and 5, is a bargain for US$10/14 for a clean single/double with phone and TV; add US$3 for air-con. The 24-room hotel also has a decent restaurant and parking. The *Hotel Virreynal* (☎ 2-23-77), on the corner of Avenida 1 and Calle 5, is also a good value. The old-style place offers large, clean rooms with fan and private bath for US$13/14.

The *Hotel Iberia* (☎ 2-13-01), at Avenida 2 No 919 (two blocks downhill from the Virreynal, then one block to the left and half a block to the right), has small, modern rooms around a courtyard with TV and fan for US$8/10. Next door at Avenida 2 No 909, the *Hotel Trescadó* (☎ 2-23-66) is very bare and basic, but costs only US$5/6 (add US$1 for parking). Both places are quite acceptable.

Stepping up in quality and price, the *Hotel Mansur* (☎ 2-60-00) on the Plaza de Armas at Avenida 1 No 301 is well kept and has an elegant lobby. Rooms with TV, phone and air-con start at US$20/21; the rooms on the 4th floor overlooking the plaza are quite nice.

The *Hotel Palacio* (☎ 2-21-88), on the corner of Avenida 3 and Calle 2, has big, air-con rooms with TV for US$17/21; be sure to get an upper room facing Pico de Orizaba, Mexico's tallest mountain. The *Hotel Real Villa Florida* (☎ 4-33-33) is at Avenida 1 No 3002 between Calles 30 and 32, 1.5 km northwest of the center, where Avenida 1 meets highway 150. It has lovely gardens, a restaurant and 82 tasteful, modern, air-con rooms for US$34/46.

Places to Eat

The Plaza de Armas portales are lined with cafés and restaurants where you can dine and drink the local coffee in a variety of venues. Prices seem to be highest at the northern end, starting with the *Café Parro-quia*; egg dishes run about US$2.50, anto-jitos US$4.50, fish US$6, and meat US$7. The restaurant's well-known pastries and sweet breads range from US$1.25 to US$2.75. Farther down, the long menu at the deservedly popular *Restaurante El Cordobés* includes meat fillets (US$3 to

US$6), spaghetti (US$2.50 to US$3) and seafood cocktails (US$3 to US$4.50). The *spaquetti a la marinera* (US$4), which they make with shrimp, scallops and squid, is very tasty. Down the road, the *Hotel Virreynal* is popular for breakfast and also for its excellent comida corrida.

Just off the Plaza de Armas, Hotel Palacio's well-lit and somewhat elegant *Restaurante Los Balcones* offers decent food; prices range from US$3 to US$7 for pasta and about US$6 for meat dishes, to US$6 to US$14 for fish and lobster entrees. But for fish go to the *Restaurant-Bar Díaz* on Calle 15 between Avenidas 5 and 7. The restaurant serves the best seafood in the region and has menus in English. Offerings include oyster and black pepper casserole (US$3), crayfish with garlic and a mild chili sauce (US$9), squid wrapped in bacon and covered in a cheesy green sauce (US$4.50), large shrimp cocktail (US$2.75), large seafood cocktail (US$4). Frog legs, king crab and smoked baby shark are also available.

The hippest restaurant in Córdoba is *Crepas Y Carnes Los 30's* on Avenida 9 between Calles 20 and 22. It's a good trek from the zócalo but worth it. As the name suggests, this restaurant is big on crêpes and beef. In colorful rooms amid large paintings of fruit, parrots and flowers, patrons feast on delicious crêpes with chicken and mole sauce, or with mango, strawberry or apple, and dozens of other varieties on the French standard. Also offered are 18 meat dishes, costing from US$3.75 to US$7. Two blocks up Avenida 9, *Restaurant Tangos* has less atmosphere but serves up good food, particularly its filet of beef (US$6) and its beef kabob (US$4).

Getting There & Away

Bus The bus station, with deluxe (UNO and ADO GL), 1st-class (ADO and Cristóbal Colón) and 2nd-class (AU) services, is at Avenida Privada 4, three km southeast of the plaza. To get to the center take a local bus marked 'Centro' or buy a taxi ticket (US$2). To Fortín de las Flores and Orizaba, it's more convenient to take a local bus from Avenida 11 than to go out to the Córdoba bus station. Long-distance buses from Córdoba include:

Jalapa – 260 km, 3½ hours; four ADO (US$6)
Mexico City (TAPO) – 305 km, 4½ hours; two UNO (US$21), four ADO GL (US$14), 14 ADO (US$12), 10 AU locales (US$11) and 13 AU de paso (US$10)
Oaxaca – 317 km, seven hours; two CC (US$13) and one AU (US$10)
Puebla – 175 km, three hours; eight ADO (US$12), two AU locales (US$6) and 26 AU de paso (US$7)
Veracruz – 125 km, two hours; 24 ADO (US$5) and 18 AU (US$20)

Train El Jarocho, the Mexico City-Veracruz train, stops at Córdoba. Fares to Veracruz are US$2.50/1.30 in primera preferente/segunda clase. See the Mexico City Getting There & Away section for more information. The station is at the corner of Avenida 11 and Calle 33 in the south part of the town.

Car & Motorcycle Toll road 150D bypasses Fortín de las Flores and Orizaba. Highway 150 continues west from Córdoba through those towns then turns southwest to Tehuacán.

FORTÍN DE LAS FLORES
pop 25,000; alt 970m; ☎ *271*

Fortín de las Flores is seven km west of Córdoba officially, but the cities have spread up against each other. Nurseries producing flowers for export is the chief local industry. April to June is the main flowering season, but most of the color is confined to the nurseries and to private gardens. There's a week-long flower festival at the end of April and into the start of May. Year round, Fortín is a weekend retreat for the Mexico City middle class.

Fortín has a big open plaza, the Parque Principal, with the Palacio Municipal in the middle and a cathedral at the south end.

Places to Stay
The *Hotel Jardín* (☎ 3-04-27), across from the municipal palace on Avenida 1 between

Calles 1 and 3, is the cheapest place in town – and looks it. For US$7, one gets a grungy, no-frills room in major need of new paint and, quite possibly, a new bed. Still, the Jardín is tolerable for a night or two.

The *Posada El Pueblito* (☎ 3-00-33) on Avenida 2 Ote, between Calles 9 and 11 Nte, offers 45 lovely, white-walled rooms with TV, fan and, outside, lots of bougainvillea. There's a swimming pool, even tennis courts. We would rave about this hotel, which offers singles/doubles for US$20/23, except that it is located too close to a coffee plant. Unless you *really* love the smell of roasting coffee, you'll find it a bit overwhelming at the Pueblito.

Down the road, on Avenida 2 Ote between Calles 5 and 7 Nte, is the *Hotel Fortín de las Flores* (3-00-55), which is the kind of place that looks better on a postcard than it does in person. A large Mediterranean-style structure, the Flores faces an inviting pool and a lovely residence across the street. But its rooms, which come with air-con, phone and TV, are well past their prime and all four that we visited smelled heavily of cleanser. Singles and doubles go for US$32.

The best place in town is the *Hotel Posada Loma* (☎ 3-03-03), on the Córdoba-Fortín road two km from the municipal palace. It consists of 11 bungalows and eight spacious rooms with fireplace, sitting area and all the comforts, located on 32,000 sq meters covered mostly with gardens. In the center of it all is a pool. The large rooms go for US$28 for one or two people, and the bungalows, which contain a handsome kitchen, two bedrooms and two private baths (perfect for four people), go for US$50. The Posada's owner speaks English and enjoys giving tours of her gardens, which include hundreds of orchids and more than 40 species of bird. Reservations are advisable.

Places to Eat

The restaurant at the *Hotel Posada Loma* is extremely popular for breakfast, especially when the sky is clear and Pico de Orizaba seemingly fills the dining-room window. The marmalade is homemade, often from fruits found on the grounds. Expect to pay about US$6 for a delicious breakfast and US$8 for a comparable dinner here.

The most popular restaurant in town is its only Chinese restaurant – *Tam*, at the corner of Calle 5 Sur and Avenida Galindo. Soups cost US$2 to US$6 (the won ton is excellent), fish and beef dishes go for US$5 and very filling meals of the day are US$8.

Colorines, on Calle 1 Nte one block north of the Palacio Municipal, is widely considered to be the best steakhouse in town – it's nothing to write home about, though. The menu features Antojitos (US$1 to US$3), beef (US$3 to US$4.50), seafood cocktails (US$3 to US$4) and fish (US$4 to US$35). Tables in the back are quieter and face a small but attractive garden.

Half a block up Calle 1 Nte from Colorines is the city's best fish restaurant, *Lolo*, which is certainly OK although not nearly the catch that Córdoba's Restaurant-Bar Díaz is, seven km away. Seafood cocktails at the Lolo range from US$3 to US$4, filets of fish from US$4 to US$5, and squid is about US$4.

Getting There & Away

Bus From Córdoba, there are frequent buses marked 'Fortín' going northwest along Avenida 11 (15 minutes; US$0.75). In Fortín, they arrive and depart from Calle 1 Sur, on the west side of the plaza.

The ADO (1st-class) office is on the corner of Avenida 2 and Calle 6, three blocks west of the plaza along Avenida 1, then one block north. There are four buses daily to Mexico City (US$11), seven to Veracruz (US$5), four to Puebla (US$7) and eight to Jalapa (US$5). They are all de paso, but some seats can be purchased in advance. UNO has two deluxe buses daily to Mexico City (US$21) and ADO GL has one (US$13).

Train Fortín is on the Mexico City-Veracruz route, 30 minutes west of Córdoba. The main train is El Jarocho – see the Mexico City Getting There & Away section for schedule information and fares to/from the capital. Fare to Veracruz is US$2.50 in primera preferente; coches dormitorios are not available between Fortín and Veracruz. Segunda-clase trains are scheduled to leave for Veracruz at 3.55 pm and Mexico City at 3.50 pm (both US$4.50). The station is two blocks north of the plaza, just past the restaurant Lolo.

ORIZABA

pop 100,000; alt 1219m; ☎ *272*

Orizaba, 16 km west of Córdoba, was founded by the Spanish to guard the Veracruz-Mexico City road. It retains a few colonial buildings and church domes, though much was lost in the 1973 earthquake. An industrial center in the late 19th century, its factories were early centers of the unrest that led to the unseating of dictator Porfirio Díaz. Today it has a big brewery and cement, textile and chemical industries. It is also home to the Veracruz State Art Museum, a must-see. The nearby mountains are spectacular on clear days.

Orientation

The central plaza, Parque del Castillo, has the Parroquia de San Miguel on its north side. The busiest streets are Madero, bordering the west side of the plaza, and Avenidas Pte 7/Ote 6, a few blocks south of the plaza.

Information

There's a tourist office (☎ 6-22-22, ext 134) in the Palacio Municipal, on Avenida Colón Pte at Nte 7 (on the 2nd floor in the northwest corner). It's open daily from 8 am to 3 pm and 5 to 7.30 pm. One member of the staff speaks English. There are banks a block south of the plaza. Post and telecommunications offices are located near the intersection of Sur 7 and Ote 2.

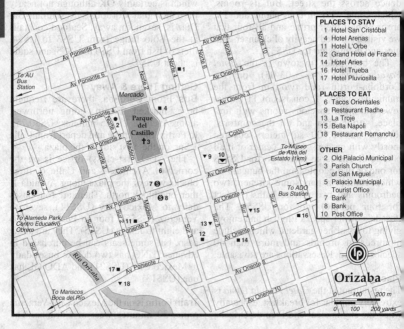

PLACES TO STAY
1 Hotel San Cristóbal
4 Hotel Arenas
11 Hotel L'Orbe
12 Grand Hotel de France
14 Hotel Aries
16 Hotel Trueba
17 Hotel Pluviosilla

PLACES TO EAT
6 Tacos Orientales
9 Restaurant Radhe
13 La Troje
15 Bella Napoli
18 Restaurant Romanchu

OTHER
2 Old Palacio Municipal
3 Parish Church
   of San Miguel
5 Palacio Municipal,
   Tourist Office
7 Bank
8 Bank
10 Post Office

Orizaba

0   100   200 m
0   100   200 yards

Things to See

The **Museo de Arte del Estado**, on Avenida Ote 4 between Calles 25 and 27, is a masterpiece. Housed in a splendidly restored colonial building dating from 1776 that has been at times a church, a hospital and a military base, the museum consists of many rooms, each of which adheres to a different theme. In one room, for example, are exquisite paintings depicting key moments in the history of Veracruz state. In another are contemporary works by regional artists. In yet another are 29 paintings by Diego Rivera, which represent his work throughout his life, from his years as a young artist in Europe until the period just before his death in 1957.

The **Parroquia de San Miguel**, the big parish church on the north side of Parque del Castillo, is mainly 17th century in style with several towers and some Puebla-type tiles. The 18th century **La Concordia** and **El Carmen** churches have Churrigue-resque façades.

The **Centro Educativo Obrero** (Workers' Education Center), on Colón between the Parque del Castillo and the Alameda park, has a 1926 mural by the great muralist José Clemente Orozco.

The dilapidated iron and steel former **Palacio Municipal**, off the northwest corner of Parque del Castillo, was the Belgian pavilion at the Paris International Exhibition in the late 19th century. Orizaba bought it for US$13,800 and had it dismantled, shipped to Mexico and reassembled. At the time of writing, its latest occupants had moved into a new municipal palace and the historic structure stood with an uncertain future.

Hiking

Hiking through the **canyon** beside the Hotel Fiesta Cascada is a free and enjoyable activity – and much less strenuous than climbing nearby Pico de Orizaba. A forest-flanked trail begins a few meters west of the hotel and descends to the canyon floor, where it forks. To the left, the trail follows the river for several km. To the right, it crosses a footbridge beside a small power station then reaches a rough road that winds northwesterly through forest and cropland for many km as it climbs up into the mountains. The best part of this trek is at the very start, where a beautiful waterfall emerging from dense forest is in clear view.

Looming over the Alameda park west of town, **Cerro del Barrego** offers brilliant views if you get to the top very early – before the mist rolls in.

If you're planning an ascent of Pico de Orizaba, see Around Orizaba.

Places to Stay

Orizaba's best budget value is the *Hotel Arenas* (☎ 5-23-61) at Nte 2 No 169. It's family-run and friendly, with a lovely courtyard garden. Clean singles/doubles with private bath are US$6/8. A close second for the same rate is the *Hotel San Cristóbal* (☎ 5-11-40) at Nte 4 No 243. Be advised that the upstairs rooms with balcony catch street noise all night long. All of the bathrooms are recently updated.

The best of the mid-range places is the *Hotel L'Orbe* (☎ 5-50-33), at Pte 5 No 3, with new beds and remodeled air-con rooms with TV for US$20/22. Rooms at the *Hotel Trueba* (Tel 4-29-30) at Ote 6 and Sur 11 cost the same but are not nearly as nice. Just behind L'Orbe in value in this price range is *Hotel Aries* (☎ 5-35-20) at Ote 6 No 265, which has newly remodeled bathrooms and 2nd-floor rooms away from the street for US$17/19. The *Hotel Pluviosilla* (☎ 5-53-00), at Pte 7 No 163, has parking and rooms for US$15/16. The *Grand Hotel de France* (☎ 5-3-11) at Ote 6 No 186 has seen better days but its rooms are OK for US$9/10 (US$13 for two beds).

The best hotel in town is the *Hotel Fiesta Cascada* (☎ 4-15-96), at Km 27.5 on the 150D Puebla-Córdoba road (look for two Pemex stations opposite each other). The Cascada is located above a gorgeous canyon (see Things to Do), and the grounds contain gardens and a nice little patch of rainforest. The rooms are charming and spacious, contain minibar, TV and phone, and look out over an inviting pool.

Singles/doubles go for a very reasonable US$25/32.

Places to Eat

Mariscos Boca del Río on Pte 7 a block or so west of the Hotel Pluviosilla is the best seafood restaurant in town and quite reasonably priced, with large shrimp and seafood cocktails, filet of fish, and squid all priced around US$5. *La Troje* at Sur 5 No 225 has lots of atmosphere and an excellent five-course comida corrida for US$3 weekdays and US$6 on Sunday. The large, popular and colorful *Restaurant Romanchu*, opposite the Hotel Pluviosilla on Pte 7, is known for its beef dishes (US$3 to US$6), as is the restaurant at Hotel Trueba (US$5 to US$7). *Restaurant Radhe* on Sur 5 offers very good, moderately priced vegetarian food. The *Bella Napoli* on Sur 7 between Ote 4 and 6 does the best pizza in town. *Tacos Orientales* at the corner of Colón and Sur 3 is very popular for its cheap and tasty tacos.

Getting There & Away

Bus The local buses from Fortín or Córdoba stop four blocks north and six blocks east of the center, around Ote 9 and Nte 14. The AU (2nd-class) station is at Zaragoza Pte 425, northwest of the center. To reach the city center from here, turn left outside the depot, cross the bridge, take the first fork right and head for the church domes. The ADO (1st-class) station is at Ote 6 No 577 between Sur 11 and 13; the deluxe services UNO and ADO GL operate out of this station. Outbound services include:

Jalapa – 240 km, four hours; 10 ADO only (US$7)

Mexico City (TAPO) – 285 km, four hours; two UNO (US$20), two ADO GL (US$13), 17 ADO (US$11) and 30 AU (US$10)

Puebla – 160 km, 2½ hours; 12 ADO (US$7) and 20 AU (US$6)

Tehuacán – 65 km, one hour; four ADO only (US$2.50)

Veracruz – 150 km, 2¼ hours; 21 ADO and 21 AU (both US$6)

There is also 1st-class service to Oaxaca, Tuxpan and Villahermosa.

Train Orizaba is on the Veracruz-Mexico City line. Fares to Veracruz on the main train, El Jarocho, are US$2.75/1.70 in primera preferente/segunda clase. See the Mexico City Getting There & Away section for the schedule and more fare information. The station is south of the city center on the corner of Pte 19 and Sur 10.

Car & Motorcycle The toll highway 150D bypasses central Orizaba, heads east to Córdoba then west, via a spectacular ascent, to Puebla (160 km). The toll-free highway 150 runs east to Córdoba and Veracruz (150 km) then southwest to Tehuacán, 65 km away over the hair-raising Cumbres de Acultzingo.

AROUND ORIZABA

Pico de Orizaba Mexico's tallest mountain (5611 meters) is located 25 km northwest of the city of Orizaba. The dormant volcano has a small crater and a three-month snowcap. From the summit, in good weather, one can see Popocatépetl, Iztaccíhuatl and La Malinche to the west and the Gulf of Mexico 96 km to the east. The only higher peaks in North America are Mt McKinley in Alaska and Mt Logan in Canada.

From Orizaba, tours of the mountain up to 4000 meters are provided by Turismo Aventura and leave from the lobby of the Hotel Trueba by 4WD every Saturday and Sunday at 9 am; price is US$20 per person. For more information, contact the hotel (☎/fax 4-29-30), which has a working relationship with Turismo Aventura.

For those wishing to climb Pico de Orizaba from Orizaba, the same outfit, Turismo Aventura, leads climbers to its peak for US$150 per person, which includes transportation from the Trueba to/from a high-elevation hut as well as guide service. The routine is: two days in Orizaba (1219 meters), two days at a hut (4440 meters), then one day for the ascent and descent. Turismo Aventura director Ricardo Demeneghi does not speak English, but one of his guides does. Expeditions should be scheduled well ahead of time.

If you wish to climb Pico from Mexico City, Mario Andrade (☎ 5-875-01-05) is *the* person to contact about leading the attempt. The bilingual Andrade is head of Coordinadores de Guías de Montaña (☎/fax 5-584-46-95), a professional group that provides qualified guides for most Mexican mountain peaks. It has its office at Tlaxcala 47 in the Colonia Roma neighborhood of Mexico City. Faxes sent to the group will be forwarded to Andrade. Andrade's fee of US$500 for one or two climbers includes his fee, transportation from your hotel in Mexico City to Pico and back, two mountain meals, non-personal equipment (radio, ropes), lodging fee, and national park entrance fee. Andrade's mailing address is PO Box M-10380, México DF, Mexico. The most popular time to climb Pico is during December and January, but the best time is in October, when there's lots of snow and the sky is clear.

Zongolica A road leads 38 km south from Orizaba to this mountain village, where isolated Indian groups make unique styles of sarapes. Buses leave from Ote 3 between Nte 12 and Nte 14 every 15 minutes.

Southern Veracruz

Southeast of the port of Veracruz is mostly a flat, hot, wet coastal plain crossed by many rivers. The exception is the region known as Los Tuxtlas ('TOOKS-lahs'), around the towns of Santiago Tuxtla and San Andrés Tuxtla. The region is hilly, green and fertile with several lakes and waterfalls, and a quiet coastline. Los Tuxtlas has one of the most agreeable climates in all Veracruz. Mexican vacationers are attracted to Catemaco, a small lakeside resort in the region.

Los Tuxtlas is also the western fringe of the ancient Olmec heartland, with interesting Olmec museums at Santiago Tuxtla and Tres Zapotes. The basalt for the huge Olmec heads was quarried from Cerro Cintepec in the east of the Sierra de los Tuxtlas

and then moved, probably by roller and raft, to San Lorenzo, 60 km to the south.

ALVARADO
pop 75,000; ☎ *297*

The busy fishing town of Alvarado, 67 km down highway 180 from Veracruz, stands on a spit of land separating the Gulf of Mexico from the Laguna de Alvarado, which is the meeting point of several rivers including the Papaloapan. The channel from the lagoon to the sea is crossed by a long toll bridge east of the town (US$2 per car).

Alvarado has a few hotels and restaurants, as well as a post office. Carnaval celebrations start here immediately after the Carnaval in Veracruz finishes. You can hire boats for trips on the lagoons or up the river to Tlacotalpan (about two hours).

TLACOTALPAN
pop 20,000; alt 155m; ☎ *288*

A very quiet old town beside the wide Río Papaloapan, 10 km south of highway 180, Tlacotalpan has some pretty streets, churches, plazas and colorful houses. The **Museo Salvador Ferrando**, open daily except Monday (US$1.50), has some 19th century furniture and artifacts. You can rent boats for river trips. Tlacotalpan's lively Candelaria festival, in late January and early February, features bull-running in the streets and an image of the Virgin floating down the river followed by a flotilla of small boats.

There are two small hotels – the *Posada Doña Lala* (☎ 4-25-80), with pleasant rooms starting at US$23/17, and the *Hotel Reforma* (no phone), from US$19. Some restaurants are along the riverfront, others near the plazas.

Highway 175 goes from Tlacotalpan up the Papaloapan valley to Tuxtepec, then twists and turns over the mountains to Oaxaca (320 km from Tlacotalpan).

SANTIAGO TUXTLA
pop 19,000; alt 285m; ☎ *272*

Santiago, founded in 1525, is a pretty valley town in the rolling green foothills of the volcanic Sierra de los Tuxtlas. It's a pleasant stopover, and worth visiting for the Olmec remains and museums in the town and at Tres Zapotes, 23 km away.

Orientation & Information

ADO buses arriving in Santiago drop you where Calle Morelos runs off the highway. Go south down Morelos a little, and the Transportes Los Tuxtlas office is on your left; turn right (west) here onto Ayuntamiento to reach the Museo Arqueológico on the south side of the zócalo. The post office is also on the zócalo, as is the Comermex bank, which changes traveler's checks.

Things to See

The **Olmec head** in the zócalo is known as the Cobata head, after the estate west of Santiago where it was found. It's thought to be a very late or even post-Olmec production, but is the biggest Olmec head found so far, and unique in that its eyes are closed.

The **Museo Arqueológico** exhibits Olmec stone carvings, including another colossal head, this one from Nestepec west of Santiago, a rabbit head from Cerro de Vigía and a copy of Monument F or 'El Negro' from Tres Zapotes, which is an altar or throne with a human form carved into it. The museum is open Monday through Saturday from 9 am to 6 pm (US$2), and Sunday 9 am to 3 pm (free).

Special Events

Santiago celebrates the festivals of San Juan (June 24) and Santiago Apóstol (St James, July 25) with processions and dances including the Liseres, in which the participants wear jaguar costumes.

Places to Stay & Eat

The family-run *Hotel Morelos* (no phone) has Morelos 12 as its address but its entrance is on Obregón, which runs off Morelos almost opposite the Transportes Los Tuxtlas bus station. Rooms cost

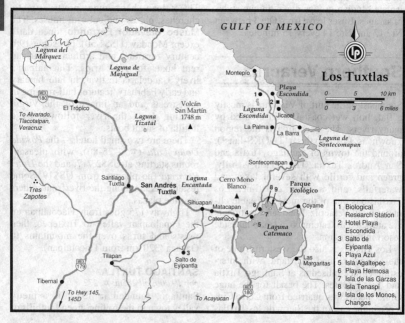

Los Tuxtlas

0   5   10 km
0   3   6 miles

1 Biological
   Research Station
2 Hotel Playa
   Escondida
3 Salto de
   Eyipantla
4 Playa Azul
5 Isla Agaltepec
6 Playa Hermosa
7 Isla de las Garzas
8 Isla Tenaspi
9 Isla de los Monos,
   Changos

US$12/14, and have fans and private bath with hot water but aren't very big. Some are brighter than others.

The modern *Hotel Castellanos* (☎ 7-02-00), in a circular building on the north side of the zócalo, is amazingly good for a small-town hotel. It has an enticing swimming pool and 48 clean, air-con rooms of varying sizes, most with fine views. Singles and doubles are US$22. Its pleasant restaurant serves egg dishes for US$1.50, meat or chicken US$3 and seafood a bit more. Cheaper eateries line up on the south side of the zócalo.

Getting There & Away
If there are no convenient services, go first to San Andrés Tuxtla by the frequent but suspension-free buses of Transportes Los Tuxtlas (US$0.75), or by taxi (US$4).

From Santiago, ADO has eight de paso buses a day to Veracruz (2½ hours; US$5), nine a day to San Andrés Tuxtla (20 minutes; US$0.75) and seven a day to Acayucan (two hours; US$3.50), as well as service to Jalapa (3½ hours; US$9), Puebla (seven hours; US$18) and Mexico City (TAPO; 8½ hours; US$23). Additionally, Cuenca, a local service that shares an office with AU on the northern edge of town, has eight daily buses to San Andrés (US$0.75) and eight to Tlacotalpan (US$2). Transportes Los Tuxtlas buses depart every 10 minutes for San Andrés Tuxtla (US$0.75), Catemaco (US$1) Veracruz (US$4.25), and hourly for Acayucan (US$3).

TRES ZAPOTES
The important late Olmec center of Tres Zapotes is now just a series of mounds in maize fields, but many interesting finds are displayed at the museum in the village of Tres Zapotes, 23 km west of Santiago Tuxtla.

History
Tres Zapotes was probably first occupied while the great Olmec center of La Venta (Tabasco) still flourished. It carried on after the destruction of La Venta (about 600 BC) in what archaeologists regard as an 'epi-Olmec' phase, when the spark had gone out of Olmec culture and other civilizations – notably Izapa – were adding their marks. Most of the finds are from this later period.

At Tres Zapotes in 1939, Matthew Stirling, the first great Olmec excavator, unearthed part of a chunk of basalt with an epi-Olmec 'were-jaguar' carving on one side and, on the other, a series of bars and dots, apparently part of a date in the Mayan Long Count dating system. Stirling decoded the date as September 3, 32 BC, which meant that the Olmecs preceded the Maya, who until then were believed to have been Mexico's earliest civilization. Much debate followed but later finds supported Stirling's discovery. In 1969 a farmer came across the rest of the stone, now called Stela C, which bore the missing part of Stirling's date.

Museum
At the Tres Zapotes museum the objects are arranged on a cross-shaped platform. On the far side is the Tres Zapotes head, dating from about 100 BC, which was the first Olmec head to be discovered in modern times; it was found by a hacienda worker in 1858. Opposite the head is Stela A, the biggest piece, with three human figures in the mouth of a jaguar. This originally stood on its end. To the right of Stela A are two pieces. One is a sculpture of what may have been a captive with hands tied behind its back. The other piece has a toad carved on one side and a skull on the other. Beyond Stela A is an altar or throne carved with the upturned face of a woman, and beyond that, in the corner, the less interesting part of the famous Stela C. (The part with the date is in the Museo Nacional de Antropología but there's a photo of it on the wall here.) The museum attendant is happy to answer questions (in Spanish). The museum is open daily from 9 am to 5 pm. Entry is US$1.50, free on Sunday.

The site these objects came from is one km away, though there's little to see. Walk back past the Sitio Olmeca taxi stand, turn left at the end of the road past the village square and go over the bridge and along the road.

Getting There & Away

The road to Tres Zapotes goes southwest from Santiago Tuxtla (a 'Zona Arqueológica' sign points the way from highway 180). Eight km down this road, you fork right onto a decent dirt track for the last 15 km to Tres Zapotes village. It comes out at a T-junction next to the Sitio Olmeca taxi stand. From here you walk to the left, then turn left again to reach the museum.

At the time of research bus service had been suspended, and there was no talk of re-establishing it. The only safe way to get to Tres Zapotes unless things change is to take a green-and-white taxi from Santiago Tuxtla (for US$1.25 if it's going *colectivo*, US$6 if you have it all to yourself). Taxis leave from the Sitio Puente Real, on the far side of the pedestrian bridge at the foot of Zaragoza, the street going downhill beside the Santiago Tuxtla museum.

SAN ANDRÉS TUXTLA
pop 100,000; alt 365m; ☎ 294

San Andrés is in the center of the Los Tuxtlas area, surrounded by countryside producing maize, bananas, beans, sugar cane and cattle – as well as tobacco, which is rolled into cigars *(puros)* in the town. There are some scenic attractions nearby, including the dormant San Martín volcano, 1748 meters high.

Orientation & Information

The ADO deluxe and AU 1st-class bus lines share a depot one km northwest of the plaza on Juárez, which runs downhill to the center. The cathedral is on the north side of the plaza, the Palacio Municipal is on the west side, and a Banamex is on the south side. Most places to stay and eat are near the plaza, and the market is three blocks west. The post office is on Lafragua; head down 20 de Noviembre directly across the plaza from the Palacio Municipal and follow it around to the left.

Things to See

The **Laguna Encantada** (Enchanted Lagoon), a lake that rises in dry weather and falls when it rains, occupies a small volcanic crater three km northeast of San Andrés. A dirt road goes there but no buses.

Twelve km from San Andrés, a 242-step staircase leads down to the 50-meter-high, 40-meter-wide **Salto de Eyipantla** waterfall. Frequent Transportes Los Tuxtlas buses (US$1) make runs to Eyipantla (about every 40 minutes). The route follows highway 180 east for four km to Sihuapan, then turns right down a dirt road.

At Cerro del Gallo near **Matacapan**, just east of Sihuapan, is a pyramid from 300 to 600 AD in Teotihuacán style. It may have been on the route to Kaminaljuyú in Guatemala, the farthest Teotihuacán outpost.

Places to Stay

For the cheapest hotels turn left when you hit the plaza from Juárez, then take the second right, Pino Suárez. The best bargain in town is the *Hotel Figueroa* (☎ 2-02-57), at the intersection of Suárez and Domínguez. It offers charming, clean rooms with hot water and fans for US$6/8; rooms 34 to 42 have vistas. At the same intersection, the *Hotel Colonial* (☎ 2-05-52) is another bargain, with clean, breezy rooms with decent beds and hot water for US$6 for one or two people (one bed; add US$2 for a second bed). Rooms 40 to 42 are best, though there's a bit of street noise in the morning.

A few doors up Domínguez from the Figueroa is the *Hotel Posada San José* (2-10-10), which offers 30 perfectly acceptable singles/doubles with TV, fan, hot water and decent beds ringing a closed courtyard for US$9/10 (add US$3 for aircon). The nearby *Hotel Catedral* (☎ 2-02-37), on the corner of Suárez and Bocangebra, offers clean rooms with fan, private bath and hot water for US$5/6, and US$7 for two beds.

Hotel San Andrés (☎ 2-04-22), at Madero 6 (turn right when you hit the zócalo from Juárez), is a fair value, with 31 clean though worn rooms with TV and bath at US$11/13 with fan, or US$14/17 with air-con. Some rooms have balconies. The *Hotel Isabel* (☎ 2-16-17) at Madero 13 offers decent rooms for US$11/13, add US$3 for air-con. The *Hotel Zamfer*, opposite the Isabel, is a total dump.

The two top places in town are the 48-room *Hotel Del Parque* (☎ 2)1-98) at Madero 5 on the zócalo, and the *Hotel De Los Pérez* (☎ 2-07-77) at Rascón 2, down the street beside the Del Parque. The newer De Los Pérez is preferable for its clean, sizable, modern, air-con rooms with TV from US$17/19. The Del Parque's rooms, also air-con and with color TV, are lighter but a little faded, for US$18/22.

Places to Eat

Cafe Winni's, just down Madero from the plaza, has soup at US$1, eggs at US$1.50, antojitos to US$2.50 and substantial main courses from US$3 to US$4. The two *Mariscos Chazaro* places, at Madero 12 just along from the Hotel San Andrés and also on the back street behind the Hotel De Los Pérez, have excellent, fresh seafood dishes like *sopa de mariscos* and seafood cocktails from US$3 to US$5.

The indoors-outdoors restaurant at the *Hotel Del Parque* is popular, affords good people-watching (it faces the plaza) and does good fish and antojitos for US$4 to US$5 and US$1 to US$2.50, respectively. For vaguely Americanized, slightly expensive fare, visit the *Cafetería California* at Rascón 2, beneath the Hotel De Los Pérez. You can get a respectable burger for under US$3 and carrot or other juices for about US$1.

Things to Buy

The Santa Lucia cigar factory at 5 de Febrero 10, 200 meters from the top of Juárez, has short, long, fat and thin cigars at factory prices. The sights and smells of cigar-making are interesting – and these are some of Mexico's best cigars.

Getting There & Away

Bus San Andrés is the transport center for Los Tuxtlas, with fairly good bus services in every direction. ADO offers deluxe service from San Andrés, AU offers 1st-class. Transportes Los Tuxtlas buses – old and bouncy but often the quickest way of getting to local destinations – leave from the corner of Cabada and Solana Nte, a block north of the market; they skirt the north side of town on 5 de Febrero (highway 180), and you can get on or off at most intersections. Departures from San Andrés include:

Acayucan – 95 km, 1½ hours; 18 ADO (US$29), one TLT every 10 minutes (US$2.50)
Campeche – 785 km, 12½ hours; one ADO only, at 10.30 pm (US$25)
Catemaco – 12 km, 20 minutes; TLT only, every 10 minutes (US$0.75)
Mérida – 965 km, 15 hours; one ADO only, at 10.30 pm (US$30)
Mexico City (TAPO) – 550 km, nine hours; one ADO at 11 pm (US$27) and three AU (US$21; at noon, 9 and 9.35 pm)
Puebla – 420 km, seven hours; one ADO at 11.35 pm (US$18) and one AU at 9.50 pm (US$17)
Santiago Tuxtla – 14 km, 20 minutes; nine ADO (US$0.75) and a TLT every 10 minutes (also US$0.75)
Veracruz – 155 km, 2¾ hours; 28 ADO (US$5.50), one AU at 9.50 pm (US$5), and TLT every 10 minutes (US$4.50)
Villahermosa – 320 km, six hours; 13 ADO (US$7.50)

Taxi A taxi to/from Catemaco or Santiago Tuxtla costs about US$5.

CATEMACO

pop 30,000; alt 370m; ☎ 294

This town on the western shore of beautiful Laguna Catemaco makes most of its living from fishing and from Mexican tourists who flood in during July and August, and for Christmas, New Year and Semana Santa. The rest of the year it's a quiet, economical place to visit. The annual convention of *brujos* (witch doctors), held on Cerro Mono Blanco (White Monkey Hill) north of Catemaco on the first Friday in March, has become more a tourist event than a supernatural one.

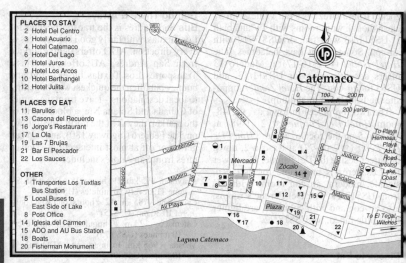

PLACES TO STAY
2 Hotel Del Centro
3 Hotel Acuario
4 Hotel Catemaco
6 Hotel Del Lago
7 Hotel Juros
9 Hotel Los Arcos
10 Hotel Berthangel
12 Hotel Julita

PLACES TO EAT
11 Barullos
13 Casona del Recuerdo
16 Jorge's Restaurant
17 La Ola
19 Las 7 Brujas
21 Bar El Pescador
22 Los Sauces

OTHER
1 Transportes Los Tuxtlas
   Bus Station
5 Local Buses to
   East Side of Lake
8 Post Office
14 Iglesia del Carmen
15 ADO and AU Bus Station
18 Boats
20 Fisherman Monument

Orientation & Information

Catemaco slopes gently down to the lake. There is no tourist office. The post office is on Mantilla, south of the Hotel Los Arcos.

You can change cash and traveler's checks on weekdays before 11.30 am at Multibanco Comermex on the zócalo. In a pinch, try at the Hotel Los Arcos, which gives low rates but is open longer hours.

Laguna Catemaco

The lake, ringed by volcanic hills, is roughly oval and 16 km long. Streams flowing into it are the source of Catemaco and Coyame mineral water. **El Tegal** is a grotto topped with a blue cross where the Virgin is believed to have appeared in the 19th century. Farther on is **Playa Hermosa**, less a beach than a thin strip of gray sand beside which people swim in murky water, and **Playa Azul**, with an upscale hotel. These can be visited in an easy walk east from Catemaco.

The lake has several islands; on the largest, Tenaspi, Olmec sculpture has been found. **Isla de los Monos**, also called Isla de los Changos (Monkey Island), has about 60 red-cheeked *Macaca arctoides* monkeys, originally from Thailand. They belong to the University of Veracruz, which uses them for research purposes. Despite pleas from the university for the animals to be left alone, boat operators bring food for them so that tourists can get close-up photos.

Farther around the north shore is the **Parque Ecológico**, where a small piece of rainforest has been preserved. A guided walk in Spanish (US$2) on a path through the reserve includes the chance to sample mineral water and test the cosmetic benefits of smearing black mud on your face. Enclosures for the not-so-wild wildlife include toucan, monkey, tortoise, peccary and raccoon enclosures. It's quite interesting, but a bit contrived, like a movie set – *The Last Eden* was filmed here. You can reach the park by road or by boat.

Places to Stay

Catemaco has lodging in all price ranges, but add 30% to 50% at peak periods.

Places to Stay – budget

Camping *Restaurant Solotepec* at Playa Hermosa, 1.5 km east of town along the road around the lake, has a small camping area/trailer park close to the water.

Hotels The *Hotel Julita* (☎ 3-00-08) at Avenida Playa 10, near the waterfront just down from the zócalo, is the best budget bargain in town, with a few basic but adequate rooms with fan, hot water and private bath for US$4.50/9 for singles/doubles. The *Hotel Acuario* (☎ 3-04-18), on the zócalo on the corner of Carranza and Boettinger, is good value with comfortable rooms with private bath at US$7/9, or US$12 for three or four people. Some rooms are better than others.

Places to Stay – middle

Hotel Los Arcos (☎ 3-00-03) at Madero 7 on the corner of Mantilla, has helpful staff, a swimming pool and clean, bright rooms with fans, private baths and wide balconies for US$20 for a single or double, US$26 for two beds and air-con. The *Hotel Juros* (☎ 3-00-84) has 23 spacious and clean rooms with TV, air-con and good beds for US$24 for a single or double; very smart suites with spa and sleeping quarters for six go for US$50.

The *Hotel Catemaco* (☎ 3-00-45) on the north side of the zócalo has a restaurant, video bar, a very inviting pool and rooms with air-con and TV for US$24/26 for one bed, US$28/31 for two beds. The lakefront *Hotel Del Lago* (☎ 3-01-60) on Avenida Playa on the corner of Abasolo has good, clean, but not very big air-con rooms with TV for US$18/25. There's a restaurant and small pool. The *Hotel Berthangel* (☎ 3-00-07) just below the zócalo has 122 rooms in a drab three-story building; rooms go for US$17/19.

The *Hotel Playa Azul* (☎ 3-00-01), 2.5 km east of town by the lake, has 80 bright, clean, modern rooms, half of them air-con, in single-story blocks around a garden. Singles and doubles go for US$27. It also offers a restaurant, a volleyball court, boat rentals and, during the high season, a discotheque. A taxi from town is around US$3.

The four-story *Hotel Del Centro* on Zaragoza just south of Carranza was being built at the time of writing. What was completed looked quite charming.

Places to Stay – top end

The lakeside *Hotel La Finca* (☎ 3-03-22), two km out of town on the Acayucan road, has 36 rooms with air-con, balconies and lake views at US$60 for a single or double. A taxi from town costs around US$3.

Places to Eat

The lake provides the specialties here, among them the *tegogolo*, a snail reputed to be an aphrodisiac and best eaten in a sauce of chili, tomato, onion and lime; *chipalchole*, a soup with shrimp or crab claws; *mojarra*, a type of perch; and *anguilas* (eels). *Tachogobi* is a hot sauce sometimes served on mojarra; eels may come with raisins and hot chilies. Many eating places can be depressingly empty out of season and tend to close early.

Two of the most popular and pleasant of Catemaco's many restaurants are right beside the lake, open-sided and breezy. They are *Jorge's Restaurant*, just west of the zócalo, and its superior neighbor, *La Ola*. Jorge's offers decent breakfasts for US$1.50 to US$3, tasty fish dishes for around US$4, beef and chicken for about US$4. There is a lovely little garden beside the restaurant. La Ola offers slightly better food for slightly more money, is more popular, and likewise affords lake views and cool breezes.

Near the plaza, the restaurant-café-video bar *Barullos* has plenty of ambiance and good food. The specialty of the house is a beef dish prepared with onions, peppers and coconut (US$5). Fish dishes range to US$7, chicken to US$5. Owner David Hernández Briszuela insists all the water served at Barullos (including the ice) is mineral water. A half block west, the *Casona del Recuerdo* has delightful balcony tables, friendly service and tasty seafood for US$4 to US$6. Its comida corrida is a good value at about US$3.

Also near the plaza, the *Hotel Catemaco* serves good food at reasonable prices – spaghetti is US$4, chicken and meat dishes US$5 to US$7, filet of sole US$5. The *Hotel Julita* has a good, budget restaurant with filling soups and meat and fish dishes from US$3.50 to US$6. A little southeast, *Las 7 Brujas* is in an interesting round building and stays open late. The lakeside *Bar El Pescador* and the cheaper *Los Sauces* are also popular restaurants.

Getting There & Away

Few long-distance buses reach Catemaco, so you may have to travel via San Andrés Tuxtla, 12 km west on highway 180, or Acayucan, 80 km south, and then take more frequent but less cozy local buses to/ from Catemaco. The 1st-class ADO buses and the 2nd-class AU buses both go from the corner of Aldama and Bravo. Transportes Los Tuxtlas (TLT) is on Cuauhtémoc near the corner of 2 de Abril. Departures from Catemaco include:

Acayucan – 80 km, 1¼ hours; four ADO (US$3), two AU (US$2.75), and a TLT every half hour (US$2.25)

Mexico City (TAPO) – 565 km, nine hours; two ADO (US$23), at 9.30 and 10 pm; and three AU (US$21), at 11.30 am and 8.20 and 9 pm

San Andrés Tuxtla – 12 km, 20 minutes; three ADO (US$0.75), three AU (US$0.60), and a TLT every 20 minutes (US$0.80)

Santiago Tuxtla – 25 km, 40 minutes; a TLT every 10 minutes (US$1)

Veracruz – 165 km, three hours; four ADO (US$6), two AU (US$5.50), and frequent TLTs (US$4.75)

Villahermosa – 310 km, 5½ hours; one ADO only, at 12.30 pm (US$10)

Getting Around

Bus To explore the villages and country east of the lake, where the mountain Santa Marta stands out, take a local bus going to Las Margaritas. They leave every hour or two from the corner of Juárez and Rayón.

Boat Boats do trips on the lake from the moorings just down from the zócalo. The posted price for a trip around the lake's main attractions with up to six people is US$23, or US$5 per person if you go as an individual. A couple of the boatmen speak English.

THE COAST NEAR CATEMACO

About four km northeast of Catemaco there's a fork; the road to the right follows the lake around past Coyame, the road to the left is sealed and scenic as it goes over the hills to **Sontecomapan**, 15 km from Catemaco. There's a basic hotel here and a couple of restaurants, and you can hire boats for trips on the lagoon. After Sontecomapan, the road is much rougher as it continues on to a seldom-visited stretch of the Gulf Coast. This is mainly ranch land and green hills rolling down to the shore.

About eight km from Sontecomapan, near La Palma, an even rougher track goes right to El Real and La Barra, near the mouth of the lagoon. There are isolated beaches but no facilities. About five km past La Palma, a sign points down another rough side road to Playa Escondida. This takes you past the long gray-sand beach of **Jicacal**, with a small, poor fishing village and one restaurant, then up to a forested headland where the *Hotel Playa Escondida* stands, two or three km from the main 'road.' This unassuming establishment has basic rooms (shower but no hot water) for US$8/9, great views and a small restaurant. **Playa Escondida** itself is another km down a steep path from the hotel.

Back on the 'road' you pass a biological research station next to one of the few tracts of unspoiled rainforest on the Gulf coast. A turnoff here leads to pretty Laguna Escondida, hidden in the mountains. The end of the road is at **Montepío**, where there's a nice beach at the rivermouth, two places to eat and the *Posada San José*, with six comfortable rooms for US$12/15.

Getting There & Away

Every half-hour or so from 6 am to 3 pm, *camionetas* (pick-up trucks with benches in the back) go from Catemaco to Montepío. The 35-km trip, with numerous stops, takes 1½ hours and costs US$2. They leave from the corner of Revolución and the Playa Azul road – from the northeast corner of the plaza, walk five blocks east and six blocks north, and look for vehicles congregating.

ACAYUCAN

pop 100,000; alt 150m; ☎ 924

Acayucan is a road-junction town where highway 180 (between Veracruz and Villahermosa) meets highway 185 (which goes south across the Isthmus of Tehuantepec to the Pacific Coast). You may have to change buses here but try to avoid it – most buses are de paso, the 1st-class bus station is not a great setup (no left-luggage storage) and the 2nd-class buses go from offices scattered in surrounding streets. The town itself has nothing of interest, but archaeology fans might want to seek out the Olmec site of San Lorenzo, 35 km to the southeast.

Orientation & Information

The bus stations are on the east side of town – to reach the central plaza, walk uphill through (or past) the market to Avenida Hidalgo, turn left and walk six blocks. The plaza has a modern church on the east side and the town hall on the west. Bancomer and Banamex, both near the plaza, have ATMs and change traveler's checks.

Places to Stay & Eat

The *Hotel Ancira* (5-00-48), on Bravo a half block southwest of the plaza, offers singles and doubles with fan, phone and private bathroom with hot water for US$5; some beds need replacing, so ask to see a room before checking in. The *Hotel Ritz* (☎ 5-00-24), between the bus stations and the central plaza at Hidalgo 7, is hardly ritzy, with grubby singles/doubles at US$7/8. On the south side of the plaza, the *Hotel Joalicia* (☎ 5-08-77) is better value with clean, sizable rooms for US$7/9, add $3 for air-con. The Joalicia's restaurant isn't bad either. The top place is the *Hotel Kinaku* (☎ 5-04-10) at Ocampo Sur 7, a block east of the plaza, where spacious, comfortable rooms with air-con and TV cost US$22/26; some rooms are better than others.

The Kinaku's restaurant, open 24 hours, is the smartest place in town; egg dishes go for US$1.50 to US$3, beef dishes from US$5 to US$7, and spaghetti (eight variations to choose from) from US$2.75 to US$3.50. *La Parrilla* restaurant, north of the plaza, offers fish dishes for up to US$6, meat dishes for up to US$5, and egg dishes for around US$3. *Los Tucanes Cafetería*, on the pedestrian street a block west of the plaza, is popular, with breakfasts going for US$4 or less, regional food for US$2.50 to US$5, and beef dishes for US$3 to US$7; open 24 hours.

Getting There & Away

Most 1st-class buses (ADO and Cristóbal Colón) are de paso, so you usually have to wait till a bus comes in before you can get a ticket out. AU, Sur and Transportes Los Tuxtlas provide 2nd-class service. UNO, a deluxe service, has some offerings. Departures include:

Catemaco – 80 km, 1¼ hours; seven AU (US$2.25) and frequent TLTs (US$2)

Juchitán – 195 km, three hours; eight ADO (US$7) and Sur buses every 30 minutes (US$6)

Mexico City (TAPO) – 650 km, 11 hours; 12 UNO (US$41), one deluxe ADO (US$31), six ADO (US$25), and six AU (US$23)

San Andrés Tuxtla – 95 km, 1½ hours; 13 ADO (US$22), two AU (US$2.75) and frequent TLTs (US$2)

Santiago Tuxtla – 110 km, two hours; one ADO at 7 am (US$4), and hourly TLTs (US$2.75)

Tapachula – 580 km, nine hours; four evening Cristóbal Colón buses (US$19) and numerous Sur buses (US$17)

Tuxtla Gutiérrez – 440 km, eight hours; one ADO at 10.45 pm (US$14) and one Cristóbal Colón at 11 pm (US$14)

Veracruz – 250 km, five hours; one UNO at 6.30 pm (US$19), one ADO deluxe at 6 pm (US$10), 18 ADO (US$8) and one AU (US$7)

Villahermosa – 225 km, 3½ hours; eight ADO (US$9) and three AU (US$8)

SAN LORENZO

The first of the two great Olmec ceremonial centers, which flourished from about 1200 to 900 BC, is 35 km southeast of Acayucan. The extraordinary main structure is a platform about 50 meters high, 1.25 km long and 700 meters wide, with ridges jutting from its sides which may have been meant to produce a bird-shaped ground plan – though recent research indicates the resemblance is coincidental.

Eight Olmec heads have been found here, and other large stone objects have been detected underground, but most of the finds are in museums elsewhere. Some heavy stone thrones, with figures of rulers carved in the side, were also found. Tools made from the black volcanic glass obsidian were imported from Guatemala or the Mexican highlands, and basalt for the heads and thrones was transported from the Sierra de los Tuxtlas. Such wide contacts, and the organization involved in building the site, show how powerful the rulers of San Lorenzo were. Other features include an elaborate stone-pipe drainage system, and evidence of cannibalism. During its dramatic destruction, which occurred around 900 BC, most of the big carvings were mutilated, dragged onto the ridges and covered with earth.

Getting There & Away

From Acayucan take a bus to Texistepec (south of the Minatitlán road), then another to San Lorenzo, a total journey of two hours. San Lorenzo proper is three km southwest of the village of Tenochtitlán. Finds have also been made at Tenochtitlán and at Potrero Nuevo, three km southeast of San Lorenzo.

MINATITLÁN & COATZACOALCOS

These two towns, 50 and 70 km respectively east of Acayucan, are bypassed by highway 180D. They mushroomed into refining centers of half a million people each during the oil boom of the late 1970s. The area is an industrial wilderness, though Coatzacoalcos retains a pleasant central plaza, and the bridge over the Río Coatzacoalcos is impressive. There are plenty of hotels here for the oil people but nothing to make anyone else want to stay.

Oaxaca State

The rugged southern state of Oaxaca ('wa-HA-ka') reaches to within just 250 km of Mexico City but, divided as it is from central Mexico by barriers of mountains, it remains a world away in atmosphere. It enjoys a slower, sunnier existence and a magical quality that has something to do with the dry, rocky landscape, the remoteness, the bright southern light and the sparse population. The high proportion of Indians in Oaxaca's population are the driving force behind the state's fine handicrafts.

Oaxaca city is a major travel destination yet remains beautiful and artistic. Around it, in the Valles Centrales (Central Valleys), are thriving village markets and spectacular ruins of pre-Hispanic Indian towns such as Monte Albán and Yagul. On the beautiful Oaxaca coast, Mexico's newest tourist resort is growing up on the lovely Bahías de Huatulco. Puerto Escondido and the Puerto Ángel area are older beach destinations that will probably always remain small scale and more laid back. The Oaxaca coast was ravaged by Hurricane Pauline in 1997, but the Bahías de Huatulco and Puerto Escondido came through with relatively little damage, and the travelers' scene around Puerto Ángel is likely to revive quickly.

The backcountry of the region is as far from Oaxaca city in culture and traveling time as Oaxaca is from Mexico City. There's enough of it to offer weeks of exploring.

Lying in a region where temperate and tropical climatic zones and several mountain ranges meet, Oaxaca has spectacularly varied landscapes and a biodiversity greater than any other Mexican state. The inland highlands still have big stands of oak and pine forest, while lower-lying areas and the Pacific-facing slopes of the southern mountains support deciduous tropical forest.

HIGHLIGHTS

- Oaxaca city – a beautiful, lively colonial city with great handicraft shopping
- Monte Albán – ruins of the ancient Zapotec capital on a superb hilltop site
- Hierve El Agua – ice-cold cliff-top swimming pools amid bizarre scenery of 'frozen waterfalls'
- Puerto Ángel area – great beaches, a laid-back scene, boat trips, snorkeling, sea turtles, dolphins, crocodiles
- Puerto Escondido – a small-scale tropical resort with superb surfing
- Lagunas de Manialtepec & Chacahua – take a boat ride through mangrove-fringed lagoons teeming with bird life
- Bahías de Huatulco – a low-key modern resort being built on a set of exquisite bays that have great snorkeling

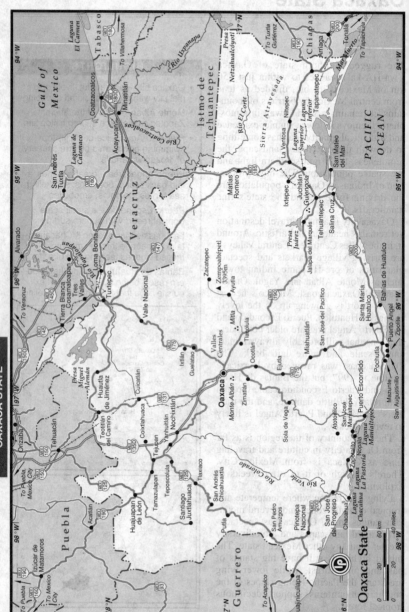

Oaxaca State

History

Zapotecs & Mixtecs Pre-Hispanic Oaxaca traded with other parts of Mexico, but its cultures were left largely undisturbed, reaching heights rivaling those of central Mexico.

The Valles Centrales have always been the hub of life here. Building began at Monte Albán about 500 BC. This became the center of the Zapotec culture, which extended its control over the Valles Centrales and other parts of Oaxaca by conquest and peaked between 250 and 750 AD. Monte Albán's decline was sudden; by about 750 AD, along with many other Zapotec sites in the Valles Centrales, it was deserted. From about 1200 those sites that remained came under growing dominance by the Mixtecs, renowned potters and metal smiths from Oaxaca's northwest uplands. Mixtec and Zapotec cultures became entangled in the Valles Centrales before they fell to the Aztecs in the 15th and early 16th centuries.

Colonial Era The Spaniards received a mixed reception in Oaxaca. They sent at least four expeditions before founding the city of Oaxaca in 1529. Cortés donated large parts of the Valles Centrales to himself and was officially named Marqués del Valle de Oaxaca. In early colonial times, the Indian population dropped disastrously. The Valles Centrales, which had about 150,000 Indians in 1568, had only 40,000 to 50,000 by the 1630s. Rebellions continued into the 20th century, but the Indian peoples rarely formed a serious threat.

Juárez & Díaz Benito Juárez, the great reforming leader of mid-19th century Mexico, was a Zapotec. He served two terms as Oaxaca state governor before being elected Mexico's president in 1861. (See the sidebar Benito Juárez.)

Juárez appointed Porfirio Díaz, son of a Oaxaca horse trainer, as state governor in 1862. Díaz, rebelling against Juárez's presidency in 1871, went on to control Mexico with an iron fist from 1877 to 1910. While his rule brought the country into the industrial age, it also fostered corruption, repression and, eventually, the revolution. In Valle Nacional in northern Oaxaca, tobacco planters set up virtual slave plantations, most of whose 15,000 workers had to be replaced annually because of deaths from disease, beating or starvation.

Oaxaca Today After the revolution about 300 *ejidos* (peasant land-holding cooperatives) were set up, but land ownership remains a source of conflict today. With little industry, Oaxaca is one of Mexico's poorest states, many of its residents leaving to work in the cities or the USA; the situation is made worse in some areas – notably in the Mixteca in the west – by deforestation and erosion. In 129 of the state's 570 municipalities, more than 60% of the people are without toilets or drainage; in 93 municipalities, more than half have no electricity. Tourism is booming in Oaxaca city and nearby villages and in Puerto Escondido, Puerto Ángel and Bahías de Huatulco, on the coast, but has little impact elsewhere.

The Ejército Popular Revolucionario (People's Revolutionary Army; EPR) is a group of rebels who emerged in neighboring Guerrero in 1996. They have been active in Oaxaca, and Bahías de Huatulco was the scene of their most violent attack that year, with 10 people dying. (The targets were the police, government and military, not tourists.) After that, EPR activity became mostly propagandistic rather than violent.

Geography & Climate

The western two-thirds of the state are rugged and mountainous; the eastern third lies on the hot, low-lying Isthmus of Tehuantepec. Oaxaca also has a thin plain along the Pacific Coast and a low-lying north central region bordering Veracruz.

The Sierra Madre del Sur (average height 2000 meters) enters Oaxaca from the west and stretches along the coast. The Sierra Madre de Oaxaca (average height 2500 meters) runs down from Mexico's central volcanic belt. The two ranges meet

Oaxaca Bus Companies
The following abbreviations for 2nd-class bus companies are used in this chapter:

AVN –   Autotransportes Valle del Norte
EB/TG –   Estrella Blanca/Transportes
          Gacela
EV/OP –   Estrella del Valle/Oaxaca
          Pacífico
FYPSA –   Fletes y Pasajes
TOI –   Transportes Oaxaca-Istmo

roughly in the center of the state. Between them, converging at the city of Oaxaca, lie the three Valles Centrales.

The Valles Centrales are warm and dry, with temperatures in the low teens on winter nights and the low 30s on summer days (both measurements in degrees Celsius). The annual rainfall of 600 mm falls mostly from June to September. On the coast and in low-lying areas it's hotter and a bit wetter.

Population & People
Oaxaca's population of 3.2 million includes about 1.25 million Indians of at least 14 different peoples. Each people has its own language but most also speak Spanish. Some Indian ways are buckling under the pressure of change – colorful traditional costumes, for instance, are seen less and less – but there's still a strong Indian presence noticeable in handicrafts, markets and festivals. Indian land and housing are often the poorest in the state. When Indian organizations campaign for land rights, the reaction of the powers-that-be has literally been murderous at times.

Some 500,000 Zapotecs live mainly in and around the Valles Centrales and on the Isthmus of Tehuantepec. You're sure to come into contact with them, though there are few obvious signs to identify them. Most are farmers, but they're also involved in trading their produce and wares, which include handicrafts and mezcal. Many have to emigrate temporarily for work.

Some 500,000 Mixtecs live around the mountainous borders of Oaxaca, Guerrero

and Puebla states, with more than two-thirds of them in Oaxaca. The state's other most numerous Indian peoples are the 190,000 or so Mazatecs in the far north, the 110,000 Mixes in the isolated highlands northeast of the Valles Centrales and the 110,000 Chinantecs around Valle Nacional, in the north.

A group you may well see in Oaxaca city – the women wearing bright red huipiles and populate craft markets – are the Triquis, from western Oaxaca. They are perhaps only 12,000 strong and have a long history of conflict with mestizos and the Mixtecs over land rights.

Dangers & Annoyances
Buses and other vehicles traveling isolated stretches of highway, including the coastal highway 200 and highway 175 from Oaxaca city to Pochutla, occasionally are stopped and robbed. The best way to avoid this risk is not to travel at night.

Oaxaca City

pop 400,000; alt 1550m; ☎ *951*

The state's capital and only sizable city is a Spanish-built place of narrow, straight streets liberally sprinkled with lovely colonial stone buildings. What's special is its atmosphere – at once relaxed and remote, energetic and cosmopolitan. Its dry mountain heat, manageable scale, old buildings and plazas and cafés help slow the pace of life. At the same time diverse Oaxacan, Mexican and international cultures create a current of excitement. There's rarely a dull moment in Oaxaca. Head for the Zócalo first to get a taste of the atmosphere. Then give yourself time to ramble and see what markets, handicrafts, cafés and festivities you come across. There are also many fascinating places within day-trip distance in the Valles Centrales.

History
The Aztec settlement here was called Huaxyacac (meaning 'In the Nose of the

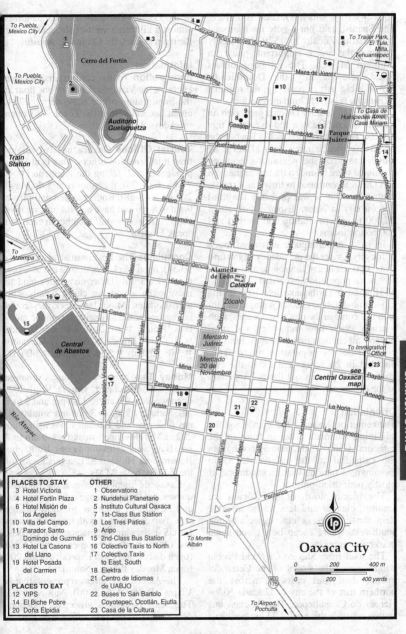

OAXACA STATE

Oaxaca City

PLACES TO STAY	OTHER
3 Hotel Victoria	1 Observatorio
4 Hotel Fortín Plaza	2 Nundehui Planetario
6 Hotel Misión de	5 Instituto Cultural Oaxaca
los Ángeles	7 1st-Class Bus Station
10 Villa del Campo	8 Los Tres Patios
11 Parador Santo	9 Aripo
Domingo de Guzmán	15 2nd-Class Bus Station
13 Hotel La Casona	16 Colectivo Taxis to North
del Llano	17 Colectivo Taxis
19 Hotel Posada	to East, South
del Carmen	18 Elektra
	21 Centro de Idiomas
PLACES TO EAT	de UABJO
12 VIPS	22 Buses to San Bartolo
14 El Biche Pobre	Coyotepec, Ocotlán, Ejutla
20 Doña Elpidia	23 Casa de la Cultura

0   200   400 m

0   200   400 yards

To Monte Albán

To Airport, Pochutla

Squash'), from which 'Oaxaca' is derived. The Spanish laid out a new town around the existing Zócalo in 1529. It quickly became the most important place in southern Mexico. The religious orders based here, notably the Dominicans, played a big part in pacifying the region's Indians by relatively humane conduct.

Eighteenth century Oaxaca grew rich on exports of cochineal, a red dye from tiny insects. The boom ended in 1783, when the Spanish crown banned debt slavery, by which many of the peasants producing cochineal were bound to traders in the city. But Oaxaca continued to thrive as a textile center: by 1796 it was probably the third biggest city in Nueva España, with about 20,000 people (including 600 clergy) and 800 cotton looms.

In 1854 an earthquake destroyed much of the city. Under the presidency of Porfirio Díaz, Oaxaca began to grow again – in the 1890s its population exceeded 30,000. In 1931 another earthquake left 70% of the city uninhabitable. Oaxaca's major expansion has come in the past two decades, with tourism, other new industries and rural poverty all encouraging migration from the countryside. Its population has roughly doubled in 20 years, and today the city sprawls well past its old limits, especially to the northwest.

Orientation

The center of Oaxaca is the Zócalo and the adjoining Alameda plaza in front of the cathedral. Calle Alcalá, running north from the cathedral to the Iglesia de Santo Domingo, a famous Oaxaca landmark, is mostly pedestrian-only.

The blocks north of the Zócalo are smarter, cleaner and less traffic-infested than those to the south, especially the southwest, where cheap hotels and some markets congregate.

The road from Mexico City and Puebla winds around the slopes of the Cerro del Fortín, then runs eastward across the northern part of the city as Calzada Niños Héroes de Chapultepec. The 1st-class bus station is beside this road, 1.75 km northeast of the Zócalo. The 2nd-class bus station is almost a kilometer west of the center, near the main market, the Central de Abastos.

Information

Immigration Tourist card extensions (see Facts for the Visitor) take about one hour at the immigration office at Periférico 2724, about one km east of the Zócalo. It's open weekdays 9 am to 2 pm.

Tourist Offices Oaxaca has two major tourist information offices. One is at Independencia 607, facing the Alameda (☎ 4-77-88, 6-01-23); the other is at 5 de Mayo 200 (☎ 6-48-28). Both are open daily from 9 am to 8 pm and have helpful, informative staff. At least one staff member in each can speak English.

Consulates The US consular agent (☎ 4-30-54), open weekdays from 9 am to 2 pm, is at Alcalá 201. Other consulates tend to move often – you can check details with tourist offices. At our last check they could be reached at the following telephone numbers: Britain ☎ 6-72-80, 3-08-65; Canada ☎ 3-37-77; France ☎ 6-35-22; Germany ☎ 3-08-65; Italy ☎ 5-31-15; Spain ☎ 8-00-31.

Money Two banks with long exchange hours are: Bancomer, García Vigil 202, open weekdays 9 am to 1.30 pm and 2 to 7 pm, Saturday 9 am to 3 pm and Sunday 10 am to 2 pm; and Banamex, Porfirio Díaz 202 at Morelos, open weekdays, 9 am to 3 pm. Bancomer gives good rates. Both, plus Banamex at Hidalgo 821, a block east of the Zócalo, have ATMs.

Casas de cambio save time in bank queues, but their exchange rates are worse – and beware of attempts to short-change you. Two central ones with reasonable rates for US dollars are: Internacional de Divisas, just off the northeast corner of the Zócalo (open daily); and Cash Express, Alcalá 201 (open Monday through Saturday).

The American Express representative is Viajes Micsa (☎ 6-27-00), Valdivieso 2. The main Telégrafos office, on Independencia next to the post office (see Post &

Communications), and the Elektra shop on 20 de Noviembre at Zaragoza both offer the Western Union 'Dinero en Minutos' money transfer service.

Post & Communications The main post office, open weekdays from 8 am to 6 pm and Saturday 9 am to 2 pm, is on the Alameda. Viajes Micsa (see Money) runs an American Express client mail service.

You can send and receive faxes at the Telégrafos office on Independencia. It's next door to the post office and open the same hours.

There are pay phones on the Zócalo and elsewhere. The many telephone casetas include two run by Computel, both with fax service, on Independencia opposite the Telégrafos office and on Trujano between JP García and 20 de Noviembre.

Cafetería Restaurant Gyros Makedonia (☎ 4-07-62), near the Zócalo at 20 de Noviembre 225, is a café-cum-telephone caseta that also has public fax, email and Internet service. At this writing email and Internet rates were cheaper at Terra Nostra (☎ /fax 6-82-92, terran@antequera.com), upstairs at Morelos 600. Terra Nostra charges US$1.30 to send an email (up to 15 minutes on the computer), US$0.70 to receive one and US$3.25 for 30 minutes on the Internet.

Travel Agencies Centroamericana de Viajes (☎ 6-37-25), at Portal de Flores 8 on the Zócalo, is a handy, efficient agent for transportation tickets of most kinds.

Bookstores Corazón El Pueblo, upstairs in Plaza Alcalá, Alcalá 307 at Bravo, has a large range of books in English about Oaxaca and Mexico. Librería Universitaria, Guerrero 108 just off the Zócalo, also has a decent range of English-language titles on Oaxaca and Mexico. Códice, Alcalá 403, has books and maps in English, French and German. Proveedora Escolar, Independencia 1001 at Reforma, has a terrific Spanish-language local history, archaeology and anthropology section upstairs. Main museums also sell books.

Libraries Oaxaca has some fine reference libraries. The Biblioteca Circulante de Oaxaca (Oaxaca Lending Library), Alcalá 305, has a sizable collection of books and magazines in English and Spanish on Oaxaca and Mexico. It's open weekdays 10 am to 1 pm and 4 to 7 pm, Saturday 10 am to 1 pm. It also has a bulletin board advertising accommodations and other useful information.

The Instituto Welte de Estudios Oaxaqueños, tucked at the back of Plaza Fray González Lucero on 5 de Mayo, has an outstanding library with titles in English and Spanish covering ethnography, archaeology, historical geography and more, including a good section on Oaxacan women. It's open weekdays from 9.30 am to 1.30 pm and 5 to 7 pm. The Instituto de Artes Gráficas de Oaxaca, Alcalá 507, has a large Spanish and English arts and architecture library, which visitors can consult.

Media The *Oaxaca Times* and *Oaxaca*, two free monthly tourist newspapers, have some useful information.

Laundry Superlavandería Hidalgo, Hidalgo at JP García, charges US$3 for same-day service wash-and-dry of up to 3.5 kg. It's open Monday through Saturday 8 am to 8 pm. Clin Lavandería, at 20 de Noviembre 605, is marginally higher.

Medical Services Dr Raúl Cruz Aguillón (☎ 6-38-40) is an English-speaking doctor recommended by locals with long experience in the tourism business. His office is at García Vigil 305. Clínica Hospital Carmen (☎ 6-26-12), Abasolo 215, open daily 24 hours, is also recommended and has at least one English-speaking doctor.

Emergency For any emergency service you can call ☎ 06. The police are at ☎ 6-27-26. The Centro de Protección al Turista (Ceprotur, ☎ /fax 6-72-80), in Plaza Santo Domingo, Alcalá 407, exists to help tourists with legal problems: if you have a complaint or have lost documents or have had things stolen, you can report it here.

OAXACA STATE

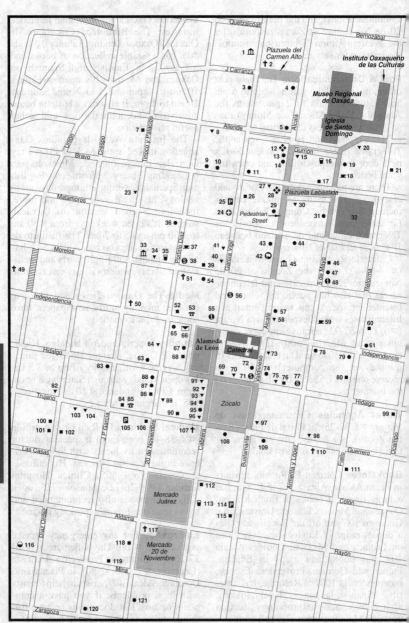

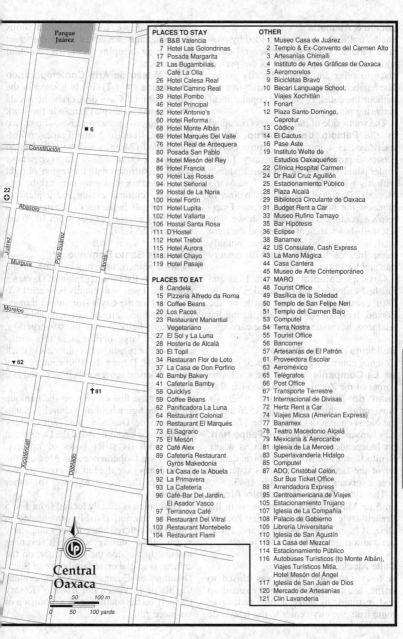

PLACES TO STAY

6 B&B Valencia
7 Hotel Las Golondrinas
17 Posada Margarita
21 Las Bugambilias,
   Café La Olla
26 Hotel Calesa Real
32 Hotel Camino Real
39 Hotel Pombo
46 Hotel Principal
52 Hotel Antonio's
60 Hotel Reforma
68 Hotel Monte Albán
69 Hotel Marqués Del Valle
76 Hotel Real de Antequera
80 Posada San Pablo
84 Hotel Mesón del Rey
86 Hotel Francia
90 Hotel Las Rosas
94 Hotel Señorial
99 Hostal de La Noria
100 Hotel Fortín
101 Hotel Lupita
102 Hotel Vallarta
106 Hostal Santa Rosa
111 D'Hostel
112 Hotel Trebol
115 Hotel Aurora
118 Hotel Chayo
119 Hotel Pasaje

PLACES TO EAT

8 Candela
15 Pizzeria Alfredo da Roma
18 Coffee Beans
20 Los Pacos
23 Restaurant Manantial
   Vegetariano
27 El Sol y La Luna
28 Hostería de Alcalá
30 El Topil
34 Restauran Flor de Loto
37 La Casa de Don Porfirio
40 Bamby Bakery
41 Cafetería Bamby
58 Quicklys
59 Coffee Beans
62 Panificadora La Luna
64 Restaurant Colonial
70 Restaurant El Marqués
73 El Sagrario
75 El Mesón
82 Café Alex
89 Cafetería Restaurant
   Gyros Makedonia
91 La Casa de la Abuela
92 La Primavera
93 La Cafetería
96 Café-Bar Del Jardín,
   El Asador Vasco
97 Terranova Café
98 Restaurant Del Vitral
103 Restaurant Montebello
104 Restaurant Flami

OTHER

1 Museo Casa de Juárez
2 Templo & Ex-Convento del Carmen Alto
3 Artesanías Chimalli
4 Instituto de Artes Gráficas de Oaxaca
5 Aeromorelos
9 Bicicletas Bravo
10 Becari Language School,
   Viajes Xochitlán
11 Fonart
12 Plaza Santo Domingo,
   Ceprotur
13 Códice
14 El Cactus
16 Pase Aste
19 Instituto Welte de
   Estudios Oaxaqueños
22 Clínica Hospital Carmen
24 Dr Raúl Cruz Aguillón
25 Estacionamiento Público
29 Plaza Alcalá
29 Biblioteca Circulante de Oaxaca
31 Budget Rent a Car
33 Museo Rufino Tamayo
35 Bar Hipótesis
36 Eclipse
38 Banamex
42 US Consulate, Cash Express
43 La Mano Mágica
44 Casa Cantera
45 Museo de Arte Contemporáneo
47 MARO
48 Tourist Office
49 Basílica de la Soledad
50 Templo de San Felipe Neri
51 Templo del Carmen Bajo
53 Computel
54 Terra Nostra
56 Tourist Office
55 Bancomer
57 Artesanías de El Patrón
61 Proveedora Escolar
63 Aeroméxico
65 Telégrafos
66 Post Office
67 Transporte Terrestre
71 Internacional de Divisas
72 Hertz Rent a Car
77 Viajes Micsa (American Express)
77 Banamex
78 Teatro Macedonio Alcalá
79 Mexicana & Aerocaribe
81 Iglesia de La Merced
83 Superlavandería Hidalgo
85 Computel
87 ADO, Cristóbal Colón,
   Sur Bus Ticket Office
88 Arrendadora Express
95 Centroamericana de Viajes
105 Estacionamiento Trujano
107 Iglesia de La Compañía
108 Palacio de Gobierno
109 Librería Universitaria
110 Iglesia de San Agustín
113 La Casa del Mezcal
114 Estacionamiento Público
116 Autobuses Turísticos (to Monte Albán),
   Viajes Turísticos Mitla,
   Hotel Mesón del Ángel
117 Iglesia de San Juan de Dios
120 Mercado de Artesanías
121 Clin Lavandería

OAXACA STATE

Zócalo & Alameda

Shady, traffic-free and surrounded by *portales* (arcades) that shelter several cafés and restaurants, the Zócalo is the perfect place to relax and watch the city go by. The adjacent Alameda, also traffic-free but without the cafés, is another popular local gathering place.

The south side of the Zócalo is occupied by the **Palacio de Gobierno**, whose stairway has a mural by Arturo García Bustos depicting Oaxacan history. In the center panel look for Benito Juárez (shown with his wife, Margarita) and José María Morelos. Porfirio Díaz appears below, in blue. At the bottom right, Vicente Guerrero's execution at Cuilapan is shown. The left wall shows ancient Mitla, and the right wall is dominated by women, notably Juana Inés de La Cruz, the 17th century nun and love poet.

Oaxaca's **Catedral**, begun in 1553 and finished (after several earthquakes) in the 18th century, stands just north of the Zócalo. Its main (west) façade, facing the Alameda, has some fine baroque carving.

Buildings near the Zócalo

Colonial churches with fine carved façades are **La Compañía**, just off the southwest corner of the Zócalo, and the popular **San Juan de Dios**, on Aldama at 20 de Noviembre, which dates from 1526 and is the oldest church in Oaxaca. The 17th century baroque **Templo de San Felipe Neri**, on Independencia at JP García, is where Benito Juárez and Margarita Maza, daughter of the family for whom his sister had been a servant, were married in 1843.

The 1903 **Teatro Macedonio Alcalá**, on 5 de Mayo at Independencia, is in the French style fashionable under Porfirio Díaz. It has a marble stairway and a five-tier auditorium that holds 1300 people.

Calle Alcalá

A few years ago Alcalá was closed to traffic, and its stone buildings cleaned up and restored, to make a fine pedestrian route from the city center to the Iglesia de Santo Domingo. Tourist-oriented shops and restaurants are dotted along the street but are in keeping with its colonial appearance.

The **Museo de Arte Contemporáneo de Oaxaca** (☎ 4-71-10) is housed in the lovely colonial Casa de Cortés, at Alcalá 202. Permanent displays include the work of five famous Oaxacan artists – Francisco Gutiérrez, Rodolfo Nieto, Francisco Toledo, Rodolfo Morales and the great Rufino Tamayo, a Oaxaca-born Zapotec whose colors are suffused with the region's bright light. There are also temporary exhibitions and other cultural events and a pleasant courtyard café in the back. The museum is open daily except Tuesday from 10.30 am to 8 pm (US$1.30).

Iglesia de Santo Domingo

Santo Domingo, four blocks north of the cathedral, is the most splendid of Oaxaca's churches. It was built mainly between 1570 and 1608 for the city's Dominican monastery. The finest artisans from Puebla and elsewhere helped with its construction. Like other large buildings in this earthquake-prone region, it has immensely thick stone walls. During the 19th century wars and anticlerical movements it was used as a stable.

Amidst the fine carving on the baroque façade, the figure holding a church is Santo Domingo de Guzmán, the 13th century Spanish monk who founded the Dominican order, with its strict vows of poverty, chastity and obedience. In Mexico the Dominicans gave the Indians some protection from the worst excesses of other colonists.

The church is usually locked from 1 to 5 pm. The interior, lavishly ornamented in gilded and colored stucco, has a magically warm glow during candlelit evening masses. Just inside the main door, on the ceiling, is an elaborate family tree of Santo Domingo de Guzmán. The 18th century Capilla de la Virgen del Rosario (Rosary Chapel), on the south side, is a profusion of yet more gilt.

Museo Regional de Oaxaca

Oaxaca's Regional Museum (☎ 6-29-91), in the old monastery buildings attached to Iglesia de Santo Domingo, has been undergoing serious remodeling, with rooms being added in wings recently vacated by the military. It's open Tuesday through Friday 10 am to 6 pm, Saturday and Sunday 10 am to 5 pm (US$1.90, free on Sunday and holidays). The museum's archaeological sections make most sense if you visit them after seeing some sites in the Valles Centrales. All explanatory matter is in Spanish.

The museum's highlight, in a room off the ground floor of the beautiful green stone cloister, is the Mixtec treasure from Tomb Seven at Monte Albán. It dates from the mid-14th century. Mixtecs reused an old Zapotec tomb to bury one of their kings and his sacrificed servants and placed with the bodies a hoard of beautifully worked silver, turquoise, coral, jade, amber, jet, pearls, finely carved jaguar and eagle bone and, above all, gold. It was discovered in 1932 by Alfonso Caso. Also on this floor is a room of other archaeological finds from 10,000 to 500 BC. Upstairs rooms are devoted to the history of Oaxaca state since the Spanish conquest and to the state's Indian peoples.

Instituto de Artes Gráficas de Oaxaca

The Graphic Arts Institute (☎ 6-69-80), at Alcalá 507, almost opposite Santo Domingo, is in a beautiful colonial house donated by the artist Francisco Toledo. It has changing exhibitions of graphic art as well as a good library. It's open daily except Tuesday from 9.30 am to 8 pm. Donations are requested when you enter.

Museo Casa de Juárez

The Juárez House Museum (☎ 6-18-60), at García Vigil 609, opposite the Templo del Carmen Alto, is where Benito Juárez found work as a boy. A Zapotec with only a few words of Spanish, he had come to Oaxaca in 1818 from the village of Guelatao, 74 km north. His employer, Antonio Salanueva,

a bookbinder, spotted the boy's potential and helped pay for an education that Juárez otherwise might not have received.

The recently renovated house shows how the early 19th century Oaxaca middle class lived. The binding workshop is preserved, along with pictures and a death mask of Juárez, some of his correspondence and other documents. Hours are Tuesday through Friday 10 am to 6 pm, Saturday and Sunday 10 am to 5 pm (US$1.30).

Museo Rufino Tamayo

This good museum (☎ 6-47-50) in a fine 17th century house at Morelos 503, was donated to Oaxaca by the famous local artist Rufino Tamayo. It focuses on the aesthetic qualities of pre-Hispanic artifacts and is arranged to trace artistic developments in the pre-conquest era. It's strong on the Preclassic era and lesser-known civilizations such as the Veracruz. Hours on Monday and from Wednesday through Saturday are 10 am to 2 pm and 4 to 7 pm; Sunday, 10 am to 3 pm (US$1.60).

Basílica de la Soledad

This 17th century church, about 3½ blocks west of the Alameda along Independencia, is much revered because it contains the image of Oaxaca's patron saint, the Virgen de la Soledad (Virgin of Solitude). The church, with a rich baroque façade, stands where the image is said to have miraculously appeared in a donkey's pack. Today the image is adorned with 600 diamonds and a huge pearl; however, its two-kg gold crown was stolen a few years ago. The adjoining convent buildings contain a religious museum.

Cerro del Fortín

This wooded hill with fine views overlooking the city from the northwest is a good place to escape the city noise and smells. From the large open-air Guelaguetza auditorium, just above the highway that winds around the hill's middle slopes, a quiet road leads up to the Cerro del Fortín observatory, with a track

Benito Juárez

Benito Juárez (1806-72) trained for the priesthood, but he abandoned it for law and worked as a lawyer for poor villagers. He became a member of the Oaxaca city council and then of the Oaxaca state government. As state governor from 1848 to 1852, he opened schools and cut bureaucracy. The conservative national government exiled him in 1853, but he returned to Mexico in the 1855 Revolution of Ayutla. The revolution ousted General Santa Anna, and Juárez became justice minister in a new liberal national government. His Ley (Law) Juárez, which transferred the trials of soldiers and priests charged with civil crimes to ordinary civil courts, was the first of the Reform laws, the laws that sought to break the power of the Catholic Church. These laws provoked the War of the Reform of 1858 to 1861, in which the liberals, after setbacks, defeated the conservatives.

Juárez was elected Mexico's president in 1861 but had only been in office a few months when France, supported by conservatives and clergy, invaded Mexico and forced him into exile again. In 1866-67, with US support, he ousted the French and their puppet emperor, Maximilian.

One of Juárez's main political achievements was to make primary education free and compulsory. He died in 1872, a year after being elected to his fourth presidential term. Today he's one Mexican hero with an unambiguous reputation. Countless statues and streets, schools and plazas preserve his name and memory, and his maxim *El respeto al derecho ajeno es la paz* (Respect for the rights of others is peace) is widely quoted. ∎

branching to the Nundehui planetarium. On foot you can reach the hill by the Escalera del Fortín, a long stairway climbing up from Crespo. It's about two km, uphill all the way, from the Zócalo to the observatory. Beyond the observatory a path leads to the top of the hill, marked by a cross, 20 to 30 minutes farther up.

Horseback Riding
Sierra Madre Adventure (☎ 5-68-64) and Rancho Sebastián (☎ 952-1-52-03) both offer rides for individuals and small groups in the countryside or mountains near Oaxaca. Guides can speak Spanish and English. Cost is around US$6.50 an hour.

Traditional Therapy
Ask at Las Bugambilias, Reforma 402 (see Place to Stay – middle), if you're interested in experiencing a *temazcal* bath. this is a purifying indigenous herbal sweat bath. It's currently undergoing a bit of fashionable revival. Las Bugambilias has a temazcal in an out-of-town location.

Courses
Language Language schools have mushroomed in Oaxaca, and there's strong rivalry among them. We have spoken to students from a number of schools, and most seem pleased with the instruction they have received. Several of the schools have websites.

The Instituto Cultural Oaxaca (☎ 5-34-04, 5-13-23, fax 5-37-28; inscuoax@antequera.com), Juárez 909, at Calzada Niños Héroes de Chapultepec, has spacious gardens and terraces where many of the classes are held. Twelve four-week courses, with seven hours' instruction five days a week, are run each year, but it's usually possible to start any Monday. Classes include cooking, craft and dance workshops and lectures on history, anthropology, archaeology and art, as well as language study. The fee for four weeks is US$450, including registration. For more information, write to Lic. Lucero Topete, Instituto Cultural Oaxaca, Apartado Postal 340, Oaxaca, Oaxaca 68000, México.

The Instituto de Comunicación y Cultura (☎ /fax 6-34-43; info@iccoax.com), upstairs in Plaza Alcalá at Alcalá 307, offers small, three-hour classes weekdays for US$100 a week or US$350 a month. Classes can start any Monday. The school focuses on the spoken language, though not exclusively. Teachers are qualified and experienced.

Becari Language School (☎ /fax 4-60-76; becari@antequera.com), Plaza San Cristóbal, Bravo 210, also offers small, three-hour classes weekdays. The regular program is US$75 a week; there are also more intensive programs.

Other places to ask about classes include the Centro de Idiomas of the Universidad Autónoma Benito Juárez de Oaxaca (UABJO, director ☎ 6-59-22), on Burgoa, and the Biblioteca Circulante de Oaxaca, at Alcalá 305. UABJO runs classes of 20 hours a week for any level. Private tutors are fairly easy to find – they often advertise on bulletin boards; one-on-one tuition generally costs US$10 an hour.

Schools can usually arrange family or hotel accommodations for students. Staying with a family costs between US$11 and US$20 a night with breakfast, more for half or full board.

Cooking Seasons of My Heart (☎ /fax 6-52-80), run by American food expert Susan Trilling at her ranch outside Oaxaca, offers a variety of classes in Mexican and Oaxacan cooking, from one-day lessons through one-week intensives. Classes incorporate market trips to buy ingredients for the feasts to be prepared. We've heard glowing reports from participants. Group day classes cost US$8.50 per person.

Organized Tours

Several companies offer day trips to places in the Valles Centrales. Four with a wide choice of itineraries are:

Viajes Turísticos Mitla (☎ 4-31-52), in the Hotel Mesón del Ángel, Mina 518, and at the Hostal Santa Rosa (☎ 4-78-00), Trujano 201
Viajes Xochitlán (☎ 4-36-28), Plaza San Cristóbal, Bravo 210

Central de Guías (☎ 6-55-44, ext 411), Hotel Calesa Real, García Vigil 306
Turismo Marqués Del Valle (☎ 4-69-62), Hotel Marqués Del Valle, on the Zócalo at Portal de Clavería s/n

A three- or four-hour trip to Monte Albán, or to El Tule, Teotitlán del Valle and Mitla, costs around US$8, but there are numerous other options.

The American-run Bicicletas Bravo no phone (wkemper@carleton.edu), Bravo 214 ; runs guided out-of-town bicycle trips. One popular day trip is to the villages of Atzompa, Arrazola and maybe Cuilapan, passing round the west side of Monte Albán. A good overnight trip is to the village of Benito Juárez in the pine-forested mountains northeast of the city. Cost is US$16 a day per person.

Special Events

Virgen del Carmen The streets around the Templo del Carmen Alto, on García Vigil at Carranza, become a fairground for a week or more before the day of the Virgen del Carmen, July 16. The nights are lit by processions and fireworks.

Guelaguetza The Guelaguetza, a brilliant feast of Oaxacan folk dance, takes place in the Auditorio Guelaguetza, a big open-air amphitheater on Cerro del Fortín. This normally happens on the first two Mondays after July 16. (The only time this differs is when July 18, the anniversary of Benito Juárez's death, falls on a Monday, in which case Guelaguetza is celebrated on July 25 and August 1.) Thousands of people flock into the city, and a festive atmosphere builds for days beforehand. On the appointed days – known as *los Lunes del Cerro* (Mondays on the Hill) – the whole hill comes alive with hawkers, food stalls and picnickers.

From about 10 am to 1 pm magnificently costumed dancers from the seven regions of Oaxaca (see the sidebar Origins of the Guelaguetza) perform a succession of dignified, lively or even comical traditional dances to live music, tossing offerings of produce to the crowd as they finish. Excitement

Origins of the Guelaguetza

The Indians of the Valles Centrales have held festivals about the same time every year on Cerro del Fortín since long before the Spanish conquest. (Guelaguetza is a Zapotec word meaning participation, cooperation, exchange of gifts.) In pre-Hispanic times the rites were in honor of maize and wind gods. After the Spanish conquest the indigenous festivities became fused with Christian celebrations of the feast of the Virgen del Carmen (July 16). In the 18th century a new tradition was established of giants and grotesquely big-headed figures dancing on the hill. Such goings-on were abolished in the 19th century, but people continued to visit the hill on the two Mondays following July 16.

Celebrations in something like their present form began in the 1930s. The first year in which the seven traditional regions of Oaxaca participated was 1957 – the seven regions are the Valles Centrales, the Sierra Juárez (northeast of the city), La Cañada (the Teotitlán del Camino and Huautla de Jiménez area), the Papaloapan area around Tuxtepec, the Mixteca, the Costa Chica (Oaxaca coast) and the Isthmus of Tehuantepec – and the amphitheater that built specifically for the celebration was opened in 1974.

Each year on the Saturday before the first Guelaguetza, delegations from the seven regions make a colorful, musical procession through the city. On the Sunday evening before each Guelaguetza, *Bani Stui Gulai* – a vibrant show of music, fireworks and dance explaining the evolution of the Guelaguetza – is staged in front of the Basílica de la Soledad. ∎

(areas). For the two nearest the stage, tickets (US$45 and US$39) go on sale several months in advance from the tourist office on Independencia. Nearer festival time they're also available at other outlets in the city. Tickets guarantee a seat, but you should still arrive before 8 am if you want one of the better ones. The two much bigger rear palcos are free and fill up early – you need to be in by 8 am to get a seat; by 10 am you'll be lucky to get even standing room. For all areas take a hat and something to drink, as you'll be sitting under the naked sun for hours.

Blessing of Animals Pets are dressed up and taken to Iglesia de La Merced, on Independencia at Doblado, at about 5 pm on August 31.

Pre-Christmas Events December 16 is the first of nine nights of **Posadas**, neighborhood processions of children and adults symbolizing Mary and Joseph's journey to Bethlehem. December 18, the **Día de la Virgen de la Soledad**, sees processions and traditional dances – including the Danza de las Plumas – at the Basílica de la Soledad. On the **Noche de los Rábanos** (Night of the Radishes), December 23, amazing figures carved from radishes are displayed in the Zócalo. You're supposed to eat *buñuelos* (a type of crisp fried pastry) and when you're finished make a wish while throwing your bowl in the air. On December 24, evening processions called **calendas**, from churches, converge on the Zócalo about 10 pm with music, floats and fireworks.

Places to Stay – budget

Most places in this range are in the noisy, crowded streets south and west of the Zócalo, but some better deals are on the other sides of town. Street-side rooms everywhere are likely to be noisy.

Camping The large, fairly shady *Oaxaca Trailer Park* (☎ 5-27-96) is 3.5 km northeast of the center on Violetas at Heroica Escuela Naval Militar. The rate for a vehicle with all hookups and two people is

climaxes with the incredibly colorful pineapple dance, by women of the Papaloapan region, and the stately, prancing Zapotec Feather Dance (Danza de las Plumas), by men wearing glorious feather headdresses. The Feather Dance is a symbolic reenactment of the Spanish conquest of Mexico.

Seats in the amphitheater (it holds perhaps 10,000) are divided into four *palcos*

US$7 to US$9. Turn north at the 'Colonia Reforma' sign on Calzada Niños Héroes de Chapultepec half a km east of the 1st-class bus station and go about seven blocks.

South of the Zócalo D'Hostel, at Fiallo 305, two blocks east and half a block south of the Zócalo, with a young and friendly management, has around 30 beds in dorms and double rooms, each at US$4 per person. It's not glamorous and is a bit cramped, though it was undergoing a major revamp when we last stopped by. The hostel has kitchen and laundry facilities, and guests gather around a big dining table in a pleasant courtyard out back. Hot water is available only in the morning and evening, and there are no lockers in the dorms. They have a few mountain bikes for rent at US$4 per day.

Hotel Aurora (☎ 6-41-45), close to the Zócalo at Bustamante 212, has singles/doubles at US$5.25/7.75. Management is friendly and the rooms are clean but cell-like. Bathrooms are shared and less clean, and the showers are cold.

Calle 20 de Noviembre has several hotels, typically consisting of a long, narrow courtyard flanked by three-story rows of boxlike rooms. Hotel Chayo (☎ 6-41-12), at No 508 opposite the Mercado 20 de Noviembre, charges US$12, single or double, for ordinary but adequate rooms with private bath. It helps if you like tangerine, pink and blue paint. Better is Hotel Posada del Carmen (☎ 6-17-79), a block farther out at No 712, which has spruced up paint and furnishings and a friendly staff. Rooms are clean and cost US$8.50 for singles, US$10 for one-bed doubles, US$15 for two-bed doubles. The desk is always attended, which makes for good security.

Hotel Pasaje (☎ 6-42-13), Mina 302, popular with travelers, has small but clean singles/doubles with private bath for US$7.75/11.

Another group of functional cheapies is on Díaz Ordaz, three blocks west of the Zócalo. Be prepared for cockroaches. Best is the Hotel Vallarta (☎ 6-49-67), Díaz

Ordaz 309, which has rooms with bath for US$11/12 and some parking spaces. Across the street at No 312, Hotel Fortín (☎ 6-27-15) has one-bed rooms that cost US$6.50 and twin-bed doubles for US$7.75. Hotel Lupita (☎ 6-57-33), No 310, has singles/doubles with shared baths for US$5.25/6.50, and doubles with private bath for US$9.25.

North of the Zócalo In the quiet, cobbled Colonia Jalatlaco, 10 minutes' walk south from the 1st-class bus station and 20 from the city center, the family-run Casa de Huéspedes Arnel (☎ 5-28-56), Aldama 404, at Hidalgo, is geared up for backpackers and deservedly popular. The small but clean rooms are on two stories around a big, jungly, parrot-inhabited courtyard. Singles/doubles/triples with private bath cost US$12/15/19; singles/doubles with shared bath are US$6/12. There are 24-hour hot water and laundry facilities. Breakfasts and evening snacks are available. Also, you can book here for buses to the coast.

In addition, Arnel runs Casa Miriam (also ☎ 5-28-56) across the street, which has more of a motel feel as well as space for parking (US$1.30 daily). Four spacious singles/doubles with bath are US$12/15, and there are apartments with kitchens for US$380 and US$450 per month. The pretty Iglesia San Matías Jalatlaco can be seen from rooms and balconies upstairs.

At Plazuela Labastida 115, four blocks north of the Zócalo, the friendly Posada Margarita (☎ 6-28-02) is a good family-run place with a surprising view of the towers of Iglesia de Santo Domingo. The 19 rooms vary in size but all are clean and have private bath; upstairs rooms are brighter. Cost is US$11/12.

Hotel Reforma (☎ 6-09-39), Reforma 102, was recently recarpeted and is fairly comfortable, with a rooftop sitting area. Rooms vary, so look first – those on the top floor have views. Singles/doubles are US$12/13.

The eccentric, rambling Hotel Pombo (☎ 6-26-73), Morelos 601, a block north of the Alameda, has 50 very varied rooms and nearly always some vacancies. It's spartan, but the better rooms are quite spacious and bright. Rates are US$7.25/8.50 with private bath, US$4.75/6 with shared bath. The latter rooms are mostly older and enclosed and sometimes damp.

Places to Stay – middle

Zócalo & Around *Hotel Marqués Del Valle* (☎ 6-36-77), on the Zócalo at Portal de Clavería s/n, has spacious, comfortable rooms, some with great views, for US$37/39 singles/doubles. *Hotel Señorial* (☎ 6-39-33), on the Zócalo at Portal de Flores 6, has more than 100 rooms, ranging from small, dark, interior ones at US$32/34 to bigger, airier ones with lots of daylight for US$37/39. The best are on the top floor, with a shared roof terrace. All are clean and have TV, and there's a restaurant and pool.

Hotel Las Rosas (☎ 4-22-17), Trujano 112, is a good value. The clean, comfy, fan-cooled rooms, with private bath, are on two levels around a pleasant courtyard. Rooms are US$17/23, and the hotel has a TV lounge, a place to wash clothes on the roof, free drinking water and, in the lobby, tea and coffee. The entrance is up a flight of stairs.

At Trujano 201, *Hostal Santa Rosa* (☎ 4-67-14) has 17 clean, pleasant rooms with color TV and bath for US$19/24, plus a restaurant. At Trujano 212, the 27-room *Hotel Mesón del Rey* (☎ 6-00-33, fax 6-14-34) is also clean and comfy. Rooms are carpeted and have TV, fan and bath for US$19/23. *Hotel Francia* (☎ 6-48-11), 20 de Noviembre 212, is a bit dark, and its rooms a bit poky, but it's clean and amiable (and DH Lawrence stayed here). Rooms have bathroom and fan for US$16/20.

Hotel Antonio's (☎ 6-72-27, fax 6-36-72), Independencia 601, has 15 nice, bright, sizable rooms at US$21 for singles, US$24 to US$28 for doubles. The best are those above the courtyard restaurant.

Hotel Real de Antequera (☎ 6-46-35), Hidalgo 807, has clean, medium-size rooms, with TV and fans, above its courtyard café. Everything is roofed over to retain the heat. Singles/doubles are US$16/18.

Hotel Trebol (☎ 6-12-56), almost hidden opposite the Mercado Juárez on the corner of Las Casas and Cabrera, has sizable, bright, clean, well-furnished rooms around a modern courtyard for US$17/23 with private bath.

North of the Zócalo The excellent *Hotel Las Golondrinas* (☎ 4-32-98, fax 4-21-26) is at Tinoco y Palacios 411, 4½ blocks north and two west of the Zócalo. Lovingly tended by friendly owners and staff and very popular with North Americans, Las Golondrinas has about 18 rooms opening onto a trio of lovely, leafy little courtyards. It's often full, so you should book ahead. Rooms vary: none are very spacious but all are tastefully decorated and immaculate. Singles are US$18, doubles US$23 to US$28. Good breakfasts are served from 8 to 10 am.

A long-running travelers' haunt still providing good rooms at a reasonable price is the *Hotel Principal* (☎ 6-25-35), 5 de Mayo 208. It's well kept, with large old rooms around a sunny, peaceful courtyard. Doubles are US$26. Only a couple of the 16 or so rooms are offered as singles (US$23), but several will function as triples (US$35). A few rooms in the less attractive rear courtyard are smaller than others.

Villa del Campo (☎ 5-96-52) at Alcalá 910, a little more than 10 blocks north of the Zócalo, compensates for its distance from the center by offering good rooms at reasonable prices, a garden, a pool and a restaurant. It also has suites. The 20 standard rooms, all with private bath, fan and TV, cost US$17/21/24 singles/doubles/triples.

Though *Hotel La Casona del Llano* (☎ 4-77-19), Juárez 701 at Humboldt, is on a busy street, the 28 clean, modern rooms with private bath are set well back from the road around a large garden. There's a restaurant too. Cost is US$27/34/40.

Bed & Breakfasts *Las Bugambilias* (☎ / fax 6-11-65; digitek@antequera.com) is a delightful B&B tucked behind Café La Olla, at Reforma 402. This beautiful colonial house has a pretty garden and a handful of individually decorated rooms with tiled bathrooms, some with terraces; there's also one apartment. Singles cost US$11 or US$25, doubles are US$30 (a bit more during December, Semana Santa and July), and the breakfast can be adjusted to suit any diet. The owner is interested in healthy eating, traditional and alternative therapies and traditional Indian life and customs.

Another attractive B&B is the charming house of the welcoming *Valencia family*, Pino Suárez 508. Cost is US$15 per person, though there's only one single. There are 10 attractive rooms, some with private bath, the best overlooking a central garden. Breakfast is served at a large table in the family dining room. The family also has two nearby apartments for rent at US$400 a month.

You'll find more B&Bs advertised in the *Oaxaca Times* and *Oaxaca* newspapers.

Apartments *Posada San Pablo* (☎ 6-49-14), Fiallo 102, once part of a convent, has 20 or so clean, stone-walled, rather dark rooms around a colonial courtyard. They're billed as apartments because each has a stove, fridge and private bath. Singles/doubles are US$16/20, or US$325/390 by the month.

The spacious, clean, well-furnished, modern apartments of *Parador Santo Domingo de Guzmán* (☎ 4-21-71, fax 4-10-19) are at Alcalá 804, 8½ blocks north of the Zócalo. Each has a bedroom with two double beds, a sitting room, a bathroom and a well-equipped kitchen. There's also hotel-style room service with clean sheets daily. You can rent by the day at US$38/42/46 for singles/doubles/triples, or by the week at US$240/264/311. Prices are lower during quiet seasons.

There are plenty more apartments and some houses to rent. Check the ads in the

Oaxaca Times and *Oaxaca*, the Spanish-language daily *Noticias*, and the notice boards at the Instituto Cultural Oaxaca language school and the Biblioteca Circulante.

Places to Stay – top end
Hostal de La Noria (☎ 4-78-44, fax 6-39-92), three blocks east of the Zócalo at Hidalgo 918, is a colonial mansion recently converted into a pleasant 43-room hotel. Centered on a pretty courtyard, it combines old-fashioned style with modern comfort, though the fan-cooled rooms are not huge and the singles have no view. If your favorite colors are tangerine and lilac, this is your place. Singles/doubles cost US$54/61, more in peak seasons. There's a restaurant/bar.

Hotel Calesa Real (☎ 6-55-44), at García Vigil 306, 2½ blocks north of the Alameda, is prettily tiled and very clean, but the mostly windowless rooms, with fan and TV, are small for US$40/50. There's a small pool.

Hotel Camino Real (☎ 6-06-11, fax 6-07-32), at 5 de Mayo 300, four blocks northeast of the Zócalo, is Oaxaca's ultimate hotel for colonial atmosphere. The entire 16th century convent of Santa Catalina was converted in the 1970s to create this hotel. The old chapel is a banquet hall, one of the courtyards contains an enticing swimming pool, and the bar is lined with books on otherworldly devotion. Thick stone walls – some still bearing original frescos – keep the place cool. There are 91 varied, well-decorated rooms starting at US$178. If you can, choose one upstairs and away from the street and kitchen noise.

Other top hotels are in the northern part of the city, well out of the center. The modern, six-story *Hotel Fortín Plaza* (☎ 5-77-77) is at Venus 118, immediately above Calzada Niños Héroes de Chapultepec. Its ambiance is low key and pleasant, with tile and marble decor. The 100 rooms are bright and fairly spacious, and those at the front have views overlooking the city. There's a pleasant pool. The hotel is used by both tour groups and independent travelers. Singles/doubles are US$51/57.

Hotel Misión de los Ángeles (☎ 5-15-00, fax 5-16-80), just north of Calzada Niños Héroes de Chapultepec at Calzada Porfirio Díaz 102, has more than 150 large, comfortable rooms in tropical gardens, plus tennis courts and a large pool. Rates are US$54/67.

Hotel Victoria (☎ 5-26-33, fax 5-24-11) stands above Calzada Niños Héroes de Chapultepec on the lower slopes of Cerro del Fortín. Many of the 150 large rooms and suites overlook the city, and the hotel has an Olympic-size pool in big gardens. Its restaurant gets good reports, too. Standard doubles cost US$81. The walk to the center is 20 to 30 minutes, but the hotel runs a regular shuttle bus.

Places to Eat
Varied new restaurants are opening all the time, and Oaxaca even boasts a few good coffee shops now. Many restaurants offer Oaxacan specialties on their menus, but two good places exclusively devoted to them are El Biche Pobre and La Casa de la Abuela (see below).

Market Meals
Cheap Oaxaqueño meals can be had in the *Mercado 20 de Noviembre*, a couple of blocks south of the Zócalo. Most of the many small comedores here serve up local specialties such as chicken in black mole. Few post prices, but a main dish typically costs US$1.30. Pick a comedor that's busy – those are the best. Many stay open until early evening, but their fare is freshest earlier in the day. There are more market comedores in the big *Central de Abastos* (see Things to Buy).

Zócalo
All the cafés and restaurants beneath the Zócalo arches are great places to watch the life of Oaxaca, but the fare and service vary widely. *Café-Bar Del Jardín*, at the southwest corner, is a favorite with locals, but it's better for a drink than food. *La Cafetería*, north along the arcade, is newer and concentrates on antojitos (US$2 to US$3), though it serves breakfasts too. *La Primavera* is a fairly good new restaurant with some vegetarian options, including whole-meal quesadillas with spinach and mushrooms (US$2.50) and whole-meal tortas.

Restaurant El Marqués, on the north side of the Zócalo, does good exotic breakfasts such as *potosinos* (US$1.90) – scrambled eggs with onions, hot peppers and tomatoes wrapped in a tortilla, topped with red mole sauce, the whole thing sitting in black mole.

Cocina Oaxaqueña
Good Oaxaqueño regional cooking is spicily delicious. Specialties include:

Amarillo con pollo – chicken in a yellow cumin and chili sauce
Chapulines – grasshoppers fried, often with onion and garlic; high in protein and good with a squeeze of lime
Coloradito – pork or chicken in a red chili and tomato sauce
Mole Oaxaqueño or *mole negro* – dark sauce made from chilies, bananas, chocolate, pepper and cinnamon, usually served with chicken
Picadillo – spicy minced or shredded pork, often used for the stuffing in chiles rellenos
Tamale Oaxaqueño – tamale with a mole Oaxaqueño and (usually) chicken filling
Tasajó – a slice of pounded beef
Tlayuda or *tlalluda* – big crisp tortilla, traditionally served with salsa and chili, but now topped with almost anything, making it into a kind of pizza
Quesillo – Oaxacan stringy cheese
Verde con espinazo – pork back in a green sauce made from beans, chilies, parsley and epazote (goosefoot or wild spinach) ■

Terranova Café, on the east side, is one of the best places on the square, serving some imaginative dishes like hotcakes with pears (US$1.70) and huitlacoche omelets (US$2.25), as well as pizzas and varied meat and chicken dishes for US$3.25 to US$6.50.

El Asador Vasco (☎ 4-47-55), above Café-Bar Del Jardín, serves good, if not cheap, Spanish, Mexican and international food. Evening diners should be prepared for musicians who serenade your table and are none too subtle about requesting a tip. Main dishes are mostly in the US$5 to US$9 range, with steaks and brochetas (kebabs) among the best choices. For a table overlooking the Zócalo, book earlier in the day.

La Casa de la Abuela (☎ 6-35-44), upstairs on the northwest corner of the Zócalo, serves some of the city's best Oaxaqueño food. The parrillada Oaxaqueña, a sort of Oaxacan mixed grill, gives you six items for US$7.75. The delicious chiles rellenos de picadillo (US$4), served with guacamole and frijoles, are a small meal. It's open daily except Friday from 1 to 6.30 pm.

El Mesón, at Hidalgo 805 just off the Zócalo, prepares tasty, mainly charcoal-grilled Mexican food at ranges in the center of the restaurant. You tick off your order on a printed list – waiters will patiently try to explain what's what. Tacos and quesadillas are the specialties, at US$1.20 to US$2.50 for a serving of two or three. Tacos alambre and tacos rajas con queso (bean tacos with cheese) are both delicious.

West of the Zócalo The clean, busy *Café Alex*, out at Díaz Ordaz 218, is well worth finding for good-value breakfasts, served from 7 am to noon daily, or an inexpensive lunch or dinner until 9 pm any day except Sunday. One breakfast possibility, for US$2, is a potato, ham, cheese, or bacon omelet with frijoles, tortillas, fresh juice and coffee. Portions are generous. There's usually a mixed Mexican and gringo crowd here, and service is quick.

A good spot for an inexpensive lunch, from 1.30 pm, is *Restaurant Colonial*, on 20 de Noviembre south of Independencia.

Locals fill the 10 or so tables daily for the US$2 comida, which includes soup, a rice dish, a good main course such as pollo a la naranja (chicken à l'orange) or costillitas de res (beef chops) and agua de fruta. *Cafeteria Restaurant Gyros Makedonia*, 20 de Noviembre 225, is run by a Greek American and doles out good Greek fare such as spanakopita (spinach and cheese pie) and pita-bread sandwiches, as well as omelets, hotcakes and more – all around US$1 to US$1.50.

Restaurant Flami, Trujano 301, an extensive, busy place with mainly Mexican customers, does a decent carnivore's comida – soup, rice, choice of three lean meat courses, agua de fruta, and coffee or dessert – for US$2.25. *Restaurant Montebello*, upstairs next door, has a similar comida minus one drink for just US$1.60. It does cheap breakfasts too.

South & East of the Zócalo The long-established *Doña Elpidia*, at Cabrera 413, 5½ blocks from the Zócalo, serves up a substantial and well-prepared comida. It's open at lunchtime only. It has just a shabby 'Restaurant' sign outside, but inside you find a green, birdsong-filled courtyard. The six-course meal, for US$4, usually starts with a botana (Oaxacan hors d'oeuvre) and proceeds to dessert by way of soup, rice and a couple of meat dishes – but they can accommodate vegetarians, too.

Restaurant Del Vitral (☎ 6-31-24), Guerrero 201, is one of Oaxaca's most elegant eateries. Upstairs in an imposing mansion, it has smooth, efficient service and a 'Oaxaca meets Europe' cuisine. You might try the lemony chapulines (grasshoppers) for starters and order flambé steak in mustard sauce for a treat to follow. You're looking at US$10 to US$15 for two courses without any drinks. Restaurant Del Vitral is open daily from 1 to 11.30 pm.

North of the Zócalo The following places are listed in approximate south-to-north order.

El Sagrario, at Valdivieso 120, half a block from the Zócalo, is a popular pizzeria/

restaurant/bar serving Mexican, Italian and international food. Most main dishes are around US$5, and there's a US$5.25 all-you-can-eat buffet daily from 1 to 5 pm.

Quicklys at Alcalá 101, 1½ blocks from the Zócalo, is a standby for a reliable and inexpensive, if bland, meal. Parrilladas – grilled vegetable and rice platters topped with melted cheese and served with tortillas and guacamole – will fill you for US$2.75 to US$3.50. Some choices have meat too. There's also a variety of burgers (including vegetarian ones) with fries, from US$2. The menú del día is lackluster.

The bright, clean *Cafetería Bamby*, at García Vigil 205, 1½ blocks north of the Alameda, is open daily except Sunday from 8 am to 10 pm and serves up sizable portions of plain but good Mexican and gringo food – salads US$1.90, spaghetti US$2.50, chicken and meats around US$3.75. If cream of carrot soup is available, order it. There's a four-course comida corrida for US$3.

Back on Alcalá, the courtyard restaurant of the *Museo de Arte Contemporáneo* offers a tasty comida (US$2.50) in very relaxed surroundings. *El Topil*, on Plazuela Labastida, serves individualistic dishes with the touch of home cooking. Tasajó with guacamole and vegetables is one specialty for US$4, and there's a range of soups – garbanzo (chickpea, US$1.90) is delicious – plus some good antojitos.

For a breakfast splurge, the all-you-can-eat buffet at the *Hotel Camino Real*, 5 de Mayo 300, costs US$9.25.

El Sol y La Luna, at Bravo 109, has three or four little rooms hung with paintings and arty photos, and there's live music most nights (see Entertainment). From 6 pm to 1 am it serves up good salads (US$2.75), pasta and pizzas (US$3.25 to US$4.75), chicken (US$4.75) and steaks and brochetas (US$6.50).

Hostería de Alcalá, at Alcalá at the Plazuela Labastida, is one of Oaxaca's classier restaurants and is always busy in mid-afternoon. Expect to pay around US$6.25 for a plato Oaxaqueño, US$4 for pasta and US$7.25 for beef dishes. A block north, *Pizzeria Alfredo da Roma*, Alcalá 400, just below the Iglesia de Santo Domingo, has fairly good Italian food. Pastas are mainly in the US$3.50 range, while pizzas come in more than 20 combinations and five sizes; those for two people are mostly around US$4.75. You can rinse it all down with sangría or wine.

Los Pacos, on Gurrión, offers good, medium-to-expensive Oaxacan and international food and friendly service in two pleasant patios, off one of which is a gallery of contemporary art. Main dishes cost from US$4 to US$7, and servings are generous.

If you're near Santo Domingo between 1 and 6 pm, a fine bet is *Candela*, at Allende 211. It has a short menu of delicious Mexican and vegetarian dishes, mostly around US$3.25, which you can eat in or take out. The US$2.50 menú del día is tasty too. There's usually a handful of quirky characters about at lunchtime. In the evenings, when Candela becomes a live music venue (see Entertainment), food quality sinks.

El Biche Pobre, Calzada de la República 600, 1.5 km northeast of the Zócalo, specializes in Oaxacan food. It's open daily from 1.30 to 6.30 pm and is an informal, friendly place with about a dozen tables, some long enough to stage lunch for an extended Mexican family. For an introduction to Oaxacan fare, you can't do better than order the US$3.50 botana surtida (assortment of snacks). This brings you a dozen tasty little items that add up to a meal.

Vegetarian Many restaurants have vegetarian options, but the following, all north of the Zócalo, have more than most.

Café La Olla, Reforma 402 (in front of Las Bugambilias), caters well to wholefood and vegetarian fans, though it also serves regional dishes and meat. The excellent food ranges from good whole-grain tortas (US$1.30) through salads and pastas (US$2.25 to US$3.75) to meat and chicken dishes (US$3.25 to US$4.75). It's open daily from 8 am to 10 pm, and the comida corrida (US$3.25) is substantial.

Restauran Flor de Loto, Morelos 509, makes a reasonable stab at pleasing a range of gringo palates, from vegan to carnivore. The crepas de espinacas (spinach pancakes) and verduras al gratin (vegetables with melted cheese) are both good, at US$2.50. The US$2.75 comida corrida, with veggie options, is a real meal.

Restaurant Manantial Vegetariano, Tinico y Palacios 303, is a welcome addition to the scene, open daily from 9 am to 10 pm, with tables in an open-air courtyard. The day starts with a range of breakfasts (US$1.10 to US$2.25), served until noon. From 1 to 6 pm the menú del día appears – salad, soup, main course, dessert and a hot drink, all for US$2.75. Evening fare, from 7 pm, consists of sweet or savory crepes or spaghetti with a choice of sauces, each around US$2.25.

Coffeehouses & Bakeries Fed up with weak coffee? The two branches of *Coffee Beans*, at 5 de Mayo 114 and 5 de Mayo 400C, offer a range of real coffee fixes, including local organic varieties, plus cakes and snacks. A straight black coffee is US$0.70, cappuccino US$1.30.

Panificadora La Luna, at Independencia 1105, east of the Zócalo, is one of the city's best bakeries, with several types of pan integral, as well as croissants. *Bamby* bakery, on García Vigil at Morelos, is a convenient stop for bolillos, pan integral and cakes.

Entertainment

Oaxaca has a lively entertainment and cultural scene, thanks mainly to its student and tourist populations. The most complete guide is the monthly *Guía Cultural*, put out in Spanish and English by the Instituto Oaxaqueña de las Culturas, Reforma 501. You can buy it (US$0.70) at La Casa de Don Porfirio (see Bars & Cafés below) and La Mano Mágica, Alcalá 203.

Music There's free music – the state band or state marimba ensemble – Sunday at noon and Monday through Saturday at 7 pm in the Zócalo. On the north side of the Zócalo, *Restaurant El Marqués* has a lively Latin band nightly from 9 pm to midnight. *Terranova Café*, on the east side of the square, has jazz, classical or mariachi groups. Nearby, *El Sagrario*, at Valdivieso 120, has good Latin music from 9 pm until 2 am in its downstairs bar. There's no cover charge, but you must spend at least US$5.25 on food or drink.

One of Oaxaca's best venues, *El Sol y La Luna*, has moved around in recent years but is now back in the center, at Bravo 109. Varied bands or musicians play from 8 or 9 pm until late most nights. Stop by to check the program. There's a cover charge of US$2.75 to sit in the central patio, where you can see the musicians. Good food is available, and there's a bar too.

Candela, Allende 211, has live music Tuesday through Saturday from 10 pm to 2 am – mainly Latin, sometimes with a rock band as support. Cover charge is US$2.75. It's popular with locals and foreigners, especially students, and is liveliest on Friday and Saturday, when you should get there early if you want a table.

Los Tres Patios, at Cosijopí 208, three blocks north of Candela, is a relaxed place with Latin music nightly (except Monday) from 11 pm to 2 am. There is space to dance. Cover is US$2. Snacks and light meals are available.

Dance Shows If you're not lucky enough to be in Oaxaca for the Guelaguetza (see Special Events), a substitute is the lively mini-Guelaguetza staged nightly from 8.30 pm at *Casa Cantera* (☎ 4-75-85), Murguía 102. Various Oaxacan dances are performed in colorful costume with live music. The charge is US$5.25, with food and drinks available. To reserve a seat, phone or stop by during the afternoon.

Another option is the 1½-hour performance of *danzas folklóricas* staged nightly at 8.30 pm at the *Hotel Monte Albán*, Alameda de León 1 (US$5.25). There's another 'Guelaguetza' Wednesday and Friday evening, with buffet dinner included, in the plush *Hotel Camino Real*, 5 de Mayo 300.

OAXACA STATE

Bars & Cafés *Pase Aste*, on Gurrión facing Santo Domingo, is a pleasant studenty bar that serves mezcal from San Lorenzo Albarradas (near Mitla) – reputedly the best in Oaxaca – at US$0.70 a shot. *La Casa del Mezcal*, one of Oaxaca's oldest bars, on Cabrera 1½ blocks south of the Zócalo, also serves good mezcal – US$0.70 for the regular stuff, US$1 for *especial*. It's more of a cantina-type place; staff say it's OK for women, though most clients are men. It has a sit-down room where food is served.

La Casa de Don Porfirio, Porfirio Díaz 208, is an arty kind of café-cum-bookstore that gets busy late in the evening. It's open daily from 3 to 11 pm or midnight. The snacks are on the expensive side, but you can stick to drinks.

Bar Hipótesis, nearby at Morelos 511A, pulls in a student/arty late-night crowd. It's open Monday through Saturday until 2 am. The two floors are packed tightly with tables. Someone may start up on the piano or a guitar. There's a range of snacks that cost around US$1.50.

Discos Oaxaca's top discos are attached to the expensive hotels in the northern part of town. *Tequila Rock*, at the Hotel Misión de los Ángeles, is one of the hottest. The *Victoria*, at the Hotel Victoria, has great views from the bar. Expect both discos to be open at least Tuesday through Saturday from about 10 pm to 2 am. Entry is around US$5 on Friday and Saturday, less on other nights. (See Places to Stay for the addresses.) *Eclipse*, at Porfirio Díaz 219, is much closer to the center, open Thursday through Sunday from 10 pm for US$2.75.

Other *Videocine MACO*, at the Museo de Arte Contemporáneo, Alcalá 202, shows free foreign and Mexican films, usually Friday through Sunday at 6 pm. You'll find the schedule in the museum's bookstore.

Art, craft or photo exhibitions, open-air or street theater, dance, music and talks are likely to pop up anywhere and anytime in Oaxaca.

Things to Buy

The state of Oaxaca has one of Mexico's richest, most inventive folk art scenes, and the city is the chief clearinghouse for the products. The finest work is generally in shops, but prices are lower in the markets. You may not pay more for Oaxaca crafts in the city than in the villages where they are made, but if you buy in the city (especially from a shop), most of the profit goes to intermediaries, and the artisan may have received next to nothing. Some artisans have grouped together to market their own products directly: MARO (see Shops) is one such enterprise; another is AMAO, with 140 women members from four Oaxaca villages, whose textiles bear the label Zenzonti.

Though many traditional techniques remain alive – the back-strap loom is used alongside the pedal loom, pottery is still often turned by hand – that doesn't stop new forms from appearing in response to the big international demand for these products. The brightly painted wood animals known as *alebrijes* were developed only a few years ago from toys that Oaxacans had been carving for their children for centuries.

Crafts to look out for include the distinctive black pottery from San Bartolo Coyotepec; blankets and rugs from Teotitlán del Valle; huipiles and other Indian clothing from anywhere (those from Yalalag and the Triqui and Amuzgo areas are among the prettiest); and stamped and colored tin from Oaxaca itself, which has been a boom business ever since someone thought of using it for Christmas decorations.

Rugs with muted colors are less likely to have been made with synthetic dyes than some of the more garish offerings. To assess rug or blanket quality you can:

- gently try to pull the fibers apart to see how tightly it's woven;
- rub your fingers or palm on it for about 15 seconds – if balls appear, the quality is poor;
- crumple it up a bit, then spread it loosely on the floor – the creases will disappear from good rugs.

A Oaxaca jewelry specialty is gold earring replicas of the Mixtec treasure from Monte Albán. The best pairs cost around US$600! Silver and precious-stone jewelry is also sold here – the best shops are on Alcalá – but most prices are a bit higher than in Mexico City or Taxco.

In the markets you'll find lots of leather, bags, hats, textiles, shoes and clothes – not necessarily local.

Markets The vast main market, the Central de Abastos (Supplies Center), is on the Periférico in the western part of town, next to the 2nd-class bus station. Saturday is the big day, but the place is a hive of activity any day. You can find almost anything if you look long enough, including handicrafts. Each type of goods has a section to itself – so you'll find 20 or so woven-basket sellers here, a couple dozen pottery stalls there and so on. The care that goes into the displays of food, particularly vegetables, puts shop windows to shame.

Nearer the city center, the indoor Mercado Juárez, a block southeast of the Zócalo, concentrates on food (more expensive than at the Central de Abastos) but also has flowers and a fair range of crafts. The Mercado 20 de Noviembre, a block farther south, is mainly taken over by comedores, but there are a few inexpensive craft stalls on its west side. The Mercado de Artesanías (Handicrafts Market), a block southwest of the Mercado 20 de Noviembre, gets few customers because it's a bit off the beaten track so you may pick up some bargains. It's strong on rugs and other textiles.

Two smaller craft markets function every day on plazas off Alcalá. On Plazuela Labastida you'll find jewelry, carved animals, leather belts and artists at work, while Plazuela del Carmen Alto has weavings, embroideries, rugs and other textiles. Triqui women weave at back-strap looms here.

Shops The shop beside the tourist office on Independencia has a good range of reasonably priced Oaxaca crafts. Also interesting is Mujeres Artesanas de las Regiones de Oaxaca (Craftswomen of the Regions of Oaxaca, MARO) 5 de Mayo 204. This sprawling store is run by a cooperative dedicated to the preservation of traditional crafts, and it's chock-full of them, with some impressive textiles.

The highest-quality crafts are found in the smart stores on and near Alcalá. Artesanías de El Patrón, Alcalá 104, is one, dealing in fine goods from Oaxaca and farther afield, especially pottery and textiles.

Other good shops, most open daily except Sunday, include the government-run Fonart, on García Vigil at Bravo; Artesanías Chimalli, García Vigil 513 (good for stamped tin and the creative pottery figures by Josefina Aguilar of Ocotlán); La Mano Mágica, Alcalá 203 (rugs and contemporary art); and El Cactus, Alcalá 401 (blankets and rugs). There are several expensive shops selling beautiful crafts, jewelry and designer clothes on 5 de Mayo opposite the Hotel Camino Real, and in Plaza Alcalá, at the corner of Alcalá and Bravo. Aripo, up at García Vigil 809, is run by the Oaxaca state government. Different rooms here are devoted to different crafts – tablecloths, clothing, pottery, tin, woodwork and so forth – and the quality is high. Weavers work at treadle looms in a back room, and the store is open Saturday morning as well as weekdays from 9 am to 7 pm.

Most craft shops will mail things home for you if you want.

The Oaxaca area is one of Mexico's chief mezcal-brewing zones, and several shops southwest of the Zócalo sell nothing but mezcal, in a variety of strange vessels. Try Mezcal Perla del Valle and El Rey de Mezcales, both on Aldama between JP García and Díaz Ordaz.

Getting There & Away

Air Mexicana and Aeroméxico between them fly direct to and from Mexico City at least five times daily (one hour, from US$75). Aviacsa has one daily flight to and from Tuxtla Gutiérrez, in Chiapas (with connections for Tapachula). Aerocaribe flies daily to and from Acapulco and operates several daily flights to and from Tuxtla Gutiérrez that go on to a variety of other destinations: Villahermosa, Mérida and Cancún twice or more daily, Palenque and Veracruz three times a week. The fare to Mérida is about US$150.

At least three airlines make the spectacular half-hour hop over the Sierra Madre del Sur to and from the Oaxaca coast, each for around US$45. Aerocaribe has at least one flight daily to and from Bahías de Huatulco; Aeromorelos flies small planes daily to and from Bahías de Huatulco and Puerto Escondido; Aerovega flies a five-seater to and from Puerto Escondido daily.

Airline offices include: Aerocaribe (☎ 6-02-66) and Mexicana (☎ 6-84-14), both at Fiallo 102; Aeroméxico (☎ 6-37-65), Hidalgo 513; Aeromorelos (☎ 6-09-74), Alcalá 501B; Aerovega (☎ 6-27-77), Hotel Monte Albán, Alameda de León 1; Aviacsa (☎ 3-18-09), Hotel Misión de los Ángeles, Calzada Porfirio Díaz 102.

Bus The recent opening of highway 135D from the north has cut journey times from Mexico City and Puebla by at least 2½ hours. The highway takes a spectacular route through sparsely populated mountains, but it has scarred the landscape badly in places.

The main 1st-class bus station, used by all UNO (deluxe) and ADO and Cristóbal Colón (deluxe or 1st-class) buses, is at Calzada Niños Héroes de Chapultepec 1036, 1.5 km northeast of the Zócalo. The main 2nd-class station, swarming with people and bus companies and with a reputation for pickpockets and thieves, is about one km west of the Zócalo along Trujano or Las Casas. The main long-distance companies here are EV/OP, FYPSA and TOI. Buses mentioned below use these two main bus stations, unless noted.

It's advisable to book a day or two in advance for some of the less frequent services, such as those to San Cristóbal de Las Casas and the better buses to the coast. The Cristóbal Colón, ADO and Sur lines have a city center booking office at 20 de Noviembre 204A, open Monday through Saturday 9 am to 2 pm and 4 to 7 pm, Sunday 9 am to 3 pm.

Oaxaca Coast You have a choice between 2nd-class buses taking the direct route down highway 175, and 1st-class Colón buses, which take the longer route via Salina Cruz.

By highway 175, EV/OP runs *directos* at 9.30 am and 10.30 pm to Pochutla (245 km, six hours, US$6) and Puerto Escondido (310 km, seven hours, US$8.75) from a terminal at Armenta y López 721, half a km south of the Zócalo. You can get tickets at the Centroamericana de Viajes travel agency, on the Zócalo.

Transportes Aragal runs a directo at 10.30 pm (Pochutla US$6, Puerto Escondido US$7.25, tickets at Hotel Trebol). There are also many EV/OP *ordinarios* to Pochutla (US$5.75) and Puerto Escondido (US$7.50), and five to Bahías de Huatulco (275 km, seven hours, US$8.50) from the 2nd-class bus station. Take care with your belongings when getting on 2nd-class buses to the coast – travelers have lost bags in the sudden crushes that happen when people are boarding.

The two or three daily Colón buses take 7½ hours to Bahías de Huatulco (US$12 to US$15), 8½ hours to Pochutla (US$14) and 10 hours to Puerto Escondido (US$16).

Other Destinations Information on buses to the Valles Centrales, the Mixteca, and northern Oaxaca state is given in the sections on those areas. Other daily buses from Oaxaca include:

Mexico City (most to TAPO; a few to Terminal Sur or Terminal Norte) – 442 km, 6½ hours; eight UNO (US$28); 22 ADO and 11 Colón (US$17 to US$20); three Sur 2nd-class from the 1st-class bus station, taking a longer nine-hour route (US$13); 13 FYPSA for US$15 (US$14 by a longer route)
Puebla – 320 km, 4½ hours; one UNO (US$20); seven ADO and five Colón (US$13 to US$15); 10 FYPSA (US$11)

San Cristóbal de Las Casas – 630 km, 12 hours; two Colón (US$18 or US$21)

Tehuantepec – 260 km, 4½ hours; 10 Colón (US$7.25 to US$8.75); many FYPSA and TOI (both US$6.25)

Tuxtla Gutiérrez – 550 km, 10 hours; three Colón (US$16 to US$19); five each by FYPSA and TOI (US$13)

Veracruz – 460 km, seven hours; one Colón (US$19); two ADO (US$17); two Cuenca 2nd-class from 1st-class bus station (US$10)

Villahermosa – 700 km, 12 hours; three ADO (US$23)

Train *El Oaxaqueño* is a reasonable way of traveling to and from Mexico City or Puebla if you don't mind its lack of sleeper or restaurant cars. Though much slower than buses, the train takes a scenic back-country route. See the Mexico City Getting There & Away section for schedules and fares. The train often arrives three or so hours late, which means that southbound you spend the morning daylight hours winding through the Sierra Madre de Oaxaca; northbound you spend them passing by a series of volcanoes on the approach to the Mexico City. Tickets are sold at Oaxaca station daily from 6.30 to 11 am and 3.30 to 7 pm. The station is at Calzada Madero 511, about two km west of the Zócalo.

Car & Motorcycle Tolls for cars from Mexico City to Oaxaca on highways 150D and 135D total US$23 (from Puebla, US$15); the trip takes about six hours. For some reason, the 135D is also numbered 131D for some stretches. The main toll-free alternative, via Izúcar de Matamoros and Huajuapan de León on highway 190, takes several hours longer.

Rental Agencies normally charge around US$40 a day for VW sedans with insurance and unlimited mileage, though Hertz is a bit higher. The airport desks may come up with some special offers. Arrendadora Express rents motorcycles too.

Arrendadora Express
    20 de Noviembre 204A (☎ 6-67-76)

Budget
    5 de Mayo 315A (☎ 6-44-45)
    Airport (☎ 1-52-52)
Hertz
    Portal de Clavería on Valdivieso, just off the Zócalo (☎ 6-24-34)
    Hotel Camino Royal, 5 de Mayo 300 (☎ 6-00-09)
    Airport (☎ 1-54-78)

Parking If your hotel doesn't offer off-street parking, it's safest to park overnight in a guarded parking lot. Estacionamiento Trujano, on Trujano 1½ blocks west of the Zócalo, is open daily from 6 am to 11 pm. An overnight stay to 7 am is US$2.50.

Getting Around

To/From the Airport Oaxaca airport is about six km south of the city off highway 175. Transportación Terrestre combi colectivos from the airport will take you to anywhere in the city center for US$1.30. A taxi costs about US$5. You could also walk the half km to the main road and pick up one of the frequent buses that pass.

You can book a place with Transportación Terrestre from the city to the airport by visiting or phoning the office (☎ 4-43-50) at Alameda de León 1G, next to the Hotel Monte Albán. It's open Monday through Saturday from 9 am to 2 pm and 5 to 8 pm.

City buses marked 'Aeropuerto' or 'Raya' go to the airport or within a couple of minutes' walk along the approach road (US$0.20). You can pick them up going south on J P García, south of Trujano, but be prepared to wait half an hour for one to come by.

Bus Most points of importance in the city are within walking distance of each other, but you might want to use buses to and from the bus and train stations.

City buses cost US$0.20. From the 1st-class bus station, a Tinoco y Palacios bus, heading left (west) along the road outside the station will take you down Tinoco y Palacios two blocks west of the Zócalo. Returning to the bus station you can catch an ADO bus going north up Crespo.

Buses between the 2nd-class bus station and the center pass slowly along crowded streets, and it may be as quick to walk. Centro buses from outside the station head toward the center along Trujano. Going out to the bus station, catch a Central bus west along Mina.

From the train station to the center, take a Centro or Independencia bus.

Taxi A taxi within the central area, or to the bus and train stations, costs US$1.30.

Bicycle Bicicletas Bravo, Bravo 214, rents bikes for town use for US$3 to US$4 a day, and heavy Mexican 'mountain bikes' for out-of-town trips at US$6.50 a day, which includes maps, helmet, pump, water, lock and chain and a puncture kit. They also do guided bike trips (see Organized Tours). Arrendadora Express (see Car & Motorcycle) rents bikes at US$1.30 an hour or US$6 a day.

Valles Centrales

Three valleys radiate from the city of Oaxaca: the Valle de Tlacolula, stretching 50 km east; the Valle de Etla, reaching about 40 km north; and the Valle de Zimatlán, stretching about 100 km south to Miahuatlán.

In these Valles Centrales, all within day-trip distance of Oaxaca city, you'll find pre-Hispanic ruins, craft-making villages and thronged country markets. The people of the valleys are mostly Zapotec.

If you fancy exploring the valleys or surrounding mountains under your own steam, Bicicletas Bravo in Oaxaca is a helpful source of information on walking and cycling routes; they also rent bikes and run guided bike trips. See Organized Tours and Getting Around in the Oaxaca City section for more information.

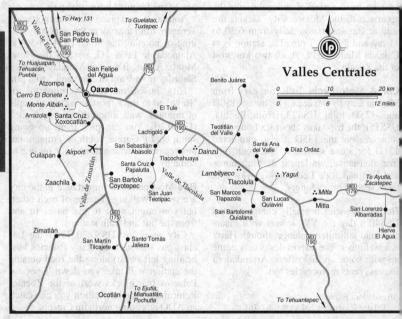

Market Days

The markets are at their busiest in the morning, and most start to wind down in early afternoon. Here are the main ones:

Sunday – Tlacolula
Monday – Miahuatlán
Wednesday – San Pedro y San Pablo Etla
Thursday – Zaachila and Ejutla
Friday – Ocotlán

Accommodations

The Oaxaca state tourism agency, Sedetur, has set up nine small self-catering units called *tourist yú'ùs* in the Valles Centrales to encourage rural tourism. ('Yú'ù,' pronounced 'you,' means 'house' in the Zapotec language.) They have no frills but are well designed. Each sleeps six people in bunks or on mattresses and bedding, towels, showers and an equipped kitchen are provided. Some are better looked after and more attractively situated than others. Cost is US$4 for one person, US$8 for two, US$12 for three and US$13 for four to six. Some have space for camping at US$1.30 per person. It's advisable to book ahead at either of the main tourist offices in Oaxaca, which can also give information on the villages where the yú'ùs are located.

You can find basic hotels in Mitla and Tlacolula.

Getting There & Away

Most of the places east of Oaxaca in the text that follows are on or within walking distance of the Oaxaca-Mitla road. South from Oaxaca, highway 175 goes through San Bartolo Coyotepec, Ocotlán, Ejutla and Miahuatlán. A separate road goes to Cuilapan and Zaachila. Monte Albán is at the top of a short road southwest from Oaxaca.

TOI's buses to Mitla, every few minutes from Gate 9 of Oaxaca's 2nd-class bus station, will drop you wherever you want along the Oaxaca-Mitla road. Further detail on bus services is given under the individual sites and villages.

An alternative to buses, costing around twice as much, is a colectivo taxi. These run to places north of Oaxaca (such as Atzompa and San Pedro y San Pablo Etla) from the street on the north side of the 2nd-class bus station and to places east, south and southwest (including El Tule, Teotitlán del Valle, Tlacolula, San Bartolo Coyotepec, Ocotlán, Arrazola, Cuilapan and Zaachila) from Prolongación Victoria just east of the Central de Abastos market. They leave when they're full (five or six people).

MONTE ALBÁN

The ancient Zapotec capital Monte Albán ('MON-te al-BAN') (White Mountain) stands on a flattened hilltop, 400 meters above the valley floor, just a few kilometers west of Oaxaca. The views over the hills and valleys for many kilometers around make it spectacular even if you're approaching ruin saturation.

History

The site was first occupied around 500 BC, probably by Zapotecs from the outset. It likely had early cultural connections with the Olmecs to the northeast.

Archaeologists divide Monte Albán's history into five phases. The years up to about 200 BC (Monte Albán I) saw the leveling of the hilltop, the building of temples and probably palaces, and the growth of a town of 10,000 or more people on the hillsides. Between 200 BC and about 300 AD (Monte Albán II) the city came to dominate more and more of Oaxaca. Buildings were typically made of huge stone blocks with steep walls.

The city was at its peak from about 300 to 700 AD (Monte Albán III), when the slopes of the main dwellings and surrounding hills were terraced for dwellings and the population reached about 25,000. Most of what we see now dates from this time. Monte Albán was the center of a highly organized, priest-dominated society. Many of the buildings were plastered and painted red, and talud-tablero architecture indicates influence from Teotihuacán. Nearly 170 underground tombs from this period have been found, some of them elaborate and decorated with frescoes. There was extensive irrigation in the valleys, where at least 200 other settlements and ceremonial centers existed. Monte Albán's people ate tortillas, beans, squashes, chili, avocado and other plants, plus sometimes deer, rabbit or dog.

Between about 700 and 950 AD (Monte Albán IV), the place was abandoned and gradually fell into ruin. Zapotec life centered on other places in the Valles Centrales. The period from 950 to 1521 (Monte Albán V) saw minimal activity, except that Mixtecs arriving in the Valles Centrales between 1100 and 1350 reused old tombs here to bury their own dignitaries. In Tumba (Tomb) 7 they left one of the richest treasure hoards in the Americas, now in Oaxaca city's Museo Regional.

Information

The site is open daily from 8 am to 5 pm (US$1.90, free on Sunday). At the entrance are a worthwhile museum (with explanations in Spanish only), a cafeteria and a good bookstore. Ask at the ticket office which tombs are open, since many main ones often aren't. (Full-size replicas of Tumba 104 and the paintings of Tumba 105 can be found in the Museo Nacional de Antropología, in Mexico City.) Official guides offer their services outside the ticket office (around US$7 for a small group), though you don't have to tour the site with a guide.

Gran Plaza

The Gran Plaza, about 300 meters long and 200 meters wide, was the center of Monte Albán. The visible structures are mostly from the peak Monte Albán III period. Some were temples, others residential. The following description takes you clockwise around the plaza.

The stone terraces of the deep, I-shaped **Juego de Pelota** (Ball Court) were probably part of the playing area, not stands for spectators. The round stone in the middle may have been used for bouncing the ball at the start of the game.

A small pillared temple stood atop the **Pirámide** (Edificio P). From the altar in front of the pyramid came a well-known jade bat-god mask, now in the Museo Nacional de Antropología. Tunnels too low for anything except crawling lead off from either side of it.

The **Palacio** (Palace) has a broad stairway and, on top, a patio surrounded by the remains of rooms typical of Monte Albán III residential buildings. Under the patio was found a cross-shaped tomb, probably from Monte Albán IV.

The big **Plataforma Sur** (South Platform), with its wide staircase, is good for a panorama of the plaza. Two or three hundred meters southeast is a big structure called **Edificio 7 Ciervo** (Building Seven Deer), from an inscription on its entrance lintel.

Edificio J, an arrowhead-shaped Monte Albán II building riddled with tunnels and inner staircases (though you can't go in), stands at an angle of 45 degrees to the other Gran Plaza structures and is believed to have been an observatory. Figures and hieroglyphs carved on its walls probably record military conquests.

The front of **Sistema M**, dating from Monte Albán III, was added, like the front of Sistema IV, to an earlier structure in an apparent attempt to conceal the plaza's lack of symmetry. (The great rock mounds on which the south and north platforms are built are not directly opposite each other.)

Edificio L is an amalgam of the Monte Albán I building that contained the famous Danzante carvings and a later structure built over it. The **Danzantes** (Dancers), some of which are seen around the lower part of the building, are thought to depict captives and Zapotec leaders. They generally have open mouths (sometimes downturned in Olmec style) and closed eyes, and in some cases blood flows where their genitals have been cut off. Hieroglyphic dates and possibly names accompanying them are the earliest known true writing in Mexico.

Sistema IV combines typical Monte Albán II construction with overlays from Monte Albán III and IV. Stela 18 (originally five meters high), just to its north, is also Monte Albán II.

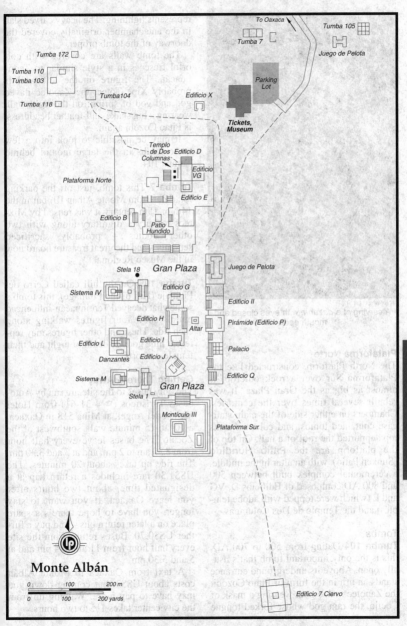

To Oaxaca

Tumba 7

Tumba 105

Juego de Pelota

Tumba 172

Tumba 110
Tumba 103

Tumba 104

Edificio X

Tumba 118

Parking Lot

Tickets, Museum

Templo de Dos Columnas

Edificio D

Edificio VG

Plataforma Norte

Edificio E

Edificio B

Patio Hundido

Gran Plaza

Juego de Pelota

Stela 18

Sistema IV

Edificio G

Edificio II

Edificio H

Altar

Pirámide (Edificio P)

Edificio L

Edificio I

Palacio

Danzantes

Edificio J

Sistema M

Palacio

Stela 1

Edificio Q

Gran Plaza

Montículo III

Plataforma Sur

Monte Albán

0   100   200 m
0   100   200 yards

Edificio 7 Ciervo

TONY WHEELER
A carving of a *dazante* with eyes closed and mouth open

Plataforma Norte

The North Platform, constructed like the Plataforma Sur over a rock outcrop, is almost as big as the Gran Plaza. It was rebuilt several times over the centuries. Chambers on either side of the main staircase contained tombs, and columns at its top supported the roof of a hall. On top of the platform are the **Patio Hundido** (Sunken Patio), with an altar in the middle, a ceremonial complex built between 500 and 800 AD composed of Edificios D, VG and E (which were topped with adobe temples) and the Templo de Dos Columnas.

Tombs

Tumba 104 Dating from 500 to 700 AD, this is the only important tomb that's usually open. Above its underground entrance stands an urn in the form of Pitao Cozobi, the Zapotec maize god, wearing a mask of Cocijo, the rain god whose forked tongue

represents lightning. The heavy carved slab in the antechamber originally covered the doorway of the tomb proper.

The tomb walls are covered with colorful frescoes in a style similar to Teotihuacán. The figure on the left wall is probably Xipe Tótec, the Zapotec flayed god and god of spring; on the right wall, wearing a big snake-and-feather headdress, is Pitao Cozobi again.

It may be possible to look into a few more tombs in the large mound behind Tumba 104.

Tumba 7 This tomb, just off the parking lot, dates from Monte Albán III, but in the 14th or 15th century it was reused by Mixtecs to bury a dignitary along with two other bodies – probably sacrificed servants – and the great treasure hoard now in the Museo Regional.

Tumba 105 On the hill called Cerro del Plumaje (Hill of the Plumage), this tomb's somewhat decayed Teotihuacán-influenced murals show four figures walking along each side. These and other figures may represent nine gods of death or night and their female consorts.

Getting There & Away

The only buses to the site are run by Autobuses Turísticos (☎ 4-31-61) from Hotel Mesón del Ángel, at Mina 518 in Oaxaca, a 10- to 15-minute walk southwest of the Zócalo. The buses leave every half hour from 8.30 am to 2 pm, and at 3 and 3.30 pm. The ride up takes about 20 minutes. The US$1.30 fare includes a return trip at a designated time, about two hours after you leave Oaxaca. If you want to stay longer, you have to hope there's a spare place on a later return bus – and pay a further US$0.70. Buses return from the site every half hour from 11 am to 4 pm and at 5 and 5.30 pm.

A taxi from Oaxaca to Monte Albán costs about US$3, but coming down you may have to pay more. Walking up from the city center takes 1½ to two hours.

OAXACA STATE

EL TULE
pop 7000

A vast *ahuehuete* tree (a type of cypress) in the churchyard at El Tule, 10 km from Oaxaca along highway 190, is claimed to have the biggest girth of any tree in the Americas. It's 58 meters around and 42 meters high, but its age is even more impressive: it's officially reckoned to be 2000 years old but may be 3000. The tree, protected by a fence, dwarfs the 17th century church. Entry to the churchyard is US$0.30.

Long revered by Oaxacans, the mighty Árbol del Tule has come under threat in recent years from new industrial plants and housing nearby, which tap the same water sources that the tree uses. Campaigners argue that the only long-term solutions are full protection of the micro-river basins from which the tree drinks and more sustainable local economic development.

AVN buses go to El Tule every 10 minutes (US$0.20) from the 2nd-class bus station in Oaxaca.

DAINZÚ

Twenty-one km from Oaxaca along the Mitla road, a track leads one km south to the small but interesting ruins of Dainzú, open daily from 8 am to 5 pm (US$1, free on Sunday and holidays). Dainzú has remains from 300 BC (or earlier) to 1000 AD.

To the left as you approach is the pyramid-like Edificio A, 50 meters long and eight meters high, built about 300 BC. Along its bottom wall are a number of engravings similar to the Monte Albán Danzantes. They nearly all show ball players – with masks or protective headgear and a ball in the right hand.

Among the ruins below Edificio A are, to the right as you look down, a sunken tomb with its entrance carved in the form of a crouching jaguar and, to the left, a partly restored ball court from about 1000 AD. At the top of the hill behind the site are more rock carvings similar to the ball players, but it's a stiff climb, and you'd probably need a guide to find them.

TEOTITLÁN DEL VALLE
pop 5000

This famous weaving village is four km north of highway 190, about 25 km from Oaxaca. The *desviación* (turnoff) is signposted. Blankets, rugs and sarapes wave at you from houses and showrooms along the road into the village (which becomes Avenida Juárez as it approaches the center), and signs point to the central **Mercado de Artesanías**, where there are hundreds more blankets, rugs and sarapes on sale. The variety of designs is enormous – from Zapotec gods and Mitla-style geometric patterns through birds and fish to imitations of paintings by Rivera, Picasso, Miró and Escher.

The weaving tradition here goes back to pre-Hispanic times: Teotitlán had to pay tributes of cloth to the Aztecs. Quality is still very high in many cases, and traditional dyes made from cochineal or indigo are still sometimes used. Prices are not necessarily lower here than in Oaxaca, but there's a bigger choice. Many shops have weavers at work.

Facing the Mercado de Artesanías on the central plaza is the **Museo Balaa Xtee Guech Gulal**, open daily except Monday from 10 am to 2 pm and 4 to 6 pm (US$0.70), with some local archaeological finds and material on textile crafts and local traditions. From the plaza, steps rise to a fine broad churchyard with the handsome 17th century **Templo de la Preciosa Sangre de Cristo** in one corner. The village's regular market, open daily, is behind the top of the churchyard.

Places to Stay & Eat

There's a tourist yú'ù on the approach to the village, 500 meters off the highway. It's not very convenient to the village, which is three km farther on. *Restaurante Tlamanalli*, at Avenida Juárez 39, open daily except Monday for lunch only, serves excellent Oaxaqueña food – soup US$2.50, chicken in mole negro US$5.25. Interest is added by exhibits on the weaving craft.

Getting There & Away

AVN buses run about 10 times daily to Teotitlán (50 minutes, US$0.40) from Gate 29 at Oaxaca's 2nd-class bus station; the last bus that comes back from the village leaves about 6 pm.

BENITO JUÁREZ

pop 2500; alt 2750m

In the cool, pine-forested mountains some 20 km north of Teotitlán by dirt road, the village of Benito Juárez is one of the most attractive tourist yú'ù sites. The well-run yú'ù is in the center of the village. A two-km walk away is a lookout at 3000 meters that affords great views – as far as the Pico de Orizaba, if you're lucky. In the village are the 17th century Templo de la Asunción (Church of the Assumption), beside which a Sunday market is held, and the 16th century Capilla del Rosario (Rosary Chapel).

Buses by Flecha de Zempoaltépetl from Oaxaca's 2nd-class bus station to various destinations, including Villa Alta and Yalalag, will drop you at the turnoff for Benito Juárez, 1¾ hours from Oaxaca. From the turnoff it's a four-km walk to the village. Most buses leave at 8 or 9 am.

LAMBITYECO

This small archaeological site is on the south side of the Mitla road, 29 km from Oaxaca. Between 600 and 800 AD Lambityeco seems to have become a sizable Zapotec place of about 3000 people. Its people may then have moved to Yagul, a more defensible site.

The interest in this site lies in two patios. In the first, immediately left of the main pyramid beside the parking lot, are two carved stone friezes, each showing a bearded man holding a bone (a symbol of hereditary rights) and a woman with Zapotec hairstyle. Both couples, plus a third in stucco on a tomb in the patio, are thought to have occupied the building around the patio and to have ruled Lambityeco in the 7th century.

The second patio has two heads of the rain god Cocijo. On one, a big headdress, spreading above his stern face, forms the face of a jaguar. Lambityeco is open daily from 9 am to 5 pm (US$1, free on Sunday and holidays).

TLACOLULA

pop 20,000

Two km beyond Lambityeco and 31 km from Oaxaca, this town holds one of the Valles Centrales' major markets every Sunday, with a strong Indian presence. The area around the church becomes a packed throng. Teotitlán blankets are among the many goods sold.

The church was one of several founded in Oaxaca by Dominican monks. Inside, the domed 16th century Capilla del Santo Cristo is a riot of golden, Indian-influenced decoration comparable with the Capilla del Rosario in Santo Domingo, Oaxaca. Martyrs can be seen carrying their heads under their arms.

Frequent TOI and FYPSA buses here from Oaxaca's 2nd-class bus station take one hour and cost US$0.50.

SANTA ANA DEL VALLE

pop 2000

Four km north of Tlacolula, Santa Ana del Valle is another village with a textile tradition going back to before the Spaniards. Today it produces woolen blankets, sarapes and bags. Natural dyes have not disappeared, and traditional designs – flowers, birds, geometric patterns – are still in use. Prices in the cooperatively run **Mercado de Artesanías**, on the main plaza, are considerably lower than in Teotitlán del Valle or Oaxaca shops. Also on the plaza are the richly decorated 17th century **Templo de Santa Ana** and the **Museo Shan-Dany**, a small community museum open daily except Monday from 10 am to 2 pm and 3 to 6 pm. The village also has a few textile shops and workshops open to visitors.

There's a good tourist yú'ù on the approach road about half a km from the village center. You can arrange horseback rides there for US$6.50 a day. Buses and minibuses run frequently from Tlacolula.

YAGUL

The ruins of Yagul are finely sited on a cactus-covered hill, 1.5 km up a paved approach from the Oaxaca-Mitla road. The signposted turnoff is 34 km from Oaxaca. The site is open daily from 8 am to 5.30 pm (US$1, free on Sunday and holidays).

Yagul became a leading Valles Centrales settlement sometime after the decline of Monte Albán. Most of what's visible is from after 750 AD and was probably built by Zapotecs, but with Mixtec influence.

Patio 4 was surrounded by four temples. On the east side is a stone-carved animal, probably a jaguar. Next to the central platform is the entrance to one of several underground **Tumbas Triples** (Triple Tombs). Steps go down to a tiny court, with three tombs off of it.

The beautiful **Juego de Pelota** (Ball Court) is the second biggest in Mesoamerica (after one at Chichén Itzá). To its west, on the edge of the hill, is **Patio 1**, with the narrow **Sala de Consejo** (Council Hall) along its north side. Behind the hall is a pathway with Mitla-style stone mosaics.

The labyrinthine **Palacio de los Seis Patios** (Palace of the Six Patios) was

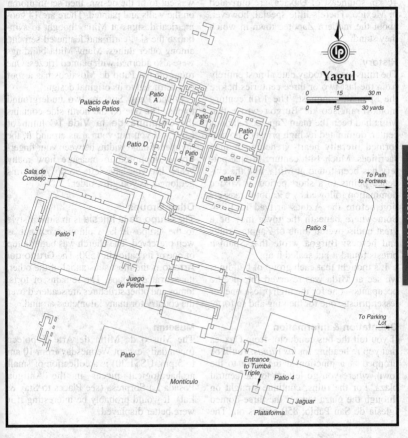

Yagul

0   15   30 m
0   15   30 yards

Palacio de los Seis Patios

Patio A

Patio B

Patio C

Patio D

Patio E

Patio F

Sala de Consejo

Patio 1

Patio 3

Juego de Pelota

To Path to Fortress

To Parking Lot

Montículo

Patio

Entrance to Tumba Triple

Patio 4

Jaguar

Plataforma

OAXACA STATE

probably the leader's residence. The walls were plastered and painted red.

It's well worth climbing the **Fortress**, the huge rock that towers above the ruins. The path passes **Tumba 28**, made of cut stone. A few steps lead down to the tomb, and you can look in. From the top of the Fortress the views are great. On the north side is a sheer drop of 100 meters or more. There are overgrown ruins of several structures up here.

MITLA
pop 10,700; ☎ *956*

The pre-Hispanic stone 'mosaics' of Mitla, 46 km southeast of Oaxaca, are unrivaled in Mexico. There's little special, however, about the modern Zapotec town in which they stand.

History
The ruins we see today date almost entirely from the last two or three centuries before the Spanish conquest. The 17th century monk Francisco de Burgoa wrote that Mitla had been the main Zapotec religious center, dominated by high priests who performed literally heart-wrenching human sacrifices. Much 14th century Mixtec pottery has been found at Mitla, and the evidence points to a short period of Mixtec domination followed by a Zapotec reassertion before the Aztecs arrived in 1494. Somewhere beneath the town may be a great undiscovered tomb of Zapotec kings and heroes; Burgoa wrote that Spanish priests found it but sealed it up.

It's thought that each group of buildings we see at Mitla was reserved for specific occupants – one for the high priest, one for lesser priests, one for the king and so forth.

Orientation & Information
If you tell the bus conductor from Oaxaca that you're heading for *las ruinas*, you'll be dropped at a junction at the entry to the town, where you go left up to the central plaza. For the ruins, continue straight on through the plaza toward the three-domed Iglesia de San Pablo, 850 meters on. The main ruins, the Grupo de las Columnas, face this church and are open daily from 8 am to 5 pm (US$1.30, free on Sunday and holidays).

Grupo de las Columnas
This group of buildings has two main patios, each lined on three sides by long rooms. Along the north side of the Patio Norte is the **Sala de las Columnas** (Hall of the Columns), 38 meters long with six thick columns. At one end of this hall, a passage leads to the additional **Patio de Mosaicos** (Patio of the Mosaics), with some of Mitla's best stonework. Each little piece of stone was cut to fit the design, then set in mortar on the walls and painted. There are 14 geometrical designs at Mitla, thought to symbolize the sky, earth and feathered serpent, among other things. Many Mitla buildings were also adorned with painted friezes. One room off the Patio de Mosaicos has a roof reconstructed to its original design.

In the Patio Sur are two underground tombs. The one on the north side contains the **Columna de la Vida** (Column of Life) – if you put your arms around it, the number of hand widths between your fingertips is supposed to measure how many years' life you have left. So do your arms get longer as you grow older?

Other Groups
The **Grupo de la Iglesia** is in similar style to the Grupo de las Columnas but not as well preserved. The church was built on top of one of its patios in 1590. The **Grupo del Arroyo** is the most substantial of the other, unexcavated groups. The remains of forts, tombs and other structures are scattered over the country for many kilometers around.

Museum
The Museo de Mitla de Arte Zapoteca (open daily except Wednesday from 10 am to 5 pm, US$1.30) is a collection of small archaeological pieces in the Antigua Posada La Sorpresa (see Places to Stay & Eat). It would probably be interesting if it were better displayed.

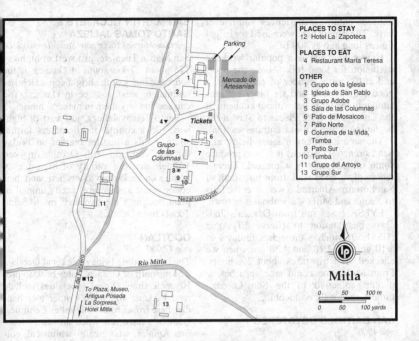

Places to Stay & Eat

Antigua Posada La Sorpresa, just off the town plaza, serves breakfast and a substantial US$5.25 comida corrida. Across the street, the very basic but friendly *Hotel Mitla* (☎ 8-01-12) has fanless singles/doubles with lumpy beds for US$6.50/9.25 and serves straightforward food at low prices. *Hotel La Zapoteca*, at 5 de Febrero 8, between the plaza and the ruins, is less decrepit, and less friendly, with bare, fanless rooms for US$9.25/11. *Restaurant María Teresa*, near the ruins, has good food at reasonable prices.

Things to Buy

Mitla's streets are spattered with shops selling mezcal and textiles, many of them made in Mitla. There's a large Mercado de Artesanías near the ruins with the same sort of stuff. Some striped rebozos are an original Mitla design.

Getting There & Away

Catch a TOI bus to Mitla from Gate 9 of Oaxaca's 2nd-class bus station. The last four km to the town are along a side road east off highway 190. Bus fare from Oaxaca is US$0.70. The last bus back to Oaxaca is about 8 pm.

HIERVE EL AGUA

Highway 179 heads east from Mitla up into the hills. Nineteen km out, a signpost points to the right to San Lorenzo Albarradas, three km away. Six km beyond San Lorenzo is Hierve El Agua, whose name means 'The Water Boils.' Here mineral springs run into icy-cold bathing pools cut from the rock atop a cliff with expansive panoramas of the mountainous countryside. The cliff and another one nearby are encrusted with petrified minerals, which give them the appearance of huge frozen waterfalls – altogether it's one of the most unusual bathing experiences you'll ever have. The waters here were used for irrigation as long ago as 400 BC.

Hierve El Agua is a popular weekend excursion for local folk. Above the pools and cliffs are a number of comedores, a good tourist yú'ù, and six other cottages similar to the yú'ù, but without kitchens, at the same prices (see Places to Stay at the beginning of the Valles Centrales section).

The area has many maguey fields, and San Lorenzo Albarradas is said to produce some of Oaxaca's best mezcal. There's reportedly a good walk from just south of San Lorenzo Albarradas west over the hills to Xaagá and Mitla – ask about it in town.

FYPSA buses run from Oaxaca's 2nd-class bus station to Hierve El Agua (US$1.50) Monday through Saturday – at 8.10 am and 2.10 and 4.30 pm when we checked. The trip takes about 2½ hours. From Mitla, you could take up a bus or pickup colectivo to the San Lorenzo turnoff, then walk or hitchhike.

SAN BARTOLO COYOTEPEC
pop 4000

All the polished, black, surprisingly light pottery you find in Oaxaca comes from San Bartolo Coyotepec, a small village about 12 km south of the city. Look for the signs to the *alfarería* (pottery workshop) of Doña Rosa, east off highway 175, open daily from 9 am to 6.30 pm. Several village families make and sell the *barro negro* (black ware), but it was Rosa Valente Nieto Real who invented the method of burnishing it with quartz stones for the distinctive shine. She died in 1979, but her family carries on. The pieces are hand-molded by an age-old technique in which two saucers play the part of a potter's wheel. Then they are fired in pit kilns; they turn black because of the iron oxide in the local clay and because smoke is trapped in the kiln.

The village also has a market where black ware is sold. Buses run to San Bartolo (US$0.30) every few minutes from a small terminal at Armenta y López 721, 500 meters south of the Oaxaca Zócalo.

SAN MARTÍN TILCAJETE & SANTO TOMÁS JALIEZA
pop (San Martín) 1600; pop (Santo Tomás) 2800

San Martín Tilcajete, just west of highway 175 about 27 km south of Oaxaca, is the source of many of the bright copal alebrijes (animal figures) you see in Oaxaca. You can see and buy them in makers' houses.

Santo Tomás Jalieza, just east of highway 175 a couple of kilometers farther south, holds a textiles market on Friday through coincide with Ocotlán market. Women weave a variety of high-quality textiles on back-strap looms here, and their cotton waist sashes have pretty animal or plant designs. Colectivo taxis run to Santo Tomás from Ocotlán.

OCOTLÁN
pop 17,000

The big, bustling Friday market at Ocotlán, 32 km south of Oaxaca, dates back to pre-Hispanic times. Local specialties include reed baskets, and there's other merchandise here from around the Valles Centrales. Ocotlán's most renowned artisan is Josefina Aguilar, who creates whimsical, colorful pottery figures of women (including, these days, Frida Kahlo) with all sorts of unusual motifs. If you'd like to see or buy some of her work, ask for *la casa de Josefina Aguilar*, which is near the center.

There are buses to Ocotlán (45 minutes, US$0.40) every few minutes from the terminal at Armenta y López 721 in Oaxaca.

EJUTLA
pop 18,000

Some 60 km from Oaxaca down highway 175, Ejutla has a Thursday market and is known for its leatherwork and engraved knives, machetes and swords – and for the mezcal from nearby Amatengo, among the best in Oaxaca. There are buses (US$0.80) every few minutes from the terminal at Armenta y López 721 in Oaxaca.

ARRAZOLA

Below the west side of Monte Albán and about four km off the Cuilapan road, Arrazola produces many of the colorful copal alebrijes that you see on sale in Oaxaca. You can see and buy them in artisans' homes.

CUILAPAN
pop 11,000

Cuilapan, 12 km southwest of Oaxaca, is one of the few Mixtec enclaves in the Valles Centrales. The main attraction is its beautiful, historic Dominican monastery, the **Ex-Convento de Santiago Apóstol** (open daily from 10 am to 6 pm, US$1.70). Begun about 1555, its pale stone seems almost to grow out of the land.

In 1831 the Mexican independence hero Vicente Guerrero was executed at the monastery by soldiers supporting the rebel conservative Anastasio Bustamante, who had just thrown the liberal Guerrero out of the presidency. Guerrero had fled by ship from Acapulco, but the captain betrayed him to the rebels at Huatulco. Guerrero was transported to Cuilapan to die.

From the entrance you first reach a long, low, elegant, unfinished church that has stood roofless since work on it stopped forever, for some reason, in 1560. Beyond is the church that succeeded it. Around its right-hand end you reach the two-story Renaissance-style cloister, whose rear ground-floor rooms have some 16th and 17th century murals. A painting of Guerrero hangs in the room where he was held, and outside, a monument stands on the spot where he was shot.

The main church is usually closed but is said to contain the Christian tombs of Juana Donají (daughter of Cocijo-eza, the last Zapotec king of Zaachila) and her Mixtec husband.

Frequent Autobuses de Oaxaca buses from Oaxaca's 2nd-class bus station (US$0.30) stop right by the monastery.

ZAACHILA
pop 15,000

This part-Mixtec, part-Zapotec village, six km beyond Cuilapan, has a busy Thursday market. At Carnaval time Zaachila is the scene of a mock battle in which masked priests defend themselves with crosses and buckets of water from whip-wielding devils. Zaachila was a Zapotec capital from about 1400 to the Spanish conquest, though under Mixtec control for at least some of that period. Its last Zapotec king, Cocijo-eza, became a Christian with the name Juan Cortés and died in 1523. Six pre-Hispanic monoliths and the village church stand on the main plaza.

Tombs

Up the road behind the church, then up a path to the right marked 'Zona Arqueológica,' are mounds containing at least two tombs used by the ancient Mixtecs. In one of them, Tumba 2, was found a Mixtec treasure hoard comparable with that of Tumba 7 at Monte Albán. It's now in the Museo Nacional de Antropología, in Mexico City. So strong was local opposition to disturbance of these relics that the famous Mexican archaeologists Alfonso Caso and Ignacio Bernal were forced to flee when they tried to dig in the 1940s and 1950s. Roberto Gallegos excavated them under armed guard in 1962.

The tombs are supposed to be open daily from 9 am to 5 pm (US$1.70, free on Sunday and holidays), but they may not be. Ask in the Palacio Municipal on the Zócalo in Oaxaca if you can't find anyone to help you. Market day is probably the best day to try.

Getting There & Away

Autobuses de Oaxaca run frequently to Zaachila (US$0.30) from Oaxaca's 2nd-class bus station. From Zaachila bus station, walk up the main street to the plaza.

ATZOMPA & AROUND
pop 11,000

Eight km northwest of Oaxaca, Atzompa is a village of potters, most of whom use a distinctive green glaze. You see and buy their work in the Casa de Artesanías, open daily. A road heads up Cerro El Bonete, the hill south of the village, which is topped by unrestored pre-Hispanic ruins. There are more abandoned ruins atop El Gallo, the hill between El Bonete and Monte Albán. All of them were associated with Monte Albán.

Choferes del Sur, at gate 39 of Oaxaca's 2nd-class bus station, runs buses every half hour to Atzompa.

Mixteca Alta & Mixteca Baja

Oaxaca's Mixteca (land of the Mixtecs) comprises three adjoining areas in the western part of the state. The northwest borderlands around Huajuapan de León are part of the Mixteca Baja, which stretches across into Puebla state at 1000 to 1700 meters altitude. The Mixteca Alta is the rugged area between the Mixteca Baja and the Valles Centrales, mostly above 2000 meters. The Mixteca de la Costa is a remote southwestern zone stretching back up into the hills from the coast.

It was from the Mixteca Alta in about the 12th century that Mixtec dominion began to spread to the Valles Centrales and Tehuantepec area. Famed as workers of gold and precious stones, the Mixtecs also developed a fine painted pottery known as Mixteca-Puebla, which, it is said, was the only type the Aztec emperor Moctezuma would eat from. The Mixteca Alta and Baja were subjugated by the Aztecs in the 15th century.

Today much of the Mixteca is over-farmed, eroded and deforested, and politics and business are dominated by mestizos. Many Mixtecs have to emigrate for work. Foreign visitors are rather a rarity here.

Things to See
The beautiful 16th century Dominican monasteries in the Mixteca Alta villages of Yanhuitlán, Coixtlahuaca and Teposcolula are among colonial Mexico's finest architecture, their restrained stonework fusing medieval, plateresque, Renaissance and Indian styles.

The most easily reached monastery, at **Yanhuitlán**, towers 120 km from Oaxaca beside highway 190, the old road to Puebla and Mexico City. It was designed to withstand earthquakes and serve as a defensive refuge. The cloister has an interesting little museum of items from the monastery (open daily from 10 am to 5 pm). The church contains valuable works of art; ask the museum caretaker to open it. A fine Mudéjar timber roof supports the choir.

The monastery in **Coixtlahuaca**, two km off highway 135D and about 115 km from Oaxaca, is, if anything, more beautiful than Yanhuitlán's. Beside the monastery church stands its graceful, ruined *capilla abierta* (open chapel), used for preaching to crowds of Indians. Enlist the caretaker of the cloister museum to open the church itself, which has a lovely rib-vaulted roof with carved keystones. At **Tejupan**, 22 km southwest on highway 190, is another giant 16th century Dominican church.

Thirteen km south of highway 190 lies **Teposcolula**, on highway 125. The monastery is beside the main plaza, which borders the road through town. Its stately capilla abierta of three open bays is immediately north of the west end of the monastery church. The cloister is a museum (open daily, 10 am to 5 pm).

Tlaxiaco, 43 km south of Teposcolula on highway 125, was known before the revolution as Paris Chiquita (Little Paris), for the quantities of French luxuries such as clothes and wine imported for its few rich land- and mill-owning families. Today the only signs of that elegance are the arcades around the main plaza and a few large houses with courtyards. The market area is off the southeast corner of the plaza – Saturday is the main day.

South of Tlaxiaco, highway 125, paved all the way, winds through the Sierra Madre del Sur to Pinotepa Nacional, on coastal highway 200. The major town on the way is **Putla**, 95 km from Tlaxiaco. Just before reaching Putla is **San Andrés**

Chicahuaxtla, in the small territory of the Triqui Indians. The Amuzgo Indians of **San Pedro Amuzgos**, 73 km south of Putla, are known for their fine huipiles.

Places to Stay & Eat

You can visit the Mixteca Alta or Baja in a long day trip from Oaxaca, but there are also basic hotels in Nochixtlán (where highways 190 and 135D meet), Coixtlahuaca, Tamazulapan (on highway 190 southeast of Huajuapan de León) and Putla, and better ones in Tlaxiaco and Huajuapan de León.

In Tlaxiaco, *Hotel Del Portal* (☎ 955-2-01-54), on the plaza, has big, clean singles/doubles with private bath around a pleasant courtyard for US$8/11. *Casa Habitación San Michell*, on Independencia, charges a little less. Cheaper is *Hotel Colón* (☎ 955-2-00-13), one block east of the plaza, on the corner of Colón and Hidalgo. There's good food at *Cafe Uni-Nuu*, next to the Hotel Del Portal, and *Restaurant En La Bohemia*, halfway between Hotel Colón and the main plaza.

Getting There & Away

Yanhuitlán, Tejupan and Huajuapan, on highway 190, are served by several 1st- and 2nd-class buses daily from Oaxaca. Yanhuitlán is 2½ hours from Oaxaca (1st-class, US$3.75). For Coixtlahuaca, a Puebla- or Mexico City-bound bus may let you off at the turnoff, or you can take a Huajuapan-bound bus to Tejupan, where colectivo taxis run to Coixtlahuaca.

For Teposcolula, Tlaxiaco and other places on highway 125, there are a couple of 1st-class Cristóbal Colón buses from Oaxaca daily, plus half a dozen 2nd-class FYPSA buses. Or you can take any bus to the junction of highways 190 and 125, where minibuses go down highway 125. Some Cristóbal Colón and FYPSA buses run south from Tlaxiaco to Putla and Pinotepa Nacional.

Buses run from Mexico City's Terminal Oriente (TAPO) to several Mixteca towns.

Northern Oaxaca

On the Río Papaloapan, 128 km from Alvarado on the Veracruz coast, **Tuxtepec** is the 'capital' of a low-lying area of northern Oaxaca which, in culture and topography, is akin to Veracruz. The rough but sometimes spectacular highway 175 winds 210 km through the mountains from Oaxaca, so Tuxtepec is on a possible coast-to-coast route. This growing town has several moderately priced hotels and is served by 1st- and 2nd-class buses from many towns in Oaxaca and Veracruz.

On the way to Tuxtepec, 74 km from Oaxaca, is **Guelatao**, birthplace of Benito Juárez, with at least two memorials and a museum devoted to him. In **Ixtlán**, five km beyond Guelatao on highway 175, is the baroque Templo de Santo Tomás, where baby Benito was baptized.

Oaxaca Coast

A laid-back stint on the beautiful Oaxaca coast – known locally as the Costa Chica (Little Coast), in contrast to the Costa Grande, farther west in Guerrero state – is the perfect complement to the inland attractions of Oaxaca city and the Valles Centrales. The trip down highway 175 from Oaxaca is spectacular: south of Miahuatlán you climb into pine forests, then you descend through ever lusher and hotter tropical forest.

Though flights and newly paved roads have brought this once isolated area closer to the rest of Mexico in the last 20 years and turned the fishing villages of Puerto Escondido and Puerto Ángel into minor resorts, the towns remain small scale and relaxed – Puerto Ángel especially so. Puerto Escondido has famous surf, while near Puerto Ángel is a series of wonderful, little-developed beaches – among them that time-honored budget travelers' hangout,

Zipolite – with plenty of low-cost accommodations. To the east, a big new tourist resort is being developed on the Bahías de Huatulco with respect for the area's lovely surroundings.

West of Puerto Escondido, nature lovers can visit the lagoons of Manialtepec and Chacahua, teeming with bird life. Another interesting trip is to one of the many coffee plantations in the forest-covered hills behind the coast. Coffee-growing here was developed by German settlers in the 19th century.

The coast is hotter and much more humid than the highlands. Most of the year's rain falls between June and September, turning everything green. From October the landscape starts to dry out, and by March many of the trees – which are mostly deciduous – are leafless. May is the hottest month.

Dangers & Annoyances

The Oaxaca coast, a rather impoverished region apart from its few tourism honey pots, has its share of crime against tourists. Be on your guard against theft in Puerto Escondido and the Puerto Ángel-Zipolite area.

The best way to avoid risk of robbery on the coastal highway 200 or highway 175 from Oaxaca is not to travel at night.

Accommodations

Room prices given in this section's text are for the high seasons, which are Christmas to Easter, and July and August. At other times prices in the three main coastal destinations come down anywhere between 15% and 50% in many places.

Getting There & Away

If you're traveling from Chiapas to this coast, or vice-versa, and can't get a convenient through bus, the alternative is to get one to Juchitán or Salina Cruz, then another bus on from there.

PUERTO ESCONDIDO

pop 35,000; ☎ 958

A haunt for surfers since long before paved roads reached this part of Oaxaca, Puerto Escondido (Hidden Port) is more resort than fishing village now, but remains relatively small and reasonably inexpensive. Scattered across a hillside above the ocean, it has few paved streets, several beaches, a range of reasonable accommodations, plenty of cafés and restaurants and a spot of nightlife.

Any breath of breeze can be at a premium, and you're more likely to get one up the hill a bit, rather than down at sea level. The wettest months here are May, June, early July and September. Until recently, at these times tourism slumped and Puerto Escondido showed its worst face in other ways too – resentment and crime against tourists seemed to increase. Now, with tourism more evenly spread over the year and a general air of increased prosperity, there seems less cause for desperate behavior.

Orientation

The town rises above the small, south-facing Bahía Principal. Highway 200 runs across the hill halfway up, dividing the upper town where the locals live and work – and buses arrive – from the lower, tourism-dominated part. Avenida Pérez Gasga, partly pedestrianized (known locally as 'adoquín,' Spanish for paving stone) is the heart of the lower town. The mall has cafés, restaurants, shops and some hotels. The west end of Pérez Gasga winds up the slope to meet the highway at a crossroads known simply as El Crucero.

Bahía Principal curves around, at its east end, to the long Playa Zicatela (great for surfing but dangerous for swimming) which is backed by loads of mostly mid-range places to stay. Other beaches line a series of bays to the west.

Information

Tourist Office The main tourist office (☎ 2-01-75) is about 2.5 km west of Pérez Gasga on the road to the airport, at the corner of Boulevard Juárez. It's a couple of palm-thatched buildings with a 'Sedetur Representación de Turismo' sign, open weekdays from 9 am to 3 pm and 6 to 8 pm, Saturday 9 am to 1 pm. This is the place to come if you have any serious problems, but far handier is the tourist information booth, with energetic English-speaking staff, at the west end of the Pérez Gasga pedestrian mall. It's open weekdays from 9 am to 2 pm and 4 to 7 pm, Saturday 9 am to 2 pm. Staff give out free maps and other printed information in English about the town and beyond. Ask here about walking tours of the town proper, often overlooked by tourists.

Money Banamex, on the corner of Pérez Gasga and Unión, changes dollars and traveler's checks weekdays from 9 am to 3 pm and has a couple of ATMs. Bancomer and Bital, also with ATMs, are in the upper part of town, on 1a Norte at 2a and 3a Poniente, respectively. Their hours are roughly weekdays 8.30 am to 2.30 pm, Saturday 10 am to 2 pm. There are several casas de cambio – all called Money Exchange – giving worse rates than the banks but typically open Monday through Saturday from 9 am to 2 pm and 4 to 7 pm: at least two of them are on the mall; another is on Playa Zicatela. in front of the Bungalows Acuario.

Post & Communications The post office is a 20- or 30-minute uphill walk from the sea front, a blue building on Oaxaca at 7a Norte. You can take a Mercado bus or colectivo taxi up Oaxaca to save your legs. It's open weekdays 8 am to 7 pm, Saturday 9 am to 1 pm.

There are a couple of pay phones on the mall and a telephone caseta with fax across the street from the Farmacia Cortés. There are more pay phones outside the Money Exchange on Playa Zicatela.

Laundry You can wash eight kg of clothes for US$2.50 at Lavamática del Centro, on Pérez Gasga a little uphill from the Hotel Nayar. Complete service (wash, dry, iron) for eight kg is US$9.50. There's another laundry at the east end of Pérez Gasga.

Dangers & Annoyances Stories of knife-point robberies and attacks were rife a few years ago, but we have noticed an easing of the problem. Steps have been taken to make Playa Zicatela – once renowned for

Hurricane Pauline

On October 7, 8 and 9, 1997, shortly before this book went to press, Hurricane Pauline caused great damage and loss of life all along the Oaxaca coast and its hinterland and on the Isthmus of Tehuantepec. At least 75 people, possibly many more, were killed, more than 50,000 homes were destroyed or damaged, most trees along the coast were downed and swathes were cut through inland forests. In all, more than 1300 sq km of plantations and cropland were devastated.

Worst hit were the poor. Thousands of their flimsy homes of wood, cardboard, adobe or tin were simply blown away by winds of up to 200 km per hour, or washed away by the floods that followed the hurricane's torrential rainfall. In some villages, barely a single home was left standing. Some isolated hill areas remained cut off and without help for at least a week after the disaster. The damage to agriculture has left many farm workers without prospect of employment for many months.

While the more solidly built resorts of Puerto Escondido and Bahías de Huatulco suffered less, there were still reports of severe damage in the poorer areas of Puerto Escondido and in villages near Huatulco. Witnesses spoke of many homes destroyed and most roofs ripped off in Puerto Ángel, and devastation in Zipolite and other nearby villages.

Detailed information on damage was nearly impossible to obtain in the aftermath of the hurricane, but obviously some places to stay and eat, and other services mentioned in this section, will no longer be operating. Travelers are likely to find the greatest differences in Zipolite, San Agustinillo and Mazunte but, even in these communities, rebuilding started within days of the disaster. Some owners are hoping to reopen within a couple of months.

Roads to the region were being restored fairly quickly after the hurricane, but it may take many months for highway 200 to be passable in the Pinotepa Nacional area, where many bridges were destroyed. ∎

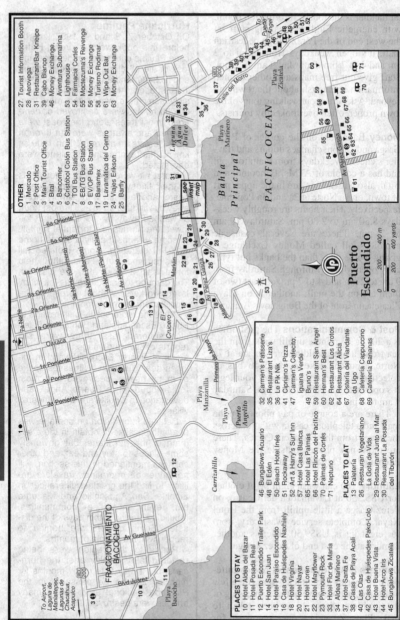

OAXACA STATE

Puerto Escondido

Bahía Principal

PACIFIC OCEAN

Bahía Marinero

Playa Principal

Playa Marinero

Playa Zicatela

Playa Manzanilla

Playa Angelito

Puerto Angelito

Carrizalillo

Playa Bacocho

El Crucero

FRACCIONAMIENTO BACOCHO

To Airport, Laguna de Manialtepec, Lagunas de Chacahua, Acapulco

Av Guelatao

Blvd Juárez

0   200   400 m
0   200   400 yards

see insert map

PLACES TO STAY
10 Hotel Aldea del Bazar
11 Hotel Posada Real
12 Puerto Escondido Trailer Park
14 Hotel San Juan
15 Hotel Paraíso Escondido
16 Casa de Huéspedes Naxhiely
18 Hotel Virginia
20 Hotel Nayar
21 Hotel Loren
22 Hotel Mayflower
23 Plymouth Rock
33 Hotel Flor de María
34 Aldea Marinero
37 Hotel Santa Fe
38 Casas de Playa Acali
40 Las Olas
42 Casa de Huéspedes Pako-Lolo
43 Hotel Buena Vista
44 Hotel Arco Iris
45 Bungalows Zicatela
46 Bungalows Acuario
48 El Edén
50 Beach Hotel Inés
51 Rockaway
52 Art & Harry's Surf Inn
57 Hotel Casa Blanca
65 Hotel Las Palmas
66 Hotel Rincón del Pacífico
70 Palmas de Cortés
71 Neptuno

PLACES TO EAT
13 Paletería
26 Restauran Vegetariano La Gota de Vida
29 Restaurant Junto al Mar
30 Restaurant La Posada del Tiburón
32 Carmen's Patisserie
35 Restaurant Liza's
36 Le Pik Nik
41 Cipriano's Pizza
47 Carmen's Cafecito, Iguana Verde
49 Bruno's
59 Restaurant San Angel
60 Herman's Best
62 Restaurant Los Crotos
64 Osteria del Viandante da Ugo
67 Restaurant Alicia
68 Cafetería Cappuccino
69 Cafetería Bananas

OTHER
1 Mercado
2 Post Office
3 Main Tourist Office
4 Bital
5 Bancomer
6 Cristóbal Colón Bus Station
7 TOI Bus Station
8 EB/TG Bus Station
9 EV/OP Bus Station
17 Banamex
19 Lavamática del Centro
24 Viajes Erikson
25 Barfly
27 Tourist Information Booth
28 Aerovega
31 Restaurant/Bar Kneipe
39 Cabo Blanco
46 Money Exchange, Aventura Submarina
53 Lighthouse
54 Farmacia Cortés
55 Moctezuma's Revenge
56 Money Exchange
58 Turismo Rodimar
61 Wipe Out Bar
63 Money Exchange

Av Pérez Gasga
Marsilin
Av Hidalgo
Av Pérez Gasga
Av Alfonso Pérez Gasga
1a Norte (Porfirio Díaz)
2a Norte (Morelos)
3a Norte (Guerrero)
4a Norte
Av Hidalgo
Oaxaca
1a Poniente
2a Poniente
3a Poniente
1a Oriente
2a Oriente
3a Oriente
4a Oriente
5a Oriente
6a Oriente
1a Norte
Primero de Mayo
Alfaro
Laguna Agua Dulce

muggings – safer, with more street lighting and police patrols on Calle del Morro, the road along the back of the beach. In general, to avoid any threat, stick to well-lit areas at night (or use taxis) and to populated places by day.

Beaches

Bahía Principal The main town beach is long enough to accommodate a few restaurants at its west end, a small fishing fleet in the middle, sun worshippers at the east end (known as Playa Marinero) and occasional flocks of pelicans winging in inches above the waves. A few hawkers wander up and down, offering textiles and necklaces. The smelly water entering the bay at times from the inaptly named Laguna Agua Dulce (Freshwater Lagoon) will put you off dipping anywhere other than Playa Marinero, but don't get too close to the rocks there.

Zicatela The waters of Zicatela, beyond the rocky outcrop at the east end of Playa Marinero, have a lethal undertow. It is for strong-swimming surfers only – though landlubbers can still enjoy the sand and the acrobatics of the board-riders on the 'Mexican Pipeline.' It's said that drownings here have essentially ceased since lifeguards began to patrol the beach. Zicatela is developing fast and now has several palapa beach bars and even small lawned gardens being planted right on the beach. Watch your back on Zicatela after dark!

Puerto Angelito The sheltered bay of Puerto Angelito, about a km west of the Bahía Principal as the crow flies, has two small beaches separated by a few rocks. On weekends and holidays it can get as busy as the Bahía Principal.

Lanchas (fast, open, outboard boats) from in front of the Palmas de Cortés on Bahía Principal will take you to Puerto Angelito for about US$2.75 per person roundtrip. The boat returns at an agreed pickup time. By land, go west along highway 200 for a few hundred meters from El Crucero. A sign points left down to Puerto Angelito. On the way down, fork

left at the Pepsi sign – altogether, it's a 30- to 40-minute walk from Avenida Pérez Gasga. A taxi from town costs about US$1.30.

Carrizalillo This small cove, just west of Puerto Angelito, is rockier but OK for swimming, with a little beach and a bar with a few palapas for shade. Lanchas from the Bahía Principal (about US$4 per person roundtrip) will bring you here too. A path down from the Puerto Escondido Trailer Park reaches the cove.

Bacocho This long, straight beach, on the open ocean just west of the Hotel Posada Real, has a dangerous undertow. The hotel has a beach bar with a few palapas.

Activities

On Playa Zicatela, Las Olas cabañas rents surfboards for US$6.50 a day. Iguana Verde, behind popular Carmen's Cafecito, charges twice as much.

You can rent snorkeling gear at the small restaurant on Puerto Angelito. Aventura Submarina (☎ 2-10-26), in front of Bungalows Acuario at Zicatela, open 9 am to 2 pm and 5 to 7 pm, has diving gear and offers diving trips. Apparently the San Andreas Fault begins somewhere straight out to sea from Zicatela!

Hotel Virginia runs fishing trips – around US$20 per hour for the boat.

Organized Tours

Several companies on the mall run trips to places along the coast to the west (see West of Puerto Escondido) and to Bahías de Huatulco (US$20 to US$23 per person, generally with a stop at Puerto Ángel). There are also horseback riding outings to Atotonilco hot springs, north of San José Manialtepec, 20 km west of Puerto Escondido (US$22), and trips to the mountain town of Nopala, with a visit to a coffee plantation (US$26).

Among trips offered by Iguana Verde, on Zicatela, is a two-hour jaunt to the Río Colotepec. They depart morning and afternoon, Monday through Saturday. You float down the river in a tire inner tube (US$10 per person). People were queueing up for the fun when we stopped by.

Special Events
Semana Santa is a big week for local partying. The Oaxaca state surf carnival is held at this time. Two international surfing competitions are held annually, in August and November. In fact, November is the big month: the national surfing championships, held around November 17 to 20, coincide with the Puerto Escondido fiesta, incorporating coastal dances, beauty contests, fishing competitions and more. On December 18 a statue of the Virgen de la Soledad is taken out to sea aboard a boat leading a religious procession.

Places to Stay
In the peak tourist seasons the most popular places in all ranges may be full. Your best chance, if you haven't booked ahead, is to ask early in the day, about 9 or 10 am.

Places to Stay – budget
Camping *Puerto Escondido Trailer Park* (☎ 2-00-77) occupies a large open area on the cliff above Playa Carrizalillo. Water and electrical hookups are included at US$10 for two people; sites with sea views cost extra. The best approach road is Avenida Guelatao.

Neptuno, on Bahía Principal, has a dirt area for camping, with electrical hookups and a big central fireplace. The communal toilets are grubby. Cost is US$1.30 per person. The better *Palmas de Cortés*, next door, has more shade but less space, charging US$2.75 per person and the same again per vehicle, with showers, electrical hookups and fireplaces.

El Edén is a pleasant small campsite at Zicatela. It's next to Bruno's restaurant on a thin strip of land leading up to a few inexpensive, basic cabañas. Coconut palms provide shade. The cost with electrical hookups is US$2.75 per person.

Playa Zicatela *Art & Harry's Surf Inn*, at the far end of the Zicatela strip, has

pleasant rooms with private bath, hot water, fans and mosquito screens for US$11 and US$13, single or double. Most rooms face the beach, and a couple have an extra sitting area. Renovations were in progress when we last visited, so prices may increase.

Bahía Principal The cabañas on Playa Marinero are mostly small, shabby (some are dirty) and crowded together in what's a pretty crowded area anyway. The best are at *Aldea Marinero*, located in a small lane going back from the beach. They have canvas beds, mosquito nets, hammocks strung out front and shared bathrooms for US$3.25/5.25 singles/doubles. It can get pretty noisy here.

Neptuno campsite has some small, basic cabañas (no nets, a few mosquitoes) for US$2.75 per person.

Avenida Pérez Gasga There are a couple of newish places with dorm beds on Libertad, the flight of stairs heading uphill just west of the mall. The attractive, friendly *Hotel Mayflower* (☎ 2-03-67) has spacious rooms with three to six beds at US$4 per person. Its other rooms, at US$20/24, are midrange. Opposite, *Plymouth Rock* has dorm beds at US$4 per person.

Hotel Virginia (☎ 2-01-76), on Alfaro off Pérez Gasga, 400 meters uphill from the mall, has 10 or so reasonable rooms with fan and private bath for US$9.25/13. The upstairs rooms are breezier and have good views.

Casa de Huéspedes Naxhiely, Pérez Gasga 301, has clean, adequate but smallish and breezeless rooms with fan and bathroom for US$12, single or double.

Places to Stay – middle
Playa Marinero & Playa Zicatela If the *Hotel Flor de María* (☎ 2-05-36) stood somewhere more exciting than a little dirt lane between Playa Marinero and the highway, it could be the best deal in town. Run by a friendly, English-speaking, Mexican/Italian couple, it has 24 ample, prettily decorated rooms with fan, two double beds

and private bath, all around a courtyard. There's a small rooftop pool, a TV room and a restaurant. Singles/doubles are US$26/33.

On Zicatela, *Casas de Playa Acali* (☎ 2-07-54) provides 17 wooden cabañas for up to four people with mosquito nets, fans, fridge, stove, private shower and toilet and filtered water. Singles/doubles/triples are US$13/20/24. There's a swimming pool.

Next along the strip, *Las Olas* has six good cabañas or bungalows with attached bath, fan, screens, fridge and stove from US$16/18 for singles/doubles – good prices for Zicatela.

Casa de Huéspedes Pako-Lolo, a favorite of surfers with a friendly English-speaking owner, was moving to beside Cipriano's Pizza when we visited. Ask for prices.

On the hillside above Cipriano's is the *Hotel Buena Vista* (☎ 2-14-74), with a range of good, basic but clean rooms with private bath, fan and mosquito screens. Balconies with splendid views catch the breeze. Cost is US$16/18; doubles with kitchen and US$24.

Just beyond here, *Hotel Arco Iris* (☎ 2-04-32, fax 2-14-94) has 20 or so big, clean, fan-cooled rooms with kitchens and balconies looking straight out to the surf, plus a large pool and a good upstairs restaurant/bar open to the breeze. A mixed crowd of surfers and others uses this friendly, relaxed hotel, where singles/doubles are US$26.60/31.

Next door, *Bungalows Zicatela* (☎ /fax 2-07-98) has 12 spacious bungalows, each with three double beds, stove, fridge and attached bath. There's a restaurant and pool. Singles/doubles are US$26/29. Twelve cheaper rooms in a two-story block go for US$18/24.

Farther along the strip, at the back of the Money Exchange, *Bungalows Acuario* has 12 comfortable wooden cabañas around a swimming pool. The cabañas have attached bath, fan, mosquito nets and cooking facilities for US$26, single or double. There are also cheaper rooms at US$20, single or double. Near the far end of the strip, *Beach Hotel Inés* (☎ 2-07-92) has a lovely pool area with a café serving excellent food, and clean, fan-cooled rooms with bath for US$32, single or double. There are also a few cabañas for US$16/20 and a couple of expensive suites. *Rockaway* (☎ 2-06-68) has good singles/doubles/triples cabañas around a pool for US$16/26/37.

Avenida Pérez Gasga & Around *Hotel Rincón del Pacífico* (☎ 2-00-56), on the mall, has 20-odd big-windowed, fan-cooled rooms around a palmy courtyard and its own café/restaurant on the beach. Though slightly dilapidated, it has cheery, helpful staff and fairly well-kept rooms at US$18/20. *Hotel Las Palmas* (☎ 2-02-30), next door, is similar but with slightly bigger rooms at US$16/20. In both places, rooms that face the street may be assailed by loud late-night music from outside.

In some ways a better bet than either of the above two is the friendly *Hotel Casa Blanca* (☎ 2-01-68), across the street at Pérez Gasga 905. It faces the street, not the beach, but has 21 good, large, modern rooms with fans, big bathrooms and, on the street side, balconies. Singles/doubles/triples are US$16/19/23. There's a pool as well.

A minute uphill from the mall, still on Pérez Gasga, is the *Hotel Loren* (☎ 2-00-57, fax 2-05-91), charging US$24, single or double, for bare but good-sized rooms. All have fan, hot water, TV and balcony – but not all catch a sea view. The similar *Hotel Nayar* (☎ 2-03-19), just up the street, gets a good breeze in its wide sitting areas/ walkways. Its 36 rooms have fans (air-con US$3.25 extra), hot water, TV and small balconies. Some have sea views. Singles/ doubles are US$15/19. Both of these hotels have pools.

The friendly *Hotel San Juan* (☎ 2-03-36), at Marklin 503 just east of Pérez Gasga and immediately below El Crucero, has 30 good rooms at various prices, starting at US$16/20. All have bathroom, fan and mosquito screens; the more expensive are bigger and have private terraces. There's a swimming pool and a great rooftop sitting area for catching sun, view or breeze.

Places to Stay – top end

The top place in the Pérez Gasga vicinity is *Hotel Paraíso Escondido* (☎ 2-04-44), on little Unión. It's a rambling whitewash-and-blue-paint place on several levels, with lots of tile, pottery and stone sculpture decoration. There's an attractive restaurant/bar/pool area. The 24 clean though moderately sized rooms have air-con. Some have stained-glass windowpanes. Prices are US$46/59 year round.

Beside the rocky outcrop that divides Playa Marinero from Playa Zicatela, *Hotel Santa Fe* (☎ 2-01-70, fax 2-02-60) has 51 rooms attractively set around small terraces and a palm-fringed pool. The stairways are tiled, and there's a lovely, airy restaurant/bar looking down Zicatela. Rooms vary in size and view, but good design – with tiles again cleverly used – makes most of them agreeable. Many have air-con as well as a fan. Singles/doubles are US$65/75 or US$75/85. There are also eight appealing bungalows with kitchen at US$79 or US$89.

Hotel Posada Real (☎ 2-01-33, fax 2-01-92), part of the Best Western group, is about 2.5 km west of town, at Boulevard Juárez 11 in the still-being-developed Fraccionamiento Bacocho, off highway 200. It has big palm-shaded gardens and 100 air-con rooms with balconies in three four-story buildings on a headland overlooking Playa Bacocho. There's a pool. Rooms are US$60 or US$90, depending on the season.

Hotel Aldea del Bazar (☎ 2-05-08), at Boulevard Juárez 7, also above Playa Bacocho, is a big, plush place in eye-catching modern Moorish style. Rooms are US$83 in the high seasons and US$45 at other times. It has all the top-end facilities, including a fine pool in extensive gardens.

Apartments

Several apartments and houses are available for short and long stays. Ask at the tourist information booth on Pérez Gasga, Carmen's Patisserie or Le Pik Nik restaurant, on Playa Marinero.

Places to Eat

Puerto Escondido's restaurants and cafés are mostly simple, semi-open-air places.

Italian food is abundant, and Escondido is a vegetarian's paradise. Be sure to sample the town's excellent ice cream, fruit drinks and *paletas* (frozen crushed fruit on a stick) at any establishment labeled *paletería* or *nevería*. There's a good one on the north side of El Crucero. Try the delicious, refreshing, chilled coconut milk (US$0.30). The main produce market is in the upper part of town (see map).

Playa Marinero & Plaza Zicatela Good whole-grain and banana breads, cakes, croissants and pastries are sold at tiny *Carmen's Patisserie*, just up from the Hotel Flor de María on the little lane leading back from Playa Marinero. Attached is a small fan-cooled palapa-style café offering good breakfasts and snacks, bottomless cups of coffee and even Twinings tea. It's open Monday through Saturday from 7 am to 6 pm. *Carmen's Cafecito*, on Zicatela, run by the same friendly Mexican/Canadian couple and offering much the same fare, does a roaring trade. It's open daily from 6 am to 9 pm.

Le Pik Nik is a popular new open-air restaurant on Playa Marinero. The French-inspired snacks, including pâté, are around US$2, and typical Mexican fish dishes cost US$4.75. There's sometimes live music at night.

The *Hotel Santa Fe* restaurant, spacious and open to the breezes, has some tasty seafood and vegetarian fare (but be ready for your choice to be unavailable). It's medium priced, with fish and seafood dishes mostly from US$4.25 to US$11 and antojitos, pasta, tofu and vegetarian offerings mostly US$3.25 to US$7.

Along Zicatela, *Cipriano's Pizza* does the best pizza we've found in town, with a thin, crisp crust and lots of good cheese, baked in a brick oven by a friendly family. There's a range of toppings, and the only size available, costing US$3.25 to US$9.25, is enough for two. They also do cheap breakfasts.

Beyond Cipriano's, the *Hotel Arco Iris* restaurant, with a good upper-story position, serves a tasty mix of Mexican and international fare to satisfy the Zicatela surfers. Pasta and antojitos go for around US$1.60 to US$3.25, fish and meat courses for US$3.25 to US$6 (though you'll probably also need, say, a salad to really fill up). Next door, the *Bungalows Zicatela* restaurant is a good value – try the burgers (meat, soy or fish), at less than US$2 including salad and fries.

Halfway down Zicatela, *Bruno's* mixes mean cocktails at its bar, perfect while you wait for your meal. The imaginative menu includes vegetarian, Asian and Italian choices. Prices run from US$2.75 to US$4.50. Special nights are devoted to different cuisines, such as Thai or Japanese. Hours are 6 to 10 pm, later if there's live music.

Many Zicatela hostelries have cooking facilities, and the town has at least four grocery stores.

Avenida Pérez Gasga There's a clutch of reasonably priced restaurants serving seafood, which we have always found to be fresh, around the west end of the mall. Several open onto the beach. *Restaurant Junto al Mar*, *Restaurant La Posada del Tiburón* and *Restaurant Los Crotos* all serve up a good meal. Most fish dishes – such as a whole juicy huachinango (snapper) with rice or fries and a little salad – go for US$4.75 to US$6. The Junto al Mar's flavorful fish soup is almost a meal in itself, with large chunks of tender fish, for US$5.

Just beyond this west end of the mall and also with a branch on Zicatela, *Restauran Vegetariano – La Gota de Vida* serves up some tasty fare. Breakfasts, tortas and large salads are each around US$2.50. Both tofu and tempeh are available – try the torta de tempeh con salsa barbacoa, a delicious tempeh burger served on grainy bread with salad and a spicy tomato sauce. There are delicious fruit and yogurt smoothies too.

Around the middle of the mall, little *Restaurant Alicia* is a good value, with seafood cocktails and excellent fish dishes from US$1.90 to US$4. It also does cheap breakfasts. Toward the east end of the mall, the good Italian-run *Ostería del Viandante*

da Ugo does a range of pasta and one-person pizzas from US$1.90 to US$6.25, and some good salads (including avocado and octopus) for US$2.25 to US$4.50. *Cafetería Cappuccino* serves excellent coffee. It also offers good bowls of yogurt, fruit salad and granola; decent crepas; and a buffet breakfast for US$2.75. Main dishes, including fish, are around US$5.50.

Restaurant San Ángel, opposite Cafetería Bananas at the east end of the mall, does good-value fish and seafood, with huachinango at US$3.75 and camarones at US$5.25.

Just beyond the east end of the mall you can enjoy cheap, tasty home cooking and the jolly humor of the cook/owner at *Herman's Best*. There are only seven tables and you might have to wait, but it's worth it. For just US$2.25, he dishes up fried fish, chicken or pork with rice, frijoles, salad and huge tortillas. Photos of satisfied customers brighten one of the walls.

Entertainment

Many Puerto Escondido evenings start during happy hour – usually about 6 to 9 pm – in café-bars such as *Wipe Out*, *Barfly*, *Cafetería Bananas* and *Hotel Las Palmas*, all on the mall; *Restaurant Liza's* on Playa Marinero; or *Cabo Blanco* and the bar at *Hotel Arco Iris*, on Playa Zicatela.

Escondido's spectacular sunsets are renowned. Then there are usually at least a couple of places with live music into the wee hours – on our last visit *Wipe Out* had a very good band playing Latin rhythms, while *Moctezuma's Revenge* featured an excellent Mexican salsa/samba band. Both places are on the mall. *Restaurant/Bar Kneipe*, at the east end of Pérez Gasga, has live music nightly. A mediocre group was thumping out '70s favorites when we checked it out. You can also dance the night away at *Tequila Sunrise*, at the west end of Bahía Principal. It gets going most nights at 9 pm and lasts until late.

Getting There & Away

Air See the Oaxaca City section for details on flights between Puerto Escondido and

Oaxaca. Mexicana flies nonstop direct to and from Mexico City at least five days a week (one hour, US$98). Ticket offices for Mexicana (☎ 2-00-98, 2-03-02) and Aero-morelos (☎ 2-06-53) are at the airport. Aerovega (☎ 2-01-51) has an office just off the west end of the mall. Turismo Rodimar (☎ 2-07-34) and Viajes Erikson (☎ 2-08-49), both on Pérez Gasga, sell air tickets.

Bus The 2nd-class EB/TG, EV/OP and TOI and bus terminals are all on Avenida Hidalgo, in the upper part of town: turn right (east) two blocks uphill from El Crucero. EB/TG directo services are almost up to 1st-class standards. Cristóbal Colón (1st-class) is on 1a Norte between 1a and 2a Oriente, two blocks north of El Crucero.

It's advisable to book ahead for some of the better and more limited services, such as the directo buses to Oaxaca and Colón buses. Daily departures include:

Acapulco – 400 km, 6½ to 7½ hours; 14 EB/TG (US$8.75 to US$11)
Bahías de Huatulco – 115 km, 2½ hours; two Colón (US$3.25), 11 EB/TG (US$2.25 to US$2.75)
Oaxaca – 310 km, seven hours; five directo (US$9.25) and several ordinario (US$7.50) by EV/OP; 2nd-class Transportes Aragal directo at 9.30 pm from TOI terminal (US$7.25); one Colón overnight via Salina Cruz (530 km, 10 hours, US$16)
Pochutla – 65 km, 1½ hours; 11 EB/TG (US$1.30 to US$1.70)

There are four daily Colón buses to Tuxtla Gutiérrez and two to San Cristóbal de Las Casas (US$19). Colón and EB/TG go daily to Salina Cruz. EB/TG and EV/OP run daily to Mexico City.

Car & Motorcycle Budget (☎ 2-03-12/15) has a rental office in the Hotel Posada Real.

Getting Around
To/From the Airport The airport is about four km west of the town center on the north side of highway 200. For two or three people, a taxi is probably the cheapest way

into town, if you can find one and agree on a reasonable price (US$2). Otherwise, colectivo combis (US$2 per person) will drop you anywhere in town. You can book them to take you back to the airport at the travel agencies on the mall. There should be no problem finding a taxi to the airport for a reasonable fare.

Taxi & Lancha Taxis wait by the barriers at each end of the pedestrian mall. Taxis and lanchas (see Beaches) are the only transportation between the central Pérez Gasga/Bahía Principal area and the outlying beaches if you don't want – or think it's unsafe – to walk. The standard taxi fare to Playa Zicatela or Puerto Angelito is US$1.30.

WEST OF PUERTO ESCONDIDO
Highway 200, heading toward Acapulco, runs along behind a coast studded with lagoons, pristine beaches and prolific bird and plant life. The people here are of mixed ancestry. In addition to the indigenous Mixtecs and the Spanish input, there are descendants of African slaves who escaped from the Spanish, of itinerant Asians and of Chileans shipwrecked on their way to the California gold rushes. The latter inspired a local folk music known as la Chilena.

Laguna de Manialtepec
This lagoon, eight km long, begins about 15 km along highway 200 from Puerto Escondido. It is home to ibis and several species of hawks, falcons, ospreys, egrets, herons, kingfishers and iguanas. The birds are most plentiful in June and July and best seen in the early morning, but even at midday in January birders we know logged 40 species. The lagoon is mainly surrounded by mangroves, but there are also tropical flowers and palms on the ocean side.

Hidden Voyages Ecotours, run by knowledgeable Canadian ornithologist Michael Malone, is operated through Turismo Rodimar, on Pérez Gasga in Puerto Escondido. It charges US$30 for excellent early morning or sunset tours to Manialtepec. Two other bird-watching tours with an English-speaking guide both cost US$20. One is with Turismo Rodimar, the other with Ana Márquez, who has a desk in the lobby of the Hotel Rincón del Pacífico.

To do it independently, take an EB/TG bus or drive to the small villages of La Alejandría or El Gallo, on the north shore of the lagoon, just off the highway. Both have restaurants with boats for hire. La Alejandría, about 16 km from Puerto Escondido, has a shady beach, camping space and some basic cabañas. *Restaurant Isla de Gallo*, a bit farther along at El Gallo, does good grilled fish and has a shaded boat for up to eight people, with a knowledgeable captain. He charges US$26 for the boat for a trip of up to 2½ hours, with a stop on the sandbar on the ocean side of the lagoon.

Lagunas de Chacahua

The area around the coastal lagoons of Chacahua and La Pastoría forms the beautiful Parque Nacional Lagunas de Chacahua. The area is of special interest to birders, during the northern winter, when birds from Alaska and Canada migrate here. Mangrove-fringed islands harbor cormorants, wood storks, herons, egrets, ibis and roseate spoonbills, as well as black orchids, mahogany trees, crocodiles and turtles. El Corral, a long waterway lined with mangroves filled with countless birds, connects the two lagoons. From the lagoons you can see huge flocks of birds skidding across the water and soaring in big blue skies with fluffy white clouds, while the contours of inland mountains shimmer in the distance.

Zapotalito A five-km road leads south from highway 200 about 60 km out of Puerto Escondido to Zapotalito, a small fishing village on the eastern edge of La Pastoría. A local tourism cooperative here runs lancha tours of the lagoons, which cost US$45 for a whole boat (about six people) for two hours. Some trips stop for a swim at Cerro Hermoso beach or the beach near Chacahua, a fishing village at the western end of the park. Colectivo boats (US$2.75 per person) also link Zapotalito with Chacahua village; when there are seven or eight passengers, they head off. The journey is about 25 km one way and takes about 45 minutes. In Zapotalito you'll find the colectivo boats (with canopies for shade) a short walk straight ahead from the departure point for the lancha tours. There are a few simple restaurants beside the lagoon.

Chacahua Chacahua village, a five minute walk from a wonderful expanse of ocean beach, is a perfect place to bliss out – for the day, a few days, weeks. There are good waves here for surfers but also strong currents – ask locals where it's safest to swim. Several places to stay, such as *Siete Mares*, facing the lagoon, offer basic cabañas for around US$5/8, singles/doubles. Cheaper cabañas can be found right on the beach, where there are also restaurants with hammocks strung in the shade; all specialize in fish, seafood and tropical fruits. The friendly *Restaurant Siete Mares*, on the beach, has big breakfasts for US$1.50 and cooks up huachinango for US$4 or camarones for US$6. Across the end of the lagoon (you can walk around it) is a crocodile farm with a sad-looking collection of creatures kept for protection and reproduction. Chacahua's croc population (not human-eating) has been decimated by hunters after their skins.

Getting There & Away Easiest is an all-day guided tour from Puerto Escondido with the same operators as for Manialtepec (US$23 to US$36 per person). It's quite an adventure to go independently: From Puerto Escondido take an EB/TG bus to Río Grande (45 minutes, US$1). Colectivo taxis (US$0.70) and vans operate between Río Grande and Zapotalito, about 15 km west. Then complete the independent mode in a colectivo lancha from Zapotalito to Chacahua, and return!

Chacahua village can also be reached by a rough road (impassable in the wet season) from San José del Progreso, 30 km away on highway 200, about 80 km from Puerto Escondido.

Pinotepa Nacional
pop 40,000; ☎ 954

The biggest town between Puerto Escondido and Acapulco has a high Mixtec population, a Sunday market and several places to stay. One of the best is *Hotel Carmona* (☎ 3-23-22), Porfirio Díaz 127, where singles/doubles with bath are US$11/13 with fan, US$15/23 with air-con. *Hotel Tropical* (☎ 3-20-10), on Pte 3 at the corner of Progreso, has singles/doubles for US$9.25/10.

POCHUTLA
pop 30,000; ☎ 958

Pochutla is the crossroads town where highway 175 from Oaxaca meets coastal highway 200.

Orientation
Highway 175 passes through Pochutla as Cárdenas, the narrow north-south main street. Hotel Izala, on the corner of Juárez, marks the approximate midpoint of Cárdenas. Bus stations cluster on Cárdenas half to one km south of the Izala. The main square, Plaza de la Constitución, is a block east of the Izala along Juárez. The market is on Allende, east of Cárdenas and two blocks north of the Izala. Highway 175 meets highway 200 about 1.5 km south of the bus stations.

Information
Bital bank, on Cárdenas a block north of the Hotel Izala, changes traveler's checks and US dollars Monday through Saturday from 8 am to 6.30 pm; Bancomer on Cárdenas at Allende does exchange weekdays from 9 am to 1.45 pm, Saturday from 10 am to 2 pm. Both banks have ATMs.

The post office, open weekdays 8 am to 7 pm and Saturday 9 am to 1 pm, is on Avenida Progreso behind Plaza de la Constitución. There are several pay phones and telephone casetas (some of the latter with fax) on Cárdenas. There's a hospital (☎ 4-02-16) on the east side of the road south of

the bus stations, though it was badly damaged by Hurricane Pauline in 1997.

Places to Stay & Eat
Hotel Santa Cruz (☎ 4-01-16), at Cárdenas 88, just north of the bus stations, has basic singles/doubles with fan and bath for US$4/8. *Hotel Izala* (☎ 4-01-19), Cárdenas 59, has reasonable rooms at US$9/14 with fan and TV, US$14/18 with air-con and TV. *Hotel Pochutla* (☎ 4-00-33), one block north and half a block east of the Izala, at Madero 102, has 32 clean rooms with fan for US$7.75/9.25. Nicest is *Hotel Costa del Sol* (☎ 4-03-18), Cárdenas 47, 1½ blocks north of the Izala, with clean rooms at US$9.25 single or double with fan, or US$11/12 singles/doubles with air-con.

One of the better places to eat in town is *Restaurant Los Ángeles*, on Allende almost opposite the market: egg dishes are US$1.30, fish or shrimp soup US$2.25, seafood cocktails US$3.25 or US$4.75. The market has some cheap comedores. *La Michoacana*, just up and across Cárdenas from the EB/TG bus station, is good for juices and licuados.

Getting There & Away
Bus The three main bus stations, in north-south order down Cárdenas, are EB/TG (2nd-class), on the west side of the street; EV/OP (2nd-class), on the east side; and Cristóbal Colón (1st-class), on the west side. Daily departures include:

Acapulco – 465 km, eight hours; four EB/TG (US$10 to US$12)
Bahías de Huatulco – 50 km, one hour; seven EB/TG (US$1); Transportes Rápidos de Pochutla every 15 minutes until 7 pm from a yard opposite EB/TG (US$1); four Colón (US$1.30)
Mazunte – 22 km, 45 minutes; same buses (US$0.60) and vans as to Puerto Ángel
Oaxaca – 245 km, 6½ hours; one EV/OP '1st-class' at 11 pm (US$7.25); hourly EV/OP 2nd-class, 5 am to 5 pm (US$5.75); 2nd-class Transportes Aragal directo at 10.30 pm (US$6), ticket office on first street east off Cárdenas above EB/TG; two Colón via Salina Cruz (465 km, 8½ hours, US$14)

Puerto Ángel – 13 km, 20 minutes; EV/OP every 20 minutes, 6 am to 8 pm (US$0.30); vans duplicate this service from the next street corner up Cárdenas above the EB/TG station

Puerto Escondido – 65 km, 1½ hours; nine Colón (US$2); 12 EB/TG (US$1.30 to US$1.70)

San Cristóbal de Las Casas – 585 km, 11 hours; two Colón (US$17)

Tuxtla Gutiérrez – 500 km, 10 hours; three Colón (US$15 to US$18)

Zipolite – 17 km, 30 minutes; same buses (US$0.40) and vans as to Puerto Ángel

Colón and EB/TG go to Salina Cruz. Colón also runs to Tehuantepec and Juchitán and has one bus overnight to Tapachula. All three main companies go to Mexico City.

Taxi Taxis wait on Cárdenas between the EB/TG and EV/OP bus stations. Up until about 8 pm they depart fairly often on a colectivo (shared) basis to Puerto Ángel for US$0.60 per person; a whole taxi costs about US$3.

PUERTO ÁNGEL
pop 10,000; ☎ *958*

The onetime coffee port of Puerto Ángel ('PWER-toh ANN-hell') is now a small fishing town and travelers' haven straggling around a little bay between two rocky headlands. There are beaches within the bay, and several others are easily accessible along the beautiful coast within a few kilometers on either side of the town – including the famous Zipolite, four km west.

Paved roads now lead to Puerto Ángel from Oaxaca, Salina Cruz and Acapulco, or you can fly to Huatulco or Puerto Escondido, but Puerto Ángel remains a hot, sleepy place where tourism is still small scale. More laid back than Puerto Escondido, it has a number of good places to stay and eat.

Though Puerto Ángel was severely hit by Hurricane Pauline in 1997, with fishing boats smashed and many homes damaged or destroyed, a lot of the accommodations and restaurants mentioned in this section were likely to be functioning near-normally again within a few months.

Orientation
The paved road from Pochutla, 13 km north, emerges at the east end of the small Bahía de Puerto Ángel, where you can see most of the village. The road winds around the back of the bay, over an often-dry arroyo (creek), up a hill, then forks – right to Zipolite and Mazunte, left down to Playa del Panteón.

Information
The Oficina del Alcalde (Mayor's Office, for tourist information) and the post office are side by side on Avenida Principal near the pier at the east end of Bahía de Puerto Ángel. The post office is open weekdays from 9 am to 8.30 pm.

The nearest bank is in Pochutla, but several hostelries and restaurants will change cash or traveler's checks at their own rates. There's a telephone caseta with fax in a little café on Vasconcelos next door to Gambusino's. Caseta Telefónica El Ángel, on Boulevard Uribe just over the arroyo, also has telephone and fax service and accepts major credit cards.

Gambusino's travel agency, at Vasconcelos 3, just up from the Hotel Soraya, books air tickets; it's open Tuesday through Saturday from 9 am to 8 pm, Monday from noon to 8 pm.

Dr Constancio Aparicio (☎ 4-30-25) is a doctor recommended by foreign residents. Ask for him in the pharmacy on Vasconcelos.

Theft and robbery can be a problem, especially on the Zipolite road at night.

Beaches
Playa del Panteón The little beach on the west side of Bahía de Puerto Ángel is shallow and calm, and its waters are cleaner than those near the fishers' pier across the bay. You can swim out to the rocky islet on the right.

Estacahuite Half a km from Puerto Ángel up the road to Pochutla, a sign points right along a path to this beach '500 meters' away. (In fact it's 700 meters.) There are

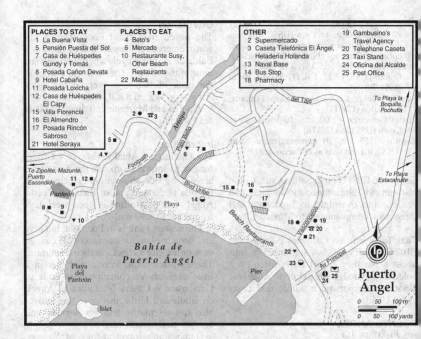

PLACES TO STAY
1 La Buena Vista
5 Pensión Puesta del Sol
7 Casa de Huéspedes
   Gundy y Tomás
8 Posada Cañon Devata
11 Hotel Cabaña
11 Posada Loxicha
12 Casa de Huéspedes
   El Capy
15 Villa Florencia
16 El Almendro
17 Posada Rincón
   Sabroso
21 Hotel Soraya

PLACES TO EAT
4 Beto's
6 Mercado
10 Restaurante Susy,
   Other Beach
   Restaurants
22 Maca

OTHER
2 Supermercado
3 Caseta Telefónica El Ángel,
   Heladería Holanda
13 Naval Base
14 Bus Stop
18 Pharmacy
19 Gambusino's
   Travel Agency
20 Telephone Caseta
23 Taxi Stand
24 Oficina del Alcalde
25 Post Office

Puerto Ángel

three tiny sandy bays, all good for snorkeling – but watch out for jellyfish. Two small shack restaurants serve good, reasonably priced seafood or spaghetti. At least one of them has a snorkel to rent.

Playa La Boquilla The coast northeast of Estacahuite is dotted with more good beaches, none of them very busy. A good one is Playa La Boquilla, on a small bay about five km out, with the good Bahía de la Luna restaurant. You can get there by a 3.5-km dirt road, very rough in parts, from a turnoff four km out of Puerto Ángel on the road to Pochutla. More fun is to go by boat – you should be able to find a fisher who will take you and pick you up later for about US$13.

Activities

You can rent snorkeling gear from some of the café-restaurants on Playa del Panteón or get a fisher to take you for a boat trip from Panteón or from the pier on the other side of the bay. A dive shop next to Hotel Cabaña rents snorkeling and diving gear and offers day trips.

Places to Stay

Places with an elevated position are more likely to catch any breeze. Mosquito screens are a big plus too. Some places have a water shortage; there's usually enough to wash yourself, but not always your clothes. What follows is in east-to-west order.

Hotel Soraya (☎ 4-30-09), on Vasconcelos overlooking the pier, is slightly run-down, but its 32 rooms with private bath, fan and screens are clean, and most of them have balcony access and good views. Singles or doubles are US$16.

Little *Posada Rincón Sabroso* (☎ 4-02-95) is up a flight of stairs to the right as you start to wind your way around the bay. It has 10 clean, fan-cooled rooms along a greenery-shaded terrace, with a hammock outside each. They have private bathrooms, but there's water for only a few hours a day. Singles or doubles are US$18. *El Almendro*, in a shady garden up a little lane a few meters past the Rincón Sabroso steps, has similarly clean rooms, but they're mostly a bit smaller and darker. Singles or doubles including breakfast are US$17. There are also a couple of bungalows for longer-term rent, and a small library.

Villa Florencia (☎ 4-30-44) has 13 pleasant but smallish rooms, each with private bath, fan and screens. There's a cool sitting area with caged parrots. Singles/doubles/triples cost US$14/21/28.

Owned by the same people as El Almendro, *Casa de Huéspedes Gundy y Tomás* (☎ 4-31-02) has a variety of rooms, from singles/doubles with shared bath for US$7.75/11 to doubles with fan and private bath for US$13. All have mosquito nets or screens. The cheaper ones are mostly higher up and feel airier. At peak times you can hang or rent a hammock for US$2.75. Good food is available, including homemade bread and vegetable juices, and there are pleasant sitting areas. There's an office safe for valuables.

To reach the excellent *La Buena Vista* (☎ /fax 4-31-04), turn right along the arroyo, then go a short way up the first track on the left. There are a dozen or so big rooms here, kept scrupulously clean, all with private bath, fans and mosquito screens and opening onto breezy balconies with hammocks. Year-round prices range from US$16/20 to US$22/26 for singles/ doubles, depending on size. There are also a couple of excellent mud-brick bungalows, one with two rooms, at US$30 to US$33. The airy terrace restaurant has really good food and a great atmosphere.

The German/Mexican-owned *Pensión Puesta del Sol* (☎ 4-30-96) is up to the right past the arroyo. Rooms are sizable and clean and have fans and screens. With shared bath, singles/doubles are US$12 and US$14; doubles with private bath are US$17 to US$20. Food is available morning and evening. A small library, satellite TV and videos are available in the sitting room, and there are a couple of breezy terraces with hammocks for relaxing.

On the road descending to Playa del Panteón is *Casa de Huéspedes El Capy* (☎ 4-30-02), with 26 clean, cool but smallish rooms with fan, private bath and mostly good views from US$7.75/11. Just beyond, up a steep path on the right, the friendly, relaxed *Posada Loxicha* has six basic rooms with the same prices as El Capy and hammocks for US$3.25. There are also a couple of cabañas at US$6.50. The very clean restaurant serves breakfast and a comida corrida, both US$2. The view up here is gorgeous.

Behind Playa del Panteón is the bigger *Hotel Cabaña* (☎ 4-31-05), with 23 clean, comfortable rooms centered on a small, plant-filled patio for US$18/24 doubles/ triples. Rooms have private bath, fan and screens.

Farther along this road and up some steps to the right, the friendly *Posada Cañon Devata* (☎ /fax 4-30-48) has a variety of attractive accommodations scattered among the foliage on a quiet hillside. This is a good place for those seeking a quiet retreat (there are morning yoga sessions for those interested). Rooms range from comfortable singles/doubles with fans and private bath at US$11/13 to a two-room, four-bed unit at US$30 for two, plus US$3.25 for each extra adult. There's also good food, mainly vegetarian. The owners have reforested the whole canyon and installed compost toilets. The posada is closed in May and June.

The recently opened *Bahía de la Luna*, out at Playa La Boquilla (see Beaches), has nice adobe bungalows with bath for US$20, single or double. It also has a good beachside restaurant-café with mid-range prices – fish is around US$5. The European owners aim to get creative arts and personal development courses going here. The address is Apartado Postal 90, Pochutla 70900, Oaxaca.

Places to Eat

The excellent restaurant at *La Buena Vista* is open for breakfast and in the evenings only (closed Sunday, except for a light breakfast). On an airy terrace overlooking the bay, it offers both Mexican and North American fare, from hotcakes (US$2.50) to delicious chiles rellenos (US$4.75). The menu is selective but varied enough to please anyone, and the food is very well prepared. A specialty is tamales with vegetarian or chicken and mole fillings for US$3.25. You don't have to be staying at La Buena Vista to eat here.

Non-guests can also eat at the *Posada Cañon Devata*, where you can enjoy a good, sizable three-course dinner served for US$5 at long tables in a lovely palm-roofed, open-sided dining room. Fare is usually vegetarian, with organically grown vegetables. It's best to book earlier in the day. From about 7.30 am to 2 pm you can get dishes such as yogurt with granola and bananas, sandwiches, enchiladas, muffins and soy burgers on excellent homemade bread.

There are numerous places to eat on the main town beach and the main street, Boulevard Uribe. They're fairly economical – breakfast around US$1.50, a big plate of spaghetti for US$1.50 to US$2, fish around US$2.50 – but none of them is very well frequented, though *Restaurant Marisol* has good-value food and cheap sunset beers. *Maca*, the little restaurant down by the pier, has good food.

The Italian restaurant at *Villa Florencia*, on Boulevard Uribe, usually manages good pasta (try the pesto) from US$2 to US$3.25, good cappuccinos (US$1.10), and pizza, seafood, Mexican fare and cheap breakfasts.

The restaurants on Playa del Panteón, including the good *Restaurante Susy*, offer fish and seafood for US$2.75 to US$5.25, plus cheaper fare such as entomatadas and eggs. Be careful about the freshness of seafood in the low season. The setting is very pretty after dark.

Two small restaurants on the road toward Playa del Panteón have reasonable food.

At *Betos* a tasty fish filet – which could be al mojo de ajo, a la veracruzana or plain – goes for just US$2.25, or there's a variety of salads and meat dishes from US$1.60 to US$3.25. Betos is open from late afternoon only. At the terrace restaurant of *Casa de Huéspedes El Capy* – cool in the evening – fish, shrimp, chicken, meat and salads are all around US$3.50.

Getting There & Away

To reach Puerto Ángel by bus, you first have to get to Pochutla, 13 km north. Frequent buses and colectivo taxis run from 6 am to 8 pm between Pochutla and Puerto Ángel. After 8 pm you need a taxi. See the Pochutla section for details.

The main bus stop in Puerto Ángel is on the main street near the naval base.

ZIPOLITE

The two km stretch of pale sand called Zipolite, beginning three km west of Puerto Ángel, is fabled as southern Mexico's ultimate place to lie back in a hammock and do as little as you like, in as little as you like, for almost as little as you like.

Zipolite was very badly hit by Hurricane Pauline in October 1997 – nearly all of its mainly flimsy buildings were blown or washed away, and many of the palm trees along the back of the beach were flattened. In the years before Pauline, fisherfolk's shacks and a proliferation of comedores and budget places to stay had come to line almost the whole length of the beach, and Zipolite had become increasingly busy – though still a great place to take it easy, its magic stemming from some combination of pounding sea and sun, open-air sleeping and, for some, the drug scene.

Rebuilding of some homes and some places to stay and eat started within a few days of the hurricane, and the Zipolite scene may well return to something approaching its former self in 1998. The details of its establishments, however, will obviously vary from the information given in this section, which was gathered before the hurricane but is retained in the belief that it's better than nothing.

Beware of the Zipolite surf: it's fraught with rip tides, changing currents, and a strong undertow, and it can be deadly. A few life-saving posts are dotted along the beach, but drownings still occur. Locals rarely swim here. Particularly from about May to August, going in deeper than your knees can be risking your life. Keep away from the rocks at both ends of the beach. If you do get swept out, your best hope is to swim calmly parallel to the shore to get clear of the current pulling you outward.

Theft is a problem at Zipolite, and it's not advisable to walk along the Puerto Ángel-Zipolite road after dark. Also take care with drugs – if you buy any, be careful who you buy them from.

Nudity is nowadays more common up at the far (west) end of the beach.

Information

There's a money exchange office with reasonable rates on the main drag as you enter Zipolite. Hours are 9 am to 5 pm. Close by are laundry facilities.

Places to Stay

Palmera Trailer Park is on the road from Puerto Ángel before you enter Zipolite.

Nearly all the palm shacks and other abodes along the beach rent small rooms and/or have hammock space for travelers. Pick one whose owner will look after, and preferably lock up, your things for you. The normal price for a rented hammock is US$2 a night, or you can sling your own for US$1.40. Rooms range upward from US$4, with many under US$10. Price depends on size and whether shower, fan or mosquito net are provided.

Among the more substantial places is *Lola's*, at the east end of the beach (nearest Puerto Ángel). It has 15 or so rooms with bath, fan and screens; the best rooms are upstairs, facing the ocean. Singles/doubles are US$11/13. Next door, *Restaurante Tomás* (with Italian/Mexican food) has cabañas at US$5.25 a person and dorm beds for US$2.75. A bit farther along, *Lyoban* has 12 basic rooms (curtains instead of doors) on two levels and lockers

for luggage. Showers are communal. Cost is US$2.75 per person. Midway along the beach, *Aris* has nine rooms from US$4 to US$6.50. Next door, *The Green Hole* has 12 bare cabañas, the best two upstairs. Cost is US$4 per person.

The three-story *Tao Zipolite*, toward the west end, has 20 simple rooms with mosquito nets and communal showers. Asking price for doubles is US$6.50. There's a bar/restaurant.

One of the most popular places is *Lo Cósmico*, with cabañas around a tall rock outcrop near the west end of the beach. A hammock in a cabaña here will cost you US$4, a hammock on a breezy terrace US$2. There are more expensive options, up to doubles for US$26, in one of the larger individually crafted cabañas. A friendly, casual atmosphere prevails. Atop the rock are the rocket-shaped huts of the amiable Mexican/Swiss couple who own the place. Good food is served in the open-air restaurant here.

The *Shambhala Posada*, an old establishment commonly known as *Casa Gloria*, after its North American owner, is on the hill at the far end of the beach – with great views back along it. It offers hammocks and tent or van space at US$2, small cabañas with bed and mosquito net for US$7.75, or larger cabañas for US$11. There are inexpensive rooms too. The shared bathrooms are decent.

Places to Eat

Few places at Zipolite have free drinking water. There are a dozen or two basic comedores along the beach, where a typical plate of fish, rice and salad costs around US$3.50. Some offer spaghetti or other variations for less.

A couple of places have greater choice and even formal menus. *Restaurante-Bar La Choza*, about halfway along the beach, has an extensive menu – an eggs breakfast is around US$1.30; fish and other seafood dishes, including prawns, are up to US$4. On a dirt road back toward the main road midway along the beach is *3 Diciembre*, a recommended vegetarian restaurant, bakery and pizzeria. It's open from 7 pm to 3 am.

Toward the west end of the beach are grouped three of the larger, most organized eateries. Their popularity testifies to their higher quality. The first, *Posada San Cristóbal*, does respectable snapper or prawns for US$4, spaghetti, sandwiches and hamburgers, each at US$2 to US$3. There's even cappuccino.

Lo Cósmico, on the rocks near the west end of the beach, has good food prepared in an impeccably clean kitchen, especially its delicious crepas (sweet and savory), from US$1.60 to US$2.50, and its salads.

Getting There & Away

The road from Puerto Ángel to Zipolite is paved. Buses and vans run every few minutes from Pochutla through Puerto Ángel to Zipolite from about 6 am to 8 pm. See Pochutla for details. Puerto Ángel to Zipolite costs US$0.30. The main Zipolite bus stop is behind the buildings about halfway along the beach, with a taxi stand 200 meters back toward Puerto Ángel. A taxi to Pochutla costs around US$3.

MAZUNTE & AROUND

West from Zipolite more glorious beaches stretch almost unbroken all the way to Puerto Escondido. In and around the villages of San Agustinillo (four km from Zipolite) and Mazunte (one km farther) are several very relaxed places to stay. Both places have fine safe beaches, and Mazunte is the site of a pioneering and very interesting village ecotourism project.

The coast between Zipolite and Puerto Escondido is one of the world's major sea turtle nesting sites. It was also, until a few years ago, the scene of a gruesome turtle industry, with some 50,000 turtles being killed per year at a slaughterhouse at San Agustinillo. Mazunte village grew up around this industry. (See the sidebar Mexico's Turtles: Not Saved Yet.) After the hunting and killing of sea turtles was officially banned in Mexico in 1990, many villagers turned to slash-and-burn agriculture, endangering the nearby forests.

In 1991, with the backing of a Mexico City-based environmental group, Ecosolar, Mazunte declared itself a Reserva Ecológica Campesina, aimed at preserving the local environment while creating a sustainable economy. Projects include printing and natural cosmetics workshops, the use of ecological toilets, garbage separation and nutrition education. Tourism is a key element. Ecosolar has an interesting Internet site (see the Website Directory).

Like Zipolite, the Mazunte and San Agustinillo area was hit very hard by Hurricane Pauline in 1997, but details of the destruction were hard to obtain before we went to press. Apart from information on the Centro Mexicano de la Tortuga, we have left this section in its pre-Pauline state, in the belief that it will serve as a partly useful guide to what will emerge as reconstruction proceeds.

Getting There & Away

A paved road now runs from Puerto Ángel and Zipolite to San Agustinillo and Mazunte, then continues on to meet highway 200. Buses and vans run every few minutes, 6 am to 8 pm, from Pochutla to Mazunte via Puerto Ángel, Zipolite and San Agustinillo. Fare to Mazunte from Puerto Ángel is US$0.40. The last one back leaves Mazunte about 7.30 pm.

San Agustinillo

West of the headland at the west end of Zipolite, the long, straight Playa Aragón – another beach in the Zipolite mold, but almost empty – stretches along to San Agustinillo. From Zipolite, footpaths to Playa Aragón cross the headland behind Casa Gloria, or you can take the road, which loops inland, then comes back down to San Agustinillo.

San Agustinillo beach is between two small rocky headlands, and its waves are often good for body surfing. It's backed by a line of comedores – US$3 to US$4 for fish, octopus or shrimp – behind which are the remains of the infamous turtle abattoir.

A few places have cabañas and rooms, with prices similar to Zipolite. Atop the

OAXACA STATE

steep slope backing Playa Aragón, *Rancho Cerro Largo* (fax 958-4-30-63) has five superior, comfortable, fan-cooled cabañas at US$40 a single or US$50 a double, including a good breakfast and dinner. It's reachable from the road.

Mazunte
☎ *958*

As you enter Mazunte by road from San Agustinillo, the Centro Mexicana de la Tortuga is on the left. A little farther along on the right is the village square, with Mazunte's helpful information kiosk, the Ecoturismo Módulo de Información (☎ 4-07-14), open daily from 8 am to 7 pm.

Mazunte's fine beach – generally safe, though the waves can be quite big – curves around to Punta Cometa, the headland at its west end.

Centro Mexicano de la Tortuga Sadly, the Mexican Turtle Center, an aquarium and research center for Mexico's many marine and freshwater turtle species, was badly damaged by Hurricane Pauline in 1997. It's anyone's guess when it will be up and running again. The government-funded center, one of Mazunte's main attractions, was opened in 1994. All seven of Mexico's marine turtle species were on view in fairly large tanks, and it was enthralling to get a close-up view of these creatures, some of which are *big*. The center was open Tuesday through Saturday from 10 am to 4.30 pm, Sunday 10 am to 2.30 pm; visits were guided (in Spanish) and cost US$1.30.

Fábrica de Cosméticos Mazunte's ecological cosmetics workshop and store is by the roadside toward the west end of the village. Set up with help from a range of organizations, including the Body Shop, this co-op of 14 people makes shampoo and cosmetics from things such as maize, coconut, avocado and sesame seeds. Also sold here are T-shirts, granola, wooden toys made by disabled people and other things produced by other Mazunte co-ops.

Activities The tourist kiosk offers lancha trips out to sea, where you can swim with turtles and dolphins (two hours, US$39 for up to 10 people); horseback riding for groups of six along Playa Ventanilla (three hours, US$16 per person); bicycle rentals (US$1.30 an hour); and trips to the lagoon at Playa Ventanilla (US$6.50 per person).

Places to Stay & Eat The tourist kiosk can set you up with a *village family* for US$12 a person in rooms with mosquito net, including meals.

Several of the beach comedores have rooms, cabañas or hammock/tent space. At *Comedor Yuri*, for instance, not far west of the Centro de la Tortuga, you can sling your own hammock or camp for US$1.30 a person, rent a hammock for US$2, take a room with bathroom for US$7.75 single or double or a cabaña with bathroom for US$12.

On a small rocky outcrop toward the west end of the beach, *Posada del Arquitecto*, run by an Italian/Mexican couple, has a handful of varied accommodations worked into the natural features of the land using only natural materials (bioarchitecture). A *tapanco* – a double bed on a rope-slung upper floor, with hammock space below – is US$13; the *casita*, a small abode cleverly built into the natural rock, is about US$27. Prices include continental breakfast. *El Rinconcito*, a little farther along the beach, has nice cabañas for US$5.25 a double. There are more places near this end of the beach, and still others near the road.

Typical beach comedor prices are US$3 for a fish filet or shrimp, US$1.20 for eggs.

Playa Ventanilla
Some 2.5 km along the road west from Mazunte, a sign points left to Playa Ventanilla, 1.2 km down a dirt track. A couple of small homes and comedores constitute the settlement here. The beach stretches west all the way to Puerto Escondido – but take care if swimming. For US$2.75 per person the locals will paddle you around a mangrove-fringed lagoon a little way down

OAXACA STATE

Mexico's Turtles: Not Saved Yet

Of the world's eight sea turtle species, seven are found in Mexican waters. Turtle nesting sites are scattered all along Mexico's coasts. Turtles usually lay their eggs on the beaches where they were born, some swimming huge distances to do so. They come ashore at night and scoop out a trough in the sand, in which they lay 50 to 200 eggs. Then they cover the eggs and go back to the sea. Six to 10 weeks later, the baby turtles hatch, dig their way out and crawl to the sea at night. Only two or three of every 100 make it to adulthood.

Playa Escobilla, just east of Puerto Escondido, is one of the world's main nesting grounds for the **olive ridley turtle** (*tortuga golfina* to Mexicans), the smallest species and the only one not endangered. Between May and January, about 700,000 olive ridleys come ashore here in about a dozen waves – known as *arribadas* – over two or three nights. Arribadas often (though not always) happen during the waning of the moon. Playa Escobilla's turtles are guarded by armed soldiers, and there is no tourist access to the beach.

The rare **leatherback** (*tortuga laud* or *tortuga de altura*) is the world's largest sea turtle – it grows up to three meters long and can weigh one ton and live 80 years. One nesting site for the leatherback is Playa Mermejita, between Punta Cometa and Playa Ventanilla, near Mazunte. Another is Barra de la Cruz beach, east of Bahías de Huatulco.

The most endangered sea turtle, the **Kemp's ridley**, or parrot turtle (*tortuga lora*), stays on Mexico's Gulf Coast, where one of its principal nesting sites, Rancho Nuevo, Tamaulipas, is protected.

The **green turtle** (*tortuga verde*) is a vegetarian that grazes on marine grasses. Most adults are about one meter long. For millennia, the green turtle has provided protein to humans in the tropics from its meat and eggs. European exploration of the globe marked the beginning of its decline. By the 19th century tinned turtle was available in London. As recently as the 1960s, the Empacadora Baja California in Ensenada, Baja California, was canning as many as 100 tons of turtle soup a season. Many green turtle nesting sites are at remote spots in Baja California and Michoacán, though there are sites on Baja's East Cape, around Bahía Los Frailes and near San José del Cabo.

The **loggerhead turtle** is famous for the vast distances it crosses between its feeding grounds and nesting sites. Loggerheads feeding off Baja California are believed to have hatched at nesting sites in Japan or even Australia. One loggerhead tagged in Baja California in 1994 turned up in a fishing net off Japan 16 months later. More recently, scientists have been satellite-tracking another loggerhead, 'Adelita,' released off Baja California in 1996. For details on Adelita's progress, check the Turtle Happenings Internet site in the Website Directory.

Other important Mexican turtle nesting sites include Mismaloya and Nuevo Vallarta, near Puerto Vallarta, Jalisco; Playa Troncones, near Zihuatanejo, Guerrero; Lechugillas,

the beach, where you'll see crocodiles and a variety of bird life (most prolific during July and August). The 1½-hour trip includes a stop on an island where you can buy coconuts to eat or drink. Three or four km farther west along the beach is a larger lagoon, which flows out to the sea from July to January. Horseback riding trips are also available.

A taxi from Mazunte to Playa Ventanilla is US$3.25.

BAHÍAS DE HUATULCO
pop 20,000; ☎ 958

Mexico's newest big coastal resort is taking shape along a series of beautiful sandy bays, the Bahías de Huatulco ('wah-TOOL-koh'), some 50 km east of Pochutla. Until the 1980s this stretch of coast had just one small fishing village and was known to only a few outsiders as a great place for a quiet swim in translucent waters. Fortunately, Huatulco's developers appear to have

Veracruz; Celestún, Yucatán, for the green and the **hawksbill turtle** *(tortuga carey)*; and Pamul and Akumal, Quintana Roo. Nesting seasons vary, but late summer – July to September – is a peak time in many places.

Mexico's seventh species, the **black turtle** *(tortuga negra)*, sticks to the Pacific coast.

Despite international conservation efforts, most turtle species are still endangered. In Mexico, illicit killing and egg-raiding still goes on – hardly surprising, since one clutch of eggs can be sold for more than a typical worker makes in a week. When the soldiers guarding Playa Escobilla temporarily left their posts in response to the 1996 EPR guerrilla attack at Bahías de Huatulco, poachers descended on the beach, slaughtering turtles and taking an estimated 800,000 to 1 million eggs. Turtle flesh and eggs are valued as food, and the eggs are believed to be an aphrodisiac. Turtle skin and shell are used to make clothing and adornments. The world's fishing boats kill many turtles by trapping and drowning them in nets.

Another major setback to Mexico's sea turtle population came in 1997, when Hurricane Pauline destroyed hundreds of thousands of nests on Pacific beaches – especially in the state of Oaxaca – wiping out a large proportion of that year's eggs.

To help the turtles that use Mexican beaches – and anyone who has seen these graceful creatures swimming at sea is likely to want to do that – consider these tips from Nayarit's Grupo Ecológico de la Costa Verde. If you find yourself at a nesting beach:

- Try to avoid nesting beaches altogether between sunset and sunrise.
- Don't approach turtles emerging from the sea or disturb nesting turtles or hatchlings with noise or lights (lights on or even near the beach can cause hatchlings to lose their sense of direction on their journey to the water).
- Keep vehicles, even bicycles, off nesting beaches.
- Don't build sandcastles, or stick umbrellas into the sand.
- Never handle baby turtles or carry them to the sea – their arduous scramble is vital to their development.
- Boycott shops or stalls selling products made from sea turtles or any other endangered species. ■

OAXACA STATE

learned their lessons from other modern Mexican resorts. Limited-scale developments are separated by tracts of unspoiled shoreline. The maximum building height is six stories, with future hotels likely to be limited to four; all wastewater is said to be recycled, and no sewage goes into the sea. At this stage of its growth, Huatulco is still an enjoyable, relatively uncrowded resort, with a succession of lovely beaches lapped by beautiful water and backed by forest.

But it's not a place to stay long if you're on a tight budget.

The solid construction of most buildings greatly restricted damage by Hurricane Pauline in 1997 at Bahías de Huatulco. The primary reported casualty in the main resort areas was the beach at Bahía Tangolunda, some of which was washed away – but is to be replaced. Destruction was apparently more severe among the flimsier buildings at Bahía San Agustín.

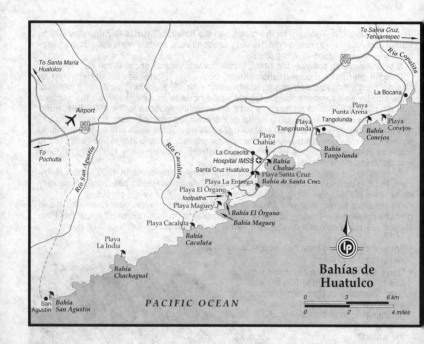

Bahías de Huatulco

Orientation

A divided road leads a few km down from highway 200 to La Crucecita, the service town for the resort, which has the bus stations, market, most of the shops, the only cheap accommodations and most of the better-value restaurants. One km south of La Crucecita, on Bahía de Santa Cruz, is Santa Cruz Huatulco, site of the original village, with some hotels and a harbor. The other main development so far is at Tangolunda, five km east, which has most of the top-end hotels.

The Huatulco bays are strung along the coast about 10 km in each direction from Santa Cruz. From west to east, they are: San Agustín, Chachacual, Cacaluta, Maguey, El Órgano, Santa Cruz, Chahué, Tangolunda and Conejos.

Bahías de Huatulco airport is 400 meters north of highway 200, 12 km west of the turnoff to La Crucecita and Santa Cruz Huatulco.

Information

Tourist Offices The Asociación de Hoteles de Huatulco (☎ 7-08-48, 7-10-37), on Boulevard Santa Cruz in Santa Cruz, provides tourist information weekdays from 9 am to 6 pm, Saturday from 10 am to 2 pm. There's also a tourist office (☎ 1-03-88, 1-01-76) on Avenida Juárez in Tangolunda, about 250 meters west of the Caribbean Village hotel, open daily from 9 am to 3 pm and 6 to 9 pm.

Money Banamex and Bancomer on Boulevard Santa Cruz in Santa Cruz change cash and traveler's checks and have ATMs. The Telecomm office next door to La Crucecita's post office, on Boulevard Chahué, has the Western Union 'Dinero en Minutos' money transfer service.

Post & Communications La Crucecita's post office is on Boulevard Chahué, 400 meters east of the Plaza Principal – open weekdays 9 am to 1 pm and 3 to 6 pm, Saturday 9 am to 1 pm. There are pay phones around the Plaza Principal at La Crucecita, and a telephone caseta with fax half a block away, at Bugambilias 505.

Laundry Lavandería Estrella, on Flamboyan at Carrizal in La Crucecita, will wash three kg of laundry for US$3.25 with same-day pickup, or for US$2.75 if you can wait until the next day.

Medical Services Some doctors speak English at the good Hospital IMSS (☎ 7-11-83), on Boulevard Chahué, halfway between La Crucecita and Bahía Chahué. The larger hotels have English-speaking doctors on call.

Beaches

All Huatulco's beaches are sandy with clear waters (though boats, Jet Skis and so forth leave an oily film here and there).

Some have coral offshore and excellent snorkeling, though visibility can be poor in the rainy season.

At Santa Cruz Huatulco the small **Playa Santa Cruz** is kept pretty clean but is inferior to most Huatulco beaches. Lanchas will whisk you out to the others from Santa Cruz's harbor. A taxi is cheaper than a lancha, but a boat ride is more fun. Tickets are sold at a hut beside the harbor. Lanchas will take you anytime between 8 am and 4 pm and collect you until 7 pm. Roundtrip rates for up to 10 people include: Playa La Entrega, US$11; Bahía Maguey or Bahía El Órgano, US$26; Bahía Cacaluta, US$33. There's also a seven-hour, nine-bay boat cruise with an open bar, leaving daily at 11 am for US$20 per person.

Playa La Entrega lies toward the outer edge of Bahía Santa Cruz, a five-minute lancha trip or 2.5 km by paved road from Santa Cruz. This 300-meter-long beach, backed by a line of seafood palapas, can get

La Crucecita

0   50   100 m

0   50   100 yards

PLACES TO STAY
2   Gran Hotel Huatulco
3   Hotel Benimar
5   Posada Michelle
9   Hotel Busanvi II
10 Hotel Flamboyant
13 Hotel Grifer
14 Hotel Las Palmas
16 Hotel Posada Del Parque
18 Hotel Suites Begonias
23 Hotel Su Casita
24 Hotel Busanvi I

PLACES TO EAT
4   El Tiburón Tragón
11 Los Portales
12 Comedores
17 Restaurant-Bar Oasis
20 Restaurant La Crucecita

OTHER
1   Transportes Rápidos de Pochutla Bus Stop
6   EB/TG Bus Station
7   Cristóbal Colón Bus Station
8   Budget Rent a Car
15 Pemex
19 Telephone Caseta
21 Bicycle Rentals
22 Lavandería Estrella
25 Post Office

To Hwy 200, Pochutla

Sabali
Pochote
Gardenia
Jazmin
Palo Verde
Palma Real
Ocotillo
Macuil
Macuilite
Guarumbo
Guanacaste
Mercado
Plaza Principal
Carrizal
Blvd Chahué
Av Bugambilias
Guamuchil
Flamboyan
Chacah
Colorin
Canal

To Santa Cruz Huatulco

To Hospital IMSS, Posada Chahué, Bahía Chahué, Tangolunda

OAXACA STATE

crowded, but it has beautiful calm water with fine snorkeling in a large area from which boats are cordoned off. 'La Entrega' means 'The Handover': here in 1831 the Mexican independence hero Vicente Guerrero was betrayed to his enemies by an Italian sea captain for 50,000 pieces of gold. Guerrero was taken to Cuilapan, near Oaxaca, and shot.

Roads to the bays farther west are, where they exist, rough tracks. A 1.5 km track accessible to cars heads off to **Bahía Maguey** from the road to La Entrega about half a km out of Santa Cruz. Maguey has a fine, 400-meter beach curving around a clear, calm, beautiful bay between forested headlands. It too has a line of seafood palapas but is less busy than La Entrega. There's good snorkeling around the rocks at the left (east) side of the bay. **Bahía El Órgano**, an inlet east of Maguey, has a 250-meter beach. You can reach it by a narrow 10-minute footpath that heads into the trees halfway along the Maguey track, where that track briefly broadens out. Maguey has clear, calm waters good for snorkeling but no comedores.

Bahía Cacaluta has a beach about one km long, protected by an island, though there can be undertow. Snorkeling is best around the island. Behind the beach is a lagoon with bird life. A narrow track that's just about drivable in dry conditions heads west off the Maguey track 200 meters above the Maguey parking area and winds 2.5 km, mostly through forest, to Cacaluta. Inaccessible by land, **Bahía Chachagual** has a headland at each end and two beaches – one of which, Playa La India, is one of Huatulco's most beautiful.

Thirteen km down a dirt road from a crossroads on highway 200, 1.7 km west of the airport, is **Bahía San Agustín**. The road is OK but it fords a river after nine km, which could be tricky after rains. The beach is long and sandy, with a long line of palapa comedores, some with hammocks to rent for overnight. It's popular with Mexicans on weekends and holidays, but quiet at other times. The waters are usually calm and the snorkeling good (some of the comedores rent gear).

A paved road runs to the bays east of La Crucecita and Santa Cruz, continuing eventually to highway 200. Currently, **Bahía Chahué** is mainly a construction site. **Bahía Tangolunda** is the site of the major top-end hotel developments to date. There's nothing to stop anyone from using the sands in front of the hotels, though the sea is sometimes rough. Tangolunda has an 18-hole golf course too. Three km farther east is the long sweep of **Playa Punta Arena**, on Bahía Conejos. Around a headland at the east end of Bahía Conejos is the more sheltered **Playa Conejos**, unreachable by road.

Two to three km beyond Bahía Conejos, the road runs down to the coast again at **La Bocana**, where there are a handful of seafood comedores at the mouth of the Río Copalita. Another long beach stretches to the east.

Activities

You can rent snorkeling gear beside the lancha kiosk at Santa Cruz harbor for US$4 a day. At Playa La Entrega you can rent a snorkel and mask from a stall for US$2 (US$4 with flippers). In high season these prices allow you an hour; at other times you'll probably get a whole day. At La Entrega you can also ride the 'banana' (US$1.30 for a half hour) or go waterskiing (US$13 for a half hour).

Numerous travel agencies, including several in hotels, can set you up for horseback riding, diving, cycling or sport fishing. The North American-run DAD Adventure Tours (☎ 1-00-97), in Hotel Club Plaza Huatulco opposite the Sheraton at Tangolunda, gets good reports. Triton Dive Center, by the harbor at Santa Cruz, has also been recommended.

Posada Michelle, in La Crucecita (see Places to Stay), offers kayak or canoe trips on the Río Copalita for US$19.

Organized Tours

DAD Adventure Tours (see Activities) does good coffee plantation trips. Jeep Safaris (☎ 1-03-23), near Restaurant La Pampa in Tangolunda, also does coffee

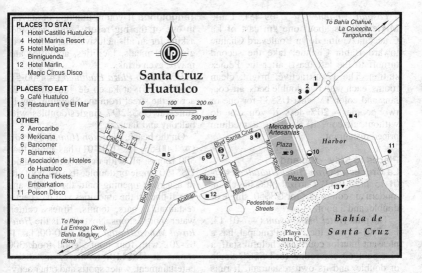

PLACES TO STAY
1 Hotel Castillo Huatulco
4 Hotel Marina Resort
5 Hotel Meigas
  Binniguenda
12 Hotel Marlin,
   Magic Circus Disco

PLACES TO EAT
9 Café Huatulco
13 Restaurant Ve El Mar

OTHER
2 Aerocaribe
3 Mexicana
6 Bancomer
7 Banamex
8 Asociación de Hoteles
  de Huatulco
10 Lancha Tickets,
   Embarkation
11 Poison Disco

Santa Cruz
Huatulco

To Bahía Chahué,
La Crucecita,
Tangolunda

Mercado de
Artesanías

Plaza

Harbor

Plaza

Plaza

Pedestrian
Streets

To Playa
La Entrega (2km),
Bahía Maguey
(2km)

Playa
Santa Cruz

Bahía de
Santa Cruz

plantation outings (US$60 per person), plus a two-day trip to San José del Pacífico in the mountains, with walks through a pine forest to a Zapotec village and to a 30-meter waterfall (around US$150).

Eco Discover Tours, opposite the Sheraton in Tangolunda, does guided bicycle tours. Several agencies in La Crucecita, Santa Cruz Huatulco and Tangolunda offer tours to Puerto Ángel, Zipolite and Mazunte.

Places to Stay – budget
All these hotels are in La Crucecita. The family-run *Hotel Benimar* (☎ 7-04-47), Bugambilias 1404 at Pochote, is a bit grubby, but it's adequate. Rooms have fan and bath; you should get one for US$10 in high season.

Hotel Busanvi II (☎ 7-08-90), Macuil 208, is a bit gloomy but all right. Rooms, with fan and hot water, are US$11/15 for singles/doubles or US$18 for two or three people in two beds. Some have TV.

Hotel Posada Del Parque (☎ 7-02-19), on the Plaza Principal, is better, with more comfortable and sizable singles/doubles with air-con and TV for US$13/16. *Hotel Grifer* (☎ 7-00-48), a block east of the

plaza at Carrizal 702, has decent fan-cooled rooms for US$16.

Places to Stay – middle
Again, most options are in La Crucecita. *Hotel Busanvi I* (☎ 7-00-56), at Carrizal 601, has plain singles/doubles with fan for US$10/20 and doubles or triples with air-con for US$24. *Hotel Su Casita* (no telephone), Chacah 207, has just a couple of apricot-colored rooms, but they're big and bright, with fans, for US$16/20 singles/doubles. *Hotel Las Palmas* (☎ 7-00-60), half a block from the plaza at Guamuchil 206, has clean but small rooms with fan, TV and private bath for US$20/24.

Posada Michelle (☎ 7-05-35), at Gardenia 8, next to the EB/TG bus station, is a friendly place with a handful of nice, clean, quite sizable rooms with private bath and TV. Singles/doubles/triples/quads are US$19/26/30/32 with fan, US$27/30/38/39 with air-con.

The small *Hotel Suites Begonias* (☎ 7-00-18, fax 7-03-90), Bugambilias 503, just off the Plaza Principal, has comfortable rooms with TV and fan opening on upstairs walkways, for US$30 single or double.

Posada Chahué (☎ 7-09-45), Calle Mixie L75, is about one km east of La Crucecita. Going down Boulevard Chahué toward Bahía Chahué, take the second turnoff to the left (east) after the Pemex station. The 12 attractive, bright, clean rooms, each with two double beds, air-con, fans and color TV, cost US$33 for one or two people – 20% less if you can do without air-con. It also has a medium priced restaurant.

Places to Stay – top end
La Crucecita *Gran Hotel Huatulco* (☎ 7-01-15, fax 7-0-83), Carrizal 1406, has clean, modern air-con rooms for US$50, single or double, and a pool.

The pink *Hotel Flamboyant* (☎ 7-01-13, fax 7-01-21), on the Plaza Principal, has a pleasant interior courtyard, helpful staff, a nice pool, air-con rooms for US$64, single or double, and its own restaurant. It runs hourly free transportation to Playa La Entrega.

Santa Cruz Huatulco The good, French-run *Hotel Marlin* (☎ 7-00-55, 800-27373; fax 7-05-46), Mitla 28, has nicely decorated, colorful rooms with TV and air-con for US$59 single or double. There are a restaurant and small central swimming pool too.

Hotel Castillo Huatulco (☎ 7-01-44, fax 7-01-31), at the east end of Boulevard Santa Cruz, has a good pool, a restaurant and 107 good-size air-con rooms for US$75 single or double. It also runs a beach club on Bahía Chahué, with free transportation.

Hotel Meigas Binniguenda (☎ 7-00-77, fax 7-02-84), on Boulevard Santa Cruz near Calle E-1a, is Huatulco's oldest hotel, dating from all of 1987. It has colonial-style decor, a nice garden-courtyard, a pool, a restaurant and coffee shop and 74 air-con rooms at US$81 single or double.

The 40-room *Hotel Marina Resort* (☎ 7-09-63, fax 7-08-30), on the east side of the harbor, charges US$92 single or double and has three pools.

Tangolunda If you're thinking of staying in one of the big resort hotels, consider asking for an all-inclusive rate, which will give you meals, facilities, activities and maybe even drinks.

Hotel Club Plaza Huatulco (☎ 1-00-51, fax 1-00-35), at Paseo de Tangolunda 23 across the street from the Sheraton, has 12 suites at US$82/97 singles/doubles with balcony and Jacuzzi.

On the beach, *Sheraton Huatulco Resort* (☎ 1-00-55, fax 1-03-01) has more than 300 rooms, all with ocean view, at about US$190 single or double. Its vast pool sits in a garden opening onto the beach, and you'll find all the amenities you'd expect – restaurants, bars, tennis, fitness center, water sports, shops. Next door is the *Hotel Royal Maeva Huatulco* (☎ 1-00-00, fax 1-02-20), with four pools, good food, 300 rooms at US$110, tennis, gym, disco, entertainment, water sports and other activities. It's much favored by package tourists, many of whom rave about it and its friendly staff.

A little farther around the bay, the *Zaashila Huatulco* (☎ 1-04-60, fax 1-04-61) has 184 rooms, some with private pools, for around US$200. Beyond the Zaashila is the elegant *Casa del Mar* (☎ 1-01-02, 800-90060; fax 1-02-02), with 25 air-con suites only, which cost US$102/112 singles/doubles.

The new, very luxurious *Hotel Quinta Real* (☎ /fax 1-04-28), at the west end of Tangolunda, has a hilltop position with 28 suites only.

The 135-room *Caribbean Village* (☎ 1-00-44, fax 1-02-21), climbing the hillside at Boulevard Juárez 8, is set back from the beach but has its own beach club next to the Sheraton.

Places to Eat
La Crucecita The very clean market has several comedores doling out decent portions of fish various ways for US$2, shrimp for US$2.75 and enfrijoladas or entomatadas for US$1.60. There's fresh fruit at the market stalls.

Restaurant-Bar Oasis, on the Plaza Principal, has good and moderately priced, if bland, fare, from tortas at US$0.80 to US$1.30 to filete de pescado at US$3.25 or steaks at US$4.75. It takes a stab at Japanese too. *Los Portales* is also good, with offerings such as four beef tacos for US$1.60, fish fillet for US$3, or meat alambres for US$4. *Restaurant La Crucecita*, Bugambilias at Chacah, a block from the plaza, is open from 7 am to 10 pm and does well-priced breakfasts and good-value meat, chicken or seafood dishes from US$2.50 to US$4. Its sincronizadas a la Mexicana (US$2) are a good antojito.

El Tiburón Tragón, next to Posada Michelle, does decent inexpensive seafood and Guerrero-style food – eggs or chicken quesadillas for US$1.20, filete empanizado or bisteck various ways for US$2, shrimp or octopus cocktails for US$2.50.

Santa Cruz Huatulco There are several eateries on Playa Santa Cruz. The food is disappointing, except at *Restaurant Ve El Mar*, at the east end, where the seafood is fine and the margaritas potent. A fish costs from US$4, octopus or shrimp US$4.75.

Café Huatulco, in the plaza near the harbor, serves good local Pluma coffee in many different ways – the capuchino frío (cold, with a dollop of ice cream) is well worth a splash at US$1.30.

Tangolunda The big hotels offer a choice of expensive bars, coffee shops and restaurants. The *Casa del Mar* hotel has one of the best restaurants, and it has a great view. Most main dishes are around US$10 to US$13. You'll spend US$30 to US$50 for a full dinner with wine.

There are also a few restaurants, medium to expensive in price, along Tangolunda's two streets. *Restaurant La Pampa Argentina*, at the west end, where the two streets meet, does very good but expensive steaks for around US$13.

Beaches The seafood palapas at La Entrega are ordinary (US$5 to US$6 for fish or seafood), but we had a fine meal at Maguey – around US$4 for a whole huachinango. The comedores at La Bocana will cook you up a tasty grilled fish with fries or salad for around US$4.

Entertainment

In Santa Cruz, the discos *Magic Circus*, beside Hotel Marlin, and *Poison*, near the harbor, are open weekends only, except at the busiest tourist times. When we checked, entry at Poison was US$17 for men, US$2.75 for women, with a free bar. Magic Circus is said to be cheaper. *Noches Oaxaqueñas*, by the traffic circle in Tangolunda, does a Guelaguetza regional dance show Friday, Saturday and Sunday evenings for US$13 with a drink or US$24 with dinner.

Getting There & Away

Air Mexicana flies twice or more daily, and Aeromar once most days, to and from Mexico City (from US$71); they also have a few flights direct to and from Los Angeles (about US$480 roundtrip). Aeromorelos and Aerocaribe both fly once or more daily to and from Oaxaca city (US$45). There are occasional cheap charters from North America.

Mexicana (☎ 7-02-23, 1-90-08 at the airport) and Aerocaribe (☎ 7-12-20, 1-90-30 at the airport) have offices next to the Hotel Castillo Huatulco in Santa Cruz. Aeromar (☎ 1-90-01) and Aeromorelos (☎ 1-90-22) are at the airport.

Bus The main bus stations are on Gardenia in La Crucecita. Some buses are marked 'Santa Cruz Huatulco,' but they still terminate in La Crucecita. Make sure your bus is *not* headed to Santa María Huatulco, which is a long way inland.

Cristóbal Colón (1st-class) is on Gardenia at Ocotillo, four blocks from the plaza. Most of its buses are de paso. EB/TG, one block farther up Gardenia at Palma Real, has primera services that are quick and fairly comfortable, though not really 1st-class, and ordinario buses, which are typical ordinario. Daily departures include:

Oaxaca – 415 km, 7½ hours; two Colón overnight via Salina Cruz (US$12 or US$15)
Puerto Escondido – 105 km, two hours; six Colón (US$3.25), 11 EB/TG (US$2.25 or US$2.75)
Pochutla – 50 km, one hour; 11 EB/TG (US$1); Transportes Rápidos de Pochutla every 15 minutes up to about 7 pm from the main road opposite Bugambilias (US$1)
Salina Cruz – 140 km, 2½ hours; several Colón (US$4.25), three EB/TG (US$3.75)

Colón also runs several buses to Tehuantepec and Juchitán and a few to Tuxtla Gutiérrez, San Cristóbal de Las Casas and Tapachula. EB/TG goes to Acapulco. Both EB/TG and Colón go to Mexico City.

Car & Motorcycle Car rental agencies include:

Advantage
    Hotel Castillo Huatulco, Santa Cruz
    (☎ 7-01-44)
Budget
    Ocotillo at Jazmín, La Crucecita (☎ 7-00-34)
    Airport (☎ 7-00-10, 1-00-20)
Dollar
    Hotel Castillo Huatulco, Santa Cruz
    (☎ 7-02-51)
    Sheraton Huatulco Resort, Tangolunda
    (☎ 1-00-55)
Fast
    Caribbean Village, Tangolunda (☎ 1-00-02, 1-00-44)
    Airport (☎ 1-90-31)
National
    Hotel Club Plaza Huatulco, Tangolunda
    (☎ 1-02-93)

Advantage and Fast both have VW Beetles for around US$45 a day with unlimited mileage, and other cars from around US$60.

Getting Around
To/From the Airport Transporte Terrestre (☎ 1-90-14, 1-90-24) provides colectivo combis for US$5.25 per person to La Crucecita or Santa Cruz, US$6 to Tango-

lunda. Get tickets at their airport kiosk. A taxi should be US$8 to La Crucecita or Santa Cruz, US$9.50 to Tangolunda.

Bus Local buses run every 15 minutes or so until about 8 pm between La Crucecita, Santa Cruz Huatulco and Tangolunda. In La Crucecita they stop on Gardenia, opposite the bus stations, and on Guamuchil just over a block from the Plaza Principal. In Santa Cruz they stop by the harbor and in Tangolunda at the traffic circle outside the Maeva hotel.

Bicycle A shop on Flamboyan a few steps off La Crucecita's Plaza Principal rents bicycles for around US$8 a day. Eco Discover Tours, opposite the Sheraton in Tangolunda, charges US$9.25 a day, US$6.50 a half day.

Taxi Taxis are common and rates fixed. La Crucecita or Santa Cruz to Tangolunda costs US$1.90; La Crucecita to Bahía Maguey is $5.50.

Isthmus of Tehuantepec

Eastern Oaxaca is the southern half of the 200-km-wide Isthmus of Tehuantepec ('teh-wan-teh-PECK'), Mexico's narrowest point. This is sweaty, flat country, but Zapotec culture is strong here. Of its three main towns, Tehuantepec is the most appealing. You may find yourself changing buses in Salina Cruz or Juchitán, each with a share of Oaxaca's limited industry. If you do spend a night or two here you'll probably be agreeably surprised by the people's liveliness and friendliness.

Fifteen km east of Juchitán, around La Ventosa, where highway 185 to Acayucan diverges from highway 190 to Chiapas, strong winds sweep down from the north and sometimes blow high vehicles off the road.

History & People
In 1496 the isthmus Zapotecs repulsed the Aztecs from the fortress of Guiengola, near Tehuantepec, and the isthmus never became part of the Aztec empire. Later there was strong resistance to the Spanish here, notably from 1524 to 1527 (by an alliance of Zapotecs, Mixes, Zoques and Chontals) and in a 1660 rebellion in Tehuantepec.

Isthmus women are noticeably open and confident and take a leading role in business and local government. Many older women still wear embroidered huipiles and voluminous printed skirts. For fiestas, Tehuantepec and Juchitán women turn out in velvet or sateen huipiles, skirts embroidered with fantastically colorful silk flowers, and a variety of odd headgear. They also deck themselves in gold and silver jewelry, a sign of wealth. Many isthmus fiestas feature the *tirada de frutas*, in which women climb on roofs and throw fruit on the men below!

TEHUANTEPEC
pop 50,000; ☎ *971*
Tehuantepec is a friendly town, often with a fiesta going on in one of its barrios.

Orientation & Information
The Oaxaca-Tuxtla Gutiérrez highway 190 meets highway 185 from Salina Cruz at a point west of Tehuantepec. It then skirts the north edge of town. All Tehuantepec's bus stations, collectively known as 'Terminal,' cluster just off highway 190 on the northeast side of town, about 1.5 km from the center. Local buses to and from Salina Cruz stop, more conveniently, where highway 190 passes the end of 5 de Mayo, only a minute's walk from the central plaza. To reach the plaza from the Terminal on foot, follow Avenida Héroes toward town until it ends at a T-junction, then go right along Guerrero for four blocks to another T-junction, then one block left along Hidalgo.

You can get some tourist information in the Ex-Convento Rey Cosijopí. A couple of banks around the central plaza have ATMs. The dark, almost medieval market is on the west side of the plaza, and the post office is on the north side.

Ex-Convento Rey Cosijopí
Down a short side street off Guerrero (a shop called Keiko is on the corner), this former Dominican monastery is now the town's Casa de la Cultura, with various classes and occasional exhibitions; it's open every day. You can admire its stout two-story construction around a central courtyard. Built in the 16th century, it's named for the local Zapotec leader of the day (who paid for it). It served as a prison before being restored in the 1970s.

Guiengola
The hillside Zapotec stronghold of Guiengola, where the king Cosijoeza rebuffed the Aztecs, is north of highway 190 from a turnoff about 11 km out of Tehuantepec. A sign points to 'Ruinas Guiengola 7' just past the 240 km marker. You can see the remains of two pyramids, a ball court, a 64-room complex known as El Palacio and a thick defensive wall. There are fine views over the isthmus.

You can get here by taking a bus bound for Jalapa del Marqués from the Terminal. Get off at Puente Las Tejas. It's a walk of about 2½ hours from there. It's best to start early, 6 am or before, to take advantage of the morning coolness. You may well be able to find a guide by asking in the Ex-Convento Rey Cosijopí.

Special Events
The Vela Guiexoba (Jasmine Vigil) festival in the third week of May includes parades in regional dress and a tirada de frutas. Each Tehuantepec barrio also holds its own fiesta for several days around its saint's day, with parades, tiradas de frutas and lots of marimba music and dancing.

Places to Stay
Hotel Donají (☎ 5-00-64), at Juárez 10, two blocks south of the east side of the

central plaza, has clean rooms with private bath (intermittent hot water) on two upper floors with open-air walkways. Singles/doubles with fan are US$7.75/11 (US$0.50 more for two beds), and with air-con US$11/16. *Hotel Oasis* (☎ 5-00-08), Ocampo 8 at Romero, one block south of the west side of the plaza, has slightly smaller fan-cooled rooms, bare and basic but with warm-water showers, for US$8/10 (US$11 with two beds). There's parking in the courtyard.

Places to Eat
El Portón, at Romero 54, 1½ blocks south of the plaza, serves cheap, simple, fresh food, with a comida corrida for US$1.60. *Cafe Colonial*, Romero 66, a little farther down the street, has generous chicken and meat dishes for US$3.25 to US$5, antojitos for US$2.25 to US$3.75 and a menú del día for US$3.

Restaurante Scarú at Leona Vicario 4, up a side street a block east of the Hotel Donají, is the most interesting place to eat. Occupying an 18th century house with a courtyard and colorful modern murals of Tehuantepec life, it serves up varied fish, seafood, meat and chicken dishes, mostly for US$3.25 to US$4.75; it's open daily from 7 am to 11 pm.

Getting There & Away
The 260-km trip from Oaxaca takes 4½ hours in a 1st-class bus. The road winds downhill for the middle 160 km. Watch for the dead vehicles on the slopes below.

Cristóbal Colón (1st-class) runs 11 daily buses to Oaxaca (US$7.25 to US$8.75) and a few each to Tuxtla Gutiérrez, San Cristóbal de Las Casas, Bahías de Huatulco, Pochutla and Puerto Escondido. There's also service to Mexico City and Tapachula. ADO (1st-class) has night buses to Villahermosa and Palenque plus services to Acayucan. Most Colón and ADO buses are de paso, often in the wee hours.

AU (2nd-class) has a few buses to Veracruz, Oaxaca and Mexico City. Sur (2nd-class) has frequent buses to Tonalá and a

few to Oaxaca (all at night), Tapachula and Mexico City. TOI (2nd-class), 50 meters east along the highway from Cristóbal Colón, has hourly buses to Oaxaca (US$6.25) around the clock, plus a few to Tuxtla Gutiérrez and Tapachula.

Across the street from Cristóbal Colón are local buses to Juchitán (25 km) and Salina Cruz (15 km). They go at least every half hour during daylight hours, taking half an hour to either place.

Getting Around
Taxis, colectivos and buses run between the central plaza and the Terminal during daylight hours. A curious form of local transportation is the *motocarro* – a kind of three-wheel buggy in which the driver sits on a front seat while passengers stand behind on a platform.

SALINA CRUZ
pop 70,000; ☎ 971
When a railway was built across the isthmus at the start of the 20th century, Salina Cruz became an important port. But a lack of major oil finds and the cutting of the Panama Canal farther south soon ended its prosperity. In recent years it has revived as an oil pipeline terminal with a big refinery. It's a windy city with a bit of a Wild West feel today.

Orientation & Information
Highway 200 from Puerto Escondido and Pochutla meets the Salina Cruz-Tehuantepec road, highway 185, on the northern edge of Salina Cruz, about two km from the center. Avenida Ferrocarril runs south from this junction to the center, with the main bus stations just off it: Estrella Blanca is on Obrero, nearly halfway to the center; Cristóbal Colón, ADO, Sur and AU are together on Laborista, three blocks past Obrero.

Avenida Ferrocarril becomes Avenida Tampico as it nears the center, passing a block west of the wide, windy plaza, which is to the left.

Banks near the main plaza have ATMs. There are pay phones and telephone casetas on the plaza and more casetas near the bus stations. The large market is on the northeast corner of the plaza.

Places to Stay

Hotel Posada del Jardín (☎ 4-01-62) at Camacho 108, a couple of blocks north of the west side of the main plaza, has clean little rooms with fan and shower, all around a leafy little courtyard, for US$5.25/7.75, or US$6.50/9.25 with TV.

At 5 de Mayo 520, 1½ blocks south of the east side of the plaza, *Hotel Altagracia* (☎ 4-07-26) has clean air-con rooms for US$17/20 and friendly management. The choice central place is the modern *Hotel Costa Real* (☎ 4-02-93, fax 4-51-11), at Progreso 22, two blocks north of the plaza and half a block east of Avenida Tampico. Carpeted, air-con singles/doubles with color TV go for US$20/24. It also has a restaurant and parking.

Places to Eat

The clean, modern *Restaurant Viña del Mar*, at Camacho 110, 1½ blocks north of the main plaza, has most main dishes at US$4 or more. *Cafe Istmeño*, on the east side of the plaza, does economical lunch platters for US$1.30 to US$2.50 and tortas from US$0.70. *Jugos Hawaii*, half a block north of the plaza on Camacho, is good to drop in for juices (US$0.70 to US$1.20), tortas (US$0.80), quesadillas or sincronizadas.

Getting There & Away

Frequent buses to Tehuantepec (30 minutes, US$0.40) and Juchitán (one hour, US$1) leave from the corner of Avenida Tampico and Progreso, one block west and two north from the plaza.

Cristóbal Colón and ADO run daily deluxe and 1st-class buses; other lines are 2nd-class. Nine Colón and four Estrella Blanca buses run daily to Bahías de Huatulco (140 km, 2½ hours, US$3.75 to US$4.25), Pochutla (190 km, 3½ hours, US$4.75 to US$5.50) and Puerto Escondido (250 km, five hours, US$6.25 to US$7.50). To Oaxaca (275 km, five hours),

there are seven daily buses by Colón (US$7.75 or US$9.50) and three by Sur (US$6.75). Colón runs two buses to Tuxtla Gutiérrez (315 km, six hours, US$9) and San Cristóbal de Las Casas (400 km, eight hours, US$12). There's also 1st-class service to Tapachula, Veracruz, Villahermosa, Palenque and Acayucan.

Getting Around

Local buses run along Avenida Ferrocarril from the bus stations to the town center. Going out to the bus stations, catch a 'Refinería' bus or walk.

JUCHITÁN

pop 70,000; ☎ *971*

A friendly town visited by few gringos, Juchitán has cultural similarities to Tehuantepec.

Orientation & Information

Prolongación 16 de Septiembre leads into Juchitán from a busy crossroads with traffic lights on highway 190 on the north edge of town. The main bus terminal is about 100 meters toward town from the crossroads. The street eventually curves to the right and divides into 5 de Septiembre (the right fork) and 16 de Septiembre (left). These emerge as opposite sides of the central plaza, Jardín Juárez, after seven blocks. There are banks on and near Jardín Juárez, some with ATMs. Several telephone casetas are across the street from the main bus terminal.

Things to See & Do

The **Jardín Juárez** is a lively central square. A busy **market** spills into the streets from one side of the plaza. It's a good place to look for hammocks, made locally.

Juchitán's **Lidxi Guendabiani** (Casa de la Cultura), on José F Gómez a block from Jardín Juárez, has an art collection with works by leading 20th century Mexican artists such as Rufino Tamayo and José Luis Cuevas and a good archaeological collection. It's housed around a big patio beside the 19th century Iglesia de San Vicente Ferrer.

Places to Stay & Eat

Hotel Malla, upstairs in the main bus station, has cool, tolerably clean singles/doubles for US$6.75/8.50. *Hotel Santo Domingo del Sur* (☎ 1-10-50, fax 1-19-59), by the highway 190 crossroads, is a step up, with air-con singles/doubles at US$14/19 and plenty of parking space. *Casa de Huéspedes Echazarreta* on Jardín Juárez is OK for its prices of US$4.75 single or double with shared bath or US$5.25 with private bath.

Restaurant La Oaxaqueña, at the highway 190 crossroads, does good carne asada for US$2.50. There are other meat and fish dishes available. It closes about 8 pm. *Café Colón*, at the rear of the gasoline station across the road, is a smarter alternative with bow-tied waiters. Pancakes and salads cost from US$2.50 to US$4, main dishes from US$4. There are a couple of 24-hour places across the street from the main bus station. The best place in town is the *Casagrande Cafe Restaurant*, with smooth service in a pleasant courtyard off Jardín Juárez. It offers all sorts of goodies, including regional 'paquetes típicos' such as Xadani, which gives you juice, stuffed pork with mole

negro and coffee for US$3.25. If you're eating you get a free plate of raw vegetables and a dip to start off with.

Getting There & Away

Cristóbal Colón and ADO (1st-class) and Sur and AU (2nd-class) use the main bus terminal on Prolongación 16 de Septiembre. Frequent Autotransportes Istmeños buses to Tehuantepec (30 minutes) and Salina Cruz (one hour) stop next door during daylight hours. FYPSA (2nd-class) has its own terminal, separated from the main one by a Pemex station. Many long-distance buses are de paso and leave in the middle of the night.

To Oaxaca (285 km, five hours) there are nine Colón, eight ADO and 19 FYPSA buses, all daily. FYPSA goes almost around the clock. Colón runs six daily buses to Bahías de Huatulco, Pochutla and Puerto Escondido. Colón and FYPSA go several times daily to Tuxtla Gutiérrez and Tapachula, and Colón goes twice to San Cristóbal de Las Casas. Sur has frequent service to Acayucan. ADO has night buses to Villahermosa and Palenque. Colón and AU run to Mexico City, Veracruz and Puebla.

EL DIABLITO

EL CORAZON

LA MANO

LA PERA

EL VIOLONCELLO

EL MUNDO

Tabasco & Chiapas

Just east of the Isthmus of Tehuantepec – Mexico's narrow 'waist' – lie the states of Tabasco and Chiapas. Their differences define them: Chiapas is rich in potential but poor in reality, whereas Tabasco is an oil-rich boomland. Chiapas is mostly mountainous and volcanic, with forests of oak and pine (although there are some low-lying parts), while Tabasco is low, well-watered and humid, and mostly covered in equatorial rainforest. Chiapas' indigenous history is Mayan, Tabasco's is Olmec and Totonac.

Despite their differences, Tabasco and Chiapas form a geographical whole. Separated from the cosmopolitan centers of Mexico City to the northwest and Mérida to the northeast, the Tabascan capital city of Villahermosa and the Chiapan capital of Tuxtla Gutiérrez generate their own isthmian society. Both with frontage on the mighty Río Usumacinta and borders with Guatemala, the two states share a cross-border history of cultural exchange and conquest.

Tabasco

Tabasco is the low-lying coastal area to the north of Chiapas, kept fertile by huge rivers that slice through the state on their way to the Gulf of Mexico. It was in this unlikely country that the Olmecs developed Mesoamerica's first great civilization. Besides its cultural wealth, Tabasco is noted for its mineral riches – particularly gaseum – which in recent years have brought great prosperity.

History

This land was once the Olmec heartland, the home to the first great Mesoamerican civilization (about 1200-600 BC), whose religion, art, astronomy and architecture would deeply influence the civilizations that followed. La Venta, the second great Olmec center (after San Lorenzo, Veracruz) was established in the western part of Tabasco. The Chontal Maya who followed the Olmecs built a great ceremonial city called Comalcalco outside present-day Villahermosa.

Cortés, who disembarked on the Gulf coast near present-day Villahermosa in 1519, initially defeated the Maya and founded a settlement called Santa María de la Victoria. The Maya regrouped and offered stern resistance until they were defeated by Francisco de Montejo, who pacified the region by 1540. This tranquillity was short-lived. The depredations of pirates forced the original settlement to be moved inland from the coast and renamed Villahermosa de San Juan Bautista.

After independence was won from Spain, various local land barons tried to assert their power over the area, causing considerable strife. The 1863 French intrusion under Maximilian of Hapsburg was strongly resisted here and led to regional solidarity and political stability. Nonetheless, the economy languished until after the Mexican Revolution, when exports of cacao, bananas and coconuts began to increase.

In the 20th century, US and British gaseum companies discovered oil, and Tabasco's economy began to revolve around the liquid fuel. During the 1970s, Villahermosa became an oil boomtown and profits from the state's export of agricultural crops added to the good times. This new-found prosperity has brought a feeling of sophistication that cuts right through the tropical heat, stamping Tabasco as different from neighboring Chiapas and Campeche.

Geography & Climate

Tabasco's topography changes from flat land near the seaside to undulating hills as you near Chiapas. Due to heavy rainfall – about 1500 mm annually – there is much swampland and lush tropical foliage. Outside Villahermosa, the state is rather sparsely populated for Mexico, with a little more than a million people inhabiting about 25,000 sq km.

Be prepared for sticky humidity in this tropical zone. Much of the substantial rainfall here occurs between May and October. Outside of Villahermosa, it can be quite bug-infested (particularly near the rivers), so bring repellent.

VILLAHERMOSA

pop 250,000; ☎ 93

Once just a way-station on the long, sweltering road from central Mexico to the savannas of Yucatán, Villahermosa was anything but the 'beautiful city' that its name implies. Its situation on the banks of the Río Grijalva was pleasant enough, but its lowland location meant it was bathed in tropical heat and humidity every day of every year.

Today, courtesy of the Tabasco oil boom, Villahermosa is indeed a beautiful city with wide, tree-shaded boulevards, sprawling parks, fancy hotels (for the oilies) and excellent cultural institutions.

If you want to see everything here, you will have to stay at least one night. The open-air Olmec archaeological museum, called the Parque-Museo La Venta, is one of Mexico's great archaeological exhibits, and it will take you most of a morning to take in its wonderful sights. The excellent Museo Regional de Antropología deserves at least an hour or two. And just a short bus ride from the city are the ruins of ancient Comalcalco.

Orientation

Villahermosa is a sprawling city, and you will find yourself walking some considerable distances – in the sticky heat – and occasionally hopping on a minibus (combi) or taking a taxi.

Budget and mid-range hotel and restaurant choices are mostly in the older commercial center of the city, which stretches from the Plaza de Armas, between Independencia and Guerrero, to the Parque Juárez, and is bound by streets named Zaragoza, Madero and Juárez. This section has been renovated in recent years and is known, because of those renovations, as the Zona Remodelada or, more poetically, as the Zona Luz. It is a lively area, busy with shoppers. Top-end hotels are on and off the main highway, which passes through the city as Avenida Ruiz Cortines. The Parque-Museo La Venta is also on Avenida Ruiz Cortines, 500 meters northwest of the intersection with Paseo Tabasco.

The Central Camionera de Primera Clase (1st-class bus station), sometimes called the ADO terminal (☎ 12-89-00), is on Mina, three long blocks south of Avenida Ruiz Cortines and about 12 blocks north of the city center. The Central de Autobuses de Tabasco (2nd-class bus station) is on Avenida Ruiz Cortines near a traffic circle marked by a statue of a fisherman; the station is one block east of Mina, five long blocks north of the 1st-class station, and about 17 long blocks from the center.

Villahermosa's Rovirosa airport (☎ 12-75-55) is 13 km east of the center on highway 186.

Information

Tourist Offices There's a small, often unstaffed tourist office next to the ticket window at the Parque-Museo La Venta, and a more reliably staffed desk at the Rovirosa Airport.

The administrative staff at the Tabasco state tourist office (☎ 16-28-89, fax 16-28-90), Paseo Tabasco 1504, in the governmental development known as Tabasco 2000, 500 meters northwest of Avenida

Ruiz Cortines, do their best to answer travelers' questions. Hours are weekdays from 8.30 am to 4 pm. Go northwest along Paseo Tabasco from Ruiz Cortines to the first huge building on the right (northeast) side. Walk along the building's monumental central corridor, down the steps, and look for the office on the right-hand side.

Money There are at least eight banks within the Zona Luz (see the Central Villahermosa map). Banking hours are generally weekdays from 9 am to 1.30 pm. Banamex (☎ 12-89-94), at the corner of Madero and Reforma, has an ATM, as does

Bancomer (☎ 12-37-00), at Zaragoza and Juárez.

Post & Communications The main post office (☎ 12-10-40) is in the Zona Luz at Saenz 131, at the corner of Lerdo de Tejada. Hours are weekdays from 8 am to 5.30 pm, Saturday 9 am to noon, closed Sunday.

Travel Agencies Viajes Villahermosa Travel Agency (☎ 12-54-56, fax 14-37-21), at 27 de Febrero 207, and Madero 422, sells international and domestic tickets; the staff speak English and can arrange excursions.

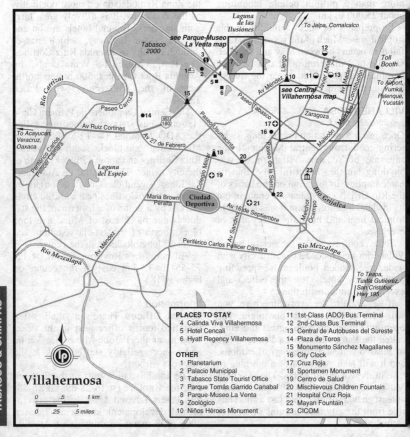

Villahermosa

0   .5   1 km
0   .25   .5 miles

PLACES TO STAY
4 Calinda Viva Villahermosa
5 Hotel Cencali
6 Hyatt Regency Villahermosa

OTHER
1 Planetarium
2 Palacio Municipal
3 Tabasco State Tourist Office
7 Parque Tomás Garrido Canabal
8 Parque-Museo La Venta
9 Zoológico
10 Niños Héroes Monument

11 1st-Class (ADO) Bus Terminal
12 2nd-Class Bus Terminal
13 Central de Autobuses del Sureste
14 Plaza de Toros
15 Monumento Sánchez Magallanes
16 City Clock
17 Cruz Roja
18 Sportsmen Monument
19 Centro de Salud
20 Mischievous Children Fountain
21 Hospital Cruz Roja
22 Mayan Fountain
23 CICOM

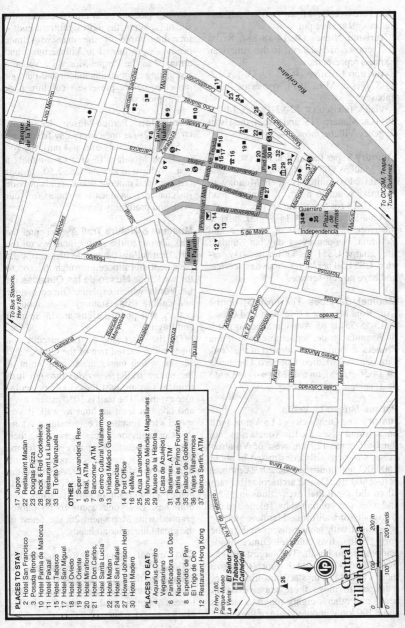

PLACES TO STAY
2   Hotel San Francisco
3   Posada Brondo
10 Hotel Palma de Mallorca
11 Hotel Pakaal
15 Hotel Tabasco
17 Hotel San Miguel
18 Hotel Oviedo
19 Hotel Oriente
20 Hotel Miraflores
21 Hotel Don Carlos;
    Hotel Santa Lucia
24 Hotel Madan
24 Hotel San Rafael
27 Howard Johnson Hotel
30 Hotel Madero

PLACES TO EAT
4   Aquarius Centro
    Vegetariano
6   Panificadora Los Dos
    Naciones
8   Expendio de Pan
    El Trigo de Oro
12 Restaurant Hong Kong

17 Jugos
22 Restaurant Madan
23 Douglas Pizza
28 Rock & Roll Cockteleria
32 Restaurant La Langosta
33 El Torito Valenzuela

OTHER
1   Super Lavandería Rex
5   Bital, ATM
7   Bancomer, ATM
9   Centro Cultural Villahermosa
13 Unidad Médico Guerrero
    Urgencias
14 Post Office
16 TelMex
25 Museo de la Historia
    (Casa de Azulejos)
26 Monumento Méndez Magallanes
29 Banamex, ATM
31 Patria es Primo Fountain
34 Palacio de Gobierno
35 Viajes Villahermosa
36 Banca Serfín, ATM

Central
Villahermosa

To Hwy 180,
Parque-Museo
La Venta

CG   El Señor de
     Tabasco
     Cathedral

TABASCO & CHIAPAS

Hours are weekdays from 9 am to 7 pm, and Saturday 9 am to 1 pm.

Turismo Nieves (☎ 14-18-88), Sarlat 202, corner of Fidencia, is the American Express representative.

Turismo Creativo (☎ 12-79-73, fax 12-85-82), is at Mina 1011, corner of Paseo Tabasco.

Viajes Tabasco (☎ 12-53-18, fax 14-27-80) is at Madero 718, and also in the Hyatt Regency Villahermosa.

Laundry Super Lavandería Rex (☎ 12-08-15), Madero 705 at Méndez, facing Restaurant Mexicanito, is open Monday to Saturday 8 am to 8 pm. A three-kg load costs US$8 for three-hour service.

Acua Lavandería (☎ 14-37-65), next to the river on the corner of Madrazo and Reforma, is open every day but Sunday; they charge US$1 per kg for two-day service, US$1.50 per kg for same-day service, and have no self-service.

Medical Services The hospital of the Cruz Roja Mexicana (Mexican Red Cross; ☎ 15-55-55) is on Avenida Sandino north of Avenida 16 de Septiembre in Colonia Primera, a short ride southwest of the Zona Luz. Unidad Médico Guerrero Urgencias (☎ 14-56-97/98), on 5 de Mayo 44 at Lerdo de Tejada, is open 24 hours.

Parque-Museo La Venta

History The Olmec city of La Venta, built on an island where the Río Tonalá runs into the Gulf some 129 km west of Villahermosa, was originally constructed in about 1500 BC, and flourished in the last centuries before 600 BC. Danish archaeologist Frans Blom did the initial excavations in 1925, and work was continued by Tulane and the University of California. Matthew Sterling is credited with having discovered, in the early 1940s, five colossal Olmec heads sculpted from basalt. The largest weighs over 24 tons and stands more than two meters tall. It is a mystery how the Olmecs managed to move these massive basalt heads and other weighty religious statues some 100 km without the use of the wheel.

When gaseum excavation threatened the site of La Venta, the most significant finds – including three of the massive Olmec heads – were moved to Villahermosa and arranged as the Parque-Museo La Venta, a fascinating combination indoor-and-outdoor museum, nature preserve, sculpture park and tropical zoo.

Admission Parque-Museo La Venta (☎ 15-22-28) is open every day from 8 am to 5 pm (last tickets sold at 4 pm); the zoo is closed Monday 'to give the animals a rest.' Admission costs US$2.50. Indoor (air-con) and outdoor snack stands provide sustenance. Plan at least two hours for your visit, and preferably three.

Museum & Nature Trail As you enter the park, detour to the spider monkeys on the left, then follow the purple tiles set in the pavement and proceed through the zoo to the well-done **Museo de las Olmecas de La Venta** which explains Olmec history and culture using statuary, scale models, pottery and photos; signs are in Spanish and English.

On the other side of the museum is a giant ceiba, sacred tree of the Olmecs and Mayas, which marks the starting point of the nature trail *(recorrido)* through lush tropical verdure past the 33 Olmec sculpture exhibits. The trail is 1050 meters long, and takes at least an hour to walk if you spend a few minutes at each exhibit. Along the way, many trees bear signs giving their names and species. Keep an eye out for the cacao tree just past the crocodile pool on the way to Monument 19: see how the cacao beans (from which chocolate is made) grow right out of its trunk and branches. Everyone wants to be photographed with Monument 26, the finest of the great Olmec basalt heads.

Zoo Animals from Tabasco and nearby regions live in habitats grouped near the entrance to the park, and at several places along the nature trail. Colorful macaws and toucans, pumas and jaguars (including black jaguars), white-tailed deer, crocodiles,

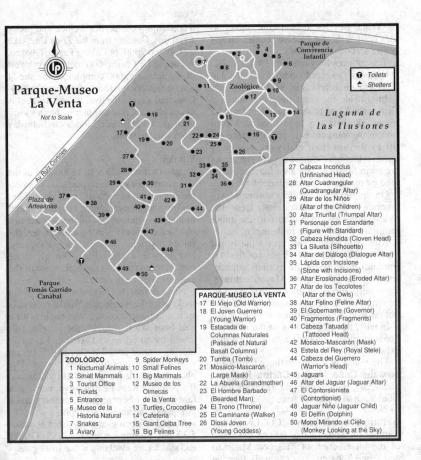

Parque-Museo La Venta

Not to Scale

Av Ruiz Cortines

Plaza de Artesanas

Parque Tomás Garrido Canabal

Parque de Convivencia Infantil

Zoológico

Laguna de las Ilusiones

- **T** Toilets
- **▲** Shelters

ZOOLÓGICO
1 Nocturnal Animals
2 Small Mammals
3 Tourist Office
4 Tickets
5 Entrance
6 Museo de la Historia Natural
7 Snakes
8 Aviary
9 Spider Monkeys
10 Small Felines
11 Big Mammals
12 Museo de los Olmecas de la Venta
13 Turtles, Crocodiles
14 Cafeteria
15 Giant Ceiba Tree
16 Big Felines

PARQUE-MUSEO LA VENTA
17 El Viejo (Old Warrior)
18 El Joven Guerrero (Young Warrior)
19 Estacada de Columnas Naturales (Palisade of Natural Basalt Columns)
20 Tumba (Tomb)
21 Mosaico-Mascarón (Large Mask)
22 La Abuela (Grandmother)
23 El Hombre Barbado (Bearded Man)
24 El Trono (Throne)
25 El Caminante (Walker)
26 Diosa Joven (Young Goddess)

27 Cabeza Inconclus (Unfinished Head)
28 Altar Cuadrangular (Quadrangular Altar)
29 Altar de los Niños (Altar of the Children)
30 Altar Triunfal (Triumpal Altar)
31 Personaje con Estandarte (Figure with Standard)
32 Cabeza Hendida (Cloven Head)
33 La Silueta (Silhouette)
34 Altar del Diálogo (Dialogue Altar)
35 Lápida con Incisione (Stone with Incisions)
36 Altar Erosionado (Eroded Altar)
37 Altar de los Tecolotes (Altar of the Owls)
38 Altar Felino (Feline Altar)
39 El Gobernante (Governor)
40 Fragmentos (Fragments)
41 Cabeza Tatuada (Tattooed Head)
42 Mosaico-Mascarón (Mask)
43 Estela del Rey (Royal Stele)
44 Cabeza del Guerrero (Warrior's Head)
45 Jaguars
46 Altar del Jaguar (Jaguar Altar)
47 El Contorsionista (Contortionist)
48 Jaguar Niño (Jaguar Child)
49 El Delfín (Dolphin)
50 Mono Mirando el Cielo (Monkey Looking at the Sky)

boa constrictors and peccaries show Tabasco's diversity of fauna. Several animals that pose little danger to humans, such as coati and agouti, roam freely throughout the jungle habitat.

Getting There & Away Parque-Museo La Venta is three km from the Zona Luz. Catch any bus or combi heading northwest along Paseo Tabasco, get out before the intersection with Avenida Ruiz Cortines, and walk northeast through the sprawling Parque Tomás Garrido Canabal, a larger park which actually surrounds Parque-Museo La Venta. A taxi from the Zona Luz costs US$1.50.

CICOM & Museo Regional de Antropología

The Center for Investigation of the Cultures of the Olmecs & Maya (CICOM) is a complex of buildings on the bank of the Río Grijalva, one km south of the Zona Luz. The centerpiece of the complex is the Museo Regional de Antropología Carlos Pellicer Cámara, dedicated to the scholar and poet responsible for the preservation of the Olmec artifacts in the Parque-Museo

La Venta. Besides the museum, the complex holds a theater, research center, an arts center and other buildings.

The anthropology museum (☎ 12-32-02) is open daily except Monday from 10 am to 3.30 pm; admission is US$1.75.

Just inside the front door is a massive Olmec head, one of those wonders from La Venta. The best way to proceed with your tour of the museum is to turn left, take the lift to the top floor and work your way down. Although the museum's explanations are all in Spanish, they are often accompanied by photos, maps and diagrams.

On the top floor, exhibits outline Mesoamerica's many civilizations, from the oldest stone-age inhabitants to the more familiar cultures of our millennium.

After you've brushed up on the broad picture, descend one flight to the 1st (middle) floor where the exhibits concentrate on the Olmec and Mayan cultures. Especially intriguing are the displays concerning Comalcalco, the ruined Mayan city not far from Villahermosa.

Finally, the ground floor of the museum holds various changing and traveling exhibits.

The house of Carlos Pellicer Cámara is now the **Casa Museo Carlos Pellicer**, Saenz 203, in the Zona Luz. It's open daily from 9 am to 6 pm, for free.

Getting There & Away CICOM is one km south of the Zona Luz, or 600 meters south of the intersection of Malecón Madrazo and Paseo Tabasco. You can walk there in 12 to 15 minutes, or catch any bus or colectivo ('CICOM' or 'No 1') traveling south along Madrazo; just say 'CICOM?' ('SEE-kom') before you get in.

Tabasco 2000 & Parque La Choca
The Tabasco 2000 complex is a testimonial to the prosperity the oil boom brought to Villahermosa, with its modern Palacio Municipal, chic boutiques in a gleaming mall, a convention center and pretty fountains. There are huge state and city government buildings, the high-rise Hotel Casa Real, chic boutiques in a gleaming mall,

a convention center, floral clock and pretty fountains. Coming from the Zona Luz, take a 'Tabasco 2000' bus along Paseo Tabasco.

Parque La Choca, 600 meters northwest of the Tabasco 2000 complex, is the site of a state fair, complete with livestock exhibitions and a crafts festival in late April. It is also a pleasant place to picnic, has a swimming pool and is open Monday to Saturday from 7 am to 9 pm.

Yumká
Yumká (☎/fax 13-23-90), 18 km east of the city (northeast of the airport), is Villahermosa's tribute to ecotourism, a one-sq-km nature interpretive center boasting spider monkeys, antelopes, wildebeests, zebras, giraffes, elephants, white rhinos, water buffaloes, ostriches, camels, caged jaguars, and maybe a crocodile. Though some metal fences partition the park, most of the animals are free to roam.

Named for the legendary dwarf who looks after the jungle, the Yumká reserve is split into three sections: you begin with a half-hour stroll through the jungle, followed by an Asian and African Savannah tour by tractor-pulled trolley and finish up with a boat trip on the large lagoon. The obligatory guided tour takes 1½ to 2 hours. It's hardly a Kenya game drive, but if you fancy a dose of open space, greenery and a glimpse of the animal kingdom, go.

Yumká is open every day from 9 am to 5.30 pm. Admission costs US$5. Drinks and snacks are available at the front gate.

Getting There & Away On weekends, shuttles go between the Parque-Museo La Venta car park and Yumká every thirty minutes from 10 am to 4 pm. On weekdays, there are supposedly combis to Yumká from Parque La Paz on Madero, yet we could find only taxis, charging US$13 for the ride.

Places to Stay – budget
Youth Hostel & Camping There is an *albergue de la juventud* (youth hostel) in the Ciudad Deportiva in the southern part of the city, but it is decrepit, inconvenient,

and not particularly economical. You're better off staying at a budget hotel in the Zona Luz.

It's sometimes possible to set up a tent or caravan/trailer at the Ciudad Deportiva. Ask at the field-house adjacent to the Olympic Stadium during the day. The Tamolte bus runs out there.

Zona Luz The Zona Luz has the best selection of cheap hotels. Keep street noise in mind when choosing accommodation.

On Lerdo de Tejada between Juárez and Madero are three small, plain, cheap hotels all in a row. *Hotel San Miguel* (☎ 12-15-00), Lerdo 315, is perhaps the best of the lot, renting its plain rooms with fan for US$7/9/11 a single/double/triple, or US$15 for a double with air-con. *Hotel Oviedo* (☎ 12-14-55), Lerdo 303, the worst of the lot, charges the same prices. *Hotel Tabasco* (☎ 12-00-77), Lerdo 317, is a step down from the San Miguel, but charges even less. *Hotel Oriente* (☎ 12-01-21), around the corner at Madero 425, is marginally better, though the front rooms are noisier.

Hotel San Francisco (☎ 12-31-98), at Madero 604 between Zaragoza and Carmen Sánchez, is considerably better for just a little more money. An elevator does away with the sweaty hike upstairs, where you'll find both rooms with ceiling fan and others with air-con for only about US$2 more.

Hotel Madero (☎ 12-05-16), Madero 301 between Reforma and 27 de Febrero, is in an old building with some character. The rooms are among the best at this price in the city, US$8/10/12 a single/double/triple with ceiling fan and private shower. Air-con costs US$2.50 more. *Hotel Palma de Mallorca* (☎ 12-01-44/5), Madero 516 between Lerdo de Tejada and Zaragoza, costs about the same, but is not as nice.

Even cheaper? Try the *Hotel San Rafael* (☎ 12-01-66), Constitución 240 off Lerdo de Tejada, where two people sharing a double bed in a room with shower and fan pay only US$7, though many rooms are noisy. *Hotel Santa Lucia* (☎ 12-24-99), on

Madero next door to (south of) the midrange Hotel Don Carlos, charges a bit more.

Posada Brondo (☎ 12-59-61), at Pino Suárez 411 between Carmen Sánchez and Mármol, has bright, clean double rooms with TV and shower for US$10. For US$14 you get a room with a small couch, refrigerator and perhaps a balcony (with street noise).

Near the ADO Bus Station *Hotel Palomino Palace* (☎ 12-84-31), Mina at Fuentes, is directly across from the main entrance to the ADO (1st-class) bus station. Its location lets it get away with charging US$16 for a basic room (with fan and shower). It's often noisy and you may be put on the 4th or 5th floor (stairs only). Even including taxi fare to and from the ADO bus station, Zona Luz hotels are cheaper.

Places to Stay – middle
Most middle-range hotels are also in the Zona Luz. The 64-room *Hotel Miraflores* (☎ 12-00-22, fax 12-04-86), Reforma 304 just west of Madero, is conveniently located, relatively quiet, and offers nicely appointed air-con rooms with bath for US$27/29/32 a single/double/triple.

Hotel Madan (☎ 12-16-50), Madero 408, has 20 modern air-con rooms with bath right in the center for US$23/single or double. *Hotel Pakaal* (☎ 12-45-01, fax 14-46-48), Lerdo de Tejada 106 at Constitución, is even newer, but charges less for air-con rooms with bath and TV. *Hotel Don Carlos* (☎ 12-24-99, fax 12-46-22), Madero 422 between Reforma and Lerdo, charges more for its older air-con rooms.

The *Howard Johnson Hotel* (☎/fax 14-46-45; hotel@Mail.Inforedmx.com.mx), Aldama 404 at Reforma, is new and has small but comfortable rooms right in the heart of the Zona Luz's pedestrian streets for US$34 single or double in one bed, US$38 in two beds.

Places to Stay – top end
As an oil boomtown, Villahermosa has no shortage of luxury lodgings. Three of the

best hotels are located near the intersection of Paseo Tabasco and Avenida Ruiz Cortines (highway 180), a pleasant 10-minute walk from Parque-Museo La Venta.

Poshest is the *Hyatt Regency Villahermosa* (☎ 15-12-34, fax 15-58-08, toll-free fax 800-23234), Calle Juárez, Colonia Lindavista, near the intersection of Avenida Ruiz Cortines and Paseo Tabasco, with all the expected luxury services, including swimming pool and tennis courts, for US$85, single or double. The food in the restaurants is particularly good here. Note that this Calle Juárez is a different street from the one in the Zona Luz, three km away.

Hotel Cencali (☎ 15-19-99, fax 15-66-00) is on Calle Juárez, Colonia Lindavista, off Paseo Tabasco next to the Hyatt. The hotel's setting, away from noisy streets amidst tropical greenery, is excellent, and its modern air-con rooms cost only US$60 single or double. There's even a swimming pool.

Calinda Viva Villahermosa (☎ 15-00-00, 800-90000, in the USA 800-221-2222; fax 15-30-73), next to the two aforementioned hotels, is a two-story motel-style white stucco building surrounding a large swimming pool. Comfortable rooms cost US$65, single or double.

Places to Eat
Budget Avenida Madero and the pedestrian streets of the Zona Luz (Lerdo, Juárez, Reforma, Aldama) have numerous snack and fast-food shops. Coffee drinkers beware! Most cheap places will serve you a cup of lukewarm water and a jar of instant coffee (sometimes decaf). If you need a quick early-morning shot of the good stuff, try KFC at Juárez 420, near Reforma.

El Torito Valenzuela, 27 de Febrero 202 at Madero, next to the Hotel Madero, is the most popular and convenient taquería, open from 8 am to midnight. Tacos made with various ingredients cost US$0.30 to US$0.60 apiece. More substantial platters range from US$3.75 to US$6, but the daily comida corrida costs less than US$3.50 for four courses.

The neighboring *Restaurant La Langosta*, despite its name, specializes in rotisserie chicken, charging US$2 for half a bird. Other dishes are good and cheap as well.

Douglas Pizza, Lerdo de Tejada 107, at Constitución opposite the Hotel Pakaal, offers a wide assortment of two-person pizzas for US$4 to US$5.50, or *grandes* for US$6 to US$7.50.

Near Parque Juárez, *Aquarius Centro Vegetariano*, Zaragoza 513 between Aldama and Juárez, is open from 9 am to 9 pm; closed Sunday. Try the granola, yogurt and honey (US$1), the soyaburger (US$1), or a special sandwich (containing alfalfa, tomatoes, onions, avocado, cheese and beans on grain bread (US$1.50). They also sell whole-wheat baked goods and vitamins.

Always packed in the late afternoon is *Rock & Roll Cocktelería* on Reforma just east of Juárez. Here you may sample a cocktel (fish, tomato sauce, lettuce, onions and a lemon squeeze) with crackers for US$4.

At the Parque Los Pajaritos (Park of the Little Birds), Zaragoza and 5 de Mayo, there are two antojito stands where tacos are US$0.20 and tortas US$0.60. The food is OK, but it's the natural shade, big trees and the enormous cage of colorful birds that makes this park a relaxing snack stop. Somehow the breeze finds its way here and the quiet roar of a water fountain drowns out most city sounds.

If you're eating or drinking on the run, try *Jugos* next to the Hotel San Miguel on Lerdo for licuados or heaping fruit platters (US$0.70), or the *Expendio de Pan El Trigo de Oro* on Mármol facing the Parque Juárez, for sweet rolls, bread and pastries. Another useful bakery is the *Panificadora Los Dos Naciones*, at the corner of Juárez and Zaragoza.

Middle There's not much in the Zona Luz. *Restaurant Madan*, on Madero just north of Reforma, is bright, modern and air-conditioned, with a genuine espresso machine hissing in one corner. But the regulars come to chat and sip coffee, not to eat, so the food suffers from lack of patronage.

Restaurant Hong Kong, 5 de Mayo 433, just off the Parque Los Pajaritos, is a Chinese restaurant on an upper floor with a six-page menu. A full meal, from won ton soup through steamed duck to fortune cookie, costs between US$6 and US$11.

You may want to coordinate a visit to the Museo Regional de Antropología with lunch at the *Restaurant Los Tulipanes* in the CICOM complex, open every day from noon to 8 pm. Seafood and steaks are their specialties and cost between US$6.50 and US$11. There is a pianist every afternoon and a Sunday buffet for US$12.

Entertainment

Teatro Esperanza Iris at the CICOM complex frequently hosts folkloric dance, theater, comedy and music performances. For information on cultural goings-on, call the Instituto de la Cultura (☎ 12-75-30) or ask at the tourist office or your hotel.

The *Centro Cultural Villahermosa*, on Madero between Mármol and Zaragoza, east of Parque Juárez, sponsors films, musical performances, and changing art and cultural exhibits. It's open from 10 am to 9 pm, for free.

Live music is featured at bars in the Calinda Viva, Hyatt and Cencali luxury hotels, open every evening except Sunday and Monday from about 10 pm. The *'Ku' Disco*, near the junction of Sandino and Ruiz Cortines, has a good reputation. Cover charge at any of these is around US$7.

Getting There & Away

Air There are nonstop or one-stop direct flights between Villahermosa and the following cities:

Chetumal – Aviacsa, daily except Saturday
Ciudad del Carmen – Aerocaribe, four days a week
Mérida – Aerocaribe, Aeroméxico, Aviacsa: daily
Mexico City – Aerocaribe, Aeroméxico, Aviacsa: daily

Oaxaca – Aerocaribe, three days a week (daily with one stop); Aeroméxico, daily
Palenque – Aerocaribe, three days weekly
Tuxtla Gutiérrez – Aerocaribe, twice daily; Aeroméxico, daily
Veracruz – Aeroméxico, daily

Aerocaribe (☎ 16-50-46, fax 16-50-47), operated by Mexicana, has its ticket office in the Centro Comercial Plaza de Atocha, Avenida Vía 3, No 20, Tabasco 2000.

Aeroméxico (☎ 12-15-28) is at Periférico Carlos Pellicer 511-2, in the CICOM complex.

Aviacsa (☎ 14-57-70, fax 12-57-74) is at Mina 1025D.

1st-Class Bus The 1st-class (ADO) bus station, Mina 297, has a luggage room (US$0.20 per hour) and a selection of little eating places.

The two main 1st-class companies are ADO and Cristóbal Colón; UNO, the deluxe line, has buses to central Mexico. Villahermosa is an important transportation point, but many buses serving it are de paso, so buy your onward ticket as far in advance as possible.

The listings below are mainly for daily 1st-class or deluxe buses that start their runs in Villahermosa; there are many more de paso buses. Prices are for 1st-class; the few deluxe ADO GL and Maya de Oro buses cost about 15% more:

Campeche – 450 km, six hours; 15 by ADO (US$14 to US$17)
Cancún – 915 km, 11 hours; three evening buses by ADO (US$28)
Catazajá – 116 km, two hours; ten ADO (US$4)
Chetumal – 575 km, eight hours; eight ADO (US$18)
Comalcalco – 55 km, one hour; three ADO (US$2.75), starting at 12.30 pm
Mérida – 700 km, nine hours; 10 ADO (US$20); one evening bus by UNO (US$32), several Autotransportes del Sur (ATS) for US$16
Mexico City (TAPO) – 820 km, 14 hours; 11 ADO (US$30); three evening UNO (US$43)
Oaxaca – 700 km, 13 hours; three ADO (US$23)
Palenque – 150 km, 2½ hours; 10 ADO (US$5); one Colón (US$5)
Playa del Carmen – 848 km, 14 hours; two nightly ADO (US$26)

San Cristóbal de Las Casas – 300 km, eight hours; one Colón (US$10); or go via Tuxtla Gutiérrez

Tapachula – 735 km, 13 hours; one Colón (US$24)

Teapa – 60 km, one hour; five Colón (US$2)

Tenosique – 290 km, four hours; nine ADO (US$6)

Tuxtla Gutiérrez – 294 km, six hours; 10 Colón (US$9), three Autotransportes Tuxtla Gutiérrez (ATG) for US$6.50

Veracruz – 480 km, eight hours; 10 ADO (US$17), one evening UNO (US$28)

2nd-Class Bus The 2nd-class Central de Autobuses de Tabasco bus station is on the north side of Avenida Ruiz Cortines (highway 180) just east of the intersection with Mina, about five blocks north of the 1st-class bus station. Use the pedestrian overpass just east of the station to cross the highway.

A number of smaller companies serve local destinations within the state of Tabasco, but most of the buses that you'll want depart from the 1st-class ADO bus station.

Car & Motorcycle Most car rental companies have desks at Rovirosa Airport. Here are the city offices:

Avis – at the airport (☎ 12-92-14)
Budget – Malecón Madrazo 761 (☎ /fax 14-37-90)
Dollar – Paseo Tabasco 600, next to the cathedral (☎ 13-68-35, fax 13-35-84)
Hertz – in the Hotel Casa Real, Paseo Tabasco Prolongación 1407, Tabasco 2000 (☎ 16-44-00)
National – in the Hyatt Regency Villahermosa, Reforma 304 (☎ 15-12-34)

Getting Around
To/From the Airport Transporte Terrestre minibuses charge US$3 per person for the trip into town; a taxi costs US$8. The trip takes about 20 minutes to the Zona Luz and 25 minutes to the top-end hotels. Buy your tickets from a counter in the terminal. From town to the airport a taxi is your only choice (US$8).

To/From the Bus Stations From the 1st-class ADO bus station, it's a 15- to 20-minute walk to the Zona Luz. Colectivo taxis depart from just outside the main entrance for the Zona Luz for US$0.40. Regular taxis charge US$1.30 to US$2 for a ride to any point in the city.

For buses and minibuses, go out the main (east) door of the ADO station, turn left, and walk two blocks north to the corner of Mina and Zozaya, where minibuses and combis stop en route to the Zona Luz and Madero, the main thoroughfare; look for 'Centro' on the windshield.

To walk to the Zona Luz, go out the side (south) door, turn left onto Lino Merino and walk five blocks to Parque de la Paz, then turn right on Madero.

Bus & Minibus A dozen municipal bus routes link the Zona Luz with outlying areas of the city; VW combi minibuses are useful as well. The fare is a few pesos (US$0.20). These vehicles travel tortuous, twisting routes which are summarized by cryptic words scrawled in their windshields: landmarks, major streets and distant *colonias* (neighborhoods). Here are some translations:

2000 – Tabasco 2000 government complex
Centro – Zona Luz
Chedraui – big department store near ADO bus station
CICOM – Anthropology Museum
Deportes – Ciudad Deportiva
Palacio Mpal – Palacio Municipal in Tabasco 2000 complex
Reloj – clock at 27 de Febrero and Calle 1, southwest of Paseo Tabasco
Tabasco – Paseo Tabasco
Terminal – ADO bus station
X 27 – via Calle 27 de Febrero

COMALCALCO RUINS
Comalcalco flourished during the Mayan Late Classic period between 500 and 900 AD, when the region's agricultural productivity prompted population expansion. The principal crop that drew Indian peasants from Palenque to this region was the cacao bean, which the Comalcalcans traded with

other Mayan settlements. It is still the chief cash crop.

Though it resembles Palenque in architecture and sculpture, Comalcalco is unique because it is built of bricks made from clay, sand and – ingeniously – oyster shells. Mortar was made with lime from the oyster shells.

As you enter the ruins, the substantial structure to your left may surprise you, as the pyramid's bricks look remarkably like the bricks used in construction today. Look on the right-hand side for remains of the stucco sculptures which once covered the pyramid. In the northern section of the Acropolis are some remains of fine stucco carvings.

Although the west side of the Acropolis once held a crypt comparable to that of Palenque's Pakal, the tomb was vandalized centuries ago and the sarcophagus stolen. Continue up the hill to the Palace, and from this elevation enjoy the breeze while you gaze down on unexcavated mounds.

Comalcalco is open daily from 9 am to 5 pm; admission costs US$1.75.

Getting There & Away
The 55-km journey from Villahermosa takes about an hour. ADO runs buses from Villahermosa daily at 12.30, 4.45 and 8.30 pm for US$2.75. Ask the driver to get you to *las ruinas*.

If you want to get an earlier start (as you should), walk along the colectivo taxi ranks on the north side of the ADO bus station. The Comalcalco colectivo leaves when all seats are filled, and charges US$4 for the ride. A private taxi trip to Comalcalco and back, with an hour's waiting time, costs US$24.

RÍO USUMACINTA
The mighty Río Usumacinta snakes its way northwest along the border between Mexico and Guatemala. A journey along the Río Usumacinta today reveals dense rainforest, thrilling bird and animal life, and ruined cities such as Bonampak and Yaxchilán (see the Chiapas section).

You can also use a tributary of the Usumacinta as your water-road into El Petén, Guatemala's vast jungle province, with its stupendous ruins at Tikal. There are three routes through the jungle between Mexico and Flores, the main jumping-off point for Tikal – see the later To El Petén section for details.

Chiapas

Mexico's southernmost state has enormous variety. At the center of Chiapas is San Cristóbal de Las Casas, a cool, tranquil hill-country colonial town surrounded by mysterious, very traditional Indian villages. Two hours' drive west – and nearly 1600 meters lower – the surprisingly modern state capital, Tuxtla Gutiérrez, has probably Mexico's best zoo, devoted entirely to Chiapas' varied fauna. Only a few km from Tuxtla is the 1000-meter-deep Cañón del Sumidero (Sumidero Canyon), through which you can take an awesome boat ride.

Three hours' drive southeast of San Cristóbal, near the border with Guatemala, with which Chiapas has always had much in common, is the lovely Montebello lakes region. Chiapas also has a steamy Pacific coast, where Puerto Arista, near Tonalá, is a very laid-back beach spot.

About four hours north of San Cristóbal are the Agua Azul waterfalls, among Mexico's most spectacular. A little farther on are the ruins of Palenque, one of the most beautiful of all ancient Mayan sites. To the east are the other fine Mayan sites of Yaxchilán and Bonampak, both deep in the Lacandón jungle, one of Mexico's largest areas of tropical rainforest. You can even go from Palenque to Flores and Tikal in Guatemala's El Petén.

History
Pre-Hispanic civilizations straddled the Chiapas-Guatemala border, and for most of the colonial era Chiapas was governed from Guatemala.

Pre-Hispanic Central and coastal Chiapas came under the influence of the Olmecs, who flourished on the Gulf Coast from about 1200 to 400 BC. Izapa, in the southern corner of Chiapas near Tapachula, was the center of a culture that peaked between 200 BC to 200 AD and is thought to be a link between the Olmec and the Maya.

During the Classic era (approximately 300-900 AD), coastal and central Chiapas were relative backwaters, but low-lying, jungle-covered eastern Chiapas gave rise to two important Mayan city-states, Palenque and Yaxchilán, which both flourished in the 7th and 8th centuries. Toniná and Chinkultic were lesser Mayan centers.

After the Classic Mayan collapse, highland Chiapas and Guatemala came to be divided among a number of often-warring kingdoms, many with cultures descended from the Maya but some also with rulers claiming central Mexican Toltec ancestry. Coastal Chiapas, a rich source of cacao, was conquered by the Aztecs at the end of the 15th century and became their most distant province, under the name Xoconochco (from which its present name, Soconusco, is derived).

Spanish Era Central Chiapas didn't come under effective Spanish control until the 1528 expedition of Diego de Mazariegos, who defeated the dominant, warlike Chiapa Indians, many of whom jumped to their death in the Cañón del Sumidero rather than be captured. Outlying areas of Chiapas were subdued in the 1530s and 1540s, though the Spaniards never gained control of the Lacandón forest, which remained a Mayan refuge.

Soconusco and inland Chiapas were administered separately, both from Guatemala, for most of the Spanish era, which meant that they lacked supervision for long periods and there was little check on colonists' excesses against the Indians. New diseases were brought by the Spaniards and one epidemic in 1544 killed about half the Indians of Chiapas.

The only light in the Indians' darkness was the work of some Spanish church figures, among them the Dominican monks. Pre-eminent was Bartolomé de Las Casas (1474-1566), appointed the first bishop of Chiapas in 1545. Las Casas had come to the Caribbean as an ordinary colonist, but in 1510 he entered the Dominican order and spent the rest of his life fighting for Indian rights in the new colonies. His achievements, including partly-observed laws reducing compulsory labor (1542) and banning Indian (but not black) slavery (1550), earned him the hostility of the colonists but the affection of the Indians.

19th & 20th Centuries In 1821, with the end of Spanish rule over Mexico and Central America, Mexico's new emperor, Agustín Iturbide, invited Spain's former Central American provinces (including Chiapas) to unite with Mexico. But Iturbide was soon overthrown, and when the Mexican congress was dissolved in 1823, the United Provinces of Central America declared their independence. A small military force under General Vicente Filísola, sent from Mexico City by Iturbide to preserve order in Guatemala City, returned home by way of Chiapas. Filísola used his power to bring Chiapas into the Mexican union, and this was approved by a referendum in 1824.

Permanent union with Mexico has not solved Chiapas' problems, however. Though quite rich in natural resources and economic potential, a succession of governors sent out from Mexico City, along with local landowners, have maintained an almost feudal control over the state – particularly in the highlands. Periodic uprisings and protests by the local indigenous peoples have borne witness to bad government, but the world took little notice until January 1, 1994, when a group calling itself the Ejército Zapatista de Liberación Nacional (EZLN, Zapatista National Liberation Army) briefly occupied San Cristóbal de Las Casas and nearby towns by military force. With world press attention riveted on Chiapas, the Mexican government was forced to take vigorous measures to restore order and to meet some of the rebels' demands. Whether the Zapatista rebellion is the one which will bring Chiapas better government and better times, or is just another in the state's long history of rebellions, remains to be seen.

Geography & Climate

Chiapas' 74,000 sq km fall into five distinct geographic bands, all roughly parallel to the Pacific Coast. The heaviest rainfall in all of them occurs from May to October.

The hot, fertile coastal plain, 15 to 35 km wide, called the Soconusco, receives quite heavy rainfall from June to October, especially in July and August.

Rising from the Soconusco is the Sierra Madre de Chiapas mountain range, mostly between 1000 and 2500 meters but higher in the south where the Tacaná volcano reaches 4092 meters. The Sierra Madre continues into Guatemala, throwing up several more volcanoes.

Inland from the Sierra Madre is the wide, warm, fairly dry Río Grijalva valley, also called the Central Depression of

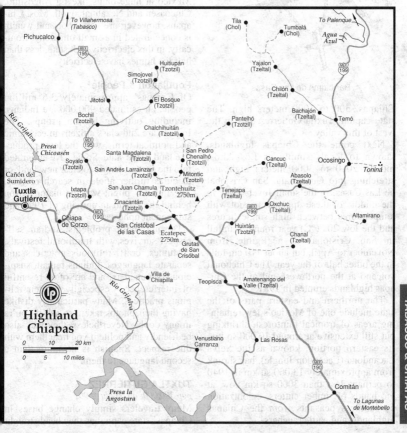

Highland Chiapas

Bartolomé de Las Casas

Chiapas, 500 to 1000 meters high. The state capital, Tuxtla Gutiérrez, lies in the west of this valley.

Next come the Chiapas highlands, known to locals simply as Los Altos, mostly 2000 to 3000 meters high and stretching into Guatemala. San Cristóbal de Las Casas, in the small Jovel valley in the middle of these uplands, is cool with temperatures between high single figures and the low 20s (°C) year round. Rainfall in San Cristóbal is negligible from November to April, but about 110 cm falls in the other half of the year. The Chichonal volcano at the northwest end of the Chiapas highlands erupted in 1981.

The northern and eastern parts of the state include one of Mexico's few remaining areas of tropical rainforest, shrinking but still extensive at around 10,000 sq km. Its eastern portion, known as the Selva Lacandona (Lacandón Jungle), has shrunk from approximately 13,000 sq km in 1940 to perhaps less than 3000 sq km now, at the hands of timber cutters, colonization by landless peasants from the Chiapas highlands, and cattle ranchers.

Economy

Chiapas has little industry but is second only to Veracruz among Mexican states in value of agricultural output, producing more coffee and bananas than any other state. The fertile Soconusco and adjacent slopes are the richest part of Chiapas and the source of much of the coffee and bananas. Tapachula is the commercial hub of the Soconusco.

Chiapas has other sources of wealth. Oil was found in northwest Chiapas in the 1970s. The Río Grijalva, which flows through the center of the state, generates more electricity than any other river in Mexico at huge dams like La Angostura, Chicoasén and Nezahualcóyotl. Most Chiapans, however, are very poor, and wealth is concentrated in a small oligarchy. Ironically, in this electricity-rich state, less than half the homes have electricity.

Population & People

Of Chiapas' approximately 3.6 million people, an estimated 900,000 are Indians, including outlying Mayan groups. The Indians are 2nd-class citizens in economic and political terms, with the least productive land in the state. Some have emigrated into the eastern jungle to clear new land, or to cities further afield in search of jobs. The Indians' plight was the major reason behind the Zapatista uprising of 1994 and subsequent upheavals.

Despite these problems, Indian self-respect survives with traditional festivals, costumes, craft, religious practices and separate languages. Indians remain suspicious of outsiders, and are often resentful of interference – especially in their religious practices. Many particularly dislike having their photos taken, so ask if you're in any doubt. Nevertheless, they may also be friendly and polite if you treat them with due respect. Spanish is no more than a second language to them.

TUXTLA GUTIÉRREZ
pop 300,000; alt 532m; ☎ 961

Many travelers simply change buses in Chiapas' state capital as they head straight

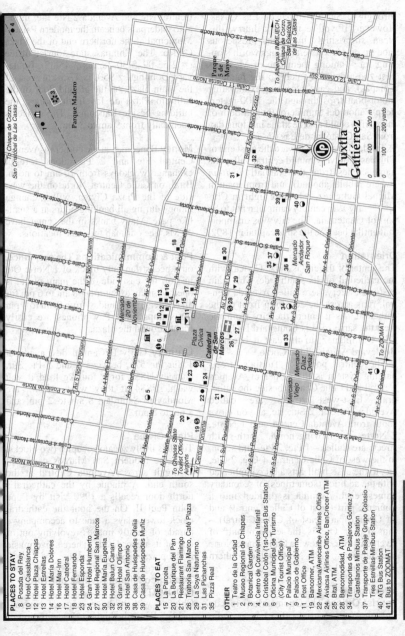

Tuxtla Gutiérrez

PLACES TO STAY
8   Posada del Rey
10 Hotel Casablanca
12 Hotel Plaza Chiapas
13 Hotel Estrellas
14 Hotel María Dolores
16 Hotel Mar-Inn
17 Hotel Catedral
18 Hotel Fernando
23 Hotel Esponda
24 Gran Hotel Humberto
27 Hotel Regional San Marcos
30 Hotel María Eugenia
32 Hotel Balún Canan
33 Gran Hotel Olimpo
36 Hotel San Antonio
39 Casa de Huéspedes Ofelia
38 Casa de Huéspedes Muñiz

PLACES TO EAT
15 La Parcela
20 La Boutique del Pan
21 Restaurant Flamingo
26 Trattoria San Marco, Café Plaza
29 La Soya Naturismo
31 Las Pichanchas
35 Pizza Real

OTHER
1   Teatro de la Ciudad
2   Museo Regional de Chiapas
3   Botanical Garden
4   Centro de Convivencia Infantil
5   Cristóbal Colón (1st-Class) Bus Station
6   Oficina Municipal de Turismo
     (City Tourist Office)
7   Palacio Municipal
9   Palacio de Gobierno
11 Post Office
19 Bancomer, ATM
22 Mexicana/Aerocaribe Airlines Office
24 Aviacsa Airlines Office, BanCrecer ATM
25 Bital, ATM
28 Bancomodidad, ATM
34 Transportes de Pasajeros Gómez y
     Castellanos Minibus Station
37 Transporte de Pasaje Grupo Colosio -
     Tres Estrellas Minibus Station
40 ATG Bus Station
41 Bus to ZOOMAT

TABASCO & CHIAPAS

through to San Cristóbal de Las Casas. However, if you're not in a hurry, this clean, surprisingly lively and prosperous modern city has several things worth stopping for – among them one of Mexico's best zoos (devoted solely to the fauna of Chiapas), and easy access to exhilarating motor-boat trips through the 1000-meter-deep Cañón del Sumidero, though both of these trips could also be made in a long day from San Cristóbal de Las Casas.

Tuxtla Gutiérrez is toward the west end of Chiapas' hot, very humid central valley. Its name comes from the Nahuatl *tuchtlan* (where rabbits abound), and from Joaquín Miguel Gutiérrez, a leading light in Chiapas' early 19th century campaign not to be part of Guatemala. The city was unimportant until it became the state capital in 1892.

Orientation

The center of the city is Plaza Cívica, with the cathedral on its south side. The main east-west artery, here called Avenida Central, runs across the zócalo in front of the cathedral. As it enters the city from the west the same road is Boulevard Dr Belisario Domínguez; to the east it becomes Boulevard Ángel Albino Corzo.

The central point for Tuxtla's street-naming system is the corner of Avenida Central and Calle Central beside the cathedral. East-west streets are called Avenidas – 1 Sur, 2 Sur, etc, as you move south from Avenida Central, and 1 Norte, 2 Norte, etc, moving north. North-south streets are Calles – 1 Pte, 2 Pte, and so on, to the west of Calle Central; 1 Ote, 2 Ote, etc, to the east. It all gets a bit complicated with the addition (sometimes) of secondary names: each Avenida is divided into a Poniente part (west of Calle Central) and an Oriente part (east of Calle Central) – thus 1 Sur Ote is the eastern half of Avenida 1 Sur. Likewise Calles have Norte and Sur parts: 1 Pte Norte is the northern half of Calle 1 Pte.

Information

Tourist Offices The Oficina Municipal de Turismo (city tourist office) is at Calle Central Nte and Avenida 2 Nte Pte, in the auto underpass beneath the modern Palacio Municipal at the northern end of the Plaza Cívica. The Chiapas state tourist office (☎ 2-55-09, 3-30-28, fax 2-45-35), Boulevard Domínguez 950, is 1.75 km west of the main plaza, on the ground floor of the Edificio Plaza de las Instituciones, the building beside Bancomer. The office is open daily from 9 am to 8 pm.

Money Bancomer, at the corner of Avenida Central Pte and 2 Pte, does foreign exchange weekdays from 10 am to noon. Bital, on Calle Central Norte on the west side of the Plaza Cívica, will exchange money during all banking hours at a snail-like pace. Many banks in the center have ATMs. See our map for some locations.

Post & Communications The post office, on a pedestrian-only block of 1 Norte Ote just off the east side of the main plaza, is open Monday to Saturday 8 am to 6 pm for all services, and Sunday from 9 am to 1 pm for stamps only. Pay phones are easily found around the plaza.

Laundry Gaily II Central de Lavado at 1 Sur Pte 575, between 4 and 5 Pte Sur, charges US$2 for a four-kg load if you wash, US$4 if they wash. Hours are Monday to Saturday, 8 am to 2 pm, and 4 pm to 8 pm.

Plaza Cívica

Tuxtla's lively zócalo occupies two blocks, with the modern San Marcos cathedral facing it across Avenida Central at the south end. A plaque by the cathedral's north door recalls a 1990 visit by Pope John Paul II. On the hour the cathedral clock tower plays a tune to accompany a parade of saintly images revolving out of one of its upper levels. There's live music in the plaza on Sunday nights.

Zoológico Miguel Alvárez del Toro (ZOOMAT)

Chiapas, with its huge range of environments, claims the highest concentration of

Indigenous Peoples of Chiapas

Nine languages are commonly spoken in Chiapas. Spanish is the language of commerce, education and government in the cities. In the countryside, the Mayan languages of Chol, Chuj, Lacandón, Mam, Tojolabal, Tzeltal, Tzotzil and Zoque can be heard, depending upon which area you visit. Although they're all derived from the ancient Mayan language, these dialects are mutually unintelligible, so local inhabitants use Spanish or the fairly widely understood Tzeltal to communicate with members of other linguistic groups.

The Indian people that travelers are most likely to come into contact with are the 310,000 or so Tzotzils around San Cristóbal de Las Casas. Tzotzil textiles are among the most varied, colorful and elaborately worked in Mexico. You may also encounter the Tzeltals, another traditional people, numbering about 334,000, who inhabit the region just east of San Cristóbal.

Other Chiapas Indians include about 150,000 Chols on the north side of the Chiapas highlands and the low-lying areas beyond, east and west of Palenque; an estimated 20,000 Mexican Mames near the Guatemalan border between Tapachula and Ciudad Cuauhtémoc, including some on the slopes of Tacaná (many more Mames – around 300,000 – are Guatemalans); and the Zoques, some 25,000 of whom used to inhabit western Chiapas, but were dispersed by the 1981 Chichonal eruption. Some have moved back to the area and there are hopes that the damage is not irreversible.

There are still a few hundred Lacandóns, the last true inheritors of ancient Mayan traditions, in the eastern Chiapas rainforest, with a language related to Yucatán Maya which they call 'Maya.' The past four decades have wrought more changes in Lacandón life than the previous four centuries: 100,000 land-hungry settlers have arrived in the forest, and missionaries have succeeded in converting some Lacandóns to Christianity. ■

---

animal species in North America – among them several varieties of big cats, 1200 types of butterfly and 641 bird species. You can see a good number of them in Tuxtla's excellent zoo, where they're kept in relatively spacious enclosures in a hillside woodland area just south of the city.

Among the creatures you'll see are an ocelot, jaguar, puma, tapir, red macaw, boa constrictor, a monkey-eating harpy eagle (aguila arpia) and some mean-looking scorpions and spiders.

The zoo is open daily except Monday from 8 am to 5.30 pm and entry is free. It has a bookstore. To get there take a 'Cerro Hueco' bus (US$0.20) from the corner of 1 Ote Sur and 7 Sur Ote. They leave about every 20 minutes and take 20 minutes to get there. A taxi – easy to pick up in either direction – will cost US$1.

Parque Madero Complex

This museum-theater-park area is 1.25 km northeast of the city center. If you don't want to walk, take a colectivo along Avenida Central to Parque 5 de Mayo on the corner of 11 Ote, then another north along 11 Ote.

The **Museo Regional de Chiapas** has fine archaeological and colonial history exhibits and costume and craft collections, all from Chiapas, plus often interesting temporary exhibitions. It's open daily, except Monday, from 9 am to 4 pm. Next door is the 1200-seat **Teatro de la Ciudad**. Nearby there's a shady **botanical garden**, with many species labeled – it's open daily except Monday from 9 am to 6 pm; entry is free.

Also in Parque Madero are a public swimming pool (US$0.30), and an open-air children's park, the **Centro de Convivencia Infantil**, which adults may enjoy too. It has models and exhibits on history and prehistory, a mini-railway, minigolf, pony and boat rides.

Places to Stay – budget

Camping *La Hacienda Hotel & Trailer Park* (☎ 2-79-86), Boulevard Domínguez

1197, on the west edge of town beside a roundabout, has a pool, cafeteria and all hookups for US$6 a double. The *Hotel Bonampak* (☎ 8-16-21, fax 8-16-22), on the highway at the western edge of town, has a trailer park as well.

Hotels Tap water in the cheaper hotels is 'al tiempo' (not heated) but, since this is a hot town, it is not cold either.

The *Villa Juvenil – Albergue INDEJECH* (☎ 3-34-05) at Boulevard Albino Corzo 1800, just under two km (17 blocks) east of the main plaza, is Tuxtla's youth hostel, though you need no hostel card to stay here. For a bed in a small, clean separate-sex dormitory you pay US$4 (plus US$2 deposit for sheets), which is not really any cheaper than you'd pay for a private room in a cheap hotel or pension. Breakfast costs US$1.75, lunch or dinner US$2. From the main plaza take a Ruta 1 colectivo east along Avenida Central to the statue of Albino Corzo beneath a yellow pedestrian overpass.

Closest to the ATG bus station is the *Casa de Huéspedes Muñiz* at 2 Sur Ote 733 (across from the north end of the bus yard). Rooms are bearable, bathrooms are shared; singles/doubles are US$5.50/8. On the

The Zapatistas

On January 1, 1994, an armed peasant group calling itself the Ejército Zapatista de Liberación Nacional (EZLN; Zapatista National Liberation Army) attacked and sacked government offices in San Cristóbal, Ocosingo and a few other towns. Troops evicted the Zapatistas within a few days, with about 150 people killed (fighting was particularly savage in Ocosingo). The rebels retreated to the Lacandón jungle, having succeeded in drawing the attention of the world's media to the situation in Chiapas. There they stayed at a remote forest base for over a year, encircled but not engaged by government forces, while a succession of attempts to negotiate came to nothing.

The EZLN's goal was to overturn the hold of Chiapas' wealthy minority on land, resources and power in the state, which had left many Indians and other peasants impoverished and lacking in education, health care and civil rights. It was often noted that the Mexican Revolution of 1910-20 never happened in Chiapas. Though the Zapatistas were militarily far outnumbered, they drew support and sympathy from many Mexicans, and their leader, a masked figure known only as Subcomandante Marcos, became something of a cult figure for many who resented the country's political stagnation.

The rebellion also provoked a social upheaval in Chiapas. In 1994, while Marcos waged a propaganda war from his jungle hideout, demanding widespread reforms of the same block, at 2 Sur Ote 643, the *Casa de Huéspedes Ofelia* (☎ 2-73-46) has no sign but '643' is visible above its doorway in the black stone façade with silver pointing. Rooms are fanless but clean and cost US$5.50/8 for a single/double. Note that Señora Ofelia goes to bed around 10 pm, so you must be in before then.

Closer to the Plaza Cívica and slightly more expensive are the many hotels on 2 Norte Ote, near the northeast corner of the main plaza. *Hotel Casablanca* (☎ 1-03-05), half a block off the plaza at 2 Norte Ote 251, is bare and basic, but exceptionally clean for the price. Rooms with fan and

shower are US$7.50/10/15 single/double/triple; with TV, air-con and twin beds, two pay US$18, or US$28 with two double beds.

The glitzy mirrored lobby of the *Hotel Plaza Chiapas* (☎ 3-83-65), 2 Norte Ote 229 at 2 Ote Norte, is deceptive as the rooms are no fancier and actually a bit cheaper than other hotels in this block.

Across the street, *Hotel María Dolores* and *Hotel Estrellas*, at 2 Ote Norte 304 and 322, have unremarkable rooms, but the *Hotel Fernando* (☎ 3-17-40), two blocks east at 2 Norte Ote 515, has spacious decent rooms with big windows for

---

Mexican political and judicial systems, peasants took over hundreds of farms and ranches around the state. The evicted landowners focused much of their wrath on Samuel Ruiz García, Bishop of San Cristóbal, who follows in the Bartolomé de Las Casas tradition of support for the poor, and has earned the nickname El Obispo Rojo (The Red Bishop) from his enemies.

In February 1995, in the wake of the peso crisis for which uncertainty caused by the Zapatistas had in part been blamed, the government sent in the army to 'arrest' Marcos and other EZLN leaders.

Marcos – whom the government had now 'unmasked' as a former university lecturer from Tampico called Rafael Guillén – and most of his followers escaped the army, fleeing into yet more remote regions, accompanied by thousands of peasants. The army however gained control of all significant towns in the region. A new standoff ensued. Marcos reemerged into contact with the world in October 1995, setting off new rounds of talks which led to an agreement on indigenous rights between the EZLN and government negotiators, reached at San Andrés Larraínzar in February 1996. The deal was to give limited autonomy to Mexico's Indian peoples by redrawing voting boundaries to create Indian majorities, which would allow them to choose their leaders by traditional methods. Indian languages were to receive official recognition and bilingual education was to become a right. The signing of a formal peace, and other favorite Zapatista topics such as reforms in agriculture, justice and democracy, were left for later talks. By mid-1997 however the government had not turned the accord into law. President Zedillo wanted changes in the law that had been drafted, saying he supported indigenous autonomy but not constitutional guarantees of territorial autonomy, which he said would raise questions about national sovereignty. The Zapatistas rejected his changes and once again there was stalemate.

There had been an amnesty, and few incidents, since 1995, but the rebels, hemmed into a remote pocket of territory near the Guatemalan border, remained surrounded (or at least confronted) by Mexican troops. They continued to wage a mainly propaganda war, using the Internet and staging a series of high-profile conventions, an 'intercontinental encounter against neoliberalism,' and they were visited by people such as film director Oliver Stone, French leftist intellectual Regis Debray, and Danielle Mitterrand, widow of the French president.

One success the Zapatistas could probably claim is a hand in the pressure for national democratic reform, which has taken significant steps forward during the Zedillo presidency. However, their action in disrupting the 1997 congressional elections in Chiapas, to prevent people from voting, suggested they thought reform had not gone nearly far enough. ∎

only US$8, about the best deal on the street.

The *Hotel San Antonio* (☎ 2-27-13) at 2 Sur Ote 540, is an amicable place, a modern building with a small courtyard and clean rooms for US$5.50/8. Surprisingly, the rambling *Gran Hotel Olimpo* (☎ 2-02-95) at 3 Sur Ote 215 charges the same rates for small, muggy rooms, but they're clean and with bath.

For the traveling foursome who enjoy space, check out the *Hotel Catedral* (☎ 3-08-24) at 1 Norte Ote 367 between 3 Ote Sur and the post office. They have enormous quadruples – two large rooms with a double bed in each are partitioned by a hallway. Bathroom, fans, hot water and cleanliness are included for US$9/10/13/16 single/double/triple/quad.

The *Hotel Mar-Inn* (☎ 2-10-54, fax 2-49-09), at 2 Norte Ote 347, has 60 decent rooms, with wide plant-lined walkways and a roof that seems to trap in humidity, but a double costs only US$12.

Places to Stay – middle

The bright, clean *Hotel Regional San Marcos* (☎ 3-19-40, fax 3-18-87), 2 Ote Sur 176 at Avenida 1 Sur, one block from the main plaza, is the best value in this group at US$18/22/25 for middle-sized rooms with tile baths.

Hotel Balun Canan (☎ 2-30-48, fax 2-82-49), Avenida Central Ote 944, has good rooms for good prices – US$18/23/25/28 single/double/triple/quad – but get one at the back, not on the noisy street.

The 51-room *Hotel Esponda* (☎ 2-00-80, fax 2-97-71), 1 Pte Nte 142, a block west of the main plaza, has middling fan-cooled rooms with big bathrooms for US$14/17/21. Its sister hotel around the corner, the aging but clean 105-room *Gran Hotel Humberto* (☎ 2-25-04, fax 2-97-71), Avenida Central Pte 180 at 1 Pte Nte, charges more – too much – for its rooms with air-con, TV, phone and vast showers.

The most elaborate and comfortable downtown hotel is the *Hotel María Eugenia* (☎ 3-37-67, fax 3-28-60), Avenida Central Ote 507 at 4 Ote, three blocks east of the main plaza. The hotel has a good restaurant and attractive air-con rooms with TV and bath for US$32/37/40/44.

Places to Stay – top end

Tuxtla's most luxurious hostelry is the five-star, 210-room *Camino Real Hotel Tuxtla* (☎ 7-77-77, fax 7-77-71), Boulevard Domínguez 1195, four km west of the main plaza. Very comfortable rooms cost US$65 to US$85, single or double. The town's other top end hotels – the *Arecas* (☎ 5-11-22, fax 5-11-21) and the *Flamboyant* (☎ 5-09-99, fax 5-00-87) are nearby.

Places to Eat

The cheapest quick bite you'll find is at one of the cookshops in the Mercado Andador San Roque, a pedestrian alley just west of the ATG bus station. The going rate is US$0.30 a taco, but the fumes may inspire vegetarian thinking. Other cheap eateries are clustered near the market at the corner of 3 Sur Pte and 1 Ote Sur.

The city's fanciest bakery is *La Boutique del Pan*, 2 Pte Nte 173, two blocks west and around a corner from the main plaza.

If you want a bag of granola, swing by *La Soya Naturismo* at 3 Ote Sur 132, just off Avenida Central. They sell vitamins, healthy snacks and health care products.

There's a row of popular restaurants on the east side of the cathedral along Callejon Ote Sur in the Edificio Plaza. Enjoy 20 varieties of pizza (US$2 to US$7) at the *Trattoria San Marco* (☎ 2-69-74), or sandwiches on baguettes (US$1.50 to US$3), or salads and *papas rellenas* (potatoes with filling), or savory *crepas*. It's open from 7 am to midnight. Next door, *Cafe Plaza* has a simpler menu, but good breakfasts (yogurt, fruit, cereal and coffee) for around US$2.

If you're looking for a big meal at a little price, try *Pizza Real*, 2 Sur Ote 557, across from the Hotel San Antonio, where a comida corrida costs only US$1.75. *La Parcela*, on 2 Ote Norte behind the Post Office, serves hotcakes, eggs or seven tacos for under US$2, or a four-course comida corrida for US$1.75.

Chiapas – Tuxtla Gutiérrez 803

It's worth making the short trek six blocks east of the zócalo to *Las Pichanchas* (☎ 2-53-51), Avenida Central Ote 857. This plant-filled courtyard restaurant has a long menu of local specialties. Try the chipilín, a cheese-and-cream soup on a maize base; and for dessert, chimbos, made from egg yolks and cinnamon. In between, have tamales, vegetarian salads (beets and carrots) or carne asada. A full dinner might cost US$5 to US$10. There's music and folk dancing nightly except Monday.

The *Restaurant Flamingo*, down a passage at 1 Pte Sur 17, is a quiet, slightly superior place with air-con. A full hotcakes breakfast is yours for US$2.50, an order of luncheon tacos or enchiladas for about the same. Meat and fish dishes cost US$3.50 to US$7.

As for a good comida corrida (US$5), one of the best for the money is served in the dining room of the *Hotel María Eugenia* (see Places to Stay).

Entertainment

There's live music in the Plaza Cívica on Sunday evenings.

Cinemas Gemelos, next to the Trattoria San Marco on the east side of the cathedral, has first-run movies.

If it's dancing you're after, Tuxtla's best disco is *Colors* in the Hotel Arecas at Boulevard Domínguez 1080, just west of the Hotel Flamboyant. Friday is the busiest night – entry costs about US$5 and drinks US$1. The mosque-like *Disco Sheik* (get it?) at the Hotel Flamboyant is reputed to be fun, as is the singles bar in the *Hotel Bonampak*. The teen and 20s crowd fills the *Tropicana Salon*, 2 Ote Sur south of Avenida Central Ote, more or less opposite the Hotel Regional San Marcos.

Getting There & Away

Air Tuxtla has two airports. Aeropuerto Llano San Juan, 28 km west of the city, handles the jets and bigger aircraft. Aeropuerto Francisco Sarabia (also called Aeropuerto Terán) (☎ 2-29-20), two km south of highway 190 from a signposted turning, about five km west of the main plaza, takes some of the smaller planes. In winter, Llano San Juan sometimes closes because of foggy conditions, with flights using Terán instead.

Aviacsa flies nonstop to Mexico City (US$110) and Tapachula. Aerocaribe/Mexicana flies nonstop to Mexico City, Oaxaca, Palenque and Villahermosa.

Aviacsa (☎ 2-80-81, 2-49-99, fax 3-50-29, 2-88-84) is at Avenida Central Pte 160, a block west of the Plaza Cívica beneath the Gran Hotel Humberto. Mexicana/Aerocaribe (☎ 2-20-53, fax 1-17-61), Avenida Central Pte 206, is a block west of the main plaza.

Bus The Cristóbal Colón terminal, at the corner of 2 Norte Pte and 2 Pte Norte, two blocks northwest of the main plaza, is the city's 1st-class bus station. ADO operates from here as well. The terminal has no baggage checkroom, but there are private ones nearby. Exit the terminal on to 2 Norte Pte and look right for the sign 'We Keep Your Objet' [sic].

Many 2nd-class bus companies have offices on 3 Sur Ote west of 7 Oriente Sur, chief of which is Autotransportes Tuxtla Gutiérrez (ATG) at 3 Sur Ote 712 just west of 7 Ote Sur; from the southeast corner of the main plaza, that's four blocks east, one south, one more east, and one south. The last block is pedestrian only, through a small market. Other companies on this street include Autotransportes Rápidos de San Cristóbal and Oriente de Chiapas.

Transporte de Pasaje Grupo Colosio-Tres Estrellas runs minibuses to San Cristóbal de Las Casas from its Tuxtla terminus at 2 Sur Ote, opposite the Hotel San Antonio.

Transportes de Pasajeros Gómez y Castellanos (abbreviated as Gómez below) runs minibuses from its Tuxtla terminal at 3 Ote Sur 380 to Cahuare and Chiapa de Corzo every 20 or 25 minutes from 5 am to 10 pm for US$0.50.

Cancún – 1100 km, 16 hours; one 1st-class by Cristóbal Colón (US$35)

Chiapa de Corzo – 12 km, 20 minutes; frequent Chiapa-Tuxtla and Gómez minibuses (US$0.50) stopping at Cahuare en route

TABASCO & CHIAPAS

Ciudad Cuauhtémoc (Guatemalan border) – 255 km, four hours; two buses by Cristóbal Colón (US$6), one by ATG (US$5.50)

Comitán – 168 km, 3½ hours; five Cristóbal Colón buses (US$5), hourly buses by ATG (US$2.75)

Mérida – 995 km, 14 hours; three by Cristóbal Colón (US$25)

Mexico City (TAPO) – 1000 km, 17 hours; three afternoon Cristóbal Colón buses (US$37), two evening ADO buses (US$37)

Oaxaca – 550 km, 10 hours; two Cristóbal Colón buses (US$16)

Palenque – 275 km, six hours; six Cristóbal Colón buses (US$9), several by ATG (US$7) and several by Oriente de Chiapas (US$6)

San Cristóbal de Las Casas – 85 km, two hours; hourly buses by Cristóbal Colón (US$2.50), ATG (US$1.50), and Oriente de Chiapas (US$1.50); frequent shared taxis (US$3.75 to US$4.50 per person) by Autotransportes Rápidos de San Cristóbal

Tapachula – 400 km, seven hours; five Cristóbal Colón buses (US$12), six ATG buses (US$10)

Villahermosa – 294 km, six hours; six Cristóbal Colón buses (US$8.75), three ATG buses for US$6.50

Car Rental companies include:

Budget – Boulevard Domínguez 2510 (☎ 5-06-72, fax 5-09-71)

Dollar – Avenida 5 Norte Pte 2260 (☎ 2-52-61, fax 2-89-32)

Gabriel Rent-a-Car – Boulevard Domínguez 780 (☎ 2-07-57, fax 2-24-51)

Getting Around

To/From the Airports Transporte Terrestre (☎ 2-15-54) runs taxis (US$10) and minibuses (US$5) from Aeropuerto Llano San Juan to the city center. Minibuses depart from the airline offices for the Aeropuerto Llano San Juan two hours before flight time. For Aeropuerto Terán, use a taxi (US$2).

Local Transport All colectivos (US$0.30) on Boulevard Domínguez-Avenida Central-Boulevard Albino Corzo run at least as far as the tourist offices and the Hotel Bonampak in the west, and 11 Ote in the east. Official stops are marked by the blue 'Ascenso/Decenso' signs but they'll some-

times stop for you elsewhere. Taxis are abundant and rides within the city usually cost around US$1.

TUXTLA GUTIÉRREZ TO VILLAHERMOSA

After traveling 30 km from Tuxtla Gutiérrez on highway 190 (beyond Chiapa de Corzo; see the following section), you come to the junction with highway 195. Go straight on to San Cristóbal de Las Casas (55 km), or turn left (north) to Villahermosa on highway 195 (264 km).

The village of **Bochil** (altitude 1272 meters, population 13,000), 94 km from Tuxtla Gutiérrez, is inhabited by Tzotzil Maya. It has two hotels: the tidy *Hotel Juárez* on the main road, and the more modest *Hotel María Isabel* set back a bit from the road. There's also a Pemex fuel station, the only one for many kilometers.

Five km before the Teapa turnoff, on the right-hand (east) side, is the **Balneario El Azufre** (Sulphur Baths); the origin of the name is immediately obvious once you descend into the valley to cross a stream and the stink of sulfur rises to meet you. The highway bypasses Teapa to the west, 60 km from Villahermosa.

CHIAPA DE CORZO

pop 50,000; alt 500m

Chiapa de Corzo, 12 km east of Tuxtla Gutiérrez, is a little colonial town on the Río Grijalva. It is the starting point for trips to the Cañón del Sumidero.

History

Chiapa de Corzo has been occupied almost continuously since about 1500 BC. It's in a crossroads area where Olmec, Monte Albán, Mayan and Teotihuacán influences were all felt, and its sequence of cultures makes it an invaluable site to archaeologists trying to trace pre-Hispanic cultural developments.

In the couple of centuries before the Spaniards arrived, the warlike Chiapa – the dominant people in western Chiapas at the time – had their capital, Nandalumí, a couple of km downstream from present-day Chiapa de Corzo, on the opposite bank of the river near the canyon mouth. When the Spaniards under Diego de Mazariegos arrived in 1528 to occupy the area, the Chiapa, realizing defeat was inevitable, apparently hurled themselves by the hundreds – men, women and children – to death in the canyon rather than surrender.

Mazariegos then founded a settlement which he called Chiapa de los Indios here, but a month later shifted his base to a second new settlement, Villa Real de Chiapa (now San Cristóbal de Las Casas), where the climate and the Indians were less hostile.

In 1863, Chiapa was the scene of the decisive battle for Chiapas between liberals supporting president Benito Juárez and pro-church conservatives supporting the French invasion of Mexico. The conservatives had taken San Cristóbal de Las Casas but were defeated by forces from Chiapa and Tuxtla Gutiérrez, organized by the liberal state governor Ángel Albino Corzo and led by Salvador Urbina. Corzo was born here and died here, and his name was added to the town's in 1888, making it Chiapa de Corzo.

Orientation & Information

Minibuses from Tuxtla stop along Calle 21 de Octubre on the north side of Chiapa's spacious plaza, named for Albino Corzo.

Chiapa's embarcadero for boat trips through the Cañón del Sumidero is two blocks south of the plaza along Calle 5 de Febrero, the street on the plaza's west side. Bital, at 21 de Octubre and 5 de Febrero, has an ATM.

Things to See

Impressive **arcades** frame three sides of the plaza, a statue of General Corzo rises on the west side, and an elaborate castle-like brick **fountain** said to resemble the Spanish crown stands in the southeastern corner. The town's ancient church, the **Templo de Santo Domingo de Guzmán**, one block south of the plaza, was built in 1572 by the Dominican order. Its adjoining convent is now the Centro Cultural, holding the **Museo de la Laca** (closed

Monday) which features the lacquered gourds that are the local artistic specialty.

Special Events

Some of Mexico's most colorful and curious fiestas, together known as the Fiesta de Enero, happen in Chiapa de Corzo every January.

From January 9, young men dressed as women and known as Las Chuntá dance through the streets nightly – a custom said to derive from a distribution of food to the poor by the maids of a rich woman of colonial times, Doña María de Angulo.

Processions and dances of the bizarre Parachicos – men with wooden masks and ixtle 'hair,' representing Spanish conquistadors – take place in daylight hours on January 15, 17 and 20.

There's a musical parade on January 19, then on the night of January 21 there's the Combate Naval – an hour-long mock battle on the river, enacted by people in canoes, with spectacular fireworks.

Places to Stay

There are plenty of places to stay in Tuxtla Gutiérrez – see the previous section for details.

Places to Eat

By the embarcadero there are eight restaurants with almost identical menus and deafening music. All are equally overpriced, though the view of the river is certainly nice.

Near the municipal market on Calle Coronel Urbina, across from the Museo de la Laca, are the standard ultra-cheap market eateries.

More appealing is the friendly *Restaurant Jardines de Chiapa*, in a garden off Madero, one block west of the plaza.

Ristorante Italiano, on the west side of the plaza, serves cheap pizza and more elaborate, moderately priced Italian-style dishes.

Restaurant Los Corredores, on Madero at 5 de Febrero, has good cheap breakfasts, and plenty of reasonably priced fish plates for lunch or dinner.

Getting There & Away

Transportes de Pasajeros Gómez y Castellanos runs minibuses from its Tuxtla terminal at 3 Ote Sur 380 to Cahuare and Chiapa de Corzo every 20 or 25 minutes from 5 am to 10 pm for US$0.50.

CAÑÓN DEL SUMIDERO

The Cañón del Sumidero (Sumidero Canyon) is a daunting fissure in the countryside a few km east of Tuxtla Gutiérrez, with the Río Grijalva (or Río Grande de Chiapas) flowing northward through it. In 1981 the Chicoasén Dam was completed at the canyon's northern end, and the canyon became a narrow, 35-km-long reservoir.

Fast passenger launches speed up the Cañón del Sumidero between sheer walls rising to heights of 1200 meters. To rent an entire boat (one to seven people) for the two to three-hour voyage to see Chiapas' most awesome scenery costs US$55 to US$60; in a colectivo boat with eight to 12 people, the fare is US$7 or US$8.

Highway 190, going east from Tuxtla Gutiérrez, crosses the canyon mouth at Cahuare, about 10 km from central Tuxtla. Just east of the bridge and about 500 meters off the highway is Cahuare embarcadero. You can board one of the fast, open-air fiberglass launches here, or at another embarcadero in Chiapa de Corzo, between roughly 8 am and 4 pm. If you don't have enough people to fill a boat, relax; even on weekdays you shouldn't have to wait more than a half-hour or so. Midday is the busiest. Bring a layer or two of warm clothing and something to shield you from the sun.

It's about 35 km from Chiapa de Corzo to the dam. Soon after you pass under highway 190 the sides of the canyon reach an amazing 1000 meters above you. Along the way you'll see a variety of bird life – herons, egrets, cormorants, vultures, kingfishers – plus probably a crocodile or two. The boat operators will point out a few odd formations of rock or vegetation, including one cliff face covered in thick, hanging moss resembling a gigantic Christmas tree.

At the end of the canyon, the fast, brown river opens out behind the dam. The water beneath you is 260 meters deep.

Cañón Lookouts

If you want to see Sumidero from the top, Transportes Cañón del Sumidero (☎ 961-2-06-49), at 1 Norte Ote 1121, eight blocks east of the Plaza Cívica in Tuxtla, will take up to six people in a minibus for a two-hour tour of miradores on the canyon edge for US$10.

SAN CRISTÓBAL DE LAS CASAS
pop 90,000; alt 2100m; ☎ *967*

The road from Tuxtla seems to climb endlessly into the clouds before descending into the small valley of Jovel where lies San Cristóbal (cris-TOH-bal), a beautiful colonial town in a temperate, pine-clad mountain valley.

In the early weeks of January 1994, world attention was riveted on San Cristóbal as the EZLN, representing Mexico's (especially Chiapas') oppressed Indians, seized the town by force of arms. Though the rebellion was suppressed by the Mexican army within a matter of weeks, it sent shock waves through the country, and attracted increased attention to the plight of Mexico's oppressed indigenous peoples. At the time of writing, an uneasy peace has returned to the region. The Mexican government has promised redress of grievances and the Zapatistas and the local Indians are waiting, restlessly, to see these promises fulfilled.

History

The Maya ancestors of the Tzotzils and Tzeltals moved to these highlands after the collapse of lowland Maya civilization. The Spaniards arrived in 1524, and Diego de Mazariegos founded San Cristóbal as their regional headquarters four years later.

For most of the colonial era San Cristóbal's Spanish citizens made their fortunes – usually from wheat – at the cost of the Indians, who lost their lands and suffered diseases, taxes and forced labor. Early on, the church gave the Indians some protection against colonist excesses. Dominican monks arrived in Chiapas in 1545 and made San Cristóbal their main base. Bartolomé de Las Casas (after whom the town is now named), was appointed bishop of Chiapas that year; he and Juan de Zapata y Sandoval, bishop from 1613 to 1621, are both fondly remembered.

San Cristóbal was the state capital from 1824, when Chiapas joined independent Mexico, to 1892, when Tuxtla Gutiérrez took over. The road from Tuxtla Gutiérrez wasn't paved until the 1940s.

Orientation

San Cristóbal is easy to walk around, with straight streets rambling up and down several gentle hills. The Pan-American Highway (highway 190) passes along the south side of town. Officially named Boulevard Juan Sabines Gutiérrez, it's called 'El Bulevar' by locals.

From the bus terminals on the highway, walk north (slightly uphill) to Plaza 31 de Marzo, which has the cathedral on its north side. From the Cristóbal Colón terminal it's six blocks up Insurgentes to this main plaza; from ATG it's five blocks up Allende, then two to the right (east) along Mazariegos.

Places to stay and eat are scattered all around town, but there are concentrations on Insurgentes, Real de Guadalupe and Madero.

Information

Tourist Offices San Cristóbal's helpful tourist office (☎ 8-04-14) is in the north end of the Palacio Municipal, on the west side of the main plaza. Hours are Monday to Saturday 8 am to 8 pm, Sunday 9 am to 2 pm. The notice board in front is plastered with flyers of the current happenings; there's a message board inside, and they will hold mail.

The Secretaría de Desarrollo Turístico (Sedetur; ☎ /fax 8-65-70) has an information office at Hidalgo 2 at Mazariegos, just north of La Galería.

There is also a little tourist information kiosk in front of the Cristóbal Colón bus station which is staffed – so it seems – on sunny days.

Money Banamex, on the main plaza, is the most efficient at currency exchange, but it's still quicker and easier to use bank ATMs (see map), or to change cash or traveler's checks at casas de cambio. Casa de Cambio Lacantún (☎ 8-25-87), Real de Guadalupe 12A, half a block from the main plaza, offers rates not much worse than at the banks. The minimum transaction is US$50 and hours are Monday to Saturday 8.30 am to 2 pm and 4 to 8 pm, Sunday 9 am to 1 pm. There are many others, so shop around. The Posada Margarita (see map) changes money at good rates without charging commission.

Post & Communications The post office (☎ 8-07-65) is on the corner of Cuauhtémoc and Crescencio Rosas, just one block west and one south of the main plaza.

TABASCO & CHIAPAS

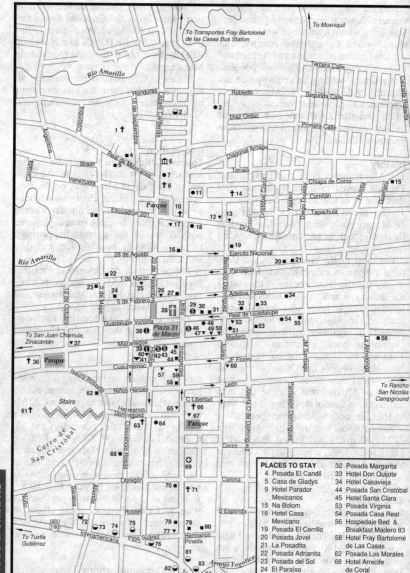

PLACES TO STAY

4 Posada El Candil	32 Posada Margarita
5 Casa de Gladys	33 Hotel Don Quijote
9 Hotel Parador	34 Hotel Casavieja
Mexicanos	44 Posada San Cristóbal
15 Na Bolom	45 Hotel Santa Clara
16 Hotel Casa	53 Posada Virginia
Mexicano	54 Posada Casa Real
19 Posada El Cerrillo	56 Hospedaje Bed &
20 Posada Jovel	Breakfast Madero 83
21 La Posadita	58 Hotel Fray Bartolomé
22 Posada Adrianita	de Las Casas
23 Posada del Sol	62 Posada Los Morales
24 El Paraíso	68 Hotel Arrecife
27 Hotel Posada Diego	de Coral
de Mazariegos	70 Posada Lucella
30 Hotel Real del Valle	78 Posada Insurgentes
31 Hotel San Martín	79 Hotel Capri
	80 Posada Vallarta

TABASCO & CHIAPAS

San Cristóbal de Las Casas

0   125   250 m

0   125   250 yards

Calzada Franz Blom

Isabel la Católica

Ejercito Nacional

Hermosal

Real de Guadalupe

✝ 35

To El Arcotete,
Tenejapa

Cerro de
Guadalupe

PLACES TO EAT
12 La Parrilla
13 La Casa del Pan
15 Na Bolom
17 Las Estrellas
25 Café-Restaurant
   El Teatro
26 Taquería La
   Salsa Verde
37 El Taquito
40 La Galería
47 Restaurant Fulano's
49 Restaurant París México
50 Restaurant Flamingo
52 Cafetería del Centro
57 Cafetería San Cristóbal
59 Restaurant Tuluc
61 Restaurant Normita
65 Madre Tierra
67 Los Merenderos
   Cookshops
77 Restaurant Tikal

OTHER
1 Church
2 Combis to San Juan
   Chamula, Tenejapa,
   Zinacantán
3 Mercado Municipal
6 Museo de Arqueología,
   Etnografía, Historia y Arte
8 Templo de Santo Domingo
10 Templo de La Caridad
11 J'pas Joloviletik
14 Church

15 Na Bolom
18 Librería Chilam Balam
28 Cathedral
29 Casa de Cambio Lacantún
35 Guadalupe Church
36 La Merced Church
38 Tourist Office, Palacio
   Municipal
39 SEDETUR Tourist Office
41 Post Office
42 Banca Serfin
43 Bancomer, ATM
46 Banamex, ATM
48 Aviacsa Airline Office
51 Lavandería Orve
55 Centro Cultural El Puente
61 Church of San Cristóbal
63 Templo del Carmen
64 Casa de Cultura/Bellas Artes
66 Templo de San Francisco
69 Hospital
71 Santa Lucía Church
72 ATG Bus Station
73 Colectivos (Shared Taxis)
   to Tuxtla Gutiérrez
74 Minibuses to Ocosingo
75 Transportes Lacandonia
   Bus Station
76 Autotransportes Andres
   Caso Bus Station
81 Cristóbal Colón Bus Station
82 Rudolfo Figueroa Bus Station
83 Autotransportes Rápidos de
   San Cristóbal Bus Station
84 Sociedad Cooperativa Altos
   de Chiapas Minibus Station

It's open weekdays from 8 am to 7 pm, Saturday, Sunday and holidays 9 am to 1 pm.

There are pay phones on the west side of the zócalo and in the Cristóbal Colón and ATG bus stations.

Bookstores & Libraries La Pared, located at Avenida Miguel Hidalgo 2, has used books in English and Spanish.

Librería Chilam Balam has a good selection of history and anthropology books, and some novels and guidebooks in English, German and French. Their larger shop is on Utrilla 33 at Dr Navarro (diagonally opposite La Caridad Church); a smaller shop is at Insurgentes 18 at León. Libros Soluna, at Real de Guadalupe 13B less than a block east of the main plaza, has a decent English section.

The 14,000 books at Na Bolom comprise one of the world's biggest collections on the Maya and their lands. Those interested can use the library Tuesday to Saturday from 9 am to 1 pm.

Laundry Lavandería Orve (☎ 8-18-02), Belisario Domínguez 5 at Real de Guadalupe, run by the Posada Margarita, offers same-day service from 8 am to 8 pm.

Lavasor has a drop-off/pick-up shop at Real de Guadalupe 26, between Utrilla and Belisario Domínguez. Same-day service costs US$3 for four kg; hours are 8 am to 10 pm daily.

Plaza 31 de Marzo
The main plaza was the old Spanish center of town, used for markets until early this century. Today it is a fine place to sit, watch the town life happen around you, or enjoy a meal in the central kiosk.

The cathedral, on the north side, was begun in 1528 but completely rebuilt in 1693. Its gold-leaf interior has a baroque pulpit and altarpiece.

The Hotel Santa Clara, on the southeast corner, was the house of Diego de Mazariegos, the Spanish conqueror of Chiapas. It's one of the few secular examples of the plateresque style in Mexico.

MARIO GALLOTTA
Templo de Santo Domingo

Templo de Santo Domingo

North of the center, opposite the corner of Cárdenas and Real de Mexicanos, Santo Domingo is the most beautiful of San Cristóbal's many churches – especially when its pink façade is floodlit at night. The church and the adjoining monastery were built from 1547 to 1560. The church's baroque façade was added in the 17th century. There's plenty of gold inside, especially on the ornate pulpit. Chamulan women conduct a daily craft market around the Templo de Santo Domingo and Templo de La Caridad (built in 1712) immediately to its south.

Weavers' Cooperatives

Each Chiapas highland village has its own distinctive woven or embroidered dress. Most of the seemingly abstract designs are in fact stylized snakes, frogs, butterflies, dog pawprints, birds, people, saints, etc.

Cooperatives of village weavers were founded to foster this important folk art for income and to preserve Indian identity and tradition. The weavers aim to revive forgotten techniques and designs, and to continue to develop dyes from plants, soil, tree bark and other natural sources.

Sna Jolobil (a Tzotzil name meaning Weavers' House; ☎/fax 8-26-46), at Cárdenas 42 by the Santo Domingo church, represents 800 women. In its showrooms, open daily except Sunday from 9 am to 2 pm and 4 to 6 pm, you can see huipiles, shawls, sashes, ponchos, hats and other craft items. Prices range from a few dollars for smaller items up to US$500 for the finest huipiles and ceremonial garments.

J'pas Joloviletik, nearby at Utrilla 43 just past La Caridad church, represents about 850 weavers from 20 Tzotzil and Tzeltal villages. It's open Monday to Saturday 9 am to 1 pm and 4 to 7 pm, and Sunday 9 am to 1 pm.

Museo de Arqueología, Etnografía, Historia y Arte

This museum, located next to the Santo Domingo church, deals mainly with the history of San Cristóbal. It's open from 10 am to 5 pm (closed Monday) for US$2. All explanatory material is in Spanish.

Templo del Carmen & Bellas Artes

El Carmen church stands on the corner of Hidalgo and Hermanos Domínguez. Formerly part of a nunnery (built in 1597), it has a distinctive tower (built in 1680) resting on an arch, erected to replace one destroyed by floods 28 years earlier. Next door is the Casa de Cultura, containing an art gallery, library and the Bellas Artes auditorium.

Centro Cultural El Puente

'El Puente' (☎/fax 8-22-50), at Real de Guadalupe 55, 2½ blocks east of the main plaza, is an information and cultural center buzzing with locals, artists and interested travelers, open every day but Sunday from 8 am to 10 pm. El Puente has a gallery with changing exhibitions and a media room busy nightly with films, lectures, music or theater (English or Spanish). The Centro's Café El Puente serves food, including vegetarian.

Mercado Municipal

The flavor of outlying Indian villages can be sampled at San Cristóbal's busy municipal market, between Utrilla and Belisario Domínguez, eight blocks north of the main plaza, open daily except Sunday till late afternoon. Many of the traders are Indian villagers for whom buying and selling is the main reason to come to town.

The Indians generally keep their distance from the mestizo population, the result of centuries of exploitation. But they are friendly and good-humored (and can drive a hard bargain!).

San Cristóbal & Guadalupe Hills

The most prominent of the several small hills over which San Cristóbal undulates are the Cerro (Hill) de San Cristóbal in the southwest quarter of town, reached by steps up from Allende, and the Cerro de Guadalupe, seven blocks east of the main plaza along Real de Guadalupe. Both are crowned by churches and afford good views, but there have been reports of attempted rapes here too.

Grutas de San Cristóbal

The grutas (caves) are in fact a single long cavern nine km southeast of San Cristóbal. The entrance is among lovely pine woods a five-minute walk south of the Pan-American Highway, in the midst of a huge army encampment set up since the EZLN rebellion in 1994.

The first 350 meters or so of the cave have a wooden walkway and are lit. You can enter for US$0.50, daily from 7 am to 5 pm. To get there take a minibus east along the Pan-American Highway and ask for 'Las Grutas' (US$0.30). Camping is allowed, and there are horses for hire.

Reserva Ecológica Huitepec & Pro-Natura

The Huitepec Ecological Reserve is a two-km interpretive nature trail on the slopes of Cerro Huitepec, about 3.5 km out of San Cristóbal on the Chamula road. The ascent, rising through various vegetation types to rare cloud forests, takes about 45 minutes.

It's open daily except Monday from 9 am to 4 pm.

Pro-Natura, an independent organization staffed by volunteers and funded by donations, offers tours for US$2. Its office is at María Adelina Flores 2 (☎ 8-40-69).

Horseback Riding

Various travel agents and hotels can arrange rides to surrounding villages or the caves. Try to find out about the animals

---

Traditional Highland Dress

Each Chiapas highland village has its own distinctive dress. In San Juan Chamula, men traditionally wear loose homespun tunics of white wool; cargo-holders – those charged with responsibility for important religious and ceremonial duties – wear black ones. The men of Zinacantan wear very distinctive red-and-white striped tunics (which appear pink), and flat, round, ribboned palm hats. Unmarried men's hats have longer, wider ribbons.

Women's costumes are more elaborately decorated than men's. Most of the seemingly abstract designs on these costumes are in fact stylized snakes, frogs, butterflies, birds, saints and other natural and supernatural beings. Some motifs have religious-magical functions: scorpions, for example, can be a symbolic request for rain, since scorpions are believed to attract lightning.

Some designs have pre-Hispanic origins: for instance, the rhombus shape on some huipiles from San Andrés Larraínzar is also found on the garments shown on Lintel 24 at Yaxchilán. The shape represents the old Maya universe, in which the earth was cube-shaped and the sky had four corners.

Other costumes are of more recent origin: the typical men's ensemble from Chamula – long-sleeved shirt, wool tunic, belt and long trousers – stems from the Spaniards, who objected to the relative nudity of the loincloth and cloak that Chamulan men used to wear.

The sacredness of traditional costume is shown by the dressing of saints' images in old and revered garments at festival times. ■

before you commit yourself: are they horses or just ponies, fiery or docile, fast or slow? Will there be a guide?

Posada Margarita, Posada Jovel and Posada Del Sol charge about US$10 for a three- to five-hour ride. José Hernández (☎ 8-10-65), at Elías Calles 10 (a dirt road two blocks northwest of Na Bolom), off Huixtla just north of Chiapa de Corzo, hires horses cheaper at US$7 a ride. The Rancho San Nicolás campground (☎ 8-18-73) also provides mounts.

Language Courses

Centro Bilingüe (☎ 8-41-57, fax 8-37-23, fax in USA 800-303-4983), a language school, has two offices. Spanish classes are given in Centro Cultural El Puente (☎/fax 8-22-50) at Real de Guadalupe 55, and English is taught at Insurgentes 57 (☎ 8-41-57).

One-on-one lessons are US$6 per hour, three-on-one lessons are US$4 per person per hour.

Homestay programs offer 15 hours of instruction (three hours per day, five days a week), at least three hours of homework every day, homestay for a full week (seven days, double occupancy) and include three meals a day (every day except Sunday). A homestay with one-on-one instruction is US$150, three-on-one is US$125 per week. If you study for more than one week, it's a bit cheaper. For US$100, you can sign up for 'lunch/breakfast with Spanish,' a five-day program which includes a meal and three hours of lessons each day.

Organized Tours

For many years, Señora Mercedes Hernández Gómez, a fluent English speaker who grew up in San Juan Chamula, has been leading fascinating tours to the villages. You can find Mercedes at 9 am near the kiosk in the main plaza, twirling a colorful umbrella. Tours are US$8 and generally last 5 to 6 hours, traveling by minibus and on foot.

Readers of this travel guide have also enjoyed the tours led by Alex and Raúl (☎ 8-37-41), whom you can find in front of

the cathedral on the main plaza daily at 9.30 am. They offer similar tours at similar prices, and also give city tours.

Travel agents in San Cristóbal offer day trips further afield for those who are short of time. Tours and average prices (per person, minimum four people) are: Indian Villages (five hours, US$12); Cañón del Sumidero (eight hours, US$22); Lagunas de Montebello, Chinkultic ruins, Amatenango del Valle (nine hours, US$20); Palenque ruins, Agua Azul, Misol-Ha (13 hours, US$26); and Toniná (six hours, US$18).

Travel agencies include:

Viajes Kanan-Ku – specializes in ecological study tours to organic farms, herbolaria, butterfly breeding areas and the jungle. Real de Guadalupe 55, 2½ blocks east of the main plaza in Centro Cultural El Puente (☎/fax 8-41-57)

Viajes Chinkultic – can arrange almost any budget trip on horseback, or by car, bus or plane. Real de Guadalupe 34 in the Posada Margarita (☎/fax 8-09-57)

Viajes Pakal – Cuauhtémoc 6 at Hidalgo (☎/fax 8-28-19)

Special Events

Semana Santa (Holy Week, before Easter), with processions on Good Friday and the burning of 'Judas' figures on Holy Saturday, is followed by the Feria de la Primavera y de la Paz (Spring & Peace Fair) with more parades, bullfights and so on. Sometimes the celebrations for the anniversary of the town's founding (March 31) fall in the midst of it all too!

Also look out for events marking the feast of San Cristóbal (July 17 to 25), the anniversary of Chiapas joining Mexico in 1824 (September 14), National Independence Day (September 15 and 16), the Day of the Dead (November 2), the Feast of the Virgin of Guadalupe (December 10 to 12) and preparations for Christmas (December 16 to 24).

Places to Stay – budget

Camping The *Rancho San Nicolás* camping and trailer park (☎ 8-00-57) is two km east of the main plaza: go east along León for a km after it becomes a dirt track. It's a friendly place with a grassy lawn, apple trees, horses grazing and hot showers. Cost is US$2 per person in a tent, US$5 in a cabin, US$4 to US$6 per person in a camper or trailer with full hookups.

Hotels & Casas de Huéspedes Several cheap hostelries are on and just off Insurgentes, the street leading from the Cristóbal Colón bus station to the main plaza.

Casas de huéspedes (guest houses) don't post their prices in this town. Don't be afraid to haggle a bit.

Na Bolom

A visit to Na Bolom, a house at Guerrero 33 on the corner of Chiapa de Corzo, six blocks north of Real de Guadalupe, is one of San Cristóbal's most fascinating experiences. For many years it was the home of Danish archaeologist Frans Blom, who died in 1963, and his wife, the Swiss anthropologist and photographer Gertrude (Trudy) Duby-Blom, who died in 1993 at age 92.

The couple shared a passion for Chiapas and particularly for its Indians. While Frans explored, surveyed and dug at ancient Mayan sites including Toniná, Chinkultic and Moxviquil, Trudy devoted much of her life to studying the tiny Lacandón Indian population of eastern Chiapas. She worked for the Lacandóns' well-being, but also attracted criticism for shielding the Lacandóns too zealously from change.

The house, whose name is Tzotzil for Jaguar House as well as a play on the owners' name, is full of photographs, archaeological and anthropological relics and books – a treasure-trove for anyone with an interest in Chiapas. Visits are by informal guided tour, conducted in Spanish at 11.30 am, and in Spanish and English at 4.30 pm, for US$2.50 (no tours on Monday). Following the tour, a film is shown on the Lacandón and Trudy Blom's work.

Na Bolom also offers meals and lodging (see Places to Stay). ∎

Insurgentes A block and a half up from the Cristóbal Colón bus station, *Hotel Capri* (☎ 8-30-13, fax 8-00-15), Insurgentes 54, has modern, clean, and fairly quiet singles/doubles round a narrow flowery courtyard for US$11/13. Across the street, *Posada Insurgentes* (☎ 8-24-35), at No 73, is even newer, at similar prices.

Posada Lucella (☎ 8-09-56), Insurgentes 55, directly across from the Santa Lucia church, has OK doubles for US$9, US$12 with private bath.

Posada Vallarta (☎ 8-04-65), half a block east off Insurgentes at Hermanos Pineda 10 (the first street to the right as you go up Insurgentes) has clean and modernish rooms with private baths and balconies for US$11/12/14 -- good value.

Real de Guadalupe *Posada Margarita* (☎ 8-09-57), Real de Guadalupe 34, 1½ blocks east of the main plaza, has long been a popular budget travelers' halt and a good meeting place. A *dormitorio* bed is (US$5), a clean bathless double US$10; there are triples and quads as well, though all rooms tend to be small and airless. The Margarita has a good cheap restaurant, a travel agency, laundry, bike rentals, and will hold mail for you.

Posada Virginia (☎ 8-11-16), Cristóbal Colón 1, between Real de Guadalupe and Madero, is tidy, with a friendly, efficient señora and even a few parking spaces. Double rooms with shower cost US$13.

On Real de Guadalupe, next to Centro Cultural El Puente, is *Posada Casa Real*. It is humble, clean and cheap at US$4 a bed.

Hotel Real del Valle (☎ 8-06-80, fax 8-39-55), Real de Guadalupe 14, is good, clean and central, with a nice courtyard and 36 rooms costing US$12/15/19. The neighboring *Hotel San Martín* (☎/fax 8-05-33), Real de Guadalupe 16, is similarly priced and pleasant.

Elsewhere Undoubtedly the best deal in town is at *Hospedaje Bed and Breakfast Madero 83* (☎ 8-04-40), Madero 83, five blocks east of the main plaza. Clean dorm beds (US$3.25), singles (US$4.50), and rooms with private baths (US$7.50 to US$11) all include breakfast of egg, beans, tortillas and coffee. For a few pesos you can use the kitchen. This place fills up.

The tidy *Posada Jovel* (☎ 8-17-34) at Paniagua 28 between Cristóbal Colón and Santiago, attracts backpackers with its friendly owners, good atmosphere and good-value rates of US$6.75/10 single/double with shared bath, US$8.50/12.50 with private bath. They rent bikes, too. If it's full, try *La Posadita* right next door at Paniagua 30.

Posada del Sol (☎ 8-04-95), Primero (1) de Marzo 22 at 5 de Mayo, three blocks west of the main plaza, has caged birds, '70s decor and great prices: US$8/10/14/15 with shared bathroom, slightly more with private bath.

For a hint of the '60s, try the easygoing *Casa de Gladys* at Real de Mexicanos 16, a colonial house with a purplish courtyard, hanging hammocks and peace posters. Waterless doubles cost US$10; coffee and purified water are free. The nearby *Posada El Candil* (☎ 8-27-55), Real de Mexicanos 7, has starkly bright, clean, simple waterless rooms for US$7/11.

Posada El Cerrillo, Belisario Domínguez 27, just north of Ejército Nacional, has a beautiful flowered courtyard and big guest rooms for US$15 double with shower. *Posada Adrianita* (☎ 8-12-83), Primero de Marzo 29 at 5 de Mayo, is similar.

Places to Stay – middle

The nice *Posada San Cristóbal* (☎ 8-68-81) at Insurgentes 3, near the main plaza, has airy, colorful rooms, set around a pleasant courtyard for US$15/19/23 single/double/triple.

The colonial *Hotel Fray Bartolomé de Las Casas* (☎ 8-09-32), Niños Héroes 2 at Insurgentes, two blocks south of the main plaza, is clean and has a variety of rooms with character for US$15/18/22. You can stay at the research institute of *Na Bolom* (☎ 8-14-18, fax 8-55-86), Guerrero 33, for US$27/30/35, with reductions when it's not busy. See the sidebar for more on Na Bolom.

Back in the 16th century, the *Hotel Santa Clara* (☎ 8-08-71, fax 8-10-41), at Avenida Insurgentes 1 (the southeast corner of the main plaza), was the home to Diego de Mazariegos, the Spanish conqueror of Chiapas. Amenities here include sizable, comfortable rooms, a pleasant courtyard that is brightened by caged red macaws, a restaurant, a bar/lounge, and a heated pool. Singles/doubles/triples/quads are US$20/22/26/30.

El Paraíso (☎ 8-00-85, fax 8-51-68), 5 de Febrero 19, three blocks west of the main plaza, has a cheery flower-filled courtyard with leather sunchairs and smiling señoras who lend it an amiable atmosphere. The comfortable rooms cost US$25/29/34. The restaurant serves Swiss and Mexican dishes.

Hotel Parador Mexicanos (☎ 8-00-55) at 5 de Mayo 38, just south of Escuadrón 201, has big comfortable rooms flanking its garden-cum-drive, at the end of which is a tennis court. A lobby lounge, restaurant and pleasant verandas make it fair value at US$15/23/28.

Posada Los Morales (☎ 8-14-72) at Allende 17 has a dozen bare white-washed two-person bungalows in a maze of gardens on a slope five blocks southwest of the plaza. Each has a fireplace, bathroom and gas stove, and rents for US$20. Some are cleaner and brighter than others, so check out a few.

Hotel Don Quijote (☎ 8-09-20, fax 8-03-46), Colón 7, between Real de Guadalupe and Adelina Flores, is among the brightest and newest in the area. Colorful maps and traditional costumes embellish the walls; rooms (US$15/18/22/25) and the upstairs restaurant are pleasing, and it has a laundry, travel service and free morning coffee.

Hotel Arrecife de Coral (☎ 8-21-25, fax 8-20-98), Crescencio Rosas 29, between Hermanos Domínguez and Obregón, reminds one of an American motel with its several buildings set amid grassy lawns. The 50 quiet, modern rooms on two floors have baths, TVs and phones, and offer great value at US$23/28/32/36.

Hotel Casavieja (☎ 8-03-85, fax 8-52-23), Adelina Flores 27, between Colón and Dujelay, is new but colonial in style, attractive and comfortable, with very friendly management. Rooms are arranged around grassy, flowered courtyards; there's a tidy restaurant. Rates are US$30/38/42.

Places to Stay – top end
Hotel Casa Mexicano (☎ 8-06-98, fax 8-26-27), 28 de Agosto at Utrilla, with its sky-lit garden, fountains, plants, and traditional art and sculptures, exudes colonial charm. Rooms are agreeable, have views of the courtyard and cost US$38/42/47 a single/double/triple; suites with whirlpool bath cost US$65.

The *Hotel Posada Diego de Mazariegos* (☎ 8-18-25, fax 8-08-27), 5 de Febrero 1, occupies two fine buildings on Utrilla one block north of the main plaza. Rooms (US$38/45/54) are tastefully furnished and most have fireplace and TV. There's a restaurant and a nightclub that offers live entertainment.

Places to Eat
The cheapest meals are from the cookshops in a complex called *Los Merenderos*, just south of the Templo de San Francisco on Insurgentes. To be safe, pick items that look fresh and hot. A full meal can be had for little over US$1.50.

A perennially popular eatery is *Restaurant Tuluc* at Insurgentes 5, 1½ blocks south of the main plaza. The Tuluc scores with its 6.15 am opening time for early breakfasts, efficient service, good food and reasonable prices. Most main courses cost US$2.50 to US$4.50.

Madre Tierra (Mother Earth), Insurgentes 19 at Hermanos Domínguez, is a vegetarian oasis in the land of carnes and aves. The menu is eclectic and appetizing with filling soups, wholemeal sandwiches, brown rice dishes, pasta, pizzas and salads. Most everything on the menu is between US$1.80 and US$4, and the daily set menu costs US$6. Excellent whole-grain bread is served with all meals. The *Panadería*

Madre Tierra next door is a wholefood bakery selling breads, muffins, cookies, cakes, quiches, pizzas and frozen yogurt.

La Casa del Pan at Dr Navarro 10 off Belisario Domínguez, serves a 'feel-great breakfast' of fruit, granola, yogurt, muffins and organic coffee (US$4), and a veggie comida corrida of soup, rice, beans, quesadilla, beverage and dessert (also US$4). There's lunch and dinner as well. You may dine in the calming courtyard or the dining room where they sell whole grain breads, bagels, brownies and cookies. Hours are 7 am to 10 pm; closed Monday.

Probably the best coffee in town, and good cakes too, are served in the little *Cafetería San Cristóbal*, on Cuauhtémoc just off Insurgentes. The clientele is mainly Mexican men who bring along chess sets and newspapers to relax.

The walls of *Las Estrellas* at Escuadrón 201 No 6B, across from La Caridad park, are covered with beautiful batiks (for sale, of course). Its menu includes pesto dishes, veggie quiches and rice plates for US$2, and pasta with garlic bread or pizza for US$2.75. Service is friendly and fast.

Restaurant París México at Madero 20, one block east of the main plaza, is an arty little café serving French and Mexican specials daily for US$4, crepas for US$2, and great coffee.

For local cooking, try the *Restaurant Normita*, JF Flores at Juárez. A big bowl of pozole, a soup of maize, cabbage, pork, radishes and onions, costs US$2, and a plato típico Coleto, a local mixed grill with pork sausage, chops, frijoles and guacamole, goes for US$4, but there is plainer, cheaper fare as well.

Cafetería del Centro, Real de Guadalupe 15, has cheap breakfasts, less than US$2 for the works: eggs, toast, butter, jam, juice and coffee. Upstairs at Hidalgo 3, *La Galería* serves pizza at popular prices.

At the humble *El Taquito*, on the corner of Mazariegos and 12 de Octubre, tacos are half the price and still good. You can also enjoy filete al queso a la parrilla (grilled meat filet with a cheese topping), or fruit cocktail with granola and honey.

Speaking of tacos, *Taquería La Salsa Verde*, 20 de Noviembre, has an open kitchen with señoras hard at work making them by hand. They're good, and not expensive at about US$1.50 a plate.

La Parrilla on the corner of Belisario Domínguez and Dr Navarro, open Sunday to Friday from 6.30 pm to midnight, serves excellent carnes and quesos al carbón (char-grilled meats and cheese). A dinner, drink and dessert will cost about US$7.

Restaurant Tikal, a block north of the Cristóbal Colón bus terminal on Insurgentes, serves generous portions of spaghetti in different styles (such as Genovesa, with cheese, nutmeg and spinach), and good guacamole with totopos, for US$2.50. Meat dishes and burgers cost a bit more.

Café-Restaurant El Teatro, upstairs at Primero de Marzo 8, near 16 de Septiembre, is among the few upscale restaurants in town. The menu, based on French and Italian cuisine, lists chateaubriand, crepes, fresh pasta, pizzas and desserts. Expect to spend US$6 to US$12 for a full dinner here.

Both *Restaurant Flamingo* and *Restaurant Fulano's* on Madero are respectable if unremarkable, with similar menus and prices: spaghetti and salads are about US$2, pizzas and main dishes are twice that.

You must reserve about two hours ahead for lunch (1.30 pm) or dinner (7 pm) at *Na Bolom* (see above), but breakfast is served any time from 7.30 to 10 am. Meals are somewhat expensive, but the ambiance is unique.

Entertainment

San Cristóbal is an early-to-bed town, and conversation in cafés, restaurants or rooms will most likely occupy many of your evenings. However there are films, cultural events, concerts and rowdy music scenes to be relished if so motivated. Check the notice boards in front of the tourist office and in El Puente for scheduled events.

Centro Cultural El Puente on Real de Guadalupe 55 has cultural programs, films, concerts or conferences nightly.

There are fairly regular musical and theatrical performances at the *Casa de Cultura/Bellas Artes* at the corner of Hidalgo and Hermanos Domínguez.

Things to Buy

Chiapas' Indian crafts are justifiably famous and there are now hosts of shops in San Cristóbal selling them. The heaviest concentrations are along Real de Guadalupe (where prices go down as you go away from the zócalo) and Utrilla (toward the market end). La Galería, at Hidalgo 3, has beautiful and expensive crafts.

Textiles – huipiles, rebozos, blankets – are the outstanding items, for Tzotzil weavers are some of the most skilled and inventive in Mexico (see the Weavers' Cooperatives section earlier). Indian women also sell textiles in the park around Santo Domingo. You'll also find some Guatemalan Indian textiles and plenty of the appealing and inexpensive pottery from Amatenango del Valle (animals, pots, jugs, etc) in San Cristóbal. Leather is another local specialty.

You can even buy black ski-mask hooded Subcomandante Marcos dolls, effigies of the popular leader of the EZLN.

You're expected to bargain unless prices are labeled (though there's no harm in trying even then). The first price quoted is traditionally much more than the going rate for the item.

Getting There & Away

Air Scheduled flights come no nearer than Tuxtla Gutiérrez. Aviacsa (☎ 8-44-41, fax 8-43-84) has an office at Real de Guadalupe 7, Pasaje Mazariegos 16. Travel agencies can make bookings on other airlines.

Chevy Suburban vans shuttle between Tuxtla Gutiérrez's Aeropuerto Llano San Juan and San Cristóbal for US$7 per person. Buy your ticket at the Aviacsa office.

Bus A new Central de Autobuses is planned in the south of the town but for the moment each company has its own terminal.

Each bus company serving San Cristóbal has various classes of service that may be called 2nd- or 1st-class or deluxe, or by proprietary names. Usually price is a surer determinant of comfort and speed than class: the more you pay, the higher the comfort and quicker the trip.

Cristóbal Colón is at the junction of Insurgentes and the Pan-American Highway, and shares the 1st-class terminal with Autobuses del Sur. There is no place to leave your luggage, but shops nearby on Insurgentes will hold it for a small fee. Look for signs reading 'Se Reciben Equipaje,' or words to that effect.

Autotransportes Tuxtla Gutiérrez (ATG) is on Allende half a block north of the Pan-American Highway. The terminal is not visible from the highway: walk up the little street opposite the Chevrolet dealership, northwest of the Supermercado Jovel, and southeast of the Policía Federal de Caminos.

Andrés Caso is on the Pan-American Highway between Hidalgo and Crescencio Rosas (1½ blocks west of Cristóbal Colón); Autotransportes Rápidos de San Cristóbal is on the Pan-American Highway half a block east of Cristóbal Colón; and Transportes Fray Bartolomé de Las Casas is on Avenida Salomon González Blanco, the continuation of Utrilla, 300 meters north of the market.

Sociedad Cooperativa Altos de Chiapas runs minibuses up and down the Pan-American Highway.

Bus departures from San Cristóbal include:

Chetumal – 700 km, 11 hours; Colón Maya de Oro (deluxe) buses at 9.30 am and 4.35 pm (US$24), which continue to Cancún (US$33 from San Cristóbal); others by Colón (US$21) at 2.30 pm and Sur (US$18) at 12.30 pm
Chiapa de Corzo – 70 km, 1½ hours; ATG (US$1.50) every half-hour, which may or may not stop at Chiapa; Altos de Chiapas minibuses or shared-taxi colectivos are a better bet (see map for station)
Ciudad Cuauhtémoc (Guatemalan border) – 165 km, three hours; seven by Colón (US$3.75);

nine by ATG (US$3); others by Andrés Caso and Altos de Chiapas. Take an early bus if you hope to get any distance into Guatemala the same day
Comitán – 83 km, 1½ hours; seven by Colón (US$1.75) from 7 am to 10 pm; many cheaper ones by other companies
Mérida – 770 km, 15 hours; one evening Colón deluxe (US$26) and a normal (US$22) at 5.30 pm; one ATG Plus (deluxe; US$21) at 6 pm
Mexico City (TAPO) – 1085 km, 19 hours; five by Colón (US$38 to US$44); more by ATG
Oaxaca – 630 km, 12 hours; two by Colón (US$18 to US$22)
Ocosingo – 92 km, 1½ hours; eight by Colón (US$2.50); most other lines run this route as well, and there are frequent minibuses (see map for departure point)
Palenque – 215 km, four hours; eight by Colón (US$6); seven by Figueroa (US$5), more by ATG, ATS and Lacandonia (US$5)
Tapachula – 350 km, eight hours; five by Colón (US$11); more by ATG and Andrés Caso (US$6)
Tuxtla Gutiérrez – 85 km, two hours; hourly by Colón (US$2.50), ATG (US$1.50), and Oriente de Chiapas (US$1.50); frequent shared taxis (US$3.75 to US$4.50 per person) by Autotransportes Rápidos de San Cristóbal (see map for station)
Villahermosa – 300 km, eight hours; one by Colón (US$10), or go via Tuxtla Gutiérrez

Getting Around

For buses to the Indian villages near San Cristóbal, see Around San Cristóbal. Taxis are fairly plentiful. One stand is on the north side of the main plaza. A typical trip within the town costs US$1.

Car Budget Rent-a-Car (☎ 8-18-71) is at Auto Rentas Yaxchilán at Mazariegos 36, 2½ blocks from the main plaza. Opening hours are Monday to Saturday from 8 am to 2 pm and 3 to 8 pm and Sunday from 8 am to noon and 5 to 7 pm. At busy periods you may need to book your car a few days in advance. The cheapest, a VW sedan, is around US$40 a day, taxes included.

Bicycle Los Pinguinos (☎ 8-02-02, fax 8-66-38), Avenida 5 de Mayo 10B, rents bikes for US$1 per hour, US$7.50 per day, including a lock, map and water bottle. They also conduct half-day bike tours for US$7 to US$11, full-day tours for US$12.50. It's a good way to explore the city and surrounding country. The guides speak English, Spanish, German and Romansh.

Also check out Bicirent, Belisario Domínguez 5B, open daily from 9 am to 8 pm, which makes similar arrangements.

AROUND SAN CRISTÓBAL

Visiting the Indian villages around San Cristóbal is among the most interesting things to do here.

Warning

Robbery Armed robbers have discovered that it's easy and profitable to hold up tourists walking between villages. Don't walk from village to village. Instead, take a horse, bus or taxi.

Photography In some villages, particularly those nearest San Cristóbal, you may be greeted with wariness, the result of centuries of oppression and the desire to preserve traditions from interference. Cameras are at best tolerated – and sometimes not even that. Photography is banned in the church and during festivals at Chamula, and banned completely at Zinacantán. You may well put yourself in physical danger if you take photos without permission. If in any doubt at all, ask before taking a picture.

Indigenous Peoples

The Tzotzils and Tzeltals of highland Chiapas – descendants of the ancient Maya – are among Mexico's most traditional Indians, with some distinctly pre-Hispanic elements in their nominally Catholic religious life, and Spanish very much a second language. Their clothing, too, marks them as the inheritors of ancient Mayan traditions.

The 150,000 or so Tzotzils occupy an area about 50 km from east to west and 100 km from north to south, with San Cristóbal at its center. Tzeltal territory is of a similar size and shape, immediately east of the Tzotzil area. Most of the people live in the hills outside the villages, which are primarily market and ceremonial centers.

Most of these Indians are poor. Many men from San Juan Chamula and Mitontic, for instance, have to spend half the year away from home working on Soconusco coffee plantations. Some Tzotzil have moved to the Lacandón forest in search of land. Despite long repression, the Tzotzils' and Tzeltals' relatively large numbers have enabled them to maintain their group pride. Tzotzils and Tzeltals figured prominently in the Zapatista rebellion of January 1994.

Markets & Special Events

The villages' weekly markets are nearly always on Sunday. Proceedings start very early and wind down by lunchtime.

Festivals often give the most interesting insight into Indian life, and there are plenty of them. Apart from fiestas for a village's patron and other saints, occasions like Carnaval (for which Chamula is famous), Semana Santa, the Day of the Dead (November 2) and the day of the Virgin of Guadalupe (December 12) are celebrated almost everywhere.

San Juan Chamula

The Chamulans put up strong resistance to the Spaniards in 1524 and launched a famous rebellion in 1869. Today they are one of the most numerous Tzotzil groups – 40,000-strong – and their village 10 km northwest of San Cristóbal is the center for some unique religious practices. A big sign at the entrance to the village says that it is strictly forbidden to take photos in the church or anywhere rituals are being performed.

From dawn on Sunday, people stream into town from the hills for the weekly market, and to go to church. The church stands on the far side of the main plaza. A sign on its door tells visitors to ask at the 'tourist office,' also on the plaza, for tickets (US$1) to enter. Inside the church, the rows of burning candles, the thick clouds of incense, the chanting worshippers kneeling with their faces to the pine needle-carpeted floor make a powerful impression. Saints' images are surrounded with mirrors and dressed in holy garments.

Next to the church, the Museo de Chamula (open 9 am to 6 pm, US$1) exhibits traditional handicrafts and wattle-and-daub construction.

Chamulans believe Christ rose from the cross to become the sun. Christian festivals are interwoven with older ones: the pre-Lent Carnaval celebrations, which are among the most important and last several days in February or March, also mark the five 'lost' days of the ancient Mayan Long Count calendar, which divided time into 20-day periods (18 of these make 360 days, which leaves five more to complete a full year). Other festivals include ceremonies for San Sebastián (mid- to late January); Semana Santa; San Juan, the village's patron saint (June 22-25); and the annual change of cargos (December 30 to January 1; see Ceremonial Brotherhoods sidebar).

On such occasions a strong alcoholic brew called *posh* is drunk and you may see groups of ceremonially attired men, carrying flags and moving slowly round in tight, chanting circles. At Carnaval, troops of strolling minstrels called *mash* wander the roads strumming guitars and wearing sunglasses (even when it's raining) and tall pointed hats.

Cargo holders wear black tunics instead of the usual white ones.

Zinacantán
pop 15,000

The road to this Tzotzil village, 11 km northwest of San Cristóbal, forks left off the Chamula road, then goes down into a valley. Photography is banned altogether here.

The men wear very distinctive red-and-white striped tunics (which appear pink), and flat, round, ribboned palm hats. Unmarried men's hats have longer, wider ribbons. A market is usually held only at fiesta times. The most important celebrations are for the town's patron saint, San Lorenzo, between August 8 and 11, and San Sebastián (January).

Zinacantecos venerate geranium, which along with pine branches is offered in rituals to bring a wide range of benefits. Zinacantán has two churches. The crosses dotting the Zinacantán countryside mostly mark entrances to the abodes of the important ancestor gods or the Señor de la Tierra (Earth Lord), all of whom have to be kept happy with offerings at the appropriate times.

Ceremonial Brotherhoods

Traditional religious brotherhoods still exist in the indigenous villages of the Chiapas highlands. In the past these fraternal organizations were the governing bodies of Mayan society, and though they still exercise limited civil powers in some Guatemalan highland towns and villages, their functions in Chiapas are mostly ceremonial.

Members of the brotherhoods – which are all male – take turns discharging the obligations of *cargos* (charges or duties). These duties normally last for one year, and include caring for the images of saints in the churches, and the masks and costumes used in religious ceremonies. Other cargos entail organizing and paying for the ceremonies, celebrations and fiestas which mark the many saints' days throughout the year.

Taking on a cargo is an honor and a burden. Only fairly prosperous villagers can afford the considerable expense of discharging a cargo; and by burdening the prosperous ones with the costs, village society ensures that the financial success of some works to the benefit of all.

Among the Tzotzils, senior cargo-holders called *mayordomos* are responsible for the care of saints' images; the *alféreces* organize and pay for fiestas; *capitanes* dance and ride horses at fiestas. After having successfully carried out the duties of a cargo several times, members enter the ranks of the *Principales*, or Village Elders.

Women are generally restricted to domestic work, including weaving. ∎

TABASCO & CHIAPAS

If you walk a few hundred meters along the road past the San Lorenzo church, you'll come to the **Museo Ik'al Ojov**, a private entity dedicated to the Earth Lord. The thatched buildings hold exhibits showing Zinacantán's traditional way of life.

Tenejapa
Tenejapa is a Tzeltal village 28 km northeast of San Cristóbal, in a pretty valley with a river running through it. There are about 20,000 Tenejapanecos in the surrounding area. A busy market fills the main street (behind the church) early on Sunday mornings. Cargo holders wear wide, colorfully beribboned hats, and chains of silver coins round their necks. Women wear brightly brocaded or embroidered huipiles.

Tenejapa has a few comedores in the main street and one basic posada, the *Hotel Molina*, which isn't always open. The main festival is for the town's patron saint, San Ildefonso, on January 23.

Amatenango del Valle
The women of this Tzeltal village, by the Pan-American Highway, 37 km southeast of San Cristóbal, are renowned potters. Amatenango pottery is still fired by the pre-Hispanic method, building a wood fire around the pieces rather than putting them in a kiln. In addition to the pots, bowls, urns, jugs and plates that the village has turned out for generations, young girls in the last 15 years or so have made animalitos, which find a ready market with tourists. These are small, appealing and cheap, if fragile. If you visit the village, expect to be surrounded within minutes by girls selling them.

The women wear white huipiles embroidered with red and yellow, wide red belts and blue skirts. Amatenango's patron saint, San Francisco, is fêted on October 4.

Other Villages
Intrepid Mayaphiles might want to make visits to some more remote villages.

San Andrés Larraínzar is a hilltop Tzotzil and mestizo village 28 km northwest of San Cristóbal (18 km beyond San Juan Chamula). A turnoff to the left, 10 km after San Juan Chamula, heads uphill through spectacular mountain scenery to the village. San Andrés was the setting for negotiations between the EZLN rebels and government officials during 1996. The patron saint's day is November 30. A weekly Sunday market is held and the people seem less reserved toward outsiders than those of other villages. People from Santa Magdalena, another Tzotzil village a few km north, attend the San Andrés market; their ceremonial huipiles are among the finest of all Chiapas Indian garments.

The plaza at **Mitontic**, a small Tzotzil village a few hundred meters left of the Chenalhó road, 23 km beyond San Juan Chamula, has both a picturesque, ruined 16th century church and a more modern working one. The patron saint, San Miguel, is honored from May 5 to 8.

San Pedro Chenalhó is a Tzotzil village in a valley with a stream running through it; it's 1500 meters high, 27 km beyond and quite a descent from Chamula. It's the center for about 14,000 people in the surrounding area. There's a weekly Sunday market. The main fiestas are for San Pedro (June 27 to 30), San Sebastián (January 16 to 22) and Carnaval.

Huixtán, 32 km from San Cristóbal on the Palenque road, is the center for roughly 12,000 Tzotzils, as it was in pre-Hispanic times. Huixtán has a 16th century church. **Oxchuc**, 20 km beyond Huixtán, is a small Tzeltal and mestizo town dominated by the large colonial church of San Tomás.

Getting There & Away
Don't walk to or between the following villages because of the threat of robbery. Ride.

There are paved roads to San Juan Chamula, Zinacantán, Amatenango del Valle and most of the way to Tenejapa. Reaching the other villages mentioned involves long stretches of fairly rough dirt track, but buses make it along them and so can a VW sedan (slowly).

Bus and colectivo schedules are geared to getting villagers into town early and back home not too late.

Combis to the villages nearest San Cristóbal leave from the northwestern corner of San Cristóbal market, between Utrilla and Cárdenas. They depart for San Juan Chamula and Zinacantán every 20 minutes or so up to about 5 pm; the fare is US$0.80. For Tenejapa they leave about half-hourly, take an hour and cost US$1. Return services from Tenejapa start getting scarce after noon.

To get to Amatenango del Valle, take a Comitán bus (see Getting There & Away in the San Cristóbal de Las Casas section). The fare is US$1.

Transportes Fray Bartolomé de Las Casas (see also Getting There & Away in the San Cristóbal de Las Casas section) operates buses to Chenalhó (US$1.50, 2½ hours) four times daily, and also to San Andrés Larráinzar (US$1.30, 2½ hours) at 2 pm. A return bus leaves from San Andrés at 7 am.

SAN CRISTÓBAL TO PALENQUE

The road to Palenque is 12 km southeast from San Cristóbal down the Pan-American Highway, then north on highway 199. The 210-km journey takes you from the cool, misty highlands to the steaming lowland jungle, and is dotted with interesting stopovers along the way.

Ocosingo, 92 km from San Cristóbal, is the jumping-off point for the little-known Mayan ruins at Toniná. The turnoff for the superb cascades of Agua Azul is about 50 km beyond Ocosingo. Another beautiful waterfall, Misol-Ha, with a good swimming hole, is two km off the road 40 km after the Agua Azul turning. Over the years, we've received occasional reports from travelers who have been robbed along the Palenque-San Cristóbal road in the vicinity of Ocosingo. Highwaymen stop buses, cars and cyclists and relieve travelers of their valuables.

Ocosingo

pop 20,000; ☎ *967*

Ocosingo is a small mestizo and Tzeltal valley town on the San Cristóbal-Palenque road. Some 14 km east of the town are the ruins of the Mayan city of Toniná. See the Toniná section later on.

Orientation & Information Ocosingo spreads downhill to the east of the main road. Avenida Central runs straight down from the main road to the zócalo. Most of the bus stations are on Avenida 1 Norte, parallel to Avenida Central a block north.

To orient yourself on the zócalo, remember that the church is on the east side and the Hotel Central on the north side. The large market – scene of some of the bloodiest fighting in the 1994 Zapatista rebellion – is three blocks east along Avenida 1 Sur Ote from the church.

None of the banks in town will change cash or traveler's checks, though this may change if Ocosingo edges onto the tourist map.

Places to Stay The *Hotel Central* (☎ 3-00-39), Avenida Central 1, on the north side of the zócalo, has simple, clean rooms with fan and bath for US$8/12/15 a single/double/triple.

Hotel Margarita (☎ 3-02-80) on Calle 1 Pte Norte, one block northwest of Hotel Central, charges US$20 a double. It isn't elaborate but it's nicer than most hotels in town; rooms have fan and bath, there is a comfortable lobby downstairs and a restaurant upstairs.

Posada Agua Azul, at 1 Ote Sur 127, two blocks south of the church, has medium-size, average rooms around a courtyard that harbors a few tightly caged anteaters, hawks and macaws. Rooms are US$9/$13.

At the really cheap end there's *Hospedaje La Palma* on the corner of Calle 2 Pte and Avenida 1 Norte Pte, just down the hill from the ATG bus station. It's a clean, family-run place; singles/doubles are US$4/US$8 with shared bathrooms. *Hotel San Jacinto* at Avenida Central 13, around the corner from the church charges US$4/9 for drab rooms with a shared bath. *Hospedaje San José* (☎ 3-00-39), Calle 1 Ote 6, half a block north of the northeast corner of the zócalo, has small, dark, but clean rooms for US$6/10.

Places to Eat Ocosingo is famous for its *queso amarillo* (yellow cheese), which comes in three-layered one-kg balls. The two outside layers are like chewy Gruyère, the middle is creamy.

Restaurant La Montura has a prime location on the north side of the zócalo, with tables on the Hotel Central's veranda. It's good for breakfast (fruit, eggs, bread and coffee for US$2.50), lunch or dinner (comida corrida for US$5 or a plate of tacos for US$2). They'll build you some sandwiches if you want to take a picnic to Toniná ruins.

Restaurant Los Portales, Avenida Central 19, facing the northeast corner of the zócalo, is a homey, old-fashioned place. Several matronly señoras will mother you here, offering traditional meals for US$2 to US$5. Los Portales proves an interesting contrast to the neighboring *Restaurant Los Arcos*, which is more modern, but not nearly so pleasant. On the opposite side of the zócalo, *Restaurant & Pizzería Troje* features the famous queso amarillo. Quesadillas are cheap (US$1.25), and pizzas of different sizes and sorts go for US$2.50 to US$7.

Restaurant Maya, two blocks west of the zócalo on Avenida Central, is a tidy, bright little eatery featuring *platos fuertes* (main-course lunch or dinner platters) for US$2.50; fruit salads and antojitos are less. The *Restaurant San Cristóbal*, Avenida Central 22, near the Town Hall, is a simple lonchería where nothing on the menu is more than US$3.

Pesebres Steak House, on Calle 1 Pte Norte above Hotel Margarita, has a nice breeze, super views and good prime rib or filet mignon for US$6.50; Mexican dishes and salads will run you less than US$3.

Getting There & Away The Autotransportes Tuxtla Gutiérrez (ATG) terminal is on Avenida 1 Norte, one block from the Palenque-San Cristóbal road. Transportes Lacandonia is on the same street a little higher up.

Autotransportes Fray Bartolomé de Las Casas (in between the previous two companies for price and comfort) is on the far side of the main road at the top of Avenida 1 Norte. They have a mixture of modern microbuses and decrepit big buses. Auto-transportes Ocosingo is at the corner of Avenida Central and the main road. Quickest are the combis that shuttle to Palenque and San Cristóbal. They leave when full from the top of Avenida Central and charge US$2.50.

Palenque – 123 km, 2½ hours; five buses (US$2.80) by ATG, two buses (US$3) by Autotransportes Fray Bartolomé de Las Casas

San Cristóbal de Las Casas – 92 km, 1½ hours; six buses (US$2) by ATG, six buses (US$1.75) by Lacandonia, five buses (US$2.30) by Autotransportes Fray Bartolomé de Las Casas

Tuxtla Gutiérrez – 193 km, 4½ hours; seven buses (US$4) by ATG, two morning buses (US$3) by Autotransportes Lacandonia, five buses (US$2) by Autotransportes Ocosingo

Villahermosa – 232 km, six hours; two morning buses (US$3) by Autotransportes Lacandonia

Toniná

The Mayan ruins at Toniná, 14 km east of Ocosingo, are relatively hard to reach and don't compare with Palenque for beauty or importance, but form a sizable, interesting site with some big structures on terraces cut from a hillside. Recent excavations have reduced Toniná's 'lost in the jungle' feel, but have revealed and explained much more of this impressive site. The ruins are open daily from 9 am to 4 pm daily for US$2.50.

Toniná was probably a city-state independent of both Palenque and Yaxchilán, though it declined at the same time as they did, around 800 AD. Dates found at the site range from 500 to 800 AD, and like Palenque and Yaxchilán, it peaked in the last 100 years or so of that period.

The caretaker may be willing to show you the site. If you have already visited Palenque or Yaxchilán, imagine a similar splendor here. Many of the stone facings and interior walls were covered in colored paint or frescos.

The track goes past the small museum, which holds quite a number of good stone carvings – statues, bas-reliefs, altars, calendar stones – then over a stream and up to a flat area from which rises the terraced hill supporting the main structures. As you face this hillside, behind you in a field are an overgrown outlying pyramid and the main ball court. The flat area contains a small ball court and fragments of limestone carvings. Some appear to show prisoners holding out offerings, with glyphs on the reverse sides.

The most interesting area of the terraced hillside is the right-hand end of its third and fourth levels. The stone facing of the wall rising from the third to fourth levels has a zigzag x-shape, which may represent Quetzalcóatl and is also a flight of steps. To the right of the base of this are the remains of a tomb, with steps leading up to an altar. Behind and above the tomb and altar is a rambling complex of chambers, passageways and stairways, believed to have been Toniná's administrative hub.

Over toward the center of the hillside are remains of the central stairway, which went much of the way up the hillside. One level higher than the top of the zigzag wall is a grave covered in tin sheeting, which you can lift to see a stone coffin beneath. Here were found the bodies of a ruler and two others. To the left on the same level is a shrine to Chac, the rain god. To the right at the foot of a crumbling temple is a carving of the earth god, labeled *monstruo de la tierra*. Higher again and to the left are two more mounds. The left-hand one, the pyramid of life and death, may have supported the ruler's dwelling. At the very top of the hill rise two more tall pyramid-temple mounds.

Getting There & Away The 14-km track from Ocosingo is dirt, and rough in parts, but crosses pleasant, flat ranchland with lots of colorful birds.

If driving, follow Calle 1 Ote south from Ocosingo church. Before long it curves left and you pass a cemetery on the right. At the fork a couple of km farther on, go left. At the next fork, the site is signposted to the right. Finally, a sign marks the entry track to Toniná at Rancho Guadalupe on the left. From here it's another km to the site itself.

Otherwise, you have the options of a taxi (about US$20 roundtrip, with an hour at the ruins), or hitching (maybe six vehicles an hour pass Toniná), or a passenger truck from Ocosingo market (several a day, most frequent from late morning, about US$1) or a bus of Carga Mixta Ocosingo from their yard near the market. There appear to be two or three buses to Guadalupe (near the ruins) and back each day. The ride costs US$1 and takes about 45 minutes. The Rancho Guadalupe sometimes puts people up for the night or allows them to camp.

Minibus day trips to Toniná with English-speaking guides are run by travel agents in Palenque and San Cristóbal.

Cascadas Agua Azul

Just 66 km south of Palenque and 4.5 km off the highway, scores of dazzling white waterfalls thunder into turquoise pools surrounded by jungle. The Agua Azul cascades are among the wonders of Mexico.

On holidays the site is thronged with local families; at other times you will have few companions. Admission is US$1.50 per car, half that for a person on foot. Note that the beautiful color which gives the place its name is often evident only in April and May. Silt clouds the waters in other months and it turns muddy during the height of the rainy season.

The temptation to swim is great but take extreme care – the current is deceptively fast and there are many invisible submerged hazards like rocks and dead trees. Use your judgment to identify slower, safer areas. Drownings are all too common, as indicated by memorials to those who have died here (including foreign travelers).

A vehicle track leads down from highway 199 to a section of the falls with a parking lot, a collection of simple eateries and, nearby, a small village.

Upstream, a trail takes you over some swaying, less-than-stable foot bridges and up through jungle.

Places to Stay & Eat There are a few spots to hang your hammock or pitch a tent, but if you are looking for a decent bed, go to Palenque. *Camping Agua Azul*, near the entrance, and *Restaurant Agua Azul*, next to the car park, rent hammocks and hammock space for a few dollars. You can leave your backpacks at Restaurant Agua Azul for US$1 per day. You'll find more solace and scenery if you camp upstream. Follow the trail up the left bank.

A five- to ten-minute walk will bring you to *Camping Casablanca*. It's far from elegant but you can hang your hammock (US$2) or rent one (US$3) in its big hollow barn. Owner Jerónimo guides three-hour (five km) hikes around the cascades for US$5 per person.

If you can gather another five minutes of walking energy, you'll find more pleasant camping at *José Antonio's*. It's the yellow house with white furniture and a Coca-Cola sign in front, a stone's throw from the water. There's a grassy lawn for tents, a palapa for hammocks, palm trees for atmosphere, and you're just steps from safe swimming. A night here will cost you US$2.

There are several restaurants and food stalls next to the car park, but the food is overpriced and average. You would be much better off packing a picnic from Palenque.

Getting There & Away The Agua Azul junction, or *crucero*, on highway 199 is 66 km south of Palenque, 57 km north of Ocosingo, and 149 km northeast of San Cristóbal. The 4.5-km walk from the crucero to the falls is OK on the way down, but the sweltering heat makes it hard on the uphill trip back out. If you want to take the risk, hitching is possible but don't rely on it.

An easy way of visiting Agua Azul and Misol-Ha is a day trip from Palenque with transport laid on. Several travel agents in Palenque offer such trips, departing daily about 9 am, returning about 4 pm, and charging between US$6 and US$8 per person including entrance fees, with typically three hours at Agua Azul and half an hour at Misol-Ha. Colectivos Chambalu and Colectivos Palenque, in Palenque, charge US$6. (For a list of Palenque travel agents, see Palenque – Organized Tours.)

Taking the organized tours, though more expensive than the bus, eliminates standing for hours on crowded buses and walking (perhaps with all your luggage) the 1.5 km in from the highway to (and back out from) Misol-Ha, and the 4.5 km walk downhill from the highway to Agua Azul proper – and then back uphill when it comes time to leave.

Alternatively you can travel by 2nd-class bus to the crucero and trust your legs and luck from there. Any 2nd-class bus between Palenque and San Cristóbal or Ocosingo will drop you there; 1st-class buses might not stop. The crucero is about three hours from San Cristóbal (US$4), one hour from Ocosingo (US$1), and one to 1½ hours from Palenque (US$1.60). Try to book ahead on these buses unless you want to stand. Catching a bus from the crucero when you leave almost certainly means standing at least part of the trip. Again, hitching is possible, but don't count on it.

Cascada Misol-Ha

About 25 km from Palenque, a waterfall drops nearly 35 meters into a beautiful, wide pool that's safe for swimming. The Misol-Ha cascade and its jungle surroundings are spectacular enough to be the setting for an Arnold Schwarzenegger thriller.

The waterfall is 1.5 km west by dirt road off highway 199 and the turn is signposted. To enter you pay US$1 per visitor.

Places to Stay & Eat You can set up a tent or hammock near the falls for US$5, or stay in one of the eight newly renovated cabins. Cabins are clean and comfortable with dark wood interiors, large bathrooms, hot water and furnished kitchenettes. Cabins with one double bed are US$16 to US$30, with two double beds US$30 to US$48. Rates vary with the seasons.

There is a small café near the entrance, but you're better off bringing food from Palenque.

PALENQUE

pop 20,000; alt 80m; ☎ *934*

Surrounded by emerald jungle, Palenque's setting is superb and its Mayan architecture and decoration are exquisite.

History

The name Palenque (Palisade) is modern Spanish and has no relation to the city's ancient name, which is uncertain. It could have been Nachan (City of Snakes), Chocan (Sculptured Snake), Culhuacán, Huehuetlapalla, Xhembobel Moyos, Otolum . . . no one knows for sure.

Evidence from pottery fragments indicates that Palenque was first occupied more than 1500 years ago. It flourished from 600 to 800 AD, and what a glorious two centuries they were! The city first rose to prominence under Pakal, a club-footed king who reigned from 615 to 683 AD. Archaeologists have determined that Pakal is represented by hieroglyphics of sun and shield. He lived to a ripe old age, possibly 80 to 100 years.

During Pakal's reign, many plazas and buildings, including the superlative Templo de los Inscripciones, were constructed within 20 sq km of the city. The structures were characterized by mansard roofs and very fine stucco bas-reliefs. Hieroglyphic texts at Palenque state that Pakal's reign was predicted thousands of years prior to his ascension and would be celebrated far into the future.

Pakal was succeeded by his son Chan-Balum, symbolized in hieroglyphics by the jaguar and the serpent. Chan-Balum continued Palenque's political and economic expansion as well as the development of its art and architecture. He completed his father's crypt in the Templo de los Inscripciones and presided over the construction of the Plaza del Sol temples, placing sizable narrative stone stelae within each. One can see the influence of Palenque's architecture in the ruins of the Mayan city of Tikal in Guatemala's Petén region, and in the pyramids of Comalcalco near Villahermosa.

Not long after Chan-Balum's death, Palenque started on a precipitous decline.

Whether this was due to ecological catastrophe, civil strife or invasion has been disputed, but after the 10th century Palenque was largely abandoned. In an area that receives the heaviest rainfall in Mexico, the ruins were overgrown with vegetation and lay undiscovered until the latter half of the 18th century.

Orientation

There are two Palenques: the town and the archaeological zone, 6.5 km apart.

Coming south from the Catazajá junction on highway 186, it's 20 km to the village of Pakal-Na, which has Palenque's train station; Palenque town is several km farther south. Buses and minibuses run between Catazajá and Palenque town fairly frequently in the morning and afternoon. A taxi from Catazajá to Palenque town costs US$7.50.

Coming northeast from Tuxtla Gutiérrez, San Cristóbal and Agua Azul, you pass the Calinda Hotel Nututum, and shortly thereafter join the town-to-ruins road. Turn right for the town.

As you approach Palenque, you come to a fork in the road marked by a huge statue of a Mayan chieftain's head (King Pakal?). East of the statue is the area called La Cañada. Go east from the statue to Palenque town (one km) or west for the ruins (5.5 km) within the national park.

Most hotels and restaurants are in the town center; the camping areas and several top-end hotels are located along the road to the ruins. There are also hotels and restaurants in La Cañada.

Though relatively small, Palenque town is spread out. It's about two km from the Mayan statue at its western limit to the Hotel Misión Palenque at the eastern end. But most of the bus offices are clustered a few hundred meters east of the Mayan statue past the Pemex fuel station on the way into town, and the walk to most hotels is 800 meters or less.

The main road from the Mayan statue into town is Avenida Juárez, which ends at the town's main square, known as el parque

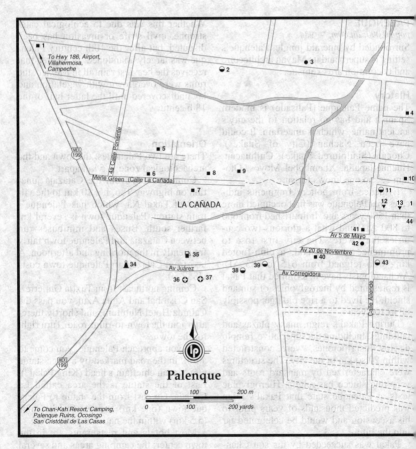

To Hwy 186, Airport, Villahermosa, Campeche

2a Calle Poniente

(MEX) 199

5

6

Merle Green (Calle La Cañada)

8

9

7

LA CAÑADA

1

2

3

4

10

11

12   13   1

44

41

42

Av 5 de Mayo

Av 20 de Noviembre

40

35

34

Av Juárez

38   39

43

Av Corregidora

36   37

Calle Allende

(MEX) 199

Palenque

0   100   200 m

0   100   200 yards

To Chan-Kah Resort, Camping, Palenque Ruins, Ocosingo San Cristóbal de Las Casas

(the park). Juárez is also the center of the commercial district.

It's always sweltering in Palenque, and there's rarely any breeze.

Information

Tourist Office Located in the Mercado de Artesanías building on Juárez, the tourist office (☎ 5-08-28) has an English-speaking staff, reliable town and trail information and a few maps. It's open daily from 8.30 am to 8.30 pm.

Money Bancomer, 1½ blocks west of the park on Juárez, changes money weekdays

from 10 to 11.30 am. Banamex, two blocks west of the park, does the exchange weekdays from 10.30 am to noon. Both banks have ATMs. Some hotels, restaurants, travel agencies and exchange shops in town will also change money, though at less favorable rates.

Post & Communications The post office, in the Casa de la Cultura on the south side of the park, is open weekdays from 9 am to 1 pm and 3 to 6 pm, and Saturday from 9 am to 1 pm (closed Sunday).

You can place long-distance telephone calls from the ADO bus station. There

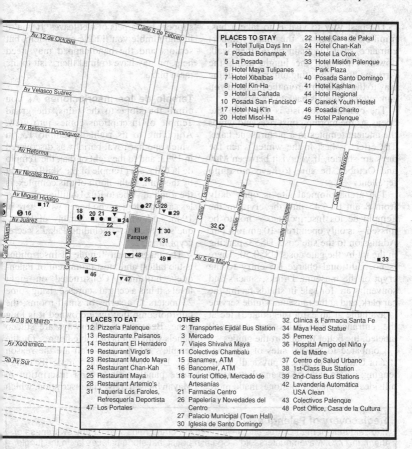

PLACES TO STAY
1 Hotel Tulija Days Inn
4 Posada Bonampak
5 La Posada
6 Hotel Maya Tulipanes
7 Hotel Xibalbas
8 Hotel Kin-Ha
9 Hotel La Cañada
10 Posada San Francisco
17 Hotel Naj K'in
20 Hotel Misol-Ha
22 Hotel Casa de Pakal
24 Hotel Chan-Kah
29 Hotel La Croix
33 Hotel Misión Palenque
    Park Plaza
40 Posada Santo Domingo
41 Hotel Kashlan
44 Hotel Regional
45 Caneck Youth Hostel
46 Posada Charito
49 Hotel Palenque

PLACES TO EAT
12 Pizzería Palenque
13 Restaurante Paisanos
14 Restaurant El Herradero
19 Restaurant Virgo's
23 Restaurant Mundo Maya
24 Restaurant Chan-Kah
25 Restaurant Maya
28 Restaurant Artemio's
31 Taquería Los Faroles,
    Refresquería Deportista
47 Los Portales

OTHER
2 Transportes Ejidal Bus Station
3 Mercado
7 Viajes Shivalva Maya
11 Colectivos Chambalu
15 Banamex, ATM
16 Bancomer, ATM
18 Tourist Office, Mercado de
    Artesanías
21 Farmacia Centro
26 Papelería y Novedades del
    Centro
27 Palacio Municipal (Town Hall)
30 Iglesia de Santo Domingo
32 Clínica & Farmacia Santa Fe
34 Maya Head Statue
35 Pemex
36 Hospital Amigo del Niño y
    de la Madre
37 Centro de Salud Urbano
38 1st-Class Bus Station
39 2nd-Class Bus Stations
42 Lavandería Automática
    USA Clean
43 Colectivos Palenque
48 Post Office, Casa de la Cultura

are also several telephone casetas on Juárez.

Bookstores Papelería y Novedades del Centro (☎ 5-07-77), at Independencia 18 and Nicolás, is a small store selling paper and books, attached to a café. Shelves hold a few English guidebooks, some Mayan literature and maps of Chiapas.

Laundry Lavandería Automática USA Clean is across from the Hotel Kashlan.

Medical Services The Hospital Amigo del Niño y de la Madre, across from the Pemex station near the Maya statue, treats all ailments, not just those of children and mothers. There's also a Centro de Salud Urbano (Urban Health Center) next door, and various other clinics and pharmacies (see map).

Palenque Ruinas
Only a few dozen of Palenque's nearly 500 buildings have been excavated. Everything you see here was built without metal tools, pack animals or the wheel. As you explore the ruins, try to picture the gray stone edifices as they would have been at the peak of Palenque's power: painted bright red.

TABASCO & CHIAPAS

The best way to visit is to take a bus, minibus or taxi to the main (upper) entrance, visit the main plaza, then walk downhill through the jungle along the Arroyo Otolum, visiting minor ruins all the way to the museum. From the museum you can catch a minibus back to town.

The best time to visit is when the site opens, as the morning mist rises and wraps the ancient temples in a picturesque haze. The effect is best in the winter when the days are shorter. If you visit between May and October, be sure to have mosquito repellent.

The archaeological site is open daily from 8 am to 4.45 pm; the crypt in the Templo de los Inscripciones – not to be missed – is only open from 10 am to 4 pm. Admission to the site costs US$3; parking in the lot by the gate costs US$0.50. There is no additional charge for entry to the crypt or the museum. Drinks, snacks and souvenirs are for sale in stands facing the car park, and at the museum. Guide service is available at an extra (negotiated) fee at the entrance. The ruins are not well labeled, the better to support the guides.

Compared to the flat sites of Chichén-Itzá or Uxmal, Palenque is physically challenging: jungle paths go up and down steep hillsides of slippery limestone, made more slippery by carpets of wet leaves. If you're fit and nimble you'll have no problem, but seniors and the handicapped may need help, or may have to limit their visit to the main plaza.

Templo de los Inscripciones As you climb the slope to the ruins, the grand Temple of Inscriptions comes into view. Adjoining to its right is Templo 13, in which another royal burial was discovered in 1993; and to the right of that, the Templo de la Calavera (Temple of the Skull). Right by the path, to the north of this complex, is the tomb of Alberto Ruz Lhuillier, the tireless archaeologist who began work here in 1945, and who revealed many of Palenque's mysteries – including Pakal's secret crypt in 1952.

The magnificent Temple of Inscriptions is the tallest and most prominent of Palenque's buildings. Constructed on eight levels, it has a central staircase rising some 23 meters to a series of small rooms; the tall roofcomb that once crowned it is long gone. Between the doorways are stucco panels with reliefs of noble figures. On the temple's interior rear wall are the reason Ruz Lhuillier gave the temple its name: three panels with a long inscription in Mayan hieroglyphs. The inscription, which

---

Rediscovery of Palenque

It is said that Hernán Cortés came within 40 km of the ruins without any awareness of them. In 1773, Mayan hunters told a Spanish priest that stone palaces lay in the jungle. Father Ordoñez y Aguilar led an expedition to Palenque and wrote a book claiming that the city was the capital of an Atlantis-like civilization.

An expedition led by Captain Antonio del Río set out in 1787 to explore Palenque. Although his report was then locked up in the Guatemalan archives, a translation of it was made by a British resident of Guatemala who was sufficiently intrigued to have it published in England in 1822. This led a host of adventurers to brave malaria in their search for the hidden city.

Among the most colorful of these adventurers was the eccentric Count de Waldeck who, in his 60s, lived atop one of the pyramids for two years (1831-33). He wrote a book complete with fraudulent drawings that made the city resemble great Mediterranean civilizations, causing all the more interest in Palenque. In Europe, Palenque's fame grew and it was mythologized as a lost Atlantis or an extension of ancient Egypt.

Finally, in 1837, John L Stephens reached Palenque with artist Frederick Catherwood. Stephens wrote insightfully about the six pyramids he started to excavate, and the city's aqueduct system. His was the first truly scientific investigation and paved the way for research by other serious scholars. ■

was dedicated in 692 AD, recounts the history of Palenque and of the temple.

Ascend the 69 steep steps to the top for access to stairs down to the tomb of Pakal (open 10 am to 4 pm). If you cannot climb the stairs up, take the path around to the side of the temple and into the jungle, emerging high up at the back of the temple. Though still difficult, this back way is easier than the front staircase. You'll still have to negotiate the slippery steps down to the crypt if you want to see it, however.

Although Pakal's jewel-bedecked skeleton and jade mosaic death mask were taken to Mexico City and the tomb recreated in the Museo Nacional de Antropología, the stone sarcophagus lid remains here. (The priceless death mask was stolen from the Mexico City museum in 1985.) The carved stone slab protecting the sarcophagus includes the image of Pakal encircled by serpents, mythical monsters, the sun god and glyphs recounting Pakal's reign. Carved on the wall are the nine lords of the underworld. Between the crypt and the staircase, a snake-like hollow ventilation tube connected Pakal to the realm of the living.

El Palacio Diagonally opposite the Templo de los Inscripciones is the Palace, an unusual structure harboring a maze of courtyards, corridors and rooms. The tower, restored in 1955, has fine stucco reliefs on its walls, but it is no longer open to visitors.

Archaeologists and astronomers believe that the tower was constructed so that Mayan royalty and the priest class could observe the sun falling directly into the Templo de los Inscripciones during the December 22 winter solstice.

Templo del Jaguar On the east side of the Templo de los Inscripciones, a steep, uphill, somewhat difficult path leads south into the jungle to the small ruined Temple of the Jaguar. Partly reclaimed from the jungle verdure, clinging romantically to a steep hillside next to a great ceiba tree, the façade of this small temple has fallen away,

down the hillside toward the rushing Arroyo Otolum stream, exposing the interior which still bears mold-covered traces of colored murals. The large pyramid behind the Templo del Jaguar is still a mere hill of rubble engulfed in jungle.

Grupo de la Cruz Although Pakal had only the Templo de los Inscripciones dedicated to him during his 68-year reign, Chan-Balum had four buildings dedicated to him, known today as the Grupo de la Cruz (Group of the Cross).

The Templo del Sol (Temple of the Sun), with the best-preserved roofcomb at Palenque, bears narrative inscriptions dating from 642, replete with scenes of offerings to Pakal, the sun-shield king.

The smaller, less well-preserved Templo 14 also has tablets showing ritual offerings – a common scene in Palenque.

The Templo de la Cruz, largest in this group, was restored in 1990, and also has narrative stones within.

On the Templo de la Cruz Foliada (Temple of the Foliated Cross), the arches are fully exposed, revealing how Palenque's architects designed these buildings. A well-preserved inscribed tablet shows a

Bust of a Mayan ruler

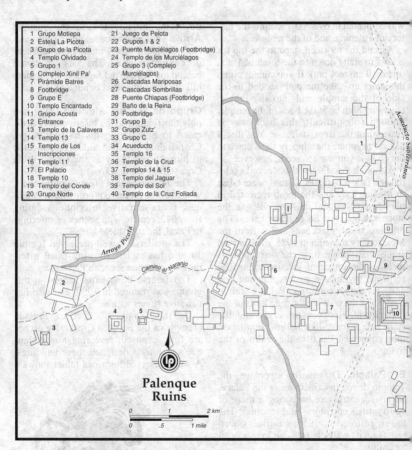

1	Grupo Motiepa
2	Estela La Picota
3	Grupo de la Picota
4	Templo Olvidado
5	Grupo 1
6	Complejo Xinil Pa'
7	Pirámide Batres
8	Footbridge
9	Grupo E
10	Templo Encantado
11	Grupo Acosta
12	Entrance
13	Templo de la Calavera
14	Templo 13
15	Templo de Los Inscripciones
16	Templo 11
17	El Palacio
18	Templo 10
19	Templo del Conde
20	Grupo Norte
21	Juego de Pelota
22	Grupos 1 & 2
23	Puente Murciélagos (Footbridge)
24	Templo de los Murciélagos
25	Grupo 3 (Complejo Murciélagos)
26	Cascadas Mariposas
27	Cascadas Sombrillas
28	Puente Chiapas (Footbridge)
29	Baño de la Reina
30	Footbridge
31	Grupo B
32	Grupo Zutz'
33	Grupo C
34	Acueducto
35	Templo 16
36	Templo de la Cruz
37	Templos 14 & 15
38	Templo del Jaguar
39	Templo del Sol
40	Templo de la Cruz Foliada

Palenque Ruins

king (most likely Pakal) with a sun-shield emblazoned on his chest, corn growing from his shoulder blades and the sacred quetzal bird atop his head.

Grupo Norte North of the Palace is the Northern Group, unrestored, and the ruins of a ball court. Crazy Count de Waldeck lived in one of the temples of the Northern Group – the Templo del Conde (Temple of the Count), built in 647 AD under Pakal.

Arroyo Otolum Continue east past the Northern Group and some service buildings to the Arroyo Otolum (Otolum

stream). Cross the stream, turn left (north) and continue into the jungle. You have a better chance of seeing wildlife here – including howler monkeys – than around the main plaza.

A flight of steep steps by the Cascada Motiepa waterfall brings you to the **Complejo Murciélagos** and **Puente Chiapas**. The ruins, thought to have been residential, are not spectacular, but the jungle setting by the waterfalls (there are two – the other is called the Baño de la Reina, or Queen's Bath) certainly is.

Grupo B is a plaza surrounded by five elongated buildings rising from terraces

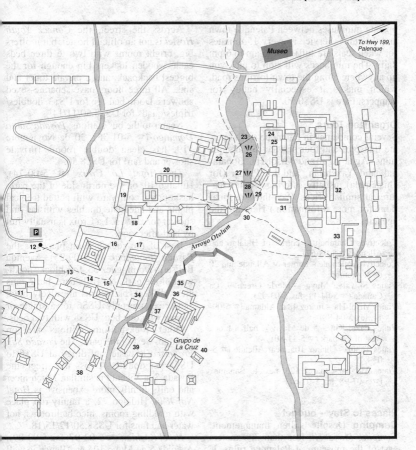

built between the Otolum and Murciélago arroyos. Residential, these buildings were thought to have been occupied around 770 to 850 AD; tombs were found beneath them.

Continue along the stream to the **Grupo de los Murciélagos** (Bat Group), another residential quarter. Descend the stairway to the **Puente Murciélago** (Bat Bridge), a suspension footbridge across the Otolum offering grand views of the waterfalls. If you've brought your bathing suit, this is where to use it, though you should be discreet, as swimming is discouraged.

Across the bridge and downstream, a path goes west to **Grupos I & II**, a short walk uphill. These ruins, only partially uncovered and restored, are at least in a beautiful jungle setting.

Returning to the river and the bridge, the main path continues north along the west bank of the river to the museum and visitor center.

Getting There & Away A paved footpath, some parts of which are shaded, runs right next to the road from the Maya head statue all the way to the museum, just about six km.

Several companies, including Colectivos Chambalu and Colectivos Palenque, operate minibuses between Palenque town and the ruins. Service is every 15 minutes (or when seats are full) from 6 am to 6 pm daily. The minibuses will stop to pick you up anywhere along the town-to-ruins road, which makes it especially handy for campers. Fare is US$0.50.

Organized Tours
Several companies in Palenque town operate transport and tour service to Palenque ruins, Agua Azul and Misol-Ha, Bonampak and Yaxchilán, and La Palma (for Guatemala), usually offering similar features at similar prices. (See those destinations for more information.) Here are the agencies:

Colectivos Chambalu – corner of Hidalgo and Allende (☎ 5-08-67)
Colectivos Palenque – corner of Allende and 20 de Noviembre
Viajes Shivalva Maya – Merle Green 9, La Cañada (☎ 5-04-11, fax 5-03-92)
Viajes Misol-Ha – Juárez 48 at Aldama (☎ 5-09-11, fax 5-04-88)
Viajes Pakal-Kin – 5 de Mayo 7, half a block west of the park (☎ 5-11-80)
Viajes Toniná – Juárez 105, near Allende (☎ 5-03-84)
Viajes Yax-ha – Juárez 123, next to Banamex (☎ 5-07-98, fax 5-07-67)

Places to Stay – budget
Camping Despite sullen management, *Camping Mayabell*, less than 300 meters east of the museum at Palenque ruins, is the best and most convenient place to camp. For US$1.75 per person you get toilets, showers, some shade, full hookups, snacks and drinks for sale. They rent cabañas as well, for US$17 for up to three people. *Camping El Panchan*, another 500 meters east, is an alternative.

Hostel & Hotels *Posada Charito* (☎ 5-01-21), 20 de Noviembre 15, two blocks southwest of the park, is quiet, well kept, and run by a friendly family. For US$7.50 you get a double with a shower, clean sheets, a ceiling fan, and a Gideon Bible (in Spanish) on your pillow.

Across the street, the *Caneck Youth Hostel* is not an official hostel, but it offers big, bright rooms with two to three beds each, wooden lockers big enough for the biggest backpack, and a private toilet and sink. All three floors have separate-sexed showers. Dorm beds go for US$3, doubles/triples/quads for US$8.50/11/14.

Nearer to the bus stations, *Posada Santo Domingo* (☎ 5-01-36), 20 de Noviembre 119, has clean double rooms (private shower and fan) for US$8.50.

The *Hotel La Croix* (☎ 5-00-14), Hidalgo 10, on the north side of the park, has a pretty courtyard with potted tropical plants and adequate doubles with fan and shower for US$13. La Croix is usually full by mid-afternoon.

Best of the rock-bottom places is the *Posada Bonampak* (☎ 5-09-25), Avenida Belisario Domínguez 33, five blocks northwest of the park. No frills here, but rooms are well kept, bathrooms are nicely tiled, and prices are only US$6 for a single or double with one bed, US$8 with two beds.

Other rock-bottom options are on Hidalgo, west of the park. The *Posada San Francisco* is basic and dingy at US$6 to US$8 per double. Across the street, the Posada San Vicente is similar. Much nicer and only slightly more expensive is *Hotel Naj K'in*, Hidalgo 72, a family-run place with middling rooms, nice bathrooms, hot water and fans for US$8.50/12/15/18.

Hotel Kashlan (☎ 5-02-97, fax 5-03-09), Avenida 5 de Mayo 105 at Allende is well located. Its decent rooms have private baths, and cost US$16/20 a single/double with fan, US$10 more with air-con. A laundry is just across the street.

The *Hotel Regional* (☎ 5-01-83), Juárez at Aldama, has adequate rooms with shower and fan around a small plant-filled courtyard priced at US$10/14/18. The *Hotel Misol-Ha* (☎ 5-00-92) is priced similarly.

La Posada (☎ 5-04-37), behind Hotel Maya Tulipanes in La Cañada, is a quiet backpackers' hangout with a grassy courtyard, table tennis, and a lobby wall covered with messages of peace, passion and travel. Average rooms with bath cost US$10/13.

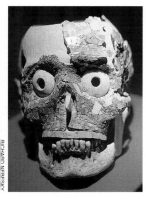

OAXACA
Above: Mixtec mask, Museo Regional de Oaxaca
Right: Looking for a gig
Below: 'House of Mezcal'

RICHARD NEBESKY

F STOPPELMAN

RICHARD NEBESKY

Top: Church, El Tule
Bottom Left: Agave, near Oaxaca
Bottom Right: Church of Coixtlahuaca, Oaxaca

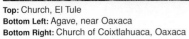

Places to Stay – middle

The *Hotel Palenque* (☎ 5-01-88, fax 5-00-39), Avenida 5 de Mayo 15, the town's oldest hotel, has been spruced up and now offers good value. Its rooms, priced at US$17/18/20 for a single/double/triple with private bath and fan, are arranged around a pretty garden courtyard which boasts a small and sometimes presentably clean swimming pool. Rooms with air-con cost US$10 more.

Hotel Chan-Kah (☎ 5-03-18, fax 5-04-89), above the restaurant of the same name, is at the corner of Juárez and Independencia overlooking the park. Lots of extras here: an elevator, insect screens, two double beds and a TV in each room, little balconies and air-con for US$30 a double.

Near the park on Juárez, the *Hotel Casa de Pakal* has 14 small double rooms with air-con and private bath for US$22.

In La Cañada, walk east from the Mayan head statue to find the *Hotel Maya Tulipanes* (☎ 5-02-01, fax 5-10-04), Calle Cañada 6, the most comfortable lodging on the street. Air-con rooms go for US$35/42; there is a small pool and a nice restaurant.

Next along the street, and under the same management as the Maya Tulipanes, is the cheaper *Hotel Kin-Ha* (☎ 5-04-46), with large air-con rooms going for US$23/29.

Across the road is the *Hotel Xibalbas* (☎ 5-04-11, fax 5-03-92), with attractive air-con rooms above Shivalva Travel Agency and in the modern A-frame next door, priced at US$20/23.

Hotel La Cañada (☎ 5-01-02) is a group of cottages at the eastern end of the street, many with huge ceramic bathtubs. This was once a favorite with archaeologists working at the ruins. Rates are US$20/23 with fan, slightly more for air-con. On the road to the ruins is *Villas Solymar Kin-Ha*, with cabañas for US$25 to US$29 with fan, US$10 more with air-con.

Places to Stay – top end

The most attractive and interesting lodgings in Palenque are at *Chan-Kah Resort*

Temple of the Sun, Palenque

TONY WHEELER

Village (☎ 5-03-18, fax 5-04-89), three km west of town and two km east of the ruins. The palapa-topped restaurant, enormous stone-bound swimming pool, lush jungle gardens and other accouterments enhance the handsome wood and stone cottages with Mayan traditional accents, private baths, ceiling fans and air conditioning, for US$60 double.

South of town 3.5 km on the road to San Cristóbal is the *Calinda Nututum Palenque* (☎ 5-01-00, fax 5-01-61). The modern motel-style buildings are set in spacious jungle gardens shaded by palm trees. Large air-con rooms with bath cost US$60 a double.

The *Hotel Misión Palenque Park Plaza* (☎ 5-02-41, fax 5-03-00), at the far eastern end of town along Hidalgo, has gardens, a pool, restaurant and bar, but is inconveniently located and overpriced at US$75 double, sometimes without air-con.

Other hotels are north of the Maya head statue, but none are conveniently located or distinguished in their services.

The *Hotel Tulija Days Inn* (☎ 5-01-04, fax 5-01-63) is closest to the Maya head statue. Doubles cost US$62. The *Best Western Plaza Palenque* (☎ 5-05-55, fax 5-03-95), 500 meters farther north, charges the same for its 100 air-con rooms surrounding a garden and swimming pool; there's a disco, bar and restaurant. Even farther north, the 72-room *Hotel Ciudad Real Palenque* (☎/fax 5-12-85, 5-13-15) has three-story motel-style lodgings that surround a central swimming pool and restaurant-bar.

Places to Eat

Cheapest fare in Palenque is at the taquerías along the eastern side of the park, in front of the church. Try *Los Faroles* or *Refresquería Deportista* for a plate of tacos at US$2 to US$3.

Restaurant Maya, at the corner of Independencia and Hidalgo on the northwest corner of the park, is the longstanding favorite since 1958, according to the menu. The food is típico and the hours long (7 am to 11 pm). Prices range from US$3 to US$7 for a full meal; the comida corrida costs US$3.50.

Next most popular is *Los Portales*, at 20 de Noviembre and Independencia, offering breakfasts for US$1.75 to US$2.50, set-priced meals for US$3 to US$3.75, and – some evenings – special two-for-one prices on drinks.

Restaurant Virgo's (☎ 5-08-83), Hidalgo 5, offers 2nd-story open-air dining one block west of the park. White pillars, a red-tile roof, plants and occasional live marimba music set the scene. Try the burritas al aguacate (US$2.25), or one of their pasta plates for about the same. Meat dishes cost around US$4. They serve wine here as well as beer.

Also good is *Restaurant Mundo Maya*, on Juárez a half block west of the park, with rustic decor and numerous set-price menus.

Restaurant Artemio's is a family-run place facing el parque. Everything on the menu seems to cost between US$2.25 and US$4.50, whether it be filete, chicken or traditional Mexican antojitos.

Several good cheap eateries are to be found along Juárez west of the park. *Restaurante Paisanos* is a tidy, cheap workers' place where everything seems to cost about US$2.25. The nearby *Restaurant El Herradero* is similar.

Pizzería Palenque on Juárez at Allende has surprisingly good pizzas ranging in price from a small cheese (US$3.25) to a large combination (US$9).

Restaurant Chan-Kah, facing el parque at the corner of Independencia and Juárez, offers a Mexican variety plate with an assortment of antojitos for US$4. Sometimes there's live music in the upstairs bar.

Getting There & Away

Air Palenque's airport terminal is little more than a shack, but Aerocaribe (☎ 5-06-18, 5-06-19) runs flights between Palenque and Villahermosa daily except Thursday (US$50); Tuxtla Gutiérrez daily except Monday (US$45); Cancún on Monday, Wednesday and Friday (US$135); and Flores, Guatemala (for Tikal) on Monday, Wednesday and Friday (US$85).

Aerolíneas Bonanza (☎ 800-03062) runs flights on Monday, Wednesday and Friday between Palenque and Tuxtla Gutiérrez, Mérida and Cancún.

Bus Some bus passengers have reported goods stolen on trips to or from Palenque. Don't leave anything of value in the overhead rack, and stay alert. Your gear is probably safest in the luggage compartment under the bus, but watch as it is stowed and removed.

Autobuses de Oriente (ADO), Cristóbal Colón and Autotransportes del Sur (ATS) share the 1st-class bus station; the 2nd-class Autotransportes Tuxtla Gutiérrez (ATG), Figueroa and Transportes Lacandonia bus stations are nearby, all on Juárez. The 1st-class terminal has a baggage check (left luggage) room for US$1 per piece per day.

It's a good idea to buy your onward ticket from Palenque a day in advance if possible. Here are some distances, times and prices:

Agua Azul Crucero – 66 km, 1½ hours; numerous 2nd-class buses (US$1.60) by ATG, Figueroa and Lacandonia. These buses go on to Ocosingo, San Cristóbal and Tuxtla Gutiérrez; seats are sold to those passengers first. Tickets to Agua Azul go on sale 30 minutes before departure, and if all seats are sold, you must stand all the way to the Agua Azul turn-off. It is easier to take an organized day trip (see the Agua Azul section and Organized Tours in this Palenque section).

Bonampak – 152 km, three hours; Autobuses Lagos de Montebello (US$5) at 3 am, 9 am, 6 pm, 8 pm

Campeche – 362 km, five hours; ADO (US$12) at 8 am; Colón (US$12) at 1.45 and 9 pm; two by ATS (US$10)

Cancún – 869 km, 13 hours; ADO (US$26) at 8 pm; Colón (US$28) at 6.50 and 10.30 pm

Catazajá – 27 km, 30 minutes; six ADO (US$1), many more local

Chetumal – 425 km, seven hours; ADO (US$15) at 8 pm; Colón (US$15) at 6.50 and 10.30 pm; one by ATS (US$12)

Flores (Guatemala) – three routes between Palenque and Flores, which can be done in a day or overnight (see the To El Petén section for details)

Mérida – 556 km, nine or 10 hours; ADO (US$18) at 8 am; Colón (US$18) at 1.45 and 9 pm; several ATS as well

Misol-Ha – 25 km, 40 minutes; see Agua Azul Crucero, above, and the Palenque Organized Tours and Agua Azul sections

Mexico City (TAPO) – 1020 km, 16 hours; ADO (US$35) at 6 pm

Oaxaca – 850 km, 15 hours; ADO (US$27) at 5.30 pm

Ocosingo – 123 km, 2½ hours; at least a dozen buses daily; four Colón (US$3.75), more by Figueroa and Lacandonia (US$2.25 to US$3.75)

Playa del Carmen – 800 km, 12 hours; ADO (US$27) at 8 pm; Colón (US$25) at 6.50 and 10.30 pm; and ATS (US$20)

San Cristóbal de Las Casas – 215 km, 4½ hours; eight by Colón (US$6), seven by Figueroa (US$6), others by ATG, ATS and Lacandonia

Tulum – 738 km, 11 hours; Colón (US$20) at 6.50 and 10.30 pm

Tuxtla Gutiérrez – 275 km, six hours; more than a dozen buses, six by Colón (US$9), seven by Figueroa (US$8), others by ATG and Oriente de Chiapas

Villahermosa – 150 km, 2½ hours; 10 by ADO (US$5); one Colón (US$5) at 11.10 pm

Getting Around

The airport is less than one km north of the Maya head statue along the road to Catazajá. Taxis wait at the park and the bus stations. Minibuses shuttle between Palenque town and ruins about every 15 minutes until 6 pm. The train station is at Pakal-Na, six km north of Palenque town, though the trains should be avoided.

BONAMPAK & YAXCHILÁN

The ruins of Bonampak – famous for frescoes – and the ancient city of Yaxchilán are accessible by bus, on organized camping excursions from Palenque, or by chartered small plane.

Bonampak and Yaxchilán have neither food nor water, so make certain you are well supplied; also bring insect repellent and a flashlight (torch). Don't leave your gear unattended, as thefts have been reported.

TABASCO & CHIAPAS

Bonampak

Bonampak, 155 km southeast of Palenque near the Guatemalan frontier, was hidden from the outside world by dense jungle until 1946. A young WWII conscientious objector by the name of Charles Frey fled the United States draft and somehow wound up here in the Lacandón rainforest. Local Indians showed him the ruins, which they used as a sacred site. Frey revealed his findings to Mexican officials and archaeological expeditions were mounted. Frey died in 1949 while attempting to save an expedition member from drowning in the turbulent Usumacinta.

The ruins of Bonampak are situated around a rectangular plaza. Only the southern edifices are preserved, however. It was the frescoes of Building 1 that excited Frey: three rooms are covered with paintings that depict ancient Mayan ceremonies and customs.

Unfortunately, some 12 centuries of weather deterioration were accelerated when the first expedition attempted to clean the murals with kerosene. On the positive side, some restoration has been undertaken and reproductions have been installed for comparison.

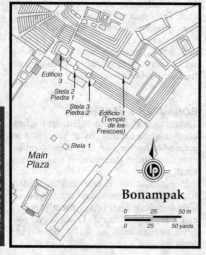

Edificio 3
Stela 2 / Piedra 1
Stela 3 / Piedra 2
Edificio 1 (Templo de los Frescoes)
Stela 1
Main Plaza

Bonampak

0   25   50 m
0   25   50 yards

Yaxchilán

Set above the jungled banks of the Usumacinta, Yaxchilán was first inhabited about 200 AD, though of the hieroglyphs found the earliest have been dated from 514 to 807 AD. Although not as well restored as Palenque, the ruins here cover a greater extent, and further excavation may yield even more significant finds.

Yaxchilán rose to the peak of its prominence in the 8th century under a king whose name in hieroglyphs is translated as Shield Jaguar. His shield-and-jaguar symbol appears on many of the site's buildings and stelae. The city's power expanded under Shield Jaguar's son, Parrot Jaguar (752-70). His hieroglyph consists of a small jungle cat with feathers on the back and a bird superimposed on the head. Building 33 on the southwestern side of the plaza has fine religious carvings over the northern doorways, and a roofcomb which retains most of its original beauty.

The central plaza holds statues of crocodiles and jaguars. A lintel in Building 20 shows a dead man's spirit emerging from the mouth of a man speaking about him, and stelae of Maya making offerings to the gods.

Be certain to walk to Yaxchilán's highest temples, still covered with trees and not visible from the plaza. Building 41 is the tallest, and the view from its top is one of the highlights of a visit to Yaxchilán. Some tour guides do not want to make the effort to show you Building 41 – insist on it!

Getting There & Away

The road from Palenque to Bonampak is being improved, and access will soon be easier and faster. At this writing, travel agencies in Palenque run two-day road and river tours to Bonampak and Yaxchilán (see Palenque, Organized Tours). A minivan takes you within seven km of Bonampak and you walk the rest of the way. (By the time you arrive the improved road may get you closer to the ruins.) Tents are provided for overnight. The next morning, you are driven to the Río Usumacinta, where a motor boat takes you through the jungle

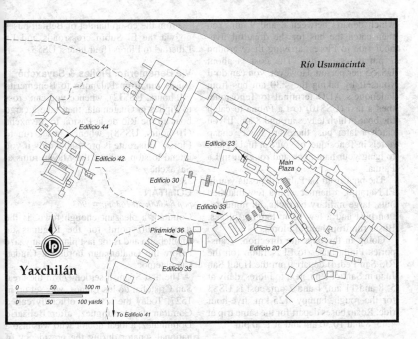

Río Usumacinta

Edificio 44

Edificio 42

Edificio 23

Main Plaza

Edificio 30

Edificio 33

Pirámide 36

Edificio 20

Yaxchilán

Edificio 35

0   50   100 m
0   50   100 yards

To Edificio 41

to Yaxchilán. The rate is US$80 to US$100 per person for the two-day venture, including transportation and all meals.

There are also one-day trips offered to Bonampak or Yaxchilán. Most travel agents charge US$50 to US$70 for a one-day excursion.

It doesn't much matter who you sign up with; you'll probably end up in the same vehicle with others booked by other agencies.

If you have camping gear and are on a tight budget, you can do the same trip by yourself on jungle buses for about half that much. Take an Autobuses Lagos de Montebello bus to Frontera Corozal (about 4½ hours). Register at the Migración office at Frontera Corozal; it's sometimes possible to bed down here for the night. Renting a boat to cruise down the Usumacinta to Yaxchilán is fairly easy. A chartered boat might cost US$60, but sometimes you can hitch a ride with a group for US$10 or so. The bus from Frontera to Palenque leaves

early in the morning; you can make the seven-km trek to Bonampak from the road turnoff if you care to.

TO EL PETÉN, GUATEMALA

There are currently three routes through the jungle from Palenque to Flores, El Petén (Guatemala), the main stepping-off point for the magnificent ruins of Tikal. Whichever way you go, make sure you clear customs and get your exit and entry stamps in your passport on both sides of the border. For details on travel in Guatemala, see Lonely Planet's *Guatemala, Belize & Yucatán: La Ruta Maya.*

Via La Palma & El Naranjo

The traditional route to El Petén is via bus to Tenosique and La Palma, then by boat along the Río San Pedro to El Naranjo, then by bus to Flores.

Travel agencies in Palenque offer to get you from Palenque to La Palma by minibus in time to catch the boat to El Naranjo,

TABASCO & CHIAPAS

which departs between 8 and 9 am. You then catch the bus for the dreadful five-hour ride to Flores, arriving there around 7 pm the same day. The cost is about US$55 per person. However, you can do it yourself by taking the 4.30 am bus from Palenque's ADO terminal to Tenosique, then a taxi (US$10) to La Palma to catch the boat, which leaves around 8 am. If you catch a later bus, there are basic, cheap hotels in Tenosique, or you can find a place to hang your hammock and rough it in La Palma.

The boat from La Palma deposits you in El Naranjo, a hamlet with a few thatched huts, large military barracks, an immigration post and a few basic lodging places. Buses run from here to Flores.

Going in the opposite direction, Transportes Pinita buses to El Naranjo (on the Río San Pedro) depart from the Hotel San Juan in Santa Elena, next to Flores, daily at 5, 8 and 11 am, 1 and 2 pm; cost is US$3 for the rough, bumpy, 125-km, five-hour ride. Rosío buses depart for the same trip at 4.45, 8 and 10.30 am and at 1.30 pm.

Via Frontera Corozal & Bethel

From Palenque, you can bus to Frontera Corozal (three hours, US$5), take a boat upstream on the Río Usumacinta (25 minutes to the Posada Maya, 35 minutes to the village of Bethel), and either stay overnight at the Posada Maya or continue on the bus to Flores. Frontera Corozal is within reach of the ruins of Bonampak and Yaxchilán (see the preceding section).

Frequent boats make the hour-long trip upriver from Frontera Corozal to Bethel on the Guatemalan side, charging from US$4 to US$12 for the voyage, depending to some extent on your bargaining power.

Palenque travel agencies may insist that you can't do this trip on your own, that you must sign up for their US$30 trip, and that there is no place to stay overnight at the border. Not so! These organized trips save you some hassle, but you can do the same thing yourself for half the price. Just be sure to hit the road as early as possible in the morning.

From the co-op hamlet of Bethel, buses go via the El Subín crossroads and La Libertad to Flores (four hours, US$3).

Via Benemerito, Pipiles & Sayaxché

Buses run from Palenque to Benemerito (10 hours, US$12), whence you can cross to Pipiles in Guatemala, then take a cargo boat up the Río de la Pasión to Sayaxché (10 hours, US$8), whence buses run to Flores. This route is preferable only if you intend to stop and see the Mayan ruins at Sayaxché.

COMITÁN

pop 84,000; alt 1635m; ☎ *963*

Comitán, a pleasant enough town, is the jumping-off point for the Lagunas de Montebello and is the last place of any size before the Guatemalan border at Ciudad Cuauhtémoc.

The first Spanish settlement in the area, San Cristóbal de los Llanos, was set up in 1527. Today the town is officially called Comitán de Domínguez, after Belisario Domínguez, a local doctor who was also a national senator during the presidency of Victoriano Huerta. Domínguez had the cheek to speak out in the senate in 1913 against Huerta's record of political murders and was himself murdered for his pains.

Orientation

Comitán is set amid hills, so you'll find yourself walking up and down, down and up.

The wide and attractive main plaza is bounded by Avenida Central on its west side and 1 Sur Ote on the south. The street numbering scheme resembles that of Tuxtla Gutiérrez in its complexity and confusion.

The 1st-class Cristóbal Colón bus station is on the Pan-American Highway, here named the Boulevard Belisario Domínguez and called simply 'El Bulevar.' It passes through the western part of town, about a 20-minute walk from the main plaza. Taxis outside the terminal charge US$1 for the short trip to the main plaza, or you can

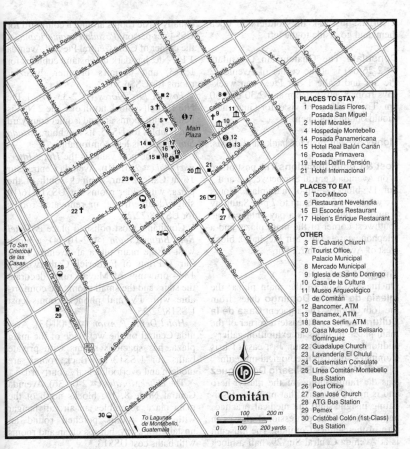

Comitán

| 0 | 100 | 200 m |
| 0 | 100 | 200 yards |

PLACES TO STAY
1 Posada Las Flores,
  Posada San Miguel
2 Hotel Morales
4 Hospedaje Montebello
14 Posada Panamericana
16 Hotel Real Balún Canán
16 Posada Primavera
19 Hotel Delfín Pensión
21 Hotel Internacional

PLACES TO EAT
5 Taco-Miteco
6 Restaurant Nevelandia
15 El Escocés Restaurant
17 Helen's Enrique Restaurant

OTHER
3 El Calvario Church
7 Tourist Office,
  Palacio Municipal
8 Mercado Municipal
9 Iglesia de Santo Domingo
10 Casa de la Cultura
11 Museo Arqueológico
  de Comitán
12 Bancomer, ATM
13 Banamex, ATM
18 Banca Serfin, ATM
20 Casa Museo Dr Belisario
  Domínguez
22 Guadalupe Church
23 Lavandería El Chulul
24 Guatemalan Consulate
25 Línea Comitán-Montebello
  Bus Station
26 Post Office
27 San José Church
28 ATG Bus Station
29 Pemex
30 Cristóbal Colón (1st-Class)
  Bus Station

cross El Bulevar in front of the bus station and catch any minibus with 'Centro' in its window. To walk to the plaza, turn left (north) out of the bus station and walk downhill, then take the first right downhill onto Calle 4 Sur Pte (but it's not marked), and walk six blocks (up and down hills), then turn left onto Avenida Central Sur and go three blocks.

The 2nd-class Autotransportes Tuxtla Gutiérrez (ATG) bus station is several blocks north of the Cristóbal Colón station. To reach the town center, walk out of the ATG station, turn left (south), then left again (east) on Calle 2 Sur Poniente and

walk six blocks to Avenida Central, then turn left (north) for one block to the plaza.

Línea Comitán-Montebello buses serving Lagunas de Montebello go from Avenida 2 Pte Sur 17B between Calles 2 and 3 Sur Pte, two blocks west and 1½ south of the main plaza.

Information
Tourist Office There's a helpful tourist office (☎ 2-40-47) in the Palacio Municipal on the north side of the main plaza, open Monday to Saturday from 9 am to 8 pm, Sunday 9 am to 2 pm. The tall iron gates to the palacio may be closed to keep out

TABASCO & CHIAPAS

terrorists; just ask the soldiers to open them, and go inside to the left.

Consulate The Guatemalan Consulate (☎ 2-26-69) is at the corner of Avenida 2 Pte Sur and Calle 1 Sur Pte, open weekdays from 8 am to 1 pm and 2.30 to 4.30 pm. Those who need visas for Guatemala should obtain them here.

Money See our map for banks and ATMs.

Post & Communications The post office is on Avenida Central Sur between 2 and 3 Sur, 1½ blocks south of main plaza. Hours are weekdays from 8 am to 7 pm, Saturday 8 am to 1 pm. There's a pay phone at the southwest corner of the main plaza, and a telephone caseta on 2 Sur Pte, half a block west of Avenida Central Sur.

Things to See
On the east side of the main plaza, the **Iglesia de Santo Domingo** dates from the 16th century. The adjacent **Casa de la Cultura**, on the southeastern corner of the main plaza, includes an exhibition gallery, auditorium and museum. Just east of it is Comitán's small archaeological museum.

Casa Museo Dr Belisario Domínguez was the family home of the martyr-hero and is now a museum that provides fascinating insights into the medical practices and the life of the professional classes in turn-of-the-century Comitán. The museum is at Avenida Central Sur 29, half a block south of the main plaza. It's open from 10 am to 6.45 pm (Sunday 9 am to 12.45 pm), closed Monday. Admission is only a peso.

Places to Stay
Comitán has several cheap posadas with small, often dingy and severely plain rooms, most of them OK for a night. *Posada Primavera*, Calle Central Pte 4, only a few steps west of the main plaza, charges US$3.25 per bed for rooms with sinks, but without bath or windows. The *Hospedaje Montebello* (☎ 2-17-70), a block farther at Calle 1 Norte Pte 10, has

equally basic rooms around a courtyard for US$4 per person. *Posada Panamericana*, at the corner of Calle Central Pte and Avenida 1 Pte Nte, has dark downstairs cubicles for US$3, and upstairs brighter, breezier rooms for US$6.50.

Posada Las Flores (☎ 2-33-34), 1 Pte Nte 15, half a block north of Calle 2 Nte, is better, with rooms around a quiet courtyard and doubles for US$5. Its neighbor, *Posada San Miguel*, is less comfortable.

About the best value is the *Hotel Internacional* (☎ 2-01-10), Avenida Central Sur 16 at Calle 2 Sur, a block south of the plaza, with older rooms for US$14/16/19 single/double/triple, or renovated rooms for US$18/22/26.

Comitán's most polished place is *Hotel Real Balún Canán* (☎ 2-10-94), a block west of the main plaza at Avenida 1 Pte Sur 7. Prints of Frederick Catherwood's 1844 drawings of Mayan ruins decorate the stairs and the small rooms are comfortable with TV and phone. Rooms cost US$18/22/25.

Hotel Delfín Pensión (☎ 2-00-13), Avenida Central on the west side of the main plaza, has spacious rooms with private baths for US$12/15. Back rooms are modern and overlook a leafy courtyard.

The *Hotel Morales* (☎ 2-04-36), Avenida Central Norte 8, 1½ blocks north of the main plaza, resembles an aircraft hangar with small rooms perched round an upstairs walkway, but it's clean and rooms with baths cost US$13.

Places to Eat
The friendly, colorful *Taco-Miteco*, on Avenida Central Norte 5 near the main plaza, serves 13 varieties of tacos for US$0.35 each, quesadillas for US$2, and a 'super-breakfast' of juice, coffee, eggs, toast and chilaquiles for US$2.25.

Several reasonable cafés line the west side of the main plaza. Prime among them is *Helen's Enrique Restaurant*, in front of the Hotel Delfín. With a porch and pretensions to decor, Helen's serves all three meals for US$2.50 to US$6. *Restaurant Acuario*, *Restaurant Yuly*, and *Restaurant*

Vicks, along the same row, are more basic and cheaper.

Restaurant Nevelandia, on the northwest corner of the main plaza, has tacos for US$0.30 to US$0.65, antojitos, spaghetti and burgers for around US$2.25, and meat dishes typically for US$4.50.

For a more expensive meal amid cosmopolitan surroundings go to the Hotel Real Balún Canán, where *El Escocés Restaurant* is open until 11 pm and the *Disco Tzisquirin* until 1 am.

Getting There & Away

Comitán is 85 km southeast down the Pan-American Highway from San Cristóbal, and 80 km north of Ciudad Cuauhtémoc. Buses are regularly stopped for document checks by immigration and army officials, both north and south of Comitán, so keep your passport handy.

Departures include:

Ciudad Cuauhtémoc (Guatemalan border) – 80 km, 1½ hours; seven by Colón (US$2.50); six by ATG (US$1.75)

Mexico City (TAPO) – 1168 km, 20 hours; two by Colón for US$40 or US$46

San Cristóbal de Las Casas – 85 km, 1½ hours; two dozen buses for US$1.25 to US$1.75

Tapachula – 260 km, seven hours (via Motozintla); seven by Colón (US$8), more by ATG (US$6.50)

Tuxtla Gutiérrez – 170 km, 3½ hours; 16 by Colón (US$4.75 to US$6), also by ATG (US$4)

LAGUNAS DE MONTEBELLO

The temperate forest along the Guatemalan border southeast of Comitán is dotted with about 60 small lakes – the Lagunas or Lagos de Montebello. The area is beautiful, refreshing, not hard to reach, and quiet. The many little-used vehicle tracks through the forest provide some excellent walks. Some Mexican weekenders come down here in their cars, but the rest of the time you'll probably see only resident villagers and a small handful of visitors. There are two very basic hostelries and a campground. At one edge of the lake district are the rarely visited Mayan ruins of Chin-

kultic. A number of Guatemalan refugee camps are in and around the lakes area.

Orientation

The paved road to Montebello turns east off the Pan-American Highway 16 km to the south of Comitán, just before the town of La Trinitaria. Running first through flat ranchland, it passes Chinkultic after 30 km, entering the forest and the Parque Nacional Lagunas de Montebello five km further on. At the park entrance (no fee) the road splits. The paved section continues three km ahead (north) to the Lagunas de Colores, where it dead-ends at two small houses 50 meters from Laguna Bosque Azul. To the right (east) from the park entrance, a dirt road leads to turnings for several more lakes and to the village and lake of Tziscao (nine km).

Chinkultic

These dramatically sited ruins lie two km along a track north off the La Trinitaria-Montebello road, 30 km from the Pan-American Highway. A sign 'Chinkultic 3' marks the turning. Doña María at La Orquidea restaurant, a km further along the road, has a map and book on Chinkultic.

Chinkultic was on the far western edge of the ancient Mayan area. Dates carved here extend from 591 to 897 AD – the last of which is nearly a century after the latest dates at Palenque, Yaxchilán and Toniná. Those years no doubt span Chinkultic's peak period, but occupation is thought to have started around 200 AD and continued until after 900 AD. Of the 200 mounds scattered over a wide area, only a few parts have been cleared, but seeing them is worth the effort.

The track brings you first to a gate with a hut on the left. From here, take the path to the left, which curves round to the right. On the overgrown hill to the right of this path stands one of Chinkultic's major structures, E23. The path reaches a long ball court where several stelae – some carved with human figures – lie on their sides, some under thatch shelters.

Follow the track back to the hut and turn left, passing what could be a parking area,

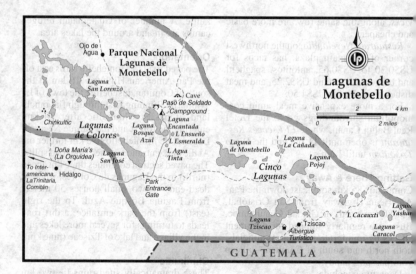

until you can spot a few stone mounds in the undergrowth to the right. On the hillside that soon comes into view is the partly restored temple called El Mirador. The path goes over a stream and steeply up to El Mirador, from which there are good views over the surrounding lakes and down into a big 50-meter-deep cenote.

The Lakes

Lagunas de Colores The paved road straight on from the park entrance leads through the Lagunas de Colores, so called because their colors range from turquoise to deep green. The first of these, on the right about two km, is Laguna Agua Tinta. Then on the left comes Laguna Esmeralda followed by Laguna Encantada, with Laguna Ensueño on the right opposite Encantada. The fifth and biggest is Laguna Bosque Azul, on the left where the road ends.

Two paths lead on from the end of the road. Straight ahead for 800 meters will bring you to the *gruta* – a cave shrine where locals make offerings (take a flashlight with you). To the left, you reach Paso de Soldado, a picnic site beside a small river after 300 meters.

Laguna de Montebello About three km along the dirt road toward Tziscao from the park entrance, a track leads 200 meters left to the Laguna de Montebello, one of the bigger lakes, with a flat, open area along its shore where the track ends. About 150 meters to the left is a stony area which is better for swimming than the muddy fringes elsewhere.

Cinco Lagunas A further three km along the Tziscao road another track leads left to these 'five lakes.' Only four of them are visible from the road, but the second, La Cañada, on the right after about 1.5 km, is probably the most beautiful of all the Montebello lakes; it's also nearly cut in half by two rocky outcrops. The track eventually reaches the village of San Antonio and is, amazingly, a bus route.

One km further along the Tziscao road from the Cinco Lagunas, you can turn down a track that leads to Laguna Pojoj, one km north.

Laguna Tziscao This comes into view on the right another km along the road. The junction for Tziscao village is a little farther, again on the right. The village has pleasant grassy streets, friendly people and a hostel.

Places to Stay & Eat

Half a km past the Chinkultic turn-off, you can camp or rent a cabin at *La Orquidea*, a small restaurant on the left of the road. The owner, Señora María Domínguez de Castellanos, better known as Doña María, has helped Guatemalan refugees by buying a nearby farm and turning it over to them. The cabins have electric light but no running water, and cost US$3; meals are less.

Inside the national park, camping is officially allowed only at Laguna Bosque Azul (no fee), the last and biggest of the Lagunas de Colores, where the paved road ends. There are toilets and water here. *Bosque Azul Restaurant*, at the Laguna Bosque Azul car park, serves eggs (US$2), chiles rellenos or meaty dishes (US$4), and drinks, chips and fruit. Outside the restaurant, local cowboys wait, eager to guide you (by horse) to the caves (US$3).

Tziscao village has a hostel – the *Albergue Turístico* – where you pay US$3 per person for a dormitory bunk or a wooden cabaña, or camp for US$1. The hostel lies on the shore of one of the most beautiful lakes – you can rent a rowboat – and Guatemala is just a few hundred meters away. Entering the village, turn right beside a corner store soon after you come level with a small church on the hill, and follow the track down toward the lake, then round to the left. The señora will cook up eggs, frijoles and tortillas (US$2) and there's a fridge full of refrescos. The toilets seem to be in permanent desperate need of a good clean.

Getting There & Away

It's possible to make a whirlwind tour of Chinkultic and the lakes in a day from San Cristóbal – either by public transport or tour, but if you prefer a pace that enables you to absorb something of your surroundings, it's better to stay at the lakes or at least at Comitán.

Buses and combis to the Lagunas de Montebello go from the yard of Línea Comitán-Montebello in Comitán. One or the other leaves every 20 or 30 minutes up to about 5 pm. Vehicles have a number of different destinations so make sure you get one that's going your way.

Most people head initially for Chinkultic, Doña María's (La Orquidea), Lagunas de Colores, Laguna de Montebello or Tziscao. The last vehicle to Tziscao (1¼ hours, US$2) is at about 2 pm. By combi, it's 45 minutes to Doña María's; a local bus can take up to 1½ hours (US$1.75). It's the same fare to the Chinkultic turnoff or Lagunas de Colores.

Returning to Comitán, the last bus leaves Lagunas de Colores at 4.30 pm.

MOTOZINTLA

The small town of Motozintla lies in a deep valley in the Sierra Madre 70 km southwest of Ciudad Cuauhtémoc. A good road leads to it from the Pan-American Highway a few km north of Ciudad Cuauhtémoc, then continues down to Huixtla near the Chiapas coast near Tapachula – a spectacular, unusual trip. Have your passport handy for identity checks.

CIUDAD CUAUHTÉMOC

This 'city' is just a few houses and a comedor or two, but it's the last/first place in Mexico on the Pan-American Highway (highway 190). Comitán is 80 km north, San Cristóbal 165 km north. Ciudad Cuauhtémoc is the Mexican border post; the Guatemalan one is three km south at La Mesilla. There are taxis (US$2), combis and trucks (US$0.50) running between the border posts.

If yours is a passport which requires only a tourist card to visit Guatemala, you can get it at the border. If you need a visa, obtain it in advance at the Guatemalan Consulate in Comitán.

There's no bank at this border. Individual moneychangers operate but may give fewer quetzals than a bank would.

Getting There & Away

Many buses and minibuses shuttle between Ciudad Cuauhtémoc, Comitán and San

Cristóbal all day. See those two cities' sections for details.

Guatemalan buses depart La Mesilla every half hour from 8 am to 8 pm for main points inside Guatemala like Huehuetenango (84 km, 1½ to two hours, US$1), Quetzaltenango (also known as Xela, 170 km, 3½ hours, US$3.35) and Guatemala City (380 km, seven hours, US$4.50). Lago de Atitlán (245 km, five hours) and Chichicastenango (244 km, five hours) both lie a few km off the Pan-American Highway. Before boarding a bus at La Mesilla, try to find out when it's leaving and when it reaches your destination. This could save you several hours of sitting in a stationary bus. For full information on traveling in Guatemala, get a copy of Lonely Planet's *Guatemala, Belize & Yucatán: La Ruta Maya*.

THE SOCONUSCO
The Soconusco is Chiapas' hot, fertile coastal plain, 15 to 35 km wide. Its climate is hot and humid all year round, with plenty of rain from June to October. The steep mountainsides of the Sierra Madre de Chiapas, sweeping up from the coast, provide an excellent climate for the cultivation of coffee, bananas and other crops. Though far less interesting than other parts of Chiapas, the Soconusco has its high points, which you might want to stop for if you're heading through this area on your way to/from Guatemala.

Arriaga
pop 40,000; alt 40m
Arriaga, where the Juchitán-Tapachula road meets the Tuxtla Gutiérrez-Tapachula road, has a few suitable lodgings and restaurants, but no good reason for you to stop.

For some reason, quite a few buses end their runs in Arriaga. Happily, the same number start their runs here. The new Central de Autobuses houses all the 1st- and 2nd-class buses serving Arriaga. Destinations include:

Juchitán – 135 km, two hours; three by Colón (US$3.30); many by Sur and Fletes y Pasajes/Transportes Oaxaca-Istmo

Mexico City (TAPO) – 900 km, 16 hours, one afternoon Cristóbal Colón bus (US$34), and a Plus at 6.30 pm (US$43), 2nd-class buses every day by Fletes y Pasajes/Transportes Oaxaca-Istmo

Oaxaca – 400 km, seven hours; a 10 pm bus by Colón (US$13), a few 2nd-class buses daily by Sur and Fletes y Pasajes/Transportes Oaxaca-Istmo

Salina Cruz – 175 km, three hours; several buses daily by Colón for US$6.25, and by Sur

San Cristóbal de Las Casas – 240 km, five hours; buses every 30 minutes (via Tuxtla) by Colón (US$6.50), several by Sur for US$6

Tapachula – 245 km, 3½ hours; seven by Colón (US$8), and by Sur and ATG

Tonalá – 23 km, 30 minutes; Transportes-Arriaga-Tonalá minibuses every few minutes for US$0.75

Tuxtla Gutiérrez – 155 km, three hours; every hour by Colón (US$4.50), others by ATG

Tonalá
Twenty-three km southeast of Arriaga on highway 200, Tonalá has only marginally more intrinsic appeal but is the jumping-off point for the laid-back beach spot of Puerto Arista. A tall pre-Hispanic stela in the Tonalá main plaza appears to depict Tláloc, the central Mexican rain god. There's also a small regional museum at Hidalgo 77, with some archaeological pieces found in the region.

The tourist office (☎ 966-3-01-01) is on the ground floor of the Palacio Municipal (look for its clock), on the Hidalgo side of the main plaza. It's open weekdays from 9 am to 3 pm and 6 to 8 pm, and Saturday 9 am to 2 pm.

Tonalá has no great accommodation deals. If you're heading for Puerto Arista, go straight there if you can.

Puerto Arista
Puerto Arista, 18 km southwest of Tonalá, is a half-km collection of palm shacks and a few more substantial buildings in the middle of a 30-km gray beach. The food's mostly fish, you get through a lot of refrescos, and nothing else happens except the crashing of the Pacific waves . . . until the weekend, when a few hundred Chiapanecos cruise in from the towns, or until

Semana Santa and Christmas, when they come in the thousands, and the residents make their money for the year.

Usually the most action you'll see is when an occasional fishing boat puts out to sea, or a piglet breaks into a trot if a dog gathers the energy to bark at it. Mosquitoes and sand fleas seem to be the only relentlessly energetic beings in town. The temperature's usually sweltering if you stray more than a few yards from the shore, and it's humid in summer.

The sea is clean here but don't go far from the beach: there's an undertow, and rip tides known as *canales* can sweep you a long way out in a short time.

TAPACHULA
pop 250,000; ☎ *962*
Most travelers come to Mexico's southernmost city only because it's a gateway to Guatemala, though for ruins buffs Izapa, 11 km east, is worth a visit.

Tapachula is the 'capital' of the Soconusco, and a busy commercial center, overlooked by the 4092-meter Tacaná volcano to its northeast, the first of a chain of volcanoes stretching southeast into Guatemala. The village of Unión Juárez, 40 km from Tapachula, supposedly provides good views of the volcano, and the surrounding country has hiking possibilities.

Orientation
The Parque Hidalgo (or Parque Central) is the main plaza, with the Sedetur tourist office, banks, and the Casa de la Cultura, formerly the Palacio Municipal.

Information
Tourist Offices The city tourist office (☎ 6-54-70, fax 6-55-22) is at Avenida 4 Nte 35, a few doors north of the Hospedaje Colonial, on the 3rd floor, and has few customers. The Sedetur office (☎ 6-87-55, fax 6-35-02) is at Avenida 8 Norte at Calle 3 Pte on the main plaza.

Consulate The Guatemalan Consulate (☎ 6-12-52) is on Avenida 9 Norte just south of Calle Central Oriente. It's open

weekdays from 8 am to 4 pm. Visas are issued quickly.

Money There are banks with ATMs around the main plaza, including Banamex on the east side and BanCrecer on the west. The Casa de Cambio Tapachula at the corner of Calle 3 Pte and Avenida 4 Nte, open Monday to Saturday 7.30 am to 7.30 pm and Sunday 7 am to 2 pm, is another option.

Post & Communications The post office is several blocks from the center on the corner of Calle 1 Ote and Avenida 9 Nte and is open weekdays from 8 am to 6 pm, Saturday 8 am to noon.

There are telephone casetas on Calle 17 Ote, 1½ blocks west of the Cristóbal Colón bus station, and in the Farmacia Monaco, which is across from Hotel Don Miguel on Calle 1 Pte.

Travel Agency Viajes Tacaná (☎ 6-87-95, fax 6-35-02) on Avenida 4 Nte 8, between Calle 1 and Calle Central, sells Aviacsa, Aeroméxico, and Mexicana tickets.

Museo Regional del Soconusco
The Soconusco Regional Museum on the west side of the Parque Hidalgo has some archaeological and folklore exhibits, including some finds from Izapa. Entry costs US$2.

Places to Stay – budget
The friendly *Hospedaje Las Américas* (☎ 6-27-57), at Avenida 10 Nte 47 north of the main plaza, has singles with fans and private bathroom for US$4.50/7 single/double. The *Hospedaje Colón* (☎ 6-91-78), on Avenida Central Nte 72, a couple of doors north of Calle 9 Ote, has small, noisy, mosquito-inhabited rooms with fans for US$7/11.

The *Hospedaje Colonial* (☎ 6-20-52), at Avenida 4 Norte 31, half a block north of Calle 3 Pte, has clean, bright rooms with private baths along a balcony for US$5.50 per person. Ring the bell to enter.

Around the corner (one block west) from the Cristóbal Colón bus station is *Hospedaje*

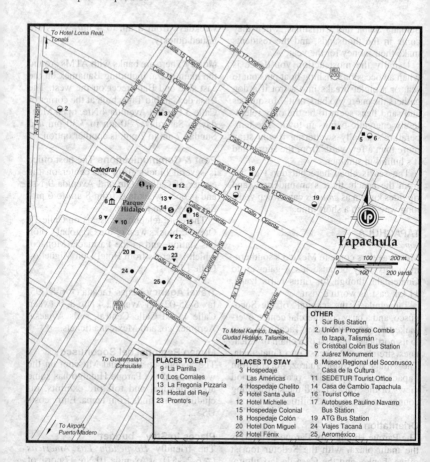

To Hotel Loma Real, Tonalá

Calle 15 Oriente

Calle 17 Oriente

Calle 13 Oriente

MEX 200

Av 14 Norte

Av 12 Norte

Av 10 Norte

Av 8 Norte

Av 5 Norte

Av 2 Norte

Av 4 Norte

■ 1

● 2

■ 3

■ 4

● 6
■ 5

Calle 11 Poniente

Catedral

Calle 9 Poniente

■ 18

Calle 9 Oriente

Parque Hidalgo

7 ▲   ● 11

■ 12

Calle 7 Poniente

● 17

Calle 7 Oriente

8 ⌂

13 ▼

14 ⓢ

● 16

● 19

9 ▼   ▼ 10

15

Calle 5 Poniente

Calle 5 Oriente

▼ 21

Calle 3 Poniente

20 ■

▼ 22

23 ▼

Av Central Norte

Calle 1 Poniente

24 ●

25 ●

Calle Central Poniente

Av 1 Norte

Av 3 Norte

To Motel Kamico, Izapa, Ciudad Hidalgo, Talismán

To Guatemalan Consulate

To Airport, Puerto Madero

MEX 18

Tapachula

0   100   200 m
0   100   200 yards

OTHER
1 Sur Bus Station
2 Unión y Progreso Combis to Izapa, Talismán
6 Cristóbal Colón Bus Station
7 Juárez Monument
8 Museo Regional del Soconusco, Casa de la Cultura
11 SEDETUR Tourist Office
14 Casa de Cambio Tapachula
16 Tourist Office
17 Autobuses Paulino Navarro Bus Station
19 ATG Bus Station
24 Viajes Tacaná
25 Aeroméxico

PLACES TO EAT
9 La Parrilla
10 Los Comales
13 La Fregonia Pizzaría
21 Hostal del Rey
23 Pronto's

PLACES TO STAY
3 Hospedaje Las Américas
4 Hospedaje Chelito
5 Hotel Santa Julia
12 Hotel Michelle
15 Hospedaje Colonial
18 Hospedaje Colón
20 Hotel Don Miguel
22 Hotel Fénix

Chelito (☎ 6-24-28), at Avenida 1 Nte 107 between Calle 15 Pte and 17 Pte. Rooms with B&W TV, fan and private bathroom cost US$11; for US$17 you get a color TV and air-con. Attached is a small café.

Places to Stay – middle
The *Hotel Santa Julia* (☎ 6-31-40), Calle 17 Ote 5, next door to the Cristóbal Colón 1st-class bus station, has clean singles/doubles with TV, telephone and private bath for US$18/26.

Hotel Fénix (☎ 5-07-55), Avenida 4 Norte 19 near the corner of Calle 1 Pte, a

block west of the main plaza, has an encouraging lobby and room service but a mixed bag of medium-sized rooms within. Some fan-cooled ones at US$18 are less dilapidated than some air-con ones at US$24.

The nearby modern and pricier *Hotel Don Miguel* (☎ 6-11-43) at Calle 1 Pte 18, is probably the best city center hotel. Rooms are clean and bright with air-con and TV for US$28/38. There's a good little restaurant here too.

Half a block east of the main plaza, at Calle 5 Pte 23, the *Hotel Michelle* (☎ 6-88-74, 5-26-40) has comely 2nd- and 3rd-story rooms with air-con, TV, big closets and desks for US$24/32 single/double.

Places to Stay – top end

The town's two top hotels, both with air-con rooms and swimming pools, are the *Motel Kamico* (☎ 6-26-40), on highway 200 east of the city (singles/doubles US$45/57), and the *Hotel Loma Real* (☎ 6-14-40), just off highway 200 on the west side of town, where rooms are US$60.

Places to Eat

Several restaurants line the south side of the main plaza. *Los Comales* serves a filling comida corrida for US$3.75, and traditional antojitos for less. *La Parrilla*, across the street on Avenida 8 Norte, is probably a better value, and open 24 hours. *Pronto's*, on Calle 1 Pte between Avenidas 4 and 2 Norte, is also open 24 hours but is pricier.

If the sun isn't glaring, you may want to sit at one of *La Fregonia Pizzaría's* sidewalk tables on the pedestrian extension of Calle 5 Pte, half a block east of the plaza. Pizzas, pastas, burgers and antojitos are all priced between US$2 and US$5.

Breakfast at *Hostal Del Rey*, Avenida 4 Norte 17 near Calle 3 Pte, with its pretty decor, quiet music, and waiters in pink bow ties and cummerbunds, is a nice way to begin the day. An early meal of hotcakes, fruit, eggs and coffee is US$3. Later in the day you may want soup and salad or antojitos for US$2.50, or aves or carne for US$4.50 to US$7.

Getting There & Away

Air Aviacsa (☎ 6-14-39, fax 6-31-59), Calle Central Norte 52B, operates daily nonstop flights from Tapachula to Tuxtla Gutiérrez and twice daily to Mexico City.

Aeroméxico (☎ 6-20-50), Avenida 2 Norte 6, has a daily nonstop flight to/from Mexico City.

Bus Cristóbal Colón, at Calle 17 Ote and Avenida 3 Norte, is five blocks east and six north of the main plaza. To reach the main plaza go west (left) along 17 Ote for two blocks, then six blocks south (left) down

Avenida Central Norte and three west (right) along Calle 5 Pte.

The main 2nd-class bus stations are Sur, at Calle 9 Pte 63, a block west of Avenida 12 Norte; Autotransportes Tuxtla Gutiérrez (ATG), at the corner of Calle 9 Ote and Avenida 3 Norte; and Autobuses Paulino Navarro, on Calle 7 Pte 5, half a block west of Avenida Central Norte.

Buses to/from the Guatemalan border are covered in the Talisman & Ciudad Hidalgo section. Other departures include:

Arriaga – 245 km, 3½ hours; eight buses by Cristóbal Colón (US$9), three afternoon buses by ATG (US$6), buses every 30 minutes by Autobuses Paulino Navarro (US$6)

Comitán – 260 km, seven hours (via Motozintla); three buses by ATG (US$12); several by Paulino Navarro (US$13)

Juchitán – 380 km, six hours; three buses by ATG (US$10), several daily by Sur

Mexico City (TAPO) – 1150 km, 20 hours; six regular Cristóbal Colón buses (US$43) and two afternoon Plus buses (US$53)

Oaxaca – 650 km, 11 hours; two by Colón (US$23), and one 2nd-class evening by Sur

Salina Cruz – 420 km, seven hours; two buses daily by ATG (US$14)

San Cristóbal de Las Casas – 350 km, eight hours; five by Colón (via Tuxtla) for US$11, more by ATG and Andrés Caso for US$6

Tonalá – 220 km, three hours; eight by Colón (US$7), three by ATG (US$5.50), several by Sur

Tuxtla Gutiérrez – 400 km, seven hours; five by Colón (US$12), six by ATG (US$10)

Train The station lies just south of the intersection of Avenida Central Sur and Calle 14. Only masochists and the hopelessly adventurous take the train.

Getting Around

Tapachula's airport is 20 km south of the city off the Puerto Madero road. Transporte Terrestre (☎ 6-12-87) at Avenida 2 Sur 40A charges US$3.25 to the airport and will pick you up from any hotel in Tapachula. A taxi is US$7.

IZAPA

If this site was in a more visited part of Mexico, it would have a constant stream of visitors, for it's not only important to archaeologists as a link between the Olmec and the Maya, but it's also interesting to walk around. It flourished from approximately 200 BC to 200 AD. The Izapa carving style – typically seen on stelae with altars placed in front – is derived from the Olmec style and most of the gods shown are descendants of Olmec deities, with their upper lips grotesquely lengthened. Early Mayan monuments from lowland north Guatemala are similar.

Northern Area
Most of this part of the site has been cleared and some restoration has been done. There are a number of platforms, a ball court, and several carved stelae and altars. The platforms and ball court were probably built sometime after Izapa was at its peak.

Southern Area
This is less visited than the northern area. Go back about 1.75 km along the road toward Tapachula and take a dirt road to the left. Where the vehicle track ends, a path leads to the right. The three areas of interest are separated by less-than-obvious foot trails and you may have to ask the caretaker to find and explain them. One is a plaza with several stelae under thatched roofs. The second is a smaller plaza with more stelae and three big pillars topped with curious stone balls. The third is a single carving of jaguar jaws holding a seemingly human figure.

Getting There & Away
Izapa is 11 km east of Tapachula on the road to Talismán. You can reach it by the combis of Unión y Progreso which depart from Calle 5 Pte, half a block west of Avenida 12 Nte in Tapachula. The main (northern) part of the site is marked on the left of the road. The second (southern) part lies less than one km back toward Tapachula on the other side of the road.

TALISMÁN & CIUDAD HIDALGO
The road from Tapachula to Guatemala heads 20 km east past Izapa to the border at Talismán bridge, opposite El Carmen, Guatemala. A branch south off this road leads to another border crossing at Ciudad Hidalgo (38 km from Tapachula), opposite Ciudad Tecún Umán. Both crossings are open 24 hours.

At the time of writing it was possible to obtain Guatemalan visas as well as tourist cards at the border, but check this in advance; availability may depend upon your nationality. There's a Guatemalan consulate at Central Ote 10 in Ciudad Hidalgo, as well as the one in Tapachula. The Guatemalan border posts may make various small charges as you go through, and they insist on being paid in either dollars or quetzals – so get some before you leave Tapachula.

Getting There & Away
Combis of Unión y Progreso shuttle between Tapachula and Talismán every few minutes. The fare is US$0.75. A taxi from Tapachula to Talismán takes 20 minutes and costs US$3.

Autobuses Paulino Navarro makes the 45-minute journey between Tapachula and Ciudad Hidalgo every hour for US$1.

There are two daily Cristóbal Colón 1st-class buses from Talismán to Mexico City for US$43.

Many of the longer-distance buses leaving the Guatemalan side of the border head for Guatemala City (about five hours away) by the coastal slope route through Retalhuleu and Escuintla. If you're heading for Lake Atitlán or Chichicastenango, you need to get to Quetzaltenango (Xela) first, for which you may have to change buses at Retalhuleu or at Malacatán on the Talismán-San Marcos-Quetzaltenango road. For details of travel in Guatemala, see Lonely Planet's *Guatemala, Belize & Yucatán: La Ruta Maya*.

The Yucatán Peninsula

When you cross the Río Usumacinta into the Yucatán Peninsula, you are crossing into the realm of the Maya. The appearance of the countryside changes, as do the houses and the people in them. Inheritors of a glorious and often violent history, the Maya live today where their ancestors lived a millennium ago. The Maya are proud to be Mexican, but even prouder to be Maya, and it is the Mayab – the lands of the Maya – that they consider their true country.

Though it's flat and hot, the Yucatán Peninsula has surprising diversity. There are archaeological sites galore, several handsome colonial cities, Mexico's most popular seaside resort and quiet coastlines populated mostly by exotic tropical birds.

The Yucatán Peninsula's rainy season is from mid-August to mid-October. During this time, afternoon showers come down most days. A good time to visit is in November and early December, when it's less crowded and less pricey.

HIGHLIGHTS

- Mérida, the 'White City,' traditional capital of the Yucatecan Maya
- Chichén Itzá, the great Maya-Toltec ceremonial center
- Uxmal, the graceful chief city of the Puuc region
- The Caribbean beaches: coral reefs, 'air-conditioned' sand and a laid-back lifestyle

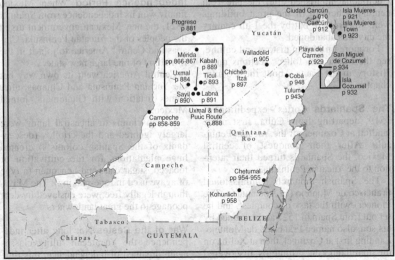

History

The Maya At the height of Mayan culture during the Late Classic Period (600 to 900 AD), the Mayan lands were ruled not as an empire but as a collection of independent but also interdependent city-states. Each city-state had its noble house, headed by a king who was the social, political and religious center of the city's life.

By the end of the Late Classic Period, the focus of Mayan civilization had shifted from Guatemala and Belize to the northern part of the Yucatán Peninsula, where a new civilization developed at Chichén Itzá, Uxmal and Labná.

In the 9th and 10th centuries classic Mayan civilization collapsed. Weakened, the Maya were prey to a wave of invaders from central Mexico. It's thought that Toltecs from Tula (near present-day Mexico City) sailed eastwards to the Yucatán Peninsula.

They were led by a fair-haired, bearded king named Kukulcán or Quetzalcóatl, who established himself in Yucatán at Uucil-abnal (Chichén Itzá). He left behind in Mexico, and then in Yucatán, a legend that he would one day return from the direction of the rising sun. The culture at Uucil-abnal flourished after the late 10th century, when all of the great buildings were constructed, but by the 14th century the city was abandoned.

For more on Mayan history and culture, see the Maya and Toltecs sections under History in the Facts About the Country chapter.

The Spaniards Cortés' expedition of 1519, departing from Cuba, first made landfall at Cozumel off the Yucatán Peninsula. After their conquest of central Mexico, the Spaniards turned their attention to the Yucatán Peninsula.

The Spanish monarch commissioned Francisco de Montejo (El Adelantado, The Pioneer) with the task of conquest, and he set out from Spain in 1527 accompanied by his son, also named Francisco de Montejo. Landing first at Cozumel, then at Xel-ha on the mainland, the Montejos discovered that the local people wanted nothing to do with them.

The Montejos then sailed around the peninsula, conquered Tabasco (1530), and established their base near Campeche, which could be easily supplied with necessities, arms and new troops from New Spain (central Mexico). They pushed inland, but after four long, difficult years were forced to retreat and to return to Mexico City in defeat.

The younger Montejo (El Mozo, The Lad) took up the cause again, with his father's support, and in 1540 he returned to Campeche with his cousin named (guess what?) Francisco de Montejo. These two Francisco de Montejos pressed inland with speed and success, allying themselves with the Xiú Maya against the Cocom Maya, defeating the Cocoms and gaining the Xiús as converts to Christianity.

The Montejos founded Mérida in 1542, and within four years had subjugated almost all of the Yucatán Peninsula to Spanish rule. The once proud and independent Maya became peons, working for Spanish masters without hope of deliverance except in heaven.

Independence Period When Mexico finally won its independence from Spain in 1821, the new Mexican government urged the peoples of the Yucatán Peninsula, Chiapas and Central America to join it in the formation of one large new state.

Central America went its own way but the Yucatán Peninsula and Chiapas, after some flirtation with Guatemala, joined Mexico.

Mayan claims to ancestral lands were largely ignored and the criollos (descendants of the Spanish colonists) created huge plantations for the cultivation of tobacco, sugar cane and henequén (a type of agave used in rope-making). The Maya, though legally free, were enslaved by debt peonage to the great landowners.

War of the Castes Not long after independence, the Yucatecan ruling classes again dreamed of independence, this time

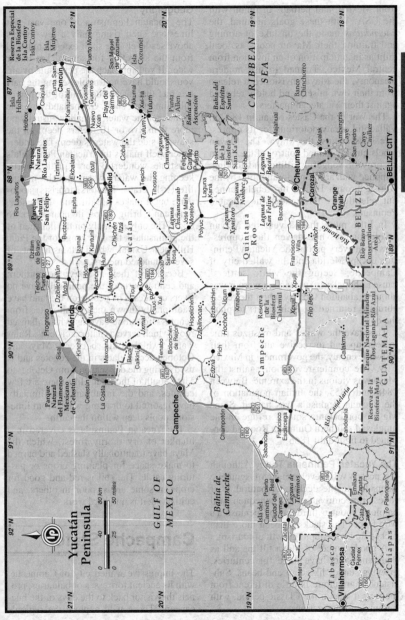

Yucatán Peninsula

from Mexico, and perhaps of union with the USA. With these goals in mind, the *hacendados* made the mistake of arming and training their Mayan peons as local militias in anticipation of an invasion from central Mexico. Trained to use modern weaponry, the Maya envisioned a release from their own misery and boldly rebelled against their Yucatecan masters.

The War of the Castes began in 1847 in Valladolid, a city notorious for its oppressive laws against the Maya. The Mayan rebels quickly gained control of the city in an orgy of vengeful killing and looting. Supplied with arms and ammunition by the British through Belize, the rebels fanned out relentlessly throughout the Yucatán Peninsula.

In little more than a year the Mayan revolutionaries had driven their oppressors from every part of the Yucatán Peninsula except Mérida and the walled city of Campeche. Seeing the white settlers' cause as hopeless, Yucatán's governor was about to abandon the city when the rebels abruptly returned to their farms to plant the corn.

This gave the whites and mestizos time to regroup and to receive aid from their erstwhile enemy, the government in Mexico City. The counter-revolution against the Maya was vicious in the extreme. Between 1848 and 1855, the Indian population of the Yucatán Peninsula was halved. Some Mayan combatants sought refuge in the jungles of southern Quintana Roo and continued to fight until 1866.

The Yucatán Peninsula Today Although the post-WWII development of synthetic fibers led to the decline of natural fiber ropes, the cultivation of henequén still employs about a third of the peninsula's workforce. The slack has been more than picked up by the rapid growth of tourism.

A good number of Maya till the soil as their ancestors have done for centuries, growing staples like corn and beans. Subsistence agriculture is little different from the way it was in the Classic period, with minimal mechanization.

Geography

The Yucatán Peninsula is one vast flat limestone shelf rising only a few meters above sea level. The shelf extends outward from the shoreline for several km under water. If you approach the peninsula by air, you should have no trouble seeing the barrier reef that marks the limit of the peninsular limestone shelf. On the landward side of the reef the water is shallow, usually no more than five or 10 meters deep; on the seaward side the water is deep. The underwater shelf makes the Yucatán Peninsula's coastline wonderful for aquatic sports, keeping the waters warm and the marine life (fish, crabs, lobsters, tourists) abundant, but it makes life difficult for traders, who can't bring ships in near shore to dock. The only anomaly on the flat shelf of the peninsula is the low range of the Puuc Hills near Uxmal, which attains heights of several hundred meters.

Because of their geology, the northern and central parts of the peninsula have no rivers or lakes. The people on the land have traditionally drawn their fresh water from cenotes, limestone caverns with collapsed roofs which serve as natural cisterns. Rainwater, which falls between May and October, accumulates in the cenotes and is used during the dry season from October to May. South of the Puuc Hills there are few cenotes, and the inhabitants traditionally have resorted to drawing water from limestone pools deep within the earth.

The Yucatán Peninsula is covered in a blanket of dry thorny forest, which the Maya have traditionally slashed and burned to make space for planting crops or pasturing cattle. The soil is red and good for crops in some areas, poor in others, and cultivating it is hot, hard work.

Campeche State

The impressive walled city of Campeche, with its ancient fortresses or baluartes, propels the visitor back to the days of the buccaneers. Those who explore the region's ancient Mayan Chenes-style ruins at Edzná may find they have the site all to themselves. With so much interest, why is Campeche the least-visited state in the Yucatán Peninsula?

For all its attractiveness, Campeche is not particularly tourist-friendly. Hotels are few, often disappointing and expensive for what you get. The fine regional museum charges a very high admission price. The beaches, such as they are, can be less than clean and transport to Edzná can be haphazard.

Even so, the state has its attractions, and you should enjoy a short stay here.

ESCÁRCEGA
pop 18,000

Most buses between Villahermosa and the Yucatán Peninsula stop in Escárcega to give passengers a refreshment break, but there is no other reason to stop in this town at the junction of highways 186 and 261, 150 km south of Campeche and 301 km from Villahermosa. Indeed, as most buses arrive in town full and depart in the same condition, you may find it difficult to get out of Escárcega if you break your trip here.

The town is spread out along two km of highway 186 toward Chetumal. It's 1.7 km between the ADO and Autobuses del Sur bus stations. Most hotels are nearer to the Autobuses del Sur bus station than to the ADO; most of the better restaurants are near the ADO bus station.

XPUJIL & VICINITY
π 981

Highway 186 heads due east from Escárcega through the scrubby jungle to Chetumal in the state of Quintana Roo, a 2½-hour ride. Right on the border between Campeche and Quintana Roo near the village of Xpujil, 153 km east of Escárcega and 120 km west of Chetumal, are several important Mayan archaeological sites: Xpujil, Becan, Chicanna and Río Bec.

These pristine, unrestored sites, largely free of tourists, will fascinate true ruins buffs, but be forewarned that those expecting park-like sites such as Uxmal and Chichén Itzá will be disappointed. Most of what you see here is jungle and rubble.

Orientation

The hamlet of Xpujil (shpu-HEEL), at the junction of the east-west and northern highways, is growing into a village, but services are still few and basic.

From the junction, the Xpujil ruins are 1.5 km west; Becan is eight km west, Chicanna is 11.5 km west, and Balamku is 60 km west. There are no services (drinks, snacks, toilets, etc) as yet at any of these sites.

Xpujil Ruins

Xpujil, 'Place of the Cattails' in Mayan, flourished during the Late Classic period from 400 to 900 AD, though there was a settlement here much earlier. The site, 200 meters north of the highway, is open from 8 am to 5 pm for US$1.50.

Edificio I (Structure I) in Grupo I (Group I), built about 760 AD, is a fine example of the Río Bec architectural style with its lofty towers (see Río Bec, later in this chapter, for a description of this style of architecture). The three towers (rather than the usual two) have traces of the impractically steep ornamental stairways reaching nearly to their tops, and several fierce jaguar masks (go around to the back of the tower to see the best one).

About 60 meters to the east is Edificio II, an elite residence.

Xpujil is a far larger site than may be imagined from these two buildings. Three other structure groups have been identified, but it may be decades before they are restored.

Becan

Becan ('Path of the Snake' in Mayan) sits atop a rock outcrop. It is well named, as a two-km fosse ('becan' in Mayan) snakes its way around the entire city to protect it from attack. Seven causeways once crossed the fosse, providing access to the city. Becan was occupied from 550 BC until 1000 AD. Today the site, 400 meters north of the highway, is open from 8 am to 5 pm for US$1.50.

This is among the largest and most elaborate sites in the area. The first building you reach, Edificio I on the Plaza Sureste (Southeast Plaza), has the two towers typical of Río Bec style. Climb a stairway on the east side of the building to get to the Plaza Sureste surrounded by four large temples, with a circular altar (Edificio III-a) on the east side.

Arrows direct you to a path which leaves the plaza's northeast corner and descends a flight of stairs, then turns left (west) and passes along a rock-walled walk and beneath a corbeled arch. At the end of the path is a huge twin-towered temple with cylindrical columns at the top of a flight of steps. This is Edificio VIII, dating from about 600 to 730 AD. The view from the top of this temple is good in all directions.

Northwest of Edificio VIII is the Plaza Central, surrounded by the 30-meter-high Edificio IX, tallest building at the site, and the better looking Edificio X.

More ruins await you in the jungle. The West Plaza, west of Edificio X, is surrounded by low buildings, one of which is a ball court.

Chicanná

Almost 12 km west of Xpujil junction and 800 meters south of the highway, Chicanná is a mixture of Chenes and Río Bec architectural styles buried in the jungle. The city flourished about 660 to 680 AD, and today is open from 8 am to 5 pm for US$1.50.

Enter through the modern palapa admission building, then follow the rock paths through the jungle to Grupo D and Edificio XX (750-830 AD) which boasts not one but two monster-mouth doorways, one above the other, the pair topped by a roofcomb.

A five-minute walk along the jungle path brings you to Grupo C, with two low buildings (Edificios X and XI) on a raised platform; the temples bear a few fragments of decoration.

The buildings in Grupo B have some intact decoration as well, and a good roofcomb on Edificio VI.

At the end of the path is Chicanná's most famous building, Edificio II (750-770 AD)

in Grupo A, with its gigantic Chenes-style monster-mouth doorway. If you photograph nothing else here, you'll want a picture of this, which is best taken in the afternoon.

Balamku

Discovered only in 1990, Balamku (also called Chunhabil), is famous for the façade of one building. The façade is decorated with a well-preserved bas relief stucco stylized figure of a jaguar flanked by two large mask designs, and topped with designs of other animals and humans. This elaborate, unusual design bears little resemblance to any of the known decorative elements in the Chenes and Río Bec styles, and has mystified archaeologists.

Balamku is 60 km west of Xpujil junction (less than three km west of Conhuas), then just under three km north of the highway along a rough unpaved road. There are no services.

Calakmul

Most Mayanists agree that Calakmul is a very important site, but at this writing little of its expanse – it's larger than Tikal – has been cleared, and few of its 6500 buildings have been consolidated, let alone restored. Access can be difficult or practically impossible during the summer rainy season, as it is 118 km southwest of Xpujil junction over very rough roads and tracks. See Tours below.

Beneath Edificio VII, archaeologists discovered a burial crypt and a funerary offering of some 2000 pieces of jade. Other jade offerings were found beneath other structures. Calakmul also has a surprising number of carved stelae, many eroded.

Hormiguero

Hormiguero (Spanish for 'anthill') is an old site, with some buildings dating from 50 to 250 AD, though it flourished during the Late Classic period.

Located 22 km southwest of Xpujil junction (six km beyond the village of Carrizal), Hormiguero has one of the most impressive buildings in the region. The 50-meter-long

Edificio II is graced by a huge Chenes-style monster-mouth doorway with much of its decoration in good condition. Though similar to the huge monster-mouths at Hochob and Chicanná, Hormiguero's is even bigger and bolder. You'll also want to see Edificio V, 60 meters to the north, and Edificio E-1 in the Grupo Oriente (East Group).

Río Bec

Río Bec is the designation for an agglomeration of small sites, 17 at last count, in a 50-sq-km area southeast of Xpujil. Of these many sites, the most interesting is certainly Grupo B, followed by Grupos I and N. These sites are difficult to reach at this writing, and require a guide. See Organized Tours below.

Río Bec gave its name to the prevalent architectural style of the region, characterized by long, low buildings that look as though they're divided into sections, each with a huge serpent-mouth for a door. The façades are decorated with smaller masks, geometric designs and columns. At the corners of the buildings are tall towers with extremely small and steep non-functional steps, topped by small temples. Many of these towers have roofcombs as well.

The best example of Río Bec architecture is Edificio I at Grupo B, a Late Classic building dating from around 700 AD. Though not restored, Edificio I has been consolidated and is in a condition certainly good enough to allow appreciation of its former glory.

At Grupo I, look for Edificios XVII and XI. At Grupo N, Edificio I is quite similar to the grand one at Grupo B.

El Raminal

These fairly impressive ruins are within walking distance of the Ejido 20 de Noviembre collective farm, reached by a road 10 km east of Xpujil junction. Look for signs, turn south and follow an unpaved ejido road for five km to the farm and its **U'lu'um Chac Yuk Nature Reserve**. As you come into the spartan village with its free-roaming livestock and thatched huts, look for the 'museum,' the fourth building

on the right-hand side of the road. Ask here for guides to show you the sights of El Raminal.

Guides from the ejido can also show you the various sites of Río Bec, about 13 km away.

The people of the ejido are building tourist bungalows with solar-heated hot water and other ecologically-sensitive features, so by the time you arrive there should even be accommodations.

Organized Tours

Xpujil's guides have formed an association, and with a 4WD vehicle a guide can show you the more remote sites such as Calakmul, Hormiguero and Río Bec for about US$30 per person. One place to book is at El Mirador Maya restaurant, from which tours depart at 8 am. Book at least a day in advance.

Places to Stay & Eat

The best choice for budget travelers is *El Mirador Maya* (no phone), one km west of Xpujil junction. Rooms with shared baths go for US$14. The little palapa-covered restaurant serves decent meals at decent prices, and there's even a little swimming pool. You can sign up for tours here (see above). This is currently the intrepid travelers' gathering place.

About 350 meters west of Xpujil junction, the *Restaurant-Hotel Calakmul* has slightly cheaper waterless rooms, but also a few rooms with private shower for US$19.

Near the junction and the ADO bus station (just east of the junction) are a few very basic eateries. We expect this area will develop very rapidly, so there should be other sleeping and eating options available by the time you arrive.

Incredibly, Xpujil has luxury accommodations in the form of the *Ramada Chicanná Ecovillage Resort* (☎ /fax 6-22-33), highway 186 at km 144, 12 km west of Xpujil junction, then 500 meters north of the highway. Large, airy rooms with private baths and ceiling fans are grouped four to a bungalow and set amid well-tended grass lawns, an odd sight here in the jungle. The

Pirates

As early as the mid-16th century, Campeche was flourishing as the Yucatán Peninsula's major port under the careful planning of Viceroy Hernández de Córdoba. Locally grown timber, chicle and dyewoods were major exports to Europe, as were gold and silver mined from other regions and shipped from Campeche.

Such wealth did not escape the notice of pirates, who arrived only six years after the town was founded.

For two centuries, the depredations of pirates terrorized Campeche. Not only were ships attacked, but the port itself was invaded, its citizens robbed, its women raped and its buildings burned. In the buccaneers' Hall of Fame were the infamous John Hawkins, Diego the Mulatto, Laurent de Gaff, Barbillas and the notorious 'Pegleg' himself, Pato de Palo. In their most gruesome assault, in early 1663, the various pirate hordes set aside their jealousies to converge as a single flotilla upon the city, where they massacred many of Campeche's citizens.

It took this tragedy to make the Spanish monarchy take preventive action, but not until five years later. Starting in 1668, 3.5-meter-thick ramparts were built. After 18 years of construction, a 2.5-km hexagon incorporating eight strategically placed baluartes surrounded the city. A segment of the ramparts extended out to sea so that ships literally had to sail into a fortress, easily defended, to gain access to the city.

With Campeche nearly impregnable, the pirates turned their attention to ships at sea and other ports. In response, in 1717, the brilliant naval strategist Felipe de Aranda started attacking the buccaneers and in time made the Gulf of Mexico safe from piracy. ■

small dining room and bar serves decent meals at fairly high prices, but this is the only place you'll find such a meal anywhere within 100 km of Xpujil. Rates are US$75 to US$95. As this is the only luxury hotel here, you should reserve your room in advance.

Getting There & Away

Xpujil is 220 km south of Hopelchén, 153 km east of Escárcega and 120 km west of Chetumal. There are four buses daily between Xpujil and Campeche, and more between Escárcega and Chetumal. No buses originate in Xpujil, so you must hope to find a vacant seat on one passing through. The bus station is 100 meters east of the highway junction in Xpujil, on the north side of the highway.

There is a Pemex fuel station dispensing both leaded and unleaded fuel five km east of Xpujil junction. Make sure you don't get overcharged.

Getting Around

Xpujil ruins are within walking distance of Xpujil junction. You may be able to hitch a ride to the access roads for Becan and Chi-

canná, but for other sites you will need to join a tour (see Organized Tours, above).

Your own wheels will get you to the sites along the highway, but you may want to abandon them and join a tour to Calakmul or Hormiguero, relying on the guide's 4WD vehicle to get you there and back.

CAMPECHE

pop 170,000; ☎ *981*

Filled with historic buildings, the center of Campeche is quite appealing. Local people make their living fishing for shrimp or digging for oil, and the prosperity brought by those two activities is apparent in the town.

History

Once a Mayan trading village called Ah Kim Pech (Lord Sun Sheep-Tick), Campeche was first entered by the Spaniards in 1517. The Maya resisted and for nearly a quarter of a century the Spaniards were unable to fully conquer the region. Colonial Campeche was founded in 1531, but later abandoned due to Mayan hostility. By 1540 the conquistadors had gained sufficient control, under the leadership of Francisco de Montejo the Younger, to found a settlement here which survived. They named it the Villa de San Francisco de Campeche.

The settlement soon flourished as the major port of the Yucatán Peninsula, but suffered from pirate attacks from an early date. After a particularly appalling attack in 1663 left the city in ruins, the Spanish crown ordered construction of Campeche's famous baluartes which put an end to the periodic carnage.

Orientation

Though the baluartes still stand, the city walls themselves have been mostly razed and replaced by the Avenida Circuito Baluartes, or Circular Avenue of the Bulwarks, which rings the city center just as the walls once did.

Besides the modern Plaza Moch-Cuouh, Campeche also has its Parque Principal, also called the Plaza de la Independencia, the standard Spanish colonial park with the cathedral on one side and former Palacio de Gobierno on another.

According to the compass, Campeche is oriented with its waterfront to the northwest, but tradition and convenience hold that the water is to the west, inland is east (we observe that rule in the following text). The street grid is numbered so that streets running north-south have even numbers, while east-west streets have odd numbers; street numbers ascend toward the south and the west.

Information

Tourist Offices The Coordinación General de Turismo (☎ 6-60-68, 6-67-67), is at Calle 12 No 153, off Calle 53. The staff are very friendly and available Monday to Saturday from 8 am to 2.30 pm and 4 to 8.30 pm; closed Sunday.

The city maintains the Coordinación Municipal de Turismo, on Calle 55 at Calle 8, just west of the cathedral facing the Parque Principal.

Money Banks are open weekdays from 9 am to 1 pm. See the map for bank and ATM locations.

Post The central post office (☎ 6-21-34), is at the corner of Avenida 16 de Septiembre and Calle 53, in the Edificio Federal. Hours are weekdays 8 am to 7 pm, Saturday 8 am to 1 pm and Sunday 8 am to 2 pm.

Walking Tour

Seven bulwarks still stand and four of them are of interest. You can see them all by following the Avenida Circuito Baluartes around the city – it's a two-km walk.

Because of traffic, some of the walk is not very pleasant, so you might want to limit your excursion to the first three or four baluartes described below, which house museums and gardens. If you'd rather have a guided tour, you can sign up for a city tour at either the Ramada Inn or Hotel Baluartes for about US$18. We'll start at the southwestern end of the Plaza Moch-Cuouh.

Half a block from the modern Palacio de Gobierno, at the intersection of Calles 8 and 65, near a ziggurat fountain, is the **Baluarte de San Carlos**. The interior of the bulwark is now arranged as the Sala de las Fortificaciones (Chamber of Fortifications) with some interesting scale models of the city's fortifications in the 18th century. You can also visit the dungeon, and look out over the sea from the roof. Baluarte de San Carlos is open from 9 am to 1 pm and 5 to 7.30 pm daily, for free.

Next, head back north along Calle 8. At the intersection with Calle 59, notice the **Puerta del Mar** (Sea Gate), which provided access to the city from the sea before the area to the northwest was filled in. The gate was demolished in 1893 but rebuilt in 1957 when its historical value was realized.

The **Baluarte de la Soledad**, on the north side of the Plaza Moch-Cuouh close to the intersection of Calles 8 and 57, is the setting for the **Museo de Estelas Maya**. Many of the Mayan artifacts here are badly weathered, but the precise line drawing next to each stone shows you what the designs once looked like. The bulwark also has an interesting exhibition of colonial Campeche. Among the antiquities are 17th and 18th century seafaring equipment and

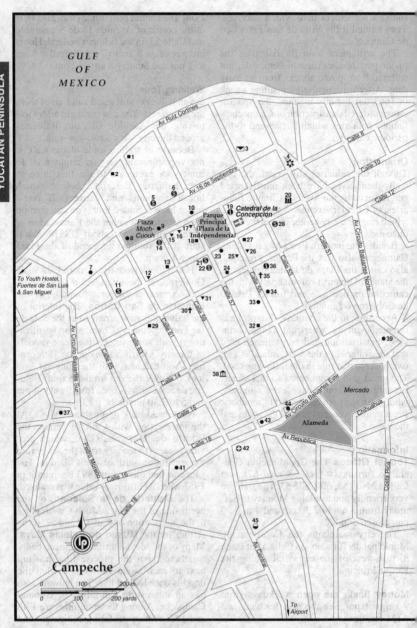

GULF
OF
MEXICO

Av Ruiz Cortines

Av 16 de Septiembre

Calle 8

Calle 10

Calle 12

Plaza
Moch-
Cuouh

Parque
Principal
(Plaza de la
Independencia)

Cathedral de la
Concepción

Av Circuito Baluartes Norte

Calle 51

Calle 53

Calle 55

Calle 57

Calle 59

Calle 61

Calle 63

Calle 65

To Youth Hostel,
Fuertes de San Luis
& San Miguel

Av Circuito Baluartes Sur

Pedro Moreno

Calle 14

Calle 16

Calle 18

Av Circuito Baluartes Este

Mercado

Chihuahua

Alameda

Av Republica

Costa Hca

Campeche

0   100   200 m
0   100   200 yards

To
Airport

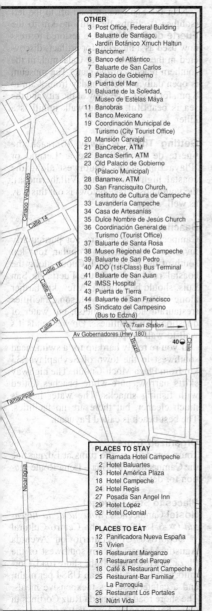

armaments used to battle pirate invaders. The museum is open Tuesday to Saturday from 9 am to 2 pm and 3 to 8 pm, Sunday from 9 am to 1 pm, closed Monday. Admission costs US$0.50.

Just across the street from the Baluarte de la Soledad is the **Parque Principal**, Campeche's favorite park. Whereas the sterile, modernistic, shadeless Plaza Moch-Cuouh was built to glorify its government builders, the Parque Principal is the pleasant place where locals go to sit and think, chat, smooch, plot, snooze, stroll and cool off after the heat of the day, or have their shoes shined. Come for the concerts on Sunday evenings.

Construction was begun on the **Catedral de la Concepción**, on the north side of the plaza, in the mid-16th century shortly after the conquistadors established the town, but it wasn't finished until 1705.

The attractive, arcaded former **Palacio de Gobierno** (or Palacio Municipal) dates only from the 19th century.

Continue north along Calle 8 several blocks to the **Baluarte de Santiago**, at the intersection of Calles 8 and 51. It houses a minuscule yet lovely tropical garden, the **Jardín Botánico Xmuch Haltun**, with 250 species of tropical plants set around a lovely courtyard of fountains. Tours of the garden are given weekdays between 5 and 6 pm. The garden is open weekdays from 8 am to 3 pm and 6 to 8.30 pm; Saturday from 9 am to 1 pm and 6 to 8 pm; Sunday 9 am to 1 pm. Admission is free.

From the Baluarte de Santiago, walk inland along Calle 51 to Calle 18, where you'll come to the **Baluarte de San Pedro**, in the middle of a complex traffic intersection which marks the beginning of the Avenida Gobernadores. Within the bulwark is the Exposición Permanente de Artesanías, a regional crafts sales center, open weekdays from 9 am to 2 pm and 5 to 8 pm. Admission is free.

To make the entire circuit, head south from the Baluarte de San Pedro along the Avenida Circuito Baluartes to the **Baluarte de San Francisco** at Calle 57 and, a block farther at Calle 59, the **Puerta de Tierra**

(Land Gate). The **Baluarte de San Juan**, at Calles 18 and 65, marks the southern-most point of the old city walls. From here you bear right along Calle 67 (Avenida Circuito Baluartes) to the intersection of Calles 14 and 67 and the **Baluarte de Santa Rosa**. From hear Avenida Circuito Baluartes leads back to Calle 8 and the Plaza Moch-Cuouh.

Evening Stroll

Walk through Campeche's streets – especially Calles 55, 57 and 59 – looking for more beautiful houses. (The Casa de Artesanías on Calle 55 is a fine one.) The walk is best done in the evening, when the sun is not blasting down and when interior lighting illuminates courtyards, salons and alleys.

Museo Regional de Campeche

The Regional Museum (☎ 6-91-11) is set up in the former mansion of the Teniente del Rey (King's Lieutenant), at Calle 59 No 36, between Calles 14 and 16. Architecture, hydrology, commerce, art, religion and Mayan science are all featured in interesting and revealing displays.

Hours are Tuesday to Saturday from 8 am to 2 pm and 2.30 to 8 pm, Sunday from 9 am to 1 pm, closed Monday. Admission is an unreasonable US\$3.

Mansión Carvajal

The Mansión Carvajal, Calle 10 between Calles 51 and 53, started its eventful history as the city residence of Don Fernando Carvajal Estrada and his wife Señora María Iavalle de Carvajal. Don Fernando was among Campeche's richest hacendados. Sometimes the building is open and you can take a quick walk around. The monogram you see throughout the building, 'RCY,' is that of Rafael Carvajal Ytorralde, Don Fernando's father and founder of the fortune.

Forts

Four km south of the Plaza Moch-Cuouh along the coast road stands the **Fuerte de San Luis**, an 18th-century fortress of which only a few battlements remain.

Near the San Luis, a road off to the left (southeast) climbs the hill one km to the **Fuerte de San Miguel**, a restored fortress now used as a museum for artifacts discovered in the excavations at Calakmul, in the southern reaches of the state. The museum is open daily except Monday from 8 am to 8 pm, for US\$1. The view of the city and the sea is beautiful, but the walk uphill is a killer.

Getting There & Away To reach the Fuerte de San Luis, take a 'Lerma' or 'Playa Bonita' bus southwest along the coastal highway (toward Villahermosa); the youth hostel (see below) is out this way as well.

Beaches

Campeche's beaches are not particularly inviting. The Balneario Popular, four km south of the Plaza Moch-Cuouh along the coastal road just past the Fuerte de San Luis, should be avoided. A few km farther along is Playa Bonita with some facilities (restaurant, lockers, toilets), but water of questionable cleanliness. On weekends it's wall-to-wall people.

If you're really hard up for a swim, head southwest to the town of Seybaplaya, 33 km from Plaza Moch-Cuouh. The highway skirts narrow, pure-white beaches dotted with fishing smacks. The water here is much cleaner, but there are no facilities. The best beach is called Payucan.

Organized Tours

Tours run daily to the ruins at Edzná. See the Campeche to Mérida – Long Route section for details.

Places to Stay – budget

Hostel Campeche's *Albergue de la Juventud* (☎ 6-18-02) is in the Centro Cultural y Deportivo Universitario on Avenida Agustín Melgar, 3.5 km southwest of the Plaza Moch-Cuouh off the shore road. Dormitory beds cost less than US\$4 per night, and a cafeteria serves inexpensive meals. The shore road is Avenida Ruiz Cortines in town, but becomes Avenida Resurgimiento as it heads toward Villahermosa. Buses marked 'Avenida Universidad' will take you there. Ask the driver to let you off at the Albergue de la Juventud. Avenida Melgar heads inland between a Volkswagen dealership and a Pemex fuel station. The hostel is about 150 meters up on the right.

Hotels The cheapest hotels – *Reforma, Roma* and the like – are dumps. The *Hotel Campeche* (☎ 6-51-83), Calle 57 No 2, above the Café y Restaurant Campeche facing the Parque Principal, is very cheap and centrally located. Rooms without running water cost a mere US$6, with cold water US$8, with hot water US$10.

Though we've heard a few complaints, beds at the *Hotel Colonial* (☎ 6-22-22), Calle 14 No 122, between Calles 55 and 57, are usually in great demand by budget travelers. Housed in what was once the mansion of Doña Gertrudis Eulalia Torostieta y Zagasti, former Spanish governor of Tabasco and Yucatán, the rooms have fans and good showers with hot water for US$10/12/15 a single/double/triple.

Posada San Angel Inn (☎ 6-77-18), Calle 10 No 307, between Calles 55 and 53, is a Swiss-style cell block: rooms are spartan, but modern and clean, with bath and fan for US$12/15/17/20 a single/double/triple/quad, US$3 more with air-con.

Places to Stay – middle

Hotel Regis (☎ 6-31-75), Calle 12 No 148, between 55 and 57, is conveniently located and serviceable, with adequate air-con rooms for US$12/18/24/28.

Hotel López (☎ 6-33-44, fax 6-24-88), Calle 12 No 189, between Calles 61 and 63, is somewhat more expensive, and not quite as nice, charging US$14/15/19/25 with fan and color TV. Air-con rooms cost a few dollars more.

Hotel América Plaza (☎ 6-45-88, fax 6-45-76), Calle 10 No 252, is a fine colonial house with large, OK rooms overlooking the interior court costing US$15/19/22 with fan.

Places to Stay – top end

The best hotel in town is the 119-room *Ramada Hotel Campeche* (☎ 6-22-33, fax 1-16-18), Avenida Ruiz Cortines No 51. Prices range from US$85 single or double for a standard room, to US$125 for a master suite.

Just south of the Ramada is its competition, the older but still comfortable *Hotel Baluartes* (☎ 6-39-11, fax 6-24-10). The Baluartes' well-used rooms are air-con and comfortable, offer sea views, and are cheaper than the Ramada at US$35/40 a single/double.

Places to Eat

Among the best eateries is the *Restaurant Marganzo* (☎ 6-23-28), Calle 8 No 265, between Calles 57 and 59, facing the sea and the Baluarte de la Soledad. Breakfast costs US$2 to US$3, regional specialties US$3 to US$5; the seafood menu, priced up to US$8, includes lots of shrimp.

The *Café y Restaurant Campeche* (☎ 6-21-28), Calle 57 No 2, opposite Parque Principal, is in the building that saw the birth of Justo Sierra, founder of Mexico's national university, but the restaurant is very simple, bright with fluorescent light bulbs and loud with a blaring TV set. The *platillo del día* usually costs less than US$3.

In the same block facing the plaza is the *Restaurant del Parque* (☎ 6-02-40), Calle 57 No 8, a cheerful little place serving fish, meat and shrimp for around US$3 a platter. It opens early for breakfast, and is open on Sunday.

If you'd just like to pick up some sweet rolls, biscuits, bread or cakes, head for the *Panificadora Nueva España*, Calle 10 at the corner of Calle 61, which has a large assortment of fresh baked goods at very low prices.

Every now and then a brave entrepreneur opens a natural foods restaurant in Campeche, only to close soon after. I hope the latest effort, the *Vivien*, beneath the Hotel Reforma at Calle 8 No 263, survives. Another place to look for whole food and vegetarian fare is *Nutri Vida*, Calle 12 No 167.

Perhaps the best known restaurant in town is the *Restaurant-Bar Familiar La Parroquía* (☎ 6-18-29), Calle 55, between 10 and 12. The complete family restaurant-café-hangout, La Parroquía serves breakfasts Monday through Friday from 7 to 10 am for US$2.25 to US$3.50; substantial lunch and dinner fare like chuleta de cerdo (pork chop), filete a la tampiqueña, shrimp cocktail or shrimp salad, and even fresh pampano, cost US$5 to US$9.

Entertainment
On Friday evenings at 8 pm (weather permitting) from September to May, the state tourism authorities sponsor *Estampas Turísticas*, performances of folk music and dancing, in the Plaza Moch-Cuouh. Other performances, sponsored by the city government, take place in the Parque Principal Thursday through Sunday evenings at around 7 pm.

Things to Buy
The Casa de Artesanías (☎ 6-90-88), Calle 55 No 25, between 12 and 14, is run by the state government. Crafts are on sale from 9 am to 2 pm, and 5 to 8 pm.

Getting There & Away
Air The airport is west of the train station at the end of Avenida López Portillo (Avenida Central), across the tracks about 800 meters away, or 3.5 km from Plaza Moch-Cuouh. You must take a taxi (US$4) to the city center.

Bus Campeche's 1st-class ADO bus terminal is on Avenida Gobernadores, 1.7 km from Plaza Moch-Cuouh, or about 1.5 km from most hotels. The 2nd-class terminal is directly behind it.

Here's information on daily buses from Campeche:

Cancún – 512 km, nine hours, US$12 to US$15, change at Mérida

Chetumal – 422 km, seven hours, US$11 to US$14, three buses

Edzná – 66 km, 1½ hours; catch bus to Pich or Hool from the Sindicato del Campesino on Avenida Central, or take a faster bus to San

Antonio Cayal (45 km) and hitch south from there

Hopelchén – 86 km, two hours, US$1.50; a dozen 2nd-class buses by Camioneros de Campeche

Mérida – 195 km (short route via Becal), 2½ to three hours; 250 km (long route via Uxmal), four hours; 33 by ADO (US$6) around the clock; every 20 or 30 minutes by ATS (US$3 to US$3.50)

Mexico City (TAPO) – 1360 km, 20 hours (US$50), two by ADO

Palenque – 362 km, five hours, one by ADO (US$12), two by Colón (US$12), two by ATS (US$10); many other buses drop you at Catazajá (Palenque turnoff), 27 km north of Palenque village

San Cristóbal de las Casas – 820 km, 14 hours; three by ADO (US$15 to US$18); one by ATS (US$14)

Villahermosa – 450 km, six hours (US$14 to US$17), 15 buses; they'll drop you at Catazajá (Palenque junction) if you like

Xpujil – 306 km, six hours, US$8; four by ATS

Train The train station is three km northeast of the city center, south of Avenida Gobernadores on Avenida Héroes de Nacozari in the district called Colonia Cuatro Caminos. Buses departing from a stop to the right (west) as you leave the station will take you to the center.

CAMPECHE TO MÉRIDA – SHORT ROUTE (HIGHWAY 180)
This is the fastest way to go and if you buy a bus ticket from Campeche to Mérida your bus will follow this route. If you'd prefer to go the long way via Edzná, Kabah and Uxmal, you must ask for a seat on one of the less frequent long-route buses. If you'd like to stop at one of the towns along the short route, catch a 2nd-class bus.

Hecelchakan, Calkini & Becal
At Hecelchakan, 77 km northeast of Campeche, is the **Museo Arqueológico del Camino Real**, where you will find some burial artifacts from the island of Jaina, as well as ceramics and jewelry from other sites. The museum is open Monday to Saturday from 9 am to 6 pm, closed Sunday. The **Iglesia de San**

Francisco is the center of festivities on the saint's day, October 4. From August 9 to 18 a popular festival called the Novenario is held, with bullfights, dancing and refreshments.

After Hecelchakan, it's 24 km to Calkini, site of the 17th century **Iglesia de San Luis de Tolosa**, with a plateresque portal and lots of baroque decoration. Each year the Festival of San Luis is celebrated on August 19.

Becal is eight km from Calkini just before you enter the state of Yucatán. It is a center of the Yucatán Peninsula's Panama hat trade. The soft, pliable hats, called *jipijapa* by the locals, have been woven by townsfolk from the fibers of the huano palm tree in humid limestone caves since the mid-19th century. The caves provide just the right atmosphere for shaping the fibers, keeping them pliable and minimizing breakage.

From Becal it's 85 km to Mérida.

CAMPECHE TO MÉRIDA – LONG ROUTE (HIGHWAY 261)

Most travelers take the long route (highway 261) from Campeche to Mérida, in order to visit the various ruin sites.

Edzná

The closest ruins to Campeche are at Edzná, south of highway 261.

Edzná means House of Grimaces as well as House of Echoes and may well have been host to both, as there has been a settlement here since about 800 BC. Most of the carvings are of a much later date: 550 to 810 AD. Though a long way from such Puuc Hill sites as Uxmal and Kabah, some of the architecture here is similar to Puuc style.

The site is open daily from 8 am to 5 pm, and admission is US$4.

Although the archaeological zone covers two sq km, the best part is the main plaza, 160 meters long and 100 meters wide, surrounded by temples. Every Mayan site has huge masses of stone, but at Edzná there are cascades of it, terrace upon terrace of bleached limestone.

The major temple here, the 30-meter-high Templo de Cinco Pisos (Temple of Five Levels), is to the left as you enter the plaza from the ticket kiosk. Built on a vast platform, it rises five levels from base to roofcomb, with rooms and some weathered decoration of masks, serpents and jaguars' heads on each level. A great central staircase of 65 steps goes right to the top. On the opposite (right) side of the plaza as you enter is a monumental staircase 100 meters wide, which once led up to the Temple of the Moon. At the far end of the plaza is a ruined temple that may have been the priests' quarters.

Getting There & Away Picazh Servicios Turísticos (☎ 6-44-26, fax 6-27-60), Calle 16 No 348 between 57 and 59 in Campeche, runs tours from Campeche to Edzná. For US$10 per person, they'll drive two or more people to Edzná ruins and back. For another US$5 per person, they'll give you a guided tour in Spanish or English. Entry to the site is not included in these prices. Join the tour at the plaza next to the Puerta de Tierra, at the eastern end of Calle 59. Tours depart daily at 9 am and 2 pm.

The Picazh tours are worth the money for convenience, but you can do it more cheaply by bus. Catch a 2nd-class village bus early in the morning headed for Edzná (66 km) from near the Sindicato del Campesino in Campeche, on Avenida Central south of the Circuito Baluartes; it may be a bus going to Pich, 15 km southeast of Edzná, or to Hool, 25 km southwest. Either bus will drop you at the access road to the site.

Coming from the north and east, get off at San Antonio Cayal and hitch or catch a bus 20 km south to Edzná.

A sign just north of the Edzná turn-off on highway 261 says 'Edzná 2 km,' but the ruins are just 500 meters beyond the sign, only about 400 meters off the highway.

When you leave you'll have to depend on hitching or buses to get you to San Antonio Cayal, from which you can hitch or catch a bus west back to Campeche or east and north to Hopelchén, Bolonchén and ultimately Uxmal.

Bolonchén de Rejón & Xtacumbilxunaan

By heading 40 km east from San Antonio Cayal, you'll reach Hopelchén, where highway 261 turns north. The next town to appear out of the flat, dry jungle is Bolonchén de Rejón, after 34 km. The local festival of Santa Cruz is held each year on May 3.

Bolonchén is near the Grutas de Xtacumbilxunaan (SHTAA-koom-beel-shoo-NAHN), located about three km south of town. You can visit the cavern by taking a 30- to 45-minute tour with the guide/caretaker for the price of a tip. The cave is 'open' when the caretaker is around, which is most of the time during daylight hours.

Highway 261 continues into Yucatán state to Uxmal, with a side road leading to the ruin sites of the Puuc Route. See the Uxmal and Puuc Route sections later in this chapter for more information.

Yucatán

The state of Yucatán is a pie slice at the northern end of the Yucatán peninsula. Until the development of Cancún and the peninsula's Caribbean coast, the state of Yucatán was the most important area of the peninsula. Historically and culturally, it still is. This is where you'll find Yucatán's most impressive Mayan ruins (Chichén Itzá, Uxmal) and its finest colonial cities (Mérida and Valladolid), as well as several small, interesting coastal communities.

MÉRIDA

pop 600,000; ☎ *99*

The capital of the state of Yucatán is a proud, charming city of narrow streets, colonial buildings and shady parks. It has been the center of Mayan culture in Yucatán since before the conquistadors arrived; today it is the peninsula's center of commerce as well. There are lots of hotels and restaurants of every class and price range and good transportation services to any part of the peninsula and the country.

Mérida seems busiest with tourists in high summer (July and August) and winter (December through March).

History

Francisco de Montejo the Younger founded a Spanish colony at Campeche in 1540. From this base he was able to take advantage of political dissension among the Maya, conquering Tihó (now Mérida) in 1542. By the end of the decade, Yucatán was mostly under Spanish colonial rule.

When Montejo's conquistadors entered defeated Tihó, they found a major Mayan settlement of lime-mortared stone which reminded them of Roman architectural legacies in Mérida, Spain. They promptly renamed the city and proceeded to build it into the colonial capital. Mérida took its colonial orders directly from Spain, not from Mexico City, and Yucatán has had a distinct cultural and political identity ever since.

During the War of the Castes (1847-55), only Mérida and Campeche were able to hold out against the rebel forces; the rest of the Yucatán Peninsula came under Indian control. On the brink of surrender, the ruling class in Mérida was saved by reinforcements sent from central Mexico in exchange for Mérida agreeing to take orders from Mexico City. Though Yucatán is certainly part of Mexico, there is still a strong feeling of local pride in Mérida, a feeling that the Mayab are a special realm set apart from the rest of the country.

Orientation

The Plaza Mayor, or main square, has been the center of Mérida since Mayan times. Most of the services you want are within five blocks of the square; the rest are on the broad, tree-lined boulevard named Paseo de Montejo.

Be advised that house numbers may progress unevenly from street to street: you cannot know whether Calle 57 No 481 and Calle 56 No 544 are one block or 10 blocks apart. Perhaps for this reason, addresses are usually given in this form: Calle 57 No 481 X 56 y 58 (between Calles 56 and 58).

RICHARD NEBESKY

TONY WHEELER

Top Left: Temple of the Warriors, Palenque
Top Right: Palenque
Middle: Temple of Inscriptions & Palace, Palenque
Bottom Left: Temple of the Inscriptions, Palenque
Bottom Right: Stela 1, La Venta, Villahermosa

Top: Tziscao village, Lagunas de Montebello
Middle Right: Lagunas de Montebello
Bottom Left: Chiapas Indian woman
Bottom Right: Templo del Carmen, San Cristóbal de Las Casas

Information

Tourist Offices There are information booths of minimal usefulness at the airport and the bus station Terminal CAME.

Your best bet for information is the Tourist Information Center (☎ 24-92-90, 24-93-89), at the corner of Calles 60 and 57, in the southwest corner of the huge Teatro Peón Contreras, less than two blocks north of the Plaza Mayor.

The city government (Ayuntamiento de Mérida) has a tourist office one block west of the Parque Hidalgo along Calle 59, at the corner of 62.

Consulates A number of countries have consulates in Mérida:

Belgium
  Calle 25 No 159, between Calles 28 and 30 (☎ 25-29-39)
Denmark
  Calle 32 No 198 at Calle 17, Colonia Garcia Ginerés (☎ 25-44-88, 25-45-27)
France
  Calle 33B No 528 between Calles 62 and 64 (☎ 25-22-91, fax 25-70-09)
Germany
  Calle 7 No 217 between Calles 20 and 20A, Colonia Chuburna de Hidalgo (☎ 81-29-76)
Honduras
  Calle 54 No 280, Fraccionamiento del Norte (☎ 27-44-74)
Netherlands
  Calle 64 No 418 between Calles 47 and 49 (☎ 24-31-22, 24-41-47)
Spain
  Calle 3 No 237, Fraccionamiento Campestre (☎ 27-15-20, fax 23-00-55)
UK
  Calle 53 No 489, at Calle 58, Fraccionamiento del Norte (☎ 28-29-62, fax 28-39-62). You can get information about travel in Belize here, weekday mornings from 9.30 am to noon.
USA
  Paseo de Montejo 453, at Avenida Colón (☎ 25-54-09, fax 25-62-19); open weekdays from 7.30 am to 3.30 pm ; it is rumored that this consulate-general will soon be downgraded, and a new consulate-general opened in Cancún.

Money Casas de cambio offer faster, better service than banks, but may charge a fee for changing money. Try the Money Marketing Centro Cambiario to the left of the Gran Hotel on Parque Hidalgo; Finex (☎ 24-18-42), Calle 59 No 498K, to the left of the Hotel Caribe; or Cambio La Peninsular, on the east side of Calle 60 between Calles 55 and 57.

In addition, there are lots of banks along Calle 65 between Calles 60 and 62, one block behind Banamex/Palacio Montejo (that is, one block south of the Plaza Mayor). Banking hours are generally weekdays from 9.30 am to 1.30 pm.

Post & Communications The main post office (☎ 21-25-61) is in the market area on Calle 65 between Calles 56 and 56A, open weekdays from 8 am to 7 pm and Saturday from 9 am to 1 pm. There are postal service booths at the airport and the bus station, open weekdays.

Pay phones are found on the Plaza Mayor, Parque Hidalgo, and at the airport, the bus station, at the corner of Calles 59 and 62 or Calles 64 and 57, or on Calle 60 between Calles 53 and 55. Yucatán is not served by a sufficient number of circuits, and you may have problems getting a line.

CDC, a private telephone company, has phones in many transport termini, hotels and pensions. Before you make a call, find out what it will cost.

Bookstores Librería Dante Peón (☎ 24-95-22), in the Teatro Peón Contreras on the corner of Calles 60 and 57, has some English, French and German books as well as Spanish ones. It's open seven days a week.

Laundry Lavamática La Fe, Calle 61 No 520, at Calle 64, can take care of your washing.

Medical Services Hospital O'Horan (☎ 24-41-00) is near the Parque Zoológico Centenario on Avenida de los Itzaes. For the Red Cross, call ☎ 24-98-13.

Dangers & Annoyances Guard against pickpockets, bag-snatchers and bag-slashers

Mérida

PLACES TO STAY
3 Hotel Los Aluxes
4 Hotel Trinidad Galería
5 Hotel Santa Lucía
6 Hotel Trinidad
9 Hotel Mérida Misión
   Park Plaza
10 Hotel Casa del Balam
11 Posada Toledo
12 Hotel Mucuy
15 Casa Mexilio
36 Gran Hotel
39 Hotel Caribe
42 Hotel Las Monjas
43 Hotel Margarita
48 Casa de Huéspedes
   Peniche
49 Hotel Sevilla
52 Hotel Dolores Alba
53 Casa Bowen
54 Posada del Angel
56 Hotel Peninsular
59 Hotel del Mayab
61 Casa Becil

in the market district, and in any crowd, such as at a performance. They see you, but you won't see them.

Plaza Mayor

The most logical place to start a tour of Mérida is in Plaza Mayor. This was the religious and social center of ancient Tihó; under the Spanish it was the Plaza de Armas, or parade ground, laid out by Francisco de Montejo the Younger. The plaza is surrounded by some of the city's most impressive and harmonious colonial buildings, and its carefully pruned laurel trees provide welcome shade. On Sunday, the adjoining roadways are off-limits to traffic.

Catedral On the east side of the plaza, on the site of a Mayan temple, is Mérida's huge, hulking, severe cathedral, begun in 1561 and completed in 1598. Some of the stone from the Mayan temple was used in the cathedral's construction.

Walk through one of the three doors in the baroque façade and into the sanctuary. The great crucifix at the east end of the nave is Cristo de la Unidad, Christ of Unity, a symbol of reconciliation between those of Spanish and Mayan stock. To your right over the south door is a painting of Tutul Xiú, cacique of the town of Maní, paying his respects to his ally Francisco de Montejo at Tihó (Montejo and Xiú jointly defeated the Cocoms; Xiú converted to Christianity and his descendants still live in Mérida).

Look in the small chapel to the left of the principal altar for Mérida's most famous religious artifact, a statue of Jesus called Cristo de las Ampollas, or the Christ of the Blisters. Local legend has it that this statue was carved from a tree in the town of Ichmul. The tree, hit by lightning, supposedly burned for an entire night without charring. The statue carved from the tree was placed in the local church where it alone is said to have survived the fiery destruction of the church, though it was blackened and blistered from the heat. It was moved to the Mérida cathedral in 1645.

PLACES TO EAT
- 2 La Casona
- 7 Pop Cafetería,
     Restaurante Portico
     del Peregrino
- 8 Restaurant Santa Lucía
- 14 Gran Almendros
- 17 Amaro
- 19 La Bella Epoca
- 21 Café Peón Contreras
- 24 Los Almendros
- 27 Lonchería Mily
- 28 Kükis by Maru
- 29 El Louvre
- 30 Pizzería de Vito Corleone
- 31 Panificadora El Retorno
- 34 Café-Restaurant Express
- 37 Giorgio's Pizza & Pasta
- 39 Cafetería El Rincón
- 40 Tiano's
- 50 Panificadora Montejo

OTHER
- 1 Anthropology Museum
     (Palacio Cantón)
- 13 Alianza Francesa
      (Alliance Française)
- 16 City Tourist Office
- 18 Universidad de Yucatán
- 20 Teatro Peón Contreras
- 21 Tourist Information Center
- 22 Parque de la Madre
- 23 Iglesia de Jesús,
      Pinacoteca del Estado
- 25 Ex-Convento de
      la Mejorada
- 26 Centro Cultural de
      los Pueblos Mayas
- 32 Pasaje Picheta
- 33 Palacio de Gobierno
- 35 Parque Hidalgo
- 38 Cine Fantasio
- 41 Museo Regional
      de Artesanías
- 44 Casa de los Artesanías
- 45 Ex-Convento de
      las Monjas
- 46 Palacio Municipal
- 47 MACAY (Contemporary
      Art Museum)
- 51 Casa de Montejo
      (Banamex)
- 55 Progreso Bus Station
- 57 Correos (Main
      Post Office)
- 58 Oriente & Noroeste
      Bus Station
- 60 Autobuses del Noreste
      en Yucatán Bus Station
- 62 Minibus to Dzibilchaltún
- 63 Iglesia de San Juan
- 64 Terminal CAME
- 65 Old Terminal
      de Autobuses
- 66 Celestún Bus Station

Train Station

To Acanceh, Mayapán

To Chichén Itzá

The rest of the church's interior is plain, its rich decoration having been stripped by angry peasants at the height of anticlerical feeling during the Mexican Revolution.

MACAY On the south side of the cathedral, housed in the former archbishop's palace, is MACAY, the Museo de Arte Contemporáneo Ateneo de Yucatán (Yucatán Contemporary Art Museum and Atheneum; ☎ 28-32-58), at Pasaje de la Revolución 1907. The attractive museum holds permanent exhibits of Yucatán's most famous painters and sculptors, as well as changing exhibits of local arts and artisanry.

MACAY is open daily except Tuesday from 10 am to 6 pm. Mexican citizens pay US$0.75 for admission, non-Mexicans pay US$3, students, teachers, workers, campesinos and seniors may enter for free. On Sunday admission is free to all. There's a cafeteria inside.

Palacio de Gobierno On the north side of the plaza, the Palacio de Gobierno houses the state of Yucatán's executive government offices. It was built in 1892 on the site of the palace of the colonial governors. The palace is open every day from 8 am to 8 pm.

See also the historical murals painted by local artist Fernando Castro Pacheco. After 25 years of work, the murals were completed in 1978.

In vivid colors, the murals portray a symbolic history of the Maya and their interaction with the Spaniards. Over the stairwell is a painting of Mayan sacred corn, the 'ray of sun from the gods.' On Sunday at 11 am, there's usually a concert (jazz, classical, pop, traditional Yucatecan) in the Salón de la Historia of the Palacio de Gobierno.

Palacio Municipal Facing the cathedral across the square, the Palacio Municipal is topped by a clock tower. Originally built in 1542, the Palacio has twice been refurbished, in the 1730s and the 1850s.

Today the building also serves as the venue for performances of Yucatecan dances (especially the *jarana*, danced to a guitar ensemble by men all in white, and women in white dresses with colorful embroidery) and music at the weekly Vaquería Regional, a regional festival that celebrates the branding of the cattle on haciendas. Performances are on Monday evenings at 9 pm.

Every Sunday at 1 pm, the city sponsors a reenactment of a colorful mestizo wedding at the Palacio Municipal.

Casa de Montejo From its construction in 1549 until the 1970s, the mansion on the south side of the plaza was occupied by the Montejo family. Sometimes called the Palacio de Montejo, it was built for the conqueror of Mérida, Francisco de Montejo the Younger. These days the great house shelters a branch of Banamex and you can look around inside whenever the bank is open (usually weekdays from 9 am to 1.30 pm).

If the bank is closed, content yourself with a close look at the plateresque façade, where triumphant conquistadors with halberds hold their feet on the necks of generic barbarians (who are not Maya, but the association is inescapable). Also gazing across the plaza from the façade are busts of Montejo the Elder, his wife and his daughter. The armorial shields are those of the Montejo family.

Walking up Calle 60

A block north of the Plaza Mayor is the shady refuge of **Parque Hidalgo**. The park's benches always hold a variety of conversationalists, lovers, taxi drivers, hammock peddlers and tourists.

At the far end of the park, several restaurants, including Café El Mesón and Tiano's, offer alfresco dining. Tiano's often has a marimba band in the evening. The city sponsors free marimba concerts here on Sunday mornings at 11.30 am as well.

Just to the north of the park rises the 17th century **Iglesia de Jesús**, also called the Iglesia El Tercer Orden. Built by the Jesuits in 1618, it is the surviving edifice in a complex of Jesuit buildings that once filled the entire city block. Always interested in education, the Jesuits founded schools that later gave birth to the Universidad de Yucatán nearby. The 19th century General Cepeda Peraza collected a library of 15,000 volumes, which is housed in a building behind the church.

Directly in front of the church is the little **Parque de la Madre**, sometimes called Parque Morelos. The modern Madonna-and-child statue, which is a common fixture of town squares in Mexico, is a copy of a statue by Lenoir that stands in the Jardin du Luxembourg in Paris.

Just north of Parque de la Madre you confront the enormous bulk of the great **Teatro Peón Contreras**, built from 1900 to 1908 during Mérida's henequén heyday. Designed by Italian architect Enrico Deserti, it boasts a main staircase of Carrara marble, a dome with imported frescos by Italian artists and, in its southwest corner, the Tourist Information Center.

The main entrance to the theater is on the corner of Calles 60 and 57. A gallery inside the entrance often holds exhibits by local painters and photographers; usual hours are weekdays from 9 am to 2 pm and 5 to 9 pm, and weekends from 9 am to 2 pm. To see the grand theater itself, you'll have to attend a performance.

Across Calle 60 from the theater is the entrance to the main building of the **Universidad de Yucatán**. Though the Jesuits provided education to Yucatán's youth for centuries, the modern university was only established in the 19th century by Governor Felipe Carrillo Puerto and General Manuel Cepeda Peraza. The story of the university's founding is rendered graphically in a mural done in 1961 by Manuel Lizama. Ask for directions to the mural.

The central courtyard of the university building is the scene of concerts and folk performances every Tuesday or Friday evening at 9 pm (check with the Tourist Information Center for performance dates and times).

A block north of the university, at the intersection of Calles 60 and 55, is the pretty little **Parque Santa Lucia**, with arcades on the north and west sides. When

Mérida was a lot smaller, this was where travelers would get into or out of the stage-coaches which bumped over the rough roads of the peninsula, linking towns and villages with the provincial capital.

Today the park is the venue for orchestral performances of Yucatecan music on Thursday at 9 pm and Sunday at 11 am. Also here on Sunday at 11 am is the Bazar de Artesanías, the local handicrafts market.

To reach the Paseo de Montejo, walk 3½ blocks north along Calle 60 from the Parque Santa Lucia to Calle 47. Turn right on Calle 47 and walk two blocks to the paseo, on your left.

Paseo de Montejo
The Paseo de Montejo was an attempt by Mérida's 19th century city planners to create a wide European-style grand boulevard, similar to Mexico City's Paseo de la Reforma or Paris' Champs Elysées. Though more modest than its predecessors, the Paseo de Montejo is still a beautiful swath of green and open space in an urban conglomeration of stone and concrete.

As the Yucatán Peninsula has always looked upon itself as distinct from the rest of Mexico, its powerful hacendados and commercial barons maintained good business and social contacts with Europe. Europe's architectural and social influence can be seen along the paseo in the surviving fine mansions built by wealthy families around the turn of the century. Many other mansions have been torn down to make way for the banks, hotels and other establishments. Most of the remaining mansions are north of Calle 37, which is three blocks north of the Museo Regional de Antropología.

Museo Regional de Antropología The great white palace on the corner of Paseo de Montejo and Calle 43 is the Museo Regional de Antropología de Yucatán, housed in the Palacio Cantón. The great mansion was designed by Enrico Deserti, also responsible for the Teatro Peón Contreras. Construction took place from 1909 to 1911. The mansion's owner, General

Francisco Cantón Rosado (1833-1917) lived here for only six years before his death. No building in Mérida exceeds it in splendor or pretension. It's a fitting symbol of the grand aspirations of Mérida's elite during the last years of the Porfiriato.

Admission to the museum costs US$5; free Sunday. It's open Monday to Saturday from 8 am to 8 pm, Sunday from 8 am to 2 pm. The museum shop is open from 8 am to 3 pm (2 pm on Sunday). Labels on the museum's exhibits are in Spanish only.

The museum covers the peninsula's history from the very beginning, when mastodons roamed here. Exhibits on Mayan culture include explanations of forehead-flattening, which was done to beautify babies, and other practices such as sharpening teeth and implanting them with tiny jewels. If you plan to visit archaeological sites near Mérida, you can study the many exhibits here – lavishly illustrated with plans and photographs – which cover the great Mayan cities of Mayapán, Uxmal and Chichén Itzá, as well as lesser sites.

Avenida Colón For more mansion-viewing, turn left (west) onto Avenida Colón. The first block west of Paseo de Montejo is Mérida's posh entertainment and shopping district serving the big hotels: Holiday Inn, Fiesta Americana, Hyatt. Beyond the hotels are several splendid turn-of-the-century mansions.

Parque Centenario
About 12 blocks west of the Plaza Mayor lies the large, verdant Parque Centenario, bordered by Avenida de los Itzaes, the highway to the airport and Campeche. There's a zoo in the park that specializes in exhibiting the fauna of Yucatán. To get there, take a bus westward along Calle 61 or 65. The park is open daily except Monday from 6 am to 6 pm; the zoo from 8 am to 5 pm. Admission is free.

Mayan Cultural Center The Centro Cultural de los Pueblos Mayas, on Calle 59 between Calles 48 and 50, six blocks east of the Plaza Mayor, holds displays of the best

of indigenous arts and crafts. Located behind the ancient ex-Convento de la Mejorada, it will satisfy your curiosity about the weaving of colorful huipiles, the carving of ceremonial masks, the weaving of hammocks and hats, and the turning of pottery. It's open for free from 8 am to 8 pm (Sunday from 9 am to 2 pm), closed Monday.

Organized Tours
You can choose from many group tours to sights around Mérida: Chichén Itzá (US$17), Chichén with dropoff in Cancún (US$29), Uxmal and Kabah (US$17), Uxmal sound-and-light (US$17), the Puuc Route (US$32) and Izamal (US$14). All prices are per person. Ask at your hotel reception desk, or in a fancier hotel, or at any of the travel agencies on Calle 60.

Special Events
Prior to Lent in February or March, Carnaval features colorful costumes and nonstop festivities. It is celebrated with greater vigor in Mérida than anywhere else in Yucatán. During the first two weeks in October, the Cristo de las Ampollas (Christ of the Blisters) statue in the cathedral is venerated with processions.

Places to Stay – budget
Prices for basic but suitable rooms in Mérida range from about US$9 to US$15 for a small but clean double room with fan and private shower only a short walk from the plaza. All hotels should provide purified drinking water, usually at no extra charge. (Sometimes the water bottles are not readily evident, so ask for agua purificada.)

Hotel Las Monjas (☎ 28-66-32), Calle 66A No 509 at Calle 63, is one of the best deals in town. All 28 rooms in this little place have ceiling fans and sinks or private baths with hot and cold water. Doubles with one bed cost US$10, with two beds US$12. One room has air-con and goes for a dollar more. Rooms are tiny and most are dark, but they're clean. Room No 12 is the best.

Hotel Margarita (☎ 23-72-36), Calle 66 No 506, between Calles 61 and 63, offers low standards for low prices, but a convenient location. Its small, fairly grubby rooms with fan and running water cost US$7/8/10/11 a single/double/triple/quad. Air-con is in some rooms for a few dollars more.

Casa de Huéspedes Peniche (☎ 28-55-18), Calle 62 No 507, between 63 and 65, is in terrible condition, but right off the Plaza Mayor, and singles/doubles without running water cost as little as US$5/6, or US$7 double with shower. If you're really broke, look at it.

Hotel Mucuy (☎ 28-51-93, fax 23-78-01), Calle 57 No 481, between Calles 56 and 58, has been serving thrifty travelers for more than a decade. It's a family-run place with 26 tidy rooms on two floors facing a long, narrow garden courtyard. Señora Ofelia Comin and her daughter Ofelia speak English; Señor Alfredo Comin understands it. Singles/doubles/triples with ceiling fans and private showers cost US$11/13/16.

Casa Bowen (☎ 28-61-09), Calle 66 No 521B, near Calle 65, is a large old Mérida house converted to a hotel. The narrow courtyard has a welcome swath of green grass. Rooms are simple, even bare, and some are dark and soiled, but all have fans and showers for US$9/11 with fan, US$19 with air-con. Staff tend to be sullen. The *Café Terraza* across the street provides quick, cheap meals.

Casa Becil (☎ 24-67-64), Calle 67 No 550C, between Calles 66 and 68 near the bus station, is a house with a high-ceilinged sitting room/lobby and small, sometimes hot guest rooms at the back. With private shower and fan, the price is US$11 to US$14 a double.

Hotel Sevilla (☎ 23-83-60), Calle 62 No 511, at the corner of Calle 65, offers a whisper of faded elegance, but most rooms are musty and dark. The price is not too bad: US$8/10/13 for a single/double/triple.

Hammocks

The fine strings of Yucatecan hammocks make them supremely comfortable. In the sticky heat of a Yucatán summer, most locals prefer sleeping in a hammock, where the air can circulate around them, rather than in a bed. Many inexpensive hotels used to have hammock hooks in the walls of all guest rooms, though the hooks are not so much in evidence today.

Yucatecan hammocks are normally woven from strong nylon or cotton string and dyed in various colors; there are also natural, undyed versions. In the old days, the finest, strongest, most expensive hammocks were woven from silk.

Hammocks come in several widths. From smallest to largest, the names generally used are: *sencillo* (about 50 pairs of end strings, US$8 to US$10), *doble* (100 pairs, US$10 to US$15), *matrimonial* (150 pairs, US$12 to US$20) and *matrimonial especial* or *cuatro cajas* (175 pairs or more, US$18 to US$30). You must check to be sure that you're really getting the width you're paying for. Because hammocks fold up small and the larger hammocks are more comfortable (though more expensive), consider the bigger sizes.

During your first few hours in Mérida you will be approached on the street by hammock peddlers. They may quote very low prices, but a low price is only good if the quality is high and street-sold hammocks are mediocre at best. Check the hammock very carefully.

You can save yourself a lot of trouble by shopping at a hammock store with a good reputation. *La Poblana* (☎ 21-65-03), at Calle 65 No 492 between Calles 58 and 60, is fairly good. Some travelers report slightly cheaper prices for good quality at El Aguacate, Calle 58 No 604 at the corner of Calle 73. El Campesino, at Calle 58 No 548 between Calles 69 and 71, is cheaper but provides less guidance – so you should really know what you are looking for and check quality.

It's interesting to venture out to the nearby village of Tixcocob to watch the hammocks being woven. A bus runs regularly from the Progreso bus station south of the main plaza at Calle 62 No 524 between Calles 65 and 67. ■

If you don't mind walking or busing a few extra blocks and you really want to save money, try the *Hotel del Mayab* (☎ 28-51-74, fax 28-60-47), Calle 50 No 536A, between 65 and 67. Streetside rooms can be noisy, but interior rooms with shower are quiet, and there's a swimming pool, all for US$8 a double with fan, US$11 with air-con.

Hotel Santa Lucía (☎ 28-26-72, 28-26-62), Calle 55 No 508, between Calles 60 and 62 facing the Parque Santa Lucía, has 51 decent, well located double rooms for US$18 with fan, or US$20 with air-con.

Hotel Trinidad (☎ 23-20-33), Calle 62 No 464 between Calles 55 and 57, is run by artists and can be funky or quirky, depending on your feelings. Modern Mexican paintings draw your eye from the peeling paint on the walls. The guest rooms, priced from US$12 to US$13 double, are all different, and exhibit both charm and squalor.

The Trinidad's sister hotel, *Hotel Trinidad Galería* (☎ 23-24-63, fax 24-23-19), Calle 60 No 456, at Calle 51, was once an appliance showroom. There's a small swimming pool, a bar, art gallery and antique shop as well as presentable rooms with fans and private showers renting for similar rates.

Hotel Peninsular (☎ 23-69-96), Calle 58 No 519 between Calles 65 and 67, is in the heart of the market district. You pass through a long corridor to find a neat restaurant and a maze of rooms, most with windows opening onto the interior spaces. It costs US$9/11/15 with private bath and fan; add a few dollars for air-con.

The neo-colonial *Posada del Angel* (☎ 23-27-54), Calle 67 No 535 between Calles 66 and 68, is three blocks northeast of Terminal CAME and is quieter than most other hotels in this neighborhood. It's convenient, and priced at US$11 to US$13 a double, US$17 with air-con.

Places to Stay – middle

Mérida's middle-range places provide surprising levels of comfort for what you pay. Most charge US$20 to US$50 for a double room with air-conditioning, ceiling fan and

private shower; and most have restaurants, bars and little swimming pools.

Hotel Dolores Alba (☎ 21-37-45), Calle 63 No 464, between Calles 52 and 54, 3½ blocks east of the plaza, is one of the top choices in Mérida because of its pleasant courtyard, beautiful swimming pool and clean, comfortable rooms for US$22/25/28 a single/double/triple, with shower, fan and air-con.

Hotel Caribe (☎ 24-90-22, 800-20003, in USA 800-826-6842; fax 24-87-33), Calle 59 No 500, at the corner of Calle 60 on the Parque Hidalgo, is a favorite with visiting foreigners because of its central location, its rooftop pool, and its two restaurants. Most rooms have air-con and range in price from US$20 for a small single with fan to US$40 for a large double with air-con.

Gran Hotel (☎ 24-77-30, fax 24-76-22), Calle 60 No 496, between Calles 59 and 61, is on the southern side of the Parque Hidalgo. Corinthian columns support terraces on three levels around the verdant central courtyard and fancy wrought-iron and carved wood decoration evoke a past age. All 28 rooms have air-con and cost US$30/40/50.

Casa Mexilio (☎ /fax 28-25-05; in USA 800-538-6802), Calle 68 No 495, between Calles 59 and 57, is Mérida's most charming pension, a well-preserved and decorated house with a small pool and quiet, comfortable rooms for US$28 to US$50 a double, breakfast included.

Posada Toledo (☎ 23-16-90, fax 23-22-56), Calle 58 No 487 at Calle 57, three blocks northeast of the main plaza, is a colonial mansion with rooms arranged on two floors around the classic courtyard, a dining room straight out of the 19th century, and small, modernized double rooms with fan or air-con for US$20 on the ground floor, or US$26 on the upper floor.

Places to Stay – top end

Top-end hotels charge between US$70 and US$150 for a double room with air-con. Each hotel has a restaurant, bar, swimming pool and probably other services like a newsstand, hairdresser, travel agency and nightclub.

If you reserve your top-end room through your travel agent at home, you're likely to pay typical international-class rates for these hotels. But if you walk in and ask about *promociones* (promotional rates), or – even better – look through local newspapers and handouts for special rates aimed at a local clientele, you can lower your lodging bill substantially.

Mérida's newest and most luxurious hotel is the 17-story, 300-room *Hyatt Regency Mérida* (☎ 42-12-34, fax 25-70-02), Avenida Colón and Calle 60, 100 meters west of Paseo de Montejo and about two km north of the Plaza Mayor. Rooms with all the comforts cost US$95 to US$135, but promotional deals can bring those prices down.

Holiday Inn Mérida (☎ 25-68-77, in USA 800-465-4329; fax 25-77-55), Avenida Colón 498 at Calle 60, half a block off the Paseo de Montejo behind the US Consulate General, is one of Mérida's most luxurious establishments. Its 213 air-con rooms cost US$65 to US$85.

Across Avenida Colón from the Hyatt and Holiday Inn is a large multi-purpose building within which you'll find the *Fiesta Americana Mérida* (☎ 42-11-11, 800-50450, in USA 800-343-7821; fax 42-11-12), a new neo-colonial luxury hotel charging US$105 to US$125 for its very comfortable rooms and junior suites.

Hotel Casa del Balam (☎ 24-88-44, in USA 800-624-8451; fax 24-50-11), Calle 60 No 488 at Calle 57, has numerous advantages: agreeable colonial decor, modern rooms and services, a central location, and a price of US$75 per room, with discounts offered when it's not busy.

For all-round quality, convenience and price, try the *Hotel Los Aluxes* (☎ 24-21-99, in USA 800-782-8395; fax 23-38-58), Calle 60 No 444, at Calle 49. This 109-room hotel, popular with tour groups, has all the services, plus modern architecture and an intriguing name: *aluxes* (ah-LOO-shess) are the Mayan equivalent of lep-

rechauns. Rates are US$65 a single/double, US$85 a triple.

The *Hotel Mérida Misión Park Plaza* (☎ 23-95-00, fax 23-76-65), Calle 60 No 491, at Calle 57, is half modern and half colonial in decor, comfortable without being particularly charming. Rates for the 150 air-conditioned rooms are US$75 for a single or double.

Places to Eat

Budget Walk two blocks south from the main plaza to Calle 67, turn left (east) and walk another two or three blocks to the market. Continue straight up the ramping flight of steps on Calle 67 just east of Calle 58. As you ascend, you'll pass the touristy Mercado de Artesanías on your left. At the top of the ramp, turn left and you'll see a row of market family-run eateries with names like *El Chimecito, La Temaxeña, Saby, Mimi, Saby y El Palon, La Socorrito, Reina Beatriz* and so forth. Comidas corridas here are priced from US$1 to US$2, big main-course platters of beef, fish or chicken with vegetables and rice or potatoes go for US$1.25 to US$2.50. The market eateries are open from early morning until early evening – some as late as 8 or 8.30 pm – every day.

El Louvre (☎ 21-32-71), Calle 62 No 499, corner of Calle 61 at the northwest corner of the Plaza Mayor, is grubby, but has a loyal local clientele who come for the daily US$1.50 comida corrida, though it's hardly a gourmet treat. Breakfast costs the same.

Cafeteria Erick's, Cafe Los Amigos, Chicken Express and *El Trapiche*, up Calle 62 from El Louvre, offer food nearly as cheap in more attractive surroundings.

Lonchería Mily, Calle 59 No 520 between 64 and 66, opens at 7.30 am and serves cheap breakfasts (US$1), a two-course comida corrida (US$2) and cheap sandwiches. It closes at 5 pm, and is closed all day Sunday.

For take-out food, try the *Pizzería de Vito Corleone* (☎ 23-68-46), Calle 59 No 508, at 62. This tiny eatery suffers from

Yucatecan Cuisine

Called by its Maya inhabitants 'the Land of the Pheasant and the Deer,' Yucatán has always had a distinctive cuisine. Here are some of the Yucatecan dishes you might want to try:

Frijol con puerco – Yucatecan-style pork and beans, topped with a sauce made with grilled tomatoes, and decorated with bits of radish, slices of onion and leaves of fresh cilantro; served with rice

Huevos Motuleños – 'Eggs in the style of Motul'; fried eggs atop a tortilla, garnished with beans, peas, chopped ham, sausage, grated cheese and a certain amount of spicy chile – high in cholesterol, fat and flavor

Papadzules – Tortillas stuffed with chopped hard-boiled eggs and topped with a sauce of marrow squash or cucumber seeds

Pavo relleno – Slabs of turkey meat are layered with chopped, spiced beef and pork and served in a rich, dark sauce (the Yucatecan *faisán* (pheasant) is actually the *pavo* [ocellated turkey])

Pibil – Meat wrapped in banana leaves, flavored with achiote, garlic, sour orange, salt and pepper, and baked in a barbecue pit called a *pib*. The two main varieties are *cochinita pibil* (suckling pig) and *pollo pibil* (chicken)

Poc-chuc – Tender pork strips marinated in sour orange juice, grilled and served topped with a spicy onion relish

Puchero – A stew of pork, chicken, carrots, marrow squash, potatoes, plantains and *chayote* (vegetable pear), spiced with radish, fresh cilantro and sour orange

Salbutes – Yucatán's favorite snack: a hand-made tortilla, fried, then topped with shredded turkey, onion and slices of avocado

Sopa de lima – 'Lime soup'; chicken broth with bits of shredded chicken, tortilla strips, lime juice and chopped lime

Venado – Venison, a popular traditional dish, might be served as a *pipián*, flavored with a sauce of ground marrow squash seeds, wrapped in banana leaves and steamed ■

---

loud street noise, so many customers take their pizzas to the Parque Hidalgo instead. Pizzas are priced from US$2 to US$8, depending upon size and ingredients. Vegetarian varieties are available.

The best cheap breakfasts can be had by picking up a selection of pan dulces (sweet rolls and breads) from one of Mérida's several *panificadoras* (bakeries). A convenient one is the *Panificadora Montejo* at the corner of Calles 62 and 63, at the southwest corner of the main plaza. Pick up a metal tray and tongs, select the pastries you want and hand the tray to a clerk who will bag them and quote a price, usually US$2 or so for a full bag. *Panificadora El Retorno*, on Calle 62 just north of 61, is a tiny, modish, version.

Kükis by Maru, Calle 61 between 62 and 64, a few doors west of El Louvre, serves fresh-baked cookies ('kükis') and cappuccino (hot or iced) for less than US$2. More substantial fare such as scones with ham and cheese, and sandwiches made with whole-grain bread, cost even less.

Middle Those willing to spend a bit more money can enjoy the pleasant restaurants of the Parque Hidalgo at the corner of Calles 59 and 60.

The least expensive, yet one of the most pleasant restaurants here, is the *Cafetería El Rincón* (the stained-glass sign above the door reads El Mesón; ☎ 21-92-32) in the Hotel Caribe. Meat, fish and chicken dishes are priced from US$4 to US$7, but sandwiches and burgers are less. El Rincón is open from 7 am to 10.30 pm.

Perhaps the most popular spot on the Parque Hidalgo is *Giorgio's Pizza & Pasta*, to the left of the Gran Hotel. This is the center of the action in the park. Come and carbo-load on plates of spaghetti for US$4, or pizzas for US$3.50 to US$7.

Right next to El Rincón is *Tiano's* (☎ 23-71-18), Calle 59 No 498, which hires a marimba group each evening to entertain its patrons as well as the dozens of hangers-on in the square. The menu bears the cheerful legend 'Please avoid ambulant sellers, touching money during meals un-hygienic, or you can choke.' Have sopa de lima, puntas de filete, dessert and a drink and your bill might be US$13 – a bit expensive for the quality of the food.

Across Calle 60, facing the Parque Hidalgo, is an old Mérida standard, the *Café-Restaurant Express* (☎ 21-37-38), Calle 60 No 502, south of Calle 59. Busy with a loyal crowd of regulars and for-eigners, Express is a bustling and noisy meeting place, and prices are just a bit too high, but the food is OK and service is fast. Hours are 7 am to midnight daily.

Amaro (☎ 28-24-51), Calle 59 No 507, between Calles 60 and 62, specializes in Yucatecan food and beer, and also offers vegetarian dishes and pizzas, daily from 9 am to 10 pm. The setting, complete with strolling troubadour, is the courtyard of the house in which Andrés Quintana Roo – poet, statesman, and drafter of Mexico's Declara-tion of Independence – was born in 1787.

A few steps north along Calle 60 from the Parque Hidalgo is the *Cafe Peón Con-treras*, attractive for its outdoor sidewalk tables. The menu is long, varied, and mod-erately priced, with breakfasts for US$2.50 to US$4, pizzas for around US$5, and a combination plate of Yucatecan specialties for US$10.

Restaurant Santa Lucia (☎ 28-59-57), Calle 60 No 479 at Calle 55, is cozy and atmospheric, with low lights and a strolling guitarist. The Yucatecan combination plate, including sopa de lima, costs US$5, though other main courses may go as high as US$13. Service is slow, and some dishes are bland.

Pop Cafetería (☎ 28-61-63), Calle 57 between 60 and 62, is plain, modern, bright, air-conditioned, and named for the first month of the 18-month Mayan cal-endar. Though the menu includes ham-burgers, spaghetti, chicken and other main-course platters for US$2.50 to US$5, most people come for breakfast (US$2 to US$4), coffee, fruit plates or pastries. It's open daily from 7 am to midnight.

Top End The secret to enjoying a dinner at *La Bella Epoca* (☎ 28-19-28), Calle 60 between 57 and 59, opposite the Parque de la Madre, is to get there early enough to get one of the five little two-person tables set out on the 2nd-floor balconies. Have an ap-petizer, pollo pibil, dessert and a beer, for US$14 per person. It's open from 7 am to 11 pm daily.

Restaurante Portico del Peregrino (☎ 28-61-63), Calle 57 No 501, between Calles 60 and 62, right next to Pop, is a 'Pilgrim's Refuge' of several pleasant, almost elegant traditional dining rooms (some are air-conditioned) around a small courtyard replete with colonial artifacts. Yucatecan dishes are the forte, but you'll find many continental dishes as well. Lunch (noon to 3 pm) and dinner (6 to 11 pm) are served every day and your bill for a full meal might be US$12 to US$20 per person.

La Casona (☎ 23-83-48), Calle 60 No 434 between Calles 47 and 49, is a fine old city house with tables set out on a portico next to a small but lush garden; dim light-ing lends an air of romance. Italian dishes crowd the menu, with a few concessions to local cuisine. Plan to spend anywhere from US$9 to US$17 per person. La Casona is open every evening for dinner; on week-ends, you might want to make reservations.

Los Almendros (☎ 28-54-59), Calle 50A No 493 between Calles 57 and 59, facing the Plaza de Mejorada, specializes in authentic Yucatecan country cuisine such as pavo relleno negro (grilled turkey with hot peppered pork stuffing), papadzul (tacos filled with egg smothered in a fiery sauce), sopa de lima (chicken broth with lime and tortillas) or Los Almendros' most famous dish, the zingy onion-and-tomato pork dish poc-chuc. Full meals cost US$9 to US$15. Some people are disappointed at Los Almendros because they go expecting delicacies; this is hearty food.

Mérida boasts two other Los Almendros locations as well, one of which is the fancier *Gran Almendros* (☎ 23-81-35), Calle 57 at Calle 50.

Entertainment

Proud of its cultural legacy and attuned to the benefits of tourism, the city of Mérida offers nightly *folkloric events* by local performers of considerable skill. Admission is free to city-sponsored events. Check with the tourist office for the schedule.

Many English-language films, some of fairly recent release, are screened in Mérida with Spanish subtitles. Buy your tickets (usually about US$2) before showtime and well in advance on weekends. There's popular *Cine Fantasio*, Calle 59 at 60 facing the Parque Hidalgo between the Gran Hotel and Hotel Caribe, the *Cinema 59*, Calle 59 between Calles 68 and 70, and the *Plaza Cine Internacional*, Calle 58 between 57 and 59.

Things to Buy

From standard shirts and blouses to Mayan exotica, Mérida is *the* place on the peninsula to shop. Purchases you might want to consider include traditional Mayan clothing such as the colorful women's embroidered tunic called a huipil, a Panama hat woven from palm fibers, local craft items and of course the wonderfully comfortable Yucatecan hammock, which holds you gently in a comfortable cotton web.

Guard your valuables extra carefully in the market area. Watch for pickpockets, purse-snatchers and slash-and-grab thieves.

Mérida's main market, the Mercado Municipal Lucas do Gálvez, is bound by Calles 56 and 56A at Calle 67, four blocks southeast of the Plaza Mayor. The market building is more or less next door to the city's main post office and telegraph office, on the corner of Calles 65 and 56. The surrounding streets are all part of the large market district, lined with shops selling everything one might need.

The Bazar de Artesanías, Calle 67 on the corner of Calle 56A, is set up to attract tourists. You should have a look at the stuff here, then compare the goods and prices with independent shops outside the Bazar.

Handicrafts The place to go for high-quality craft and art items is the Casa de los Artesanías, Estado de Yucatán on Calle 63 between 64 and 66; look for the doorway marked 'Dirección de Desarrollo Artesanal DIF Yucatán.' It's open weekdays from 8 am to 8 pm, Saturday from 8 am to 6 pm. This is a government-supported marketing effort for local artisans. The selection of crafts is very good, quality is usually high and prices reasonable.

You can also check out locally made crafts at the Museo Regional de Artesanías on Calle 59 between Calles 50 and 48. The work on display is superb, but the items for sale are not as good. Admission is free and it's open from 8 am to 8 pm Tuesday to Saturday and from 9 am to 2 pm Sunday.

Panama Hats Panama hats are woven from jipijapa palm leaves in caves and workshops in which the temperature and humidity are carefully controlled, as humid conditions keep the fibers pliable when the hat is being made. Once blocked and exposed to the relatively drier air outside, the panama hat is surprisingly resilient and resistant to crushing. The Campeche town of Becal is the center of the hat-weaving trade, but you can buy good examples of the hatmaker's art in Mérida.

The best quality hats have a very fine, close weave of slender fibers. The coarser the weave, the lower the price should be. Prices range from a few dollars for a hat of basic quality to US$20 or more for top quality.

Hammocks You will be approached by peddlers on the street wanting to sell you hammocks about every hour throughout your stay in Mérida (every five minutes in Parque Hidalgo). Check the quality of the hammocks on offer carefully. You can save yourself a lot of trouble by shopping at a hammock store with a good reputation – see the sidebar on hammocks for more information.

Getting There & Away

Air Mérida's modern airport is a 10 km, 20-minute ride southwest of the Plaza Mayor off highway 180 (Avenida de los Itzaes). The airport has car rental desks and a tourist office that can help with hotel reservations.

Most international flights to Mérida are connections through Mexico City or Cancún. The only nonstop international services are Aeroméxico's two daily flights from Miami and Aviateca's flights to Guatemala City. Domestic flights are operated mostly by smaller regional airlines, with a few flights by Aeroméxico and Mexicana.

Aerocaribe – flies between Mérida and Cancún (morning and evening flights, US$55 one way, US$100 round-trip excursion), Havana (Cuba), Chetumal, Mexico City, Oaxaca, Tuxtla Gutiérrez (for San Cristóbal de Las Casas), Veracruz and Villahermosa. Paseo de Montejo 476A (☎ 24-95-00, 23-00-02)

Aerolíneas Bonanza – flies round trips daily from Mérida to Cancún, Chetumal and Palenque. Calle 56A No 579, between Calles 67 and 69 (☎ 26-06-09, fax 27-79-99)

Aeroméxico – has a few flights. Paseo de Montejo 460 (☎ 27-95-66, 27-92-77)

Aviacsa – flies nonstop to Cancún, Villahermosa and Mexico City. The airport (☎ 26-32-53, 26-39-54, fax 26-90-87)

Aviateca – flies to Tikal and Guatemala City several times a week. The airport (☎ 24-43-54)

Litoral – flies to Ciudad del Carmen, Veracruz and Monterrey. Based in Veracruz (☎ 800-29020)

Mexicana – has nonstop flights to and from Cancún and Mexico City. Calle 58 No 500 (☎ 24-66-33)

Bus Mérida is the bus transport hub of the Yucatán peninsula. If you take an all-night bus, don't put anything valuable in the overhead racks, as there have been several reports of gear being stolen at night.

Bus Stations Mérida has several bus stations. Here's a rundown of stations and companies that serve them (see Bus Companies and Bus Routes, below, for points served):

Terminal CAME – Mérida's main bus terminal, seven blocks southwest of the Plaza Mayor at Calle 70 No 555 between 69 and 71, is known as Terminal CAME (KAH-meh). It handles ticketing and departures for ADO, one of Mexico's biggest bus companies. Come here if you're headed for Campeche, Palenque, Villahermosa, Tuxtla Gutiérrez, San Cristóbal de Las Casas, or points in the rest of Mexico. Buses run by Línea Dorada and UNO depart from CAME, but their ticket counters are in the old Terminal de Autobuses around the corner on Calle 69. CAME has pay phones and a hotel desk. Look through the flyers offering hotel room discounts (see Places to Stay).

Terminal de Autobuses – The old bus terminal, around the corner from CAME, has ticket counters for Línea Dorada and UNO, and also for Autotransportes de Oriente, Autotransportes del Sur, Omnitur del Caribe and Transportes Mayab. Come here for buses to points in the state and peninsula of Yucatán, and some beyond.

Parque de San Juan – The Parque de San Juan, on Calle 69 between 62 and 64, is the terminus for Volkswagen minibuses going to Dzibilchaltún Ruinas (US$0.55), Muna, Oxkutzcab, Peto, Sacalum, Tekax and Ticul (US$1.75).

Oriente & Noroeste – Autotransportes de Oriente and Autotransportes del Noroeste en Yucatán share a terminal at Calle 50 No 527A, between Calles 65 and 67.

Autotransportes del Sur (ATS) – Though most ATS buses depart from the old Terminal de Autobuses, the company also runs buses to Celestún from its old terminal at Calle 50 No 531 at Calle 67.

Progreso – The separate bus terminal for Progreso is at Calle 62 No 524, between Calles 65 and 67.

Bus Companies Here's a quick rundown on the companies and the destinations they serve:

Autobuses de Oriente (ADO) – long-haul 1st-class routes to Campeche, Palenque, Villahermosa, Veracruz, Mexico City and beyond

Autotransportes de Oriente (Oriente) – buses every hour from 5.15 am until 12.15 am between Mérida and Cancún stopping at Chichén Itzá and Valladolid; buses between Mérida and Cobá, Izamal, Playa del Carmen and Tulum

Autotransportes del Sur (ATS) – hourly buses to Cancún and buses every 20 to 40 minutes to Campeche. They also run buses to Bolonchén de Rejón, Cancún, Celestún, Chiquilá, Ciudad del Carmen, Emiliano Zapata, Hecelchakan, Hopelchén, Izamal, Ocosingo, Palenque, Playa del Carmen, San Cristóbal de Las Casas, Tizimin, Tulum and Valladolid. Special buses serve the Ruta Puuc, and Uxmal for the evening sound-and-light show; see Uxmal, below, for details.

Línea Dorada – a deluxe line serving Felipe Carrillo Puerto and Chetumal.

Noroeste – service to many small towns in the northeastern part of the peninsula, including Río Lagartos (two buses daily, US$4.50) and Tizimin

Omnitur del Caribe (Caribe) – deluxe service between Mérida and Chetumal via Felipe Carrillo Puerto; ticket counter in the old Terminal de Autobuses

Transportes Mayab (Mayab) – buses to Cancún, Chetumal, Felipe Carrillo Puerto, Peto and Ticul; ticket counters and departures in the old Terminal de Autobuses

Transportes de Lujo Línea Dorada (LD) – deluxe service to Felipe Carrillo Puerto and Chetumal; ticket counter in the old Terminal de Autobuses, departures from Terminal CAME

UNO – super-deluxe service on major routes, such as Mérida to Cancún and Mérida to Villahermosa and Mexico City.

Bus Routes
Here's information on daily trips to and from Mérida:

Campeche – 195 km (short route via Becal), 2½ to three hours; 250 km (long route via Uxmal), four hours; ATS has buses every 20 to 30 minutes for US$3 to US$3.50; 33 by ADO (US$6) around the clock

Cancún – 320 km, four to 6 hours; Oriente has hourly buses from 5.15 am to 12.15 am for US$7; ATS runs buses hourly from 4 am to midnight for US$7; ADO has 21 deluxe buses daily for US$8.75; UNO has morning and evening super-deluxe buses for US$11

Celestún – 95 km, 1½ to two hours, US$1.75; 12 buses from 5 am to 8 pm, departing the Unión de Camioneros de Yucatán terminal on Calle 71 between 62 and 64, then stopping at the Autotransportes del Sur terminal at Calle 50 No 531 at Calle 67

Chetumal – 456 km, eight hours; deluxe Caribe buses at 12.30, 9 and 10.30 pm for US$13; LD and Mayab have buses for less

Chichén Itzá – 116 km, 2½ hours, US$2.75 to US$3.50, ten buses; those by Oriente stop right at the Chichén ruins. A special round-trip (US$6.75) excursion bus by Oriente departs from Mérida at 8.45 am and returns from Chichén Itzá at 3 pm.

Dzibilchaltún – 15 km, 30 minutes, US$0.55; minibuses and colectivo taxis depart when full from the Parque de San Juan (see above), and go all the way to the ruins; the alternative is a bus from the Progreso terminal, which drops you on the highway at the Dzibilchaltún access road, five km west of the ruins.

Felipe Carrillo Puerto – 310 km, 5½ to six hours; Caribe, LD and Mayab run for US$6.50 to US$8; see Chetumal

Izamal – 72 km, 1½ hours, US$1; 20 buses by Oriente from its terminal at Calle 50 between 65 and 67

Kabah – 101 km, two hours, US$2; buses on the 'chenes' or inland route between Mérida and Campeche may stop at Kabah on request

Mexico City (TAPO) – 1550 km, 20 hours; five buses by ADO (US$45)

Palenque – 556 km, nine or 10 hours; two each (morning and evening) by ATS (US$15) and ADO (US$17) go directly to Palenque; many more drop you at Catazajá, the main highway junction 27 km north of Palenque Town. From Catazajá you can hitchhike or catch a bus or colectivo to Palenque.

Playa del Carmen – 385 km, seven hours; nine by ADO (US$10 to US$12), several others by ATS (US$8) and Mayab (US$10)

Progreso – 33 km, 45 minutes, US$0.70; Auto-progreso buses every six minutes from 5 am to 9.45 pm from the Progreso bus terminal (see above)

Ticul – 85 km, 1½ hours, US$2; Mayab runs frequent buses, or you can take a minibus from the Parque de San Juan (see above)

Tizimin – 210 km, four hours, US$3.75; Noroeste, Oriente and ATS have a few buses daily, or take a bus to Valladolid and change there for Tizimin

Tulum – 320 km, five hours via Cobá or 450 km, seven hours via Cancún; Oriente (US$7) and ADO (US$8.25) have a few buses

Tuxtla Gutiérrez – 995 km, 14 hours; three by Colón (US$25), or change at Palenque or Villahermosa

Uxmal – 80 km, 1½ hours; six by ATS, including two special excursions. The Ruta Puuc excursion (US$4.50) departs Mérida's old Terminal de Autobuses at 8 am, goes to Uxmal, Kabah and several other sites, departing Uxmal on the return journey to Mérida at 2.30 pm. The sound-and-light excursion (US$3.75) departs Mérida at 6.15 pm, and Uxmal at 10 pm.

Valladolid – 160 km, three hours, US$5; many buses, especially ADO, Oriente and ATS; see Cancún

Villahermosa – 700 km, nine hours; ADO (US$20) runs 10 buses, UNO (US$32) one; ATS (US$16) has several buses as well

Train Buses are preferable to trains in that they are faster and safer. Rail robberies in some areas (between Mérida, Campeche and Palenque in particular) have reached epidemic proportions. There are no *dormitorios* to lock on trains traveling this route – just vulnerable 1st- and 2nd-class seating.

If you really want to ride a Yucatecan train, sign up for the special excursion by train from Mérida to Izamal; see the Izamal section later in this chapter for details.

If you still want to get between Mérida and other points by rail, a train with no diner departs at midnight for Campeche, Palenque and ultimately Mexico City (two days journey). The station is at Calle 55 between Calles 46 and 48, about nine blocks northeast of the main plaza. Tickets should be bought several hours in advance.

Car & Motorcycle Rental car is the optimal way to tour the many archaeological sites south of Mérida, especially if you have two or more people to share costs.

Assume you will pay a total of US$40 to US$60 per day (tax, insurance and gas included) for the cheapest car offered, usually a bottom-of-the-line Volkswagen or Nissan.

Mexico Rent a Car (☎/fax 27-49-16, 23-36-37), Calle 62 No 483E between Calles 59 and 57, owned and operated by Alvaro and Teresa Alonzo and their children, offers good service and value. The Alonzos also have a desk on Calle 60 at the car park entrance next to the Hotel del Parque, just north of the Parque Hidalgo. Several friends of one of our authors have used them for years with no complaints.

Several other car rental companies have offices on Calle 60 just north of the Teatro Peón Contreras.

Dollar (☎ 28-67-59, fax 25-01-55), Calle 60 No 491, between 55 and 57

Hertz (☎ 24-28-34, fax 84-01-14), Calle 60 No 486D between 55 and 57

National (☎ 28-63-08), Calle 60 No 486F, between 55 and 57

Getting Around

To/From the Airport Bus 79 ('Aviación') travels infrequently between the airport and the city center for US$0.40. Most arriving travelers use the Transporte Terrestre minibuses (US$9.50) to go from the airport to the center; to return to the airport you must take a taxi (US$6.50).

To/From CAME Bus Station To walk from CAME to the Plaza Mayor, exit the terminal, turn left, then right onto Calle 69; the old Terminal de Autobuses will be on your right. Walk straight along Calle 69 for four blocks, passing the Church of San Juan de Dios and a park, to Calle 62. Turn left on Calle 62 and walk the remaining three blocks north to the plaza.

Bus Most parts of Mérida that you'll want to visit are within five or six blocks of the Plaza Mayor and are thus accessible on foot. Given the slow speed of city traffic, particularly in the market areas, travel on foot is also the fastest way to get around.

City buses are cheap at US$0.20 per ride (US$0.30 in a minibus), but routes are confusing. Most routes start in suburban neighborhoods, meander through the city center, and terminate in another distant suburban neighborhood.

To travel between the Plaza Mayor and the upscale neighborhoods to the north along Paseo de Montejo, catch a 'Tecnológico' bus or minibus on Calle 60 and get out at Avenida Colón; to return to the city center, catch almost any bus – López Mateos, Chedraui, etc – along Paseo de Montejo.

The bus system is supplemented by colectivo minibuses, which are easier to use as they run shorter and more comprehensible routes. The one you're liable to find most useful is the Ruta 10 (US$0.40) which departs the corner of Calles 58 and 59, half a block east of the Parque Hidalgo and travels along the Paseo de Montejo to Itzamná.

Taxi Most taxi rides within the city center, including from the CAME bus terminal to the Plaza Mayor, and from the Plaza Mayor to the Holiday Inn or Hyatt off Paseo de Montejo, should cost around US$1.50 or US$2.

DZIBILCHALTÚN

Dzibilchaltún (Place of Inscribed Flat Stones) is a large site. It was the longest continuously utilized Mayan administrative and ceremonial city, serving the Maya from 1500 BC or earlier until the European conquest in the 1540s. At the height of its greatness, Dzibilchaltún covered 80 sq km. Archaeological research in the 1960s mapped 31 sq km of the city, revealing some 8500 structures.

Though the site itself is far less exciting today than Chichén Itzá or Uxmal, there is a fine museum, the interesting little Temple of the Seven Dolls, and the cenote swimming pool.

Dzibilchaltún is open from 8 am to 5 pm every day for US$3, but the museum is closed Monday. Parking costs US$0.75; there's a US$4 fee for use of a video camera.

You enter the site along a nature trail, which ends at the modern, air-conditioned Museo del Pueblo Maya, featuring artifacts from throughout the Mexican-Mayan region. Exhibits explaining Mayan daily life and beliefs, from ancient times until the present, are in Spanish and English.

Beyond the museum, a path leads to the central plaza, with an open chapel dating from early Spanish times (1590-1600).

The Temple of the Seven Dolls (Templo de las Siete Muñecas), which got its name from seven grotesque dolls discovered here during excavations, is a one-km walk from the central plaza. While still a good distance away from the temple, note that you can see right through the building's doors and windows on the east-west axis. But when you approach, this view is lost. The temple's construction is such that you can't see through from north to south at all. The rising and setting sun of the equinoxes 'lit up' the temple's windows and doors, making them blaze like beacons and signaling this important turning-point in the year. Thus the temple is impressive not for its size or beauty, but for its precise astronomical orientation and its function in the Great Mayan Time Machine.

The Cenote Xlacah, now a public swimming pool, is over 40 meters deep. In 1958, an expedition sponsored by the US National Geographic Society sent divers down and recovered some 30,000 Mayan artifacts, many of ritual significance. The most interesting of these are now on display in the site's small but good museum. But enough history – plunge in and cool off!

Getting There & Away

Minibuses and colectivo taxis depart frequently from Mérida's Parque de San Juan, on Calle 69 between Calles 62 and 64, for the village of Dzibilchaltún Ruinas (15 km, 30 minutes, US$0.55), only a little over one km from the museum.

PROGRESO

pop 40,000; ☎ 993

This is a seafarers' town, the port for Mérida and northwestern Yucatán. The Yucatecan limestone shelf declines so gradually into the sea that a *muelle* (pier) 6.5 km long had to be built to reach the deep water.

This same gradual slope of land into water affects Progreso's long beach: the waters are shallow, warm and safe from such dangers as riptide and undertow, though usually murky with seaweed and swirling sand. The beach is nearly shadeless, having lost its palm trees to hurricanes. The few small shelters are inadequate for the crowds, so you bake and burn. The beach at Yucalpeten, a 10-minute bus ride west, is much better.

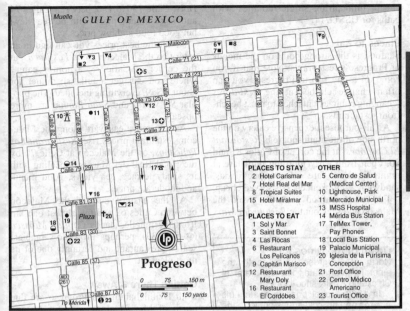

PLACES TO STAY
2 Hotel Carismar
7 Hotel Real del Mar
8 Tropical Suites
15 Hotel Miralmar

PLACES TO EAT
1 Sol y Mar
3 Saint Bonnet
4 Las Rocas
6 Restaurant
    Los Pelícanos
9 Capitán Marisco
12 Restaurant
    Mary Doly
16 Restaurant
    El Cordóbes

OTHER
5 Centro de Salud
    (Medical Center)
10 Lighthouse, Park
11 Mercado Municipal
13 IMSS Hospital
14 Mérida Bus Station
17 TelMex Tower,
    Pay Phones
18 Local Bus Station
19 Palacio Municipal
20 Iglesia de la Purísima
    Concepción
21 Post Office
22 Centro Médico
    Americano
23 Tourist Office

Progreso is normally a sleepy little town, but on weekends, especially in summer, it seems as if all of Mérida is here.

Orientation

Progreso is long and narrow, stretched out along the seashore. Though it has an apparently logical street grid, it is illogically subject to two numbering systems fifty numbers apart. One system has the city center's streets numbered in the 60s, 70s and 80s, another has them in the 10s, 20s and 30s. Thus you might see a street sign on Calle 30 calling it Calle 80, or on a map Calle 10 might also be referred to as Calle 60. We've included both systems on our map.

The bus stations are near the main square. It's six short blocks from the main square to the Malecón and the muelle.

Places to Stay

Progreso is looked upon as a resort, if a modest one, so rooms here tend to be a bit more expensive than in other Yucatecan towns. On Sundays in July and August, the cheapest hotels fill up.

Hotel Miralmar (☎ 5-05-52), Calle 77 No 124 at the corner of Calle 76, offers rooms with private shower, fan and one double bed for US$11, with two beds for US$14. Rooms on the upper floor are preferable – they're not as dungeon-like as the ground-floor rooms.

At the corner of the Malecón and Calle 70 are two more hotels. *Tropical Suites* (☎ 5-12-63) has tidy rooms with showers and fans going for US$18 to US$35 a double. Some rooms have sea views.

Hotel Real del Mar (☎ 5-07-98), between Calles 70 and 72 behind the Restaurant Los Pelícanos, is an older hostelry which looks its age sometimes, but is still a good deal as it's right on the Malecón. Rooms with shower and fan cost US$11 single, US$14 double in one bed, US$15 double in two beds, and US$18 in a double with sea view.

Hotel Carismar (☎ 5-29-07), Calle 71 No 151 between Calles 78 and 80, has cheap, uninspiring singles/doubles with baths for US$11/14.

Places to Eat

Seafood is the strong point on the menus of Progreso's restaurants. Note that if you come on a day trip to Progreso, you can often change clothes at the *vestidores* (changing cubicles) attached to most beach-front restaurants.

An all-purpose inexpensive eatery on the north side of the main square is *Restaurant El Cordóbes*, at the corner of Calles 81 and 80, open from early morning until late at night. Standard fare – tacos, enchiladas, sandwiches, chicken, etc – is served cheap.

For cheap seafood you must avoid the Malecón and seek out the *Restaurant Mary Doly*, Calle 75 No 150, between Calles 74 and 76, a homey place with no sea view, but good food and low prices.

About the best prices you can find in an eatery on the Malecón are at *Las Rocas*, at the corner of Calle 78, a homey eatery where you can get a full fish dinner for about US$9, everything included. The popular *Sol y Mar* and *Saint Bonnet* are more upscale.

As you move eastward along the Malecón, restaurant prices rise. *Restaurant Los Pelícanos*, on the Malecón at Calle 70 by the Hotel Real del Mar, is appealing with its shady terrace, sea views, good menu, and moderate prices.

At the eastern end of the Malecón between Calles 62 and 60, almost one km from the muelle, stands *Capitán Marisco* (☎ 5-06-39), perhaps Progreso's fanciest seafood restaurant and certainly one of its most pleasant.

Getting There & Away

Both Dzibilchaltún and Progreso are due north of Mérida along a fast four-lane highway that's basically a continuation of the Paseo de Montejo. If you're driving, head north on the Paseo and follow signs for Progreso.

Progreso is 18 km (20 minutes) beyond the Dzibilchaltún turnoff. Autoprogreso buses depart the Progreso bus terminal, 1½ blocks south of the main plaza in Mérida at Calle 62 No 524 between Calles 65 and 67, every six minutes from 5 am to 9.45 pm. The fare is US$0.70 one-way, US$1.25 round-trip.

CELESTÚN

pop 1500; ☎ 993

Famed as a bird sanctuary, Celestún makes a good beach-and-bird day trip from Mérida. Although this region abounds in anhingas and egrets, most bird-watchers come here to see the flamingos.

The town is located on a spit of land between the Río Esperanza and the Gulf of Mexico. Brisk westerly sea breezes cool the town on most days. The white-sand beach is appealing, but on some days fierce

---

> ### Death of the Dinosaurs
> North of Progreso, underneath the emerald-green water, lies the crater of Chicxulub (CHIK-shoo-LOOB).
>
> In 1980, Nobel prize laureate Luis Alvarez and his colleagues put forth the theory that the tremendous impact caused by an asteroid or small comet hitting the earth about 65 million years ago caused climatic changes so severe that they resulted in the extinction of the dinosaurs. In 1991 the huge Chicxulub crater, some 200 km in diameter and the largest yet discovered on Earth, was identified as the most likely candidate for the site of impact.
>
> Numerous scientific expeditions have added to the evidence. Some scientists now believe that the celestial missile came in from the southwest at a low angle of about 30 degrees. If this is true, North American flora and fauna would have suffered the most from the impact.
>
> In 1996, scientists think they may have found tiny pieces of the original meteor or comet. Work continues, and will no doubt lend support to the contentions of many out-of-work nuclear-bomb makers that the world needs a massive, well-funded effort to develop an enormous nuke to vaporize the next meteor that threatens to smack our planet. ■

afternoon winds swirl clouds of choking dust through the town. The dust makes the sea silty, and therefore unpleasant for swimming in the afternoon. Row upon row of fishing boats outfitted with twin long poles line the shore.

Given the winds, the best time to see birds is in the morning. Hire a lancha from the bridge on the highway one km east of the town. The rental should run to about US$20; a boat may take up to eight people at high tide, but perhaps only four at low tide, lest it run aground. The voyage to the flamingo area takes about 30 minutes; after another 30 minutes of viewing, the boat begins the 30-minute voyage back to Celestún. Don't let your boat approach too near the birds, or attempt to make them fly.

Orientation
You come into town along Calle 11, past the marketplace and church (on your left/south) to Calle 12, the waterfront street.

Places to Stay
Hotels are few, and filled on weekends. A daytrip from Mérida is the best way to visit, but you can try for a room at the places listed below:

Turn left (south) along Calle 12 from Calle 11 to find the *Hotel Gutiérrez* (☎ in Mérida 99-28-04-19, 99-28-69-78), Calle 12 No 22, at Calle 13, the top budget choice, with well-kept rooms with fan and bath costing US$15. *Hotel María del Carmen*, just south of it, is similar; enter from Calle 15.

Turn right (north) from Calle 11 along Calle 12 to find the *Hotel San Julio* (☎ 1-85-89), at Calle 12 No 92, by Calle 9,

where singles/doubles cost US$9/12, with fan and bath.

Places to Eat
Celestún's specialty is crab claws, and of course fresh fish. The junction of Calles 11 and 12 has many small restaurants, including the *Celestún*, *Playita*, *Boya* and *Avila*, most with sea views. Locals in the know favor *La Palapa* (☎ 6-20-04). The cheaper eateries, as always, are inland.

Getting There & Away
Buses from Mérida start 12 times daily between 5 am and 8 pm from the Unión de Camioneros de Yucatán terminal on Calle 71 between 62 and 64, then stop at the Autotransportes del Sur station on Calle 50 No 531 at Calle 67. To be assured of a seat, get on board at the terminal on Calle 71. The 95-km trip takes about 1½ to two hours and costs US$1.75.

Cultur (☎ in Mérida 99-24-96-77), the cultural department of the Yucatán state government, organizes minibus tours to Celestún every Wednesday, Friday and Sunday, departing Mérida's Parque de Santa Lucia at 9 am, returning by 4.30 pm. Ask at your hotel or any travel agency.

UXMAL
Set in the Puuc Hills, which lent their name to the architectural patterns in this region, Uxmal ('oosh-MAL') was an important city during the Late Classic period (600-900 AD) in a region that encompassed the satellite towns of Sayil, Kabah, Xlapak and Labná. Although Uxmal means 'thrice built' in Maya, it was actually reconstructed five times.

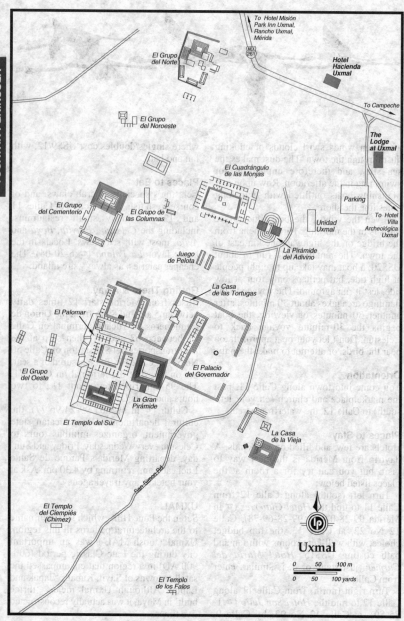

El Grupo
del Norte

To Hotel Misión
Park Inn Uxmal,
Rancho Uxmal,
Mérida

Hotel
Hacienda
Uxmal

To Campeche

El Grupo
del Noroeste

The Lodge
at Uxmal

El Cuadrángulo
de las Monjas

Parking

El Grupo
del Cementerio

El Grupo
de las Columnas

Unidad
Uxmal

To Hotel Villa
Archeológica
Uxmal

Juego
de Pelota

La Pirámide
del Adivino

La Casa
de las Tortugas

El Palomar

La Casa
de las Tortugas

El Grupo
del Oeste

El Palacio
del Governador

La Gran
Pirámide

El Templo
del Sur

La Casa
de la Vieja

El Templo
del Ciempiés
(Chimez)

San-Simon Rd

Uxmal

0   50   100 m
0   50   100 yards

El Templo
de los Falos

That a sizable population ever flourished in this area is a mystery, as there is precious little water in the region. The Mayan cisterns (chultunes) must have been adequate.

History

First occupied in about 600 AD, the town was architecturally influenced by highland Mexico, and features the well-proportioned Puuc style, which is unique to this region.

Given the scarcity of water in the Puuc Hills, Chac the rain god was of great significance. His image is ubiquitous here in stucco monster-like masks protruding from façades and cornices.

There is much speculation as to why Uxmal was abandoned around 900 AD. Drought conditions may have reached such proportions that the inhabitants had to relocate. One widely held theory suggests that the rise to greatness of Chichén Itzá drew people away from the Puuc Hills.

Rediscovered by archaeologists in the 19th century, Uxmal was first excavated in 1929 by Frans Blom. Although much has been restored, there is still a good deal to discover.

Orientation & Information

As you come into the site from the highway, the big new Lodge at Uxmal hotel is on the left, with the Hotel Villa Arqueológica beyond it; the site parking lot is to the right (US$0.75 per car).

You enter the site through the modern Unidad Uxmal building, which holds the air-conditioned Restaurant Yax-Beh. Also in the Unidad Uxmal are a small museum, shops selling souvenirs and crafts, the auditorium Kit Bolon Tun, and toilets. The Librería Dante has a good selection of travel and archaeological guides in English, Spanish, German and French, though imported books are very expensive.

The archaeological site at Uxmal is open daily from 8 am to 5 pm; admission costs US$5, free on Sunday. The Unidad Uxmal building stays open till 10 pm because of the 45-minute Luz y Sonido (Light & Sound) show, held each evening in English

(US$5.50) at 9 pm and in Spanish (US$4) at 8 pm.

If you come for the day and want to stay for the evening sound-and-light show, plan to have dinner and a swim at one of the restaurants; most hotels allow restaurant patrons to use their pools.

As you pass through the turnstile and climb the slope to the ruins, the rear of the Pyramid of the Magician comes into view.

Pyramid of the Magician

The Pyramid of the Magician (Pirámide del Adivino), 39 meters high, was built on an oval base. The smoothly sloping sides have been restored; they date from the temple's fifth incarnation. The four earlier temples were covered in the rebuilding, except for the high doorway on the west side, which has been retained from the fourth temple. Decorated in elaborate Chenes style, the doorway proper takes the form of the mouth of a gigantic Chac mask.

The ascent to the doorway and the top is best done from the west side. Heavy chains serve as handrails to help you up the very steep steps.

From the top of the pyramid, you can survey the rest of the archaeological site. Directly west of the pyramid is the Nunnery Quadrangle. On the south side of the quadrangle, down a short slope, is a ruined ball court. Further south stands the great artificial terrace holding the Governor's Palace; between the palace and the ball court is the small House of the Turtles. Beyond the Governor's Palace are the remains of the Great Pyramid, and next to it are the House of the Pigeons and the South Temple. There once were many other structures at Uxmal, but most have been recaptured by the jungle and are now just verdant mounds.

Nunnery Quadrangle

Archaeologists guess that the 74-room Nunnery Quadrangle (Cuadrángulo de las Monjas) might actually have been a military academy, royal school or palace complex. The long-nosed face of Chac appears everywhere on the façades of the four

RICHARD NEBESKY
Detail of the Nunnery Quadrangle

separate temples which form the quadrangle. The northern temple, grandest of the four, was built first, followed by the south, east and west temples.

Several decorative elements on the façades show signs of Mexican, perhaps Totonac, influence. The feathered serpent (Quetzalcóatl) motif along the top of the west temple's façade is one of these. Note also the stylized depictions of the *na*, or Mayan thatched hut, over some of the doorways in the northern and southern buildings.

Ball Court
Pass through the corbeled arch in the middle of the south building of the quadrangle and continue down the slope to the ball court, which is much less impressive than the great ball court (Juego de Pelota) at Chichén Itzá.

House of the Turtles
Climb the steep slope up to the artificial terrace on which stands the Governor's Palace. At the top on the right is the House of the Turtles (La Casa de las Tortugas), which takes its name from the turtles carved on the cornice. The frieze of short columns or 'rolled mats' which runs around the top of the temple is characteristic of the Puuc style. Turtles were associated by the Maya with the rain god Chac. According to Mayan myth, when the people suffered from drought so did the turtles, and both prayed to Chac to send rain.

Governor's Palace
The magnificent façade of the Palacio del Gobernador, nearly 100 meters long, has been called 'the finest structure at Uxmal and the culmination of the Puuc style' by Mayanist Michael D Coe. Buildings in Puuc style have walls filled with rubble, faced with cement and then covered in a thin veneer of limestone squares; the lower part of the façade is plain, the upper part festooned with stylized Chac faces and geometric designs, often lattice-like or fretted. Other elements of Puuc style are decorated cornices, rows of half-columns and round columns in doorways. The stones forming the corbeled vaults in Puuc style are shaped like boots.

Great Pyramid
Adjacent to the Governor's Palace, the 32-meter Gran Pirámide has been restored only on the northern side. There is a quadrangle at the top which archaeologists theorize was largely destroyed in order to construct another pyramid above it. This work, for reasons unknown, was never completed. At the top are some stucco carvings of Chac, birds and flowers.

House of the Pigeons
West of the great pyramid sits a structure whose roofcomb is latticed with a pigeonhole pattern – hence the building is called House of the Pigeons (El Palomar). The nine honeycombed triangular belfries sit on top of a building that was once part of a quadrangle. The base is so eroded that it is difficult for archaeologists to guess its function.

Places to Stay & Eat – budget

As there is no town at Uxmal, only the archaeological site and several top-end hotels, you cannot depend upon finding cheap food or lodging.

Campers can pitch their tents five km north of the ruins on highway 261, the road to Mérida, at *Rancho Uxmal* (☎ 47-80-21) for US$2.50 per person. The *Parador Turístico Cana Nah* next door has a 'trailer park' camping lot as well.

Rancho Uxmal has 28 basic, serviceable guestrooms with shower and fan for US$25 a double, expensive for what you get, but this is Uxmal. There's a restaurant. It may take you 45 to 55 minutes to walk here – in the hot sun – from the ruins, but there's some possibility of hitching a ride.

Other than the Rancho Uxmal, there's no cheap lodging in the area. If you don't want to return to Mérida for the night, make your way to Ticul.

The *Salon Nicté-Ha*, just across the highway from the road to the ruins, on the grounds of the Hotel Hacienda Uxmal, is an informal air-con restaurant open from 1 to 8.30 pm daily offering sandwiches (US$3.75 to US$4.50), fruit salads and similar fare at prices higher than those at the Yax-Beh. The beer is cold. There's a swimming pool for restaurant patrons.

Places to Stay & Eat – top end

Mayaland Resorts' *Hotel Hacienda Uxmal* (☎ 23-02-75, in USA 800-235-4079; fax 23-47-44), 500 meters from the ruins across the highway, originally housed the archaeologists who explored and restored Uxmal. High ceilings with fans, good cross-ventilation and wide, tiled verandahs set with rocking-chairs make this an exceptionally pleasant and comfortable place to stay. The beautiful swimming pool is a dream come true on a sweltering hot day.

Simple rooms in the annex cost US$38 a single or double; the nicer rooms in the main building range from US$50 to US$90 a single, US$60 to US$100 a double. Meals are unremarkable and moderately priced. You can supposedly make reservations in Mérida at the Mérida Travel Service

in the Hotel Casa del Balam (☎ 24-88-44), at the corner of Calles 60 and 57, but they seem not to know the correct room prices and have always told us the hotel is full, even if it isn't.

The Lodge at Uxmal (☎ 23-02-75, in USA 800-235-4079; fax 23-47-44), another Mayaland Resort just opposite the entrance to the Unidad Uxmal and the archeological site, is Uxmal's newest, most luxurious hotel, and the closest to the ruins. Air-con rooms with all the comforts cost US$94/111 a single/double.

Hotel Villa Arqueológica Uxmal (in Mérida, ☎ /fax 99-28-06-44, Apdo Postal 449), run by Club Med, is an attractive modern hotel with swimming pool, tennis courts, a good French-inspired restaurant and air-con guestrooms for US$45/55/65 a single/double/triple.

The *Hotel Misión Park Inn Uxmal* (☎ / fax 24-73-08) is set on a hilltop two km north of the turn-off to the ruins. Many rooms have balcony views of Uxmal, but are overpriced at US$75 a single or double.

Getting There & Away

Air An airstrip is under construction near Uxmal. When it is finished, routes from Cancún will be developed, making it possible for Cancúnites to visit Uxmal on a day excursion.

Bus From Mérida's Terminal de Autobuses, it's 80 km (1½ hours) to Uxmal. The inland route between Mérida and Campeche passes Uxmal, and most buses coming from the cities will drop you at Uxmal. But when you want to leave, buses may be full and not stop.

The Ruta Puuc excursion (US$4.50) run daily by Autotransportes del Sur departs Mérida's old Terminal de Autobuses at 8 am, goes to Uxmal, Kabah and several other sites, and departs from the parking lot of Uxmal archaeological site on the return journey to Mérida at 2.30 pm, returning to Mérida by 4 pm. If you're going to Ticul, hop on a bus heading north, get off at Muna and get another bus eastwards to Ticul.

YUCATÁN PENINSULA

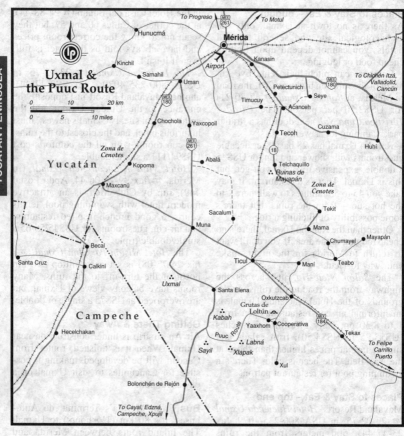

Uxmal & the Puuc Route

0   10   20 km

0   5   10 miles

For buses to Kabah, the Puuc Route turnoff and points on the road to Campeche, flag down a bus at the turnoff to the ruins.

THE PUUC ROUTE

Uxmal is undoubtedly the finest Mayan city in the Puuc Hills, but the ruins at Kabah, Sayil, Xlapak and Labná, and the Grutas de Loltún, offer a deeper acquaintance with the Puuc Maya civilization. The Codz Poop (Palace of Masks) at Kabah and El Palacio at Sayil are especially worth

seeing. The Grutas de Loltún (Loltún Caves) are also impressive.

Cultur (☎ in Mérida 99-24-96-77), the cultural department of the Yucatán state government, organizes Puuc Route tours every day, departing Mérida's Parque Santa Lucia at 9 am, visiting Sayil, Xlapak and Labná, and after lunch the Grutas de Loltún. There are stops at the market in Oxkutzcab and in Ticul before returning to Mérida by 7 pm, but the tour does not visit Kabah or Uxmal. There is also a special Ruta Puuc bus operated by Autotransportes del Sur. See Getting There & Away in the Uxmal section above for details.

Kabah

The ruins of Kabah, just over 18 km southeast of Uxmal, are right astride highway 261. The sign says 'Zona Arqueológica Puuc.' The site is open from 8 am to 5 pm. Admission costs US$2, free on Sunday.

The guard shack and souvenir shop are on the east side of the highway as you approach. Cold drinks and junky snacks are sold.

The most impressive building here is the **Codz Poop** (Palace of Masks), set on its own high terrace on the east side of the highway. It's an amazing sight, with its façade covered in nearly 300 masks of Chac, the rain god or sky serpent.

To the north of the Palace of Masks is a small **pyramid**. Further north is **El Palacio**, with a broad façade having several doorways; in the center of each doorway is a column, a characteristic of the Puuc architectural style. Walk around the north side of El Palacio and follow a path into the jungle for several hundred meters to the **Tercera Casa**, also called the Temple of Columns, which is famous for the rows of semi-columns on the upper part of its façade.

Cross the highway to the west of El Palacio, walk up the slope and on your right you'll pass a high mound of stones that was once the **Gran Teocalli**, or Great Temple. Continue straight on to the sacbe, or cobbled and elevated ceremonial road, and look right to see a ruined monumental arch with the Mayan corbeled vault (two straight stone surfaces leaning against one another, meeting at the top). It is said that the sacbe here runs past the arch and through the jungle all the way to Uxmal, terminating at a smaller arch; in the other direction it goes to Labná. Once, all of the Yucatán Peninsula was connected by these marvelous 'white roads' of rough limestone.

Beyond the sacbe, about 600 meters farther from the road, are several other complexes of buildings, none as impressive as

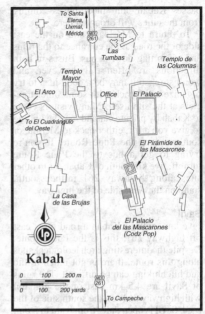

Kabah

what you've already seen. The **Cuadrángulo del Oeste** (Western Quadrangle) has some decoration of columns and masks. North of the quadrangle are the **Temple of the Key Patterns** and the **Temple of Lintels** (Templo de los Dinteles); the latter once had intricately carved lintels of tough sapodilla wood.

Places to Stay The quiet, well-kept *Camping Sacbé* (no phone) on the south side of the village of Santa Elena, 3.5 km north of Kabah, has simple (waterless) but clean rooms for US$8 to US$10 single or double; one room has a private shower, the rest are shared. Camping amid the orchards costs US$2.50 per person. Good breakfasts and dinners are served at low prices.

Getting There & Away Kabah is 101 km from Mérida, a ride of about two hours, and just over 18 km south of Uxmal. The inland route between Mérida and Campeche passes Kabah, and most buses coming from the cities will drop you here.

To return to Mérida, stand on the east side of the road at the entrance to the ruins and try to flag down a bus. Buses in both directions are often full, however, and won't stop, so it may be a good idea to try organize a lift back with some other travelers at the site itself. Many visitors come to Kabah by private car and may be willing to give you a lift, either back to Mérida, or southward on the Puuc Route. If you're trying to get a bus to the Puuc Route turnoff, five km south of Kabah, or to other sites along highway 261 farther south, stand on the west side of the highway.

Sayil

Five km south of Kabah a road turns east off highway 261: this is the Puuc Route. Despite the interesting archaeological sites along this route, there is not much traffic and hitchhiking can be difficult. The ruins of Sayil are 4.5 km east of the junction with highway 261, on the south side of the road. Sayil is open daily from 8 am to 5 pm; admission costs US$2, but is free on Sunday.

El Palacio Sayil is best known for El Palacio, the huge three-tiered building with a façade some 85 meters long that makes one think of the Minoan palaces on Crete. The distinctive columns of Puuc architecture are used here over and over, as supports for the lintels, as decoration between doorways and as a frieze above the doorways, alternating with huge stylized Chac masks and 'descending gods.'

Climb to the top level of the Palacio and look to the north to see several *chultunes*, stone-lined cisterns in which precious rainwater was collected and stored for use during the dry season. Some of these chultunes can hold more than 30,000 liters.

El Mirador If you take the path southwards from the palace for about 800 meters you come to the temple named El Mirador, with its interesting rooster-like

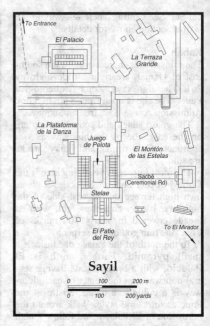

Sayil

To Entrance
El Palacio
La Terraza Grande
La Plataforma de la Danza
Juego de Pelota
El Montón de las Estelas
Sacbé (Ceremonial Rd)
Stelae
El Patio del Rey
To El Mirador

0   100   200 m
0   100   200 yards

roofcomb once painted bright red. About 100 meters beyond El Mirador by the path to the left is a stela beneath a protective palapa. It bears a relief of a phallic god, now badly weathered.

Xlapak

From the entrance gate at Sayil, it's six km east to the entrance gate at Xlapak ('shla-PAK'). The name means Old Walls in Maya and was a general term among local people for ancient ruins, about which they knew little. The site is open from 8 am to 5 pm; admission is US$1.50, free on Sunday.

The ornate palace at Xlapak is smaller than those at Kabah and Sayil, measuring only about 20 meters in length. It's decorated with the inevitable Chac masks, columns and colonnettes and fretted geometric latticework of the Puuc style. To the right is the rubble of what were once two smaller buildings.

YUCATÁN PENINSULA

Labná

From the entrance gate at Xlapak, it's 3.5 km east to the gate at Labná. The site here is open from 8 am to 5 pm; admission costs US$2.

El Arco Labná is best known for its magnificent arch, once part of a building that separated two quadrangular courtyards. It now appears to be a gate joining two small plazas. The corbeled structure, three meters wide and six meters high, is well preserved and stands close to the entrance of Labná. The mosaic reliefs decorating the upper façade are exuberantly Puuc in style.

If you look at the ornate work on the northeastern side of the arch, you will make out mosaics of Mayan huts. At the base of either side of the arch are rooms of the adjoining building, now ruined, including upper lattice patterns constructed atop a serpentine design.

El Mirador Standing on the opposite side of the arch and separated from it by the limestone-paved sacbe is a pyramid with a temple atop it called El Mirador. The pyramid itself is poorly preserved, being largely stone rubble. The temple, with its five-meter-high roofcomb, true to its name, looks like a watchtower.

Palacio Archaeologists believe that at one point in the 9th century, some 3000 Maya lived at Labná. To support such numbers in these arid hills, water was collected in chultunes. At Labná's peak there were some 60 chultunes in and around the city; several are still visible.

The palace, the first edifice you come to at Labná, is connected by a sacbe to El Mirador and the arch. One of the longest buildings in the Puuc Hills, its design is not as impressive as its counterpart at Sayil. There's a ghoulish sculpture at the eastern corner of the upper level of a serpent gripping a human head between its jaws. Close to this carving is a well preserved Chac mask.

Grutas de Loltún

From Labná it's 15 km eastward to the village of Yaaxhom, surrounded by lush orchards and palm groves, which are surprising in this generally dry region. From Yaaxhom a road goes another four km northeast to Loltún.

Loltún Caves, the most interesting *grutas* in Yucatán, provided a treasure trove of data for archaeologists studying the Maya. Carbon dating of artifacts found here reveals that the caves were first used by humans some 2500 years ago.

Loltún is open from 9 am to 5 pm daily, for US$4. To explore the 1.5-km labyrinth, you must take a scheduled guided tour at 9.30 or 11 am, or at 12.30, 2 or 3 pm, but these may depart early if enough people are waiting. The guides may be willing to take you through at other hours if you offer a few dollars' tip. Occasionally there is a guide on the premises who speaks English – check to see if the tour will be in a language you understand. The guides, who are not paid by the government, expect a tip at the end of the hour-long tour.

For refreshments there's the *Restaurant El Guerrero* near the exit of the caves, a walk of eight to 10 minutes (600 meters) along a marked path from the far side of the parking lot near the cave entrance. Once you get to the restaurant you'll find that their comida corrida costs about US$7. Icy-cold drinks are served at high prices.

Getting There & Away Loltún is on a country road leading to Oxkutzcab ('Oshkootz-KAHB'; eight km) and there is usually some transport along the road. Try hitching, or catch one of the colectivos – often a *camioneta* (pickup truck) or *camión* (truck or lorry) – which ply this route, charging about US$0.50 for the ride. A taxi from Oxkutzcab may charge US$6 or so, one way, for the eight-km ride.

Buses run frequently every day between Mérida and Oxkutzcab via Ticul.

If you're driving from Loltún to Labná, drive out of the Loltún car park, turn right and take the next road on the right, which passes the access road to the restaurant. Do not take the road marked for Xul. After four km you'll come to the village of Yaaxhom, where you turn right to join the Puuc Route westwards.

TICUL
pop 30,000; ☎ 997

Ticul, 30 km east of Uxmal, is the largest town south of Mérida in this ruin-rich region. It has several serviceable hotels and restaurants, and good transport. It's also a center for fine huipil weaving – the embroidery on these dresses is extraordinary. For both quality and price, Ticul is a good place to buy this traditional Mayan garment. Ticul's main street is Calle 23, sometimes called the Calle Principal, going from the highway northeast past the market and the town's best restaurants to the main plaza.

Places to Stay
Hotel Sierra Sosa (☎ 2-00-08, fax 2-02-82), Calle 26 No 199A, half a block northwest of the plaza, has very basic rooms for US$9 with fan, US$12 with air-con. A few

rooms at the back have windows, but most are dark and dungeon-like. Be sure the ceiling fan works.

Similarly basic but even cheaper is the *Hotel San Miguel* (☎ 2-03-82), Calle 28 No 195, near Calle 23 and the market. Singles at the San Miguel cost US$5, doubles US$6 to US$7, with fan and bath.

Ticul's better hotels don't really offer too much more in the way of comfort and both are on the highway on the outskirts of town, an inconvenient two-km walk from the center, but fine if you have a car.

Best in town is the *Hotel Las Bougambillias* (☎ 2-07-61), 23 Calle No 291A near the junction of the western end of Calle 25 and the highway to Muna and Mérida. The darkish rooms are simple but newer and far cleaner than the competition's. Prices are US$8 for two in one bed, US$12 for two in two beds.

A hundred meters northwest of the Bougambillias on the opposite side of the highway is the older *Hotel-Motel Cerro Inn*. Set in more spacious, shady grounds, the Cerro Inn has nine well-used rooms with private shower and ceiling fan going for US$8 to US$10 a double.

Places to Eat
Ticul's lively market provides all the ingredients for picnics and snacks. It also has lots of those wonderful market eateries where the food is good, the portions generous and the prices low. For variety, try out some of the loncherías along Calle 23 between Calles 26 and 30.

For bread and sweet rolls, there's *El Buen Samaritano*, on Calle 23 west of Calle 26.

For a sit-down meal, there's the cheap *Restaurant El Colorín* (☎ 2-03-14), Calle 26 No 199B, close to the Hotel Sierra Sosa half a block northwest of the plaza. Have a look at the *Carmelita*, on the opposite side of the Hotel Sierra Sosa, as well.

Pizza La Góndola, Calle 23 at Calle 26A, is tidy, with two-person pizzas cooked to order for US$5 to US$8. *Chan Ki-Huic* on Calle 23 west of Calle 28 is new, bright and clean. The *Lonchería Mary*

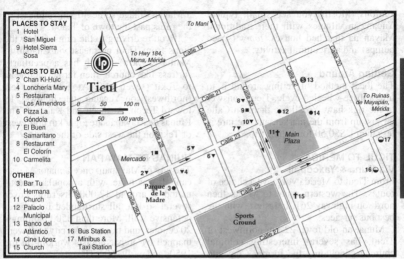

PLACES TO STAY
1 Hotel
   San Miguel
9 Hotel Sierra
   Sosa

PLACES TO EAT
2 Chan Ki-Huic
4 Lonchería Mary
5 Restaurant
   Los Almendros
6 Pizza La
   Góndola
8 El Buen
   Samaritano
8 Restaurant
   El Colorín
10 Carmelita

OTHER
3 Bar Tu
   Hermana
11 Church
12 Palacio
   Municipal
13 Banco del
   Atlántico
14 Cine López
15 Church
16 Bus Station
17 Minibus &
   Taxi Station

Ticul

To Maní
To Hwy 184,
Muna, Mérida
To Ruinas
de Mayapán,
Mérida

Mercado
Parque
de la
Madre
Main
Plaza
Sports
Ground

on Calle 23 east of Calle 28 is a clean, family-run place.

Restaurant Los Almendros (☎ 2-00-21), Calle 23 No 207, between 26A and 28, is set up in a fortress-like townhouse with a large courtyard and portico. The air-con restaurant, open every day from 10 am to 9 pm, is fairly plain, but the food is authentically Yucatecan. The *combinado yucateco* (Yucatecan combination plate), with a soft drink or beer, costs less than US$7.

Getting There & Away

Bus Ticul's bus station is behind the massive church off the main square. Autotransportes Mayab makes the 85 km, 1½-hour run between Mérida and Ticul for US$2. There are also three buses to Felipe Carrillo Puerto (US$7), frequent ones to Oxkutzcab (US$1), and nine a day to Chetumal (6½ hours, US$7).

You can catch a minibus (combi) from the intersection of Calles 23 and 28 in Ticul to Mérida's Parque de San Juan (or vice-versa – see Getting There & Away in the Mérida section), or to Oxkutzcab, 16 km away, and from Oxkutzcab a minibus or pickup truck to Loltún (eight km); ask

for the camión to Xul ('shool'), but get off at Las Grutas de Loltún.

Minibuses to Santa Elena (15 km), the village between Uxmal and Kabah, also depart from the intersection of Calles 23 and 28, taking a back road and then leaving you to catch another bus northwest to Uxmal (15 km) or south to Kabah (3.5 km). You may find it more convenient to take a minibus or bus to Muna (22 km) on highway 261 and another south to Uxmal (16 km).

Car Those headed eastwards to Quintana Roo and the Caribbean coast by car can go via highway 184 from Muna and Ticul via Oxkutzcab to Tekax, Tzucacab and Peto. At Polguc, 130 km from Ticul, a road turns left (east), ending after 80 km in Felipe Carrillo Puerto, 210 km from Ticul, where there are hotels, restaurants, fuel stations, banks and other services. The right fork of the road goes south to the region of Lago de Bacalar.

From Oxkutzcab to Felipe Carrillo Puerto or Bacalar there are few services: very few places to eat (those that exist are rock-bottom basic), no hotels and few fuel stations. Mostly you see small, typical Yucatecan villages with their traditional Mayan na thatched houses, *topes* (speed bumps) and agricultural activity.

Getting Around

The local method of getting around is to hire a three-wheeled cycle, Ticul's answer to the rickshaw. You'll see them on Calle 23 just up from the market, and the fare is less than US$0.50 for a short trip.

TICUL TO MÉRIDA
Via Muna & Yaxcopoil

From Ticul to Mérida you have a choice of routes. The western route to Muna, then north on highway 261, is fastest, with the best bus services.

Muna, an old town 22 km northwest of Ticul, has several interesting colonial churches, including the former Convento de la Asunción and the churches of Santa María, San Mateo and San Andrés.

The hacienda of Yaxcopoil, 29 km north of Muna on the west side of highway 261, has numerous French Renaissance-style buildings which have been restored and turned collectively into a museum of the 17th century (open from 8 am to 6 pm, Sunday from 9 am to 1 pm; US$5). This vast estate specialized in the growing and processing of henequén. Walking around, you can see much of the estate without paying the high museum fee.

From Yaxcopoil it's 16 km north to Uman, and then another 17 km to the center of Mérida.

Via Ruinas de Mayapán

The eastern route north follows Yucatán state highway 18 from Ticul via the ruins of Mayapán to Tecoh, Acanceh and Mérida. Transport on this route is difficult without your own car. Buses and colectivos run fitfully, so you should plan the better part of a day, with stops in Ruinas de Mayapán and Acanceh, to travel the route by public transport.

Those taking this route should be careful to distinguish between Ruinas de Mayapán, the ruins of the ancient city, and Mayapán,

a Mayan village some 40 km southeast of the ruins past the town of Teabo.

If you're driving to the ruins, follow the signs from Ticul northeast via Chapab to Mama (25 km), which has a peculiarly fortress-like church, then farther northeast to Tekit (seven km). At Tekit, turn left (northwest) on Yucatán state highway 18 toward Tecoh, Acanceh and Kanasin. The Ruinas de Mayapán are eight km northwest of Tekit on the west side of the road.

RUINAS DE MAYAPÁN

The city of Mayapán, once a major Mayan capital, was huge, with a population estimated at around 12,000. Its ruins cover several sq km, all surrounded by a great defensive wall. More than 3500 buildings, 20 cenotes, and traces of the city wall were mapped by archaeologists working in the 1950s and early '60s. The city's workmanship was inferior to the great age of Mayan art; though the Cocom rulers of Mayapán tried to revive the past glories of Mayan civilization, they succeeded only in part.

History

Mayapán was supposedly founded by Kukulcán (Quetzalcóatl) in 1007, shortly after the former ruler of Tula arrived in Yucatán. His dynasty, the Cocom, organized a confederation of city-states which included Uxmal, Chichén Itzá and many other notable cities. Despite their alliance, animosity between the Cocoms and the Itzaes during the late 1100s led to the storming of Chichén Itzá by the Cocoms, which forced the Itzá rulers into exile. The Cocom dynasty under Hunac Ceel Canuch emerged supreme in all of the northern Yucatán Peninsula and obliged the other rulers to pay tribute.

Cocom supremacy lasted for almost 2½ centuries, until the ruler of Uxmal, Ah Xupán Xiú, led a rebellion of the oppressed city-states and overthrew Cocom hegemony. The great capital of Mayapán was utterly destroyed and remained uninhabited ever after.

But there was no peace in Yucatán after the Xiú victory. The Cocom dynasty recovered and frequent struggles for power erupted until 1542, when Francisco de Montejo the Younger founded Mérida. The ruler of the Xiú people, Ah Kukum Xiú, submitted his forces to Montejo's control in exchange for a military alliance against the Cocoms. The Cocoms were defeated and – too late – the Xiú rulers realized that they had willingly signed the death warrant of Mayan independence.

Ruins

At the caretaker's hut 100 meters in from the road, pay the admission fee of US$1.50 and enter the site any day between 8 am and 5 pm.

Jungle has returned to cover many of the buildings, but you can visit several cenotes (including Itzmal Chen, a main Mayan religious sanctuary) and make out the large piles of stones which were once the Temple of Kukulcán and the circular Caracol. Though the ruins today are far less impressive than those at other sites, Mayapán has a stillness and a loneliness (usually undisturbed by other tourists) that seems to fit its sorrowful later history.

RUINAS DE MAYAPÁN TO MÉRIDA

About two km north of the Ruinas de Mayapán is **Telchaquillo**. Beneath the village plaza is a vast cenote filled with rainwater, which is still used as a water source during the dry months.

From Telchaquillo it's 11 km north to **Tecoh**, with its church and well-kept Palacio Municipal separated by a green soccer field. From Tecoh it's only 35 km to Mérida, but you should plan a short stop in Acanceh.

The road enters **Acanceh** and goes to the main plaza, which is flanked by a shady park and the church. To the left of the church is a partially restored pyramid (admission US$1.50), and to the right are market loncherías if you're in need of a snack. In the park, note the statue of the smiling deer; the name Acanceh means Pond of the Deer. Another local sight of interest is the cantina Aqui Me Queda (I'm Staying Here), a ready-made answer for

husbands whose wives come to urge them homeward.

Continuing northwest you pass through Petectunich, Tepich, San Antonio and Kanasin before coming to Mérida's periférico (ring road).

HACIENDA TEYA

The *casa principal* (main house) at the Hacienda San Ildefonso Teya (☎ 99-28-50-00, fax 99-28-18-89), 13 km east of Mérida on the Chichén Itzá road, was built in 1683 with its own chapel. More than three centuries have passed, and the grand house and lush gardens look better than ever.

The elegant Casa de Maquinas (machinery house), facing the main house, was built in 1905 to harbor the high-tech of its day: an oily assemblage of engines, gears, pulleys and belts which worked harder than the hacienda's oppressed peasantry at processing henequén.

Today the ground floor of the Hacienda Teya houses the elegant *Restaurant La Cava*, serving Yucatecan cuisine from noon to 6 pm daily. The specialty is a stone platter bearing an assortment of Yucatecan specialties for US$10.

Upstairs are a handful of period rooms for guests, updated with air-con, whirlpool baths and minibars, and priced at US$50 to US$65 double.

Another fine old hacienda, the Hacienda Katanchel near San Bernardino on the Mérida-Chichén Itzá road, is also being restored, and may be open by the time you arrive.

IZAMAL

pop 40,000

In ancient times, Izamal was a center for the worship of the supreme Mayan god Itzamná and the sun god Kinich Kakmó. A dozen temple pyramids in the town were devoted to these or other gods. Perhaps this Mayan religiosity is why the Spanish colonists chose Izamal as the site for an enormous and very impressive Franciscan monastery.

Today Izamal is a small, quiet provincial town with the atmosphere of life in another century. Its two principal squares are surrounded by impressive arcades painted in the town's signature yellow, and dominated by the gargantuan bulk of the Convento de San Antonio de Padua. This *Ciudad Amarilla* (Yellow City), as it's known, has a few small, cheap hotels and eateries.

Convento de San Antonio de Padua

When the Spaniards conquered Izamal, they destroyed the major Mayan temple, the Popul-Chac pyramid, and in 1533 began to build from its stones one of the first monasteries in the Western Hemisphere. The work was finished in 1561.

The monastery's principal church is the Santuario de la Virgen de Izamal, approached by a ramp from the main square. Walk up the ramp and through an arcaded gallery to the Atrium, a spacious arcaded courtyard in which the fiesta of the Virgin of Izamal takes place each August 15.

Entry to the church is free. The best time to visit is in the morning, as it may be closed during the afternoon siesta. The monastery and church were restored and spruced up for the papal visit of John Paul II in 1993.

If you wander around town, you may come across remnants of the other 11 Mayan pyramids. The largest is the temple of Kinich Kakmó; all are unrestored piles of rubble.

Getting There & Away

Oriente runs 20 buses daily between Mérida and Izamal (72 km, 1½ hours, US$1) from its terminal in Mérida on Calle 50 between Calles 65 and 67; there are buses from Valladolid (155 km, two hours, US$3) as well. Coming from Chichén Itzá, you must change buses at Hóctun. If you're driving from the east, turn north at Kantunil.

On Sundays at 8 am, you can board a special train at Mérida's railroad station for a day excursion to Izamal, arriving in the Yellow City at 9.50 am. You then have a city tour (in Spanish), lunch, and a folklore show before reboarding the train at 3 pm, arriving back in Mérida at 5 pm.

There's also a minibus tour from Mérida every Tuesday, Thursday and Saturday,

departing Mérida's Parque de Santa Lucia at 9 am, returning by 5 pm.

Most travel agencies can reserve your place; or call Cultur (☎ in Mérida 99-24-96-77), the cultural department of the Yucatán state government, which sponsors the excursions.

CHICHÉN ITZÁ
☎ 985

The most famous and best restored of the Yucatán Peninsula's Mayan sites, Chichén Itzá will awe even the most jaded of visitors. Many mysteries of the Mayan astronomical calendar are made clear when one understands the design of the 'time temples' here. But one astronomical mystery remains: why do most people come here from Mérida and Cancún on day trips, arriving at 11 am, when the blazing sun is getting to its hottest point, and departing around 3 pm when the heat finally begins to abate? You'd do better to stay the night nearby and do your exploration of the site either early in the morning or late in the afternoon.

Should you have the good fortune to visit Chichén Itzá on the vernal equinox (March 20 to 21) or autumnal equinox (September 21 to 22), you can witness the light-and-shadow illusion of the serpent ascending or descending the side of the staircase of El Castillo. The illusion is almost as good in the week preceding and the week following the equinox.

History

Most archaeologists agree that Chichén Itzá's first major settlement, during the Late Classic period, was pure Mayan. In about the 9th century, the city was largely abandoned for unknown reasons.

The city was resettled around the late 10th century, and shortly thereafter, Chichén seems to have been invaded by Toltecs who had moved down from their central highlands capital of Tula, north of Mexico City. Toltec culture was fused with that of the Maya, incorporating the cult of Quetzalcóatl (Kukulcán in Maya). (See the Toltecs section of History in Facts about

ALLAN A PHILIBA

TONY WHEELER

TONY WHEELER

Top Left: Temple of the Warriors, Chichén Itzá
Top Right: Detail, Chichén Itzá
Middle Left: Chac-Mool & Pyramid of Kukulcán, Chichén Itzá
Bottom: Tzompantli, Temple of Skulls, Chichén Itzá

TONY WHEELER

This Page
Top: Playa del Carmen, Quintana Roo
Bottom Left: Hombre, Mérida
Bottom Right: Taking the plunge, Quintana Roo

Opposite Page
Top Left: Isla Mujeres ferry
Top Right: Tropical drinks, Cancún
Middle Left: Roadside cross, Yucatán
Bottom Left: Cafe, Isla Mujeres
Bottom Right: Cancún beach scene

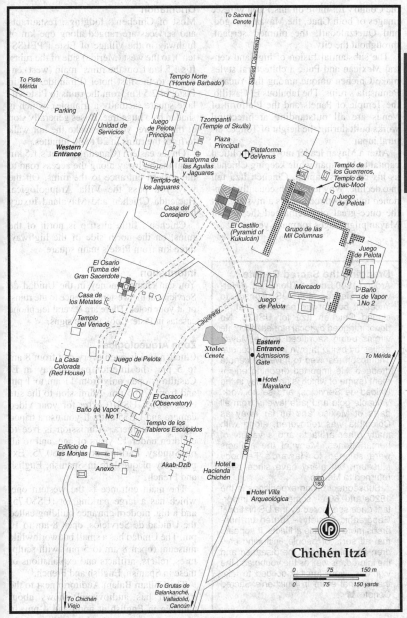

Chichén Itzá

To Piste,
Mérida

Parking

Western
Entrance

Unidad de
Servicios

Juego
de Pelota
Principal

Templo Norte
('Hombre Barbado')

Tzompantli
(Temple of Skulls)

Plaza
Principal

Plataforma
de Venus

To Sacred
Cenote

Sacred Causeway

Plataforma de
las Águilas
y Jaguares

Templo de
los Jaguares

Casa del
Consejero

El Castillo
(Pyramid of
Kukulcán)

Templo de
los Guerreros,
Templo de
Chac-Mool

Juego
de Pelota

Grupo de las
Mil Columnas

Juego
de Pelota

El Osario
(Tumba del
Gran Sacerdote)

Casa de
los Metates

Templo
del Venado

La Casa
Colorada
(Red House)

Juego de Pelota

Baño de Vapor
No 1

El Caracol
(Observatory)

Templo de los
Tableros Esculpidos

Edificio
de las
Monjas

Anexo

Akab-Dzib

Xtoloc
Cenote

Causeway

Mercado

Juego
de Pelota

Baño
de Vapor
No 2

Eastern
Entrance
Admissions
Gate

Hotel
Mayaland

Old Hwy

To Mérida

Hotel
Hacienda
Chichén

MEX
180

Hotel Villa
Arqueológica

To Chichén
Viejo

To Grutas de
Balankanché,
Valladolid,
Cancún

0   75   150 m
0   75   150 yards

the Country for more on this.) You will see images of both Chac, the Mayan rain god, and Quetzalcóatl, the plumed serpent, throughout the city.

The substantial fusion of highland central Mexican and Puuc architectural styles make Chichén unique among the Yucatán Peninsula's ruins. The fabulous El Castillo, the Temple of Panels and the Platform of Venus are all outstanding architectural works built during the height of Toltec cultural input.

After a Mayan leader moved his political capital to Mayapán while keeping Chichén as his religious capital, Chichén Itzá fell into decline. Why it was subsequently abandoned in the 14th century is a mystery, but the once-great city remained the site of Mayan pilgrimages for many years.

Dredging the Sacred Cenote

Around 1900 Edward Thompson, a Harvard professor and US Consul to Yucatán, bought the hacienda that included Chichén Itzá for US$75. No doubt intrigued by local stories of female virgins being sacrificed to the Mayan deities by being thrown into the cenote, Thompson resolved to have the cenote dredged. He imported dredging equipment (some of which is on display in the Unidad de Servicios) and set to work. Valuable gold and jade jewelry from all parts of Mexico and as far away as Colombia was recovered, along with many other artifacts and a variety of human bones. Many of the artifacts were shipped to Harvard's Peabody Museum, but many have since been returned to Mexico.

Subsequent diving expeditions in the 1920s and '60s – some of them important ones sponsored by the US National Geographic Society – turned up hundreds more valuable artifacts. It appears that all sorts of people, including children and old people, the diseased and the injured, as well as the young and the vigorous, were forcibly obliged to take that eternal swim in Chichén's Sacred Cenote. ■

Orientation

Most of Chichén's lodgings, restaurants and services are ranged along one km of highway in the village of Piste ('PEESS-teh'), to the west (Mérida) side of the ruins. It's 1.5 km from the ruins' main (west) entrance to the first hotel (Pirámide Inn) in Piste, or 2.5 km from the ruins to Piste village square (actually a triangle), which is shaded by a huge tree. Buses generally stop at the square; you can make the hot walk to/from the ruins in 20 to 30 minutes.

On the eastern (Cancún) side, it's 1.5 km from the highway along the access road to the eastern entrance to the ruins. On the way you pass the Villa Arqueológica, Hacienda Chichén and Mayaland luxury hotels.

Chichén's little airstrip is north of the ruins, on the north side of the highway, three km from Piste's main square.

Information

You can change money in the Unidad de Servicios at the western entrance to the ruins, or at your hotel. There are several telephone casetas in Piste. Look for the signs.

Zona Arqueológica

Chichén Itzá is open every day from 8 am to 5 pm; the interior passageway in El Castillo is open only from 11 am to 1 pm and from 4 to 5 pm. Admission to the site costs US$5; US$10 extra for your video camera and US$5 extra if you use a tripod with your camera. Admission is free to children under 12 years of age, and to all on Sunday. Parking costs US$0.75. Explanatory plaques are in Spanish, English and French.

The main entrance is the western one, which has a large parking lot (US$0.75) and a big, modern entrance building called the Unidad de Servicios, open 8 am to 10 pm. The Unidad has a small but worthwhile museum (open 8 am to 5 pm) with sculptures, reliefs, artifacts and explanations of these in Spanish, English and French.

The Chilam Balam Auditorio next to the museum has audiovisual shows about Chichén in English at noon and 4 pm. In the central space of the Unidad stands a scale model of the archaeological site, and off toward the toilets is an exhibit on Thompson's excavations of the sacred cenote in 1923. There are two bookstores with a good assortment of guides and maps; a currency exchange desk (open 9 am to 1 pm); and a *guardarropa* at the main ticket desk where you can leave your belongings (US$0.35) while you explore the site.

A sound-and-light show lasting 45 minutes begins each evening in Spanish at 7 pm in summer and 8 pm in winter for US$3.75. The English version (US$5) starts at 9 pm year round.

El Castillo As you pass through the turnstiles from the Unidad de Servicios into the archaeological zone, El Castillo rises before you in all its grandeur. Standing nearly 25 meters tall, the 'castle' was originally built before 800 AD, prior to the Toltec invasion. Nonetheless, the plumed serpent was sculpted along the stairways and Toltec warriors are represented in the doorway carvings at the top of the temple. No doubt this is grist to the mill of those inconvenient historians who believe that the Toltec capital Tula, near Mexico City, was influenced from Chichén Itzá, rather than vice-versa as conventional wisdom has it.

Climb to the top for a view of the entire site. This is best done early in the morning or late in the afternoon, both to avoid the heat and to see Chichén without the crowds.

The pyramid is actually the Mayan calendar formed in stone. Each of El Castillo's nine levels is divided in two by a staircase, making 18 separate terraces which commemorate the 18 20-day months of the Vague Year. The four stairways have 91 steps each; add the top platform and the total is 365, the number of days in the year. On each façade of the pyramid are 52 flat panels, symbolizing the 52 years in the Calendar Round.

Most amazing of all, during the spring and autumn equinoxes (around March 21 and September 21), light and shadow form a series of triangles on the side of the north staircase which mimic the creep of a serpent. The illusion lasts three hours and 22 minutes.

This pyramid holds more surprises: there's another pyramid *inside* El Castillo. When archaeologists opened it, they found the brilliant red jaguar throne with inlaid eyes and spots of shimmering jade which still lies within. The inner sanctum also holds a Toltec chac-mool figure.

The inner pyramid is only open from 11 am to 1 pm and 4 to 5 pm. Entry is not a good idea for claustrophobes or those who hate close, fetid air.

Principal Ball Court The principal ball court, the largest and most impressive in Mexico, is only one of the city's eight courts, indicative of the importance the games held here. The court is flanked by temples at either end and bound by towering parallel walls with stone rings cemented up high.

There is evidence that the ball game may have changed over the years. Some carvings show players with padding on their elbows and knees and it is thought that they played a soccer-like game with a hard rubber ball, forbidding the use of hands. Other carvings show players wielding bats; it appears that if a player hit the ball through one of the stone hoops, his team was declared the winner. It may be that during the Toltec period the losing captain, and perhaps his teammates as well, were sacrificed.

Along the walls of the ball court are some fine stone reliefs, including scenes of decapitations of players. Acoustically the court is amazing – a conversation at one end can be heard 135 meters away at the other end, and if you clap, you hear a resounding echo.

Temple of the Bearded Man & Temple of the Jaguars The structure at the northern end of the ball court, called the Temple of the Bearded Man (Templo del Barbudo) after a carving inside it, has some finely sculpted pillars and reliefs of flowers, birds and trees. The Temple of the Jaguars

(Templo de los Jaguares), to the southeast, has some rattlesnake-carved columns and jaguar-etched tablets. Inside are faded mural fragments depicting a battle.

Tzompantli The tzompantli, a Toltec term for 'temple of skulls,' is between the Temple of the Jaguars and El Castillo. You can't mistake it because the T-shaped platform is festooned with carved skulls and eagles tearing open the chests of men to eat their hearts. In ancient days this platform held the heads of sacrificial victims.

Platform of the Jaguars & Eagles Adjacent to the Temple of Skulls, this platform's (Plataforma de las Aguilas y Jaguares) carvings depict jaguars and eagles gruesomely grabbing human hearts in their claws. It is thought that this platform was part of a temple dedicated to the military legions responsible for capturing sacrificial victims.

Platform of Venus Rather than a beautiful woman, the Toltec symbol for the planet Venus is a feathered serpent bearing a human head between its jaws, and you can see many examples of this image on this structure (the Plataforma de Venus), just north of El Castillo.

Carving of a jaguar eating a human heart, Platform of the Jaguars & Eagles

Sacred Cenote A 300-meter rough stone road runs north (a five-minute walk) to the huge sunken well that gave this city its name. The Sacred Cenote is an awesome natural well, some 60 meters in diameter and 35 meters deep. The walls between the summit and the water's surface are ensnared in tangled vines and other vegetation. There are ruins of a small steam bath next to the cenote, as well as a modern drinks stand with toilets.

Although some of the guides enjoy telling visitors that female virgins were sacrificed by being thrown into the cenote to drown, divers in 1923 brought up the remains of men, women and children.

Skeletons were not all that was found in the Sacred Cenote. Artifacts and valuable gold and jade jewelry from all parts of Mexico were recovered.

The artifacts' origins show the far-flung contacts the Maya had (there are some items from as far away as Colombia). It is believed that offerings of all kinds, human and otherwise, were thrown into the Sacred Cenote to please the gods.

Group of the Thousand Columns Comprising the Temple of the Warriors (Templo de los Guerreros), Temple of Chac-Mool (Templo de Chac-Mool) and Sweat House or Steam Bath (Baño al Vapor), this group takes its name (Grupo de las Mil Columnas) from the forest of pillars in front.

The platformed temple greets you with a statue of the reclining god, Chac, as well as stucco and stone-carved animal deities. The temple's roof, once supported by columns entwined with serpents, disappeared long ago.

Archaeological work in 1926 revealed a Temple of Chac-Mool beneath the Temple of the Warriors. You may enter via a stairway on the north side. The walls inside have badly deteriorated murals that are thought to portray the Toltecs' defeat of the Maya.

Just east of the Temple of the Warriors lies the rubble of a Mayan sweat house, with an underground oven and drains for the water. The sweat houses were regularly used for ritual purification.

Ossuary The Ossuary (El Osario) otherwise known as the Bonehouse or High Priest's Grave, is a ruined pyramid. As with most of the buildings in this southern section, the architecture is more Puuc than Toltec.

La Casa Colorada Spaniards named this building La Casa Colorada (The Red House) for the red paint of the mural on its doorway. This building has little Toltec influence and its design shows largely a pure Puuc Maya style. Referring to the stone latticework at the roof façade, the Maya named this building Chichán-Chob, or House of Small Holes.

El Caracol Called El Caracol (The Giant Conch Snail) by the Spaniards for its interior spiral staircase, this observatory is one of the most fascinating and important of all of Chichén Itzá's buildings. Its circular design resembles some central highlands structures, although, surprisingly, not those of Toltec Tula. In a fusion of architectural styles and religious imagery, there are Mayan Chac rain god masks over four external doors that face the cardinal directions.

The windows in the observatory's dome are aligned with the appearance of certain stars at specific dates. From the dome the priests decreed the times for rituals, celebrations, corn-planting and harvests.

Nunnery & Annex Thought by archaeologists to have been a palace for Mayan royalty, the Nunnery (Edificio de las Monjas), with its myriad rooms, resembled a European convent to the conquistadors, hence their name for the building. The Nunnery's dimensions are imposing: its base is 60 meters long, 30 meters wide and 20 meters high. The construction is Mayan rather than Toltec, although a Toltec sacrificial stone stands in front. A small building added onto the west side is known as the Annex (El Anexo). These buildings are in the Puuc-Chenes style, particularly evident in the lower jaw of the Chac mask at the opening of the Annex.

Akab-Dzib On the path east of the Nunnery, the Akab-Dzib is thought by some archaeologists to be the most ancient structure excavated here. The central chambers date from the 2nd century. Akab-Dzib means Obscure Writing in Maya and refers to the south-side Annex door whose lintel depicts a priest with a vase etched with hieroglyphics. The writing has never been translated, hence the name. Note the red fingerprints on the ceiling, thought to symbolize the deity Itzamna, the sun god from whom the Maya sought wisdom.

Chichén Viejo Chichén Viejo (Old Chichén), comprises largely unrestored ruins, scattered about and hidden in the bush south of the Nunnery. The predominant architecture is Mayan, with Toltec additions and modifications. Though trails lead to the most prominent buildings, you may want to hire a guide.

Grutas de Balankanché

In 1959 a guide to the Chichén ruins was exploring a cave on his day off. Pushing against a cavern wall, he broke through into a larger subterranean opening. Archaeological exploration revealed a path that runs some 300 meters past carved stalactites and stalagmites, terminating at an underground pool.

The Grutas de Balankanché are six km east of the ruins of Chichén Itzá, and two km east of the Hotel Dolores Alba on the highway to Cancún. Second-class buses heading east from Piste toward Valladolid and Cancún will drop you at the Balankanché road. You'll find the entrance to the caves 350 meters north of the highway.

As you approach the caves, you enter a pretty botanical garden displaying many of Yucatán's native flora, including many species of cactus. In the entrance building is a little museum, a shop selling cold drinks and souvenirs, and a ticket booth. Plan your visit for an hour when the compulsory tour and light-and-color show will be given in a language you can understand: the 40-minute show (minimum six people, maximum 30) is given in the cave at 11 am,

1 and 3 pm in English, at 9 am, noon and 2 and 4 pm in Spanish, and at 10 am in French. Tickets are available daily between 9 am and 4 pm (last show). Admission costs US$5 (US$2.50 Sunday).

Places to Stay

Most of the lodgings convenient to Chichén are in the middle and top-end price brackets. No matter what you plan to spend on a bed, be prepared to haggle in the off season (May, June, September and October) when prices should be lower at every hotel.

Places to Stay – budget

Camping There's camping at the *Pirámide Inn* (see below). For US$4 per person you can pitch a tent, enjoy the Pirámide Inn's pool and watch satellite TV in the lobby. There are hot showers and clean, shared toilet facilities. Those in vehicles pay US$12 for two for full hook-ups.

Hotels *Posada Olalde*, two blocks south of the highway by Artesanías Guayacan, is the best of Piste's several small pensions: clean, quiet and attractive, but somewhat more expensive than the others at US$19/28 a double/triple.

Posada Chac-Mool, just east of the Hotel Misión Chichén on the opposite (south) side of the highway in Piste, charges US$12 for a double with shower and fan. *Posada Novelo*, on the west side of the Pirámide Inn, charges the same for similar basic accommodations, but you can use the Pirámide's pool.

Hotel Posada Maya, a few dozen meters north of the highway (look for the sign), also charges US$12 for double rooms with shower and fan, but only US$4 to hang your hammock. It's a bit quieter, but drab. *Posada Poxil*, at the western end of town, charges the same for relatively clean, quiet rooms.

Places to Stay – middle

Hotel Dolores Alba (☎ in Mérida 99-21-37-45), on hwy 180 at Km 122, is just over three km east of the eastern entrance to the ruins and two km west of the road to Bal-

ankanché, on the highway to Cancún. (Ask the bus driver to stop here.) There are more than a dozen rooms surrounding a small swimming pool. The dining room is good (breakfasts US$3 to US$4, dinner US$10), which is important as there is no other eating facility nearby. They will transport you to the ruins, but you must take a taxi, bus or walk back. Singles/doubles/triples with shower and air-con cost US$22/25/28.

Stardust Inn (☎ /fax 1-01-22), next to the Pirámide Inn in Piste and less than two km west of the ruins, is an attractive place with two tiers of rooms surrounding a palm-shaded swimming pool and restaurant. Air-con rooms with TV cost US$38 single or double.

The *Pirámide Inn* (☎ /fax 1-01-14), next door, has been here for years. Its gardens have had time to mature, and its swimming pool is a blessing on a hot day. There's a selection of different rooms, some older, some newer (look before you pay), all air-conditioned and priced at US$25/30/40/50. Here, you're as close as you can get to the archaeological zone's western entrance.

Places to Stay – top end

All of these hotels have beautiful swimming pools, restaurants, bars, well-kept tropical gardens, comfortable guest rooms and tour groups coming and going. Several are very close to the ruins. If you are going to splurge on just one expensive hotel in Mexico, this is a good place to do it.

Hotel Mayaland (☎ in Mérida 99-25-21-22, in USA 800-235-4079; fax 99-25-70-22), a mere 200 meters from the eastern entrance to the archaeological zone, is the oldest (1923) and most gracious at Chichén. From the lobby you look through the main portal to see El Caracol framed as in a photograph. Room rates are US$88/100 a single/double.

Hotel Hacienda Chichén (☎ in Mérida 99-24-21-50, in USA 800-624-8451; fax 99-24-50-11), a few hundred meters farther from the ruins on the same eastern access road, was where the archaeologists lived when excavating Chichén. Their bungalows have been refurbished and new ones built. Rooms in the garden bungalows, priced at US$60 single or double, US$70 triple, have ceiling fans, air-con, and private baths, but no TVs or phones. The dining room serves simple meals at moderate prices.

The *Hotel Villa Arqueológica* (☎ 6-28-30; Apdo Postal 495, Mérida), is a few hundred meters east of the Mayaland and Hacienda Chichén on the eastern access road to the ruins. Run by Club Med, it's a modern layout with a good restaurant, tennis courts and swimming pool. Rooms are fairly small but comfortable and air-conditioned and priced at US$55/60/75.

On the western side of Chichén, in the village of Piste, the *Hotel Misión Chichén* (☎ 1-00-22, in USA 800-648-7818; fax 1-00-23) is comfortable without being distinguished. Its pool is refreshing, its vast restaurant often filled with bus tours. Air-con rooms cost US$75, single or double.

Places to Eat

The cafeteria in the *Unidad de Servicios* at the western entrance to the archaeological zone serves mediocre food at high prices in pleasant surroundings.

The highway through Piste is lined with more than 20 restaurants. The cheapest places are the entirely unatmospheric little market eateries on the main square opposite the huge tree. The others, ranged along the highway from the square to the Pirámide Inn, are fairly well tarted up in a Mayan villager's conception of what foreign tourists expect to see.

Los Pajaros and *Cocina Económica Chichén Itzá* are among the cheapest ones, serving sandwiches, omelets, enchiladas and quesadillas for around US$2.50. *Restaurant Sayil*, facing the Hotel Misión Chichén, offers good value: bistec, cochinita or pollo pibil for US$2. Another simple little eatery with wooden benches and tables is the *Restaurant Parador*.

Prices are higher at the larger, more atmospheric restaurants such as the *Pueblo Maya*, *Carrousel*, and *Fiesta*. *Restaurant Ruinas* serves big plates of fruit for

US$1.50, tuna salad with mango for US$4, and hamburgers, sandwiches, fried chicken, and spaghetti plates for around US$4.

The big *Restaurant Xaybe*, opposite the Hotel Misión Chichén, has decent food and prices, about US$10 per person. Customers of the restaurant get to use its swimming pool for free, but even if you don't eat here, you can still swim for about US$2.

The luxury hotels all have restaurants, with the Club Med-run *Villa Arqueológica* serving particularly distinguished cuisine. If you try its French-inspired Mexican-Mayan restaurant, it'll cost you about US$15 per person for a four-course comida corrida, and almost twice that much if you order à la carte – but the food is good.

Getting There & Away

Air Aerocaribe runs same-day roundtrip excursions by air from Cancún to Chichén Itzá in little planes, charging US$99 for the flight. Aerocozumel runs a similar service from Cozumel to Cancún for US$109.

Bus The fastest buses between Mérida, Valladolid and Cancún travel by the Cuota (toll highway), and do not stop at Chichén Itzá.

Autotransportes de Oriente has a ticket desk right in the souvenir shop in Chichén's Unidad de Servicios. The Oriente bus station is a small building just west of the Pirámide Inn.

Here are some bus routes daily from Piste:

Cancún – 205 km, two to 3½ hours, US$4.50 to US$7, 10 buses
Cobá – 148 km, 2½ hours, US$4, one bus
Izamal – 95 km, 2 hours, US$3.50, change buses at Hóctun
Mérida – 116 km, 2½ hours, US$2.75 to US$3.50, ten buses; those by Oriente stop right at the Chichén ruins. A special roundtrip (US$6.75) excursion bus by Oriente departs from Mérida at 8.45 am and returns from Chichén Itzá at 3 pm
Playa del Carmen – 272 km, four hours, US$6 to US$9, five buses
Tulum – 402 km, 6½ hours, US$5, one bus
Valladolid – 42 km, 30 to 45 minutes, US$1; 10 buses

Getting Around

Be prepared for walking at Chichén Itzá: from your hotel to the ruins, around the ruins, and back to your hotel, all in the very hot sun and humidity. For the Grutas de Balankanché, you can set out to walk early in the morning when it's cooler (it's eight km from Piste, less if you're staying on the eastern side of the ruins) and then hope to hitch a ride or catch a bus for the return.

A few taxis are available in Piste and sometimes at the Unidad de Servicios car park at Chichén Itzá, but you cannot depend on finding one unless you've made arrangements in advance.

VALLADOLID

pop 80,000; ☎ 985

Valladolid is only 40 km (half an hour) east of Chichén Itzá and 160 km (about two hours) west of Cancún but as it has no sights of stop-the-car immediacy, few tourists do stop here; most prefer to hurtle on through to the next major site. It's just as well, for this preserves Valladolid for the rest of us who want to enjoy it.

History

The Mayan ceremonial center of Zací was here long before the Spaniards arrived. The initial attempt at conquest in 1543 by Francisco de Montejo, nephew of Montejo the Elder, was thwarted by fierce Mayan resistance, but the Elder's son Montejo the Younger ultimately conquered the Maya and took the town. The Spanish laid out a new city on the classic colonial plan.

Throughout much of the colonial era, Valladolid's distance from Mérida, its humidity and the surrounding forests kept it isolated from royal rule and thus relatively autonomous. Banned from even entering this town of pure-blooded Spaniards, the Maya rebelled, and in the War of the Castes of 1847 they made Valladolid their first point of attack. Besieged for two months, Valladolid's defenders were finally overcome; many of the citizens fled to the safety of Mérida and the rest were slaughtered by the Mayan forces.

Orientation & Information

The old highway goes right through the center of town, though all signs will direct you to the toll highway north of town. To follow the old highway eastbound, follow Calle 41; westbound, Calle 39 or 35. The bus terminal is on Calle 37 between Calles 54 and 56, eight blocks from the plaza.

Recommended hotels are on the main plaza, called the Parque Francisco Cantón Rosado, or just a block or two away from it.

The post office is on the east side of the main plaza at Calle 40 No 195A. Hours are weekdays from 8 am to 6 pm, Saturday 9 am to 1 pm.

Templo de San Bernardino & Convento de Sisal

Although Valladolid has a number of interesting colonial churches, the Church of San Bernardino de Siena and the Convent of Sisal, 1.5 km southwest of the plaza, are said to be the oldest Christian structures in Yucatán. Constructed in 1552, the complex was designed to serve a dual function as fortress and church.

If the convent is open, go inside. Apart from the miracle-working Virgin of Guadalupe on the altar, the church is relatively bare. During the uprisings of 1847 and 1910, angry Indians stripped the church of its decoration.

To get to the church, walk west on Calle 41 one km, then turn left and walk 500 meters to the convent. If you're riding a bicycle to the Cenote Dzitnup, you can stop at the convent on your way.

Cenotes

Cenotes, those vast underground limestone sinkholes, were the Maya's most dependable source of water. The Spaniards used them also. The Cenote Zací, Calle 36 between Calles 39 and 37, is the most famous.

Set in a pretty park which also holds the town's museum, an open-air amphitheater and traditional stone-walled thatched houses, the cenote is vast, dark, impressive and covered with a layer of scum. It's open daily from 8 am to 8 pm; admission costs US$2 for adults, half-price for children.

YUCATÁN PENINSULA

Valladolid

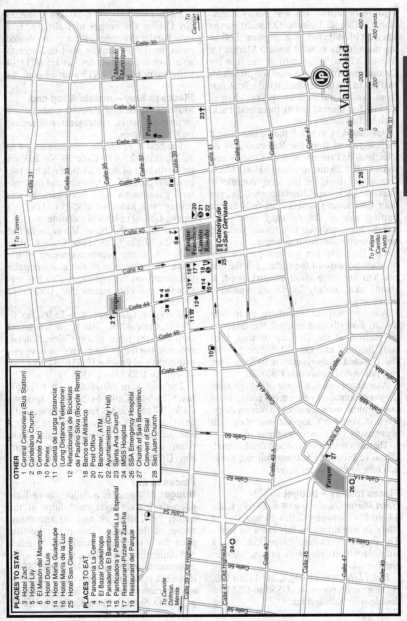

To Cancún

To Tizimín

To Temax

To Cenote Dzitnup,
Mérida

To Cenote Dzitnup

To Felipe
Carrillo
Puerto

Calle 30

Calle 32

Calle 34

Calle 36

Calle 37

Calle 38

Calle 39

Calle 40

Calle 41

Calle 42

Calle 43

Calle 44

Calle 45

Calle 46

Calle 47

Calle 48

Calle 49

Calle 50

Calle 51

Calle 52

Calle 41A (Old Highway)

Calle 41 (Old Highway)

Calle 39 (Old Highway)

Calle 31

Calle 33

Calle 35

Mercado
Municipal

Parque

Parque

Parque
Francisco
Cantón
Rosado

Catedral de
San Gervasio

Parque

N

0   200   400 m
0   200   400 yards

PLACES TO STAY
3   Hotel Zaci
5   Hotel Lily
6   El Mesón del Marqués
8   Hotel Don Luis
14 Hotel María Guadalupe
16 Hotel María de la Luz
25 Hotel San Clemente

PLACES TO EAT
4   Panadería La Central
7   El Bazar Cookshops
13 Panadería El Bambino
15 Panificadora y Pastelería La Especial
17 Restaurant-Pizzería Zazil-ha
19 Restaurant del Parque

OTHER
1   Central Camionera (Bus Station)
2   Candelaria Church
9   Cenote Zaci
10 Pemex
11 Caseta de Larga Distancia
    (Long Distance Telephone)
12 Refaccionaria de Bicicletas
    de Paulino Silva (Bicycle Rental)
18 Banco del Atlántico
20 Post Office
21 Bancomer, ATM
22 Ayuntamiento (City Hall)
23 Santa Ana Church
24 IMSS Hospital
26 SSA Emergency Hospital
27 Church of San Bernardino,
    Convent of Sisal
28 San Juan Church

More beautiful, but less easily accessible, is Cenote Dzitnup (Xkakah), seven km west of Valladolid's main plaza. Follow the main highway west toward Mérida for five km. Turn left (south) at the sign for Dzitnup and follow the road for just under two km to get to the site, on the left. A taxi from Valladolid's main plaza charges US$10 for the excursion there and back, with half an hour's wait.

Another way to reach the cenote is on a bicycle rented from the Refaccionaría de Bicicletas de Paulino Silva, on Calle 44 between Calles 39 and 41, facing Hotel María Guadalupe; look for the sign 'Alquiler y Venta de Bicicletas.' Rental costs US$2 per hour. Check out your bike carefully before putting money down. They rent some wrecks here, and you don't want yours to break down miles from nowhere.

The first five km are not particularly pleasant because of the traffic, but the last two km are on a quiet country road. It should take you only 20 minutes to pedal to the cenote.

Another way to get there is to hop aboard a westbound bus, ask the driver to let you off at the Dzitnup turning, then walk the final two km (20 minutes) to the site. Cenote Dzitnup is open daily from 7 am to 6 pm. Admission costs US$1.50.

As you approach, a horde of village children will surround you, each wanting to be your 'guide' to the cenote, 10 meters away. Even if you don't appoint one, they will accompany you down into the cave.

There's a restaurant and soft drinks stand. If you've brought a bathing suit and towel you can go for a swim here.

Places to Stay – budget
Hotel María Guadalupe (☎ 6-20-68), Calle 44 No 188, between Calles 39 and 41, is a study in modernity in this colonial town. The simple rooms here go for US$7/9/13 a single/double/triple with private shower and fan.

Hotel Lily (☎ 6-21-63), Calle 44 No 190, is cheap and very basic: US$8 to US$12 a double with bath and fan.

Hotel Don Luis (☎ 6-20-08), Calle 39 No 191, at the corner of Calle 38, is a motel-style structure with a palm-shaded patio, murky swimming pool and acceptable rooms priced as low as US$8/11/14 with fan, or US$10/13/15 with air-con.

Places to Stay – middle & top end
Most of Valladolid's better places have swimming pools, restaurants and secure parking facilities.

The best is *El Mesón del Marqués* (☎ 6-20-73, fax 6-22-80), Calle 39 No 203, on the north side of the main plaza. It has two beautiful colonial courtyards, and modernized guestrooms with both air-con and ceiling fans. Rates are US$45 to US$58 a single, US$50 to US$70 a double.

Next best is the *Hotel María de la Luz* (☎ 6-20-70, fax 6-20-71) on Calle 42 near Calle 39, at the northwest corner of the plaza. Boasting one of the more popular restaurants on the square, it also has serviceable air-con rooms for US$16 to US$20.

Hotel San Clemente (☎ 6-22-08, fax 6-35-14), Calle 42 No 206 at the southwest corner of the main plaza. Colonial decor abounds, but the 64 double rooms have private baths and fans for US$16 to US$22, or air-con for US$20 to US$28.

The well-kept *Hotel Zací* (☎ 6-21-67, fax 6-25-94), Calle 44 No 191, between Calles 37 and 39, has rooms built around a quiet, long and narrow courtyard with a swimming pool. You may choose from rooms with fan (US$15/22/28) or with air-con (US$18/25/32).

Places to Eat
Budget *El Bazar* is a collection of little open-air market-style cookshops at the corner of Calles 39 and 40 (northeast corner of the plaza). This is our favorite place for a big cheap breakfast. At lunch and dinnertime, comidas corridas of soup, main course and drink cost less than US$4 – if you ask prices before you order. There are a dozen eateries here – Doña Mary, El Amigo Panfilo, Sergio's Pizza, La Rancherita, El

Amigo Casiano, etc – open from 6.30 am to 2 pm and from 6 pm to about 9 or 10 pm.

For a bit more you can dine at the breezy tables in the *Hotel María de la Luz*, overlooking the plaza. The breakfast buffet costs only US$3, a lunch time *comida corrida* the same.

The *comida* costs even less at the old-fashioned, high-ceilinged *Restaurant del Parque*.

Restaurant-Pizzería Zazil-ha, Calle 42 on the west side of the plaza, has been fixed up and now offers good, cheap pizza, and rock music at ear-splitting volume.

Valladolid has several good bakeries, including *Panificadora y Pastelería La Especial*, on Calle 41 less than a block west of the plaza, and *Panadería El Bambino* on Calle 39 a half block west of the plaza. There's also *Panadería La Central* next door to the Hotel Lily on Calle 44.

Middle Best is the *Hostería del Marques*, the dining room of the Hotel El Mesón del Marqués, Calle 39 No 203 on the north side of the main plaza. Start with gazpacho, continue with pork loin Valladolid-style (in a tomato sauce) or grilled pork steak, and finish up with a slice of cake for US$7 to US$11 per person.

Getting There & Away

Bus The bus terminal is on Calle 37 between Calles 54 and 56, eight blocks from the plaza. It has a telephone caseta with fax service. The main companies are Autotransportes de Oriente Mérida-Puerto Juárez (1st- and 2nd-class) and Expresso de Oriente. Here are the daily departures:

Cancún – 160 km, 1½ to two hours, US$4 to US$8; seven *local* (originating here), hourly de paso from 6 am to 9 pm

Chichén Itzá – 42 km, 30 to 45 minutes, US$1; 10 buses

Chiquilá (for Isla Holbox) – 155 km, 2½ hours, US$5; at least one bus daily

Cobá – 106 km, two hours, US$3; one bus at 2.30 pm

Izamal – 115 km, two hours, US$3; Autobuses del Centro del Estado de Yucatán operates five buses

Mérida – 160 km, three hours, US$5; seven *local* (originating here), hourly de paso from 6 am to 9 pm

Motul – 156 km, three hours, US$5; Autobuses del Noreste runs five buses via Dzitas, Tunkas, Izamal and Tixcocob

Playa del Carmen – 213 km, 3½ hours, US$7; five by ADO (US$6), four by ATS (US$5)

Río Lagartos – 103 km, two hours, US$3.50; the 10 am bus to Tizimin continues to Lagartos; or change buses at Tizimin

Tizimin – 51 km, one hour, US$2; Autobuses del Noreste en Yucatán operates hourly buses

Tulum – 156 km, three hours, US$7; one bus at 2.30 pm

Taxi A quicker, more comfortable, but more expensive way to Cancún is by taking one of the shared taxis that are parked outside the bus station and leave as soon as all seats are filled. The trip costs approximately twice the bus fare.

TIZIMIN
pop 65,000; ☎ *986*

Many travelers bound for Río Lagartos change buses in Tizimin (Place of Many Horses), the second-largest city in the state of Yucatán. There is little to warrant an overnight stay, but the main plaza is pleasant.

Two great colonial structures, the Convento de los Tres Reyes Magos (Monastery of the Three Wise Kings) and the Convento de San Francisco de Asis (Monastery of Saint Francis of Assisi) are worth a look. Five lengthy blocks from the plaza, northwest on Calle 51, is a modest zoo, the Parque Zoológico de la Reina.

The Banco del Atlantico, next to the Hotel San Jorge on the southwest side of the plaza, changes money weekdays between 10 am and noon. Banco Internacional is open from 9 am to 1.30 pm.

Places to Stay
The *Hotel San Jorge* (☎ 3-20-37), Calle 53 No 411, has basic but serviceable rooms with private bath and fan for US$15/20 for a double with fan/air-con. *Hotel San Carlos* (☎ 3-20-94), Calle 54 No 407, is

built like a motel, and charges identical prices.

Posada María Antonia (☎ 3-23-84), Calle 50 No 408, on the east side of the Parque de la Madre, also has comfy rooms at these prices. Doubles with air-con cost US$22. The reception desk is also a telephone caseta.

Places to Eat

The market, a block northwest of the bus station, has the usual cheap eateries. *Panificadora La Especial* is on Calle 55, down a little pedestrian lane from the plaza.

Restaurant Los Tres Reyes (☎ 3-21-06), on the corner of Calles 52 and 53, opens early for breakfast and is a favorite with town notables who take their second cup of coffee around 9 am. Lunch or dinner costs US$3 to US$5, and is well worth it.

Facing the plaza are several simple places good for a quick, cheap bite, including the *Los Portales, La Parrilla, Tortas Económicas La Especial*, and the *Cocina Económica Ameli*.

Pizzería Cesar's, at the corner of Calles 50 and 53, serves pizza and pasta (US$2.50 to US$5) in air-conditioned comfort from 5.30 to 11 pm.

Getting There & Away

Autobuses del Noreste en Yucatán operates hourly buses from Valladolid to Tizimin (51 km, one hour, US$2). From Cancún and Puerto Juárez, there are several direct buses to Tizimin (212 km, three hours, US$4). There are several daily 1st- and 2nd-class buses between Tizimin and Mérida (210 km, four hours, US$3.75) via Valladolid. For Río Lagartos there are three 1st-class departures and five daily 2nd-class buses which continue to San Felipe.

RÍO LAGARTOS
pop 900; ☎ 986

It is well worth going out of your way to this little fishing village, 103 km north of Valladolid and 52 km north of Tizimin, to see the most spectacular flamingo colony in Mexico. The estuaries are also home to snowy egrets, red egrets, great white herons

and snowy white ibis. Although Río Lagartos (Alligator River) was named after the once substantial alligator population, don't expect to see any, as hunting has virtually wiped them out.

The town of Río Lagartos itself, with its narrow streets and multihued houses, has little charm, though the panorama of the boats and the bay is pleasant. Were it not for the flamingos, you would have little reason to come here. Although the state government has been making noise about developing the area for tourism, this has not happened yet.

At the center of town is a small triangular plaza, a town hall and the Conasupo store.

Flamingos

When you approach a horizon of hundreds of these brilliant red-pink birds, you will fully understand why they are called flamingos. The name is derived from the Spanish word *flamenco*, which means 'flaming.' When the flock takes flight, the sight of the suddenly fiery horizon makes the long hours on the bus to get here all worthwhile. However, in the interests of the flamingos' well-being, convince your local guide not to frighten the birds into flight. Being frightened away from their habitat several times a day can't be good for them, however good it may be for the guide's business.

Everybody in town will offer to set you up with a boat. Haggling over price is essential. In general, a short trip (two to three hours) to see a few nearby local flamingos and to have a swim at the beach costs US$20 to US$30 for a five-seat boat. The much longer voyage (four to six hours) to the flamingos' favorite haunts costs US$60 or so for the boat, or about US$12 per person for a full load.

Places to Stay & Eat

The forlorn *Hotel María Nefertiti*, Calle 14 No 123, is currently closed for lack of trade.

The cavernous palapa-shaded *Restaurant Los Flamingos* at the back is equally empty most of the time. The *Restaurant Familiar Isla Contoy*, just down from Los Flamingos on the water, is perhaps a better bet. There's also the *Restaurant Los Negritos* facing a little park with a statue of Benito Juárez, two blocks inland from the main square.

It is sometimes possible to rent a bed or a pair of hammock hooks in a local house, which brings down considerably the cost of sleeping.

Getting There & Away
Autobuses del Noreste en Yucatán operates hourly buses from Valladolid to Tizimin (51 km, one hour, US$2). Several buses go on to Río Lagartos (103 km, two hours, US$4). There is also one direct bus daily between Tizimin and Mérida.

SAN FELIPE
pop 400; ☎ 98
This tiny fishing village of painted wooden houses on narrow streets, 12 km west of Río Lagartos, makes a nice day trip from Río Lagartos. While the waters are not Caribbean turquoise and there's little shade, in spring and summer scores of visitors come here to camp. Other than lying on the beach, bird-watching is the main attraction in San Felipe, as just across the estuary at Punta Holohit there is abundant bird life.

Places to Stay & Eat
The proprietor of the Floresita grocery store not far from the pier can rent you a spartan room above the Cinema Marrufo. Campers are ferried across the estuary to islands where they pitch tents or set up hammocks.

Otherwise, there's the new *Hotel San Felipe de Jesús* (☎ 63-37-38), Calle 9 between 14 and 16, renting quite nice rooms for US$15. There's a good restaurant as well.

For cheap fish, try *El Payaso*. Even cheaper eats, such as chicken and turkey soups and tacos, are available from vendors.

Getting There & Away
Some buses from Tizimin to Río Lagartos continue to San Felipe and return. The 12-km ride takes about 20 minutes.

Quintana Roo

In the past two decades, Mexico's once-sleepy Caribbean coastline has been subject to furious development. From being one of the country's most backward and sparsely populated areas, Quintana Roo is well on the way to becoming just the opposite.

Why? Long stretches of beautiful beach, warm water, luxuriant undersea coral reefs, interesting islands and a lust for bucks. The Quintana Roo coast is nature in the service of Mammon.

CANCÚN
pop 600,000; ☎ 98
In the 1970s Mexico's ambitious tourism planners decided to build a brand new world-class resort on a deserted sand spit offshore from the little fishing village of Puerto Juárez. The island sand spit was shaped like a lucky '7.' The name of the place was Cancún.

The Yucatán Peninsula's major international airport is here, as are doctors, modern hospitals, consular representatives, rental car agencies and many other services.

Dozens of mammoth hotels march along the island's shore as it extends from the mainland nine km eastward, then 14 km southward, into the turquoise waters of the Caribbean. At the north end the island is joined to the mainland by a bridge leading to Ciudad Cancún; at the south end a bridge joins a road leading inland to the international airport.

The Mexican government built Cancún as an investment in the tourism business. Cancún's raison-d'être is to shelter plane-loads of tourists who fly in (usually on the weekend) to spend one or two weeks in a resort hotel before flying home again (usually on a weekend). They have a good time. This is the business of tourism.

Orientation
Ciudad Cancún is a planned community on the mainland, divided into *super manzanas*

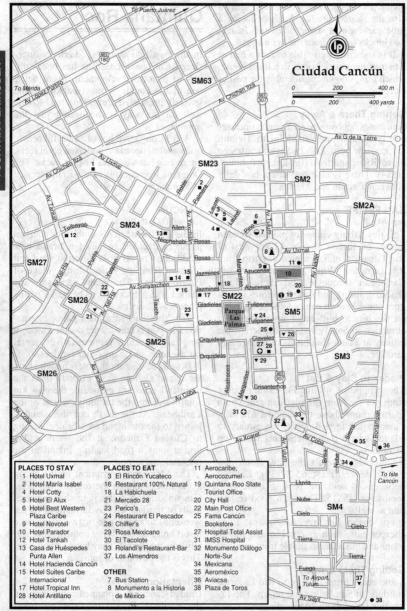

Ciudad Cancún

PLACES TO STAY
1 Hotel Uxmal
2 Hotel María Isabel
4 Hotel Cotty
5 Hotel El Alux
6 Hotel Best Western
   Plaza Caribe
9 Hotel Novotel
10 Hotel Parador
12 Hotel Tankah
13 Casa de Huéspedes
   Punta Allen
14 Hotel Hacienda Cancún
15 Hotel Suites Caribe
   Internacional
17 Hotel Tropical Inn
28 Hotel Antillano

PLACES TO EAT
3 El Rincón Yucateco
16 Restaurant 100% Natural
18 La Habichuela
21 Mercado 28
23 Perico's
24 Restaurant El Pescador
26 Chiffer's
29 Rosa Mexicano
30 El Tacolote
33 Rolandi's Restaurant-Bar
37 Los Almendros

OTHER
7 Bus Station
8 Monumento a la Historia
   de México

11 Aerocaribe,
   Aerocozumel
19 Quintana Roo State
   Tourist Office
20 City Hall
22 Main Post Office
25 Fama Cancún
   Bookstore
27 Hospital Total Assist
31 IMSS Hospital
32 Monumento Diálogo
   Norte-Sur
34 Mexicana
35 Aeroméxico
36 Aviacsa
38 Plaza de Toros

(SM; super blocks), and the SM number sometimes given in addresses. On the 23-km-long sandy island is the Zona Hotelera, or Zona Turística, with its towering hotels, theme restaurants, convention center, shopping malls, golf course and so on.

Several landmarks will help you find your way around this vast resort. In Ciudad Cancún, the main north-south thoroughfare is called Avenida Tulum; it's a tree-shaded boulevard lined with banks, shopping centers, noisy hotels, restaurants and touts selling time-share condominiums.

Coming from Ciudad Cancún, the main road to Isla Cancún is Boulevard Kukulcán (sometimes called Avenida or Paseo Kukulcán), a four-lane divided highway that goes east along the top of the '7.' The youth hostel and the few moderately priced hotels are located on the first few km of Boulevard Kukulcán. After nine km, the road reaches the convention center near Punta Cancún, and turns south for another 14 km to Punta Nizuc and then rejoins the mainland.

With the exception of the overpriced youth hostel, there are no budget hotels in the Zona Hotelera.

Cancún international airport is about eight km south of Avenida Tulum. Puerto Juárez, the port for passenger ferries to Isla Mujeres, is about three km north of the intersection of Avenida Tulum and Avenida López Portillo. Punta Sam, the dock for the slower car ferries to Isla Mujeres, is about two km farther north.

Information

Tourist Office The state tourist office for Quintana Roo (☎ 84-04-37), 26 Avenida Tulum, is next to the Multibanco Comermex, left of the municipality.

Consulates If your consulate or agent is not listed here, call your consulate in Mérida, or your embassy in Mexico City.

Belize
    Calle Rosas 22, SM 22 (☎ 84-65-98, 84-85-46)
Canada
    Avenida Tulum 200, Plaza México 312, 2nd floor (☎ 84-37-16, fax 87-67-16)

France
    Instituto de Idiomas de Cancún, Avenida Xel-ha 113 (☎ 84-60-78, fax 87-33-62)
Germany
    Punta Conoco 36, SM 24 (☎ 84-18-98)
Italy
    Calle Alcatraces 39 (☎ 83-12-61, fax 84-54-15)
Netherlands
    Hotel President Inter-Continental (☎ 83-02-00, fax 83-25-15)
Spain
    Oasis Building, Boulevard Kukulcán km 6.5 (☎ 83-24-66, fax 83-28-70)
United Kingdom
    Royal Caribbean in the Zona Hotelera (☎ 85-11-66 ext 462, fax 85-12-25)
USA
    Plaza Caracol shopping center, 3rd floor, in the Zona Hotelera (☎ 83-02-72); it is said that the consulate general will soon move from Mérida to Cancún.

Money Banks on Avenida Tulum are open from 9 am to 1.30 pm, but many limit foreign exchange transactions to between 10 am and noon. Casas de cambio usually are open from 8 or 9 am to 1 pm and again from 4 or 5 pm till 7 or 8 pm; some casas are open seven days a week. ATMs are numerous throughout Ciudad Cancún and the Zona Hotelera.

Post & Communications The main post office (Oficina de Correos, Cancún, Quintana Roo 77500) is at the western end of Avenida Sunyaxchén, which runs west from Avenida Yaxchilán; the post office is four or five short blocks from Avenida Yaxchilán. Hours for buying stamps and picking up Lista de Correos (poste restante) mail are weekdays from 8 am to 7 pm, and Saturday and holidays from 9 am to 1 pm. For international money orders and registered mail, hours are weekdays from 8 am to 6 pm, Saturday and holidays from 9 am to noon, closed Sunday.

Now that Mexico has opened telephony up to competition, the situation is in flux. Telmex phones are numerous, on street corners and in large public buildings, as are other sorts of phones aimed at foreigners, especially North Americans. Before

YUCATÁN PENINSULA

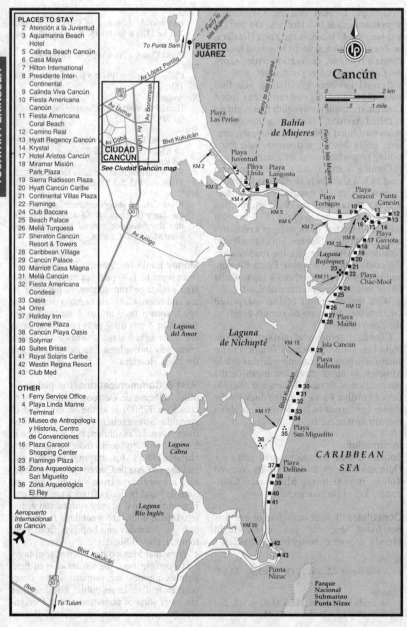

PLACES TO STAY
2 Atención a la Juventud
3 Aquamarina Beach Hotel
5 Calinda Beach Cancún
6 Casa Maya
7 Hilton International
8 Presidente Inter-Continental
9 Calinda Viva Cancún
10 Fiesta Americana Cancún
11 Fiesta Americana Coral Beach
12 Camino Real
13 Hyatt Regency Cancún
14 Krystal
17 Hotel Aristos Cancún
18 Miramar Misión Park Plaza
19 Sierra Radisson Plaza
20 Hyatt Cancún Caribe
21 Continental Villas Plaza
22 Flamingo
24 Club Baccara
25 Beach Palace
26 Meliá Turquesa
27 Sheraton Cancún Resort & Towers
28 Caribbean Village
29 Cancún Palace
30 Marriott Casa Magna
31 Meliá Cancún
32 Fiesta Americana Condesa
33 Oasis
34 Omni
37 Holiday Inn Crowne Plaza
38 Cancún Playa Oasis
39 Solymar
40 Suites Brisas
41 Royal Solaris Caribe
42 Westin Regina Resort
43 Club Med

OTHER
1 Ferry Service Office
4 Playa Linda Marine Terminal
15 Museo de Antropología y Historia, Centro de Convenciones
16 Plaza Caracol Shopping Center
23 Flamingo Plaza
35 Zona Arqueológica San Miguelito
36 Zona Arqueológica El Rey

To Punta Sam

Ferry to Isla Mujeres

PUERTO JUÁREZ

Av López Portillo

Av Uxmal

MEX 180

Av Bonampak

Av Coba

Av Tulum

CIUDAD CANCÚN

See Ciudad Cancún map

Blvd Kukulcán

Playa Las Perlas

Playa Juventud

Playa Linda

Playa Langosta

KM 2

KM 3

KM 4

KM 5

KM 6

KM 7

Ferry to Isla Mujeres

Ferry to Isla Mujeres

Bahía de Mujeres

Cancún

0   1   2 km
0   .5   1 mile

Playa Tortugas

Playa Caracol

Punta Cancún

KM 8

KM 10

Playa Gaviota Azul

Laguna Bojórquez

KM 11

Playa Chác-Mool

KM 12

Playa Marlin

KM 15

Isla Cancún

Playa Ballenas

Blvd Kukulcán

MEX 307

Av Amigo

Laguna del Amor

Laguna de Nichupté

Laguna Cabra

Laguna Río Inglés

Aeropuerto Internacional de Cancún

Blvd Kukulcán

(toll)

MEX 307

To Tulum

KM 17

Playa San Miguelito

36

35

30
31
32
33
34

37

38
39

40
41

Playa Delfines

KM 20

42
43

Punta Nizuc

CARIBBEAN SEA

Parque Nacional Submarino Punta Nizuc

you call, check the rates; they can be very high – up to US$6 per minute.

Bookstores Fama Cancún, Avenida Tulum 105, near the corner with the southern end of Tulipanes, has periodicals and books in several languages.

Laundry The Lavandería María de Lourdes, near the hotel of the same name, is on Calle Orquideas off Avenida Yaxchilán. You might also try the Lavandería y Tintorería Cox-Boh, Avenida Tankah 26, SM 24. Walk toward the post office along Avenida Sunyaxchén; in front of the post office, bear right onto Avenida Tankah and Cox-Boh is on the right-hand side of the street.

The Cox-Boh charges US$3.50 per kg for bulk service (such as a traveler's three or five kg bag of washing). To have a pair of trousers washed and ironed costs US$3.50, or $6.50 for dry cleaning. Washing and ironing a shirt costs US$2.25. Cox-Boh is open every day except Sunday.

Medical Services Cancún's many hospitals include the large IMSS (Social Security, ☎ 84-23-42), Avenida Cobá at Avenida Tulum; the Cruz Roja (Red Cross, ☎ 84-16-16), Avenida Labná 1; Hospital Americano (☎ 84-64-30, 84-60-68), Calle Viento 15; and Hospital Total Assist (☎ 84-10-92, 84-81-16), Calle Claveles 22, adjacent to the Hotel Antillano just off Avenida Tulum.

Zona Arqueológica El Rey
These Mayan ruins, on Isla Cancún, are fairly unimpressive – a small temple and several ceremonial platforms. Heading south along Boulevard Kukulcán from Punta Cancún, watch for the marker for km 17. Just past the marker there's an unpaved road on the right which leads to the ruins, open from 8 am to 5 pm every day; admission costs US$2.

For just a quick glimpse, continue on Boulevard Kukulcán 700 meters past the km 17 marker and up the hill. At the top of the hill, just past the restaurant La Prosperidad de Cancún, you can survey the ruins without hiking in or paying the admission charge.

The tiny Mayan structure and chac-mool statue set in the beautifully kept grounds of the Sheraton Hotel are actually authentic ruins found on the spot.

Museo de Antropología y Historia
This archaeological museum, next to the Centro de Convenciones in the Zona Hotelera, has a limited collection of Mayan artifacts. Although most of the items, including jewelry, masks and skull deformers, are from the Postclassic period (1200-1500), there is a Classic-period hieroglyphic staircase inscribed with dates from the 6th century as well as the stucco head which gave the local archaeological zone its name of El Rey (The King).

Hours are 9 am to 7 pm (Sunday 10 am to 5 pm), closed Monday. Admission costs US$1.50. But on our last visit, the museum was closed, and there was no indication of when – or if – it might reopen.

Beaches
The dazzling white sand of Cancún's beaches is light in weight and cool underfoot, even in the blazing sun. That's because it is composed not of silica but rather of microscopic plankton fossils called disco-aster (a tiny star-shaped creature). The coolness of the sand has not been lost on Cancún's ingenious promoters, who have dubbed it 'air-con.' Combined with the crystalline azure waters of the Caribbean, it makes for beaches that are pure delight.

All of these delightful beaches are open to you because all Mexican beaches are public property. Several of Cancún's beaches are set aside for easy public access, but you should know that you have the right to walk and swim on any beach at all. In practice it may be difficult to approach certain stretches of beach without going through a hotel's property, but few hotels will notice you walking through to the beach in any case.

Starting at Ciudad Cancún and heading out to Isla Cancún all the beaches are on the left-hand side of the road; the lagoon is on your right. The beaches are: Playa Las Perlas, Playa Linda, Playa Langosta, Playa Tortugas, Playa Caracol, and then Punta Cancún, the point of the '7.' South from Punta Cancún are Playa Gaviota Azul, Playa Chac-Mool, Playa Marlin, Playa Ballenas (km 15), Playa San Miguelito, and Playa Delfines (km 18).

Beach Safety Cancún's Rescate 911 ambulance crews respond to as many as a dozen near-drownings per week. The most dangerous beaches seem to be Playa Delfines and Playa Chac-Mool.

As any experienced swimmer knows, a beach fronting on open sea can be deadly dangerous and Cancún's eastern beaches are no exception. Though the surf is usually gentle, undertow is a possibility and sudden storms (called *nortes*) can blacken the sky and sweep in at any time without warning. The local authorities have devised a system of colored pennants to warn beachgoers of potential dangers. Look for the colored pennants on the beaches where you swim:

Blue	Normal, safe conditions
Yellow	Use caution, changeable conditions
Red	Unsafe conditions, swim in a pool

Getting There & Away To reach the beaches from Ciudad Cancún, catch any bus marked 'Hoteles' or 'Zona Hotelera' going south along Avenida Tulum or east along Avenida Cobá. The cost of a taxi depends upon how far you travel. For details, see Getting Around at the end of the Cancún section.

Places to Stay

If you want to stay right on the beach, you must stay in the Zona Hotelera, out on the island. With the exception of the youth hostel, there are no budget accommodations here. You can choose from among the few older, smaller, moderately priced hotels, or the many new, luxurious, pricey hotels.

Places to Stay – budget

Though there are more than 20,000 hotel rooms in Cancún, this resort offers the low-budget traveler the worst selection of cheap accommodation at the highest prices of any place in Mexico.

To make your room search as easy as possible, we've arranged our hotel recommendations on walking itineraries starting from the bus station. If you arrive by air and take a minibus into town (see Getting Around), your minibus driver will drop you at your chosen hotel at no extra charge.

In general, budget rooms range from US$14 to US$38 a double, tax included, in the busy winter season. Prices drop 15% to 20% in the less busy summer months. Except for the cheapest places, this gets you a room with private bathroom, fan and probably air-conditioning and the hotel might even have a small swimming pool.

Hostel Four km from the bus station, the local youth hostel is called *Atención a la Juventud* (☎ 83-13-37). It's at Boulevard Kukulcán km 3.2, on the left (north) side of the road as you come from Ciudad Cancún.

Built decades ago as a modern 600-bed complex in honor of youth, it is now sadly dilapidated, though still functioning. The staff is friendly, but it's overpriced for what you get: a single-sex dorm bed for US$11 (plus a US$7 deposit). (Two people can usually find a decent hotel room with bath in Ciudad Cancún for the same US$22 – or less.) Camping on the beach costs US$6 per person, with a locker and use of the hostel's facilities, as there are none for the camping area itself. The beach is silty and shallow here.

Avenida Uxmal All of Cancún's cheap hotels are in Ciudad Cancún and many are within a few blocks of the bus station. Go northwest on Avenida Uxmal and you'll come to the following cheap lodgings.

Hotel El Alux (☎ 84-06-62, 84-05-56), Avenida Uxmal 21, is only a block from the bus station. Air-con rooms with shower go for US$15 to US$20 single, US$20 to

US$25 double. An *alux*, by the way, is the Mayan version of a leprechaun.

Across from El Alux on the south side of Uxmal is the 38-room *Hotel Cotty* (☎ 84-13-19, 84-05-50), at No 44, a motel-style place that's more or less quiet. It's seen better days, but it's certainly cheap: rooms with shower and air-con cost US$15/20/25 a single/double/triple or quad. There's off-street parking.

A few steps farther along Uxmal is Calle Palmera and the *Hotel María Isabel* (☎ 84-90-15), Palmera 59, a tiny, clean place with a quieter location. Rooms with private shower and air-con cost US$18/22 a single/double. This is perhaps the best value close to the bus station.

From Avenida Uxmal, walk south along Avenida Yaxchilán and turn right after one block at Calle Punta Allen to find the quiet *Casa de Huéspedes Punta Allen* (☎ 84-02-25, 84-10-01), Punta Allen 8. This family-run guesthouse has several double rooms with bath and air-con for US$18 to US$22, light breakfast included.

Farther west along Uxmal, on the left side just before the corner with Avenida Chichén Itzá, stands the *Hotel Uxmal* (☎ 84-22-66, 84-23-55), Uxmal 111, a clean, family-run hostelry where US$24 will buy you a double room with fan and/or air-con, TV and off-street parking.

Avenidas Sunyaxchén & Tankah Staying here puts you close to the post office and Mercado 28 with its good, cheap eateries.

Just off Avenida Yaxchilán stands the *Hotel Hacienda Cancún* (☎ 84-36-72, fax 84-12-08), Sunyaxchén 39-40, on the right (north) side. It's popular with Mexican tour groups. For US$25 to US$32 (single or double) you get an air-con room with color TV and private bath, use of the hotel's pretty swimming pool and patio, and a good location.

Continue along Sunyaxchén to the post office and bear right onto Avenida Tankah. Watch on the right side of the street for the *Hotel Tankah* (☎ 84-44-46, 84-48-44), Tankah 69, charging US$18 for a double with fan, US$7 more with air-con.

Farther North Several cheap hotels are hidden away on quiet residential streets 1200 meters north of the bus terminal. Go north on Avenida Tulum past the large San Francisco de Asis store (on the right/east side), and just after the road narrows turn right on Calle 6 Oriente. (If you take a bus, get off opposite the big Plaza Cancún 2000 shopping center, which is on the left/west side of the street.) Go three short blocks east, then turn left onto Calle 7 Oriente, and the *Hotel Piña Hermanos* (☎ 84-21-50) is on the right-hand side. Rooms with fan and private bath on this quiet street cost US$10/14 a single/double. If it's full, look at the similarly priced *Hotel Mary Tere* (☎ 84-04-96) nearby.

Places to Stay – middle

Mid-range hotel rooms cost from US$30 to US$65 in the busy winter season, somewhat less during the summer. During the very slow times (late May to early June, October to mid-December), prices may be only half those quoted here, particularly if you haggle a bit. These hotels offer air-con rooms with private bath and color cable TV, a swimming pool, restaurant and perhaps some other amenities such as a bar, elevators and shuttle vans from the hotel to the beach.

Near the Bus Station Directly across from the bus station is the *Hotel Best Western Plaza Caribe* (☎ 84-13-77, in the USA 800-528-1234; fax 84-63-52), offering very comfortable air-con rooms and all the amenities for US$60 a double in summer, US$85 in winter.

Avenida Tulum Around the corner from the bus station on Avenida Tulum is the *Hotel Novotel* (☎ 84-29-99, fax 84-31-62), Tulum 75 (Apdo Postal 70). Rooms in the main building have air-con and cost US$30 to US$38, single or double; front rooms can be noisy. Rooms in cabañas behind the main building around the pool have fans only, are quiet, and cost US$22 to US$28. They have triples and quad rooms as well.

Across Avenida Tulum from the Novotel is the *Hotel Parador* (☎ 84-13-10, fax 84-97-12), Tulum 26, a modern building with 66 rooms, each with two double beds, costing US$30 to US$45.

The *Hotel Antillano* (☎ 84-15-32, fax 84-18-78), Calle Claveles just off Avenida Tulum, has 48 good guestrooms and all the mid-range services for US$35/50/65 a single/double/triple in winter.

Avenida Yaxchilán *Hotel Tropical Inn* (☎ 84-30-78, fax 84-34-78), Avenida Yaxchilán 31, corner of Jazmines, has 87 nice rooms with two double beds priced at US$35/50/65 a single/double/triple in winter. It's popular with foreign tour groups.

Across Yaxchilán from the Tropical Inn is the *Hotel Suites Caribe Internacional* (☎ 84-39-99, fax 84-19-93), Sunyaxchén 36 at Avenida Yaxchilán. The 80 rooms here include normal double rooms, but also junior suites with two beds, sofa, kitchenette with cooker and refrigerator, and a living room. Prices for doubles are similar to the Tropical Inn, with the suites a bit higher.

Places to Stay – top end

Cancún's top places range from comfortable but boring to luxurious full-service hostelries of an international standard. Prices range from US$90 to US$250 and up for a double room in winter. All the top places are located on the beach, many have vast grounds with rolling lawns of manicured grass, tropical gardens, swimming pools (virtually all with swim-up bars – a Cancún necessity) and facilities for sports such as tennis, handball, waterskiing and sailboarding. Some are constructed in whimsical fantasy styles with turrets, bulbous domes, minarets, dramatic glass canopies and other architectural megalomania. Guestrooms are air-con, and equipped with minibar and TV linked to satellite receivers for US programs.

To get the most advantageous price at any of these luxury hotels, sign up before you come for an inclusive tour package that includes lodging.

If you have not come with a group, you can find the best value for money at the following hotels on Boulevard Kulkulcán (listed from north to south). *Aquamarina Beach Hotel* (☎ 83-14-25, fax 83-17-51, Apdo Postal 751), Km 3.5, was built with tour groups of young adult sunlovers in mind. Rooms go for under US$100 in summer, US$135 in winter. Some rooms have kitchenettes and refrigerators.

Calinda Beach Cancún (☎ 83-16-00, 800-90000, in USA 800-221-2222; fax 83-18-57) at Km 4 facing the Playa Linda Marine Terminal, has a decor of red tiles, white stucco and modern muted colors, all with a light, airy feel. Rooms cost US$110 in summer, US$155 in winter.

Calinda Viva Cancún (☎ 83-08-00, 800-90000, in USA 800-221-2222; fax 83-20-87) at Km 8, has 210 rooms and rates very similar to the aforementioned Calinda Beach Cancún.

Hotel Aristos Cancún (☎ 83-00-11, in USA 800-527-4786; fax 83-00-78) at Km 9, has about the best rates in the neighborhood: US$90 double in summer, US$130 in winter, lunch and tax included.

If no rooms are available in those establishments, you can also look for good value at the following. At Km 8, *Fiesta Americana Cancún* (☎ 83-14-00, in the USA 800-343-7821) is an oddity, resembling nothing so much as an old-city streetscape, an appealing jumble of windows, balconies, roofs and other features.

Hyatt Regency Cancún (☎ 83-12-34, in the USA 800-233-1234; fax 83-16-94, hyattreg@cancun.rce.com.mx) at Km 8.5 is a gigantic cylinder with a lofty open court at its core and 300 guestrooms arranged around it. Situated right on Punta Cancún by the Centro de Convenciones, virtually all of its rooms have excellent views. The beach is right outside the building. Rates in winter are US$185 to US$245, in summer US$160 to US$205, the higher rates being for Regency Club rooms.

Hyatt Cancún Caribe (☎ 83-00-44, in USA 800-233-1234; fax 83-15-14), Km 10.5, has a good variety of accommodations.

Its 198 rooms and suites include ground-level rooms with private terraces, upper-level rooms with fine sea views, and Regency Club villas surrounding their own clubhouse, with private pools and Jacuzzi. Rooms and villas cost US$205 to US$242 in summer, US$286 to US$331 in winter.

At Km 14, *Cancún Palace* (☎ 85 05 33, in USA 800-346-8225; fax 5-15-93) works extra hard to offer good value to guests. The 421 rooms and suites have all the amenities you'd expect, including balconies with water views and all the services.

Places to Eat

Nowhere in Mexico have we found more mediocre food at higher prices than in Cancún. If you don't expect too much from Cancún's restaurants, you'll be pleasantly surprised when you get a memorable meal (and you will have at least a few).

Budget As usual, market eateries provide the biggest portions at the lowest prices. Ciudad Cancún's market, near the post office, is set back from the street in a building that's emblazoned with the name Mercado Municipal Artículo 115 Constitucional. Called simply Mercado 28 (that's 'Mercado Veinte y Ocho') by the locals, it has shops selling fresh vegetables, fruits and prepared meals.

In the second courtyard in from the street are the eateries: *Restaurant Margely, Cocina Familiar Económica Chulum, Cocina La Chaya*, etc. These are pleasant, simple eateries with tables beneath awnings and industrious señoras cooking away behind the counter. Most are open for breakfast, lunch and dinner, and all offer full meals (comidas corridas) for as little as US$2.50, and sandwiches for less.

El Rincón Yucateco, Avenida Uxmal 24, across from the Hotel Cotty, serves good Yucatecan food. Service is from 7 am to 10 pm every day. Main courses cost US$2.50 to US$4.

El Tacolote, on Avenida Cobá across from the big red IMSS hospital, is brightly lit and attractive with dark wood benches.

Tacos – a dozen types – are priced from US$1 to US$3. El Tacolote (the name is a pun on taco and *tecolote*, owl) is open from 7 to 11.30 am for breakfast, then till 10 pm for tacos.

Chiffer's, in the big San Francisco de Asis department store on the east side of Avenida Tulum, has welcome air-conditioning. You can spend as much as US$13 for a full, heavy meal with dessert and drink, but most people keep their bill below US$6. It's open from 7 am to 11 pm daily.

Middle Most of the moderately priced restaurants are located in the city center. If you're willing to spend between US$12 and US$20 for dinner you can eat fairly well in Cancún.

The *Restaurant El Pescador* (☎ 84-26-73), Tulipanes 28, has been serving dependably good meals since the early days of Cancún. The menu lists lime soup and fish ceviche for starters, then charcoal-grilled fish, red snapper in garlic sauce and beef shish kebab. El Pescador is open for lunch and dinner (closed Monday).

Rolandi's Restaurant-Bar (☎ 84-40-47), Avenida Cobá 12, between Tulum and Nader just off the southern roundabout, is an attractive Italian eatery open every day. It serves elaborate one-person pizzas (US$5 to US$10), spaghetti plates and more substantial dishes of veal and chicken. Watch out for the high drink prices. Hours are 1 pm to midnight (Sunday, 4 pm to midnight).

Every visitor to Cancún makes the pilgrimage to *Los Almendros* (☎ 87-13-32), Avenida Bonampak at Calle Sayil across from the bullring, the local incarnation of Yucatán's most famous restaurant. Started in Ticul in 1962, Los Almendros set out to serve *platillos campesinos para los dzules* (country food for the bourgeoisie, or townfolk). The chefs at Los Almendros (The Almond Trees) claim to have created pocchuc, a dish of succulent pork cooked with onion and served in a tangy sauce of sour orange or lime. If you don't know what to order, try the *combinado yucateco*, or

Yucatecan combination plate. A full meal here costs about US$16 per person. Come any day for lunch or dinner.

Restaurant 100% Natural (☎ 84-36-17), Avenida Sunyaxchén at Yaxchilán, is an airy café. Though the menu lists several natural food items such as fruit salads and juices, green salads and yogurt, they also serve hamburgers, enchiladas, wine and beer at moderate prices. There are branches in the Plaza Terramar (☎ 83-11-80) and Kukulcán Plaza (☎ 85-29-04) shopping centers in the Zona Hotelera.

Top End Traditionally, Mexican restaurants have followed the European scheme of simple decor and elaborate food. Cancún, however, caters mostly to the sort of sun-baked North Americans who seem to prefer simple food served in elaborate surroundings. Half the menus in town are composed of such grill-me items as steak, jumbo shrimp, fish fillet and lobster tail. Thus Cancún's expensive restaurants are elaborate, with rhapsodic menu prose, lots of tropical gardens, mirrors, waterfalls, paraphernalia, even fish tanks and aviaries of exotic birds. The food can be good, forgettable or execrable. If the last, at least you'll have pleasant music and something to look at as you gnaw and gag.

Perico's (☎ /fax 84-31-52), Avenida Yaxchilán 71 at Calle Marañón, is quintessential Cancún, a huge thatched structure stuffed with stereotypical Mexican icons: saddles, enormous sombreros, baskets, bullwhips, etc. An army of señores and señoritas dressed in Hollywood-Mexican costumes doesn't serve so much as 'dramatize your dining experience.' In other words, if you're in the mood for dinner à la Disney, Perico's will do. The menu is heavy with macho fare: filet mignon, jumbo shrimp, lobster, barbecued spareribs. After the show, fork over US$20 to US$30 per person to pay your bill. It's supposedly open from noon to 2 am, but may in fact serve only dinner.

One exceptional place is *Rosa Mexicano* (☎ 84-63-13), a long-standing favorite at Calle Claveles 4 in Ciudad Cancún. This is

the place to go for unusual Mexican dishes in a pleasant hacienda decor. There are some concessions to Cancún such as tortilla soup and filete tampiqueña, but also squid sautéed with three chiles, garlic and scallions and shrimp in a *pipián* sauce (ground pumpkin seeds with spices). Dinner, served daily from 5 to 11 pm, goes for US$20 to US$30.

Another dependable favorite (since 1977) is *La Habichuela* (☎ 84-31-58), Margaritas 25, just off Parque Las Palapas in a residential neighborhood of Ciudad Cancún. The menu tends to dishes easily comprehended and easily perceived as elegant: shish kebab flambé, lobster in champagne sauce, jumbo shrimp and beef tampiqueña: US$25 to US$38 per person for dinner. Hours are 1 pm to about 11 pm, every day of the year. La Habichuela ('LAH-b'CHWEH-lah') means The Stringbean.

Entertainment

Most of the nightlife is loud and bibulous, as befits a supercharged beach resort. If the theme restaurants don't do it for you, take a dinner cruise on a mock pirate ship.

The local Ballet Folklórico performs some evenings at various halls for about US$40 per person, which includes dinner. The dancers come on at 8.30 pm. Don't expect the finesse and precision of the performances in Mexico City.

Spectator Sports

Bullfights (four bulls) are held each Wednesday afternoon at 3.30 pm in the Plaza de Toros at the southern end of Avenida Bonampak, across the street from the Restaurant Los Almendros, about one km from the center of town. Tickets cost about US$15 and can be purchased from any travel agency.

Getting There & Away

Air Cancún's international airport is the busiest in southeastern Mexico. Upon arrival, don't change money until after you've passed through customs and immigration as the rate of exchange is terrible. Then, if you really want the best rate, walk two minutes to the *departures* area and look for inconspicuous exchange windows in back corners – they have the best rates.

The arrivals area has lockers big enough for a briefcase or small suitcase, but not for a stuffed backpack; US$3 for 24 hours.

For information on transport to or from the airport see the following Getting Around section.

Cancún is served by many direct international flights (see the Getting There & Away chapter), and the main domestic airlines, Aeroméxico and Mexicana, link it to Mexico City and other major Mexican cities. Aerocaribe offers a special fare deal called the Mayapass, good for a series of flights at reduced prices. Aerocaribe has flights to points in Yucatán and beyond, in small and medium-sized planes at these regular prices (one-way): Chetumal US$60, Cozumel US$30, Mérida US$50, Mexico City US$120, and Villahermosa US$90. Excursion fares offer better deals than these one-way fares.

Aviacsa flies from Cancún to Mérida, Mexico City, Oaxaca, Tapachula, Tuxtla Gutiérrez, Villahermosa and points in Guatemala.

Aviateca, Guatemala's national airline, runs flights from Cancún to Flores (for Tikal), and onward to Guatemala City, on Monday, Wednesday, Saturday and Sunday, returning on Tuesday, Friday, Saturday and Sunday.

Airline contact addresses are:

Aerocancún
   Oasis building, Boulevard Kukulcán (☎ 83-24-75)
Aerocaribe/Aerocozumel
   Avenida Tulum 29, Plaza América, at the roundabout intersection with Avenida Uxmal (☎ 84-20-00; at the airport ☎ /fax 86-00-83)
Aeroméxico
   Avenida Cobá 80, between Tulum and Bonampak (☎ 84-35-71, fax 84-70-05)
American Airlines
   Cancún airport (☎ 86-00-55, fax 86-01-64)
Aviacsa
   Avenida Cobá 37 (☎ 87-42-14, fax 84-65-99)
Aviateca
   Plaza México, Avenida Tulum 200 (☎ 84-39-38, fax 84-33-28)

Continental
   Cancún airport (☎ 86-00-06, fax 86-00-07)
LACSA
   Edificio Atlantis, Avenida Bonampak at Avenida Cobá (☎ 87-31-01)
Mexicana
   Avenida Cobá 39 (☎ 87-44-44)
Northwest
   Cancún airport (☎ 86-00-46)
TAESA
   Avenida Yaxchilán 31 (☎ 87-43-14, fax 87-33-28)

Bus The confusing bus station on Avenida Uxmal just west of Avenida Tulum has two separate parts under the same roof; look in both. Companies include Autobuses de Oriente (ADO), Autotransportes de Oriente, Transportes de Lujo Línea Dorada (a mainly 2nd-class line despite its pompous name), Autotransportes del Sur, Autobuses del Noroeste and Autobuses del Centro. Services are 2nd, 1st or any of several deluxe flavors.

Across from the bus station entrance is the ticket office of Playa Express, which runs shuttle buses down the Caribbean coast to Tulum and Felipe Carrillo Puerto at least every 30 minutes all day, stopping at major towns and points of interest along the way.

Here are some major routes (daily):

Chetumal – 382 km, six hours, US$10 to US$14; 23 buses
Chichén Itzá – 205 km, two to 3½ hours; 10 buses, US$4.50 to US$7
Mérida – 320 km, four to six hours, US$7 to US$12; buses at least every half hour; Super Expresso buses take less than four hours
Mexico City (TAPO) – 1772 km, 22 hours, US$48 to US$57; six buses daily
Playa del Carmen – 65 km, one hour, US$1.75; Playa Express buses every 30 minutes; others 12 times daily
Puerto Morelos – 36 km, 40 minutes, US$1; Playa Express buses every 30 minutes; others 12 times daily
Ticul – 395 km, six to eight hours, US$10; five buses by Línea Dorada
Tizimín – 212 km, three hours, US$4; six daily via Valladolid
Tulum – 132 km, two hours, US$3 to US$4; Playa Express buses every 30 minutes; other buses about every two hours

Valladolid – 160 km, 1½ to two hours, US$4 to US$8; same as Mérida
Villahermosa – 915 km, 11 hours, US$28; three by ADO

Getting Around

To/From the Airport Orange-and-beige airport vans (Transporte Terrestre, US$7.50) monopolize the trade to/from the airport, charging taxi fare for a van ride with other travelers. If you want taxi service (ie, the van or car to yourself, direct to your hotel), the cost is an outrageous US$25 (just a bit less than airfare to Cozumel). A taxi back to the airport from Ciudad Cancún costs about US$8.

The route into town is invariably via Punta Nizuc and north up Isla Cancún along Boulevard Kukulcán, passing all of the luxury beach-front hotels before reaching the youth hostel and Ciudad Cancún. If your hotel is in Ciudad Cancún, the ride to your hotel may take as long as 45 minutes.

If you walk out of the airport and follow the access road, you can often flag down a taxi which will take you for less because the driver is no longer subject to the expensive regulated airport fares. Walk the two km to the highway and you can flag a passing bus, which is very cheap.

To return to the airport you must take a taxi, or hop off a southbound bus at the airport junction and walk the two km to the terminal.

Bus Although it's possible to walk most everywhere in Ciudad Cancún, to get to the Zona Hotelera, catch a Ruta 1 'Hoteles-Downtown' local bus heading southward along Avenida Tulum. The fare depends upon distance traveled, and ranges from US$0.50 to US$1.25.

To reach Puerto Juárez and the Isla Mujeres ferries, take a Ruta 13 bus ('Pto Juárez' or 'Punta Sam').

Taxi Cancún's taxis do not have meters so you must haggle over fares. Generally, the fare between Ciudad Cancún and Punta Cancún (Hyatt, Camino Real and Krystal hotels and the Centro de Convenciones) is

US$4 or US$5. To the airport costs US$8 (from Ciudad Cancún) to US$12 (from Punta Cancún). To Puerto Juárez you'll pay about US$3.

Ferry There are frequent passenger ferries from Puerto Juárez to Isla Mujeres (see that section for details). Local buses (Ruta 13, US$0.60) take about 20 minutes from stops on Avenida Tulum to the Puerto Juárez ferry dock. Taxis cost about US$3. See the Isla Mujeres section for more details.

ISLA MUJERES

pop 13,500; ☎ 987

Isla Mujeres (Island of Women) has a reputation as a backpackers' Cancún, a place where one can escape the high-energy, high-priced mega-resort for the laid-back life of a tropical isle – at bargain prices. Though this was true for many years, it is less true today. Cancún has been so successful that its version of the good life has spilled over onto its neighboring island.

The chief attribute of Isla Mujeres is its relaxed social life in a tropical setting with surrounding waters that are turquoise blue and bathtub warm. If you have been doing some hard traveling through Mexico, you will find many travelers you met along the way taking it easy here. Others make it the site of a one- to two-week holiday.

History

Although it is said by some that the Island of Women got its name because Spanish buccaneers kept their lovers here while they plundered galleons and pillaged ports, a less romantic but still intriguing explanation is probably more accurate. Juan de Grijalva's expedition stopped at the island twice in 1518. Hernández de Córdoba's ships were forced by high winds into the island's harbor in the same year. When the crew reconnoitered, they found a Mayan ceremonial site filled with clay female figurines. Cortés, stopping by a year later, destroyed the idols, and picked up Jerónimo de Aguilar, who had been shipwrecked nearby in 1511. Having lived among the Maya for eight years, Aguilar

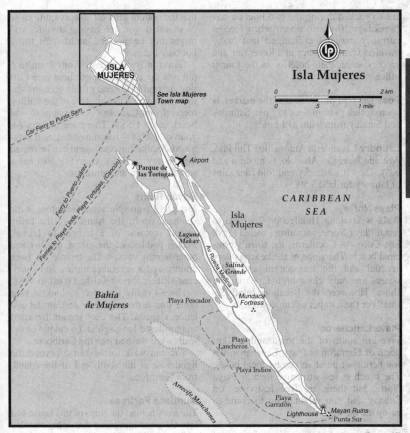

Isla Mujeres

could speak their language, and proved invaluable to Cortés as an interpreter.

Today, some archaeologists believe that the island was a stopover for the Maya en route to worship their goddess of fertility, Ixchel, on the island of Cozumel. The clay idols are thought to represent the goddess.

Orientation

The island is about eight km long and anywhere from 300 to 800 meters wide. The good snorkeling and some of the better swimming beaches are on the southern part of the island along the western shore; the

eastern shore is washed by the open sea and the surf is dangerous. The ferry docks, the town and the most popular sand beach (Playa Norte) are at the northern tip of the island.

Information

Tourist Office The Delegación Estatal de Turismo (State Tourist Department, ☎ 7-03-16) faces the basketball court in the main plaza.

Money The island's Banco del Atlantico at Juárez 5 and Banco Serfin, at Juárez 3, are so packed during the two hours a day (weekdays 10 am to noon) when foreign currency may be exchanged that many travelers change money at a lower rate at a grocery store, their hotel or at the tourist office.

Post The post office, next to the market, is open weekdays from 8 am to 7 pm, Saturday and Sunday from 9 am to 1 pm.

Laundry Lavandería Automática Tim Phó, Avenida Juárez at Abasolo, is modern and busy. They'll wash, dry and fold four kilos of laundry for US$3.50.

Playa Norte

Walk west along Hidalgo or Guerrero to reach Playa Norte, sometimes called Playa Los Cocos or Cocoteros, the town's principal beach. The slope of the beach is very gradual and the transparent and calm waters are only chest-high far from the shore. However, the beach is relatively small for the number of sunseekers.

Playa Lancheros

Five km south of the town and 1.5 km north of Garrafón is Playa Lancheros, the southernmost point served by local buses. The beach is less attractive than at Playa Norte, but there are free festivities on Sunday and you might want to come to enjoy the music.

Playa Garrafón

Although the waters are translucent and the fish abundant, Garrafón is perhaps a bit overrated. Hordes of daytrippers from Cancún fill the water most of the day, so you are more often ogling fellow snorkelers than aquatic life. Furthermore, the reef is virtually dead, which makes it less likely to inflict cuts but reduces its color and the intricacy of its formations.

The water can be extremely choppy, sweeping you into jagged areas. When the water is running fast, snorkeling is a hassle and can even be dangerous. Those without strong swimming skills should be advised

that the bottom falls off steeply quite close to shore; if you are having trouble, you might not be noticed amidst all those bobbing heads.

Garrafón is open daily from 8 am to 5 pm and the earlier you get here (see Getting Around at the end of this section), the more time you will have free of the milling mobs from Cancún. Admission to the beach costs US$4. There are lockers for your valuables – recommended as a safeguard. Snorkeling equipment can be rented for the day at US$8. Garrafón also has a small aquarium and museum.

Mayan Ruins

Just past Parque Nacional Garrafón, at the southern tip of the island, are the badly ruined remains of a temple to Ixchel, Mayan goddess of the moon, fertility and other worthy causes. The temple has been crumbling for several centuries, and Hurricane Gilbert almost finished it off in 1988.

There's really little left to look at here other than a fine sea view and, in the distance, Cancún. The clay female figurines were pilfered long ago and a couple of the walls were washed into the Caribbean.

You can walk to the ruins, beyond the lighthouse at the south end of the island, from Garrafón.

Mundaca Fortress

The story behind the ruins of this house and fort are more intriguing than what remains of them. In the 1600s, a slave-trading pirate, Fermín Antonio Mundaca de Marechaja, fell in love with a visiting Spanish beauty. To win her, the rogue built a two-story mansion complete with gardens and graceful archways as well as a small fortress to defend it. While Mundaca built the house, the object of his affection's ardor cooled and she married another islander. Brokenhearted, Mundaca died and his house, fortress and garden fell into disrepair.

The Mundaca fortress (Fuerte de Mundaca) is east of the main road near Playa Lancheros, about four km south of the town. Look for signs.

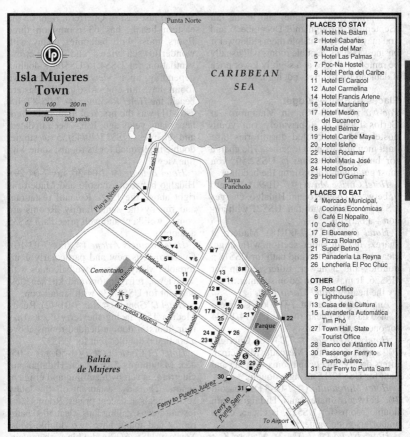

Isla Mujeres Town

Punta Norte

CARIBBEAN SEA

0   100   200 m
0   100   200 yards

Zazil-Ha

Playa Norte

Playa Pancholo

Av Carlos Lazo

Guerrero

Hidalgo

Juárez

López Mateos

Matamoros

Abasolo

Madero

Av Rueda Medina

Cementerio

Bahía de Mujeres

Pedestrian Mall

Parque

Morelos

Bravo

Allende

Uribe

Ferry to Puerto Juárez

Ferry to Punta Sam

To Airport

PLACES TO STAY
1   Hotel Na-Balam
2   Hotel Cabañas
     María del Mar
5   Hotel Las Palmas
7   Poc-Na Hostel
8   Hotel Perla del Caribe
11 Hotel El Caracol
12 Autel Carmelina
14 Hotel Francis Arlene
16 Hotel Marcianito
17 Hotel Mesón
     del Bucanero
18 Hotel Belmar
19 Hotel Caribe Maya
20 Hotel Isleño
22 Hotel Rocamar
23 Hotel María José
24 Hotel Osorio
29 Hotel D'Gomar

PLACES TO EAT
4   Mercado Municipal,
     Cocinas Económicas
6   Café El Nopalito
10 Café Cito
17 El Bucanero
21 Pizza Rolandi
25 Panadería La Reyna
26 Lonchería El Poc Chuc

OTHER
3   Post Office
9   Lighthouse
13 Casa de la Cultura
15 Lavandería Automática
     Tim Phó
27 Town Hall, State
     Tourist Office
28 Banco del Atlántico ATM
30 Passenger Ferry to
     Puerto Juárez
31 Car Ferry to Punta Sam

Scuba Diving

Diving to see sunken ships and beautiful reefs in the crystalline waters of the Caribbean is a memorable way to pass time on Isla Mujeres. If you're a qualified diver, you'll need a license, rental equipment and a boat to take you to the good spots. Arrangements made at any of the island's several dive shops range from US$50 to US$100 depending upon how many tanks you use up.

A regular stop on the dive boat's route is the Sleeping Shark Caves, about five km north of the island and at 23 meters' depth,

where the otherwise dangerous creatures are alleged to be lethargically nonlethal due to the low oxygen content of the caves' waters. Veteran divers say it's foolish to test the theory: you could become shark bait. It's far better to explore the fine reefs off the island like Los Manchones, La Bandera, Cuevones or Chital.

Places to Stay

During the busy seasons (late December to March and midsummer), many island hotels are booked solid by noon; at these times prices are also highest. Prices are lower in late spring (May to June) and in the fall (September through mid-December), and you may be able to haggle them still lower if business is slack. Double rooms will usually be rented as singles at a slightly lower price if demand for rooms is not high.

Places to Stay – budget

Poc-Na (☎ 7-00-90), on Matamoros at Carlos Lazo, is a privately run youth hostel. The fan-cooled dormitories take both men and women together. The charge for bunk and bedding is US$2.50; you must put down a deposit on the bedding.

Hotel Caribe Maya (☎ 7-01-90), Madero 9, between Guerrero and Hidalgo, charges US$16 a double with fan, US$21 with air-con – a bargain.

Hotel Osorio (☎ 7-00-18), Madero at Juárez, has an older section with huge, clean rooms with fan and bath for US$18 a double; and a newer, tidier section for US$26. It may be closed in summer. If so, try the nearby *Hotel María José*.

Autel Carmelina (☎ 7-00-06), Guerrero 4, also has OK cheap rooms: US$14/17/24 for one/two/three beds.

Hotel Las Palmas (☎ 7-04-16), Guerrero 20, across from the Mercado Municipal, offers dreary but cheap rooms with fan and bath for US$12/15 a single/double.

Hotel Marcianito (☎ 7-01-11), Abasolo 10, between Juárez and Hidalgo, with double rooms for US$12, is cheap, clean and offers good value.

Hotel Isleño (☎ 7-03-02), Madero 8 at the corner of Guerrero, has rooms with ceiling fans and good cross-ventilation, without/with bath for US$14/20 a double. There's a shared bathroom for every three guestrooms. Get a room on the upper floor if you can.

Places to Stay – middle

Moderately priced rooms have private baths, and usually (but not always) air-con, perhaps a balcony and/or a nice sea view, restaurant, bar and swimming pool.

The *Hotel Perla del Caribe* (☎ 7-04-44, in USA 800-258-6454; fax 7-00-11), on

Madero just east of Guerrero, right on the eastern beach, has 63 rooms on three floors, most with balconies, many with wonderful sea views and good cross-ventilation, for US$4 to US$65 a double, depending upon view; most expensive rooms have air-con. Also on the eastern beach, the *Hotel Rocamar* (☎ 7-05-87, fax 7-01-01) was the first real hotel to be built here many years ago. It has been updated, and charges US$35/40/45/55 a single/double/triple/quad for its rooms, some with fine views.

Hotel Belmar (☎ 7-04-30, fax 7-04-29), Hidalgo between Abasolo and Madero, is right above the Pizza Rolandi restaurant and run by the same family. Rooms are comfy, well kept and well priced at US$35 a double.

Hotel Francis Arlene (☎ /fax 7-03-10), Guerrero 7, is new and particularly comfortable. Many rooms have balconies with sea views, refrigerators and kitchenettes, and rent for US$28/34 with fan/air-con.

Hotel D'Gomar (☎ /fax 7-01-42), Rueda Medina 150, facing the ferry docks, has four floors of double-bedded rooms above a boutique; doubles rent for US$32.

Hotel El Caracol (☎ 7-01-50, fax 7-05-47), Matamoros 5, between Hidalgo and Guerrero, is run by a smiling and efficient señora. The tidy restaurant off the lobby serves meals at decent prices. Rooms have insect screens, ceiling fans, clean tiled bathrooms and many have two double beds. You pay US$26/32 a double with fan/air-con. Watch out for disco noise from across the street. *Hotel Mesón del Bucanero* (☎ 7-02-10, fax 7-01-26), Hidalgo 11, between Abasolo and Madero, is above the restaurant of the same name. Rooms are pleasant enough at US$25 to US$28 a double.

Places to Stay – top end

Hotel Na-Balam (☎ 7-02-79, fax 7-05-93, nabalam@cancun.rce.com.mx), Calle Zazil-Ha 118, faces Playa Norte at the northern tip of the island. Most of the 12 spacious junior suites have fabulous sea views. There are numerous nice touches, such as the bathroom vanities made of colorful travertine. Prices for suites with balcony are US$105 to US$120 a double in season, US$85 to US$105 off season.

Near Na-Balam is *Hotel Cabañas María del Mar* (☎ 7-01-79, in USA 800-223-5695; fax 7-02-13), on both sides of Avenida Carlos Lazo, also right on the beach. The 12 cabañas and 51 hotel rooms are priced from US$55 to US$61 a double in low season, to US$83 to US$90 in the winter season, light breakfast included. There are many services, such as a restaurant and swimming pool.

Places to Eat

Beside the market are several *cocinas económicas* (economical kitchens) serving simple but tasty and filling meals at the best prices on the island. Prices are not marked, so ask before you order. Hours are usually (and approximately) 7 am to 6 pm.

Another cocina económica is *Lonchería El Poc Chuc*, a tiny hole-in-the-wall eatery on Juárez at Madero, offering a ham-and-eggs breakfast for a mere US$2, poc chuc and other meals for US$2.75.

Super Betino, the food store on the plaza, has a little cafeteria serving tacos and fruit plates for US$0.75, and sometimes cheap breakfasts.

Panadería La Reyna, on Madero at Juárez, is the place for breakfast buns, picnic breads and snacks.

Most of the island's restaurants fall into the middle category. Depending upon what you order, breakfast goes for US$2.50 to US$4, lunch or dinner for US$7 to US$15 per person, unless you order lobster.

Café Cito, a small place at Juárez and Matamoros, offers croissants, fruit, 10 varieties of crepes and the best coffee in town. The menu is in English and German. Come for breakfast (8 am to noon, about US$5), or supper (6 to 10 pm, about US$10).

Café El Nopalito, on Guerrero near Matamoros, serves delicious set breakfasts from 8 am to noon and daily special plates for US$5 to US$7, specializing in healthful but fancy food.

El Bucanero (☎ 7-02-36), Avenida Hidalgo 11 between Abasolo and Madero, has a long menu: breakfast omelets of ham and cheese (US$3.50), fried chicken or fish (US$5) and Mexican traditional foods (enchiladas, tacos, etc) for about the same. Besides the usual, they serve offbeat things like asparagus au gratin with whole-meal bread.

Pizza Rolandi (☎ 7-04-30), across the street, serves pizzas and calzones cooked in a wood-fired oven, and pastas with various sauces, for US$5 to US$9 per person. The menu includes fresh salads, fish and some Italian specialties. Hours are 1 pm to midnight daily, 6 pm to midnight on Sunday.

Entertainment

The first place to go is the main plaza, where there's always something to watch (a soccer match, a basketball or volleyball game, an impromptu concert or serenade) and lots of people watching it.

As for discos, Tequila Video Bar (☎ 7-00-19), at the corner of Matamoros and Hidalgo, is a favorite with locals that draws foreigners as well. Hours are 9 pm to 3 am every day except Monday.

Getting There & Away

There are four points of embarkation from the mainland by ferry to Isla Mujeres, 11 km off the coast.

Puerto Juárez From Ciudad Cancún, take a Ruta 13 bus heading north on Avenida Tulum (US$0.30) or a taxi (US$2.50) to Puerto Juárez, about three km north.

Transportes Marítimos Magaña operates boats every 30 minutes from 6 to 8.30 am; and every 15 minutes from 8.30 am to 8.30 pm, for a fare of US$2.25 per person one way.

The boats named *Sultana del Mar* and *Blanca Beatriz* run about every hour from 7 am to 5.30 pm, taking 45 minutes to Isla, for US$1 per person.

Punta Sam Car ferries (which also take passengers) depart from Punta Sam, about five km north of Avenida Tulum and 3.5 km north of Puerto Juárez. The car ferry is more stable but less frequent and slower, taking 45 minutes to an hour to reach the island.

Ferries leave Punta Sam at 8 and 11 am, and 2.45, 5.30 and 8.15 pm. Departures from Isla Mujeres are at 6.30 and 9.30 am, and 12.45, 4.15 and 7.15 pm. Passengers pay US$1.50; a car costs US$6 to US$8. If you're taking a car, be sure to get to the dock an hour or so before departure time. Put your car in line and buy your ticket early.

Playa Linda Terminal Four times daily, The Shuttle (☎ 98-84-63-33, 98-84-66-56) departs from Playa Linda on Isla Cancún for Isla Mujeres. Voyages from Playa Linda are at 9 and 11.15 am, 4 and 7 pm; return voyages depart Isla Mujeres at 10 am, 12.30, 5 and 8 pm. The round-trip fare is US$14, but this includes free beer and soft drinks on board.

Show up at the Playa Linda Marine Terminal, Boulevard Kukulcán km 5 on Isla Cancún, just west of the bridge, between the Aquamarina Beach and Calinda Cancún hotels, at least 30 minutes before departure so you'll have time to buy your ticket and get a good seat on the boat.

Playa Tortugas Isla Mujeres Shuttle (☎ 98-83-34-48) departs from Fat Tuesday's on Playa Tortugas beach at 9.15 and 11.30 am, and 1.45 and 3.45 pm for Isla, returning from Isla at 10 am and 12.30, 2.30 and 5 pm, for US$10 per person each way.

Getting Around

Bus & Taxi By local bus from the market or dock, you can get within 1.5 km of Garrafón; the terminus is Playa Lancheros. The personnel at Poc-Na youth hostel can give you an idea of the bus' erratic schedule. Locals in league with taxi drivers may tell you the bus doesn't exist.

If you walk to Garrafón, bring drinking water – it's a hot, two-hour, six-km walk. By taxi, it costs about US$2 to Garrafón, just over US$1 to Playa Lancheros. Rates are set by the municipal government and

are posted at the ferry dock, though the sign is frequently defaced by the taxi drivers.

Bicycle & Moped Bicycles can be rented from a number of shops on the island, including Sport Bike, on the corner of Juárez and Morelos, a block from the ferry docks. Before you rent, compare prices and the condition of the bikes in a few shops; arrive early in the day to get one of the better bikes. The costs are US$3 to US$5 for four hours, only a bit more for a full day; you'll be asked to plunk down a deposit of US$8 or so.

When renting mopeds, shop around, compare prices and look for new or newer machines in good condition, full gas tanks and reasonable deposits. Cost per hour is usually US$5 or US$6 with a two-hour minimum, US$22 all day, or even cheaper by the week. Shops away from the busiest streets tend to have better prices, but not necessarily better equipment.

When riding, remember that far more people are seriously injured on motorbikes and the like than in cars. Your enemies are inexperience, speed, sand, wet or oily roads and other people on motorbikes. Don't forget to slather yourself with sun block before you take off. Be sure to do your hands, feet, face and neck thoroughly, as these will get the most sun.

ISLA CONTOY BIRD SANCTUARY

You can take an excursion from Isla Mujeres by boat to tiny Isla Contoy, a national bird sanctuary (Reserva Especial de la Biosfera Isla Contoy), about 25 km north of Isla Mujeres. It's a treasure trove for bird watchers, with an abundance of brown pelicans, olive cormorants and red-pouched frigates, as well as frequent visits by flamingos and herons. There is good snorkeling both en route and just off Contoy.

Getting There & Away

For a one-day excursion (about US$30 per person), ask at the Sociedad Cooperativa Transporte Turística 'Isla Mujeres' (☎ 987-7-02-74) on Avenida Rueda Medina to the north of the ferry docks.

ISLA HOLBOX

If you're looking to be close to nature, Isla Holbox ('HOHL-bosh') might appeal to you, but note that the most basic facilities are in short supply and the beaches are not Cancún-perfect strips of clean, air-con sand. To enjoy Isla Holbox, you must be willing to rough it.

The 25-km by three-km island has sands that run on and on, as well as tranquil waters where you can wade out quite a distance before the sea reaches shoulder level. Moreover, Isla Holbox is magic for shell collectors, with a galaxy of shapes and colors. The fishing families of the island are friendly – unjaded by encounters with exotic tourists or the frenetic pace of the urban mainland.

However, the seas are not the translucent turquoise of the Quintana Roo beach sites, because here the Caribbean waters mingle with those of the darker Gulf. Seaweed can create silty waters near shore at some parts of the beach. While there are big plans to develop Isla Holbox one day, at the time of writing there is only one modest hotel, the aptly named *Hotel Flamingo* (with doubles for US$12) and a few snack shops. Most travelers camp or stay in spartan rooms rented from locals.

Getting There & Away

To reach Isla Holbox, take the ferry from the unappealing port village of Chiquilá on Quintana Roo's north coast. Buses make the 2½-hour trip three times a day from Valladolid to Chiquilá (US$5) and in theory the ferry is supposed to wait for them. However, it may not wait for a delayed bus or may even leave early (!) should the captain feel so inclined. If you're coming from Cancún, you'll probably need to change buses at the highway junction to Chiquilá.

It is therefore recommended that you reach Chiquilá as early as possible. The ferry is supposed to depart for the island at 8 am and 3 pm, and takes an hour. Ferries return to Chiquila at 2 and 5 pm. The cost is US$2.50.

Try not to get stuck in Chiquilá, as it is a tiny, fairly dismal place with no hotels, no decent camping and very disappointing food.

PUERTO MORELOS

pop 600; ☎ *987*

Puerto Morelos, 34 km south of Cancún, is a sleepy fishing village known principally for its car ferry to Cozumel. There is a good budget hotel here and travelers who have reason to spend the night here find it refreshingly free of tourists. A handful of scuba divers come to explore the splendid reef 600 meters offshore, reachable by boat.

Only a few km from the town, just off the highway, the Jardín Botánico Dr Alfredo Barrera gives you a look at the flora (and also some fauna) of the Yucatán peninsula for US$3 per person between 9 am and 5 pm daily.

Places to Stay & Eat

The *Posada Amor* (☎ 1-00-33, fax 1-01-78), Apdo Postal 806, 77580 Cancún, south of the center, is the longtime lodging here. Rooms with fan, shared bathroom and a double bed are expensive at US$22, or US$28 with two beds, single or double. Meals are served.

Hotel Hacienda Morelos (☎ /fax 1-00-15), 150 meters south of the plaza on the waterfront, has nice sea-view, sea-breeze rooms for US$50, single or double, and a decent restaurant called El Mesón as well.

Farther to the south beyond the ferry terminal, *Rancho Libertad* (☎ 1-01-81, in USA 800-305-5225, 800-730-4322) has several small two-story thatched bungalows with a guestroom on each floor. Upstairs rooms are priced at US$65, downstairs US$55, single or double, all with private bath, buffet breakfast included. Lower rates are offered when it's not busy. Scuba diving and snorkeling gear is available for rent, as are bicycles.

The *Caribbean Reef Club* (☎ 1-01-91, in USA 800-322-6286; fax 1-01-90), right next to the aforementioned Rancho Libertad, is a beautiful, very comfortable, quiet resort hotel right on the beach. Lots of water sports activities and helpful owners are the bonuses when you pay the rates: US$110 to US$140 from mid-December to late April, about 30% cheaper in summer.

Right next door to Hacienda Morelos is *Las Palmeras*, a good restaurant, though the best is *Los Pelícanos*, just off the southeast corner of the plaza.

Getting There & Away

Playa Express buses running between Cancún and Playa del Carmen drop you on the highway, two km west of the center of Puerto Morelos. All 2nd-class and many 1st-class buses stop at Puerto Morelos coming from, or en route to, Cancún, 36 km (45 minutes) away.

The car ferry *(transbordador*; ☎ in Cozumel 987-2-09-50, 987-2-09-50) to Cozumel leaves Puerto Morelos at noon on Tuesday, at 8 am on Monday and Wednesday, and at 6 am on other days. Departure times are subject to change from season to season, and according to the weather.

Unless you plan to stay for awhile on Cozumel, it's hardly worth shipping your vehicle. You must get in line up to 12 hours before departure time and hope there's enough space on the ferry for you. Fare for the 2½ to four-hour voyage is US$30 per car, US$4.50 per person.

Departure from Cozumel is from the dock in front of the Hotel Sol Caribe, south of town along the shore road.

PLAYA DEL CARMEN

pop 20,000; ☎ 987

For decades Playa was just a simple fishing village on the coast opposite Cozumel. With the construction of Cancún, however, the number of travelers roaming this part of Yucatán increased exponentially. Now Playa has taken over from Cozumel as the preferred resort town in the area. Playa's beaches are better and nightlife groovier than Cozumel's, and the reef diving is just as good. On the beaches, tops are optional everywhere; nudity is optional about a km north of Playa town center.

What's to do in Playa? Hang out. Swim. Dive. Stroll the beach. Get some sun. Catch the Playa Express shuttle to other points along the coast. In the evening, Avenida Quinta, the pedestrian mall, is the place to sit and have a meal or a drink, or stroll and watch others having meals and drinks. Early evening happy hour (5 to 7 pm), with two drinks for the price of one, is an iron rule. We found it impossible to order a single beer. The waiter automatically brought two.

Places to Stay

Playa del Carmen is developing and changing so fast, that almost anything written about it is obsolete by the time it's printed. Expect many new hotels by the time you arrive, and many changes in the old ones. The room prices given below are for the busy winter season. Prices are substantially lower at other times.

Places to Stay – budget

The youth hostel, or *Villa Deportiva Juvenil*, 1.2 km from the ferry docks, is a modern establishment offering the cheapest clean lodging in town, but it's quite a walk to the beach and you sleep in single-sex dorm bunks. It's cheap at US$3 per bunk.

Camping-Cabañas La Ruina (☎ 2-14-74, fax 2-15-98), on Calle 2 just off the beach, offers several cheap ways to sleep. Pitch your own tent for US$3 per person, or hang your hammock beneath their palapa for slightly more; or rent a hammock from them; or a simple cabaña with two cots and ceiling fan for US$8 to US$11; or a more comfortable cabaña with private bath for US$15 to US$40. Be careful to secure your stuff from roaming thieves. La Ruina rents lockers, but it's best to have your own sturdy lock.

Posada Lily, on Avenida Juárez (Avenida Principal) just a block inland from the main square, offers clean rooms with private shower and fan for US$16 a double.

Posada Yumil-Kin (no phone), Calle 1 between Avenidas 5 and 10, is simple, clean, convenient and cheap at US$15 for a double with fan.

At *Cabañas Nuevo Amanecer* (☎ 3-00-30), Calle 4 between Avenidas 5 and 10, each cabaña has a shady little porch complete with hammock. Waterless, the cabañas go for US$18, or US$26 with private bath.

Tour groups sometimes fill the *Hotel Mar Caribe* (☎ 3-02-07), Avenida 15 at

Top: Beach at Tulum
Bottom: Temple entrance on the Pyramid of the Magician, Uxmal

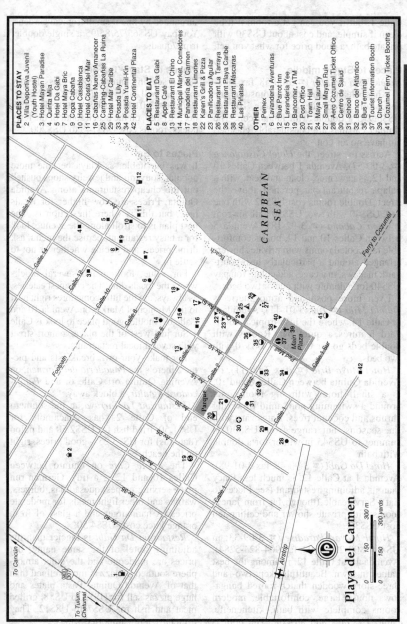

PLACES TO STAY
2 Villa Deportiva Juvenil
   (Youth Hostel)
3 Hotel Mayan Paradise
4 Quinta Mija
5 Hotel Da Gabi
7 Hotel Maya Bric
9 Copa Cabana
10 Hotel Casablanca
11 Hotel Costa del Mar
16 Cabañas Nuevo Amanecer
25 Camping-Cabañas La Ruina
29 Hotel Mar Caribe
33 Posada Lily
34 Posada Yumil-Kin
42 Hotel Continental Plaza

PLACES TO EAT
5 Restaurant Da Gabi
8 Apple Café
13 Restaurant El Chino
14 Municipal Market, Comedores
17 Panadería del Carmen
18 Restaurant Limones
22 Karen's Grill & Pizza
23 Panificadora Aguilar
26 Restaurant La Tarraya
36 Restaurant Playa Caribe
38 Restaurant Mascaras
40 Las Piñatas

OTHER
1 Pemex
6 Lavandería Aventuras
12 Blue Parrot Inn
15 Lavandería Yee
19 Bancomer, ATM
20 Post Office
21 Town Hall
24 Maya Laundry
27 Small Mayan Ruin
28 Aero Cozumel Ticket Office
30 Centro de Salud
31 School
32 Banco del Atlántico
35 Bus Terminal
37 Tourist Information Booth
39 Church
41 Cozumel Ferry Ticket Booths

Playa del Carmen

Calle 1, but if you can get a room it'll be clean if simple, and cost about US$30 with private bath, a good price for what you get.

Places to Stay – middle

Hotel Costa del Mar (☎ 3-00-58, fax 2-02-31) has clean, attractive rooms on the beach on Avenida 1 at Calle 10, for US$55/75 a double with fan/air-con. The simpler cabañas are considerably cheaper, but have no air-con.

Across the street, the *Hotel Casablanca* (☎ 3-00-57), Avenida 1 between Calles 10 and 12, is new, nice, clean and neat, with a palapa restaurant-bar perched above the street. Double rooms cost US$32 with one bed, US$40 with two, US$50 with air-con.

Copa Cabaña (☎ 3-02-18), Avenida 5 between Calles 10 and 12, boasts comfortable fan-cooled rooms with private showers arranged around a particularly lush courtyard; macaws, in a cage, add color. You pay US$40 for a double with one or two beds.

Even more posh and atmospheric is *Quinta Mija* (☎ /fax 3-01-11), Avenida 5 at Calle 14, where the lush tropical courtyard features a quiet bar. Rooms with double beds go for US$50, or US$70 with two beds.

Hotel Maya Bric (☎ /fax 3-00-11), on Avenida Quinta between Calles 8 and 10, is a small hotel with big rooms, set around a swimming pool amid flowering shrubs and coconut trees. Rates vary with the seasons, but range from US$30 in summer to US$45 in winter for a double with bath.

Hotel Da Gabi (☎ 3-00-48, fax 3-01-98), Avenida 1 at Calle 12, is much less fancy than its adjoining restaurant (see Places to Eat). Serviceable (though far from fancy) rooms with private shower and ceiling fan cost US$35.

Hotel Mayan Paradise (☎ 3-09-33; in USA ☎ 800-217-2192, fax 904-824-5284), Avenida 10 at Calle 12, is among the best values in town. Beautifully kept two- and three-story wooden thatch-roofed bungalows house large, comfortable, modern rooms complete with bath, kitchenette, cable TV, fans and air-con. The pool is

surrounded by fine if small tropical gardens. You pay US$65/75/85/95 a single/double/triple/quad.

Places to Stay – top end

Those seeking international-class luxury lodging will like the *Hotel Continental Plaza* (☎ 3-01-00, in USA 800-882-6684; fax 3-01-05), on the beach south of the ferry docks; rooms cost US$140 to US$200.

Places to Eat

It was inevitable: as Playa became more popular, souvenir and jewelry shops pushed out the cheap restaurants along Avenida Quinta. Prices are now higher for meals here, but this is where the action is. The best plan is to stroll along the avenue, look for a busy restaurant, peruse the menu, ask drink prices, and decide whether or not to settle in.

For value, look inland several blocks where the locals dine. The cheapest eateries, as always, are the little comedores right next to the Municipal Market on Avenida 10 and Calle 6. Another good place to look is Calle 1 Sur just west of the plaza, a short street with several local restaurants.

For make-your-own breakfasts and picnics, there's the *Panadería del Carmen*, on Avenida Quinta off Calle 6, and *Panificadora Aguilar*, a block away.

Restaurant La Tarraya, at the southern end of Calle 2, has guacamole for US$1.50, fried fish for US$2.50 and pulpo (octopus) for US$3.25 – good prices, right on the beach.

The *Apple Café* on Quinto between Calles 10 and 12 is a tidy, German-run place serving crepes, quesadillas, burgers, waffles and other light meals for moderate prices. A hamburger and a glass of fresh orange juice costs US$4.50.

Restaurant Da Gabi is fancier than the adjoining hotel of the same name, but prices are moderate and the quiet atmosphere soothed by jazz is more refined than that of Avenida Quinta. Pasta plates and huge pizzas sell for US$5 to US$8, grilled meat and fish for US$7 to US$12. They even have a few imported wines.

Because it's farther from the beach and Avenida Quinta, *Restaurant El Chino*, Calle 4 between Avenidas 10 and 15, has lower prices and better food, but also a pleasant setting and decent service. A full meal of soup, ceviche or grilled fish and dessert might cost US$10 or US$12, drinks and tip included.

Of the more expensive places, the *Restaurant Máscaras*, on the main plaza, is the most famous and long-lived. The pizzas (US$4 to US$7) are dependably good, the more complex dishes less so, but it's the company you come for. Drinks are expensive. *Las Piñatas*, downhill from Máscaras, has the best sea view.

A better choice as far as the food is concerned is the *Restaurant Limones*, Avenida Quinta at Calle 6, where the atmosphere is more sedate than jolly. Though you can pay up to US$19 for their 'Symphony of Seafood' with lobster, shrimp and conch, most fish dishes cost around US$5, and filet mignon costs US$12.

Restaurant Playa Caribe on Avenida Quinta seems to be a bit cheaper than the other places. A big, varied Mexican combination plate costs US$7.50.

Entertainment
The evening happy hour is more certain than death and taxes in Playa. When the sun goes down, the sound of beer bottles being opened is louder than the crash of surf. Avenida Quinta is the epicenter. *Karen's Grill & Pizza* often has marimba music in the evenings, and the Red & Black Bar at *Restaurant Limones* features live jazz, but the bar at the *Blue Parrot Inn* is among the cooler places, with an international clientele.

Getting There & Away
Air Playa's little airstrip handles mostly small charter, tour and air taxi flights. Aero Cozumel (☎ 3-03-50), part of Mexicana, has an office next to Playa's airstrip, as does Aero Saab. They'll fly you to Cozumel for US$70 (up to five people), or round-trip to Chichén Itzá for US$120 per person.

Bus ADO, Autotransportes del Sur (ATS), Cristóbal Colón, Mayab and Autotransportes de Oriente (Oriente) serve Playa's bus terminal at the corner of Avenida Juárez and Avenida Quinta. Playa Express buses run up and down the coast every 20 minutes, charging US$1.75 from Playa to either Tulum or Cancún.

Cancún – 65 km, one hour; frequent buses by ADO, Playa Express and Oriente for US$1.75

Chetumal – 315 km, five hours; seven by ADO (US$10 to US$12), one by Colón (US$10), and three by Mayab (US$6.50)

Chichén Itzá – 272 km, four hours, US$6 to US$9; five buses

Cobá – 113 km, two hours; four by Oriente (US$2.50) and one by ATS (US$2.75)

Mérida – 385 km, seven hours; nine by ADO (US$10 to US$12), several others by ATS (US$8) and Mayab (US$10)

Palenque – 800 km, 12 hours; one each by ADO (US$27), Colón (US$25) and ATS (US$20)

San Cristóbal de las Casas – 990 km, 18 hours; one each by ADO (US$30), Colón (US$27) and ATS (US$24)

Tulum – 63 km, one hour; Playa Express (US$2.25) every 20 minutes, and four by ATS (US$1.50)

Valladolid – 213 km, 3½ hours; five by ADO (US$6), four by ATS (US$5); many buses going to Mérida via Cancún stop at Valladolid, but it's faster to go on the *ruta corta* (short route) via Tulum and Cobá (see Cobá)

Boats to Cozumel Approach the dock and you can't miss the ticket booths for *México*, *México II* and *México III*, charging US$4 one way to Cozumel. Together they make a dozen runs (30 minutes) daily.

COZUMEL
pop 175,000; ☎ *987*
Cozumel (Place of the Swallows) floats in the midst of the Caribbean's crystalline waters 71 km south of Cancún. Measuring 53 km long and 14 km wide, it is the largest of Mexico's islands. Cozumel's legendary Arrecife Palancar (Palancar Reef) was made famous by Jacques Cousteau and is a lure for divers from all over the world.

YUCATÁN PENINSULA

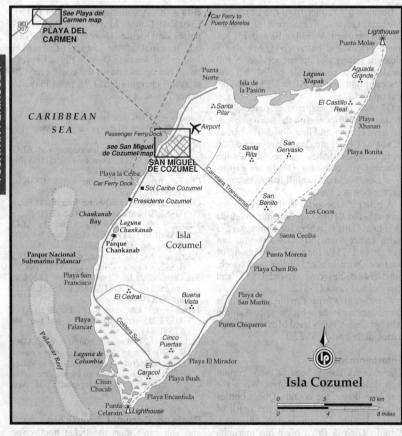

See Playa del
Carmen map

Car Ferry to
Puerto Morelos

PLAYA DEL
CARMEN

Lighthouse
Punta Molas

Punta
Norte

Aguada
Grande

Laguna
Xlapak

Isla de
la Pasión

El Castillo
Real

Santa
Pilar

Playa
Xhanan

**CARIBBEAN
SEA**

Airport

Passenger Ferry Dock

see San Miguel
de Cozumel map

San
Gervasio

Playa Bonita

SAN MIGUEL
DE COZUMEL

Santa
Rita

Playa la Ceiba

Car Ferry Dock

Sol Caribe Cozumel

Presidente Cozumel

San
Benito

Los Cocos

*Chankanab
Bay*

Laguna
Chankanab

Santa Cecilia

**Parque
Chankanab**

Isla
Cozumel

Punta Morena

**Parque Nacional
Submarino Palancar**

Playa Chen Río

Playa San
Francisco

El Cedral

Buena
Vista

Playa de
San Martín

Playa
Palancar

Costera Sur

Punta Chiqueros

Palancar Reef

Laguna de
Columbia

Cinco
Puertas

Playa El Mirador

El
Caracol

Playa Bush

Chun
Chacab

Playa Encantada

Punta
Celarain   Lighthouse

Isla Cozumel

0   5   10 km

0   4   8 miles

Though it has that beautiful offshore reef, Cozumel does not have many good swimming beaches. The western shore is mostly sharp, weathered limestone and coral, and the eastern beaches are too often pounded by dangerous surf.

History
Mayan settlement here dates from 300 AD. During the Postclassic period, Cozumel flourished both as a commercial center and as a major ceremonial site. The Maya sailed here on pilgrimages to shrines dedicated to

Ixchel, the goddess of fertility and the moon.

Although the first Spanish contact with Cozumel in 1518 by Juan de Grijalva was peaceful, it was followed by the Cortés expedition in 1519. Cortés, en route to his conquest of the mainland, laid to waste Cozumel's Mayan shrines. The Maya offered staunch military resistance until they were conquered in 1545. The coming of the Spaniards brought smallpox to this otherwise surprisingly disease-free place. Within a generation after the conquest, the island's population had dwindled to only 300 souls, Maya and Spaniards.

While the island remained virtually deserted into the late 17th century, its coves provided sanctuary and headquarters for several notorious pirates, including Jean Lafitte and Henry Morgan. Pirate brutality led the remaining populace to move to the mainland and it wasn't until 1848 that Cozumel began to be resettled by Indians fleeing the War of the Castes.

At the turn of the century, the island's population, which was now largely mestizo, grew thanks to the craze for chewing gum. Cozumel was a port of call on the chicle export route and locals harvested chicle on the island. Although chicle was later replaced by synthetic gum, Cozumel's economic base expanded with the building of a US air force base here during WWII.

When the US military departed, the island fell into an economic slump and many of its people moved away. Those who stayed fished for a livelihood until 1961, when underwater scientist Jacques Cousteau arrived, explored the reef and told the world about Cozumel's beauties. A resort destination was born.

Orientation

It's easy to make your way on foot around the island's only town, San Miguel de Cozumel. The airport, two km north of town, is accessible only by taxi or on foot.

The waterfront boulevard is Avenida Rafael Melgar; along Melgar south of the ferry docks (officially called Muelle Fiscal) there is a narrow but usable sand beach. The main plaza is just opposite the ferry docks.

Lockers are for rent at the landward end of the Muelle Fiscal for US$2 per day, but they're not big enough for a full backpack.

Information

Tourist Office The local tourist office (☎ 2-09-72) is on the 2nd floor of a building facing the main square to the north of Bancomer. It's open weekdays from 9 am to 3 pm and 6 to 8 pm.

Money For currency exchange, Banamex and Banca Serfin (see map) have ATMs. Bancomer and Banco del Atlantico, off the main plaza, change money only on weekdays from 10 am to 12.30 pm, and the queues are long. Banpaís, facing the ferry docks, will change your traveler's checks weekdays from 9 am to 1.30 pm for a 1% commission.

The casas de cambio around the town are your best bets for long hours and fast service, though they may charge as much as 3.5% commission. Most of the major hotels, restaurants and stores will change money at a less advantageous rate when the banks are closed.

Post & Communications The post office (☎ 2-01-06) is south of Calle 7 Sur on the waterfront just off Avenida Melgar. Hours are weekdays from 9 am to 1 pm and 3 to 6 pm, and Saturday from 9 am to noon.

The Telmex telephone office is on Salas between Avenidas 5 and 10 Sur. There are pay phones in front, and they sell telephone cards in the office.

Bookstore The Gracia Agencia de Publicaciones, on the southeast side of the plaza 40 meters from the clock tower, next to Bancomer, is open seven days a week selling English, French, German and Spanish books, and English and Spanish magazines and newspapers.

Laundry Margarita Laundromat, Avenida 20 Sur 285, between Salas and Calle 3 Sur, is open Monday to Saturday from 7 am to 9 pm, Sunday from 9 am to 5 pm, and charges US$1.50 to wash a load (US$0.40 extra if you don't bring your own detergent), US$0.70 for 10 minutes in the dryer. Ironing and folding cost extra. There's also the Lavandería Express, Salas at Avenida 10 Sur.

Museo de la Isla de Cozumel

This museum, on Avenida Melgar between Calles 4 and 6 Norte, has nautical exhibits covering the history of the island.

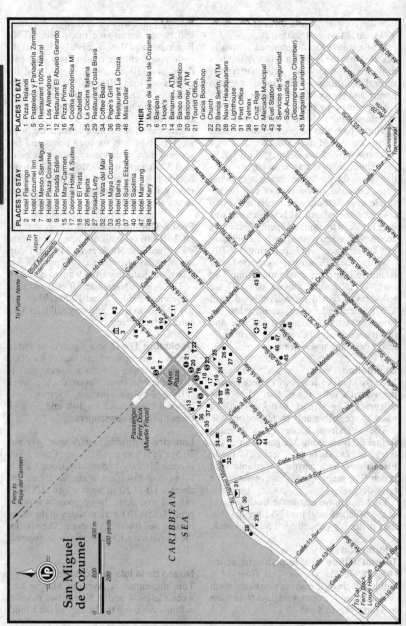

PLACES TO STAY

2 Hotel Flamingo
4 Hotel Cozumel Inn
7 Hotel Mesón San Miguel
8 Hotel Plaza Cozumel
9 Hotel Posada Edém
15 Hotel Mary-Carmen
17 Colonial Hotel & Suites
18 Hotel El Pirata
26 Hotel Pepita
27 Posada Letty
32 Hotel Vista del Mar
33 Hotel Bahía
35 Hotel Maya Cozumel
37 Hotel Suites Elizabeth
40 Hotel Saolima
47 Hotel Marruang
48 Hotel Kary

PLACES TO EAT

1 Pizza Rolandi
5 Pastelería y Panadería Zermatt
10 Restaurant 100% Natural
11 Los Almendros
12 Restaurant El Abuelo Gerardo
16 Pizza Prima
24 Cocina Económica Mi Chabelita
25 La Cocina Italiana
29 Restaurant Costa Brava
34 Coffee Bean
36 Pepe's Grill
39 Restaurant La Choza
46 Miss Dollar

OTHER

3 Museo de la Isla de Cozumel
6 Banpaís
13 Hook's
14 Banamex, ATM
19 Banco del Atlántico
20 Bancomer, ATM
21 Tourist Office,
   Gracia Bookshop
22 Church
23 Banca Serfín, ATM
28 Naval Headquarters
30 Lighthouse
38 Post Office
41 Cruz Roja
42 Mercado Municipal
43 Fuel Station
44 Servicios de Seguridad
   Sub-Acuatica
   (Decompression Chamber)
45 Margarita Laundromat

San Miguel
de Cozumel

CARIBBEAN SEA

It's open from 10 am to 6 pm for US$3; closed Saturday.

Scuba Diving

For equipment rental, instruction and/or boat reservations, there are numerous dive shops on Avenida Melgar along San Miguel's waterfront. Generally, a two-tank, full-day scuba trip will cost US$50 to US$65, an introductory scuba course US$60, and a full certification course US$300.

Cozumel has over 60 dive shops. Here are a few names and addresses:

Black Shark Dive Shop (☎ 2-03-96, fax 2-56-57), Avenida 5 Sur between Salas and Calle 3 Sur

Blue Bubble Divers – Avenida 5 Sur and Calle 3 Sur (☎ /fax 2-18-65)

Caballito del Caribe – Avenida 10 Sur No 124B (☎ 2-14-49)

Caribbean Divers – Avenida Melgar at Calle 5 Sur (☎ 2-10-80)

Dive Paradise (Paraíso del Buceo) – Avenida Melgar 601 (☎ 2-10-07, fax 2-10-61)

Pascual's Scuba Center – Salas 176 (☎ /fax 2-54-54)

Pro Dive – Salas 198 at Avenida 5 Sur (☎ /fax 2-41-23)

Yucatech Expeditions – specializes in diving Yucatán's cenotes. Avenida 15 Sur between Salas and Calle 1 Sur (☎ 2-46-18, 4-78-35)

The local hyperbaric chamber is Servicios de Seguridad Sub-Acuatica (☎ 2-23-87, 2-14-30, fax 2-18-48), Calle 5 Sur No 21B, open 24 hours.

The most prominent scuba destinations are: the five-km-long Arrecife Palancar (Palancar Reef), where stunning coral formations and a 'horseshoe' of coral heads in 70-meter visibility offer some of the world's finest diving; Maracaibo Reef, for experienced divers only, which offers a challenge due to its current and its aquatic life; Paraíso Reef, famous for its coral formations, especially brain and star coral; and Yocab Reef, shallow yet vibrantly alive and great for beginners.

Snorkeling

You can go out on a half-day boat tour for US$20 to US$30 or, far cheaper, rent gear for about US$8 and snorkel at the following places: Chankanab Bay, Playa San Francisco, Playa La Ceiba near the car ferry dock (where a plane was purposely sunk for the film *Survive*), the Presidente Hotel and Palancar.

Glass-Bottom Boat Rides

You can enjoy the coral formations and aquatic life by taking a tour on a glass-bottom boat, the *Palapa Marina* (☎ 2-05-39), Calle 1 Sur No 177, between Avenidas 5 and 10. The boat departs the Sol Caribe pier, south of San Miguel near the car ferry dock, daily at 9 am and 1 pm. The fare is US$15 per person.

Places to Stay – budget

Camping To camp anywhere on the island you'll need a permit from the island's naval authorities. Permits are obtainable 24 hours a day, for free, from the naval headquarters south of the post office on Avenida Rafael Melgar. The best camping places are along the relatively unpopulated eastern shore of the island.

Hotels All rooms described below come with private bath and fan, unless otherwise noted.

Hotel Flamingo (☎ 2-12-64), Calle 6 Norte No 81, off Melgar, is not the cheapest, but it's run efficiently and undoubtedly is the best value for money. The 21 rooms go for US$20 to US$35 a double, depending upon the season.

Hotel Marruang (☎ 2-16-78, 2-02-08) at Salas 440 is entered from a passageway across from the municipal market. A clean room with one double and one single bed costs US$16 to US$24.

Hotel Cozumel Inn (☎ 2-03-14), Calle 4 Norte No 3, has rooms for only US$20/24 a double with fan/air-con in summer.

Hotel Posada Edém (☎ 2-11-66), Calle 2 Norte 12, between Avenidas 5 and 10 Norte, is uninspiring but inexpensive at US$12/18 a single/double.

Posada Letty (☎ 2-02-57), on Avenida 15 Sur near Calle 1 Sur, is among the cheapest lodgings in town at US$14 in summer, US$19 in winter.

Hotel Saolima (☎ 2-08-86), Salas 268 between Avenidas 10 and 15 Sur, has clean, pleasant rooms in a quiet locale that cost US$14/18 a double/triple in the summer.

Hotel Kary (☎ 2-20-11), Salas at Avenida 25 Sur, is five blocks east of the plaza and a bit out of the way, but has a pool. Rooms are US$17 for a double with fan and US$24 with air-con.

Places to Stay – middle

Most middle-range hostelries offer air-conditioning and swimming pools. All have private bathrooms.

Hotel Vista del Mar (☎ 2-05-45, fax 2-04-45), Avenida Melgar 45, at Calle 5 Sur, has a small swimming pool, restaurant, liquor store, rental car and travel agency. Some rooms have balconies with sea views. The price in summer is US$40 a double, rising to US$50 in winter.

Tried and true, clean, comfortable lodgings are yours at the *Hotel Mary-Carmen* (☎ 2-05-81), Avenida 5 Sur 4, half a block south of the plaza. The 27 tidy air-con rooms cost US$28 double in summer, US$40 in winter. Equally pleasant and even cheaper is the *Hotel Suites Elizabeth* (☎ 2-03-30), at Salas 44. Air-con bedrooms have kitchenettes here.

Hotel Pepita (☎ 2-00-98, fax 2-02-01), Avenida 15 Sur No 120, corner of Calle 1 Sur, has well maintained rooms around a delightful garden for US$25 in summer, US$35 in winter. Most rooms have two double beds, insect screens, fans and little refrigerators as well as the air-con, and there's free morning coffee.

Colonial Hotel & Suites (☎ 2-40-34, fax 2-13-87), Avenida 5 Sur No 9, has studios and one-bedroom suites (some of which can sleep up to four people) with kitchenette, air-con and pretensions to decor for US$42 to US$52 double.

The similar *Hotel Bahía* (☎ 2-02-09, fax 2-13-87), facing the sea on Avenida Melgar at Calle 3 Sur, under the same management, charges slightly more.

Hotel El Pirata (☎ 2-00-51), Avenida 5 Sur 121, offers decent rooms with private bath and fan for US$19 double in summer, US$28 with air-con.

Hotel Maya Cozumel (☎ 2-00-11, fax 2-07-18), Calle 5 Sur No 4, has good TV-equipped rooms and a pool surrounded by grass and bougainvillea for US$35/40/45 a single/double/triple in winter, about US$5 less per room in summer.

Hotel Plaza Cozumel (☎ 2-27-11, fax 2-00-66), Calle 2 Norte 3, just off Avenida Melgar a block north of the plaza, is a modern hotel with a rooftop swimming pool, color TV, and prices of US$50 in summer, US$75 in winter.

Hotel Mesón San Miguel (☎ 2-03-23, fax 2-18-20), Avenida Juárez 2B, on the north side of the plaza, has a little pool, blissful air-con, a restaurant and 100 rooms with balconies. There's also a separate beach club with water sports facilities seven blocks from the hotel on the water. Rates are US$55/80 a double in summer/winter.

Places to Stay – top end

Several km south of town are the big luxury resort hotels of an international standard, which charge US$150 to US$300 for a room during the winter season. North of town along the western shore of the island are numerous smaller, more modest resort hotels, usually cheaper than the big places, but catering mostly to package tour groups.

South of town, the *Presidente Cozumel* (☎ 2-03-22, fax 2-13-60), Carretera a Chankanab km 6.5, is hard to miss with its 259 rooms, many with sea views, set amidst tropical gardens.

Sol Caribe Cozumel (☎ 2-07-00, fax 2-13-01), Playa Paraíso km 3.5 (Apdo Postal 259), has 321 luxurious rooms and a lavish layout with tropical swimming pool complete with a large 'island.' For reservations at either the Presidente or Sol Caribe, call ☎ 800-343-7821 in the USA.

Meliá Mayan Cozumel (☎ 2-04-11, fax 2-15-99), Playa Santa Pilar, is a 200-room resort with a full list of water sport equipment. Another Meliá hotel, the *Sol Cabañas del Caribe* (☎ 2-01-61, 2-00-17, fax 2-15-99) caters mostly to divers. For reservations, call ☎ 800-336-3542 in the USA.

Places to Eat

Budget Cheapest of all eating places, with fairly tasty food, are the market loncherías located next to the Mercado Municipal on Salas between Avenidas 20 and 25 Sur. All of these little señora-run eateries offer soup and a main course for less than US$3, with a large selection of dishes available. Hours are 6.30 am to 6.30 pm daily.

Restaurant Costa Brava, on Avenida Melgar just south of the post office, is among the more interesting – read funky – places to dine on the island. Cheap breakfasts (US$2 to US$3), and such filling dishes as chicken tacos, grilled steak and fried fish or chicken for US$3 to US$7, are served daily from 6.30 am to 11.30 pm.

Restaurant La Choza, Salas 198, specializes in authentic Mexican traditional cuisine, which is not all tacos and enchiladas. Have the pozole, a filling, spicy meat-and-hominy stew. With a soft drink, you pay US$6 for a huge bowl.

The *Cocina Económica Mi Chabelita*, Avenida 10 Sur between Calle 1 Sur and Salas, is a tiny, fairly cheap eatery run by a señora who serves up decent portions of decent food for US$3 or less. It opens for breakfast at 7 am and closes at 7 pm.

The forthrightly named *Miss Dollar* earns its money by providing meals to take out. The *Coffee Bean*, Calle 3 Sur just off Avenida Melgar, serves up the latest trendy java recipes.

Restaurant 100% Natural, Calle 2 Norte at Avenida 10 Norte, serves meals for as low as US$6 – and it's all natural.

For pastries, try the *Pastelería y Panadería Zermatt*, Avenida 5 Norte and Calle 4 Norte.

Middle Our favorite is *Pizza Prima* (☎ 2-42-42), Salas 109 between Avenidas 5 and 10 Sur, open from 1 to 11 pm (closed Wednesday). The American owners produce home-made pasta and fresh pizza (US$5 to US$12) as well as excellent Italian specialties (US$8 to US$15). Dine streetside, or upstairs on the patio.

Pizza Rolandi, Avenida Melgar between Calles 6 and 8 Norte, serves good one-person (20-cm diameter) pizzas for US$7 to US$9. It's open from 11.30 am to 11.30 pm; closed Sunday.

Restaurant El Abuelo Gerardo (☎ 2-10-12), Avenida 10 Norte No 21, is attractive, with locally made crafts for decoration and lively salsa music. The menu is extensive, and prices moderate: US$3 for chicken, US$6 for beef, US$5 to US$9 for seafood. The guacamole and chips are on the house.

La Cocina Italiana, Avenida 10 Sur No 121, at Calle 1 Sur, has rustic wooden tables and rustic pizzas and pastas, but prices straight out of central Roma: US$6 to US$8 for pizzas, US$10 to US$13 for meat or fish.

Los Almendros, the famous Yucatecan restaurant which originated in Ticul, has branches in Mérida, Cancún, and now Cozumel, at Avenida 10 Norte and Calle 2 Norte. Go here for authentic Yucatecan dishes at moderate prices.

Top End Cozumel's traditional place to dine well and richly is *Pepe's Grill* (☎ 2-02-13), Avenida Melgar at Salas. Flaming shrimps, grilled lobster, caesar salad and other top-end items can take your bill to the lofty heights of US$25 to US$40 per person.

Entertainment

Nightlife in Cozumel is pricey, but if you want to dance, the most popular disco is *Neptuno Dance Club*, five blocks south of the post office on Avenida Melgar at Calle 11 Sur. Cover charge is US$5, with drinks (even Mexican beer) for US$3 and up. Another hot spot, similarly priced, is *Hook's* at the intersection of Avenida Melgar and Salas. For Latin salsa music, try *Los Quetzales*, Avenida 10 Sur at Calle 1 Sur, a block from the plaza. It's open every evening from 6 pm.

Getting There & Away

Air Cozumel has a surprisingly busy international airport, with numerous direct flights from other parts of Mexico and the USA. Flights from Europe are usually routed via the USA or Mexico City. There are direct flights on Continental (☎ 2-02-51) and American (☎ 2-08-99) from Dallas, Houston, and Raleigh-Durham, with many flights from other US cities via these hubs. Mexicana (☎ 2-02-63) has nonstops from Miami and direct flights from Mérida and Mexico City.

Aero Cozumel (☎ 2-09-28, 2-05-03), with offices at Cozumel airport, operates flights between Cancún and Cozumel about every two hours throughout the day for US$50 one way. Reserve in advance.

Ferry Passenger ferries run from Playa del Carmen, car ferries run from Puerto Morelos. See those sections for details.

Getting Around
To/From the Airport The airport is about two km north of town. You can take a minibus from the airport into town for less than US$2, slightly more to the hotels south of town, but you'll have to take a taxi (US$4) to return to the airport.

Bus & Taxi Cozumel's taxi drivers have a lock on the local transport market, defeating any proposal for a convenient bus service. Fares in and around town are US$3 per ride. From the town to Laguna Chankanab is US$7.

Car & Motorcycle Rates for rental cars are upwards of US$40 to $55 per day, all inclusive. You could probably haggle with a taxi driver to take you on a tour of the island, drop you at a beach, come back and pick you up, and still save money. If you do rent, observe the law on vehicle occupancy. Usually only five people are allowed in a vehicle (say, a Jeep). If you carry more, the police will fine you.

The island has one fuel station, on Avenida Juárez five blocks east of the main square.

Rented mopeds are popular with those who want to tour the island on their own. It seems that every citizen and business in San Miguel – hotels, restaurants, gift shops, morticians – rents mopeds, generally for US$25 to US$32 per day (24 hours), though

some rent from 8 am to 5 pm for US$18. Insurance and tax are included in these prices. It's amusing that a 24-hour rental of two mopeds (for two people) almost equals the cost of renting a car (for up to four people) for the same period of time.

You must have a valid driving license, and you must use a credit card to rent, or put down a hefty deposit (around US$50).

The best time to rent is first thing in the morning, when all the machines are there. Choose a good one, with a working horn, brakes, lights, starter, rear-view mirrors, and a full tank of fuel; remember that the price asked will be the same whether you rent the newest, pristine machine or the oldest, most beat-up rattletrap. (If you want to trust yourself with a second-rate moped, at least haggle the price down significantly.) You should get a helmet and a lock and chain with the moped; the law requires that you wear a helmet.

Don't plan to circumnavigate the island with two people on one moped. The well-used and ill-maintained machine may well break down under the load, stranding you a long way from civilization with no way to get help.

When riding, keep in mind that you will be as exposed to sunshine on a moped as if you were roasting on a beach. Slather yourself with sun block (especially the backs of your hands, feet and neck, and your face), or cover up, or suffer the consequences. Also, be aware of the dangers involved. Of all motor vehicle operators, the inexperienced moped driver on unfamiliar roads in a foreign country has the highest statistical chance of having an accident, especially when faced by lots of other inexperienced moped drivers. Drive carefully.

AROUND COZUMEL
In order to see most of the island (except for Chankanab Bay) you will have to rent a bicycle, moped or car, or take a taxi (see the previous Getting Around section). The following route will take you south from the town of San Miguel, then counterclockwise around the island.

Chankanab Bay Beach

This bay of clear water and fabulously colored fish is the most popular on the island. It is nine km south of San Miguel.

You used to be able to swim in the adjoining lagoon, but so many tourists were fouling the water and damaging the coral that Chankanab lagoon was made a national park and decreed off-limits to swimmers. Don't despair – you can still snorkel in the sea here and the lagoon has been saved from destruction.

Snorkeling equipment can be rented for US$7 per day. Divers will be interested in a reef offshore; there is a dive shop at the beach, and scuba instruction is offered.

There is also a restaurant and snack shop. The beach has dressing rooms, lockers and showers, which are included in the US$3 admission price to the national park, open 9 am to 5 pm daily. The park also has a botanical garden with 400 species of tropical plants.

Playa San Francisco & Playa Palancar

Playa San Francisco, 14 km from San Miguel, and Playa Palancar, a few km to the south, are the nicest of the island's beaches. San Francisco's white sands run for more than three km, and rather expensive food is served at its restaurant. If you want to scuba dive or snorkel at Arrecife Palancar, you will have to sign on for a day cruise or charter a boat.

El Cedral

To see these small Mayan ruins, the oldest on the island, go 3.5 km down a paved road a short distance south of Playa San Francisco. Although El Cedral was thought to be an important ceremonial site, its minor remnants are not well preserved.

Punta Celarain

The southern tip of the island has a picturesque lighthouse, accessible via a dirt track, four km from the highway. To enjoy truly isolated beaches en route, climb over the sand dunes. There's a fine view of the island from the top of the lighthouse.

East Coast Drive

The eastern shoreline is the wildest part of the island and highly recommended for beautiful seascapes of rocky coast. Unfortunately, except for Punta Chiqueros, Chen Río and Punta Morena, swimming is dangerous on Cozumel's east coast due to potentially lethal riptides and undertows. Be careful! Swim only in coves protected from the open surf by headlands or breakwaters. There are small eateries at both Punta Morena and Punta Chiqueros and a hotel at Punta Morena. Some travelers camp at Chen Río.

El Castillo Real & San Gervasio

Beyond where the east-coast highway meets the Carretera Transversal (cross-island road) that runs to San Miguel, intrepid travelers may take the sand track about 17 km from the junction to the Mayan ruins known as El Castillo Real. They are not very well preserved and you need luck or a 4WD vehicle to navigate the sandy road.

There is an equally unimpressive ruin called San Gervasio on a bad road from the airport. 4WD vehicles can reach San Gervasio from a track originating on the east coast, but most rental car insurance policies do not cover unpaved roads such as this. The jungle en route is more interesting than the ruins.

Punta Molas Beaches

There are some fairly good beaches and minor Mayan ruins in the vicinity of the northeast point, accessible only by 4WD vehicle or foot.

BEACHES – CANCÚN TO TULUM

Some of the world's most beautiful beaches lie between Cancún and Tulum.

Xcaret (Km 290)

Once a communal turkey farm, Xcaret (SHKAR-et; ☎ 98-83-31-43, fax 98-83-33-24), 'Nature's Sacred Paradise,' has been heavily Disneyfied. The beautiful inlet *(caleta)* filled with tropical marine life is surrounded by several minor Mayan ruins and has a cenote for swimming, a restaurant, and an evening show of 'ancient Mayan ceremonies' worthy of Las Vegas. Package tourists from Cancún fill the place everyday, arriving in a caravan of special Xcaret buses and happily paying the US$25 admission fee, plus additional fees for many attractions and activities such as swimming with dolphins (US$50). It is typical of our time that such an overdeveloped, hypercommercialized amusement can be called an 'eco-archaeological park.'

Pamul (Km 274)

Although Pamul's small rocky beach does not have long stretches of white sand like some of its Caribbean cousins, the palm-fringed surroundings are inviting. If you walk only about two km north of Pamul you will find an alabaster sand beach to call your own. The least rocky section is the southern end, but watch out for spiked sea urchins in the shallows offshore.

Giant sea turtles come ashore here at night in July and August to lay their eggs. Why they return to the same beach every year is a mystery not understood by zoologists. If you run across a turtle during your evening stroll along the beach, keep a good distance from it and don't use a light, as this will scare it. Do your part to contribute to the survival of the turtles, which are endangered: let them lay their eggs in peace.

Places to Stay & Eat *Hotel Pamul* offers basic but acceptable rooms with fan and bath for US$16 a single and US$26 a double. There is electricity in the evenings until 10 pm. The friendly family that runs this somewhat scruffy hotel and campsite also serves breakfast and seafood at their little restaurant.

The fee for camping is US$6 for two people per site. There are showers and toilets.

Puerto Aventuras (Km 269.5)

The Cancún lifestyle spreads inexorably southward, dotting this previously pristine coast with yet more sybaritic resort hide-aways. One such place is the *Puerto Aventuras Resort* (☎ 987-2-22-11), PO Box 186, Playa del Carmen, Quintana Roo, a modern luxury complex of hotel rooms, swimming pools, beach facilities and other costly comforts.

Xpu-ha (Km 264)

Xpu-ha (Shpoo-HA) offers camping and moderately-priced cabañas on a beautiful stretch of beach just north of the Club Robinson resort accessed by an unpaved road. Bonanza Beach has the best camping – that is, until the developers drive us out. Walk 15 minutes north to find Laguna Tin-ha and Cenote Manatee.

Laguna Yal-ku (Km 256.5)

Laguna Yal-ku, once a well kept secret of snorkeling enthusiasts, has been discovered. Access is now by taxi from the northernmost of the Akumal hotels, thereby providing rich income for local drivers. Bring your own refreshments and snorkeling gear.

Akumal (Km 255)

Famous for its beautiful beach, Akumal (Place of the Turtles) does indeed see giant turtles come ashore to lay their eggs during the summer.

Activities There are two dive shops here where you can rent snorkeling gear. The best snorkeling is at the north end of the bay; or try Laguna Yal-ku, 1.5 km north of Akumal.

World-class divers come here to explore the Spanish galleon *Mantancero* which sank in 1741. You can see artifacts from the galleon at the museum at nearby Xel-ha. The dive shops will arrange all your scuba excursion needs. Beginners' scuba instruction can be provided for less than US$120; if you want certification, the dive shops offer three-day courses. They will also arrange deep-sea fishing excursions.

Places to Stay Lodgings at Akumal can be reserved by calling ☎ in the USA 800-448-7137.

The least expensive hotel is the *Hotel-Club Akumal Caribe Villas Maya*, where basic two-person air-conditioned cabañas with bath and the amenities of tennis and basketball courts cost US$90 to US$125 a double.

The *Hotel Akumal Caribe* on the south end of the beach is an attractive two-story modern lodge with swimming pool, boat rental and night tennis. Spacious air-con rooms equipped with refrigerators cost US$110. These can sleep six people.

On the north side of the beach you will find the cabañas of *Las Casitas Akumal* (☎ 987-2-25-54) consisting of a living room, kitchen, two bedrooms and two bathrooms. Bungalows cost US$160 in the busy winter season, US$110 in summer.

Places to Eat Even the shade-huts near the beach are expensive for light lunches and snacks, considering what you get. Just outside the walled entrance of Akumal is a grocery store patronized largely by the resort workers; if you are daytripping here, this is your sole inexpensive source of food. The store also sells tacos.

Las Aventuras (Km 250)

Developers got the first chance at Las Aventuras, which now has a planned community of condominiums, villas and the beautiful *Aventuras Akumal Hotel*, which has double rooms for about US$115.

Chemuyil (Km 248)

Here there's a beautiful sand beach shaded by coconut palms, and good snorkeling in the calm waters with exceptional visibility. Admission costs US$2.

Chemuyil is being developed, with some condos already built. During winter's high season there are a fair number of campers here (US$3.75 per person).

The cheap accommodation is spartan screened shade huts with hammock hooks. Inquire about availability at the bar; they cost US$20, and showers and toilets are communal.

Local fare is prepared at the bar, including some seafood.

Xcacel (Km 247)

Xcacel ('shkah-CELL') has no lodging other than camping (US$2.50 per person), no electricity and only a small restaurant stall. You can enjoy this patch of paradise for a day-use charge of US$1.50.

For fine fishing and snorkeling, try the waters north of the campground. The rocky point leads to seas for snorkeling, and the sandy outcropping is said to be a good place to fish from. Swimming, like snorkeling, is best from the rocky point to the north end of the beach.

Xcacel offers good pickings for shell collectors, including that aquatic collector, the hermit crab. There are also some colorful and intricate coral pieces to be found. When beachcombing here, wear footgear.

Take the old dirt track which runs two km north to Chemuyil and three km south to Xel-ha, and you may spy parrots, finches or the well-named clockbird (mot-mot) with its long tail.

Xel-ha Lagoon (Km 245)

Once a pristine natural lagoon brimming with iridescent tropical fish, Xel-ha ('SHELL-hah') is now a national park with landscaped grounds, changing rooms, restaurant-bar and ripoff prices. The fish are regularly driven off by the dozens of busloads of sun-oiled daytrippers who come to enjoy the beautiful site and to swim in the pretty lagoon.

Should you visit Xel-ha? Sure, so long as you come off-season (in summer), or in winter either very early or very late in the day to avoid the tour buses. Bring your own lunch, as the little restaurant here is overpriced. Entry to the lagoon area costs US$12 (US$7 for children under 12); it's open from 8 am to 6 pm daily. You can rent snorkeling gear; the price is high and the equipment may be leaky.

Ruinas de Xel-ha There is a small archaeological site on the west side of the highway 500 meters south of the lagoon entry road, open from 8 am to 5 pm for US$1.50. The ruins, which are not all that impressive, date from Classic and Postclassic periods, and include El Palacio and the Templo de los Pájaros.

TULUM
☎ 987

The ruins of Tulum (City of the Dawn, or City of Renewal), though well preserved, would hardly merit rave notices if it were not for their setting. And what a setting: the grey-black buildings of the past sit on a palm-fringed beach, lapped by the turquoise waters of the Caribbean.

Don't come to Tulum expecting majestic pyramids or anything comparable to the architecture of Chichén Itzá or Uxmal. The buildings here, decidedly Toltec in influence, were the product of Mayan civilization in decline.

Tulum's proximity to the tourist centers of Cancún and Isla Mujeres makes it a prime target of tour buses. The press of crowds threatened to damage the temples, so it is now not permitted to approach them closely or to climb atop them. To best enjoy the ruins, visit them either early in the morning or late in the day. The ruins are open from 8 am to 5 pm.

Recent development has turned the site into a money-sucking machine: you pay to park your car (US$1.50), then pass through a warren of shops to get to the mini-train (US$1.30) which takes you the 800 meters to the site entrance (US$3). Inside the site, the buildings aren't marked, so you'll need a guide (US$15 to US$22). The cost for a couple to tour Tulum can thus mount to around US$30 – and this for a second-rate site in which you can't even get close to the buildings.

History
Most archaeologists believe that Tulum was settled in the early Postclassic period (900-1200). When Juan de Grijalva's expedition sailed past Tulum in 1518, he was amazed by the sight of this walled city with its buildings painted a gleaming red, blue and white, and a ceremonial fire flaming atop its seaside watchtower.

The ramparts that surround three sides of Tulum (the fourth side being the sea) leave little question as to its strategic function as a fortress. Averaging nearly seven meters in thickness and standing three to five meters high, the walls protected the city during a period of considerable strife between Mayan city-states.

The city was abandoned about three-quarters of a century after the Spanish conquest. Mayan pilgrims continued to visit over the years and Indian refugees from the War of the Castes took shelter here from time to time.

Orientation
There are many Tulums: Tulum Crucero is the junction with highway 307 and the old access road to the ruins (the new entrance to the Zona Arqueológica is 400 meters south of Tulum Crucero); Tulum Ruinas is the ruins, 800 meters southeast of Tulum Crucero; Tulum Pueblo is the modern settlement 3.5 km south of Tulum Crucero; and Tulum Zona Hotelera is the assortment of beach cabañas from one to seven km south of the ruins. The Zona Hotelera is reached by an access road two km south of Tulum Crucero (1.5 km north of Tulum Pueblo), opposite the Cobá road.

South of the Zona Hotelera, the unpaved road enters the Reserva de la Biosfera Sian Ka'an, and continues for some 50 km past Boca Paila to Punta Allen.

El Castillo
Tulum's tallest building (Structure 1) is a watchtower fortress overlooking the Caribbean, appropriately named El Castillo by the Spaniards. Note the Toltec-style serpent columns at the temple's entrance, echoing those at Chichén Itzá.

Temple of the Descending God
The Temple of the Descending (or Diving) God (Templo del Dios Descendente) is named for the relief figure above the door, a diving figure, partly human, which may be related to the Mayas' reverence for bees. This figure appears at several other east coast sites, as well as at Cobá.

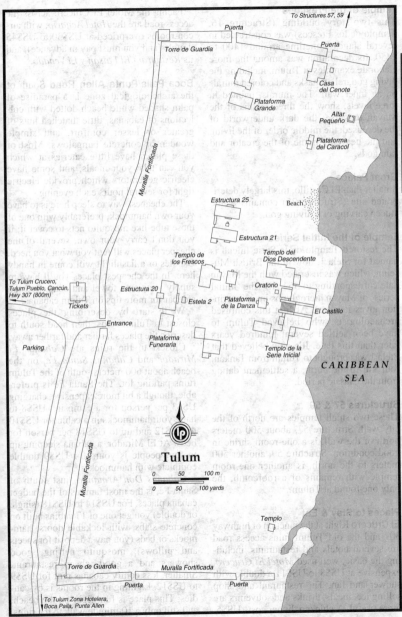

To Structures 57, 59

Puerta

Torre de Guardia

Puerta

Puerta

Casa
del Cenote

Plataforma
Grande

Altar
Pequeño

Plataforma
del Caracol

Muralla Fortificada

Estructura 25

Beach

Estructura 21

Templo de
los Frescos

Templo del
Dios Descendente

Oratorio

Estructura 20

Estela 2

Plataforma
de la Danza

El Castillo

To Tulum Crucero,
Tulum Pueblo, Cancún,
Hwy 307 (800m)

Tickets

Entrance

Parking

Plataforma
Funeraria

Templo de la
Sene Inicial

CARIBBEAN
SEA

Muralla Fortificada

Tulum

0   50   100 m
0   50   100 yards

Templo

Torre de Guardia

Muralla Fortificada

To Tulum Zona Hotelera,
Boca Paila, Punta Allen

Puerta

Puerta

Temple of the Frescoes

This two-story building (Structure 16, Templo de los Frescos) was constructed in several stages sometime around 1400 to 1450. Its decoration was among the more elaborate examples at Tulum, including the diving god, relief masks and colored murals on an inner wall. The murals, painted in three levels, show the three realms of the Mayan universe: the dark underworld of the deceased, the middle order of the living and the heavenly home of the creator and rain gods.

Great Palace

Smaller than El Castillo, this largely deteriorated site (Structure 25) contains a fine stucco carving of a diving god.

Temple of the Initial Series

The restored Templo de la Serie Inicial is named for Stela 1, now in the British Museum, which was inscribed with the Mayan date corresponding to 564 AD (the 'initial series' of Mayan hieroglyphs in an inscription gives its date). At first this confused archaeologists, who believed Tulum to have been settled several hundred years later than this date. It's now believed that Stela 1 was brought to Tulum from Tankah, four km to the north, a settlement dating from the Classic period.

Structures 57 & 59

These two small temples are north of the city wall. Structure 57, about 500 meters north of the wall, is a one-room shrine in good condition. Structure 59, another 500 meters to the north, is another one-room temple with remains of a roofcomb, the only one found at Tulum.

Places to Stay & Eat

El Crucero Right at the junction of highway 307 and the old Tulum ruins access road are several hotels and restaurants, including the basic, well used *Motel El Crucero*, expensive at US$8 to US$11 a double with shower and fan. The restaurant and shop selling ice, meals, drinks and souvenirs are more useful. A chicken dinner costs US$5.

Facing the Motel El Crucero across the access road are the *Hotel Acuario*, with air-con rooms overpriced at US$30 to US$45 double (and you must pay in advance), and its *Restaurant El Faisan y El Venado*.

Boca Paila/Punta Allen Road South of the archaeological zone is a paradise of palm-shaded white beach dotted with collections of cabañas, little thatched huts of greater or lesser comfort, and simple wooden or concrete bungalows. Most of these places have little eateries at which you can take your meals, and some have electric generators which provide electric light for several hours each evening.

The cheapest way to sleep here is to have your own hammock, preferably with one of those tube-like mosquito nets to cover it; if you don't carry your own, several of the cheaper places will rent you what you need. Candles or a flashlight will come in handy here. In the cheapest places you'll have to supply your own towel and soap. See the sidebar for more tips on Tulum cabañas.

We'll start by describing the places closest to Tulum ruins, then head south to describe the places farther and farther away.

Closest to the ruins are *Cabañas El Mirador* and *Cabañas Santa Fe*, on the beach about 600 meters south of the Tulum ruins parking lot. The Santa Fe is preferable, though a bit more expensive, charging US$3 per person for a campsite, US$8 to hang your hammocks in a cabin, or US$10 to US$12 and up to US$18 per person for beds. At El Mirador, a cabaña sleeping up to four people is yours for US$9 double complete with hammocks.

Cabañas Don Armando, just south of Santa Fe, is the most famous of the budget cabaña places. For US$14 to US$18 (single or double) you get one of 17 cabins built on concrete slabs, with lockable doors, hammocks or beds (you pay a deposit for sheets and pillows), mosquito netting, good showers and a good, cheap restaurant. Smaller, less comfy cabañas rent for US$9 to US$12. Lighting in the rooms is by candles. This place is fun, right on the beach, and still only a 10-minute walk to the ruins.

The *Hotel El Paraíso* (☎ 1-21-42, fax 1-20-07), 1.5 km south of the ruins, approaches a conventional hotel in its services. The newer rooms, with two double beds and private bath, cost US$38, the nicer cabañas US$55. There's a restaurant with sea view, and electricity until 10 pm. *Gato's Cabañas*, 700 meters south, charges slightly less.

One km south of the junction with the access road from highway 307 is a cluster of lodgings. *La Conchita* is simple and cheap, as is *Punta Piedra*, with cabañas for US$12.

Cabañas Nohoch Tunich, just south of Punta Piedra, has older but still serviceable cabañas for US$10 to US$18, and comfortable modern ones for US$40 to US$55. *La Perla*, Apdo Postal 77, Tulum, Quintana Roo 77780, has quite good rooms for US$35 to US$45; some are newer than others, so look at several if possible.

Zamas, Apdo Postal 49, Tulum, Quintana Roo 77780 (☎ in USA 415-387-9806,

fax 415-668-1226) fronts on a beach accented by dramatic rock formations. Rooms range from US$25 for a double with shared bath to US$50 for one with two double beds and private bath.

Piedra Escondida (☎ /fax 1-20-92), Apdo Postal 128, Tulum, Quintana Roo 77780, is the nicest accommodation in the area, with modern, stylish two-story thatched cabañas renting for US$60 to US$80 with one or two double beds. The management is Italian.

Just south of this cluster the paved road gives way to a good sand track.

Osho Oasis Retreat (☎ 4-27-72, in USA 707-778-1320; fax 3-02-30 ext 174), Apdo Postal 99, Tulum, Quintana Roo 77780, is a resort for plain living and high thinking. There's a meditation hall and facilities for yoga, Zen, kundalini and massage, as well as the beach. Cabañas cost US$50 to US$70 a double in high season; meals are US$7/6/14 for breakfast/lunch/dinner.

Tulum Cabañas

Everybody's heard about the cabañas south of Tulum as a little bit of paradise. Here's what you need to know to pass through the Pearly Gates safely and thriftily:

- All of the cabañas are full by 10 or 11 am every day during the winter season (mid-December through March) and in July and August. You must get here very early to get one, or make a reservation the night before. But if you have your own hammock and mosquito net, you'll be able to find some place to sleep without too much problem.
- If you take an afternoon or evening bus to the Tulum Crucero or Zona Arqueológica entrance, then a taxi to the cabañas, the taxi driver knows there are no rooms available but won't tell you this because he doesn't want to lose the fare. Besides, after you have discovered that there are no rooms, he'll get another fare taking you back to the highway.
- There is great variety in the cabañas: comfortable, secure ones, ramshackle ones; some with hammocks provided, others where you must bring your own hammock or rent one; some with sea views and good beds, others with neither. Most will be full when you arrive, so you'll have to take whatever's vacant, at least for the first night or two.
- Cheapest are the rustic cabañas made of sticks and providing hammocks. These are about one km south of Tulum ruins along the old road, and include El Mirador, Santa Fe, and Don Armando's.
- Supposedly, you can reserve cabañas in advance, but reservations are only dependable with the more expensive ones.
- Security is a big problem here. Few of the flimsy, primitive cabañas can be reliably secured. Thieves lift the poles in the walls to gain entrance, or burrow beneath through the sand, or jimmy the locks. You may even have your beach towel stolen from a drying line. Consider security carefully when you choose a place to stay. ■

Los Arrecifes, south of Osho, has fairly rustic cabañas (some of sticks, others of cinder block) for US$28, single or double.

About 3.5 km south of the access road intersection (seven km south of the ruins), *Cabañas de Ana y José* (☎ in Cancún 98-80-60-22, fax 98-80-60-21), has older bungalows for US$40, or newer ones for US$50 a double, and a sand-floor restaurant-bar.

Just south is *Cabañas Tulum* (☎ 25-82-95), Apdo Postal 63, Tulum, Quintana Roo 77780, where older concrete bungalows look out through palms to the sea and the beach. The rate is US$36 per night, single or double, in summer, US$40 in winter. There's a restaurant and bar. The electric generator runs (if it's working) from dusk to 10 pm each evening.

Getting There & Away

You can walk from Tulum Crucero to the ruins (800 meters), or take the mini-train for a fee.

Reaching the cabañas is more difficult. The closest are one km from Tulum Crucero on foot, or at least six km on the road, and there is no public transport except taxis. Though you may occasionally be able to hitch a ride, you can depend only upon your own two feet or a taxi to get you to your lodgings, and from your lodgings to the ruins.

There is a small ADO bus station at the southern end of Tulum Pueblo. When leaving Tulum, you can wait at Tulum Crucero for a Playa Express bus or regular intercity bus. Here are some distances and travel times:

Cancún – 132 km, two hours, US$3 to US$4
Chetumal – 251 km, four hours, US$5 to US$7
Chichén Itzá – 402 km, 6½ hours, US$5; one bus
Cobá – 45 km, one hour
Felipe Carrillo Puerto – 98 km, 1¾ hours
Mérida – 320 km, five hours via Cobá or seven hours via Cancún; Oriente (US$7) and ADO (US$8.25) have a few buses
Palenque – 738 km, 11 hours; two by Colón (US$20)
Playa del Carmen – 63 km, one hour
Punta Allen – 57 km, 1½ hours
Valladolid – 156 km, three hours, US$7

TULUM TO BOCA PAILA & PUNTA ALLEN

The scenery on the 50-km stretch from Tulum Ruinas past Boca Paila to Punta Allen is the typically monotonous flat Yucatecan terrain, but the land, rich with wildlife, is protected as the Reserva de la Biosfera Sian Ka'an. The surfy beaches are not spectacular, but there's plenty of privacy.

A minivan makes the trip from Tulum Pueblo to Punta Allen more or less daily, taking anywhere from two to four hours for the trip, depending upon the condition of the road.

It's important to have plenty of fuel before heading south from Tulum as there is no fuel available on the Tulum-Punta Allen road.

Reserva de la Biosfera Sian Ka'an

Over 5000 sq km of tropical jungle, marsh, mangrove and islands on Quintana Roo's coast have been set aside by the Mexican government as a large biosphere reserve. In 1987 the United Nations appointed it a World Heritage Site – an irreplaceable natural treasure.

A trip into Sian Ka'an (Where the Sky Begins) reveals thousands of butterflies as well as varied fauna: howler monkeys, foxes, ocelots, pumas, vultures, caimans (crocodiles), eagles, raccoons, giant land crabs and – if you're very lucky – a jaguar. Unrestored Mayan ruins are everywhere. Though small and mostly unimpressive, it's still a thrill to visit one of these quiet sites which has lain here unheeded for centuries.

Treks into the reserve are run from Cancún and Playa del Carmen. For details on the reserve, contact Amigos de Sian Ka'an (☎ 98-84-95-83, 98-87-30-80), Plaza América, Avenida Cobá 5, 3rd Floor, Suites 48-50, Cancún, Quintana Roo 77500.

Boca Paila

Boca Paila is 25 km south of Tulum. One of the two hotels on the road to Punta Allen is *La Villa de Boca Paila*, where luxury cabañas complete with kitchens cost about US$90 per double, including two meals.

The clientele is predominantly affluent American sport fishers. For reservations write to Apdo Postal 159, Mérida, Yucatán.

Ten km south of Boca Paila you cross a rickety wooden bridge. Beyond it is *El Retiro Cabañas*, where you can hang hammocks or camp for a few dollars.

Punta Allen

Once a pocket of wealthy lobster fishers in a vast wilderness, Punta Allen suffered considerable damage from the ferocious winds of Hurricane Gilbert in 1988. The hurricane and overfishing have depleted lobster stocks, but a laid-back ambiance reminiscent of the Belizean cayes gives hope for a touristic future.

Punta Allen does have some rustic lodgings. The *Cruzan Inn* (fax 983-4-03-83) has cabañas with hammocks for about US$25 a double. The couple who run it prepare breakfast and lunch at a cost of US$6.50 per person and charge US$14 for dinner. They can arrange snorkeling and fishing expeditions, or visits to the offshore island of Cayo Colibri, known for its bird life. To write for reservations, the address is Cruzan Inn, c/o Sonia Lillvik, Apdo Postal 703, Cancún, Quintana Roo 77500.

The *Bonefishing Club of Ascension Bay*, run by Jan Persson, specializes in guided fishing expeditions, but also has two rooms for rent in the house that is its headquarters. Family-style meals are served.

Let It Be Inn has three thatched cabañas with comforts such as private bath (with

Catching lobsters

hot water) and sea-view porches hung with hammocks. For reservations write to Rick Montgomery, Let It Be Inn, Apdo Postal 74, Tulum, Quintana Roo 77780.

If you wish to camp on Punta Allen's beach, simply ask the Maya in front of whose house you would be sleeping for permission.

COBÁ

Perhaps the largest of all Mayan cities, Cobá, 50 km northwest of Tulum, offers the chance to explore mostly unrestored antiquities set deep in tropical jungles.

History

Cobá was settled earlier than Chichén or Tulum, its heyday dating from 600 AD until the site was mysteriously abandoned about 900 AD. Archaeologists believe that this city once covered 50 sq km and held 40,000 Maya.

Cobá's architecture is a mystery; its towering pyramids and stelae resemble the architecture of Tikal, several hundred km away, rather than the much nearer sites of Chichén Itzá and the northern Yucatán Peninsula.

Some archaeologists theorize that an alliance with Tikal was made through marriage to facilitate trade between the Guatemalan and Yucatecan Maya. Stelae appear to depict female rulers from Tikal holding ceremonial bars and flaunting their power by standing on captives. These Tikal royal females, when married to Cobá's royalty, may have brought architects and artisans with them.

Archaeologists are also baffled by the network of extensive sacbeob (stone-paved avenues) in this region, with Cobá as the hub. The longest runs nearly 100 km from the base of Cobá's great pyramid Nohoch Mul to the Mayan settlement of Yaxuna. In all, some 40 sacbeob passed through Cobá. The sacbeob were parts of the huge astronomical 'time machine' that was evident in every Mayan city.

The first excavation was by the Austrian archaeologist Teobert Maler. Hearing rumors of a fabled lost city, he came to Cobá

COBÁ VILLAGE
1 Villa Arqueológica
   Cobá
2 Restaurante
   Bocadito
3 Parking
4 Restaurants
5 Tickets

Cobá

0   250   500 m

0   250   500 yards

∴Chacne

Mirador ✳

To
Nuevo
Xcan

To
Tulum

∴Pyramid

Nohoch ∴
Mul

**COBÁ
VILLAGE**

1 ■ ▼2
  3 ○ ▼4
     ● 5

Laguna
Cobá

Grupo
Las
Pinturas ∴

To Chan
Mul

∴ Grupo Cobá

Laguna
Macanxoc

Uitzil Mul

Grupo ∴
Macanxoc

Laguna
Xkanha

Grupo
Zacakal
∴

Kitamna ∴

Laguna
Zacalpuc

Laguna
Sina A Kal

small, simple, cheap lodging and eating places. At the lake, turn left for the ruins, right for the upscale Villa Arqueológica Cobá hotel.

Cobá archaeological site is open from 8 am to 5 pm; admission costs US$2.50, free on Sunday.

Be prepared to walk at least five to seven km on jungle paths. Dress for heat and humidity, and bring insect repellent. It's also a good idea to bring a canteen of water; it's hot and there are no drinks stands within the site, only at the entrance. Avoid the midday heat if possible. A visit to the site takes two to four hours.

Grupo Cobá

Walking just under 100 meters along the main path from the entrance brings you to the Temple of the Churches (Templo de las Iglesias), on your right, the most prominent structure in the Cobá Group. It's an enormous pyramid, and from the top you can get a fine view of the Nohoch Mul pyramid to the north and shimmering lakes to the east and southwest.

Back on the main path, you pass through the Juego de Pelota, 30 meters farther along. It's now badly ruined.

Grupo Macanxoc

About 500 meters beyond the Juego de Pelota is the turning (right) for the Grupo Macanxoc, a group of stelae which bore reliefs of royal women thought to have come from Tikal.

Grupo de las Pinturas

One hundred meters beyond the Macanxoc turning, a sign points left toward the Conjunto de las Pinturas, or the Temple of Paintings. It bears easily recognizable traces of glyphs and frescoes above the door, and traces of richly colored plaster inside.

You approached the Temple of Paintings from the southwest. Leave by the trail at the northwest (opposite the temple steps) to see several stelae. The first of these is 20 meters along beneath a palapa. A regal figure stands over two others, one of them kneeling with his hands bound behind him.

alone in 1891. There was little subsequent investigation until 1926, when the Carnegie Institute financed the first of two expeditions led by J Eric S Thompson and Harry Pollock. After their 1930 expedition not much happened until 1973, when the Mexican government began to finance excavation. Archaeologists now estimate that Cobá contains some 6500 structures of which just a few have been excavated and restored.

Orientation

The small village of Cobá, 2.5 km west of the Tulum-Nuevo Xcan road, has several

Sacrificial captives lie beneath the feet of a ruler at the base. Continue along the path past another badly weathered stela to the Nohoch Mul path, and turn right.

Nohoch Mul – The Great Pyramid
A further walk of 800 meters brings you to Nohoch Mul. Along the way, just before the track bends sharply to the left, a narrow path on the right leads to a group of badly weathered stelae. Farther along, the track bends between piles of stones – obviously a ruined temple – before passing Temple 10 and Stela 20. The exquisitely carved stela bears a picture of a ruler standing imperiously over two captives. Eighty meters beyond the stela stands the Great Pyramid.

At 42 meters high, the huge Great Pyramid is the tallest of all Mayan structures in the Yucatán Peninsula. Climb the 120 steps, observing that the Maya carved shell-like forms where you put your feet.

There are two diving gods carved over the doorway of the Nohoch Mul temple at the top, similar to the sculptures at Tulum. The view is spectacular.

From Nohoch Mul, it's a 1.4-km, 30-minute walk back to the site entrance.

Places to Stay & Eat
There are several small restaurants among the souvenir shops by the car park. The staff at the drinks stand right by the entrance tend to be surly, so buy your drinks at either the *Restaurant El Faisan* or the *Restaurant El Caracol*, both of which serve cheap meals. In the village of Cobá, *Restaurant Lagoon* is nearest the lake, with good views and friendly service. The *Restaurant Isabel* and *Restaurant Bocadito* are also popular.

The Bocadito rents rooms with bath for US$8/12 a single/double, though I've heard a complaint of fleas. Meals are overpriced.

As for camping, there's no organized spot, though you can try finding a place along the shore of the lake.

For upscale lodging and dining the choice is easy: there's only the *Villa Arqueológica Cobá* (☎ in Cancún 98-84-25-74, in the USA 800-528-3100). The pleasant

hotel has a swimming pool and good restaurant. Air-conditioned rooms cost US$50/65/75 a single/double/triple. Lunch or dinner in the good restaurant might cost US$12 to US$20.

Getting There & Away
Numerous buses trace the route between Tulum and Valladolid. Be sure to mention to the driver that you want to get out at Cobá junction; the road does not pass through the village.

Leaving Cobá is problematic, as most buses are full when they pass here. If you're willing to stand for the 50 km to Tulum or the 50 km to Nuevo Xcan (120 km to Valladolid), you have a better chance.

A more comfortable, dependable but expensive way to reach Cobá is by taxi from Tulum Crucero. Find some other travelers interested in the trip and split the cost, about US$18 or US$25 roundtrip, including two hours (haggle for three) at the site.

By the way, many maps show a road from Cobá to Chemax, but this road is impassable.

FELIPE CARRILLO PUERTO
pop 17,000; ☎ *983*
Now named for a progressive governor of Yucatán, this town was once known as Chan Santa Cruz, the dreaded rebel headquarters during the War of the Castes.

History
In 1849 the War of the Castes turned against the Maya of the northern Yucatán Peninsula, who made their way to this town seeking refuge. Regrouping their forces, they were ready to sally forth again in 1850, just when a 'miracle' occurred. A wooden cross erected at a cenote on the western edge of the town began to 'talk,' telling the Maya they were the chosen people, exhorting them to continue the struggle against the whites, and promising victory. The talking was actually done by a ventriloquist who used sound chambers, but the people nonetheless looked upon it as the authentic voice of their aspirations.

YUCATÁN PENINSULA

Time Among the Maya

The history of the Talking Cross is not over. Every year on May 3, the Feast of the Holy Cross, Mayas gather in Felipe Carrillo Puerto – known as Noh Cah Santa Cruz Balam Na to them – to celebrate the cross as the symbol of ancient Mayan traditions, and specifically the Talking Cross as the last great symbol of Mayan independence.

Just a short drive inland from Carrillo Puerto, Mayan villagers observe many aspects of traditional life, including even the use of the ancient Mayan calendar.

In the mid-1980s, English writer Ronald Wright came here in search of Mayas who still understood the Long Count and lived by the dictates of the tzolkin, the ancient Mayan almanac. Wright wrote about his experiences in a fascinating book, *Time Among the Maya*, in 1989.

Wright found what he was seeking in X-Cacal Guardia and nearby villages, where descendants of the survivors of the 19th-century War of the Castes settled. Enveloped in the Yucatecan jungle, away from the wealth and centers of power which the government in Mexico City sought to control, they guard their ancient crosses and religious beliefs while accepting innovations like electric light, automobiles and Coca-Cola.

The 25-meter-long church at X-Cacal Guardia is guarded by men with rifles, its inner sanctum to be entered only by the Nohoch Tata (Great Father of the Holy Cross) himself. It may be that Chan Santa Cruz's famous Talking Cross, spirited away from the doomed city by the Mayas retreating from the last battle of the War of the Castes, has come to rest here. This is Ronald Wright's guess. ∎

The oracular cross guided the Maya in battle for more than eight years, until their great victory in conquering the fortress at Bacalar. For the latter part of the 19th century, the Maya in and around Chan Santa Cruz were virtually independent of governments in Mexico City and Mérida. In the 1920s a boom in the chicle market brought prosperity to the region and the Maya decided to come to terms with Mexico City, which they did in 1929. Some of the Maya, unwilling to give up the cult of the talking cross, left Chan Santa Cruz to take up residence at small villages deep in the jungle, where they still revere the talking cross to this day. You may see some of them visiting the site where the cross spoke, especially on May 3, the day of the Holy Cross.

You can visit the **Sanctuario del Cruz Parlante** (Sanctuary of the Talking Cross) five blocks west of the Pemex fuel station on the main street (highway 307) in the commercial center of town. Besides the cenote and a stone shelter, there's little to see in the park, though the place reverberates with history.

Places to Stay & Eat

El Faisán y El Venado (☎ 4-07-02), Juárez 781 across from the Pemex station 100 meters south of the traffic circle, has 13 air-con rooms with private showers and ceiling fans for US$8/16/18 a single/double/triple. They have a restaurant with surprisingly good food and service.

Just a few dozen meters to the south is the *Restaurant 24 Horas*, which is a bit cheaper.

South of the 24 Horas is the *Hotel San Ignacio*, with air-con rooms for US$12 to US$16, and an air-con restaurant with the odd name of *Danburguer Maya*.

Restaurant Familiar La Cozumeleño is a tidy family-run place, cheaper than the others.

For breads and pastries, check out the *Panadería Mar y Sol*.

Getting There & Away

Buses running between Cancún (230 km, four hours, US$8) and Chetumal (155 km, three hours, US$4 to US$6) stop here, as do buses traveling from Chetumal to Valladolid (160 km, three hours, US$6) and Mérida (310 km, 5½ to six hours, US$6.50 to US$8). There are also a few buses between Felipe Carrillo Puerto and Ticul (200 km, 3½ hours, US$8); change at Ticul or Muna for Uxmal. Bus fare between FCP and Tulum is US$3.75.

Note that there are very few services such as hotels, restaurants or fuel stations between Felipe Carrillo Puerto and Ticul.

XCALAK & COSTA MAYA

The coast south of the Reserva de la Biosfera Sian Ka'an to the small fishing village of Xcalak ('shka-LAK') is known as the Costa Maya. Unknown and difficult to access until 1981, it is now drawing handfuls of adventurous travelers in search of that fast-disappearing natural asset, the undeveloped stretch of coastline.

Travel services are few, and accommodations are often full. Unless you have advance reservations, be prepared to pitch your own tent or hang your own hammock, or return on the same bus that brought you. There are no banks, and currently the local economy runs on cash US dollars, not pesos, though this must change soon.

Several dive shops offer instruction and certification for scuba divers, rent snorkeling and scuba gear, and provide boat transportation to Chinchorro Reef.

Places to Stay & Eat

The six-room *Hotel Caracol* is currently the village's only cheap place to stay, offering cold-water rooms with fans for US$7/9 single/double. Look for the owner next door to the hotel. No doubt these prices will rise, and new small lodging places will open, as word of Xcalak's beauties spreads around the world.

Costa de Cocos (☎ in USA 800-538-6802), Apdo Postal 62, Chetumal, Quintana Roo, 1.5 km north of Xcalak, has eight thatched cabañas with private baths and solar hot water, and 24-hour electricity. There's a restaurant-bar.

Villa Caracol (☎ 983-8-18-72), km 45, Carretera Majahual-Xcalak, has six comfortable air-con rooms and two cabañas, each with two queen-size beds, purified water, private baths, and 24-hour electricity.

Several small restaurants – Capitan Caribe, Conchitas and El Caracol – serve cheap, good seafood dinners.

Getting There & Away

From highway 307, turn east at Cafetal, 68 km south of Felipe Carrillo Puerto and 46 km north of Bacalar, for Majahual (58 km). South of Majahual is an all-weather road to Xcalak (58 km).

Sociedad Cooperativa del Caribe buses depart Chetumal's main bus terminal for Majahual and Xcalak (200 km, five hours, US$3) daily at 6 am and 3.30 pm. There are also minibuses from Chetumal, departing the corner of Avenida 16 de Septiembre and Mahatma Gandhi near the Restaurant Pantoja, at 7 am, and departing from Xcalak at 1 pm.

There are plans for a daily ferry service to link Chetumal, Xcalak and San Pedro, Ambergris Caye, Belize.

LAGUNA BACALAR

Nature has set a turquoise jewel in the midst of the scrubby Yucatecan jungle – Laguna Bacalar. A large, clear fresh-water lake with a bottom of gleaming white sand, Bacalar comes as a surprise in this region of tortured limestone.

The small, sleepy town of Bacalar, just east of the highway some 125 km south of Felipe Carrillo Puerto, is the only settlement of any size on the lake. It's noted mostly for its old fortress and its swimming facilities.

The fortress was built over the lagoon to protect citizens from raids by pirates and Indians. It served as an important outpost for the whites in the War of the Castes. In 1859, it was seized by Mayan rebels who held the fort until Quintana Roo was finally conquered by Mexican troops in 1901. Today, with formidable cannon still on its ramparts, the fortress remains an imposing sight. It houses a museum exhibiting colonial armaments and uniforms from the 17th and 18th centuries. The museum is open daily from 8 am to 1 pm for US$1.

A divided avenue runs between the fortress and the lakeshore northward a few hundred meters to the balneario. Small restaurants line the avenue and surround the balneario, which is very busy on weekends.

YUCATÁN PENINSULA

Costera Bacalar & Cenote Azul

The road that winds southward along the lakeshore from Bacalar town to highway 307 at Cenote Azul is called the Costera Bacalar. It passes a few lodging and camping places along the way.

Hotel Laguna (☎ 983-2-35-17 in Chetumal), 3.3 km south of Bacalar town along the Costera, is only 150 meters east of highway 307, so you can ask a bus driver to stop there for you. Clean, cool and hospitable, it boasts a wonderful view of the lake, a swimming pool, a breezy terrace restaurant and bar. Rooms cost US$20 to US$30 a single or double with fan, good cross-ventilation and private bath.

Only 700 meters past the Hotel Laguna along the Costera is *Los Coquitos* camping area on the shore run by a family who live in a shack on the premises. You can camp in the dense shade of the palm trees, enjoy the view of the lake from the palapas, swim from the grassy banks, all for US$4 per couple. Bring your own food and drinking water, as the nearest supplier is the restaurant at the Hotel Laguna.

The Cenote Azul is a 90-meter-deep natural pool on the southwestern shore of Laguna Bacalar, 200 meters east of highway 307. (If you're approaching from the north by bus, get the driver to stop and let you off here.) Since this is a cenote there's no beach, just a few steps leading down to the water from the vast palapa which shelters the restaurant. You might pay US$8 to US$12 for the average meal here. A small sign purveys Mayan wisdom: 'Don't go in the cenote if you can't swim.'

Getting There & Away

Coming from the north, have the bus drop you in Bacalar town, at the Hotel Laguna, or at Cenote Azul, as you wish; check before you buy your ticket to see if the driver will stop.

Heading west out of Chetumal, you turn north onto highway 307; 15.5 km north of this highway junction is a turn on the right marked for the Cenote Azul and Costera Bacalar.

Catch a minibus from Chetumal's minibus terminal on Primo de Verdad at Hidalgo. Departures are about every 20 minutes from 5 am to 7 pm for the 39-km (40 minutes, US$2) run to the town of Bacalar; some northbound buses (US$1.25) departing from the bus terminal will also drop you near the town of Bacalar. Along the way they pass Laguna Milagros (14 km), Xul-ha (22 km) and the Cenote Azul (33 km), and all four of these places afford chances to swim in fresh water. The lakes are beautiful, framed by palm trees, with crystal clear water and soft white limestone-sand bottoms.

CHETUMAL

pop 130,000; ☎ *983*

Before the Spanish Conquest, Chetumal was a Mayan port for shipping gold, feathers, cacao and copper from this region and Guatemala to the northern Yucatán Peninsula. After the conquest, the town was not actually settled until 1898 when it was founded to put a stop to the illegal trade in arms and lumber carried on by the descendants of the War of the Castes rebels. Dubbed Payo Obispo, the town's name was changed to Chetumal in 1936. In 1955, Hurricane Janet virtually obliterated Chetumal.

During the rebuilding, the city planners laid out the new town on a grand plan with a grid of wide boulevards. In times BC (Before Cancún), the sparsely populated territory of Quintana Roo could not support such a grand city, even though Quintana Roo was upgraded from a territory to a state in 1974. But the boom at Cancún brought prosperity to all, and Chetumal is finally fulfilling its destiny as an important capital city.

Chetumal is also the gateway to Belize. With the peso so low and Belize so expensive, Belize nearly empties out on weekends with shoppers coming to Chetumal's markets.

Orientation

Despite Chetumal's sprawling layout, the city center is easily manageable on foot.

Once you find the all-important intersection of Avenida de los Héroes and Avenida Alvaro Obregón, you're within 50 meters of several cheap hotels and restaurants. The best hotels are only four or five blocks from this intersection.

Information
Tourist Office A tourist information kiosk (☎ 2-36-63) on Avenida de los Héroes at the eastern end of Aguilar, can answer questions. Hours are 8 am to 1 pm and 5 to 8 pm daily.

Consulates The Guatemalan consulate (☎ 2-85-85) is at Avenida Héroes de Chapultepec 354, nine blocks (just over one km) west of Avenida de los Héroes. Look for the blue-and-white flag on the left (south) side of the street. It's open weekdays from 9 am to 2 pm and offers quick visa service.

The Belizean consulate (☎ 2-01-00), Avenida Obregón 226A, between Juárez and Independencia, is open weekdays from 9 am to 2 pm, and 5 to 8 pm; Saturday from 9.30 am to 2 pm; closed Sunday.

Money See the map for locations of currency exchange offices and banks with ATMs.

Post The post office (☎ 2-00-57) is at Plutarco Elías Calles 2A.

Museo de la Cultura Maya
This museum is the city's claim to cultural fame, a bold block-long air-conditioned showpiece designed to draw visitors from as far away as Cancún.

The exhibits cover all of the Mayab (lands of the Maya), not just Quintana Roo or Mexico, and seek to explain the Mayan way of life, thought and belief. There are beautiful scale models of the great Mayan buildings as they may have appeared; replicas of stelae from Copán, Honduras; and reproductions of the murals found in Room 1 at Bonampak, as well as artifacts discovered at sites in Quintana Roo.

The museum is organized into three levels, as was Mayan cosmogony based on the 'World Tree': the main floor represents this world, the upper floor the heavens, and the lower floor Xibalba, the underworld. All exhibits are labeled in Spanish and English. It's open from 9 am to 7 pm (closed Monday) for US$2.50, half-price for children.

Places to Stay – budget
Instituto Quintanarroense de la Juventud y El Deporte (☎ 2-05-25), the youth hostel, on Calzada Veracruz near the corner with Avenida Obregón, is the cheapest place in town. It has a few drawbacks: single-sex dorms, 11 pm curfew, and a location five blocks east of the intersection of Héroes and Obregón. The cost is US$5 for a bunk in a room with four or six beds and shared bath, or US$2.50 per person to camp. Breakfast costs US$1.75 and lunch or dinner US$2.50 in the cafeteria.

Hotel María Dolores (☎ 2-05-08), Avenida Obregón 206 west of Héroes above the Restaurant Sosilmar, is the best for the price, with tiny, stuffy rooms for US$7/9/11/13 single/double/triple/quad with fans and private bath. Some rooms sleep up to six.

Hotel Ucum (☎ 2-07-11), Avenida Gandhi 167, is a large place with lots of rooms around a bare central courtyard and a good cheap little restaurant. Plain rooms with fan and shower cost US$8/10/12 single/double/triple, or US$11 double with air-con.

Hotel Cristal (☎ 2-38-78), Colón 207, between Juárez and Belice, is run by an energetic señora who offers clean rooms for US$7/9/11 a single/double/triple with fan, US$14 a double with air-con.

Want a very clean, quiet room with good cross-ventilation, fan, air-con, TV and private bath for only US$14? Then find your way to the *Posada Pantoja* (☎ 2-17-81), Lucio Blanco 95, one km northeast of the tourist info kiosk in a peaceful residential area. Ask at the Restaurant Pantoja for directions.

Bahía Chetumal

PLACES TO STAY
1 Posada Pantoja
3 Hotel Cristal
6 Hotel Ucum
10 Holiday Inn Chetumal Puerta Maya
15 Hotel Los Cocos
20 Hotel El Cedro
30 Hotel María Dolores
33 Hotel Caribe Princess
34 Instituto Quintanarroense de la
   Juventud y El Deporte (Youth Hostel)

PLACES TO EAT
6 Restaurant Ucum
7 Restaurant Pantoja
15 Hotel Los Cocos Sidewalk Café
17 Restaurant Vegetariano La Fuente
22 Restaurant Típico El Taquito
24 Café-Restaurant Los Milagros
29 Pollo Brujo
30 Restaurant Sosilmar,
   Panadería La Muralla
32 Sergio's Pizzas, Maria's Restaurant
37 Panadería y Pastelería La Invencible

OTHER
2 Minibus Terminal
4 ADO Bus Ticket Office
5 Museo de la Cultura Maya
8 Mercado Ignacio Manuel Altamirano
9 Clinica de Chetumal
11 Tourist Information Kiosk
12 Hospital Morelos
13 Cruz Roja
14 Centro de Salud
16 TelMex
18 Banco Mexicano
19 Banpaís, BanCrecer, ATMs
21 Post Office
23 Chetumal Express Casa de Cambio
25 Banca Serfin, ATM
26 Belizean Consulate
27 Banamex, ATM
28 Banamex
31 Easy Money Casa de Cambio
35 Bital
36 Banco del Atlántico
38 Palacio de Gobierno

Chetumal

| 0 | 100 | 200 m |
| 0 | 100 | 200 yards |

Hotel El Cedro (☎ 2-68-78), on Avenida de los Héroes between Plutarco Elías Calles and Cárdenas, has acceptable rooms for US$19 double with air-con, TV and private baths.

The quiet *Hotel Caribe Princess* (☎ 2-09-00), Avenida Obregón 168, has lots of marble and good air-con rooms for US$18/20/23.

Two blocks (200 meters) south of the Nuevo Mercado and buses to Belize, the *Hotel Nachancan* (☎ 2-32-32), Calzada Veracruz 379, offers decent, more-or-less quiet rooms with air-con and TV for US$15/18/21. The *Hotel Posada Rosas del Mar*, Calzada Veracruz 407, is directly across from the market, and is cheap at US$8 double, but is nothing special.

One km north of the Museo Maya on the way to the bus terminal, the *Hotel Principe* (☎ 2-47-99, fax 2-51-91), Avenida de los Héroes 326, has decent rooms, a restaurant, and even a small swimming pool. Rooms cost US$20 double with air-con.

Places to Stay – middle
Hotel Los Cocos (☎ 2-05-44, fax 2-09-20), Avenida de los Héroes at Avenida Heroes de Chapultepec, has a nice swimming pool set in grassy lawns, guarded car park and popular sidewalk restaurant. Air-con rooms with TV, rich in nubby white stucco, cost US$38 to US$55 single or double.

Two blocks north of Los Cocos along Avenida de los Héroes, near the tourist information kiosk, is the *Holiday Inn Chetumal Puerta Maya* (☎ 2-11-00, 2-10-80, in USA 800-465-4329; fax 2-16-76), Avenida de los Héroes 171. Its comfortable rooms overlook a small courtyard with a swimming pool set amid tropical gardens; there's a restaurant and bar. Rates are US$66, single or double. This is the best in town.

Places to Eat
Across from the Holiday Inn and the tourist information kiosk is the Mercado Ignacio Manuel Altamirano and its row of small, simple market eateries purveying full meals for US$2 or US$3.

YUCATÁN PENINSULA

Restaurant Sosilmar, on Avenida Obregón below the Hotel María Dolores, is bright and simple, with prices listed prominently. Filling platters of fish or meat go for US$3 to US$5.

Next door is the *Panadería La Muralla*, providing fresh baked goods for bus trips, picnics and make-your-own breakfasts. An even grander pastry shop is the *Panadería y Pastelería La Invencible* on Carmen Ochoa de Merino west of Avenida de los Héroes.

West of the Sosilmar is *Pollo Brujo*, where a roasted half chicken is yours for US$2.50. Take it with you, or dine in their air-con salon.

Restaurant Vegetariano La Fuente, Cárdenas 222 between Independencia and Juárez, is a tidy meatless restaurant next to a homeopathic pharmacy. Healthy meals cost US$4 or less.

Café-Restaurant Los Milagros, on Zaragoza between Héroes and 5 de Mayo, serves meals for US$3 to US$4 indoors or outdoors, and there's a book exchange with numerous English titles. It's a favorite place for Chetumal's student and intellectual set.

The family-owned *Restaurant Pantoja* (☎ 2-39-57), Avenida Gandhi 181 at 16 de Septiembre, is a neighborhood favorite which opens for breakfast early, and later provides a comida corrida for US$2.50, enchiladas for US$2, and meat plates such as bistec or *higado encebollado* (liver and onions) for US$3. The nearby *Restaurant Ucum*, in the Hotel Ucum, also provides good cheap meals.

To sample the typical traditional food of Quintana Roo, head for the *Restaurant Típico El Taquito*, Plutarco Elías Calles 220 at Juárez. You enter past the cooks, hard at work, to an airy, simple dining room where good, cheap food is served. Tacos cost US$0.50 each, slightly more with cheese. There's a daily comida corrida for US$2.75. This is a good place to go with a jolly group of friends.

Maria's (☎ 2-04-91) and *Sergio's Pizzas* (☎ 2-23-55), Avenida Obregón 182, a block east of Héroes, are actually the same full-service restaurant with two wood-paneled, air-conditioned dining rooms

open from 1 pm to midnight daily. Look for the stained-glass windows, enter to low lights and soft classical music. In Maria's, order one of the many wines offered, then any of the Mexican or continental dishes, such as seafood, or beef cordon bleu (US$7), finishing up with sacher torte. In Sergio's, order a cold beer in a frosted mug and select a pizza priced from US$3 (small, plain) to US$14 (large, fancy).

For people-watching (especially in the evening), try the sidewalk café at the Hotel Los Cocos, where a full lunch or dinner is yours for US$6 to US$12. Drinks are expensive here.

Getting There & Away

Air Chetumal's small airport is less than two km northwest of the city center along Obregón and Revolución.

Mexicana's regional carrier Aerocaribe (☎ /fax 2-66-75), Avenida Héroes 125, Plaza Baroudi Local 13, operates flights between Chetumal and Cancún, Cozumel, Flores (Petén, Guatemala) and Palenque.

Aviacsa (☎ 2-76-76, fax 2-76-54; at the airport ☎ 2-77-87, fax 2-76-98) flies nonstop to Villahermosa and direct to Mexico City.

For flights to Belize City (and on to Tikal) or to Belize's cayes, cross the border into Belize and fly from Corozal.

Bus The Terminal de Autobuses de Chetumal is three km north of the center (Museo de la Cultura Maya) at the intersection of Avenida de los Insurgentes and Avenida Belice. ADO, Autotransportes del Sur, Cristóbal Colón, Omnitur del Caribe, Línea Dorada and Unimaya provide service. The terminal has lockers, a tourism information kiosk, bookstore, newsstand, post office, international phone and fax services, and shops. Next to the terminal is a huge San Francisco de Asis department store.

You can buy ADO tickets in the city center on Avenida Belice just west of the Museo de la Cultura Maya.

Many local buses, and those bound for Belize, depart from the Nuevo Mercado Lázaro Cárdenas, on Calzada Veracruz at

Regundo, 10 blocks (1.5 km) north of the Museo Maya along Avenida de los Héroes, then turn at the Jeep dealership and go three blocks east.

The Minibus Terminal at the corner of Avenida Primo de Verdad and Hidalgo, has minibuses to Bacalar and other nearby destinations.

Bacalar – 39 km, 45 minutes; minibuses from the Minibus Terminal for US$2; nine 2nd-class buses from the bus terminal for US$2.50

Belize City – 160 km, four hours, US$5; express three hours, US$6; Batty's runs 12 north-bound buses from Belize City via Orange Walk and Corozal to Chetumal's Nuevo Mercado from 4 am to 11.15 am; 12 southbound buses from Chetumal's Nuevo Mercado run from 10.30 am and 6.30 pm. Venus Bus Lines has buses departing from Belize City every hour on the hour from noon to 7 pm; departures from Chetumal are hourly from 4 to 10 am.

Campeche – 422 km, seven hours, US$11 to US$14; three buses

Cancún – 382 km, six hours, US$10 to US$14; 23 buses

Corozal (Belize) – 30 km, one hour with border formalities, US$1.75; see Belize City schedule

Felipe Carrillo Puerto – 155 km, three hours; 23 buses for US$4 to US$6

Flores (Guatemala) – 350 km, nine hours, US$35; Servicio San Juan operates a bus at 2.30 pm daily from Chetumal's main bus terminal to Flores and Tikal

Kohunlich – 67 km, 1¼ hours; take a bus heading west to Xpujil or Escárcega, get off just before the village of Francisco Villa and walk nine km (1¾ hours) to site

Mérida – 456 km, eight hours, US$9 to US$13; 12 buses

Orange Walk (Belize) – 91 km, 2¼ hours; Urbina's and Chell's each run one bus daily (US$4), departing Chetumal's Nuevo Mercado around lunchtime; see also Belize City

Palenque – 425 km, seven hours; one ADO (US$15) at 10.20 pm; two Colón (US$15); one ATS (US$12) at 8.15 pm; see also Villahermosa

Playa del Carmen – 315 km, five hours; seven by ADO (US$10 to US$12), one by Colón (US$10), three by Mayab (US$6.50)

San Cristóbal de las Casas – 700 km, 11 hours; two by Colón (US$21 to US$24), two by ATS (US$18), plus several ADO buses (US$22) de paso

Ticul – 352 km, 6½ hours, US$7; nine buses

Tikal (Guatemala) – 351 km, 11 hours, US$40; see Flores

Tulum – 251 km, four hours, US$5 to US$7; at least 12 buses

Villahermosa – 575 km, eight hours, US$18; eight buses; get off at Catazajá for Palenque

Xcalak – 200 km, five hours, US$3; Sociedad Cooperativa del Caribe runs buses at 6 am and 3.30 pm from the Minibus Terminal

Xpujil – 120 km, two hours, US$3 to US$4; eight buses

Getting Around

Official taxis from the bus terminal to the center overcharge. Rather, walk out of the terminal to the main road, turn left, walk to the traffic circle and catch a regular cab.

AROUND CHETUMAL

West of Chetumal along highway 186 is rich sugar cane and cattle country; logging is still important here, as it was during the 17th and 18th centuries.

Kohunlich Ruins

The archaeological site of Kohunlich is only partly excavated, with many of its nearly 200 mounds still covered in vegetation. The surrounding jungle is thick, but the archaeological site itself has been cleared selectively and is now a delightful forest park. Admission to the site costs US$1.50, and is open from 8 am to 5 pm daily. Drinks are sometimes sold at the site. The toilets are usually locked and 'under repair.'

These ruins, dating from the late Pre-classic (100-200 AD) and early Classic (AD 250-600) periods, are famous for the great Pirámide de los Mascarones (Pyramid of the Masks): a central stairway is flanked by huge, three-meter-high stucco masks of the sun god. The thick lips and prominent features are reminiscent of Olmec sculpture. Though there were once eight masks, only two remain after the ravages of archaeology looters. The masks themselves are impressive, but the large thatch coverings that have been erected to protect them from further weathering also obscure the view; you can see the masks

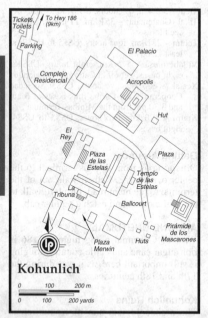

Kohunlich

```
0    100    200 m
0    100    200 yards
```

only from close up. Try to imagine what the pyramid and its masks must have looked like in the old days as the Maya approached it across the sunken courtyard at the front.

The hydraulic engineering used at the site was a great achievement; nine of the site's 21 hectares were cut to channel rainwater into Kohunlich's once-enormous reservoir.

Getting There & Away At the time of writing, there is no public transport running directly to Kohunlich. To visit the ruins without your own vehicle, start early in the morning, and take a bus heading west from

Chetumal to Xpujil or Escárcega, then watch for the village of Nachi-Cocom some 50 km from Chetumal. About 9.5 km past Nachi-Cocom, just before the village of Francisco Villa, is a road on the left (south) which covers the nine km to the archaeological site. Have the bus driver stop and let you off here, and plan to walk and hope to hitch a ride from tourists in a car; hold up this guidebook for the driver to see.

Developers plan to build a luxury hotel on the Kohunlich access road, which may result in better public transportation as well.

To return to Chetumal or head westward to Xpujil or Escárcega you must hope to flag down a bus on the highway; not all buses will stop.

SOUTH TO BELIZE & GUATEMALA
Corozal, 18 km south of the Mexican/Belizean border, is a pleasant, sleepy, laid-back farming and fishing town, and an appropriate introduction to Belize. There are several decent hotels catering to a full range of budgets, and restaurants to match. For complete details on travel through, within and beyond Belize, get hold of Lonely Planet's *Guatemala, Belize & Yucatán: La Ruta Maya* and/or *Central America*.

Buses run directly from Chetumal's market to Belize City via Corozal and Orange Walk. From Belize City you can catch westward buses to Belmopan, San Ignacio, and the Guatemalan border at Benque Viejo, then onward to Flores, Tikal and other points in Guatemala.

A special 1st-class bus service operated by Servicio San Juan goes directly between Chetumal's bus terminal and Flores (near Tikal in Guatemala) once daily (350 km, nine hours, US$35).

Glossary

AC – *antes de Cristo* (before Christ); equivalent to BC

adobe – sun-dried mud brick used for building

aduana – customs

agave – family of plants including the *maguey*

aguardiente – literally 'burning water'; strong liquor usually made from sugar cane

Alameda – name of the formal parks in several Mexican cities

albergue de juventud – youth hostel; often dormitories in a *villa juvenil*

alfarería – potter's workshop

alfíz – rectangular frame around a curved arch; an Arabic influence on Spanish and Mexican buildings

Altiplano Central – dry plateau stretching across north central Mexico between the two Sierra Madre ranges

amate – paper made from tree bark

Ángeles Verdes – Green Angels: government-funded mechanics who patrol Mexico's major highways in green vehicles; they help stranded motorists with fuel, spare parts and service

Apdo – abbreviation for *Apartado* (Box) in addresses; hence *Apdo Postal* means Post Office Box

arroyo – brook, stream

artesanías – handicrafts, folk arts

atlas (s), **atlantes** (pl) – sculpted male figure(s) used instead of a pillar to support a roof or frieze; a *telamon*

atrium – churchyard, usually a big one

autopista – expressway, dual carriageway

azulejo – painted ceramic tile

bahía – bay

balneario – bathing-place, often a natural hot spring

baluarte – bulwark, defensive wall

barrio – neighborhood of a town or city, often a poor neighborhood

billete – bank note

boleto – ticket

brujo, -a – witch-doctor, shaman, similar to *curandero, -a*

burro – donkey

caballeros – literally 'horsemen,' but corresponds to 'gentlemen' in English; look for it on toilet doors

cabaña – cabin, simple shelter

cabina – Baja Californian term for a telephone *caseta*

cacique – Aztec chief; in more recent times used to describe a provincial warlord or political strongman

calle – street

callejón – alley

calzada – grand boulevard or avenue

camarín – chapel beside the main altar in a church; contains ceremonial clothing for images of saints or the Virgin; also, a type of sleeping compartment on a train

camión – truck or bus

camioneta – pickup truck

campesino, -a – country person, peasant

capilla abierta – open chapel; used in early Mexican monasteries for preaching to large crowds of Indians

casa de cambio – exchange house; place where currency is exchanged, faster to use than a bank

caseta de larga distancia – public telephone call station, often in a shop

caseta de teléfono – see *caseta de larga distancia*

caseta telefónica – see *caseta de larga distancia*

cazuela – clay cooking-pot; usually sold in a nested set

cenote – a limestone sinkhole filled with rainwater, used in Yucatán as a reservoir and sometimes for ceremonial purposes

central camionera – bus terminal

cerro – hill

Chac – Mayan rain god

chac-mool – pre-Hispanic stone sculpture of a hunched, belly-up figure; the stomach may have been used as a sacrificial altar

charreada – Mexican rodeo

charro – Mexican cowboy

Chilango, -a – citizen of Mexico City

chinampas – Aztec gardens built from lake mud and vegetation; versions still exist at Xochimilco, Mexico City

chingar – literally 'to fuck'; it has a wide range of colloquial usages in Mexican Spanish equivalent to those in English

chultún – cement-lined brick cistern found in the *chenes* (wells) region in the Puuc hills south of Mérida

Churrigueresque – Spanish late-baroque architectural style; found on many Mexican churches

cigarro – cigarette

clavadistas – the cliff divers of Acapulco and Mazatlán

Coatlicue – mother of the Aztec gods

colectivo – minibus or car that picks up and drops off passengers along a predetermined route; can also refer to other types of transport, such as boats, where passengers share the total fare

Coleto, -a – citizen of San Cristóbal de Las Casas

colonia – neighborhood of a city, often a wealthy residential area

comedor – literally 'eating place,' usually a sit-down stall in a market or a small, cheap restaurant

comida corrida – fixed-price menu with several courses, offered in restaurants; cheaper than eating à la carte

completo – no vacancy, literally 'full up'; a sign you may see at hotel desks

conasupo – government-owned store that sells many everyday basics at subsidized prices

conde – count (nobleman)

conquistador – early Spanish explorer-conqueror

cordillera – mountain range

correos – post office

coyote – person who smuggles illegal Mexican immigrants into the USA

criollo – Mexican-born person of Spanish parentage; in colonial times considered inferior by peninsular Spaniards (see *gachupines, peninsulares*)

Cristeros – Roman Catholic rebels of the late 1920s

cuota – toll; a *vía cuota* is a toll road

curandero, -a – literally 'curer,' a medicine man or woman who uses herbal and/or magical methods and often emphasizes spiritual aspects of disease

damas – ladies; the sign on toilet doors

danzantes – literally 'dancers'; stone carvings at Monte Albán

DC – *después de Cristo* (after Christ); equivalent to AD

de lujo – deluxe; often used with some license

delegación – a large urban governmental subdivision in Mexico City comprising numerous *colonias*

descompuesto – broken, out of order

DF – Distrito Federal (Federal District); about half of Mexico City lies in the DF

ejido – communal landholding

embarcadero – jetty, quay

encomienda – a grant made to a *conquistador* of labor by or tribute from a group of Indians; the conquistador was supposed to protect and convert the Indians, but usually treated them as little more than slaves

enramada – thatch-covered, open-air restaurant

enredo – wrap-around skirt

entremeses – hors d'oeuvres; also theatrical sketches, such as those performed during the Cervantino festival in Guanajuato

escuela – school

esq – abbreviation of *esquina* (corner) in addresses

estación de ferrocarril – train station

estípite – long, narrow, pyramid-shaped, upside-down pilaster; the hallmark of Churrigueresque architecture

ex-convento – former convent or monastery

excusado – toilet

faja – waist sash used in traditional Indian costume

feria – fair

ferrocarril – railway

ficha – locker token at bus terminals

fonda – eating stall in a market; small restaurant

fraccionamiento – subdivision, housing development; similar to a *colonia*, often modern

frontera – border between political entities

gachupines – derogatory term for the colonial *peninsulares*

giro – money order

gringo, -a – North American (and sometimes European, Australasian, etc) visitor to Latin America; can be used derogatorily

grito – literally 'shout'; the Grito de Dolores was the 1810 call to independence by parish priest Miguel Hidalgo, which sparked the struggle for independence from Spain

gruta – cave, grotto

guarache – also *huarache*, woven leather sandal, often with tire tread as the sole

guardería de equipaje – room for storing luggage, eg, in a bus station

guayabera – also *guayabarra*; man's shirt with pockets and appliquéd designs up the front, over the shoulders and down the back; worn in place of a jacket and tie in hot regions

güero, -a – fair-haired, fair-complexioned person; a more polite alternative to *gringo*

hacha – flat carved-stone object from the Classic Veracruz civilization; connected with the ritual ball game

hacendado – *hacienda* owner

hacienda – estate; Hacienda (capitalized) is the Treasury Department

hay – there is, there are; you're equally likely to hear *no hay* (there isn't, there aren't)

henequén – agave fiber used to make sisal rope; grown particularly around Mérida in Yucatán

hombres – men; sign on toilet doors

huarache – see *guarache*

huevos – eggs; also slang for testicles

huipil, -es – Indian woman's sleeveless tunic(s), usually highly decorated; can be thigh-length or reach the ankles

Huizilopochtli – Aztec tribal god

iglesia – church

INAH – Instituto Nacional de Antropología e Historia; the body in charge of most ancient sites and some museums

indígena – indigenous, pertaining to the original inhabitants of Latin America; can also refer to the people themselves

INI – Instituto Nacional Indígenista; set up in 1948 to improve the lot of Indians and to integrate them into society; sometimes accused of paternalism and trying to stifle protest

ISH – *impuesto sobre hospedaje*; lodging tax on the price of hotel rooms

isla – island

IVA – *impuesto de valor agregado*, or 'ee-bah'; a 15% sales tax added to the price of many items

ixtle – maguey fiber

jaguar – panther native to Central America; principal symbol of the Olmec civilization

jai alai – the Basque game *pelota*, brought to Mexico by the Spanish; a bit like squash, played on a long court with curved baskets attached to the arm

Jarocho, -a – citizen of Veracruz

jefe – boss or leader, especially a political one

jipijapa – Yucatán name for a Panama hat

jorongo – small poncho worn by men

Kukulcán – Mayan name for the plumed serpent god Quetzalcóatl

Lada – short for *larga distancia*

Ladatel – the long-distance telephone system operated by the former monopoly Telmex

ladino – more or less the same as *mestizo*

lancha – fast, open, outboard boat

larga distancia – long-distance; usually refers to telephones

latifundio – large landholding; these sprang up after Mexico's independence from Spain

latifundista – powerful landowner who usurped communally owned land to form a *latifundio*

libramiento – road, highway

licenciado – university graduate, abbreviated as Lic and used as an honorific before a person's name; a status claimed by many who don't actually possess a degree

licuado – drink made from fruit juice, water or milk, and sugar

lista de correos – literally 'mail list,' a list displayed at a post office of people for whom letters are waiting; similar to General Delivery or Poste Restante

lleno – full, as with a car's fuel tank

machismo – Mexican masculine bravura

madre – literally 'mother,' but the term can be used colloquially with an astonishing array of meanings

maguey – a type of agave, with thick pointed leaves growing straight out of the ground; *tequila* and *mezcal* are made from its sap

malecón – waterfront street, boulevard or promenade

mañana – literally 'tomorrow' or 'morning'; in some contexts it may just mean 'some time in the future'

maquiladora – assembly-plant operation in a Mexican border town or city; usually owned, at least in part, by foreigners and allowed to import raw materials duty-free on condition that the products are exported

mariachi – small ensemble of street musicians playing traditional ballads on guitars and trumpets

marimba – wooden xylophone-type instrument, popular in Veracruz and the south

Mayab – the lands of the Maya

mercado – market; often a building near the center of a town, with shops and open-air stalls in the surrounding streets

Mesoamerica – the ancient Mexican and Mayan cultures

mestizaje – 'mixedness,' Mexico's mixed-blood heritage; officially an object of pride

mestizo – person of mixed (usually Indian and Spanish) ancestry, ie, most Mexicans

metate – shallow stone bowl with legs, for grinding maize and other foods

Mexican Hat Dance – a courtship dance in which a girl and boy dance around the boy's hat

mezcal – strong alcoholic drink produced from maguey cactus

milpa – peasant's small cornfield, often cultivated by the slash-and-burn method

mirador, -es – lookout point(s)

Montezuma's revenge – Mexican version of Delhi-belly or travelers' diarrhea; referred to as *turista* by Mexicans

mordida – literally 'little bite,' a small bribe to keep the wheels of bureaucracy turning; giving a mordida to a traffic policeman may ensure that you won't have to pay a bigger fine later

mota – marijuana

Mudéjar – Moorish architectural style, imported to Mexico by the Spanish

mujeres – women; sign on toilet doors

municipio – small local-government area; Mexico is divided into 2394 of them

na – Mayan thatched hut

NAFTA – North American Free Trade Agreement (see *TLC*)

Nahuatl – language of the Nahua people, descendants of the Aztecs

naos – Spanish trading galleons

norteamericanos – North Americans, people from north of the US-Mexican border

Nte – abbreviation for *norte* (north), used in street names

Ote – abbreviation for *oriente* (east), used in street names

Paceño, -a – person from La Paz, Baja California Sur

palacio de gobierno – state capitol, state government headquarters

palacio municipal – town or city hall, headquarters of the municipal corporation

palapa – thatched-roof shelter, usually on a beach

palma – long, paddle-like, carved-stone object from the Classic Veracruz civilization; connected with the ritual ball game

panadería – bakery, pastry shop

panga – fiberglass skiff for fishing or whale-watching in Baja California

parada – bus stop, usually for city buses

parado – standing up, as you often are on 2nd-class buses

parque nacional – national park; an environmentally protected area in which human exploitation is supposedly banned or restricted

parroquia – parish church

paseo – boulevard, walkway or pedestrian street; also the tradition of strolling in a circle around the plaza in the evening, men and women moving in opposite directions

Pemex – government-owned petroleum mining, refining and retailing monopoly

peña – evening of Latin-American folk songs, often with a political protest theme

peninsulares – those born in Spain and sent by the Spanish government to rule the colony in Mexico (see *criollo, gachupines*)

periférico – ring road

pesero – Mexico City's word for *colectivo*

petate – mat, usually made of palm or reed

peyote – a hallucinogenic cactus

pinacoteca – art gallery

piñata – clay pot or papier-mâché mold decorated to resemble an animal, pineapple, star, etc; filled with sweets and gifts and smashed open at fiestas, particularly children's birthdays and Christmas

playa – beach

plaza de toros – bullring

plazuela – small plaza

Poblano, -a – person from Puebla, or something in the style of Puebla

pollero – same as a *coyote*

Porfiriato – Porfirio Díaz's reign as president-dictator of Mexico for 30 years, until the 1910 revolution

portales – arcades

presidio – fort or fort's garrison

PRI – Partido Revolucionario Institucional (Institutional Revolutionary Party); the political party that has ruled Mexico since the 1930s

propina – tip; different from a *mordida*, which is closer to a bribe

Pte – abbreviation for *poniente* (west), used in street names

puerto – port

pulque – thick, milky drink of fermented maguey juice; a traditional intoxicating drink that is also nutritious

quechquémitl – Indian woman's shoulder cape with an opening for the head; usually colorfully embroidered, often diamond-shaped

quetzal – crested bird with brilliant green, red and white plumage, native to Central and northern South America; quetzal feathers were highly prized in pre-Hispanic Mexico

Quetzalcóatl – plumed serpent god of pre-Hispanic Mexico

rebozo – long woolen or linen shawl covering the head or shoulders

Regiomontano, -a – person from Monterrey

reja – wrought-iron window grille

reserva de la biosfera – biosphere reserve; an environmentally protected area where – unlike in parques nacionales – human exploitation is allowed to continue but is steered towards ecologically unharmful activities

retablo – altarpiece; or small painting on wood, tin, cardboard, glass, etc, placed in a church to give thanks for miracles, answered prayers, etc

río – river

s/n – *sin número* (without number); used in street addresses

sacbe (s), **sacbeob** (pl) – ceremonial avenue(s) between great Mayan cities

sanatorio – hospital, particularly a small private one

sanitario(s) – toilet(s), literally 'sanitary place'

sarape – blanket with opening for the head, worn as a cloak

Semana Santa – holy week, the week before Easter; Mexico's major holiday period, when both accommodations and transport get very busy

servicios – toilets

sierra – mountain range

sitio – taxi stand

stela, -ae – standing stone monument(s), usually carved

supermercado – supermarket; anything from a small corner store to a large, North American-style supermarket

Sur – south; often seen in street names

taller – shop or workshop; a *taller mecánico* is a mechanic's shop, usually for cars; a *taller de llantas* is a tire-repair shop

talud-tablero – stepped building style typical of Teotihuacán, with alternating vertical (*tablero*) and sloping (*talud*) sections

Tapatío, -a – person born in the state of Jalisco

taquería – place where you buy tacos

taquilla – ticket window

telamon – statue of a male figure, used instead of a pillar to hold up the roof of a temple; see also *atlas*

telar de cintura – backstrap loom; the warp (lengthwise) threads are stretched between two horizontal bars, one of which is attached to a post or tree and the other to a strap around the weaver's lower back, and the weft (crosswise) threads are then woven in

teleférico – cable car

templo – church; anything from a wayside chapel to a cathedral

teocalli – Aztec sacred precinct

tequila – vodka-like liquor; like *pulque* and *mezcal*, it is produced from maguey cactus

Tex-Mex – Americanized version of Mexican food

Tezcatlipoca – multifaceted pre-Hispanic god, lord of life and death and protector of warriors; as a smoking mirror he could see into hearts, as the sun god he needed the blood of sacrificed warriors to ensure he would rise again

tezontle – light-red, porous volcanic rock used for buildings by the Aztecs and conquistadors

tianguis – Indian market

típico, -a – characteristic of a region; particularly used to describe food

Tláloc – Pre-Hispanic rain and water god

TLC – Tratado de Libre Comercio, the North American Free Trade Agreement (NAFTA)

topes – anti-speed bumps; found on the outskirts of many towns and villages, they are only sometimes marked by signs

trapiche – mill; in Baja California usually a sugar mill

tzompantli – rack for the skulls of Aztec sacrificial victims

UNAM – Universidad Nacional Autónoma de México (National Autonomous University of Mexico)

universidad – university

viajero, -a – traveler

villa juvenil – youth sports center, often the location of an *albergue de juventud*

voladores – literally 'flyers,' the Totonac Indian ritual in which men, suspended by their ankles, whirl around a tall pole

War of the Castes – bloody 19th century Mayan uprising in the Yucatán peninsula

were-jaguar – half-human, half-jaguar being, portrayed in Olmec art

yácata – ceremonial stone structure of the Tarascan civilization

yugo – U-shaped carved-stone object from the Classic Veracruz civilization; connected with the ritual ball game

zaguán – vestibule or foyer, sometimes a porch

zócalo – main plaza or square; a term used in some (but by no means all) Mexican towns

Zona Rosa – literally 'Pink Zone'; an area of expensive shops, hotels and restaurants in Mexico City frequented by the wealthy and tourists; by extension, a similar area in another city

EL SOL

LA SANDIA

EL GALLO

EL BANDOLON

EL CAMARON

LA ESTRELLA

Spanish for Travelers

Pronunciation

Pronunciation of Spanish is not difficult, given that many Spanish sounds are similar to their English counterparts, and there is a clear and consistent relationship between the pronunciation and spelling.

Vowels Spanish has five vowels: **a**, **e**, **i**, **o** and **u**. They are pronounced something like the highlighted letters of the following English words:

a as in 'f**a**ther'
e as in 'm**e**t'
i as in 'f**ee**t'
o as in '**o**r'
u as in 'b**oo**t'

Diphthongs A diphthong is one syllable made up of two vowels each of which conserves its own sound. Here are some diphthongs in Spanish, and their approximate English pronunciations:

ai as in 'h**i**de'
au as in 'h**ow**'
ei as in 'h**ay**'
ia as in '**ya**rd'
ie as in '**ye**s'
oi as in '**boy**'
ua as in '**wa**sh'
ue as in '**we**ll'

Consonants Many consonants are pronounced in much the same way as in English, but there are some exceptions.

c is pronounced like 's' in 'sit' when before 'e' or 'i'; elsewhere it is like 'k'
ch as in 'choose'
g as the 'g' in 'gate' before 'a,' 'o' and 'u'; before 'e' or 'i' it is a harsh, breathy sound like the 'h' in 'hit.' Note that when 'g' is followed by 'ue' or 'ui' the 'u' is silent, unless it has a dieresis (ü), in which case it functions much like English 'w':
guerra 'GEH-rra'
güero 'GWEH-ro'
h always silent
j a harsh, guttural sound similar to the 'ch' in Scottish 'loch'

ll as the 'y' in 'yellow'
ñ nasal sound like the 'ny' in 'canyon'
q as the 'k' in 'kick'; always followed by a silent 'u'
r is a very short rolled 'r'
rr is a longer rolled 'r'
x is like the English 'h' when it comes after 'e' or 'i,' otherwise it is like English 'x' as in 'taxi'; in many Indian words (particularly Mayan ones) 'x' is pronounced like English 'sh'
z is the same as the English 's'; under no circumstances should 's' or 'z' be pronounced like English 'z' – that sound does not exist in Spanish

There are a few other minor pronunciation differences, but the longer you stay in Mexico, the easier they will become. The letter **ñ** is considered a separate letter of the alphabet and follows 'n' in alphabetically organized lists and books, such as dictionaries and phone books.

Stress There are three general rules regarding stress:

- For words ending in a vowel, 'n' or 's' the stress goes on the penultimate (next-to-the-last) syllable:

  naranja na-RAN-ha   *joven* HO-ven   *zapatos* sa-PA-tos

- For words ending in a consonant other than 'n' or 's' the stress is on the final syllable:

  estoy es-TOY   *ciudad* syoo-DAHD   *catedral* ka-teh-DRAL

- Any deviation from these rules is indicated by an accent:

  México MEH-hee-ko   *mudéjar* moo-DEH-har   *Cortés* cor-TESS

Gender

Nouns in Spanish are either masculine or feminine. Nouns ending in 'o,' 'e' or 'ma' are usually masculine. Nouns ending in 'a,' 'ión' or 'dad' are usually feminine. Some nouns take either a masculine or feminine form, depending on the ending; for example, *viajero* is a male traveler, *viajera* is a female traveler. An adjective usually comes after the noun it describes and must take the same gender as the noun.

Greetings & Civilities

Hello/Hi.	*Hola.*
Good morning/Good day.	*Buenos días.*
Good afternoon.	*Buenas tardes.*
Good evening/Good night.	*Buenas noches.*
See you.	*Hasta luego.*
Good-bye.	*Adiós.*
Pleased to meet you.	*Mucho gusto.*
How are you? (to one person)	*¿Como está?*
How are you? (to more than one person)	*¿Como están?*
I am fine.	*Estoy bien.*
Please.	*Por favor.*
Thank you.	*Gracias.*
You're welcome.	*De nada.*
Excuse me.	*Perdóneme.*

People

I	*yo*	they (f)	*ellas*
you (familiar)	*tú*	my wife	*mi esposa*
you (formal)	*usted*	my husband	*mi esposo*
you (pl, formal)	*ustedes*	my sister	*mi hermana*
he/it	*el*	my brother	*mi hermano*
she/it	*ella*	Sir/Mr	*Señor*
we	*nosotros*	Madam/Mrs	*Señora*
they (m)	*ellos*	Miss	*Señorita*

Useful Words & Phrases

For words pertaining to food and restaurants, see the Food and Drinks sections of the Facts for the Visitor chapter.

Yes.	*Sí.*	I am . . .	*Estoy . . .*
No.	*No.*	(location or temporary condition)	
What did you say?	*¿Mande?* (colloq)	here	*aquí*
good/OK	*bueno*	tired (m/f)	*cansado/a*
bad	*malo*	sick/ill (m/f)	*enfermo/a*
better	*mejor*		
best	*lo mejor*	I am . . .	*Soy . . .*
more	*más*	(permanent state)	
less	*menos*	a worker	*trabajador*
very little	*poco* or *poquito*	married	*casado*

Buying

How much?	*¿Cuánto?*
How much does it cost?	*¿Cuánto cuesta?* or *¿Cuánto se cobra?*
How much is it worth?	*¿Cuánto vale?*
I want . . .	*Quiero . . .*
I do not want . . .	*No quiero . . .*
I would like . . .	*Quisiera . . .*
Give me . . .	*Deme . . .*
What do you want?	*¿Qué quiere?*
Do you have . . . ?	*¿Tiene . . . ?*
Is/are there . . . ?	*¿Hay . . . ?*

Nationalities

American (m/f)	*(norte)americano/a*	English (m/f)	*inglés/inglesa*
Australian (m/f)	*australiano/a*	French (m/f)	*francés/francesa*
British (m/f)	*británico/a*	German (m/f)	*alemán/alemana*
Canadian (m & f)	*canadiense*		

Languages

I speak . . .	*Yo hablo . . .*
I do not speak . . .	*No hablo . . .*
Do you speak . . . ?	*¿Habla usted . . . ?*
Spanish	*español*
English	*inglés*
German	*alemán*
French	*francés*
I understand.	*Entiendo.*
I do not understand.	*No entiendo.*
Do you understand?	*¿Entiende usted?*
Please speak slowly.	*Por favor hable despacio.*

Crossing the Border

birth certificate	*certificado de nacimiento*
border (frontier)	*la frontera*
car-owner's title	*título de propiedad*
car registration	*registración*
customs	*aduana*
driver's license	*licencia de manejar*
identification	*identificación*
immigration	*inmigración*
insurance	*seguro*
passport	*pasaporte*
temporary vehicle import permit	*permiso de importación temporal de vehículo*
tourist card	*tarjeta de turista*
visa	*visado*

Getting Around

street	*calle*	forward, ahead	*adelante*
boulevard	*bulevar, boulevard*	straight ahead	*todo recto* or *derecho*
avenue	*avenida*	this way	*por aquí*
road	*camino*	that way	*por allí*
highway	*carretera*	north	*norte*
corner (of)	*esquina (de)*	south	*sur*
corner/bend	*vuelta*	east	*este*
block	*cuadra*	east (in an address)	*oriente* (or *Ote*)
to the left	*a la izquierda*	west	*oeste*
to the right	*a la derecha*	west (in an address)	*poniente* (or *Pte*)

Where is . . . ?	*¿Dónde está . . . ?*
the bus station	*el terminal de autobuses/central camionera*
the train station	*la estación del ferrocarril*
the airport	*el aeropuerto*
the post office	*el correo*
a long-distance phone	*un teléfono de larga distancia*
bus	*camión* or *autobús*
minibus	*colectivo, combi* or (in Mexico City) *pesero*
train	*tren*
taxi	*taxi*
ticket sales counter	*taquilla*
waiting room	*sala de espera*
baggage check-in	*(Recibo de) Equipaje*
toilet	*sanitario*
departure	*salida*
arrival	*llegada*
platform	*andén*
left-luggage room/checkroom	*guardería* (or *guarda*) *de equipaje*
How far is . . . ?	*¿A qué distancia está . . . ?*
How long? (How much time?)	*¿Cuánto tiempo?*
short route (usually a toll highway)	*vía corta*

Driving

gasoline	*gasolina*	full	*lleno; 'ful'*
fuel station	*gasolinera*	oil	*aceite*
unleaded	*sin plomo, Magna Sin*	tire	*llanta*
regular/leaded	*regular/con plomo, Nova*	puncture	*agujero*
fill the tank	*llene el tanque; llenarlo*		

How much is a liter of gasoline?	*¿Cuánto cuesta el litro de gasolina?*
My car has broken down.	*Se me ha descompuesto el carro.*
I need a tow truck.	*Necesito un remolque.*
Is there a garage near here?	*¿Hay un garaje cerca de aquí?*

Highway Signs

Though Mexico mostly uses the familiar international road signs, you should be prepared to encounter these other signs as well:

road repairs	*camino en reparación*
keep to the right	*conserve su derecha*
do not overtake	*no rebase*
dangerous curve	*curva peligrosa*
landslides or subsidence	*derrumbes*
slow	*despacio*
detour	*desviación*
slow down	*disminuya su velocidad*
school (zone)	*escuela, zona escolar*
men working	*hombres trabajando*
road closed	*no hay paso*
danger	*peligro*
continuous white line	*raya continua*
speed bumps	*topes* or *vibradores*
road under repair	*tramo en reparación*
narrow bridge	*puente angosto*
toll highway	*vía cuota*
short route (often a toll road)	*vía corta*
have toll ready	*prepare su cuota*
one-lane road 100 meters ahead	*un solo carril a 100 m*

Accommodations

hotel	*hotel*	shower	*ducha* or *regadera*
guesthouse	*casa de huéspedes*	hot water	*agua caliente*
inn	*posada*	air-conditioning	*aire acondicionado*
room	*cuarto, habitación*	blanket	*manta*
room with one bed	*cuarto sencillo*	towel	*toalla*
room with two beds	*cuarto doble*	soap	*jabón*
room for one person	*cuarto para una persona*	toilet paper	*papel higiénico*
		the check (bill)	*la cuenta*
room for two people	*cuarto para dos personas*	What is the price?	*¿Cuál es el precio?*
		Does that include taxes?	
double bed	*cama matrimonial*		*¿Están incluidos los impuestos?*
twin beds	*camas gemelas*	Does that include service?	
with bath	*con baño*		*¿Está incluido el servicio?*

Money

money	*dinero*
traveler's checks	*cheques de viajero*
bank	*banco*
exchange bureau	*casa de cambio*
credit card	*tarjeta de crédito*
exchange rate	*tipo de cambio*
I want/would like to change some money.	*Quiero/quisiera cambiar dinero.*
What is the exchange rate?	*¿Cuál es el tipo de cambio?*
Is there a commission?	*¿Hay comisión?*

Telephones

telephone	*teléfono*
telephone call	*llamada*
telephone number	*número telefónico*
area or city code	*clave*
prefix for long-distance call	*prefijo*
local call	*llamada local*
long-distance call	*llamada de larga distancia*
long-distance telephone	*teléfono de larga distancia*
coin-operated telephone	*teléfono de monedas*
telephone-card phone	*teléfono de tarjetas telefónicas*
long-distance telephone office	*caseta de larga distancia*
tone	*tono*
operator	*operador(a)*
person to person	*persona a persona*
collect (reverse charges)	*por cobrar*
dial the number	*marque el número*
please wait	*favor de esperar*
busy	*ocupado*
toll/cost (of call)	*cuota/costo*
time & charges	*tiempo y costo*
don't hang up	*no cuelgue*

Times & Dates

Monday	*lunes*	Saturday	*sábado*
Tuesday	*martes*	Sunday	*domingo*
Wednesday	*miércoles*	yesterday	*ayer*
Thursday	*jueves*	today	*hoy*
Friday	*viernes*		

tomorrow (also at some point, or maybe)	*mañana*
right now (meaning in a few minutes)	*horita, ahorita*
already	*ya*
morning	*mañana*
tomorrow morning	*mañana por la mañana*
afternoon	*tarde*
night	*noche*
What time is it?	*¿Qué hora es?*

Numbers

0	*cero*	14	*catorce*	60	*sesenta*
1	*un, uno* (m), *una* (f)	15	*quince*	70	*setenta*
2	*dos*	16	*dieciséis*	80	*ochenta*
3	*tres*	17	*diecisiete*	90	*noventa*
4	*cuatro*	18	*dieciocho*	100	*cien*
5	*cinco*	19	*diecinueve*	101	*ciento uno*
6	*seis*	20	*veinte*	143	*ciento cuarenta y tres*
7	*siete*	21	*veintiuno*	200	*doscientos*
8	*ocho*	22	*veintidós*	500	*quinientos*
9	*nueve*	30	*treinta*	700	*setecientos*
10	*diez*	31	*treinta y uno*	900	*novecientos*
11	*once*	32	*treinta y dos*	1000	*mil*
12	*doce*	40	*cuarenta*	2000	*dos mil*
13	*trece*	50	*cincuenta*		

Mexican Slang

Think you know enough Spanish? If you still don't understand what your *cuates* are saying, here's a quick rundown on some of the colorful colloquialisms you may hear while traveling. Many of these words and phrases are used all around Mexico, while others are particular to Mexico City.

¡Quiúbole!	Hello!
¿Qué onda?	What's up? What's happening?
¿Qué pex?	What's up?
¿Qué pasión? (Mexico City only)	What's up? What's going on?
¡Qué padre!	How cool!
fregón	really good at something, way cool, awesome
Este club está fregón.	This club is way cool.
El cantante es un fregón.	The singer is really awesome.
ser muy buena onda	to be really cool, nice
Mi novio es muy buena onda.	My boyfriend is really cool.
Eres muy buena onda	You are really cool (nice).
estar de pelos	to be super, awesome
La música está de pelos	The music is awesome.
unas serpientes bien elodias	some freezing cold beers (sounds like *unas cervezas bien heladas*)
pomo (in the south)	booze
pisto (in the north)	booze
alipús	booze
echarse un alipús, echarse un trago	to go get a drink
Echamos un alipús/trago	Let's go have a drink.
dar un voltión	go cruising, drive around
tirar la onda	try to pick someone up, flirt
ligar	to flirt
irse de reventón	go partying
¡Vámonos de reventón!	Let's go party!
reven	a 'rave' – huge party, lots of loud music and wild atmosphere
un toquín	an informal party with live music

un desmadre	a mess
Simón.	Yes.
Nel.	No.
Naranjas Dulces.	No.
No hay tos.	No problem. (literally 'there's no cough.')
¡Órale! – positive	'Sounds great!' (responding to an invitation)
¡Órale!- negative	'What the *#*!?' (exclamation)
¿Te cae?	Are you serious?
Me late.	Sounds really good to me.
Me vale.	I don't care, 'Whatever.'
Sale y vale.	I agree. Sounds good.
¡Paso sin ver!	I can't stand it! No thank you!
¡Guácatelas! ¡Guácala!	How gross! That's disgusting!
¡Bájale!	Don't exaggerate! Come on!
¡¿Chale?! (Mexico City only)	Really?! No way!
¡Te sales!, ¡Te pasas!	That's it! You've gone too far!
¿Le agarraste?	Did you understand? Do you get it?
un resto	a lot
lana	money, dough
carnal	brother
cuate, cuaderno	buddy
chavo	guy, dude
chava	girl, gal
jefe	father
jefa	mother
la tira, la julia	the police
chapusero	a cheater (at cards, for example)

Website Directory

TOURIST & TRAVEL INFORMATION

A good website to start with is *Mexico An Endless Journey*, the official site of SECTUR, Mexico's Ministry of Tourism. This has detailed information on about 200 natural wonders (click on 'Attrac. Activ.' then 'Natural Wonders'), 60-odd beaches and some 300 major buildings and museums. There's also some good Mexico information on *Excite City.Net*.

Lonely Planet's own site has a Destination Mexico page with succinct information on the country and its major destinations, plus tips from recent travelers and links to other Mexico sites.

One of the better Mexican regional travel sites is the official *Guía Turística del Estado de Oaxaca* (Oaxaca State Tourist Guide) – but at the time of writing this is only in Spanish. There is however an excellent independent English-language guide called *The Pacific Coast of Oaxaca*.

Driving Regulations in Mexico
www.mexonline.com/drivemex.htm

Excite City.Net
city.net/countries/mexico/

Guía Turística del Estado de Oaxaca
oaxaca-travel.gob.mx/

Lonely Planet
www.lonelyplanet.com/

Mexico An Endless Journey (SECTUR)
mexico-travel.com/

The Pacific Coast of Oaxaca
www.eden.com/~tomzap/index.html#main

DISCOUNT AIRFARES

ETN Discount Airfares Home Page
www.discountairfares.com

Expedia
expedia.com

Flifo
www.flifo.com

Travelocity
www.travelocity.com

DISABLED TRAVELERS

A good site for disabled travelers to check is:
www.access-able.com

Mobility International USA
www.miusa.org/

ART & ARCHAEOLOGY

Frida freaks will love *The Original Frida Kahlo Home Page* and its many links to other Kahlo sites. Rivera fans will find links to lots of Diego sites on *WWW's Riverinos*. Archaeology fans could make a start with *A Mesoamerican Archaeology WWW Page*.

A Mesoamerican Archaeology WWW Page
copan.bioz.unibas.ch/meso.html

The Original Frida Kahlo Home Page
www.cascade.net/kahlo.html

WWW's Riverinos
www.chapingo.mx/cultura/Capilla/www-riv.html

When calling up websites, don't forget to precede the addresses given with **http://**.

EMBASSIES & CONSULATES
There are several sites with links to the homepages of Mexican embassies and consulates, and of foreign embassies in Mexico City. Many of these have data on tourist cards, visas, travel with minors, and so on – they don't all agree with each other, so you should back up your Internet information with a phone call or two.

Links to homepages of Mexican embassies and consulates and some foreign embassies in Mexico City, can be found on:

Embajadas y Consulados
mexico.web.com.mx/mx/embajadas.html

Universidad Nacional Autónoma de Mexico
serpiente.dgsca.unam.mx/rubrica/
    gobierno/gobConsul.html

Consulado General de Mexico en Nueva York
www.quicklink.com/mexico/sremain.htm

ENVIRONMENT
Eco Travels in Mexico is an interesting North American site with articles and information on places, as well as links to other info sources including ecotravel companies and environmental organizations. The *Reservas de la Biosfera* site gives lots of detail on protected natural areas (in Spanish) provided by INE and CONABIO, two arms of Mexico's environment ministry, SEMARNAP.

Ecosolar Mazunte
www.laneta.apc.org/mazunte/

Eco Travels in Mexico
www.txinfinet.com/mader/ecotravel/
    mexico/mexinterior.html

SEMARNAP (Mexico's environment ministry)
semarnap.conabio.gob.mx

Turtle Happenings – Sea Turtle News & Information
www.vex.net/~honu/happen2.htm

FOREIGN GOVERNMENT INFORMATION SITES
For foreign government warnings on the latest hazards of Mexico travel, plus some less alarming travel tips and health information, you can visit US, Canadian and British government sites. The US State Department Bureau of Consular Affairs site gives you travel warnings, consular information sheets, US embassy and consulate home pages, US customs and passport information, travel health and more.

Centers for Disease Control & Prevention (US Department of Health)
www.cdc.gov/

British Foreign Office Travel Advice Notices
www.fco.gov.uk/reference/travel_advice

Know Before You Go! (US Customs information)
travelhealth.com/uscustoms.htm

Canadian Dept of Foreign Affairs & International Trade – Travel Information Report Mexico
www.dfait-maeci.gc.ca

US State Department Bureau of Consular Affairs
travel.state.gov/index.html

When calling up websites, don't forget to precede the addresses given with **http://**.

NEWS
For Mexican news in English, read the Internet edition of the Mexico City English-language daily paper, *The News*. *Latino Link* is also good for Latin American news and other information.

Latino Link
www.latino.com

The News
www.novedades.com.mx/the-news.htm

DIRECTORIES & SEARCH ENGINES OF MEXICO-RELATED SITES

Mexico's Index
www.trace-sc.com/index1.com

Mexico Web Guide
mexico.web.com.mx/

Mexsearch Yellow Pages
nic.yellow.com.mx/

WWW in Mexico
serpiente.dgsca.unam.mx/rectoria/htm/mexico.html

STUDY & WORK IN MEXICO
Many language schools in Mexico have Internet sites. Search for them by the name of the school.

Council on International Educational Exchange, New York
www.ciee.org.

Earthwatch
www.earthwatch.org/

National Registration Center for Study Abroad, Milwaukee
www.nrcsa.com

TOUR COMPANIES
The following directories have some interesting links:

Eco Travels in Mexico
www.txinfinet.com/mader/ecotravel/mexico/mexinterior.html

**GORP
(Great Outdoor Recreation Pages)**
www.gorp.com

Metropark Travel Services
www.metropark.com/list/services/travel.html

Vacations Worldwide
www.vacations-ww.com/

MISCELLANEOUS
To find out what the EZLN rebels are all about, check their site *¡Ya Basta!*, which has lots of interesting links.

Canada Direct (telephone service)
www.stentor.ca/canada_direct

Libraries in Mexico
www.web-strategies.com/amabp/libraries.cgi

***Tiempo Libre* Mexico City gay guide**
www.tiempolibre.com.mx/gay/

***Tiempo Libre* (Mexico City's entertainment listings magazine)**
www.planet.com.mx/tiempolibre

UNAM (Universidad Autónoma de México, Mexico City)
serpiente.dgsca.unam.mx

¡Ya Basta! (EZLN)
www.ezln.org

When calling up websites, don't forget to precede the addresses given with **http://**.

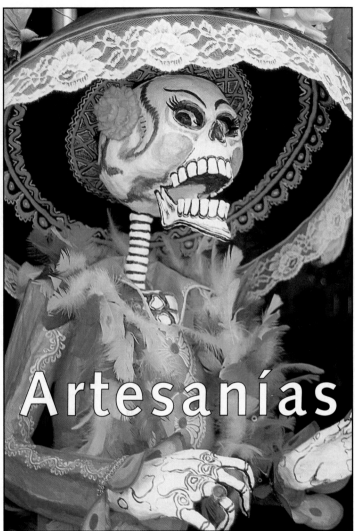

Artesanías

Artesanías

Mexico is so richly endowed with appealing *artesanías* (handicrafts) that even the most hardened non-hunter of souvenirs finds it hard to get home without at least one pair of earrings or a little model animal. There's such a huge and colorful range of arts and crafts, many of them sold at reasonable prices, that virtually every visitor is irresistibly attracted to something, somewhere along the way.

Because the tourist and collectors' market in folk art has been a growing money-earner for Mexican artisans since before WWII, it's easy to forget that bringing in foreign tourist dollars is only one of the roles handicrafts play in Mexican life. For one thing, Mexicans themselves are eager buyers and collectors of such handicrafts. More fundamentally, Mexicans have been producing artesanías for millennia: Many modern Mexican crafts are easily traced to their pre-Hispanic origins, and some techniques, designs and materials have remained

JAMES LYON
Talavera pottery from
Dolores Hidalgo, Guanajuato

unchanged since long before the arrival of Europeans. In a way, the colorful, highly decorative artesanías that catch the eye in shops and markets today are counterparts to the splendid costumes, beautiful ceramics and elaborate jewelry used by the nobility in Aztec, Mayan and other pre-Hispanic cultures. On a more mundane level, even though Mexico has undergone rapid modernization, contemporary Mexican artisans turn out countless handmade objects for everyday use – pots, hats, baskets, toys, clothes, sandals, to name but a few – just as they did centuries before the Spanish came.

When they arrived, the Spanish brought their own artistic methods, styles and products, and although these mingled to some extent with older traditions, indigenous crafts were generally regarded as inferior during the colonial period. But with the search for a national identity after the Mexican Revolution in the early 20th century, a new interest – inspired partly by artists such as Frida Kahlo and Diego Rivera – arose in older, specifically Mexican, craft traditions. A lot of craftwork today shows a clear fusion of pre-Hispanic and Spanish inspirations, and sometimes eclectic modern influences too. Because many of Mexico's Indian peoples still maintain age-old skills and traditions, it's no surprise that the areas producing the most exciting artesanías are often those with prominent Indian populations, in states such as Chiapas, Guerrero, México, Michoacán, Nayarit, Oaxaca, Puebla and Sonora.

BUYING HANDICRAFTS

Though you can buy items intended for sale to tourists or collectors in the villages where they are produced, they also make their way to shops and markets in urban centers, where you'll find a wide range of wares, usually of the best quality. Some bigger towns and cities also have workshops where you can see artisans at work, though that should not stop you from traveling to a village whose products or techniques you're particularly interested in.

Prices are not necessarily higher in the bigger centers – on occasion they may even be lower than in the villages. For example, in Oaxaca city, which is the major clearinghouse for handicrafts from all over the state of Oaxaca, the number of stores and markets selling crafts helps keep prices competitive. What's more, goods from Oaxaca become more expensive when they're transported to Mexico City or elsewhere. But it's worth bearing in mind that if you buy crafts in the villages where they are made, rather than from shops or large centralized craft markets, a lot more of the profit will go to the usually poor people who created them.

City shops devoted to artesanías will give you a good overview of what's available. Some towns and cities – notably those with large numbers of long-staying foreigners or craft-aware tourists, such as Mexico City, Guadalajara, San Miguel de Allende, Puerto Vallarta and Oaxaca – have stores offering handicrafts from all over the country. In shops in other cities you'll find wares from all around the local region. Even if you don't buy in these stores, they'll show you good-quality crafts and give you a basis for price comparisons.

Museums can also be good for information and examples of handicrafts. Many towns have artesanías museums showing local crafts and techniques, sometimes with items for sale. The upper floor of the Museo Nacional de Antropología, in Mexico City, is devoted to the modern lifestyles of many of Mexico's Indian peoples, and it's interesting to compare the displays on their handicrafts with the artifacts of their pre-Hispanic ancestors in the ground-floor archaeological sections of the museum.

RICK GERHARTER

Colorful blankets at a Tijuana market

Markets, of course, are a major source of handicrafts. A few cities have special markets devoted exclusively to crafts, but ordinary daily or weekly markets always have some handicrafts on sale – often regional specialties that attract buyers from farther afield, as well as the everyday pots, baskets etc used by local people. The quality of market goods may not be as high as in stores, but you'll normally pay less – bargaining is expected in markets, whereas shops generally have fixed prices.

Specific shops, markets, villages and museums with interesting handicrafts are listed in this book's regional sections.

TEXTILES
Traditional Costume

Though traditional Indian clothing is rarely worn in towns nowadays, if you get out into some of Mexico's Indian villages you won't fail to be intrigued by the variety of colorful everyday attire, which differs from area to area and often from village to village. In general, the more remote and the less open an area is to outside influences, the more

MARK HONAN

Traditional Huichol dress

intact its costume traditions tend to be. One town where you will come across Indians in traditional dress is San Cristóbal de Las Casas, in Chiapas, which is visited every day by numerous Indians from nearby villages.

Traditional costume – more widely worn by women than men – serves as a mark of the community to which a person belongs and may also have specific meanings related to a person's status in the community, or to religious or spiritual beliefs. A great deal of laborious, highly skilled work goes into creating such clothing. Many of the garments and the methods by which they are made – and even some of the designs worked into them – are little changed since before the Spanish reached Mexico, and Indian clothing is a reminder of the continued identity of these peoples. The following four types of women's garment have been in use since long before the Spanish conquest:

Huipil – a sleeveless tunic, often reaching as low as the thighs or ankles, though some are shorter and may be tucked into a skirt. The huipil is now mainly found in the southern half of the country.

Quechquémitl – a shoulder cape with an opening for the head, now mainly worn in the center and north of the country

Enredo – a wraparound skirt, almost invisible if worn beneath a long huipil

Faja – a waist sash that holds the enredo in place

Blouses, introduced by Spanish missionaries who thought the quechquémitl immodest when worn without a huipil, are now often embroidered with just as much care and detail

DAVE G HOUSER

Sarapes for sale in a Cancún market

ARTESANÍAS

as the more traditional garments. They have caused quechquémitls to shrink in size and have replaced huipiles in some places.

The *rebozo*, which also probably appeared in the Spanish era, is a long shawl that may cover the shoulders or head or be used for carrying.

Indian men's garments are less traditional than women's. In Spanish times modesty was encouraged by the church, so loose shirts and *calzones* (long baggy shorts, often held up by a woolen sash) were introduced. Indian men may carry shoulder bags, because their clothes lack pockets, though many of them have adopted ordinary modern clothing. The male equivalent of the rebozo, also dating from the Spanish era, is the *sarape*, a blanket with an opening for the head.

Most eye-catching about Indian clothing – especially women's – are the colorful, intricate designs woven into or embroidered on them. Some garments are covered with a multicolored web of stylized animal, human, plant and mythical shapes, which can take months to complete.

The basic materials of Indian weaving are cotton and wool, which were once home-produced and home-spun. Today, however, labor-saving factory yarn, including synthetic fibers, is increasingly common.

Colors too are often synthetic – Mexicans use bright modern shades in some highly original combinations – but some natural dyes are still in use, among them deep blues from the indigo plant; reds and browns from various woods; reds, pinks and purples from the cochineal insect (chiefly used in Oaxaca state); and purples and mauves from a secretion of the *caracol púrpura* (purple sea snail), found on rocks along the southwestern coast of Oaxaca and used by some Mixtec weavers in that region. Cloth with natural dyes is highly valued, but it's very difficult for the untrained eye to tell the difference between natural and artificial colors. Thread dyed from the caracol púrpura, however, is said to always retain the smell of the sea.

The basic Indian weaver's tool – invented before the Spanish conquest and, now as then, used only by women – is the *telar de cintura* (back-strap loom). In simple terms, the warp (long) threads are stretched between two horizontal bars, one of which is fixed to a post or tree, while the other is attached to a strap that goes around the weaver's lower back; the weft (cross) threads are then woven in. The length of a cloth woven on a back-strap loom is almost unlimited, but the width is restricted to the weaver's arm span.

A variety of sophisticated weaving techniques, including tapestry and brocading, is used to create amazing patterns in the cloth. Embroidery of already-woven cloth – either homemade or bought – is another widespread decorative technique. The intricacy of some final products has to be seen to be believed. Huipiles, skirts, blouses, sashes, quechquémitls and other garments and cloth are decorated in these ways.

Among Mexico's most intricate and eye-catching garments are the huipiles worn by Indian women in some villages and towns in the south and southeast of the country. In the state of Oaxaca the Mazatecs, Chinantecs, Triquis, the coastal Mixtecs and some Zapotecs,

NANCY KELLER
Detail of an embroidered dress

in villages such as Yalalag, create some of the finest, most colorful designs. The Amuzgos, whose communities straddle the southern part of the Oaxaca-Guerrero border, are superb textile artisans as well. In Chiapas the most skilled weavers are the highland Tzotzils, and the Maya of the Yucatán Peninsula also create some attractive huipiles.

The variety of color and pattern in the clothing of different Indian peoples is immense. There may even be big differences in the styles of neighboring villages. That is especially noticeable around San Cristóbal de Las Casas, in Chiapas, where each of the dozen or so Indian villages within about 30 km of the

town has an entirely distinct clothing design. Differences also exist between everyday huipiles and special ceremonial huipiles, and each individual huipil is likely to have its own unique features.

Some especially beautiful embroidered blouses and quechquémitls are created by Nahua women in Puebla state, the Mazahua in the western part of México state, and by the Huichol people who live in a remote region on the borders of Nayarit, Jalisco and Durango states.

An exception to the generally less elaborate design of Indian men's clothing is the garb of the Tacuate Indian people in the southwestern portion of Oaxaca, which is embroidered with hundreds of tiny, colorful birds, animals and insects – an idea now widely copied on clothing commercially produced elsewhere.

The care that goes into embellishing Indian clothing is not just for simple joy in decoration. Costume and its patterning may also have a magical or religious role, usually of pre-Hispanic origin. In some cases the exact significance has been forgotten, but among the Huichol, for instance, waist sashes are identified with snakes, which are themselves symbols of rain and fertility, so the wearing of a waist sash is a symbolic prayer for rain. To some Indian weavers of Chiapas, scorpion motifs serve a similar function, as scorpions are believed to attract lightning. Diamond shapes on some huipiles from San Andrés Larrainzar, in Chiapas, represent the universe of the ancient Maya, ancestors of these villagers, who believed that the earth was a cube and the sky had four corners. Wearing a garment with a saint's figure on it is also a form of prayer, and the sacred nature of traditional costume in general is shown by the widespread practice of dressing saints' images in old, revered garments at festival times.

JAMES LYON

Intricately embroidered cloth from the San Pueblita area, Cholula

Indian costume is not something you're likely to buy for practical use, but collectors purchase many items as works of art, which the finest examples certainly are. Outstanding work doesn't come cheap: several hundred dollars are asked for the very best huipiles in shops in Oaxaca and San Cristóbal de Las Casas. A less expensive representation of Mexican costume comes in the form of the cloth dolls found in several parts of the country; some are quite detailed in their reproduction of Indian dress.

Other Textiles

One textile art that's practiced by men is weaving on a treadle loom, introduced to Mexico by the Spanish and operated by foot pedals. This machine can weave wider cloth than the back-strap loom and tends to be used for blankets, rugs and wall hangings, as well as rebozos, sarapes and skirt material. Like the back-strap loom, it's capable of great intricacy in design. Mexico's most famous blanket- and rug-weaving village is Teotitlán del Valle, near Oaxaca city, which produces, among other things, fine textile copies of pre-Hispanic and modern art, including versions of works by Picasso, Escher, Rivera and Miró, as well as pre-Hispanic-influenced geometric patterns. Some appealing wall hangings, depicting simple village and other scenes, are woven in Jocotepec, near Lago de Chapala, Jalisco, and sold in local towns.

JOHN NOBLE
Rug from Teotitlán del Valle,
Oaxaca, with pre-Hispanic motif

Also suitable as a wall hanging is the cloth embroidered with multitudes of highly colorful birds, animals and insects by the Otomí Indians of San Pablito, a remote, traditional village in northern Puebla state. This cloth is found in many shops and markets around central Mexico.

Though not textiles per se, the 'yarn paintings' of the Huichol Indians – created by pressing strands of wool or acrylic yarn onto a wax-covered board – make colorful and unique decorations. The scenes resemble visions experienced under the influence of the hallucinatory cactus peyote, which is a central part of Huichol culture as it is believed to put people in contact with the gods. Huichol crafts are mainly found in the states of Nayarit and Jalisco, on whose remote borders the Huichol live. There's a museum in Zapopan, Guadalajara, where you can buy Huichol crafts,

JAMES LYON
Oaxacan rug colored with
natural dyes

LEE FOSTER
Oaxacan rug colored with
bright synthetic dyes

and Huichol artisans can be watched while working most of the year at the Centro Huichol, in Santiago Ixcuintla, Nayarit. Some of the galleries in Puerto Vallarta also deal in Huichol artwork.

Not to be forgotten beside the more authentic textile products is the wide range of commercially produced clothing based to varying degrees on traditional designs and widely available in shops and markets throughout Mexico. Some of these clothes are very attractive and of obvious practical use.

Also useful and decorative are the many tablecloths and shoulder bags found around the country. Commercially woven tablecloths can be a good buy, as they're often reasonably priced and can serve a variety of purposes. Attractive ones are found in Oaxaca and Michoacán, among other places. Bags come in all shapes and sizes, many incorporating pre-Hispanic or Indian-style designs. Those produced and used by the Huichol are among the most authentic and original.

MARK HONAN

Huichol yarn painting

CERAMICS

Mexicans have been making ceramics of both simple and sophisticated designs for several millennia. Owing to its preservability, pottery has told us a great deal of what we know about Mexico's ancient cultures. Wonderful human, animal and mythical ceramic figures are to be seen in almost any archaeological museum.

Today the country has many small-scale, often one-person, potters' workshops, turning out anything from the plain, everyday cooking or storage pots that you'll see in markets to elaborate decorative pieces that are really works of art.

SCOTT DOGGETT
Juan Quezada, a potter from Mata Ortiz, Chihuahua, poses with his work

Some village potters work without a wheel: molds are employed by some; others use a board resting on a stone, or two upturned dishes, one on top of the other, as devices for turning their pots. Two villages producing attractive, inexpensive, and unique styles of unglazed pottery by these methods are Amatenango del Valle, near San Cristóbal de Las Casas, and San Bartolo Coyotepec, near Oaxaca city. Amatenango women make jars and plates turned on boards, but the village is best known for its *animalitos* (tiny animal figures), many of which are made by children. (Young potters will surround you with baskets of their creations if you set foot in the village.) Amatenango pottery is painted with colors made from local earths mixed with water; it's fired by the pre-Hispanic method of burning a mound of wood around a pile of pots.

San Bartolo is the source of all the shiny, black, surprisingly light pottery you'll see in Oaxaca and, increasingly, farther afield. It comes in hundreds of shapes and forms – candlesticks, jugs and vases, decorative animal and bird figures, you name it. Turning is by the two-dish method. The distinctive black color is achieved by firing pottery in pit-kilns in the ground, which minimizes oxygen intake and turns the iron oxide in the local clay black. Burnishing and polishing give the shine.

JOHN NOBLE
Animalitos from Amatenago del Valle, Oaxaca

A more sophisticated and highly attractive type of Mexican pottery is Talavera, named after a town in Spain whose pottery it resembles. Talavera has been made in the city of Puebla since colonial times; Dolores Hidalgo is another Talavera production center. Talavera comes in two main forms – tableware and tiles. Bright colors (blue and yellow are often prominent) and floral designs are typical, but tiles in particular may bear any kind of design. In Puebla, Talavera tiles, some painted with people or animals, adorn the exteriors of many colonial-era buildings. The basic Talavera method involves two firings, with a tin and lead glaze and the painted design applied between the two.

Another of Mexico's distinctive ceramic forms is the *árbol de la vida* (tree of life). These elaborate candelabra-like objects, often a meter or more high, are molded by hand and decorated with numerous tiny figures of people, animals, plants and so on. Trees of life may be brightly or soberly colored. The most common themes are Christian, with the Garden of Eden a frequent subject, but trees of life may be devoted to any theme the potter wishes. The works of Herón Martínez, a renowned potter from Acatlán de Osorio, in Puebla state, are among the best; others are produced in Izúcar de Matamoros, also in Puebla, and in Metepec, in the state of México. Artesanías shops in several major centers sell trees of life, as well as the striking clay suns, sometimes painted with brilliant colors, from Metepec.

The Guadalajara suburbs of Tonalá and Tlaquepaque are two other renowned Mexican pottery centers. Tonalá is actually the source of most of the better work, and its products are sold in both places, as well as farther afield. The towns produce a wide variety of ceramics;

JAMES LYON

Talavera pottery from Puebla

DAVE G HOUSER

Distinctive black pottery from San Bartolo Coyotepec, Oaxaca

Tiles adorn many colonial buildings

JAMES LYON   JAMES LYON

Tiles from Dolores Hidalgo, Guanajuato

the outstanding work is the heavy 'stoneware' of Jorge Wilmot – mostly tableware in delicate blue colors, fired at very high temperatures.

One truly eye-catching method of decoration, employed by the Huichol Indians, practitioners of so many unusual craft techniques, is to cover the ceramics in dramatic, bright patterns of glass beads pressed into a wax coating. The Huichol also use this technique on masks and gourds and even to create pictures.

A walk around almost any Mexican market or craft shop will reveal interesting ceramics. All kinds of decorative animal and human figurines, often with strong pre-Hispanic influence, are sold around the country. Copies of pre-Hispanic pottery can be attractive too, a notable example being figures of the pudgy, playful, hairless *Tepezcuintle* dogs that formed part of the diet of ancient western Mexicans. Many pottery Tepezcuintles have been unearthed around the city of Colima, and skillful reproductions of them are sold in several places in the city.

Mexican ceramics make pleasing souvenirs, but before you go overboard on buying pottery, remember that it all needs very careful packing if you want to get it home in one piece.

SUSAN KAYE

Bright ceramic suns

NANCY KELLER
Huichol beadwork iguana, Galería
Pyrámide, Puerto Vallarta, Jalisco

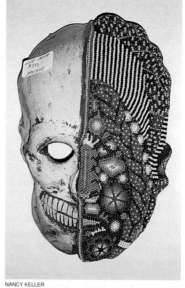

NANCY KELLER
Huichol beadwork mask,
Galería Pyrámide, Puerto Vallarta, Jalisco

MASKS & HEADDRESSES

Like so many other Mexican crafts, mask-making dates back to pre-Hispanic times. In authentic use, masks were and are worn for magical and religious purposes in dances, ceremonies and shamanistic rites: the wearer temporarily becomes the creature, person or deity depicted by the mask. The exact meanings of some masked dances performed in Indian festivals today may be forgotten, but often the dances enact a mythical story intended to bring fertility or scare away enemies or other evil forces. These dances often have a curious mixture of pre-Hispanic and Christian or Spanish themes. In some cities traditional dances, some with masks, are regularly performed in *folklórico* shows for tourists.

A huge range of masks is employed, differing from region to region and dance to dance. Though masks obviously have much more life when in use, you can still admire their variety and artistry at museums in cities such as San Luis Potosí, Zacatecas, Morelia and Colima, and at artesanías shops and markets around the country. The southern state of Guerrero has produced probably the most varied range of fine masks.

JOHN NOBLE
Miniature wooden 'tiger' mask

Wood is the usual basic material of masks, but papier-mâché, clay, wax and leather are also used. A mask will often be painted or embellished with real feathers, hair, teeth or other adornments. 'Tigers' – often looking more like leopards or jaguars – are fairly common, as are other animals and birds, actual and mythical. Christs and devils are also numerous; so are masks depicting Europeans, whose pale, wide-eyed, usually mustachioed features may look as bizarre and comical to visitors today as the original Europeans in Mexico looked to the native Mexicans.

Today masks are also made for hanging on walls. While these may not have the mystique that surrounds genuine ceremonial masks, some of which are of considerable age, they're often brighter and in better condition. Even miniature masks can be attractive. Distinguishing genuine dance masks from imitations can be nearly impossible for the uninitiated. Some new masks are even treated so that they will look old. There's also a steady, quite separate business in papier-mâché masks of cartoon and movie characters, animals and so on, which can be fun for children.

Unless you know something about masks or have expert guidance, the best policy when buying them is simply to go for what you like – if the price seems right.

JAMES LYON
European-faced mask

Another spectacular element of some dance costumes is the brilliant feathered headdress, recalling the famous ones that adorned the Aztec emperor Moctezuma and other ancient Mexican nobles. Unless you're lucky enough to be present at a festival in Puebla state where the *Danza de los Quetzales* (Quetzal Dance) is being performed, or in Oaxaca state for the Zapotec Indians' stately *Danza de las Plumas* (Feather Dance), the best chance you'll have of seeing these magnificent creations is at folklórico dance shows. The *conchero* dance, frequently staged by informal groups in the Mexico City Zócalo to the accompaniment of loud, upbeat drumming, features feathered headdresses that are not quite as superb, but still are eye-catching. Huichol Indians also adorn some of their hats with impressive feather arrays.

LEE FOSTER

Ceramic mask
from Zihuatanejo

JAMES LYON

Brilliant Totonac headdress

DAVE G HOUSER

Eye-catching gourds from Oaxaca

LACQUERWARE & WOODWORK

Gourds, the hard shells of certain squash-type fruits, have been used in Mexico since time immemorial as bowls, cups and small storage vessels. Today they're turned to many other uses, including children's rattles, maracas and even hats. Since pre-Hispanic times, too, gourds have been decorated. The most eye-catching technique is the lacquer process, in which the outside of the gourd is coated with layers of paste or paint, each left to harden before the next is applied. The final layer is painted with the artisan's chosen design, then coated with oil, or sometimes varnish, to seal the lacquer. All this makes the gourd non-porous and to some extent heat resistant. The painted designs often show birds, plants or animals, but the possibilities are infinite.

Wood too can be lacquered, and today the majority of lacquerware you'll see in Mexico – sold all over the central and southern portions of the country – is pine or a sweetly scented wood from the remote village of Olinalá, in the northeastern part of Guerrero state. Characteristic of Olinalá crafts are boxes, trays, chests and furniture lacquered by the *rayado* method, in which designs are created by scraping off part of the top coat of paint to expose a different-colored layer below. Other lacquering centers

JOHN NOBLE

Detail of a lacquered wooden tray from Olinalá, Guerrero

ARTESANÍAS

NANCY KELLER
Wood carver plying his trade in
Mazatlán, Sinaloa

are the towns of Chiapa de Corzo, in
Chiapas, and Uruapan and Pátzcuaro, in
Michoacán state. Some lacquer artists
in Uruapan practice the *embutido* method, in which they scrape a design into the
top layer of lacquer and fill in the resulting
depressions with different colors, sometimes with beautiful results.

Among the finest wooden crafts
made in Mexico are the polished *palo
fierro* (ironwood) carvings created by the
Seri Indians of the northwestern state of

DAVE G HOUSER
Marionettes on display in a handicrafts
market, Cancún, Quintana Roo

Sonora. The hard wood is worked into a variety of dramatic human, animal and sea-
creature shapes. Seris sell their work in Hermosillo, Kino Viejo and Kino Nuevo.

Other attractive woodcrafts are the brightly painted copal animals, dragons and
other imaginary beasts produced by villagers in San Martín Tilcajete, Arrazola and La
Unión Tejalapan, near Oaxaca city. Multitudes of these creatures, called *alebrijes*, are
arrayed in shops and markets in Oaxaca. The craft emerged as a form of souvenir only in
the late 1980s, from toys the local people had been carving for their children for generations. It has brought relative wealth to many families in the villages concerned.

The Tarahumara Indians of the Barranca del Cobre (Copper Canyon) area, in northwest Mexico, produce dolls, toys and animals. Quiroga, near Pátzcuaro in Michoacán, is
known for its brightly painted wooden furniture. San Miguel de Allende and Cuernavaca
are other centers for wooden furniture.

Musical Instruments

Mexico's finest guitars are produced in Paracho, near Uruapan in Michoacán, which also turns out violins, cellos and other instruments. There are many shops and workshops in the town, which holds a guitar festival every August. The Tarahumara Indians also make violins.

Elsewhere you'll come across maracas, tambourines, whistles, scrape boards and a variety of drums in markets and shops. Interesting to look out for, though not particularly common, are 'tongue drums' – hollowed-out pieces of wood, often cylindrical in shape and attractively carved or decorated, with two central tongues of wood, each giving a different note when struck.

BARK PAINTINGS

Colorful paintings on *amate*, paper made from tree bark, are sold in countless souvenir shops. While many are cheap, humdrum productions for an undiscriminating tourist market, others certainly qualify as art, showing village life in skillful detail.

Bark paper has been made in Mexico since pre-Hispanic times, when some codices – pictorial manuscripts – were painted on it. It has always been held sacred. The skill of making amate survives only in one small, remote area of central Mexico where the states of Hidalgo, Puebla and Veracruz converge. A chief source of the paper is the Otomí Indian village of San Pablito, where Christianity has only a toehold and non-Christian nature deities are still believed to control life. The paper is made by women, who boil the bark, then lay out the fibers and beat them till they blend together. The resulting paper is dried in the sun. Most of it is then bought by Nahua Indian villagers from the state of Guerrero, who have been creating bark paintings since the 1960s. More recently, San Pablito villagers have taken up bark painting, some producing unorthodox designs representing San Pablito's traditional deities.

JOHN NOBLE

Maraca, tambourine, miniature tongue drum, and guiro fashioned from a hallowed out gourd

NANCY KELLER

Amate painting

Shamans in San Pablito still use bark paper cutouts portraying the same deities for fertility and medicinal rites, and some of these highly unusual works are also sold.

LEATHER

Leather belts, bags, *huaraches* (sandals), shoes, boots and clothes are often of good quality in Mexico and usually much cheaper than at home. They're widely available in shops and markets all over the country, but towns and cities in the northern and central ranching regions – such as Zacatecas, Jerez, Hermosillo, Monterrey, Saltillo, León and Guadalajara – have some especially well crafted gear. These towns are also the places to look if you want to make a present of a Mexican cowboy saddle or pair of spurs to your steed back home.

León is renowned as Mexico's shoe capital and does indeed have dozens of shoe stores, but in fact every other sizable city has plenty of good ones too. Check quality and fit carefully before you buy. Mexicans use metric footwear sizes.

DAVE G HOUSER

Leather sandals on display at a Oaxaca market

JEWELRY & METALWORK

Some ancient Mexicans were expert metal smiths and jewelers, as museum exhibits show. The Spanish fever for Mexico's reserves of gold and silver led to Indians' being banned from working those metals for a time during the colonial period, during which European styles of jewelry predominated. Indigenous artisanry was revived in the 20th century, however – most famously in the central Mexican town of Taxco by the American William Spratling, who initiated a silver-craft industry that now boasts more than 300 shops in Taxco. Silver is much more widely available than gold in Mexico, in all manner of styles and designs and with artistry ranging from the dully imitative to the superb. Earrings are particularly popular. It's quite possible to buy good pieces at sensible prices – see the Taxco section in this book's Around Mexico City chapter for hints on judging and buying silver

JAN BUTCHOFSKY-HOUSER
Handmade jewelry crafted from locally mined silver, Copala, Sinaloa

jewelry. For gold, including some delicate filigree work, Oaxaca and Guanajuato cities are two of the best places to look.

Necklaces of a wide variety of materials, including glass or stone beads, wood, seeds and coral, are worn by many Mexican women and are quite easy to come by. Many original jewelry creations, mostly from inexpensive materials, are also sold at the weekend market in the Mexico City suburb of Coyoacán and by vendors in travelers' haunts such as Oaxaca city and San Cristóbal de Las Casas.

Precious stones are much less common than precious metals. True jade, beloved of ancient Mexicans, is a rarity; most 'jade' jewelry is actually jadeite, serpentine or calcite. One abundant stone is the opal, mined in Querétaro state, where the town of San Juan del Río, near Tequisquiapan, has become quite a gem and jewelry center.

Though silver- and goldsmithing are probably Mexico's two most prominent metal crafts, others stand out in a few specific areas. The town of Santa Clara del Cobre, near Pátzcuaro in Michoacán, is a center for copperware, turning out shining plates, pots, candlesticks, lamps and more from dozens of workshops.

Oaxaca city is the scene of a thriving craft in tin plate, stamped into low relief and painted, with hundreds of attractive, colorful, small shapes – birds, people, mermaids, fruits, animals, churches, suns, moons, fish, butterflies.

JAMES LYON
Beaten copper basins from the Bajío area, in Mexico's Northern Central Highlands

NANCY KELLER
Silver earrings

ARTESANÍAS

RETABLOS

An engaging Mexican custom is the practice of adorning the sanctuaries of specially revered saints or holy images with *retablos*, small paintings giving thanks to the saint in question for answered prayers. Typically done on small sheets of tin, but sometimes on glass, wood, cardboard or another material, the retablos depict these miracles in touchingly literal images painted by their beneficiaries. They may show a cyclist's hair-breadth escape from a hurtling bus, a sailor's survival of a shipwreck, or an invalid rising from a sickbed, beside a representation of the saint and a brief message along the lines of, 'Thanks to San Milagro for curing my rheumatism – María Suárez González, 6 June 1990.' The Basílica de Guadalupe in Mexico City; the Santuario de Plateros near Fresnillo, in Zacatecas; and the church at Real de Catorce in San Luis Potosí state all have fascinating collections of retablos. Diego Rivera was among the first to treat these works as real folk art, and the Museo Frida Kahlo in Coyoacán, Mexico City, the former home of his artist wife, displays some of his collection.

BASKETS, HATS & HAMMOCKS

Handmade baskets of multifarious shapes and sizes are common in Mexican markets. If you take a liking to one or two and are in a buying mood, at least you can use them to carry other souvenirs home. Materials used to make baskets include cane, bamboo, and rush or palm-leaf strips. The latter may be wound around a filling of grasses. The more pliable materials enable a coiled construction, but weaving is most common. Many baskets are attractively patterned or colored.

JAMES LYON
Colorful, straw baskets
(above and below)

The classic wide-brimmed, high-crowned Mexican *sombrero* is now largely a thing of the past, except on a few mariachi musicians and in a few souvenir shops. Contemporary everyday men's hats are smaller but still often woven from palm strips, either in factories or by hand. The best are considered to be the *jipijapas* (Panama hats) made in caves at Becal, Campeche, where the humidity prevents the fibers from becoming too brittle during the production process. Mérida, in the adjacent state of Yucatán, is a good place to buy a jipijapa.

Another Mexican product of practical use to many travelers is the hammock. Hammocks can be the most comfortable and economical places to sleep in many hot, southern areas. Generally made of cotton or nylon, they come in a variety of widths and an infinite number of color patterns. Notable places where they're made or sold include Mérida, in Yucatán state; Palenque, in Chiapas; and Mitla and Juchitán, in Oaxaca. You can watch them being made in the village of Tixcocob, near Mérida. Some useful information for anyone thinking of buying a hammock can be found in the Mérida section of this book's Yucatán Peninsula chapter.

DAVE G HOUSER

DAVE G HOUSER

Panama hats on display in Cozumel, Quintana Roo

FESTIVAL CRAFTS

Some Mexican crafts are produced for specific events. The national obsession with skull and skeleton motifs, by which Mexicans continually remind themselves of their own mortality, reaches a crescendo in the weeks before *Día de los Muertos* (Day of the Dead), November 2, when the souls of the dead are believed to revisit the earth and people gather in graveyards with gifts for them. As Day of the Dead approaches, families build altars in their homes, and shops and markets fill with countless toy coffins and paper, cardboard and clay skeletons, many of them engaged in lively activities such as riding a bicycle, playing music or getting married. Most amazing are the rows of chocolate and candy skulls, skeletons, and coffins that appear in market stalls – an obvious indication of the almost joyful nature of the festival, which reunites the living with their dead.

JOHN NOBLE

Candy skulls for the Day of the Dead

Most Mexican children's birthdays would be incomplete without a piñata, a large, brightly decorated papier-mâché star, animal, fruit or other figure, constructed around a clay pot or papier-mâché mold. At party time the piñata is stuffed with small toys, sweets and fruit and suspended on a rope. Blindfolded children take turns at bashing it with a stick until it breaks open and, with luck, showers everyone with the gifts inside. Piñatas are also broken after the traditional pre-Christmas processions called posadas, which are still held in some towns.

ARTESANÍAS

NADA EN ESTE MUNDO DURA
FENECEN BIENES Y MALES
UNA TRISTE SEPULTURA
A TODOS NOS HACE IGUALES

JOHN NOBLE
Day of the Dead altar at the Templo Mayor, Mexico City

Another Christmas craft is the creation of *nacimientos*, nativity scenes, in homes or town plazas. Clay or wood figures of the personages in these scenes may be reused year after year. Some larger-scale nacimientos even feature live sheep and goats.

BOOKS ON MEXICAN HANDICRAFTS

There are countless books on the subject, but two fairly recent works by Chloe Sayer are excellent sources if you want to delve into the field. *Arts and Crafts of Mexico* is a general introduction covering almost every craft you could think of, and it's a good starting point for further research. *Costumes of Mexico* (published in Britain as *Mexican Costume*) concentrates on the textile arts and will answer most questions you could ask about the bewildering array of techniques, materials, styles and designs employed in Mexican Indian clothing.

Index

TEXT

Map references are in **bold** type.

Acanceh 895
Acapulco 496-509, **497, 500**
    accommodations 502-5
    beaches 501
    entertainment 506-7
    history 499
    La Quebrada 499
    orientation 496-7
    places to eat 505-6
    transportation 507-9
Acatepec 242-3
Acatlán de Osorio 245, 987
Acaxochitlán 670
Acayucan 709
accidents 116
accommodations 92-3
Acolman 212
Actopan 219
Aeropuerto Internacional Benito
    Juárez 193, 201
Africans 658, 758
Agua Prieta 333
Aguascalientes 596-601, **597**
Ahuizotl 22
air travel 733
    airfares 103-4, 111
    airlines 105, 193-4
    around Mexico 111
    from Australia 105
    from Canada 103-4
    from Central & South
        America 105
    from Europe 104-5
    to/from Mexico City 193-4
    from USA 103-4
Ajijic 537
Akumal 940-1
Alamos 344-9, **345**
Aldama 404
Allende, Ignacio 22

Alvarado 701
Alvarado, Pedro de 22
Amatenango del Valle 820
Amecameca 223
Amozoc 245
Amuzgo Indians 749
Angahuan 569
Angangueo 549
Ángeles Verdes 201
anthropology 159
antojitos 94-5
Aquismón 665
Arareko, Complejo Ecoturístico
    360
archaelogical sites
    Balamku 854
    Balcón de Montezuma 407
    Becan 853-4
    Bonampak 836, **836**
    Calakmul 854
    Calixtlahuaca 276
    Chicanná 854
    Chichén Itzá 21, 850,
        896-904, **897**
    Chinkultic 794, 841-2
    Cholula 241, **240**
    Cobá 947-9, **948**
    Comalcalco 792-3
    Dainzú 741
    Edzná 863
    El Cedral 939
    El Raminal 855
    El Rey, Cancún 913
    El Tajín 669, 672-5, **673**
    Hormiguero 854
    Izapa 847-8
    Kabah 889-90, **889**
    Kohunlich 957-8, **958**
    Labná 891, **891**
    Lambityeco 742
    Madera 375-6
    Mayapán 894-5

Mitla 744-5, **745**
    Palenque 825-35, **830-1**
    Paquimé 374
    San Lorenzo 709
    Sayil 890, **890**
    Teotihuacán 17-8, 120,
        212-7, **213**
    Tlateloco 162
    Toniná 822-3
    Tres Zapotes 703
    Tula 210-1, **210**
    Tulum 942-6, **943**
    Xel-ha 941
    Xlapak 890
    Xochicalco 263
    Xpujil 853
    Yagul 743-4, **743**
    Yaxchilán 794, 836-7, **837**
    Zaachila tombs 747
    Zempoala 676-7, **676**
archaeology 16
    museums 159, 169, 680
architecture 52-4
    books 73
area codes 71
Arrazola 747, 994
Arrecife Palancar 931
Arriaga 844
Arroyo de Cuchujaquihas 349
Arroyo los Monos 375
artesanías 230, 977-1000
    books 73, 1000
    buying handicrafts 978-80
    Seri people 339
arts 50-5, 73
    Mayan 19
    rock paintings 304
Atl. *See* Murillo, Gerardo
Atlixco 245
ATMs 66
Atotonilco 645
Atotonilco el Grande 220

SIDEBARS

THANKS

Terhi Aaltonen, Elinor T Abdulla, Audria Abel & Jimmy Davies, Edward Abse, Campamento Adame, Felix Adank, Beatrice Aebi & annina Zwicky, Bob Agnew, Heidi Albert & Gareth Lowndes, David Alexander, Karen Alexopoulos, Carl Allen, Judy Almeranti, Fred Ameling, Gail Anderman, Marion Anrys, Caroline & Joëlle Apter, Regina Aragon, Jan E Arctander, Jacqueline K Atkinson, Jörg Ausfelt, Maik Aussendorf, Barbara Avery, Susan & Art Bachrach, john F Barimo, Sophie Barker, Ruth Barnard, Steven Barr, Susan Barreau, David Baum & Julie Blumenfeld, P Beauchamp, Guy Beauregard, Victoria Behm, Michael Beier, James Bell, Charles Bennett, Caryl Bergeron, Marianna Berkley, Howard Bernstein, Hiro Bhojwani, Sarah Billyack, Stéphane Éric Bisson, Jessica Björklund, Shenais BockNelson, Tove Bøe, Ulrike Böhm, Nicole Boogaers, Ian Booth, Stephanie D Bormann, Theo Borst, Erik Botsford, Robert J Bowker, Jeanie Bowman, Cat Brandon, Sarah Kate Bridgewater & Vicky Scrivens, Elizabeth Briggs, Katharina Bringold, Iden Bromfield,

Frank Bron, Mike & Lisa Bryan, Jill Buckingham, Anthony Bullock, Jan Bulman, Adrian Burden, Andrew Burns, Matthew Butler, Dermot Byrne, Richard Cain, Eric Calder, Heather Cameron, Lila Campbell & Fred Hart, Timothy JC Cannon, Jeff Cardille, Anna Cassilly, Annick Ceuppens, Rick Chandler & Heidi Pankoke, François & Claudette Chevassus, Harrell G Chotas, James L Citron, Barbara Cochrane, Flora S Cockburn, Jane Cockburn, Rachel Cohen, Valerie P Cohen, Lynette Conder, Sue Conrad, Peter Converse, Dennis Conway, Geoff Cook, Peter Cook, Steve Cook & Esmé-Jane Lippiatt, Kathleen Cooke, Pamela Cooper, Maggie Copping, Abigail Cottrell, Louise Coulthard, Rob Craig, Leo Crofts, Lyn Crowl, Jorge Penagos Cruz, Virginia & Victor Cruz, Laurence Cuscó, Patty & Rosario D'Alessandro, Ulysses D'Aquila, Mike Darcy, Rob & Georgie Davidson, J Davies, Richard Davies, Simon Davis, Neal A Davis & Tatiana Blackington, Paul de Brem & Isabelle Vial, CJ de Quartel, A de Vries, Anthony De'Angelis, Alberto Deacon-Morey, Paul Dickerson, Kathy Didier,

Martin Dillig, Joanne Dinsmore de López, Wendy Dison, Carsten Dittmann, MG Dixon, Clement Djossen & lotta Andersson, Cy & Dee Donaldson, William J Doris, Brooke Douglas, J Winslow Dowson, Sally Drake, Erika Drucker, Bridget Drury, Eddie Dry, Desmond Dubbin, Alex Dunne, AC Earl, Tom Earle, Gerlinde Ecker & Helmut Lifka, Jenny Edwards, Libby Edwards, Donald Eischen, Naomi Eisenstein, Caroline Elliott, David Ellis, Kari Eloranta, Jean-Pierre Estéve, Vladimir Estrada, Nia Evans &Michael Jense, Craig Faanes, Clint & Ina Ferguson, Jesse Ferris & Ilanit Evron, Lee Fields, Krisztina Filep, Daniel Finke, Hedy Fischer & Randy Shull, Charles A Fisher, Janice M Flaherty, AJ Fleming & L Bell, Tom Fletcher Jr, Harmony Folz, Rudi Forster, Donna Franklin, Bill & Caroll Fraser, Jürg Furrer, Dick Gabriel, Tim Gagan, Anna & Tomasz Galka, Yvonne Garry & Ryan Parenteau, Alison Gaylord, Gary Geating & Rob Stokes, Dolores Gende, J George, Werner Ginzky, Maria Giribaldi & Robert Noparast, Sarah Gleave, Jan Kees Glynis, Matthew

Goh, Catherine Gold, Katherine Golder, Adam Goldstein, Peter Goltermann, Kate Gomberg, Victor M Jiménez González, Wolf Gotthilf, Rachel Grant, Carrol Greenbaum, Anne Grimes, Camilla Gustafsson, Noah Guy, Kenneth R Haag, Sven Haberer, Suzette Hafner & Joseph-Ambroise Desrosiers, Oliver Hagemann, Steve & Em Hahoney, Mirén Haines, Marc Hale, MA Hall, Susan Hall, Cindy Halvorson, Rhonda Hankins, Andy Hanssen, Mabel Haourt, Murray R Hasson, Ilana Hatch, Rhonda Haukins, Lewis Haupt, Kendra Hawke, Gaye Haworth, Sharon & Alvin Hazelrigg, John Heaton, Robert J Heerekip & Simone de Haan, Ruth Hellier, Allen & Dale Hermann, R Hethey, Marcel Heutmekers, Ken & Cheryl Hickson, John Hildebrand, Graeme Hind, Allan Hindmarch, John J Hoffman, Duane & Liz Hohling, Jennifer Holleyman, Pete Hollings, Mark Hollis, Victoria Holtchis, Victoria Holtehib, Joe Holzer & Elisabeth Julia Jilek, Jeff Hopkins, Edward Horne, Gavin Imhof, Steve Immel, Deb Inglis, Ted Jacobson, Sarah Jain, Victor M Jiménez, Martin Jirman, Tim Johnson, Miguel A Julia, Stefan Justi, Jane Kaluta, Sarah Kavasharov, Dietmar Kenzle, Barnabas John Kerekes, David Kerkhoff, Michael S Kero & William A Bachmaier, Ian Kerr, Adriaan Kievit, Erik King, Peggie Klekotka, Christoffel Klimbie & Gracia Reijnen, Spencer Knight, David Knox, Steven Koenig, Simone Koliwyzer, Robert Kozak, Raghu Krishnan, Jørgen Kristensen, Svend Haakon Kristensen, Sandra Küenzi, Lena Landegren, Louise Lander, Leah Larkin, Anne Larsen, Dean Larsen, Robert & Laura Larson, Peter Laurence, Norma Lauring, Michal Lavi & Aviv Fried, William H Lawrence, Cale Layton, Steve Leavitt & Amanda Lines, Daniel Lebidois, Adam Leibowitz, Scott Leonard, Marina Lewis, Frederico Lifsichtz, Piotr Ligaj, Paul Linnebach, Dana Lissy, David Lloyd, Bill Lordge, Gaute Losnegard, Anthony Lott, Markus J Low, Carey Luff, Susan Lynch, Hemming Lyrdal, Freya Maberly, W Iain Mackay, Brian MacNamee & Isabel Hernandez, Steve & Em Mahoney, Glenn D Mair, Catherine Mao, Joe & Joan Margel, Richard Marks, Dina Marshall, Zeus Marofo & Roberto Alcalar, Stephane Martinez, Julian Mason, Steve Mathias, Brent Matsuda, Eduardo

Maubert, Chris S Maun, Regina F & Andreas Mayer, Steve Mayer, Leonard G Mazzone, Chris McCauley, Nell McCombs, Dave McConnell & Jim Justice, Barrie McCormick, Bruce McGrew, Cheryl & Bruce McLaren, Cameron McPherson, Annalise Mellor, M Michael Menzel, Nathan Meyer, Margrit Meyer, Marie Meyer, Ben Miller, Allen C Miller, Suzzanne Miller, Jason Milligan, Stephanie Mills, Carolina A Miranda, Ramon Mireles, Bill Mitchell, Paul Mixon, Lester H Moffatt, Duane & Liz Mohling, Erick Molenaar, Hans Molenaar, Peter Møller, Thais Morales & Laia Pol, Alexis Morgan, Pauline Mourits, Ashish Mukharji, Sandra Müller, Barbara Müller, Michael Müller, Mark Mulligan & Ana Smallwood, Todd Munro, Roberta Murray, Pat & Mary Murray, Marian Nadler, Mark Nicklas, David Nielsen, Karen Nienaber & Ann Smith, Rob Nieuwenhuis, Anna Nilsson, Larry Norris, Peter O'Brien, Zeyn O'Leary, Helen O'Reilly, Lynn Oakerbee, John Oakes, Kevin Okell & Janine Bentley, David Olson, Karin Oyevaar, Robert Pacholski, Giovanni Paganini, Axel B Pajunk, Schoro Pantschev, Pierre-Joseph Paoli, Steven Parsa, Steve Patterson, C J Paulet, Patrik Paulis, Caroline Peene, Ben Pelle, Richard W Pennington, Linda Peregrine, Patricia Perret, Stefano Piazzardi, Darlene S Pinch, Tobias Platzen, Liz Plumb, Andreas Poethen, Olver Pollux, annette & Edgar Portillo, Lucille Poulin & Chris Osterbauer, Bonnie Pressinger, Michael Prest, Philip Preston, Shelley Preston, M Philippe Queriaux, Hugh E Quetton, Ann Rabin, Jean Radosevich, Hanna Rajalahti, Dave Randall & Craig Rokes, Clare Ranger, Carol Ann Raphael, Kathleen Reagan & Ronny Haklay, Clarence E Redberg, George Redman, C Reed, Julian Remnant, Kevin Reynolds, José R Rivera, Richard Robinson, Mauricio & Mayra Rodriquez, William Roemmich, Steve Rogowski, Jens Rohark, Patrick Römer, Susan Rose-Dick, Wolfgang Rosenthal, Linnéa Rowlatt, Lauren Roycroft & Ralf Tieken, Sente Rudi, James Russell, Mark Rutkowski, Piotr & Magda Rybka, Julie Sadigursky, Jeff Samboy, Marcelo Sanchez, Fernando Sanchez Cuenca, Marietta Sander, Alexandra Savage, Michael Schaich, Ralph Schmens, Jörg Schmidt, Marius Schoenberg, Lee & Brenda Schussman, Thomas Schwarz, Devin Scott, Bryan Scott, Heather J Seaton,

Shelly Selin, Katie Shannon, Jan Sharkey-Dodds & Ian Yeagne, Florence & Peter Shaw, Ken Shaw, Rebecca C Shell, P Shenkin, Graham Shuley, David & Linda Simmonds, Richard Simpkins, S Skerritt, Lisa Smailes, George & Shirley Smith, Ali Smookler, Dick Snyder, Göran Söderberg, Janne Solpark, Skeen Möller Sörensen, Leopold Soucy, Patrick Spanjaard, Anne Spencer, Hermine Spitz, Detlef Spötter, Janice St Marie, Lionel & Lucienne St Pierre, Imelda Stack, Dirk Stadtmann, Paul Stang, David Stanle, Roland Steffen, Marc Stegelmann, Laura Stegeman, Jack Steinberg, Edel Stephenson, Richard Stockwell, Suzanne N Strauss, Else Strømman, Mitja Strukelj, Tigridia EB Syme, Allan Taylor, Richard Antonio Tejidor, Detlef Thedieck, Bill Thomas, Tom Thomas, Aled Thomas & Kate Douglas, Peter Thompson, Jackie Thompson, Keith & Birgid Thompson, George Thorsen, Sören Tiedemann, Clark Timmins & Cynthia Sorensen, Mark Tipping, Betsy L Tipps, Bill &Norma Titheridge, Dan Treecraft, Beatrix Trojer, Jada Tullos, Salome Turberger, Myrna Turkewitz, Hideaki Ueda, Michael Uleck, Jens Christian Ulrich, Alfie Urencio Del Río, Martin T Valezquez, Anne van Acker, Sandra van der Pas & Erik Agterhuis, Onno van der Salm, AH & SJ Boon van Ostade, Phyllis Vaughn, Kay Veenandaal, Esther Veenendaal & Auke van Stralen, Martin T Velazquez, David M Vella, Sabine Verhelst, R Vermaire, Michael Vestergaard & Helle Bjerre, Javier Perez Vicente, Michel Villeneuve, Erica Visser, Johan & Marie Von Matern, David Voyzey, Anna Wakeley, Veronica Walker, Veronica Wallace, Clifford Wallis, Dympna Walsh, Stephen Warren, Nicola Watson, DC Webster, Pascal Weel, N S Welch, Don & Alicia Welker, A Went, Anders Westlund, Sharon Westmorland & Derek Bromley, Sarah Wharton & Michael Nielsen, A White, Nishi Whiteley, Darnell & Elaine Whitley, Beth Whitman, Vincent Wiers, Eleanore Wilde, John D Wildi, Scott Wilhelm, Derek Williams, Dave & Ann Williams, Erica Wilson, Angela Wit, Julia Wood, Holly Yasui, Geoff Yeandle, RA Zambardino, Fred Zanger, Jerry & Barbara Zaninelli, Patrick A Zebedee, Perry V Zizzi, Jolee Zoła, Andrea & Agar Zuin

LONELY PLANET PRODUCTS

Lonely Planet is known worldwide for publishing practical, reliable and no-nonsense travel information in our guides and on our web site. The Lonely Planet list covers just about every accessible part of the world. Currently there are eight series: *travel guides, shoestring guides, walking guides, city guides, phrasebooks, audio packs, travel atlases* and *Journeys*–a unique collection of travel writing.

EUROPE

Amsterdam • Austria • Baltic States & Kaliningrad • Baltic States phrasebook • Britain • Central Europe on a shoestring • Central Europe phrasebook • Czech & Slovak Republics • Denmark • Dublin • Eastern Europe on a shoestring • Eastern Europe phrasebook • Finland • France • French phrasebook • Germany • German phrasebook • Greece • Greek phrasebook • Hungary • Iceland, Greenland & the Faroe Islands • Ireland • Italy • Italian phrasebook • Lisbon • London • Mediterranean Europe on a shoestring • Mediterranean Europe phrasebook • Paris • Poland • Portugal • Portugal travel atlas • Prague • Romania & Moldova • Russia, Ukraine & Belarus • Russian phrasebook • Scandinavian & Baltic Europe on a shoestring • Scandinavian Europe phrasebook • Slovenia • Spain • Spanish phrasebook • St Petersburg • Switzerland • Trekking in Greece • Trekking in Spain • Ukrainian phrasebook • Vienna • Walking in Britain • Walking in Italy • Walking in Switzerland • Western Europe on a shoestring • Western Europe phrasebook

NORTH AMERICA

Alaska • Backpacking in Alaska • Bahamas • Baja California • Bermuda • California & Nevada • Canada • Chicago • Deep South • Florida • Hawaii • Honolulu • Los Angeles • Mexico • Mexico City • Miami • New England • New Orleans • New York City • New York, New Jersey & Pennsylvania • Pacific Northwest USA • Rocky Mountain States USA • San Francisco • Seattle • Southwest USA • USA phrasebook • Washington, DC & The Capital Region

CENTRAL AMERICA & THE CARIBBEAN

Bahamas, Turks & Caicos • Central America on a shoestring • Costa Rica • Cuba • Eastern Caribbean • Guatemala, Belize & Yucatán: La Ruta Maya • Jamaica

SOUTH AMERICA

Argentina, Uruguay & Paraguay • Bolivia • Brazil • Brazilian phrasebook • Buenos Aires • Chile & Easter Island • Chile travel atlas • Colombia • Ecuador & the Galápagos Islands • Latin American Spanish phrasebook • Peru • Quechua phrasebook • Rio de Janeiro • South America on a shoestring • Trekking in the Patagonian Andes • Venezuela

Travel Literature: Full Circle: A South American Journey

AFRICA

Arabic (Moroccan) phrasebook • Africa on a shoestring • Africa The South • Cape Town • Cairo • Central Africa • East Africa • Egypt & the Sudan • Egypt travel atlas • Ethiopian (Amharic) phrasebook • Kenya • Kenya travel atlas • Malawi, Mozambique & Zambia • Morocco • North Africa • South Africa, Lesotho & Swaziland • South Africa travel atlas • Swahili phrasebook • Trekking in East Africa • West Africa • Zimbabwe, Botswana & Namibia • Zimbabwe, Botswana & Namibia travel atlas

Travel Literature: The Rainbird: A Central African Journey • Songs to an African Sunset: A Zimbabwean Story

ISLANDS OF THE INDIAN OCEAN

Madagascar & Comoros • Maldives & Islands of the East Indian Ocean • Mauritius, Réunion & Seychelles

Also Available: Travel with Children • Traveller's Tales

MAIL ORDER

Lonely Planet products are distributed worldwide. They are also available by mail order from Lonely Planet, so if you have difficulty finding a title please write to us. North American and South American residents should write to Embarcadero West, 155 Filbert St, Suite 251, Oakland CA 94607, USA; European and African residents should write to 10A Spring Place, London NW5 3BH, UK; and residents of other countries to PO Box 617, Hawthorn, Victoria 3122, Australia.

NORTH-EAST ASIA

Beijing • Cantonese phrasebook • China • Hong Kong • Hong Kong, Macau & Canton • Japan • Japanese phrasebook • Japanese audio pack • Korea • Korean phrasebook • Mandarin phrasebook • Mongolia • Mongolian phrasebook • North-East Asia on a shoestring • Seoul • Taiwan • Tibet • Tibet phrasebook • Tokyo

Travel Literature: Lost Japan

MIDDLE EAST & CENTRAL ASIA

Arab Gulf States • Arabic (Egyptian) phrasebook • Central Asia • Central Asia phrasebook • Iran • Israel & the Palestinian Territories • Israel & the Palestinian Territories travel atlas • Istanbul • Jerusalem • Jordan & Syria • Jordan, Syria & Lebanon travel atlas • Lebanon • Middle East • Turkey • Turkey travel atlas • Turkish phrasebook • Trekking in Turkey • Yemen

Travel Literature: The Gates of Damascus • Kingdom of the Film Stars: Journey into Jordon

INDIAN SUBCONTINENT

Bengali phrasebook • Bangladesh • Delhi • Goa • Hindi/Urdu phrasebook • India • India & Bangladesh travel atlas • Indian Himalaya • Karakoram Highway • Nepal • Nepali phrasebook • Pakistan • Rajasthan • Sri Lanka • Sri Lanka phrasebook • Trekking in the Indian Himalaya • Trekking in the Karakoram & Hindukush • Trekking in the Nepal Himalaya

Travel Literature: In Rajasthan • Shopping for Buddhas

SOUTH-EAST ASIA

Bali & Lombok • Bangkok • Burmese phrasebook • Cambodia • Ho Chi Minh • Indonesia • Indonesian phrasebook • Indonesian audio pack • Jakarta • Java • Laos • Lao phrasebook • Laos travel atlas • Malay phrasebook • Malaysia, Singapore & Brunei • Myanmar (Burma) • Philippines • Pilipino phrasebook • Singapore • South-East Asia on a shoestring • Thailand • Thailand's Islands and Beaches • Thai phrasebook • Thailand travel atlas • Thai audio pack • Thai Hill Tribes phrasebook • Vietnam • Vietnamese phrasebook • Vietnam travel atlas

ANTARCTICA

Antarctica

AUSTRALIA & THE PACIFIC

Australia • Australian phrasebook • Bushwalking in Australia • Bushwalking in Papua New Guinea • Fiji • Fijian phrasebook • Islands of Australia's Great Barrier Reef • Melbourne • Micronesia • New Caledonia • New South Wales & the ACT • New Zealand • Northern Territory • Outback Australia • Papua New Guinea • Papua New Guinea phrasebook • Queensland • Rarotonga & the Cook Islands • Samoa • Solomon Islands • South Australia • Sydney • Tahiti & French Polynesia • Tasmania • Tonga • Tramping in New Zealand • Vanuatu • Victoria • Western Australia

Travel Literature: Islands in the Clouds • Sean & David's Long Drive

THE LONELY PLANET STORY

Lonely Planet published its first book in 1973 in response to the numerous 'How did you do it?' questions Maureen and Tony Wheeler were asked after driving, bussing, hitching, sailing and railing their way from England to Australia.

Written at a kitchen table and hand collated, trimmed and stapled, *Across Asia on the Cheap* became an instant local best seller, inspiring thoughts of another book.

Eighteen months in South-East Asia resulted in their second guide, *South-East Asia on a shoestring*, which they put together in a backstreet Chinese hotel in Singapore in 1975. The 'yellow bible', as it quickly became known to back-packers around the world, soon became the guide to the region. It has sold well over half a million copies and is now in its 9th edition, still retaining its familiar yellow cover.

Today there are 240 titles, including travel guides, walking guides, language kits & phrasebooks, travel atlases and travel literature. The company is the largest independent travel publisher in the world. Although Lonely Planet initially specialized in guides to Asia, today there are few corners of the globe that have not been covered.

The emphasis continues to be on travel for independent travelers. Tony and Maureen still travel for several months of each year and play an active part in the writing, updating and quality control of Lonely Planet's guides.

They have been joined by over 70 authors and 170 staff at our offices in Melbourne (Australia), Oakland (USA), London (UK) and Paris (France). Travelers themselves also make a valuable contribution to the guides through the feedback we receive in thousands of letters each year and on our website.

The people at Lonely Planet strongly believe that travelers can make a positive contribution to the countries they visit, both through their appreciation of the countries' culture, wildlife and natural features, and through the money they spend. In addition, the company makes a direct contribution to the countries and regions it covers. Since 1986 a percentage of the income from each book has been donated to ventures such as famine relief in Africa; aid projects in India; agricultural projects in Central America; Greenpeace's efforts to halt French nuclear testing in the Pacific; and Amnesty International.

'I hope we send people out with the right attitude about travel. You realize when you travel that there are so many different perspectives about the world, so we hope these books will make people more interested in what they see. Guidebooks can't really guide people. All you can do is point them in the right direction.'

– Tony Wheeler

LONELY PLANET PUBLICATIONS

Australia
PO Box 617, Hawthorn 3122, Victoria
☎ (03) 9819 1877 fax (03) 9819 6459
e-mail talk2us@lonelyplanet.com.au

USA
155 Filbert St, Suite 251
Oakland, California 94607
☎ (510) 893 8555, TOLL FREE (800) 275 8555
fax (510) 893 8563
e-mail info@lonelyplanet.com

UK
10A Spring Place, London NW5 3BH, UK
☎ (0171) 428 4800 fax (0171) 428 4828
e-mail go@lonelyplanet.co.uk

France
71 bis rue du Cardinal Lemoine, 75005 Paris
☎ 01 44 320620 fax 01 46 347255
e-mail 100560.415@compuserve.com

World Wide Web: www.lonelyplanet.com